Criminal EVIDENCE

tenth edition

Jefferson L. **Ingram**

University of Dayton

John C. Klotter Justice Administration Legal Series

Criminal Evidence, Ninth Edition

Copyright © 1971, 1975 W.H. Anderson Company
1980, 1987, 1992, 1996, 2000, 2004, 2007, 2009
Matthew Bender & Company, Inc., a member of the LexisNexis Group

Phone 877-374-2919
Web Site www.lexisnexis.com/anderson/criminaljustice

Library of Congress Cataloging-in-Publication Data

Ingram, Jefferson..
    Criminal evidence / Jefferson L. Ingram. – 10th ed.
      p. cm.
    Includes index.
    ISBN 978-1-4224-6141-9 (softbound)
    1. Evidence, Criminal–United States. I. Title.
KF9660.K57 2009
345.73'06–dc22

                 2009038517

Cover design by Tin Box Studio, Inc.

EDITOR   Elisabeth Roszmann Ebben
ACQUISITIONS EDITOR   Michael C. Braswell

Preface

In revising *Criminal Evidence*, Tenth Edition, the author continued to honor John Klotter's extensive work on criminal evidence and to continue the excellent approach he followed by updating evidentiary themes, trends, and cases, while remaining true to the original organization and presentation. The book remains primarily a textbook with illustrated cases for those involved in the study of criminal evidence and in the administration of justice. It should prove especially valuable to those who are preparing for careers in criminal justice or related areas of study. For those reasons, the emphasis continues to be placed on the rules and principles of evidence that primarily affect criminal cases.

This book has been prepared as a textbook for individuals teaching or learning about the evidentiary framework in the administration of criminal justice. The materials presented cover general evidence law in use by the states and the federal justice system. The text makes frequent reference to the Federal Rules of Evidence as a benchmark of how the law of evidence applies in particular situations. Although differences exist in the way a rule of evidence is administered in the various American jurisdictions, there is significant uniformity because many states have adopted versions of the Federal Rules of Evidence or the Uniform Rules of Evidence. As state courts follow their particular adaptations of the Federal Rules of Evidence, they place significant emphasis and reliance on the way the federal courts interpret the Rules while occasionally recognizing an interpretation of a rule that reflects a state's individual needs.

For the reader or instructor, the book retains its familiar organization with related ancillary materials, including the glossary, a current version of the Federal Rules of Evidence, and the table of contents of the Uniform Rules of Evidence. As a method of organization, the text portion of this book roughly follows the current organizational order of the Federal Rules of Evidence and includes portions of particular rules in box format within the chapters. In Part II, where cases demonstrate some of the evidentiary principles, the author has added several newer legal cases that explain the evolving principles of evidence in a contemporary case context. While several landmark cases are presented in Part II, this version of the book retained some older cases in which the judicial writers offered particularly excellent explanations of legal principles. After Part II, the glossary permits the reader to find definitions and learn many principles that may be unique to the study of the law of evidence. Although the text portion of this book does not deal with every section of the Federal Rules of Evidence, Appendix I contains a copy of the Federal Rules of

Evidence that incorporates all of the new rule changes that became effective in December 1, 2008.

Constitutional reinterpretations by the Supreme Court of the United States often change the admissibility of evidence. Forty-three years ago, the Miranda revolution altered the way in which criminal justice professionals could obtain and use some types of evidence. A few terms ago, the Supreme Court of the United States reinterpreted the Sixth Amendment right of confrontation in a way that affected the admissibility of hearsay evidence by requiring more in court testimony. Just this year, the Supreme Court revised the admissibility of evidence seized from automobile searches in particular arrest contexts. Recognizing that the law of evidence evolves, the author made every effort to recognize changes in evidence law and to incorporate the new material into the text discussion of the principles.

The study of criminal evidence involves some understanding of collateral legal subjects like constitutional law and criminal law. In this book, evidentiary principles are embedded in criminal cases and in textual references involving murder, robbery, assault, battery, and other crimes. Using a criminal prosecution context, this book presents the traditional rules of evidence that most often affect criminal cases that lawyers, police, and criminal justice professionals will encounter.

To assist instructors, an Instructor's Guide and a PowerPoint presentation covering the text section of this book are available.

Jefferson Ingram, University of Dayton, August, 2009.

Table of Contents

Preface   iii

PART I   1

History and Approach to Study   3

Chapter 1
History and Development of Rules of Evidence   5

Section
1.1	Introduction	7
1.2	Early Attempts to Determine Guilt or Innocence	7
1.3	Modern Legal Systems—Romanesque System	11
1.4	—Anglican System	12
1.5	Development of the Rules of Evidence in the United States	14
1.6	Application of the Rules of Evidence in State and Federal Courts	16
1.7	Future Development of the Rules of Evidence	18
1.8	Summary	20

Chapter 2
Approach to the Study of Criminal Evidence   21

Section
2.1	Introduction	23
2.2	Definitions	24
2.3	Reasons for the Rules of Evidence	28
2.4	Reasons for Excluding Evidence	29
2.5	Rules of Evidence in Criminal Cases Compared to Rules of Evidence in Civil Cases	31
2.6	Pretrial Flow of Evidence	33
2.7	Use of Evidence at the Trial	35
2.8	Consideration of Evidence on Appeal	36
2.9	Use of Evidence at the Probation Hearing	37
2.10	Use of Evidence When Considering Parole	37
2.11	Summary	38

Proof by Evidence and Substitutes   **41**

Chapter 3
Burden of Proof   43

Section
3.1   Introduction   45
3.2   Definitions and Distinctions   46
3.3   Preponderance of the Evidence   49
3.4   Clear and Convincing Evidence   50
3.5   Beyond a Reasonable Doubt   52
3.6   Burden on the Prosecution   56
3.7   Burden to Prove All Elements of the Crime   58
3.8   Burden on the Accused   60
3.9   Burden of Proving Affirmative Defenses—General   63
3.10   —Alibi   64
3.11   —Insanity   66
3.12   —Self-Defense   69
3.13   Sufficiency of Evidence   72
3.14   Summary   73

Chapter 4
Proof via Evidence   75

Section
4.1   Introduction   77
4.2   Pretrial Motions Pertaining to Evidence   78
4.3   General Approach to Admissibility   79
4.4   Order of Presenting Evidence at the Trial   81
4.5   Procedure for Offering and Challenging Evidence   83
4.6   Role of the Trial Judge in Evidence Matters   85
4.7   Function of the Jury   88
4.8   Role of Witnesses   89
4.9   Prosecuting Attorney's Responsibilities   91
4.10   Defense Attorney's Responsibilities   94
4.11   Admissibility and Weight of Direct and Circumstantial Evidence   97
4.12   Summary   103

Chapter 5
Judicial Notice   105

Section
5.1   Introduction   107
5.2   Judicial Notice Defined   108
5.3   Judicial Notice of Facts   111
5.4   —Matters of General Knowledge   113
5.5   —History and Historical Facts   116

5.6	—Geography and Geographical Facts	117
5.7	—Facts Relating to Nature and Science	119
5.8	—Language, Abbreviations, and Symbols	121
5.9	Judicial Notice of Laws	123
5.10	—Law of the Forum	124
5.11	—Federal Law	124
5.12	—Law of Sister States	125
5.13	—Law of Foreign Countries	126
5.14	—Municipal Ordinances	127
5.15	—Administrative Regulations	128
5.16	—Jurisdiction of Courts	129
5.17	Judicial Notice Process	130
5.18	Judicial Notice in Criminal Cases	132
5.19	Summary	133

Chapter 6
Presumptions, Inferences, and Stipulations   135

Section

6.1	Introduction	137
6.2	Definitions and Distinctions	138
6.3	Reasons for Presumptions and Inferences	144
6.4	Presumptions of Law	146
6.5	Presumptions of Fact	147
6.6	Classes of Presumptions	148
6.7	Specific Presumption Situations	151
6.8	—Innocence	152
6.9	—Sanity	156
6.10	—Suicide	159
6.11	—Possession of Fruits of Crime	160
6.12	—That a Person Intends the Ordinary Consequences of His or Her Voluntary Acts	163
6.13	—Knowledge of the Law	167
6.14	—Flight or Concealment	168
6.15	—Unexplained Absence as Death	171
6.16	—Regularity of Official Acts	173
6.17	Constitutionality Tests for Presumptions and Inferences	175
6.18	Stipulations	180
6.19	—Polygraph Tests	183
6.20	Summary	185

General Admissibility Tests 187

Chapter 7   189
Relevancy and Materiality

Section
7.1	Introduction	191
7.2	Relevancy and Materiality Defined	192
7.3	Admissibility of Relevant Evidence	196
7.4	Reasons for Exclusion of Relevant and Material Evidence	199
7.5	Relevancy of Particular Matters	206
7.6	—Identity of Persons	207
7.7	—Identity of Things	210
7.8	—Circumstances Preceding the Crime	211
7.9	—Subsequent Incriminating or Exculpatory Circumstances	213
7.10	—Defenses	217
7.11	—Character Evidence	221
7.12	—Proof of Other Crimes, Wrongs, or Acts	224
7.13	—Experimental and Scientific Evidence	229
7.14	Summary	231

Chapter 8
Competency of Evidence and Witnesses   233

Section
8.1	Introduction	235
8.2	Definitions	236
8.3	General Categories of Incompetent Evidence	236
8.4	Competency of Evidence—Documentary Evidence	238
8.5	—Tests and Experiments	238
8.6	—Conduct of Trained Dogs	240
8.7	—Telephone Conversations	243
8.8	Negative Evidence as Competent Evidence	245
8.9	Evidence Competent for Some Purposes but Not for Others	247
8.10	Competency of Witnesses	248
8.11	—Mental Incapacity	251
8.12	—Children	254
8.13	—Husband and Wife	258
8.14	—Conviction of Crime	262
8.15	—Religious Belief	264
8.16	Competency of Judge as Witness	265
8.17	Competency of Juror as Witness	267
8.18	Summary	271

Evidence via Witness Testimony **273**

Chapter 9
Examination of Witnesses 275

Section
9.1	Introduction	277
9.2	Essential Qualities of a Witness	278
9.3	Oath or Affirmation Requirement	281
9.4	Judicial Control of Testimony	283
9.5	Separation of Witnesses	285
9.6	Direct Examination of Witnesses	288
9.7	—Leading Questions	289
9.8	—Refreshing Memory—Present Memory Revived	293
9.9	—Past Recollection Recorded	297
9.10	Cross-Examination of Witnesses	300
9.11	Redirect and Recross-Examination	305
9.12	Impeachment of Witnesses	306
9.13	—Own Witness	308
9.14	—Bias or Prejudice	310
9.15	—Character and Conduct	312
9.16	—Conviction of Crime	316
9.17	—Prior Inconsistent Statements	321
9.18	—Defects of Recollection or Perception	323
9.19	—Use of Confession for Impeachment Purposes	324
9.20	Rehabilitation of Witness	326
9.21	Summary	328

Chapter 10
Privileges 331

Section
10.1	Introduction	333
10.2	Reasons for Privileged Communications	337
10.3	Communications Between Husband and Wife	338
10.4	Communications Between Attorney and Client	351
10.5	Communications Between Physician and Patient	362
10.6	Communications to Clergy	368
10.7	Confidential Informant Privilege	372
10.8	State Secrets and Other Official Information	376
10.9	News Media-Informant Privilege	380
10.10	Summary	386

Chapter 11
Opinions and Expert Testimony   389

Section
11.1   Introduction   391
11.2   Definitions and Distinctions   392
11.3   Admissibility of Nonexpert Opinions   394
11.4   Subjects of Nonexpert Opinions   397
11.5   Opinions of Experts   411
11.6   Qualifications of an Expert   415
11.7   Selection of Expert Witness   417
11.8   Examination of Expert Witness   419
11.9   Cross-Examination of Expert Witness   422
11.10   Subjects of Expert Testimony   425
11.11   Experts From Crime Laboratories   443
11.12   Summary   444

Chapter 12
Hearsay Rule and Exceptions   447

Section
12.1   Introduction   449
12.2   Definitions and Statement of the Hearsay Rule   452
12.3   History and Development of the Hearsay Rule   458
12.4   Exceptions to the Hearsay Rule—General   459
12.5   —Spontaneous and Excited Utterances   460
12.6   —Business and Public Records   466
12.7   —Family History and Records (Pedigree)   473
12.8   —Former Testimony   477
12.9   —Dying Declarations   480
12.10   —Declarations Against Interest   484
12.11   —Other Exceptions—Residual Exceptions   490
12.12   Nontestimonial Utterances   494
12.13   Summary   497

Evidence via Documents and Real Evidence   499

Chapter 13
Documentary Evidence   501

Section
13.1   Introduction   503
13.2   Authentication   504
13.3   Self-Authentication   510
13.4   Methods of Authentication   515

13.5   Specific Examples of Documentary Evidence   517
13.6   Best Evidence Rule   522
13.7   Secondary Evidence   525
13.8   Summaries   530
13.9   Learned Treatises   534
13.10   Summary   535

Chapter 14
Real Evidence   537

Section
14.1   Introduction   539
14.2   Admissibility Requirements   541
14.3   Exhibition of Person   548
14.4   Articles Connected with the Crime   549
14.5   View of the Scene   560
14.6   Photographs   562
14.7   Motion Pictures and Videotapes   571
14.8   X-rays   575
14.9   Sound Recordings   576
14.10   Diagrams, Maps, and Models   580
14.11   Courtroom Demonstrations and Experiments   582
14.12   Preservation and Disclosure of Evidence Favorable to the Defense   583
14.13   Summary   584

Chapter 15
Results of Examinations and Tests   587

Section
15.1   Introduction   589
15.2   Examination of the Person   593
15.3   Intoxication Tests   594
15.4   Blood Grouping Tests and Blood Comparisons   603
15.5   Polygraph Examinations   604
15.6   "Truth Serum" Results   612
15.7   Fingerprint Comparisons   615
15.8   Ballistics Experiments   618
15.9   Speed Detection Readings   620
15.10   Neutron Activation Analysis   625
15.11   Deoxyribonucleic Acid (DNA) Tests   627
15.12   Other Examinations and Tests   630
15.13   Summary   632

Exclusion of Evidence on Constitutional Grounds **635**

Chapter 16
Evidence Unconstitutionally Obtained   637

Section
16.1   Introduction   639
16.2   Development of the Exclusionary Rule   640
16.3   Search and Seizure Exclusions   642
16.4   Exclusion of Evidence Obtained by Illegal Wiretapping
        or Eavesdropping   665
16.5   Exclusion of Confessions Obtained in Violation   668
        of Constitutional Provisions   668
16.6   Self-Incrimination and Related Protections   676
16.7   Due Process Exclusions   679
16.8   Right to Counsel as it Relates to the Exclusion of Evidence 680
16.9   Summary   684

PART II
Judicial Decisions Relating to Part I   **687**

Table of Cases in Part II   689

Glossary   **861**

Appendix I
Federal Rules of Evidence for United States Courts and Magistrates   **871**

Appendix II
Table of Jurisdictions in which Uniform Rules of Evidence
have been Adopted—2009   **895**

Appendix III
Table of Contents
Uniform Rules of Evidence with 2005 Amendments   **897**

Table of Cases   **901**

Index   **947**

PART I

History and Approach to Study

History and Development of Rules of Evidence

1

The fundamental basis upon which all rules of evidence must rest—if they are to rest upon reason—is their adaptation to the successful development of the truth.

Funk v. United States, 290 U.S. 371 (1933)

Chapter Outline

Section

1.1   Introduction

1.2   Early Attempts to Determine Guilt or Innocence

1.3   Modern Legal Systems—Romanesque System

1.4   —Anglican System

1.5   Development of the Rules of Evidence in the United States

1.6   Application of the Rules of Evidence in State and Federal Courts

1.7   Future Development of the Rules of Evidence

1.8   Summary

§ 1.1 Introduction

Observers of criminal trials are often confused by the procedures concerning the admission and exclusion of evidence. The form of the objections offered and the arguments presented only add to the confusion. Logically assuming that the purpose of a trial is to seek the truth, the lay observer is likely to be bewildered by objections to the introduction of apparently relevant evidence. Sometimes evidence that could have a direct bearing on the case is, in fact, excluded at the trial. To understand why certain evidence is admitted and other evidence is excluded, it is necessary to study the history and evolution of the rules of evidence.

§ 1.2 Early Attempts to Determine Guilt or Innocence

Through the ages, humankind has sought fair methods of reaching the truth in criminal cases. Each culture arrived at a method that was congenial to that culture. Some of these systems of determining guilt or innocence were ridiculous and often barbaric. However, history has helped succeeding generations to develop systems that are more workable.

Every tribe and every people devised a system for protecting the lives and property of its citizens. Authorities noted, however, that there were only a few that developed a well-defined, organized, continuous body of legal ideas and methods that could be called a legal system. According to Wigmore, 16 legal systems developed to a stage at which they could be recognized as a legal system: Egyptian, Mesopotamian, Chinese, Hindu, Hebrew, Greek, Maritime, Roman, Celtic, Germanic, Church, Japanese, Mohammedan, Slavic, Romanesque, and Anglican.[1] Although all of these systems had some effect on modern evidence rules, only a few of the older systems have been selected for discussion, because they represent systems that were adopted in part by other cultures and eventually led to our judge-jury system, which in turn was responsible for our rules of evidence. Some of the procedures that developed under these systems are gone, while some remain.

A. Egyptian Legal System

In the Egyptian system (the oldest of the systems listed above) the court was made up of 30 judges chosen from the states that constituted Egypt. The defendant was advised in writing of the charges against him or her, and he or she was authorized to answer each charge in writing by: (1) asserting that he or she did not do it; (2) stating that if he or she did it, it was not wrongful; or (3) if it was wrongful, it should bear a lesser penalty than that advocated by his or her accusers. It is interesting to note that at this time (beginning at approximately 4000 B.C.) all formal proceedings of the court were conducted without speeches from advocates. It was believed that speeches of advocates would cloud the legal issues, and those speeches, combined with the cleverness of the speakers, the spell of their delivery, and the tears of the accused, would influence many persons to ignore the strict rules of law and the standards of truth.[2]

The Greek historian Diodorus describes the procedure developed by the Egyptians as follows:

> After the parties had thus twice presented their case in writing, then it was the task of the thirty judges to discuss among themselves their judgment and of the chief justice to hand the image of truth to one or the other of the parties.[3]

B. Mesopotamian Legal System

Under the early Mesopotamian system, the king was the fountain of justice, receiving the law from divine guidance. But under King Hammurabi, approximately 2100 B.C., the system envisioned the king as the source of law under which the king could personally administer justice or allow local governors or courts of law to handle the matters.[4] The Mesopotamian system did not operate with police or a prosecutor, but the judges, who were originally royal priests, found the facts from the evidence and applied the law.[5] A record of the trials of this period indicates that the judges called upon the accusers to "produce

---

[1]　For a complete, interesting, and informative study of the world's legal systems, see WIGMORE, A PANORAMA OF THE WORLD'S LEGAL SYSTEMS (1928).

[2]　WIGMORE, A PANORAMA OF THE WORLD'S LEGAL SYSTEMS (1928).

[3]　KOCOUREK & WIGMORE, SOURCES OF ANCIENT AND PRIMITIVE LAW, EVOLUTION OF LAW SERIES (1915).

[4]　99 MIL. L. REV. 1 (1983).

[5]　Id.

witnesses or instruments to show guilt." The judges then examined the facts and reached a conclusion as to guilt or innocence. This perhaps was the origin of the modern use of testimony and real evidence.[6]

C. Hebrew Legal System

Under the Hebrew legal system, in the early periods rabbis developed the law. The law was tied closely to religion and the judges were considered to act with divine authority. The Pentateuch, which consists of the five books collectively known as the Torah, served as the central foundation of the Hebrew legal system from approximately 1200 B.C. to 300 B.C.[7] When the Jewish people came under the control of the Persian, Greek, and Roman rulers, they continued to have their own court system. Individual jurists made the decisions because there appears to be no record of the use of a jury, or of counsel to represent the defendant.[8]

D. Chinese Legal System

One of the earliest recorded legal systems in the world is the Chinese legal system, beginning before 2500 B.C. It is unique in that it is the only system that survived for approximately 4,500 years, until the country was taken over by the communists during the twentieth century. Under the ancient Chinese system, there was little difference between civil law and criminal law, because the Chinese believed in the existence of the natural order of things, or the law of nature, and considered the written law good only if it was a correct translation of the law of nature. One person—from emperor down to magistrate—made the decision concerning guilt or innocence. Under the Chinese system, there was little distinction between morality and law, and in determining guilt or innocence. The Chinese legal system employed no lawyers as we know them now. There were notaries and brokers, but no licensed professional class. Only judges made the decisions, but higher courts were permitted to review these decisions.[9]

E. Greek Legal System

Unlike the systems previously discussed, under the early Greek legal system a jury determined whether a person charged with a crime was guilty. According to the records, in Athens in approximately 500 B.C., a jury list of about 6,000 names was drawn up. Ordinarily a panel of 201 names was drawn by lot, but for special cases a panel might consist of as many as 1,000 or 1,500

---

6   Wigmore, *supra* note 2.

7   Summum v. City of Ogden, 152 F Supp. 2d 1286, 2001 U.S. Dist. Lexis 12760, n. 10 (2001). *See* The Panorama of the World's Legal Systems at 104 and 107.

8   Wigmore, *supra* note 2.

9   *Id.*

people. At the trial of Socrates in approximately 400 B.C., 501 jurors voted and found a verdict of guilty by a majority of only 60. In one period in Greek history, the decision of guilt or innocence was entirely in the hands of nonprofessionals. The presiding magistrate was selected by lot and the jurors were drafted from the whole citizen body. Under this system, the defendant conducted his or her own defense and presented his or her own evidence. There was no presiding judge to declare the law, and there was no appeal.[10]

F. Roman Legal System

The Roman instinct for constitutional and legal ideas produced the best and most well-developed system of law. Because this system had the greatest influence on modern evidence law, it is discussed in greater detail.

The Roman legal system can be divided into three periods: the Period of the Republic, the Period of the Early Empire, and the Period of the Later Empire. During the Period of the Republic, the Romans began a code that was chiefly procedural. Even this early period, approximately 400 B.C., has influenced the law of the present day. During this period, the lay courts were made up of judges both of law and of fact, there was little judicial discretion, and there was no appeal. Under this early system, the decision of the tribunal that first tried the case was final.

During the Early Empire Period, professional judges and jurors came to the forefront, while the culmination of Roman judicial science was reached in the second and third centuries A.D. By this time, the Roman legal system had developed far beyond that of any earlier civilization. The administration of justice was separated from general political administration, and schools of law were started for the training of lawyers. Also during this period records of cases were kept and, according to Wigmore, these court records were of a type strikingly similar to those later kept in England.

During the Period of the Later Empire (approximately 550 A.D.), Justinian undertook to reduce the enormous bulk of laws to manageable form. The results were the famous *Pandects* (or *Digest*), the *Code*, the *Institute*[11] and the *Novels*. *Black's Law Dictionary* defines the *Pandects* as "[t]he 50 books constituting Justinian's *Digest* (one of the four works making up the *Corpus Juris Civilis*) first published in A.D. 533."[12] The *Code* collected the laws and constitutions of the Emperor Justinian and contained 12 books. The Code is another of the four works that are part of the *Corpus Juris Civilis*.[13] The *Institute* was an "elementary treatise on Roman law in four books."[14] The Institute was also one of the four component parts of the *Corpus Juris Civilis*. The *Novels* are a collection of

---

[10] *Id.*

[11] *Id.*

[12] *See* BLACK'S LAW DICTIONARY (2004).

[13] *Id.*

[14] *Id.*

168 of the constitutions issued by Emperor Justinian and subsequent emperors that collectively make up the final component of the *Corpus Juris Civilis*.[15]

Jurisprudence had been one of the most advanced of Roman sciences, and it perished with the fall of the Roman government. As other civilizations appeared and evolved, the legal concepts developed by the Romans, including the use and admissibility of evidence, strongly influenced the later legal procedures. As a matter of fact, Quintilian's teachings, recorded about A.D. 68 to 88, contained legal precepts that are pertinent today and reveal how little the nature of legal practice has changed in 2,000 years. Some of the evidence rules, such as those relating to the testimony of witnesses and preparation of real and documentary evidence, are still valid today.

Thus we have examples of ancient systems in which guilt or innocence was determined by professional judges without the assistance of a jury, and examples of procedures in which the determination was made entirely by laypersons who were not instructed in the law. In some civilizations, the legal systems were well developed, while in others the administration of justice was a farce, with the person or group in power making decisions concerning life and liberty without guidelines or precedent.

Not only have the experiences of other cultures affected our own evidence rules today, but they have also served as guides for other modern systems and surely will be considered during future attempts to reach just and fair methods of administering justice.

§ 1.3   Modern Legal Systems — Romanesque System

From the world's 16 systems as described by Wigmore, three primary world systems exist today. These systems have spread beyond the country and people of their origin. These are the Romanesque, the Anglican, and the Mohammedan. The two that are most dominant in modern times and of most importance in Western civilization are the Romanesque and Anglican.

Approximately five centuries after the Roman Empire fell, the law texts that were prepared by Roman scholars were resurrected and became the basis of the legal system in Italy, then in many other countries in Europe, and finally far beyond Europe. In Italy, the city of Bologna became the center of the study of the Roman law, and legal scholars arrived from all over Europe. During the 1200s, 1300s, and 1400s, thousands of foreign students carried the new advanced ideas of the Roman law to the countries of Europe. Faculties of law sprang up in Spain, France, Germany, and the Netherlands. Roman law, or a modification of it, was codified and nationalized.

In the early 1800s, after three centuries of effort, France completed civil, criminal, and commercial codes and developed rules of civil and criminal

---

[15]   *Id.*

procedure. Freedom of contract, recognition of private property and family solidarity were the three ideological pillars of the *Code Napoleon*.[16] Napoleon himself presided at many of the debates and his wishes shaped the code.[17] This so-called Code Napoleon was soon translated into almost every language, and set the fashion in the other European countries. The Code Napoleon of 1804 served as the basis for Louisiana law[18] and remains a strong influence both in principles and in legal terminology. It was adopted in Austria in 1811, the Netherlands in 1838, Italy in 1865, Spain in 1888, Germany in 1898, and Switzerland in 1907. The Code had taken eight centuries from the resurrection of the Roman law in the 1100s to the final formation of the Romanesque law in the 1800s.

When the Romanesque system was first developed, the judges established the rules for gathering and admitting evidence and were the finders of fact as well as the law. At first there were few rules of evidence, but eventually a complex set of rules for obtaining and weighing evidence evolved. As often happens, these rules became merely restrictive—that is, they were not guides, but self-sufficient formulas.

The restrictive rules of evidence became so overdeveloped that they were abolished as being a mere hindrance. To replace this system, the continental nations of France, Germany, and Italy adopted a system that allowed a judge to hear and weigh any evidence, without limitations. Although certain rules have developed in recent times to limit the type and amount of evidence to be considered in this judge-directed system, there are no elaborate controlling rules, such as have been developed in the Anglo-American system. A main reason for this is that the judge's discretion, even when a jury is used, largely determines what evidence will be admitted.

The Romanesque system is now used in many countries throughout the world, from Quebec to Cairo and Budapest to Buenos Aires. Millions of people now live under this system, and of the three world systems today, the Romanesque system is the most extensive. In 1928, it governed almost one-sixth of the world's inhabitants.[19]

§ 1.4   – Anglican System

Unlike the other countries of Europe, England rejected the Romanesque legal system. Like other systems, the Anglican legal system developed in several phases. The first of these was the Period of Building a Common Law; the second was the Period of Rejection of the Romanesque Law; the third was the Period of Cosmopolitanization and Expansion.

---

[16]   Gallo v. Gallo, 861 So. 2d 168, 173, 2003 La. LEXIS 3448, n.6 (2003).

[17]   WIGMORE, A PANORAMA OF THE WORLD'S LEGAL SYSTEMS (1928), at 1031.

[18]   Madisonville Boatyard, Ltd. v. Poole, 2001 U.S. Dist. LEXIS 20589 (E.D. La. 2001). *See also* Pepper v. Triplet, 864 So. 2d 181, 189, 2004 La. LEXIS 151 (2004).

[19]   WIGMORE at Chapter XV.

The early methods of determining guilt or innocence in England were crude by our modern standards. For example, one kind of trial known as "trial by battle" was brought to the British Isles by William the Conqueror in 1066. Instead of a formal trial before a judge, the accused was required to fight his or her victim or the victim's representative. This method of trial continued until the 1800s, when Parliament finally passed an act abolishing it.[20] The case that finally brought trial by battle to the attention of Parliament involved a man who was accused of murdering his sweetheart. He claimed the right of trial by battle. The judges, after considering the law in the matter, agreed that this type of trial had never been abolished. They therefore allowed the accused to select this type of trial. The brother of the deceased refused to fight the accused, and the accused went free.

Following the Norman Conquest, the Norman judges organized the jury to assist in their investigation. However, jurors were not selected as unbiased triers of fact, as is the practice today, but were selected because they had knowledge of the case. An ordinance of Henry II in the twelfth century provided that a certain number of jurors should be selected in criminal cases; it specified that jurors be knights.[21] In contrast to modern procedure, the prospective juror was excused if he was ignorant of the facts of the case. The jurors were first left to their own discretion in the use of evidence and were allowed to go among the people in the community and ask for information outside of court. During this period, the jurors were forbidden to call in outside witnesses. However, starting in approximately 1500, witnesses were used more frequently, and gradually the requirement that the triers of the facts possess knowledge of the crime came to be less important. By the end of the 1600s, the jury was allowed to receive no information except that which was offered in court. Initially, the jury served as a substitute for trial by battle, compurgation, and ordeal,[22] but during this period, it evolved into a body that listened to evidence and used logic to render a verdict. Thus, in a period of three or four hundred years, there was a complete reversal of the juror's role.

Given the development of the jury system and the English tradition of protecting the rights of the individual, the need for guidance was obvious. Both the judges and the laymen who participated in the trial recognized that the jurors must have guidance to prevent them from being misled by false testimony or by evidence that was not relevant to the issue. Accordingly, in the 1600s and 1700s, numerous exclusionary rules were developed that kept certain kinds of evidence from the jurors unless the evidence met various tests,

---

[20]   Tracy, Handbook of the Law of Evidence (1952).

[21]   *Id.*

[22]   Crist v. Bretz, 437 U.S. 28, 36, 1978 U.S. LEXIS 107, n.12 (1978). Black's Law Dictionary (2004) refers to compurgation as a trial where a defendant could bring friends, frequently numbering 11, to state that they believed the defendant was telling the truth. It explains that ordeal was a "primitive form of trial in which an accused person was subjected to a usually dangerous or painful physical test, the result being considered a divine revelation of the person's guilt or innocence."

as determined by the judge. These rules of admissibility were based upon long judicial experience with parties, witnesses, and jurors. The purpose of these rules was to allow the jury to consider only evidence that was as free as possible from the risks of irrelevancy, confusion, and fraud.[23]

The Anglican system is now followed in England, Scotland, and Ireland; Sri Lanka, Hong Kong, and some other countries in Asia; to a great extent in India and some African countries; Canada and, of course, the United States. From the very beginning, the American colonies followed English law. For example, part of Virginia's plan in 1606 was that "the disposing of all causes happening within the colonies should be done as near to the common law of England and the equity thereof as may be."[24]

§ 1.5   Development of the Rules of Evidence in the United States

During the past two centuries, a system of rules for the presentation of evidence has been established in the United States. In some instances, the rules are the result of centuries of deep thought and experience. In other instances, the rules have been established in a haphazard manner without much thought. Although the United States inherited the English system, rules concerning the admissibility of evidence have taken separate developmental paths and are not the same in the two countries. Federal evidence rules are not necessarily the same in the various states within the United States and even states that have adopted a version of the Federal Rules of Evidence have some different interpretations. Due to legislation and court decisions, some of which interpret constitutional provisions, the rules for obtaining and weighing evidence are now more restrictive in the United States than in England.

Certainly the rules are not perfect and are always subject to change— either by the courts or by statute. As stated in *Funk v. United States*:

> The fundamental basis upon which all rules of evidence must rest if they are to rest upon reason is their adaptation to the successful development of the truth. And, since experience is of all teachers the most dependable, and since experience also is a continuous process, it follows that a rule of evidence at one time thought necessary to the ascertainment of the truth should yield to the experience of a succeeding generation whenever that experience has clearly demonstrated the fallacy or unwisdom of the old rule.[25]

The rules of evidence are changed not only by court decisions, but also by congressional or legislative enactments. For example, in 1878, Congress

---

[23]   WIGMORE ON EVIDENCE 5 (1935).

[24]   *Id.*

[25]   290 U.S. 371 (1933). *See* case in Part II.

changed federal law to allow a defendant in a federal criminal case to be a witness at his own request, but included a provision that where a defendant did not desire to testify, no negative presumption could be drawn.[26] In Illinois, the legislature provided, under the Sexually Dangerous Persons Act, that evidence of a defendant's prior crimes and punishments, if any, may be admitted against a defendant[27] despite a general rule against admitting a defendant's past criminal acts in a subsequent proceeding. More recently, Congress has enacted specific legislation relating to the admissibility of confessions, wiretap evidence, and eyewitness testimony.[28]

A. *Adoption of the Federal Rules of Evidence*

In an effort to obtain more uniformity in court procedures, the United States Supreme Court in 1972 adopted the Rules of Evidence for United States Courts and Magistrates. Congress initially blocked their effective use until it was satisfied with the wording of the rules. Subsequently, in 1987, the scope of these rules was extended to include proceedings before United States bankruptcy judges.[29]

A study of the development and application of this set of rules demonstrates how rules of evidence are changed by legislative action. The Supreme Court order of November 20, 1972, directed the federal district courts and United States magistrates to follow these rules after July 1, 1973. However, in accordance with federal laws, the proposed rules were required to be transmitted to Congress for approval. The House Judiciary Committee wrestled with the provisions for nearly a year, and finally approved a modified version in early 1974 by a vote of 377 to 130. Before approving the Supreme Court draft of the rules of evidence, the House Judiciary Committee changed provisions concerning privileged communications. The current enhancement of the Federal Rules of Evidence became effective in December 2006; however, some revisions are pending but not yet effective.

In explaining the purpose and construction of the Federal Rules of Evidence, the drafters included this comment:

> These rules shall be construed to secure fairness in administration, elimination of unjustifiable expense and delay, and promotion of growth and development of a law of evidence to the end that the truth may be ascertained and proceedings justly determined.[30]

---

[26] *See* Reagan v. United States, 157 U.S. 301, 305 (1878). "By the Act of March 16, 1878, c. 37, 20 Stat. 30, a defendant in a criminal case may, 'at his own request but not otherwise, be a competent witness.'" The modern version can be found at 18 U.S.C. § 3481 Competency of accused. (2006).

[27] *See* 725 ILCS 205/5 (2006).

[28] *See* 18 U.S.C. §§ 2515 and 2518 (2006).

[29] Federal Rules of Evidence, Title 28 United States Code (1972). These rules, updated through 2005 by Congress, are included as Appendix I and are referred to throughout this text.

[30] FED. R. EVID. 102.

The adoption of the Federal Rules of Evidence has contributed to establishing a uniform body of law. However, there is some doubt that the adoption of the rules has achieved the goal of simplicity that its drafters envisioned.[31]

B. *Uniform Rules of Evidence*

As Congress worked toward adoption of the Federal Rules of Evidence, the National Conference of Commissioners on Uniform State Laws prepared new Uniform Rules of Evidence patterned after the Federal Rules. In 1999, the Commissioners approved an updated draft of the Uniform Rules of Evidence that reflected recent amendments to the Federal Rules. This codification of evidence laws was designed and suggested for adoption by the state legislatures and has been periodically revised to keep it in fair conformity with the Federal Rules,[32] which federal courts have followed since 1975.

To avoid confusion and encourage uniformity, the numbering systems for the two sets of rules are consistent. As the Federal Rules have been changed by Congress, the Commissioners on Uniform State Laws have made an effort to bring the Uniform Rules into conformity.

As the evidence rules followed in the federal and state courts of the United States today are products of a combination of legislative acts (as discussed in previous paragraphs) and court decisions, a study of evidence requires an examination of federal and state legislation and the cases interpreting the rules.

§ 1.6   Application of the Rules of Evidence in State and Federal Courts

The history of the United States and the separation of powers concept have influenced the legislative bodies and courts in establishing evidence rules. As a general rule, questions of evidence are governed by the laws of the forum, i.e., the state rules of evidence apply in state courts, and the federal rules apply in federal courts. If the state has jurisdiction over the parties and the cause of action, the rules of evidence and the laws of that state generally will apply.

The United States Constitution gives Congress the power to make regulations guiding the Supreme Court and to create tribunals inferior to the Supreme Court. The rules of evidence established by Congress are to be followed in federal courts. However, no codification of rules can be applied without court interpretation. Therefore, one must carefully examine federal cases, especially United States Supreme Court cases, in applying the law governing the admissibility of evidence in federal courts.

---

[31]   WIGMORE ON EVIDENCE § 6.5 (1988).

[32]   Uniform Rules of Evidence (1999). National Conference of Commissioners on Uniform State Laws. The Table of Contents for the Uniform Rules of Evidence is included in the Appendix.

While the legislation of each jurisdiction is supreme, and state rules of evidence provide general guides in state courts, legislation is subject to such limitations as may be prescribed in federal constitutional provisions applicable to the states. For example, the United States Supreme Court has determined that a state rule requiring that a defendant desiring to testify in a criminal case must do so prior to the admission of any other defense testimony violates the Fifth Amendment to the Constitution and the due process clause of the Fourteenth Amendment.[33] Also, where constitutional authority exists, Congress may establish rules relating to the admissibility of evidence in state courts. Demonstrative of such principle is the Omnibus Crime Control and Safe Streets Act of 1968—Title 18 of the United States Code—which provides that evidence relating to a wire or oral communication that has been intercepted in violation of that section shall not be used "in or before any court, grand jury, department . . . or other authority of the United States, state or political subdivision thereof."[34]

Even though the adoption of the Federal Rules of Evidence and the Uniform Rules of Evidence has not achieved the goal of simplicity that the drafters envisioned, these rules have produced more uniformity and consistency. Because the Federal Rules of Evidence regulate evidentiary matters in all federal courts of the United States, including bankruptcy courts and proceedings held before United States magistrate judges, uniformity has been accomplished to a substantial degree in the federal system. With recognition that our nation is based on a federalist system, there naturally is far less uniformity among the states. At one point, only 36 jurisdictions had adopted evidence codes that followed the model of the Federal Rules and/or the Uniform Rules patterned after the Federal Rules.[35] Currently, 42 states as well as Guam, Puerto Rico, the Virgin Islands, and the United States military have adopted evidence codes based partially or completely on the Federal Rules of Evidence.[36] California, Georgia, Illinois, Kansas, Massachusetts, Missouri, New York, and Virginia have not adopted a version of the Federal Rules.[37] The District of Columbia has not adopted the Federal Rules of Evidence for the District's courts, but the Federal Rules, of course, apply in federal courts sitting within the District of Columbia.[38]

---

[33] Brooks v. Tennessee, 406 U.S. 605 (1972).

[34] For a more thorough discussion of the powers of the federal and state governments, see Kanovitz & Kanovitz, Constitutional Law, ch. 1 (11th ed. 2008).

[35] Charles W. Gamble, *Drafting, Adopting and Interpreting the New Alabama Rules of Evidence: A Reporter's Perspective*, 47 Ala. L. Rev. 1, n. 55 (1995).

[36] See 6-T Weinstein's Federal Evidence, "Table of State and Military Adaptations of Federal Rules of Evidence." (Matthew Bender 2006). The Appendix contains a list of states that have adopted the Uniform Rules of Evidence with the effective dates and the statutory citations.

[37] *Id.*

[38] *Id.*

Because the Federal Rules of Evidence have had a major impact on state laws and evidence rules, and because the states have increasingly looked to federal decisions for interpretations, provisions of the Federal Rules of Evidence and federal cases interpreting the Federal Rules are cited throughout this text.[39]

The Federal Rules and the Uniform Rules have generated a reform of the evidence rules. However, the states have not given up their independence on evidence issues. State courts are free to interpret evidentiary rules in a manner different from federal courts and interpretations offered by the courts of sister states. To develop a more comprehensive understanding of the rules, state cases as well as federal cases are cited and examined. Nevertheless, because some state evidence rules differ from both the Federal Rules and the Uniform Rules, it is necessary to consult the laws and decisions of the state that has jurisdiction over the parties.[40]

§ 1.7　Future Development of the Rules of Evidence

In studying rules of criminal evidence, it must be recognized that our rules are a product of progressive growth and adaptation to new circumstances. The rules of evidence will continue to change and, in fact, probably will change more rapidly in the next several years as judicial officials and members of legislatures attempt to fashion a more effective system to meet the needs of an evolving society. Evidence rule changes may reflect some new pressing social needs such as allowing admission into evidence of prior sexual offenses by a defendant when other offenses might not be admissible.[41] Alterations to the Dead Man's statutes indicate that the old fears of fraud by witnesses against the dead have been overblown and the usual avenues of cross-examination may work perfectly well.[42] It may be that admitting evidence of prior sex offenses will be seen as unfair and will later be rejected, while changes to the Dead Man's statutes will be seen as appropriate for the ages and will have lasting effects.

Demonstrative of evolutionary development of the rules and interpretations of the rules of evidence is the change made to the marital testimonial privilege recognized by federal courts. Prior to *Trammel v. United States*,[43] both husband and wife were considered holders of the testimonial privilege and could prevent the other from testifying against a defendant spouse. The original theory involved the protection and promotion of marital harmony. The Supreme Court reasoned that if "one spouse is willing to testify against the other in a criminal proceeding—whatever the motivation—their relationship

---

[39]　The Federal Rules of Evidence, as amended, are included in Appendix I.

[40]　For a comprehensive coverage of the differences in state rules and interpretations, see Joseph & Saltzburg, Evidence in America, the Federal Rules in the States (1994).

[41]　29 HAMLINE L. REV. 177 (2006).

[42]　53 CLEV. ST. L. REV. 75 (2005).

[43]　444 U.S. 40, 1980 U.S. LEXIS 84 (1980).

is almost certainly in disrepair; there is probably little in the way of marital harmony for the privilege to preserve."[44] In such a situation, in federal courts, the old rule had to give way to the modern interpretation of the marital testimonial privilege favoring admissibility of the testimony offered by a willing witness spouse.

The application of the rules of evidence to the administration of the law is and should be within the sound discretion of the judiciary. However, contrary to statements made in some cases, recent decisions of reviewing courts appear to require more strict application of the rules of evidence, thus leaving lower courts with less discretion concerning the administration of the business of the court and the admissibility of evidence.

Acts of Congress have effects on the admission of evidence and executive branch orders may have some similar effects in other types of proceedings. Following the attacks of September 11, 2001, Congress passed the USA PATRIOT Act, which changed some of the ways in which the federal government is permitted to collect and use evidence.[45] Although the PATRIOT Act was designed to make the nation safer from terrorist activity, some civil libertarians became concerned that the new powers granted to federal law enforcement could have the effect of curtailing some civil rights. Among other things that affect the use or admission of evidence in some cases, the President of the United States issued an Executive Order that limited some indictments, jury trials, and other civil liberties of some non-citizen individuals accused of terrorist activities.[46] The same Executive Order directed that the defense secretary issue orders that purported to limit admission of evidence in special tribunals in cases of trials of international terrorists.[47] However, the Foreign Intelligence Surveillance Act of 1978 authorized some evidentiary searches prior to obtaining a warrant, but the statute anticipated that a warrant would be forthcoming in most cases. The Act excluded the use of any evidence unlawfully obtained through illegal electronic searches and surveillance.[48] Congress passed the Omnibus Crime Control and Safe Streets Act of 1968, which included a Title III section that regulated the manner in which wiretap evidence could be admitted in court. As part of Title III, the Congress provided that evidence seized illegally in violation of the statute would not be admissible in courts or other venues.[49] In another adjustment of search and seizure law, the Congress amended the Foreign Intelligence Surveillance Act by passing relevant provisions of the Patriot Act that had the effect of limiting the use of the Foreign Intelligence Surveillance Act for domestic law enforcement purposes.[50] In summary, the Congress has adjusted

---

[44]   *Id.* at 52.
[45]   PUB. L. NO. 107-56, 115 STAT. 272 (2001).
[46]   51 AM. U.L. REV. 1081 (2002).
[47]   *Id.*
[48]   82 B.U.L. REV. 555 (2002).
[49]   *Id.*
[50]   28 HARV. J.L. & PUB. POL'Y 319 (2005).

the admission of seized evidence through statutory enactments that mirrored public policy initiatives of interest groups and to accommodate the needs of the executive branch. The general thrust has been to allow more evidence to be admitted into court when the legal proceeding involved terrorism or related criminal matters.

Have the restrictive rules of evidence become overdeveloped? Perhaps our society has reached the point where some of the rationales for exclusionary rules are no longer valid and the rules no longer provide appropriate results. However, it would prove unwise to abolish our system entirely, as was done in France in the 1700s. Appropriate changes should be made by the courts and legislatures after careful study and with regard to the objectives to be achieved. Therefore, not only is it necessary that all who are involved in the criminal justice system be aware of the rules of evidence as they exist today, but everyone must also be familiar with the history of the rules, keep up with changes as they occur, and take an active part in recommending improvements when time and events have dictated that changes need to be made to some of the current rules of evidence.

§ 1.8 Summary

In every society efforts have been made to determine the guilt or innocence of a person charged with violating the rules of that society. Some of the world's legal systems were built on sound foundations and have continued for many centuries. However, other legal systems disappeared when the governments responsible for developing them were overthrown, or when governments developed other methods for determining guilt or innocence. The experience of history has proven to be a strong teacher that has preserved evidence of prior legal systems so that nations today can harness the knowledge of the past to help the law of evidence evolve in a productive path toward the future.

In England, after centuries of experimentation, a system for determining guilt or innocence developed by utilizing parts of earlier systems. With the development of the jury system, a complex set of rules for determining the admissibility of evidence gradually developed. Although a jury system patterned after that of England was adopted by the United States, the rules for admitting the evidence have been changed by our courts and legislative bodies. Today, the rules of exclusion are stricter in the United States than in England.

The rules for determining the admissibility of evidence have changed and will continue to evolve. In this country, judges, legislators, and other criminal justice personnel must work together to seek better methods for determining guilt and protecting society, while at the same time protecting the rights of the individual.

Approach to the Study
of Criminal Evidence   2

The word "evidence" is applied to that which renders evident; and is defined to be any matter of fact, the effect, tendency, or design of which is to produce in the mind a persuasion, affirmative or disaffirmative, of the existence of some other matter of fact.

State v. Ward, 61 Vt. 153, 17 A. 483 (1889)

Chapter Outline

Section
2.1   Introduction
2.2   Definitions
2.3   Reasons for the Rules of Evidence
2.4   Reasons for Excluding Evidence
2.5   Rules of Evidence in Criminal Cases Compared to Rules of Evidence in Civil Cases
2.6   Pretrial Flow of Evidence
2.7   Use of Evidence at the Trial
2.8   Consideration of Evidence on Appeal
2.9   Use of Evidence at the Probation Hearing
2.10 Use of Evidence When Considering Parole
2.11 Summary

§ 2.1   Introduction

Before searching the cases and statutes for evidence guidelines on specific issues such as the admissibility of hearsay evidence or the exclusionary effect of evidentiary privileges, developing an understanding of the general concepts and definitions will prove invaluable. Rational thought and history have shaped the rules regulating the admissibility of evidence, while similar reasoning and fairness have provided the justifications for excluding pertinent evidence. The overall goal of the rules of evidence is to produce the truth while reducing the chance for falsehood. A knowledge of these rules and the rationale used by the courts in framing the rules that exclude some evidence assists immeasurably in understanding the specific rules of evidence. Under the Anglican system (with the jury deciding the facts), evidence is not admitted when it would be unfairly prejudicial to the accused.

Although the rules of evidence generally apply in both civil and criminal cases, there are some important differences that are of special interest to those involved in criminal justice. These differences are discussed in this chapter. In addition, the flow and use of evidence from the time it is located, processed, and analyzed by the investigator to the time it is considered by the parole board are discussed. In Chapter 4 the use of evidence at the trial is more particularly considered.

§ 2.2 Definitions

In order to fully understand the discussion of the rules of evidence, it is necessary to define some of the words and phrases used. Other words or phrases are defined in future chapters as they are discussed.

A. Evidence

Evidence has been defined as *the means employed for the purpose of proving an unknown or disputed fact*, and it is either judicial or extrajudicial. Every determination of the judgment, whatever its subject may be, is the result of evidence.[1] Evidence is any information upon which a person can base a decision. For example, before a used car is purchased, the car dealer is questioned as to the condition of the car, and in some instances, the car is taken to another mechanic for an inspection. All of this information, or evidence, is then considered before a decision is reached as to whether the purchase will be made.

B. Legal Evidence

Legal evidence is defined in *Black's Law Dictionary* as "[a]ll admissible evidence, both oral and documentary, of such a character that it reasonably and substantially proves the point, rather than merely raising suspicion or conjecture."[2] Legal evidence is that which is used or is intended to be used at the trial or at inquiries before courts, judges, commissioners, referees, etc. To state this more succinctly, evidence as used in law means "that which demonstrates or makes clear or ascertains the truth of the very fact or point in issue, either on the one side or the other."[3]

C. Direct Evidence

Direct evidence is "evidence that is based on personal knowledge or observation and that, if true, proves a fact without inference or presumption."[4] Direct evidence has been defined as "evidence that demonstrates the existence or non-existence of a precise fact and issue without the need to draw inferences or apply presumptions."[5] For example, a witness testifies that he saw the acts that constituted the precise fact to be proved. If, in a homicide case, the witness testifies that he saw the accused stab the victim, this would be direct evidence.

---

[1]   RICE, LAW OF EVIDENCE (1893).

[2]   BLACK'S LAW DICTIONARY (8th ed. 2004).

[3]   Leonard v. State, 100 Ohio St. 456, 127 N.E. 464 (1919), quoting Blackstone. (3 BLACKSTONE'S COMMENTARIES 367).

[4]   BLACK'S LAW DICTIONARY (8th ed. 2004).

[5]   Yancy v. State, 2009 Ala. Crim. LEXIS 38 (Ala. 2009), quoting J. COLQUITT, ALABAMA LAW OF EVIDENCE § 1.0 at 2 (1990).

D. Circumstantial Evidence

Circumstantial evidence, sometimes called indirect evidence, is so called because the truth is discovered through inferences of probabilities arising from an association of facts. Circumstantial evidence has been defined as "that which is applied to the principal fact, indirectly, or through the medium of other facts, from which the principal fact is inferred."[6] One judge stated that the only difference between direct and circumstantial evidence is that direct evidence is more immediate and has fewer links in the chain of connection between the premise and the conclusion. An example of circumstantial evidence would be the testimony of a police officer that he apprehended a subject who had a bag of money that had been covered in red dye from an exploding dye pack. It should be noted that circumstantial evidence has the same value, force, and weight as direct evidence.[7]

E. Testimony

Testimony is evidence that comes to the court through witnesses speaking under oath or affirmation. In some instances, the word *testimony* is used synonymously with the word *evidence*. It is obvious when considering the two words, however, that testimony is limited to that which is oral, while evidence includes writings, physical objects, and other forms. Evidence is the broader term and includes testimony, which is only one type of evidence.[8]

F. Documentary Evidence

Documentary evidence consists of tangible objects that have the capacity to convey a fact or to establish the truth or untruth of a proposition at issue. Documentary evidence includes all types of traditional documents, records, photographs, pictures, X-ray images, drawings, audio- and videotapes, as well as writings that are not objectionable under the various exclusionary rules.[9] Modern methods of storing information have expanded the concept of documentary evidence to include e-mail, computer diskettes, memory sticks, flash drives, hard drives, and optically stored information. With documentary evidence, it is the object or thing that speaks to offer evidence. "Evidence supplied by a writing or other document, which must be authenticated before the evidence is admissible."[10] A ransom note in a kidnapping case and a printout from a Web site in a child pornography prosecution are examples of documentary evidence.

---

[6]   People v. Smith, 168 Cal. App. 4th 7, 2008 Cal. App. LEXIS (Cal. 2008), quoting People v. Rivera, 109 Cal. App. 4th 1241, 1244, 2003 Cal. App. LEXIS 903 (Cal. 2003).

[7]   United States v. Ortiz, 447 F.3d 28, 32, 2006 U.S. App. LEXIS 10961 (1st Cir. 2006).

[8]   31 C.J.S. *Evidence* § 3 (1964).

[9]   *See* Fed. R. Evid. 1001.

[10] BLACK'S LAW DICTIONARY (8th ed. 2004).

G. Real Evidence

Real evidence, or "physical" evidence, has been defined as *a fact, the existence of which is perceptible to the senses*. As compared to an intangible concept, real evidence possesses a physical essence and existence that can be observed, touched, and handled. A clearer definition is "physical evidence (such as a knife wound) that itself plays a direct part in the incident in question."[11] Real evidence also includes weapons or implements used in the commission of a crime as well as evidence of the physical appearance of a place (as obtained by a jury when the members are taken to view a crime scene).

H. Prima Facie Evidence

Prima facie evidence is the body of evidence that, if unexplained, uncontradicted, or not called into question, is sufficient to carry a case to the jury and to sustain a verdict in favor of the issue that it supports. Prima facie evidence will support a ruling in favor of the offering party if no contrary evidence is produced by the opposing side.[12] The phrase *prima facie* means "at first sight" or "on the first appearance" or "on the face of it." Prima facie evidence is "evidence that will establish a fact or sustain a judgment unless contradictory evidence is produced."[13] For example, where there was testimony that a defendant was observed at the crime scene, such testimony, if believed, would be prima facie evidence that the defendant was present. Such prima facie evidence exists unless or until contradictory evidence is introduced by the opposing side.

I. Proof

Proof is the effect of evidence; that is, it is *the establishment of fact by evidence*. Even though the terms *proof* and *evidence* are sometimes used synonymously, they are different. Properly speaking, evidence is only the medium of proof; proof is the effect of evidence. Proof implies persuasion and proof has been defined as "the conviction or persuasion of the mind of a judge or a jury, by the exhibition of evidence, of the reality of a fact alleged."[14]

J. Cumulative Evidence

Cumulative evidence is *that which goes to prove what has already been established by other evidence*. Montana offers this definition: " 'Cumulative evidence' is additional evidence of the same character to the same point."[15] In legal phraseology, it means evidence from the same or a new witness that simply repeats, in substance and effect, or adds to, what has already been

---

[11] *Id.*

[12] Krinsky v. Doe, 159 Cal. App. 4th 1154, 2008 Cal. App. LEXIS 180 (Cal. 2008).

[13] BLACK'S LAW DICTIONARY (8th ed. 2004).

[14] Ellis v. Wolfe-Shoemaker Motor Co., 227 Mo. 508, 55 S.W.2d 309 (1932).

[15] MONT. CODE ANNO., 26-1-102 (2007). (Current through April 14, 2009).

offered in court. For example, where 10 people witnessed a defendant assault a person on a public street, to have all 10 come to court and render virtually the exact same story identifying the defendant could be considered cumulative evidence. Having two or three witnesses explain what was observed would generally be appropriate and not be considered cumulative evidence.

K. Corroborative Evidence

Corroborative evidence is *evidence that is supplementary to evidence already given in court*. It tends to strengthen or confirm previously admitted evidence. It is additional evidence of a different character, but it seeks to prove the same point as the earlier evidence. (For example, historically, a conviction cannot stand based solely upon a defendant's confession without corroborating evidence.) Such corroborating evidence may be the testimony of a witness who saw the accused at the scene of the crime. Similarly, evidence from a conspirator made during the existence of the conspiracy may provide corroborating evidence of the crime that will permit the use of the confession.

L. Relevant Evidence

Relevant evidence is *evidence that has any tendency to make the existence of any fact that is of consequence to the determination of the action more probable or less probable than it would be without the evidence*.[16] Kansas defined relevant evidence as "evidence having any tendency in reason to prove any material fact."[17] To be considered relevant, the evidence must help one party prove or disprove a fact while not being unfairly prejudicial to the opposing party's case. Evidence of a past conviction to help prove guilt might help the prosecution gain a conviction, but the admission of the evidence of the prior conviction might result in a conviction because the jury thought the defendant was a bad person.

M. Material Evidence

Material evidence is *that which goes to the substantial matters in dispute or has a legitimate and effective influence or bearing on the decision of the case*. Material evidence has been defined as "[e]vidence having some logical connection with the facts of consequence or the issues."[18] A Tennessee court noted that "substantial and material evidence has been defined as such relevant evidence as a reasonable mind might accept to support a rational conclusion and such as to furnish a reasonably sound basis for the action under consideration."[19]

---

[16] FED. R. EVID. 401; For further discussion concerning relevant evidence, see Chapter 7.

[17] K.S.A. § 60–401(b) Definitions. (2008).

[18] BLACK'S LAW DICTIONARY (8th ed. 2004).

[19] Webster v. Univ. of Tennessee, 2008 Tenn. App. LEXIS 413 (Tenn. 2008), citing Jones v. Bureau of Tennecare, 94 S.W.3d 495. 500, 501 (Tenn. 2002). Internal quotation marks omitted.

N. Competent Evidence

Although the terms *relevancy*, *competency*, and *materiality* are frequently used conjunctively, a matter may be relevant and material to an issue but still be incompetent, and therefore inadmissible under the established rules of evidence. Competent evidence is *evidence that, in legal proceedings, is admissible for the purpose of proving a relevant fact*. The competency of evidence depends on whether it is of the sort or type that may be accepted on any issue to which it is relevant.[20] Evidence may be made competent (or incompetent) by legislation or judicial construction.[21]

O. Hearsay Evidence

"'Hearsay' is *a statement, other than one made by the declarant while testifying at the trial or hearing, offered in evidence to prove the truth of the matter asserted*."[22] An in-court witness's statement based upon what someone else has told him or her outside of court, and not from personal observation or knowledge of the original facts, constitutes hearsay evidence. In Virginia, hearsay has been defined as oral testimony or written evidence of a statement presented in-court but made out of court, where the statement is being presented to show the truth of the matter being asserted and resting its value on the credibility of the out-of-court declarant.[23] As a general rule, hearsay evidence is not admissible unless it meets an exception to the rule that excludes such evidence. Where an eyewitness has explained to a police officer that the witness observed the defendant breaking into a store, the officer would generally not be permitted to tell the court what the witness told the officer because such testimony would constitute hearsay evidence if offered by the police officer for proof of its truth.

§ 2.3   Reasons for the Rules of Evidence

By the seventeenth century, the evolution of the jury function was well advanced, and the jury depended on the testimony of witnesses for facts on which to base a verdict. Members of juries were generally ordinary laypeople, impressionable and unacquainted with the law; it was therefore recognized that specific rules for filtering the evidence were necessary. To protect the accused, rules were gradually developed to help assure that evidence was dependable, credible, and trustworthy before it could be considered. Evidentiary rules developed, in part, to keep out untrustworthy evidence or

---

[20]   Maddox v. News Syndicate Co., 176 F.2d 897 (2d Cir. 1949).

[21]   Funk v. United States, 290 U.S. 371, 64 S. Ct. 212, 78 L. Ed. 2d 369 (1933).

[22]   FED. R. EVID. 801(c); For further definitions of hearsay and terms related to hearsay evidence, *see* Chapter 12.

[23]   Baker v. Commonwealth, 2009 Va. App. LEXIS 75 (Va. 2009). Unpublished opinion.

unfairly prejudicial evidence. To achieve order and decorum it was necessary for courts to establish rules to carry out the proceedings in an efficient manner. To meet these objectives, courts and legislatures have formulated our present-day evidentiary rules.

Efforts have been made to state in more specific terms the reasons for the rules of evidence and to account for the many varied rules that must be interpreted by the courts. As these rules have been developed by gradual evolution and in fact are still developing, it is difficult to categorize them and to explain why each rule exists. Although it appears that in some instances there is an effort to rationalize or justify an outmoded or outdated rule, there is logic to the explanations given for most of the specific rules of evidence.

§ 2.4   Reasons for Excluding Evidence

Much evidence is excluded even though it would help the jury or the court in determining the true facts concerning the matters at issue. The reasons for excluding the evidence have been numerous and they are phrased in many ways. An effort is made here to categorize these reasons in order to make them more meaningful and understandable. The general reasons for excluding otherwise pertinent evidence are listed below.

A. Protect Interests and Relationships

A court weighs the value of having all of the facts before the court against the protection of certain interests and relationships, and it may decide to exclude relevant evidence. Such interests and relationships are regarded, rightly or wrongly, as having sufficient social importance to justify some incidental sacrifice of sources of fact needed in the administration of justice.[24] Protecting interests and relationships by the exclusion of otherwise relevant evidence may also harm the search for the truth. Examples of evidence excluded on the basis of this public policy of protection of relationships are:

1. Evidence protected by the husband and wife confidential communication privilege.
2. Evidence protected by the husband and wife testimonial privilege.
3. Evidence protected by the attorney-client privilege.
4. Evidence protected by the penitent-confessor privilege.[25]

B. Avoid Undue Prejudice to the Accused

Some evidence that would be relevant to the issue is not admitted because of the risk that it might create undue or unfair prejudice to the defendant's

---

[24] McCORMICK, EVIDENCE § 72 (4th ed. 1992).
[25] Testimonial privileges are discussed in Chapter 10.

case. For example, the criminal record of the accused generally is not admitted, except to impeach the testimony of the accused, because to admit this evidence would unfairly and unduly prejudice the accused in the minds of the jurors. Evidence that might indicate the guilt of the accused would be appropriate for admission, but to allow evidence of prior crimes might cause the jury to convict based on the evidence of the prior crimes and not on evidence concerning the case presently in court. In some situations, evidence might have such a low level of relevance that to allow its admission would create undue prejudice by changing the outcome in a defendant's case.[26] In some cases, gruesome photographs may be excluded from evidence, even though relevant, because admitting them might inflame the jury with unfair prejudice against the accused.

C. Prohibit Consideration of Unreliable Evidence

Evidence considered to be unreliable is generally excluded from admission in court, even though it might have a bearing on the case. This category of evidence includes hearsay evidence and most lay witness opinion evidence.[27] To illustrate, the testimony of a police officer that a bystander told him that the accused was driving the car that had been involved in a bank robbery is not admissible. Such evidence is considered hearsay and, although it possesses some relevance, is not considered sufficiently reliable for use in court.

D. Reduce Violations of Constitutional Safeguards

In order to ensure respect for constitutional provisions regulating search and seizure as well as to ensure respect for other constitutional rights, the Supreme Court of the United States, in the latter half of the twentieth century, developed rules of exclusion to be applied when evidence has been illegally seized. Until the beginning of the previous century, it was almost universally accepted that evidence was admissible even though it was obtained illegally.[28] However, because of later interpretations of the federal and state constitutions, the courts now reason that such evidence secured by an illegal search and seizure, evidence obtained in violation of the self-incrimination provisions, or evidence taken in violation of the right-to-counsel provisions, should generally be excluded, even though relevant to the case. In fact, such evidence might provide the only basis for a conviction.[29] The rationale for excluding such evidence has not been consistent, but generally, exclusion has been justified on the ground that by rejecting such evidence, there will be little incentive for law enforcement officials to violate the Constitution in an effort to obtain incriminating evidence.

---

[26] *See* State v. Anthony, 218 Ariz. 439, 2008 Ariz LEXIS 123 (Ariz. 2008). *See* case in Part II.

[27] These rules are discussed in Chapters 11 and 12.

[28] *See* Weeks v. United States, 232 U.S. 383 (1914).

[29] Constitutional rationales for excluding evidence are discussed more thoroughly in Chapter 16.

E. Conserve Time

Cumulative evidence is evidence that is unnecessary and repetitive, and thus may be excluded upon proper objection by one of the parties or upon the court's own motion. The admission of cumulative evidence would otherwise constitute a waste of the court's time as well as the time of the individuals involved. Rejection of cumulative evidence is consistent with and follows the principle of judicial economy.

There have been arguments that some of the historical reasons for excluding relevant evidence have long since disappeared, leaving the technical rules without a logical basis. In some instances, so many exceptions have developed that the rules are no longer meaningful. However, most of the justification for the rules is still valid and should be carefully considered, because understanding the reasons behind the rules can help one to understand their application.

§ 2.5   Rules of Evidence in Criminal Cases Compared to Rules of Evidence in Civil Cases

An early English court stated that there is no distinction between the rules of evidence in criminal and civil cases. The court continued:

> What may be received in the one case, may be received in the other; and what is rejected in the one ought to be rejected in the other. A fact must be established by the same evidence, whether it is to be followed by a criminal or civil consequence.[30]

In some states, the civil rules of evidence have been made applicable in criminal cases by case law or by statute unless otherwise provided.[31] For example, a Washington statute holds that "[t]he rules of evidence in civil actions, so far as practicable, shall be applied to criminal prosecutions."[32] The Federal Rules of Evidence "govern proceedings in the courts of the United States and before bankruptcy judges and United States magistrate judges,"[33] subject to some exceptions. There are, however, some differences in the current rules and in the application of the rules of evidence that arise solely, or more frequently, in criminal cases. Constitutional law cases that regulate how and when a suspect or arrestee may be questioned have produced rules relating to admission or exclusion of evidence in criminal cases that have no comparable

---

[30]   Rex v. Watson, 2 Stark. 116 (1817); Lord Melville's Case, 29 How. St. Tr. 763 (1806).

[31]   MCLS. § 768.22 (1) Rules of evidence; applicability of criminal and quasi criminal proceedings; evidence of prior conviction. (Matthew Bender 2009). "The rules of evidence in civil actions, insofar as the same are applicable, shall govern in all criminal and quasi criminal proceedings except as otherwise provided by law."

[32]   REV. CODE WASH. (ARCW) § 10.58.010 (Matthew Bender 2009).

[33]   FED. R. EVID. 101.

place in civil cases.[34] In addition, evidence produced by searches and seizures may be excluded on federal or state constitutional grounds where police conduct failed to meet constitutional standards.[35]

In civil cases, the contending parties negotiate through the legal process on terms of approximate equality, with no legal presumption favoring the plaintiff or defendant. In criminal cases, the law seeks to protect the person accused of a crime, and a presumption accompanies him or her from the time of apprehension to the moment of conviction: the presumption that he or she is innocent until proven guilty. Throughout the trial, the burden of proof remains on the state, and the prosecution must prove guilt beyond a reasonable doubt, rather than by a preponderance of the evidence.[36] Because of this presumption of innocence, courts have developed special rules for overcoming the presumption.

In addition to requiring the government to meet a higher (or greater) standard of proof in a criminal prosecution, the rules differ in a few other instances. For example, where a victim in a homicide case makes a statement concerning the manner in which death-threatening injuries were received and who caused the injuries, older rules indicated that the dying declarations were only available in prosecutions for the homicide. However, the newer rules, based on the Federal Rules of Evidence, do not require that the victim actually die and the declaration is also admissible in civil cases.[37] The doctor-patient privilege operates differently in many jurisdictions depending on whether the case is civil or criminal and, to some degree, whether the need for the evidence is great.[38]

Although many state civil juries operate with fewer than 12 jurors, the majority of criminal cases operate with 12 jurors and require unanimous verdicts. Although the degree of proof is higher in criminal cases, except for some affirmative defenses,[39] the accused must be found guilty by all 12 members of the jury, but in civil cases, a unanimous decision may not be required. Logic suggests that it should be easier to obtain a money judgment against a defendant in a civil case than to send a defendant to jail or prison in a criminal case. For example, a defendant who has been acquitted in a criminal assault prosecution may be found liable for a monetary judgment in a subsequent civil case brought by the original victim based on the conduct that was the subject of the criminal case.

---

[34]   *See* Miranda v. Arizona, 384 U.S. 436, 1966 U.S. LEXIS 2817 (1966).

[35]   *See* Mapp v. Ohio, 367 U.S. 643, 1961 U.S. LEXIS 812 (1961).

[36]   Apprendi v. New Jersey, 530 U.S. 466 at 483 (2000).

[37]   OHIO EVID. R. 804(B)(2) (Matthew Bender 2009).

[38]   *See* O.R.C. ANN. § 2317.02 (Matthew Bender 2009). *See also* Wyo. Stat. § 1-12-101 (2008).

[39]   *See* Johnson v. Louisiana, 406 U.S. 356 (1972), which upheld a conviction in a criminal case in which the state statute provided that 9 of 12 jurors may find the defendant guilty. *But see* Burch v. Louisiana, 441 U.S. 130 (1979), which held that a state defendant who has been placed on trial for a nonpetty offense and is subsequently convicted by a nonunanimous six-person jury has been denied his right to a trial by jury.

Although the distinction between criminal evidence and civil evidence may be slight when defining the rules, from a practical standpoint there is a great deal of difference. While a jury may accept weak evidence in determining the rights of parties in a civil case, the members of the jury are less likely to accept such evidence when life or liberty is at issue. To the prosecutor, this means that evidence must be presented that will be given great weight by the jury, and sufficient evidence must be presented in court to overcome any reasonable doubt on the part of the jury or judge. In a criminal case, the judge must protect the rights of the defendant. Circumstances or conduct that may call a judge's impartiality into question may result in an appellate court reversing a conviction.[40]

§ 2.6   Pretrial Flow of Evidence

Although much valuable evidence is made available in court by laypersons who are not connected with the criminal justice process, in most instances police officers and investigators are responsible for discovering, evaluating, protecting, analyzing, and presenting evidence. If the officer does not present the evidence herself, she is still primarily responsible for guiding the flow of evidence, at least until the indictment or information stage.

The officer must develop and preserve the evidence in such a way as to maximize its usefulness in subsequent proceedings. For example, at the beginning of an investigation, if names and addresses of witnesses to a crime are not recorded by the officer, this information may be lost forever. The techniques of sound criminal investigation are outside the scope of this text, but it bears repeating that the failure to properly gather and preserve the available evidence affects all subsequent proceedings.

The Federal Rules of Criminal Procedure and the rules of criminal procedure of all states require an officer making a warrantless arrest to take the arrestee before the nearest available judicial official without unnecessary delay.[41] The officer at this first appearance is not required to present sufficient evidence to convict, but must produce sufficient evidence for the judge or magistrate to determine whether there is probable cause[42] to believe that an offense has been committed and that the accused committed the offense.[43]

Following a review of the evidence, if the judicial official determines that there is probable cause to hold the arrestee for further proceedings or to have

---

[40]   State v. Tody, 2009 Wisc. LEXIS 21 (Wis. 2009). Appellate court reversed when judge's mother sat as a juror in the judge's court.

[41]   See County of Riverside v. McLaughlin, 500 U.S. 44 (1991); *see also* Fed. R. Crim. P. 5.

[42]   Probable cause has been shown "If the facts and circumstances before the officer are such as to warrant a man of prudence and caution in believing that the offense has been committed, it is sufficient." Carroll v. United States, 267 U.S. 132, 161, 1925 U.S. LEXIS 361 (1925).

[43]   *See* Chapter 16 for a discussion of evidence needed to determine probable cause for the issuance of a search warrant.

the case presented to a grand jury in a felony case, the officer must make available all of the evidence that he or she has collected, together with names and pertinent information, to the prosecutor. Although the prosecutor may and should enter into the case at an earlier time, this is usually the step where the prosecutor takes charge.

In many jurisdictions, in order to move the case toward trial, the prosecutor must present the evidence to a grand jury in order to procure an indictment. With the consent of the arrested defendant, the prosecution may be initiated with the use of an information. Prosecutors in many states are not required to obtain a grand jury indictment, but may file an information against the defendant. The prosecution must have sufficient evidence to demonstrate probable cause for a grand jury, and in the case of using an information, the prosecutor must believe that the evidence indicates the existence of probable cause. One might argue—and with justification—that the process of determining probable cause before a judge or magistrate and then presenting the evidence to a grand jury for a probable cause determination seems redundant. The first presentation of the evidence involved the judicial system making the initial determination of probable cause rather than allowing a suspect to be held to answer for a crime solely by the executive branch in the absence of judicial involvement.

The prosecutor controls the proceedings in front of the grand jury proceeding, but again, he or she must, in almost every case, call on the officer-investigator and other witnesses to offer testimony before the grand jury. While sufficient evidence must be presented to a grand jury that will allow it to conclude that probable cause exists to believe a particular person has committed a particular crime, the formal evidence rules are not followed when presenting evidence to the grand jury.[44] However, sufficient admissible evidence must be presented to convince the grand jury (usually 12 to 23 persons) that an offense against the state has been committed by the person accused.

In some states, where neither the state constitution nor state law requires a grand jury indictment, process by way of information can substitute for the grand jury hearing. The prosecutor, using the evidence presented by officers and other witnesses, evaluates the evidence to determine whether probable cause exists. Where probable cause exists and where the prosecutor concludes that a prosecutable case exists, the prosecutor makes the decision to prepare the information, files it with the proper court, and serves notice to the accused of the specific charge.

Following the return of the indictment or the preparation of the information, the defendant appears personally before the judge. Here, the defendant is arraigned (informed of the charges against him or her), defense counsel may be appointed, and the defendant may enter a plea. Because probable cause is not an issue to be proved at arraignment following a grand jury indictment,

---

[44] *See* United States v. John Doe, 481 U.S. 102 (1987).

there is no need for the judge to admit or evaluate evidence except when the case originated with the filing of an information. However, at the conclusion of the arraignment, the judge may suggest a time for a preliminary hearing or set a date to hear pretrial motions.

At the pretrial hearing, the defense and the prosecution may present some evidence concerning pretrial motions. Where admission of evidence at trial depends on the manner in which the evidence was seized, both sides will normally present evidence to support their respective positions. Police officers and the defendant may offer evidence of the facts surrounding the search and seizure of evidence so that the judge can determine the legality of the procedure and rule on the trial admissibility of the evidence. Often, the outcome of the suppression hearing determines the fate of both the accused and of the prosecution's case. If, for example, the judge determines that police obtained a confession illegally or that they unconstitutionally seized illegal drugs in the possession of the arrestee, the prosecutor may decide to drop the charge if the judge suppresses the evidence. Conversely, if the judge rules against the defendant at the suppression hearing, the defendant's attorney may advise him or her to consider a negotiated plea or enter a guilty plea. If there are no more pretrial motions or legal issues to be resolved, the case is ready for trial.

§ 2.7   Use of Evidence at the Trial

Even before the trial, the evidence acquired by the police officer, the prosecutor, or by other means, already has been considered several times. Assuming that there has been sufficient evidence to indict the defendant, the case eventually comes before the court and the jury at the trial. By this time, there is a good possibility that some evidence has been found inadmissible by the court. If so, the prosecutor must determine whether there is still enough admissible, relevant evidence to meet the burden of proof beyond a reasonable doubt.

In addition to the parties on each side, the court is made up of the judge, jury, witnesses, prosecutor, and defense attorney.[45] In early English proceedings, the jurors were the only witnesses and were called upon by the judge to give information concerning the case because they had knowledge of the facts. However, the modern juror ideally should have no knowledge of the case, and certainly no firsthand knowledge of the facts. The jury determines what facts have been proved after it has heard the evidence presented by the witnesses, evaluated the facts judicially noticed by the judge, and has considered the inferences and presumptions as instructed by the court.

The trial judge has the duty, upon proper objection, to determine whether a particular item of evidence is relevant, material, and competent, and whether the item should be admitted or excluded from jury consideration. Generally,

---

[45]   State v. Perkins, 130 W. Va. 708, 45 S.E.2d 17 (1947). In Chapter 4, the procedure for introducing and considering evidence at trial is presented in more detail.

a judge may ask questions of a witness, but the judge must be careful not to appear to favor one party over the other.[46] At the close of the case, when all the evidence has been heard, the trial judge's duty is to instruct the jury concerning the law applicable to the case. In a bench trial (without a jury), the judge continues to make evidentiary rulings and takes on the additional role of the trier of fact in determining guilt or innocence.

The prosecutor has the responsibility to evaluate all evidence presented to him or her, to determine the legality of the evidence, to arrange the evidence in sequence so that it is best suited to achieve the objective, to identify the witnesses for the prosecution, to examine the witnesses, and to cross-examine defense witnesses.

Finally, the defense attorney is responsible for seeking evidence with which to present a defense for the accused. The defense attorney also arranges the evidence in the sequence most likely (in his or her opinion) to convey the defendant's legal position to the finders of fact. Defense counsel has the opportunity to introduce, examine, and cross-examine witnesses. Even in a case that from the beginning appears to be hopeless, the defendant has the right to "put the prosecution to its proof" by pleading not guilty and going to trial.

§ 2.8   Consideration of Evidence on Appeal

If the jury or the judge acquits the defendant at the trial, the state has no right to appeal the acquittal in a way that would affect any rights of the defendant.[47] The prohibition against double jeopardy mandates this result. If, however, the defendant is convicted, he or she may appeal the conviction, and the appellate court may examine what occurred in the trial court and reverse the conviction, with or without granting the state the opportunity to retry the defendant. As a general rule, "The presumptions on appeal are all in favor of the validity of the judgment of the trial court,"[48] and, therefore, an appellate court will uphold the guilty verdict unless there were clear legal errors or the evidence was insufficient to meet the government's burden of proof. However, if evidence has been wrongly admitted or improperly excluded in a manner that may have affected the outcome of the trial, an appellate court will often reverse the conviction with directions to retry the case. When a defendant succeeds in having a conviction overturned on appeal, the state may appeal to a higher appellate court in an effort to overturn the lower appellate court and have the trial verdict reinstated. Changes in the application of the rules of evidence change gradually and may result in different outcomes as newer cases

---

[46]   *See* Craft v. State, 274 Ga. App. 410, 2005 Ga. App. LEXIS 778 (Ga. 2005). *See* case in Part II.
[47]   *See* Benton v. Maryland, 395 U.S. 784, 1969 U.S. LEXIS 1167 (1969).
[48]   Hoffman v. Gregory, 2005 Ark. LEXIS 135 (Ark. 2005).

reach appellate courts. For example, in *Trammel v. United States*, the Supreme Court approved a change in the old rule that a spouse could not testify against another spouse without that spouse's consent.[49] When the Court revisited the logic behind the rule that a defendant spouse could prevent the other's adverse testimony, it approved the new interpretation offered by the trial court.

§ 2.9   Use of Evidence at the Probation Hearing

Even after the determination of guilt or innocence, the judge may make additional use of evidence in determining whether the person who has been found guilty will be placed on probation or incarcerated. In many jurisdictions, a probation/parole officer will conduct a presentence report. The general rules of evidence that limit the use of evidence at the trial do not apply to the use of the presentence report by the judge. Although this presentence report should be factual, evidence such as hearsay evidence is not excluded from the report. However, it is obvious that this evidence is available only for determining the disposition of the person who has been convicted of a crime and that it cannot be used in determining guilt or innocence. Where a person has been granted probation that may have to be revoked, similar evidentiary policies control the use of evidence at a revocation hearing. When revoking federal probation, the rules of evidence, except those governing privileges, have no application.[50]

While in most states the probation report or presentence investigation report is confidential and available only to the judge, some jurisdictions require that the pre-sentence report be made available for inspection by the offender or by the defense attorney.[51]

§ 2.10   Use of Evidence When Considering Parole

State parole boards consider evidence when determining whether a person who has served time in an institution merits conditional release under the supervision of a parole officer. After making a complete investigation in the field, a parole officer prepares a report that covers the personal position of the convict and his or her history while in custody, among other factors. Once a person has been granted parole, the individual must meet the conditions of release. When the parolee fails to adhere to the required conditions, the conditional freedom may be revoked, consistent with due process. Since parole revocation hearings

---

[49]   Trammel v. United States, 445 U.S. 40, 1980 U.S. LEXIS 84 (1980). *See* case in Part II.

[50]   United States v. Aspinall, 389 F.3d 332, 344, 2004 U.S. App. LEXIS 23954 (2d Cir. 2004) and FED. R. EVID. 1101(d)(3).

[51]   *See* CARLSON, CRIMINAL JUSTICE PROCEDURE (7th ed. 2005).

are not considered criminal prosecutions, the rules of evidence do not apply at those types of hearings[52] or reports,[53] the information compiled serves as important evidence that assists a parole board.

§ 2.11 Summary

In a criminal case, the objective is to gather all of the evidence, whether favorable or unfavorable to the prosecution, that will help the trial court and the reviewing courts to reach the truth and dispose of the case according to law. Although it would appear that all relevant evidence should be admitted, after long empirical investigation, the courts have determined that certain evidence should be excluded. The rules for excluding evidence are generally justified on the grounds that they prevent waste of time and confusion, protect certain interests and relationships, avoid undue and unfair prejudice to the accused, prevent the jury from considering unreliable evidence, and enforce constitutional safeguards.

Generally, there is little distinction between the rules of criminal evidence and rules of civil evidence. However, because the prosecution must prove the accused guilty beyond a reasonable doubt and because the jury verdict usually must be unanimous, a higher degree of evidence is required for proof of guilt in a criminal case.

The importance of recognizing, protecting, preserving, and evaluating evidence begins at the time that the crime is committed. Even prior to trial, the evidence plays a very important part in determining whether there are sufficient grounds for the judicial official to bind the defendant over to the grand jury and for the grand jury to determine whether there is sufficient evidence for an indictment. In some jurisdictions, an information may be filed by the prosecutor as an alternative to an indictment.

The evidence has been filtered, challenged, and evaluated prior to the time that the trial begins, but it is at the trial that evidence is of greatest importance. In a criminal case, the prosecution must introduce sufficient evidence that, together with facts judicially noticed and legal presumptions and inferences, will justify the fact finders in finding the defendant guilty beyond a reasonable doubt. At the trial, the judge, jury, witnesses, prosecutor, and defense attorney are all concerned with the admissibility and weight of evidence.

Even after the trial, reviewing courts often consider the record of evidence presented at the trial in order to determine whether a conviction should be set aside for one reason or another. A reviewing court does not reweigh the evidence, but generally confines its review to matters of law.

---

[52] State v. Abd-Rahmaan, 154 Wash. 2d 280, 111 P.3d 1157, 2005 Wash. LEXIS 461 (2005). *See* this case in Part II. *See also* Peters v. State, 984 So. 2d 1227, 2008 Fla. LEXIS 757 (Fla. 2008).

[53] Simpson v. Florida Parole Commission, 2006 U.S. Dist. LEXIS 18068 (2006).

Evidence that could not be admitted in court, as well as legally acquired evidence, may be considered by the judge to determine whether a defendant who has been convicted should be placed on probation. This evidence may also influence the judge in determining the conditions on which probation should be granted. Although the strict rules of evidence do not apply to the probation officer when obtaining information for the judge, evidence should be acquired that will help the judge to make an intelligent decision concerning the advisability of granting probation.

Finally, in jurisdictions that still allow early release on parole, evidence is again considered by the parole board in making a determination concerning whether the person who has served time in institutional custody should be granted early release. Once again, the evidence considered by the board need not meet the rules of evidence followed by a court in a trial on the merits. According to the Supreme Court of the United States, the federal exclusionary rule, which helps enforce the Fourth Amendment, does not prohibit a state parole board's use of evidence seized in violation of a parolee's rights.[54]

In the chapters that follow, the many general admissibility tests and special tests for the use of evidence are discussed more comprehensively.

---

[54] Pennsylvania Board of Probation and Parole v. Scott, 524 U.S. 357, 1998 U.S. LEXIS 4037 (1998). *And see* O'Neal v. Renico, 2005 U.S. Dist. LEXIS 31045 (E.D. Mich. 2005).

Proof by Evidence
and Substitutes

Burden of Proof 3

The term "burden of proof" imports the duty of ultimately establishing any given proposition. This phrase marks the peculiar duty of him who has the risk of any given proposition on which the parties are at issue, who will lose the case if he does not make this proposition out, when all has been said and done.

Thayer, Evidence (1898)

Chapter Outline

Section

3.1   Introduction

3.2   Definitions and Distinctions

3.3   Preponderance of the Evidence

3.4   Clear and Convincing Evidence

3.5   Beyond a Reasonable Doubt

3.6   Burden on the Prosecution

3.7   Burden to Prove All Elements of the Crime

3.8   Burden on the Accused

3.9   Burden of Proving Affirmative Defenses—General

3.10   —Alibi

3.11   —Insanity

3.12   —Self-Defense

3.13   Sufficiency of Evidence

3.14   Summary

§ 3.1 Introduction

In approaching the study of evidence logically and progressively, one starting point is to consider the task of producing evidence with which to prove the truth of a given proposition. No attorney takes a civil or criminal case to court unless there is a good chance that the ultimate proposition can be established by the proper level of proof. In a criminal case, the state has the burden of proving the guilt of the accused beyond a reasonable doubt. Therefore, the "burden of proof" is on the prosecution throughout the trial and this burden never shifts. The term denotes the duty of establishing the truth of the charge against the accused. Ascertaining the truth then becomes an important, if not the most important, objective of the court and jury.

In the criminal justice process, it is necessary that those involved understand the considerations and obligations of the parties in presenting sufficient evidence and the consequences of failing to do so. Failure on the part of the prosecution to introduce sufficient evidence, or failure to properly explain the evidence, will make it impossible for the jury (or judge, when the case is tried without a jury) to determine the truth and thus will result in a miscarriage of justice. Therefore, a thorough knowledge of the concept of burden of proof is an essential starting point on which to build an understanding of the rules of evidence.

In a civil case, the party who has the burden of establishing the truth of a given proposition is a private individual, corporation or, in some instances, a governmental unit. In a criminal case, however, the prosecution has the responsibility of establishing the truth of the charges stated in the indictment or information. The rule that imposes the burden of proving guilt of the accused beyond a reasonable doubt upon the state in criminal cases does not apply in civil actions. Therefore, the burden of proof becomes even more important when considering criminal cases than when considering civil cases.

In a criminal case, the investigator must compile evidence sufficient to convince the jury not only that the accused is guilty by a "preponderance of the evidence" but "beyond a reasonable doubt"—that is, the prosecution or the state has the burden of proving the existence of every element of the crime charged.

Recognizing this requirement, the defense can be expected to deliver an attack against the weak links in the chain, because the defense knows that if even one of the elements is not proved beyond a reasonable doubt, there can be no conviction on that specific charge.

Because there has been some confusion concerning the term burden of proof, the pertinent terms are comprehensively defined and explained in the following sections of this chapter. In other sections of the chapter, the obligation of the prosecution to prove guilt and the obligation of the accused to produce evidence in a criminal trial are discussed.

In Chapters 4, 5, and 6, rules relating to the process for establishing or ascertaining truth at the trial are defined, explained, and considered.

§ 3.2   Definitions and Distinctions

A statement of what the burden of proof is not makes it easier to frame a positive definition. First, the burden of proof does not relate to the number of witnesses, but rather to the merit and weight of the evidence produced—whether by one or many witnesses. Second, the fact that evidence is admissible in conformity with the general principles regarding admissibility, relevancy, materiality, and competency does not necessarily mean that it will be given such weight as to sustain the burden of proof. The testimony of one well-prepared, reliable witness or evidence of a documentary or real nature may result in better proof than testimony from a large number of witnesses whose credibility is suspect.

Generally, the phrase burden of proof denotes the duty of establishing the truth of a given proposition or issue. Because the term has been used somewhat loosely by some courts, the definition of burden of proof as used in law requires further explanation. To avoid confusion, the phrases burden of going forward and burden of persuasion are also defined.

A. Burden of Proof

This term is defined as "[a] party's duty to prove a disputed assertion or charge."[1] The burden of proof may also be defined as the duty upon one party to establish the truth of an issue that is important to the case by the quantum

---

[1]   BLACK'S LAW DICTIONARY (8th ed. 2004).

of evidence demanded by law. *Black's Law Dictionary* notes that the burden of proof also "includes both the burden of persuasion and the burden of production."[2] The burden of persuasion means that one party must convince the judge or jury to see the facts in a manner that favors the party who introduced the evidence, while the burden of production means that the party has a duty to introduce evidence to attempt to prove a particular point or issue. In a criminal case, the burden of proof means that the prosecution has the duty of proving the guilt of the accused beyond a reasonable doubt. This duty or burden never shifts during the course of the trial, but remains with the prosecution throughout the trial. The emphasis is on the ultimate result rather than on individual issues or questions within the case.

B. Burden of Going Forward

At the start of a criminal trial, the prosecution has the obligation to introduce evidence that will move toward meeting the burden of proof. The burden of going forward has been defined as "[a] party's duty to introduce enough evidence on an issue to have the issue decided by the factfinder, rather than decided against the party . . ."[3] This is a way of saying that the government possesses the initial burden of going forward by initiating its presentation of evidence. In a sense, at the beginning of the legal contest, the government begins the case and must start by introducing evidence that will build toward and eventually reach the level of proof beyond a reasonable doubt. If the prosecution meets the burden of going forward with the evidence and survives a defendant's request for a directed verdict, the burden of going forward with the evidence shifts to the defense to begin building its case. Demonstrative of the principle that the burden of going forward was met is a case in which the defendant had been accused of rape of a child. The prosecution, during its case-in-chief, had introduced evidence that the defendant had blood on his clothes, the child had blood in her diaper, the victim had torn flesh in the private area, and technicians found the defendant's DNA profile on a diaper. At the close of the prosecution's case, the defendant requested a directed verdict of acquittal on the theory that the prosecution had failed to meet its burden of going forward with the evidence. The reviewing court upheld the trial court's denial of the motion because the evidence, both circumstantial and direct, was sufficient for conviction of child rape if a jury would choose to believe the evidence.[4] If the defendant, in meeting the burden of going forward with the evidence, succeeds in creating a reasonable doubt in the prosecution's case, the burden of going forward will shift to the prosecution at the close of the defendant's case-in-chief. In the case of a defendant who pleads an affirmative defense such as alibi, self-defense, mistake of fact, insanity, or another legal theory,

---

[2]   *Id.*
[3]   BLACK'S LAW DICTIONARY (8th ed. 2004).
[4]   Terry v. State, 2006 Ark. LEXIS 326 (Ark. 2006).

the burden of going forward with the evidence supporting the defense initially rests on the defendant. Similarly, in a case involving a felon in possession of a firearm,[5] the defendant had the burden of going forward with evidence that he had been pardoned or had otherwise had his right to bear firearms restored. If the defendant succeeds in going forward with evidence sufficient to meet any burden of proof for that affirmative defense, the burden of going forward shifts to the prosecution to negate the defendant's proof of the defense. This is often expressed by the term burden of evidence.[6]

C. Burden of Persuasion

The burden of persuasion refers only to the burden of convincing the fact-finder of the collective truth of evidence produced by one side or the other. When the burden of persuasion has been met, the attorney will be able to refer to the evidence during closing arguments to assist the jury in understanding why his or her party should prevail and to demonstrate that his or her client's version is the truth.

When the term burden of proof is used in the following sections, the definition as stated in subsection A, *supra*, is applied.

In meeting the burden of proof, the amount of evidence varies depending on whether the case is criminal or civil and whether the case involves an affirmative defense. Generally, in a civil case, the party who initiated the lawsuit possesses the duty of establishing the truth of specific propositions and must do so by a preponderance of the evidence. However, there are some issues in civil cases that must be proved by higher degrees of proof—clear and convincing or beyond a reasonable doubt.

For example, in a civil case in which a state wants to keep a mentally ill person in custody following the end of a criminal sentence, the burden of proof required in order to meet minimal due process requirements must be greater than a preponderance of the evidence that an offender remains a dangerous person.[7] Minnesota permits sexually dangerous predators to be committed to civil custody beyond a prison term when there was clear and convincing evidence that the subject had demonstrated a "habitual course of misconduct in sexual matters and an utter lack of power to control sexual impulses."[8] Viewing matters a bit differently, Kansas chose to use the criminal burden of proof in civil cases in which it desired to commit dangerous pedophiles to civil custody beyond their criminal sentences.[9] The Kansas statute committing sexually violent predators uses the same burden of proof that the prosecution has

---

[5]   State v. Kelly, 210 Ariz. 460, 112 P.3d 682, 2005 Ariz. App. LEXIS 70 (Ariz. 2005).

[6]   *Id.* at 464 and 686.

[7]   Addington v. Texas, 411 U.S., 418, 432, 1979 U.S. LEXIS 93 (1979).

[8]   In re Civil Commitment of Barber, 2005 Minn. LEXIS 355 (Minn. 2005).

[9]   In re Care and Treatment of Ward, 131 P.3d 540, 547, 2006 Kan. App. LEXIS 296 (Kan. 2006).

in proving guilt in criminal cases—beyond a reasonable doubt.[10] These three degrees of proof are discussed and distinguished in the following sections.

§ 3.3 Preponderance of the Evidence

The plaintiff in a civil case possesses the burden of proof, which requires that the truth of the plaintiff's claim be established by a fair preponderance of the credible evidence when considered with the defendant's evidence. The preponderance standard means by the greater weight of evidence and has been stated to be anything more than 50 percent of the believable evidence, although a mathematical model often does not provide a precise analogy. The concept of preponderance of the evidence does not mean the greater number of witnesses or the greater length of time taken by either side. The phrase preponderance of the evidence refers to the quality of the evidence, i.e., its ability to convince and the weight and the effect it has on the jurors' minds.

In order for the civil plaintiff to prevail, the evidence that supports the claim must appear to the jury at least slightly more believable than the evidence presented by the opposing party. If the evidence presented by the plaintiff fails to be more believable than the defendant's evidence, or if the evidence from both sides weighs so evenly that the jurors are unable to say that there is a preponderance on the plaintiff's side, the jury must resolve the question in favor of the defendant. Because the plaintiff has the burden of proof by a preponderance of evidence in civil cases, a failure to meet the burden means that the opposing party prevails due to a failure of proof.

Some civil cases that use the preponderance standard may seem more like criminal cases in some contexts. For example, California permits persons being held civilly as sexually violent predators after the completion of that person's prison term to petition for unconditional release. The burden of proof by a preponderance has been placed on the civil detainee to prove that he or she is no longer dangerous and is entitled to release from post-conviction civil confinement.[11] The appellate court found no violation of any constitutional right in requiring an alleged sexually violent petitioner to bear the burden of demonstrating his fitness for release.

Although the preponderance of the evidence standard finds primary application in civil cases, some criminal cases use the standard for different purposes. In a California case in which the defendant pled legal insanity, the burden of persuasion for the defendant to prove insanity was only proof by a preponderance of the evidence, because insanity was not considered an element

---

[10]   Kohlsaat v. Parkersburg & Marietta Sand Co., 266 F. 283 (4th Cir. 1920) and In re Winship, 397 U.S. 358 (1970) for proof beyond a reasonable doubt as a federal constitutional requirement.

[11]   *See* People v. Force, 170 Cal. App. 4th 797, 2009 Cal. App. LEXIS 85 (Cal. 2009).

of the crime. According to the California reviewing court, the civil burden was appropriate even though the defendant argued that the prosecution should have to prove his sanity beyond a reasonable doubt.[12] In Arizona, when a defendant has introduced some evidence supporting a statute of limitations defense, the prosecution shoulders the burden by the standard of a preponderance of the evidence that the prosecution is not time barred.[13] In the death penalty phase of a capital case, North Carolina permitted the defendant to bring for jury consideration any evidence of mitigation that had been proved by the defendant by a preponderance of the evidence. This creates a reduced standard that a convicted defendant might more easily meet in avoiding the death penalty.[14] Similarly, in Ohio, to prevail using an insanity defense or any other affirmative defense, a defendant must introduce evidence to prove the existence of that defense by meeting the burden of proof by a preponderance of the evidence.[15] In approving the use of the preponderance standard for a defendant's burden in an insanity defense, the Supreme Court in Patterson v. New York noted that:

> [O]nce the facts constituting a crime are established beyond a reasonable doubt, based on all the evidence, including the evidence of the defendant's mental state, the State may refuse to sustain the affirmative defense of insanity unless demonstrated by a preponderance of the evidence.[16]

In essence, civil cases primarily use the preponderance of the evidence standard for decision-making purposes, but in a variety of contexts the civil standard has application in criminal cases, especially concerning affirmative defenses.

§ 3.4   Clear and Convincing Evidence

While the level of proof required for civil cases has been described as proof by a preponderance (greater weight) of the evidence, some aspects of civil litigation dictate a greater level of proof known as clear and convincing evidence. As one court noted, "to be clear and convincing, is somewhere between the rule in ordinary civil cases and the requirement of criminal procedure—that is, it must be more than a mere preponderance but not beyond a reasonable doubt."[17]

---

[12] People v. Farris, 130 Cal. App. 4th 773, 780 30 Cal. Rptr. 3d 426, 430, 2005 Cal. App. LEXIS 1017 (2005).
[13] See State v. Aguilar, 218 Ariz. 25, 178 P.3d 497, 2008 Ariz. App. LEXIS 44 (Ariz. 2008).
[14] State v. McNeill, 360 N.C. 231, 249, 624 S.E.2d 329, 341, 2006 N.C. LEXIS 1 (2006).
[15] O.R.C. Ann. 2901.05 (2009), State v. Hancock, 108 Ohio St. 3d 57, 62, 2006 Ohio 160, 840 N.E.2d 1032, 1043, 2006 Ohio LEXIS 215 (2006). See also Martin v. Ohio, 480 U.S. 228 (1987).
[16] Patterson v. New York, 432 U.S. 197, 206 (1977).
[17] In the Interest of B.D.-Y., a Child under the Age of 18, 286 Kan.686, 693, 187 P.3d 594, 599, 2008 Kan. LEXIS 343 (Kan. 2008).

Clear and convincing evidence is that degree of proof that "will produce in the mind of the trier of facts a firm belief or conviction as to the allegations sought to be established. It is intermediate, being more than a mere preponderance, but not to the extent of such certainty as is required beyond a reasonable doubt as in criminal cases."[18] Another way of describing the clear and convincing standard suggests that the level of proof should be evidence that:

> will produce in the mind of the trier of fact a firm conviction as to each essential element of the claim and a high probability as to the correctness of the conclusion. Proof by clear and convincing evidence requires a level of proof greater than a preponderance of the evidence or the substantial weight of the evidence, but less than beyond a reasonable doubt.[19]

The clear and convincing standard of proof defies precise definition. A Tennessee court noted that

> While it is more exacting than the preponderance of the evidence standard, it does not require such certainty as the beyond a reasonable doubt standard. Clear and convincing evidence eliminates any serious or substantial doubt concerning the correctness of the conclusions to be drawn from the evidence. It should produce in the fact-finder's mind a firm belief or conviction with regard to the truth of the allegations sought to be established.[20]

The use of the clear and convincing standard of proof was first applied to actions for fraud or deceit.[21] The rationale for employing a higher standard of proof in civil cases in which fraud or criminal conduct has been alleged implicates other concerns. Alleged civil fraud or other wrongdoing suggests that more than money may be involved in a civil case. For example, the defendant's reputation may be at risk in a defamation case or a state may be moving to terminate parental rights to an allegedly abused or neglected child based on this standard.[22]

In the case of *Addington v. Texas*, Chief Justice Warren Burger wrote "the intermediate standard, which usually employs some combination of the words 'clear,' 'cogent,' 'unequivocal,' and 'convincing,' is less commonly used, but nonetheless is no stranger to civil law."[23]

---

[18] State v. West, 2008 Ohio 1391, 2008 Ohio App. LEXIS 1210 (Ohio 2008), quoting Cross v. Ledford, 161 Ohio St. 469, 120 N.E.2d 118 (Ohio 1954).

[19] CODE OF ALA. § 25-5-81 (2008).

[20] Department of Children's Services v. K.B., 2008 Tenn. App. LEXIS 122 (Tenn 2008) quoting O'Daniel v. Messier 905 S.W.2d 182, 1995 Tenn App. LEXIS (Tenn 1995).

[21] *Appellate Review in the Federal Courts of Findings Requiring More Than a Preponderance of the Evidence,* 60 HARV. L. REV. 119 (1946).

[22] *See* In the Matter of S.H., 2008 Tenn App. LEXIS 262 (Tenn. 2008). *See also* ALASKA STAT. § 47.10.088, Involuntary termination of parental rights and responsibilities (2006).

[23] Addington v. Texas, 441 U.S. 418, 99 S. Ct. 1804, 60 L. Ed. 2d 323 (1979).

In distinguishing the levels of proof, the Supreme Court of New Jersey noted that the state's rules of evidence set forth at least "three standards of proof: a preponderance of the evidence, clear and convincing evidence, and proof beyond a reasonable doubt."[24] The court mentioned that, as a general rule, the preponderance standard applies in civil cases in which the litigant must show that the desired inference is more likely than not to be true.[25] According to the court, the second standard, clear and convincing, denotes a higher standard than proof by a preponderance and less than proof beyond a reasonable doubt.[26] This second standard should produce in the mind of the finder of fact a firm belief concerning the facts sought to be proven. In defining the beyond a reasonable doubt standard, a different court stated that it means that the evidence is sufficient that the facts asserted are almost certainly true.[27]

Lawsuits involving significant interests beyond money, such as a suit to correct a mistake in a deed or other writing, disputes involving an oral contract to make a will, to establish the terms of a lost will, and for the specific performance of an oral contract frequently dictate that sufficient proof requires clear and convincing evidence. In some states, the termination of parental rights generally requires proof by clear and convincing evidence.[28] Jurisdictions that desire to commit dangerous sexual predators to mental facilities following completed prison terms typically require the state to use a heightened level of proof, such as clear and convincing evidence.[29] Following an assassination attempt on President Reagan in 1984, Congress strengthened the federal insanity defense by requiring federal criminal defendants to prove the affirmative defense of insanity by clear and convincing evidence.[30]

§ 3.5　Beyond a Reasonable Doubt

In criminal cases, where freedom or life itself may hang in the balance, the federal constitution has been interpreted to require the highest level of proof, known as proof beyond a reasonable doubt.[31] This demanding level of certainty

---

[24]　*See* N.J. R. EVID. 101(b)(1).

[25]　Liberty Mutual Ins. Co. v. Land, 186 N.J. 163, 169, 892 A.2d 1240, 1243, 2006 N.J. LEXIS 375 (N.J. 2006).

[26]　*Id.*

[27]　Riley Hill General Contractor v. Tandey Corp., 757 P.2d 595 (Or. 1987).

[28]　State v. Sonya, 270 Neb. 870, 880, 708 N.W.2d 786, 795, 2006 Neb. LEXIS 5 (Neb. 2006). A higher standard of proof beyond a reasonable doubt is required for termination of parental rights for Indian children. *See* R.R.S. Neb. § 43-279.01 (2006).

[29]　See In the Matter of the Care and Treatment of John W. Morgan v. State, 2009 Mo. App. LEXIS 8 (Mo. 2009). See also Commonwealth v. Allen, 269 Va. 262, 609 S.E.2d 4, 2005 Va. LEXIS 23 (2005).

[30]　18 U.S.C. §§ 17, 4241–4247, and *see* § 3.11.

[31]　Clark v. Arizona, 548 U.S. 735, 2006 U.S. LEXIS 5184 (2006), quoting In re Winship, 397 U.S. 358, 1970 U.S. LEXIS 56 (1970).

requires that the prosecution prove that the accused is guilty by introducing strong and overwhelming evidence of guilt beyond a reasonable doubt. The proof presented by the prosecution must have sufficient believability and substance to rebut the strong constitutional presumption of innocence. In legal theory this means that each and every element of the offense charged in the indictment, as well as any aggravating circumstances that affect a sentence, must be proved beyond a reasonable doubt.[32] Otherwise, the accused generally must be acquitted of the charge.[33] The reality is that a jury considers all the evidence together and reaches a verdict without close judicial scrutiny concerning what the jury found on each and every element.

In 1970, the United States Supreme Court traced the history of the "beyond a reasonable doubt" requirement and concluded that this standard of proof is indispensable to command the respect and confidence of the community in applications of criminal law. In recognizing this constitutional requirement, the Court emphasized:

> Lest there remain any doubt about the constitutional stature of the reasonable-doubt standard, we explicitly hold that the Due Process Clause protects the accused against conviction except upon proof beyond a reasonable doubt of every fact necessary to constitute the crime with which he is charged.[34]

In some states, the exact wording of the charge to the jury explaining the criminal standard of proof is stated by statute. In other states, there is no requirement to explain the concept of proof beyond a reasonable doubt[35] and some do not allow any instruction on reasonable doubt. However, where a state statute contains an appropriate jury instruction, if a court reads it to a jury, it should be read exactly as it appears in the statute. For example, a California statute explaining the concept of reasonable doubt provides that:

> It is not a mere possible doubt; because everything relating to human affairs, and depending on moral evidence, is open to some possible or imaginary doubt. It is that state of the case, which, after the entire comparison and consideration of all the evidence, leaves the minds of jurors in that condition

---

[32] *See* Ring v. Arizona, 536 U.S. 584, 2002 U.S. LEXIS 4651 (2002), Scalia, J., concurring.

[33] An acquittal is not always required in federal courts where the error was harmless beyond a reasonable doubt. In Neder v. United States, 527 U.S. 1, 1999 U.S. LEXIS 4007 (1999), the Court held that failure to include an element of the crime in the charge to the jury did not necessarily result in an unfair trial.

[34] In re Winship, 397 U.S. 358, 90 S. Ct. 1068, 25 L. Ed. 2d 368, 1970 U.S. LEXIS 56 (1970). *See* case in Part II. See also Clark v. Arizona, 548 U.S. 735, 2006 U.S. LEXIS 5 (2006) in which the Court notes that all elements of criminal cases and juvenile adjudications that involve acts that would be crimes if committed by adults must be proved beyond a reasonable doubt.

[35] *See* Padilla v. State, 254 S.W.3d 585, 2008 Tex. App. LEXIS 2719 (Tex. 2008). *See also* Ex parte Gillentine, 2006 Ala. Crim. App. LEXIS 107 (2006), in which the court held that a trial judge must give an instruction on reasonable doubt and failure to do so constitutes reversible error.

that they cannot say they feel an abiding conviction, to a moral certainty, of the truth of the charge.[36]

In conveying the reasonable doubt concept to a jury, the Michigan Supreme Court voiced approval for an instruction that phrased the criminal burden of proof as:

> A reasonable doubt is exactly what it infers. A reasonable doubt is a fair, honest doubt growing out of the evidence or lack of evidence in this case; or growing out of any reasonable or legitimate inferences drawn from the evidence or lack of evidence. It is not merely an imaginary doubt or a flimsy, fanciful doubt. But, rather, it is a fair, honest doubt based upon reason and common sense.[37]

However, other courts hold not only that there is also no error in refusing to give an instruction explaining reasonable doubt, but that it constitutes reversible error to instruct the jury on the meaning of reasonable doubt. In a Wyoming arson case, the defendant attempted to have his conviction reversed because the prosecutor mentioned the concept during closing arguments when court interpretations prohibited any jury instruction covering reasonable doubt. The Supreme Court of Wyoming upheld the conviction on the theory that the prosecutor was not instructing the jury but was merely saying that there was no precise formula for reasonable doubt.[38]

In a case in which the trial judge failed to offer a jury instruction covering the concept of reasonable doubt, the defendant was convicted on lesser homicide offenses. The circuit court eventually vacated his conviction on the ground that the original trial contained "structural error" and was a nullity because the trial court failed to give the reasonable doubt instruction. The reviewing court affirmed the circuit court decision, sending the case back for a new trial.[39] When the Michigan, Wyoming, and Alabama views on reasonable doubt are considered, the result is that state courts are nowhere near a consensus on the correct way to deal with the concept of reasonable doubt in jury instructions.

Where a court offers a reasonable doubt jury instruction, whether it is required to do so by a state law or rule, the court must give the jury an instruction that meets federal constitutional standards. In *Sullivan v. Louisiana*, the United States Supreme Court decided that giving a constitutionally flawed reasonable doubt instruction is not subject to a harmless-error standard of review and requires a reversal.[40] In this first-degree murder case, the prosecution agreed that the instruction did not comply with the requisite instruction mandated by a previous case,[41] but argued that the error was harmless.

---

[36] CAL. PEN. CODE § 1096 (Deering 2008).

[37] Michigan v. Allen, 466 Mich. 86, 87, n. 1, 643 N.W.2d 227, 229, n.1 (2002).

[38] Callen v. State, 2008 WY 107, 146, 192 P.3d 137, 2008 Wyo. LEXIS 111 (Wyo. 2008).

[39] Ex parte Gillentine, 2006 Ala. Crim. App. LEXIS 107 (2006).

[40] Sullivan v. Louisiana, 508 U.S. 275, 113 S. Ct. 2078, 124 L. Ed. 2d 182 (1993).

[41] Cage v. Louisiana, 498 U.S. 39, 111 S. Ct. 328, 112 L. Ed. 2d 339 (1990).

The Supreme Court first reaffirmed that:

> What the factfinder must determine to return a verdict of guilty is prescribed by the Due Process Clause. The prosecution bears the burden of proving all elements of the offense charged, … and must persuade the factfinder "beyond a reasonable doubt" of the facts necessary to establish each of these elements. This beyond-a-reasonable-doubt requirement, which was adhered to by virtually all common law jurisdictions, applies in state, as well as federal, proceedings.

> It is self evident, we think, that the Fifth Amendment requirement of proof beyond a reasonable doubt and the Sixth Amendment requirement of a jury verdict are interrelated. It would not satisfy the Sixth Amendment to have a jury determine that the defendant is probably guilty, and then leave it to the judge to determine whether he is guilty beyond a reasonable doubt. In other words, the jury verdict required by the Sixth Amendment is a jury verdict of guilty beyond a reasonable doubt.[42]

Rejecting the prosecution's argument that the reasonable doubt instruction error was harmless, the Supreme Court reversed the judgment of the Louisiana court and remanded the case. If a federal constitutional error is to be held harmless, the reviewing court must be able to declare its conviction that the error was harmless beyond a reasonable doubt. Where a court has not been convinced beyond a reasonable doubt, the conviction under review must be reversed.

Referring to the landmark case of *In re Winship*, and reiterating that the government must prove beyond a reasonable doubt every element of a charged offense, in *Victor v. Nebraska* the United States Supreme Court in 1994 acknowledged that the proof beyond a reasonable doubt requirement of our criminal justice system defies any easy explanation. The *Victor* Court noted that both cases, *In re Winship* and *Cage v. Louisiana*, involved appeals arising from two attempts to define the concept of reasonable doubt.[43] The United States Supreme Court first restated that the "beyond a reasonable doubt" standard is a requirement of due process, but the Constitution neither prohibits trial courts from defining a reasonable doubt nor requires them to do so as a matter of course.[44] The Constitution does not require any particular form or words to be used in advising the jury of the government's burden of proof. However, when a court gives a jury instruction, it must correctly convey the concept of reasonable doubt to the jury. In addition, a jury instruction must not have the effect of shifting the burden of proof to the defendant because such an instruction relieves the prosecution of proving the case beyond a reasonable doubt.[45]

---

[42] *Sullivan* at 227, 228.
[43] Victor v. Nebraska, 511 U.S. 1, 114 S. Ct. 1239, 127 L. Ed. 2d 583 (1994). *See case* in Part II.
[44] *Id*. The syllabus of this case is included in Part II. The instructions to the jurors are included in the case.
[45] Sandstrom v. Montana, 442 U.S. 510, 523 (1979).

In *Victor v. Nebraska*, the instruction included, "[y]ou may find the accused guilty upon the strong probabilities of the case, provided such probabilities are strong enough to exclude any doubt of his guilt that is reasonable." The instruction also included, "A reasonable doubt is an actual and substantial doubt arising from the evidence." In evaluating the merits of the defendant's objection to the jury instruction, the Court noted:

> So long as the court instructs the jury on the necessity that the defendant's guilt be proved beyond a reasonable doubt, the Constitution does not require that any particular form of words be used in advising the jury of the govern-ment's burden of proof. Rather, "taken as a whole, the instructions [must] correctly convey the concept of reasonable doubt to the jury.[46]

A state or federal prosecutor is not required to prove the defendant guilty beyond all possible doubt and the Constitution of the United States does not require that any particular form or words be used in advising the jury of the gov-ernment's burden of proof or to advise the jury at all concerning the reasonable doubt standard. However, if the jury is erroneously instructed in such a manner that effectively relieves the prosecution of its burden to establish every element of guilt, automatic reversal is often required, "because it is constitutionally man-dated that the prosecution prove guilt beyond a reasonable doubt, an erroneous jury instruction on reasonable doubt is never harmless."[47] In a Maryland case, the reviewing court reversed the defendant's conviction of first-degree murder because his trial attorney failed to object to an erroneous jury instruction. The way the judge phrased the jury instruction on reasonable doubt, it could have permitted the jury to convict the defendant by a preponderance of the evidence standard or some standard lower than proof beyond a reasonable doubt.[48]

From the time a law enforcement official begins investigating and prepar-ing a criminal case, the focus is directed toward gathering sufficient evidence to meet the trial evidentiary standard of proof beyond a reasonable doubt. The standard not only applies at the trial, but also influences appellate courts reviewing a case, because they may reverse a conviction if a review of the trial court indicates an absence of proof beyond a reasonable doubt. The high level of proof necessary in criminal cases constitutes one of the fundamental differ-ences between criminal and civil cases.[49]

§ 3.6   Burden on the Prosecution

From the initiation of the prosecution and throughout the trial, the govern-ment has the burden of proof and the obligation to convince the jury or the court

---

46   *Victor*, at 5.
47   State v. McClellan, 2006 Md. App. LEXIS 103 (2006).
48   *Id.*
49   Jackson v. Virginia, 443 U.S. 307, 99 S. Ct. 2781, 61 L. Ed. 2d 560 (1979).

of the guilt of a defendant beyond a reasonable doubt. Because the due process clause of the Fifth and the Fourteenth Amendment requires the prosecution to introduce evidence that proves a defendant's guilt beyond a reasonable doubt, trial judges must be vigilant in offering jury instructions concerning proof beyond a reasonable doubt lest the instructions contain defects that might allow a jury to convict on a lower standard of proof. Although not all jurisdictions require that a trial judge give a detailed definition of proof beyond a reasonable doubt, where a judge is required or decides to offer such an instruction, it must properly explain the concept of reasonable doubt. The explanation of the standard must be offered to the jury in a way that ensures that a jury does not convict a defendant where the prosecution has introduced insufficient proof.[50] Where the crime requires proof of criminal intent, or mens rea, the responsibility rests with the prosecution to introduce evidence to prove intent. No defendant has any burden to prove innocence and a prosecutor must not imply that the defendant has any duty to disprove the case. For example, in a New York prosecution for driving while impaired, the prosecutor asked the defendant whether he asked to take a breath test in order to prove his innocence. The trial court judge overruled the defendant's objection to the question. The reviewing court reversed the conviction because the prosecutor's question improperly implied that the defendant had a burden to prove his innocence.[51] The prosecutor has a duty that prevents the government from effectively reducing its burden of proof. With the exceptions of affirmative defenses, no defendant possesses any burden of proof in a criminal trial and no defendant ever has a duty to prove that he or she did not commit the crime. Defendants do have some responsibilities during criminal trials—these will be discussed in future sections.

If the defendant pleads not guilty to a criminal charge, the defendant's plea necessarily imposes upon the government the burden of introducing proof of all the elements of the crime beyond a reasonable doubt.[52] The due process clause of the federal Constitution requires that the prosecution bear the burden of proving all of the elements of each offense charged.[53] In addition to the elements, the prosecutor must prove that the court has jurisdiction of the case and that the case is being tried in the proper venue.[54] Additionally, there must be proof that the alleged crime violated the law of the particular jurisdiction and the defendant was the person who committed the crime.[55]

The burdens on the prosecution become most clear when an appeal alleges that the government failed to prove all the elements of a crime. In an Ohio

---

[50] Arizona v. Fulminante, 499 U.S. 279, 291 (1991).

[51] People v. Handwerker, 2006 N.Y. Slip Op. 26119, 12 Misc. 3d 19, 816 N.Y.S.2d 824, 2006 N.Y. Misc. LEXIS 662 (2006).

[52] In re Winship, 397 U.S. 358 (1970); State v. Sullivan, 34 Idaho 68, 199 P. 647 (1921). See also Unif. R. Evid. 303(b) (1999).

[53] Sullivan v. Louisiana, 508 U.S. 275, 113 S. Ct. 2078, 124 L. Ed. 2d 182 (1993). See also Perkins v. State, 441 S.E.2d 511 (Ga.1994).

[54] State v. Miller, 2003 Utah App. 76, 2003 Utah App. LEXIS 247 (2003).

[55] See People v. Moreland, 226 Ill. Dec. 814, 686 N.E.2d 597 (1997).

case where the defendant had been convicted of trademark counterfeiting, she successfully contended that the prosecution's expert failed to compare the appearance of the allegedly infringing product with how a genuine article appeared. Because proof of an element of the crime was missing, the case had to be reversed.[56] Generally an appellate court will uphold a conviction where a rational finder of fact could have determined that the state proved all the essential elements of the crime.[57]

§ 3.7　Burden to Prove All Elements of the Crime

"As a matter of due process the prosecution must prove beyond a reasonable doubt every fact necessary to constitute the crime with which the defendant is charged."[58] To win a conviction, the prosecutor must introduce sufficient believable evidence that proves all the elements of the charged crime beyond a reasonable doubt. For example, in the common law crime of burglary, there are seven elements: (1) trespass, (2) breaking, (3) entering, (4) the dwelling house, (5) of another, (6) at night, and (7) with intent to commit a felony. Meeting the duty of the prosecutor involves introducing proof of each of these elements of common law burglary with sufficient evidentiary weight the meet the burden of proof. Evidence that the defendant interfered in the property rights of another would meet the "trespass" standard, as proof that the defendant applied force to make entry shows a "breaking." But where the evidence also demonstrated that the defendant had permission to stay the night at the bed and breakfast inn, the element of "trespass" would be negated and no conviction for common law burglary would be proper.

Both state and federal courts have consistently reversed convictions after determining that the prosecution did not prove one of the elements of the crime charged. For example, in a New York case, *People v. Sandoval*, the reviewing court reversed the defendant's conviction for burglary because a jury instruction that was erroneous had the effect of relieving the prosecution of the duty to prove that the defendant had unlawfully entered the apartment building, a crucial element in a burglary prosecution.[59]

An appellate court reversed a defendant's conviction of endangering a child where the defendant had been charged with willfully allowing a minor child to enter or remain in a building where the defendant knew that methamphetamine was stored. Under appellate review, the court determined that the defendant was entitled to a jury instruction that covered all the elements of the

---

[56]　State v. Troisi, 2008 Ohio 6062, 2008 Ohio App. LEXIS (Ohio 2008).

[57]　State v. Butler, 2008 La. App. LEXIS 1388 (La. 2008). *See also* United States v. Lopez, 443 F.3d 1026, 1030, 2006 U.S. App. LEXIS 9560 (8th Cir. 2006).

[58]　29 AM. JUR. 2D *Evidence* § 168.

[59]　People v. Sandoval, 56 A.D.3d 253, 866 N.Y.S.2d 656, 2008 N.Y. App. Div. LEXIS 8238 (NY 2008).

crime. In this particular case the trial judge, in failing to instruct the jury that it must find that the defendant willfully permitted the child to enter the drug storage building, committed reversible error because the jury may have convicted the defendant without making a determination that the defendant knowingly allowed the child to enter the drug house.[60] Where one of the elements of a crime was not proved beyond a reasonable doubt, a reviewing court must reverse the conviction.

Many jurisdictions will reverse a conviction where one element has not been proved, where the existence of the element was in dispute, and a trial court omitted a jury instruction requiring proof of the element. In a Connecticut case, a defendant had been charged with possession of cocaine in his automobile and in a jacket alleged to belong to the defendant. The defendant disputed the allegation that the cocaine was in his possession and the trial court omitted to instruct the jury on the element that the defendant had to have knowledge that the substance was cocaine. The reviewing court reversed the trial court and held that harmless error could not be found because the issue of knowledge was in dispute.[61] On different facts, a Kentucky appellate court upheld a conviction for robbery in the first degree that required a threat while armed with a deadly weapon. The judge failed to instruct the jury that it first had to find that the defendant's gun was a deadly weapon before it could convict him of first-degree robbery. Over the defendant's objection that his case was not proved beyond a reasonable doubt because one element was missing, the Supreme Court of Kentucky held that the jury would most certainly have found that the gun was a deadly weapon and it applied the harmless error standard of review to uphold the conviction.[62]

In contrast to state practices, federal courts treat a neglected element somewhat differently. In one case in which the trial court failed to instruct the jury that the element, materiality, in a mail and wire fraud case was an element of both crimes, the Supreme Court allowed the conviction to stand. According to the Court, a jury instruction that omits an element of the crime does not necessarily result in a fundamentally unfair trial and should be judged on the harmless error standard. Even though the jury did not consider all the elements in the case, the Court upheld the convictions that resulted.[63] Normally, factors that must be found for sentence enhancements must be determined by the jury and are treated like elements of the crime. In federal prosecutions, where the government must prove sentencing factors beyond a reasonable doubt and fails to do so, they can be treated just like elements of the crime that were not proven and can be measured by the harmless error standard. In a case in which the jury in a domestic assault case found that the defendant had assaulted his

---

[60]   Granzer v. State, 2008 WY 118, 193 P.2d 266, 2008 Wyo. LEXIS 124 (Wyo. 2008).
[61]   State v. Gooden, 89 Conn. App. 307, 319, 873 A.2d 243, 251, 2005 Conn. App. LEXIS 202 (2005).
[62]   Thacker v. Commonwealth, 194 S.W.3d 287, 2006 Ky. LEXIS 174 (2006).
[63]   Neder v. United States, 527 U.S. 1 (1999).

wife with a deadly weapon, the trial court enhanced the sentence because the proof in the case showed that the deadly weapon was a firearm even though the jury verdict form only mentioned a "deadly weapon." The Supreme Court believed that even though the jury had not specifically found that a firearm was used, and the verdict was for a "deadly weapon," the harmless error standard should be applied and the defendant should have been sentenced as if the jury had found that he used a firearm.[64]

If the prosecution fails to prove one element of the crime beyond a reasonable doubt, the accused may sometimes be found guilty of a lesser degree of that crime or a lesser included offense. For example, under some statutes, a person may be found guilty of burglary in the second degree if the prosecution failed to prove that the breaking and entering occurred at night. In such instances, of course, the penalty is less severe. Similarly, if a sentencing factor is not proved in a state case, the sentence enhancement should not be imposed.

§ 3.8   Burden on the Accused

As a strong general rule, no defendant has any duty to present any evidence, to introduce any witnesses, or to testify personally because a defendant has no burden to prove or disprove anything.[65] A defendant need not prove anything in order to prevail in a criminal trial. In fact, a strong general rule exists that "[i]t is improper for a prosecutor to suggest that a defendant shoulders the burden of proof in a criminal trial."[66] This concept is such a universal principle of American criminal justice that if a prosecutor were to hint or inadvertently imply during opening or closing statements that any burden rests on the defense, that suggestion could result in a reversal of a conviction on appeal. In a Florida case involving a defendant's arrest for leaving her baggage unattended at an airport, she testified that the deputies who arrested her were unreasonably rough during the booking process and left bruises on her arm. Defendant allegedly battered a police officer, which brought additional charges that she denied. During cross-examination at the battery trial, the prosecutor asked the defendant whether she had any photographs of her injuries. The prosecutor emphasized the lack of photographs during cross-examination and while making closing arguments. According to the reviewing court, this emphasis on the defendant's lack of evidence amounted to an improper shifting the burden of proof and placing it on the accused and required a reversal of her conviction.[67] The court upheld the principle that a defendant does not have

---

[64]   Washington v. Fecuenco, 548 U.S. 212, 2006 U.S. LEXIS 5164 (2006).

[65]   Generally, a defendant has no burden of proof unless the defendant has pled an affirmative defense.

[66]   Stephenson v. State, 742 N.E.2d 463 (Ind. 2001).

[67]   Ramirez v. State, 2009 Fla. App. LEXIS 739 (Fla. 2009). *See also* People v. Johnson, 218 Ill. 2d 125, 140, 842 N.E.2d 714, 723, 2005 Ill. LEXIS 2072 (2005).

to prove anything and that she did not have to introduce other evidence of her oral theory of the incident. Therefore, the prosecution committed reversible error in implying that the defendant had any burden of proof.

An accused, in constructing a defense, may make some issues logically and legally relevant by pleading an affirmative defense where the burden of proof at some level may rest on the defendant. In the case of an insanity defense, the defendant may have the burden of proof by a preponderance, by clear and convincing evidence, or the defendant may merely have to raise the issue of insanity and introduce some slight evidence of insanity to meet the required affirmative burden. Once the defendant has met whatever burden was required in the jurisdiction, the burden of going forward with the evidence will fall on the prosecution to negate insanity or to introduce evidence to contradict the defendant's claim.

When pleading an affirmative defense, such as coercion, self-defense, entrapment, statute of limitations, or mistake, all of which would absolve a defendant of liability, the defendant generally has the responsibility of "going forward with the evidence." Because the allocation of the burden of persuasion varies in many jurisdictions, the burden of proving affirmative defenses may fall on either the government or the defendant as determined by state or federal statute or court decision. For example, New York[68] and Ohio[69] require affirmative defenses to be proved by the defendant by a preponderance of the evidence. Once the prosecution has proved the elements of the crime, the defendant must prove the existence of the affirmative defense by a preponderance. Where the burden of proof has been allocated to the defendant who has asserted an affirmative defense, the reality is that, in order to prevail, the defendant need only introduce sufficient believable evidence to create a reasonable doubt. To warrant submission of the defense to the jury, the defendant must produce substantial evidence to support the particular defense theory sufficient to create a reasonable doubt.[70]

The Supreme Court of California explained that where a defendant presented sufficient evidence that, if believed by the jury, could support an affirmative defense, the trial court must offer the jury an instruction explaining the concept of affirmative defenses and how they operate. The court reversed a conviction for selling unregistered securities because one defendant offered a sufficient evidentiary foundation that he personally did not know that the securities he was selling were required to be registered prior to sale. Because the defendant made a proper showing of evidence that could support an affirmative defense, the trial court committed reversible error in not giving the jury an instruction on affirmative defenses.[71] If the defense introduces a

---

68 *See* N.Y. C.L.S. PENAL § 25.00 Defenses; burden of proof (2006).
69 State v. Stephens-Tun, 2008 Ohio 3491, 2008 Ohio App. LEXIS 2951 (Ohio 2008).
70 State v. Babers, 514 N.W.2d 79 (Iowa 1994).
71 People v. Salas, 37 Cal. 4th 967; 127 P.3d 40, 38 Cal. Rptr. 3d 624, 2006 Cal. LEXIS 1900 (2006).

sufficient foundation showing an affirmative defense, the defendant is entitled to an appropriate jury instruction on the affirmative defense.

Because the prosecution possesses the burden of proof for each element of the crime, there is no lawful way to shift that burden to a defendant through a jury instruction or a prosecutor's final argument. For example, in a Montana drunk driving case, a judge gave the jury an instruction that indicated a defendant's refusal to submit to a test to detect alcohol or drugs could be a factor that the jury might consider in determining whether the defendant was under the influence at the time of his arrest. The Supreme Court of Montana rejected the defendant's contention that the jury instruction and a prosecutor's mention of the refusal constituted a reversal of the burden of proof.[72] The court noted that the government and not the defendant had the burden of proof on all the elements of impaired driving.

Statutory wording or the effect of jury instructions in allegedly altering or shifting the burden of proof has been attacked in a variety of cases. The Supreme Court accepted a case, *Sandstrom v. Montana,* which involved a jury instruction involving an inference that allegedly shifted the burden of proof from the prosecution to the defendant.[73] In this case, the state charged the defendant with deliberate homicide, and the question of the defendant's intent was crucial to both the defense and the prosecution. At the trial, the defendant's attorney informed the jury that, although his client admitted to killing the victim, he did not do so "purposely or knowingly," and he was, therefore, not guilty of a deliberate crime but rather of a lesser crime. The defendant's counsel objected to the instruction that "the law presumes that a person intends the ordinary consequences of his voluntary act." He argued that this instruction had the effect of shifting the burden of proof on the issue of purpose or knowledge to the defendant, and it was therefore impermissible because it was in violation of the constitutional guarantee of due process of law. The Supreme Court, in reversing the decision, reasoned that:

> [A] reasonable jury could have interpreted the presumptions as "conclusive," i.e., not technically as a presumption at all, but rather an irrebuttable direction by the court to find intent once convinced of the facts triggering the assumption. Alternatively, the jury may have interpreted the instruction as a direction to find intent upon proof of the defendant's voluntary actions, unless the defendant proved the contrary.[74]

Under either interpretation, according to the Court, the burden of persuasion on the element of intent effectively shifted to the defendant. The Court then stated:

> We conclude that under either of the two possible interpretations of the instruction set out above, precisely that effect (relieving the state of the

---

[72] State v. Slade, 2008 MT 341, 346 Mont. 271, 194 P.3d 677, 2008 Mont. LEXIS 574 (Mont. 2008).

[73] Sandstrom v. Montana, 442 U.S. 510, 1979 U.S. LEXIS 113 (1979).

[74] *Id.* at 517.

burden of proof) would result, and that the instruction therefore represents constitutional error.[75]

To summarize, the defendant has the burden of going forward with the evidence to show an affirmative defense such as alibi or insanity; however, an instruction that tends to require the defendant to prove his or her innocence, or any instruction that relieves the prosecution of proving an element of the crime, violates the due process requirement that the prosecution must prove every element of the offense beyond a reasonable doubt.

§ 3.9   Burden of Proving Affirmative Defenses — General

Once the prosecution has introduced sufficient evidence that, if believed, would permit a finding of guilt beyond a reasonable doubt on every element of the charge, in order to avoid a conviction, the accused may be obliged to respond with evidence that raises or permits a reasonable doubt that he or she is guilty as charged.[76] In most instances, the defense has only to introduce sufficient evidence to raise a reasonable doubt in the minds of the jury.

Some states follow a slightly different path and allocate a higher burden to the prosecution where a defendant introduced evidence in support of an affirmative defense. Demonstrative of this theory, when a defendant has made a prima facie showing of an affirmative defense, the government has the burden of proving beyond a reasonable doubt that the affirmative defense did not exist.[77] States following this theory hold that the prosecution bears the burden of proving the defendant's guilt beyond a reasonable doubt concerning the issue raised by affirmative defense evidence. Other jurisdictions place the burden of proof firmly on the defendant to prove the affirmative defense by a preponderance of the evidence and place no burden on the prosecution.[78] In a federal prosecution for illegally purchasing firearms, the defendant contended that her affirmative evidence of duress should force the prosecution to disprove duress beyond a reasonable doubt. The Supreme Court rejected her position because a majority of the Court presumed that the Congress intended a defendant accused of firearms offenses to bear the burden of proving duress by a preponderance of the evidence.[79] In a prosecution for illegally purchasing firearms, this was especially the case because the elements of the crime, if proved, show guilt, while duress constitutes an excuse for the crime but does not negate an element of the crime.

---

[75] *Id.* at 521.

[76] People v. Gonzalez, 275 Cal. Rptr. 729, 800 P.2d 1159 (1990).

[77] *See* Fields v. State, 998 So. 2d 1185, 2008 Fla. App. LEXIS 11871 (Fla. 2008).

[78] State v. Ray, 290 Conn. 24, 37, 961 A.2d 947, 2009 Conn. LEXIS 5 (Conn. 2009).

[79] Dixon v. United States, 548 U.S. 1, 2006 U.S. LEXIS 4894 (2006).

Allocating the burden of proving an affirmative defense by statute does not violate due process even where the burden is placed on the defendant to prove insanity beyond a reasonable doubt.[80] Using a lower standard, Congress reformed the federal insanity defense requiring a defendant to prove insanity by clear and convincing evidence.[81]

In the sections that follow, some of the more common affirmative defenses are discussed, including alibi, self-defense, justification, excuse, and other affirmative defenses, with special emphasis on the question of burden of proof.

§ 3.10 — Alibi

In the alibi defense, the defendant admits that the crime occurred, but alleges that he or she was not present to commit the crime because he or she was at a different location and otherwise had no connection to the alleged crime, whether in planning or in execution. Some jurisdictions hold that the presentation of an alibi constitutes an affirmative defense, and when it is asserted, the defendant has the burden of proof by a preponderance of the evidence.[82] Georgia law takes an opposite view and in an armed robbery case that alleged the defendant was the robber, a fact he disputed, the burden of proof remained on the prosecution to prove the defendant's presence beyond a reasonable doubt.[83] A third view, represented by Delaware, holds that an alibi defense in not an affirmative defense and the defendant holds no burden of proof. Under the Delaware theory, an alibi instruction informs the jury that if the defendant's alibi evidence creates a reasonable doubt, the jury must acquit the defendant.[84] Because the defense of alibi denies any connection with the crime, a successful albi defense requires that the defendant be acquitted.

In order to prevent unfair prejudice to the case of the prosecution, most jurisdictions require by rule or statute that the defense give the prosecution pretrial notice of an intention to present an alibi defense. For example, within 20 days of arraignment, New York permits the prosecution to request notice of whether the defendant intends to assert an alibi defense. The defendant must respond within eight days and allege the place where the defendant was located at the time of the crime and offer the names and addresses of proposed alibi witnesses.[85] In a situation where the defendant fails to serve the

---

[80] Leland v. Oregon, 343 U.S. 790, 1952 U.S. LEXIS 1955 (1952).

[81] United States v. Freeman, 804 F.2d 1574 (11th Cir. 1986). *See also* People v. Spry, 68 Cal. Rptr. 2d 691 (1997). As of 2006, the Supreme Court has never accepted a case to review the constitutionality of the federal insanity defense statute.

[82] State v. Stump, 254 Iowa 1181, 119 N.W.2d 210 (1963).

[83] Hill v. State v. State, 290 Ga. App. 140, 658 S.E.2d 863, 241, 2008 Ga. App. LEXIS 272 (2008).

[84] *See* Brown v. State, 958 A.2d 833, 2008 Del. LEXIS 468 (Del. 2008).

[85] NY CLS CPL § 250.20 Notice of Alibi (2008). *See also* Conn. Practice Book § 40–21. Defense of Alibi; Notice by Defendant (2008). The Connecticut rule requires that the defendant give notice to the prosecutor within 20 days following the prosecutor's demand.

prosecution with a signed alibi and the names of witnesses upon whom he or she plans to rely, the trial court may refuse to allow the alibi witnesses to present evidence.[86] Connecticut follows a similar rule and excludes evidence of alibi when the notice requirement has been violated. The reasons for this exclusion, according to a Connecticut case, is that exclusion is a sanction for failure to obey the notice rules; that otherwise, the state could suffer surprise at trial because it would not have time to investigate the witnesses; and that it was proper for the trial court to view late identification of alibi witnesses with suspicion.[87]

If a defendant fails to file and serve a copy of the alibi notice as generally required, a trial court may exclude defense witness evidence offered for the purpose of providing an alibi, except the defendant may give personal alibi testimony whether or not notice was given.[88] Consistent with this principle, the Supreme Court of New Jersey in *State v. Bradshaw* upheld reversal of the defendant's conviction because the trial court had abused its discretion in not allowing the defendant to testify concerning his alibi even though he had not complied with the notice of alibi requirement.[89]

In explaining the burden of proof requirement in alibi cases in a state that does not view such a defense as an affirmative defense, the Supreme Court of Delaware indicated that the defendant does not have the burden of proving his alibi. All that is demanded of the defendant who presents an alibi defense is that he or she introduce evidence that raises a reasonable doubt concerning presence of the accused at the time and place where the crime was committed.[90]

In *Dat Pham v. Beaver*, a New York court charged the jury that the government had to prove that the defendant was the individual who committed the crime and that the government had to disprove the defendant's alibi beyond a reasonable doubt. The appeals court approved the jury charge and refused to disturb the defendant's conviction[91] because the charge correctly explained New York law, which required the prosecution to rebut evidence of alibi by proof beyond a reasonable doubt.

---

[86]   *See* N.J. Court Rules, R. 3:12–2 (2009) and Fla. R. Crim. P. 3.200 Notice of Alibi (2006). *See also* McEwing v. State, 2006 Ark. LEXIS 332 (Ark. 2006).

[87]   *See* State v. Salters, 89 Conn. App. 221; 872 A.2d 933; 2005 Conn. App. LEXIS 200 (2005). *See also* State v. Lewis, 391 N.W.2d 726 (Iowa 1986), which held that a trial court's exclusion of the defendant's alibi witness was an abuse of discretion when the defense counsel filed a notice of alibi one day after he heard of the existence of witnesses, witnesses were made available for all informal interviews or depositions before the trial, and the state had one week before the trial to investigate the alibi defense, but chose to do nothing, even declining interviews with witnesses.

[88]   McKenny v. State, 967 So. 2d 951, 2007 Fla. App. LEXIS 15581 (Fla. 2007). *See also* Fla. R. Crim. P. 3.200 Notice of Alibi (2008).

[89]   State v. Bradshaw, 195 N.J. 493; 950 A.2d 889; 2008 N.J. LEXIS 873 (N.J. 2008).

[90]   Brown v. State, 958 A.2d 833, 839, 2008 Del. LEXIS 468 (Del. 2008).

[91]   2006 U.S. Dist. LEXIS 46109 (W.D.N.Y. 2006).

A court is generally required to instruct the jury on the alibi if the defendant requests the instruction and has presented some credible evidence to support the alibi.[92] However, an alibi instruction is appropriate only when the defense evidence demonstrates the defendant's presence elsewhere for the entire period during which the government's evidence shows he or she was involved in criminal activity.[93]

§ 3.11 — Insanity

Related to but separate from legal insanity is the issue of competency of a defendant to stand trial. Every defendant comes to court with a presumption that he or she is competent to stand trial, to enter a plea, and to receive a sentence. Where a question of competency to stand trial arises, as a general rule the burden of proof is on the defendant to prove by a preponderance of the evidence that he or she is not competent.[94] In determining a defendant's competence, a court considers whether a defendant can consult with his or her lawyer with a reasonable degree of rationality and whether the defendant has an understanding of nature of the criminal proceedings and is able to assist in his or her defense. This type of mental difficulty affecting competency is different from legal insanity and a person may be competent but still legally insane.

A defendant comes to court with not only a presumption of competency, but also with a presumption of sanity. Unless the defendant takes step to make sanity an issue in the case, the prosecutor has no special duty to prove sanity. Although the prosecution has the ultimate burden of proof on sanity if it does not does not become an issue, the prosecutor will have to offer no evidence proving insanity. To raise the issue of sanity, the defendant has the burden of introducing evidence sufficient to evoke the possibility that, as a result of mental disease or defect, he or she lacked a substantial capacity to appreciate the wrongfulness of his or her conduct or to conform his or her conduct to the requirements of the law. If the defendant places sanity at issue, there are several ways that different jurisdictions handle the issue. One group of states requires that the defendant raise the issue and offer some proof toward insanity and then the burden of proof shifts to the prosecution to prove sanity either by a preponderance or in some cases beyond a reasonable doubt. Other jurisdictions require the defendant to raise the issue and to affirmatively prove insanity by either clear and convincing evidence or proof beyond a reasonable doubt.

The rule followed by most state courts (and federal courts until 1984) requires that when the defendant introduces substantial evidence of his or her insanity, the issue of his or her capacity to commit the offense becomes a

---

[92] Brown v. State, 958, A.2d 833, 838, 2008 Del. LEXIS 468 (Del. 2008).
[93] Bright v. United States, 698 A.2d 450 (D.C. App. 1997).
[94] State v. Were, 118 Ohio St.3d 448, 2008 Ohio 2762, 890 N.E.2d, 2008 Ohio LEXIS 1615 (Ohio 2008).

question of proof, and the prosecution's burden of going forward with the evidence requires it to introduce sufficient evidence on the issue of sanity to preclude a verdict of acquittal for the defendant.[95] However, the defendant must introduce sufficient evidence to meet the burden of proof required in that particular jurisdiction to prove insanity. In a prosecution in which the defendant alleged legal insanity as a defense and offered proof, the judge rejected the defense because, as a matter of law, the evidence directed toward proving insanity failed to meet the clear and convincing level of proof. According to the reviewing court, "[t]he clear and convincing standard requires a quantum of proof greater than a preponderance of the evidence, but less than proof beyond a reasonable doubt"[96] and requiring clear and convincing proof did not violate standards of due process.

The legislatures of a large number of states have taken a somewhat different approach to the insanity defense and have provided that the defense is a true affirmative defense and the burden of proof rests on a defendant by a preponderance of the evidence.[97] The statutes in these states allocate the burden of proof for legal insanity to the party asserting insanity[98] by a preponderance of the evidence.[99] For example, in California, when a defendant pleads not guilty by reason of insanity, the defendant has the burden of proof by a preponderance of the evidence to prove that he or she was insane at the time he or she committed the act.[100] The United States Supreme Court in several instances has determined that placing this burden on the defendant does not violate the Constitution of the United States[101] even where the burden is on the defendant to prove insanity beyond a reasonable doubt.[102]

In 1984, as part of the Comprehensive Crime Control Act, Congress enacted legislation titled "Insanity Defense Reform Act of 1984." Section 17 of Title 18 of the United States Code defines the scope of the insanity defense for federal offenses and shifts the burden of proof to the defendant. This section provides:

> (a) Affirmative Defense. It is an affirmative defense to a prosecution under
> any Federal statute that, at the time of the commission of the acts constituting

---

[95] United States v. Westerhausen, 283 F.2d 844 (7th Cir. 1960).

[96] People v. Clay, 361 Ill. App. 3d 310, 332, 836 N.E.2d 872, 882, 2005 Ill. App. LEXIS 994 (2005).

[97] REV. CODE WASH. (ARCW) § 10.77.030 (2008). Establishing insanity as a defense.

[98] CAL. EVID. CODE § 522 (2008). See also Turner v. Arkansas, 2005 Ark. App. LEXIS 237 (2005).

[99] A.C.A. § 5-1-111 (d)(1) Burden of Proof—Defenses and affirmative defenses—Presumptions (2008).

[100] People v. Farris, 130 Cal. App. 4th 773, 30 Cal. Rptr. 3d 426, 2005 Cal. App. LEXIS 1017 (Calif. 2005).

[101] Patterson v. New York, 432 U.S. 197, 97 S. Ct. 2319, 53 L. Ed. 2d 281 (1977). Leland v. Oregon, 343 U.S. 790, 72 S. Ct. 1002, 96 L. Ed. 1302 (1952). See also Fleenor v. State, 622 N.E.2d 140 (Ind. 1993), in which the court held that instructing the jury that a capital murder defendant was required to prove insanity at the time of the offense by a preponderance of the evidence, if the state proved that the defendant knowingly killed the victim, was proper.

[102] See Leland v. Oregon, 343 U.S. 790 (1952).

the offense, the defendant, as a result of a severe mental disease or defect, was unable to appreciate the nature and quality or the wrongfulness of his acts. Mental disease or defect does not otherwise constitute a defense.

(b) Burden of Proof. The defendant has the burden of proving the defense of insanity by clear and convincing evidence.[103]

The clear and convincing evidence standard is a higher standard than a mere preponderance of the evidence and remains lower than Oregon's current standard for its insanity defense of proof beyond a reasonable doubt.[104] The design of the revised federal insanity defense was to eliminate the confusing spectacle of competing expert witnesses testifying to directly contradictory conclusions as to the ultimate legal issue to be found by the trier of fact. Under the revised insanity defense, expert psychiatric testimony is limited to presenting and explaining the diagnosis of the psychiatrist. In federal criminal trials, expert witnesses may not "state an opinion as to whether the defendant did or did not have the mental conditions constituting an element of the crime charged. Such ultimate issues are matters for the trier of fact alone."[105]

Another provision of the Crime Control Act relates to the disposition of a person found not guilty by reason of insanity.[106] This section of the Act provides:

> If a person is found not guilty only by reason of insanity at the time of the offense charged, he shall be committed to a suitable facility until such time as he is eligible for release pursuant to subsection (e).

Subsection (d) of the Act relates to burden of proof. It provides that:

> In a hearing pursuant to subsection (c) of this section, a person found not guilty only by reason of insanity of an offense involving bodily injury to, or serious damage to property of, another person, or involving a substantial risk of such injury or damage, has the burden of proving by clear and convincing evidence that his release would not create a substantial risk of bodily injury to another person or serious damage of property of another due to present mental disease or defect. With respect to any other offense, the person has the burden of proof by the preponderance of the evidence.

Following the enactment of the Insanity Defense Reform Act, defendants attacked its constitutionality and claimed that placing the burden of this affirmative defense on a defendant by clear and convincing evidence violated due process. The Supreme Court had noted that placing the burden of persuasion

---

[103] 18 U.S.C. § 17 (2006).
[104] People v. Clay, 361 Ill. App. 3d 310, 325, 836 N.E.2d 872, 885, 2005 Ill. App. LEXIS 994 (2005).
[105] FED. R. EVID. § 704(b).
[106] 18 U.S.C. § 4243 (2006).

on a defendant to prove insanity, whether by a preponderance of the evidence, or to some more convincing degree, does not violate the Constitution.[107] Many states have adopted the federal burden of proof in modernizing their individual insanity defense statutes. Demonstrative of following the federal standard is the state of Illinois, which holds that "the burden of proof is on the defendant to prove by clear and convincing evidence that the defendant is not guilty by reason of insanity."[108] Louisiana follows a lower standard by giving defendants who plead insanity "the burden of establishing the defense of insanity at the time of the offense by a preponderance of the evidence."[109] However, the burden of proof remains on the prosecution to prove every element beyond a reasonable doubt.

In summary, the United States Congress established that the burden of proof of insanity in federal courts would rest upon the defendant and require him or her to prove the insanity defense by clear and convincing evidence. In some states, where the defendant has raised a mental defense, the issue of whether a defendant possessed the proper mental capacity to be convicted of a crime requires the prosecution to introduce sufficient evidence to avoid a verdict of acquittal in the defendant's favor. In other states, the defendant must not only go forward with the evidence, but has the ultimate burden to prove insanity by a preponderance of the evidence. A third group of states places the burden of proof on the defendant using the standard of clear and convincing evidence. In any situation, to have any chance of prevailing on an insanity defense, the defendant who claims insanity has at least a minimal burden to go forward with evidence to overcome the presumption of sanity and constitutionally may have the burden completely placed on him- or herself by proof beyond a reasonable doubt.

§ 3.12 — Self-Defense

In criminal prosecutions involving violence to the alleged victim, justifiable self-defense may be set up as a complete defense to, or exoneration from, liability for the act charged. Preservation from harm, whether the danger rises to the level of defense of life or of defense from lesser physical harms, is generally recognized as proper conduct if the defender is not committing any wrong.[110] As a general rule, during the presentation of a homicide case, the

---

[107] *See* Clark v. Arizona, 548 U.S. 735, 2006 U.S. LEXIS 5184 (2006).

[108] See § 720 ILCS 5/6-2. Insanity (2009). "All defendants are presumed sane and a defendant must prove by clear and convincing evidence that he was not guilty by reason of insanity." People v. Houseworth, 2008 Ill. App. LEXIS 1290 (Ill. 2008).

[109] La. C.Cr.P. Art. 652 (2008). *See also* State v. Coleman, 976 So. 2d 268, 2008 La. App. LEXIS 142 (2008).

[110] *See* People v. Lee, 131 Cal. App. 4th 1413, 32 Cal. Rptr. 3d 745, 2005 Cal. App. LEXIS 1278 (2005), where victim fired gun at two menacing dogs.

prosecution has the burden of establishing the death of a human caused by the defendant under circumstances in which it did not appear that the defendant acted in self-defense. If the defendant alleged self-defense in this hypothetical homicide case, the burden of proving this affirmative defense requires the defendant to go forward with proof of facts that indicate that the defendant had a right of self-defense and used no more force than was appropriate under the circumstances. Proof of the defense dictates that the defendant must introduce proof that the he or she did not provoke the incident and killed the other while under an actual or reasonable apprehension of death or serious bodily injury from the aggressor.[111]

A few states place the ultimate burden of proof for affirmative defenses squarely on the defendant. For example, Ohio law states "[t]he burden of going forward with the evidence of an affirmative defense, and the burden of proof, by a preponderance of the evidence, for an affirmative defense, is upon the accused."[112] Demonstrative of this principle, in Ohio a woman had been convicted of killing her husband with a firearm despite pleading self-defense. She appealed, contending that the Ohio procedure that required her to prove her affirmative defense by a preponderance violated the due process clause of the Fourteenth Amendment by requiring her to prove her innocence. The Supreme Court rejected her contention and held that the allocation of the burden of proof to a defendant did not require a defendant to prove her innocence. Ohio's definition of aggravated murder required the prosecution to prove that she had both purposely and with prior calculation and design caused her husband's death. According to the Supreme Court, the fact that evidence offered to support self-defense might negate a purposeful killing by prior calculation and design does not mean that elements of the crime and self-defense impermissibly overlap. Evidence that could create a reasonable doubt about one element of the crime necessary for a finding of guilt could easily fall far short of proving self-defense by a preponderance of the evidence.[113] Where a reasonable doubt appears in the state's proof or by the defendant's presentation of an affirmative defense, the defendant would have to be acquitted. The United States Supreme Court agreed that neither Ohio law nor the instructions concerning self-defense violate the due process clause of the Fourteenth Amendment by shifting to the petitioner the state's burden of proving the elements of the crime. The court went on to note that the "mere fact that all but two States have abandoned the common-law rule that affirmative defenses, including self-defense, must be proved by the defendant does not render the rule unconstitutional."

Instead of placing the burden on a defendant to prove self-defense, some jurisdictions have helped prospective defendants present self-defense claims by giving a defender a positive presumption without the introduction of any evidence. Within the past several years, several states enacted affirmative

---

[111]   40 AM. JUR. 2D *Homicide* § 141 (2006).

[112]   OHIO REV. CODE ANN. § 2901.05 Burden and degree of proof (2009).

[113]   Martin v. Ohio, 480 U.S. 228, 107 S. Ct. 1098, 94 L. Ed. 2d 267 (1987). *See* case in Part II.

presumptions that presume a defendant was acting in self-defense in particular situations. Ohio has determined that a person is presumed to have acted in self-defense or in defense of another person when a different person has unlawfully invaded the home or motor vehicle of the person using the defending force.[114] The presumption in favor of self-defense is rebuttable by the opposing party. In a similar fashion, Florida statutes indicate that a person is presumed to have a reasonable fear of imminent death or great injury to himself or others when he uses defensive force that is calculated to cause death or serious bodily injury when the force used was against a person who was in the process of entering a dwelling, residence, or occupied vehicle of the defending person.[115]

While a state statute requiring the defendant to prove self-defense does not have an unconstitutional burden-shifting result, some states require only that the defendant raise some evidence tending to prove self-defense. For example, in Texas criminal prosecutions where a defendant pleads self-defense, the defendant has the duty to introduce some evidence to support the alleged claim of self-defense. Then the state has the burden of disproving self-defense beyond a reasonable doubt.[116]

An Alaska decision followed prior case law in applying the rule that when a defendant has presented some evidence of self-defense, it becomes the prosecution's duty to disprove the defendant's evidence of self-defense beyond a reasonable doubt.[117] In this case, the prosecution's evidence showed that the defendant had hit the victim in the forehead with his hand, punched her in the face, dragged her to the floor, and choked her. The defendant's evidence was that the woman was the aggressor and that he held her on the floor to prevent her from harming him. The self-defense claim failed, but the defendant's evidence was sufficient to force the prosecution to disprove self-defense beyond a reasonable doubt and to obtain a jury instruction on self-defense.

To summarize, in some states when the accused offers the affirmative defense of self-defense and produces some evidence in support of the self-defense theory, the burden rests on the prosecutor to prove beyond a reasonable doubt that the accused did not act in self-defense. Procedurally, the defendant must raise the issue and offer some evidence that shifts the burden of proof to the prosecution. In other states, the accused not only has the initial burden of going forward with evidence of self-defense, but also carries the ultimate burden of proof by a preponderance of the evidence that he or she acted in self-defense. While imposing any burden of proof on a defendant might appear to raise constitutional issues, state statutes allocating the ultimate burden of proof to the defense have been determined not to run afoul of the requirements of the Constitution.

---

[114] OHIO REV. CODE ANN. § 2901.05 (B) (2009).
[115] FLA. STAT. § 776.013 (2008).
[116] London v. State, 2008 Tex. App. LEXIS 9039 (Tex. 2008).
[117] Ross v. State, 2006 Alaska App. LEXIS 41 (2006).

§ 3.13 Sufficiency of Evidence

Once a court or jury has rendered a decision, there is a strong presumption of regularity and that the case was properly determined. When a defendant appeals a conviction, he or she must contend that serious defects exist in the case sufficient to warrant a reversal of the judgment. A Texas reviewing court noted that in considering the sufficiency of the evidence to support a criminal conviction, "we view the evidence in the light most favorable to the verdict and examine whether a rational fact-finder could have found the essential elements of the crime beyond a reasonable doubt."[118] A reviewing court, on appeal or in a habeas corpus action, may determine that the evidence was insufficient to support the finding of guilt even though, technically, an appellate court does not reweigh the evidence or reconsider the credibility of the witnesses.[119] In *Jackson v. Virginia*, the United States Supreme Court, in confirming the authority of a federal court to review a state court decision on the sufficiency of the evidence, made this comment:

> Yet a properly instructed jury may occasionally convict even when it can be said that no rational trier of fact could find guilt beyond a reasonable doubt, and the same may be said of a trial judge sitting as a jury.[120]

Once it is recognized that a reviewing court can look behind the decision of the jury to determine whether there was sufficient evidence to justify a finding of guilt beyond a reasonable doubt, the question then becomes: What is the test of sufficiency?

In *Jackson*, the United States Court of Appeals for the Fourth Circuit determined that an appellate court should uphold a state court decision so long as there was any evidence in the record to support it. Following this theory, if there is absolutely no evidence to justify the jury in finding guilt, then the court will reverse the conviction as a violation of due process. But if there is any evidence to support the conviction, as there was in *Jackson*, the case will be affirmed.

The defendant in *Jackson* appealed to the United States Supreme Court, claiming that the "any evidence rule" was inadequate to protect against misapplication of the constitutional standards of reasonable doubt. The United States Supreme Court agreed, stating that the rule that should have been applied was not the "any evidence rule," but rather the rule that was stated in *In re Winship*,[121] which held that a federal habeas corpus court must consider not whether there was any evidence to support a state conviction, but whether there was sufficient evidence to justify a rational trier of fact to find guilt beyond a reasonable doubt. The Supreme Court in *Jackson* first held that the "any evidence rule"

---

[118]   Everson v. State, 2008 Tex. App. LEXIS 4834 (Tex. 2008).
[119]   United States v. Zavala, 2006 U.S. App. LEXIS 15848 (3d Cir. 2006).
[120]   443 U.S. 307, 317, 1979 U.S. LEXIS 10 (1979).
[121]   In re Winship, 397 U.S. 358, 90 S. Ct. 1068, 25 L. Ed. 2d 368 (1970). *See* case in Part II.

is simply inadequate to protect against misapplications of the constitutional standard of proof beyond a reasonable doubt. That Court then insisted:

> Instead the relevant question is whether after reviewing the evidence in the light most favorable to the prosecution, any rational trier of fact could have found the essential elements of the crime beyond a reasonable doubt.

In affirming that a federal court can and will apply the *Winship* sufficiency rule, the Court in *Jackson* made this conclusion as to the rules to be followed:

> We hold that in a challenge to a state criminal conviction … the appellant is entitled to habeas corpus relief if it is found that upon the record evidence adduced at the trial no rational trier of fact could have found proof of guilt beyond a reasonable doubt.

After a review on the new standard, the Court found on the merits that Jackson's case would not be reversed. The Court said that from the evidence in the record, it was clear that the judge could reasonably have found beyond a reasonable doubt that Jackson did possess the necessary intent at or before the time of the killing to justify the first-degree murder conviction.

To summarize the sufficiency-of-the-evidence rule, in a criminal case the prosecutor must introduce relevant and otherwise admissible evidence sufficient for the trier of fact to find the defendant guilty beyond a reasonable doubt. Although an appellate court does not reweigh the evidence, the reviewing court may set aside a conviction if that reviewing court finds that no rational trier of fact could logically have found the defendant guilty beyond a reasonable doubt.

§ 3.14   Summary

In every criminal case, the ultimate burden of proof rests with the prosecution to prove every element of a charged crime beyond a reasonable doubt. This burden of proof or burden of persuasion rests on the prosecution from the start of a trial to the end and it never shifts to the defendant. By asserting an affirmative defense, a defendant may, depending on the jurisdiction, have an ultimate burden of proof concerning the defense. The burden of going forward with the evidence initially rests on the prosecution but may shift to the defense if the prosecution succeeds in introducing evidence that, if believed by the jury or judge, would result in a conviction. To avoid an adverse result, the defendant must meet the burden of going forward with the evidence and introduce evidence that either creates reasonable doubt or establishes an affirmative defense. Constitutional interpretations dictate that that proof beyond a reasonable doubt must be used in criminal cases while civil plaintiffs only need to meet the burden of proving their case by a preponderance of the evidence.

Depending upon the nature of the case, there are three degrees of proof required. These are: a preponderance of the evidence, clear and convincing evidence, and beyond a reasonable doubt. While in a civil case the plaintiff is usually only required to establish his or her claim by a preponderance of the evidence. Some civil cases go beyond this standard and require proof by clear and convincing evidence because other important interests, like reputation, may be at stake. The use of the higher beyond a reasonable doubt standard in criminal cases has been justified because life, freedom, and liberty may be at risk—not merely money. In a criminal case, however, there is no doubt that the accused retains the presumption of innocence until his or her guilt is established beyond a reasonable doubt.

The burden is on the prosecution in a criminal case to show affirmatively the existence of every material fact, including each element of the crime, the identity of the person who committed the crime, and that the crime was perpetrated in violation of the penal laws of the place where it took place.

Even though the burden of proving the elements in a criminal case rests solely with the prosecution, the accused be allocated a burden of proof when the accused gives notice of asserting an affirmative defense. For example, when a defendant alleges an affirmative defense such as coercion, self-defense, entrapment, or mistake, the burden of proof may rest with the defendant to prove the defense, usually by a preponderance of the evidence. Some jurisdictions require that a defendant raise the issue of an affirmative defense and present some evidence in order to require the prosecution to disprove the affirmative defense beyond a reasonable doubt. In some jurisdictions, an affirmative defense may not be proven but the evidence may create a reasonable doubt, which has the same effect as a successful affirmative defense.

Even though alibi, strictly speaking, is not an affirmative defense, because the defendant merely offers evidence that the defendant had no involvement in the crime, the defendant must affirmatively introduce evidence to substantiate this alibi claim. If the defense is insanity, the law in some jurisdictions requires that the defendant prove his or her legal insanity by a preponderance of the evidence or by clear and convincing evidence, and even proof beyond a reasonable doubt has been approved. When evidence is introduced to show self-defense to justify an otherwise criminal act, the defendant may be required to offer proof by a preponderance of the evidence that he or she acted in self-defense.

All criminal justice personnel need to recognize the additional evidentiary burden placed on the prosecution in criminal cases and must be aware that sufficient evidence should be gathered to convince the jury or the judge not only that the accused is probably guilty of the offense charged, but that the proof must meet or exceed the beyond a reasonable doubt standard. Those involved in the criminal justice process should also recognize that the defense will make every effort to create reasonable doubt in the minds of the jury and need only create a reasonable doubt concerning one element for the defense to prevail.

A study of the burden of proof accentuates the need to become familiar with other evidence rules that bear upon the admissibility of evidence. Much of the remainder of the book is devoted to a discussion of these rules.

Proof via Evidence 4

At the trial of a person charged with murder, the fact of death is provable by circumstantial evidence, notwithstanding that neither the body nor any trace of the body has been found and that the accused has made no confession of any participation in the crime. Before he can be convicted, the fact of death should be proved by such circumstances as render the commission of the crime morally certain and leave no ground for possible doubt; the circumstantial evidence should be so cogent and compelling as to convince a jury that upon no rational hypothesis other than murder can the facts be accounted for.

Rex v. Horry, 1952 N.Z.L.R. 111

Chapter Outline

Section

4.1   Introduction

4.2   Pretrial Motions Pertaining to Evidence

4.3   General Approach to Admissibility

4.4   Order of Presenting Evidence at the Trial

4.5   Procedure for Offering and Challenging Evidence

4.6   Role of the Trial Judge in Evidence Matters

4.7   Function of the Jury

4.8   Role of Witnesses

4.9   Prosecuting Attorney's Responsibilities

4.10 Defense Attorney's Responsibilities

4.11 Admissibility and Weight of Direct and Circumstantial Evidence

4.12 Summary

§ 4.1 Introduction

The previous chapter cited and discussed cases that clearly indicated the prosecution possesses the burden of proving guilt in criminal cases. The prosecutor must introduce evidence and/or use other evidentiary tools that will meet the standard of proof beyond a reasonable doubt.

To prove a criminal case, it is not absolutely essential that the prosecution actually present to the jury or judge each fact or bit of knowledge in the form of direct evidence. To save time and to avoid placing an unnecessary burden on the parties, the judge may take judicial notice of certain facts and may advise the jury that they may make certain presumptions and inferences. The factfinders may also consider facts stipulated by the parties. Therefore, the jury or other factfinders may make a decision from: (1) facts presented in the form of evidence; (2) information judicially noticed by the judge; (3) legal presumptions; (4) judicially approved inferences; and (5) accepted stipulations. This chapter presents the method of proving facts by the courtroom introduction of evidence.

After considering the procedure relating to pretrial motions to exclude evidence, this chapter discusses general admissibility tests. This is followed by a section describing the order of presenting evidence at the trial. Also, the role of the judge, jury, witness, prosecuting attorney, and legal counsel for the defense in relation to the introduction and evaluation of evidence is explained. Finally, the rules relating to the admissibility and weight of direct and circumstantial evidence are comprehensively considered.

In Chapters 5 and 6, "substitutes for evidence"—judicial notice, presumptions, inferences, and stipulations—are defined and examples of each are offered.

§ 4.2 Pretrial Motions Pertaining to Evidence

Rule 104

Preliminary Questions

(a) Questions of admissibility generally

Preliminary questions concerning the qualification of a person to be a witness, the existence of a privilege, or the admissibility of evidence shall be determined by the court, subject to the provisions of subdivision (b). In making its determination, it is not bound by the rules of evidence except those with respect to privileges.

(b) Relevancy conditioned on fact

When the relevancy of evidence depends upon the fulfillment of a condition of fact, the court shall admit it upon, or subject to, the introduction of evidence sufficient to support a finding of the fulfillment of the condition.[1]

* * *

During the pretrial stage of a criminal prosecution, either party may file motions that challenge the evidence that an opposing party is expected to introduce at the trial. As a general rule, any procedural defense or evidentiary objection that can be determined without a trial of the general issues should be raised by a pretrial motion. The rationale behind determining some procedural or evidentiary issues during the pretrial stage is that the resolution could make a trial unnecessary but, in any event, it resolves issues that would otherwise disrupt the smooth flow of the trial. These pretrial motions include challenges to the court's jurisdiction, competence or fairness of the tribunal, the statement of the charges, the competency of the defendant to stand trial, the legality of the way in which police gathered evidence, flaws in a grand jury indictment, and constitutional challenges, such as double jeopardy, speedy trial, and search and seizure issues, to name a few.

As a general rule, the motion to suppress evidence must be made within a reasonable time prior to the scheduled trial, but the failure to challenge the evidence in a timely manner may be excused by the court for good cause. If the defense offers a motion to suppress evidence, a hearing will be scheduled within a reasonable time where the attorneys for each party generally present evidence and argue the merits of their respective positions. Police officers and the defendant may be called as witnesses in support of each party's legal theory. If the judge agrees with the defendant's legal position, the evidence, even if relevant to the issues, will not be admitted at the trial.

One of the most common pretrial motions to exclude evidence is that which challenges the use of evidence illegally seized in violation of either the

---

[1] FED. R. EVID. 104(a) and (b).

Fourth Amendment to the United States Constitution or the search and seizure provisions of state constitutions. For example, if the defendant alleges that law enforcement officials obtained evidence by conducting a warrantless search and seizure of the defendant's home in violation of the defendant's Fourth Amendment rights, the defense attorney will file a pretrial motion to suppress the evidence. At the hearing, the prosecutor will have the burden of proving that the warrantless search was lawful while the defense counsel will present evidence to support the seizures as having been unlawful. If the accused can demonstrate that the evidence was obtained by an unlawful search and seizure, and such evidence does not come within an exception to the exclusionary rule recognized by the courts, the evidence will be suppressed from introduction at the trial.[2] But if the prosecutor can show that the evidence was obtained without violating the defendant's rights under the Constitution, or that the search was within one of the recognized exceptions to the exclusionary rule,[3] or that the social costs of applying the rule outweigh the benefits,[4] the motion to suppress will be denied, and the evidence will be admitted unless excluded for some other evidentiary reason.

Evidence may also be challenged as having been secured in violation of other constitutional provisions. For example, if the self-incrimination provisions of the Fifth Amendment, the right-to-counsel provisions of the Sixth Amendment, the due process clause of the Fifth or Fourteenth Amendments, or the principles of the *Miranda* warnings have been violated by law enforcement personnel, the evidence may be inadmissible.[5]

§ 4.3 General Approach to Admissibility

As a general proposition, all evidence is admissible unless a particular rule of evidence requires its exclusion. Therefore, all evidence offered in a criminal case carries with it a presumption of admissibility unless there is a timely and specific objection by the opposing party. Following an appropriate objection, the trial judge will be required to entertain the basis for the objection and make a ruling concerning the admissibility of the questioned evidence. When one party asks a question of a witness and the opposing party offers an objection to it, the objection normally will be based on either the form or phrasing of the question that was asked or on the substance of the expected answer. A helpful way to approach the rules of evidence is to keep

---

[2] Mapp v. Ohio, 367 U.S. 643 (1961), Wong Sun v. United States, 371 U.S. 471, 1963 U.S. LEXIS 2431 (1963).

[3] *See* Massachusetts v. Sheppard, 468 U.S. 981, 1984 U.S. LEXIS 154 (1984) and Dickerson v. United States, 530 U.S. 428, 2000 U.S. LEXIS 4305 (2000).

[4] Hudson v. Michigan, 2006 U.S. LEXIS 4677, 74 U.S.L.W. 4311 (2006).

[5] *See* Chapter 16 for more comprehensive coverage of the exclusion of illegally obtained evidence.

these simple tests concerning form and substance in mind as each rule of evidence is discussed.

A. Objections as to Form

In order to avoid confusing the witness, the court will require that a question be clear and intelligent. Judges will not permit questions to be asked of witnesses where the questions are confusing, compound, improperly phrased, misleading, or argumentative where an objection has been raised by opposing counsel. In fact, the judge will often ask that such questions be rephrased. Questions that are phrased in such a way that there can be no definite answer will, of course, mislead the witness as well as the jury.

Questions that have two parts, called compound questions, are generally objectionable as to form because it may impossible to answer both parts with one answer and if one answer is given, there is no way to know to which question the answer responded. Other questions that are sometimes objectionable as to form, especially during direct examination, are classified as leading questions.[6] Such questions generally suggest the desired answer by the manner in which they are phrased.

B. Objections as to Substance

If there is no objection as to form, or if an objection is made and settled, the test of substance is then applied. One easy way to understand the test of substance is to imagine three hurdles erected between the evidence and the court. Before the evidence can be admitted into court, all three hurdles must be cleared. They are: relevancy, materiality, and competency.

The concept of relevancy concerns whether the information has a tendency to prove or disprove one or more of the facts at issue in the case. To be relevant, the information must have a tendency to establish or disprove matters at issue in the case.[7] In other words, will the matter at issue be more or less likely to be believed or disbelieved if the jury hears the evidence than if it does not hear the evidence? If the evidence affects the probabilities of belief, it will be considered relevant evidence. Materiality involves the relative importance of evidence. Evidence is material only when it affects a fact or issue of the case in a significant way. The definition of competency is more elusive. Competent evidence is that which is legally adequate and sufficient. The competency test is a catch-all for the exclusionary rules. For example, evidence obtained by an illegal search in violation of the Constitution is inadmissible not because it is immaterial or irrelevant, but because of its legal inadequacy or incompetency.

If the proposed evidence meets the tests of form and substance, it is admitted into court. The weight or the importance to be given to the evidence by the jury or the judge depends on many other factors.

---

[6] Leading questions are discussed in Chapter 9.

[7] The relevancy and materiality rules and examples are comprehensively discussed in Chapter 7.

§ 4.4   Order of Presenting Evidence at the Trial[8]

The judge has a great deal of discretion in establishing court procedures, but he or she generally follows the procedures that have been developed over a period of years and have become standard. The usual order of procedure in presenting the case is as follows:[9]

1.   Prosecution's case-in-chief.
2.   Defendant's case-in-chief.
3.   Prosecution's case in rebuttal.
4.   Defense's case in rejoinder.

Each of these steps is discussed in some depth to point out its scope and limitations.

A. Prosecution's Case-in-Chief

At the beginning of the trial, because the prosecution has the burden of going forward with the evidence and has the ultimate burden of proof, it introduces evidence on behalf of the state. The prosecutor may call as many witnesses as necessary and may introduce exhibits, photographs, documents, or other types of evidence that may help the jury in determining the guilt or innocence of the accused—provided that the evidence meets the admissibility tests. During this phase of the procedure, the prosecutor is "carrying the ball," "calling the plays," and going forward with the presentation of evidence. The lead prosecutor determines which of the potential witnesses for the government will actually testify, decides the order in which the witnesses are presented to the court, and guides the flow of evidence. Each prosecution witness is questioned by the prosecutor first[10] and subsequently the defense has an opportunity to cross-examine the prosecution witnesses. At this stage, the defense cannot introduce its own witnesses and—according to the majority view—must limit cross-examination to subject matters mentioned during the direct examination.

When the prosecuting attorney has presented the case-in-chief and has met the burden of going forward with the evidence or what he or she feels is sufficient evidence to make a case against the defendant by proof beyond a reasonable doubt, he or she signifies the completion of the case-in-chief by stating, "The prosecution rests," or other words to that effect.

B. Defendant's Case-in-Chief

After the prosecution rests, if the defense believes that the prosecution evidence failed to meet the government's burden of proof, the defense may

---

[8]   For a more comprehensive explanation of criminal procedure from arrest to final release, *see* CARLSON, CRIMINAL JUSTICE PROCEDURE (7th ed. 2005).

[9]   McCORMICK, EVIDENCE 7.

[10] The procedure to be followed in the examination of witnesses is discussed in Chapter 9, *infra*.

ask the judge for a "directed verdict" of acquittal. If the judge believes that no rational jury could convict on the basis of the evidence presented, the judge will order an acquittal. Is this situation, the case ends and no retrial is possible because the judge's decision operates as a verdict on the merits of the case. If this motion by the defense attorney fails, the defense has the opportunity to present its evidence or case-in-chief. However, the defendant is not required t o put on a defense, because the burden of proof remains with the prosecution. The defendant may present evidence in denial of the prosecution's claim; he or she may introduce evidence designed to destroy the prosecutor's proof of one of the elements of the offense; the defendant may attempt to establish an alibi or one of the other affirmative defenses through the use of witnesses. The defendant has a Fifth Amendment privilege not to become a witness in his or her own behalf, but all defendants have an opportunity to personally become a witness. If so, the defendant is usually the first witness to take the stand at this stage of the proceedings.[11] As in the case of the prosecution, the defense counsel conducts direct examination of each defense witness and then immediately following the direct examination of each witness, he or she may be cross-examined by the prosecution. When the defense counsel has completed the presentation of the evidence, the defendant's attorney states, "The defense rests."

C. State's Case in Rebuttal

The prosecution now has the opportunity to rebut or refute the evidence presented by the defense. At this stage, the prosecution may not present witnesses that merely support the allegations of the indictment. That should have been done when the prosecution presented its case-in-chief. At this point, the prosecution is limited to the introduction of testimony or other evidence that is directed toward refuting the evidence that has been offered by the defense. New witnesses may be called at this time, but only if they can rebut, contradict, or cast doubt upon the evidence presented by the defendant. For example, if the defense raises the question of insanity, the prosecution may offer evidence to show that the defendant was not insane as defined by law. In this stage, as in other stages, the witness may not only be examined directly, but may also be cross-examined by opposing counsel.

D. Defense's Case in Rejoinder

The defense also has the opportunity to introduce evidence contrary to that introduced by the prosecution during its case in rebuttal. This phase of the trial is called the defense case in rejoinder. With a view to narrowing the subject matter, the evidence is limited to refuting or discrediting the evidence presented by the prosecution during the state's case in rebuttal. Returning to the example above,

---

[11] In 1972, the United States Supreme Court held that requiring the defendant to testify before other defense witnesses violates the self-incrimination provisions of the Constitution. Brooks v. Tennessee, 406 U.S. 605, 92 S. Ct. 1891, 32 L. Ed. 2d 358 (1972). State v. Glover, 636 So. 2d 976 (La. 1994).

where the state has offered evidence to demonstrate that the defendant may not have been legally insane, the defendant has the opportunity to offer testimony to correct the evidence offered by the prosecution that the defendant was insane, according to the legal definition. If the prosecution managed to introduce new evidence that "opened the door" to new material, the defense is permitted to rebut the new material with relevant evidence during this stage of the case.

There are instances when the case may continue with the prosecution and the defense each having the opportunity to refute the evidence presented by the other. However, it is obvious that this becomes more and more limited and, in the usual case, both parties will have presented all the evidence that they intend to present by the end of the defendant's rejoinder.

When both parties have announced that they have rested their cases, the hearing on the facts comes to an end, and the trial proceeds with the arguments of counsel and the court's instructions to the jury.

§ 4.5   Procedure for Offering and Challenging Evidence

Rule 103

Rulings on Evidence

(a) Effect of erroneous ruling. Error may not be predicated upon a ruling which admits or excludes evidence unless a substantial right of the party is affected, and

    (1) Objection. In case the ruling is one admitting evidence, a timely objection or motion to strike appears of record, stating the specific ground of objection, if the specific ground was not apparent from the context; or

    (2) Offer of proof. In case the ruling is one excluding evidence, the substance of the evidence was made known to the court by offer or was apparent from the context within which questions were asked.

(b) Record of offer and ruling. The court may add any other or further statement which shows the character of the evidence, the form in which it was offered, the objection made, and the ruling thereon. It may direct the making of an offer in question and answer form.[12]

* * *

For a variety of reasons and in the interests of justice, courts will not admit all evidence offered by either party. The courts follow a complex set of rules in determining what evidence should be admitted and what evidence should be

---

[12]   FED R. EVID. 103. The Federal Rules of Evidence, effective Jan. 2, 1975 (Pub. L. No. 93-595), apply to United States federal courts, judge magistrate proceedings, and bankruptcy courts. Portions of these rules, as well as the committee comments thereto, are inserted when relevant to the text discussion. The complete rules as approved through 2008 appear in the Appendix, *infra*.

excluded. A significant portion of the remainder of this book will be devoted to the rules that have been developed for judicial application in determining the admissibility of evidence. Most of these rules are rules of exclusion, which the parties will argue are inapplicable in a particular situation, depending on which side desires the admission of the evidence.

The usual way of offering and eliciting oral testimony involves placing the witness on the stand and asking the witness a question or series of questions. If either the prosecution or the defense believes a question is improper, an objection is made and the court then decides whether the answer should be allowed. The party making the objection must state the ground for the objection, unless the context makes the reason obvious. The opposing counsel may offer the judge the legal rationale concerning why the objection should be overruled and the evidence admitted. If the judge sustains an objection that keeps evidence from being presented, the attorney for that party should make an offer of proof (a proffer) of what the evidence, if it had been allowed, would have shown. An offer of proof must show three things: (1) "what the evidence would be, (2) the purpose and object of the evidence, and (3) each fact essential to establishing its admissibility."[13] The offer of proof allows the trial court properly to consider the arguments for admissibility while preserving the record for appeal.

If the judge makes what one party considers an erroneous ruling, this can be challenged on appeal, provided that the opposing counsel made a proper and timely objection. In general, however, reversible error will not be predicated upon an erroneous ruling unless the error was sufficiently substantial to have affected the outcome of the trial. If an error did not rise to this level it is called "harmless error" and does not constitute error sufficient to reverse the case.

To avoid an unnecessary expenditure of trial time, the rules in virtually all states provide that the formal exception procedure is unnecessary,[14] but the objecting attorney must have made an appropriate objection, stating the legal grounds, in order to preserve the trial record for appellate purposes.

In the case of real evidence, such as bullets, guns, articles of clothing, and similar evidence, the party offering the evidence, after having it identified or authenticated by a witness, submits it to the opposing counsel for inspection. When this has been done, it is presented to the judge and, depending upon the type of evidence, it may be presented to each juror individually or to the jury as a whole.

In a North Carolina case that involved a state version of Rule 103, in order to preserve for appellate review, either the admission or exclusion of evidence, the significance of the admitted or excluded evidence must appear in the record and a specific offer of proof must have been made to the court unless its significance is obvious or apparent from the record. If a defendant alleges error in the exclusion of testimony but has failed to offer proof for the

---

[13] State v. Childs, 257 S.W.3d 655, 658, 2008 Mo. App. LEXIS 975 (Mo. 2008).

[14] Texas Rules of Appellate Procedure, Rule 33(c)(1), Preservation of Appellate Complaints (Matthew Bender 2008).

record, there is no issue on which an appellate court may rule.[15] However, an appellate court may use the concept of "plain error" as the standard for review as a way to allow an appeal where a party failed to make an appropriate Rule 103 objection.[16]

The requirement that the objecting party offer specific grounds for an objection permits the judge to understand the objection, its purpose, and the legal basis. It allows the opposing counsel to properly meet the objection and address it. Also, a precise objection allows the judge correct any errors by making an informed and appropriate decision that has the effect of preserving the record for appeal.[17]

§ 4.6 Role of the Trial Judge in Evidence Matters

In the English and American systems, the trial judge is responsible for controlling the courtroom while ensuring that the trial is administered in an orderly way and that it progresses efficiently and smoothly. When a defendant has requested a jury trial, the jury evaluates the evidence and determines which facts have been established beyond a reasonable doubt; however, the judge still plays an important role in relation to the admission and exclusion of evidence. Some of these duties are enumerated and explained below. The judge:

- *During pretrial hearings, determines whether some of the evidence will be admissible at the trial*—In the first instance, the judge determines, after listening to arguments from both sides, what evidence will be admitted during the trial and what evidence will be suppressed. If a motion to suppress is made before the trial starts, generally the judge's decision stands for the duration of the trial. In most situations, the judge's pretrial evidence rulings will stand, although the prosecution may appeal a ruling suppressing evidence where the matter is crucial to the prosecutor's case. Where the pretrial ruling effectively ends the prosecution's case, the prosecutor must decide to either drop the case or pursue an immediate pretrial appeal.

- *Acts on motions and objections regarding evidence during the trial*—If a party challenges the admission of evidence as being irrelevant, immaterial, incompetent, or otherwise excludable under the rules of evidence, the judge determines whether the evidence will be admitted or excluded and announces that ruling in court.

---

[15]   State v. Cousar, 660 S.E.2d 902, 905, 2008 N. C. App. LEXIS 1076 (N.C. 2008).

[16]   FED. R. EVID. 103(d). According to the Tenth Circuit, to establish plain error, an appellant must demonstrate "To establish plain error, a defendant must show that: (1) an error; (2) that is plain and obvious, (3) that affects substantial rights, and (4) seriously affects the fairness or public reputation of the judicial proceeding. United States v. Vazquez, 2009 U.S. App. LEXIS 2473 (10th Cir. 2009).

[17]   75 AM. JUR. 2D *Trial* § 312 (2008). *See also* Gbur, Executrix v. Golio, 2009 Pa. LEXIS 177 (2009).

As a general rule, trial judges have the inherent power to admit or exclude evidence at trial and a trial judge's decisions concerning the admissibility of evidence are reviewable only under the abuse of judicial discretion standard.[18] Putting this in somewhat different terms, a federal appeals court observed that a trial judge has broad discretion in ruling on the admissibility of evidence, and an appellate court will not reverse a trial judge's decision unless a clear abuse of discretion was demonstrated.[19]

- *Makes decisions concerning the constitutionality of law enforcement activities*—A motion to exclude evidence obtained in violation of the Constitution generally must be made at a pretrial hearing on a motion to suppress or may be made during the trial if the issue first surfaces at that point. To decide this challenge properly, the judge must be familiar with the decisions regarding such matters as search and seizure, confessions, right to counsel, self-incrimination, and due process. If a motion is made to exclude evidence because these provisions were violated and the judge admits the evidence that has been obtained in violation of the Constitution, the reviewing court on appeal can and probably will reverse the decision unless the error is harmless.

- *Protects the witnesses from overzealous examination and cross-examination by counsel*—Overzealous counsel sometimes browbeat witnesses by continuing to ask questions that have been answered or by harshly or unnecessarily cross-examining a witness. Because the judge has the duty to control the courtroom and the manner in which witnesses are questioned, the judge may intervene on his or her own motion or from objections made by counsel for the parties.

- *Takes judicial notice*—The judge plays a very important role in judicially noticing facts that may be considered by the jury in making the decision.[20] Some facts are so well known that to require proof via witnesses would constitute a waste of a trial court's time. For example, requiring proof that water boils at 100 degrees Centigrade is a universally known scientific fact. Having a physicist or other expert prove the boiling point of water would certainly waste the court's resources. The judge may accept without proof that water boils at 100 degrees and both parties would generally have no legal objection.

- *Determines competency of the witness to testify*—The judge determines whether the witness meets the requirements of competency.[21] "The general rule is that every witness is presumed to be competent

---

[18]   Jones v. State, 780 N.E.2d 373 at 376 (Ind. 2002). *See also* Grace v. City of Cheyenne, 2006 U.S. App. LEXIS 15182 (10th Cir. 2006).
[19]   United States v. Fuller, 2006 U.S. App. LEXIS 14852 (5th Cir. 2006).
[20]   Judicial notice is discussed in Chapter 5.
[21]   Competency of witnesses is discussed in Chapter 9, *and see* Commonwealth v. Judd, 2006 Pa. Super. 84, 2006 Pa. Super. LEXIS 538 (2006).

to be a witness"[22] unless the opposing party can demonstrate otherwise. For example, where the witness possessed sufficient memory of the facts and would tell the truth, an appellate court held that the trial court did not abuse its discretion in holding that the challenged witness was competent to testify.[23] Judicial determinations of competency are reviewable on appeal based on an abuse of discretion standard.

- *Rules on issues of law*—In addition, the judge instructs the jury concerning the law to be applied to the facts that the jury determined, advises the jury as to what facts may be considered, and provides alternatives with respect to lesser included offenses in returning its verdict.

- *Acts a finder of fact in some cases*—Finally, when a trial takes place without a jury, such as when the defendant waives the Sixth Amendment right to jury, the judge has the role as the factfinder. In this instance, the judge performs a dual role; he or she acts in the normal capacity as a judge managing the case and ruling on evidentiary matters and the judge performs the function of the jury in deciding which facts have been properly proven.

A criminal trial judge is not an advocate for either party, but serves as a neutral referee placed between the parties and their attorneys and commits error if he or she acts as an advocate for either party.[24] Generally, a trial judge has discretion to comment on the evidence presented at trial and to make other comments during the course of a trial,[25] but some jurisdictions do not permit the judge to comment on the evidence.[26] Where permitted, judicial comments to the jury concerning evidence must be done with great care so that unfair prejudice to either party is avoided.[27]

While a trial judge must avoid any actual or apparent partisanship to, for, or against a party, the judge must be actively engaged in overseeing the trial. In *Brown v. State*, the trial judge denied a defense request for a mistrial because the prosecution had not notified the defense of some evidence that the prosecution had to disclose.[28] The judge properly recognized that the prosecution was not being unfair because the prosecution notified the defense as soon as it became aware of the evidence. The judge remained impartial in ruling on the case. In different case, a judge abandoned this impartial role where he made jokes, light-hearted comments, and generally had an irreverent attitude

---

[22] *Id. See also* A.R.E. Rule 601 General rule of competency (Ark. 2008).
[23] People v. Watson, 245 Mich. App. 572 at 583, 629 N.W.2d 411 at 420 (2001).
[24] Commonwealth v. Baumhammers, 960 A.2d 59, 2008 Pa. LEXIS 2078 (Pa. 2008).
[25] United States v. Zidar, 2006 U.S. App. LEXIS 11858 (9th Cir. 2006).
[26] State v. Francisco, 148 Wash. App. 168, 179, 2009 Wash App. LEXIS 22 (Wash 2009).
[27] United States v. Frederick, 406 F.3d 754, 2005 U.S. App. LEXIS 7770 (6th Cir. 2005).
[28] Brown v. State, 897 A.2d 748, 2006 Del. LEXIS 163 (Del. 2006). *See* case in Part II.

during a murder trial. He joked about not wanting to be there and told lawyer jokes during trial. The appellate court, in reversing the murder conviction that resulted, noted that:

> The trial judge has primary responsibility for maintaining order and decorum in the courtroom and must control criminal proceedings so as to insure that justice is done. We recognize that the trial judge's intent in the instant case may have been to create a casual atmosphere to put jurors at ease and make them feel welcome; however, the trial judge not only failed to maintain order and decorum but also actively contributed to creating an aura of jocularity inappropriate to the gravity of the proceedings.[29]

During deliberations, when a jury appears to be confused about a legal issue and needs additional guidance, and when a resolution of the question is not apparent from earlier instructions, a trial judge has a responsibility to give the jury additional guidance by a clear statement of relevant legal criteria.[30] As a general rule, after a jury has retired to deliberate and desires to be informed on a point of law, after consultation with the parties, the judge may offer additional instructions to the jury.[31]

§ 4.7   Function of the Jury

In a criminal trial, the jury has the duty to resolve conflicts in the evidence and determine the truth based on the facts that both parties have been presented. A jury faces a host of challenges when evaluating the evidence and rendering a decision because almost every case presents contradictory, and sometimes confusing testimony, as well as physical evidence. The criminal justice system has given the jurors the challenge of determining the credibility of witnesses and what evidence should be given the most weight. In a jury trial, the ultimate goal is to determine whether the prosecution has proven the defendant is guilty beyond a reasonable doubt. Following the presentation of all of the evidence by the prosecution and the defense and after the attorneys have presented their closing arguments, the jury retires to deliberate. No judge, attorney, or other court employee meets with the jury; the case decision rests entirely with the jury.

The jury need not resolve difficult questions of law because it is the duty of the judge to make legal decisions and resolve legal disputes during the trial. Immediately prior to retiring to deliberate, the judge instructs the jury concerning the law to be applied by giving the jury what amounts to a lesson in law that covers the case the jury has just heard. The charge by the judge, or jury instruction, attempts to educate the jury concerning the law and the jury instruction needs to have sufficient particularity that the jury can understand

---

[29]   State v. Langley, 896 So. 2d 200, 207, 2004 La. App. LEXIS 3177 (2004).
[30]   United States v. Evans, 431 F.3d 343, 347, 2005 U.S. App. LEXIS 27403 (8th Cir. 2005).
[31]   Howard v. State, 2008 Miss. App. LEXIS 478 (Miss. 2008).

and apply the law. In a nutshell, the trial judge is required to explain the law correctly to the jury so that it may apply the law to the facts and determine a defendant's guilt with respect to every element of the crime.[32] In jury trials, the jurors have the exclusive responsibility to find the facts, and the trial court may not interfere with this function.

In determining what actually happened, the jurors must have the opportunity to see and hear the prosecution and defense witnesses and some jurisdictions permit jurors to ask questions of the witnesses,[33] including the defendant if the defendant has taken the stand. Based on the questions asked by counsel, the answers given by the witnesses, the documentary and real evidence, the demeanor of the witnesses, and their own knowledge of people, the jurors must reach a decision based on the evidence and substitutes for evidence that have been made available at the trial. Jurors must make decisions only on the evidence obtained by virtue of courtroom presentations and a juror's private investigation beyond the courtroom can be grounds for a reversal.[34]

In one case, a defendant argued that his conviction for homicide should be reversed because of alleged juror misconduct by using knowledge that had not been introduced at court. In determining the defendant's intent, there was some evidence that the defendant had fired a gun at one of the victims but two of the jurors noted that when a gun is fired it does move upward and to the left, evidence that had never been introduced at trial. The reviewing court held that the jurors had not conducted themselves improperly, they were just relying on their knowledge and common sense in evaluating the evidence.[35] A reversal is not appropriate if the juror's conduct constituted nothing more than applying everyday perceptions and common sense to evaluating the issues presented at trial. In an Arizona case involving an allegation of jury misconduct, the court noted that a reversal warrants a new trial only if the defendant can demonstrate both juror misconduct and actual prejudice or prejudice that could be assumed from the facts. Where jurors observed a witness hug a homicide victim's relative and where a newspaper that did not address the case was found in the jury room, these episodes did not result in a reversal of the homicide conviction.[36]

§ 4.8 Role of Witnesses

In presenting evidence in a criminal trial, witness testimony proves to be an absolute necessity because no actual evidence can be introduced without a

---

[32] 47 Am. Jur. 2d *Jury* § 15 (West 2008). *See also* People v. Miller, 164 Cal. App. 4th 653, 662. 2008 Cal. App. LEXIS 971 (Cal. 2008).

[33] Amos v. State, 896 N.E.2d 1163, 1170, 2008 Ind. App. LEXIS 2544 (Ind. 2008). *See also* Ex parte Malone, 2008 Ala. LEXIS 271 (2008).

[34] State v. Cook, 2006 Kan. LEXIS 361, (2006).

[35] Robinson v. Woodford, 2006 U.S. App. LEXIS 6009 (9th Cir. 2006).

[36] State v. Cruz, 218 Ariz. 149, 2008 Ariz. LEXIS 49 (2008), *cert. denied,* Cruz v. Arizona, 2009 U.S. LEXIS 428 (2009).

witness.[37] Witnesses may be classified as either lay or expert, with lay witnesses generally answering "who," "what," "where," and "when" types of questions while expert witnesses are permitted to offer opinions. Criminal cases usually involve criminal justice officials like police officers, parole and probation officers, and correctional officers who offer testimony based on their respective first-hand knowledge of the facts of a particular case. These and other witnesses offer the court and jury important facts and assist in introducing narrative evidence of what they observed at the crime scene or other relevant location. Witnesses serve as the essential link in bringing physical and documentary evidence to the court for jury consideration. When properly presented, the witnesses' testimony "paints" a picture of the operative facts of the prosecution or the defense case. The jury must evaluate the testimony of the witnesses for truthfulness, and therefore it is important to recognize that it is not only what is said by the witnesses, but also how it is said and the demeanor with which it is said, that jurors consider. For this reason, a trial witness must have some concern about his or her demeanor, the method of presenting the facts, voice, and even his or her dress. Although the direction of witness interrogation falls to the attorneys, it is important that all witnesses give answers that are responsive to the questions actually asked and to explain fully each piece of evidence in context so that the jury can understand its significance.[38]

The importance of witnesses in the judicial process has long been recognized by the courts. Under constitutional and statutory provisions, including the Sixth Amendment to the federal constitution, persons accused of crime have the right to have compulsory process for obtaining courtroom attendance of witnesses on their behalf. The defendant, with a few exceptions,[39] has the Sixth Amendment right to confront and cross-examine adverse witnesses.[40] In a New Jersey case, a defendant had properly requested that an incarcerated witness testify for the defense, but the authorities did not produce the witness. The Supreme Court of New Jersey reversed the lower court and remanded the case to determine whether the proposed witness's testimony would have been favorable to the defendant because the defendant had the right to have the government's assistance in using compulsory process to produce the witness.[41] The Sixth Amendment guarantee to confront and cross-examine witnesses and to call witnesses as well as the right to interrogate such favorable witnesses in one's own behalf have long been recognized as essential to due process.[42]

---

[37] A court may take judicial notice of facts as a substitute for evidence. *See* Chapter 5, Judicial Notice.

[38] *See* Chapter 9 for a discussion of the examination of witnesses.

[39] People v. Bunyard, 2009 Cal. LEXIS 1102 (Cal. 2009). Confrontation right was not enforced where witness disappeared, state made good faith effort to find witness, and defendant previously had opportunity to confront and cross-examine.

[40] Marshall v. State, 2009 Ala. Crim. App. LEXIS 16 (Ala. 2009).

[41] State v. Garcia, 195 N.J. 192, 201, 2008 N.J. LEXIS 771 (N.J. 2008).

[42] 21A AM. JUR. 2D *Criminal Law* §1072 (West 2008).

§ 4.9   Prosecuting Attorney's Responsibilities

As a representative of the executive branch, prosecutors have a dual role in the administration of justice because they are advocates for the government's position and are also administrators of justice who are charged with seeing that a defendant has a fair trial and will not be convicted unless competent and admissible evidence has been introduced.[43] In a federal prosecution, a court of appeals noted that the courts have no authority to interfere with a prosecutor's decision to prosecute and that a prosecutor can choose to add charges to a prosecution by the use of a superseding indictment without any judicial intervention.[44] In a landmark case, the Supreme Court of the United States held that a prosecutor could actually procure an additional indictment under the habitual offender statute where the defendant refused to accept a plea bargain.[45] A Michigan court of appeals noted that a prosecutor has the discretion to bring any charges supported by the evidence and that reviewing courts have only a narrow power of review of such decisions. A court could only grant relief if a prosecutor's acts were unconstitutional, illegal, or beyond the power of a prosecutor.[46] In fact, some prosecutors have the discretion to charge offenders who have committed the same crimes under separate statutes that provide for different punishments.[47]

In a criminal case, a prosecuting attorney represents a state government or the government of the United States and has the duty to bring criminal cases for which sufficient evidence exists and to decline to prosecute cases for which evidence is insufficient.[48] The prosecutor generally has the power to dismiss cases when the interests of justice require it. Above all, the prosecutor has the duty to see that justice is done, not that the government merely secures convictions. To carry out these responsibilities, the prosecutor's duties include the collection of physical evidence, interviewing witnesses, and preparing the case for trial.

With respect to evidence, the prosecutor must decide not only what evidence is to be introduced, but how that evidence is to be produced and consider the appropriate time during the trial when each item should be introduced. Legal cases that support admission should be available to present to the court in the event that opposing counsel challenges an item of evidence as violating one of the many rules of exclusion.

The prosecutor guides the case for the state by putting prosecution witnesses on the stand and proving the state's case-in-chief. After asking questions,

---

[43]   People v. Williams, 170 Cal. App. 4th 587, 2009 Cal. App. LEXIS 78 (Cal. 2009).

[44]   United States v. Banner, 442 F.3d 1310, 1315, 2006 U.S. App. LEXIS 5967 (11th Cir. 2006).

[45]   *See* Bordenkircher v. Hayes 434 U.S. 357, 1978 U.S. LEXIS 56 (1978).

[46]   People v. Green, 2009 Mich. App. LEXIS 311 (Mich. 2009).

[47]   People v Wilkinson, 102 Cal. App. 4th 72, 125 Cal. Rptr. 2d 294 (2002).

[48]   63C Am. Jur. 2d *Prosecuting Attorneys* § 20.

the prosecutor must be so familiar with the evidence that appropriate follow-up questions may be directed to the witness during redirect examination to clear up any possible misconceptions. It is not enough for prosecutors to be familiar with the state's case—the prosecutor should be aware of the accused's defense and have questions prepared for cross-examination of the defendant's witnesses.

In presenting the case, part of the prosecutor's duties involves making opening and closing statements or arguments. During the opening statement, the prosecutor explains what the state intends to prove and how the state will present its evidence. Ideally, the opening statement provides a "road map" for the jury that predicts the manner in which the prosecution's case will be presented. In the closing statement or argument, the prosecutor summarizes the evidence that has been presented in such a way as to cast it in the light most favorable to the prosecution. The prosecutor must anticipate the defense closing argument and because, following the closing argument of the defense, the prosecution has a final opportunity to counter it during the prosecution's closing rebuttal.

Constitutionally, the prosecutor has some responsibilities to the defense, and to a possibly innocent defendant, to make exculpatory evidence available upon request. In the interests of justice, there is a general duty to disclose evidence that might be exculpatory to the defendant and would include any evidence that might help impeach a prosecution witness. It is reversible error for the prosecutor to use evidence that he or she knows—or should know—is untrue, to use evidence that was acquired in violation of the law, or to withhold evidence favorable to the defense.[49] In the 1963 case of *Brady v. Maryland*, the United States Supreme Court held that suppression by the prosecution of evidence favorable to the accused, upon request, violates due process where the evidence is material either to guilt or to punishment, irrespective of good faith or bad faith on the part of the prosecution. In interpreting the *Brady* decision in a 1999 case, the United States Supreme Court noted that:

> There are three components of a true *Brady* violation: The evidence at issue must be favorable to the accused, either because it is exculpatory, or because it is impeaching; that evidence must have been suppressed by the State, either willfully or inadvertently; and prejudice must have ensued.[50]

The Court pointed out that in order to prevail on a claim under *Brady*, it must be shown that the prosecution violated its duty to disclose information favorable to the defendant, which affected the outcome of the trial. A "*Brady* violation does not exist unless the nondisclosure was so serious that there [was] a reasonable probability that the suppressed evidence would have produced a different verdict."[51]

---

[49] Maddox v. Montgomery, 718 F.2d 1033 (11th Cir. 1983). *See* case in Part II. Brady v. Maryland, 373 U.S. 83, 83 S. Ct. 1194, 10 L. Ed. 2d 215 (1963).

[50] Strickler v. Greene, 527 U.S. 263, 281–282 (1999).

[51] *Id*. at 282.

The duty to disclose exculpatory evidence becomes demonstrably critical, both for the defendant and for the non-disclosing attorney. In a New Orleans murder case, a man and his date were leaving a restaurant in the French Quarter when one of three subjects shot the man in the face, resulting in his death. When police questioned his date, she indicated that she had not been wearing her contacts or her glasses and as a result she did not get a good look at the killer and could only see patterns and shapes. However, three weeks later, she made a positive identification of the eventual defendant by picking him from a police lineup. The prosecutor shared the woman's story about not seeing the perpetrator well on the night of the murder and the defense had one police report that the witness needed corrective lenses to see properly, but a second police report three days later that expanded on her need for corrective lenses was never shared with the defense. The defendant's conviction and death sentence were reversed and the prosecutor received sanctions from the Louisiana bar for violating the Rules of Professional Conduct because he had failed to share exculpatory impeachment evidence with the defense, possibly causing the wrong person to be convicted of murder.[52] Finding that the prosecutor had improperly withheld exculpatory evidence from the defendant that there existed a reasonable probability that the conviction might not have resulted but for the prosecutor's wrongdoing, the Supreme Court of Louisiana sanctioned the prosecuting attorney. The Court noted that:

> By withholding material exculpatory evidence from a criminal defendant, respondent violated a duty owed to the public. As a prosecutor, respondent is charged with a high ethical standard and may not carelessly skirt his obligation. [Citation omitted.] Although neither *Brady* [*v. Maryland*] or Rule 3.8 [of Professional Responsibility] incorporates a mental element, Rule XIX, § 10(C) does. Based on the testimony of respondent and the character evidence discussed below, we find that respondent knowingly withheld *Brady* evidence. As to the element regarding actual injury, this Court reversed [the defendant's] conviction on other grounds and granted him a new trial. However, this Court's actions in reversing the conviction does not vitiate the potential injury to the criminal justice system, or to [the defendant], caused by respondent's actions, and warrants serious consideration and discipline by this Court.[53]

Although the defendant's conviction had been reversed prior to the sanction applied to the prosecutor by the Supreme Court of Louisiana, the Court noted that a prosecutor's duty "to disclose is imbedded in the principle that a criminal defendant is deprived of a fair trial when the state withholds exculpatory evidence that is material to guilt or punishment."[54]

Thus, where a state prosecutor failed to share information that was important to either guilt or innocence with the defendant, a violation of the due process

---

[52]   In re Roger W. Jordan, 913 So. 2d 775; 2005 La. LEXIS 2104 (2005).

[53]   *Id.*

[54]   *Id.*

clause of the Fourteenth Amendment occurs. Although the defendant had his murder conviction reversed on other grounds other than the misconduct of the prosecutor, the prosecutor's conduct created a reasonable probability that the verdict might have been different if the material had been properly shared. Even when the prosecutor has a duty to share exculpatory evidence and merits a disciplinary sanction, a reviewing court will not reverse a conviction unless the false evidence was material to guilt or punishment and a different result would probably have occurred but for the error.

§ 4.10 Defense Attorney's Responsibilities

When the Bill of Rights was adopted as part of our Constitution in 1791, the right to counsel was included as part of the Sixth Amendment. The Amendment reads in part:

> In all criminal prosecutions the accused shall enjoy the right. . . . to have the assistance of counsel for his defense.

In addition to the federal Constitution, all of the states require by their respective constitutions that the accused shall have the right to appear in person and be represented by counsel.

The right to counsel entitles criminal defendants to have effective assistance of counsel, a standard that contemplates the services of an attorney with the customary skills and diligence that a reasonably competent attorney would perform under similar circumstances.[55] According to the Supreme Court, "In assessing attorney performance, all the Federal Courts of Appeals and all but a few state courts have now adopted the "reasonably effective assistance of counsel" standard in one formulation or another."[56] In a landmark case, *Strickland v. Washington*, Justice O'Connor wrote, "The benchmark for judging any claim of ineffectiveness must be whether counsel's conduct so undermined the proper functioning of the adversarial process that the trial cannot be relied on as having produced a just result."[57] *Strickland* required a complaining defendant to demonstrate that (1) the defense counsel's performance was deficient and (2) that the deficient performance prejudiced the defense in a way that adversely affected the outcome of the trial.[58] As a general rule, reviewing courts must imply a strong presumption that counsel's conduct falls within the wide range of reasonable professional assistance. The primary function of a defendant's trial attorney is to force the prosecution to introduce sufficient evidence of the alleged offenses and to assure that the defendant's legal and constitutional rights have not been violated. Pretrial preparation is

---

[55] United States v. Boone, 437 F.3d 829, 839, 2006 U.S. App. LEXIS 3531 (8th Cir. 2006).

[56] Strickland v. Washington, 466 U.S. 668 at 683, 1984 U.S. LEXIS 79 (1984).

[57] *Id.* at 686.

[58] *Id.* at 687.

essential and includes consulting with the prosecutor and preparing the case for trial. Pretrial preparation includes researching and filing pretrial motions and, where necessary, pretrial conferences with the defendant and interviews with all defense witnesses.

In preparing the case, the defense attorney has the duty to prepare the defendant for the trial by explaining the procedures that the court will follow and what the prosecutor's role will be. A good defense attorney will not tell the defendant what to say, but will advise the defendant on courtroom demeanor and cover the topics for which the defendant might have a constitutional right not to answer. Proper preparation of the defendant as a witness, including previewing expected questions and answers, is an essential defense counsel task. The defense attorney will have investigated the case, will have prepared questions for the defendant and other witnesses, and will be ready to introduce the witnesses in such a manner that the evidence has its maximum force and impact for the defense. He or she has a responsibility to cross-examine the prosecution's witnesses and to introduce evidence to rebut the testimony of such witnesses and, where possible, to impeach their credibility.

A violation of the Sixth Amendment right to effective counsel can result in a new trial where the error may have had an effect on the outcome of the trial. In an Illinois case,[59] the defendant was a houseguest in another person's apartment. Police requested consent from the apartment holder to conduct a search of the apartment for illegal drugs. Without a warrant, police conducted a search of the apartment, including a separate bedroom that the defendant occupied, and discovered controlled substances within the guest's bedroom. The guest never gave any permission to search the bedroom she occupied. Her defense counsel did not effectively pursue a motion to suppress evidence, even in the face of a fairly clear constitutional error by the police in warrantlessly searching the bedroom and in seizing the controlled substance. Her appeal contended that she received ineffective assistance of counsel. In order to prevail on this legal theory the defendant generally must demonstrate that her counsel's performance was objectively unreasonable and the attorney failed to meet the prevailing professional norms. If the defendant can also demonstrate that the outcome would likely have been different had the counsel met proper legal standards, the conviction should be reversed. According to the reviewing court, there was a great probability that, had a motion to suppress been filed, it would have been granted, and in that event, there would have been no controlled substance evidence with which to proceed to a trial. Accordingly, the appellate court reversed the conviction and remanded the case based on incompetency of legal counsel.[60]

In determining standards for evaluating the Sixth Amendment right to counsel, the Rhode Island Supreme Court stated that it would reject an allegation of ineffective assistance of counsel unless "the attorney's representation

---

[59]   People v. Givens, 384 Ill. App. 3d 101, 2008 Ill. App. LEXIS 684 (Ill. 2008).
[60]   *Id.* at 115.

was so lacking that the trial has become a farce and a mockery of justice."[61] A New Jersey appellate court noted that "[t]he benchmark for judging ineffective assistance of counsel claims is whether the defense attorney's professional errors 'materially contributed' to the defendant's conviction."[62] As a general rule, in order to obtain a reversal of a conviction due to ineffective assistance of counsel, the defendant must demonstrate that counsel's performance was deficient and that that deficient performance created such prejudice to the case that the defendant was deprived of a fair trial.[63] In order to prevail on an ineffective assistance of counsel claim, "The defendant must show that there is a reasonable probability that, but for counsel's unprofessional errors, the result of the proceeding would have been different. A reasonable probability is a probability sufficient to undermine confidence in the outcome."[64] Just because the attorney was appointed a few weeks prior to trial does not demonstrate ineffective assistance of counsel.[65] Ineffective assistance of counsel was not demonstrated in a multiple murder case in which the evidence clearly established that defendants were busy stealing cattle from a couple's farm at the time the defendants killed the farmer and his wife. Counsel's failure to request that some information about a prior conviction be removed from a police report before it was introduced as evidence did not qualify as ineffective assistance of counsel.[66] In other words, if a case had been tried with adequate representation and the outcome of the case would have been different, the error was not harmless and a new trial should be ordered. However, where there would have been no change in outcome with different counsel, the harmless error rule should be applied and the conviction sustained.

In an overall sense, the Sixth Amendment demands that defense counsel effectively represent the defendant in a criminal case by taking advantage of the available legal tools, including pleading affirmative defenses. In an Alabama case,[67] where a defendant had been charged with murder involving a fight among several people, on the night prior to the start of the murder trial, his defense attorney suggested that he lie about stabbing the deceased and tell the jury that he did stab the deceased. This defense plan of perjury had the effect of giving up a viable self-defense argument because at the moment the victim was stabbed, the defendant was trying to get away from the affray. At a hearing for a new trial, the original defense counsel admitted getting the defendant to commit perjury concerning the stabbing. Giving up a viable claim of self-defense suggested by the defense attorney constituted ineffective assistance of counsel because a proper assertion might have resulted in an acquittal

---

61　　Moniz v. State, 933 A.2d 691, 696, 2007 R.I. LEXIS 100 (2007).

62　　New Jersey v. Velez, 329 N.J. Super. 128 at 134, 746 A.2d 1073 at 1077 (2000).

63　　State v. Brownlow, 2003 Ohio 1819, 2003 Ohio App. LEXIS 1721 (2003), quoting State v. Cassano, 96 Ohio St 3d. 94, 2002 Ohio 3751 (2002).

64　　Strickland at 694.

65　　Id.

66　　Rousan v. Roper, 436 F.3d 951, 959, 2006 U.S. App. LEXIS 3003 (8th Cir. 2006).

67　　McCombs v. State, 2008 Ala. Crim. App. LEXIS 139 (Ala. 2008).

based on self-defense. The appellate court reversed the conviction and granted a new trial.

Finally, the defense attorney has the responsibility to make opening statements following the prosecution's opening statements. The defense counsel may defer an opening statement until the start of the defense case-in-chief so that the preview of the defense theory or "road map" of the case will be presented to the jury at a more appropriate time. The defense attorney also has the right to give a closing statement immediately prior to the final statement given by the prosecutor. In the closing statement, the defense attorney reviews and summarizes the evidence presented by defense witnesses, emphasizes inconsistencies in the prosecution's case, focuses on credibility issues of the prosecution's witnesses, and explains the evidence in such a way as to be most favorable to the defendant.

§ 4.11　Admissibility and Weight of Direct and Circumstantial Evidence

The responsibilities of the prosecutor and the defense attorney include introducing evidence at the trial in an effort to cause the factfinders to be convinced that certain acts occurred or did not occur or that facts did or did not exist. In a criminal case, the prosecutor has the responsibility to prove beyond a reasonable doubt that the defendant committed the acts charged, and that these acts violated the law. Creating a reasonable doubt is the goal of the defense attorney, a task that can be accomplished by the introduction of evidence that calls into question the facts presented by the prosecutor, by casting doubt on the credibility of the prosecution witnesses, of by the presentation of an affirmative defense.

In the process of introducing sufficient proof of guilt, the both parties may use both direct and circumstantial evidence. A combination of direct evidence and circumstantial evidence or either one alone may prove sufficient to meet the burden of proof because most courts hold that direct and circumstantial evidence carry equal weight.[68] Demonstrative of this equality is the fact that in considering a defendant's motion for acquittal following the prosecution's case-in-chief, courts give equal weight to direct and circumstantial evidence.[69] One court noted that circumstantial evidence in a murder case could sustain a conviction when the defendant's fingerprint was found on the deceased's identification card and another witness told of driving the defendant to the home of the deceased on the day of the homicide.[70] Rape convictions have been

---

[68]　United States v. Wiggins, 146 Fed. Appx. 437; 2005 U.S. App. LEXIS 19120 (11th Cir. 2005).

[69]　United States v. Bailey, 169 Fed. Appx. 815, 821, 2006 U.S. App. LEXIS 3402 (5th Cir. 2006).

[70]　State v. Roubideaux, 2008 S.D. 81, 2008 S.D. LEXIS 119 (S.D. 2008).

upheld when the victim was unconscious at the time of the crime and the only evidence available was the defendant's DNA recovered from the victim.[71]

While some academic doubt may exist in the minds of legal scholars as to the admissibility, weight, and sufficiency of circumstantial evidence, many cases have reached a judgment of guilt in the absence of direct evidence. The basic difference between direct and circumstantial evidence is that in the case of direct evidence, the witness testifies concerning his or her own personal knowledge of the facts; in the case of circumstantial evidence, the witness gives evidence to establish one fact and the use of logic allows the jury to decide whether a second fact naturally follows from proof of the first fact. As categories of evidence, both direct and circumstantial evidence carry equal weight and the elements of a crime may be established by either direct or circumstantial evidence.[72]

There is a classic story that helps explain the difference. In a case in which a witness testified that he observed a fight where one man was accused of "biting off" the other fighter's ear. When he testified that the one man "bit off" the other man's ear, the testimony was that he was present when it happened and he saw the fight. On cross-examination, the witness was asked whether he actually observed the one bite the other's ear, he stated that he did not actually see it being bitten but that he saw the defendant spit out the ear. Although he did not see the biting event, circumstantial evidence told him and the court that the defendant must have bitten the ear during the fight because there is no other logical explanation concerning how it got in the one man's mouth. In this context, it is difficult to argue that circumstantial evidence would not have the full force and effect of direct evidence.

The mere fact that evidence is characterized as either direct or circumstantial may indicate that one type may be superior to the other with respect to reliability. As part of California's jury instructions, the wording might suggest to jurors that circumstantial evidence might be worth less than direct evidence. The jury instructions state that:

> a finding of guilt as to any crime may not be based on circumstantial evidence unless the proved circumstances are not only (1) consistent with the theory that the defendant is guilty of the crime, but (2) cannot be reconciled with any other rational conclusion.[73]

Taking a position slightly different from California, Ohio rejected any distinction between the two types of evidence. An Ohio court of appeals noted that direct and circumstantial evidence carry equal weight and that because circumstantial and direct evidence are no different so far as the jury's fact-finding mission is concerned, all that a jury must do is to weigh all the evidence, both

---

[71] Bartman v. State, 2009 Alaska LEXIS 17 (Alaska 2009).

[72] 29A AM JUR.2D *Evidence* § 1391 (2008).

[73] *See* Caljic 2.01, California Jury Instructions (2005).

direct and circumstantial, against the reasonable doubt standard and come to a conclusion.[74]

Although it is true that, all things being equal, direct evidence probably carries more weight with juries, circumstantial evidence has a definite place in the trial of criminal cases because the case law is replete with examples of convictions based exclusively on circumstantial evidence and many others in which direct evidence proved insufficient for a conviction.

The need for circumstantial evidence appears obvious because criminals generally prefer cover and often do not commit their activities in plain view. For this reason, the use of some circumstantial evidence is usually a necessity, especially in stealth-type crimes, such as burglary, larceny, and embezzlement. In a variety of criminal cases, without the use of circumstantial evidence, a prosecutor would have a difficult task in obtaining convictions.

There is often the mistaken belief that circumstantial evidence fails to carry sufficient weight to result in a criminal conviction, or at least calls into question a conviction based wholly or primarily on circumstantial evidence. In a capital murder case involving the death of a child whose body was covered in cuts and bruises and puncture wounds, all in different states of healing, the appellate court upheld the conviction based on circumstantial evidence.[75] No one observed the child receiving injuries although the defendant claimed the child had fallen in a bathtub and fallen down a stairway. On appeal, the defendant contended that because no one had seen her injure the child and because she was not the only person with access at the time of the injury, the circumstantial evidence was insufficient to sustain a conviction for capital murder. The Texas Court of Appeals noted that circumstantial evidence can be used to prove a culpable mental state as well as prove the other elements of capital murder beyond a reasonable doubt.

Before continuing with the discussion of admissibility, weight, and sufficiency of direct and circumstantial evidence, some definitions and explanations are in order.[76]

A. *Direct Evidence*

" 'Direct evidence' is that which proves a fact without an inference or presumption and which in itself, if true, establishes that fact.' "[77] It is evidence that is applied immediately and directly to the fact to be proved—without the aid of any intervening fact or reasoning process. For example, in a trial for murder, a witness positively testifies that he saw the accused inflict the fatal wound. Evidence is declared to be direct and positive when the very acts in dispute are communicated by persons who have actual knowledge of the facts.

---

[74]   State v. Roberts, 2008 Ohio 5750, 2008 Ohio App. LEXIS 4821 (Ohio 2008).

[75]   Williams v. State, 2009 Tex. App. LEXIS 1045 (Tex. 2009).

[76]   *Id.*

[77]   MONT. CODE ANNO., 26-1-102(5) (2009).

When direct evidence is introduced, it is not necessary that the factfinders make any inferences or deductions of fact, or that there be any presumptions flowing from the evidence to connect it with the crime. Where the witness is believable, the factfinder will find that the existence of the fact has been established, unless and until other contrary evidence of equal credibility is introduced.

B. *Circumstantial Evidence*

"Circumstantial evidence is evidence that, if found to be true, proves a fact from which an inference of the existence of another fact may be drawn."[78] Another definition of circumstantial evidence is "evidence that, without going directly to prove the existence of a fact, gives rise to a logical inference that such fact does exist."[79] Circumstantial evidence is "testimony not based on actual personal knowledge or observation of the facts in controversy, but of other facts from which deductions are drawn, showing indirectly the facts sought to be proved."[80] While circumstantial evidence may not always be given the recognition by a jury that it deserves in all situations, Justice Kennedy noted that, "[c]ircumstantial evidence may be as probative as testimonial evidence."[81] The Supreme Court of Virginia noted that "circumstantial evidence is competent and is entitled to as much weight as direct evidence[,] provided that the circumstantial evidence is sufficiently convincing to exclude every reasonable hypothesis except that of guilt."[82]

After observing the differences between direct evidence and circumstantial evidence, it must be noted that all that is required of the jury is that it weigh all of the evidence—direct and circumstantial—against a standard of reasonable doubt. This was made clear in an Ohio case in which the defendant contended that the evidence presented by the state was insufficient because it was based on circumstantial evidence of intent. The appellate court noted:

> The elements of an offense may be established by direct evidence, circumstantial evidence, or both. Circumstantial and direct evidence are of equal probative value. When reviewing the value of circumstantial evidence, we note that the weight accorded an inference is fact-dependent and can be disregarded as speculative only if reasonable minds can come to the conclusion that the inference is not supported by the evidence.[83]

When evaluating whether the weight and sufficiency of circumstantial evidence should justify a determination of guilt, the United States Supreme

---

[78] Caljic 2.00, Calfifornia Jury Instructions (2005).

[79] Bland v. Fox, 172 Neb. 662, 111 N.W.2d 537 (1961), quoting C.J.S. *Evidence* §2.

[80] Ajaxo, Inc. v. E'Trade, 135 Cal. App. 4th 21, 51, 37 Cal. Rptr. 3d 221, 244, 2005 Cal. App. LEXIS 1950 (2005).

[81] Siegert v. Gilley, 500 U.S. 226 at 236 (1991), Justice Kennedy concurring.

[82] Finney v. Commonwealth, 277 Va. 83, 89, 2009 Va. LEXIS 12 (2009), quoting Dowden v. Commonwealth, 260 Va. 459, 468, 536 S.E.2d 437, 441 (2000).

[83] Ohio v. Thomas, 2002 Ohio 7333, 2002 Ohio App. LEXIS 7226 (2002).

Court, in the landmark case of *Holland v. United States*,[84] clearly stated that circumstantial evidence alone will support a conviction. In unambiguous language, the *Holland* Court did more than reject the jury instruction that, in circumstantial evidence cases, the evidence must be such as to exclude every reasonable hypothesis other than that of guilt; it clearly stated that "where the jury is properly instructed on the standards for reasonable doubt, such an additional instruction on circumstantial evidence is confusing and incorrect."[85] In a recent case that followed the rationale indicated in the Holland case, a federal district court in a habeas corpus case refused to disturb a conviction for attempted aggravated kidnapping. The defendant alleged that the prosecution failed to prove its case because the evidence was circumstantial when it showed him chasing two children and attempting to grab one child's leg. The court noted that, "Circumstantial evidence alone, however, may be sufficient to support a criminal conviction."[86]

The federal courts have consistently held that the proof of guilt by the use of circumstantial evidence alone "may be sufficient to support a conviction, and it is not necessary that the evidence preclude every reasonable hypothesis except that of guilt"[87] that some state courts require. Consistent with this view, recently the Tenth Circuit Court of Appeals reiterated that circumstantial evidence should be given the same weight as direct evidence and noted, that "[t]o sustain a criminal conviction [based on circumstantial evidence], the Government's evidence must be 'substantial' or raise more than a 'mere suspicion of guilt,' but it need not disprove every other reasonable theory of the case."[88]

Although most states follow the reasoning of the federal courts that circumstantial evidence is of equal weight to direct evidence, some states still hold that the jury instruction must contain the language "it must exclude every other reasonable hypothesis consistent with innocence," only if the case rests wholly on circumstantial evidence. In *Terry v. State*, an Arkansas case involving the rape of a child, the father appealed his conviction on the ground that the trial court erred when it refused to grant his motion for a directed verdict based on a failure of proof. The father had been left alone with his infant daughter, who was in good health. When the child's mother returned after a short absence, the father was standing over the infant with blood on his chest and on the victim's clothing. He stated that he had cut his cuticle, but the baby had a significant amount of red blood in her private area when her mother checked. A medical exam indicated tears in her private area and the doctor suspected sexual abuse. Two semen stains on the baby's diaper matched the defendant's DNA profile. Following his conviction and life sentence, he appealed, contending that

---

[84]   Holland, *supra.*

[85]   Holland, *supra,* 139.

[86]   Sparrow v. Lindamood, 2006 U.S. Dist. LEXIS 9640 (M.D. Tenn. 2006).

[87]   United States v. Hardman, 2005 U.S. Dist. LEXIS 28923 (M.D. Tenn. 2005) and United States v. Barnett, 398 F.3d 516, 522, 2005 U.S. App. LEXIS 2644 (6th Cir. 2005).

[88]   United States v. Winder, 2009 U.S. App. LEXIS, 3647 (10th Cir. 2009).

circumstantial evidence used to convict must exclude every other reasonable hypothesis consistent with innocence and that only conjecture by the jury that he was the perpetrator supported the conviction. According to the Supreme Court of Arkansas:

> Circumstantial evidence may constitute substantial evidence to support a conviction. The longstanding rule in the use of circumstantial evidence is that, to be substantial, the evidence must exclude every other reasonable hypothesis than that of the guilt of the accused. The question of whether the circumstantial evidence excludes every other reasonable hypothesis consistent with innocence is for the jury to decide. Upon review, this court must determine whether the jury resorted to speculation and conjecture in reaching its verdict. [Internal citations omitted.][89]

The Supreme Court of Arkansas affirmed his conviction over his contention that there was no direct proof of what caused the baby's trauma. The reviewing court noted that the jury could have found the circumstantial evidence to be substantial and there was DNA evidence that the defendant was the guilty party.[90]

Some states follow a slightly different view of the manner in which circumstantial evidence should be evaluated. Florida holds that a judgment of acquittal should be granted in a case in which proof of one or more of the elements of an offense depends completely on circumstantial evidence. The prosecutor does not have to rebut every conceivable variation of events that could potentially be inferred from the facts presented; it need just present evidence that is inconsistent with the defendant's reasonable hypothesis of innocence. In a case that applied the above principle, Florida charged a defendant with uttering a forged check drawn on another person's account. The account holder took the witness stand and denied writing the check. The defendant's testimony was that he had performed automobile repairs for a person who had been referred to him by another client. The new customer paid with a check that the defendant tried to cash that turned out to be a forgery. The prosecution's theory was that the defendant knew the check was forged and that he tried to cash it, while the defendant's position was that he had a reasonable explanation concerning why and how he had acquired the check. Even though nothing in the prosecution's completely circumstantial proof contradicted the defendant's story, the trial court denied defendant's motion for acquittal and the defendant's conviction resulted. On appeal, the reviewing court reversed the conviction on the strength of the Florida rule that requires a prosecutor to present evidence to contradict a defendant's hypothesis of innocence in a circumstantial evidence prosecution. The reviewing court ruled that the trial court should have granted the defendant's motion for acquittal.[91]

---

[89]   Terry v. State, 2006 Ark. LEXIS 326 (2006).

[90]   *Id.*

[91]   Linn v. State, 921 So. 2d 830, 2006 Fla. App. LEXIS 3040 (2006).

Notwithstanding some disagreement concerning the "hypothesis of innocence" instruction, courts all hold that a conviction may be based solely on circumstantial evidence. Whether a prosecutor introduced sufficient evidence to meet the constitutional standard for "the sufficiency of the evidence is whether, upon viewing the evidence in the light most favorable to the prosecution, any rational trier of fact could conclude that the state proved the essential elements of the crime beyond a reasonable doubt."[92] This measure of evidence sufficiency applies in cases involving both direct and circumstantial evidence.

§ 4.12 Summary

The prosecutor in a criminal case has the responsibility of introducing evidence sufficient to prove guilt beyond a reasonable doubt. The defense attorney has the responsibility to introduce evidence that challenges the sufficiency of the state's evidence while offering evidence to substantiate the defendant's theory of the case, including evidence of affirmative defenses. Over the years, courts and legislatures have established rules for the admissibility of evidence and for the procedure to be followed in presenting evidence in court.

To promote a smooth and orderly flow of evidence at trial, pretrial evidentiary motions may be made by the parties to exclude or suppress certain types of evidence. When a motion to suppress is presented, the burden is on the party making the motion to show that there is a legal reason the evidence should not be admitted.[93]

For all practical purposes, the rules of evidence are rules of exclusion. All evidence is admissible as a general rule unless it is excluded based on an objection or upon the court's own motion. Objections may be based on the form of the question. For example, if the attorney's questions are confusing, improperly phrased, misleading, argumentative, or compound, the opposing party may object based on the form. Objections may also be made based upon the substance of the question asked by the opposing counsel. If the objection is made because the evidence is irrelevant, immaterial, or incompetent, the complaining party should offer a legal theory to support the objection.

The usual order for presenting evidence is for the state to present its case-in-chief, followed by the defendant's case-in-chief. The prosecution then has the opportunity to introduce evidence to rebut the evidence presented by the defense. The defense may, if it deems necessary, follow up with evidence contrary to that introduced by the prosecution during the rebuttal. When both parties have rested their cases, the hearing on the facts comes to an end, and the trial proceeds with the closing arguments and the court's instructions to the jury.

---

[92] State v. Singleton, 922 So. 2d 647, 650, 2006 La. App. LEXIS 115 (La. 2006).

[93] Where a defendant files a motion to suppress evidence and no arrest or search warrant was used, the burden of proving a valid search or arrest is placed on the prosecution.

The customary method of offering evidence involves having the party place its witness on the stand and conducting direct examination by asking a series of non-leading questions. The opposing party, through counsel, may challenge any question before an answer is given by making a specific objection. The attorneys must be ready to offer grounds for their respective positions. The court considers the contentions of both parties and then determines whether the answer should be allowed into evidence. In order to preserve an objection to admission or exclusion of evidence for appeal, the objection or motion must have been timely and made with sufficient specificity that the trial judge was aware of the complaint and the court must have actually made a ruling on the objection or motion. In some cases, the attorney who lost the objection or motion may make an offer of proof to preserve the record for appeal.

In English and American courts, the trial judge, jury, witnesses, prosecuting attorney, and defense attorney all have specific functions. The judge determines whether evidence is admissible and gives instructions to the jury. The jury determines the facts from the evidence and applies the law to the facts, using the instructions given by the judge. The witnesses are the eyes and ears of the court. The prosecuting attorney guides the case for the state by producing witnesses on behalf of the state, and the defense attorney represents the accused by challenging prosecution witnesses and by presenting evidence designed to counter the prosecutor's case.

Although a few American jurisdictions question the weight and sufficiency of circumstantial evidence as compared to direct evidence, most jurisdictions hold that circumstantial evidence has equal weight when compared to direct evidence. A case built entirely upon circumstantial evidence may meet the prosecutor's burden of proof beyond a reasonable doubt. Juries may give circumstantial evidence somewhat less weight than direct evidence, but as long as the jury is satisfied that the total weight of all the evidence demonstrates the defendant's guilt beyond a reasonable doubt, a conviction is appropriate.

All who are involved in the criminal justice process, whether they are directly or indirectly involved in collecting, preserving, presenting, or evaluating the evidence, should be aware of the process by which evidence is introduced, challenged, and evaluated during the trial.

Judicial Notice

5

Judicial notice takes the place of proof, and is of equal force. As a means of establishing facts, it is therefore superior to evidence. In its appropriate field, it displaces evidence, since, as it stands for proof, it fulfills the object which evidence is designed to fulfill, and makes evidence unnecessary.

State v. Maine, 69 Conn. 123, 36 L.R.A. 623,
61 Am. St. Rep. 30, 37 A. 80 (1897)

Chapter Outline

Section
5.1   Introduction
5.2   Judicial Notice Defined
5.3   Judicial Notice of Facts
5.4   —Matters of General Knowledge
5.5   —History and Historical Facts
5.6   —Geography and Geographical Facts
5.7   —Facts Relating to Nature and Science
5.8   —Language, Abbreviations, and Symbols
5.9   Judicial Notice of Laws
5.10   —Law of the Forum
5.11   —Federal Law
5.12   —Law of Sister States
5.13   —Law of Foreign Countries
5.14   —Municipal Ordinances
5.15   —Administrative Regulations
5.16   —Jurisdiction of Courts
5.17   Judicial Notice Process
5.18   Judicial Notice in Criminal Cases
5.19   Summary

§ 5.1 Introduction

Near the close of a criminal trial, the judge has the duty to educate the jury concerning the law to be applied to the particular facts that will be determined by the jury. In this phase of the trial, it is said that the judge "instructs the jury," which means that the judge explains to the members of the jury that they are to determine, from the facts presented at the trial consistent with the explanations of the applicable law given by the judge, the guilt or innocence of the accused. Generally, the prosecution and the defense have the burden of establishing facts by producing sworn witnesses, authenticated documents, or real evidence. However, the courts, recognizing that it would be unreasonable to require the opposing parties to introduce evidence for every fact considered by the jury or the judge in a bench trial, have made some exceptions. Criminal trials can be lengthy affairs under our present system, and it would be unwise to require the parties to prove facts that are so well known that their truth is not in any dispute.

To save the time of the court and for procedural convenience, by virtue of legislative enactment and through case law, formal procedures that serve as substitutes for evidence have evolved. The first substitute for evidence is judicial notice. The principle of judicial notice authorizes the court to accept appropriate facts as true without requiring one of the parties to offer formal proof and not permitting the other party to introduce evidence that would dispute the judicially noticed fact. For example, a court would judicially notice and would not require formal proof that the excess alcohol consumption degrades human motor skills, or that gravity causes an object to fall to earth.

The second substitute for evidence is the category called presumptions and inferences. Based on court decisions and through statutory enactments, when a particular basic fact has been proven, the existence of another fact may be deduced from the proof of the basic fact, thereby relieving parties of the burden of presenting evidence to prove a particular fact. One way to consider the difference between a presumption and an inference is to consider that in the case of a presumption, once the basic fact has been proven, the deduction of fact must be made, while in the case of an inference, once the basic fact has been proven, the trier of fact may make the deduction, but is not required to do so. In any event, in a criminal case, a jury or judge is not required to make the deduction of fact from either a presumption or an inference and may choose to ignore it.

Stipulations are the third substitute for evidence. The stipulation serves the goal of judicial economy by saving the court's time and by allowing the court to continue its business without requiring proof of a fact or issue over which the parties have no disagreement. The agreed stipulation renders proof unnecessary as to the matters stipulated. The remainder of this chapter is devoted to a discussion of specific examples of judicial notice of facts and judicial notice of laws. In the following chapter, the other substitutes for evidence—presumptions, inferences and stipulations—are explained.

§ 5.2   Judicial Notice Defined

Judicial notice may be defined as the recognition and acceptance of certain facts that are reasonably undisputable that a judge, under the rules of evidentiary procedure, may properly take or act upon without proof—either because the facts noticed are indisputable as a matter of notorious common knowledge or are capable of being immediately verified by consultation with standard reference works. "Judicial notice is a method of dispensing with the necessity for taking proof, and is intended to avoid the formal introduction of evidence in limited circumstances where the fact sought to be proved is so well known that evidence in support thereof is unnecessary."[1] Facts that are well known to the general population, or are well known to those within the relevant field of knowledge, or are common knowledge within the jurisdiction's geographic area, may be the proper subject of judicial notice. When a court takes judicial notice of a fact, the court is dispensing with requiring proof of a fact where the fact is one of public knowledge or is of sufficient notoriety to be known by all well-informed persons within the court's jurisdiction.

Judicial notice involves the acceptance as true of certain facts and laws without the necessity of introducing evidence. Judges will not close their minds to obvious truths that that other reasonable people see and understand, but a judge does not necessarily have to have personal knowledge of a fact judicially noticed.[2] When a fact is judicially noticed by the court as true, the

---

[1]   29 Am. Jur. 2d *Evidence* § 24.

[2]   A judge may not use her personal experience as a substitute for evidence that was not a proper subject for judicial notice. *See* State v. Sarnowski, 2005 Wis. App 48, 280 Wis. 2d 243, 251, 694 N.W.2d 498, 502, 2005 Wis. App. LEXIS 150 (2005).

party requesting judicial notice need not introduce any evidence in support of the fact and the opposing party is generally prevented from introducing evidence to contradict the judicially noticed fact.

In using judicial notice as a substitute for evidence, courts generally are permitted to take judicial notice at a pretrial hearing,[3] during a trial,[4] and at the appellate stage[5] of a criminal case. In federal courts, judicial notice may be taken at any time during any stage of a proceeding.[6] A limitation on matters that may be judicially noticed by any court is a requirement that the fact, concept, or principle must be relevant to the issues in the case. For example, although a state court may take judicial notice of court records within the state, the court records must be relevant to the issues in the case or judicial notice would be inappropriate.[7]

In taking judicial notice, what passes for common knowledge will vary with the geographic area where the court sits and does not necessarily depend upon the actual knowledge of the judge. A court may take judicial notice of a fact if that fact is not subject to reasonable dispute in that it is "(1) generally known within the territorial jurisdiction of the trial court, or (2) capable of accurate and ready determination by resort to sources whose accuracy cannot reasonably be questioned."[8] For instance, a judge might not understand the exact science involved in DNA testing, but could judicially notice the accuracy of the scientific principle where there was general acceptance of the principle by those with knowledge in the field. In other fields of knowledge, a judge may consult authoritative sources to verify the validity of taking judicial notice. For example, in making a decision, a court properly could take judicial notice of the English language and consult "[r]epresentative authoritative sources for verification [of facts that] include such materials as historical works, science and art books, language and medical journals and dictionaries, calendars, encyclopedias . . ."[9]

Although the judge has discretion in taking judicial notice, the power of judicial notice must be exercised with caution. If there is any doubt whatever, either as to the fact itself or as to its being a matter of common knowledge, evidence should be required. Generally speaking, matters of judicial notice meet at least two basic requisites and one final consideration: (1) a matter must be of common and general knowledge to those in the relevant field of knowledge; and (2) it must be authoritatively settled, not subject to reasonable dispute, and not uncertain.[10] Finally, because judicial notice is a substitute for evidence and

---

[3]   United States v. Haque, 2009 U.S. App. LEXIS 4231 (6th Cir. 2009).

[4]   United States v. Dedman, 527 F.3d 577, 583, 2008 U.S. App LEXIS 11407 (6th Cir. 2008).

[5]   *See* United States v. Elashyi, n.9, 554 F.3d 480, 2008 U.S. App LEXIS 27088 (5th Cir. 2008).

[6]   FED. R. EVID. 201(f).

[7]   29 AM. JUR. 2D *Evidence* § 25.

[8]   FED. R. EVID. 201(b).

[9]   Stokes v. Commonwealth, 2008 Ky. LEXIS 321 Ky. 2008), quoting RICHARD H. UNDERWOOD & GLEN WEISSENBERGER, KENTUCKY EVIDENCE 2005–2006 COURTROOM MANUAL 44 (2005).

[10]   State v. Shanks, 640 A.2d 155 (Conn. 1994).

only relevant evidence is admissible, a court will not take judicial notice of facts that are not relevant in the particular case.[11]

The judge may take judicial notice upon the request of either party, or upon his or her motion, even in the absence of a request.[12] In deciding whether to judicially notice a fact, the judge may consult statutes and case law, as well as review legal encyclopedias, in seeking sources of information regarding the appropriateness of taking judicial notice. A judge may seek assistance in reaching the decision by consulting any authoritative source of information that serves the purpose. The judge may decline to take notice where the defendant has failed to provide information to support the request.[13] In a California homicide case, where the defendant contended that a recent change in California law altered the death penalty to where almost anyone in a gang would be responsible for any murder done by the gang and argued that the change would have the effect of widening and not narrowing the class of people eligible for the death penalty. The appellate court noted that because the defendant had failed to provide any sources from which the court could take judicial notice of the defendant's contention, the trial court properly declined to take judicial notice.[14]

With respect to the topics of proper judicial notice in criminal cases, one North Carolina court consulted a leading legal encyclopedia that suggested the existence of a wide range of miscellaneous facts that may be the subject of judicial notice, including:

> the laws of nature; human impulses, habits, functions and capabilities; the prevalence of a certain surname; established medical and scientific facts; well-known practices in farming, construction work, transportation, and other businesses and professions; the characteristics of familiar tools and appliances, weapons, intoxicants, and poisons; the use of highways; the normal incidence of the operation of trains, motor vehicles, and planes; prominent geographical features such as railroads, water courses, and cities and towns; population and area as shown by census reports; the days, weeks, and months of the calendar; the effect of natural conditions on the construction of public improvements; the facts of history; important current events; general economic and social conditions; matters affecting public health and safety; the meaning of words and abbreviations; and the results of mathematical computations.[15]

While these categories are not all-inclusive and some courts might reject some of them, they represent many topics on which courts take judicial

---

[11] People v. Young, 34 Cal. 4th 1149, 1171, 105 P.3d 487, 499, 24 Cal. Rptr. 3d 112, 126, 2005 Cal. LEXIS 1017 (2005).

[12] FED. R. EVID. 201(c).

[13] People v. Herrera, 2007 Cal. App. Unpub. LEXIS 3965 (2007).

[14] Id.

[15] Haynes Mall v. Central Carolina, 2006 N.C. App. LEXIS 175 (N.C. 2006), quoting 1 KENNETH S. BROUN, BRANDIS AND BROUN ON NORTH CAROLINA EVIDENCE § 27, at 104–09 (5th ed. 1998).

notice of facts on an ongoing basis. For convenience, the rules concerning judicial notice are often categorized as judicial notice of facts and judicial notice of laws. In the following sections, the two categories are discussed and distinguished.

§ 5.3 Judicial Notice of Facts

> ### Rule 201
>
> #### Judicial Notice of Adjudicative Facts
>
> (a) Scope of rule. This rule governs only judicial notice of adjudicative facts.
>
> (b) Kinds of facts. A judicially noticed fact must be one not subject to reasonable dispute in that it is either (1) generally known within the territorial jurisdiction of the trial court or (2) capable of accurate and ready determination by resort to sources whose accuracy cannot reasonably be questioned.
>
> (c) When discretionary. A court may take judicial notice, whether requested or not.
>
> (d) When mandatory. A court shall take judicial notice if requested by a party and supplied with the necessary information.[16]
>
> * * *

Rule 201 of the Federal Rules of Evidence addresses only judicial notice of "adjudicative facts" and does not cover legislative facts. Adjudicative facts that are appropriate for judicial notice are the facts that are specific and unique to a particular case and are facts that will determine the result of the case. These facts can be established by judicial notice but are usually proved by the introduction of actual evidence. These are the facts that will prove or disprove elements of the crime or defense. Adjudicative facts that have been the subject of judicial notice permits the jury to accept them as true without requiring formal proof by the introduction of evidence.[17] In accordance with Subdivision (b) of Rule 201, a court may take judicial notice of the facts that are well-known within the territorial jurisdiction of the trial court, or the judge determines by reference to an authoritative source that the fact is not subject to reasonable dispute.

As indicated in Subdivision (c) of Rule 201, a court may take judicial notice without a formal request from either counsel. According to the general rule, a judge may take judicial notice at any time, whether during the trial or whether for the first time on appeal,[18] so long as judicial notice would

---

[16] FED. R. EVID. 201.

[17] 29 AM. JUR. 2D *Evidence* § 29.

[18] Crooks v. Lynch, 2009 U.S. App. LEXIS 4020 (8th Cir. 2009).

have been appropriate at the trial. The judge is required to take judicial notice if asked by a party and supplied with the necessary information. In a North Carolina case, the appellant requested that the reviewing court take judicial notice of the existence of an arrest warrant for the first time during the appeal. Since a warrant was a public record and the court had been supplied with the necessary information, the court judicially noticed the warrant.[19] As a general rule, courts are not required to initiate research to discover indisputable sources of information and if the information supplied to a trial or appellate court is not sufficient, the court is entitled to refuse to take judicial notice of the matter requested. In a California case where the defendant alleged that a constitutional flaw existed in death penalty legislation, the court refused to take judicial notice of the flaw because the defendant failed to demonstrate on the record, or through sources of which the court could have taken judicial notice, that his claims were empirically accurate.[20]

In most states, the code or statute pertaining to evidence provides the rules that must be followed by the court relating to judicial notice of facts.[21]

Judicial notice of facts is not dependent on the extrajudicial or personal knowledge of the judge; what the judge knows and what facts the judge may judicially notice are not identical. Court rules are quite clear that the private knowledge of the judge is not a sufficient basis for taking judicial notice of facts.[22] In most courts, a judge must take judicial notice of facts regardless of whether the judge personally is aware of the fact for which notice has been requested. In *State v. Vejvoda*,[23] the reviewing court, after explaining the limits on the use of judicial notice, decided that the trial court improperly took judicial notice of the fact that the defendant was driving in a city within the county of prosecution when the arresting officer's testimony referred only to street names, but not their location. The fact that the judge was aware that the streets were probably in the county of prosecution did not cure the failure to introduce evidence. In a different case, the Ninth Circuit Court of Appeal held that a judge should not have relied upon his personal knowledge in commenting on the location of stop signs, the fact that the area at issue was extremely or rural, and that there was not a lot of traffic on a particular road after 1030 at night. The Court of Appeals noted that a judge is prohibited from taking judicial notice when he or she relies upon personal experience to support the taking of judicial notice.[24]

Courts do not always reach predictable results when asked to take judicial notice. California appellate courts generally do not take judicial notice of

---

[19]   State v. Tyson, 658 S.E.2d 285, 287, 2008 N.C. App. LEXIS 652 (N.C. 2008).

[20]   People v. Michaels, 28 Cal. 4th 486, 541, 49 P.3d 1032, 122 Cal. Rptr. 2d 285 (2002).

[21]   *See* Appendix II for a list of states that follow the Uniform Rules of Evidence.

[22]   *See* 29 AM. JUR. 2D *Evidence* § 35. *See also* United States v. Lewis, 833 F.2d 1380 (9th Cir. 1987) and Vaughn v. Shelby-Williams of Tenn., Inc., 813 S.W.2d 132 (Tenn. 1991).

[23]   *See also* State v. Vejvoda, 231 Neb. 668, 438 N.W.2d 461 (1989). See case in Part II.

[24]   United States v. Berber-Tinoco, 510 F3d. 1083, 1091, 2007 U.S. App. LEXIS 29301 (9th Cir. 2007), *cert. denied*, 2008 U.S. LEXIS 7266 (2008).

matters that were neither presented nor requested of a trial court[25] and do not take judicial notice of documents that were not presented to the trial court.[26] Other jurisdictions seem quite comfortable in taking judicial notice in post conviction proceedings.[27] Even though courts are not in complete agreement as to what facts must be judicially noticed and when to take notice and what facts may be judicially noticed on request, some matters traditionally have been considered proper topics for consideration. These are discussed in the sections that follow. However, the examples given are merely demonstrative of the general principles and are not meant to be exhaustive.

§ 5.4   — Matters of General Knowledge

While it is accepted practice to take judicial notice of facts of common knowledge, and such facts need not be proved by the opposing party, determining what facts can be classified as common knowledge may prove to be a challenge in some situations. A fact is said to be generally recognized or known when it is not open to reasonable dispute. A fact that possesses sufficient notoriety will be deemed to be a proper subject for judicial notice. All that is necessary is that a matter be familiar to the majority of humankind or to those persons familiar with a particular matter in question. For example, the fact that whiskey and rum are intoxicating liquors is generally known and their qualities are not subject to any reasonable dispute.[28] This does not mean that everyone must be aware of the fact, because scarcely any fact is known by everyone. When the matter depends upon uncertain testimony or rests on speculation, it becomes a disputable item in court and ceases to fall under the heading of common knowledge and should not be judicially recognized. For example, in a criminal case that arose from a domestic violence episode, that criminal judge took judicial notice that the judge in the domestic violence case determined that the defendant could not have arrived on the scene in time to have committed the violence. In the criminal case, it was reasonably disputed whether the defendant committed the violent acts and the criminal court erred in taking judicial notice of the decision of the judge who refused to issue a domestic restraining order.[29]

In many instances, facts that may be properly judicially noticed involve matters of purely local knowledge that are open and notoriously known to people who live in a local geographical area. These facts might include where intersecting streets serve as an accepted center of a city, or indicate where a

---

[25]   People v. Suehr, 2008 Cal. App. Unpub. LEXIS 2713 (Cal. 2008).

[26]   The Termo Company v. Luther, 169 Cal. App. 4th 394, 404, 2008 Cal. App. LEXIS 2430 (Cal. 2008).

[27]   Trotter v. State, 392 So. 2d 1045, 1048, 2006 Fla. LEXIS 940 (Fla. 2006).

[28]   *See* State v. Aiken, 121 Ohio Misc. 2d 7, 2002 Ohio 6436, 779 N.E.2d 1105, 2002 Ohio Misc. LEXIS 44 (Ohio 2002).

[29]   State v. Silva, 394 N.J. Super. 270, 2007 N.J. Super. LEXIS 200 (N.J. 2007).

statue dedicated to a war hero is located or the name of the major street that runs through a city. For example, a federal court sitting in Georgia took judicial notice of the identity of the new county sheriff in a civil rights case where the new sheriff's name had to be substituted for name of the former sheriff.[30] In one suit, a federal district court took judicial notice of the fact that Operation Iraqi Freedom did not begin until March 19, 2003 and took notice that there was a long standoff that preceded military operations.[31] The date of the military operation was in the current memory of many people and was subject to easy verification and served as an appropriate fact for judicial notice.

Courts may take judicial notice of notorious nationally known facts that are not the subject of reasonable dispute. For example, one court took judicial notice that because the E-Bay auction process had been in business longer than ten years, its methods of operation constituted a matter of common knowledge concerning how the bidding and selling operated.[32] Another court took judicial notice that, in litigation concerning the Star Wars series of movies, Luke Skywalker was nurtured by Obi-Wan Kenobi.[33] Because it is a well-known fact that tobacco products pose disease-related risks, including lung cancer, it is proper for a court to take notice of the harm of tobacco.[34] But a different court decided "that reasonable minds could differ as to whether public knowledge about the health risks of developing disease and nicotine addiction from smoking cigarettes was so certain and generally known" at a particular time in history that judicial notice was not appropriate.[35]

Concerning the proper subjects of judicial notice, courts have held that the judge may take judicial notice of mortality tables as proof of life expectancy.[36] Other examples of instances in which courts have taken judicial notice of matters of general knowledge are these: firearms serve as the tools of the trade to substantial dealers in narcotics,[37] a pistol is a deadly weapon,[38] farmers in South Dakota produce significant amounts of seed corn[39] the capitol building of the state of Utah is located on State Street,[40] Tiffany & Co. is a very

---

[30] Young v. Graham, 2005 U.S. Dist. LEXIS 20882 (2005).

[31] Lynch v. Robertson, 2007 U.S. Dist. LEXIS 60835 (W.D. Pa. 2007).

[32] Choice Auto Brokers, Inc. v. Dawson, 274 S.W.3d 172, n. 1, 2008 Tex. App. LEXIS 7236 (Tex. 2008).

[33] Twentieth Century Fox Film Corp. v. Marvel Enterprises, 155 F. Supp. 2d 1, 41, 2001 U.S. Dist. LEXIS 11568 (S. Dist. N.Y. 2001).

[34] Spain v. Brown and Williamson Tobacco, 363 F.3d 1183, 1194, 2004 U.S. App. LEXIS 5792 (11th Cir. 2004).

[35] Smith v. Brown & Williamson Tobacco Corp., 2007 Mo. App. LEXIS 1144 (Mo. 2007).

[36] Tobin v. Liberty Mutual, 2007 U.S. Dist. LEXIS 23680 (D. Mass. 2007), aff'd, 553 F.3d 121, 2009 U.S. App. LEXIS 1278 (1st Cir. 2009).

[37] United States v. Riley, 452 F.3d 160, 165, 2006 U.S. App. LEXIS 15584 (2d Cir. 2006).

[38] State v. Taylor, 182 S.W. 159 (Mo. 1916).

[39] Braun v. E.I. du Pont de Nemours & Co., 2006 U.S. Dist. LEXIS 37431 (D.S.D 2006).

[40] Utah Gospel Mission v. Salt Lake City, 316 F. Supp. 2d 1201, 2004 U.S. Dist. LEXIS 12966 (2004).

well-known jewelry store;[41] and a defendant nearly always wants his or her trial to be postponed.[42]

In discussing judicial notice, a Georgia court explained that the courts will generally take judicial notice of a fact if the fact is of common knowledge that all people of average intelligence are presumed to know and that is certain and indisputable.[43] A Maryland court noted that it was appropriate for a court to take judicial notice that most men do not carry purses.[44] A Florida court took judicial notice that a well-known local Christian school was a school for purposes of state law because the trial judge should not be compelled to force the school's principal to spend valuable time at the courthouse confirming a status that seemed to be common knowledge.[45] Although perhaps not well-known by most people, one court took judicial notice in a fraud case "that when one consumes telephone service, one is consuming an applied form of electricity that uses an electric current to transmit the human voice—is a fact readily discernable from a variety of sources . . ."[46]

On the other hand, the courts have held that certain facts are not presumed to be known by the court. Bringing case law to a court's attention has been held not to be a proper topic for judicial notice[47] and in a criminal case, the specific findings of a domestic violence judge will not be considered a proper topic for judicial notice.[48] Courts have refused to take judicial notice of a pardon,[49] that all of the detainees from Iraq and Afghanistan at Guantanamo Bay were "enemy combatants,"[50] and that a non-law-abiding citizen is always a perjurer.[51] A federal district court could not properly take judicial notice that seven victims of a defendant had suffered any number of losses as a result of a defendant's actions when the notice was based on the judge's own professional experience.[52] A Florida court improperly took judicial notice of the value of a non-working motor vehicle based on a reference value book because the reference book considered only vehicles that were operable.[53] A court should not take judicial notice of the age of a juvenile because that fact was an element of the charge of underage alcohol consumption.[54] Because many people have knowledge of events around them that may affect everyday lives, judicial

---

[41]   Correa v. Comm'r of Corr., 101 Conn. App. 554, 557, 2007 Conn. App. LEXIS 225 (Conn. 2007).

[42]   Sam v. State, 265 P. 609 (Ariz. 1928).

[43]   Weems v. State, 485 S.E.2d 767 (Ga. 1997).

[44]   Ransome v. State, 2003 Md. LEXIS 39 (Md. Ct. App. 2003).

[45]   Cox v. Florida, 764 So. 2d 711, 713, 2000 Fla. App. LEXIS 7516 (2000).

[46]   State v. Howard, 2008 Wis. App. LEXIS 807 (Wis. 2008).

[47]   Hyde v. Paskett, 383 F. Supp. 2d 1256, 2005 U.S. Dist. LEXIS 23165 (D. Idaho 2005).

[48]   State v. Brown, 394 N.J. Super. 492, 507, 2007 N.J. Super. LEXIS 247 (N.J. 2007).

[49]   State v. Garrett, 188 S.W. 58 (Tenn. 1916).

[50]   Rasul v. Bush, 215 F. Supp. 2d 55, 67, 2002 U.S. Dist. LEXIS 14031 (D.D.C. 2002).

[51]   State v. Baird, 195 S.W. 1010 (Mo. 1917).

[52]   United States v. Gregory, 2009 U.S. App. LEXIS 1970 (11th Cir. 2009).

[53]   Walentukonis v. Florida, 2006 Fla. App. LEXIS 9766 (2006).

[54]   State v. K.N., 124 Wash. App. 875, 103 P.3d 844, 2004 Wash. App. LEXIS 3135 (2004).

notice of contemporary happenings and events may be the subject of judicial notice. For instance, it is common knowledge that there has been an increase in the number of serious crimes committed by persons less than 18 years of age. The judge may take judicial notice of economic facts, such as the constant increase in the cost of living and the decrease in the purchasing power of the dollar. In such instances, the facts are noticed judicially without proof by either side.

§ 5.5 — History and Historical Facts

The collection of historical facts that make up the history of the states and our nation are either well-known to contemporary members of society or have been recorded in works of history. As such, these facts are either common knowledge or are subject to ready verification by consulting standard reference works. In taking judicial notice of historical facts or events, courts simply recognize the reasonably irrefutable facts of our history that, if proof were required by a court, would constitute a waste of time. Most Americans vividly remember the historic events that occurred on September 11, 2001. In a case in which a parole hearing was not held in a timely fashion on September 11, 2001, due to the terrorist attacks in Pennsylvania and the governor's response, a court took judicial notice of the events of that day in recognizing that a sufficient reason existed for the hearing to be rescheduled later than the time demanded by administrative regulations.[55] According to a case cited by the court, "matters of history, if sufficiently notorious to be subject to general knowledge, will be judicially noticed."[56] The financial history of the United States, including events such as the 1929 stock market collapse and the depression of the 1930s, are proper matters for judicial notice. In a bankruptcy matter, a court can take judicial notice of the average rate of a 30-year mortgage at a particular time by consulting the *Wall Street Journal*.[57] The price of listed stocks on recognized exchanges constitutes historical data that cannot be subject to any serious dispute and can be the subject of judicial notice.[58] The day of the week on which a particular date fell, the date on which war was declared or ended, the destructive character of a flood or other disaster—all can be matters of judicial notice. The court, in an action to declare life insurance policies in force, judicially noticed the flight of refugees from Castro's Cuba to Miami, Florida, and their acceptance, encouragement, and support by the United States.[59]

---

[55]   Wiley v. Commonwealth, 801 A.2d 644, 2002 Pa. Commw. LEXIS 510 (2002).

[56]   *See generally* Fatemi v. Fatemi, 371 Pa. Super. 101, 537 A.2d 840 (Pa. Super. 1988).

[57]   In re Chaing, 274 B.R. 295, 305, 2002 Bankr. LEXIS 170 (D. Mass. 2002).

[58]   Grimes v. Navigant Consulting, 185 F. Supp. 2d 906, 913, 2002 U.S. Dist. LEXIS 1708 (N.D. Ill. 2002).

[59]   Blanco v. Pan-American Life Ins. Co., 221 F. Supp. 219 (S.D. Fla. 1963); Perez v. Department of Revenue, 778 P.2d 326 (Colo. Ct. App. 1989).

In criminal cases as well as civil cases, the court may take judicial notice of historical facts of a national character, such as the fact that 97 percent of the population of Iraq is Muslim,[60] that a political disturbance and civil war existed in Croatia after it declared independence in 1991[61] and, in a modern environmental suit, that the decade following 1953 was one of heightened military concern in the United States.[62]

The judge does not have to be personally aware of historical facts to take judicial notice of them. It would be asking too much for the judge to be aware of all the details of history. He or she may refer to properly authenticated official public documents, encyclopedias, history books, periodicals, or even newspaper articles. However, in taking judicial notice, a judge is limited to what is appropriate in his or her judicial capacity and may not take notice of historical facts known only to the judge and not generally known by the public. Historical facts within historical documents that may themselves be subject to dispute as historical facts are not proper subjects for judicial notice.[63] Although a court may take judicial notice of historical facts, the court is not required to do so unless the party so requesting supplies the necessary information.[64]

§ 5.6   – Geography and Geographical Facts

Although the prosecutor must introduce evidence to show that the court has jurisdiction in the case during the initial stages, he or she does not have to introduce evidence to show, for example, that Chicago is in Cook County, Illinois, or that the Mississippi River flows generally from the north to the south. In Florida, courts are permitted to take judicial notice "of the prominent geographical and natural features of the country, such as the large lakes and rivers; the division of the country into states; the existence, location, and population of political subdivisions; and distances between well-known points."[65] It is permissible for Florida courts to take judicial notice of the territorial limits of the United States"[66] and of the prominent geographical and natural features of the country that are common knowledge, such as lakes and other bodies of water, and whether the body of water is tidal water or whether it can be navigated;[67] In a similar way, a federal district court sitting in the District of Columbia can take judicial notice that the geographic locations mentioned

---

[60]   Sulieman v. Roswell Park Cancer Inst., 2007 U.S. Dist. LEXIS 46599 (W.D. N.Y. 2007).

[61]   Abrambasic v. Ashcroft, 403 F. Supp. 2d 951, 958, 2005 U.S. Dist. LEXIS 31713 (D. S.D. 2005).

[62]   Gould Electronics v. United States, 2002 U.S. Dist. LEXIS 262 (E.D. Pa. 2002).

[63]   New York v. Shinnecock Indian Nation, 523 F. Supp. 2d 185, 262, 2007 U.S. Dist. LEXIS 80443 (E.D N.Y. 2007).

[64]   State v. Hofland, 151 N.H. 322, 327, 857 A.2d 1271, 1276, 2004 N.H. LEXIS 146 (N.H. 2004).

[65]   23 FLA. JUR. *Evidence and Witnesses* § 40 (2008). *See also* TEX. WATER CODE § 49.066 (2007).

[66]   *Id.*

[67]   *Id.* § 41.

in the testimony are in the District of Columbia as a way to find venue and jurisdiction.[68] In a cocaine case involving possession too near a school, a Texas court noted that courts "may take judicial notice of the location of cities, counties, boundaries, dimensions, and distances, because geographical facts such as these are easily ascertainable and capable of verifiable certainty."[69] But a federal judge is prohibited from relying on his own experience to support the taking of judicial notice of the locations of stop signs or the narrow features of a road within his jurisdiction.[70]

Topography of the land and geographic features change very slowly, which makes judicial notice quite appropriate in many cases. Municipal boundaries may change more frequently due to annexation and consolidation, but the exact area and location of a municipal border can be discerned by reference to topographical maps, reference works, and common knowledge. "Trial courts are generally permitted to take judicial notice of any geographic facts that are common knowledge within its jurisdiction."[71] In one case involving well-known geography, the court took judicial notice that "Suffolk County . . . is the easternmost county on Long Island, separated from Connecticut on the north by Long Island Sound and bordered on the west by Nassau County."[72] In these cases, the facts were notorious and well-known within the judicial district or were subject to verification by unimpeachable sources. However, it would be improper for a judge to take judicial notice that a particular road had "a very tapered grass shoulder road [that went] into a heavy ditch in low lying swamp ground."[73] Such a description was subject to some reasonable dispute and the court noted that "if there is even a mere possibility of dispute as to whether the fact asserted is accurate, or of common knowledge, judicial notice is inappropriate and evidence is required to establish the fact."[74]

A court may take judicial notice that a geographical area of a city has a well-known reputation as a location for particular purposes. A federal appellate court upheld a lower court determination under judicial notice that it is common knowledge that there are strip clubs in Buffalo, New York.[75] Other geographical facts that have been judicially noticed include the fact that a traffic stop occurred within the jurisdiction of the police officer,[76] and the question of whether an alleged crime occurred within "particular geographic boundaries

---

[68]   Long v. United States, 940 A.2d 87, 99, 2007 D.C. App. LEXIS 667 (D.C. Cir. 2007).

[69]   Lovelady v. State, 65 S.W.3d 810, 813, 2002 Tex. App. LEXIS 378 (2002) and New Process Steel, L.P. v. Sharp Freight System, n.5, 2006 Tex. App. LEXIS 2967 (2006).

[70]   United States v. Berber-Tinoco, 510 F.3d 1083, 1091, 2007 U.S. App. LEXIS 29301 (9th Cir. 2007).

[71]   State v. Davis, 2004 Ohio 5680, 2004 Ohio App. LEXIS 5144 (2004).

[72]   Town of Suffolk v. Town of East Hampton, 406 F. Supp. 2d 227, 232, 2005 U.S. Dist. LEXIS 41036 (2005).

[73]   State v. Smith, 2006 Del. C.P. LEXIS 34 (Del. 2006). See case in Part II.

[74]   Id.

[75]   Singh v. Mukasey, 553 F.3d 207, 212, 2009 U.S. App. LEXIS 966 (2d Cir. 2009)

[76]   State v. Burkhalter, 2006 Ohio 1623, 2006 Ohio App. LEXIS 1520 (2006).

is proper subject for judicial notice.[77] Similarly, a federal magistrate judge who was holding court within Yosemite National Park could properly take judicial notice that to travel between two points in the park along a park road required travel entirely within the national park.[78]

§ 5.7 — Facts Relating to Nature and Science

Facts relating to nature and science can be the subject of judicial notice where the facts are reasonably undisputable. According to a Maryland court, "A trial court may take judicial notice of the reliability of scientific techniques and methodologies that are widely accepted within the scientific community."[79] Even where the general public does not understand a fact of nature or a principle of science, courts may take judicial notice of the truth of facts that can readily be determined by references to accurate sources. In some cases, courts may have to hear expert testimony before taking notice, where a scientific fact or principle proves complicated. In novel areas of scientific inquiry, where there may initially be some dispute concerning the fact or principle, and before the fact or principle has reached the level of near-universal acceptance, the new scientific principles or facts must have their validity established by expert testimony before courts may take judicial notice. As a particular scientific fact or process gains general acceptance and becomes reasonably undisputed by those in the field, a court may judicially notice the fact and dispense with formal proof. In some cases, trial and appellate courts have taken judicial notice of scientific literature even when neither party presented any supporting information.[80] Such practice, however, may pose a danger if the court misapplies the principle or the scientific conclusion.

Consistent with the proper use of judicial notice, courts frequently take notice of the elementary principles of physics, such as the force of gravity or the laws of thermodynamics. Also, facts relating to the climate of the state and the climate elsewhere may be judicially noticed. Of special significance in criminal cases is the fact that the courts may take judicial notice of scientific facts that have a bearing on the case, and scientific facts that have been well established by authoritative scientists and are generally accepted as irrefutable. For example, the general reliability of expert medical testimony based on reasoning from epidemiological data is generally considered a proper subject for judicial notice.[81] With respect to judicial notice of weather, courts usually

---

[77] United States v. Kelly, 535 F.3d 1229, 2008 U.S. App. LEXIS 16572 (10th Cir. 2008), *cert. denied,* 2009 U.S. LEXIS 1053 (2009).

[78] United States v. Couchavlis, 260 F.3d 1149, 2001 U.S. App. LEXIS 18363 (9th Cir. 2001).

[79] Montgomery Mutual v. Chesson, 399 Md. 314, 327, 2007 Md. LEXIS 331 (Md. 2007).

[80] Mata v. State, 46 S.W.3d 902, 910, 2001 Tex. Crim. App. LEXIS 45 (Tex. 2001).

[81] Knight v. Kerby Inland Marine, Inc., 363 F. Supp. 2d 859, 2005 U.S. Dist. LEXIS 10615 (2005).

take judicial notice of historical weather conditions because past weather conditions are not subject to reasonable dispute.[82] In an unpublished opinion, a federal judge took judicial notice concerning the weather conditions on a prison yard in a suit brought by a dissatisfied prisoner.[83]

The scope of judicial notice in science and nature is not static and changes as new discoveries are made, expanding the human knowledge base. A number of these scientific areas are of special interest in the criminal justice process. For example, ballistic identification for firearms was once unacceptable because the scientific principle behind the process was not generally accepted, but presently, the validity of ballistic identification techniques is a proper subject for judicial notice. Likewise, courts were reluctant to admit DNA identification evidence because the science was not well known by scientists or understood by courts, but as the science became accepted in the relevant scientific community, courts recognized the principle that human DNA is unique to each person.[84] A California court, when faced with an appeal contending that the principles of DNA testing were not proved, noted just the opposite and observed the acceptability of DNA evidence by stating, "the record provides no basis to conclude that a challenge to the admissibility of the DNA evidence would have been successful."[85] In the California case, representative of state cases everywhere, the court took judicial notice of the accuracy of the PCR [polymerase chain reaction] method of using DNA to make accurate identifications.[86] In a different situation, courts have been "been known to take judicial notice that improperly performed DNA tests have resulted in wrongful convictions."[87] An Ohio reviewing court noted with approval that a trial court took judicial notice of the scientific accuracy and reliability of a laser speed measuring device.[88] Judicial notice may be appropriate in recognizing the scientific validity of the principle underlying the horizontal gaze nystagmus (HGN) test, used as a diagnostic tool to identify alcohol-impaired drivers. In a Maine prosecution for driving while intoxicated, the state's top court approved the use of the HGN test as circumstantial evidence of impairment.[89] As a general rule, courts have been unwilling to take judicial notice of the scientific validity of the polygraph or to admit the results in criminal cases due to concerns about

---

[82] Easy Sportswear, Inc. v. Am. Econ. Ins. Co., 2008 U.S. Dist. LEXIS 51402 (W.D. Pa. 2008). Memorandum opinion.

[83] Conn v. Jack Does 1-40 et al., 2008 U.S. Dist. LEXIS 17733 (D.N.J.2008).

[84] DNA profiles are unique except for identical twins.

[85] Campbell v. Rice, 408 F.3d 1166, 1171, 2005 U.S. App. LEXIS 9221 (9th Cir. 2005).

[86] *Id.*

[87] Brown v. Farwell, 525 F.3d 787, 796–97 (9th Cir. 2008).

[88] State v. Kim, 2008 Ohio 6928, 2008 Ohio App. LEXIS 5814 (Ohio 2008). *Contra,* State v. Miko, 2008 Ohio 1991, 2008 Ohio App. LEXIS 1703 (Oh. 2008).

[89] State v. Just, 2007 ME 91, 2007 Me. LEXIS 92 (Me. 2007). *But see* People v. McKown, 226 Ill.2d 245, 2007 Ill. LEXIS 1163 (2007), where the court rejected judicial notice for the principle behind the horizontal gaze nystagmus test.

reliability or relevancy,[90] but some courts will take judicial notice of reliability of the polygraph due to the fact that it is used extensively by police agencies.[91]

Courts often take judicial notice of facts involving a mix of science and law. In one case, where a prisoner complained of inappropriate medical care, a federal district court took judicial notice that treating a specific ailment involved using an approved drug, doxycycline, was a medically acceptable course of treatment.[92] A Texas trial court judicially noticed "the Controlled Substances Act, which lists hydrocodone as a Schedule II drug, and took judicial notice of the fact that Vicodin and Lortab both contain hydrocodone.[93] An Arizona appellate court took judicial notice of the legislative determination and of the expert scientific opinion concerning the effects and harmfulness of marijuana.[94]

When considering nature and science as topics for judicial notice, it "is generally limited to matters of public record and to matters of common knowledge that cannot reasonably be disputed."[95] These subjects include notice of a date on a calendar, the principle of gravity, or an unquestioned law of mathematics.[96] Notice should be taken of scientific principles and authoritative treatises that are generally known and accepted or are readily verifiable from sources of indisputable accuracy. However, courts generally will not take judicial notice of scientific facts or principles that remain of questionable validity. For example, in an assault case, an Ohio appellate court refused to take judicial notice of a defendant's offering of a complicated scientific formula that he alleged computed the rate of the acceleration of falling objects, which the prosecution contended injured other people. The court believed that the formula did not represent a proven scientific principle that was so well understood as to be part of the common knowledge of every person.[97]

§ 5.8 — Language, Abbreviations, and Symbols

Judges may take judicial notice of commonly used words, phrases, symbols, and slang words having a clearly fixed meaning, where the language has a settled community meaning by the group that uses the terminology. The

---

90 United States v. Ramirez-Robles, 386 F.3d 1234, 1248, 2004 U.S. App. LEXIS 21847 (9th Cir. 2004). The Fourth Circuit Court of Appeals continues to enforce a per se ban on polygraph evidence. *See* United States v. Prince-Oyibo, 320 F.3d 494, 501, 2003 U.S. App. LEXIS 3568 (4th Cir. 2003).

91 State v. Domicz, 377 N.J. Super 515, 2005 N.J. Super. LEXIS 161 (N.J. 2005).

92 Banks v. County of Allegheny, 2008 U.S. Dist. LEXIS 107544 (2008).

93 Smith v. State, 2008 Tex. App. LEXIS 4779 (2008).

94 State v. Hardesty, 2008 Ariz. App. LEXIS 121 (Ariz. 2008). Review granted, 2009 Ariz. LEXIS 22 (Ariz. 2009).

95 Timm v. Reitz, 39 P.3d 1252, 1258, 2001 Colo. App. LEXIS 2019 (2001).

96 Johnson v. Commonwealth, 12 S.W.3d 258, 267, 1999 Ky. LEXIS 159 (1999).

97 State v. Mendez, 2004 Ohio 3107, 2004 Ohio App. LEXIS 2755 (2004).

personal knowledge of judges does not qualify them to take judicial notice merely because they have an extensive knowledge of words and phrases; they may take judicial notice of usual words that are known by the community, even if not known personally by the judge. Where a word or phrase has a plain meaning to those in the relevant field, but not understood by the judge, a judge may consult a generally accepted dictionary "to aid in the ascertaining of such meaning."[98] Judges may consult dictionaries directed to specific fields such as a medical dictionary in determining the meaning of a particular word.[99] In a case where the language or meaning of a statute is ambiguous, a court may take judicial notice of the legislative history in evaluating the meaning of a word or phrase.[100]

Ordinarily, the court may not take judicial notice of the meaning of obscure slang words or expressions common to a small group. However, if the word has come into such frequent use as to convey a particular meaning, and it no longer can be considered as simply the language of slang that is understood only by a certain segment of the population, the court may take judicial notice of the word. For example, a federal court took judicial notice of the slang term "booty" and recognized that it served as a common term for human buttocks.[101] Idioms that have acquired a special meaning may be judicially noticed. The term "Democrat" may be judicially noticed as meaning the members and candidates of the Democratic party, and the court may take judicial notice that "pig" has come to be used as a derogatory name for the police.[102]

The corporate and institutional use of graphics and symbols can be proper subjects for judicial notice. Trademarks, logos, and similar graphic representations convey identifying messages to interested persons. Corporations frequently use symbols to make a company image or product recognizable to the public. In one case, the court took judicial notice that Microsoft's trademarks were valid and properly registered.[103] The designs of badges assigned to police officers are generally unique to the particular department. In an unpublished opinion in a case alleging impersonation of an officer, one court took judicial notice of the design, writing, and symbols incorporated into a genuine badge carried by a bona fide police officer.[104]

The courts may take judicial notice of the meaning of abbreviations generally known and in common use, such as abbreviations for days and months. But judicial notice may not be taken of the meaning of abbreviations, symbols, or initials when the meaning is not generally known or

[98] Service Corporation of Westover Hills v. Guzzetta, 2007 Del. Ch. LEXIS 84 (Del. 2007).

[99] *See* Stokes v. Commonwealth, 2008 Ky. LEXIS 321 (Ky. 2008).

[100] *See* County of Orange v. Superior Court of Orange County, 155 Cal. App. 4th 1253, 2007 Cal. App. LEXIS 1649, n.1 (2007).

[101] Requa v. Kent School District No. 415, 492 F. Supp. 1272, 2007 U.S. Dist. LEXIS 40920 (W.D. Wash. 2007).

[102] St. Petersburg v. Waller, 261 So. 2d 151 (Fla. 1972).

[103] Microsoft v. Atek 3000 Computer, 2008 U.S. Dist. LEXIS 56689 (E.D.N.Y. 2008).

[104] People v. Diaz, 2005 Cal. App. Unpub. LEXIS 3559 (2005).

when they have no meaning without explanation. A court, for example, may take judicial notice that the initials "M.D." refer to a physician,[105] and that "Chas." is an abbreviation for "Charles,"[106] or that the abbreviation "G.I." refers to a soldier.[107]

§ 5.9 Judicial Notice of Laws

While courts often take judicial notice of facts, judicial notice of law follows from the same basic premise of allowing for the notice of undisputable facts. Because the statutory law has been written by legislative bodies and is easily accessed and brought to the attention of a court or of opposing counsel, to require a party to produce evidence to prove that laws that are currently in force would be a waste of time. A court must take judicial notice of the statutory law applicable in its own individual jurisdiction as well as the laws of the state in which it sits. A federal appellate court recently quoted an old case, noting that "The law of any state of the Union, whether depending upon statutes or upon judicial opinions, is a matter of which the courts of the United States are bound to take judicial notice, without plea or proof."[108] Many states permit judicial notice of the laws of sister states and some will allow notice of foreign law on a proper occasion. To facilitate judicial notice of law, counsel usually brings the judge's attention to statutes or citations in references to decisions applicable to the case being tried. An Ohio court noted that it could take judicial notice of a sister state's public statutory or case law within the United States and "may inform itself in such manner as it deems proper."[109]

State trial courts judicially notice federal law, and a federal court will judicially notice the law of every state. In fact, when sitting in a diversity jurisdiction case, the federal court is acting as if it were a state court and will follow state law concerning judicial notice as precisely as possible. However, when the United States Supreme Court reviews the decision of a state court, it will not take judicial notice of the law of another state unless the state court below could have done so.[110]

The following sections (§§ 5.10 through 5.16), specifically discuss the extent to which courts take judicial notice of laws prevailing within the forum, the laws of other states, and foreign nations.

---

[105] State v. Brady, 223 Or. 433, 354 P.2d 811 (1960).

[106] Cumbol v. State, 205 Tenn. 260, 326 S.W.2d 454 (1959).

[107] Still v. Secretary of the Commonwealth, 73 Pa. D. & C. 106; 1950 Pa. D. & C. LEXIS 247 (1950).

[108] Unites States v. Dedman, 527 F.3d 577, 586, 2008 U.S. App. LEXIS 11407 (6th Cir. 2008), quoting Lamar v. Micou, 114 U.S. 218, 1885 U.S. LEXIS 274 (1885).

[109] Ohio v. Turner, 105 Ohio St. 3d 331, 341, 2005 Ohio 1938, 826 N.E.2d 266, 278, 2005 Ohio LEXIS 961 (2005).

[110] Hanley v. Donoghue, 116 U.S. 1, 6 S. Ct. 242, 29 L. Ed. 535 (1885).

§ 5.10 — Law of the Forum

It goes without saying that all courts must take judicial notice of the law prevailing within the forum, i.e., the law that exists within the state or that applies to the particular federal jurisdiction. One of the reasons for having state and federal laws is that they are to be used and adjudicated by the courts. It would be foolish to permit courts to take judicial notice of federal laws and laws of other states and countries without taking judicial notice of their own laws. A court sitting in a particular state must take judicial notice of the law of its own state, including both statutory and case law.[111] In addition to notice of laws, courts generally take judicial notice of their own court records and from court records generated by other courts in the state. For example, California courts may judicially notice the records of any court in the state.[112]

If prior case law has established a particular principle, a trial court may judicially notice the principle and the trial court is not required to hold a pretrial hearing before taking judicial notice. For example, an Illinois appeals court determined that it was unnecessary to hold a pretrial hearing prior to admitting deoxyribonucleic acid (DNA) identification testimony if case law had established the validity of the principle in a previous case.[113] The court could take judicial notice of DNA identification as an accepted scientific procedure based on prior rulings. But a court could not judicially notice a denial of a motion to suppress that occurred in a case that was dismissed and later refiled. In a Wisconsin case the judge improperly took notice that the defendant's motion to suppress had previously been denied in a prior proceeding and, when the case was refiled, the prior suppression decision was not a proper subject of judicial notice because the earlier proceeding had not concluded on the merits.[114]

§ 5.11 — Federal Law

Article VI of the United States Constitution provides that the "Constitution, and the laws of the United States which shall be made in Pursuance thereof, and all Treaties made, or which shall be made under the Authority of the United States, shall be the supreme Law of the Land; the Judges in every State shall be bound thereby . . ." Accordingly, all federal and state courts must take judicial notice of the provisions of the federal Constitution, its amendments, and the laws of the United States made pursuant to the Constitution. In regard

---

[111]   Carmona v. Warden, 2007 Conn. Super. LEXIS 3425 (Conn. 2007).

[112]   *See* People v. Young, 34 Cal. 4th 1149; 105 P.3d 487; 24 Cal. Rptr. 3d 112; 2005 Cal. LEXIS 1017 (2005) (In n.3, the court noted its power to judicial notice of all state court records under the authority of CAL. EVID. CODE § 452(d).

[113]   People v. Johnson, 199 Ill. Dec. 931, 634 N.E.2d 1285 (1994). *See also* United States v. Martinez, 3 F.3d 1191 (8th Cir. 1993).

[114]   State v. Wasserman, 2008 Wis. App. 148, 2008 Wis. App. LEXIS 669 (Wis. 2008).

to congressional enactments, judicial notice is not limited to their existence, wording, and interpretation, but extends to all matters connected therewith.[115] For example, a federal district court may properly take judicial notice that a drug was classified as a Schedule I drug.[116] In addition to traditional federal law, federal courts have found that records and reports of administrative bodies are proper subjects of judicial notice because administrative bodies create administrative law by promulgating rules and regulations.[117]

§ 5.12   – Law of Sister States

Many states have adopted a version of the Uniform Judicial Notice of Foreign Law Act. Wisconsin's version provides that "Every court of this state shall take judicial notice of the common law and statutes of every state, territory and other jurisdiction of the United States."[118] Under Wisconsin law, it permits a state court to inform itself "of such laws in such manner as it may deem proper, and the court may call upon counsel to aid it in obtaining such information."[119]

Typical of many states, Ohio law requires a party who plans to rely on the law of a sister American state to give notice in the pleadings or other reasonable written notice. The court may consider any reasonable source to determine the substance of foreign law.[120] The reasonable notice requirement is to assure fairness and avoid undue surprise to the opponent when a party plans to rely on laws of other jurisdictions by using judicial notice. In an expansive view of notice of law, a Kansas statute requires that the courts of that state take judicial notice of the "common law, constitutions, and public statutes in force in every state, territory and jurisdiction of the United States."[121] Florida follows a similar plan but mandates that a court take judicial notice of the laws of sister states where a party has given a "written notice of the request, proof of which is filed with the court, to enable the adverse party to prepare to meet the request."[122]

Public laws of general application are clearly included within the term "statutes." This term also fairly includes other states' constitutions and rules of procedure and evidence having force of law throughout each such state, even though some of the "law" consists of rules that were adopted by the highest

---

[115] Gardner v. Barney, 73 U.S. (6 Wall.) 499, 18 L. Ed. 890 (1868).

[116] United States v. Arroyo, 2009 U.S. App. LEXIS 4165 (7th Cir. 2009).

[117] United States v. 14.02 Acres of Land, 530 F.3d 883, 894, 2008 U.S. App. LEXIS 13309 (9th Cir. 2008).

[118] Wis. Stat. § 902.02(1) (2008).

[119] Id. at § 902.02(2).

[120] State v. Turner, 105 Ohio St. 3d 331, 341, 2005 Ohio 1938, 826 N.E.2d 266, 2005 Ohio LEXIS 961 (2005).

[121] K.S.A. 60–409(a) (2007).

[122] See Fla. Stat. Ann. § 90.203(1), (2) (Matthew Bender 2009).

court of the state. These materials are usually accessible through state codes and through verifiable Internet sites, and because they are in the general nature of public laws, these laws and rules should be judicially noticed. In a Texas case that concerned a breach of contract, the trial court took judicial notice of Illinois case law in resolving the controversy.[123] Although not a sister state, a federal court may take judicial notice of state law where appropriate. In fact, judicial notice may not even be required in the future because the Sixth Circuit has recently explained that "we used to allow judicial notice of state law, [but] now we consider that state law is simply a matter for the judge to determine."[124] In a federal drug prosecution in which the defendant was attempting to suppress evidence, a federal district court took notice of the Nebraska and California requirements for display of vehicle license plates, which helped determine whether a vehicle stop was legal.[125]

§ 5.13 — Law of Foreign Countries

As a practical matter, foreign civil and criminal law has an infrequent, but not necessarily unimportant, usage in criminal cases in either federal or state courts. United States federal courts may take judicial notice of the laws of foreign countries where a party has given written notice to raise the issue.[126] The Federal Rules of Criminal Procedure require that one party give notice to the other party that a matter of foreign law will be an issue at the trial.[127] The trial judge is then permitted to consider relevant material, whether offered by the prosecution or by the defense. Following modern logic, federal courts will be required to take judicial notice where a federal law or a treaty specifically requires it.[128] State courts often judicially recognize foreign law and parties may introduce into evidence statutes or case law to support judicial notice.[129] Massachusetts also takes a progressive approach and requires its courts to take judicial notice of the "law . . . of a foreign country whenever the same shall be material."[130] Ohio law serves as a typical model where it requires a party who plans to rely on the law of a foreign country to give notice in the pleadings or other reasonable notice.[131] The court may consider any reasonable source to determine the substance of foreign law.[132] Although many state courts will not

---

[123] Orion Ref. Corp. v. UOP, 259 S.W.3rd 749 (Tex. 2007).

[124] United States v. Dedman, 527 F.3d 577, 587 (6th Cir. 2008).

[125] United States v. Molson, 2006 U.S. Dist. LEXIS 2292 (D. Neb. 2006).

[126] Eshelman v. Orthoclear Holdings, 2009 U.S. Dist. LEXIS 19293 (N.D. Cal. 2009).

[127] *See* FED. R. CRIM. P. 26.1.

[128] Baxter v. Baxter, 423 F.3d 363; 2005 U.S. App. LEXIS 19825 (3d Cir. 2005), n. 4.

[129] K&K Leasing v. Tech Logistice, 2008 Iowa App. LEXIS 1107 (Iowa 2008).

[130] ANN. LAWS MASS. GL ch. 233, § 70 (Matthew Bender 2008).

[131] *See* OHIO CIV. R. 44.1 (Matthew Bender (2009).

[132] OHIO CIV. R. 44.1 is incorporated by OHIO CRIM. R. 27 (Matthew Bender 2009).

be required to take judicial notice of laws in foreign countries,[133] some states allow their courts to judicially notice foreign law as a substitute for proof. In Texas, when the law of a foreign jurisdiction could have been introduced in the pleadings or requested on motion, but was not, the courts take an interesting approach by assuming that the foreign jurisdiction's laws are the same as Texas law.[134] A Wisconsin statute under the Uniform Judicial Notice of Foreign Law Act holds that the laws of foreign nations shall be an issue for the trial court but are not subject to the state provisions concerning judicial notice.[135]

§ 5.14 — Municipal Ordinances

State and local courts are often required to take judicial notice of local government ordinances passed by any subdivision of a state that has power to enact ordinances. For example, in Pennsylvania, all courts must take judicial notice of the ordinances of all the municipal corporations within the Commonwealth. The courts are permitted to request assistance of the parties and may inform themselves in any proper manner.[136] For example, a California appeals court took judicial notice, where the trial court could have, of both the municipal ordinances at issue but also took notice of the legislative history of the ordinances.[137] In a case involving litigation against a street gang,[138] a California appellate court took judicial notice of the Oxnard codified ordinances as required by state statute allowing courts to take notice of "[r]egulations and legislative enactments issued by or under the authority of the United States or any public entity in the United States."[139] In some jurisdictions, reviewing courts may be required to exercise that same judicial notice over municipal ordinances as is required or allowed by the municipal courts themselves. The court may obtain information sufficient to take judicial notice of ordinances in any manner it may deem appropriate and may consult with counsel for assistance in obtaining the information. As a general rule, when municipal courts are permitted to take judicial notice, they do so under the same rules that apply to courts of general jurisdiction and appellate courts.[140]

Although many jurisdictions either allow or require their courts to take judicial notice of the municipal ordinances, some states require proof of the

---

[133] Kearney v. Savannah Foods, 350 F. Supp. 85 (S.D. Ga. 1972).

[134] Gerdes v. Kennamer, 155 S.W.3d 541, 548, 2004 Tex. App. LEXIS 10945 (2004).

[135] WIS. STAT. §902.02, Uniform judicial notice of foreign law act (2008).

[136] 42 PA. C. S. § 6107 (Judicial notice of certain [Pennsylvania] local government ordinances) (2008).

[137] *See* Friends of Lagoon Valley v. City of Vacaville, 154 Cal. App.4th 807, 2007 Cal. App. LEXIS 1424 (Cal. 2007).

[138] People v. Totten, 156 Cal. App. 4th 31, n.9, 2007 Cal. App. LEXIS 1697 (Ca. 2007).

[139] CAL. EVID. CODE § 452 (2009).

[140] *See* PA. R. E. 201 (Judicial Notice of Adjudicative Facts) (Pa. 2008).

ordinance. Georgia retains the rule that municipal ordinances "must be alleged and proved by production of the original or of a properly certified copy."[141] In a case involving the City of Atlanta, a Georgia reviewing court noted that neither a trial court nor appellate court can take judicial notice of municipal ordinances.[142] Although not representative of the modern trend on judicial notice, in Georgia, when a prosecutor or defendant wants to rely on the provisions of a municipal ordinance, it must be alleged and proved in the trial court because the state has a well-established principle that judicial notice cannot be taken by superior and appellate courts.[143] Louisiana has a slightly different approach from actually requiring proof and allows judicial notice to be taken of parish ordinances when a copy of the ordinance is filed with the court with a judicial notice request.[144]

Demonstrative of modern practice, Ohio requires criminal courts to take judicial notice of the rules of the supreme court of the state and of the decisional, constitutional, and public statutory law of the state. If a party intends to rely upon a municipal ordinance, to obtain judicial notice, it must give the opposing party notice in the pleadings.[145] The modern practice of allowing judicial notice of municipal ordinances and rules enhances the concept of judicial economy and appears to demonstrate a trend in this direction.

§ 5.15   — Administrative Regulations

Under Federal Rule of Evidence 201(b), administrative regulations, acts, orders, and records of federal agencies fall within the category of facts that are capable of accurate and simple determination by consulting sources whose accuracy cannot reasonably be questioned[146] and for which judicial notice proves appropriate. Federal courts have held that records and reports of administrative bodies are proper subjects of judicial notice because administrative bodies create administrative law by promulgating rules and regulations.[147]

In addition, the Uniform Rules of Evidence provide that judicial notice may be taken of the published regulations of governmental subdivisions or agencies of the state. Administrative regulations published in the Federal Register must be judicially noticed by all federal courts, and many state courts also notice such regulations in the interest of judicial economy. In an unpublished opinion, the Tenth Circuit Court of Appeals observed that a

---

[141]   Bailey v. City of Atlanta, 2009 Ga. App. LEXIS 306 (2009).

[142]   Latimore v. City of Atlanta, 289 Ga. App. 85, 86, 2008 Ga. App. LEXIS 2 (Ga. 2008).

[143]   Flippen Alliance v. Brannan, 267 Ga. App. 134, 136, 601 S.E.2d 106, 109, 2004 Ga. App. LEXIS 460 (2004).

[144]   Bayou Liberty Association v. St. Tammany Parish Council, 2006 La. App. LEXIS 1378 (2006).

[145]   Ohio Civ. R. 44.1 (Anderson 2009). *See also* OHIO CRIM. R. 27 (2009). Rule 27 notes that it incorporates Civil Rules 44 and 44.1 involving judicial notice.

[146]   Toth v. Grand Trunk Railroad, 306 F.3d 335, 2002 U.S. App. LEXIS 19169 (6th Cir. 2002).

[147]   United States v. 14.02 Acres of Land, 530 F.3d 883, 894, 2008 U.S. App. LEXIS 13309 (9th Cir. 2008).

federal court sitting under its diversity jurisdiction may judicially notice that state's administrative regulations.[148] Naturally, a federal court can take judicial notice of reports of the federal Department of Health and Human Services and of relevant Ohio Administrative Code provisions.[149]

In 2008, a federal district court, in a deportation proceeding of a convicted illegal alien, properly took judicial notice of federal immigration regulations and took judicial notice of a prior federal deportation order.[150] In California, a trial court took judicial notice of regulations requiring death row prisoners to provide the state with blood and saliva samples containing DNA.[151] In a challenge to the proper promulgation of the Indiana Administrative Code in a driving under the influence case, the reviewing court upheld the manner in which the administrative rule had been established and held that the trial court acted properly in taking judicial notice of the code's provisions.[152]

Where courts have taken judicial notice of state and federal administrative regulations and orders, logic dictates that such notice is appropriate because matters addressed under administrative law are capable of easy verification from official printed sources whose accuracy cannot reasonably be disputed.

§ 5.16 — Jurisdiction of Courts

As a general rule, courts have limited territorial jurisdiction and generally, but not always, have a limited subject matter jurisdiction. For a criminal conviction to withstand appellate challenge, the court trying a defendant must have possessed subject matter jurisdiction covering the alleged crime and the operative facts of the crime must have occurred within the court's territorial jurisdiction. A criminal conviction must be reversed where the evidence or substitutes for proof failed to provide evidence that the offense was committed within the jurisdiction of the court. A court has power to take judicial notice that an alleged crime occurred within the territorial jurisdiction of the court[153] and must judicially notice the "limits of its own subject matter jurisdiction.[154] However, a juvenile court cannot take judicial notice of its jurisdiction where part of the requirement of jurisdiction depends on the age of the juvenile; the juvenile's age must be proven in the case as part of jurisdiction.[155] In a

---

[148] Samson Resources v. Wamsutter, 117 Fed. Appx. 641, 644, 2004 U.S. App. LEXIS 22795 (10th Cir. 2004).

[149] Gamble v. Ohio Department of Job and Family Services, 2006 U.S. Dist. LEXIS 968 (S.D. Ohio 2006).

[150] United States v. Gutierrez-Casada, 553 F. Supp.2d 1259, 2008 U.S. Dist. LEXIS 39406 (D. Kan. 2008).

[151] Alfaro v. Terhune, 98 Cal. App. 4th 492, 120 Cal. Rptr. 2d 197, 2002 Cal. App. LEXIS 4116 (2002).

[152] Disabato et al. v. State, 840 N.E.2d 1, 4, 2005 Ind. App. LEXIS 2390 (2005).

[153] See United States v. Troupe, 2008 U.S. App. LEXIS 24941 (4th Cir. 2008).

[154] 29 Am. Jur. 2d Evidence § 39.

[155] State v. K.N., 124 Wash. App. 875, 877, 103 P.3d 844, 845, 2004 Wash. App. LEXIS 3135 (2004).

delinquency case, the prosecution must prove that the offense was committed within the territorial jurisdiction of the court and a failure to prove jurisdiction or have judicial notice taken of jurisdiction may reverse the case.[156] A court may also take judicial notice of the fact that a particular milepost or interchange of an interstate highway is within the court's territorial jurisdiction.[157]

The courts have been consistent in holding that a court may take judicial notice of its own jurisdiction. In one case, an officer observed a driver speeding on the opposite side of the road. When he stopped the speeder and when he initially observed him, the speeder was in a different city because the city and court boundary ran down the middle of the road. The officer cited the driver for speeding as well as driving while intoxicated, but the trial court took judicial notice that the defendant had not been driving within the city over which it had territorial jurisdiction. When the defendant requested that the judge take judicial notice that the defendant had committed no offense within the court's jurisdiction, the court agreed and dismissed the case due to the judicial notice it took concerning the limits of its jurisdiction.[158]

§ 5.17 Judicial Notice Process

Rule 201

Judicial Notice of Adjudicative Facts

* * *

(c) when discretionary. a court may take judicial notice, whether requested or not.

(d) when mandatory. a court shall take judicial notice if requested by a party and supplied with the necessary information

(e) Opportunity to be heard. A party is entitled upon timely request to an opportunity to be heard as to the propriety of taking judicial notice and the tenor of the matter noticed. In the absence of prior notification, the request may be made after judicial notice has been taken.

(f) Time of taking notice. Judicial notice may be taken at any stage of the proceeding.

(g) Instructing jury. In a civil action or proceeding, the court shall instruct the jury to accept as conclusive any fact judicially noticed. In a criminal case, the court shall instruct the jury that it may, but is not required to, accept as conclusive any fact judicially noticed.[159]

---

[156] In the Interest of A. C., 263 Ga. App. 44, 45, 587 S.E.2d 210, 211, 2003 Ga. App. LEXIS 1087 (2003).

[157] State v. Scott, 3 Ohio App. 2d 239, 32 Ohio Op. 2d 360, 210 N.E.2d 289 (1965).

[158] City of North Ridgeville v. Stack, 2006 Ohio 1177, 2006 Ohio App. LEXIS 1063 (2006).

[159] FED. R. EVID. 201.

In proving or disproving a criminal case, the attorneys introduce evidence of adjudicative facts that the fact finder must either believe or disbelieve. These types of facts normally concern questions involving what a defendant did, where the events occurred, what actually happened, and how the alleged crime was accomplished. The evidence that supports or refutes these facts must be determined by the fact finder and proof of some of the facts may come from the use of judicial notice.

When one of the parties desires a judge to take judicial notice of a particular point, principle, or fact, the attorney for that party makes a request and offers the reasons that support the taking of judicial notice. The request is sometimes made in open court but is often made out of the hearing of the jury. Once a request has been made and prior to the judge's decision, the opposing party is entitled, on timely request, to have an opportunity to be heard—outside the hearing of the jury—on the propriety of taking judicial notice and on the nature of the matter proposed to be judicially noticed.

Because a jury in a criminal case serves as the ultimate finder of fact, it is free to adopt as true or reject as false any fact judicially noticed. A federal court of appeals stated that "[j]udicial notice is a doctrine that authorizes the finder of fact to waive proof of facts that cannot reasonably be contested."[160] Under this doctrine and without hearing evidence, a jury could accept [or reject] as a fact that a particular drug was considered a Schedule I controlled substance.[161] In one case, the judge instructed the jury, that using judicial notice, the judge accepted as proved that a marriage between a grandfather and his adopted granddaughter is illegal under the law of the state.[162]

Under the process of taking judicial notice, how does a jury become aware that it may consider facts judicially noticed by the court? When a party requests by motion or in open court that the judge take judicial notice of a particular matter and where the judge agrees that taking notice is proper, the judge will state in open court to the jury that such fact is noticed. Also, upon the court's own motion, it may determine that a particular fact will be judicially noticed and so advise the jury.

Once a matter is judicially noticed, a court will not admit evidence to dispute the fact noticed. One court noted that it would not "accept as true allegations that contradict matters properly subject to judicial notice."[163] To allow evidence to contradict judicially noticed facts would be contrary to the rationale on which judicial noticed is based. However, a court commits error if it takes judicial notice of a fact where the fact is doubtful, uncertain, or subject to reasonable dispute. In a criminal case, the jury is not required to accept the fact as conclusive. Demonstrative of general judicial notice practice,

---

[160]   United States, 2009 U.S. App. LEXIS 4165 (7th Cir. 2009).
[161]   United States v. Arroyo, 2009 U.S. App. LEXIS 4165 (7th Cir. 2009).
[162]   United States v. Dedman, 527 F.3d 577, 584, 2008 U.S. App. LEXIS 11407 (6th Cir. 2008).
[163]   Brown v. Hawai'i, 2009 U.S. Dist. LEXIS 10546 (D. Hawai'i 2009).

Ohio criminal courts "shall instruct the jury that it may, but is not required to, accept as conclusive any fact judicially noticed."[164]

In some states, the rules relating to the procedure followed in judicial notice situations are spelled out by rule or statute. For example, in Oregon,[165] the procedures for taking judicial notice permit the court to take notice on its own motion or upon request of one of the parties. The court must take judicial notice upon request and after being supplied with the necessary information. The judge may desire to hear from the attorney who wants the court to take notice and the opposing counsel is entitled to offer objections prior to the taking of notice or after. A court may judicially notice a fact, concept, or principle at any time during a case, even during the appellate stage.

§ 5.18 Judicial Notice in Criminal Cases

As a general rule, criminal trial courts may take judicial notice of court records of any state or federal jurisdiction,[166] the hour of sunrise on a particular day,[167] the scientific accuracy of laser speed detection,[168] the speed limit on a highway,[169] the fact that a defendant has prior convictions,[170] legislative history of state law,[171] and a variety of other verifiable facts. In a Texas case, the punishment was enhanced following the trial court's judicial notice of the defendant's prior felony conviction for aggravated robbery. On appeal, the defendant argued that the taking of judicial notice of his prior convictions and their finality for appellate purposes was improper. The reviewing court determined that taking notice of the prior conviction and its finality was not an abuse of the trial court's discretion because a silent record allows a court to presume that a conviction is final.[172] However, some courts are more reluctant to permit the use of judicial notice in criminal cases than in civil cases. The taking of judicial notice proved to be improper in a Florida case where a criminal court ordered restitution based on the value of a Dodge truck that it determined from a standard reference book on vehicle values. Normally, judicial notice would have been proper, but in this case the truck was missing its engine and

---

[164] *See* OHIO R. EVID. 201(G) Judicial Notice of Adjudicative Facts (Matthew Bender 2009).

[165] ORS §§ 40.070–40.080 (Or. 2007).

[166] Schwab v. State, 969 So. 2d 318, 2007 Fla. LEXIS 2011 (Fla. 2007). *See also* FLA. STAT. § 90.202(6) (2009).

[167] Swafford v. Florida, 828 So. 2d 966 at 967, 2002 Fla. LEXIS 789 (2002).

[168] State v. Williamson, 144 Idaho 597, 602, 2007 Idaho App. LEXIS 43 (Ida 2007).

[169] Hicks v. Jones, 2008 U.S. Dist. LEXIS 104274, n.5 (N.D. Ok. 2008).

[170] United States v. Perkins, 548 U.S. App. 510, 515, 2008 U.S. App. LEXIS 23678 (7th Cir. 2008).

[171] People v. Acosta, 29 Cal. 4th 105 at 120, 52 P.3d 624 at 634, 124 Cal. Rptr. 2d 435 at 447 (2002).

[172] Figueroa v. State, 250 S.W.3d 490, 504, 2008 Tex. App. LEXIS 2028 (Tex. 2008).

transmission and the remaining value was subject to reasonable dispute and was not the proper subject for judicial notice.[173]

Judicially noticed facts are treated differently depending on whether the case is civil or criminal. Rule 201(g) of the Federal Rules of Evidence notes that a court shall instruct the jury to accept as conclusive any fact judicially noticed in civil cases, but in criminal cases the rule requires that a court instruct the jury that it may, but is not required to, accept as conclusive any fact judicially noticed. Because every defendant has the right to have the jury or the judge serve as factfinder and recognizing that taking judicial notice of a fact, a principle, or other matter has the effect of removing the issue from the jury's consideration, in close cases where there might be an argument against judicial notice, judges are often reluctant to take judicial notice. It is better practice to prepare traditional evidence that would prove the fact or concept that might be the subject of judicial notice. This proof would assist a judge either in taking judicial notice or in cases where judicial notice was declined, it allows the matter to be introduced and proved in court.

§ 5.19 Summary

Although the usual procedure is for the parties to introduce evidence to prove a fact in dispute, in some instances such evidence is unnecessary because the court will take judicial notice of certain facts. This procedure is necessary and reasonable in order to save the time of the court, the parties, and the attorneys.

Judicial notice involves the court recognizing the existence of certain facts and laws without requiring the parties to introduce proof. For convenience, the rules concerning judicial notice are often categorized as judicial notice of facts and judicial notice of laws. Rule 201 of the Federal Rules of Evidence relates only to the taking of judicial notice of adjudicative facts.

The general rule is that the trial judge may take judicial notice without motion of counsel or take judicial notice of fact following a formal request. The judge, in fact, is given a great deal of discretion concerning judicial notice, and an appellate court will not disturb the taking of judicial notice unless there is a clear abuse of discretion. Where a trial court could have taken judicial notice on its own motion, but did not, or where a trial court could have taken judicial notice, but declined, generally an appellate court may take judicial notice.[174] Many appellate courts will not judicially notice a fact where a trial court could have done so, but declined for appropriate reasons within the limits of a trial court's discretion.

---

[173]   Walentukonis v. State, 932 So. 2d 1136, 1137, 2006 Fla. App. LEXIS 9766 (Fla. 2006).
[174]   In re Solis, 2008 Tex. App. LEXIS 7529 (Tex. 2008).

In the interests of judicial economy, it is obvious that there are many facts that are commonly known and need not be proved in court. Examples of these include historical facts, geographical facts, scientific facts, and other facts that are generally known to the ordinary person. A judge may take notice of facts that may be ascertained by consulting standard reference works. In addition to facts, the judge may take judicial notice of certain laws, such as the Constitution of the United States, administrative regulations, laws of the several states, and in some instances, municipal ordinances and foreign law.

While judicial discretion permits a judge to take notice of certain facts and certain laws, it is not a certainty that a judge will always view the suggestion in a favorable manner to the party requesting it. Judges in criminal cases often err on the side of caution when faced with a request for judicial notice. If there is any doubt concerning the appropriateness of the fact to be introduced or proved in court, traditional proof should be acquired and made ready for court presentation. The availability of traditional evidence to present to the judge may assist or prompt the judge to take judicial notice of certain facts.

Presumptions, Inferences, and Stipulations 6

The use of presumptions and inferences to prove an element of the crime is indeed treacherous, for it allows men to go to jail without any evidence on one essential ingredient of the offense. It thus implicates the integrity of the judicial system.

Barnes v. United States, 412 U.S. 837, 93 S. Ct. 2357 (1973)
(Douglas, J., dissenting)

Chapter Outline

Section
6.1   Introduction
6.2   Definitions and Distinctions
6.3   Reasons for Presumptions and Inferences
6.4   Presumptions of Law
6.5   Presumptions of Fact
6.6   Classes of Presumptions
6.7   Specific Presumption Situations
6.8   —Innocence
6.9   —Sanity
6.10   —Suicide
6.11   —Possession of Fruits of Crime
6.12   —That a Person Intends the Ordinary Consequences of His or Her
         Voluntary Acts
6.13   —Knowledge of the Law
6.14   —Flight or Concealment
6.15   —Unexplained Absence as Death
6.16   —Regularity of Official Acts
6.17   Constitutionality Tests for Presumptions and Inferences
6.18   Stipulations
6.19   —Polygraph Tests
6.20   Summary

§ 6.1 Introduction

Chapter 4 described the process of introducing evidence in criminal cases. In the typical criminal case, to the extent that a party has a burden of proof,[1] each party has the obligation of introducing evidence to establish facts from which a judge or jury will make a decision. However, in some instances, the jury may consider facts other than the facts that have actually been introduced in court by the parties. One way of distinguishing this information source from actual evidence is to designate it as a substitute for evidence.

Judicial notice, discussed in Chapter 5, is one of several substitutes for evidence. The chapter included discussion of the legal reasoning that permits a trial or appellate judge to take notice of certain facts and laws. In addition, the chapter introduced case decisions and statutes limiting the use of judicial notice. This chapter considers three additional substitutes for evidence—the presumption, the inference, and the stipulation.

The use of inferences and presumptions in criminal trials, while based on logic and predictability, have the effect of relieving one party or the other from actually proving facts and elements of the crime. The use of an inference to help prove that a defendant possessed sufficient knowledge to commit the crime or that a defendant possessed a particular criminal intent may only be proved by the use of circumstantial evidence because no one can really know

---

[1] Generally, a defendant has no burden of proof and the burden of proof beyond a reasonable doubt rests with the prosecution. Where a defendant pleads an affirmative defense such as self-defense, insanity, alibi, mistake of fact, or some other affirmative defense, there may be a burden of proof on a defendant to establish the defense by a preponderance of the evidence, by clear and convincing evidence, or beyond a reasonable doubt.

what another person was thinking. Whether a defendant knowingly possessed recently stolen property or whether a defendant possessed a specific intent to defraud in a forgery case can only be inferred by considering surrounding facts and making that deduction from those facts. Ultimately, the use of presumptions and inferences relieves a party of the burden of presenting evidence to prove a particular fact where the fact can be inferred or deduced from proof of other facts.

This chapter defines, distinguishes, and demonstrates how presumptions, inferences, and stipulations affect criminal trials. In addition, the chapter discusses the theoretical basis for allowing presumptions and inferences, as well as the types of presumptions recognized by the courts and legislatures. This chapter gives detailed attention to specific examples of common presumptions and inferences and explains how they play an important role in the trial process. Finally, this chapter defines and explains the remaining substitute for evidence—the stipulation—and demonstrates some significant specific examples of how attorneys use stipulations.

§ 6.2　Definitions and Distinctions

> **Rule 301**
>
> **Presumptions in General
> in Civil Actions and Proceedings**
>
> In all civil actions and proceedings not otherwise provided by Acts of Congress or by these rules, a presumption imposes on the party against whom it is directed the burden of going forward with evidence to rebut or meet the presumption, but does not shift to such party the burden of proof in the sense of the risk of nonpersuasion, which remains throughout the trial upon the party on whom it was originally cast.[2]
>
> * * *

A.　Presumptions

When the Federal Rules of Evidence were being written, the committee that considered Rule 301 intended to limit the scope of the rule to civil actions and proceedings and declined to have the rule cover federal criminal proceedings. The committee chose not to consider the thorny questions of presumptions in criminal cases and therefore limited Rule 301 to civil actions. In criminal cases, the parties must look to state statutes and state court decisions as well as federal court decisions for answers to questions relating to presumptions. Because the federal Constitution has been interpreted to require

---

[2]　FED. R. EVID. 301.

proof beyond a reasonable doubt for criminal cases, presumptions cannot be designed to allow a conviction due to the use of a presumption that shifts the burden of proof. Presumptions can be created only by courts or legislatures and they are based on considerations of fairness, public policy, and the probability that some events or facts follow other events or facts.[3]

The term *presumption* has been used by courts and legal writers to describe several different consequences that flow from the introduction of evidence in a trial. Under the California Evidence Code, "[a] presumption is an assumption of fact that the law requires to be made from another fact or group of facts found or otherwise established in the action."[4] In Illinois, "[a] presumption is a legal device that permits or requires the fact finder to assume the existence of an ultimate fact, after certain predicate or basic facts have been established."[5] A presumption is a rule of law that allows a jury in a criminal case to infer or deduce the existence of a second fact from the proof of the first, or basic, fact. Demonstrative of this concept is a section of the penal code in California that provides that when a victim of a crime dies beyond three years from receiving injuries, there is "a rebuttable presumption that the killing was not criminal."[6] In Texas, when there is independent proof of a burglary, unexplained possession of recently stolen goods connected to the burglary may provide sufficient evidence for a conviction.[7] However, "[m]ere possession of stolen property does not give rise to a presumption of guilt; rather, it will support an inference of guilt regarding the offense during which the property was stolen."[8] In other words, a presumption draws a particular conclusion as to the existence of one fact, not actually known, arising from its usual connection with another fact or facts that are known or proved.

Some courts and legislative enactments hold that a true legal presumption is in the nature of evidence and is to be weighed as such. Other jurisdictions hold that a presumption is not considered evidence, but is a substitute for evidence[9] and may be treated as if it were evidence and accepted as fact or disregarded.

Mandatory presumptions in criminal cases are generally unconstitutional because they relieve the prosecution of having to prove all the elements beyond a reasonable doubt and have the effect of calling into question the presumption of innocence. Therefore, a statutory presumption that considered that a renter of personal property, who did not return it within five days after receiving a

---

[3] *See* 23 FLA. JUR. *Evidence and Witnesses* § 97 (2008).

[4] CAL. EVID. CODE § 600 (Matthew Bender 2008).

[5] People v. Cazacu, 373 Ill. App. 3d 465, 2007 Ill. App. LEXIS 484 (Ill. 2007), citing People v. Woodrum, 223 Ill. 2d 286, 308, 2006 Ill. LEXIS 1633 (Ill. 2007), *cert. denied*, Woodrum v. Illinois, 2007 U.S. LEXIS 4140 (2007).

[6] CAL. PENAL CODE § 194 (Matthew Bender 2009).

[7] Nimitz v. State, 2008 Tex. App. LEXIS 8341 (Tex. 2008).

[8] *Id.*

[9] *See* Ament v. Reassure America Life Insurance Co., 2009 Ohio 36, 2009 Ohio App. LEXIS 23 (Ohio 2009) and Cal Evid Code § 600 (Matthew Bender 2008).

demand for the return of the property, had unlawfully converted it to his own use could not stand because of its mandatory nature.[10]

B. Inferences

One state defines an inference as "a deduction of fact that may logically and reasonably be drawn from another fact or group of facts established by the evidence"[11] Phrased in a slightly different manner, an inference has been defined as a deduction of fact that a jury may make but that a criminal jury cannot be required to make. "Whether the inferred fact is found to exist will be decided by the trier of fact."[12] In accepting the existence of one fact and making a deduction from that fact that another fact exists, the jurors are free to make the deduction or to not make the deduction and, thus, reject the inference.

Although the terms *presumption* and *inference* are sometimes used synonymously, the courts have attempted to distinguish between them as to both their origin and effect. According to some courts, an inference should be recorded as a permissible deduction from the evidence before the court, which the jury may accept or reject. A presumption, as contrasted with an inference, is a rule of law, relatively fixed or relatively defined in scope and effect, that attaches to certain evidentiary facts and produces a specific procedural consequence. To state this more simply, a presumption is a mandatory deduction that the law expressly requires, while an inference is no more than a permissible deduction that the trier of fact may adopt. Any criminal jury is free to disregard the finding of the deduced or inferred fact because the jury has the sole power to determine the facts in a criminal case. Concerning the historical facts of the case, it would almost be true to state that, in criminal cases, only inferences may exist because presumptions of fact cannot be enforced. In adopting this view concerning inferences and presumptions, the Supreme Court of Pennsylvania noted that:

> Inferences and presumptions are staples of our adversary system of factfinding. It is often necessary for the trier of fact to determine the existence of an element of the crime—that is, an "ultimate" or "elemental" fact—from the existence of one or more "evidentiary" or "basic" facts. Nevertheless, to the extent that these logical tools impede rather than assist in the jury's exercise of its factfinding function, they cannot be employed to prove the elements of a crime. Hence, "virtually all so-called 'criminal presumptions' are really no more than . . . inferences." Commonwealth v. DiFrancesco, 458 Pa. 188, 329 A.2d 204, 207 n. 3 (Pa. 1974).[13]

---

[10]   Sherrod v. State, 280 Ga. 275, 275, 627 S.E.2d 36, 37, 2006 Ga. LEXIS 145 (Ga. 2006).

[11]   Bowlin v. Chrones, Warden, 2008 U.S. Dist. LEXIS (E.D. Cal. 2008), citing CALJIC 2.00.

[12]   CHARLES W. EHRHARDT, FLORIDA EVIDENCE § 301.1 at 89–90 (2003 ed.), quoted in Palmas y Bambu v. E.I Dupont, 881 So. 2d 565; 2004 Fla. App. LEXIS 7372 (Fla. 2004).

[13]   Commonwealth v. Salter, 2004 Pa. Super. 318, 858 A.2d 610, 615, 2004 Pa. Super. LEXIS 2687 (2004).

In a Georgia murder case,[14] the reviewing court noted with approval a jury charge that stated, "[y]ou may infer, if you wish to do so, that the acts of a person of sound mind and discretion are the product of that person's will. A person of sound mind and discretion intends the natural and probable consequences of those acts. That's the second thing that you can infer."[15] According to the appellate court, the wording of this jury instruction creates a lawful permissive inference and fails to require a jury to draw any particular conclusion. Because the jury has a free choice, no constitutional errors exist with this type of inference. In another case, the court made this distinction concerning the difference between an inference and a presumption:

> Presumptions are one thing; inferences another. Presumptions are assumptions of fact which the law requires to be made from another fact or group of facts; inferences are logical deductions or conclusions from an established fact. Presumptions deal with legal processes, whereas inferences deal with mental processes.[16]

In the court's view, an inference is simply a logical deduction or conclusion that the law allows, but does not require, following the establishment of the basic facts.

A jury or trial court may "draw inferences from circumstantial evidence so long as the inferences are rationally related to the proven fact."[17] That is, a rational connection must exist between the initial fact proven and the fact later inferred. According to the Supreme Court of the United States, a jury may properly infer from one fact the existence of another fact that is essential to guilt, if reason and experience support the inference.[18] However, finding an inferred fact from an earlier inferred fact has its limits because, at some point, inferences become so removed from the original fact that supported the first inference that the final conclusion may not be accurate. A federal court of appeals cautioned that "reasonable inferences supported by other reasonable inferences which have an evidentiary basis may warrant a conviction. Nonetheless, where a conviction appears to be based on multiple and successive inferences, we must exercise caution"[19] to ensure that a conviction rests upon more than conjecture.

---

[14]   Smith v. State, 284 Ga. 33, 2008 Ga. LEXIS 540 (Ga. 2008).

[15]   *Id.*, 36.

[16]   State v. Jackson, 112 Wash. 2d 867, 774 P.2d 1211 (1989). *See* case in Part II. *See also* State v. Parks, 245 Neb. 205, 511 N.W.2d 774 (1994), in which the court held that a "presumption" is a fact inferred from another proved or established fact or facts, while an "inference" is a conclusion on the existence of a particular fact reached by considering other facts in the usual course of human reasoning, and thus an "inference" is a deduction that the factfinder may draw in his discretion, but is not required to draw as a matter of law.

[17]   State v. Germany, 2006 Wash. App. LEXIS (Wash. 2006).

[18]   Tot v. United States, 319 U.S. 463, 63 S. Ct. 1241, 87 L. Ed. 2d 1519 (1943).

[19]   United States v. Michel, 446 F.3d 1122, 1128, 2006 U.S. App. LEXIS 11665 (10th Cir. 2006).

When a state revises its evidence code, a state legislature may create statutory inferences that follow logic and, so long as there is a predictable relationship between the fact proved and the fact to be inferred and no mandatory requirements, the statute should withstand litigation. For example, Florida has a statute that provides that "[p]roof of the purchase or sale of stolen property at a price substantially below the fair market value, unless satisfactorily explained, gives rise to an inference that the person buying or selling the property knew or should have known that the property had been stolen."[20]

While a court may give instructions regarding inferences that can be drawn from proven facts, an instruction that permits the jurors to infer an element of the crime charged is constitutional only if the presumed fact follows beyond a reasonable doubt from the proven fact. In the case of *State v. Jackson*, the Supreme Court of Washington held that, when the charge is attempted second degree burglary, a trial court cannot instruct the jury that it may infer that the defendant acted with intent to commit a crime within a building when the evidence supports the finding that the defendant may have attempted to enter the building, when there exist other equally reasonable conclusions that follow from the circumstances.[21] In this case, an officer saw the defendant kicking the front door of a shop. When the door was examined, it was found that about 10 inches of Plexiglas had been pushed inward and that part of the wood stock around the Plexiglas was broken out of its frame. The judge instructed the jury that it might infer that the defendant acted with intent to commit a crime within the building. In reversing the conviction, the court noted that an inference shall not exist when other reasonable conclusions exist that could follow from the circumstances. Applying this reasoning, the court determined that the instruction was improper because the jury might have inferred that the defendant intended to commit a crime within the building when he might have had different plans.

A proper inference cannot be mandatory and still meet approval under the Constitution of the United States. Therefore, a jury instruction that permits a jury either to draw an inference of an element of a crime or to choose not to draw the inference will survive an attack based on constitutional grounds. In a Florida case, to prove enhancements to the charged crime, proof of prior driving while intoxicated (DUI) convictions could be proved by admitting as evidence official Florida records.[22] The records were sufficient in themselves to prove a prior conviction for DUI, but the statute allowed that evidence to be contradicted or rebutted by other evidence that a defendant might want to introduce. According to the reviewing court:

> The statute authorizes the prosecution to offer into evidence the records of the Department of Highway Safety and Motor Vehicles showing that the defendant has been previously convicted of the offense of driving under the

---

[20]   FLA. STAT. § 812.022, Evidence of theft or dealing in stolen property (2009).

[21]   State v. Jackson, *supra* note 16.

[22]   Ibarrondo v. State, 2008 Fla. App. LEXIS 20619 (Fla. 2008).

influence. If the State does so, the record evidence is "sufficient by itself" to establish the prior convictions. The statute says only that the introduced records are prima facie evidence of that element of the offense.[23]

The court took the view that because the statute permitted a defendant to rebut the inference that the prior record has been proved, the inference is permissive and not mandatory and creates only a rebuttable inference that the defendant has prior offenses.

In summary, when the finder of fact is free to ignore an inference or to accept it, whether or not the defendant introduces any evidence, the inference will be determined to be permissive and will not offend either the federal or the Florida constitution.

C. Stipulations

As another substitute for evidence, the stipulation is less difficult to define and understand than presumptions and inferences. When the parties stipulate to a fact, it simply means that they have agreed that proof of the matter will not be required. A stipulation implies that both parties have conceded to the existence or nonexistence of a fact, the contents of a document, the testimony of a witness, or other matter that has an important connection to the case. When the parties have agreed to a stipulation, the effect is to remove the fact as an issue in the case because the parties no longer have any dispute as to the fact, document, principle, or testimony. A stipulation may be in writing or offered orally, and normally the trial judge will consent to entering the stipulation on the record.[24] The liberal use of stipulations is generally encouraged by judges so that parties have agreed to the admissibility of exhibits and stipulations of fact prior to trial. Once parties have agreed to stipulate to a particular fact, the stipulation remains binding on both parties. A stipulation authorizes the court to find the existence of such a fact and to consider that fact without any further proof. The triers of fact are not, however, bound to accept the fact as true and may find to the contrary if persuaded by other evidence. A stipulation of fact between the parties will not automatically be accepted by the trial judge and sentencing courts are not bound by stipulations of fact in plea bargains.[25] Many courts refuse to accept polygraph evidence even where both the prosecutor and defendant have stipulated prior to the examination to agree concerning the admissibility of the test results.[26]

---

[23]　*Id.*

[24]　*See* Briceno v. Scribner, 555 F.3d 1069, 2009 U.S. App. LEXIS 3524 (9th Cir. 2009), in which an oral stipulation was read to the jury and United States v. Miranda-Lopez, 532 F.3d 1034, 1036, 2008 U.S. App. LEXIS 15200 (9th Cir. 2008), in which a written stipulation was entered in the record.

[25]　United States v. Evans-Martinez, 530 F.3d 1164, 2008 U.S. App. LEXIS 13972 (9th Cir. 2008) and United States v. Toepfer, 2008 U.S. App. LEXIS 14811 (11th Cir. 2008), unpublished opinion.

[26]　*See* People v. Muniz, 190 P.3d 774, 786, 2008 Colo. App. LEXIS 237 (Cal. 2008).

When the parties have stipulated concerning a fact or facts, such agreement authorizes the court to find the existence of such a fact and to consider the fact proven beyond a reasonable doubt. In a murder case, the parties agreed to a stipulation of many facts, including the fact that the defendant admitted to committing the killings. The stipulations of fact indicated that the defendant and the prosecution were in agreement concerning the facts of the case and no proof was necessary.[27] In a different case, the prosecution and the defense stipulated that a government expert witness would have testified to the presence of cocaine base in a sample that had been tested.[28] The stipulations in the two cases were proper because neither side had any disagreement with the other on the stipulated facts or issues.

While the general rule is that parties are bound by their stipulations, a trial court has the discretion to consider issues not actually covered in a pretrial stipulation. A trial court, for good cause shown, may allow a party to withdraw a stipulation, but where the stipulation survives the trial, a reviewing court is usually bound by the stipulation.[29]

§ 6.3   Reasons for Presumptions and Inferences

The use of presumptions and inferences in criminal trials plays an important part in expediting the judicial process even though many disagreements among judges, prosecutors, and defense attorneys exist concerning their application in a particular case. In many jurisdictions, inferences and presumptions serve as a substitute for evidence, and take the place of actual proof. In allowing the use of inferences and presumptions as circumstantial evidence, the courts hold that they possess the same theoretical evidentiary weight as direct evidence.[30] In jurisdictions that do not consider them to be substitutes for evidence, the operative effect is quite similar with respect to the importance and the effect of their use. In countless appellate court decisions, the rule that circumstantial evidence based on inferences or presumptions is sufficient by itself, in the absence of any direct evidence, to prove the most serious crime.[31] Naturally, in criminal cases, the finder of fact may choose to accept or to ignore any presumption or inference. In the final analysis, when presented with an inference or presumption, most jury members will probably make the deduction of fact suggested by proof of the basic fact because much everyday reasoning and decisionmaking follows a similar path of logic.

---

[27] Johnson v. Wilson, 2006 U.S. App. LEXIS 15479 (6th Cir. 2006).

[28] United States v. Anderson, 450 F.3d 294, 2006 U.S. App. LEXIS 14177 (7th Cir. 2006).

[29] State v. Stegman, 2009 Kan. App. LEXIS 124 (Kan. 2009).

[30] State v. Nulf, 2008 Wash. App. LEXIS 2278 (Wash. 2008). *See also* State v. Roberts, 2008 Ohio 5750, 2008 Ohio App. LEXIS 4821 (Ohio 2008), noting that "direct and circumstantial evidence carry equal weight."

[31] United States v. Stackhouse, 2009 U.S. App. LEXIS 2760 (8th Cir. 2009), quoting United States v. Wesseh, 531 F.3d 633, 636 (8th Cir. 2008).

A. *Procedural Technique*

Most presumptions serve as rules of evidence that provide for a particular result in a case unless the opposing party introduces evidence that refutes the presumption. The evidentiary effect of proving the basic fact in a presumption is to shift the burden of going forward with the evidence to the opposing party to introduce evidence that displaces the circumstantial conclusion offered by the presumption.[32] These are not absolute rules because a jury in a criminal case has no duty to follow the logic proposed by a presumption or inference. Without the use of presumptions, it would be difficult in some instances for the trial to go forward. One purpose of the presumption is to place the burden on the party who alone is in possession or in control of the facts with respect thereto. To make it possible to go forward with the trial, the presumption assumes a certain condition to exist until the contrary is shown.

The use of a presumption as a substitute for evidence alters the burden of offering evidence. As noted, the effect of a presumption is that the existence of the presumption shifts the burden of going forward with the evidence to the opposing party.[33] Once the presumption exists, the existence of the presumed fact remains proved unless and until the opposing party introduces evidence that casts doubt on the truth of the presumed fact. When rebuttal evidence is introduced, the finder of fact must determine whether the rebuttal evidence was sufficiently strong as to negate the existence of the presumed fact and ignore the presumption, or decide whether the presumed fact remains.[34] As the Supreme Court of Indiana noted, "[w]hen the party against whom the presumption operates introduces evidence that disputes the presumed fact, the presumption ceases to operate, disappears from the case, and no longer remains to assist any party."[35] Therefore, whether a presumption remains operative in the face of contrary evidence or disappears altogether under the "bursting bubble theory," it has the operative effect of placing the burden of going forward with the evidence on the party best able to produce the evidence on that point.[36]

B. *Public Policy*

Some presumptions of law are sanctioned by the courts and legislatures for public policy purposes. Because most children born to a married couple are the children of the husband, Maryland law states "[t]here is a rebuttable presumption that the child is the legitimate child of the man to whom its mother was married at the time of conception."[37] Public policy promotes a finding of

---

[32]　BLACK'S LAW DICTIONARY (8th ed. 2004).

[33]　Gross v. FBL Financial Services, Inc., 526 F.3d 356, 359, 2008 U.S. App. LEXIS 10355 (8th Cir. 2008).

[34]　Barnes v. Yoshikawa, 2002 Cal. App. Unpub. LEXIS 12095 (Cal. 2002).

[35]　Bonilla v. Commercial Services of Perry, Inc., 900 N.E.2d 22; 2009 Ind. App. LEXIS 112 (Ind. 2009), quoting Schultz v. Ford Motor Co., 857 N.E.2d 977, 982 (Ind. 2006).

[36]　Green v. Ransor, Inc. 175 S.W.3d 513, 516, 2005 Tex. App. LEXIS 8125 (2005).

[37]　MD. FAMILY LAW CODE ANN. § 5-1027 (Matthew Bender 2008).

legitimacy and this presumption serves that purpose. Similarly, when a child is born or conceived during wedlock, the child is presumed to be legitimate, with the husband of the wife being the presumed father.[38]

An example of a presumption of law that is often stated is that it is generally presumed that everyone knows the law[39] and that presumption applies with equal force to trial judges.[40] Likewise, criminal defendants are presumed to be innocent until the contrary may be proved.[41] When a government agent has authority to exercise discretion, such as a federal prosecutor in bringing a criminal charge, the presumption is that the prosecutor acted in good faith in making a decision to prosecute.[42] Therefore, in a criminal case where a prosecutor exercises discretion or in when a governmental agent makes a decision, a strong presumption exists that the official possesses legitimate grounds for the action taken and is acting with regularity.[43]

C. Allowance of Normal Governmental Activities

Presumptions such as honest and proper conduct by public officials allow normal governmental activities to be accepted at face value. Without this presumption, it would be burdensome, if not impossible, for prosecutors and defendants to prove affirmatively each and every routine record that is material to a case. Consequently, there is a general presumption "that trial judges know the law and apply it properly is of long standing, and [the presumption] springs from multiple sources. One of these sources is the strong presumption that judges, like other public officers, perform their duties properly."[44] It would be virtually impossible to prove a record when, for example, the clerk who made the entry has died, or due to the heavy caseload of the trial court, no one in the court or clerk's office can personally remember anything about the case in question. The presumption that the government acted in good faith and with proper conduct proves to be quite strong and a person who wishes to prove differently must have sufficient evidence to actually prove bad faith.[45]

§ 6.4 Presumptions of Law

A presumption of law is "[a] legal assumption that a court is required to make if certain facts are established and no contradictory evidence is

---

[38] Stubbs v. Colandrea et al., 154 Md. App. 673, 682, 841 A.2d 361, 366, 2004 Md. App. LEXIS 9 (Md. 2004).

[39] State v. Blunt, 2008 ND 135, 2008 N.D. LEXIS 137 (N.D. 2008).

[40] United States v. Saddler, 538 F.3d 879, 2008 U.S. App. 17211 (8th Cir. 2008).

[41] Mejia v. Garcia, 534 F.3d 1036, 1042, 2008 U.S. App. LEXIS 15933 (9th Cir. 2008).

[42] United States v. Abdelaziz et al., 2008 U.S. Dist. LEXIS 49076 (W.D. Tex. 2008).

[43] Hartman et al. v. Moore, 126 S. Ct. 1695, 1705, 164 L. Ed. 2d 441, 456, 2006 U.S. LEXIS 3450 (2006).

[44] White et al. v. The Pines Community Improvement Assn., 173 Md. App. 13, 2007 Md. App. LEXIS 23 (Md. 2007).

[45] United States v. Case, 2008 U.S. Dist. LEXIS 33891 (S.D. Miss. 2008).

produced."[46] Presumptions of law may be rebutted by the introduction of evidence that contradicts the original presumption and effectively replaces that presumption with a different conclusion. Examples of presumptions of law are the presumption of innocence, the presumption in favor of sanity, and the presumption that people do not act with criminal intent. Naturally, every person is presumed to intend the natural and probable consequences of his or her acts, but such a presumption may be rebutted.

Generally, there is a presumption that regularly enacted laws are constitutional,[47] but this is a rebuttable presumption. Following a similar rationale, a judge's findings or rulings carry with them a presumption of correctness[48] and a properly performed voir dire of a jury will assure the seating of a fair and impartial jury.[49] However, not all presumptions of law presume regularity. For example, the presumption of law is that prejudice to a defendant's case has resulted if the judge spoke with the jury without the defense counsel's knowledge.[50] With respect to Congress, there is a presumption of law that the plain language used by Congress in enacting a statute properly expresses congressional intent.[51]

A presumption of law is a rule of law that allows a judge or jury to assume that a fact is true until such time as the opposing party introduces other evidence that disproves or outweighs the presumed fact. When a presumption of law exists, such as the presumption of innocence in favor of the defendant, it has sufficient strength and will support an acquittal unless the prosecutor overcomes the presumption to a reasonable and moral certainty.[52]

In distinguishing between a presumption of law and a presumption of fact, one reviewing court noted, "There can be presumptions of law or presumptions of fact. Presumptions can be artificial or logical. Artificial presumptions are those created because of considerations of public policy. Logical presumptions are those where there is a 'rational connection' on the basis of 'logical probability' between the elemental fact and the evidentiary fact."[53]

§ 6.5 Presumptions of Fact

One court defined a presumption of fact as being "an inference of the existence of one fact from the existence of some other fact, or an inference as to the existence of a fact not actually known, arising from its usual connection

---

[46] Black's Law Dictionary (2004).
[47] Smith v. Doe, 538 U.S. 84, 110, 2003 U.S. LEXIS 1949 (2003).
[48] Lacaze v. Leger, 2008 U.S. Dist. LEXIS 37107 (W.D. La. 2008).
[49] Ross v. State, 954 So. 2d 968, 988, 2007 Miss. LEXIS 235 (Miss. 2007).
[50] Wells v. State, 2009 Ga. App. LEXIS 384 (Ga. 2009).
[51] United States v. Clintwood Elkhorn Mining Co., 128 S. Ct. 1511, 1518, 2008 U.S. LEXIS 3472 (2008).
[52] Stoltie v. People, 501 F. Supp.2d 1252, 2007 U.S. Dist. LEXIS 53333 (C.D. Cal. 2007).
[53] Wasserman v. Parciasepe, 377 N.J. Super. 191, 198, 871 A.2d 781, 784, 2004 N.J. Super. LEXIS 4 (N.J. 2004).

with another which is known."[54] When a particular fact has been established and where a conclusion naturally follows from proof of that fact, it is permissible for a jury to infer or presume the truth of the deducted fact. The terms *presumption of fact* and *inference* seem to be used more frequently when the deduced fact is permissive in nature and rebuttable if contrary facts exist. A presumption of fact generally must be used only where the proof of the basic fact has been founded on direct evidence and not upon another inference or presumption.[55] This concept is intended to prevent inferences or presumptions from becoming too uncertain or being based on improper speculation or conjecture.[56] To say this differently, presumptions do not create their own foundations. Presumptions of fact are derived from circumstances in a particular case, by using ordinary logic and reasoning.

Presumptions of fact may be permissible "if there is a sound and rational connection between the proved and inferred facts and when proof of one fact renders the existence of another fact so probable that it is sensible and time-saving to assume the truth of the inferred fact until the adversary disproves it. . . ."[57] Destroying the presumption may be accomplished by refuting the basic fact upon which the presumption of fact rests or by demonstrating that the fact presumed is not true. For example, an inference of fact arises that a properly mailed letter arrived at its destination when the sender demonstrated that she properly addressed, stamped, and mailed the letter.[58] This inference or presumption of fact could be rebutted where the recipient demonstrated that the letter never arrived.

§ 6.6 Classes of Presumptions

For purposes of discussion, presumptions are further divided into conclusive (irrebuttable) presumptions and rebuttable presumptions. A conclusive presumption (presumption *juris et de jure*) is a rule of substantive law rather than a rule of evidence. A disputable or rebuttable presumption is a species of evidence that may be accepted and on which reliance may be placed when there is no other evidence to refute the contention it stands for.

A statute may make a presumption conclusive; in which case, the presumption cannot be destroyed or overcome by evidence. However, in criminal cases, conclusive presumptions have been held to violate the Constitution and no longer may be used in criminal cases. In *Sandstrom v. Montana*, the

---

[54] State v. Narron, 666 S.E.2d 860, 2008 N.C. App. LEXIS 1758 (N.C. 2008), quoting Bryant v. Burns-Hammond Const. Co., 197 N.C. 639, 1929 N.C. LEXIS 321 (1929).

[55] 42 OH. JUR. *Evidence and Witnesses* 110.

[56] *Id.*

[57] USX Corp. v. Barnhart, 395 F.3d 161, 171, 2004 U.S. App. LEXIS 26868 (3d Cir. 2004), quoting Sec'y of Labor v. Keystone, 331 U.S. App. D.C. 422 (D.C. Cir. 1998).

[58] *See* Rothwell v. Yeager, 2008 Ark. Appl. LEXIS (Ark. 2008).

United States Supreme Court held that mandatory conclusive presumptions are unconstitutional because they conflict with the presumption of innocence.[59] In California, a conclusive presumption once existed where:

> Intent to commit theft by fraud is presumed if one who has leased or rented the personal property of another pursuant to a written contract fails to return the personal property to its owner within 20 days after the owner has made written demand by certified or registered mail following the expiration of the lease or rental agreement for return of the property so leased or rented. Cal. Penal Code Ann. § 484(b) (West 1988).

The Supreme Court of the United States reversed a California conviction of grand theft auto because the statute created an impermissible mandatory conclusive presumption in violation of the due process clause of the Fourteenth Amendment as prohibited by *Sandstrom v. Montana*. When faced with the proof of the basic fact that a defendant had not returned personal property within the statutory time limit, a conclusive presumed fact arose that the defendant possessed an intent to commit theft by fraud.[60]

An example of a traditional conclusive presumption held that a child born in wedlock was conclusively presumed to be a legitimate child, but modern court decisions hold that the presumption is rebuttable. Even so, a Hawai'i court of appeals noted that the presumption of legitimacy for a child born to a married couple is "one of the strongest and most persuasive known to the law."[61] In days before the availability of reliable blood and DNA testing, traditionally courts would uphold the conclusive presumption of fatherhood and not permit the husband or another man to introduce evidence to contest or to support the possibility of paternity. However, all modern evidence codes allow the admission of contrary evidence of paternity when certain conditions are present, making the presumption rebuttable. The advent of irrefutable genetic testing dictated that the conclusive presumption of paternity had to be reconsidered.[62] Demonstrative of this change is an Indiana case in which the court noted that:

> "[a] child born during marriage is presumed legitimate. This presumption is not conclusive although it may be rebutted only by direct, clear, and convincing evidence."[63]

---

[59] Sandstrom v. Montana, 442 U.S. 510, 523 (1979).
[60] *See* Carella v. California, 491 U.S. 263 (1989).
[61] Inoue v. Inoue, 118 Haw. 86, 101, 2008 Haw. App. LEXIS 50 (Hawai'I 2008). *See also* G.M.H. v. J.L.H., 700 S.W.2d 506 (Mo. Ct. App. 1985), which reaffirmed that at common law the presumption that a child born in wedlock is conclusively presumed to be legitimate, but indicated that today the presumption is rebuttable, is an evidentiary presumption, and is overcome by a showing of substantial evidence to the contrary.
[62] D.F. v. Department of Revenue, 823 So. 2d 97, 98, 2002 Fla. LEXIS 1162 (2002).
[63] State v. Black, 877 N.E.2d 1239, 1242, 2007 Ind. App. LEXIS 2762 (Ind. 2007).

But definitive genetic testing has resulted in a new conclusive presumption in favor of paternity in some situations. Rhode Island law provides that "[i]f the results of the blood or tissue typing tests duly admitted into evidence establish a ninety-seven percent (97%) or greater probability of inclusion that a party is the biological father of the child, then that probability shall constitute a conclusive presumption of paternity."[64] If a jury chose to disregard this presumption in a criminal case, it would have the power to do so, despite the statutory language that the presumption is conclusive.

A rebuttable presumption (presumption *juris tantum*) requires the trier of fact to consider the deduction as true until disproved by contrary evidence. An example of a rebuttable presumption of law is the presumption that states that an accused person is presumed to be innocent, but a prosecutor's presentation of evidence to a guilty verdict negates the presumption of innocence, as does a guilty plea.[65] In Georgia, proof that a defendant had control of his automobile gave rise to the presumption that he had possession and control of any contraband found in the vehicle. This presumption was rebuttable by proof that other persons had equal access to the contraband that would overcome the strength of the presumption.[66]

In some jurisdictions, presumptions are evidentiary devices that are categorized into two groups—mandatory and permissive. According to a federal district court, a mandatory presumption tells a jury that it must find that an element of the crime has been proved if the prosecution proves certain basic or predicate facts.[67] A mandatory presumption of this nature violates due process because it relieves the prosecution of the burden of persuasion on an element of an offense. However, a "permissive presumption" in a criminal case allows, but does not require, the trier of fact to infer an elemental fact from proof of a basic fact.

A "permissive inference" or presumption allows but does not require the finder of fact to infer the fact while it places no burden on the defendant to rebut it. The judge or jury can accept the existence of the inferred fact or reject it. In a Florida burglary case in which the defendant was found in possession of property taken from the victim's residence, the judge charged the jury that "[p]roof of possession of recently stolen property, unless satisfactorily explained, gives rise to an inference that the person in possession of the property knew or should have known that the property had been stolen."[68] The standard jury instruction, despite the defendant's allegation, did not create a mandatory presumption by suggesting to the jury that it might infer that the defendant knew the property was stolen but was free to decide otherwise. In a

---

[64]   R.I. GEN. LAWS § 15-8-11 (Matthew Bender 2009).

[65]   United States v. Madoff, 2009 U.S. App. LEXIS 5985 (2d Cir. 2009).

[66]   Hamilton v. State, 293 Ga. App. 297, 298, 2008 Ga. App. LEXIS 926 (Ga. 2008).

[67]   Nicholson v. Kane, 2009 U.S. Dist. LEXIS 21889 (N.D. Ga. 2009).

[68]   Walker v. State, 896 So. 2d 712, 714, 2005 Fla. LEXIS 361 (Fla. 2005), quoting Fla. Std. Jury Instr. (Crim.) 14.1.

burglary case, a Georgia reviewing court upheld a similar jury instruction in a theft case, citing that "[e]vidence of recent, unexplained possession of stolen goods may be sufficient to give rise to an inference that the defendant committed the burglary."[69]

Regardless of whether a presumption is categorized as conclusive, rebuttable, mandatory, or permissive, a presumption will generally be considered unconstitutional if it relieves the prosecution from having to prove every element of the crime.[70] For example, where a statute notes that a person who fails to return a rental car within five days after the lease expires, a presumption arises that the person embezzled the vehicle, but such mandatory presumption violates the due process clause of the Fourteenth Amendment because it relieves the prosecution of proving part or all of the crime.[71] A mandatory presumption may not shift the burden of proof on any element of the offense; to do so conflicts with the overriding presumption of innocence and invades the fact-finding function of the judge or jury.

§ 6.7   Specific Presumption Situations

A study of the most common presumptions used in criminal cases will produce a clear understanding of their purposes and limitations. A strong general rule is that the finder of fact is never bound by a presumption in a criminal case and may choose to ignore a presumption completely. In studying presumptions, it is important to appreciate the legal reasoning that supports the concept of a presumption and understand the statutory and constitutional limitations that apply to specific presumptions. State legislatures have created some presumptions by statute while others have developed as a result of state and federal court decisions. When presumptions have been created as examples of public policy by a legislature, virtually all of them may be rebutted with the presentation of substantial evidence to the contrary. One clear limitation on a presumption is that it cannot have the effect of shifting the burden of proof to a criminal defendant.

One view of presumptions holds that a presumption is not evidence of anything and merely determines which party should go forward and produce evidence pertaining to the matters at issue. Along with this position is the collateral view that a presumption should not be treated as evidence and should not be placed on the scale of justice to be weighed with actual evidence when making a decision.[72] As a Pennsylvania court held, "[a]ffirmative

---

[69]   Butler v. State, 294 Ga. App. 540, 2008 Ga. App. LEXIS 1228 (Ga. 2008), quoting Davis v. State, 275 Ga. App. 714, 715–716, 2005 Ga. App. LEXIS 1099 (Ga. 2005).

[70]   United States v. Haberek, 2006 U.S. Dist. LEXIS 44670 (N.D. Ill. 2006); United States v. Edelkind, 2006 U.S. Dist. LEXIS 41056 (W.D. La. 2006).

[71]   People v. Laughlin, 137 Cal. App. 4th 1020, 1024, 40 Cal. Rptr. 3d 737, 739, 2006 Cal. App. LEXIS 388 (2006).

[72]   Mullin v. Brown, 210 Ariz. 545, 548, 115 P.3d 139, 142, 2005 Ariz. App. LEXIS 83 (2005).

evidence of a material element of the crime charged may never be displaced by a mere evidentiary presumption; nor may that presumption substitute for evidence."[73] The principle that a presumption is not evidence has not gained universal acceptance because some jurisdictions hold that a presumption actually serves as a substitute for evidence. In a North Dakota case, the court noted that where a presumption has been established by credible evidence, the presumption serves as evidence until such time as it is rebutted."[74] Some courts have held that "a presumption has the effect of evidence"[75] and must be given the same force and effect unless rebutted or called into question.

Presumptions in criminal cases have limitations and are scrutinized very carefully by reviewing courts to determine whether they place an unconstitutional burden on the accused. Moreover, statutory presumptions must not have the effect of creating a mandatory presumption in a criminal case or have the effect of reversing the normal burden of proof of any element of a crime.[76]

The number of statutory presumptions and judicial presumptions is extensive and find most of their use in civil cases; those presumptions will not be discussed in detail. Some examples of presumptions used in civil cases are: (1) a private transaction has been fair and regular; (2) the ordinary course of business has been followed; (3) a promissory note or a bill of exchange was given or endorsed for a sufficient consideration; and (4) a writing is accurately dated.

Although presumptions possess a more limited usage in criminal cases, presumptions play an important role in criminal cases and are often litigated on appeal. The following sections discuss and demonstrate the most significant and important presumptions related to criminal cases.

§ 6.8 — Innocence

As a matter of well-settled law, it is uniformly agreed that the defendant in a criminal case is presumed innocent from the time the prosecution begins and retains this presumption forever or until a finder of fact returns a guilty verdict. This rebuttable presumption of innocence places upon the prosecution the burden of proving the defendant guilty beyond a reasonable doubt. This presumption exists until the time the finder of fact renders a guilty verdict.[77] Upon a conviction, a defendant's presumption of innocence ends because it has been overcome by the evidence presented by the government.[78]

---

[73]   Commonwealth v. Salter, 2004 Pa. Super. 318, 858 A.2d 610, 614 2004 Pa. Super. LEXIS 2687 (Pa. 2004).

[74]   Kortum v. Johnson, 2008 ND 154, 2008 N.D. LEXIS 161 (N.D. 2008). *See also* N.D.R. Ev. Rule 301(a) (2008).

[75]   People v. Niene, 8 Misc. 3d 649, 652, 798 N.Y.S.2d 891, 894, 2005 N.Y. Misc. LEXIS 981 (N.Y. 2005).

[76]   Gross v. Jackson, 2008 U.S. Dist. LEXIS 37095 (S.D. Ohio 2008). *See also* People v. Illinois, 2009 Ill. App. LEXIS 45 (Ill. 2009).

[77]   State v. Halls, 2006 Utah App. 142, 549 Utah Adv. Rep. 21, 2006 Utah App. LEXIS 136 (2006).

[78]   United States v. Medina, et al., 430 F.3d 869, 2005 U.S. App. LEXIS 26772 (2005).

The so-called presumption of innocence is not, strictly speaking, a presumption in the sense of a deduction from a given premise or basic fact. It does not involve the proof of a basic fact from which a deduction may be drawn; it is a fact that exists until sufficient proof to the contrary appears. More accurately, the "presumption of innocence serves as a procedural doctrine that allocates the burden of proof in criminal trials."[79]

A Maryland trial court explained that the presumption of innocence covers a defendant at the start and throughout the trial, whereby a:

> defendant is presumed to be innocent of the charges – charges. This presumption remains with the defendant throughout every stage of the trial and is not overcome unless you are convinced beyond a reasonable doubt that the defendant is guilty. The State has the burden of proving the guilt of the defendant beyond a reasonable doubt. This burden remains on the State throughout the trial. The defendant is not required to prove his innocence. However, the State is not required to prove guilt beyond all possible doubt or to a mathematical certainty, nor is the State required to negate every conceivable circumstance of innocence. A reasonable doubt is a doubt founded upon reason. It is not a *fanciful doubt*, a *whimsical doubt*, or a *capricious doubt*. Proof beyond a reasonable doubt requires such proof as would convince you of the truth of a fact to the extent that you would be willing to act upon such belief without reservation in an important matter in your own business or personal affairs. However, if you are not satisfied of the defendant's guilt to that extent, then reasonable doubt exists and the defendant must be found not guilty.[80] [Emphasis added.]

The reviewing court rejected the defendant's contention that by using the words *fanciful*, *whimsical*, and *capricious doubt*, the trial court probably misled the jury in understanding the meaning of reasonable doubt because the words were not included in the Maryland jury instructions. The fact that a judge deviates in some manner from approved jury instructions covering the presumption of innocence does not necessarily indicate a reduction in the protections offered by the presumption of innocence principle.

In an appeal based partly on an alleged jury instruction error, the Third Circuit Court of Appeals in *United States v. Dufresne*,[81] rejected the defendant's contention that the trial court improperly instructed the jury on the presumption of innocence. The judge's instructions told the jurors that:

> after careful and impartial consideration of all of the evidence in the case, have a reasonable doubt that a defendant is guilty, you must find the defendant not guilty. If, members of the jury, you view the evidence in the case as reasonably permitting either of two conclusions, one of innocence, the

---

[79] United States v. Scott, 2006 U.S. App. LEXIS 14182 (9th Cir. 2006).

[80] Turner v. State, 181 Md. App. 477, 481, 2008 Md. App. LEXIS 106 (Md. 2008).

[81] United States v. Dufresne, 58 Fed. Appx. 890, 2003 U.S. App. LEXIS 2126 (3d Cir. 2003), *cert. denied,* 538 U.S. 1064, 2003 U.S. LEXIS 4193 (2003).

other of guilt, then you *should* of course adopt the conclusion of innocence. [Emphasis added.][82]

According to the reviewing court, the use of the word "should" did not dilute the presumption of innocence. So long as the trial judge informed the jury about the concept of guilt beyond a reasonable doubt, including properly covering the presumption of innocence in the jury instruction, due process has been satisfied. The jury instruction additionally indicated that the presumption of innocence can be sufficiently strong that it will permit an acquittal where the prosecution's evidence fails to establish a prima facie case.[83]

Generally, judges offer a jury instruction that covers the presumption of innocence and some earlier decisions suggested that failure to give a specific instruction on the presumption of innocence was reversible error. However, in a major case, *Kentucky v. Whorton*, the Supreme Court held that failure to give a requested instruction on the presumption of innocence did not in and of itself violate the Constitution.[84] In this case, the defendant was charged with committing several armed robberies in three separate indictments. At the conclusion of all the evidence, the defendant's counsel asked that the jury be instructed on the presumption of innocence. The instruction requested was:

> The law presumes an accused to be innocent of crime. He begins a trial with a clean slate, with no evidence against him. And the law permits nothing but legal evidence presented before the jury to be considered in support of any charge against the accused. So the presumption of innocence alone is sufficient to acquit an accused unless the jury members are satisfied beyond a reasonable doubt of the accused's guilt from all of the evidence in the case.[85]

The judge refused this instruction, but gave one to the effect that the jury could return a verdict of guilty only if they found beyond a reasonable doubt that the defendant, with the requisite criminal intent, had committed the acts charged in the indictment. The jury found the defendant guilty on numerous counts and he appealed. The Supreme Court of Kentucky held that the failure to give the instruction concerning the presumption of innocence was reversible error. The commonwealth attorney appealed to the Supreme Court of the United States.

In reversing the top Kentucky court and reinstating the convictions, the Supreme Court of the United States found that an instruction on the presumption of innocence is not required in all cases. Accordingly, the *Whorton* Court held that:

> In short, the failure to give a requested instruction on the presumption of innocence does not in and of itself violate the Constitution.[86]

---

[82] *Id.*

[83] *Id.*

[84] Kentucky v. Whorton, 441 U.S. 786, 99 S. Ct. 2088, 60 L. Ed. 2d 640 (1979).

[85] *Id.* at 788, n.1.

[86] *Id.* at 789.

The Court went on to explain that failure to give a specific instruction on innocence should be evaluated in light of the totality of the circumstances, including the jury instructions, arguments of the attorneys, the strength of the evidence and any other relevant factor. In a later case, the Supreme Court noted that "[a] jury instruction on the presumption of innocence is not constitutionally required in every case to satisfy due process, because such an instruction merely offers an additional safeguard beyond that provided by the constitutionally required instruction on reasonable doubt."[87]

While a precise jury instruction supporting the presumption of innocence need not be given in every case to meet federal due process standards, trial courts strive to offer jury instructions that are fair, even if not all instructions speak directly to the presumption of innocence. In a habeas corpus case,[88] a federal judge reviewed the trial proceedings of a state case involving a murder at a crack house. Evidence in the case included eyewitness testimony and proved overwhelming. Both the prosecutor and the defendant's attorney had received proposed jury instructions from the judge in which the judge omitted any mention of the presumption of innocence. Despite his lack of objection, the defendant contended that the writ of habeas corpus should be granted because of the trial court's inadvertent omission of the presumption of innocence. The trial judge did charge the jury on the burden of proof, which in some ways performs a similar task to an instruction on the presumption of innocence. The trial judge stated:

> The standard of proof required in every criminal case is proof of guilt beyond a reasonable doubt. … So, proof of guilt beyond a reasonable doubt, what is it? It does not require the People to prove an accused guilty beyond all possibility of doubt or beyond a shadow of a doubt. It requires the People to establish the accused guilty beyond a reasonable doubt. Therefore, before you may convict the accused, each of you must be satisfied that the credible evidence, the evidence that you accept, is sufficient to convince you beyond a reasonable doubt that the accused is, in fact, guilty and that the accused is, in fact, the person who committed the crimes charged. Therefore, before you may convict the accused, each of you must be satisfied that the credible evidence, the evidence that you accept, is sufficient to convince you beyond a reasonable doubt that the accused is, in fact, guilty and that the accused is, in fact, the person who committed the crimes charged.[89]

The federal district court refused to grant the writ on the grounds that, while the presumption of innocence was not explicitly stated, the jury charge, taken as a whole, was more than sufficient to give the defendant due process. The district court was following the reasoning of *Kentucky v. Whorton*, in which the jury instruction must be viewed in its entirety. By requiring the

---

[87]   Arizona v. Fulminante, 499 U.S. 279, 291, 1991 U.S. LEXIS 1854 (1991).

[88]   Williams v. McGinnis, 2006 U.S. Dist. LEXIS 29400 (E.D. N.Y. 2006).

[89]   *Id.*

state prosecutor to prove guilt beyond a reasonable doubt, by implication, the defendant is presumed to be innocent until proven otherwise.

In a different case, a defendant objected to the trial judge's jury instruction concerning reasonable doubt and contended that the instruction diminished the presumption of innocence. Part of the jury instruction stated that "[t]he law presumes a defendant to be innocent of crime. Thus, the defendant, although accused, begins the trial with a clean slate with no evidence against him."[90] The defendant contended that the phrase "clean slate" implied that the prosecution and the defendant started the case on equal ground, thus making the presumption of innocence less forceful. The Tenth Circuit Court of Appeals rejected the argument, noting that similar language had previously been approved and did not have the effect of reducing the protections of the presumption of innocence.

The universal rule is that in an appeal following a conviction, "the presumption of innocence no longer avails and [an appellate court views] the evidence in a light most favorable to the verdict"[91] When an appellate court reviews a case, it begins its work with the presumption that the trial court was correct in its verdict and that the defendant is guilty. In a Tennessee case, *State v. Lee*, in explaining the effect that a guilty verdict has on the presumption of innocence, the court noted, "[a] guilty verdict removes the presumption of innocence and replaces it with a presumption of guilt, and on appeal the defendant has the burden of illustrating why the evidence is insufficient to support the jury's verdict."[92]

§ 6.9 — Sanity

"The presumption of sanity is equally universal in some variety or other, being (at least) a presumption that a defendant has the capacity to form the *mens rea* necessary for a verdict of guilt and the consequent criminal responsibility," according to the Supreme Court of the United States.[93] Therefore, a prosecutor does not have to prove sanity as one of the elements in every crime. On the strength of this rebuttable presumption, a judge may offer a jury instruction that states that every person is presumed sane until the contrary is shown by the evidence. The presumption of sanity is a rule of law that stands in the place of evidence, unless evidence is introduced to rebut the presumption. In some states, the presumption is considered so strong that even if there were a unanimous opinion by expert witnesses, the presumption still retains evidentiary value.[94]

---

[90]   United States v. Smith, 531 F.3d 1261; 2008 U.S. App. LEXIS 14797 (10th Cir. 2008).
[91]   Parker v. State, 2009 Ga. App. LEXIS 319 (Ga. 2009).
[92]   2009 Tenn. Crim. App. LEXIS 177 (2009).
[93]   Clark v. Arizona, 2006 U.S. LEXIS 5184 (2006).
[94]   Commonwealth v. Chiero, 24 Mass. L. Rep. 376, 2008 Mass. Super. LEXIS 245 (Mass. 2008).

The concept of competency to stand trial, while related to legal insanity, involves different considerations. The presumption of capacity to stand trial exists so long as a defendant understands the nature and importance attached to a trial and is able materially to assist in his or her defense. For example, in Illinois, to be mentally fit for trial, a defendant must have "sufficient present ability to consult with defense counsel with a reasonable degree of rational understanding and . . . has both a rational and factual understanding of the proceedings."[95] In Alabama, where the issue of lack of competency has been raised, the trial judge preliminarily reviews reports of medical personnel. The judge schedules a hearing if he or she believes competency may be at issue.[96] Each party may present evidence at the hearing that relates to the defendant's ability or inability to assist in his or her defense. Generally, a finding of competency, once made, permits the state to move forward with prosecution of the appropriate crimes.[97]

Under the insanity defense provisions of the 1984 Comprehensive Crime Control Act, mental disease or defect constitutes a defense in federal criminal trials where the defendant proves "the defense of insanity by clear and convincing evidence"[98] and that, "at the time of the commission of the acts constituting the offense, the defendant, as a result of a severe mental disease or defect, was unable to appreciate the nature and quality or the wrongfulness of his acts."[99] If the defendant fails to meet the burden of proving insanity by clear and convincing proof, the presumption of sanity has not been rebutted and the defendant fails to have the benefit of this affirmative defense.

Although some states have adopted a state version of the federal insanity defense, federal law concerning the insanity defense applies only in federal courts. The states are free to enact their respective insanity defenses and related presumptions without regard to federal law or to choose not to recognize any insanity defense.[100] In some states, after the defendant has presented some credible evidence that supports a defense of insanity, the burden of proof with the evidence shifts and the prosecution is given "the burden of proving sanity beyond a reasonable doubt."[101] In those states, if the evidence is legally sufficient to raise the issue of insanity and rebut the presumption of sanity and if the prosecution offers no evidence of sanity, there is no factual issue for the jury, and the defendant is entitled to a directed verdict of acquittal.

The nature and quantum of evidence that the prosecution must produce to meet the burden of proof of sanity, in order to justify an instruction to the jury on the issue of sanity, varies with both the jurisdiction and with the nature and

---

[95] People v. Schoreck, 384 Ill. App.3d 904, 916, 2008 Ill. App. LEXIS 829 (Ill. 2008).

[96] *See* ALA. R. CRIM. P. 11.6 (Matthew Bender 2009).

[97] O.C.G.A. § 17-7-130 (g). Official Code of Georgia (2008).

[98] 18 U.S.C. § 17(b).

[99] *Id.,* § 17(a).

[100] Medina v. California, 505 U.S. 437, 449, 1992 U.S. LEXIS 3696 (1992).

[101] People v. Grenier, 200 P.3d 1062, 2008 Colo. App. LEXIS 356 (Colo. 2008).

quantum of evidence indicating mental illness. For example, in Pennsylvania, insanity is considered an affirmative defense that requires a defendant to both raise the issue and to prove insanity by a preponderance of the evidence.[102] California takes a similar position to Pennsylvania under its penal code, which states that the insanity defense "shall be found by the trier of fact only when the accused person proves by a preponderance of the evidence that he or she was incapable of knowing or understanding the nature and quality of his or her act and of distinguishing right from wrong at the time of the commission of the offense."[103] A judge will offer a jury instruction concerning insanity where the defendant has presented evidence, that, if believed, would establish insanity by the defendant but is not obligated to give a jury instruction where a defendant has not raised legally sufficient evidence.

In support of an insanity defense, lay testimony may be sufficient to satisfy the defendant's burden of proving insanity according to the Supreme Court of New Hampshire.[104] New Hampshire provided that a defendant alleging an insanity defense "shall have the burden of proving the defense of insanity by clear and convincing evidence."[105] According to a Texas court, lay witness opinion may be admitted when an insanity defense has been pled and such opinion "may be sufficient to raise the defense of insanity"[106] even in the absence of expert testimony.

In 1984, Congress completed a comprehensive overhaul of the insanity defense as applied in the federal courts. Under the provisions of the Insanity Defense Reform Act, Congress gave defendants the burden of proving the defense of insanity by clear and convincing evidence.[107] Legal challenges attacked the revised federal insanity defense by alleging that the law violated the due process clauses of the Fifth and Fourteenth Amendments.[108] In a case heard before the United States Court of Appeals for the Eleventh Circuit, the defendant alleged that placing the burden of proof of insanity by clear and convincing evidence violated his rights under the Fifth Amendment. The Eleventh Circuit noted that several states had constitutionally placed the burden of insanity defenses on defendants without creating any due process violations. Two other federal circuits that had addressed the due process claim involving similar state insanity statutes had also rejected the theory that placing a burden on an insanity defendant violated the federal Constitution.[109] Similar to the federal

---

[102] *See* 18 PA. C. S. § 315 (2008).

[103] CAL. PENAL CODE § 25(b) (Matthew Bender 2008).

[104] State v. Fichera, 2006 N.H. LEXIS 76 (N.H. 2006).

[105] N.H. REV. STAT. ANN. 628:2 (Matthew Bender 2009).

[106] Johnson v. State, 2008 Tex. App. LEXIS 5476 (Tex. 2008).

[107] 18 U.S.C. § 17(b) and § 4242(b).

[108] *See* for example, United States v. Freeman, 804 F.2d 1574, 1986 U.S. App. LEXIS 34268 (11th Cir. 1986). As of 2009, the Supreme Court of the United States has not directly ruled on the constitutionality of the Insanity Defense Reform Act of 1984.

[109] United States v. Wattleton, 296 F.3d 1184, 2002 U.S. App. LEXIS 13686 (11th Cir. 2002); United States v. Amos, 803 F.2d 419 (8th Cir. 1986).

insanity defense, Illinois presumes that sanity is a default mental state and requires that defendants who allege insanity introduce evidence to rebut the general presumption of sanity. Illinois law provides that: "the burden of proof is on the defendant to prove by clear and convincing evidence that the defendant is not guilty by reason of insanity."[110] Against a defendant's contention that the elevated burden of proof needed to rebut the presumption of sanity violated due process by being "irrational, unfair, and contrary to contemporary practice," an Illinois reviewing court affirmed his conviction. It held that the Illinois statute did not violate due process, even if only seven jurisdictions used such a high burden of proof in insanity cases.[111]

§ 6.10   — Suicide

The presumption against suicide stems from and is raised by our common knowledge and experience that most sane persons possess a natural love of life and an instinct for self-protection that effectively deters them from suicide or the self-infliction of serious bodily injury. In support of this concept, "[t]here is a rule of law that presumes that an unexplained death by violence requires the conclusion that death was not self-imposed until credible evidence of suicide is offered in rebuttal."[112] Most jurisdictions recognize the existence of an affirmative presumption of death by accidental means and recognize a presumption against suicide,[113] but the presumption is not universally recognized.[114]

The presumption against suicide may be overcome by affirmative evidence of suicide, which effectively rebuts the presumption. When it was shown that a prisoner died two days after his arrival at a federal prison transfer center, the prison contended that he had committed suicide. The guards found the decedent's blood-soaked body hanging in his cell from torn bed sheets affixed to a ceiling vent. Oklahoma has a presumption against suicide, but it has been described as a procedural tool for ordering proof and is not considered affirmative evidence. In a suit between the federal government and the estate of the deceased, the government offered sufficient evidence to rebut the presumption against suicide by showing that the deceased had been locked alone in a cell and his injuries appeared to be self-inflicted.[115]

---

[110]   Ill. Comp. Stat. Ann. 720 ILCS 5/6-2 (Matthew Bender 2009).

[111]   People v. Clay, 361 Ill. App. 3d 310, 836 N.E.2d 872, 2005 Ill. App. LEXIS 994 (Ill. 2005), *appeal denied*, 2006 Ill. LEXIS 164 (Ill. 2006).

[112]   23 Fla. Jur. *Evidence and Witnesses* 146.

[113]   Estate of Norman Holly v. American Family Life Assurance, 2005 Ohio 2281, 2005 Ohio App. LEXIS 2190 (2005).

[114]   New Mexico does not recognize a presumption against suicide. Solorzano v. Bristow, 136 N.M. 658 N.M. 658, 662, 2004 NMCA 136; 103 P.3d 582, 586, 2004 N.M. App. LEXIS 121 (2004).

[115]   Estate of Trentadue ex rel. Aguilar v. United States, 397 F.3d 840, 863, 2005 U.S. App. LEXIS 1811 (10th Cir. 2005).

The "presumption against suicide is not evidence and cannot be treated as evidence by the jury in reaching a verdict, and an instruction that such presumption has the effect of affirmative evidence is erroneous"[116] and should not be weighed as such. However, courts in several states follow the minority view that the presumption is itself evidence or has evidentiary weight.[117] This presumption against suicide and in favor of accident or natural cause operates procedurally once a case gets to trial. In one case in which the deceased had multiple serious medical problems and was taking a variety of very strong drugs, she died from multiple drug intoxication, which could indicate suicide.[118] Her administrator, in seeking a reversal of a medical examiner's determination, contended that the decedent had not committed suicide because she was a former nun who remained deeply religious and was enthusiastic about enjoying life with her two adopted children. Although decedent had a history of depression and her blood concentration indicated a high level of antidepressant drugs, the evidence indicated that she would never have wanted to expose her children to discovering her body or to leave them with a renewed legacy of abandonment. When the reviewing court determined that the trial court erred in dismissing the petition to change the cause of death, it reversed the lower court's determination. According to the court, even though the decedent died from drug intoxication, the evidence was insufficient to rebut the strong presumption against suicide.[119]

In the majority of cases, it will prove to be a tall order to rebut the strong presumption against suicide, but where "death by external violence is shown by facts or circumstances, inconsistent with accident, the presumption against suicide is displaced, and no longer continues to operate in favor of the plaintiff."[120] In Texas, like many other jurisdictions, the presumption against suicide must fall when contrary evidence proves otherwise and the only reasonable inference is death by suicide.[121]

§ 6.11 — Possession of Fruits of Crime

When there is proof that the accused possessed recently stolen property and for which there was no satisfactory explanation, an inference of guilt may arise, but this inference or presumption is not conclusive and maybe rebutted

---

[116] City of Indianapolis v. Taylor, 707 N.E.2d 1047, 1051, 1999 Ind. App. LEXIS 456 (Ind. 1999).

[117] Under North Dakota law, the presumption that death was accidental has the weight of affirmative evidence. Dick v. New York Life Ins. Co., 359 U.S. 437, 79 S. Ct. 921, 3 L. Ed. 2d 935 (1959).

[118] Matter of Infante v. Dignan, 865 N.Y.S.2d 167, 169 2008 N.Y. App. Div. LEXIS 7118 (N.Y. 2008).

[119] *Id.*

[120] Elrod et al. v. J.C. Penny Life Insurance Company, 2000 Tenn. App. LEXIS 407 (Tenn. 2000).

[121] 35 TEX. JUR. *Evidence* § 141.

by contrary evidence. Generally, there must be actual proof that the property was recently stolen or this inference should not be applied. In some jurisdictions, this inference may be sufficient for a conviction, but in others additional proof will be required. Upon proof of possession of recently stolen property, a jury may make this inference of guilt or of guilty knowledge but when other evidence in a case has been considered, the jury may decline to make the inference.[122]

In *State v. Draine*, a case in which the defendant had been convicted of theft of a tractor and trailer, the defendant had been found in possession of the recently stolen property and had possession of the keys to operate the property.[123] The Court of Criminal Appeals mentioned that Tennessee recognizes that when a person is found in possession of recently stolen property, the situation gives rise to an inference that the defendant has stolen the property or possesses knowledge that the property is stolen. In this case, the reviewing court emphasized that the "defendant was in possession of the recently stolen property, based upon his possession of the keys, the inference that he had stolen it or had knowledge that the property was stolen arose. The proof established that the theft occurred no more than three days prior to the time in which the defendant was in control of the tractor."[124] In addition, the defendant had no rational explanation concerning why he possessed the recently stolen property. The reviewing court upheld the conviction and found no legal or constitutional problem with the use of the inference.

The strength of such an inference or presumption, which the possession of stolen property raises, depends upon the circumstances surrounding the case. The defendant's possession must be exclusive, and it must have occurred within a relatively short time after commission of the crime. The longer the period from the crime to the point at which the defendant was found in possession of the stolen property, the weaker the presumption becomes.

Although some appellate defendants have occasionally gained success in getting convictions reversed on state or federal constitutional grounds, the doctrine of knowledge or guilt based on possession of recently stolen property remains strong in many jurisdictions. In *Kerr v. State*, a Florida appellate court noted that from proof of possession of recently stolen property, two rebuttable presumptions may arise, depending on the surrounding facts.[125] The first presumption is that the possessor of the stolen property is the guilty party and the second is that the possessor knew that the property was recently stolen. In the *Kerr* case, the owner of a car had been working on it in front of his place of residence, but found it missing when he returned from inside his home. The next

---

[122]   *See* 23 FLA. JUR. *Evidence and Witnesses* 130.
[123]   2008 Tenn. Crim. App. LEXIS 623 (Tenn. 2008).
[124]   *Id.*
[125]   954 So. 2d 692, 693, 2007 Fla. App. LEXIS 5617 (Fla. 2007). This Florida court seems to use inference and presumption as rough synonyms probably because a jury is not bound to find the deduced fact from the first proven fact.

day, police encountered the defendant in possession of the car while removing some parts from it. The defendant stated to the officer that he had purchased the BMW for $500 but had no paperwork concerning the sale and he did not know the identity of the person from whom he alleged he had purchased the car. The reviewing court found the defendant's explanations incredible and not worthy of belief and noted that he lied to the police officer concerning his identity. The court upheld the conviction on the strength of the inferences and because of the defendant's lack of believable rebuttal, prima facie proof of the charge remained.

In contrast to the above cases, California treats the presumption or inference relating to possession of recently stolen property as having a much weaker evidentiary effect. California courts instruct juries that mere possession, without some corroboration, is not sufficient to prove a defendant's guilt of the particular offense. The typical California jury instruction counsels jurors that:

> If you find that a defendant was in [conscious] possession of recently [stolen] [extorted] property, the fact of that possession is not by itself sufficient to permit an inference that the defendant is guilty of the crime of [which crime]. Before guilt may be inferred, there must be corroborating evidence tending to prove defendant's guilt. However, this corroborating evidence need only be slight, and need not by itself be sufficient to warrant an inference of guilt.[126]

The Supreme Court of California, in *People v. Parson*, a capital murder case in which the defendant was found in possession of a variety of property belonging to the victim, rejected the defendant's contention that the above jury instruction was erroneous because it reduced the prosecution's burden of proof so that the prosecution no longer had to establish guilt beyond reasonable doubt.[127] The prosecution introduced proof that, following the victim's death, the defendant possessed and used the decedent's ATM card following a burglary and a robbery. During the trial, the court informed the jury that it should consider additional attributes of possession such as time, place, and manner, which might connect a defendant to a charged crime. The Supreme Court of California held that the jury instruction given did not create a presumption or inference in a way that violated due process. According to the court, commonsense reasoning justified the conclusion that if the defendant possessed the decedent's recently stolen ATM card, although not sufficient to permit an inference of guilt, other factors presently existed that tended to corroborate the stolen property and the defendant's guilt of robbery and burglary. In upholding the convictions, the Supreme Court of California noted that the jury instructions on recently stolen property were also accompanied by the other typical instructions covering reasonable doubt, the presumption of innocence, and the prosecutor's overall burden of proof.[128]

---

[126] CALJIC 2.15, Possession of Stolen Property (West Group 2005).
[127] 44 Cal. 4th 332, 355, 2008 Cal. LEXIS 8243 (Cal. 2008).
[128] *Id.* at 356.

The net effect of the California jury instruction covering possession of recently stolen property weakened the traditional inference or presumption concerning knowledge that property was stolen, but still permits the jurors to use natural and logical reasoning.

In summary, where the presumption or inference concerning recently stolen property is applied, these conditions must be met: (a) the possession must be unexplained by any innocent origin; (b) the possession must be fairly recent; and (c) the possession must be exclusive,[129] as a general rule, although many jurisdictions will find that joint possession is sufficient. As noted above, some states require some corroboration with the inference in order to allow a conviction.

§ 6.12 — That a Person Intends the Ordinary Consequences of His or Her Voluntary Acts

In most situations, humans do particular acts and intend or expect fairly certain results. Where criminal activity is concerned, similar considerations and expectations occur so that it would be fair to state that a person intends to have the usual and predicted result happen given the criminal act that the person performed. Recognizing this connection, state and federal courts have used various methods to convey to a jury the proposition that, from a legal perspective, "a person is presumed to intend the natural and probable consequences of one's actions."[130] The presumption mentioned, often delivered by a jury instruction or in closing argument, cannot be phrased in terms that appear mandatory or require that the presumption be given complete effect. Otherwise proof that a person did a physical act would effectively transfer the burden of proof to a defendant who must prove lack of guilt in order to prevail, a procedural effect that is unconstitutional.

The United States Supreme Court considered the effects of this type of jury instruction in the case of *Sandstrom v. Montana* in 1979,[131] in which the Court recognized the principle that a jury instruction that has the effect of shifting the burden of proof to a defendant on a required element of the crime violates due process. Sandstrom had been convicted of deliberate homicide in that he purposely or knowingly caused the victim's death. At the trial, the defendant admitted killing the victim, but contended that he did not do so purposely or knowingly, and, therefore was not guilty of deliberate homicide.

The trial court instructed the jury that "the law presumes that a person intends the ordinary consequences of his voluntary acts,"[132] but was not told

---

[129] Constructive possession is sufficient to allow the presumption. *See* Ahmed v. Yates, 2006 U.S. Dist. LEXIS 18549 (N.D. Cal. 2006) and Ferguson v. State, 920 So. 2d 838, 840, 2006 Fla. App. LEXIS 2283 (2006).

[130] Boldin v. State, 373 Ark. 295, 300, 2008 Ark. LEXIS 277 (Ark. 2008).

[131] Sandstrom v. Montana, 442 U.S. 510, 99 S. Ct. 2450, 61 L. Ed. 2d 39 (1979).

[132] *Id.* at 515.

that the presumption could be rebutted or that the jury did not have to accept the presumption. The defendant's attorney argued that the instruction had the effect of shifting the burden of proof on the issue of purpose or knowledge to the defense and that the instruction was impermissible under the federal Constitution as a violation of due process of law.

Following a guilty verdict, despite Sandstrom's trial objections, he appealed to the Supreme Court of Montana. That court upheld the conviction, conceding that cases cited by the defense prohibited shifting the burden of proof to the defendant by means of the presumption, but held that the cited cases permit placing some "burden of proof to the defendant under certain circumstances."[133] The court also found that, because the defendant had only the burden of producing some evidence that he did not intend the ordinary consequences of his voluntary act, but not to disprove that he acted purposely or knowingly, the burden of proof had not shifted.

The Supreme Court of the United States reasoned that it was possible for the jury to interpret this instruction as conclusive on the issue of intent. The Court agreed that the instruction violated the Fourteenth Amendment's requirement that the state prove every element of a criminal offense beyond a reasonable doubt. The Court therefore found that the instruction "that the law presumes a person intends the ordinary consequences of his voluntary acts"[134]—in this case, at least—was improper and unconstitutional.

In *Sandstrom v. Montana*, the United States Supreme Court held that the due process clause of the Fourteenth Amendment was violated by a jury instruction inferring that the law presumes that a person intends the ordinary consequences of his voluntary acts in the absence of an instruction that noted that the presumption could be rebutted. The Court expressly left open the question whether, if a jury is so instructed, the error can be held harmless.

Following *Sandstrom*, courts took different approaches to the harmless error problem, and the Supreme Court considered the matter again in 1983 in *Connecticut v. Johnson*.[135] In the *Johnson* case, the defendant was convicted of robbery and attempted murder following a jury instruction that noted a person intended the ordinary consequences of his voluntary act. The jury was permitted to use a conclusive presumption without examining the element of intent necessary for the convictions. The trial court's charge to the jury, which was challenged, included instructions regarding the presumption of innocence and the state's burden of proving guilt beyond a reasonable doubt for all elements of the crime. The trial judge instructed the jury on the issue of intent and stated "a person's intention may be inferred from his conduct and every person is conclusively presumed to intend the natural and necessary consequences of his act."[136] With respect to attempted murder, the court again spoke of a conclusive presumption.

---

[133]   Sandstrom v. Montana, 176 Mont. 492, 497, 580 P.2d 106, 109 (1978).
[134]   Sandstrom v. Montana, 442 U.S. 510, 525, 99 S. Ct. 2450, 61 L. Ed. 2d 39 (1979).
[135]   Connecticut v. Johnson, 460 U.S. 73, 1983 U.S. LEXIS 131 (1983).
[136]   *Id*. at 78.

The respondent argued on appeal that the conclusive presumption language in the jury instructions on intent rendered the instructions unconstitutional under *Sandstrom*. Over the state's contention that any error was harmless, the Supreme Court of Connecticut affirmed some of the other convictions, but reversed the convictions for attempted murder and robbery on the grounds that the jury instructions included a conclusive presumption that shifted the burden of proof concerning intent. The court concluded that the "unconstitutional conclusive presumption language in the general instruction was not cured by the specific instructions on attempted murder and robbery."

When the defendant appealed to the United States Supreme Court, that Court agreed with the state supreme court that the proposition "every person is conclusively presumed to intend the natural and necessary consequences of his act," constituted error violating the Fourteenth Amendment's due process clause. The Supreme Court further explained that "an erroneous presumption on a disputed element of the crime renders irrelevant the evidence on the issue because the jury may have relied upon presumptions rather than upon that evidence."[137] If the instruction is given on the presumption, especially the conclusive presumption, the concern is that the jury will look no further in determining the intent, which is an element of the crime.

In *Connecticut v. Johnson*, the Supreme Court indicated, "[t]here may be rare situations in which the reviewing court can be confident that a *Sandstrom* error did not play any part in the jury's verdict. For example, if the instruction had no bearing on the offense for which the defendant . . . was convicted, it would be appropriate to find the error harmless."[138] However, the Court explained that, in the *Johnson* case, the conclusive presumption instruction permitted the jury to convict the respondent using what amounted to a conclusive presumption. According to the Court, such an error deprived the respondent of "constitutional rights so basic to a fair trial that their infraction can never be treated as harmless error."[139]

In a California case in which the defendant had been convicted of killing his former wife's boyfriend after a plea of not guilty and not guilty by reason of insanity, the Ninth Circuit Court of Appeals reversed the conviction.[140] The bifurcated, or two-stage, trial involved a guilt phase in which the jury had been informed, for the purposes of that phase, that the jury was to conclusively presume that the defendant was sane. At the second phase, the jury found the defendant sane as well. The reviewing court reversed the conviction on the basis that the trial judge had given a jury instruction containing a conclusive presumption that relieved the prosecution of proving the crucial element of mental state for guilt of murder. The Court of Appeals followed the *Sandstrom* rationale and concluded "[t]hat the jury instruction in this case violated the

---

[137] *Id.* at 85, 86.

[138] *Id.* at 87.

[139] *Id.* at 88, citing Chapman v. California, 386 U.S. 18, 23, 1967 U.S. LEXIS 2198 (1967).

[140] Stark v. Hickman, 455 F.3d 1070, 1077, 1078, 2006 U.S. App. LEXIS 19296 (9th Cir. 2006).

Due Process Clause of the Fourteenth Amendment and that the error was not harmless."[141]

Sandstrom and related cases held that the due process clause bars the state from using evidentiary presumptions that effectively relieve the state of its burden of persuasion beyond a reasonable doubt as to every essential element of the crime. A permissive presumption, which suggests a possible conclusion but does not require it to be drawn, does not shift the burden of proof and is permissible as long as the conclusion follows logically from the predicate. But a mandatory presumption, even a rebuttable one, is prohibited if it relieves the state of the burden of persuasion as to an element of the offense.

While United States Supreme Court decisions involving inferences or presumptions of ordinary consequences have not proved to be models of clarity, the decisions appear to indicate that where jury instructions relating to intent create a mandatory presumption that unconstitutionally shifts the burden of persuasion on an important element of the crime to the defendant, the instruction violates due process. As a general rule, such decisions should not survive judicial scrutiny, but some state decisions may not be following the principle in every case. However, where the inference is clearly rebuttable and does not change the ultimate burden of proof, a jury instruction may not always, in every case, be objectionable, and some state courts may not be following the *Sandstrom* case properly. As an Arkansas court observed, "[i]ntent or state of mind is seldom capable of proof by direct evidence and must usually be inferred from the circumstances of the crime."[142]

Accordingly, courts have generally allowed the prosecution to introduce indirect evidence to show intent. For example, an Arkansas appeals court held that "[d]ue to the difficulty in ascertaining a defendant's intent or state of mind, a presumption exists that a person intends the natural and probable consequences of his or her acts"[143] A Virginia court permitted the measuring of a defendant's intent by considering the natural and probable consequences of the defendant's acts.[144] The Georgia code provides that "[a] person of sound mind and discretion is presumed to intend the natural and probable consequences of his acts but the presumption may be rebutted."[145] In an unpublished opinion in an attempted murder case, a Minnesota court permitted a jury instruction that allowed the jury to infer that the defendant intended the natural and probable consequences of his act.[146] And in a Maryland first and second degree assault case, the reviewing court approved a jury's inference that "one intends the natural and probable consequences of his act."[147] From a review of the

---

[141] *Id.* at 1080.

[142] Taylor v. State, 77 Ark. App. 144, 150, 72 S.W.3d 882, 885 (Ark. 2002).

[143] Jones v. State, 2009 Ark. App. LEXIS 109 (Ark. 2009).

[144] Thornburgh v. Commonwealth, 2006 Va. App. LEXIS 90 (Va. 2006).

[145] O.C.G.A. § 16-2-5 (2008).

[146] State v. Johnson, 2006 Minn. App. Unpub. LEXIS 560 (Minn. 2006).

[147] Brown v. State, 182 Md. App. 138, 179, 2008 Md. App. LEXIS 121 (Md. 2008).

above cases, it may become somewhat apparent that many courts regularly come dangerously close to violating the principles announced in *Sandstrom v. Montana*. However, because most cases are not litigated to the state supreme court level and almost never reach the Supreme Court of the United States, some deviation from the black-letter case law occurs.

§ 6.13　—Knowledge of the Law

A society that operates on the rule of law requires that the individuals within the society make strong efforts to obey the law, whether civil or criminal. "The general rule that ignorance of the law or a mistake of law is no defense to criminal prosecution is deeply rooted in the American legal system."[148] Therefore, as a legal principle, all persons are presumed to know the general public laws of the nation, state, and locality where they reside and to know the legal effects of their acts. The maxim that "[a]ll persons are conclusively presumed to know the law"[149] is necessary for the functioning of an orderly society. For example, a federal court held that the defendant was presumed to know that an American Indian cannot kill a bald eagle without a federal permit[150] and federal courts can include the phrase "ignorance of the law is no excuse" in jury instructions.[151] While a number of decisions have held that the presumption that one knows the law is a conclusive presumption, it is recognized that no single person knows all the law or even comes close to understanding all its meanings. One federal court of appeals noted that the concept that "everyone knows the law" is based on an "embarrassing tenacity of legal fictions."[152] If everyone really always knew the law, no court cases would ever be reversed because the judges would know the law and would apply it properly and no police officer would ever make an illegal arrest.

As a general rule, trial judges are presumed to know the law and to follow it properly when making sentencing decisions,[153] and "police officers are charged with knowledge of the law"[154] and defendants are presumed to know the law they have been charged with breaking and to know the consequences.[155]

While the presumption extends to judicial decisions, police officers are not charged with knowing how a court will construe a law or when or if a

---

[148]　United States v. Hancock, 231 F.3d 557, 561, 2000 U.S. App. LEXIS 26827 (9th Cir. 2000), quoting Cheek v. United States, 498 U.S. 192, 199, 1991 U.S. LEXIS 348 (1991).

[149]　24 Tex. Jur. *Criminal Law* 3407.

[150]　United States v. Friday, 525 F.3d 938, 2008 U.S. App. LEXIS 9919 (10th Cir. 2008), *cert. denied,* 2009 U.S. LEXIS 1548 (2009).

[151]　United States v. Turcotte, 405 F.3d 515, 525, 2005 U.S. App. LEXIS 6710 (7th Cir. 2005).

[152]　Atwell v. Lisle Park District, 286 F.3d 987, 2002 U.S. App. LEXIS 6775 (8th Cir. 2002).

[153]　United States v. McGlothen, 2009 U.S. App. LEXIS 3600 (10th Cir. 2009).

[154]　Sneed v. State, 876 So. 2d 1235, 1238, 2004 Fla. App. LEXIS 8390 (Fla. 2004).

[155]　State v. Robbins, 986 So. 2d 828, 835, 2008 La. App. LEXIS 862 (La. 2008).

court will declare a law to be in violation of a state or the federal constitution. In one case, an Illinois police officer was permitted to follow and enforce an Illinois law that was later ruled unconstitutional. Even though a police officer is presumed to know the law, the officer cannot foresee how a court will construe the law in future litigation.[156] In fact, prisoners gain no exemption from the maxim "everyone is presumed to know the law" when they pursue post-conviction relief in state and federal appellate courts. This presumption is so strong that governments need not assist a prisoner in negotiating the complex matrix of post-conviction relief past the first appeal of right.[157] Consequently, when prisoners fail to file briefs or other responses in attempts to gain writs of habeas corpus or other remedies, these failures do not normally serve as an adequate excuse.[158]

A person is not presumed to know the laws of a sister state or foreign country, but he or she is presumed to know that laws are subject to change, and is presumed to know of the changes.[159]

§ 6.14   – Flight or Concealment

"Evidence that the accused fled after the offense, intentionally absented himself or herself from court to avoid trial, concealed himself or herself, or made an attack on a peace officer in an endeavor to escape from jail is admissible as an indication of guilt."[160] Even though law enforcement officers assume that flight after a crime tends to prove guilt, human conduct is often ambiguous. The same response to one situation may not result in the same inference when the same response occurs in a different context. This evidence rule deserves careful attention because the factual situation of each crime might result in different conclusions being drawn from similar conduct. When a defendant departs the scene of a crime, it can be considered flight if the facts indicate that the defendant left the crime scene with the design of avoiding capture or apprehension. For flight to have evidentiary consequences, the defendant need not necessarily be in hiding or fleeing or attempting to flee from custody. A New Jersey court explained that to judicially recognize conduct as flight, the circumstances must indicate leaving accompanied by no rational explanation. This gives rise to an inference that the defendant possessed a consciousness of guilt and desired to avoid capture or apprehension for the alleged crime.[161] Alternatively, a suspect's flight from a crime scene or from a police officer could indicate a consciousness of guilt of some completely different offense

---

[156] *See* Illinois v. Krull, 480 U.S. 340 (1987).

[157] *See* Nehls v. Norris, 2008 U.S. Dist. LEXIS 101820 (E.D. Ark. 2008).

[158] *See* Allen v. Houston, 2008 U.S. Dist. LEXIS 72474 (D. Neb. 2008) and Dean v. Houston, 2006 U.S. Dist. LEXIS 2544 (D. Neb. 2006).

[159] *See* 31A C.J.S. *Evidence* 4 147 (1996).

[160] 18 TEX. JUR. *Criminal Law* 278

[161] State v. Ingram, 196 N.J. 23; 951 A.2d 1000, 2008 N.J. LEXIS 879 (N.J. 2008).

or of a desire not to be involved in a police investigation. Evidence of flight need not prove that a suspect fled immediately following the alleged crime but evidence that a person fled months later when the police efforts focused on the defendant. The strength of the evidence of flight depends upon all the facts and circumstances, because flight may show consciousness of guilt or may indicate nothing. The defendant may introduce evidence in an attempt to offer an innocent explanation concerning why flight or concealment occurred, but an innocent explanation does not negate a jury's ability to infer a consciousness of guilt.[162]

In a federal prosecution involving a felon in possession of a firearm and ammunition, state agents attempted to serve a search warrant, which the defendant initially resisted. The eventual search revealed a gun and ammunition and indicated that the defendant was the only resident. He admitted to owning the gun and the ammunition. The gun's presence resulted in a referral for federal prosecution and, after agreeing to surrender in Rhode Island, the defendant absconded and was not arrested for several years. The fact that the defendant had agreed to surrender and did not and then fled, permitted the trial judge to allow evidence of flight without unfairly prejudicing the defense. In approving the admission of flight evidence, the Court of Appeals noted:

> In the case at hand, the appellant's resistance to the execution of the search warrant, his admissions on that occasion, and the unfulfilled promise of self-surrender formed a sufficient factual predicate for the introduction of the flight evidence. This predicate substantially diminished the possibility that the jury might infer guilt solely on the basis of the appellant's flight. To cinch matters, the court's cautionary instructions, twice repeated, mitigated any risk that the jury might give the flight evidence undue weight.[163]

Here, the evidence of flight explained the long delay from the date of indictment to the trial date and added to the inference of consciousness of guilt.[164]

In a California case[165] in which the defendant contested the giving of a jury instruction concerning flight, he contended that when he left the state and committed serious crimes in Arizona following an alleged multiple murder case in California, the act of leaving the state to travel to Arizona could not be construed as flight. He contended that the giving of the standard jury instruction allowed the jury to draw impermissible inferences concerning his thought processes. The trial court gave the usual jury instruction, which read:

> The [flight] [attempted flight] [escape] [attempted escape] [from custody] of a person [immediately] after the commission of a crime, or after [he] [she] is

---

162 People v. Brown, 2009 Cal. App. Unpub. LEXIS 1600 (Cal. 2009). Unpublished opinion.
163 United States v. Benedetti, 433 F.3d 111, 116, 2005 U.S. App. LEXIS 28490 (1st Cir. 2005).
164 *Id.* at 118.
165 People v. Loker, 80 Cal. Rptr. 3d 630, 2008 Cal. LEXIS 9275 (Cal. 2008).

accused of a crime, is not sufficient in itself to establish [his] [her] guilt, but is a fact which, if proved, may be considered by you in the light of all other proved facts in deciding whether a defendant is guilty or not guilty. The weight to which this circumstance is entitled is a matter for you to decide.[166]

The California reviewing court noted that the facts and the jury instruction did not address the defendant's specific mental state at the time of the alleged crime or of his guilt of any crime, but did allow the jury to consider the circumstances suggesting the defendant's consciousness that he had committed some offense.

While California law requires a flight instruction in cases in which the defendant has removed him or herself from the scene, judges in other states may have to evaluate the fact situation to determine whether a defendant's acts actually constitute flight due to a consciousness of guilt. One Florida reviewing court held that flight from a police officer did not have sufficient connection to any crime to make the flight instruction proper.[167] The defendant was near a shopping center during a hurricane when a police officer encountered him standing by a boarded up window that had a couple of boards missing. The defendant ran because his companion ran and there was no proof of when the boards were removed from the storefront or even if a human removed them. In reversing the defendant's conviction for attempted burglary, the appellate court noted that the defendant's "flight from the police is equivocal, since a plausible explanation is that the flight inferred consciousness of a curfew violation, and not a guilty mind over an attempted burglary."[168]

In referring to flight instructions, a federal district court instructed the jury that it could consider a defendant's flight from police to infer consciousness of guilt.[169] Police noticed the defendant driving without a buckled safety belt and attempted a traffic stop. The defendant, who had prior felony convictions, sped away, but police eventually captured him, discovering a gun and drugs. As a general rule, a flight instruction may be given when the evidence warrants it. The trial court told the jury, "[y]ou may also consider any evidence of flight by the defendant, along with all of the evidence in the case, and you may consider whether this evidence shows a consciousness of guilt and determine the significance to be attached to any such conduct."[170] Because the jury instruction allowed an inference of guilt but did not require such a deduction, the reviewing court held that the giving of the flight instruction was proper.

Flight need not come immediately following the crime or its discovery, but may occur months later. In an Indiana child molestation case, the defendant complained on appeal that the trial court erred in admitting evidence

---

[166] CALJIC 2.52.
[167] Remor v. State, 991 So. 2d 957, 2008 Fla. App. LEXIS 14242 (Fla. 2008).
[168] *Id.* at 961.
[169] United States v. Webster, 442 F.3d 1065, 1066, 2006 U.S. App. LEXIS 8061 (8th Cir. 2006).
[170] *Id.* at 1067.

concerning the his initial failure to appear for trial, the state's investigation to find the defendant, his use of an assumed identity, and evidence of his flight to Mississippi 18 months after being charged. He contended that flight had to occur immediately following the crime or its discovery.[171] The appellate court rejected his argument that his alleged "flight" was not a flight and stated "[t]he evidence of Bennett's flight and assumption of false identity are indicative of a guilty mind and were properly before the jury."[172]

If evidence of flight is used to infer consciousness of guilt, a flight instruction may be given by the court. Reciprocal fairness would seem to dictate that an instruction on lack of flight should be given, but case law does not require a lack of flight instruction.[173] Courts appear reluctant to offer an absence of flight instruction because the conduct of staying at the crime scene or area is ambiguous at best. In this situation, a suspect may not realize that he or she is soon to be a defendant or believe that staying may be viewed as innocence or that remaining on the scene is indicative of actual innocence.[174]

The decision concerning whether to give a jury instruction on flight is generally left to the discretion of the trial judge. There should be unexplained actual flight and the flight instructions should be given only where the evidence of flight has considerable probative value. Evidence of flight should neither be admitted nor a jury instruction given when there is an independent justification for flight for reasons that cannot be explained to the jury because of a separate prejudicial effect.[175] Typically, the trial judge will advise the jury that flight may be prompted by a variety of motives, and best practice suggests that the judge should instruct the jury to consider all evidence before making an inference of guilt from the fact of flight.

§ 6.15 — Unexplained Absence as Death

Pursuant to traditional common law rules and the statutes of many states, "a presumption of death arises from the continued and unexplained absence of a person from his or her home or place of residence without any intelligence from or concerning him or her for a period of seven years."[176] Upon a petition by an interested party and upon proof of absence, that no person has seen the missing person, and that there is no explanation other than death, a court will enter a decree finding a presumption of death.[177] Absentee individuals who

---

[171] Bennett v. State, 883 N.E.2d 888, 892, 2008 Ind. App. LEXIS 713 (Ind. 2008).

[172] *Id.*

[173] State v. Williams, 2004 Tenn. Crim. App. LEXIS 191 (Tenn. 2004).

[174] *See* Commonwealth v. Hanford, 2007 PA Super 345 (Pa. 2007).

[175] Walker v. State, 913 So. 2d 198, 232, 2005 Miss. LEXIS 216 (Miss. 2005).

[176] *See* 22A Am. Jur. 2d *Death* § 428.

[177] Cavanagh v. Lentz, 2005 Conn. Super. LEXIS 2731 (Conn. 2005). Due to proof that a woman's husband was missing, had severe mental problems, and had tried to commit suicide at a prior time, the coroner was ordered to prepare a presumptive death certificate.

have been declared dead prior to the statutory period have often been involved in suicide, accidents, shipwrecks, aircraft accidents, or similar occurrences in which the body would not likely have been found and in which there was a high likelihood of death.

In one New York case, the trial court ruled that the missing person was deceased. The evidence showed that he had told his business partner and his wife that he was intent on ending his life. When he left the marital home, he did not take his driver's license, credit cards, or any personal effects. Medically, he had terminal heart disease, suffered from shortness of breath, and had been diagnosed as an alcoholic. The court took testimony that about 70 percent of individuals with his heart disease do not live five years. Significantly, the missing man's diagnosis was a late-term diagnosis of cardiomyopathy that indicated he needed a heart transplant. A search of all the usual databases, including Social Security, Board of Elections, and others disclosed no activity. The court concluded that the missing man was dead as of the date of his disappearance.[178]

The cases are not in agreement with respect to the presumed death of a fugitive from justice because that person, if alive, has a good reason to be absent. A good reason or motive for a person's absence may provide a satisfactory reason sufficient to determine that the individual is not deceased. Absence to avoid a criminal prosecution may constitute a sufficient reason to conclude that a person has not died but is absent to avoid potential incarceration.[179] A surety on a defendant's bail bond attempted to avoid forfeiture of bail and introduced evidence that the defendant had disappeared after leaving his car at an airport, and that an intensive search failed to locate him. Other evidence indicated that the defendant had been indicted, was a member of a group on whom a murderous assault had been made, and had a good reason for flight. The court upheld the forfeiture on the ground that, where a motive or where doubt about the reason for the absence exists, the presumption of continued life remains.[180]

The legal effect that the presumption that a person, missing seven years, with his or her location being unknown and undetermined, is dead can have important consequences for those who would inherit by will or intestate distribution. In many states and in Indiana, the common law presumption of death requires a seven-year absence that is inexplicable.[181] This term has been interpreted by Indiana courts to mean missing from the usual place of residence and no intelligence concerning the missing person has been received by relatives or friends. Washington follows a similar presumption,

---

[178]   Matter of Bennett, 2006 N.Y. Slip Op. 50889U (N.Y. 2006).

[179]   Starr et al. v. Old Line Life Insurance Co., 104 Cal. App. 4th 487, 496, 128 Cal. Rptr. 2d 282, 288, 2002 Cal. App. LEXIS 5174 (2002).

[180]   People v. Niccoli, 102 Cal. App. 2d 814, 228 P.2d 827 (1951).

[181]   Malone v. ReliaStar Life Ins. Co., 2009 U.S. App. LEXIS 5106 (7th Cir. 2009). For probate purposes, Indiana uses a five year absence.

but presumes that the missing person remains alive. Under the statute, the presumptive heirs and legatees may petition for a distribution of the presumed deceased person's estate. When the court is satisfied that the statutory requirements have been met, an order of final distribution of the estate can be entered.[182]

In many states the statutory period has been reduced to five years of absence or less. The rationale and logic for following a period shorter than the traditional seven years makes sense in the present environment given the access to large computer databases and the search abilities available on the Internet. Under present circumstances, disappearing is more difficult than ever, in the absence of actual death. Representative of many jurisdictions, California holds that a person missing for five years creates a presumption that the death occurred at the end of the statutory period unless there is contrary evidence of the date of death,[183] a fact that may create problems for insurance eligibility. New York has shortened the period for a presumption of death to a continuous absence of three years but allows proof of death in fewer than three years.[184]

§ 6.16   — Regularity of Official Acts

"The government is always presumed to act in good faith"[185] and this presumption extends to its appointed and elected officials. This rebuttable presumption of regularity supports the official acts of public officials and police officers, and courts presume that public officials have properly discharged their official duties, in the absence of clear evidence to the contrary.[186] When a person wishes to prove that a public official has not performed his or her duties properly, that person must meet and overcome the strong presumption that administrators and other public officials have discharged their duties in good faith.[187] To rebut the presumption of proper conduct, the moving party will have to meet the burden by clear and convincing evidence to the contrary[188] or, as one court phrased it, "competent and substantial evidence."[189]

---

[182]   REV. CODE WASH. 11.80.100 (Matthew Bender 2009).

[183]   *See* CAL. PROB. CODE 12401(2008).

[184]   *See* NY CLS EPTL 2-1.7 (Matthew Bender 2009). *See also* Matter of Philip v. Lieberman, 851 N.Y.S.2d 141, 2008 N.Y. App. Div. LEXIS 57 (2008), declaring a woman dead after the World Trade Center bombing of 2001.

[185]   Long Lane Limited Partnership v. Bibb, 159 Fed. Appx. 189; 2005 U.S. App. LEXIS 26912 (Fed. Cir. 2005).

[186]   Butler v. Principi, 244 F.3d 1337, 201 U.S. App. 5270 (Fed. Cir. 2001); United States v. Chemical Foundation, Inc., 272 U.S. 1, 47 S. Ct. 1, 71 L. Ed. 131 (1926); Charleston Television, Inc. v. South Carolina Budget and Control Bd., 373 S.E.2d 890 (S.C. 1988).

[187]   Hill v. Geren, 2009 U.S. Dist. LEXIS 10237 (D.C. D.C. 2009).

[188]   Tecom, Inc. v. United States, 66 Fed. Cl. 736, 768, 2005 U.S. Claims LEXIS 195 (2005).

[189]   Harrell v. City of Gastonia, 2009 U.S. Dist. LEXIS 6542 (W.D.N.C. 2009).

As a general rule, the presumption that governmental officials have acted properly extends to grand jury proceedings.[190] For example, in *United States v. Exson*,[191] the reviewing court refused to dismiss the indictment on the strength of the defense allegation that the prosecution misled the grand jury on material matters. According to the Court of Appeals, even if there were some irregularities in a grand jury proceeding, a dismissal would not be appropriate. The court noted that:

> The proceedings of a grand jury are afforded a strong presumption of regularity, and a defendant faces a heavy burden to overcome that presumption when seeking dismissal of an indictment. See *United States v. Hintzman*, 806 F.2d 840, 843 (8th Cir. 1986). Dismissal due to errors in grand jury proceedings is appropriate only if the defendant shows actual prejudice, see *United States v. Kouba*, 822 F.2d 768, 774 (8th Cir. 1987), and "the petit jury's guilty verdict rendered [any] errors harmless." *Id.*[192]

The presumption of regularity attending official acts applies to the acts of most public officials. One court may presume that another court properly performed its duties until the contrary has been shown and therefore a rebuttable presumption of regularity attaches to a defendant's prior convictions.[193] The Court of Appeals for the Seventh Circuit noted that there is a presumption that a federal trial court acted properly when it admitted evidence and there is a presumption that the evidence has been properly secured by police since its seizure.[194] Unless there has been some showing of fraud, deceit, or other misconduct by the affiant, the police, the prosecutor, or the judge, a presumption of regularity attaches to the obtaining of a warrant from a court.[195] Unless there is some particularized proof of misconduct, grand jury proceedings are given a presumption of regularity.[196] Trial jurors are considered public officials for purposes of this presumption and are presumed to have followed jury instructions properly and in good faith.[197] As an officer of the court, a prosecutor's decisions are granted a presumption of regularity unless a defendant can demonstrate that a prosecutor acted with an improper animus toward a defendant.[198]

---

[190]   United States v. Diaz, 2006 U.S. Dist. LEXIS 46315 (N.D. Ga. 2006) and United States v. Lucarelli, 2006 U.S. Dist. LEXIS 39664 (D. Conn. 2005).

[191]   United States v. Esxon, 328 F.3d 456, 459, 2003 U.S. App. LEXIS 8836 (8th Cir. 2003).

[192]   *Id.* at 459.

[193]   Montana v. Kvislen, 2003 Mont. 27, 314 Mont. 176, 2003 Mont. LEXIS 26 (2003).

[194]   United States v. Prieto, 549 F.3d 513, 524, 2008 U.S. App. LEXIS 24323 (7th Cir. 2008).

[195]   In re Directives Pursuant to Section 105b of the Foreign Intelligence Surveillance Act, 2008 U.S. App. LEXIS 27417 (Fed. Cir. 2008).

[196]   United States v. Davis, 2009 U.S. Dist. LEXIS 19404 (S.D. N.Y. 2009). *See also* Culp v. State, 2005 Miss. LEXIS 828 (Miss. 2005).

[197]   United States v. McCuiston, 2006 U.S. App. LEXIS 16292 (5th Cir. 2006).

[198]   United States v. Woods, 2009 US. App. LEXIS 93 (4th Cir. 2009). Unpublished opinion.

§ 6.17 Constitutionality Tests for Presumptions and Inferences

Criminal cases require the prosecution to prove all the elements of any charged crime beyond a reasonable doubt, but when inferences and presumptions are presented in a case, the prosecution may be proving one fact and not actually proving the inferred fact. A legislature may create inferences and presumptions by providing that "certain facts shall be prima facie or presumptive evidence of other facts."[199] Even though a legislature may have created an inference or presumption, due process clauses in the Fifth and Fourteenth Amendments require that legislation meet a fundamental fairness standard in a criminal trial. If the legislation requires a jury to make a mandatory deduction from proof of a basic fact, this violates due process. A law or jury instruction that might allow a jury to interpret a presumption as conclusive or mandatory violates due process.[200] Even allowing or permitting the jury to make the deduction or inference constitutionally requires a close logical connection between the basic fact and the presumed fact.

Early decisions of the United States Supreme Court set forth a number of different standards to measure the validity of statutory presumptions. One test was whether there was a "rational connection" between the basic fact and the presumed fact. A second was whether the legislature might have made it a crime to do the thing from which the presumption authorized an inference. A third was whether it would be more convenient for the defendant or for the prosecution to adduce evidence of the presumed fact.

However, in *Tot v. United States*,[201] the Court singled out one of these tests as controlling, and the *Tot* rule has been followed in the two subsequent cases in which the issue has been presented. The *Tot* Court had before it a federal statute that, as construed, made it a crime for a person previously convicted of a crime of violence to receive any firearm or ammunition that had been transported in interstate or foreign commerce. The statute further provided that "the possession of a firearm or ammunition by any such person shall be presumptive evidence that such firearm or ammunition was shipped or transported or received, as the case may be, by such person in violation of this Act."[202] Proof of possession and a prior violent crime equaled guilt with the presumption carrying half the burden of proof. The *Tot* Court noted that the "due process clauses of the Fifth and Fourteenth Amendments set limits upon the power of Congress or that of a state legislature to make the proof of one fact or group of facts evidence of the existence of the ultimate fact on which guilt is predicated."[203]

---

[199] 29 AM. JUR. 2D Evidence 7.
[200] *See* Sandstrom v. Montana, 442 U.S. 510, 1979 U.S. LEXIS 113 (1979).
[201] Tot v. United States, 319 U.S. 463, 1943 U.S. LEXIS 531 (1943).
[202] 15 U. S. C. 902 (f).
[203] *Tot* at 467.

The Court held the presumption unconstitutional and decided that the controlling test for determining the validity of a statutory presumption was that there be a rational connection between the fact proved and the fact presumed. The Court stated:

> Under our decisions a statutory presumption cannot be sustained if there be no rational connection between the fact proved and the ultimate fact presumed, if the inference of the one from proof of the other is arbitrary because of lack of connection between the two in common experience. This is not to say that a valid presumption may not be created upon a view of relation broader than that a jury might take in a specific case. But where the inference is so strained as not to have a reasonable relation to the circumstances of life as we know them, it is not competent for the legislature to create it as a rule governing the procedure of courts.[204]

Two subsequent cases, which remain good law, in which the Supreme Court evaluated the constitutionality of criminal presumptions, *United States v. Gainey*[205] and *United States v. Romano*,[206] involved companion sections of the Internal Revenue Code dealing with illegal alcohol stills. The presumption in *Gainey* that the person's presence at an illegal distillery permitted, but did not require, a jury to infer that Jackie Gainey was "carrying on" the business of a distiller, unless the defendant explained being present at the still to the satisfaction of the jury. The trial judge told the jury that the presumption was permissive and did not require the jury to convict even if he were proved to be present at the still. The Supreme Court held that the *Gainey* presumption should be tested by the "rational connection" standard announced in the *Tot* case, and sustained the statutory presumption and the conviction. The presumption of "carrying on" the business carried weight because few illegal distillers would allow strangers to observe the illegal still. The *Gainey* Court recognized that, in enacting the statutory presumption, Congress allowed the unexplained evidence to have its natural probative value.

The presumption under attack in the *Romano* case was identical to that in *Gainey*, except that the *Romano* jury was authorized to conclude from the defendant's presence at an illegal still that he or she had possession, custody, or control of the still. In the *Romano* case, the trial judge explained to the jury that proof of the defendant's presence at the still would be sufficient evidence to support a conviction. The Court held this presumption invalid on the ground that "absent some showing of the defendant's function at the still, its connection with possession is too tenuous to permit a reasonable inference of guilt; the inference of the one from proof of the other is arbitrary"[207] and not

---

[204] *Id.* at 467–468.
[205] United States v. Gainey, 380 U.S. 63, 1965 U.S. LEXIS 1733 (1965).
[206] United States v. Romano, 382 U.S. 136, 1965 U.S. LEXIS 207 (1965).
[207] Tot v. United States, 319 U.S. 463, 467, 1943 U.S. LEXIS 531 (1943).

based on good probabilities. In effect, presence did not indicate possession, although sometimes presence might indicate "carrying on" the business of distiller. Though quite similar to the *Gainey* presence at the still, the *Romano* case had a different outcome based on the manner in which the Supreme Court interpreted the two presumptions and the judges' jury instructions.

A "statutory presumption for criminal cases must be regarded as 'irrational' or 'arbitrary' and thus unconstitutional, unless it can at least be said with substantial assurance that the presumed fact is more likely than not to follow from the proof of the proved fact on which it is made to depend."[208] The Supreme Court applied this legal standard in *Leary v. United States*, when the Court overturned a federal statute that authorized juries to infer from the defendant's possession of marijuana that the defendant knew that the marijuana had been illegally imported into the United States. The presumption of knowing that marijuana was imported from proof of mere possession was invalid under the due process clause because there was no proof that typical marijuana possessors are generally aware that their marijuana was locally grown or aware that their marijuana was likely to have been imported or knew that it actually was imported.[209]

In the year following the *Leary* decision, the Supreme Court considered the constitutionality of instructing a jury that it may infer from the defendant's possession of heroin and cocaine that the defendant knew that the drugs had been illegally imported.[210] The Court noted that there was a reason for the logic of the presumption of knowledge of importation from proof of possession.

> It may be that the ordinary jury would not always know that heroin illegally circulating in this country is not manufactured here. But Turner and others who sell or distribute heroin are in a class apart. Such people have regular contact with a drug which they know cannot be legally bought or sold; their livelihood depends on its availability; some of them have actually engaged in the smuggling process.[211]

The Court held that the inference with regard to heroin was valid, judged by either of the two tests stated in the *Tot* decision.

As a general rule when dealing with statutory presumptions that declare that, on proof of one fact, another fact may be inferred or presumed, such a statute is probably constitutional, provided that there is a rational relationship between the basic fact proved and the fact presumed, that the presumed fact proved from the original fact cannot be arbitrary or unreasonable, and that the finder of fact may give the presumed fact the weight as it believes appropriate.[212] In New Jersey, state law presumes that any time a firearm is found in

---

[208] Leary v. United States, 395 U.S. 6, 36, 1969 U.S. LEXIS 3271 (1969).

[209] *Id.*

[210] Turner v. United States, 396 U.S. 398, 1970 U.S. LEXIS 3146 (1970).

[211] *Id.* at 416.

[212] 29 Am. Jur. 2d *Evidence* 7.

a vehicle, the individual in the vehicle is presumed to be in possession of the firearm and that where more than one person is in the vehicle, the presumption is that all persons possess the firearm.[213] Any person who possesses a handgun is presumed to possess the firearm illegally, according to New Jersey law, because of the state's strong licensing requirements. The New Jersey statutes on presumptions involving firearms appear to be in compliance with the *Tot* standard on presumptions in that it is more likely than not that a person possessing a gun in New Jersey does so illegally.

In a case involving similar reasoning concerning presumptions, police approached a vehicle that matched the description of a car whose occupants were suspected of criminal activity. When the driver saw the officer approaching, he attempted to get into the car to leave. A struggle ensued and the police prevailed. At that time an officer discovered a handgun wedged between the driver's seat and the console. Under New York law, the presence of a firearm in an automobile serves as presumptive evidence of its illegal possession by all persons then occupying the vehicle. The officers testified that none of the defendants was ever actually seen handling the gun, but they observed the defendant as one of the occupants of the vehicle. The driver's testimony that he alone possessed the gun failed to rebut the presumption of New York law that implicated all the passengers in possession. The evidence showed that the occupants of the car had been traveling together for several weeks and must have known about the gun. The Appellate Division of the Supreme Court believed that the presumption of possession by all of the vehicle occupants was entirely rational. Because it was more likely than not that all occupants possessed the gun and the presumption had not been rebutted, the reviewing court upheld the conviction for criminal possession of a gun.[214] The result was consistent with the *Tot* rationale covering the constitutionality of presumptions, and the New York jury rationally could have determined that the passenger did not have possession of the firearm, if it believed that the evidence rebutted the presumption and that the defendant-passenger was not also in possession of the gun.

In an Illinois case involving a presumption that a driver had been proven to be under the influence of alcohol, the Supreme Court reversed a double homicide conviction. In accordance with then-existing Illinois law, the trial court instructed the jury with language from 9-3(b) of the Illinois code and rephrased it into a jury instruction that stated: "If you find from your consideration of all the evidence that the defendant was under the influence of alcohol at the time of the alleged violation, such evidence shall be presumed to be evidence of a reckless act unless disproved by evidence to the contrary."[215] Other

---

[213] N.J. STAT. 2C:39-2 (2009).

[214] People v. Tabb, 12 A.D.3d 951, 952, 785 N.Y.S.2d 193, 194, 2004 N.Y. App. Div. LEXIS 14284 (N.Y. 2004), *appeal denied*, 4 N.Y.3d 768, 2005 N.Y. LEXIS 419 (2005).

[215] People v. Pomykala, 2003 Ill. LEXIS 7 (2003).

jury instructions assisted the jury in finding that the defendant was under the influence of alcohol when there had been proof that his blood-alcohol level was .08 or greater, but the instructions did not require such a finding. The court instructed the jury that:

> If you find beyond a reasonable doubt that at the time the defendant drove a vehicle that the amount of alcohol concentration in the defendant's blood or breath was 0.08 or more, you may presume that the defendant was under the influence of alcohol. You never are required to make this presumption. It is for the jury to determine whether the presumption should be drawn. You should consider all the evidence in determining whether the defendant was under the influence of alcohol. Illinois Pattern Jury Instructions, Criminal, No. 23.30 (4th ed. 2000).[216]

According to the Supreme Court of Illinois, because a reasonable juror could conclude that the jury instruction mandated a finding of recklessness without any factual connection between the intoxication and the reckless act, the statute had created a mandatory presumption. The effect of this mandatory presumption improperly and unconstitutionally shifted the burden of disproving recklessness to the defendant, which required a reversal of the homicide convictions.[217]

In a Virginia case, the law provided that a person who possessed rental property and failed to return the property within five days of the agreed date of return will be deemed guilty of larceny.[218] The statute appeared to create a mandatory presumption, but the defendant could introduce evidence that would rebut the prima facie case created by the failure to return. In one case, a defendant rented a car from Rent-a-Wreck and failed to return it consistent with the rental agreement. He told the company that he was in a hospital following a suicide attempt and could not return it, but told the company where to find it. Following his conviction, the defendant appealed, contending that Virginia law concerning the presumption of his fraudulent intent to commit larceny, based on a failure to return the car, had been rebutted by his hospitalization for attempted suicide. The Court of Criminal Appeals rejected the defendant's contention and noted that the statute operated to allow a prima facie presumption of fraudulent intent upon failure to return and that the evidence failed to rebut the deduction contemplated by the statute.[219]

One California case appeared to create a mandatory presumption that would be inconsistent with due process and the cases decided by the Supreme Court of the United States. A trial court convicted a California defendant of

---

[216] *Id.*

[217] *Id.*

[218] Va. Code Ann. 18.2-117 (Matthew Bender 2009).

[219] Newport v. Commonwealth, 2005 Va. App. LEXIS 152 (Va. 2005). For a decision overturning a conviction based on a mandatory presumption, *see* Carella v. California, 491 U.S. 263, 109 S. Ct. 2419, 105 L. Ed. 2d 218 (1989).

possessing hydriodic acid with intent to manufacture methamphetamine. State law provided that when a person possessed sufficient amounts of red phosphorus and iodine, the person would be deemed to have possessed hydriodic acid, even if no acid had ever been synthesized. The defendant contended on appeal that the statute created a mandatory presumption that if one possesses the two precursor chemicals that one was guilty of possessing hydriodic acid. The effect of the law permitted the government to convict for possession of hydriodic acid without any proof of possession of hydriodic acid. In a decision by the Supreme Court of California, the court held that there was no presumption at issue, but that the language that appeared to be a mandatory presumption was really a "valid exercise of the Legislature's power to create substantive law and define crimes."[220] The defendant's intent to manufacture methamphetamine required proof of possession of hydriodic acid, which she did not possess. The Supreme Court of California upheld the conviction[221] and the Supreme Court of the United States refused to review the decision.[222]

To summarize, when determining the constitutionality of statutory presumptions, the court must find a rational connection between the basic fact and the presumed fact, and it must find that there is a reasonable possibility in the ordinary course of events that the conclusion required by the presumption is in accord with human experience. The presumed fact must more likely than not flow from the basic fact to meet constitutional standards. Second, a presumption that has the effect of shifting the burden to the defense to disprove an element of the crime is unconstitutional.

§ 6.18   Stipulations

A stipulation "is an agreement, admission, or concession made in a judicial proceeding by the parties or their attorneys."[223] The stipulation serves as a substitute for evidence that has the effect of removing some issues from the lawsuit because the parties have clearly indicated that they have no disagreement or dispute concerning the subject or matter covered by the agreement. A stipulation amounts to a concession by both parties to the existence or nonexistence of a fact, an agreement concerning the contents of a document, or an agreement over what a witness would have said if the witness had actually testified. An Ohio court noted suggested that a stipulation is a substitute for evidence that does away with the need for evidence and is actually considered evidence.[224]

---

[220] People v. McCall, 32 Cal. 4th 175, 179, 82 P.3d 351, 354, 8 Cal. Rptr. 3d 337, 340, 2004 Cal. LEXIS 8 (Cal. 2004).

[221] *Id*.

[222] McCall v. California, 542 U.S. 923, 2004 U.S. LEXIS 4451 (2004).

[223] 73 AM. JUR. 2D *Stipulations* 1.

[224] State v. Scott, 2008 Ohio 1862, 2008 Ohio App. LEXIS 1579 (Ohio 2008).

The parties may make stipulations orally or in writing, but the agreement must clearly be part of the court record. While stipulations may be encouraged, the opposing side is not obligated to stipulate, which would otherwise have the effect of preventing that party from presenting part of its case with actual evidence. In one case involving aggravated domestic violence, the defendant complained that the prosecution should have accepted his offer to stipulate to prior domestic violence convictions. Because no party can be required to stipulate to any fact and because the prosecutor wanted the jury to hear some evidence concerning the prior crimes and not just that the convictions existed, the prosecutor properly refused to stipulate.[225] If a defendant dissents from his counsel's offer to stipulate to a matter, the stipulation cannot be accepted.[226]

A stipulation authorizes the court or jury to find the existence of such a fact and to consider that fact without any further proof. A judge does not have to allow the stipulation when the stipulation would create a potential for unfair prejudice to one party or would be against public policy. The triers of fact in criminal cases are not, however, bound to accept the stipulated fact as true. In spite of this fact, California jury instructions indicate that stipulations between the parties are binding on the jury.[227] California juries are told that "if the attorneys have stipulated or agreed to a fact, you must regard that fact as proven,"[228] but juries hearing criminal cases may choose to disregard the stipulation and are permitted find to the contrary if persuaded by other evidence or for any reason or for no reason.

In some situations, stipulated testimony merely amounts to a mutual agreement by both parties that if a certain person were present, he or she would testify under oath to the facts contained within the agreed stipulation. Once a stipulation is agreed upon, as a general rule, the stipulation may not be unilaterally withdrawn.[229] Following this principle, in a Washington case, a defendant was not permitted to withdraw his trial stipulation that he had been properly given his *Miranda* warnings even after a police officer testified that the officer had not been the one who gave the warnings.[230] Similarly, in a Texas murder case, the defendant entered a written stipulation at his first trial that he had stabbed and killed his wife, among other facts. When the trial court declared a mistrial, an issue for the second murder trial involved whether the stipulation from the first trial should be binding on the defendant for the second trial on the same issues. The trial judge admitted the stipulation at the second trial, noting that it had originally been made for trial and it would be admitted as a valid stipulation. On appeal, the reviewing court upheld the

[225]　State v. Newman, 208 Ariz. 507, 95 P.3d 950, 2004 Ariz. App. LEXIS 118 (2004).

[226]　People v. Lee, 379 Ill. App. 3d 533, 538, 2008 Ill. App. LEXIS 117 (Ill. 2008).

[227]　CALJIC 1.02, California Jury Instructions (West Group 2005).

[228]　*Id.*

[229]　State v. McCullough, 2008 Ohio 3055; 2008 Ohio App. LEXIS 2574 (Oh. 2008).

[230]　State v. Howell, 2008 Wash. App. LEXIS 799 (2008). Unreported opinion.

trial court decision that admitted the stipulation at the second trial,[231] noting that the defendant had placed no limitation on its use and the stipulation had never been withdrawn.

While the courts have indicated that stipulations should be encouraged, a party is not required to accept the adversary's offer and a trial court cannot require that one party stipulate to evidence when the other party wants to present evidence. In an Alabama murder case, the defendant contended that the trial court had committed error when it refused to require the prosecution to disclose any mitigating circumstances evidence and to stipulate for the jury that these mitigating circumstances were to be considered in determining whether to impose the death penalty. The appellate court rejected the defendant's contention and noted that, in Alabama, no party is required to accept the opponent's offer to stipulate and may insist that the opposing party introduce facts to prove the offered stipulation.[232] However, a court in a different jurisdiction held that a party may be required to stipulate. In a case involving a felon who possessed a gun under a disability and who was charged with aggravated assault, the defendant offered to stipulate that he was not permitted to possess firearms due to his prior felony conviction. The prosecution refused because it wanted to introduce evidence of his prior aggravated assault convictions rather than allow the defendant merely to admit that he was a felon. The reviewing court reversed the conviction because the facts underlying the prior felony proved to be unduly prejudicial when the probative value was considered and where the defendant admitted to being a felon.[233] The rule seems to be that where an element of a crime requires proof of a prior felony and the defendant offers to stipulate to the felony, a prosecutor may be forced to agree to a stipulation of the felony where some prejudice to the defendant's case might otherwise result.

A stipulation is also used as a means of determining whether certain evidence will be admitted into court. In criminal cases in which the parties have stipulated to the admissibility of certain evidence, that evidence is admissible to corroborate other evidence of the defendant's participation in the crime charged. In the absence of any claim that the stipulation was entered into by mistake, inadvertence, fraud, or misrepresentation, counsel may stipulate regarding evidence that may be received. As a general rule, once a stipulation has been the subject of agreement and has been filed with the court, one of the parties may not withdraw from the stipulation without the consent of the other[234] and usually consent of the court will be required. Judges typically require that the application for withdrawal be made in a timely manner and an effort to withdraw a stipulation on appeal will not usually be considered timely.[235] In a

---

[231] Carrasco v. State, 154 S.W.3d 127, 128, 2005 Tex. Crim. App. LEXIS 76 (2005).

[232] Lewis v. State, 2007 Ala. Crim. App. LEXIS 201 (Ala. 2007).

[233] Ferguson v. State, 2005 Ark. LEXIS 361 (Ark. 2005).

[234] 73 AM. JUR. 2D *Stipulations* 11.

[235] Malutin v. State, 198 P.3d 1177, 2009 Alaska App. LEXIS 5 (Alaska 2009).

death penalty case,[236] an Arizona trial court properly accepted a defendant's stipulation, which served as an aggravating circumstance, that he had been convicted of a crime where a sentence of life imprisonment was imposable. Because he made the stipulation and made no contemporaneous objection, the reviewing court found that there was no error regarding the stipulation.

There are limitations on the use of stipulations. It is clear that a stipulation amounting to a complete concession by the defense to the prosecutor's case would be inconsistent with a plea of not guilty and should not be permitted. A stipulation that is clearly erroneous should not be accepted, and its acceptance probably would be justification for reversal on constitutional grounds. Also, the court is not required to admit a stipulation as a substitute for evidence that may be detrimental to the defendant's case.[237]

As a general rule, a stipulation may be withdrawn, but doing so generally requires the trial court's consent. Granting relief from a stipulation may be granted where the agreement was made as the result of inadvertence, mistake, or excusable neglect as long as the opposing party has not been damaged by relying on the stipulation.[238] Once withdrawn, a stipulation ceases to be effective for any purpose. The withdrawal of a stipulation, however, would be a reasonable basis for a continuance in order for the opposing party to have time to prepare evidence concerning matters formerly embraced by the stipulation and avoid undue surprise.

§ 6.19 — Polygraph Tests

As a general rule, the results of polygraph examinations are not admissible in criminal cases, although there are a few examples where the results will be admissible. For example, where the prosecutor, defense counsel, and the defendant all stipulate to the admissibility prior to the examination, Nevada will permit the admission of the test results.[239] Where all parties agree to the admissibility of the results, there seems to be no reason to exclude them even though many courts believe that the polygraph produces unreliable evidence and may involve possible dangers of undue prejudice to one of the parties. Jurisdictions, represented by Nevada, have determined that the admissibility is appropriate when the parties agree. The changes brought to scientific evidence admissibility after the *Daubert v. Merrell Dow Pharmaceutical* case in 1993 have caused some federal courts to retreat from a general exclusion

---

[236] State v. Tucker, 215 Ariz. 298, 308, 2007 Ariz. LEXIS 64 (Ariz. 2007), *cert. denied*, Tucker v. Arizona, 128 S. Ct. 296, 2007 U.S. LEXIS 10884 (2007).

[237] United States v. Grassi, 602 F.2d 1192 (5th Cir. 1979).

[238] 73 Am. Jur. 2d *Stipulations* 13.

[239] Houston v. Schomig, 533 F.3d 1076, 1086, 2008 U.S. App. LEXIS 16251 (9th Cir. 2008) citing Jackson v. State, 116 Nev. 334, 2000 Nev. LEXIS 35 (Nev. 2000).

of polygraph evidence and the old per se rule of exclusion has retreated to some extent.[240]

Recognizing the changes in scientific evidence admission after *Daubert*, the Fifth Circuit Court of Appeals follows a three-step analysis to determine polygraph admissibility.[241] Courts must first determine whether the polygraph evidence possesses sufficient reliability to be admissible as scientific, technical, or other specialized knowledge, Next, the court must determine whether the offered evidence is relevant to any issue in the trial. Finally, the court must decide whether the polygraph evidence will have an unusually prejudicial effect when considered with its probative value (ability to make issues more clear). This does not mean that every polygraph exam result will be admitted, but it opened the door to the prospect that more test results could find admissibility. A majority of jurisdictions hold that polygraph evidence is generally inadmissible. Representative of the majority view, Louisiana holds that polygraph evidence is not admissible for any reason at a criminal trial because it encourages jury speculation and usurps the jury's role.[242] An Illinois appellate court reversed a conviction for first-degree murder on the ground that prejudicial error occurred when the trial judge permitted the prosecution, during its case-in-chief, to mention that the defendant had been driven by police to take a polygraph examination. An officer testified that during the drive to the testing station, she stated that she had fear that the test results would not help the defendant's case and the officer noted that the defendant made some inculpatory statements to the officer. In reversing the conviction, the reviewing court noted, "[t]he State's suggestion of reliability of the defendant's statement based on her anticipated failure of the polygraph test is an improper purpose for the admission of polygraph evidence."[243] When witnesses inadvertently mention polygraph testing, the refusal, or offer to take, this does not automatically result in a reversal of a resulting conviction, especially where a defense attorney improperly asked a polygraph-related question.[244]

Although 27 states have a complete ban on admitting results of polygraph testing,[245] a substantial minority of courts admit polygraph evidence upon stipulation of the parties.[246] New Jersey prohibits the admission of polygraph results in virtually all cases but permitted it in one case in which the defendant told the jury in mid-trial from the witness stand that he would take a polygraph

---

[240]   140 A.L.R. FED. 525.

[241]   Ulmer v. State Farm, 897 F. Supp. 299, 302, 1995 U.S. Dist. LEXIS 13295 (W.D. La. 1995).

[242]   State v. Franklin, 956 So. 2d 823, 2007 La. App. LEXIS 901 (La. 2007), *writ denied*, 2008 La. LEXIS 86 (2008). *See also* Cook v. State, 928 So. 2d 589; 2006 La. App. LEXIS 242 (La. 2006).

[243]   People v. Washington, 363 Ill. App. 3d 13, 20, 842 N.E.2d 1193, 1199, 2006 Ill. App. LEXIS 24 (Ill. 2006).

[244]   State v. Stewart, 265 S.W.3d 309, 316, 2008 Mo. App. LEXIS 1098 (Mo. 2008).

[245]   *See* Lee v. Martinez, 136 N.M. 166, 2004 N.M. LEXIS 378 (N.M. 2004), for a list of states as of 2004 that refuse to admit polygraph testing results.

[246]   *Id*. Case offers a list of states admitting polygraph results upon stipulation.

test. The test results were admitted, but upon very unusual facts.[247] Georgia generally prohibits the admission of polygraph evidence, but Georgia courts will admit the results where the parties have stipulated in favor of admission.[248] Some states have statutes that provide for the admissibility of polygraph results by stipulation, while others accomplish this result by court decision.

The California Evidence Code provides that:

> Notwithstanding any other provision of law, the results of a polygraph examination, the opinion of a polygraph examiner, or any reference to an offer to take, failure to take, or taking of a polygraph examination, shall not be admitted into evidence in any criminal proceeding, including pretrial and post conviction motions and hearings, or in any trial or hearing of a juvenile for a criminal offense, whether heard in juvenile or adult court, unless all parties stipulate to the admission of such results.[249]

A California court held that the stipulation statute that withholds admission unless all parties agree, does not violate the defendant's constitutional rights where the defendant wanted polygraph results admitted at his trial but the prosecutor would not stipulate to admission.[250] The defendant unsuccessfully alleged that the statute violated his due process right to introduce relevant evidence and that the statute was unconstitutional.

§ 6.20 Summary

To save the time of the court and to achieve results that the courts and legislatures have determined are necessary in the administration of justice, presumptions and inferences are utilized. The presumption takes the place of evidence in certain instances and, until facts that overcome the presumption are shown, the presumptive facts are accepted as true.

Presumptions are classified as rebuttable presumptions and conclusive presumptions. A rebuttable presumption may be overcome by evidence to the contrary; a conclusive presumption cannot be rebutted.

There are many specific examples of both rebuttable and conclusive presumptions. Presumptions are used sparingly in criminal cases and are looked at very carefully by reviewing courts to determine whether they place an unreasonable burden on the accused. Some of the specific presumptions that are prevalent in criminal cases are: the presumption that a person is innocent until proven guilty beyond a reasonable doubt; the presumption that a person is sane; the presumption that a person in possession of recently stolen property

---

[247] State v. A.O., 2009 N.J. LEXIS 51 (N.J. 2009).
[248] Hortman v. State, 293 Ga. App. 803, 807, 2008 Ga. App. LEXIS 1082 (Ga. 2008).
[249] CAL. EVID. CODE 351.1 (2008).
[250] People v. Richardson, 77 Cal. Rptr. 3d 163, 221, 2008 Cal. LEXIS 6208 (Cal. 2008).

knows that the property was stolen; and the presumption that all people know the general public laws of the state and country in which they reside.

Legislative bodies are not without controls when determining what presumptions are effective in law. The due process clauses of the Fifth and Fourteenth Amendments set limits upon legislatures when making proof of one fact or a group of facts serve as proof of a deduced or presumed fact. There is the danger that a presumption may subtly shift the burden of proof in an unconstitutional manner. Particularly in recent years, statutory presumptions have been subject to review on the grounds that they are unconstitutional. A presumption that was arbitrary, irrational, or shifted the burden of proof would violate the due process clauses of the Constitution.

Another means of relieving the parties of the necessity of introducing evidence is the use of the stipulation. The stipulation, which should be used more often by the courts, indicates that the parties are willing to agree to the truth of certain allegations, leaving only the truly disputed facts to be determined by the jury or court.

It is a mistake for those involved in the criminal justice process to rely heavily on presumptions. Countervailing evidence may be offered when the presumption is in favor of the prosecution, and the prosecution must be prepared to reinforce the presumption. The prosecution must also be prepared to rebut presumptions that are favorable to the defense.

Although stipulations are excellent ways of assuring judicial economy, their improper use can lead to acquittal of guilty individuals and retrials for some. Many prosecutors have gone to trial unprepared because of misinterpretation of the effect of a stipulation. To avoid this pitfall, the investigator and prosecutor should be prepared with admissible evidence in the event that the opposing party disputes the fact that a stipulation was made, or if mistake or fraud is claimed.

General Admissibility Tests

Relevancy and
Materiality

7

There is a principle—not so much a rule of evidence as a presupposition involved in the very conception of a rational system, as contrasted with the old formal and mechanical systems—which forbids receiving anything irrelevant, not logically probative. ... The two leading principles should be brought into conspicuous relief, (1) that nothing is to be received which is not logically probative of some matter requiring to be proved; and (2) that everything which is thus probative should come in, unless a clear ground of policy or law excludes it.

THAYER, EVIDENCE (1898)

Chapter Outline

Section
7.1   Introduction
7.2   Relevancy and Materiality Defined
7.3   Admissibility of Relevant Evidence
7.4   Reasons for Exclusion of Relevant and Material Evidence
7.5   Relevancy of Particular Matters
7.6   —Identity of Persons
7.7   —Identity of Things
7.8   —Circumstances Preceding the Crime
7.9   —Subsequent Incriminating or Exculpatory Circumstances
7.10   —Defenses
7.11   —Character Evidence
7.12   —Proof of Other Crimes, Wrongs, or Acts
7.13   —Experimental and Scientific Evidence
7.14   Summary

§ 7.1 Introduction

This chapter and Chapter 8 focus on general admissibility tests (relevancy, materiality, and competency) for evidence that are applied by the courts when considering whether to admit or exclude evidence. This chapter concerns the concepts of general relevancy and materiality and their effect on admission and exclusion of evidence, while Chapter 8 explains competency of evidence and witnesses.

Because the primary objective and purpose in a criminal trial is to determine the truth regarding the issues presented, the general rule considers all evidence admissible unless, upon proper objection, it is subject to exclusion under the established evidence rules. In times past, the attorney offering an objection raised a general objection, contending that the proposed evidence was irrelevant, immaterial, incompetent, or not relevant. Better and more common practice suggests that the objecting party offer a specific objection such as a hearsay objection, an objection to a compound question, or an objection that a question assumes facts not yet in evidence, so that the judge has a clear basis for making a ruling. Unless the reason for the objection is obvious from the context, the judge may ask that the challenger offer a reason that supports the claim that the evidence should be excluded from trial consideration.

For those involved in the criminal justice process, it is important to understand these relevancy and materiality rules. In many instances, evidence that has been laboriously obtained and prepared for introduction is excluded because it does not meet the relevancy and materiality tests.

§ 7.2   Relevancy Defined

Rule 401

Definition of "Relevant Evidence"

"Relevant evidence" means evidence having any tendency to make the existence of any fact that is of consequence to the determination of the action more probable or less probable than it would be without the evidence.[1]

One way to analyze the concept of relevancy involves dividing it into two separate concepts: logical relevancy and legal relevancy. One Missouri court noted that "[e]vidence must be both logically and legally relevant to be admissible."[2] An item of evidence may meet the logical relevancy test if it sways the trier of fact concerning the existence or nonexistence of any important fact. As one court noted, "[e]ach piece of logically relevant evidence need not be a slam-dunk; it must only be evidence which makes a fact of consequence more probable than not."[3] Even though a proposed item of evidence is logically relevant, that item of evidence may be excluded where it lacks legal relevancy. For example, a series of gruesome color photographs might be logically relevant because they prove death or some other issue. When the fact of death has not been disputed, it is possible to contend that the introduction of photographs of the deceased person should be excluded because they may have the tendency to cause the jury to render a decision based on emotion rather than logic. Although most photos in this category are admitted, some cases will exclude some after a careful scrutiny by a trial judge. In this type of case, the photographs can be classified as logically relevant because they prove one or more issues in the case, but some of the photographs may be excluded as legally irrelevant because the photograph presents the unfair danger of inflaming the jury.[4]

In an older case, a Connecticut court clearly explained the connection between logical and legal relevancy when it stated:

> It is not logical relevance alone, however, that secures the admission of evidence. Logically relevant evidence must also be legally relevant . . . that is, not subject to exclusion for any one of the following prejudicial effects: (1) where the facts offered may unduly arouse the jury's emotions, hostility or sympathy, (2) where the proof and answering evidence it provokes may create a side issue that will unduly distract the jury from the main issues,

---

[1]   FED. R. EVID. 401.

[2]   Crow v. Crawford, 259 S.W.3d 10, 2008 Mo. App. LEXIS 666 (Mo. 2008) and Murrell v. State (In re Murrell), 215 S.W.3d 96, 2007 Mo. LEXIS 21 (Mo. 2007).

[3]   State v. Miller, 208 S.W.3d 284, 2006 Mo. App. LEXIS 1737 (Mo. 2006).

[4]   As a practical matter, gruesome photographs are often admitted. *See, e.g.,* State v. Bowman, 289 Conn. 809, 2008 Conn. LEXIS 565 (Conn. 2008). *See also* Franklin v. Bradshaw, 2009 U.S. Dist. LEXIS 23715 (W.D. Ohio 2009).

(3) where the evidence offered and the counterproof will consume an undue amount of time, and (4) where the defendant, having no reasonable ground to anticipate the evidence, is unfairly surprised and unprepared to meet it.[5]

As a general rule, logically relevant evidence may be excluded by a judge as legally irrelevant where "the probative value is substantially outweighed by the danger of unfair prejudice, confusion of the issues, or misleading the jury, or by considerations of undue delay, waste of time, or needless presentation of cumulative evidence."[6]

A. *Relevant Evidence*

Black's Law Dictionary defines relevant evidence as "[e]vidence tending to prove or disprove a matter in issue."[7]

Relevant evidence has also been described as "evidence that in some degree advances the inquiry, and thus has probative value and is prima facie admissible."[8]

In *Corpus Juris Secundum*, logical relevancy is defined as "the existence of such a relationship in logic between the fact of which evidence is offered and a fact in issue that the existence of the former renders probable or improbable the existence of the latter."[9]

A California case noted that the "[t]est of relevance is whether the evidence tends, logically, naturally, and by reasonable inference to establish material [important] facts such as identity, intent, or motive."[10]

Other definitions include:

- Evidence that is "relevant" will, by definition "prejudice" the other side.[11]

- Relevant evidence is evidence that has a logical tendency to aid the trier [of fact] in the determination of an issue.[12]

- The usual test for relevancy is whether the evidence offered renders a material fact . . . more probable than it would be without the evidence.[13]

- Relevant evidence is evidence having any tendency in reason to prove any material fact.[14]

---

[5] Connecticut v. Crnkovic, 68 Conn. App. 757, 793 A.2d 1139, 2002 Conn. App. LEXIS 159 (2002), quoting Connecticut v. Joly, 219 Conn. 234, 593 A.2d 96 (1991).

[6] FED. R. EVID. 403.

[7] BLACK'S LAW DICTIONARY (8th ed. 2004).

[8] MCCORMICK, LAW OF EVIDENCE 319.

[9] 31A C.J.S. *Evidence* § 198 (1996).

[10] People v. Wilson, 38 Cal. 4th 1237, 1245, 2006 Cal. LEXIS 8228 (Cal. 2006).

[11] United States v. Kapp, 2003 U.S. Dist. LEXIS 4178 (N.D. Ill. 2003).

[12] State v. Mungroo, 104 Conn. App. LEXIS 668, 2007 Conn. App. LEXIS 436 (Conn. 2007).

[13] State v. Kelly, 2009 Conn. Super. LEXIS 172 (Conn. 2009).

[14] Kansas Annotated Statutes, K.S.A. § 60–401 (2006).

In a evaluating the concept of relevancy, a Florida court did not abuse its discretion in excluding, as not relevant, evidence of the defendant's arrest and possession of a .22 caliber weapon eight months after the murder for which he was then on trial.[15] The crime scene evidence indicated that .25 and .380 caliber firearms were used in the murder and the other caliber firearm had nothing whatsoever to do with the murder prosecution. Simply stated, there was no probative evidence that a .22 caliber weapon was involved in the murder, indicating that the .22 caliber gun had no probative value. In a different case, discussing the definition of relevancy, the Court of Appeals for the Ninth Circuit held that the trial court had allowed irrelevant evidence to be admitted against a defendant in a case in which the defendant had been charged with interstate travel to have sexual relations with a minor. A police detective had been chatting with the defendant in an Internet chat room and the defendant agreed to meet the "police officer/child" in Las Vegas. The police arrested the defendant and discovered numerous stories of adults having sex with children, especially incest, on the defendant's PDA (personal digital assistant). The trial court admitted five of these stories against the defendant. On appeal, the Ninth Circuit held that the sex stories on the PDA were not relevant because the stories were not inextricably linked to the charged crimes and the stories were not part of the activity that led to the defendant's arrest.[16]

A trial court's decision concerning logical relevancy, and consequently admissibility or exclusion based on legal relevancy, falls under judicial discretion. The decision to admit or exclude evidence will not be disturbed on appeal absent proof of an abuse of the trial judge's discretion. In a Kentucky child sexual abuse case, the trial court properly admitted some evidence of the defendant's involvement with the minor children.[17] However, during the trial, witnesses for the prosecution were permitted to testify concerning the defendant's possession of marijuana and pornography, ownership of sex toys, and taking trips to strip clubs. In ordering a new trial, the reviewing court found that the evidence about the pornography and sex toys in the house, trips to the strip club, and marijuana use was not legally relevant to prove any issue in the case and that the evidence was improperly introduced for the purpose of showing bad character and failed to demonstrate any sexual intent toward the children and a new trial was warranted.

B. *Material Evidence*

Black's Law Dictionary defines material evidence as "[e]vidence having some logical connection with the facts of consequence or the issues."[18] Evidence that does not have a clear relationship to a matter at issue is immaterial.

---

[15]   Joyner v. State, 2009 Fla. App. LEXIS 1492 (Fla. 2009).

[16]   United States v. Curtin, 443 F.3d 1084, 1093, 2006 U.S. App. LEXIS 8071 (9th Cir. 2006).

[17]   Jenkins v. Commonwealth, 275 S.W.3d 226, 229, 2008 Ky. App. LEXIS 377 (Ky. 2008).

[18]   BLACK'S LAW DICTIONARY (8th ed. 2004).

Materiality concerns the importance of evidence. Evidence is material only when it significantly affects the matter or issue in a case. As one court noted, "[t]he concept of materiality does not relate to the weight of evidence. Rather, it involves the relationship between the proposition that the evidence is offered to prove the issues in the case.[19] The concept boils down to this question: Would the evidence offer a substantially important fact in this case to prove or disprove a charge against the defendant without being unfairly prejudicial to the defendant?

In describing material evidence, courts have noted that:

- Material evidence is evidence, fact, statement, or information that, if believed, would tend to influence or affect the issue under determination.[20]

- Material evidence is that which reasonably could be taken to put the whole case in such a different light as to undermine the confidence in the jury's verdict.[21]

- Material evidence may include evidence that is wholly impeaching if the result of the proceeding would have been different had the evidence been disclosed.[22]

Material evidence that would otherwise be considered relevant may lose its probative value when it becomes too far removed from the event in question. For example, the fact that a testifying defendant had a poor reputation for truthfulness 25 years ago may be excluded as not having any current probative value concerning his present reputation for honesty. The decision to exclude evidence due to its remote character is a matter left to the sound discretion of the trial judge.[23]

C. Materiality and Relevancy Distinguished

In making any meaningful distinction between materiality and relevancy, it must be noted that the two concepts have clear similarities, with both concepts being used to regulate the admission or exclusion of evidence. Material evidence must have a sufficiently close relationship to issues that need to be proved in the case, and evidence that is described as material must help prove or disprove one of these issues. In a similar manner, relevant evidence also must possess a close connection to facts or principles that need to be proved

[19]   In re Estate of Bean, 2005 Tenn. App. LEXIS 754 (Tenn. 2005).
[20]   United States v. Bonsu, 291 Fed. App. 505, 2008 U.S. App. LEXIS 17998 (4th Cir. 2008).
[21]   State v. Monda, 198 P.3d 784, 2009 Kan. App. LEXIS 28 (Kan. 2009).
[22]   State v. Macdonald, 122 Wash. App. 804, 810, 95 P.3d 1248, 1251, 2004 Wash. App. LEXIS 1859 (Wash. 2004).
[23]   People v. Owens, 183 P.3d 568, 574, 2007 Colo. App. LEXIS 884 (Colo. 2007).

or disproved by one party in the suit. Even though some fact or principle may need to be proved or disproved and meets the definition of relevancy, some evidence may be deemed too unfairly prejudicial to be admitted and will be excluded by the trial judge.

Although evidence may be relevant, it is not necessarily material.[24] For example, if a party wanted to impeach a defendant with proof of the defendant's poor reputation for truthfulness dating from 25 years ago when the defendant was attending college, the evidence might arguably meet a test for logical relevancy but could be arguably immaterial (legally irrelevant) because the evidence was so remote in time. If a proposition of fact is not required to be proved under applicable rules of substantive law governing a case, that evidence is not material (not logically relevant) under Rule 401 and should be excluded from admission to evidence. Evidence introduced solely to prove or disprove an inconsequential or collateral fact could be called immaterial and/or irrelevant and should be excluded.[25] Although evidence may be relevant because it relates to or has some bearing on the case, it may have such slight relevancy as to be labeled immaterial.

In making these fine distinctions between relevancy and materiality, it is important to note that in actual practice the distinction is not always clear and in most cases when the terms *material* or *immaterial* are used by attorneys and judges, the terms may be used interchangeably or linked with the terms *relevant* or *irrelevant*.[26]

§ 7.3   Admissibility of Relevant Evidence

Rule 402

**Relevant Evidence Generally Admissible;
Irrelevant Evidence Inadmissible**

All relevant evidence is admissible, except as otherwise provided by the Constitution of the United States, by Act of Congress, by these rules, or by other rules prescribed by the Supreme Court pursuant to statutory authority. Evidence which is not relevant is not admissible.[27]

According to Federal Rule of Evidence 402, all relevant evidence is admissible, but this rule is subject to a variety of exceptions and some evidence

---

[24]   Another way to say the same thing is to say that an item of evidence may be logically relevant but not legally relevant due to its risk of unfair prejudice to the opposing party.

[25]   *See* United States v. Goodson, 2009 U.S. App. LEXIS 6013 (4th Cir. 2009).

[26]   *See* United States v. Robinson, 2008 U.S. Dist. LEXIS 102689 (S.D. Fla. 2008) and State v. Stout, 2008 Mont. Dist. LEXIS 233 (Mont. 2008).

[27]   FED. R. EVID. 402.

that has logical relevance may still be excluded from introduction in court. If an item of evidence tends to prove or disprove any fact or principle that is at issue in the case, it will be admissible unless one of the parties makes an objection. If the proposed item of evidence is only barely logically relevant, the trial judge might exclude it when other evidence also proves or disproves the point with equal or greater emphasis. If the item of evidence does not possess logical relevance and has little or no chance of assisting the jury or the judge in determining an important fact that is at issue, it will be excluded from evidence. Similarly, when the admission of the evidence would create a risk of confusion of the issues or has the effect of wasting time, the judge, upon appropriate objection, will refuse to admit the evidence from consideration because it is deemed legally irrelevant.

All evidence that is logically and legally relevant is admissible, unless the constitution of the federal or a state government, a statute, or a rule of law excludes evidence for a specific reason. As the California Evidence Code provides, "All relevant evidence is admissible unless prohibited by statute."[28] If an objection is made to the admissibility of arguably relevant evidence, the burden is on the party making the objection to show that unfair prejudice occurred as a result of the admission.

An appellate court will review the admission of evidence based on considerations of whether the trial judge abused his or her discretion in admitting the evidence.[29] In undertaking a review of a trial court's decision on admission or exclusion, one federal court of appeals noted that the trial courts generally have broad discretion in admitting or excluding evidence and that appellate courts should be mindful that a trial judge has a much better position than an appellate court does to evaluate the probative value of evidence relative to potential unfair prejudice.[30] The reviewing court agreed that a trial court's decision concerning relevancy should stand unless a trial court's decision was arbitrary and irrational.

The Federal Rules of Evidence positively state that evidence should be admitted unless a specific rule or interpretation forbids the admission of the evidence. Many states have adopted variations of the federal evidence rules when formulating their own rules, but have adopted the rules with some modifications that reflect state considerations. For example, in the Utah Rules of Evidence, Rule 402 states that "[a]ll relevant evidence is admissible, except as otherwise provided by the Constitution of the United States or the Constitution of the state of Utah, statute, or by these rules, or by other rules applicable in courts of this state. Evidence which is not relevant is not admissible."[31] State interpretations of evidence rules, including variants of

---

[28]   CAL. EVID. CODE § 351 (Matthew Bender 2009).
[29]   State v. Baker, 287 Kan. 345, 363, 2008 Kan. LEXIS 694 (Kan. 2008).
[30]   United States v. Washington, 100 Fed. App. 39, 2004 U.S. App. LEXIS 11453 (2d Cir. 2004).
[31]   UTAH R. EVID. 402 (Matthew Bender 2008).

Rule 402, may have some local interpretations that vary somewhat from the federal interpretation.

When interpreting federal evidence provisions, recent decisions of federal courts have followed the reasoning that all evidence should be admissible unless it comes within one of the specific exceptions. In a prosecution for being a felon in possession of a firearm, a federal district court abused its discretion by finding an exception when it prevented the defendant, a member of a racial or ethnic minority group, from cross-examining a prosecution witness about the witness's swastika tattoos. The trial judge apparently considered the fact that the prosecution witness exhibited swastika tattoos as logically irrelevant on any matter before the court. The reviewing court viewed the situation differently and held that an inquiry into the tattoos was appropriate because it might indicate bias by the witness against the defendant that might affect the witness's credibility. Although the appellate court found that the exclusion of the evidence constituted harmless error, it held that the tattoo evidence should have been admissible under Rule 402.[32]

Although the federal rules contemplate admitting most evidence, when the collection of the evidence transgresses federal law and federal constitutional interpretations, the evidence, though otherwise legally and logically relevant, may be excluded. In a federal prosecution for armed bank robbery and other charges, United States marshals arrested a defendant but failed to take him in front of a United States magistrate for almost 30 hours following his arrest, in violation of the federal rules of criminal procedure.[33] During that period, the defendant offered a confession that the trial court admitted in evidence against him on the theory that a different federal law permitted admission. The Supreme Court of the United States reversed the conviction and rejected the prosecution's argument that Rule 402 should make evidence admissible despite other statutory and court interpretations that might allow or require exclusion.[34]

Evidence that helps establish elements of the crime or a defense is generally considered relevant and admissible unless excludable on some other theory. In a prosecution for possession of a firearm by a felon, when the defendant stated that he thought a .30 caliber rifle was a .177 caliber BB gun, the judge properly allowed the prosecutor to introduce BB gun ammunition and .30 caliber ammunition for the jury's inspection even though none of the ammunition had been taken from the defendant. In deciding that the ammunition had relevance, the court believed that the contrast in ammunition styles would make it more likely that the defendant's assertion that he thought the gun was a BB gun was not a truthful statement.[35]

---

[32]   United States v. Figueroa, 548 F.3d 222, 229, 2008 U.S. App. LEXIS 23697 (2d Cir. 2008). Affirmed as harmless error.

[33]   *See* FED. R. CRIM. P. 5.

[34]   Corley v. United States, 2009 U.S. LEXIS 2512 (2009).

[35]   United States v. Scott, 267 F.3d 729 (7th Cir. 2001).

§ 7.4   Reasons for Exclusion of Relevant and Material Evidence

> ### Rule 403
>
> ### Exclusion of Relevant Evidence on Grounds of Prejudice, Confusion, or Waste of Time
>
> Although relevant, evidence may be excluded if its probative value is substantially outweighed by the danger of unfair prejudice, confusion of the issues, or misleading the jury, or by considerations of undue delay, waste of time, or needless presentation of cumulative evidence.[36]

Although relevant evidence is generally admissible, there are some rules of exclusion. Evidence that may be described as logically relevant may be excluded as legally irrelevant when there is the danger of unfair prejudice, the admission of the evidence could confuse the issues being litigated, the jury could become confused by the evidence, or the presentation of the evidence would be unduly time-consuming or constitute a waste of time. The Federal Rules of Evidence enumerate and codify some of these exclusions, but the practitioner must look to the cases for explanations that apply to specific fact situations. Some of the reasons for excluding relevant evidence are discussed here.

A. *The Probative Value is Substantially Outweighed by the Danger of Unfair Prejudice*

Probative value concerns the tendency of an item of evidence to help prove or refute a disputed fact or principle that is at issue in a criminal case. Where the probative value of the evidence, though relevant, is of marginal value but is highly and unfairly prejudicial, the trial court should exclude the offered evidence so that the jury never hears it.[37] When a cause is tried to a judge, an objection to the admission of evidence must still be made and the judge must make a ruling, but the judge presumably will not consider any evidence that the judge rules as inadmissible due to the danger of unfair prejudice, even though the judge is aware of the evidence. An item of evidence may be logically relevant and would help prove or disprove a fact at issue and yet it still may be excluded from admission to evidence. When the probative value of offered evidence is outweighed by the danger of unfair prejudice or would tend to confuse the issues, mislead the jury, or unduly waste the time of the court by presentation of cumulative evidence, the evidence may be refused.[38]

---

[36]   FED. R. EVID. 403.

[37]   State v. Patel, 949 A.2d 401, 413 (R.I. 2008).

[38]   Culver v. State, 2008 Ala. Crim. App. LEXIS 107 (Ala. 2008).

The crucial aspect of evaluating prejudice involves "undue prejudice," because most relevant evidence offered by one party is designed to harm the merits of the opposing side's case. Under Rule 403, concern is directed only at prejudice that is unfair under the circumstances.[39] The concept of "undue prejudice" "applies to evidence which uniquely tends to evoke an emotional bias against the defendant as an individual and which has very little effect on the issues."[40]

In one Tennessee murder case, the trial court committed error when it permitted gruesome photographs of the deceased to be admitted at the capital sentencing proceeding for the purpose of demonstrating the presence of an aggravating factor. The reviewing court noted that the photographs were extremely unpleasant and gruesome in varying degrees in that they depicted the victim's body in a state of decomposition. The court held that the prejudicial value of the photographs outweighed the probative effect, but it did not overturn the sentence. The reviewing court viewed the photographic evidence as harmless error that did not affect the judgment of the jury because it did not sentence the defendant to death.[41] In another case, involving prosecution for possession of sexually explicit photographs of minors, the trial court erred in admitting two sexually explicit violent narratives involving rape and torture found on the defendant's computer. The probative value of the explicit literary narratives was outweighed by prejudicial effect because the defendant had been charged with possession of child pornography found on his computer; however, the pornographic pictures did not involve violence, but had illegal sexual content only.[42] In the Tennessee murder case and the child pornography case, the evidence was arguably logically relevant to each prosecution, but the unfair harm to each defendant's case outweighed the effect that the evidence could have presented.

In interpreting the unfair prejudice portion of Ohio Rule of Evidence 403, an Ohio court of appeals approved a trial judge's decision to admit evidence of the defendant's prior rape and murder conviction of his wife at his trial for conspiracy to commit murder of his wife's sister. Normally, a defendant's prior criminal acts would not be logically relevant to proof of a new crime or, if the prior acts were considered logically relevant, the prejudicial value would exclude the evidence. Allegedly, the defendant, who was in prison, wanted his wife's sister murdered in the exact same way that he had previously killed his wife, so that it would look as though he were not guilty of his wife's death. The trial judge admitted the prior crime evidence to show the defendant's motive and plan for engaging in the conspiracy to have the sister murdered. The reviewing court upheld allowing the prior crime evidence because it held that the probative value to help prove the conspiracy outweighed any unfair

---

[39]   United States v. Bennafield, 287 F.3d 320, 202 U.S. App. LEXIS 8009 (4th Cir. 2002), *cert. denied,* 537 U.S. 961, 2002 LEXIS 7487 (2002).

[40]   People v. Cotton, 2002 Cal. App. Unpub. LEXIS 421 (2002).

[41]   State v. Banks, 2004 Tenn. Crim. App. LEXIS 793 (2004).

[42]   United States v. Grimes, 244 F.3d 375 (5th Cir. 2001).

prejudicial effect on the defendant's case.[43] In a prosecution for aiding and abetting the distribution of crack cocaine, evidence of other related crimes was admitted after the judge conducted an on-the-record review of the case law, evaluated the probative value of the evidence, and weighed the potential prejudice to the defendant. A second federal court, in interpreting this provision, explained that in the context of the balancing test for exclusion of evidence whose probative value is outweighed by its prejudicial effect, "unfair prejudice" means the undue tendency to suggest a decision on an improper basis.[44]

Unfair prejudice, which may justify exclusion of otherwise probative evidence, speaks to the capacity of some concededly relevant evidence to lure the fact-finder into declaring guilt on different grounds from proofs specific to the offense charged. The critical issue is the degree of unfairness of the prejudicial evidence and whether it tends to support a decision on an improper basis.[45] In the federal prosecution of a leader of the Outlaws motorcycle gang, the government managed, over the defendant's objection, to have portions of the gang's constitution shown to the jury. The Outlaws' constitution mentioned that membership was open only to white men, an irrelevant fact that the defendant believed would create an unfair prejudice to his case in the minds of the jury. The federal court of appeals held that the probative value of allowing the jury to see racism of the gang's policies did not outweigh the clear danger of unfair prejudice. Despite the error, the conviction was not reversed, because under the circumstances of the case, the error was held to have been harmless.[46]

While the trial judge has broad authority in weighing the testimony's probative value against the possible prejudicial effect, his or her determination is subject to review by an appeals court. For example, the Ninth Circuit Court of Appeals held that where the evidence possesses very slight, if any, probative value, it is an abuse of discretion to admit it if there is even a modest likelihood of unfair prejudice or small risk of misleading the jury.[47]

B. Introduction of the Evidence Would Confuse the Issues

The right of any party to introduce evidence favorable to the position of that party that is logically relevant has been clearly established but the introduction of relevant evidence is not without limit and may be restricted or curtailed where the evidence could confuse the jury or might detract from the main issues of the case.[48] Because the introduction of confusing evidence may introduce unimportant side issues in a criminal case, a judge may exclude that

[43]   State v. Bloomfield, 2004 Ohio 749, 2004 Ohio App. LEXIS 692 (2004).
[44]   United States v. Sills, 120 F.3d 917 (8th Cir. 1997).
[45]   United States v. Payne, 119 F.3d 637 (8th Cir. 1997).
[46]   United States v. Bowman, 302 F.2d 1228, 1239, 1240, 2002 U.S. App. LEXIS 17165 (2002).
[47]   United States v. Hitt, 981 F.2d 422 (9th Cir. 1992).
[48]   Clark v. Arizona, 548 U.S. 735, 2006 U.S. LEXIS 5184 (2006).

evidence from a jury trial. However, an objection on the ground that evidence would be confusing would not normally be offered in a bench trial because the implication would be that the attorney seeks to prevent the judge from becoming confused, a suggestion that would not help the client's case.[49] Evidence of prior crimes by the accused is often inadmissible even though material and logically relevant, because such evidence would tend to confuse the issues by bringing up previous wrongdoing by the same defendant. Similarly, when a defendant wanted to introduce evidence in his methamphetamine possession trial that another man had been convicted of similar crimes arising out of the same underlying conduct for which the defendant was on trial, the trial judge refused to admit the evidence of the other man's difficulties with the law. The judge's theory was that the other evidence was not relevant and, even if it had been somewhat relevant, the other case evidence posed a danger of confusing the jury.[50] Trial and appellate courts attempt to ensure that evidence introduced at trial does not distract the jury from the case being tried or risk having the jury find guilt for the wrong reason. Consistent with Federal Rule 403 and similar state rules, evidence may have some logical relevance and still be excluded from a criminal trial.

When considering the "confusion of the issues" provision of Rule 403 in a burglary and aggravated assault case, a Texas court permitted a pretrial cellmate to testify that the defendant told him that the defendant would have been better off if he had just killed his ex-girlfriend victim. The defendant admitted he illegally entered the apartment because he entered through a window without her consent. On appeal, the defendant contended that the cellmate's evidence about how he should have killed her had the tendency to confuse or distract from the issues in the case and confuse the jury. In upholding the admission of the cellmate's testimony, the reviewing court noted that the evidence negated the defendant's contention of self-defense and shed light on his intent for being inside her home.[51] In a different case, a trial court improperly permitted the admission of evidence that the defendant, who was on trial for murder, had been convicted in a prior murder, even though the two cases had some connection.[52] A primary issue in the second trial involved whether the defendant had conspired with his half-brother to kill the victim in the second case. The appellate court's concern was the fear that the introduction of the evidence of the first murder case might cause the jury to blend the details of the first murder with the details in the second murder prosecution, thereby creating confusion.

---

[49]   People v. Rogelio, 2005 Cal. Unpub. LEXIS (Cal. 2005), in which the court noted, "The trial court observed that in a bench trial, factors such as the inflammatory nature of the crime, confusion of the issues, and the consumption of time involved in addressing the prior offenses were less significant than they would have been in a jury trial."

[50]   United States v. Darling, 238 Fed. App. 258, 2007 U.S. App. LEXIS 15650 (9th Cir. 2007).

[51]   Padilla v. State, 254 S.W.3d 585, 594, 2008 Tex. App. LEXIS 2719 (Tex. 2008).

[52]   State v. Pona, 948 A.2d 941, 2008 R.I. LEXIS 69 (R.I. 2008).

C. The Evidence Would Mislead the Jury

Where evidence might have the tendency to mislead the jury to an incorrect conclusion or decision, the trial judge should refuse to admit the evidence. For example, in an Arkansas prosecution for rape and sexual assault, the trial judge permitted the prosecution to introduce 1,022 pornographic images taken from the defendant's computer that were placed on a compact disc for the jury to consider.[53] According to the appellate court, the trial court should have weighed the probative value against the possibility of unfair prejudice and considered whether the photographs could mislead the jury in making a wrong decision. According to the reviewing court, the images depicted a wide range of pornographic materials beyond the charged offenses and their inflammatory nature of the images was readily apparent. While some of them were relevant in corroborating the complaining witness's allegations, the overall effect was, among other things, to mislead the jury.[54] In determining whether evidence would mislead the jury, in a federal felon in possession of a firearm case, the trial court refused to exclude evidence that the defendant shot and killed an alleged aggressor with the firearm that he allegedly illegally possessed.[55] Over the defendant's contention that the mention of the witness's death was irrelevant or might be confusing, the trial court determined that evidence of the deceased's death was probative because it offered a complete picture of the alleged offense and explained why the key witness was not testifying in the case.

However, in another case in which the possibility of the jury being misled by evidence seemed strong, the federal district judge properly prevented the prosecution from introducing prior acts of the defendant.[56] A defendant had been indicted for aggravated child sexual abuse and the prosecution wanted to introduce into evidence prior uncharged instances of sexual assault by the defendant. The dates and times and precise details were lacking or were not sufficiently specific for the admission of the evidence. In one situation, the alleged prior victim never reported the crime until much later and one woman reported the molestation of her sister. The third woman could not recall how many times the defendant molested her and there were some differences between the new charges and the older allegations. Following the philosophy of Rule 403 of the Federal Rules, the trial court considered how forcefully the prior acts had been proved and how important the prior evidence would be to the prosecution. Additionally, in making such an evaluation, the trial judge should consider how seriously the prior evidence is disputed and how much the prior evidence would distract the jury and how much time the prior act proof would consume. In this case, the trial judge determined that, although the evidence would be helpful, the risks that the jury might convict the defendant based on the

---

[53]   Blanchard v. State, 104 Ark. 31, 35, 2008 Ark. App. LEXIS 775 (Ark. 2008).

[54]   *Id.*

[55]   United States v. Williams, 2008 U.S. Dist. LEXIS 36623 (M.D. Fla. 2008).

[56]   United States v. Begay, 2009 U.S. App. LEXIS 2577 (10th Cir. 2009).

evidence of the prior allegations and the confusion that the introduction of the evidence of prior molestations might create, the evidence should have been excluded. The reviewing court upheld the trial determination and noted that it would only reverse if the trial judge had abused his discretion, which the court did not find.

D. *The Evidence Would Unduly Delay the Trial of the Case, Waste Time, or Needlessly Present Cumulative Evidence*

Evidence that might be relevant and could assist the jury in making a decision may still be excluded when a judge determines that admission of the evidence could cause a delay in the trial proceedings. The judge, at his or her discretion, may exclude relevant evidence if its admission unnecessarily wastes time or could be considered cumulative.[57] For example, in a mail and computer fraud case, the prosecution alleged that the defendant had committed the crimes while working for the government as a civilian computer specialist. One of the defendant's supervisors testified how the defendant's fraudulent schemes operated. In an effort to impeach the supervisor, the defendant wanted to cross-examine the supervisor concerning the supervisor's financial problems 10 years ago. At that time, the defendant had lent money to the supervisor, violating government policy. In an unpublished opinion, the reviewing court held that the exclusion of this line of cross-examination by the trial court was proper because the evidence would have been a waste of time even if it could have been somewhat relevant.[58] Against a defendant's argument under Rule 403 that the trial court had allowed the government to introduce cumulative evidence against him, the appellate court upheld the ruling of the trial judge. In a drug-selling prosecution, police had arrested a defendant after he threw a bag of cocaine out a window. Subsequently, police arrested him again for dropping a jar of rock cocaine out a window as police were entering the apartment. Later, the defendant was arrested a third time after police observed a known drug seller enter an apartment occupied by the defendant. At his trial for possession with intent to distribute 50 grams or more of cocaine base, he contended that bringing evidence of the first and third arrests for drug possession was improper because the government had more than sufficient evidence to prove the case and, therefore, the proof of the other crimes was unfairly prejudicial. The Court of Appeals for the Eighth Circuit held that the evidence was not improperly cumulative because the other crime evidence helped establish knowledge that he possessed cocaine base and that it tended to prove that he had the intent to distribute cocaine products.[59] In a criminal prosecution for, among other things, firearm and drug offenses, the defendant was permitted

---

[57]   People v. Brooks, 2008 Mich. App. LEXIS 1581 (Mich. 2008). Unpublished opinion.
[58]   United States v. Benjamin, 125 Fed. Appx. 438, 440, 2005 U.S. App. LEXIS 3943 (2005).
[59]   United States v. Gipson, 446 F.3d 828, 2006 U.S. App. LEXIS 11040 (2006).

to offer evidence of an alternative source for the firearm found where he was staying.[60] His theory was that another man was upset that the defendant was staying with a particular woman and such fact indicated that the firearm might have been accidentally left in the apartment or planted by the other man. The court prohibited the defendant from introducing evidence of the other man's prior arrests for firearm and crack possession. In upholding the trial court's limitation on introducing the other man's legal difficulties, the appellate court noted that cumulative or remote or speculative evidence may be excluded by the trial court under Rule 403 to avoid confusing or misleading the jury. Evidence is considered cumulative when it adds nothing to what the jury has already heard or adds to proof that does not need reproving. An Indiana appellate court noted that:

> Cumulative evidence is " '[a]dditional evidence that supports a fact established by the existing evidence (especially that which does not need further support).' " *Witte v. Mundy ex rel. Mundy*, 820 N.E.2d 128, 135 (Ind. 2005) (quoting *Black's Law Dictionary* 596 (8th ed. 2004)).[61]

Evidence that is not needed or would duplicate the existing evidence or would delay the trial needlessly or might confuse the jury may be excluded upon proper objection by the opposing counsel.

E. The Evidence Would Unfairly and Harmfully Surprise a Party Who Has Not Had Reasonable Opportunity to Anticipate That Such Evidence Would Be Offered

In the interests of fairness and due process, many courts will refuse to admit evidence where the opposing party had a duty and failed to give prior notice of an intention to introduce unanticipated evidence such as evidence of an affirmative defense.[62] Some courts advocate the exclusion of evidence if the opposing party is caught by unfair surprise. The reasoning behind this is that if the opponent has been unfairly surprised by unanticipated evidence and has received no warning or could not have logically anticipated that such evidence would be offered, then the evidence should be excluded, even though relevant. Confusion surrounding this rule has generated concern by many writers who suggest that the situation should be addressed by judicial instructions offered to the jury at the trial stage. In some jurisdictions, if an allegation of unfair surprise occurs, the complaining party must ask for a continuance or the objection concerning surprise is deemed to have been waived.[63]

---

[60]   United States v. Lucas, 499 F.3d 769, 2007 U.S. App. LEXIS 20076 (8th Cir. 2007).

[61]   Gaddie v. Manlief (In re H.R. M.), 864 N.E.2d 442, 2007 Ind. App. LEXIS 775 (Ind. 2007).

[62]   *See* Payne v. Tennessee, 501 U.S. 808 (1991) and Ransom v. State, 919 So. 2d 887, 888, 2005 Miss. LEXIS 595 (Miss. 2005), *cert. denied,* 2006 U.S. LEXIS 4985 (2006).

[63]   Burns v. State, 2005 Tex. App. LEXIS 1772 (Tex. 2005).

For example, in a case where the defendant had been charged with operating a motor vehicle without a license plate, the trial evidence demonstrated that the defendant had been towing a trailer that had no license plate. According to the reviewing court, a reversal of the conviction was necessary. Nothing in the accusation indicated that the defendant would have to defend against towing a trailer without a tag and it would subject the defendant to unfair surprise to allow the prosecution to introduce evidence to prove a crime that was allegedly committed in a completely different manner.[64] In a different case, in a murder trial, no unfair surprise occurred when the state introduced a 911 call that the defendant had made, and that the government had taped, in which he stated that he stabbed and killed the victim.[65] Because the defendant made the call and knew its content, admission of the 911 tape was within the sound discretion of the trial judge, despite the defendant's contention that he was unaware that 911 calls were routinely taped.

§ 7.5 Relevancy of Particular Matters

In previous sections of this chapter, the focus of the material centered on the general concepts relating to relevancy and materiality and how those concepts affected admission and exclusion of evidence. These rules apply in situations in which a party to a criminal action offers evidence for introduction. However, there are some particular instances in which not only the general rules apply, but also specific rules that relate to particular situations.

Evidence necessary to prove the essential elements of a case, as well as the preliminary facts, such as identity, jurisdiction of the court, and the mental condition of the accused, must generally be admitted under one legal theory or another. However, trial and appellate challenges to admissibility or exclusion frequently occur regarding character evidence, evidence of prior crimes, identification issues, scientific testing evidence, the use of real evidence (especially in criminal cases), and other particular matters; these are discussed in detail in the sections that follow.

Logically relevant evidence is sometimes excluded by rape shield laws that are designed to protect complaining witnesses from having prior or subsequent sexual history divulged in court and to encourage the reporting of sexual crimes. Legislatures in many states have made legislative determinations that inquiries into a victim's prior sexual history might be somewhat logically relevant but carry a significant danger of unfairly prejudicing and misleading a jury and should be deemed to be legally irrelevant or immaterial.[66] This is not to say that the prior history of a victim of a sexual assault can never

---

[64]   Younger v. State, 293 Ga. App. 20, 2008 Ga. App. LEXIS 898 (Ga. 2009).

[65]   People v. Nickson, 2006 Mich. App. LEXIS 2911 (Mich. 2006).

[66]   CAL. EVID. CODE § 1103 (Matthew Bender 2009).

be determined to be legally relevant or material, but a defendant must make a strong showing of both logical and legal relevance to have such evidence admitted. In a teenage rape prosecution, the Supreme Court of New Mexico upheld a lower court reversal of the conviction because the victim's prior sexual history gave a reason to doubt her story.[67] The defendant alleged that the victim gave consent for sexual activities while she told others a different story later. Her rather religious parents had previously punished the alleged victim for engaging in sexual activity with a different boy in the past. The defendant contended that she may have been lying to avoid punishment by her parents for a second episode of sexual activity, this time with the defendant. Her prior sexual history was deemed relevant to her bias and credibility, central issues in the case.

§ 7.6   — Identity of Persons

In order to ensure that the proper persons are tried and, if guilty, have appropriate sentences imposed, it is essential that those who are prosecuted in criminal cases be positively identified as the perpetrators. Therefore, courts allow a great deal of latitude in admitting evidence designed to prove identity, and appellate courts are reluctant to second-guess. A Georgia court noted that a pretrial photographic identification and a later identification at trial will only be set aside if the identification procedure was so impermissibly suggestive to give rise to the possibility of irreparable misidentification.[68] An Arkansas court noted that it would not reverse a trial court ruling on the admissibility "of an in-court identification, unless the ruling [was] clearly erroneous under the totality of the circumstances."[69]

When evaluating the admissibility of evidence to prove identity, the court must consider not only the relevancy test, but in some instances constitutional grounds, like due process violations or the lack of counsel at lineups, or other similar arguments. If the proposed evidence relates to the actual observation of the accused or others by the witness, the evidence is generally admissible. For example, the witness proposes to testify that, "I know the accused from high school. I saw him enter the bank with nothing and exit rapidly with some bags that had the bank's logo on them." This is relevant evidence and generally admissible. Other challenges may be in order, such as the credibility of the witness, but the testimony would probably not be challenged on constitutional grounds.

Identification may become more complicated when the witness did not know the person he or she saw at the crime scene, but indicates that he or she

---

[67]   144 N.M. 360, 2008 N.M. LEXIS 391 (2008).

[68]   Fuller v. State, 295 Ga. App. 349, 441, 2009 Ga. App. LEXIS 8 (Ga. 2009).

[69]   *See* Rodgers v. State, 2008 Ark. App. LEXIS 552 (Ark 2008).

could identify him at a lineup, a showup, a photographic array, or a PowerPoint presentation. Here the evidence must meet the relevancy test, but it may be challenged if law enforcement agents performed the pretrial identification procedure in an unduly suggestive manner that may have contaminated the in-court identification of the witness.[70] The witness may be testifying from his or her memory of the identification procedure and not the crime scene observation.

In a landmark case concerning eyewitness identification decided by the Supreme Court of the United States, *Neil v. Biggers*, the Court offered a test to determine whether an identification has been made accurately. The *Neil* five-factor totality of the circumstances test considered "the opportunity of the witness to view the criminal at the time of the crime, the witness' degree of attention, the accuracy of the witness' prior description of the criminal, the level of certainty demonstrated by the witness at the confrontation, and the length of time between the crime and the confrontation."[71] In the *Neil* case, the rape victim had been in close proximity to her attacker for a considerable length of time, had paid attention to his appearance, had given police an accurate prior description, had not misidentified any other person, was very certain of her identification, and the elapsed time since the crime had been about six months. She made her identification at a one-person "walk by" in the police station recognizing his voice. The *Neil* Court approved the identification process under the five-factor test, and held that the woman's identification of her attacker satisfied relevancy and due process standards when the totality of the circumstances test has been met.[72] In another case, a woman was properly permitted to identify her rapist following the rape, but the identification occurred on a public street immediately following the attack. When she ran for help following the rape, she encountered a man who helped find her clothing and called police. Subsequently, she observed her attacker leave the basement and enter another apartment. Her spontaneous identification was held to have been properly made, done without undue suggestiveness, and was accomplished without any police involvement.[73]

When a pretrial identification procedure has been unnecessarily suggestive in that it involved "steering" by police or lineups in which a suspect appeared in several successive lineups or photo arrays or was otherwise unfair, the identification evidence at the trial is not challenged with arguments concerning relevancy, but with the possible violation of due process.

---

[70]   *See* Neil v. Biggers, 409 U.S. 188, 1972 U.S. LEXIS 6 (1972) for five factors used to evaluate the accuracy of eyewitness identification. *See also* WALKER AND HEMMENS, LEGAL GUIDE FOR POLICE: CONSTITUTIONAL ISSUES (8th ed. 2008), Chapter 8, for a comprehensive discussion of pretrial identification procedures.

[71]   Neil v. Biggers, 409 U.S. 188, 199–200, 1972 U.S. LEXIS 6 (1972).

[72]   *Id.*

[73]   State v. McElroy, 29 Kan. App. 2d 990, 992–993, 35 P.3d 283, 286–287 (2001).

Is evidence of a suspect's past activities admissible to show identity, even though this may include evidence of other crimes? Evidence of a defendant's prior crimes or crimes subsequent to the one for which he or she is currently on trial may never be used solely for the purpose of suggesting that a defendant has a criminal disposition, but under certain circumstances it may be offered to prove other facts of consequence such as identity. In a Hawai'i case involving an armed robbery with the use of a baseball bat by two assailants, the trial court permitted the prosecution to introduce evidence that the defendant had pleaded guilty to a subsequent armed robbery while using a baseball bat under similar circumstances.[74] One of the issues in the case concerned the identity of the defendant wielding the baseball bat. The Intermediate Court of Appeals of Hawai'i approved of the admission of the conviction, but only where it could be linked to motive or plan. Many jurisdictions would have permitted the introduction of the other criminal conviction to show identity because the two crimes are so clearly similar and would not have required any other purpose for the evidence.

More than mere general similarity between factual situations being compared will be required to use a separate crime in order to show identity under the similar crimes theory of proving identity.[75] There must be identifiable points of similarity that pervade both fact situations and demonstrate significant similarity, and the points of similarity must have some special character or be so unusual as to point to the defendant's identity. In an unreported California case,[76] the defendant had robbed a Greyhound bus station attendant at gunpoint 20 years earlier, accompanied by a male companion. In the original robbery, one defendant ordered an employee into the back room, where a safe was located. According to the trial judge, the only difference in the current case was that the defendant now knew about the safe in the back room because he was one of the original robbers years earlier. Although the newest crime of robbery of the bus station attendants occurred more than two decades after the first one (the defendant definitely committed the earlier one because he pled no contest), the court permitted evidence of the earlier robbery case to be admitted for purposes of identification because it was almost identical to the one for which the defendant was currently on trial. The defendant had not been charged with robberies since the first one because he had spent 20 years in prison for the first robbery.

The results of scientific tests may be considered relevant in proving a defendant's identity. In a Colorado case,[77] evidence technicians recovered a semen sample from a sweatshirt and a headband that the female victim had *not* been wearing at the time of a sexual assault; the clothing was merely on her bed or in her bedroom. There was no DNA material deposited on the clothing worn

---

[74]   *See* State v. Yamada, 116 Haw. 422, 2007 Haw. App. LEXIS 663 (Haw. 2007).

[75]   Wimberly v. State, 2005 Ala. Crim. App. LEXIS 103 (2005).

[76]   People v. Hill, 2008 Cal. App. Unpub. LEXIS 3341 (Cal 2008).

[77]   See People v. Clark, 2009 Colo. App. LEXIS 365 (Colo. 2009).

by the victim. Investigators discovered a link between the defendant's DNA and the sample of the victim's unworn clothing because his DNA was on file due to prior criminal activity. The reviewing court held that the semen sample found on the victim's unworn clothing had no other logical source other than the defendant and such evidence was sufficient to prove his identity as the perpetrator of the sexual assault. Naturally, DNA testing must be conducted by properly trained technicians, according to accepted standards, and introduced in court by a qualified witness. When properly done, DNA test results offer circumstantial evidence that the defendant's identity has been properly established.[78]

§ 7.7   — Identity of Things

Subject to some exceptions, evidence that helps prove the identity of things or objects connected to a crime is generally considered relevant by a court. Items of personal property associated with a victim or a defendant may be relevant because they may have the effect of placing a particular person at a particular place or suggesting that property may have been used in a particular way. For example, for the purpose of identifying the accused as perpetrator of a double homicide and to support intent, evidence that the defendant possessed old coins that one of the deceased was known to collect and that other old coins remained at the crime scene, helped prove what the defendant had done and for what purpose.[79] In an unpublished California case in which the defendant denied that he was one of the robbers, he was found in possession of all the proceeds of the robbery while wearing the jacket and pants worn by the actual robber, and had the gun used to intimidate the robbery victims, the evidence was sufficient to establish his identity as the perpetrator.[80]

Other examples of relevant, tangible evidence against a defendant are found in the following cases: In a North Carolina capital murder case, the reviewing court held that blood found on the defendant's pants that he wore on the night of the homicide, which matched the blood type of the decedent, was properly admitted. In addition, the fact that evidence technicians recovered DNA evidence from the pants of the defendant that indicated that the decedent was the source of the DNA also helped tie the defendant to the crime scene and helped prove the government's case.[81] In an Ohio murder case, the trial court properly admitted evidence of a defendant's DNA found within bite marks on the homicide victim's body, which indicated that the defendant was present at or near the time of death.[82] Victim bite mark evidence that compares

---

[78] Commonwealth v. Gaynor, 443 Mass. 245, 266, 820 N.E.2d 233, 251, 2005 Mass. LEXIS 7 (2005).

[79] *See* People v. Zamudio, 43 Cal. 4th 327, 2008 Cal. LEXIS 4431 (Fla. 2008).

[80] People v. Wardell, 2005 Cal. App. Unpub. LEXIS 11539 (2005).

[81] Daughtry v. Polk, 2006 U.S. App. LEXIS 17962 (4th Cir. 2006).

[82] State v. Charley, 2007 Ohio 1108, 2007 Ohio App. LEXIS 1029 (Ohio 2007).

to a defendant's teeth impressions that is offered by qualified experts[83] has been admitted in many cases in which scientific, technical, or other specialized knowledge would assist the trier of fact. In a Texas murder case, where the deceased victim had five visible bite marks on her arm, the trial court permitted a forensic odontologist to compare the bite marks on the victim with impressions taken of the defendant's mouth. The forensic odontologist, who was qualified as an expert witness, offered the opinion within a reasonable medical certainty that the defendant made two of the five bite marks. Because the marks appeared to have been made about the time of death, such evidence was relevant to prove that the defendant was in close proximity to the victim.[84]

In a California case involving the possession of marijuana with intent to sell, a police officer detailed at trial that, in the defendant's motel room, the officer discovered a quantity of marijuana, a digital scale, approximately 35 small baggies that were often used to package controlled substances, and a radio scanner, among other items.[85] Because a firearm and ammunition were also discovered within the motel room, when taken together, all these items tended to indicate that the defendant was distributing in marijuana. In an Eighth Circuit case, the court approved the introduction of a prerecorded 20-dollar "bait" bill found on a defendant following a drug transaction. The appellate court upheld the introduction into evidence of scales used to weigh drugs found in the defendant's trailer home that was used to prove the defendant's intention to distribute 50 or more grams of cocaine. Police found pre-bagged rock cocaine in the home, a factor that also helped establish the intent to distribute cocaine base.[86]

§ 7.8 — Circumstances Preceding the Crime

A defendant's preparation, planning, and calculation undertaken prior to the alleged criminal act may be relevant in establishing criminal intent or other elements of the crime. Following a crime, efforts to escape detection or apprehension, if planned prior to the crime, may also have the effect of providing circumstantial evidence of a defendant's proper *mens rea*. The purchase of items necessary for the commission of the crime and arranging to arrive at the appropriate place at the proper time will be of interest to the prosecution. Similarly, any efforts to disguise the crime or the crime scene or destroy

---

[83] Meadows v. Commonwealth, 178 S.W.3d 527, 536, 2005 Ky. App. LEXIS 131 (2005). "Forensic dentists are experts on identifying persons based on unique characteristics of their teeth, which may include determining the identity of an unknown deceased person based on dental records, determining the age of a person based on his or her teeth, and determining who made a bite based on an analysis of the bite mark and the suspect's teeth."

[84] Villa v. State, 2008 Tex. App. LEXIS 1025 (Tex. 2008).

[85] People v. Ward, 2009 Cal. App. Unpub. LEXIS 1023 (Cal. 2009).

[86] United States v. Johnson, 439 F.3d 947, 955, 2006 U.S. App. LEXIS 6040 (8th Cir. 2006), *motion to vacate denied,* Johnson v. United States, 2009 U.S. Dist. LEXIS 8363 (E.D. Mo. 2009).

evidence, as well as efforts involving escape or escape of detection, may assist a prosecutor in proving a defendant's knowledge as an element of a crime. Conduct that is inconsistent with innocence and affirmative actions that tend to demonstrate a consciousness of guilt will normally be relevant and admissible against the accused. Witnesses may have observed the crime as it occurred and other witnesses may have overheard threats directed toward a victim. Other witnesses may have conveyed a firearm or sold the defendant items used in the commission of the crime. Evidence of circumstances preceding the crime may be derived from e-mail accounts, web sites, social networking sites, thumb drives, hard drives, cell phone data from cell carriers, and metadata from all these sources. Most of these types of evidence, whether they involve physical objects, human conduct, or oral evidence, should be considered relevant and generally admissible against an accused individual.

The best test of the relevance of testimony and evidence of antecedent circumstances is whether the evidence of prior planning or engaging in specific activities would help prove or disprove any element of the charged crime. If the evidence affects the probabilities, a court will generally consider that proof to be relevant evidence. In an unpublished California case, circumstances indicated that the defendant's wife wanted him to move out of her residence because the marriage was in disarray. The defendant procured a sharp knife from the kitchen and entered her bedroom, locking the door behind him after unplugging all the telephones in the apartment. The defendant's activities preceding his stabbing of his sleeping wife with the kitchen knife tended to indicate that he possessed the *mens rea* for attempted murder.[87]

Evidence of prior planning in a Florida capital murder case involved an attempted robbery of men who ran a check-cashing business.[88] Prior to the shooting, the felons had stolen two sport-utility vehicles that were to be used to "box in" the victims' car, which carried the large amount of cash. The defendants had previously scouted the schedule of the business owner with respect to his bank visits. A firefight between the armed businessmen and the armed felons erupted when the masked felons stopped the money car using the vehicles. The felons killed one of the occupants of the money car. Proof of the planning was sufficient to prove the intent necessary for the attempted robbery conviction which, in turn, supported the first-degree murder conviction under the felony-murder rule.

Activities that precede the crime may occur very briefly prior to the actual act and still be considered relevant evidence of planning the crime. In an unpublished Michigan case, evidence that preceded the crime of murder helped prove both premeditation and malice on the part of the defendant. In rejecting the defendant's appeal that the jury should have been instructed on manslaughter, the court noted that the defendant had a chance to reflect

---

[87] *See* People v. Huerta, 2008 Cal. App. Unpub. LEXIS 2827 (Cal. 2008).
[88] *See* San Martin v. State, 995 So. 2d 247, 2008 Fla. LEXIS 1460 (Fla. 2008).

or decide to control his passions after he obtained a kitchen knife during his walk to his girlfriend's bedroom. His acts of slashing her throat and windpipe demon strated that he had the intent to kill and had time during his walk to the bedroom to premeditate. His behavior helped prove two elements of the crime of first-degree murder.[89]

Evidence of prior difficulties between a defendant and the victim may be admissible in a murder case where it may help establish motive or one or more elements of the crime. Where the defendant had beaten his "off and on" girl-friend two weeks prior to her death, such circumstance could be admissible at his later murder trial.[90] A confrontation between the defendant and the victim a week prior to her death involved disagreements that led to the defendant jumping on the hood of the victim's car and refusing to leave. The defendant's prior behavior on the day of the murder, when he procured a butcher knife from his sister's kitchen, was also antecedent conduct that was admissible at his murder trial for stabbing his girlfriend.

The defendant may also introduce evidence of events preceding the crime. For example, a defendant in a manslaughter case may introduce evidence that the deceased entered defendant's real property, appeared drunk, and tossed the defendant around like a rag doll and threw the defendant to the ground. The defendant was permitted to introduce evidence that he followed the alleged victim away from his property to tell him to wait for the police. Evidence demonstrated that the alleged victim choked the defendant almost to unconsciousness after threatening to kill him before the defendant stabbed the victim twice with a knife, with fatal results to the alleged victim.[91] Prior conduct of an alleged victim may be relevant to a defendant's plea of self-defense as well as the alleged victim's reputation for violence if that evidence suggests that the alleged victim may have been the aggressor.

§ 7.9 — Subsequent Incriminating or Exculpatory Circumstances

Following suspicious activity, the actions or conduct of a suspect may assist in establishing a defense or may provide the prosecution with evidence that helps prove guilt. As one Kentucky court noted, the "common-law rule is based on the inference that the guilty run away but the innocent remain."[92] For example, evidence of flight, resisting arrest, concealment, assuming a false name, and criminal conduct during flight for the purpose of financing and accomplishing further flight is admissible in a criminal prosecution. An

---

[89]   People v. Benore, 2005 Mich. App. LEXIS 2718 (Mich. 2005).

[90]   *See* State v. Johnson, 284 Kan. 18, 2007 Kan. LEXIS 328 (Kan. 2007).

[91]   *See* Behanna v. State, 985 So. 2d 550, 2007 Fla. App. LEXIS 19318 (Fla. 2007), *review denied,* 988 So. 2d 622, 2008 Fla. LEXIS 1338 (Fla. 2008).

[92]   Rodriguez v. Commonwealth, 107 S.W.3d 215, 219, 2003 Ky. LEXIS 138 (Ky. 2003).

Ohio court of appeals held that no error occurred when the trial court allowed the introduction of evidence of defendant's use of a false name to law enforcement officers. Additionally, with approval, the court referenced an earlier case that noted, "[i]t is today universally conceded that the fact of an accused's flight, escape from custody, resistance to arrest, concealment, assumption of a false name, and related conduct, are admissible as evidence of consciousness of guilt, and thus of guilt itself."[93] While flight and other such conduct do not raise a legal presumption of guilt, the jury may consider these circumstances together with other facts in evidence and give the evidence the weight it thinks the evidence deserves, given the facts presented.[94]

According to the Supreme Court, when an individual sees police officers and flees immediately, such conduct may be relevant to criminality and deserves some investigation by police to determine whether the flight reflected a consciousness of guilt.[95] As then-Chief Justice Rehnquist noted, "Headlong flight—wherever it occurs—is the consummate act of evasion: it is not necessarily indicative of wrongdoing, but it is certainly suggestive of such."[96] As a general rule, unexplained flight can be admissible as evidence to infer consciousness of guilt, according to a Connecticut court. In a case in which an accused fled to Puerto Rico within three or four days following the victim's allegations against him for sexual abuse and before police could interview him, evidence of flight was properly admitted. The defendant testified in his own defense but he offered no rebuttal explanation of why he needed to go to Puerto Rico at that specific time and why he remained there for six years.[97]

There are limitations on the weight of such evidence. In a very old case, the United States Supreme Court in *Hickory v. United States*[98] set aside a conviction because the trial judge had charged the jury that flight created a presumption of guilt. The Court concluded that flight and concealment "are mere circumstances to be considered and weighed in connection with other proof with that caution and circumspection which their inconclusiveness when standing alone require."[99] Flight following a criminal act constitutes a type of circumstantial evidence of consciousness of guilt, but its probative value usually depends on all of the surrounding facts and circumstances. The inference of consciousness of guilt upon flight has been subject to considerable judicial criticism on the ground that common experience does not always support the

---

[93]   State v. Stribling, 2009 Ohio 1444, 2009 Ohio App. LEXIS 1240, citing State v. Eaton, 19 Ohio St.2d 145, 150, 2, 1969 Ohio LEXIS 348 (Ohio 1969), citing 2 WIGMORE, EVIDENCE (3 Ed.) 111, Section 276.

[94]   Connecticut v. Beverly, 72 Conn. App. 91, 104, 805 A.2d 95, 104 (2002).

[95]   Illinois v. Wardlow, 528 U.S. 119 (2000).

[96]   *Id.* at 124.

[97]   State v. Gonzalez, 272 Conn. 515, 530, 864 A.2d 847, 857, 2005 Conn. LEXIS 20 (Conn. 2005).

[98]   160 U.S. 408, 16 S. Ct. 327, 40 L. Ed. 474 (1896).

[99]   *Id.* at 417.

assumption. In recognition of this concept and consistent with the *Hickory* case above, one court charged the jury that "the government bore the burden of showing that the appellant had intentionally fled and that flight does not create a presumption of guilt but, to the contrary, may be completely consistent with innocence."[100] Essentially it was up to the jury to make the determination of what inference, if any, to draw from proof of flight.

The length of time between the crime and the flight may have a bearing on both the admissibility and the weight of the flight evidence. Where a defendant in a murder case fled from police at a traffic stop seven days after the crime, the court held that evidence of consciousness of guilt could still exist and was not too remote in time to be properly associated with the crimes of murder and kidnapping. Defendant's explanation of flight seven days after the crime was held to go to the weight of flight evidence rather than its admissibility.[101]

When evidence of flight has been introduced in a case, the judge normally will assist the jury in evaluating the importance to give evidence of flight by offering a jury instruction. In California, in any case where there is evidence of flight, the judge must instruct the jury that flight following a crime is never sufficient to prove guilt, but is only a factor the jury may consider in light of all the other evidence in a case. The jury is additionally told that the flight does not require a person to reach any particular place, just indicate a purpose to avoid being seen or arrested. It is completely up to the jury to consider what weight to give flight evidence.[102]

In further amplification of jury instructions regarding flight, in a federal prosecution for having a firearm under a disability, in *United States v. Webster*, the trial court permitted the prosecution to introduce evidence that when the defendant was ordered to stop his car for a seatbelt violation, he sped away in an attempt to elude the officer. When the police viewed the interior of the car, they found a bag of marijuana and a semiautomatic pistol. The judge charged the jury that:

> You may also consider any evidence of flight by the defendant, along with all of the evidence in the case, and you may consider whether this evidence shows a consciousness of guilt and determine the significance to be attached to any such conduct.
>
> Whether or not evidence of flight shows a consciousness of guilt and the significance to be attached to any such evidence are matters exclusively within the province of the jury. In your consideration of the evidence of flight you should consider that there may be reasons for this which are fully consistent with innocence.[103]

---

[100] United States v. Benedetti, 433 F.3d 111, 116, 2005 U.S. App. LEXIS 28490 (1st Cir. 2005).

[101] United States v. Young, 2003 U.S. App. LEXIS 7432 (8th Cir. 2003).

[102] Connecticut v. Crnkovic, 68 Conn. App. 757, 766–767, 793 A.2d 1139, 1147, 2002 Conn. App. LEXIS 159 (2002).

[103] United States v. Webster, 442 F.3d 1065, 1067, 2006 U.S. App. LEXIS 8061 (8th Cir. 2006).

The Eighth Circuit Court of Appeals approved the jury instruction because it allowed the jury either to infer or not concerning whether the defendant had a consciousness of guilt after it considered the defendant's explanation offering an innocent reason for flight.[104]

If flight may indicate an inference of guilt, engaging in a standoff with a SWAT team after being cornered and disposal of a murder weapon following flight, may also indicate a desire not to face arrest and trial due to a consciousness of guilt. Against an argument that the evidence should not have been admitted against the defendant, a California reviewing court concluded that "the [trial] court did not abuse its discretion in allowing the evidence of [the defendant's] SWAT standoff as probative of his consciousness of guilt."[105]

Just as evidence of escape may be admitted to allow a jury to consider whether an inference of consciousness of guilt should be drawn,[106] a suicide attempt may be a form of avoidance of responsibility and should be admissible for any weight a jury might want to give it. In a case involving an allegation of rape of a 15-year-old girl by the man she considered her father, the defendant apparently attempted to kill himself with an overdose of drugs on several occasions after his arrest on the charges.[107] The trial judge allowed the evidence of attempted suicide by drug overdose to be admitted for whatever value the jury might see fit to give the evidence. The Arkansas reviewing court upheld the admission of the overdose evidence with the comment, "we cannot say that the circuit court erred in permitting testimony regarding [the defendant's] overdose attempts. In light of the case law from other jurisdictions, as well as our holdings regarding flight, refusal to submit to testing, and escape from incarceration, we cannot say that the circuit court abused its discretion."[108] Attempts by a defendant to intimidate or threaten witnesses can be evidence of consciousness of guilt. In a New York robbery case, the trial court permitted police officers to testify concerning the defendant's threatening hand gestures toward witnesses during trial. According to the reviewing court, "[e]vidence of threats made by defendant to witnesses may be "probative of defendant's consciousness of guilt" and thus may be admissible on that ground."[109]

In some instances, comments made by the defendant following custody for a crime are admissible. Demonstrative of this point is the case in which the defendant possessed an awareness of guilt as evidenced by his words to a television reporter during his transport from a sheriff's office to a county jail. When asked whether the defendant had been attempting to commit a robbery when the alleged victim was shot, the defendant replied, "No comment." The reviewing court approved the introduction of the defendant's answer because

---

[104]   *Id.*

[105]   People v. Garcia, 168 Cal. App. 4th 261, 292, 2008 Cal. App. LEXIS 2050 (Cal. 2008).

[106]   Bigby v. Dretke, 402 F.3d 551, 557, 2005 U.S. App. LEXIS 3815 (5th Cir. 2005).

[107]   Strong v. State, 372 Ark. 404, 416, 2008 Ark. LEXIS 112 (Ark. 2008).

[108]   *Id* at 416, 417.

[109]   People v. Lee, 868 N.Y.S.2d 453, 456, 2008 N.Y. App. Div. LEXIS 8768 (N.Y. 2008).

it was not asked by police and the defendant's comments were freely offered. Post-arrest silence following the giving of *Miranda* warnings cannot be used against a defendant because the defendant may simply exercising the rights that the warnings cover.[110] In a situation that was the opposite of speech, a North Dakota appellate court noted that "a prosecutor's use of a defendant's post-arrest silence after receiving *Miranda* warnings to impeach a defendant's exculpatory story, told for the first time at trial, violates the defendant's right to due process."[111]

Other instances in which courts have considered the activities of the suspect following the crime are: (1) the assumption of a false name after the commission of a crime; (2) the suspect's giving of a false statement; (3) concealment of evidence; and (4) growing a moustache or beard. In a Connecticut case, *State v. Pascal*, the defendant offered a false name and a false date of birth to police. These deceptions were admitted and the jury was permitted to place whatever probative value that it deemed proper on the falsities. Despite the defendant's contention that the admission of the evidence was improper, the reviewing court upheld the convictions that resulted.[112] In one bank robbery case, the accused gained weight after his arrest, shaved his beard, and began to wear glasses in an apparent effort at frustrating courtroom identification by tellers. The court charged the jury that it could consider the defendant's change of appearance to indicate a fear of being identified by tellers and that the change could help prove consciousness of guilt,[113] but it was up to the jurors to determine how much weight to give the evidence.

§ 7.10 — Defenses

While relevancy is the requirement for admitting evidence against a defendant, the same standards generally apply when the defense wants to negate or rebut the prosecution's case. Although a criminal defendant need not introduce any evidence in order to prevail, most defendants attempt to challenge the prosecution's evidence with proof that attempts to rebut the prosecution's case. A defense in a criminal case may involve presenting evidence through defense witnesses or by cross-examining prosecution witnesses, or from a combination of the two. Alternatively, a defendant may choose to present evidence of an affirmative defense, such as alibi, entrapment, self-defense, or insanity, and on these generally, the defendant has the burden of proof in many jurisdictions. As a general rule, defense evidence must meet the

---

[110] State v. Butler, 2008 N.C. App. LEXIS 1645 (N.C. 2008).

[111] State v. Rivet, 2008 ND 145, 2008 N.D. LEXIS 144 (N.D. 2008).

[112] State v. Pascal, 109 Conn. App. 45, 72, 2008 Conn. App. LEXIS 352 (Conn. 2008).

[113] United States v. Carr, 362 U.S. App. D.C. 303, 373 F.3d 1350, 1353, 2004 U.S. App. LEXIS 14305 (D.C. Cir. 2004). Post-conviction relief denied at United States v. Carr, 2006 U.S. Dist. LEXIS 6368 (D.D.C. 2006).

same tests for relevancy and materiality as the prosecution's evidence. Such evidence is usually admissible if it meets general admissibility tests, but there may be additional requirements in some situations. Several commonly offered defenses are discussed here.[114]

A. *Insanity*

A defendant may have a defense of lack of mental capacity if he or she can prove that at the time of the criminal act, he or she was too mentally deficient to be held responsible for the act. Additionally, in a situation in which the defendant is unable to assist the defense attorney in preparing and presenting a defense, the evidence may show that the defendant is not competent to stand trial. In both cases the defendant's mental condition becomes relevant. Evidence that proves the defendant met or failed to meet the jurisdiction's test for legal insanity will be relevant and admissible to either prove or disprove the mental condition of the defendant. In many jurisdictions, the insanity defense is considered an affirmative defense and the burden of proof is placed on the defendant. The defendant may have to introduce evidence that proves insanity beyond a reasonable doubt or by clear and convincing evidence. The second issue concerning mental health occurs at the time of trial and requires that the defendant possess sufficient mental competency to meaningfully assist and communicate with his or her attorney in presenting a defense.

The concept of legal insanity is recognized as a defense in most jurisdictions, while temporary insanity is recognized as a defense in some jurisdictions. Some jurisdictions allow a verdict of guilty but insane or guilty except for insanity.[115] Arizona recently restricted the insanity defense under the traditional *M'Naghten* rule by removing the part of the test that addressed cognitive capacity and leaving the basic "right-wrong" part of the test.[116] Although not a favored defense, some states recognize the concept of temporary insanity that may have arisen from the chemical effects of drugs or alcohol and will permit evidence in court to prove this defense.[117] Some states recognize a type of temporary insanity caused by voluntary intoxication but use it in

---

[114] See POLLOCK, CRIMINAL LAW (9th Ed. 2009) for a discussion of defenses in criminal cases. *And see* Abbe Smith, *Promoting Justice through Interdisciplinary Teaching, Practice, and Scholarship: The Difference in Criminal Defense and the Difference it Makes,* 11 WASH. U. J.L. & POLICY 83 (2003). *See also* Daniel S. Medwed, *Actual Innocents: Considerations in Selecting Cases for a New Innocence Project,* 81 NEB. L. REV. 1097 (2003).

[115] *See* 720 ILCS 5/6-2 (Il. 2009). *See also* OR. REV. STAT. §§ 161.319, 161.295 (2007).

[116] *See* Clark v. Arizona, 548 U.S. 735, 2006 U.S. LEXIS 5184 (2006).

[117] People v. Washington, 2009 Mich. App. LEXIS 308 (Mich. 2009). *See* § 3.11 of this book for a discussion of the burden of proving sanity. *See also* 18 U.S.C.S. § 17 (Matthew Bender 2008), Insanity Defense, for the text of the insanity defense available in federal criminal trials.

mitigation of the penalty attached to the offense for which the defendant has been convicted.[118] States that do not recognize temporary insanity may allow evidence of the condition to be used as mitigating factors that can be asserted during a capital or other sentencing proceeding.[119] As a general rule, to qualify for the defense of temporary insanity based on alcohol consumption, there must be some evidence to show that the insanity was caused by intoxication and a judge commits error if the judge offers a jury instruction in the absence of evidence of voluntary intoxication.[120]

B. *Voluntary Intoxication*

Intoxication is a voluntary insanity, and, as a general rule, a defendant's own conduct in becoming intoxicated will not excuse that individual from criminal responsibility. The Texas Code is representative of most jurisdictions when it states "[v]oluntary intoxication does not constitute a defense to the commission of crime."[121] It is generally accepted that a defendant's voluntary intoxication is neither an excuse for the commission of crime, nor a defense to a prosecution for it,[122] but may provide some mitigation of the penalty.[123] This general rule of the common law is contained in the statutes of many states and exists by judicial decision in the federal courts, but some state and federal jurisdictions recognize limited exceptions.

An exception to the general rule exists in some jurisdictions when a defendant has been accused of a crime that involves some specific intent or requires the operation of a more complicated mental process such as deliberation or premeditation. If the evidence discloses that a defendant was extremely intoxicated to the point that the correct *mens rea* could not be formed, some jurisdictions will take the lack of a specific intent into consideration either as demonstrating that a particular crime has not been committed or will use intoxication as a mitigating factor. For example, in Alabama, voluntary intoxication may be a defense in a battery case where the intoxication amounts to insanity and incapacitates a person to the extent that he or she cannot form the proper intent.[124]

Not all jurisdictions agree that voluntary intoxication may operate as a mitigator or as a partial defense. In Arizona, the statute states that "[t]emporary

---

[118] TEX. PENAL CODE § 8.04 (2009).

[119] Williams v. State, 273 S.W.3d 200, 2008 Tex. Crim. App. LEXIS 692 (Tex. 2008). See also TEX. PENAL CODE § 8.04(b) (2009).

[120] Sakil v. State, 2008 Tex. App. LEXIS 4230 (Tex. 2008).

[121] TEX. PENAL CODE § 8.04 (a) (2009).

[122] Leppla v. State, 277 Ga. App. 804, 811, 627 S.E.2d 794, 800, 2006 Ga. App. LEXIS 75 (Ga. 2006).

[123] TEX. PENAL CODE § 8.04 (b) (2009).

[124] Saunders v. Alabama, 2007 Ala. Crim. App. LEXIS 236 (Ala. 2007).

intoxication resulting from the voluntary ingestion, consumption, inhalation or injection of alcohol, an illegal substance . . . or other psychoactive substances or the abuse of prescribed medications does not constitute insanity and is not a defense for any criminal act or requisite state of mind."[125] In a Florida case,[126] a defendant failed to win a reversal of his murder conviction because the reviewing court found that his intoxication, although based partly on prescription medication, involved consumption far beyond the prescribed dosages and involved significant consumption of alcoholic beverages and was characterized as voluntary intoxication. Florida law provides that "[v]oluntary intoxication resulting from the consumption, injection, or other use of alcohol or other controlled substance . . . is not a defense to any offense proscribed by law."[127] The statute also refuses to consider what effect voluntary intoxication might have on *mens rea* or any required intent. Taking a similar approach, an Ohio reviewing court refused to reverse a vandalism conviction where the intoxicated defendant used a bulldozer to smash the windshield and the hood of a police cruiser.[128] The defendant was heavily intoxicated (.244 on a Breathalyzer test) on alcohol, but could operate the bulldozer and had control over it. The state's law did not take into consideration what effect intoxication might have on a required mental state. The approach demonstrated by these two examples is consistent with the position of the Supreme Court of the United States under its holding that a state can prohibit a criminal defendant from offering evidence of voluntary intoxication to negate the requisite *mens rea* without violating the due process clause of the Fourteenth Amendment.[129]

Where intoxication is recognized as a defense to a specific intent crime, the result may not always be acquittal, but rather conviction of a lesser degree of the offense for which no proof of specific intent is necessary. In a prosecution for aggravated sodomy by a drunk defendant, the reviewing court noted that the crime involved a specific intent and that a conviction could not stand unless there was proof of the proper intent.[130] The court upheld the conviction on the strength that the jury could have found the presence of a specific intent.

C. Other Defenses

Evidence of other affirmative defenses may be relevant if introduced for the purpose of establishing defenses such as entrapment, alibi, self-defense, defense of others, mistake of fact, mistake of law, lack of knowledge sufficient to commit the crime, and others. The evidence to support these defenses must meet the other tests of admissibility in addition to the relevancy and materiality tests.

---

[125]   Ariz. Rev. Stat. § 13-503 (2008). Effect of alcohol or drug use.

[126]   Stimus v. State, 995 So. 2d 1149, 1151, 2008 Fla. App. LEXIS 18376 (Fla. 2008).

[127]   FLA. STAT. § 775.051 (2009).

[128]   State v. Armstrong, 2007 Ohio 6405, 2007 Ohio App. LEXIS 5609 (Ohio 2007).

[129]   Montana v. Egelhoff, 518 U.S. 37, 56, 1996 U.S. LEXIS 3878 (1996).

[130]   State v. Langholz, 2009 Kan. App. LEXIS 60 (Kan. 2009). Unpublished opinion.

§ 7.11 — Character Evidence

Rule 404

**Character Evidence Not Admissible to Prove Conduct;
Exceptions; Other Crimes**

(a) Character evidence generally. Evidence of a person's character or a trait of character is not admissible for the purpose of proving action in conformity therewith on a particular occasion, except:

(1) Character of accused. In a criminal case, evidence of a pertinent trait of character offered by an accused, or by the prosecution to rebut the same; * * *.

(2) Character of victim. In a criminal case, * * * evidence of a pertinent trait of character of the alleged victim of the crime offered by an accused, or by the prosecution to rebut the same, or evidence of a character trait of peacefulness of the victim offered by the prosecution in a homicide case to rebut evidence that the victim was the first aggressor; * * *.

(3) Character of witness. Evidence of the character of a witness, as provided in rules 607, 608, and 609.[131]

* * *

The character of a defendant should assist a jury or judge in making determinations about a defendant. In ordinary social and business situations, people make judgments about others based on character, a trait of character, or reputation. This approach works quite well in ordinary human affairs where money or relationships may be involved. However, when evaluating whether someone might be guilty of a crime, reliance on character evidence could mislead a finder of fact into making an erroneous decision that affects the freedom of the accused. Merely because a person has a bad reputation for a particular character trait does not necessarily mean that he or she always follows that trait or that he or she followed the trait on a particular occasion. Clearly, a good reputation should not be used to assist a defendant when a jury might ignore some evidence and acquit due to proof of a good reputation. Alternatively, justice might not be served if we partially substitute character for more demanding and more reliable evidence of criminality. If the state were permitted to prove that a person's character is bad, it could be contended that this fact would have some slight probative value in determining whether that person actually committed the charged offense. The reputation of an accused for a particular character trait arguably might be relevant, but the jury might use the reputation for that trait to convict in a close case where, in the absence of the evidence, it would have acquitted. As is sometimes stated in legal circles, proof of character might prove too much and the jury might convict to punish the defendant

---

[131] FED. R. EVID. 404.

for his bad character rather than the issues presented at trial. In order to protect the accused from the possibility of conviction based on bad character, a general rule has evolved that evidence showing the bad character of the accused is usually not admitted.

Federal Rule 404(a) codifies the common law rule that evidence that tends only to show a propensity to act in a particular manner or shows evidence of a criminal defendant's general bad character or a witness's good character is not admissible.[132] This basic prohibition is often called the "propensity" rule. Under this rule and under the general evidence provisions, a person's character or propensity to act in a certain way may not be offered as a basis for the inference that on a specific occasion a person acted in conformity with the propensity or the character trait. The prosecution may not use evidence of a negative character trait of a defendant to show that the defendant may have a propensity to commit the crime for which the defendant is currently on trial.[133] While the text of Federal Rule 404(a) generally excludes character evidence of the defendant or of a victim, the rule recognizes exceptions where the defendant offers evidence of personal character.[134]

While the prosecution cannot introduce evidence of the bad character of the accused during its case-in-chief, the courts apply a different rule when the criminal defendant places his or her character at issue by introducing evidence in support of good character. Because a jury might give a defendant with good character the benefit of the doubt in a close case, he or she has the opportunity to introduce evidence of general good character to show that it was improbable that he or she committed the charged crime. If a defendant introduces evidence of good character by inquiring of a witness concerning the witness's knowledge of the defendant's good reputation in the community, the defense has "opened the door" to the issue of character and the prosecution may inquire into the matter using the same type of evidence.[135]

Where the defense offers evidence of good general character, the prosecutor may offer evidence that disputes the good character evidence. Therefore, if a defendant asks a witness during cross-examination if she was aware of the defendant's reputation in the community, the prosecution may ask about specific instances of the defendant's misconduct to test the witness's credibility.[136] A prosecutor may inquire about a defendant's character only after a defendant places it at issue. It was error for a South Carolina trial court to permit an inquiry into some of the defendant's prior difficulties with the legal system after the defendant testified that he hated to see a woman cry.[137] Such testimony permitted an inquiry concerning defendant's prior crimes involving

---

[132] State v. Buie, 671 S.E.2d 351, 353, 2009 N.C. App. LEXIS 48 (N.C. 2009).

[133] Ohio v. Bronner, 2002 Ohio 4248; 2002 Ohio App. LEXIS 4413 (2002).

[134] *See* 24 TEX. JUR. *Criminal Law* § 3468 (2008) and FED. R. EVID. 404(b).

[135] State v. Braswell, 2008 Tenn. Crim. App. LEXIS 43 (Tenn. 2008). *See also* FED. R. EVID. 405(a).

[136] *Id.*

[137] State v. Young, 378 S.C. 101, 106, 2008 S.C. LEXIS 153 (S.C. 2008).

dishonesty as impeachment, but did not "open the door" to permit inquiry concerning criminal domestic violence and criminal sexual conduct, identical crimes for which he was currently on trial.

Even when the defendant has not "opened the door" to his or her character and the prosecution improperly reveals to the jury that the defendant had a prior felony conviction, any resulting conviction will not automatically be reversed. If there is overwhelming evidence of guilt or if the judge issues an immediate curative jury instruction, the conviction will not be disturbed based solely on a violation of erroneous admission of character evidence against an accused.[138]

While the prosecution generally cannot introduce adverse character evidence about the defendant during its case-in-chief, a defendant may bring forth relevant evidence of the alleged victim's character for a particular trait. Federal Rule 404 generally excludes character evidence from admission, but provides an exception for "evidence of a pertinent trait of character of the victim of the crime offered by an accused."[139] For example, when a defendant wife claimed self-defense in a domestic homicide case, the trial judge refused to allow her to introduce evidence that her deceased husband had a reputation as a violent and dangerous man. On appeal, the defendant contended that the trial court erred when it prevented her from introducing proof that her husband had a violent character. Specifically, the court excluded evidence that the victim-husband, who was previously angry at a car dealership, broke several windows of cars held as inventory on the dealer's lot. In self-defense cases, the victim's violent character becomes relevant only to the extent that it relates to the defendant's fear of harm from the victim. The reviewing court granted the defendant a new trial because the trial court should have allowed the introduction of evidence of the victim's violent character, including specific instances of violence, because it was clearly relevant to the issue of self-defense.[140]

The character of the ordinary witness—one who is not accused, including the victim—can also be shown by evidence if it bears upon the case. As a general rule, every person who testifies as a witness places his or her character for truthfulness at issue. If a defendant testifies, the credibility of the defendant becomes relevant and subject to impeachment. As in the case of other types of character evidence, once the door is opened, the other side may introduce evidence to rebut the evidence introduced by the first party.

The reason a defendant can always introduce evidence good general character is that such evidence may be sufficient to create reasonable doubt concerning whether a defendant is guilty of the crime charged. The defendant is permitted to present evidence that he or she possesses a positive general reputation, but the defendant cannot introduce evidence that is irrelevant to general reputation. For example, a trial judge properly excluded a defendant's offer,

---

[138] Nickleson v. State, 2005 Tex. App. LEXIS 6658 (2005).
[139] FED. R. EVID. 404(a)(1).
[140] State v. Everett, 630 S.E.2d 703, 2006 N.C. App. LEXIS 1302 (2006).

through his witnesses, to prove that he was an honest person when the defendant had not taken the witness stand and the case involved a murder prosecution.[141]

In referring to Alaska's version of Federal Rule 404(a)(1), a state trial court noted that the accused in a criminal case has an option to introduce evidence of his or her good character by personal testimony or through other defense witnesses, but the prosecution may meet the evidence of defendant's good general character with proof of specific incidents that have the effect of rebutting the defendant's evidence.[142] In the case involving sexual abuse of girls, the defendant had testified that he had a benevolent nonsexual attitude toward children and had been employed as a counselor to teenagers who had been victims of sexual abuse. The trial court properly allowed the Alaska prosecutor to introduce evidence that the defendant had made sexual comments about 10- to 14-year-old girls as rebuttal evidence.[143] Every defendant who testifies places his or her credibility at issue and is subject to efforts to impeach like any other testifying witness, but merely testifying does not place at issue all other sorts of character traits or the defendant's general reputation.[144]

§ 7.12 — Proof of Other Crimes, Wrongs, or Acts

Rule 404

Character Evidence not Admissible to Prove Conduct; Exceptions; Other Crimes

* * *

(b) Other crimes, wrongs, or acts.

Evidence of other crimes, wrongs, or acts is not admissible to prove the character of a person in order to show action in conformity therewith. It may, however, be admissible for other purposes, such as proof of motive, opportunity, intent, preparation, plan, knowledge, identity, or absence of mistake or accident, provided that upon request by the accused, the prosecution in a criminal case shall provide reasonable notice in advance of trial, or during trial if the court excuses pretrial notice on good cause shown, of the general nature of any such evidence it intends to introduce at trial.[145]

* * *

Federal Rule 404(b) in essence restates the general rule that evidence of other crimes, wrongs, or acts may not be admissible to prove the character

---

141   Marschke v. State, 185 S.W.3d 295, 307, 2006 Mo. App. LEXIS 280 (2006).

142   Bryant v. State, 115 P.3d 1249, 1253, 2005 Alaska   App. LEXIS 62 (2005).

143   *Id.* at 1254.

144   Gage v. State, 2005 Tex. App. LEXIS 531 (2005).

145   Fed. R. Evid. 404(b).

of a person in order to show action and conformity therewith. It may, however, be admissible against a defendant for other purposes, such as proof of motive, opportunity, intent, preparation, plan, knowledge, identity, or absence of mistake or accident.[146] Federal Rule 404(b) was amended in 1991 to provide for a notice requirement to criminal defendants where use of character evidence was contemplated.

When a trial court is faced with deciding whether to admit prior acts against a defendant currently on trial, the judge must make sure that the prior acts are not admitted to prove that the defendant has a predisposition to commit the charged crime or that the evidence proves the defendant is a bad person. In a District of Columbia prosecution against a defendant who had been selling counterfeit compact discs, the prosecution wanted to prove that the defendant knew that the discs were counterfeit. The jewel cases that contained the discs had a thin piece of paper inside that indicated the artist for each disc and the jewel cases were wrapped in plastic wrap. Because the defendant had previously been convicted of selling compact discs without a vending license from the district under circumstances in which it was clear that he knew the compact discs were counterfeit, the prosecution wanted to admit the prior offense. The reviewing court noted that evidence of prior acts and crimes was presumptively inadmissible due to the danger of unfair prejudice, but in this case the court approved the admission of prior crime evidence because it tended to show that the defendant had knowledge that the compact discs were counterfeit.[147] The two crimes were so similar in many aspects that proof of one tended to prove the other.

As a general rule, evidence of prior misconduct is inadmissible as part of the evidence to suggest that the defendant might be guilty of a crime for which the defendant is presently standing trial. In a case in which a minor adopted child had accused her father of sexual offenses, it was error to permit allegations by the defendant's adult daughters from a prior marriage that, 30 years ago, the defendant had sexually abused them by touching them inappropriately. In reversing the convictions, the reviewing court noted that "[e]vidence is legally relevant if its probative value outweighs its costs."[148] In this case, the earlier allegations took place too long ago and allegedly involved only touching, while in the present prosecution the allegation involved statutory rape and sodomy. To be admissible, evidence of prior uncharged sexual activities must be nearly identical to the crime charged in the current case and so unusual that the prior acts operate as a virtual signature of the defendant's method of committing the crime. The prejudicial value of the prior 30-year-old uncharged acts outweighed any probative effect in the present case, so the appellate court reversed the convictions.[149]

---

[146] Idaho v. Siegel, 137 Idaho 538, 541, 50 P.3d 1033, 1036, 2002 Idaho App. LEXIS 30 (2002).
[147] Jackson v. United States, 856 A.2d 1111, 1114, 2004 D.C. App. LEXIS 413 (D.D.C. 2004). *See* case in Part II.
[148] State v. Berwald, 186 S.W.3d 349, 359, 2005 Mo. App. LEXIS 1917 (2005).
[149] *Id.*

Evidence of other crimes or prior misconduct by the defendant is generally not admissible to prove that a defendant is guilty of a crime for which he or she is currently on trial. Where an exception to this general rule applies, the evidence of prior crimes may be admissible if the evidence demonstrates a defendant's knowledge sufficient to commit the crime, common scheme or plan, motive, intent, or lack of mistake. In an Arkansas case[150] in which the defendant had been accused of selling methamphetamine to an undercover officer, the trial court permitted the prosecution to admit evidence that he had made a similar sale to an undercover officer 10 days prior to the date of the sale for which he was on trial. The defendant's identity was not at issue and the sale was a routine sale of methamphetamine. According to the defendant, none of the reasons for admitting prior crimes supported admission in his case and if the prior sale evidence were relevant, he contended that the prejudicial value outweighed the probative effect. The Supreme Court of Arkansas reversed the defendant's drug sale conviction because it could not perceive a valid reason for admitting that prior drug sale other than to show that he was a drug dealer likely to have sold drugs on the particular day for which he was being tried. Over a dissenting opinion, the court noted, "[t]his is precisely the type of evidence that Rule 404(b) was designed to exclude."[151] It should be stressed that many courts would take a different view and would hold that the crimes are so similar that the earlier crime evidence should have been admitted under a common scheme or plan exception.

When the prosecution introduces evidence of other crimes, wrongs, or acts committed by the defendant under Rule 404(b) or the state equivalent, the burden of proof of the fact of the prior act must be clear and convincing[152] and have a logically relevant connection to the crime for which the defendant is on trial. For example, in a North Carolina case[153] where the defendant had been charged with selling methamphetamine to a police officer working undercover, he alleged that proof of two prior sales to the same officer were erroneously introduced by the prosecution. The defendant argued that the sales were far apart and not necessarily related. One sale occurred six days prior to the date of the sale for which he was on trial and one occurred 10 months prior to the other sale. In upholding the trial court's admission of prior bad acts, the reviewing court noted that in this case the sales were made to an undercover female officer, the sale occurred in the same neighborhood as the other sales, the defendant was identified as the seller, and all three sales were made by a man standing on the street to the officer sitting in a car and the quantity of methamphetamine was the same, as was the price. The court noted, "[i]n sum, after careful review, we hold that the trial court did not abuse its discretion by admitting the challenged evidence under Rule 404(b) for the limited purpose of showing defendant's intent, identity, and common plan or scheme."[154]

---

[150]   Phavixay v. State, 373 Ark. 168, 2008 Ark. LEXIS 234 (Ark. 2008).

[151]   *Id*. at 171.

[152]   State v. Stokes, 673 S.E.2d 434, 2009 S.C. LEXIS 35 (S.C. 2009).

[153]   State v. Welch, 666 S.E.2d 826, 829, 830, 2008 N.C. App. LEXIS 1741 (N.C. 2008).

[154]   *Id*. at 831.

In determining whether a trial court properly admitted evidence of other acts under Rule 404(b), the United States Court of Appeals for the Tenth Circuit considers four factors: "(1) whether the evidence is offered for a proper purpose, (2) whether the evidence is relevant, (3) whether the probative value of the evidence is substantially outweighed by its prejudicial effect, and (4) whether a limiting instruction is given if the defendant so requests."[155] The Court of Appeals for the Fifth Circuit employs a slightly different test for admissibility of other act evidence, but overall a similar result will emerge. According to the Fifth Circuit, it employs a two-pronged analysis for the admissibility of evidence under Rule 404(b). First, the evidence of "other crimes, wrongs, or acts" must be relevant to an issue other than the defendant's character[156] and, second, the other crimes or acts evidence must possess probative value that is not outweighed by the danger of unfair prejudice to the defendant.[157] An example of a state test for other act evidence is demonstrated by Idaho, where its courts follow a two-pronged test in determining whether to admit the evidence.[158] The court first asks whether there is a sufficient level of evidence to establish the fact of the prior act and then the court must determine relevance to a disputed issue in the crime for which the defendant is presently being charged. In all of these tests for prior act admission or exclusion, the courts are attempting to screen out earlier crimes and acts that, in all fairness, should not be admitted against a defendant in an unrelated trial while allowing admission of prior acts that have sufficient relevance to the current case.

In 1988, in *Huddleston v. United States*, the Supreme Court was asked to clarify the application of Rule 404(b).[159] In this case, the petitioner had been charged under federal law with knowledge of the possession and sale of stolen videotapes. At the trial, the district court allowed the government to introduce, as evidence of "similar acts" under Rule 404(b), evidence of the petitioner's involvement in a series of sales of allegedly stolen televisions and appliances from the same suspicious source as the tapes. On appeal, the defendant conceded that "similar acts" evidence was admissible to show his knowledge that the tapes had been stolen, but he argued that the grave potential of "similar acts" evidence for causing undue prejudice calls for a preliminary determination by the court that the defendant committed such acts before the jury should be allowed to hear that evidence. In a footnote to that case, the Supreme Court noted that there was inconsistency in the circuit courts, because six circuits apparently required a preliminary finding of the trial court that the government has proven commission of the similar act.

The United States Supreme Court then decided that the evidence of the prior acts was properly admitted by the trial court. According to the Court, there is no need for a preliminary finding by the trial court that the government

---

[155] United States v. Parker, 553 F.3d 1309, 1314, 2009 U.S. App. LEXIS 359 (10th Cir. 2009).
[156] United States v. Percel, 553 F.3d 903, 912, 2008 U.S. App. LEXIS 26428 (5th Cir. 2008).
[157] *Id.*
[158] State v. Palmer, 2009 Ida. App. LEXIS 17 (Ida. 2009).
[159] Huddleston v. United States, 485 U.S. 681, 108 S. Ct. 1496, 96 L. Ed. 2d 771 (1988).

has proven the commission of the similar acts and that such a requirement is inconsistent with the legislative history behind Rule 404(b). In referring to the relevancy issue, the court included this statement:

> Evidence is admissible under Rule 404(b) only if it is relevant. "Relevancy is not an inherent characteristic of any item of evidence but exists only as a relation between an item of evidence and a matter properly provable in the case." In Rule 404(b) context, similar act evidence is relevant only if the jury can reasonably conclude that the act occurred and that the defendant was the actor.[160]

Many states have adopted rules that are either identical or fairly similar to Federal Rule 404. Each year, cases that interpret these rules reach state reviewing courts. Some of these decisions, which state the rules of the respective states and explain the reasoning of the courts in applying the rules, are included in Part II of this book.

The philosophy underlying the general rule excluding evidence of other crimes or other bad acts committed by the accused "is meant to prevent the State from punishing people for their character."[161] If most prior misconduct is allowed into evidence, its admission "endangers the defendant of being convicted because he or she is a person of bad character generally, or has criminal tendencies.[162]

Applying the general rules relating to other acts evidence, the Supreme Court of Rhode Island reversed a defendant's second murder conviction because the trial court admitted evidence that the defendant had been convicted of murder in a prior case.[163] At the second murder trial, the judge permitted mention of the fact that some of defendant's property, a pager, and fingerprints related to the first murder conviction, which inescapably led the second jury to conclude that the defendant had committed an earlier murder. While there was some connection between the two murder cases, the primary effect of the introduction of the evidence from the first murder was to brand the defendant as a murderer who might have a propensity for criminal activity or, in particular, murder. The other crime evidence introduced at the second trial deprived the defendant of a fair trial.

However, prior crimes and misconduct may be excluded when the connection to the charged crime is largely irrelevant and unfairly prejudicial. In an Indiana case in which the victim, wearing brass knuckles, initiated a fight with the defendant, who used a knife to puncture the victim's heart, the defendant objected to the use of prior act evidence at his homicide trial. The trial judge permitted the prosecutor to introduce evidence that the defendant used marijuana, had rolling papers, had Xanax and alcohol in his blood, and had

---

[160] *Id.*
[161] Bassett v. State, 795 N,E.2d 1050, 1053, 2003 Ind. LEXIS 750 (2003).
[162] Samaniego-Hernandez v. State, 839 N.E.2d 798, 802, 2005 Ind. App. LEXIS 2450 (2005).
[163] State v. Pona, 948 A.2d 941, 2008 R.I. LEXIS 69 (R.I. 2008).

indicated that he wanted to cut another man's throat at a different time. In reversing the homicide conviction, the appellate court held that the other crime and misconduct evidence was not properly admitted to show the defendant's state of mind or to refute self-defense. The other evidence involved different people and occurred at different times from the fatal altercation and had the effect of unfairly showing that the defendant had a criminal propensity and may have engaged in the illegal conduct.[164]

§ 7.13 — Experimental and Scientific Evidence

While the progress of science and its application to crime-solving in the criminal justice field cannot be overemphasized, the concepts involving relevancy require additional attention to assure the admission of scientific results. Scientific evidence that is excluded from trial does not assist the party seeking to introduce it. The most prominent recent development in science that has positively influenced criminal justice professionals involves variations of DNA testing for identification purposes. The professionals conducting criminal investigations must be aware of the rules regarding the care, custody, and admissibility of scientific evidence and evidence resulting from experiments. This includes tests covering such evidence as weapons and ammunition identification, fingerprints, DNA collection and care protocols, photographs, motion pictures, X-rays, tape recordings, maps, drawings, blood-alcohol tests, and results from computer hard drive examinations. Collection of evidence using specialized tracking software to gather data from the Internet and the use and interpretation of metadata from e-mail and web sites has become necessary in some investigations. Without proper understanding of the processes, such evidence may not be properly secured for introduction in court. While most experiments and scientific test results will be conducted by experts and introduced in court by expert witnesses, in some situations, specially trained technicians who may not precisely fit the traditional definition of "expert" may present the evidence in court. These types of evidence will be discussed more thoroughly in other chapters under specific headings, especially in Chapter 14, Real Evidence.

When properly conducted, the admissibility of all scientific or technical evidence should be a foregone conclusion because the results contain no bias and only reveal truth. The contention could be made that the introduction of scientific evidence should always be admissible because of relevancy in criminal cases. Each scientific result must meet individual tests of logical and legal relevancy prior to being considered for admission and the expert witness must be qualified as an expert. The trial judge, in the exercise of discretion, may exclude some scientific evidence to avoid possible unfair prejudice

---

[164]   Gillespie v. State, 832 N.E.2d 1112, 1117, 2005 Ind. App. LEXIS 1505 (2005).

to the accused. Moreover, the court may impose a limit on the prosecution's demonstrations to avoid procedures that may unduly arouse, mislead, or confuse the jury. The admission or exclusion of scientific or technical evidence rests with the trial judge, whose decision will not be disturbed by an appellate court unless it finds a clear abuse of discretion.

As a preliminary matter concerning the admissibility of the results of scientific tests or experiments, the trial court must determine whether the results will meet the tests for relevancy. According to Federal Rule of Evidence 702, "[i]f scientific, technical, or other specialized knowledge will assist the trier of fact to understand the evidence or to determine a fact in issue, a witness qualified as an expert by knowledge, skill, experience, training, or education, may testify thereto in the form of an opinion or otherwise." The burden of proving admissibility of evidence under Rule 702 is placed on the party offering evidence by the standard of clear and convincing evidence.[165] As a general rule, before scientific evidence is admitted, the party seeking to introduce the evidence must lay a foundation for the evidence by introducing proof that "[1.] the underlying theory is generally accepted as valid; [2.] the procedures used are generally accepted as reliable if performed properly; [and] [3.] the procedures were applied and conducted properly in the present instance."[166]

After reviewing the *Frye* test[167] for admissibility for scientific evidence as established in previous cases, the United States Supreme Court in 1993 reconsidered whether the *Frye* test had continued usefulness in federal courts. Under the *Frye v. United States* standard,[168] courts required that a scientific principle and its related tests had gained "general acceptance" in the particular scientific or technical field before a court should consider admitting the results. The *Frye* standard gradually gained acceptance in federal and many state jurisdictions. The adoption of the Federal Rules of Evidence brought some challenges to the *Frye* standard, and in *Daubert v. Merrell Dow Pharmaceuticals*,[169] the Supreme Court determined that *Frye* should no longer be followed in federal courts.

Daubert established the following nonexclusive list of factors to guide lower federal courts in assessing the reliability of scientific evidence:

1. Whether a scientific theory or technique can be (or has been) tested;
2. Whether the theory or technique has been subjected to peer review or publication;
3. The known or potential rate of error and the existence and maintenance of standards controlling the technique's operation;
4. Whether the technique is generally accepted. (But it is not an absolutely necessary precondition to the admissibility of scientific evidence.)

---

[165] Frankenfield v. State, 2008 Tex. App. LEXIS 7920 (Tex. 2008).

[166] State v. Escobido-Ortiz, 109 Haw. 359, 367, 126 P.3d 402, 410, 2005 Haw. App. LEXIS 520 (2005).

[167] Frye v. United States, 54 D.C. App. 46, 293 F. 1013, 1923 U.S. App. LEXIS 1712 (1923).

[168] Id.

[169] Daubert v. Merrell Dow Pharmaceuticals, Inc., 509 U.S. 579, 1993 U.S. LEXIS 4408 (1993).

The Court in *Daubert* emphasized that the inquiry in determining the reliability of scientific evidence is flexible and should focus on the principles and methodology offered as evidence. Where the evidence would assist the finder of fact and has sufficient reliability, the evidence should be admitted, even under circumstances when the *Frye* test would have excluded the scientific evidence.[170] In effect, following the *Daubert* rule, judges serve a "gate-keeping" role and must determine whether the expert's proffered testimony of scientific, technical, or other specialized knowledge will help the trier of fact to understand or determine a fact or principle at issue.[171]

§ 7.14 Summary

In a criminal trial, the primary objective is to determine the truth as to the issues presented. Over the years, the courts have developed rules of exclusion, including rules concerning relevancy and materiality. If the evidence does not meet the tests of relevancy and materiality, it will not be admitted. Evidence that has even a slight tendency to prove or disprove a pertinent fact in issue will be considered relevant, but some relevant evidence may be excluded if its tendency to prove or disprove a fact at issue is unfairly prejudicial. Evidence that goes to substantial matters in dispute and has an effective influence or bearing on the decision of the case is material.

The trial court has great latitude in determining the admissibility of the evidence and whether it has legal relevancy or materiality. The court's interpretation as to what evidence is relevant is usually given great weight, and its determination will be final unless there is a clear abuse of discretion.

State constitutions and the federal constitution, along with state and federal court decisions and relevant statutes, must be considered in determining what evidence meets the relevancy and materiality tests. The following general rules have been developed through this procedure:

- Evidence that tends to establish the identity of persons involved is admissible as being relevant and material. This, of course, is subject to the other rules of admissibility.

- Evidence that concerns the identity of things connected with the crime is considered relevant, although there are some exceptions.

- Evidence that helps prove or disprove elements of the crime will be considered relevant and material.

- Generally, evidence that relates to the circumstances and events that precede or follow the crime is admissible as relevant to the issues.

---

[170] *See* Chapter 15 for a comprehensive discussion of the admissibility of the results of examinations and tests.

[171] Burton v. CSX Transportation, 269 S.W.3d 1, 2008 Ky. LEXIS 236 (Ky. 2008).

- Evidence relating to the defenses claimed by the defendant, such as mental disease, coercion, self-defense, and alibi is generally admissible if it meets the other admissibility tests in addition to the relevancy and materiality tests.

- Although evidence regarding the character and reputation of the accused, as well as other evidence concerning the commission of other crimes, is sometimes recognized as relevant and material, it is often excluded because of overriding dangers of unfair prejudice to the defendant's case. For this reason, only certain evidence of this type is admissible.

- Evidence of other crimes, wrongs, or acts is not admissible to show criminal propensity, but may be admissible to show the existence of a continuing or common plan, scheme, motive, intent, identity, lack of mistake, lack of knowledge, or conspiracy of which the crime charged is a part.

- Evidence concerning experimental and scientific evidence is also usually considered relevant, but it must pass other tests before it can be admitted into court.

It is obvious that even though the parties may succeed in excluding evidence that is irrelevant and immaterial, there is certainly no reciprocal assurance that evidence that is relevant and material necessarily will be admitted. In future chapters, some of the other requirements will be discussed, and relevancy and materiality as they relate to specific types of evidence will be explored in more detail.

Competency of Evidence and Witnesses

8

The terms "relevancy," "competency," and "materiality" are frequently used conjunctively in such manner as to suggest that they are synonymous, yet it is obvious upon second thought that a matter which may be relevant to an issue of the case may be rendered incompetent and inadmissible as to the established rules of evidence, such as the rule which excludes hearsay evidence or requires the production of the best evidence. ... In other words evidence must be not only logically relevant, but of such a character as to be receivable in courts of justice.

20 Am. Jur. Evidence 253

Chapter Outline

Section
8.1   Introduction
8.2   Definitions
8.3   General Categories of Incompetent Evidence
8.4   Competency of Evidence—Documentary Evidence
8.5   —Tests and Experiments
8.6   —Conduct of Trained Dogs
8.7   —Telephone Conversations
8.8   Negative Evidence as Competent Evidence
8.9   Evidence Competent for Some Purposes but Not for Others
8.10   Competency of Witnesses
8.11   —Mental Incapacity
8.12   —Children
8.13   —Husband and Wife
8.14   —Conviction of Crime
8.15   —Religious Belief
8.16   Competency of Judge as Witness
8.17   Competency of Juror as Witness
8.18   Summary

Key Terms and Concepts

competency of evidence   negative evidence
competency of witnesses

§ 8.1   Introduction

While the preceding chapters discussed some of the rules concerning relevancy and materiality, the focus of this chapter involves competency of both witnesses and evidence. Even when evidence has been deemed to be relevant and material or logically relevant and legally relevant, it still must cross the third hurdle of competency before it can be considered admissible. Evidence is inadmissible if it is incompetent, but evidence may be admissible when it is competent[1] and when it meets the standards of relevancy and materiality.[2]

Evidence that is competent, relevant, and material is admissible. The application of the rules concerning competency of evidence and witnesses has troubled courts, judges, and attorneys with its complexity, and for that reason, many writers and even some legal encyclopedias fail to adequately explain the competency restrictions. Therefore, this chapter will consider the rules relating not only to the competency of witnesses, but also to the competency of evidence. The fact that a witness meets the threshold of competency to testify does not necessarily mean that the evidence that the witness may offer meets the standard of competency. Similarly, evidence may meet the tests of relevancy, materiality, and competency, but the witness who wishes to offer the evidence may not be competent as a witness.[3]

---

[1] Peterson v. State, 274 Ga. 165, 167 (2001); State v. Stanley, 131 N.M. 368, 373, 37 P.3d 85, 91 (2001).

[2] State v. Martinez, 149 N.C. App. 553, 560, 561 S.E.2d 528, 533 (2002); Robbins v. State, 88 S.W.3d 256, 259, 2002 Tex. Crim. App. LEXIS 208 (2002).

[3] *See* Ill. Comp. Stat. Ann. § 735 ILCS 5/8-201. Dead-Man's Act (Matthew Bender 2006) and Cal. Veh. Code § 40803 Admissibility of speed trap evidence (Matthew Bender 2006).

§ 8.2 Definitions

Black's Law Dictionary defines competent evidence as "evidence that is relevant and is of such a character (e.g., not unfairly prejudicial or based on hearsay) that the court should receive it."[4] Competent evidence is also defined as evidence that tends to establish the fact in issue and does not rest on mere surmise or conjecture.[5]

Perhaps the definition of competent evidence can be better understood if incompetent evidence is defined. In *Black's Law Dictionary*, incompetent evidence is defined as "evidence that is for any reason inadmissible."[6] A Kentucky court recognized that evidence was defective and thus incompetent where the proof indicated that a defendant was a persistent felony offender. Because the evidence proving the persistent offender status had not been properly authenticated at the trial and the incompetent evidence had been introduced against the defendant, the penalty had to be reversed.[7] Here, if the trial judge had determined that the evidence failed the test of competency, the court would have excluded the evidence from admission.

In seeking answers about what evidence should be deemed incompetent, and therefore inadmissible, many avenues are open and volumes of material are available. Much of this book is devoted to determining what evidence is considered incompetent and therefore inadmissible in court.

§ 8.3 General Categories of Incompetent Evidence

If evidence is found to be incompetent, it is usually because the courts have found that it comes within one of the three general categories discussed below.

A. *Wrongfully Obtained Evidence*

Evidence that has been obtained in violation of the Constitution, such as that obtained by an illegal search, often will not be admitted because the courts have reasoned that admitting such evidence would encourage the state to disregard the constitutional rights of citizens. Demonstrative of this principle, the Supreme Court held that where the police operated roadblocks to screen all drivers for crime, in the absence of individualized suspicion, the practice violated the Fourth Amendment.[8] Evidence obtained directly or indirectly as a result of an involuntary confession should not be admitted because the

---

[4]   BLACK'S LAW DICTIONARY (8th ed. 2004).

[5]   31A C.J.S. *Evidence* § 3 (1996).

[6]   BLACK'S LAW DICTIONARY (8th ed. 2004).

[7]   Merriweather v. Commonwealth, 99 S.W.3d 448, 2003 Ky. LEXIS 39 (2003). *See also* Young v. Commonwealth, 47 Va. App. 616; 625 S.E.2d 691; 2006 Va. App. LEXIS 42 (2006).

[8]   *See* City of Indianapolis v. Edmond, 531 U.S. 32 (2000). *See also* Mapp v. Ohio, 357 U.S. 643 (1961).

process used in obtaining the evidence violated the due process clauses of the Constitution.[9] A conviction cannot stand where police violate the principles of *Miranda v. Arizona* to obtain evidence in a manner that is inconsistent with the intent of the required custody warnings.[10] Evidence seized due to illegal police activity is inadmissible, not because it is irrelevant or immaterial, but because it is incompetent as determined by the courts.

B. Statutory Incompetency

Some evidence is admissible as competent evidence because a statute provides that it is competent evidence and, similarly, some evidence is not admissible because a state or federal statute prohibits the admission of the evidence. For example, § 2515 of the Omnibus Crime Control and Safe Streets Act of 1968,[11] as amended, provides that evidence obtained by wiretapping or eavesdropping, when conducted in violation of the statute, is inadmissible in any court or other official proceeding. Similarly, an Ohio statute provides that a police officer is incompetent to testify as a witness in a misdemeanor prosecution against a driver charged with violating the vehicle or traffic laws if the officer, at the time of the arrest or citation, was using a motor vehicle that was not properly marked and did not have a flashing light mounted outside the police vehicle.[12] Some states have statutes that protect the interests of decedents' estates when the law specifically states that some people are not competent as witnesses in listed legal actions.[13] Evidence produced in contravention of these and similar statutes will be excluded from court use, not because it is irrelevant or immaterial, but because the statutes specifically provide that the evidence is not admissible or usable in court.

C. Evidence Excluded Because of a Court-Established Rule

Although many rules of evidence have now been codified, most evidence is excluded because the courts, over a period of years, have established certain rules regarding the admissibility of evidence. Some excellent examples, which will be discussed more thoroughly in forthcoming chapters, are rules that prohibit the admission of certain opinion testimony, hearsay evidence, and privileged communications. The Federal Rules of Evidence prevent a judge who is sitting in the case from being a witness in that case, and a juror who is hearing

---

[9]   *See* Arizona v. Fulminante, 499 U.S. 279 (1991); the exclusion of illegally obtained evidence is discussed in Chapter 16. *See also* Kanovitz & Kanovitz, Constitutional Law (11th ed. 2008) and Walker and Hemmens, Legal Guide for Police: Constitutional Issues (7th ed. 2005).

[10]   State v. Seibert, 542 U.S. 600, 2004 U.S. LEXIS 4578 (2004).

[11]   Title III of the Omnibus Crime Control and Safe Streets Act of 1968, 18 U.S.C. § 2510 *et seq.*

[12]   City of Parma Heights v. Nugent, 92 Ohio Misc. 2d 67, 700 N.E.2d 430, 1998 Ohio Misc. LEXIS 32 (1998); *see* Ohio Rev. Code § 4549.14 in conjunction with Ohio Rev. Code § 4549.13 (Matthew Bender 2006) and Ohio R. Evid. 601(C) (Matthew Bender 2006).

[13]   *See* Burns Ind. Code Ann. § 34-45-2-4, When executor or administrator is party.

a case is considered incompetent as a witness in the same case.[14] Where court rules exclude evidence, the courts generally have a sound reason for rejecting the evidence, whether the purpose involves the public policy of supporting confidential relationships or preventing the admission of evidentiary errors involving hearsay evidence.

§ 8.4 Competency of Evidence — Documentary Evidence

Legal evidence includes not only oral testimony given under oath by witnesses in open court and physical objects introduced in evidence by witnesses, but also all kinds of documents and records. The concept of document includes traditional writings, as well as films, videotapes, CD and DVD data, electronically stored documents, jump drive documents, Web pages, and stored cell phone data. These methods of storing information and of observing them are roughly classified as documentary evidence. Evidence meeting the definition of documentary evidence is subject to the same rules of relevancy, materiality, and competency as other types of evidence. Documentary evidence must pass all of the competency tests, such as the hearsay test, the opinion evidence test, and the various constitutional tests. In addition, documentary evidence must meet other qualifications before it is admissible. The party desiring to offer documentary evidence must authenticate the document by demonstrating that it is genuine. Documentary evidence must also meet the requirements of the best evidence rule and comply with requirements that are peculiar to "questioned documents."[15]

§ 8.5 — Tests and Experiments

The results of scientific tests and experiments may assist the trier of fact in evaluating the evidence in a criminal case and assist the jury in reaching a correct verdict. Evidence showing the outcome of an experiment or test may be admissible to aid in determining the issues in a case in which it is shown that the conditions under which the experiment or test was made are substantially similar to the circumstances prevailing at the time of the occurrence. Evidence obtained as a result of tests and experiments made during a trial or conducted out of the courtroom has been challenged as being incompetent evidence based on alleged improper administration, improper conduct, and testing under different circumstances.[16] Generally, where it is necessary

---

[14] *See* FED. R. EVID. 605 and 606.
[15] The rules relating to the admissibility of documentary evidence are discussed fully in Chapter 13.
[16] Holt v. State, 2006 Tenn. Crim. App. LEXIS 107 (2006).

to show the condition or quality of a certain article or substance, the item itself may be introduced in evidence to supplement the testimony of the witness, or as direct evidence when properly identified. Some scientific tests are designed to reveal the identity of a substance, a chemical, or drug, while other tests reconstruct how an event occurred or connect people or objects to a crime. The actual objects tested may be introduced as evidence, but in some cases only the results of testing are available. For instance, most drug analysis tests and some experiments may prove destructive to the item being tested, a factor that will prevent the actual object or item from being introduced as physical evidence.

Determining whether the results of a test or experiment should be admitted as evidence requires a trial court to evaluate whether the test will produce relevant evidence that is reliable and fair. Until the Supreme Court of the United States decided the *Daubert v. Merrell Dow Pharmaceuticals* case (1993), a great number of courts, both federal and state, followed the old *Frye* standard. The *Frye* case (1923) generated a test for admissibility of scientific evidence suggested by the District of Columbia Court of Appeals that other state and federal courts adopted. In determining whether to admit scientific evidence and tests, the *Frye* Court considered that:

> Just when a scientific principle or discovery crosses the line between the experimental and demonstrable stages is difficult to define. Somewhere in this twilight zone, the evidential force of the principle must be recognized, and while courts will go a long way in admitting expert testimony deduced from a well-recognized scientific principle or discovery, the thing from which the deduction is made must be sufficiently established to have gained general acceptance in the particular field in which it belongs.[17]

In *Daubert v. Merrell Dow Pharmaceuticals*, the issue arose concerning whether the *Frye* standard governed in federal cases or whether the Federal Rules of Evidence should take precedence because the Federal Rules were enacted long after the *Frye* decision. According to *Daubert*, Federal Rule 702 generally controls the admissibility of scientific or technical knowledge in federal courts.[18] Rule 702, Testimony of Experts, states:

> If scientific, technical, or other specialized knowledge will assist the trier of fact to understand the evidence or to determine a fact in issue, a witness qualified as an expert by knowledge, skill, experience, training, or education, may testify thereto in the form of an opinion or otherwise, if (1) the testimony is based upon sufficient facts or data, (2) the testimony is the product of reliable principles and methods, and (3) the witness has applied the principles and methods reliably to the facts of the case.

---

[17] 54 D.C. App. at 47, 293 F. at 1014, 1923 U.S. App. LEXIS 1712 (D.C.C.A. 1923).

[18] Daubert v. Merrell Dow Pharmaceuticals, Inc., 509 U.S. 579, 1993 U.S. LEXIS 4408 (1993).

Even though the *Frye* test was displaced upon adoption of the Federal Rules of Evidence, it did not mean that Rule 702 placed no limits on the admissibility of scientific evidence and tests. The trial judge must be certain that any and all scientific evidence admitted is both relevant and reliable. While Rule 702 does not mention the "general acceptance" standard of *Frye*, many of the evaluations performed by a judge in deciding whether to admit evidence of scientific tests and experiments under Rule 702 will consider some of the following factors as a commonsense approach: (1) whether the scientific evidence has been tested and the methodology by which it has been tested; (2) whether the evidence has been subjected to peer review or publication; (3) whether the potential rate of error is known; (4) whether the evidence is generally accepted in the scientific community; and (5) whether the experts' research in the field has been conducted independent of litigation.[19] Consistent with the concept of federalism, courts that follow a state adoption of the Federal Rules of Evidence are free to interpret them differently from the *Daubert* decision and could follow a state version of the *Frye* standard or some other version consistent with due process. Examples of scientific tests and experiments that may be admissible are: blood grouping tests, blood-alcohol testing, fingerprint comparisons, ballistics experiments, and DNA tests.[20]

§ 8.6 — Conduct of Trained Dogs

Evidence produced by observing the conduct of trained dogs may be admissible against a defendant in a variety of contexts. Law enforcement officials may use dogs to discover the identity of a suspect, to discover the suspect, to find lost objects, to detect the presence of controlled substances, to alert to the presence of arson accelerants, to discover cadavers, and to identify objects containing explosives. The training for each dog in a particular field tends to be unique considering a drug-detection dog may be trained to scratch, a feature that would not be advisable in an explosives-detection dog. In order to be admissible, a foundation detailing the particular animal's training is generally required.

In a firearm possession by a felon case initiated by a Virginia state police officer and his dog, the animal alerted to the presence of drugs in a lawfully stopped motor vehicle. No drugs were ever found, giving the defendant a basis for arguing that the dog evidence was erroneous and did not establish probable cause to search his car. In denying the defendant's motion to suppress the drug evidence, the federal prosecutor constructed a foundation for the admission of the dog-produced evidence. A trainer at the Virginia State Police academy testified concerning the procedures followed when training a canine officer and a particular dog. In addition, the state trooper who handled the particular dog in

---

[19]   State v. Begley, 956 S.W.2d 471 (Tenn. 1997).
[20]   The rules relating to admissibility of evidence concerning tests and experiments are discussed in detail in Chapter 15.

question explained how he and the dog received training together. The Virginia program involved the officer and the dog completing a 13-week, 520-hour, canine and canine handler drug detector course. Before being allowed to actually work out on the street with the police officer, the dog had to pass a certification test with his police officer handler. The dog and officer team then must complete four hours of field training every week as well as three full days of training at the Virginia State Police training academy under the supervision of a certified dog trainer. The handling officer indicated that the particular dog and occasionally failed to find narcotics but had not offered false positives in any training scenario. In admitting the evidence of the firearm, the judge determined that probable cause existed even though no drugs were ever discovered. The general rule is that if a drug-sniffing dog is reliable, the positive reaction to the presence of drugs produces probable cause for a search of the controlled substance. In this case, the extensive training of the dog and his human handler were deemed sufficient to support the search and the admission of the evidence.[21]

The conduct of a dog in tracking a suspect, as interpreted by the animal's handler, has been held to produce competent and admissible evidence in both civil and criminal cases.[22] "[M]any courts have ruled that in general, evidence of tracking a defendant is admissible, subject to establishment of a proper foundation"[23] to assist in proving identity as long as a proper foundation regarding the animal's training and the handler's skills with the dog have been proven. For example, Washington requires that the party offering the dog-tracking evidence establish foundation requirements. A precondition for dog-tracking evidence to be admitted requires that:

> (1) the handler was qualified by training and experience to use the dog, (2) the dog was adequately trained in tracking humans, (3) the dog has, in actual cases, been found by experience to be reliable in pursuing human track, (4) the dog was placed on track where circumstances indicated the guilty party to have been, and (5) the trail had not become so stale or contaminated as to be beyond the dog's competency to follow.[24]

Washington courts generally require that the dog tracking evidence have some minimal corroboration to be admissible. Dog tracking evidence should include a cautionary jury instruction that dog tracking evidence by itself cannot support a conviction in the absence of other evidence.[25]

---

[21] *See* United States v. Brooks, 589 F. Supp. 2d 618, 2008 U.S. Dist. LEXIS 102201 (E.D. Va. 2008).

[22] Washington v. Loucks, 98 Wash. 2d 563, 656 P.2d 480, 1983 Wash. LEXIS 1333 (1983); *see also* Washington v. Hunotte, 2001 Wash. App. LEXIS 1941 (2001) and Commonwealth v. Hill, 52 Mass. App. 147, 153 (2001).

[23] *See* Jay M. Zitter, Annotation, *Evidence of Trailing by Dogs in Criminal Cases,* 81 A.L.R. 5th 563 (Updated 2004).

[24] State v. Lathim, 2006 Wash. App. LEXIS 936 (2006).

[25] State v. Burnice, 2006 Wash. App. LEXIS 45 (2006).

Evidence of the conduct of a dog in tracking the accused from the scene of a crime to the place where the police arrested him has been found competent and admissible. In a Connecticut case where the defendant had been charged with armed robbery, a police dog followed a human scent from the crime scene to a cap and then on to a car in which the defendant was sitting. After a break for water, the dog again went from the cap to the car where the defendant had previously been sitting. Over the defendant's objection that some extensive scientific foundation must be provided to explain dog scent tracking, the trial court refused to suppress the circumstantial evidence of identity. The court noted that properly trained dogs have been used in Connecticut for an extensive period and that courts have routinely admitted dog-tracking evidence. In this particular case, the dog had sufficient training, making the evidence properly admissible.[26]

The Court of Criminal Appeals of Alabama approved the use of trained dogs for identifying persons suspected of a store burglary. The owner of the store fired several shots at the departing men he knew to be the guilty parties. Shoes and socks believed to belong to the culprits were found in the parking lot and were used to give the canines a sniff of the goal of their search. Four miles down the road, the dogs identified the defendant's odor as matching the scent from the clothing at the parking lot. The prosecution appealed a trial court order suppressing the canine identifications on the ground that dog-tracking evidence cannot establish probable cause to arrest. In overturning the trial court's decision on the motion to suppress, the reviewing court held that such evidence could equal probable cause if the training and reliability of the dog is established, the trainer/handler has proper qualifications, and the circumstances indicate reliability of the evidence. Citing cases that extended over a century, the court held that dog-tracking evidence was admissible for identification purposes.[27]

Canine detection of accelerants used in arson cases has been approved in appropriate cases. In a Tennessee case in which fire investigators suspected the use of an accelerant in a fire and fatality in a trailer home, they procured the assistance of a dog trained to alert to the presence of hydrocarbons.[28] The investigator testified that he had been with the dog nearly nine years; that the dog had worked hundreds of fire scenes; and that the dog and the investigator trained 365 days a year. The investigator indicated that the dog alerted to the presence of hydrocarbons in two specific places indicating that an ignitable fluid had been on the floor area. The dog's conclusions were corroborated by a state investigatory agency. The reviewing court upheld the admission of the dog evidence of accelerants and the conviction for aggravated arson and felony murder.

---

[26]   *See* State v. Kelly, 2009 Conn. Super. LEXIS 98 (2009). *See also* Jones v. Commonwealth, 277 Va. 171, 2009 Va. LEXIS 10 (Va. 2009).

[27]   State v. Montgomery, 2006 Ala. Crim. App. LEXIS 36 (2006).

[28]   *See* State v. Virga, 2009 Tenn. Crim. App. LEXIS 161 (Tenn. 2009).

§ 8.7 — Telephone Conversations

The fact that a telephone call has been made may be considered competent and admissible as evidence along with other data that a call generates. The data, the fact of the conversation, and the content must be relevant to be admissible in court. In the case of voice recordings of phone conversations pursuant to a lawful wiretap or other recording, the voice must be authenticated as being genuine. The concept of authentication means that the party wishing to introduce evidence of a telephone conversation must be able to prove who was actually talking on the telephone and, in some cases, prove the identities of all parties to the conversation. Identification of the speakers may occur by the use of either direct evidence offered by one of the parties to the conversation who knew with whom he or she was speaking, or by facts and circumstantial proof that indicates the identity of one or more of the speakers. In addition, where the conversation evidence has been obtained by wiretap, relevant federal and state laws must have been properly observed or the evidence may be excluded.[29] Beyond the data generated by traditional phones, newer phone systems and cell phones generate tremendous amounts of nonverbal data and metadata that are routinely stored for long periods by the cell phone carrier and in the handset. Most cell phones store text messages, pictures, web pages, information on personal contacts, as well as calendar and appointment data and global positioning information. Most of this data is also linked to the time and date of the activity. Police and prosecutors have just begun to mine this nonverbal data, and that process and the results will generate new admissibility issues as these new technologies are exploited.

For evidence of telephone conversation contents to be admitted, the identities of participants must be authenticated. Such identity may be proved through voice identification, where the recipient is familiar with the caller's voice, or through circumstantial evidence, where the caller gives sufficient specific information that only he or she would know, such as a name, telephone number, address, and Social Security number.[30] Proper authentication of a telephone conversation can be deemed sufficient when evidence shows that a call was made to the number assigned by the telephone company to a particular person under circumstances, including self-identification by the recipient, indicating that the person answering is the person who was called.[31] In one case, conversations between drug traffickers, where the defendant denied knowing the other person or talking to him, were authenticated where the cooperating drug trafficker explained 16 intercepted phone calls between him and the defendant. During the calls, the two discussed using a hidden

---

[29] 18 U.S.C. § 2511 *et seq.*, Title III of the Omnibus Crime Control and Safe Streets Act of 1968, as periodically amended, generally prohibits the interception of wire, electronic, and oral communications by anyone, unless done in compliance with the Act.

[30] Angleton v. State, 686 N.E.2d 803 (Ind. 1997).

[31] Broadhead v. State, 981 So. 2d 320, 326, 2007 Miss. App. LEXIS 809 (Miss. 2007).

compartment in a motor vehicle and payment options for the drugs allegedly supplied by the defendant to the cooperating drug trafficker. The substance of the conversation and specialized knowledge had the effect of authenticating the caller as being the defendant.[32] Telephone conversations may be authenticated where one party to the conversation recognizes a person based on distinctive accents or speech patterns. The requirement of direct voice recognition is not an absolute requirement for authentication, but where the caller or the person called can recognize the other, this tends to authenticate the other party to the conversation.

When a caller places a call to another person who does not recognize the caller's voice, the fact that the caller self-identified does not serve as sufficient authentication of the identity of the caller[33] unless the recipient recognized the voice. Caller Identification (Caller ID), a device that, for the person called, displays the number and other data related to the incoming call, may play a role in authenticating a caller. Although Caller ID may be admitted to prove the source of the call, and while Caller ID cannot authenticate the identity of the caller, it may be admissible to prove the location and source of the call. In a Tennessee murder case, the defendant's girlfriend testified that the defendant called her from the victim's home because she had Caller ID on her phone and the readout indicated that the call originated from the victim's phone. Naturally, because she was intimately familiar with the voice of her boyfriend, the combination of the Caller ID and his voice authenticated the call as being from her boyfriend using the soon-to-be homicide victim's telephone.[34] Thus, in conjunction with other information, Caller ID may provide the additional information necessary to authenticate a caller and disclose the origination location.

In a prosecution for second-degree rape of a child, the defendant appealed his conviction based on the admission of a telephone conversation that he allegedly had with one of his young victims because it had allegedly not been properly authenticated. When adults became aware of allegations that the defendant had consummated sexual relations with one or more children, one adult had one of the victims call the defendant's telephone number and engage him in incriminating conversation that implicated the defendant in the crimes for which he was later convicted. The trial court permitted the adult to relate to the jury the substance of the conversation that the adult witness overheard between the victim and the defendant. The appellate court agreed that the adult could authenticate the defendant as being the voice on the telephone making incriminating statements because the defendant and the adult witness were neighbors, the witness was familiar with the quality of the defendant's voice, and the victim dialed the defendant's number in full view of the adult witness.[35]

---

[32]   United States v. Avila, 557 F.3d 809, 2009 U.S. App. LEXIS 4940 (7th Cir. 2009).

[33]   Wells v. Liddy, 37 Fed. Appx. 53, 2002 U.S. App. LEXIS 3356 (4th Cir. 2002).

[34]   *See* State v. Flannel, 2008 Tenn. Crim. App. LEXIS 821 (Tenn. 2008).

[35]   State v. Brown, 2006 Wash. App. LEXIS 1092 (2006).

Related to audio telephone conversations are text messages that are sent from one cell phone to another. As often is the case, these messages may be stored on a cell phone computer server and/or sent directly and immediately to the recipient's cell phone. These activities create significant metadata that is available for authentication purposes that will assist in authentication if traditional avenues of authentication are not sufficient. In order to introduce these text messages, they must be authenticated to show that the message is what it purports to be. As an Indiana court noted, "We see no reason why the writings or recordings generated and saved inside of a cellular telephone should be exempted from the . . . authentication requirement."[36] In a case involving making terroristic threats and felony domestic assault, a Minnesota court concluded that text messages received by the victim had been properly authenticated when the recipient indicated that the number associated with the text messages came from the telephone number assigned to the defendant. She possessed knowledge of the defendant's phone number because she once dated him and had had lived with him for a period of time. In addition, the defendant helped authenticate the text messages because in one of them he displayed an intimate knowledge of the domestic situation by ridiculing her for getting law enforcement involved.[37]

In summary, telephone and text messages must be properly authenticated as being genuine prior to their admissibility into evidence. As long as the method of authentication proves that the message is what it purports to be, it should be admitted where otherwise relevant.

§ 8.8　Negative Evidence as Competent Evidence

In *Black's Law Dictionary*, *negative evidence* is defined as "evidence suggesting that an alleged fact does not exist, such as a witness's testifying that he or she did not see an event occur."[38] Evidence is negative when the witness states that he or she did not see or know of the existence of a certain circumstance or fact.[39] Courts have recognized that negative evidence can be admitted where the surrounding circumstances indicate that it has some probative force, such as indicating something did not occur or what a witness did not see or hear when there would have been an opportunity for the witness to have seen or heard.[40] Trial courts have broad discretion to admit evidence that something did not happen[41] and must determine whether the probative value outweighs the prejudicial nature of the evidence. Testimony concerning negative evidence is

---

[36]　Hape v. State, 903 N.E.2d 977, 2009 Ind. App. LEXIS 637 (Ind. 2009).

[37]　*See* State v. Haines, 2008 Minn. Unpub. LEXIS 1479 (Minn. 2008). Unpublished opinion.

[38]　BLACK'S LAW DICTIONARY (8th ed. 2004).

[39]　31A C.J.S. *Evidence* § 165 (1994).

[40]　29 AM JUR. 2D *Evidence* § 327 (West Group 2008).

[41]　Brown v. Classic Inns, 2002 Wis. App 134, 255 Wis. 2d 832, 646 N.W.2d 854 (2002).

admissible where the circumstances demonstrate that the negative evidence has some probative force; the proponent establishes the competency of the witness; and the witness has personal knowledge that something did not occur.[42]

An effective use of negative evidence involves allowing an opposing witness to testify freely and completely concerning matters within his or her knowledge and noting, for later cross-examination purposes, matters that he or she would logically have related to others at a prior time. If the witness added new matters during the direct examination covering new topics that he or she had not discussed earlier, bringing out his or her previous silence on that topic, or absence of evidence, has the effect of impeaching the witness's direct testimony. In one case involving alleged sexual misconduct, a complaining witness noted to police and on direct examination that she wrote in her diary concerning the acts that the defendant perpetrated against her. On cross-examination, the defense attorney elicited from the witness that the existing diaries did not mention the alleged sexual assault. The absence of mention in the diaries would indicate that perhaps her recent testimony was fabricated.[43] The prior silence in the diaries appeared to be inconsistent with the recent trial testimony, suggesting that the trial testimony might be a recent contrivance by the witness. Questions arise when the witness fails to mention the substance of the testimony at a time when it would have been natural to speak on the topic. Therefore, the absence of evidence—negative evidence—may be relevant and competent to prove a recent fabrication by the witness.[44]

The failure of a drug-sniffing dog to alert to the presence of controlled substances within a motor vehicle constitutes negative evidence, providing an indication that drugs were not present, and the lack of evidence does not help in developing probable cause to search. A subsequent false positive indication by the canine in the same vehicle to the presence of recreational drugs is similarly negative evidence of the presence of the prohibited substances.[45]

Some writers and courts have noted that, as a general rule of evidence, all other things being equal, positive evidence carries more weight than negative evidence,[46] but to instruct the jury that positive evidence should be given greater weight is error.[47] To indicate that negative evidence carries less weight than positive evidence invades the province of the jury. One court indicated that where there are two witnesses of equal credibility in direct contradiction on a question of fact, the positive testimony will be given preference.[48]

---

[42]   29A AM. JUR. 2D *Evidence* § 318 (1994).

[43]   State v. Arcia, 111 Conn. App. 374, 379, 380, 2008 Conn. App. LEXIS 529 (Conn. 2008). On redirect as a method of rehabilitation, the prosecutor had the witness tell that she had other diaries that were in police custody that did contain statements of sexual abuse by the defendant.

[44]   Connecticut v. Vines, 71 Conn. App. 359, 371 A.2d 918, 926, 2002 Conn. App. LEXIS 406 (2002).

[45]   Longshore v. State, 399 Md. 486, 531, 532, 2007 Md. LEXIS 344 (Md. 2007).

[46]   29A AM. JUR. *Evidence* § 1438 (1994); *see also* Randall v. Norfolk S. Ry. Co., 800 N.E.2d 951, 959, 2003 Ind. App. LEXIS 2406 (2003).

[47]   Tafoya v. Chapin, 2003 Neb. App. LEXIS 64 (2003).

[48]   State v. Bentley, 499 So. 2d 581 (La. 1987); 29A AM. JUR. 2D *Evidence* § 318 (1994).

In summary, while negative evidence is regarded by some authorities as entitled to less weight than positive evidence, negative evidence is valuable and admissible when a proper foundation has been laid, provided that the competency of the witness and his or her knowledge of the matter are established.

§ 8.9 Evidence Competent for Some Purposes but Not for Others

When evidence may be admissible based upon one theory and excludable under another, generally courts have decided that the evidence is admissible but the opposing party may request a limiting instruction that restricts the use of the evidence to its proper scope.[49] If, however, the evidence has so strong a prejudicial value as to upset the balance of the advantages of receiving the evidence, a judge has discretion in deciding whether to admit or refuse it. When evidence is logically relevant and admissible under one theory but inadmissible under a different theory, in admitting the evidence, the judge should advise the jury in an instruction during the trial that the evidence can be considered for one purpose but not for another.[50] There is contrary authority that a judge should not give a cautionary instruction in the absence of a request because "a party might well intentionally forego a limiting instruction as part of its deliberate strategy."[51] If desired, a second cautionary instruction can be requested by the defendant's counsel prior to jury deliberations. The Federal Rules of Evidence note that when evidence is admissible for one purpose but not another, "the court, upon request, shall restrict the evidence to its proper scope and instruct the jury accordingly."[52]

Demonstrative of this rule, in an Iowa case the prosecution played audio recordings of the defendant's interrogation by law enforcement officials. The defendant's answers were considered substantive evidence but the questions and comments of the police officers were not evidence that could be considered for the truth and were admissible only to give context to the defendant's statements. Because the evidence was admissible for one purpose and not for other purposes, the judge erred by not giving a limiting instruction to the jury that it should not consider the police comments as evidence.[53]

---

[49] *See* TEX. EVID. R. 105 (Matthew Bender 2009). *See also* Arcement v. State, 2009 Tex. App. LEXIS 1096 (Tex. 2009).

[50] Mackey v. Russell, 148 Fed. Appx. 355, 2005 U.S. App. LEXIS 16933 (6th Cir. 2005). *See also* Ohio Evid. R. 105, which states, "When evidence which is admissible as to one party or for one purpose but not admissible as to another party or for another purpose is admitted, the court, upon request of a party, shall restrict the evidence to its proper scope and instruct the jury accordingly."

[51] Oursbourn v. State, 259 S.W.3d 159, 180, 2008 Tex. Crim. App. LEXIS 686 (Tex. 2008).

[52] FED. R. EVID. 105.

[53] State v. Esse, 2005 Iowa App. LEXIS 1199 (Iowa 2005).

Constitutional reasons may have the effect of excluding evidence when offered for one purpose but permitting admission of that evidence as competent when used for a different purpose. In a New York criminal case, the prosecution was prevented from using the defendant's statements made after his arrest due to a *Miranda* warning violation. When the defendant took the witness stand in his own defense and offered a story that was inconsistent with his post-arrest statement over defendant's objection, the trial court permitted the prosecution to introduce the inconsistent post-arrest statement for the limited purpose of impeaching the defendant and not to prove his guilt.[54] According to Chief Justice Burger, "[t]he shield provided by *Miranda* cannot be perverted into a license to use perjury by way of a defense, free from the risk of confrontation with prior inconsistent utterances."[55] If the Court had suppressed the post-arrest statement from evidence, the effect would have been to permit the defendant to commit perjury without suffering any adverse consequences.

Before moving to the discussion of the competency of witnesses, it should be mentioned that there are many other evidentiary rules of exclusion that are not addressed here, not because they are not pertinent, but because they are discussed in detail in other chapters.

§ 8.10　Competency of Witnesses

Rule 601

General Rule of Competency

Every person is competent to be a witness except as otherwise provided in these rules. However, in civil actions and proceedings, with respect to an element of a claim or defense as to which State law supplies the rule of decision, the competency of a witness shall be determined in accordance with State law.[56]

* * *

The Federal Rules of Evidence start with the presumption that all witnesses are competent to offer testimony unless a particular rule of evidence provides otherwise or there exists some defect in the four elements of competency of the witness that renders the witness incapable of offering proper evidence.[57] Because federal courts often sit as state civil courts in diversity of citizenship cases, Rule 601 defers to state law to determine whether a witness is competent when adjudicating state cases. Ohio's enhanced version of Rule 601 holds that every "person

---

[54]　*See* Harris v. New York, 401 U.S. 222 (1971).

[55]　*Id.* at 226.

[56]　FED. R. EVID. 601.

[57]　*Id.*

is competent as a witness except"[58] that "[a] spouse testifying against the other spouse charged with a crime"[59] unless the trial concerns crimes against the child or testifying spouse or unless the spouse elects to testify against the other spouse. In state courts, witnesses are generally presumed to be competent and the party alleging otherwise has the burden of proving that a witness is incompetent. In the interests of clarity, a distinction must be made between the competency of a witness and the competency of evidence. A witness may meet the personal tests of competency and yet not be authorized to testify concerning evidence that is incompetent, such as certain hearsay evidence or illegally seized evidence.

One of the common tests of witness competency looks to see whether four factors have been met. Every witness must take the oath or a substitute, have original perception, be able to remember the facts, and have an ability to communicate to the court. A collateral test of the competency of a witness requires that the witness be able to communicate relevant material and that the witness have the ability to understand that there is an obligation to communicate truthfully. When considering the issue of a witness's competency, "[p]recedence instructs that the question of a witness's competency is to be determined by the trial judge, and a reviewing court may not disturb that determination absent a clear abuse of discretion."[60] The question of competency is almost always one of fact, and thus will not be reversed unless clearly erroneous.[61] Although witness competency involves a question of law for the judge to determine, the credibility of any particular witness and the evidence that the witness offers is for the jury to determine.[62]

In determining whether the witness is competent to testify at the trial, the better practice is to make the determination prior to the trial and out of the hearing of the jury[63] in order to avoid a chance that a jury might believe that a court had determined that a witness was to be believed rather than determined minimally competent to testify. Where the trial is to the judge, a determination of witness competency may be done at the time the witness is called to the witness stand.[64]

When a person has been called as a witness to give testimony in front of a grand jury, the usual tests for competency apply, but a witness's competency is rarely contested because a grand jury meets in secret with no opposing

---

[58] OHIO EVID. R. 601 (Matthew Bender 2009). Ohio's Rule 601 also provides for some other situations involving incompetency.

[59] *Id.*

[60] People v. Harris, 2009 Ill. App. LEXIS 118 (Ill. 2009).

[61] Commonwealth v. Garmache, 35 Mass. App. 805, 626 N.E.2d 616 (1994). *See also* United States v. Gates, 10 F.3d 765 (11th Cir. 1993), in which the court held that the court has the power to rule that the witness is incapable of testifying, and in an appropriate case it has a duty to hold a hearing to determine that issue.

[62] *See* Barrientos v. State, 1 So. 3d 1209, 2009 Fla. App. LEXIS 793 (Fla. 2009).

[63] Norman v. Georgia, 269 Ga. App. 219, 223, 603 S.E.2d 737, 742, 2004 Ga. App. LEXIS 1120 (2004). *See also* Medina v. Diguglielmo, 373 F. Supp. 2d 526; 2005 U.S. Dist. LEXIS 10672 (E.D. Pa. 2005).

[64] *See* Ohio v. Cotterman, 2001 Ohio App. LEXIS 3322 (2001).

party to offer an objection. In one New York case, an indictment was quashed because the prosecutor made no attempt to determine whether the four-year-old complaining witness met the requirements of competency,[65] even though a prosecutor presenting a case to a grand jury has the power to make a ruling on the competency of a grand jury witness as if the prosecutor were a trial judge.[66] As one court noted, "[a] more stringent standard than that applied to trial proceedings certainly cannot be applied to determine competency of a witness to testify before a Grand Jury, whose function is primarily investigative."[67] In the grand jury context, one state considers children competent to testify without taking the oath, as long as the jurors are aware that the witness was not under oath but met the other requirements for competency.[68] The tests for determining competency of a witness before a grand jury are: (1) the witness must understand the obligation of an oath and the obligation to tell the truth before the grand jury; and (2) the witness must be capable of giving a reasonably correct account of the matters that he or she has seen or heard in reference to the questions being asked. Where the competency of a grand jury witness has been raised, these two issues must be determined by the court's own examination and upon the testimony of witnesses who may be called by the prosecution or by the witness's counsel. This is a duty that the court cannot avoid merely by referring to or quoting from the statements of the medical experts. The court must make its own determination and its own examination. The court must be assured that the physical and mental health of the witness will not be damaged, impaired, or harmed in any significant way.[69] Because the defendant has no representation at a grand jury proceeding, questions about the competency of grand jury witnesses do not frequently arise, and where they do, the witness often raises the issue.

Where the competency of expert witnesses is at issue, courts generally have broad discretion in determining whether to allow the testimony. The issue of competency and qualifications where expert witnesses are concerned appear to overlap somewhat. Every witness must meet the traditional standards of competency but an expert needs to meet additional standards. The California Evidence Code provides that "[a] person is qualified to testify as an expert if he has special knowledge, skill, experience, training, or education sufficient to qualify him as an expert on the subject to which his testimony relates. Against the objection of a party, such special knowledge, skill, experience, training, or education must be shown before the witness may testify as an expert."[70] The judge's determination that a person is qualified as an expert witness is binding on the jury, but the weight to be assigned to the expert's testimony rests with the finder of fact.

---

[65]   People v. Esaw, 2002 N.Y. Slip Op. 40045U, 2002 N.Y. Misc. LEXIS 201 (N.Y. 2002).

[66]   *See* NY CLS CPL § 190.30(6) Grand jury; rules of evidence (Matthew Bender 2009).

[67]   In re Loughran, 276 F. Supp. 393, 430, 1967 U.S. Dist. LEXIS 7589 (C.D. Cal. 1967).

[68]   People v. Miller, 295 A.D.2d 746, 747, 2002 N.Y. App. Div. LEXIS 6511 (2002).

[69]   *Id.*

[70]   CAL. EVID. CODE § 720 (Matthew Bender 2008).

In the sections immediately following, the specific grounds for challenging the competency of witnesses are discussed.

§ 8.11 — Mental Incapacity

In state and federal courts, feeble-mindedness, mental illness, and insanity are not enough to prevent a witness from being considered competent. However, in evaluating the mental status of witnesses, "there are few particularized standards governing the assessment of a person's mental capacity."[71] In the Notes of Advisory Committee on (federal) Rules, the committee noted that "[a] witness wholly without capacity is difficult to imagine."[72] Therefore, a teenage witness who was suffering from post-traumatic stress disorder related to sexual abuse can be considered a competent witness where she had the capacity to perceive, recollect, and understand the necessity of telling the truth. Nothing indicated that her mental challenges had any effect on her testimony and the trial judge concluded that she possessed capacity as a witness.[73]

The basic standard or rule applied when considering the mental capacity of an adult witness to testify is the one first announced by the United States Supreme Court in *District of Columbia v. Armes*:

> The general rule is that a lunatic or a person affected with insanity is admissible as a witness if he has sufficient understanding to apprehend the obligation of an oath, and to be capable of giving a correct account of the matters which he has seen or heard in reference to the questions at issue; and whether he has that understanding is a question to be determined by the court, upon examination of the party himself, and any competent witnesses who can speak to the nature and extent of his insanity.[74]

In *Armes*, the Court upheld the admissibility of the testimony of an acute melancholic who was confined to an asylum and had attempted suicide several times. The Court stressed that "the existence of partial insanity does not prevent individuals so affected . . . from giving a perfectly accurate and lucid statement of what they have seen or heard."[75]

Not only is mental competency an issue with adult witnesses, it clearly arises in juveniles as well. In an Illinois case involving alleged aggravated sexual abuse by a juvenile, the state's witnesses were all children who attended a therapeutic school with the defendant. One of the witnesses was placed in a psychiatric institution shortly after the alleged delinquent acts took place.

---

[71]   Bornstad v. Honey Brook Twp., 2005 U.S. Dist. LEXIS 19573 (E.D. Pa. 2006).

[72]   FED. R. EVID. 601, Notes of Advisory Committee on Rules.

[73]   *See* United States v. Street, 531 F.3d 703, 2008 U.S. App. LEXIS 14729 (th Cir. 2008), *cert. denied*, 129 S. Ct. 432, 2008 U.S. LEXIS 7688 (2008).

[74]   107 U.S. 519, 2 S. Ct. 840, 27 L. Ed. 618 (1882).

[75]   *Id.*

To determine the competency of the juvenile witnesses, the child facing delinquency accusations questioned the competency of the government's juvenile witnesses and wanted to have the judge conduct an *in camera* review of their school records in order to determine whether competency was at issue. Because the juvenile court refused to conduct any review of the witness's records, the appeals court reversed the finding of delinquency based on the concern that the undisclosed school records may have contained crucial evidence relevant to competency.[76]

Even though a trial court or jury might accept arcane psychiatric concepts of mental condition or illness as a basis for measuring criminal capacity and responsibility, a judge will not blindly accept such theoretical concepts when evaluating the competency of witnesses. Despite mental difficulties, the test of a witness's competency includes the capacity to communicate relevant material and to understand the obligation to do so truthfully. In upholding the admission of evidence offered by a witness in a murder case, an Illinois court noted that having bipolar disorder and a significant history of drug abuse did not disqualify a witness.[77] This history would be disqualifying only where the drug use or mental illness significantly impaired the witness's mental capacity to the extent that the witness could not meet the traditional requirements of a witness. In Illinois, a person is disqualified as a witness when he or she is not capable of expressing the matter in an understandable manner or fails to understand the duty to tell the truth.[78]

Most courts in state and federal cases allow testimony of a witness even though the witness has been found to be drug addicted and taking psychiatric medicine for mental problems. This has been reflected in the Federal Rules of Evidence as interpreted by various courts. For example, in one federal trial, a prosecution witness was permitted to testify that she was a drug addict and she admitted to having smoked significant quantities of crack cocaine on the day when she was a witness to several crimes. The witness had suffered a gunshot wound to her head and had auditory and visual hallucinations. She was also under a doctor's care, which resulted in multiple psychiatric medications being prescribed. With all of these problems that might relate to her competency, the trial court properly permitted her to testify against the defendant.[79] In a different federal case, the judge ordered the prosecution's principal witness to be examined by a court psychiatrist because there was some concern about his capacity.[80] The doctor reported that the proposed witness has a history of being hospitalized for mental illness and that he had a "severe personality disorder" and a "character disturbance," but had no present mental illness. In considering the witness's competency, the examining doctor noted that the witness

---

[76]   People v. K.S., 387 Ill. App. 3d 570, 2008 Ill. App. LEXIS 1333 (Ill. 2008).

[77]   People v. Nowicki, 385 Ill. App. 3d 53, 87, 88, 2008 Ill. App. LEXIS 869 (Ill. 2008).

[78]   *See* 725 ILCS 5/115-14. Witness Competency (Matthew Bender 2009).

[79]   United States v. Williams, 445 F.3d 724, 728 2006 U.S. App. LEXIS 9639 (4th Cir. 2006).

[80]   Bryant v. United States, 859 A.2d 1093, 1101, 2004 D.C. App. LEXIS 526 (Dist. Col. 2004).

had previously been diagnosed as a paranoid schizophrenic with conduct and adjustment disorders, but that the doctor did not believe such problems would affect competency. The trial judge's decision in favor of competency of this mentally challenged witness was not disturbed on appeal.

In making a determination of competency of a witness, the fact that a proposed witness had substance abuse issues and an unspecified learning disability would not by itself disqualify a person as a witness. Even where the witness was also suffering from severe bipolar disorder, which required long-term medical care, such fact would not necessarily indicate that the individual lacked competency.[81] When a person has been adjudicated as an incompetent in the sense of managing his or her own affairs, the individual may still qualify as a witness where the person has knowledge of the facts of the case and understands the duty to tell the truth.[82]

However, there are occasions when mental illness and psychiatric problems may require a trial court to conduct close scrutiny of how the mental challenges affect a particular witness capacity. In a case involving a juvenile adjudication of delinquency for an act that would have been rape if committed by an adult, the trial court committed error when it failed to conduct a more complete competency hearing.[83] The complaining witness was a 12-year-old girl who attended special education classes, had imaginary friends, had been previously diagnosed with schizophrenia, and her ability to remember even routine information proved to be limited. The juvenile court conducted an examination of the witness, but failed to follow up on answers that might have created doubt considering her competency. In reversing the adjudication, the reviewing court noted:

> There is no indication in the record that the court questioned B.D. regarding her capacity to recount the events accurately or even that she understood the nature of the proceedings. After the trial court questioned B.D. regarding routine questions such as the day, month, and year and received inaccurate or confusing responses from her, the court merely proceeded to the next set of questions without delving further into the key issue of competency.

> The lack of more detailed evidence supporting or refuting B.D.'s competency should be clear on the record. Since such evidence is lacking, we find that the trial court abused its discretion in failing to conduct a more complete competency hearing.[84]

As a general matter of procedure, when the competency of a witness arises, the trial judge must make a preliminary determination concerning competency. When the judge finds a proposed witness competent, the jury must evaluate

---

[81]   Witherspoon v. United States, 2008 U.S. Dist. LEXIS 94601 (W.D.N.C. 2008).

[82]   *Id.*

[83]   In re J.M., 2006 Ohio 1203; 2006 Ohio App. LEXIS 1088 (2006).

[84]   *Id.*

credibility of the witness and the jury determines the value to be assigned to the testimony.[85] Concerning the procedure in making an evaluation of a challenged witness, a Maryland court, under state Rule 601, commented that holding a competency hearing outside of the hearing of the jury is not required but is up to the sound discretion of the trial judge. The court believed that as long as the trial judge was satisfied with the competency of a challenged witness, competency was sufficiently established[86] and the value of the testimony rested with the finder of fact.

In summary, a witness is generally considered competent to testify unless evidence is introduced to show that incompetency exists. Where one party has concerns that an adverse witness may lack some of the elements of competency, many state statutes or evidence codes provide that "the burden of proof shall be on the moving party"[87] to establish that the witness lacks competency. To meet that burden, the challenging party must establish the inability to understand the obligation of the oath and to comprehend the obligation imposed by it, or a lack of understanding of the consequences of false swearing, or the inability to perceive accurate impressions and to retain them.

§ 8.12 – Children

Where the competency of a child to be a witness becomes an issue for either party, the trial judge has the duty to evaluate whether the child possesses the elements of competency. Even where neither party objects to the competency of a child witness, the trial judge generally has the discretion to determine whether competency exists.[88] In most jurisdictions, a child may not be required to take a formal oath as long as the duty and ability to tell the truth can be established.[89] As one court noted, "trial judges are required to make a preliminary determination as to the competency of all witnesses, including children, and that absent an abuse of discretion, competency determinations of the trial judge will not be disturbed on appeal."[90] According to a reviewing court, one trial judge conducted a proper examination of a six-year-old child witness when the judge's questions to the child were:

> sufficient to establish the child was capable of "receiving just impressions of the fact and transactions" and "relating them truly." Although [she] showed some confusion about the actual terms "right" and "wrong" and "truth" and

---

[85]   United States v. Phibbs, 999 F.2d 1053 (6th Cir. 1993). *See* case in Part II.

[86]   *See* Perry v. State, 381 Md. 138, 848 A.2d 631, 2004 Md. LEXIS 246 (2004).

[87]   ILL. COMP. STAT. ANN., 725 ILCS 5/115-14 (c) Witness Competency (Matthew Bender 2009).

[88]   Haycraft v. State, 760 N.E.2d 203, 209, 2001 Ind. App. LEXIS 2225 (2001).

[89]   10 DEL. C. § 4302 Competency to testify (2009). "No child under the age of 10 years may be excluded from giving testimony for the sole reason that such child does not understand the obligation of an oath. Such child's age and degree of understanding of the obligation of an oath may be considered by the trier of fact in judging the child's credibility."

[90]   In re J.M., 2006 Ohio 1203, 2006 Ohio App. LEXIS 1088 (2006).

"lie", she clearly demonstrated she knew the difference between telling the truth and telling a lie, and knew the consequences of telling a lie.[91]

While some state statutes are similar to Ohio's in providing that "children under ten years of age, who appear incapable of receiving just impressions of the facts respecting which they are examined, or of relating them truly"[92] are incompetent as witnesses, there is no fixed age at which a child is considered to be a competent witness. In fact, in Arkansas the rules of evidence state that "[e]very person is competent to be a witness except as otherwise provided"[93] in other parts of the evidence code. When making determinations of the competency of a particular witness, an Arkansas reviewing court suggested that "[t]he criteria for determining whether a witness is competent to testify are: (1) the ability to understand the obligation of an oath and to comprehend the obligation imposed by it; or (2) an understanding of the consequences of false swearing; or (3) the ability to receive accurate impressions and to retain them, to the extent that the capacity exists to transmit to the fact finder a reasonable statement of what was seen, felt, or heard."[94] Using this standard, the reviewing court upheld allowing an eight-year-old girl to testify about a defendant's acts of slamming her 23-month-old sister into a wall.[95] The trial court had spoken to the eight-year-old concerning the duty to tell the truth and she appeared to understand the difference between truth and falsity and that lies were wrong and could merit punishment. On this record, the reviewing court found no abuse of discretion on the part of the trial court.

In an old case involving a question of a minor's competency as a witness, speaking for federal courts, the United States Supreme Court in *Wheeler v. United States*,[96] said:

> That the boy was not by reason of his youth (five and one-half years), as a matter of law, absolutely disqualified as a witness is clear. While no one would think of calling as a witness an infant only two or three years old, there is no precise age which determines the question of competency. This depends on the capacity and intelligence of the child, his appreciation of the difference between truth and falsehood, as well as of his duty to tell the former. The decision of this question rests primarily with the trial judge, who sees the proposed witness, notices his manner, his apparent possession or lack of intelligence, and may resort to any examination which will tend to disclose his capacity and intelligence as well as his understanding of the obligations of an oath. As many of these matters cannot be photographed into the record the decision of the trial judge will not be disturbed on review, unless from that which is preserved, it is clear that it was erroneous.

---

[91]   State v. Patterson, 2005 Ohio 6703; 2005 Ohio App. LEXIS 6050 (2005).

[92]   Ohio R. Evid. 601(A) (Matthew Bender 2006).

[93]   A.R.E. 601 (2008).

[94]   Lyons v. State, 2008 Ark. App. LEXIS 430 (Ark. 2008).

[95]   *Id.*

[96]   159 U.S. 523, 16 S. Ct. 93, 40 L. Ed. 244 (1895).

In a variety of cases, children much younger than 10 years of age have been considered competent witnesses while other cases have refused to allow some young children to testify. A determination of competency of child witnesses depends upon the facts in each case and on the maturity of the individual child. In Pennsylvania, all witnesses are considered competent, including children, but witnesses under 14 years of age may face special scrutiny. In one case involving juvenile sexual abuse by an adult, the trial court permitted a six-year-old girl to testify.[97] Against the presumption of competency, the defendant must first demonstrate some defect in competency to cause the court to hold a "taint" hearing. This process examines whether events or other people have tainted the child's memory and perception. In evaluating whether a defendant has presented evidence sufficient to hold the "taint" hearing, the court considers the totality of the circumstances surrounding the child's allegations, including:

> (1) the age of the child; (2) the existence of a motive hostile to the defendant on the part of the child's primary custodian; (3) the possibility that the child's primary custodian is unusually likely to read abuse into normal interaction; (4) whether the child was subjected to repeated interviews by various adults in positions of authority; (5) whether an interested adult was present during the course of any interviews; and (6) the existence of independent evidence regarding the interview techniques employed.[98]

Where a Pennsylvania defendant fails to produce sufficient evidence to warrant a "taint" hearing, the trial court will permit the child's testimony without additional analysis or consideration.

While Pennsylvania's "taint" hearing appears to be a different approach from most jurisdictions, in determining a child's competency as a witness, most courts consider the child's ability to perceive just impressions of the facts at the time that the events occurred and evaluate his or her capacity to communicate them at the time of the trial. Of crucial importance is the child's competency or incompetency as of the date that the child is offered as a witness, and not at the time that the incidents originally occurred.

On occasion, courts have permitted very young children to serve as witnesses following a determination of competency. In the District of Columbia, a trial court permitted a six-year-old boy to testify concerning injuries that a defendant inflicted upon his mother when the boy was only five years old.[99] The child was able to recall that the attack took place at night and that the attacker was the defendant. He remembered that the attack on his mother took place in his bedroom and in a nearby bathroom and that he had attempted to defend her using a toy plastic sword. In approving the admission of the boy's

---

[97] Commonwealth v. Judd, 2006 Pa. Super. 84, 897 A.2d 1224, 2006 Pa. Super. LEXIS 538 (2006).

[98] *Id.* at 1230.

[99] Scott v. United States, 953 A.2d 1082, 1092, 1093 (Dist. Col. 2008).

testimony, the District of Columbia Court of Appeals noted that competency of a child required that there be proof of an ability to recall the events in question and that the child understand the difference between truth and falsehood and appreciate the need to tell the truth.

A Mississippi court noted that the test for admissibility of child testimony required that the trial judge: "determine that the child witness (1) has the ability to perceive and remember events, (2) understand and answer questions intelligently, and (3) comprehend and accept the importance of truthfulness."[100] In that case, the child had been six years of age at the time of the crime but was eight at the time of the proposed testimony and knew her birthday, where she went to school, her teachers' names, and she recounted her home telephone number. Additionally, the girl stated that it was a bad thing to tell a lie. Not only did the judge observe the child answering the questions, he observed her carriage and demeanor, all factors in reaching the conclusion that the child was competent as a witness.[101]

The preferable course is to accept a child's testimony if the competency tests are met. However, the testimony should not be allowed if evidence indicates that the child lacks competency. For example, an Ohio appellate court reversed a conviction for two counts of gross sexual imposition involving two children, one a three-year-old and a child who had just turned four years old at the time of the alleged crime. The trial court failed to conduct a competency hearing or voir dire exam of the children prior to allowing them to testify. The prosecutor's examination revealed numerous defects in memory and recollection and demonstrated a general lack of understanding of events or an understanding of the concept of time. One child did not know when she would have her next birthday and did not know the year she was born. The court of appeals reversed the conviction on the basis of plain error in permitting the testimony of children who had not been determined to be competent as witnesses.[102]

To be considered a competent witness, a child need not understand the concept of perjury but must know the difference between telling a lie and telling the truth. In an Arkansas prosecution for sexual crimes against a child who was five years old at the time of the offense and seven at the time of trial, the judge conducted a competency hearing with the child. Outside of the presence of the jury, the prosecutor asked the child witness about the difference between a lie and the truth and gave several examples that the child understood. From the prosecutor's questions, it appeared that the child knew her colors, the difference between a dog and a cat, understood the need to tell the truth, and seemed to understand the significance of an oath. In upholding the trial judge's

---

[100]   Borsarge v. State, 786 So. 2d 426, 430, 2001 Miss. App. LEXIS 227 (2001).

[101]   *Id.*

[102]   State v. Holland, 2008 Ohio 3450, 2008 Ohio App. LEXIS 2914 (Ohio 2008); *see Competency and Credibility: Double Trouble for Child Victims of Sexual Offenses,* 9 SUFFOLK J. TRIAL & APP. ADV. 113 (2004) for a discussion of problems involving competency of children in sexual assault cases.

decision to allow the child to testify, the appellate court noted that, "[a]s long as the record is one upon which the trial judge could find a moral awareness of the obligation to tell the truth and an ability to observe, remember, and relate facts, we will not hold there has been a manifest error or abuse of discretion in allowing the testimony."[103]

In summary, children as witnesses present challenges to determine whether they are competent. Individual determinations based on the unique facts of each child and each case will assist the court in evaluating each proposed child witness. When the child meets the elements of competency of original perception and recollection, and is able to communicate the story to the finder of fact, the judge should rule that the particular child is a competent witness. In the case of children, the final element of competency, the oath, is generally excused as long as the judge is satisfied that the child understands the duty to tell the truth.

§ 8.13 — Husband and Wife

The common law rule held that husbands and wives were incompetent as witnesses for or against each other because the spouse had an interest in the case and could not serve as an unbiased witness. The rule appears to have its genesis in medieval times and seems to have developed "from two canons of medieval jurisprudence: first, the rule that an accused was not permitted to testify in his own behalf because of his interest in the proceeding; second, the concept that husband and wife were one, and that since the woman had no recognized separate legal existence, the husband was that one."[104] Additional justification suggested by the Supreme Court in *Hawkins v. United States* that "the rule rested mainly on a desire to foster peace in the family and on a general unwillingness to use the testimony of witnesses tempted by strong self-interest to testify falsely."[105]

Courts began to erode this early rule, however, when the logic and philosophy supporting the concept began to fail, especially when the rule gave protection to the wrong interests. Thus, in the 1839 federal case of *Stein v. Bowman*, the United States Supreme Court noted that the rule of spousal incompetency "is subject to some exceptions; as where the husband commits an offence against the person of his wife."[106] Consistent with this logic, modern law in all states considers one spouse to possess competency to testify against

---

[103] Warner v. State, 2005 Ark. App. LEXIS 875 (Ark. 2005).

[104] People v. Sinohui, 28 Cal. 4th 205, 210, 47 P.3d 629, 2002 Cal. LEXIS 3777 (2002), quoting Trammel v. United States, 445 U.S. 40, 44 (1980). *See* 1 COKE, COMMENTARY UPON LITTLETON 6b (19th ed. 1832). *See also* Chapter 10 for a discussion of the husband-wife marital testimonial privilege.

[105] Hawkins v. United States, 358 U.S. 74, 75, 1958 U.S. LEXIS 115 (1958).

[106] 38 U.S. 209, 221, 1839 U.S. LEXIS 431 (1839).

the other where one spouse has been charged with a crime against the person or property of the other or has been charged with a crime against a child of either spouse or a crime involving the child's property.[107]

In 1933, the United States Supreme Court rejected the common law rule that excluded testimony by spouses in favor of each other,[108] but the new interpretation of the common law rule applied only to federal actions. In *Hawkins v. United States*, the Court:

> recognized that the basic reason underlying the exclusion [of one spouse's testimony on behalf of the other] had been the practice of disqualifying witnesses with a personal interest in the outcome of a case. Widespread disqualifications because of interest, however, had long since been abolished both in this country and in England in accordance with the modern trend which permitted interested witnesses to testify and left it for the jury to assess their credibility. Certainly, since defendants were uniformly allowed to testify in their own behalf, there was no longer a good reason to prevent them from using their spouses as witnesses. With the original reason for barring favorable testimony of spouses gone the Court concluded that this aspect of the old rule should go too.[109]

While spouses were considered competent to testify as interested individuals, the jury could evaluate the value of the testimony and the credibility of the spouse-witness, recognizing that the evidence came from an interested individual.

Marriage does not make the spouse incompetent in civil or criminal cases, and spouses may testify freely unless prevented by defects in the elements of competency: oath, original perception, recollection, and an ability to communicate. Typical of the modern trend, the Maine Revised Statutes hold that "[t]he husband or wife of the accused is a competent witness except in regard to marital communications."[110] What has emerged is that the spouses are generally considered competent for all purposes, but some marital privileges exist that may have the effect of allowing one spouse to refuse to give testimony. In some instances a defendant spouse may still be able to prevent the other from testifying even when the proposed witness spouse is fully willing to testify against the defendant spouse.[111]

Spousal competency as witnesses has been accepted in all jurisdictions, but spousal testimony may be rejected where a marital testimonial or confidential communication privilege exists. For example, in a murder case in which

---

[107] Wis. Stat. § 905.05(3)(b) (2006) and Va. Code Ann. § 8.01-398 (2006).

[108] Funk v. United States, 290 U.S. 371, 54 S. Ct. 212, 78 L. Ed. 369 (1933). *See* this case in Part II in Cases Relating to Chapter 1.

[109] 358 U.S. 74, 76 (1958).

[110] 15 M.R.S. § 1315 (2005).

[111] This is most likely to occur in a situation in which the defendant spouse has communicated with the proposed witness spouse under circumstances in which the defendant spouse was relying on the intimate and close marital relationship.

the defendant spouse had been accused of killing the victim and his DNA had been found on the woman's body, the prosecution wanted his then-wife to testify against him concerning his whereabouts on the night of the victim's death. It was a foregone conclusion that the then-wife was a competent witness, but the defendant argued that a marital privilege, the confidential communication privilege, prevented her from telling the jury that he left their home in the middle of the night in question. The trial court held that the defendant's act of leaving the marital home did not qualify as a confidential communication with his then-wife because it was not much of a communication and it was not done in confidence because other people outside the marital home would have been able to view his presence outside the home. Thus, because no privilege prevented her testimony and her competency was not an issue, the witness spouse properly testified against her husband.[112]

Statutes in most states permit spouses to testify against each other in prosecutions for only certain types of crimes. For example, under Ohio law, a husband and wife are competent to testify on behalf of each other in all criminal prosecutions and against each subject to the law that recognizes exceptions to statutory privileges. Under Ohio law, spouses are considered competent witnesses who may give testimony against each other in: (1) prosecutions for personal injury of either by the other, bigamy, rape of one by the other, other sexual offenses against each other, and in cases involving violations of personal protection orders; (2) prosecutions for bigamy; and (3) prosecutions for failure to provide for, for neglect of, or for cruelty to their minor children under 18 or their physically or mentally handicapped children under 21 years of age.[113]

Following a similar legal theory, the Georgia code provides that both husband and wife are competent to testify against the other in any criminal proceeding. The spouses cannot be compelled to offer testimony against the other except where either the husband or wife has been charged with a crime against any minor child.[114] In interpreting this statute, the Court of Appeals of Georgia noted that the trial court committed error when it virtually required a wife to testify against her spouse in a case in which her husband had been accused of assaulting his girlfriend. Under the Georgia statute, the witness spouse is considered competent to give evidence against a spouse but cannot be compelled to do so.[115] In a Georgia case involving a homicide witnessed by the defendant's wife, the court allowed the prosecutor to question the wife about the events despite her assertion of the statutory privilege. Although competent as a witness, the court failed to recognize the wife's marital privilege not to

---

[112] State v. Bates, 2003 Me. 67; 822 A.2d 1129; 2003 Me. LEXIS 77 (2003).

[113] OHIO REV. CODE ANN. § 2945.42 (Matthew Bender 2009).

[114] O.C.G.A. § 24-9-23 Compellability of testimony by defendant's spouse (Matthew Bender 2009).

[115] Phillips v. State, 278 Ga. App. 439, 441 629 S.E.2d 130, 132 2006 Ga. App. LEXIS 350 (2006).

testify against her spouse. The reviewing court reversed the conviction and remanded the case for additional proceedings.[116] According to Georgia law, as interpreted, the spouse is competent to testify against the accused in a criminal case, but to require such testimony would constitute error due to her spousal privilege not to testify.

The Texas Rules of Evidence follow a similar legal theory used by Georgia and grant a privilege to the spouse of the accused not to be called as a witness for the prosecution, but does not prohibit voluntary spousal testimony on behalf of the prosecution. In Texas, the potential witness spouse, though competent as a witness, is a holder of a privilege not to testify against the other spouse.[117] The rule allows the spouse to testify voluntarily for the state about non-confidential matters—even over the objection of the accused, but contains some exceptions that require adverse spousal testimony.[118] In a case involving an exception, *Jackson v. State*, the prosecution won a conviction against the defendant, who contended that error had occurred when his wife was forced to testify against him for criminal trespass of her individual apartment. Jackson argued that the apartment was community property under state law and he had an equal right to possession. The reviewing court held that he had no property interest in his wife's separate apartment because she had the lease in her name only, they did not live together, and because the crime was against her property, the privilege not to testify against her husband had no application.[119] Under the current Texas rule of evidence, the wife was competent as a witness and was properly compelled to testify against her husband.

In Pennsylvania criminal proceedings, competent spouses have a privilege not to testify against a current spouse but the witness spouse may waive the testimonial privilege. However, the privilege does not apply in some circumstances involving an alleged crime against the spouse or children or their property committed by the defendant spouse or when the defendant spouse has been charged with murder or rape.[120]

Federal evidence rules do not address in any detail the concept of marital privileges;[121] a federal court of appeals has noted that the marital privilege recognized by federal courts really involves two privileges. The first is the marital testimonial privilege, which permits a witness spouse from having to testify against the defendant spouse during the existence of the marriage; the second privilege allows one spouse to prevent the other from giving testimony relating to confidential communications made between them during the existence of the marriage.[122] As one Indiana court noted, the purpose of the marital

---

[116]   Webb v. State, 284 Ga. 122, 127, 2008 Ga. LEXIS 564 (Ga. 2008).

[117]   Tex. R. Evid. 504(b) Husband-Wife Privileges (Matthew Bender 2009).

[118]   *Id*. Rule 504(b)(4).

[119]   2005 Tex. App. LEXIS 3631 (Tex. 2005).

[120]   42 Pa. Cons. Stat. § 5913 (2005).

[121]   *See* Fed. R. Evid. 501.

[122]   United States v. Montague, 421 F.3d 1099, 1103, 2005 U.S. App. LEXIS 14593 (10th Cir. 2005).

privileges are "grounded at least in significant part not on a policy of promoting disclosure but on concern for the health of the ongoing relationship between husband and wife and the policy of preventing further conflict between them by forcing one to testify against the other."[123]

Modern legal theory holds that spouses are competent to testify for or against each other. Even though legal competency exists, through the exercise of the marital testimonial and confidential communication privileges, either spouse may refuse to testify against the other. These privileges are subject to some exceptions involving crime against the person of the other spouse, the children, or the property of either. The ability to exercise a privilege to testify for or against the other spouse depends on case law and the provisions of federal or state statutes. Although spouses may testify on behalf of each other in all jurisdictions, some jurisdictions do not require one spouse to testify against the other spouse in any criminal case, while in others the spouse is required by statute to testify against the accused spouse when the spouse is accused of specified crimes. If the statute makes wives and husbands competent to testify against each other regarding a specific crime, and there is no privilege to assert, then a spouse may be compelled to testify. Under these circumstances, if the spouse refuses to testify, he or she may be found to be in civil contempt of court.

§ 8.14 — Conviction of Crime

Under English common law, a person convicted of a felony was considered incompetent to testify as a witness in court.[124] In the Republic of Texas, prior to its admission into the federal union, the English common law was followed and all persons who had been convicted of a felony anywhere were considered incompetent as witnesses. This practice continued following statehood.[125] Nevada followed this theory and refused to admit testimony from felons during the 1800s.[126] States gradually removed this disability on the theory that a felony conviction did not by itself make an individual an untruthful person for all time.

Pursuant to state law and in agreement with the common law, a Tennessee appellate court reversed a conviction for assault with intent to commit murder because one of the prosecution witnesses had previously been convicted of petit larceny. The appellate court ordered a new trial in 1872 because the state of the law at that time was such that people who had been convicted of specific crimes were deemed to be incompetent as witnesses in courts. "The rule of exclusion grew out of the common law doctrine that a party to the record, or one interested in the result, with certain exceptions, which were engrafted upon

---

[123]   Glover v. State, 836 N.E.2d 414, 421, 2005 Ind. LEXIS 983 (2005).
[124]   Logan v. United States, 144 U.S. 263, 1892 U.S. LEXIS 2080 (1892).
[125]   Logan v. United States, 144 U.S. 263, 299, 1892 U.S. LEXIS 2080 (1892).
[126]   State v. Foley, 15 Nev. 64, 1880 Nev. LEXIS 16 (1880).

the rule from supposed necessity, was not competent as a witness, because of the temptation to perjury."[127]

In states following the English common law theory, a felony conviction meant that the individual was incompetent to testify as a court witness. As times changed, the legal theory supporting legal incompetency evolved. More than 91 years ago, the United States Supreme Court decided that "the dead hand of the common law rule," disqualifying a witness who had been convicted of crime, should no longer be applied in criminal cases in the federal courts.[128] Under modern legislation, states have acted legislatively and have removed any defect in competency from those who have criminal records. Demonstrative of this principle, Arizona legislation provides that "[a] person shall not be incompetent to testify because he is a party to an action or proceeding or interested in the issue tried, or because he has been indicted, accused or convicted of a crime . . . ."[129]

Legislation may make a person presumptively competent as a witness, but defects in the elements of competency may defeat this presumption. Aside from competency, issues relating to credibility are matters to be determined by the trier of fact. Because some crimes may, by their nature, lead to questions about a person's honesty or credibility, proof of some prior crimes committed by a witness, including a defendant-witness, may be permitted based on the theory that prior convictions may have a legitimate bearing on the jury's perception of the witness's truthfulness. Most jurisdictions permit a showing of the fact of a witness's felony conviction or conviction of a crime of moral turpitude for the purpose of impeaching the credibility of the witness.[130]

State and federal statutes enacted during the past 70 years, as well as court interpretations, have made it quite clear that a criminal conviction does not render a witness incompetent to testify but may create concerns about a witness's credibility. Demonstrative of this concept, New York provides that a person who has been convicted of a crime is a competent witness; but the conviction may be proved, for the purpose of affecting the weight of his testimony, either by cross-examination, upon which he shall be required to answer any relevant question, or by the record."[131] The general rule is that prior convictions of a witness affect the weight and credibility of the witness's testimony, but do not disqualify the witness.[132]

---

[127] State v. Kennedy, 85 S.C. 146, 150, 67 S.E. 152, 1910 S.C. LEXIS 219 (1910).

[128] Rosen v. United States, 245 U.S. 467, 1918 U.S. LEXIS 2150 (1918).

[129] ARIZ. REV. STAT. § 12-2201 Persons who may be witnesses (Matthew Bender 2008).

[130] For the rules regarding impeachment of witness, see Chapter 9. *See also* Federal Rule of Evidence 609, Impeachment by Evidence of Conviction of Crime.

[131] NY CLS CPLR § 4513, Competency of person convicted of crime (Matthew Bender 2009).

[132] United States v. Reynolds, 2006 U.S. App. LEXIS 18115 (4th Cir. 2006). *See also* People v. Hinton, 37 Cal. 4th 839, 887, 126 P.3d 981, 1018, 38 Cal. Rptr. 3d 149, 193, 2006 Cal. LEXIS 336 (Cal. 2006).

§ 8.15 — Religious Belief

Fears that nonbelievers would have no incentive to be truthful led to the old practice in many American jurisdictions of preventing persons who had no religious belief from serving as witnesses in court. In an old case, the Supreme Court of Kansas once noted that, "[u]nder the common law, as well as in some of the states, atheists and persons without religious belief are deemed insensible to the obligations of an oath and incompetent as witnesses."[133] But the Supreme Court of Alabama noted in an earlier (1841) case that oaths had nothing to do with Christianity because they were more ancient than the Christian religion.[134] Under modern law, state constitutions or state and federal statutes affirmatively provide that no person shall be rendered incompetent to testify as a witness on account of his or her religious opinions or for want of any religious belief.[135] Consistent with this view is Federal Rule of Evidence 610, which holds "[e]vidence of the beliefs or opinions of a witness on matters of religion is not admissible for the purpose of showing that by reason of their nature the witness's credibility is impaired or enhanced." If the witness is able to understand the obligation of an oath and the consequences of false swearing, the witness is competent, even if there is no evidence that he or she has a religious background.[136] Also improper is using religion as a tool to bolster a witness's credibility. Assuredly, it would be error to enhance witness testimony to suggest in a closing argument in a drug case that the police officer walked into a hotel "alone, armed *with a cross on his belt* and a gun on his side, into the belly of the beast like a surgeon aiming for the cancer as he came across it."[137]

However, "[n]ot all religious inquiries are forbidden"[138] if an aspect of religion might have an effect on bias or motive for impeachment purposes. However, it would be improper to state in a closing argument that a defendant "had the nerve to tell (the jury) 'I pray.' "[139] Massachusetts allows persons other than Christians to be sworn as witnesses according to the ceremonies of their respective religion. However, a person with a belief in some notion of a supreme being and "[a] person not a believer in any religion shall be required to testify under the penalties of perjury" and the "evidence of his disbelief in the existence of God may not be received to affect his credibility as a witness."[140]

---

[133] Atchison, T. & S. F. R. Co. v. Potter, 60 Kan. 808, 811, 58 P. 471, 1899 Kan. LEXIS 143 (1899).

[134] Blocker v. Burness, 2 Ala. 354, 355, 1841 Ala. LEXIS 357 (Ala. 1841).

[135] Gillars v. United States, 182 F.2d 962 (D.C. Cir. 1950). Under Rule 610, Religious Beliefs or Opinions, evidence of the beliefs or opinions of a witness on matters of religion is not admissible for the purpose of showing that by reason of their nature the witness's credibility is impaired or enhanced. See also United States v. Teicher, 987 F.2d 112 (2d Cir. 1993).

[136] Chapell v. State, 710 S.W.2d 214 (Ark. 1986).

[137] United States v. Rogers, 556 F.3d 1130, 1141, 2009 U.S. App. LEXIS 5236 (10th Cir. 2009) (Emphasis added.)

[138] Slagle v. Bagley, 2006 U.S. App. LEXIS 20240, 2006 Fed. Appx. 0283P (6th Cir. 2006).

[139] *Id.*

[140] Annotated Laws of Massachusetts, ALM GL ch. 233 § 19 (Matthew Bender 2009).

The courts and state statutes have been consistent in providing that one's religious belief or lack thereof should not be a basis upon which a court or jury should evaluate testimonial capacity or credibility.[141] Michigan takes a strong stand against interjecting religion into trials and has "determined that when religious beliefs and their relationship to the veracity of a defendant or witness have been improperly raised by a prosecutor during trial, reversal is necessitated regardless of whether there is a demonstration of prejudice because of the questioning."[142]

§ 8.16   Competency of Judge as Witness

Rule 605

Competency of Judge as Witness

The judge presiding at the trial may not testify in that trial as a witness. No objection need be made in order to preserve the point.[143]

* * *

For some years, the matter of whether a judge should be incompetent to testify as a witness in a trial over which he or she presides has been debated. The argument has been offered that where a judge both sits as a judge in the very case where the judge will serve as a witness calls into question the impartiality of the judge.[144] Some authorities advocate that this matter should be left to the discretion of the judge, and in some states this is the rule that is followed.[145] Additional issues would arise when a judge served as a witness, especially those involving who should rule on objections, who would compel the judge to answer questions, and what would occur during cross-examination. A party attorney could be reluctant to attempt impeachment of a judge because that attorney would have future cases before that judge, an obvious conflict of interest. However, these issues have been rendered moot by 28 U.S.C. § 455, which mandates that federal judges disqualify themselves in cases in which they are or have been material witnesses or in which they may have bias or

---

[141] *See* MICH. COMP. LAWS § 600.1436 (Matthew Bender 2009), which removed any religious test for competency and provided that religion-related interrogation of the witness could not be the subject of inquiry.

[142] People v. Bell, 2008 Mich. App. LEXIS 2307 (Mich. 2008).

[143] FED. R. EVID. 605.

[144] Elmore v. State, 13 Ark. App. 221, 227, 682 S.W.2d 758, 762, 1985 Ark. App. LEXIS 1735 (1985). The failure of a witness judge to recuse him- or herself does not always constitute reversible error. *See also* 22 A.L.R.3d 1198 (2003).

[145] *See* cases collected in Annotation, *Judge as a Witness in a Case on Trial Before Him,* 157 A.L.R. 315. *See also* MORRIS, FEDERAL PRACTICE, including the advisory committee's note on Rule 605.

prejudice.[146] Rule 605 of the Federal Rules of Evidence follows the federal statute that deems federal judges incompetent to testify in cases in which they are sitting. This rule has been so well followed that a Texas court was prompted to state, "[n]ot surprisingly, there are few reported federal or state cases involving Rule 605 violations."[147]

A federal case that did involve a Rule 605 violation occurred when a transcript of a suppression hearing, in which the judge offered some conclusions concerning a defendant's suppression witness, was admitted at the trial on the merits.[148] At a pretrial motion to suppress, the trial judge expressed his opinion concerning the credibility of a defense witness in fairly clear terms. The same judge permitted the prosecutor at trial to read part of the suppression hearing transcript, which included the judge's comments concerning the lack of credibility of the defense witness. According to the reviewing court, "the introduction of the trial judge's suppression-hearing comments amounted to impermissible judicial testimony"[149] and effectively made the judge a witness in the very trial over which he was presiding, violating Rule 605.

A violation of Rule 605, or a comparable state rule, does not require an automatic reversal of any verdict. In a federal case involving a border crossing re-entry into the United States by an illegal alien, a judge interjected some his own knowledge regarding the location and number of the stop signs along the border road where the aliens were captured and the narrowness of the road. The judge stated these facts at a time in the suppression hearing when these facts had yet to be introduced to the record. The real effect in this case was that the judge was testifying as an unsworn witness. The Court of Appeals concluded that the suppression judge violated Rule 605 making judges incompetent to testify when the judge is presiding over the proceeding but noted that the error could be judged on the harmless error standard. Because sufficient admissible evidence was present to convict the illegal alien of re-entry, the court upheld the conviction.[150]

Many states have adopted the federal rule either by statute or by court decision. For example, a Nebraska statute that mirrors federal Rule 605 provides that a judge may not testify in a any trial over which the judge is presiding.[151] Generally, a defendant cannot use Rule 605 to force a judge to recuse him- or herself from a trial or from a post-conviction proceeding by placing the judge on a witness list.[152] Even though the judge is not considered competent

---

[146]   28 U.S.C. § 455 (2006). Disqualification of justice, judge, or magistrate (magistrate judge).

[147]   Bradley v. State ex rel. White, 990 S.W.2d 245, 248, 1999 Tex. LEXIS 33 (1999).

[148]   *See* United States v. Blanchard, 542 F.3d 1133, 2008 U.S. App. LEXIS 19151 (7th Cir. 2008).

[149]   *Id.* 1149.

[150]   United States v. Berber-Tinoco, 510 F.3d 1083, 1091, 2007 U.S. App. LEXIS 29301 (9th Cir. 2007), *cert. denied,* 2008 U.S. LEXIS 7266 (2008). *See also* Henderson v. State, 2005 Tenn. Crim. App. LEXIS 667 (2005).

[151]   State v. Sims, 272 Neb 811, 826, 827, 2006 Neb. LEXIS 185 (Neb. 2006).

[152]   *Id.* 816, 817.

as a witness in the case over which the judge presides, judges may testify in separate, but related proceedings. In one case where the parties came to a settlement in the presence of the judge, but the agreement was not immediately reduced to a writing, the judge can be called as a witness in a separate proceeding to give evidence concerning the agreement.[153]

§ 8.17 Competency of Juror as Witness

Rule 606

Competency of Juror as Witness

(a) At the trial.—A member of the jury may not testify as a witness before that jury in the trial of the case in which the juror is sitting. If the juror is called so to testify, the opposing party shall be afforded an opportunity to object out of the presence of the jury.

(b) Inquiry into validity of verdict or indictment.— Upon an inquiry into the validity of a verdict or indictment, a juror may not testify as to any matter or statement occurring during the course of the jury's deliberations or to the effect of anything upon that or any other juror's mind or emotions as influencing the juror to assent to or dissent from the verdict or indictment or concerning the juror's mental processes in connection therewith. But a juror may testify about (1) whether extraneous prejudicial information was improperly brought to the jury's attention, (2) whether any outside influence was improperly brought to bear upon any juror, or (3) whether there was a mistake in entering the verdict onto the verdict form. A juror's affidavit or evidence of any statement by the juror may not be received on a matter about which the juror would be precluded from testifying.[154]

* * *

Although many older cases are to the contrary, the general rule is that a juror may not testify as a witness in the trial of a case in which he or she is sitting. According to the Tenth Circuit Court of Appeal,

> The rule against impeachment of a jury verdict by juror testimony as to internal deliberations may be traced back to "Mansfield's Rule," originating in the 1785 case of *Vaise v. Delaval*, 99 Eng. Rep. 944 (K.B. 1785). Faced with juror testimony that the jury had reached its verdict by drawing lots, Lord Mansfield established a blanket ban on jurors testifying against their own verdict.[155]

In preventing most juror testimony, "[c]onsiderations that bear upon the permissibility of testimony are similar to those invoked when a judge is called

---

[153] McMillin v. Davidson Industries, 2005 Ohio 224, 2005 Ohio App. LEXIS 221 (2005).
[154] FED. R. EVID. 606.
[155] United States v. Benally, 546 F.3d 1230, 1233, 2008 U.S. App. LEXIS 23555 (10th Cir. 2008).

as a witness."[156] The juror could argue against any personally impeaching evidence and rehabilitate his or her testimony in the perception of other jurors in a way not open to other witnesses. A witness juror would have an unfettered opportunity to unfairly sway the jurors with personal historical knowledge of the case that may have been inadmissible at trial. The chances are too great that the testimony of the juror would have an undue influence on the verdict. This rule of exclusion was codified in the Federal Rules of Evidence, which, without exception, prohibit the members of a jury from testifying in the case in which they sit as jurors. If an attorney attempted to call a sitting juror, objection may be made outside the hearing of the jury.[157]

Section (b) of Federal Rule 606 generally holds that jurors are incompetent as witnesses; however, the Rule allows jurors to testify about whether outside influences improperly affected jury deliberations. This rule makes a juror incompetent to testify not only concerning the facts to prove the case, but also covers activities that took place during the jury's deliberations. This incompetency stems from the old maxim that "a juror may not impeach his own verdict." The rule has been justified on a variety of theories including the need for the preservation of the secrecy of internal jury deliberations and to protect the verdict against attack for corrupt reasons.[158] Significant considerations support the rationale of Rule 606 (b) that "include verdict finality, maintaining the integrity of the jury system, encouraging frank and honest deliberations, and the protection of jurors from subsequent harassment by a losing party."[159]

Were this rule to permit inquiry into the mental deliberations and processes of the jurors, every verdict would be susceptible to being undermined by post-trial jury tampering and harassment of jurors. One court noted that if every defendant had the power to make former jurors into witnesses against a previous verdict, the procedure "would allow defendants to launch inquiries into jury conduct in the hope of discovering something that might invalidate the verdicts against them"[160] and result in the destruction of openness and freedom of discussion in the jury room. Under federal evidence rules, the protection from making jurors into witnesses extends to each of the components of the deliberation, including arguments, statements, discussions, mental and emotional reactions, and any other feature of the deliberation process.[161] Interestingly, where the inquiry of reasoning and deliberation concern the judge and improper extraneous factors used in reaching a verdict in a bench trial, no prohibition on an investigation of judicial reasoning exists.[162]

---

[156] Notes of Advisory Committee on Rules. Subdivision (a). of Rule 606.

[157] Fed. R. Evid. 606(a).

[158] People v. Grider, 246 Cal. App. 2d 149, 153, 54 Cal. Rptr. 497, 501, 1966 Cal. App. LEXIS 1013 (1966).

[159] United States v. Delatorre, 572 F. Supp. 2d 967, 2008 U.S. Dist. LEXIS 77787 (N. D. Ill. 2008).

[160] United States v. Siegelman, 2009 U.S. App. LEXIS 5369 (11th Cir. 2009).

[161] United States v. Crosby, 294 F.2d 928 (2d Cir. 1961).

[162] Stewart v. Southwest Foods, 688 So. 2d 733, 735, 1996 Miss. LEXIS 643 (1996).

In a case in which a trial judge improperly allowed a juror to testify that during jury deliberations, the jury foreman had made racist claims about native Americans.[163] The native American defendant had been convicted of forcibly assaulting a Bureau of Indian Affairs officer while using a dangerous weapon. The day after the verdict, a juror approached the defense counsel with information that two jurors had not been honest when asked during *voir dire* about their prior experiences with native Americans. In the jury room these two jurors indicated their belief that all native Americans got drunk and then became violent. The Court of Appeals reversed the trial judge's determination that the defendant deserved a new trial based on the juror testimony because the court determined that the juror's evidence concerning internal misconduct was not admissible under Rule 606(b). Since the only evidence of juror misconduct was not admissible, the defendant was left with no evidence with which to demonstrate or argue that any illegality or misconduct occurred.[164]

Rule 606(b) makes an exception that authorizes the juror to testify on the question of whether extraneous prejudicial information was improperly brought to the jury's attention or whether any outside influence was improperly brought to bear upon any juror. The purpose of this is to allow the courts to determine whether there were any irregularities, such as the introduction of a prejudicial newspaper account, into the jury room, or statements by the bailiff concerning the case. Mistakes and misconduct of the jury during its deliberations that do not involve external influences are not generally subject to inquiry.[165]

In a Wisconsin case, there was an allegation that some of the jury members had become extrajudicially aware that the defendant had prior criminal convictions. At post-conviction relief hearings, the defense counsel alleged that there had been jury misconduct that required a reversal and new trial. As the reviewing court noted, pursuant to Wisconsin law "the party seeking to impeach the verdict must demonstrate that a juror's testimony is admissible by establishing that: (1) the juror's testimony concerns extraneous information (rather than the deliberative process of the jurors), (2) the extraneous information was improperly brought to the jury's attention, and (3) the extraneous information was potentially prejudicial."[166] Under this daunting procedure, if the appellant establishes that the juror is permitted to testify, the appellant then must next demonstrate that one or more jurors heard the statements or engaged in the alleged conduct and, finally, the court must then determine whether sufficient prejudice occurred to justify overturning the conviction.[167] In this case, the defendant managed to meet the first three hurdles, but the court did not

---

[163]   *See* United States v. Benally, 546 F.3d 1230, 2008 U.S. App. LEXIS 23555 (10th Cir. 2008).

[164]   *Id.*

[165]   Williams v. Price, 343 F.3d 223, 2003 U.S. App. LEXIS 18662 (3d Cir. 2003).

[166]   State v. Searcy, 288 Wis. 2d 804; 709 N.W.2d 497; 2005 Wis. App. LEXIS 1124 (2005).

[167]   *Id.* at 828, 507.

find by clear and convincing evidence that any jurors were exposed to the prejudicial information about the defendant's prior convictions. Therefore, the reviewing court refused to disturb the jury verdict. Simply stated, the process to overturn a jury verdict based on outside influence almost always proves unsuccessful to any criminal appellant.

In a suit for damages allegedly at the hands of the police, one officer, who had been found civilly liable, wanted to introduce an affidavit from a juror that concerned internal juror misconduct. The court first considered whether the affidavit concerned the type of misconduct for which evidence may be entertained under Federal Rule of Evidence 606(b). The officer alleged that the jury improperly determined a verdict amount concerning punitive damages in the first phase and that decision constituted an "extraneous influence" that affected the second phase of jury deliberations. Because the allegations of misconduct did not allege that outside influence was brought to bear upon any juror and no extraneous evidence or information was allegedly brought to the jury's attention, the court determined that no evidentiary hearing was necessary to determine whether a new trial was needed.[168]

While not competent to be witnesses at the trial in which jurors are sitting, following their discharge by the judge, jurors may discuss the case with anyone and everyone. During the trial, a strong general rule exists that prohibits jurors from talking about the case with anyone or with each other until they begin their deliberations. In implementing this rule, judges routinely order jurors not to discuss the case at any time with anyone other than with fellow jurors during regularly scheduled deliberations and may remind the jurors during the trial.[169] Once a trial has concluded and the jurors have been officially discharged, they are free to speak with attorneys in the case as well as print, broadcast, and Internet media, or to choose not to speak with anyone or any organization. In this context, information concerning the internal deliberations, discussions, and behaviors of the jury may be revealed at the individual discretion of the juror. Courts are under no general duty to make jurors available to interested persons and may take some affirmative steps to protect personal matters of the jurors from unwarranted harassment.[170]

Because discharged jurors have the right to refuse any comment concerning a case, states are permitted to keep much juror information private and can refuse to disclose it unless a defendant-appellant makes a strong case for disclosure.[171] In an attempted arson case,[172] the appellant wanted to have the court identify a juror who initially seemed equivocal when the juror was polled after the verdict. The trial judge refused to release the juror information because the

---

[168]   Helena v. City of San Francisco, 2006 U.S. Dist. LEXIS 27 (N.D. Cal. 2006).

[169]   United States v. Camacho, 555 F.3d 695, 704, 2009 U.S. App. LEXIS 3592 (8th Cir. 2009).

[170]   *See* United States v. Scrushy, 2005 U.S. Dist. LEXIS 42127 (N.D. Ala. 2006).

[171]   *See* CAL. CODE CIV. PROC. § 206. Right of jurors not to discuss deliberations or verdict; Petition for access to personal juror information (Matthew Bender 2009).

[172]   People v. Carrasco, 163 Cal. App. 4th 978, 991, 2008 Cal. App. LEXIS 844 (Cal. 2008).

judge, after questioning the juror at the time of polling, was convinced that the juror acted properly. The trial court refused to disclose the personal information of the juror because it found a compelling need to keep the juror's identity secret under a California statute.[173] The statute allows some protection for jurors against unreasonable contact with the defendant or someone working on behalf of the defendant because the identity is sealed unless a judge orders a different result.[174] Similarly, under Florida law, a party who believes a verdict may be subject to legal attack, must notify the court to request an order permitting the party to interview a juror or jurors to determine if the belief is supported by facts.[175] According to the Florida criminal rules, following "notice and hearing, the trial judge, upon a finding that the verdict may be subject to challenge, shall enter an order permitting the interview, and setting therein a time and a place for the interview of the juror or jurors, which shall be conducted in the presence of the court and the parties."[176] Essentially, following the trial, jurors are free to discuss the case at any and all levels or to remain silent. Some jurisdictions limit contact, unless judicially approved, if the initiator is the defendant, counsel, or another person connected to the original case.

§ 8.18 Summary

To be admissible in a trial in a criminal case, evidence must be competent in that it meets the tests of logical and legal relevancy. The item of evidence must help prove or disprove a fact in issue and the probative value of the evidence must be greater than its prejudicial effect. The evidence is then considered competent. Even though the evidence has passed the relevancy and materiality tests, it will be excluded if the court finds that it is incompetent for other legal reasons, such as a statutory or constitutional violation.

Care must be taken to avoid confusion concerning the rules regarding competency of the evidence and competency of the witness. A witness may be competent by meeting the four elements of competency, and yet the evidence to be introduced by the witness may be ruled incompetent, and thus excludable.

From a general point of view, evidence is incompetent if: (1) law enforcement officials have obtained it wrongfully or illegally; or (2) a statute declares it to be incompetent; or (3) it has been declared incompetent by the courts, or (4) it has insufficient or no connection to the case.

Documentary evidence must meet the usual competency tests so that it possesses sufficient connection to the case, but it also must comply with special requirements. For example, it must be authenticated to show that it is

---

[173] *See* CAL. CODE CIV. PROC. § 206 Right of jurors not to discuss deliberations or verdict; Petition for access to personal juror information and § 237. Names of qualified jurors made available to public; Petition for access to records; Notice; Hearing; Violations (Matthew Bender 2009).

[174] *Id.*

[175] *See* FLA. R. CRIM. P. 3.575. Motion to Interview Juror (Matthew Bender 2009).

[176] *Id.*

genuine. Likewise, real evidence may be excluded as incompetent if specific requirements are not met.

Through court decisions and statutes, rules have evolved that require a witness to meet the four elements of competency: oath (or a substitute), original perception, recollection, and an ability to communicate prior to being permitted to testify in court. While competency rules have been liberalized in recent years, there are still certain requirements that, if not met, may make a witness incompetent to testify in court or may prevent a prospective witness from testifying through reliance on a privilege.

Even though a person may not have normal mental capacity, he or she may be allowed to testify if he or she can understand the obligation of an oath and can give a correct account of the matters seen or heard. Some jurisdictions hold that a child is generally presumed competent to testify, while other jurisdictions hold that below a specified age, the presumption is against competency. As a general rule, a child can be proved to be competent where the child demonstrates the capacity to observe events and to recollect and communicate them, and has the ability to understand questions and to make intelligent answers with the understanding of the duty to speak the truth.

At common law, neither husband nor wife was permitted to testify for or against the other. All states by statute have made both husband and wife competent to testify on behalf of an accused spouse, but with some exceptions that vary, depending on the jurisdiction. It is generally provided that the prosecution may not force a spouse to testify against the accused spouse.

A criminal conviction for a felony generally does not render a witness or a defendant incompetent to testify. While considered competent to testify, a defendant who has been previously convicted of a crime, especially a felony, can choose to forgo testifying because it opens the door to evidence of prior felonies and misdemeanors involving moral turpitude being introduced as an impeachment device. However, certain convictions may be relevant if they are introduced to show that the defendant had a common scheme or plan, motive, intent, identity, knowledge sufficient to commit the crime, or lack of mistake in committing the crime.

The competency of the presiding judge to testify as a witness in a case the judge is presently hearing has severe limitations. Under the modern rules of evidence, and consistent with Rule 605 of the Federal Rules of Evidence, judges in federal courts and states that have adopted a state version of the Federal Rules are incompetent to testify as to any matter in a trial over which the judge presides. A juror is incompetent to act as a witness at the trial of a case while serving as a juror in that case. Under Federal Rule 606, jurors also may not testify about the verdict or the manner in which the jury decided the case except when the inquiry relates to external influence or external prejudicial information that may have been improperly brought to the jurors' attention.

As a practical matter, justice personnel should be fully aware of the rules that make testimony or other evidence inadmissible because of competency rules. In some instances, a case may be resolved based on one piece of real evidence or testimony that an attorney attempts to get the court to admit or exclude.

Evidence via Witness Testimony

Examination
of Witnesses

9

For two centuries past, the policy of the Anglo-American system of Evidence has been to regard the necessity of testimony by cross-examination as a vital feature of the law. The belief that no safeguard for testing the value of human statements is comparable to that furnished by cross-examination, and the conviction that no statement (unless by special exception) should be used as testimony until it has been probed and sublimated by that test, has found increasing strength in lengthening experience.

WIGMORE, EVIDENCE, Vol. 5, § 1367 (3d ed. 1940)

Chapter Outline

Section
9.1   Introduction
9.2   Essential Qualities of a Witness
9.3   Oath or Affirmation Requirement
9.4   Judicial Control of Testimony
9.5   Separation of Witnesses
9.6   Direct Examination of Witnesses
9.7   —Leading Questions
9.8   —Refreshing Memory—Present Memory Revived
9.9   —Past Recollection Recorded
9.10   Cross-Examination of Witnesses
9.11   Redirect and Recross-Examination
9.12   Impeachment of Witnesses
9.13   —Own Witness
9.14   —Bias or Prejudice
9.15   —Character and Conduct
9.16   —Conviction of Crime
9.17   —Prior Inconsistent Statements
9.18   —Defects of Recollection or Perception
9.19   —Use of Confession for Impeachment Purposes
9.20   Rehabilitation of Witness
9.21   Summary

§ 9.1 Introduction

Most evidence in a criminal trial must be introduced to the court through the testimony of witnesses who orally describe what happened and what that witness observed. The physical evidence that may pertain to a criminal case, such as a firearm or knife or the results of a chemical test, are all brought to the court through the testimony of witnesses. While a couple of substitutes for evidence do exist, such as judicial notice, inferences, presumptions and stipulations, it would be impossible to present a criminal case without the use of trial witnesses. The function of the witness is to present the evidence to the trier of fact so that it may make a determination of what these facts indicate or what deductions may be made from the facts. Properly presented, the evidence will indicate what happened, whether a crime occurred, and whether or not that person should be held criminally responsible. On the assumption that a criminal trial has as its sole purpose the determination of whether an accused person is guilty or innocent of the crime charged it would seem appropriate to assume that all evidence related to the case should be admissible where there is any possible connection to the particular case in front of the court. However, there are various constitutional, statutory, and sound public policy reasons that limit some of the evidence that is highly related to the crime, and yet the evidence may be prohibited from admission and never revealed to the trier of fact.

In conducting the criminal trial, the normal procedure is first for the prosecution to present evidence that tends to prove the offense charged by the level of proof known as *beyond a reasonable doubt*. In so doing, the prosecution calls a series of witnesses and then proceeds to ask questions of the witnesses. The defendant may cross-examine the prosecution's witnesses and the prosecution may do the same to the defense witnesses. After the prosecution has presented its case, the defense has an opportunity to put its own witnesses on the stand and introduce evidence that follows the defense's theory of the case. As a preliminary matter, each witness must be qualified as a witness, but there is a presumption that all witnesses meet the minimum requirements. The qualifications of a witness include that the witness take an oath to tell the truth, have personal knowledge of the historical facts of the case, have memory and recollection of those facts, and have an ability to communicate. Even after the witnesses have been qualified, their testimony is subject to many rules that will be discussed in this chapter and in future chapters.

This chapter focuses on the general rules regulating the qualification of witnesses and witness examination by the prosecution and the defense. Specifically, the sections in this chapter cover the qualifications of the witnesses, the requirement of the oath or affirmation, separation of witnesses, direct and cross-examination of witnesses, and the process of witness impeachment and rehabilitation. Later chapters will discuss in great detail the rules that limit the admissibility of testimonial evidence, while giving due recognition to some of the more complex and arcane rules and their exceptions. This category includes the testimonial privileges, opinion testimony, and the hearsay rule, with its exceptions.

§ 9.2   Essential Qualities of a Witness

> **Rule 602**
>
> **Lack of Personal Knowledge**
>
> A witness may not testify to a matter unless evidence is introduced sufficient to support a finding that the witness has personal knowledge of the matter. Evidence to prove personal knowledge may, but need not, consist of the witness' own testimony. This rule is subject to the provisions of Rule 703, relating to opinion testimony by expert witnesses.[1]

In order to meet the threshold witness requirements and to be eligible to testify, a witness must have a personal connection with the relevant occurrence, coupled with mental and physical faculties sufficient to be able to observe and understand the events at the time of their occurrence and to recollect and relate them to the jury or a court in a manner that renders the testimony relevant.[2] In

---

[1]   FED. R. EVID. 602. Rule 703, which is referred to in Rule 602, provides that the expert witness need not have personal knowledge of facts or dates.

[2]   People v. Hooker, 253 Ill. App. 3d 1075, 625 N.E.2d 1081 (1993).

other words, the witness must be qualified. Normally, "in any criminal trial every person is competent to be a witness,"[3] but when an issue arises that questions the competency of a particular witness, the witness may be required to demonstrate that the witness had original perception, remembers what happened, can communicate this knowledge, and is willing to take the oath or a substitute. When a judge makes a determination about competency, the witness is either competent or incompetent, because there are no degrees of competency where one witness would have more competency than another.[4]

The rationale for Federal Rule 602 is based on the concept that lay testimony that is not based on personal information is useless for proof of guilt, and a witness cannot provide information about a matter about which the witness has no knowledge.[5] In a prosecution for illegally selling the drugs, Oxymetholone and Testosterone, the defendant moved to have an indictment quashed because the witnesses had no knowledge that what the defendant was alleged to have sold the witnesses contained any particular drug. According to the court, the witness had insufficient experience and no qualification to identify the pills alleged to be Oxymetholone or the liquid alleged to be Testosterone and was not a competent witness concerning the identity of the alleged pharmaceuticals.[6]

The requirement of firsthand knowledge or original knowledge will prevent a person from being considered competent as a witness for a particular case. In a case in which an altercation arose in a parking garage, a security guard was watching a video console where he could observe the altercation in real time.[7] Other security guards watched the tape later and concluded that the defendant was one of the perpetrators of the violence. A few days later, the defendant and his attorney viewed the videotape, but the portion containing the incident had been taped over with a television show. The trial court allowed the security guards who had only observed a replay of the tape to testify against the defendant over his objection that they were incompetent because they did not observe the incident, but only later watched it on a security playback monitor. Essentially, the argument was that the guards possessed no personal knowledge. The appellate court reversed the judgment on the ground that none of the security guards who observed the videotape were competent witnesses and because they had been permitted to testify, the verdict had to be reversed.

As a general rule, the party offering the testimony must prove that the witness had an opportunity to observe the incident about which he or she is

---

[3]　A.R.S. § 13-4061 Competency of witness (Ariz. 2006). *See also* Fed. R. Evid. 601.

[4]　Hawai'i v. Jones, 98 Haw. 294, 2002 Haw. App. LEXIS 65 (2002).

[5]　United States v. Allen, 10 F.3d 405 (7th Cir. 1993).

[6]　People v. Forgione, 2008 NY Slip Op 28365, 2008 N.Y. Misc. LEXIS 5659 (N.Y. 2008). The indictment was upheld based on sufficient grounds unrelated to the competency issue presented here.

[7]　Frazer v. El-Amin, 2004 Minn. App. LEXIS 1015 (2004).

testifying. This does not necessarily mean that a witness must have observed every facet of the event in question, especially when the witness may be considered an expert. For example, in a stabbing altercation outside an apartment complex, the court permitted a responding police officer to testify that the victim's stab wounds were consistent with someone fleeing an aggressor.[8] An emergency room doctor testified to the same conclusion, although neither the doctor nor the officer observed the fight. They obtained their personal knowledge by observing the situation and the victim and coming to a conclusion. The appellate court approved the admission of evidence by the two witnesses on the theory that each one was an expert and was properly allowed to offer a conclusion even though neither one observed the fight. The police officer had specific training as a police officer and had additional training as a military police officer.

Personal knowledge may be somewhat fleeting and still meet the requirements of firsthand knowledge. In a case in which the defendant took flight in his motor vehicle when police indicated that he should stop, he had a collision with another vehicle. At the conclusion of the vehicle chase, the witness indicated that she had an excellent opportunity to observe the defendant. She testified that she looked directly at the driver of the white Mitsubishi as he careened into the left front fender of the witness's vehicle. The witness testified that the lighting was good and that she never took her eyes off of the defendant. While the cars were crumpled together, the witness watched the defendant while he appeared to be searching for something in his car. She also observed as the police officer removed the defendant from his vehicle and she continued her observation as the two men struggled until the defendant got away. The woman identified the defendant from a photo array the first time that police showed her pictures of possible defendants. Under the circumstances, the reviewing court held that the woman witness had sufficient firsthand information to be found competent as a witness under Rhode Island's version of Rule 602.[9]

In criminal cases, witnesses are frequently called upon to testify about events that they only casually observed, such as when making an identification or recounting events that were not thought to be important at the time of observation. It is permissible under the firsthand knowledge requirement for a witness to testify that to the best of the witness's belief, the defendant committed the criminal act, while acknowledging that he or she may be mistaken as to the identity of the defendant. Where a witness has testified to an event about which he or she possessed no firsthand knowledge, without objection from the opposing side, the evidence is admitted.

---

[8]   Vasquez v. State, 2006 Tex. App. LEXIS 500 (2006).
[9]   State v. Hall, 940 A.2d 645, 2008 R.I. LEXIS 7 (R.I. 2008).

§ 9.3   Oath or Affirmation Requirement

Rule 603

Oath or Affirmation

Before testifying, every witness shall be required to declare that the witness will testify truthfully, by oath or affirmation administered in a form calculated to awaken the witness' conscience and impress the witness' mind with the duty to do so.[10]

As a general rule, every witness is required to take an oath or make a clear affirmation that he or she will offer the truth. Consequently, as one of the elements of competency, every witness, including child witnesses, is required to state that he or she will testify truthfully and with an awareness of the importance of offering truth. As one court phrased it, courts require that the prospective witness take an oath[11] or offer some form of affirmation that is "calculated to awaken the witness' conscience and impress the witness' mind with the clear duty"[12] to tell the truth. Using an affirmation in place of an oath does not itself weaken the weight of the testimony of a witness, but it may have some bearing on the weight given that testimony by some members of a jury.

Most states have statutes that allow the witness to make an affirmation rather than an oath. The affirmation need not take a particular form; the concept of affirmation is designed to afford some flexibility when dealing with religious adults or children.[13] This alternative to the formal oath is provided for those who lack the requisite belief in God, and for those who are forbidden by conscientious scruples to take an oath. Under these statutes, the witness must explicitly state that the scruple exists.

Because of First Amendment protection of the freedom of religion, federal courts do not require the witness to swear or to affirm to God in the court's administered oath. In a case in which a Mennonite defendant swore the oath to tell the truth prior to offering his trial testimony, but later complained of the process during a post-trial motion, the reviewing court noted that if he were morally opposed to swearing, he could have affirmed to tell the truth instead of swearing the oath and had, therefore, waived any right that he had in the matter.[14]

---

[10] FED. R. EVID. 603.

[11] The person administering the oath generally must be someone empowered under local law to administer oaths or the statements offered thereafter will not be deemed to be under oath. *See* State v. Lawson, 2002 Tenn. Crim. App. LEXIS 468 (2002).

[12] Esguerra v. State, 2005 Alaska App. LEXIS 2 (2005).

[13] North Carolina v. Beane, 146 N.C. App. 220, 225, 226, 552 S.E.2d 193, 196, 197, 2001 N.C. App. LEXIS 852 (2001).

[14] Izac v. United States, 2008 U.S. Dist. LEXIS 80013 (N.D.W.VA. 2008).

If the witness claims a First Amendment right not to be sworn, the court's interest in administering the precise form of oath must yield to the witness's First Amendment rights.[15] In the case of *United States v. Ward*, the reviewing court held that the defendant had a right to substitute the phrase "fully integrated honesty" for the word "truth" in taking the oath and that the rule governing the form of the oath was sufficiently flexible to permit modifications of the oath. Rule 603 and similar state statutes were developed with a view to affording flexibility when dealing with adults, atheists, conscientious objectors, mentally challenged persons, and children.[16]

When a potential witness refuses to take an oath to tell the truth and completely refuses to testify in any form, trial courts face a problem. If the potential witness made an out-of-court statement, that statement might provide needed evidence. However, a constitutional problem arises under this situation because the defendant is denied the right under the Sixth Amendment to confront the adverse witness. These types of situations have no easy answer and may result in evidence that is inadmissible.[17]

In the exercise of judicial discretion, a court may dispense with the formal oath when one of the parties presents a young child as a witness. As a substitute for the oath, the court must be satisfied that a young witness understands the consequences of not telling the truth. In California, in the judge's discretion, a child under the age of 10 may testify where the child promises to tell the truth.[18] The competency of a child witness can be demonstrated by testimony that the child understands the importance of telling the truth and understands the concept of a lie. One court noted that it was not necessary that a child understand the nature of an oath, the legal concept of false swearing or why someone holds up a hand, as long as the child demonstrates a moral awareness of the obligation to tell the truth.[19]

An oath may not be required in some other judicial proceedings that do not involve young children. For example, in a capital case, an Ohio court permitted a death-eligible convicted defendant to offer an unsworn statement to the court in an effort to present mitigating evidence to avoid the death penalty.[20] Under the criminal rules in Ohio, any criminal defendant has a right to make an unsworn statement at the time of sentencing or to present other unsworn evidence of mitigation of punishment.[21]

Rule 603 of the Federal Rules of Evidence requires that every witness declare "that he or she will testify truthfully by oath or affirmation, administered

---

[15] United States v. Ward, 989 F.2d 1015 (9th Cir. 1992).

[16] *See* the advisory Notes accompanying Federal Rule 603.

[17] *See* Crawford v. Washington, 541 U.S. 36, 2004 U.S. LEXIS 1838 (2004).

[18] CAL. EVID. CODE § 710 (Matthew Bender 2008).

[19] Warner v. State, 2005 Ark. App. LEXIS 875 (2005). *See* § 8.12 for a discussion of the competency of child witnesses.

[20] State v. Turner, 105 Ohio St. 3d 331, 2005 Ohio 1938, 826 N.E.2d 266, 2005 Ohio LEXIS 961 (2005).

[21] OHIO CRIM. R. 32 (2006).

in a form calculated to awaken the witness' conscience and impress the witness' mind with the duty to do so."[22] All jurisdictions states have adopted this or follow a similar rule. Where a witness has neither taken the oath nor otherwise affirmed to tell the truth, a failure to object immediately by the opposing party has generally been viewed as a waiver. In one California case, a prosecution witness refused to take the oath, even though the judge indicated that the witness had been told to swear to tell the truth. The prosecution offered questions to the witness that the witness answered. The reality was that the witness never took the oath or any substitute. The reviewing court held that the defendant has waived any complaint concerning the lack of oath and that the witness's evidence had been properly admitted.[23]

§ 9.4 Judicial Control of Testimony

Rule 611

Mode and Order of Interrogation and Presentation

(a) **Control by court.** The court shall exercise reasonable control over the mode and order of interrogating witnesses and presenting evidence so as to (1) make the interrogation and presentation effective for the ascertainment of the truth, (2) avoid needless consumption of time, and (3) protect witnesses from harassment or undue embarrassment.[24]

* * *

The responsive answer by a sworn witness to the questions posed by one party's attorney serves as the usual manner of introducing evidence in a criminal trial. Whether the testimony takes the form of a narrative response to a fairly open-ended question or an individual response to specific questions is ultimately a matter to be decided by the trial judge under the particular circumstances. Usually, the judge does not interfere with the attorney's approach unless there is some danger that improper or incompetent evidence might be admitted. The judge has the authority and, in fact, the responsibility to exercise reasonable control over the mode and order of interrogating witnesses and presenting evidence. Proper judicial oversight and control facilitate the interrogation process and assist in a presentation effective for the ascertainment of the truth, for avoiding needless consumption of time, and for the protection of witnesses from undue harassment.

The trial judge enjoys wide discretion in ruling on the forms of questions and how the attorneys examine the witnesses. The judge may not only rule on

---

[22] FED. R. EVID. 603.

[23] People v. Prentiss, 2008 Cal. App. Unpub. LEXIS 8119 (Cal. 2008). Unpublished opinion.

[24] FED. R. EVID. 611.

objections to questions, but also may instruct a witness to answer the questions as asked. A judge may order that witnesses not argue with the attorneys or the judge and give answers that are responsive to the actual question asked. The judge has the ultimate responsibility for the orderly reception or rejection of evidence, and a reviewing court will usually uphold judicial decisions in relation to the control of testimony unless there is a clear abuse of discretion.

Under Federal Rule of Evidence 614 and similar state rules,[25] judges have the right to ask questions of either party's witnesses and to call witnesses on the judge's own motion. Following this procedure, in a federal prosecution for selling cocaine base, the trial judge asked questions of two prosecution witnesses.[26] The judge interjected questions during the defense cross-examination of the government's drug purchaser, but the questions appeared to be of a clarifying nature. The judge also asked questions of a police officer involved in the sting drug purchase about how the police officer originally met the cooperating drug purchaser. The reviewing court held that the questions were not the kind that would have prejudiced the defendant unfairly, even though it expressed some concern that the judge placed the defense counsel in an awkward position to accept the judge's questions or to challenge the judge's impartiality in front of the jury.

A federal appellate court observed "[f]ederal judges have wide discretion to determine the role that they will play during the course of a trial."[27] Wide discretion in controlling court activity does not imply unfettered freedom, and appellate courts may reverse if the discretion is abused. For example, in an Eighth Circuit case, the defense counsel wished to inquire about a mental disability of a prosecution witness. It was known to the defense attorney that the witness had a short-term memory problem. When the witness answered that he had "diabetes" as a disability, the trial court refused to allow additional inquiry relative to mental disability. The court refused to hear any evidence of the witness's mental disability and limited the cross-examination by the defendant. On appeal, the court held that the refusal to inquire about a mental disability of the prosecution witness violated the defendant's right of confrontation necessitating a reversal of the conviction[28] under the abuse of discretion standard.

Rule 611 of the Federal Rules of Evidence and similar adoptions by the states make it clear that the judge exercises control over the examination of witnesses in determining what evidence shall be admitted and in what order. In a case heard by the Intermediate Court of Appeals of Hawai'i, the prosecution concluded its case abruptly and approximately a day earlier than was anticipated by all the parties.[29] The trial judge insisted that the defense begin its presentation immediately, over the protests of defendant's counsel that he had

---

25 State v. Dougherty, 2009 N.C. App. LEXIS 485 (N.C. 2009).
26 *See* United States v. McCray, 437 F.3d 639, 2006 U.S. App. LEXIS 3116 (7th Cir. 2006).
27 United States v. Washington, 417 F.3d 780, 783–784 (7th Cir. 2005).
28 United States v. Love, 2003 U.S. App. LEXIS 10756 (8th Cir. 2003).
29 118 Haw. 522, 2008 Haw. App. LEXIS 388 (Haw. 2008).

no witnesses present. The judge suggested that the defendant testify because the defendant was present but the defendant's legal counsel noted that the defendant had the right not to testify and might not testify depending upon the other witnesses' evidence. In exercising his control over the mode in order of presentation, the trial judge ordered that the defendant testify or waived his right to take the witness stand. Even though the reviewing court remanded this case and a final resolution still awaits, it represents a situation in which the judge may have exercised his discretion improperly by forcing the defendant to begin its presentation when it was not prepared with witnesses.

§ 9.5   Separation of Witnesses

Rule 615

Exclusion of Witnesses

At the request of a party, the court shall order witnesses excluded so that they cannot hear the testimony of other witnesses, and it may make the order of its own motion. This rule does not authorize exclusion of (1) a party who is a natural person, or (2) an officer or employee of a party which is not a natural person designated as its representative by its attorney, or (3) a person whose presence is shown by a party to be essential to the presentation of the party's cause, or (4) a person authorized by statute to be present.[30]

Statutes or court rules in all jurisdictions authorize trial judges to exclude persons who are expected to be called to testify from being in the courtroom except when that witness has been actually called to testify. Some court orders may allow witnesses who have completed their testimony to remain within the courtroom following their testimony, especially when the witnesses are not subject to recall. The procedure is variously called separation, exclusion, sequestration, or "putting witnesses under the rule." The Federal Rules of Evidence and state derivatives take the position that sequestration of witnesses is a matter of right; the rule states "[a]t the request of a party the court shall order witnesses excluded so that they cannot hear the testimony of other witnesses."[31] The purpose of the sequestration rule is to prevent witnesses from hearing the testimony of other witnesses and subsequently adjusting their testimony,[32] whether consciously or inadvertently. Other purposes of Rule 615 are "to discourage and expose fabrication, inaccuracy, and collusion and to minimize the opportunity that each witness will have to tailor testimony to the testimony of other witnesses."[33]

---

[30]   FED. R. EVID. 615.

[31]   *Id.*

[32]   Tennessee v. Coleman, 2002 Tenn. Crim. App. LEXIS 84 (2002).

[33]   *See Exclusion of Witnesses under Rule 615 of Federal Rules of Evidence,* 181 A.L.R. FED. 549 (March 2003).

Pursuant to Rule 615, several categories of persons are excluded from an order of sequestration. Natural persons who are parties to the action cannot be excluded from the courtroom because excluding them would violate the Sixth Amendment right of confrontation and create Fifth or Fourteenth Amendment due process problems. In most instances, police officers who have been in charge of an investigation are allowed to remain in court despite the fact that they may be called as witnesses.

In a federal prosecution in which the judge had placed the other witnesses "under the rule" by ordering them to be sequestered, the defendant complained at trial and on appeal that one of the arresting officers had been permitted to stay at the counsel table with the federal prosecutors.[34] The defendant argued that the officer was not absolutely necessary for the presentation of the government's case. In rejecting the defendant's argument, the Court of Appeals for the First Circuit held that Rule 615 permitted the government to designate the officer as the officer or an employee of a party that is not a natural person and to remain in the courtroom.

In interpreting Rule 615 of the Kentucky rules of evidence, the Supreme Court of Kentucky held that reversible error had occurred in a robbery case when the trial court permitted two investigating officers to remain in the courtroom during the presentation of the commonwealth's case-in-chief. Rule 615 automatically allows one officer to remain under subsection (2) of the rule, but a second officer's presence cannot be justified under subsection (3), which allows a "person whose presence is shown by a party to be essential to the presentation of the party's case." In this case, one officer testified first, while the second (and improperly present) officer was able to observe the testimony of the first and make any needed adjustments to his future testimony. When the second officer took the stand, his memory would have been completely refreshed concerning all the minute and important details. The Supreme Court of Kentucky reversed the conviction.[35]

In determining whether a witness can be excluded from a sequestration order, the judge has some discretion. In a case involving possession of an unregistered submachine gun that the defendant claimed malfunctioned and should have only fired in semi-automatic mode, he wanted his firearms expert witness to hear the government's experts testify during the prosecution's case-in-chief.[36] Because an expert may render an opinion based on facts or data made known to the expert during trial, the defendant argued that the presence of his firearms expert was essential to the presentation of his case. In the exercise of discretion, the trial judge rejected that argument and sequestered the defendant's firearms expert. In upholding the trial judge's decision, the Seventh Circuit Court of Appeals held that even if an expert may base his opinion upon matters known at trial, that argument alone did not exempt the

---

[34]   United States v. Charles, 456 F.3d 249, 2006 U.S. App. LEXIS 19619 (1st Cir. 2006).

[35]   Mills v. Commonwealth, 95 S.W.3d 838, 840, 841, 2003 Ky. LEXIS 11 (2003).

[36]   United States v. Olofson, 2009 U.S. App. LEXIS 9433 (7th Cir. 2009).

expert from the Rule 615 exclusion. Additionally, the defendant had indicated that he would "like to have" his expert present, but that was insufficient to indicate that the expert was central to the presentation of the defendant's case. As a general rule, the exemption of an expert witness from the sequestration order is up to the discretion of the trial judge, especially where the judge finds that the presence of the expert witness is crucial to the presentation of one of the parties.[37]

For a witness to meet the requirements of the exception to sequestration indicated in Rule 615(3), a party must demonstrate that the presence of a witness is essential to the presentation of the party's case. In a pretrial order, granting a defense motion under Rule 615, a federal judge decreed that the prosecution could have only one representative (the case agent) in the courtroom with the rest of the prosecution's witnesses removed from court except when testifying.[38] The judge rejected the prosecution's suggestion that it be allowed to have two agents present in the courtroom and noted that the weight of authority allows only one representative.

In a federal prosecution for fraud, conspiracy, and illegal firearm possession, where the witnesses were sequestered, a government agent who was not expected to testify remained in the courtroom during part of the proceeding.[39] Pursuant to Rule 615, another agent had been permitted to remain within the courtroom as a person essential to the case and to testify as a witness. As the testimony developed, the agent who had not been expected to testify actually took the witness stand and testified. On appeal, the government claimed that the trial court properly exercised its discretion in allowing the testimony but the appellate court determined that if this was error, it was harmless error.

In criminal cases, the defense witnesses will generally be allowed to testify even if they failed to follow the rules, although courts may consider sanctions.[40] For example, in one federal case, some of the prosecution's witnesses violated the sequestration order.[41] The judge prevented the prosecution from admitting some evidence through a witness who had not previously testified and could have received courtroom information. The judge also instructed the jury that in considering witness credibility, they could consider the fact of the violation of the sequestration order. Even though the defense contended that the judge should have taken stronger action, the appellate court affirmed the trial judge's actions.

---

[37] *See* Hernandez v. State, 4 So. 3d 642, 2009 Fla. LEXIS 149 (Fla. 2009) for a discussion of the principles prior to the adoption of the Florida version of the Federal Rules of Evidence and the changes brought by the new rules.

[38] United States v. Blackman, 2006 U.S. Dist. LEXIS 70147 (E.D.N.C. 2006).

[39] United States v. Etienne, 293 Fed. Appx. 977, 2008 U.S. App. LEXIS 20382 (4th Cir. 2008).

[40] People v. Melendez, 102 P.3d 315; 2004 Colo. LEXIS 1006 (2004). *See* case in Part II.

[41] United States v. Ruiz Solorio, 337 F.3d 580, 592, 2003 U.S. App. LEXIS 14585 (6th Cir. 2003).

In summary, where there has been a violation of a judge's sequestration order that is not affirmatively attributable to either the prosecution or the defense, a trial court will be reluctant to exclude the testimony, especially where the exclusion may do more harm to justice than any other remedy. Under the theory of judicial discretion, reviewing courts will normally uphold the decision of a lower court in rulings dealing with exclusion of witnesses under Rule 615. If an exclusion effectively removes a defendant's ability to mount a defense, a trial court will be most reluctant to apply such a remedy and would apply a different remedy.

§ 9.6   Direct Examination of Witnesses

When a witness is called to offer testimony and where there is no objection to the competency of the witness, as a general rule the witness will be allowed to give evidence in response to questions. Where there is an initial objection to the witness's competency or other challenge to giving testimony,[42] the judge will have to make an inquiry and make a determination concerning competency. After the court has determined that a witness is qualified to testify, the witness has observed any sequestration order as required, and the witness has been administered the oath or affirmation, the direct examination of the witness begins. Direct examination usually begins by having the party who called the witness ask the witness his or her name, address, and occupation. Even though everyone in the courtroom may know this information, it is necessary to complete the court records. After these preliminary background questions are completed, the general questioning of the witness begins.

If the witness cannot understand or speak English or for some other reason is not able to communicate in the usual manner, a language or sign interpreter will assist in helping the witness communicate with the attorneys and the jury. According to Rule 604, the interpreter must meet the qualifications of an expert and must take an oath to make a correct translation. An interpreter may also translate documentary evidence for admission into evidence.[43] The interpreter is not permitted to give his or her individual conclusions with respect to the answers of the witness, but must give a literal interpretation of the language employed by the witness.[44]

Even after the case has progressed to this stage, there are still rules that apply during the direct examination of the witness. For example, leading questions, those that suggest the desired answer, are usually not authorized

---

[42]   Other challenges to a witness could involve one of the marital privileges, attorney-client privilege, Fifth Amendment privilege, or a challenge under the Fourth Amendment.

[43]   Boim v. Quranic Literacy Inst., 340 F. Supp. 2d 885, 916, 2004 U.S. Dist. LEXIS 22745 (N.D. Ill. 2004).

[44]   FED. R. EVID. 604.

on direct examination, although some leading questions may be permitted concerning preliminary matters and when speaking with child witnesses. Limiting procedures have evolved regarding allowing a witness to refer to records in an effort to revive memory, or to use memoranda of past recollection as a substitute for memory. These are discussed in the sections that follow.

§ 9.7 — Leading Questions

Rule 611

**Mode and Order of Interrogation
and Presentation**

(c) Leading questions. Leading questions should not be used on the direct examination of a witness except as may be necessary to develop the witness' testimony. Ordinarily leading questions should be permitted on cross-examination. When a party calls a hostile witness, an adverse party, or a witness identified with an adverse party, interrogation may be by leading questions.[45]

The use of leading questions on direct or redirect examination is, with certain exceptions, not proper, and the opposing counsel has the right to object to such questions.[46] The reason for this rule is that the suggestive powers of leading questions have the effect of allowing the questioner to testify by having a witness adopt the substance of the examiner's questions. However, courts have some discretion in allowing the use of leading questions on direct examination[47] where necessary to develop a particular witness's testimony. This is especially true where the witness is an adverse party, a hostile witness, or a witness identified with an adverse party.[48]

"A 'leading question' is a question that suggests to the witness the answer that the examining party desires."[49] In order to elicit the facts, a trial lawyer may find it necessary to direct the attention of a witness to the specific matter about which his or her testimony is desired, and if the question does not suggest the answer, it is not leading. Even though the question may call for a "yes" or "no" answer, it is not impermissibly leading[50] unless it is so worded that, by permitting the witness to answer yes or no, the witness would be testifying in the language of the interrogator rather than his or her

---

[45] Fed. R. Evid. 611.
[46] For reasons that will be explained in later sections, leading questions are permitted on cross-examination.
[47] Williams v. State, 733 N.E.2d 919, 922 (2000).
[48] Lamkins v. State, 778 N.E.2d 1248, 1250, 2002 Ind. LEXIS 892 (2002).
[49] Cal. Evid. Code § 764 (Matthew Bender 2008).
[50] Goudeau v. Texas, 2002 Tex. App. LEXIS 5612 (2002).

own language.[51] A leading question suggests to the witness "how to answer or puts into his mouth words to be echoed back."[52]

The alternative form of question, "State whether or not . . ." or "Did you or did you not . . ." is free of this defect of form because both affirmative and negative answers are presented for the witness's equal choice. Nevertheless, such a question may become leading insofar as it rehearses lengthy details that the witness may not otherwise have mentioned, and thus supplies him or her with full suggestions, which he or she would incorporate—without any effort—by the simple answer, "I did" or "I did not." Such a question may or may not be improper, according to the amount of palpably suggestive detail that it embodies.[53]

As a general rule, the "decision whether to permit leading questions on direct examination is left to the discretion of the trial court,"[54] but the general rule against leading questions allows the trial judge discretion for the purposes of allowing an attorney an opportunity to develop a witness's testimony.[55] However, the fact that a prosecutor used several leading questions on direct examination that sparked objections that the judge sustained, does not constitute sufficient prosecutorial misconduct sufficient to require a retrial.[56] A leading question was proper in directing a witness to identify a defendant sitting at the counsel table because a computer monitor blocked the witness's original view of the complete courtroom.[57] In one case, a prosecutor conducted the state's case-in-chief by consistently using leading questions by paraphrasing the testimony of the witnesses as he moved to the next leading question. This leading question tactic, coupled with other errors, can contribute to a reversal of a criminal conviction.[58]

Although the general rule is that leading questions may not be used on direct examination, there are well-known exceptions to this rule. These exceptions are based upon necessity, and the right to lead is given only to the extent reasonably required to meet the necessity. The best-known exceptions are as follows:

A. Introductory Matters

Leading questions relating to the name of the witness, his or her address, and other matters that are introductory such as age, family, and school or work

---

[51] *See* Newsome v. State, 829 S.W.2d 260 (Tex. 1992), in which the court held that the mere fact that a question may be answered by a simple "yes" or "no" will not render it impermissibly leading. The question is impermissibly "leading" only when it suggests which answer is desired or when it puts into the witness's mouth words to be echoed back.

[52] Ohio v. Boden, 2002 Ohio 5043, 2002 Ohio App. LEXIS 5060 (2002), quoting BLACK'S LAW DICTIONARY (6th ed. 1990) 888.

[53] State v. Scott, 20 Wash. 2d 696, 149 P.2d 152 (1944).

[54] State v. Laveck, 2005 Ohio 62, 2004 Ohio App. LEXIS 6743 (2004).

[55] Moore v. State, 2005 Ark. LEXIS 245 (2005).

[56] State v. Serrano, 91 Conn. App. 227, 232, 880 A.2d 183, 188, 2005 Conn. App. LEXIS 390 (2005).

[57] People v. Williams, 2008 Cal. App. Unpub. LEXIS 7807 (Cal. 2008).

[58] Chambers v. State, 924 So. 2d 975, 977, 2006 Fla. App. LEXIS 5058 (Fla. 2006).

are authorized. One Minnesota court approved the use of leading questions on preliminary matters and noted that "[a]n attorney is allowed some scope in examination, particularly as to preliminary matters."[59] These permissible, introductory leading questions, however, must always stop short of an inquiry into the disputed facts.

B. Hostile Witnesses

Anyone who has watched television court battles recognizes the rule that leading questions are authorized whenever the party has called a hostile witness, an adverse party, or a witness identified with an adverse party, even though he or she is the witness of the party that called the witness.[60] Where the witness, although called by the prosecution, is related to the defendant and has exhibited a change in testimony to assist the defendant's case, leading questions can be posed to the hostile witness to the extent deemed necessary.[61]

The rule permitting leading questions of hostile witnesses is of special significance in criminal matters in which the state must often rely on reluctant or hostile witnesses to prove its case. As a general rule and upon objection, the trial judge must rule that the witness is hostile or reluctant before leading questions may be asked, but "where the record shows that a witness has reason to be adverse to the calling party, no formal declaration of a witness's hostility is required."[62]

The rule, as explained by a Mississippi appeals court, is that when a party must call a witness as its own but the witness is really allied and supports the other side, the party may ask the judge for a ruling that the witness is hostile.[63] Alternatively, following an objection on grounds of using leading questions, the attorney may ask that the judge rule on whether the witness is hostile. In the Mississippi case, the government prosecuted the defendant for carjacking, kidnapping, and armed robbery and the prosecution had to call the defendant's girlfriend as a government witness. Under such circumstances, a judge commits no error in allowing leading questions[64] because the girlfriend did not want to help the prosecution.

In determining whether a witness is a reluctant or an unwilling or a hostile witness, the judge takes into consideration many factors. In some instances, it is apparent that the witness is hostile and the determination is not difficult; in others, the judge must take into consideration the demeanor and actions of the

---

59   State v. Nankoo, 2009 Minn. App. Unpub. 68 (Minn. 2009). Unpublished opinion.
60   Lampkins v. Indiana, 778 N.E.2d 1248, 1250, 2002 Ind. LEXIS 892 (2002).
61   *See* State v. Clay, 2009 Ohio 1204, 2009 Ohio App. LEXIS 1012 (Ohio 2009), in which the reviewing court held that the trial court has the discretion to allow leading questions during direct exam when the witness was the defendant's good friend and has altered his testimony to be favorable to the defendant.
62   North Carolina v. Robinson, 2002 N.C. App. LEXIS 2403 (2002).
63   Brassfield v. State, 905 So. 2d 754, 760, 2004 Miss. App. LEXIS 1108 (2004).
64   *Id.*

witness. For example, in a prosecution for felonious assault, a witness gave a couple of statements to police, one of which indicated that the defendant had threatened her if she testified and stated that he would find her. At trial, the witness had a poor memory about the events and attributed it to being drunk on the night of the crime, but her memory had been better in earlier statements and in court proceedings. The trial court properly held that the witness was hostile and permitted the prosecutor to use leading questions to develop her testimony.[65]

C. Obviously Erroneous Statements

Where it appears that the witness has inadvertently answered a question incorrectly, or that he or she did not understand the question, a leading question may be used on direct examination to afford the witness an opportunity to correct the mistake.[66] For example, if a police witness, in answer to a question, inadvertently gave a date as 1989, the prosecutor would be allowed to say, "You mean 1999, don't you?" According to a federal district court, "[a] trial court has discretion to permit a prosecutor to ask leading questions on direct examination to develop and clarify testimony."[67]

Applying this rationale, a North Carolina court determined that a trial judge using discretion may allow the prosecutor, during the direct examination of a hostile witness, to ask leading questions as if on cross-examination, for the purpose of refreshing his or her recollection or awakening his or her conscience, thus enabling him or her to testify correctly.[68]

The exception to the rule that disallows leading questions also applies when the questions are asked by the defense attorney. When the witness made erroneous statements in a federal case, the reviewing court found no problem with the lower court allowing defense counsel to ask leading questions of the defendant on cross-examination when the prosecution had been "particularly egregious" in questioning the witness, causing the witness to misunderstand the prosecutor's questions.[69]

D. Child Witnesses, Mentally Handicapped Witnesses, and Witnesses with Slight Command of the English Language

While most witnesses who do not regularly testify in court find themselves stressed, worried, and feeling out of their element in the unusual and unfamiliar setting of a courtroom, this discomfort applies especially to children who have been victims of sexual or other crimes and persons with mental disabilities or

---

65   State v. Butcher, 2007 Ohio 5911, 2007 Ohio App. LEXIS 5203 (Ohio 2007).
66   *See* State v. White, 259 S.E.2d 281 (N.C. 1979), which held that a witness may be interrogated with leading questions on direct examination when it appears that the witness has exhausted his or her memory or has trouble understanding the questions.
67   Williams v. Senkowski, 2001 U.S. Dist. LEXIS 10843 (S.D.N.Y. 2001).
68   State v. Smith, 289 N.C. 143, 221 S.E.2d 247 (1976).
69   Woods v. Lecureux, 110 F.3d 1215 (6th Cir. 1997).

illness. Extremely shy witnesses or witnesses who will be asked embarrassing questions may have difficulty giving testimony when questioned under direct examination. Out of necessity, virtually all courts will allow use of leading questions in order to obtain testimony from children or witnesses who have difficulty testifying in the absence of the prompting leading questions.[70]

In a North Dakota case, the court allowed the prosecutor to question the child witnesses in a sexual abuse case through the use of leading questions.[71] The two children were questioned with leading questions and adopted, as their answers, words written on a board in the courtroom. Even with this procedure, one of the victims never verbalized the sexual acts that the defendant made her perform. The reviewing court noted that it had previously held that the use of leading questions was appropriate to develop the testimony of sexually abused children, especially concerning the physiological details of the assaults. Included in this category where leading questions may be used are witnesses who are mentally handicapped but not incompetent to testify. In a Michigan case, the trial court allowed the use of leading questions in a rape case where the 21-year-old victim was mentally disabled and had the mental development of a nine-year-old with an IQ of 56. The reviewing court cautioned the use of so many leading questions on direct examination but expressed the view that the practice in a case like this was permissible. In upholding the rape convictions, the court noted that leading questions were necessary to develop her testimony because of her level of retardation.[72]

A Mississippi appellate court ruled that the trial court did not abuse its discretion when it permitted a child who was almost five years of age to testify through the use of leading questions.[73] The defendant, who had been charged with murdering the child-witness's brother, contended that he did not get a fair trial because the prosecution used more than 40 leading questions to develop the child's testimony. The reviewing court found no unfair prejudice to the defendant and noted that the situation involving children is a classic example of a situation where leading questions may be necessary.

§ 9.8 — Refreshing Memory — Present Memory Revived

Rule 612

Writing Used To Refresh Memory

Except as otherwise provided in criminal proceedings by section 3500 of Title 18, United States Code, if a witness uses a writing to refresh memory for the purpose of testifying, either—

---

[70]   *See* Wallace v. Arkansas, 2003 Ark. App. LEXIS 15 (2003), in which the court approved using leading questions directed to a child victim of sexual abuse.

[71]   United States v. Lohnes, 554 F.3d 1166, 1169 2009 U.S. App. LEXIS 3599 (8th Cir. 2009).

[72]   People v. West, 2007 Mich. App. LEXIS 1344 (Mich. 2007). Unpublished opinion.

[73]   Osborne v. State, 2006 Miss. App. LEXIS 134 (2006).

> (1) while testifying, or
>
>   (2) before testifying, if the court in its discretion determines it is necessary in the interests of justice,
>
>   an adverse party is entitled to have the writing produced at the hearing, to inspect it, to cross-examine the witness thereon, and to introduce in evidence those portions which relate to the testimony of the witness. If it is claimed that the writing contains matters not related to the subject matter of the testimony, the court shall examine the writing in camera, excise any portions not so related, and order delivery of the remainder to the party entitled thereto. Any portion withheld over objections shall be preserved and made available to the appellate court in the event of an appeal. If a writing is not produced or delivered pursuant to order under this rule, the court shall make any order justice requires, except that in criminal cases when the prosecution elects not to comply, the order shall be one striking the testimony or, if the court in its discretion determines that the interests of justice so require, declaring a mistrial.[74]

To a greater or to a lesser extent, all memory fades with the passage of time and many witnesses experience difficulty recalling all the relevant details that were once fresh in their mind. Despite preparation by the attorneys, trial witnesses frequently do not remember all the facts, especially after a long period between the events and the trial. Memory may be additionally complicated by witnesses who are not as intelligent as average persons, were under the influence of drugs at the relevant time, or have injury or disease that has complicated memory. It is also apparent that referring to a written statement may revive the memory of an experience. In other words, by referring to statements or other past experiences, the recollection of the witness may be refreshed to the point that a witness is able to testify from present memory. If the witness has absolutely no recollection regarding the matters being contested, he or she obviously is not competent to testify concerning those matters. However, if the witness remembers the transaction in general but not the essential details, or if he or she remembers that he or she recorded the transaction, some evidence concerning the transaction is admissible. This process involves two concepts that have become known as present memory revived or present memory refreshed and past memory recorded or past recollection recorded. These two concepts differ in theory and therefore the tests for admissibility differ. In the first instance, where present memory has been refreshed, the witness is able to testify from present memory, which is the evidence and not the not the writing or other reference used to refresh memory. In the second instance, where the witness originally recorded the event in writing at a time when it was fresh in the witness's memory, the writing is the evidence and not the oral testimony.

---

[74] FED. R. EVID. 612.

In this section, the first of these two concepts—present memory revived or, as it is sometimes called, present memory refreshed—will be discussed. In the next section, we will address the concept of past recollection recorded.

In many instances, the trial court allows a witness to refer to records, accounting sheets, or reports while testifying. Generally, doctors, engineers, accountants, and other experts, as well as criminal justice officials, are allowed to refer to data on their reports while they are testifying as a means of refreshing their memory. As a practical matter, it is impossible for law enforcement personnel, who make daily investigations of alleged violations of law, to remember the names, dates, and what took place without referring to notes made by them at the time or immediately thereafter. However, trial courts must exercise caution to assure that the witness is testifying from present memory that has recently been refreshed. The court should be careful to ensure that the memorandum is not a written summary made specifically for use in court and that the law enforcement officer is not merely testifying from the written record but from a refreshed memory.

When a witness has a lapse of memory while testifying, the court allows him or her to refer to some form of memorandum to refresh or revive his or her recollection of the facts. A witness is "permitted to refresh and assist his memory, by the use of a written instrument, memorandum or entry in a book, and may be compelled to do so if the writing is present in court. It does not seem to be necessary that the writing should have been made by the witness himself, nor that it should be an original writing, provided, after inspecting it, he can speak to the facts from his own recollection."[75] After the witness's memory is revived or refreshed and he or she presently recollects the facts and swears to them, his or her testimony, and not the writing, is the evidence. When a party uses an earlier statement of his or her own witness to refresh the witness's memory, the only evidence recognized as such is the testimony so refreshed.

Documents shown to a witness for the purpose of reviving his or her recollection may not be read by the witness to the court under the pretext of refreshing the memory of the witness or shown to the jury, because the documents themselves are not evidence and have no independent evidentiary value. The fact that a defense attorney might seek to introduce that material on cross-examination rather than the prosecutor on direct examination is not a difference of significance. The fact that a tape-recording rather than a written document is involved also does not affect the result.[76]

In one case involving aggravated sexual abuse of a child, the trial court allowed the mother of the complaining witness to testify after having her memory refreshed by reviewing a transcript of her previous interview with law enforcement officers.[77] Before reading the transcript, the witness could not

---

[75] Brockenbrough v. Commonwealth, 2003 Va. App. LEXIS 243 (2003), quoting Harrison v. Middleton, 52 Va. 527, 544 (1854).

[76] United States v. McKeever, 271 F.2d 669 (2d Cir. 1959); *see also* United States v. Booz, 451 F.2d 719 (3d Cir. 1971); People v. Parks, 485 P.2d 257 (Cal. 1971).

[77] State v. Cook, 2009 N.C. App. LEXIS 268 (N.C. 2009).

remember all of the details, but following in her review of the transcript, she testified from present memory. The reviewing court rejected the defendant's argument that she was really testifying from the document because her memory had not truly been refreshed. In another use of present memory refreshed, an Ohio murder defendant complained that both the coroner and a DNA expert both consulted their written reports during their direct examination by the prosecutor.[78] The coroner referred to his report to refresh his memory of the decedent's age while the DNA expert consulted his report concerning the genetic profile obtained from an examination of the defendant's right shoe. When a convicted defendant makes a contention of this nature, the court must determine whether the witness had an independent recollection of the event and was merely using the memorandum to refresh details or is using a memorandum as a testimonial crutch for something beyond the witness's recollection. In both cases the witnesses testified from present memory that had been refreshed. According to the reviewing court, the defense attorney was not deficient in not objecting at trial and the failure to object did not prove any ineffective assistance of counsel.

In some cases in which a witness or victim possesses no present recollection, the use of hypnosis has been approved. For example, the Louisiana Supreme Court has determined that the testimony of a witness who has had his memory refreshed through hypnosis should be treated as other "recollection refreshed" testimony and the fact of hypnosis affects the weight and not the admissibility of the evidence.[79] A set of guidelines, mentioned by the Supreme Court of the United States, suggests that hypnosis be performed by a psychologist or psychiatrist who has received special training and who is independent of the investigation, that the hypnosis procedure occur in a neutral setting, and only the subject and the hypnotist should be present.[80] Although the court has discretion in determining whether hypnotically refreshed testimony is admitted, a per se rule excluding all hypnotically refreshed testimony infringes impermissibly on a criminal defendant's right to testify on his or her own behalf.[81]

In an effort to regulate hypnotic-related evidence, California, by statute, provides that hypnotic evidence for recollection can be admitted where it follows state law. Among other things, California limits the revived testimony to matters that the witness recalled and related prior to the hypnosis. Additionally, the law mandates that the pre-hypnotic memory be preserved in some written or taped form; that a written record is made of the memory of the event prior to hypnosis; that the witness gave consent; that the pre- and post-hypnosis interviews be videotaped; and that the sessions be conducted by a licensed medical doctor, psychologist, or social worker trained in hypnosis.[82]

In all cases of refreshed memory, the trial judge has a duty to prevent a witness from putting into the record the contents of an otherwise inadmissible

---

[78] State v. Neeley, 2006 Ohio 418 2006 Ohio App. LEXIS 349 (2006).

[79] Louisiana v. Smith, 809 So. 2d 556, 565, 2002 La. App. LEXIS 221 (2002).

[80] See Rock v. Arkansas, 483 U.S. 44, 107 S. Ct. 2704, 97 L. Ed. 2d 37 (1987).

[81] *Id.*

[82] *See* CAL. EVID. CODE § 795 (2008).

writing under the guise of refreshing recollection. Counsel should lay a foundation for the necessity of refreshing the witness's memory, show the witness the writing, remove the writing from the witness, and ask questions about the refreshed memory. Under this theory, showing the witness the writing should be all that is required to refresh the memory.[83] When using a writing to refresh memory, the defendant has the right to compel the production of the document used to refresh the witness's memory. Where the document is not produced, the judge may order the refreshed memory testimony to be stricken, even where the document could not be introduced as evidence.

In interpreting Rule 612 of the Federal Rules of Evidence, which provides in general terms that the adverse party is entitled to have the writing produced, a federal district court explained that it is not every time a witness looks at any document in preparation for the trial that such document must be disclosed to the other side. In determining whether the document must be disclosed, the court should consider the extent to which the documents were consulted and relied upon, and the extent to which the opinions and conclusions were reflected therein, as opposed to factual recitations.[84] The judge has much discretion in exercising control over the introduction of such evidence and in interpreting the rules.[85]

In supporting the concept that a writing used to refreshed memory must be available for inspection by the opposing counsel, the Supreme Court of Indiana ruled that the trial judge should have permitted the defendant's counsel to review and inspect that writing.[86] Prior to offering testimony against the defendant, the police officer studied his police report to refresh his memory concerning the details of the defendant's arrest and the drugs that were found with him and also used the writing during the officer's testimony. If a witness refreshes his or her memory prior to testifying, it is up to the court's discretion whether to allow the adverse party to inspect the writing. In this case, the officer used the report during his time on the witness stand and, therefore, the trial judge committed error in not allowing the defendant to inspect the reports. The case was not reversed on this basis because the reviewing court found this to be harmless error.

§ 9.9　—Past Recollection Recorded

Rule 803

Hearsay Exceptions; Availability of Declarant Immaterial

The following are not excluded by the hearsay rule, even though the declarant is available as a witness:

(5) Recorded recollection.—A memorandum or record concerning a matter about which a witness once had knowledge but now has insufficient

---

[83]　Tennessee v. Pylant, 2003 Tenn. Crim. App. LEXIS 405 (2003).

[84]　In re Comair Air Disaster Litigation, 100 F.R.D. 350 (1983).

[85]　United States v. Terry, 729 F.2d 1063 (6th Cir. 1984).

[86]　Gault v. State, 878 N.E.2d 1260, 1263, 2008 Ind. LEXIS 43 (Ind. 2008).

> recollection to enable the witness to testify fully and accurately, shown to
> have been made or adopted by the witness when the matter was fresh in the
> witness' memory and to reflect that knowledge correctly. If admitted, the
> memorandum or record may be read into evidence but may not itself be
> received as an exhibit unless offered by an adverse party.[87]

When a witness's memory cannot be refreshed by any technique and
where the evidence has been recorded by some permanent method, the recording or writing may become a substitute for the witness's memory and, where
it meets all the requirements, be introduced as substantive proof of the facts
that it contains. However, the proponent of the recorded memory must lay a
foundation before the writing will be admitted.

To meet the accepted standards of admissibility, an Ohio court noted that:

> foundational requirements for the use of a past recollection recorded include
> a showing that: (1) the witness has insufficient memory to accurately testify
> to crucial information; (2) that the witness can show through their testimony
> that the past recollection recorded was made or adopted when the matter was
> fresh in the witness's memory; and (3) that the past recollection recorded cor-
> rectly reflects the knowledge the witness had at the time it was recorded.[88]

The trial judge must be satisfied that the writing was made from firsthand
knowledge at a time when the events were fresh in the writer's mind, and the
witness must verify the writing's authenticity and truthfulness. If the witness
cannot say that there is insufficient memory to testify fully, the foundation has
not been made. In a rape case in which the prosecution attempted to have a
videotape recollection of a child witness admitted, because the child could not
testify that the videotape correctly reflected her knowledge of the events in
question on the date it was recorded, the trial court properly excluded the record
under the state version of Rule 803(5) dealing with past recollection recorded.[89]

In *Wilson v. State*, a Texas murder case, an eyewitness to significant details
of the crime recorded her statement when she had a clear and accurate memory
of the details under police direction.[90] She testified that she had a good perspective for observing the details and she would not have signed a statement unless
it was true and correct when she gave it. She indicated that her present memory
of the events was not especially good because she was "very strung out" back
then. The witness identified the document and her signature and indicated she
didn't have sufficient present memory. The witness was present and submitted
herself for cross-examination. The Texas appellate court concluded that no

---

[87] FED. R. EVID. 803(5).
[88] Ohio v. Perry, 147 Ohio App. 3d 164, 170, 171, 768 N.E.2d 1259, 1264, 2002 Ohio App.
      LEXIS 1169 (2002).
[89] *Id.*
[90] Wilson v. State, 2009 Tex. App. LEXIS 2954 (Tex. 2009).

error had occurred and that the document had properly been admitted under the Texas version of Rule 803(5).

Under modern police practice, the document may not have ever been written in the traditional manner; it may have originally been an entry by an officer on a computer system. In *North Carolina v. Love*, the complaining witness spouse told police that her husband had repeatedly threatened to beat her. This information, as well as other relevant data, was recorded by a police officer using a computer. He allowed the witness to review what she had told him in order to correct any errors in typing by the officer. She stated at the time that the report was accurate and that she did not wish to change anything. At trial, the witness could not remember what she had told the officer, but she did remember making a statement to police that was read back to her and she stated that it was true when made. The appellate court approved the trial court decision allowing the officer to read to the trier of fact the statement made by the complaining witness.[91]

Neither the federal rules nor federal courts have developed a set rule concerning precisely when the evidence must be recorded following an event.[92] An Iowa appellate court approved the use of past recollection recorded when the witness recorded the information in a writing 31 days after observing the facts of the case.[93] In one federal case, the officer interviewed the defendants but did not make a written memorandum of the interview until 11 days later. The trial court allowed the officer to read from the memorandum and the court of appeals approved. As the appellate court noted:

> Rule 803(5) requires that the memorandum be made by the witness "when the matter was fresh in the witness' memory," but we have declined to adopt any bright-line rule to measure whether a particular delay is too long. Instead, we have held that the trial court may consider the lapse of time along with other circumstances that may be relevant in determining the likelihood that the witness had an accurate memory of the event at the time the record was prepared.[94]

Despite arguments to the contrary, the application of past recollection recorded does not deprive the accused of the opportunity to cross-examine the witness as guaranteed by the Sixth Amendment[95] because the witness with the faulty memory will be in court and testifying about the making of the writing. Cross-examination may be somewhat limited given the faulty memory of the

---

[91] North Carolina v. Love, 576 S.E.2d 709, 712, 713, 2003 N.C. LEXIS 114 (2003)

[92] *See* Isler v. United States, 2003 D.C. App. LEXIS 291 (2003), in which the appeals court permitted admission of past recollection recorded when it was first recorded at the first trial of the issue some five months after the event occurred.

[93] Iowa v. Stevenson, 2001 Iowa App. LEXIS 752 (2001).

[94] United States v. Green, 258 F.3d 683, 688, 2001 U.S. App. LEXIS 16770 (7th Cir. 2001).

[95] United States v. Dingle, 2007 U.S. Dist. LEXIS (D. Conn. 2007). Witness had a drinking problem, but the tape of information was made on the same date as the observed crime.

witness, but the right to confront and cross-examine the witness will generally not pose a problem of constitutional dimensions. In applying the rule concerning past recollection recorded, the Supreme Court of Oregon held that a checklist used by a police officer in the operation of a breath analysis machine was admissible in a prosecution for drunk driving although the witness had a present recollection of the subject matter, of which the checklist was a record.[96] The witness had identified the checklist, had recalled making it at the time of the event—when his recollection was fresh—and had testified to its accuracy. And the trial court properly allowed parts of the witness's statement to be read into the record where the witness had remembered making a statement, but did not remember what she had said when the record was made at a time when the matter was fresh in her memory and reflected her knowledge correctly.[97] The United States Court of Appeals for the Seventh Circuit held that a memorandum of a telephone conversation between an Internal Revenue Service (IRS) agent and a tax defendant was properly admitted at trial.[98] The court indicated that it "would seem, as the government argues, that the report satisfies the criteria for admissibility as a recorded recollection under F.R. Ev. 803(5)." The agent, in laying a foundation, had testified that the history sheet was prepared immediately after the conversation, but that he no longer recalled the details of the conversation.

§ 9.10   Cross-Examination of Witnesses

Rule 611

Mode and Order of Interrogation and Presentation

* * *

(b) Scope of cross-examination. Cross-examination should be limited to the subject matter of the direct examination and matters affecting the credibility of the witness. The court may, in the exercise of discretion, permit inquiry into additional matters as if on direct examination.[99]

* * *

The right to confront and question adverse witnesses is a critical component in fact-finding at trial[100] and the right of confrontation is guaranteed by the

---

[96]   State v. Sutton, 450 P.2d 748 (Or. 1969).
[97]   United States v. Porter, 986 F.2d 1014 (6th Cir. 1993), *cert. denied*, 510 U.S. 933, 114 S. Ct. 347, 126 L. Ed. 2d 312 (1993).
[98]   United States v. Sawyer, 607 F.2d 1191 (7th Cir. 1979); *see also* United States v. Ray, 768 F.2d 991 (8th Cir. 1985).
[99]   FED. R. EVID. 611(b).
[100] United States v. McKeithan, 2002 U.S. App. LEXIS 23408 (3d Cir. 2002).

Sixth Amendment to the Constitution of the United States.[101] Every witness places his or her credibility at issue by taking the witness stand and offering testimony.[102] The rationale for allowing comprehensive cross-examination of witnesses has been noted in both federal and state cases and is designed, among other things, to assist in discerning whether witnesses have been truthful in their testimony. As a federal district judge noted concerning the reasons for allowing cross-examination:

> Basic to the right of cross-examination is the opportunity to impeach adverse witnesses. Impeachment is a challenge to the witness's inclination to tell the truth and her ability to do so. The cross-examiner must be allowed to examine defects in the witness's ability to perceive and remember events, clear up ambiguities, test the witness's ability to communicate accurately, and explore character defects or motives that might induce the witness to shade her testimony or to lie. The Sixth Amendment's Confrontation Clause guarantees the accused the right to cross-examine adverse witnesses to uncover possible biases and expose the witness's motivation for testifying.[103]

As the Supreme Court noted in an old case, cross-examination as part of the confrontation in a lawsuit presupposes:

> personal examination and cross-examination of the witness in which the accused has an opportunity, not only of testing the recollection and sifting the conscience of the witness, but of compelling him to stand face to face with the jury in order that they may look at him, and judge by his demeanor upon the stand and the manner in which he gives his testimony whether he is worthy of belief.[104]

The right to observe or to see one's accusers is of little value unless one can question the accuser. For that reason, the right of cross-examination is included in the Sixth Amendment right of an accused to confront adverse witnesses.[105] No one experienced in trying lawsuits would deny the critical value of cross-examination in exposing falsehood and revealing the facts. The fact that this right appears in the Sixth Amendment to the Constitution reflects the framers' belief in those liberties and safeguards whereby confrontation was a fundamental right essential to a fair trial in a criminal prosecution.

A full cross-examination of a witness on the subjects of his or her direct examination is a right and not a mere privilege of the party against whom the

---

[101] The Sixth Amendment applies to the states. South Carolina v. Mizzell, 349 S.C. 326, 563 S.E.2d 315, 2002 S.C. LEXIS 68 (2002), quoting Pointer v. Texas, 380 U.S. 400, 402 (1965).

[102] Pearce v. Commonwealth, 53 Va. App. LEXIS 113, 2008 Va. App. LEXIS 545 (Va. 2008).

[103] Vanlandingham v. McGhee, 2008 U.S. Dist. LEXIS 67934 (E.D. Mich. 2008).

[104] Mattox v. United States, 156 U.S. 237, 242, 15 S. Ct. 337, 339, 39 L. Ed. 409, 411, 1895 U.S. LEXIS 2131 (1895).

[105] United States v. Villarman-Oviedo, 325 F.3d 1, 2003 U.S. App. LEXIS 5694 (1st Cir. 2003).

witness is called. The denial of this right is reversible error except in certain limited circumstances. For example, in the usual case where the defendant has no opportunity to confront his accuser, the evidence should not be admitted. In *Giles v. California*, the defendant could not cross-examine his accuser because she had died by the time of the trial. The evidence that the deceased victim offered to police officers prior to her death should not have been admitted against the defendant. The Supreme Court did not accept the prosecutor's contention that the defendant had forfeited the right of cross-examination because he had murdered his accuser and, therefore, it was his fault that he could not cross-examine her. However, the denial of this right is not necessarily reversible error when a witness, having given his or her direct testimony, dies prior to cross-examination. The judge often allows the direct examination to stand and gives precautionary instructions to the jury in such cases. Where the cross-examination has been curtailed following proper direct examination covering material issues because of a witness's valid claim of privilege, the trial court may strike the witness's direct testimony in an effort to preserve the Sixth Amendment right of confrontation and cross-examination.[106]

The extent of cross-examination, with respect to an appropriate subject of inquiry, is within the sound discretion of the trial judge. He or she may exercise broad discretion in determining when the subject is exhausted or when it moves in an improper direction. The court has discretion regarding how long and in what direction a cross-examination may proceed. As a general rule, a cross-examiner possesses fairly wide latitude, but it does not mean that the cross-examiner may make all the decisions about examination because a judge may place reasonable limits on the examination related to relevance and repetition.[107]

However, effective cross-examination in a criminal case is the primary means by which the credibility and truthfulness of witnesses can be tested. The trial judge does not have the discretion to grant or withhold such right completely.[108] The trial court may not preclude all inquiry into a subject appropriate for cross-examination, but it may and should exercise such control over the scope of the examination as is necessary to prevent the parties from unduly burdening the record with cumulative or irrelevant matters.[109]

The determination of whether and to what extent to cross-examine a particular witness rests with the defendant's counsel. Where the attorney for the defendant chooses, as a part of trial strategy, not to cross-examine a witness, the effect is to waive the Sixth Amendment right of cross-examination.[110]

Cross-examination is generally limited in scope to the subject matter of the direct examination of the witness, but also extends to matters affecting

---

[106] Combs v. Kentucky, 74 S.W.3d 738, 744, 2002 Ky. LEXIS 98 (2002).
[107] United States v. Green, 2008 U.S. App. LEXIS 18678 (2d Cir. 2008).
[108] State v. Toole, 640 A.2d 965 (R.I. 1994).
[109] FED. R. EVID. 611(b).
[110] United States v. McKeithan, 2002 U.S. App. LEXIS 23408 (3d Cir. 2002).

the credibility of the witness.[111] A long-established rule has been that cross-examination of a witness is limited to the scope of the direct examination. One exception to this rule is that cross-examination may be permitted to test the capacity of the witness to observe, remember, and recount, and to test the sincerity and truthfulness of the witness. This may be done with respect to subjects not strictly relevant to the testimony given by the witness on direct examination. Inquiry may be made concerning bias, interest, or prejudice of the witness as long as it goes to testing credibility.

Although under the traditional rules of the limited scope of cross-examination, the prosecution usually may not cross-examine on matters not brought out on direct examination, the attorney may and should make the opposing witness the prosecution's witness at the proper time, and ask additional questions of the witness if necessary to get all the facts before the court. However, Rule 611(b) allows a trial court, in the exercise of discretion, to permit questioning on matters beyond the scope of direct examination, but the questioner must inquire as if on direct examination. When direct examination opens a particular subject, the consequent cross-examination may probe into any related area covered on direct examination and may inquire into specific facts developed by the opposing counsel on direct examination. The cross-examination is not restricted to identical details developed during the direct examination, but extends to the entire related subject matter limited by the concepts or relevance.[112]

In a case before the United States Court of Appeals for the Seventh Circuit, the court agreed that the trial court has the discretion to impose reasonable limitations on cross-examination of witnesses in a criminal trial, based upon concerns regarding harassment, confusion of issues, and repetitive or marginally relevant interrogation.[113] The court cautioned that, even though the Sixth Amendment guarantees a defendant the right to cross-examine hostile witnesses and defense counsel should be afforded every opportunity to effectively cross-examine a government witness, this does not mean that the right to cross-examination is unlimited. In this case, after the defense counsel had cross-examined the witness for most of the afternoon and evening, and had exposed facts showing virtually every possible motive or bias that the witness might have for testifying against the defendant, the court properly terminated the cross-examination.

One common exception to the rule that cross-examination should be limited to subject matter brought out on direct examination is the exception

---

[111]   Illinois v. Millbratz, 323 Ill. App. 3d 206, 211, 751 N.E.2d 650, 2001 Ill. App. LEXIS 541 (2001).

[112]   Stotler v. Florida, 834 So. 2d 940, 943, 2003 Fla. App. LEXIS 445 (2003).

[113]   United States v. Spivey, 841 F.2d 799 (7th Cir. 1988). *See* case in Part II. *See also* State v. Jackson, 212 Wis. 2d 203, 567 N.W.2d 920 (1997), in which the court held that reasonable limits may be placed upon inquiry into matters affecting the prosecution witness's credibility based on concerns about, among other things, harassment, prejudice, confusion of the issues, witness safety, or repetitiveness, especially when the attack on the witness's credibility falls under the rape shield law.

that permits cross-examination on matters relating to the names and addresses of witnesses. Under virtually all circumstances, this information must be divulged.[114] Because the witness's name and address open countless avenues of in-court examination and out-of-court investigation, the name and address of the witness generally must be given when the witness testifies at trial. In *Smith v. Illinois*, the Supreme Court held that when "the credibility of a witness is in issue, the very starting point in 'exposing falsehood and bringing out the truth' through cross-examination must necessarily be to ask the witness who he is and where he lives. The witness's name and address open countless avenues of in-court examination and out-of-court investigation. To forbid this most rudimentary inquiry at the threshold is effectively to "emasculate the right of cross-examination itself."[115] The purpose of the inquiry regarding the witness's address and present employment is to make known to the jury the setting or context in which to judge the character, veracity, or bias of the witness, and it is necessary to show that the witness was in custody in order to make such inquiry, even if there may be some danger to the witness or his family.

As is true with many rules of evidence, this rule is not without alternatives. Where there is a threat to the life of the witness, the pretrial right of the defendant to have the witness's true name, address, and place of employment is not absolute.[116] When a threat to the life of a witness is shown, the prosecution must disclose relevant information to the judge in his or her chambers. Various judicial and legal tools exist to prevent or minimize threats to witnesses, such as the use of housing relocation, establishing new identities, state witness protection programs, and transfer of an incarcerated witness to a different prison or a different jurisdiction. States may use a state witness protection program. Typical of many state laws, to protect California witnesses, a statute enhances murder convictions to life without parole when a witness has been killed to prevent testimony or in retaliation for having served as a witness.[117] When a request has been made to keep a witness's identity private, a trial judge must determine whether the witness's true name, address, and place of employment must be disclosed in order to protect the right to effective cross-examination. If the trial judge concludes that the defendant does not have the right to ask the witness's exact address and place of employment, the defendant is entitled to ask any other relevant questions that may aid the jury in weighing the witness's credibility.[118]

The rules relating to cross-examination for purposes of impeachment are discussed in other sections of this chapter.

---

[114] State v. Craft, 149 Ohio App. 3d 176, 180, 776 N.E.2d 546, 548, 2002 Ohio App. LEXIS 4647 (2002).

[115] Smith v. Illinois, 390 U.S. 129, 131 (1968).

[116] United States v. Varelli, 407 F.2d 735 (7th Cir. 1969); United States v. Smaldone, 484 F.2d 311 (10th Cir. 1973); *see e.g.,* OHIO CRIM. R. 16. Discovery and Inspection (Matthew Bender 2009).

[117] CAL. PENAL CODE § 190.2 (10) (Matthew Bender 2009).

[118] United States v. Palermo, 410 F.2d 468 (7th Cir. 1969).

§ 9.11   Redirect and Recross-Examination

After a witness has been cross-examined, the party calling the witness may, by redirect examination, afford the witness the opportunity to make a full explanation of his or her testimony during cross-examination, allowing him or her to rebut the discrediting effect of his or her testimony on cross-examination and to correct any improper impressions that may have been created. On redirect examination, a witness may give the reasons for his or her actions in order to refute unfavorable inferences from matters brought out on cross-examination. He or she may state the circumstances of the inquiry covered on cross-examination, even where the facts revealed on redirect examination may be detrimental to the other party. As explained in a Florida case, under the doctrine of completeness, redirect testimony is admissible to qualify, limit, or explain testimony given on cross-examination.[119]

Considering the scope and extent of redirect examination, a trial judge enjoys wide discretion in allowing or excluding evidence during redirect examination, but this discretion is not unlimited. The general rule in many jurisdictions holds that the scope of redirect examination is "largely within the discretion of the trial court, [and] it is limited to matters brought out during cross-examination."[120]

Redirect examination may be appropriate where the "door has been opened" by an attorney for one of the parties on cross-examination, by pursuing a line of inquiry that exceeded the scope of the direct examination. For example, in a case in which the defendant was being prosecuted for a homicide, the defense counsel during cross-examination inferred through his questioning of prosecution witnesses that some of the witnesses might have recently fabricated their trial stories.[121] It was then appropriate for the prosecution to bolster the testimony of the witnesses whose credibility had been called into question. The fact was that the defense attorney opened the door to such testimony during the cross-examination because otherwise bolstering the witnesses' credibility would have been beyond the scope of the cross-examination and inappropriate. Under the circumstances the court hearing the defendant's habeas corpus motion believed that the prosecutor's introduction of new matter, which would have otherwise be beyond the scope of cross-examination, was appropriate.

Although it is beyond dispute that a defendant has a constitutional right to cross-examine adverse witnesses and that the extent of cross-examination is based on the sound discretion of the trial judge, there is not any general constitutional right to conduct recross-examination.[122] The decision whether to allow recross-examination is typically left to the discretion of the judge and is normally limited to new matters brought out on redirect examination. If a

---

[119]   Pacheco v. State, 698 So. 2d 393 (Fla. 1997).

[120]   Christmas v. State, 2009 Miss. LEXIS 144 (Miss. 2009).

[121]   Warren v. Conway, 2008 U.S. Dist. LEXIS 106309 (E.D. N.Y. 2008).

[122]   Poole v. United States, 929 A.2d 413, 2007 D.C. App. LEXIS 470 (2007).

court refused to allow recross-examination on new matters developed during redirect examination, the party is effectively denied any cross-examination covering the new matter. While a court should not by rule prohibit recross-examination of a witness about new matters brought out on redirect examination, a court should refuse to permit recross-examination where no new material was developed on redirect examination.[123]

§ 9.12 Impeachment of Witnesses

> ### Rule 607
>
> ### Who May Impeach
>
> The credibility of a witness may be attacked by any party, including the party calling the witness.[124]

In determining the credibility of witnesses, the task rests with the trier of fact, whether it is a judge or a jury. Because only witnesses can be subject to impeachment, a non-testifying defendant cannot be impeached by evidence that he or she might be untruthful.[125] The task of giving the trier of fact the information necessary to evaluate the worth of the testimony of each witness falls to the parties, who must offer sufficient information concerning the believability and reliability of each witness. The judge or jury must determine whether to believe any witnesses and which witnesses to believe.[126] One case referred to *McCormick on Evidence*, which suggests:

> Impeachment is a technique used to attack the truth-telling capacity of a witness. Impeachment may be accomplished by demonstrating the witness' bias, self-contradiction, poor character, defect in perceptive capacity, prior convictions or bad acts, or by contradicting the witness on specific facts in her testimony.[127]

Impeachment has also been defined as the process of attempting to diminish the credibility of a witness by convincing the jury or court that the testimony of the particular witness should be considered untruthful or unreliable.[128] Every

---

[123]   Kelly v. Florida, 843 So. 2d 223, 2003 Fla. App. LEXIS 4732 (2003).
[124]   FED. R. EVID. 607.
[125]   *See* State v. Johnson, 2008 VT 135, 2008 Vt. LEXIS 200 (Vt. 2008).
[126]   Brown v. Maryland, 368 Md. 320, 327, 793 A.2d 561, 565, 2002 Md. LEXIS 95 (2002).
[127]   Colorado v. Trujillo, 49 P.3d 316, 2002 Colo. LEXIS 569 (2002), citing 1 JOHN W. STRONG, MCCORMICK ON EVIDENCE § 33 (5th ed. 1999).
[128]   State v. Dale, 874 S.W.2d 446 (Mo. 1994). *See also* State v. Johanesen, 319 Or. 128, 873 P.2d 1065 (1994), in which the court stated that "impeachment" refers to elicitation or presentation of any matter for the purpose of impairing or destroying the credibility of the witness in the estimation of the trier of fact.

witness who takes the oath to tell the truth places his or her credibility at issue and relevant evidence that affects the credibility should generally not be excluded.[129] There are various methods and techniques of impeaching adverse witnesses, some of which will be discussed in the following sections.

A party's decision to impeach a witness in a criminal case is subject to a discretionary limitation by the trial judge,[130] but a judge should not unfairly limit the process. In determining whether the trial judge abused his or her discretion in limiting a defendant's impeachment of the complaining witness, the pertinent issue is whether the rejection of a defendant's efforts to impeach the credibility of the a trial witness withheld from the jury information necessary to make a discriminating appraisal of the witness's trustworthiness. Thus, denying impeachment of the complaining witness by refusing to allow a defendant to inquire about swastikas tattooed on the person of a prosecution witness was an abuse of discretion affecting substantial rights of the defendant. The tattooed witness may have harbored feelings against other racial or ethnic minority groups, one of which the defendant was a member. Based on a failure to allow proper impeachment, the reviewing court reversed the conviction.[131] In any case, a party may impeach any witness who has felony convictions involving dishonesty or false statement.[132]

A witness may not be impeached by evidence that merely contradicts his or her testimony on an issue or matter that is collateral (and is not legally relevant) to any issue in the trial.[133] For example, where a prosecution witness has stated that the defendant was wearing a blue shirt at the crime scene, impeachment by a defense witness that the defendant was wearing a red shirt demonstrates an example of collateral evidence that could be excluded. The rule precluding impeachment of a witness by otherwise admissible evidence directed to collateral issues serves policies such as the prevention of confusion, waste of time, and surprise.

Every criminal defendant who takes the stand to testify in his or her own defense becomes subject to cross-examination to the same extent as any other witness[134] and must face the possibility of impeachment as may any other witness[135] unless, under the particular circumstances of the case, specific questions should be excluded because their probative value as to the issue of the defendant's credibility is negligible when compared with their possible

---

[129] Commonwealth v. Maddox, 955 S.W.2d 718 (Ky. 1997).

[130] Connecticut v. Abernathy, 72 Conn. App. 831, 836, 837, 806 A.2d 1139, 1145, 1146, 2002 Conn. App. LEXIS 519 (2002).

[131] United States v. Figueroa, 548 F.3d 222, 227, 2008 U.S. App. LEXIS 23697 (2d Cir. 2008).

[132] *Fed. R. Evid.* 609(b).

[133] State v. Merida, 2008 R.I. LEXIS 118, n.14 (R.I. 2008).

[134] North Carolina v. Boekenoogen, 147 N.C. App. 292, 297, 554 S.E.2d 848, 851, 2001 N.C. App. LEXIS 1143 (2001).

[135] Robinson v. Texas, 2000 Tex. App. LEXIS 5792 (2000) and Hampton v. Texas, 2003 Tex. App. LEXIS 3984 (2003).

prejudicial impact on the jury[136] or where there are overriding constitutional or statutory provisions that limit such impeachment.[137] For example, the defendant may have a Fifth Amendment privilege with respect to other uncharged crimes, the questions may relate to illegally seized wiretap evidence, or may involve a confidential marital communication.

§ 9.13　— Own Witness

The traditional rule holds that a party vouches for the credibility of witnesses it may call to offer evidence. Under this theory, a party may not impeach his or her own witness under the theory that a party would not call a witness if there were doubts about credibility. However, modern evidence theories as well as Rule 607 of the Federal Rules of Evidence permit any party to attack the credibility of its own witnesses without showing any proof of surprise, hostility on the part of the witness, or that the witness is allied with the opposing side.

With respect to state evidence law, some jurisdictions follow provisions identical or similar to Rule 607, while other states follow the traditional rule.[138] A federal appeals court, following the reasoning of Rule 607, stated that in determining the admissibility of testimony that the government elicits to impeach its own witness, the government's motive in eliciting such testimony is irrelevant.[139] Under Florida law, any party may impeach any witness, including the party who called that witness, when the witness's testimony involves a prior inconsistent position or the testimony shows that the witness may be biased, and several other methods.[140] The witness may be impeached by any party without regard to whether the witness's testimony constitutes surprise to the calling party. In contrast, a New York statute follows the traditional rule and does not permit the party who called the witness to impeach unless the witness in a criminal case gives evidence that tends to be adverse to the party calling the witness. In that event, the surprised party may introduce evidence that the witness has previously given an oral or written statement under oath that contradicts the witness's in-court testimony.[141] In New York "[a] party may impeach its own witness only if that witness gives testimony upon a material issue of the case which tends to disprove the position of such party, such party may introduce evidence that such witness has previously

---

[136]　Raffel v. United States, 271 U.S. 494, 46 S. Ct. 566, 70 L. Ed. 1054 (1926); Sharp v. United States, 410 F.2d 969 (5th Cir. 1969); United States v. McMurray, 20 F.3d 831 (8th Cir. 1994). *See also* Chandler v. State, 702 So. 2d 186 (Fla. 1997).

[137]　Lopez v. Texas, 990 S.W.2d 770, 777, 1999 Tex. App. LEXIS 871 (1999).

[138]　For example, compare N.Y. Crim. Proc. Law § 60.35(1) (demonstrating the limited situations in which a party may impeach its own witness), with Fed. R. Evid. 607 (allowing any party to impeach any witness—including its own—for any reason or no reason).

[139]　United States v. Logan, 121 F.3d 1172 (8th Cir. 1997).

[140]　FLA. STAT. § 90.608 (Matthew Bender 2009).

[141]　N.Y. CRIM. PROC. LAW § 60.35 (2009).

made" under oath an oral or written statement that is contradictory to the recent testimony.[142] The reality seems to be that a party may impeach a witness when unexpected hostility or surprise becomes evident, with the result that under either general theory, it will be a rare case in which the outcome is based on the type of policy that is followed regarding the impeachment of one's own witness.

One technique that appears to involve impeaching one's own witness may be considered damage control rather than impeachment. When a prosecutor plans to place a witness on the stand and the witness has been cooperative in exchange for certain leniencies from the government, the prosecutor may wish to disclose a plea bargain or other favorable deal between the prosecution's witness and the government. Any plea agreement with a cooperating witness may be required to be disclosed to the defendant under discovery rules and, demonstrative of this principle, Minnesota requires that the prosecution reveal this potential impeachment evidence to the defendant.[143] Sharing this evidence displays honesty on the part of the prosecution so the jury does not learn of a plea bargain for the first time when revealed by the defense counsel on cross-examination.[144] Open disclosure may benefit either party in a criminal case and is usually the most appropriate path to follow when using a witness who has prior legal problems.

In a criminal case, the government may impeach its own witness by presenting his or her prior inconsistent statements; however, there are limits on this authority. A federal prosecutor may not use impeachment by showing a prior inconsistent statement by calling a witness for the purpose of impeaching the witness to obtain evidence in front of the jury that would not normally be admissible.[145] In addition, the government also may not impeach its own witness merely because the witness refused to give testimony that the government hoped he or she would give.[146]

Impeachment of one's own witnesses is not permissible if the questioning is a means of subterfuge to expose the jury to otherwise inadmissible evidence.[147] However, the state may impeach its own witness to lessen the blow of a cross-examination by the defense attorney. For example, where the government informant's past would likely have come out on cross-examination, the government had a legitimate reason to explore the subject on direct examination.[148]

---

[142]   N.Y. Crim. Proc. Law § 60.35 (1) (2009).

[143]   State v. Miller, 754 N.W.2d 686, 706, 707, 2008 Minn. LEXIS 424 (Minn. 2008).

[144]   United States v. Valuck, 286 F.3d 221 (5th Cir. 2002).

[145]   *See* United States v. Letner, 273 Fed. App. 491, 2008 U.S. App. LEXIS 8375 (6th Cir. 2008). *See also* King v. State, 2008 Miss. App. LEXIS 765 (Miss. 2008), where the prosecution used impeachment of its own witnesses to bring otherwise inadmissible evidence into court. The conviction was reversed.

[146]   United States v. Ince, 21 F.3d 576 (4th Cir. 1994).

[147]   *Id.*

[148]   *Id.*

§ 9.14 — Bias or Prejudice

One of the most effective ways to impeach a witness is to show bias on the part of that witness. "Bias is a term used in the 'common law of evidence' to describe the relationship between a party and a witness which might lead the witness to slant, unconsciously or otherwise, his testimony in favor of or against a party. Bias may be induced by a witness' like, dislike, or fear of a party, or by the witness' self-interest."[149] In criminal cases, great latitude is generally permitted in cross-examination of a witness in order to test his or her credibility and to develop facts that may tend to show bias, prejudice, or any other motive that the witness may have for giving testimony. It is a well-established principle that the bias of a witness is subject to inquiry at trial and is almost always considered relevant as potentially discrediting the witness or otherwise affecting the weight of his or her testimony.[150] A court commits constitutional error if it unreasonably limits a defendant's cross-examination of a prosecution witness regarding that witness's bias, interest, prejudice, or motive for testifying.[151] However, reasonable limits may be placed on cross-examination where it may constitute harassment of the witness, confuse the issues, or waste the court's time. Examples of situations in which cross-examination was allowed to show bias follow.

In a California case involving a defendant who was a gang member and had been convicted of murder and shooting into an occupied motor vehicle, he argued on appeal that his right to due process had been violated by the trial court when it instructed the jury that it could consider evidence of gang activity and membership in evaluating witness credibility. According to the reviewing court, "it is well established that gang membership evidence may be used to evaluate witness credibility when the gang membership is relevant on such issues as the witness's fear or bias."[152] Generally, the use of gang member ship evidence for witness impeachment proves appropriate because the gang membership creates a reason why a witness might be untruthful due to gang retaliation or gang fellowship.

As a general rule, a prosecution witness may be cross-examined to show bias if promises of leniency were made by the prosecution. A witness may have a bias or an interest when he has a pending criminal charge or even when there is a prospect of criminal charges, and this is true even if he has made no plea bargain with the prosecutor. In a Louisiana armed robbery case, the court prohibited the defendant from inquiring about a pending criminal charge that one of the witnesses faced. The reviewing court noted that it was clear error in limiting the cross-examination of the witness with respect to his pending

---

[149] Coles v. United States, 808 A.2d 485, 489, 2002 D.C. App. LEXIS 556 (2002).

[150] Wilson v. State, 950 A.2d 634, 2008 Del. LEXIS 263 (Del. 2008).

[151] People v. Gonzales-Quevedo, 203 P.3d 609, 614, 615, 2008 Colo. App. LEXIS 1832 (Colo. 2008).

[152] People v. Flowers, 2009 Cal. App. Unpub. LEXIS 525 (Cal. 2009).

criminal charge but that under the circumstances the error was categorized as harmless.[153] As a general rule, the attorney attempting to impeach a witness by demonstrating bias must have a reasonable and well-founded suspicion that the evidence of bias has a basis in fact. The bias should be reasonably inferable from the facts presented by the attorney.[154]

Examples of cases in which evidence has been allowed to show bias are many. A few are briefly summarized here. When a defense witness who possessed exculpatory evidence prior to trial and knew of the defendant's legal difficulties immediately and never attempted to convey the information to the police and only offered the evidence at trial, that witness could be impeached by a showing of bias in favor of the defendant based on recent fabrication of exculpatory evidence.[155] Clear instances of possible bias occur when the witness is a spouse of a defendant or other close relative, or a fellow fraternity member, or when a witness is in business with the defendant.

Because a trial court has discretion in admitting impeachment evidence concerning bias, it may refuse to admit evidence for which a case could be made. In an aggravated assault case, the defendant wanted to call the victim's mother as a witness to question her about her offer, on her son's behalf, to receive $25,000 in exchange for her son (the assault victim) dropping all charges against the defendant. The court refused to allow the evidence of the monetary offer to show the witness's bias against the defendant. The bias theoretically developed because the defendant rejected the offer to compromise the criminal case and no money changed hands. The court reasoned that the offer could have been to settle civil issues between the victim and the defendant and therefore had no bearing on the criminal case.[156]

In another case involving bias against a defendant, evidence of a victim's reluctance to testify against a defendant in an attempted murder case arguably displayed fear of the defendant, a bias, interest or prejudice that may have helped the prosecution.[157] Over the defendant's contention that a mistrial should have been declared when the witness/victim took the Fifth Amendment and refused to testify additionally against the defendant, the trial court refused to grant the motion. The victim was eventually coaxed into testifying. On appeal, the defendant contended that the victim's assertion of the Fifth Amendment privilege denied him a fair trial because it unfairly suggested to the jury that it could infer that the witness/victim invoked his privilege because he feared future harm from defendant if he testified fully, and that the reason for such fear was that defendant had brutally beaten and stabbed the witness/victim. From this view, the jury could view the defendant guilty as charged. The reviewing

---

[153] State v. Bradley, 995 So. 2d 1230, 1235, 2008 La. App. LEXIS 1307 (La. 2008).

[154] Joyner v. United States, 818 A2d 166, 172, 2003 D.C. App. LEXIS 133 (2003).

[155] Massachusetts v. Cintron, 435 Mass. 509, 522, 759 N.E.2d 700, 711, 2001 Mass. LEXIS 771 (2001).

[156] Gavin v. Mississippi, 767 So. 2d 1072, 1077, 2000 Miss. App. LEXIS 454 (2000).

[157] State v. VanNguyen, 222 Ore. App. 55, 2008 Ore. App. LEXIS 1141 (Ore. 2008).

court refused to reverse on this ground because during opening statements, the prosecutor informed the jury that this particular witness was a reluctant prosecution witness and his conduct only confirmed that fact.

§ 9.15   — Character and Conduct

Rule 608

Evidence of Character and Conduct of Witness

(a) Opinion and reputation evidence of character. The credibility of a witness may be attacked or supported by evidence in the form of opinion or reputation, but subject to these limitations: (1) the evidence may refer only to character for truthfulness or untruthfulness, and (2) evidence of truthful character is admissible only after the character of the witness for truthfulness has been attacked by opinion or reputation evidence or otherwise.

(b) Specific instances of conduct. Specific instances of the conduct of a witness, for the purpose of attacking or supporting the witness' character for truthfulness, other than conviction of crime as provided in rule 609, may not be proved by extrinsic evidence. They may, however, in the discretion of the court, if probative of truthfulness or untruthfulness, be inquired into on cross-examination of the witness (1) concerning the witness' character for truthfulness or untruthfulness, or (2) concerning the character for truthfulness or untruthfulness of another witness as to which character the witness being cross-examined has testified.

The giving of testimony, whether by an accused or by any other witness, does not operate as a waiver of the accused's or the witness' privilege against self-incrimination when examined with respect to matters that relate only to character for truthfulness.[158]

As a general rule, the prosecution may not introduce evidence of a defendant's character or habit. However, if a defendant places his or her general reputation at issue by introducing what is loosely described as a "character" witness, or from the witness stand personally offers character evidence, he or she places his or her character at issue and is said to have "opened the door" for the prosecution to test the credibility of the witness. The prosecution may inquire on cross-examination whether the witness had knowledge of specific facts that, if known generally, would tend to detract from the summary of the defendant's reputation offered by the character witness. Allowing the character witness's knowledge of the defendant's character to be tested by such means is fraught with great danger. Unless circumscribed by rules of fairness and grounded in good faith on the part of the prosecution, the result may be unfairly prejudicial to the defendant, thus causing a miscarriage of justice.

---

[158] FED. R. EVID. 608.

If the prosecution attempts to attack the observations offered by a character witness or to cast doubt on the credibility of the defendant's character witnesses, there should be a prior demonstration, out of the hearing of the jury, establishing to the trial judge's satisfaction the truth of the basis for such inquiry. Moreover, cautionary instructions should be given to the jury, preferably at the time of the inquiry and in the jury instructions at the close of the case.

In *Michelson v. United States*,[159] the United States Supreme Court carefully considered the manner and extent of cross-examination of character witnesses in criminal cases. The Court stated:

> Wide discretion is accompanied by heavy responsibility on trial courts to protect the practice from any misuse. The trial judge was scrupulous to so guard it in the case before us. He took pains to ascertain, out of the presence of the jury, that the target of the question was an actual event, which would probably result in some comment among acquaintances if not injury to defendant's reputation. He satisfied himself that counsel was not merely taking a random shot at a reputation imprudently exposed or asking a groundless question to waft an unwarranted innuendo into the jury box.

Where the defendant's character witnesses have been cross-examined through inquiry about whether the witnesses had knowledge of specific facts that, if generally known, would tend to detract from the character testimony, the jury must be carefully cautioned that the testimony refers solely to reputation and not to the truth of collateral facts.[160] The prosecution may explore the basis and scope of the witness's knowledge of the defendant's reputation by asking the witness whether he or she has heard various reports about the defendant, provided that the questions have a foundation; for example, in the sense that arrests or accusations have been rumored and discussed. Past instances of misconduct mentioned on cross-examination must directly concern truthfulness or untruthfulness. If the prior conduct was merely improper, illegal, or immoral, then the evidence should not be permitted under Rule 608(b). For example, cross-examination of a witness concerning whether she ever attempted to strike another person with a stick should not be allowed, because the act, even if it occurred, has nothing to do with the honesty or believability of the witness.[161] The prosecution's cross-examination regarding specific instances of conduct has limitations. It is permitted to evaluate only the character witness's credibility and knowledge of a defendant and cannot be used to prove the prosecution's case against a defendant.[162] The prosecutor may not simply ask a question without any basis in fact; the government must have a good faith

---

[159]   335 U.S. 469, 69 S. Ct. 213, 93 L. Ed. 168 (1948).

[160]   Gross v. United States, 394 F.2d 216 (8th Cir. 1968); United States v. Lewis, 482 F.2d 632 (D.C. Cir. 1973).

[161]   Tennessee v. Neblett, 2003 Tenn. Crim. App. LEXIS 429 (2003).

[162]   United States v. Chan, 2002 U.S. Dist. LEXIS 1221 (S.D.N.Y. 2002).

belief that the specific instances of misconduct occurred. The danger lurking in this impeachment process is that in constructing an intelligible question, the cross-examiner's query often gives details of specific misconduct affecting general reputation, which would not otherwise be admissible.[163]

Because a defendant's character witnesses generally convey the collective community opinion concerning the defendant's overall character, the prosecutor may inquire on cross-examination whether a defendant's character witness "has heard" of the defendant's prior arrests or convictions. Some jurisdictions allow questions concerning whether the witness "knows" of any of the defendant's misdeeds. Such cross-examination is not admitted to establish the truth that such events took place, but only to test the foundations and reliability of the witness's testimony. Under Rule 608 it is inadmissible to establish the defendant's bad character or his or her propensity to commit the crime charged, but the evidence might be admissible under a different legal theory. The typical rationale for permitting such questions, even when they refer to a defendant's prior arrests, is that they enable the jury to better evaluate the character testimony that has been offered. If a witness has heard these damaging rumors and adheres to his or her statement that the defendant's reputation is good, some light and some doubt will have been shed upon the standards the witness has employed; alternatively, if he or she has not heard of these rumors that have some basis in fact, some doubt will have been cast upon his or her ability to speak on behalf of the collective opinion of the community. Because of this method of impeachment, some potential witness for a defendant may not be called in court. In a Texas case, involving an appeal concerning alleged ineffective assistance of counsel, the attorney for the defense had purposely not called some potential defense witnesses because the defendant's attorney knew the prosecutor would ask the "have you heard?" type of questions concerning specific instances of the defendant's conduct. The attorney believed that the answers would not benefit the defendant's case and the appellate court affirmed the conviction.[164]

In one case in which the prosecution's character witness was to be cross-examined, the court found no prejudicial error in refusing to permit questions concerning whether the witness had been involved in drug dealing because "drug dealing is not the type of conduct that necessarily bears on a witness's character for truthfulness."[165] Alternatively, when a defendant had testified on direct examination, the prosecutor properly used the defendant's prior convictions for writing a check on insufficient funds, defrauding an innkeeper, writing a check when he had no bank account, and tax fraud for impeachment evidence.[166]

---

[163] *See* North Carolina v. Calloway, 2002 N.C. App. LEXIS 2438 (2002), in which the appellate court held that cross-examination concerning prior acts of the defendant was not proper under Rule 608(b), but was admissible under North Carolina Evidence Rule 404(b), dealing with exceptions to proof of other crimes to prove conduct.

[164] Bean v. State, 2007 Tex. App. LEXIS 8914 (Tex. 2007).

[165] United States v. Walker, 47 Fed. Appx. 639, 2002 U.S. App. LEXIS 19817 (4th Cir. 2002).

[166] United States v. Arhebamen, 2006 U.S. App. LEXIS 24564 (6th Cir. 2006).

The credibility of a witness may be attacked or supported by evidence in the form of reputation or opinion, but this is subject to several limitations. Under Rule 608(a), the evidence may refer only to character for truthfulness or untruthfulness, and evidence of truthful character is admissible only after the truthfulness of the witness has been attacked by opinion or reputation evidence or otherwise. Where a witness denies specific instances of personal misconduct, other than for conviction of crime, no additional inquiry may be made under Rule 608(b). Thus, specific instances of dishonesty or untruthful prior conduct committed by a witness that are introduced for the sole purpose of attacking the witness's character or reputation for truthfulness may not be proven by extrinsic evidence. Although courts will allow inquiry into specific instances of untruthful conduct on cross-examination, the adverse party is stuck with the answer given by the witness. As a strong general rule, extrinsic evidence cannot be introduced to prove the collateral issue that the witness has denied.[167]

In applying the rules relating to the admissibility of evidence concerning character and conduct of the witness, the time element is normally given consideration when the conviction occurred more than 10 years prior. However, in a federal prosecution, the judge ruled that a defendant attorney's older convictions involving income tax issues would be permitted to be introduced by the prosecution. The defendant chose to introduce them during his direct examination. On appeal, the court held that the defendant had waived his right to complain by introducing the impeaching evidence on his direct examination, despite the fact that the judge had stated that the prosecution could use the more-than-10-year-old convictions as impeachment evidence.[168] In a case in which a police officer lied to the defendant during interrogation, the trial court properly refused to allow cross-examination concerning the officer's lies. Generally, a witness's credibility may be attacked by specific instances of conduct if they are probative of the witness's character for truthfulness or untruthfulness. In this case, the trial court held that because the use of false statements by police during questioning is a routine practice, the evidence was not admissible to impeach the police officer's testimony at trial. According to the court, it had not found any authority suggesting that use of deception as a police interrogation tactic implicated an officer's credibility under oath.[169]

In further defining the limits placed on the use of character evidence, a Pennsylvania federal court refused to allow the prosecution to impeach an embezzlement defendant using a prior felony car theft conviction as a method of questioning his character for honesty if the defendant took the witness stand. The trial judge had concerns that proof of the car theft conviction would have little probative value concerning whether the defendant committed embezzlement. The objection to using the earlier felony was that the jurors

---

[167] Heartland Surgical Specialty Hosp., LLC v. Midwest Division, 2007 U.S. Dist. LEXIS 53216 (D. Kan. 2007).

[168] United States v. McConnet, 2006 U.S. App. LEXIS 23230 (10th Cir. 2006).

[169] Minnesota v. Martinez, 657 N.W.2d 600, 602, 603, 2003 Minn. App. LEXIS 252 (2003).

might base their decision on something other than the evidence presented in the case.[170] Other judges might weigh this case differently because dishonesty is involved in both embezzlement and theft.

If evidence of prior crimes is admissible to impeach, the defendant cannot prevent the prosecution from introducing evidence to that effect by offering to stipulate to the existence of the prior felony convictions. In another case involving a felon in possession of a firearm, the defendant stipulated that he had prior felony convictions.[171] Once the defendant became a witness in his own defense, he placed his character trait for honesty at issue and the district court did not abuse its discretion in allowing the prosecution to cross-examine the defendant concerning his prior felony convictions.

§ 9.16   — Conviction of Crime

Rule 609

Impeachment by Evidence of Conviction of Crime

(a) General rule. For the purpose of attacking the character for truthfulness of a witness,

(1) evidence that a witness other than an accused has been convicted of a crime shall be admitted, subject to Rule 403, if the crime was punishable by death or imprisonment in excess of one year under the law under which the witness was convicted, and evidence that an accused has been convicted of such a crime shall be admitted if the court determines that the probative value of admitting this evidence outweighs its prejudicial effect to the accused; and

(2) evidence that any witness has been convicted of a crime shall be admitted regardless of the punishment, if it readily can be determined that establishing the elements of the crime required proof or admission of an act of dishonesty or false statement by the witness.

(b) Time limit. Evidence of a conviction under this rule is not admissible if a period of more than ten years has elapsed since the date of the conviction or of the release of the witness from the confinement imposed for that conviction, whichever is the later date, unless the court determines, in the interests of justice, that the probative value of the conviction supported by specific facts and circumstances substantially outweighs its prejudicial effect. However, evidence of a conviction more than 10 years old as calculated herein, is not admissible unless the proponent gives to the adverse party sufficient advance written notice of intent to use such evidence to provide the adverse party with a fair opportunity to contest the use of such evidence.

---

[170] United States v. Miller, 2004 U.S. Dist. LEXIS 23299 (E.D. Pa. 2006).

[171] United States v. Kilgore, 151 Fed. Appx. 799, 802, 2005 U.S. App. LEXIS 20690 (11th Cir. 2005).

(c) Effect of pardon, annulment, or certificate of rehabilitation. Evidence of a conviction is not admissible under this rule if (1) the conviction has been the subject of a pardon, annulment, certificate of rehabilitation, or other equivalent procedure based on a finding of the rehabilitation of the person convicted, and that person has not been convicted of a subsequent crime that was punishable by death or imprisonment in excess of one year, or (2) the conviction has been the subject of a pardon, annulment, or other equivalent procedure based on a finding of innocence.

(d) Juvenile adjudications. Evidence of juvenile adjudications is generally not admissible under this rule. The court may, however, in a criminal case allow evidence of a juvenile adjudication of a witness other than the accused if conviction of the offense would be admissible to attack the credibility of an adult and the court is satisfied that admission in evidence is necessary for a fair determination of the issue of guilt or innocence.

(e) Pendency of appeal. The pendency of an appeal therefrom does not render evidence of a conviction inadmissible. Evidence of the pendency of an appeal is admissible.[172]

As a general rule, because a case should be decided on relevant evidence that either proves or fails to prove the crime charged, it would be unfair to introduce evidence to show that a suspect in a criminal case had previously committed other crimes. The concern when a judge admits evidence of a prior crime or crimes is that a jury might, in a close case, convict the defendant because the defendant had committed prior crimes. A jury might determine that if the defendant had committed one prior crime, then he or she might be guilty of the crime presently charged. The concern with prior crime evidence is that juries might use a defendant's prior convictions as evidence of the defendant's propensity to commit crime.[173] When a witness takes the stand and testifies, he or she puts her credibility directly at issue.[174] The ordinary witness may usually be asked, for purposes of impeachment, whether he or she has been convicted of a felony, infamous crime, or crime involving moral turpitude. A defendant witness places his credibility at issue by testifying. If a defendant testifies in his or her own defense, evidence that the defendant had been convicted of prior felony offenses may be admitted for whatever effect the prior offenses might have on his credibility. In a Texas driving under the influence case, the defendant took the witness stand in his own defense and denied drinking alcohol. Subsequently, the prosecution introduced evidence of his two previous felony convictions and the fact that he was still on parole. Pursuant to the Texas version of Rule 609, the trial court properly admitted the evidence of his

---

[172] Fed. R. Evid. 609.
[173] North Dakota v. Stewart, 2002 N.D. 102, 646 N.W.2d 712, 715, 2002 N.D. LEXIS 140 (2002).
[174] United States v. Murphy, 172 Fed. Appx. 461, 462, 2006 U.S. App. LEXIS 7827 (3d Cir. 2006). *See also* Thomas v. State, 2009 Miss. App. LEXIS 192 (Miss. 2009).

earlier convictions and offered a limiting instruction that the jury could only consider the felonies for judging the defendant's credibility.[175] The reason for exposing a criminal record is to call into question the reliability and credibility of the witness for telling the truth.

Under Rule 609, criminal offenses that are remote in time to the current trial may be excluded where they are older than 10 years or are considered too remote in time, even if within the 10-year period. In determining whether a prior conviction's probative value outweighs its prejudicial effects, a Texas court listed five factors to consider:

> whether a prior conviction's probative value outweighs its prejudicial effect: (1) the impeachment value of the prior crime; (2) the temporal proximity of the past crime relative to the charged offense and the witness's subsequent history; (3) the similarity between the past crime and the offense being prosecuted; (4) the importance of the defendant's testimony; and (5) the importance of the credibility issue.[176]

The court considered crimes involving deception or dishonesty to have a greater impeachment value than a crime of violence.[177]

As a general rule, a witness may not be impeached by inquiry into prior misdemeanors unless those misdemeanors involve dishonesty that can be equated as involving moral turpitude. In a Virginia case, the appellate court held that a trial court erred when it allowed the prosecution to impeach the defendant with a crime not involving moral turpitude. According to the court, a prior conviction of contributing to the delinquency of a minor was not a crime involving moral turpitude and evidence of the prior crime should not have been admitted into evidence.[178] Where a prior misdemeanor involved a crime of moral turpitude such as theft, such a crime involves dishonesty and may be used for impeachment purposes. According to an Illinois appellate court, in a case in which the credibility of the defendant was crucial to guilt or innocence, "theft is a crime that speaks directly to a person's truthfulness," and the jury should have been allowed to fully assess his credibility.[179] In a federal prosecution for having a firearm under a disability, the defendant wanted to introduce the driving while intoxicated convictions for both of the officers who were the primary witnesses in the case. One of the officers lied about drinking when initially stopped by the other police. The judge excluded the DUI evidence on the theory that the police officer's misdemeanor convictions were not relevant to their credibility.[180]

---

[175]   Myers v. State, 2009 Tex. App. LEXIS 8191 (Tex. 2008).

[176]   Mixon v. State, 2007 Tex. App. LEXIS 4310 (Tex. 2007).

[177]   *Id.*

[178]   Jarrell v. Commonwealth of Virginia, 2002 Va. App. LEXIS 353 (2002).

[179]   Illinois v. Diehl, 335 Ill. App. 3d 693, 704, 783 N.E.2d 640, 650, 2002 Ill. App. LEXIS 1060 (2003).

[180]   United States v. Edwards, 156 Fed. Appx. 954, 956, 2005 U.S. App. LEXIS 26786 (9th Cir. 2005). Contra North Carolina v. Gregory, 154 N.C. App 718, 722, 572 S.E.2d 838, 840, 841, 2002 N.C. App. LEXIS 1534 (2002).

A witness generally may not be impeached by the introduction of evidence regarding a pending charge that has not been tried, but not all jurisdictions follow this rule. When the prosecutor asked a defense witness questions concerning the fact that he was about to stand trial for murder, kidnapping, and robbery, the question was not only erroneous, but also unduly prejudicial to the defendant. His constitutional right to a fair trial was violated.[181] However, in some cases the credibility of a prosecution witness may be impeached by introducing evidence that he or she has pending criminal charges.[182] The fact that a witness is facing criminal charges and cooperating with the government may indicate pro-prosecution bias and is something a jury should be permitted to evaluate.

In federal cases, the district court judge initially determines whether the probative value of admitting evidence outweighs its prejudicial effect (Rule 609 (a)(1)). The trial judge's decision will not be disturbed unless there is a clear abuse of discretion.

For example, the Eighth Circuit Court of Appeals upheld the admission of prior felonies against a defendant for the purpose of impeachment.[183] The defendant had been charged with being a felon in possession of a firearm based on a shooting at a home where he had been attending a party. The judge permitted prosecutors to question the defendant concerning the fact of his three prior violent felonies during cross-examination. Although the judge did not make a record of balancing the probative value of the impeachment evidence against the danger of unfair prejudice, the reviewing court assumed that the judge made the appropriate analysis.

Whether in state or federal courts, trial judges have broad discretion to determine the admissibility of evidence relating to prior convictions. Rule 609 must be read by the trial court in conjunction with Rule 403, which requires that the trial judge balance the probative value of the impeachment evidence against the risk of unfair prejudice. In a case involving Rule 609, a trial court refused to permit a defendant to attempt to impeach a government witness concerning the witness's past criminal activity, and the appellate court upheld the decision.[184] The government's witness had a misdemeanor conviction that was more than 10 years old and did not involve dishonesty. The felony conviction similarly dated more than a decade ago and the district court determined that the probative value of admitting the witness's prior felony was exceeded by the danger of unfair prejudice to the government. Courts are especially hesitant to admit evidence relating to convictions of witnesses that occurred long before the crime that is the subject of a current trial.

State courts have followed much of this same theory and philosophy when interpreting their respective versions of Rule 609. In an Alaska theft case, a trial court permitted the prosecutor to introduce the defendant-witness's prior

---

[181]   Moore v. Commonwealth, 634 S.W.2d 426 (Ky. 1982).
[182]   People v. Reyes, 2007 Cal. App. Unpub. LEXIS 10300 (Cal. 2007). Unpublished opinion.
[183]   United States v. Headbird, 461 F.3d 1074, 2006 U.S. App. LEXIS 22326 (8th Cir. 2006).
[184]   Unites States v. Loma, 2006 U. S. App. LEXIS 24599 (9th Cir. 2006).

conviction for theft by receiving stolen equipment.[185] The defendant had taken the stand in his own defense to explain that his company allowed any employee to borrow equipment at any time. The appellate court found no abuse of discretion under Rule 609 and upheld the admission on cross-examination of the defendant's prior crime involving a prior conviction for theft of property. Once a defendant takes the stand in his or her defense, the defendant places the defendant's credibility at issue.

Below are a few examples of cases in which criminal convictions were used for the purpose of attacking a witness's credibility. In a prosecution for possession of more than five grams of cocaine, the trial court did not abuse its discretion in admitting the defendant's prior conviction for conspiracy to import heroin and aiding and abetting the distribution of heroin.[186] There was no abuse of discretion in admitting evidence of two prior convictions for possession of unauthorized weapons when the defendant was on trial for two counts of distributing crack cocaine.[187] According to the Supreme Court of North Dakota, evidence of the defendant witness's prior convictions for felony unauthorized use of a motor vehicle, unlawful possession of a firearm by a felon, and reckless endangerment were considered probative of the defendant's character for truthfulness and admissible for impeachment purposes in a prosecution for driving under the influence and aggravated reckless driving involving a death.[188] A Minnesota court properly admitted evidence of a defendant's prior robbery conviction that occurred less than six years before as impeachment evidence in a trial for attempted second-degree murder. The appellate court noted that the evidence of the robbery conviction helped the jury obtain a better view of the whole person in assessing his truthfulness.[189]

Although subject to many exceptions, Rule 609 generally prohibits the use of evidence of a conviction when the person has been pardoned or the conviction is the subject of annulment or certificate of rehabilitation. In *United States v. McMurrey*, convictions for which the witness had been pardoned to restore rights of citizenship were inadmissible as impeachment evidence even though the pardons were not based on rehabilitation or innocence.[190] However, according to the comments associated with Rule 609, a pardon granted solely for the purpose of restoring the defendant's civil rights lost by virtue of a felony conviction has no relevance where a party desires to inquire into the character of the pardoned individual. If the pardon or other proceeding includes a finding of rehabilitation, the result under federal Rule 609, and many state jurisdictions,

---

[185] Damitz v. State, 2005 Alaska App. LEXIS 26 (2005).

[186] United States v. Conway, 53 Fed. Appx. 872, 876, 877, 2002 U.S. App. LEXIS 26341 (10th Cir. 2002).

[187] United States v. Broadwater, 2003 U.S. App. LEXIS 10873 (7th Cir. 2003).

[188] North Dakota v. Stewart, 2002 N.D. 102, 646 N.W.2d 712, 715, 716, 2002 N.D. LEXIS 140 (2002).

[189] State v. Flores, 2006 Minn. App. Unpub. LEXIS 390 (2006).

[190] United States v. McMurrey, 827 F. Supp. 424 (S.D. Tex. 1993), *aff'd,* 48 F.3d 149 (1993). *See also* State v. Baker, 956 S.W.2d 8 (Tenn. 1997).

is to render the conviction inadmissible for impeachment purposes.[191] An alternative policy could allow each party to introduce proof of the conviction and rehabilitation, but this procedure presents challenges with respect to reasons of policy, economy of time, and difficulties of evaluating the pardon and whether rehabilitation has occurred. Due process requires that federal courts give full credit to state pardons.

The examiner, in his or her inquiries about a conviction, generally may not go beyond the name of the crime, the time and place of conviction, and the punishment. Additional details, such as the name of the victim and aggravating circumstances, may not be included in the inquiry. A substantial number of states, while not opening the door to a retrial of the previous conviction, permit the witness to make a brief and general statement of explanation, mitigation, or denial of guilt, and other states recognize the discretion of the trial judge to permit the witness to do so.[192]

§ 9.17   — Prior Inconsistent Statements

Rule 613

Prior Statements of Witnesses

(a) **Examining witness concerning prior statement.** In examining a witness concerning a prior statement made by the witness, whether written or not, the statement need not be shown nor its contents disclosed to the witness at that time, but on request the same shall be shown or disclosed to opposing counsel.

(b) **Extrinsic evidence of prior inconsistent statement of witness.** Extrinsic evidence of a prior inconsistent statement by a witness is not admissible unless the witness is afforded an opportunity to explain or deny the same and the opposite party is afforded an opportunity to interrogate the witness thereon, or the interests of justice otherwise require. This provision does not apply to admissions of a party-opponent as defined in Rule 801(d)(2).[193]

The testimony of a witness may be impeached by showing prior declarations, statements, or testimony from another case made by that witness (and never another person) that contradict or are inconsistent with the witness's testimony offered at trial. Prior inconsistent statements include written statements actually signed by the maker, statements adopted or approved by a witness or a party-witness, mechanical recordings of statements or their exact transcription, and accurate statements recited in a continuous narrative form.[194] Under the Federal

---

[191] FED. R. EVID. 609: History; Ancillary Laws and Directives.

[192] Wittenberg v. United States, 304 F. Supp. 744 (D. Minn. 1969); United States v. Bray, 445 F.2d 178 (5th Cir. 1971).

[193] FED. R. EVID. 613.

[194] Ohio v. Linder, 2002 Ohio 5077, 2002 Ohio App. LEXIS 5113 (2002).

Rules, the statement need not be shown or played for the witness, but on request shall be shown or disclosed to opposing counsel. The witness should be informed of the statements and the conditions, time, place, and circumstances under which they were made. In a rape prosecution, the trial court admitted into evidence a prior recorded conversation between the defendant's ex-wife and the complaining victim. The ex-wife testified that the victim had apologized for making false accusations against the defendant concerning the alleged rape and the ex-wife denied making a phone call to the victim supporting her ex-husband's prosecution for rape. Outside of the jury's presence, the prosecution played the tape of the phone conversation and upon retaking the stand, the ex-wife stated that she was lying on the tape-recording of the phone call. The reviewing court upheld the trial court's allowing the jury to hear the tape of the prior inconsistent conversation to determine whether the ex-wife's testimony at trial was truthful and did not allow the jury to consider the out-of-court phone conversation as substantive evidence.[195]

In interpreting a state version of Rule 613 in a prosecution for two counts of rape, the defendant contended that the prosecution failed to notify the defense attorney that the victim once told a police officer that the defendant "did not put anything in her" when her position at trial was that the defendant had completed the rapes.[196] The appellate court reversed the rape convictions because it believed that the impeachment evidence, if offered in court, created a reasonable probability that the result of the trial would have been different if the complaining witness had been impeached with the prior inconsistent statement.

Previous contradictory statements introduced for the purpose of impeachment generally are not admissible as substantive evidence due to their nature as hearsay evidence. Many jurisdictions hold that it is incumbent on the defendant to request a cautionary statement from the judge that the prior inconsistent statement can only be used to evaluate the credibility of that particular witness.[197] However, contradictory statements may become substantive evidence if the witness recants the testimony that he or she gave at the grand jury or at trial and admits that his or her prior statements contained the truth. Such an admission would make the prior statements a part of the witness's present testimony[198] and the witness would be available for cross-examination. In an exception to the general rule holding that prior inconsistent statements are for impeachment use only, Colorado permits the use of a prior inconsistent statement as substantive proof if the witness, while testifying, "was given an opportunity to explain or deny the statement or is still available to give further

---

[195] Winkle v. State, 374 Ark. 128, 134, 2008 Ark. LEXIS 433 (Ark. 2008).
[196] State v. Scheidel, 165 Ohio App. 3d 131; 2006 Ohio 195; 844 N.E.2d 1248; 2006 Ohio App. LEXIS 166 (2006).
[197] Polk v. Indiana, 783 N.E.2d 1253, 1267, 1258, 2003 Ind. App. LEXIS 313 (2003).
[198] Commonwealth v. Ragland, 72 Mass. App. Ct. 815, 2009 Mass. App. LEXIS 1039 (Mass. 2008).

testimony in the trial"[199] and the previous inconsistent statement purports to contain information within the witness's personal knowledge.

State courts generally construe their adaptations of the Federal Rules of Evidence with similar reasoning and often follow the logic and jurisprudence advanced by federal court decisions. After stating that the trial court is vested with broad discretion regarding what evidence may be admitted as a prior inconsistent statement for impeachment purposes, a Connecticut appeals court noted that one of the roles of the trial court is to determine whether two statements are inconsistent, including content and considering omission, and whether the prior statement should be admitted.[200]

§ 9.18   — Defects of Recollection or Perception

An effective method of impeaching a witness involves demonstrating to the judge or jury that a witness had a defect in perception, recording of facts, recollection, narration, or perception concerning matters about which he or she testified. The trier of fact has the duty to determine the weight to be given to defects in memory or perception.[201] For example, a witness whose hearing or eyesight is impaired may be impeached by calling the impairment to the attention of the jury or judge or by demonstrating it in court. The opposing party may attempt to impeach the witness's testimony by showing that he or she has a poor memory and was unable to recall events of similar importance. The use of contradiction to impeach, while different from prior inconsistent statement as an impeachment tool, involves evidence that shows a different prior witness's testimony may not be accurate due to misperception or an erroneous conclusion derived from observed facts.[202] As in other matters involving admitting challenged evidence, the trial judge has discretion in determining whether to admit and the trier of fact has the duty to determine the weight to be given to defects in memory or perception, as well as to determine the impeachment value of inconsistencies or contradictions.[203]

A witness's consumption of alcohol or drugs at the time the witness perceived events or immediately prior to testifying can be introduced as impeachment evidence, if the consumption impaired the witness's memory and perception of the event.[204]

---

[199] C.R.S. 16-10-201. Inconsistent statement of witness—competency of evidence (2008).

[200] Connecticut v. Francis D., 75 Conn. App. 1, 17, 18, 815 A.2d 191, 203, 204, 2003 Conn. App. LEXIS 64 (2003).

[201] Singleton v State, 2009 Miss. App. LEXIS 169 (2009).

[202] McCarter v. Commonwealth of Virginia, 38 Va. App 502, 506, 507, 566 S.E.2d 868, 869, 870, 2002 Va. App. LEXIS 393 (2002).

[203] Singleton v State, 2009 Miss. App. LEXIS 169 (2009).

[204] Maynard v. Government of the Virgin Islands, n.17, 2009 U.S. Dist. LEXIS 35132 (D.V.I. 2009).

In attempting to impeach a witness, the party is permitted to test the credibility of that witness by delving into the testimony of the witness to test the witness's ability to perceive and to test the ability to remember the facts. However, judges have wide latitude in determining limits in the attempt to impeach a witness to prevent harassment of the witness, prejudice to either party, or confusion of the issues.[205]

§ 9.19 — Use of Confession for Impeachment Purposes

A free and voluntary confession, properly offered, that has been recanted prior to or at trial allows the prosecution to use the earlier confession as an impeachment tool and as substantive evidence as an exception to the hearsay rule.[206] Since the *Miranda v. Arizona* decision in 1966, a body of law has developed concerning the use of improperly taken confessions when offered solely for impeachment purposes. In the *Miranda* case, the Supreme Court of the United States held that when an individual is taken into custody and is not free to leave under circumstances in which police wish to question him or her, the police must inform the arrestee that he or she has the right to consult with an attorney and does not have to speak with police about the reason for the arrest.[207] In that decision, the Court indicated that unless such warnings were properly given at the time when custody and the desire to interrogate coexisted, and when proper waiver has been demonstrated by the prosecution at trial, no direct evidence and most derivative evidence obtained as a result of interrogation may be used against the defendant. When a defendant understands the warning and remains silent, that fact of silence cannot be used against him or her at trial because the defendant was merely following the *Miranda* principles by remaining silent.[208] Were the decision otherwise, the defendant would be informed that he has the right of silence, but the reality of the silence would be that the exercise of that right would prove costly if the prosecution could use the fact of silence as a tool against the defendant by asking a testifying police officer about the defendant's silence or mentioning it during a closing argument.

When a defendant in custody made an unwarned confession in violation of *Miranda* and realized the prosecution could not use the confession to prove

---

[205]   Newton v. Kemna, 354 F.3d 776, 781, 2004 U.S. App. LEXIS 232 (8th Cir. 2004).

[206]   A voluntary confession is generally admissible against a defendant, whether as an exception to the hearsay rule or as non-hearsay by definition. Under Federal Rule 801, a voluntary confession or a prior statement by definition is not considered hearsay and will be admitted unless some other legal doctrine calls for exclusion under the circumstances.

[207]   Miranda v. Arizona, 384 U.S. 436, 86 S. Ct. 1602, 16 L. Ed. 2d 694 (1966). The Supreme Court reaffirmed the *Miranda* case in 2000 when it ruled that the warnings were required by the constitution and that Congress could not overturn the *Miranda* decision by changing federal law. Dickerson v. United States, 530 U.S. 428, 2000 U.S. LEXIS 4305 (2000).

[208]   Doyle v. Ohio, 426 U.S. 610, 96 S. Ct. 2240, 49 L. Ed. 2d 91 (1976).

guilt, the defendant believed he could tell a different story at trial, secure in the knowledge that his prior inconsistent confession would not be admitted. The prosecution used his earlier unwarned confession to impeach him. However, in upholding the conviction, in *Harris v. United States*, the Supreme Court determined that an extrajudicial confession obtained without properly administering the *Miranda* warnings could be used for impeachment purposes.[209] The Court reasoned that a defendant, having voluntarily taken the stand, has an obligation to speak truthfully and accurately, and the prosecution properly introduced the non-Mirandized confession as impeachment evidence. If the trial court had excluded the unwarned statement, it would have given the defendant immunity from perjury when he told one story to police and a separate untruthful story to the court.

If a confession has been taken in violation of *Miranda* or has been secured from the arrestee by less than free and voluntary means, it may not be used for impeachment purposes or as substantive proof. In *Mincey v. Arizona* (1978) the Supreme Court refused to extend the *Harris* reasoning to a confession obtained in violation of the free and voluntary rule.[210] If voluntary confessions have been obtained without administering the *Miranda* warnings or in violation of the right to counsel under the Sixth Amendment, they may be used only for impeachment purposes when the defendant takes the witness stand and directly contradicts the known confession. In *Kansas v. Ventris*, the prosecution placed an informant into the defendant's cell and obtained the defendant's admission/confession to a burglary and robbery.[211] The Supreme Court upheld the use of the cell block confession for use as impeachment evidence to counter the defendant's inconsistent trial testimony. Under these circumstances, the evidence will be received not as substantive evidence of guilt, but solely as impeachment evidence. If the statement has been obtained involuntarily, it would not be inadmissible for any purpose due to doubts concerning its reliability.

While the *Miranda* case excludes unwarned custodial answers to questions, police may not make an end run around the warning requirement. For example, in one case an officer interrogated the suspect without giving any warnings while the subject was in custody. After she confessed to murder, the officer took a break for a short time and returned to give the *Miranda* warnings for the first time. The officer managed to get the subject to confess to murder for a second time. This process violated *Miranda* and the confession, though voluntary by traditional standards, violated the requirement mandated by the original *Miranda* case.[212]

A defendant's post-*Miranda* silence cannot be used to convict, impeach or otherwise call into question his or her assertion of a constitutional right, but the silence must be the exercise of a constitutional right and not a conspiracy of

---

[209] Harris v. New York, 401 U.S. 222, 91 S. Ct. 643, 28 L. Ed. 2d 1 (1971); *see also* Oregon v. Hass, 420 U.S. 714, 915 S. Ct. 1215, 43 L. Ed. 2d 570 (1975).

[210] Mincey v. Arizona, 437 U.S. 385, 1978 U.S. LEXIS 115 (1978).

[211] Kansas v. Ventris, _____ U.S _____, 2009 U.S. LEXIS 3299 (2009).

[212] Missouri v. Seibert, 542 U.S. 600, 2004 U.S. LEXIS 4578 (2004).

silence among criminals. The concept was followed in case in which one arrestee told a confederate to remain silent when the police attempted to question the confederate. Such speech did not constitute silence and could be admitted against the speaker. Introducing evidence that one defendant tried to silence another defendant does not indicate the exercise of the rights under *Miranda*; instead, it demonstrated the opposite, a desire not to remain silent. The appellate court approved the trial court's admission of evidence that one drug arrestee tried to influence the other to remain silent in the face of police attempts at interrogation.[213]

Not every instance in which a government witness or prosecutor mentions that a defendant remained silent after being given the *Miranda* warnings will result in the reversal of a conviction. In a child abuse case, police asked some questions of the accused, who was not in custody.[214] During the interview, the accused told police that he wanted to talk to his father before speaking further. The mention of this type of silence did not run afoul of the rule prohibiting comment on silence because the accused was not in custody and was not subject to *Miranda* warnings. However, later in the trial, the prosecutor asked a special agent on the witness stand if the defendant had declined to be interviewed after his arrest and after the *Miranda* warnings had been given. The agent answered in the affirmative. This type of exchange violated the principle that post-arrest, post-*Miranda* evidence of silence cannot be admitted against that defendant. However, in this case, the judge immediately issued a cautionary instruction to the jury, admonished the witness and the prosecutor, and told the jury to disregard the question and answer. The reviewing court held that this use of silence evidence constituted harmless error.

In summary, statements that have been taken properly and qualify as admissions or confessions may be used impeachment purposes and present no problem when the evidence is admitted against the person who uttered it. However, if the statement has been taken in violation of the principles of *Miranda* or has been taken involuntarily, the admission or confession is prohibited from admission to prove guilt. Where the statement was voluntarily offered, even though the *Miranda* warnings should have been offered or the right to counsel was violated, the statement may only be used for impeachment purposes when the defendant gives a contradictory statement during the defense case-in-chief. The fact that a subject exhibited silence before the *Miranda* warnings were necessary is admissible, but after the warnings are required, the fact of silence should not bring a comment from a government witness or prosecutor because it constitutes error.

§ 9.20   Rehabilitation of Witness

When evidence has been offered to impeach a witness, other evidence that is consistent with the witness's trial testimony may be offered to counteract the

---

[213]   United States v. Lopez-Lopez, 282 F.3d 1, 2002 U.S. App. LEXIS 2896 (1st Cir. 2002).

[214]   United States v. One Star, 2006 U.S. App. LEXIS 25417 (8th Cir. 2006).

effects of the impeaching evidence. For example, in Pennsylvania, a court may permit the introduction of a prior consistent statement of a witness for the purpose of rehabilitation where the statement is being presented to rebut an inference of recent fabrication, improper motive, or faulty memory.[215] Consistent with this theory, in a Colorado case, when a defendant impeached a prosecution witness with a number of prior inconsistent statements, the trial court permitted the prosecution to play a videotape of one of the witness's prior statements to police that was consistent with his trial testimony as a method of rehabilitating the prosecution witness.[216] In a federal racketeering prosecution involving a homicide, a prosecution witness had been impeached by allegations that he and a cellmate concocted a story while housed together in jail that was adverse to the defendants. The appellate court approved the trial use of the witness's prior statement, which had been made long before the witness had been housed with his cellmate. Because the prior statement was consistent with the witness's trial testimony, the trial court properly admitted the prior consistent statement as rehabilitation evidence.[217]

In a case involving sexual assault and indecency with a child, the defendant's attorney carefully questioned the prosecuting child witness concerning inconsistencies between her trial testimony and a videotaped interview given near the time of the alleged attack. The trial judge allowed the prosecution to bring the child's former babysitter/teacher to offer her opinion concerning the child's reputation for truthfulness as rehabilitation of the child witness. The conviction was reversed because the evidence of prior inconsistent statements in this case did not imply that the child was untruthful but that perhaps her memory of events was faulty and rehabilitation was not proper.[218] Not every instance of a prior inconsistent act, statement, or writing indicates a problem with truthfulness.

However, rehabilitation may be appropriate when the defendant implies that a prosecution witness has recently fabricated portions of his or her testimony. At a trial involving a potential death sentence for murder and rape, the defense suggested that a statement made by a witness, quoting the defendant as saying, "I'd like to have a piece of that," was untrue and had been recently devised. The prosecution was properly permitted to introduce evidence (as a prior consistent statement) that the witness had made nearly identical statements to an investigating police officer immediately after the murder occurred.[219]

In some instances, the court may admit evidence of the reason or explanation for a prior inconsistent statement or writing as part of the rehabilitation process when there been an attack on the witness's credibility. For example, in a homicide case, a witness whose testimonial evidence had been impeached

---

[215] *See* Pa. R. E. 613 Prior statements of witnesses (2008).
[216] *See* People v. Elie, 2006 Colo. App. LEXIS 1487 (2006).
[217] United States v. Rivera, 51 Fed. Appx. 47, 2002 U.S. App. LEXIS 24036 (2d Cir. 2002).
[218] Michael v. State, 235 S.W.3d 723, 725, 2007 Tex. Crim. App. LEXIS 1267 (Tex. 2007).
[219] Woodall v. Kentucky, 63 S.W.3d 104, 131, 2001 Ky. LEXIS 142 (2002).

by the use of two prior inconsistent prison letters that contradicted his trial testimony was permitted to rehabilitate himself by explaining why the earlier letters were inconsistent with his trial testimony.[220] In a Nebraska case, the reviewing court indicated that the admission of evidence of a witness's reputation for truthfulness after impeachment because of prior inconsistent statements made by the witness is within the discretion of the trial court.[221]

As a general rule, when a witness's credibility has been attacked by the opposing party, evidence that tends to rehabilitate that witness will be admissible. In a Wyoming murder case, the defense offered the theory that both prosecution witnesses had lied from the outset and falsely implicated him in the murder to get personal leniency from the prosecutor. Here, the witnesses' credibility was attacked when the defendant characterized them as untruthful when they implicated the defendant in the murder. In order to rehabilitate the prosecution witnesses the judge allowed a police officer to relate what the prosecution witnesses had stated to him at the beginning of the murder investigation, facts that were consistent with the prosecution witnesses' trial testimony.[222] Rehabilitation of a witness by the use of appropriate evidence may be viewed as according due process to the opposing side with a view to ensuring each party a fundamental opportunity to meet the evidence offered by the other side.

§ 9.21 Summary

Although the testimony of witnesses is essential in criminal cases, not all witnesses who have information about the facts of the case are permitted to testify. Moreover, witnesses who are authorized to testify are limited as to the manner and extent of the testimony they may give. The trial judge has a responsibility to apply the rules of evidence in determining whether a witness may testify at all and, if so, the extent of his or her testimony. Usually the trial judge has a great deal of discretion in making this determination and a reviewing court will not reverse a trial judge except on abuse of discretion.

Generally, to be eligible to testify, a witness must have a personal connection with the relevant occurrence, coupled with mental and physical faculties sufficient to observe the events at the time of their occurrence, and must be able to recollect and relate the events to the jury or court in a manner that renders the testimony relevant. Before the witness gives substantive information, he or she is required to state under oath or affirmation that he or she will testify truthfully.

To prevent witnesses from being influenced by the testimony of other witnesses, the judge has the discretion to separate the witnesses during the

---

[220] Commonwealth v. Young, 73 Mass. App. Ct. 479, 484, 2009 Mass. App. LEXIS 15 (Mass. 2009).

[221] State v. King, 197 Neb. 729, 250 N.W.2d 655 (Neb. 1977).

[222] Proffit v. State, 2008 WY 103 191 P.3d 974, 982, 2008 Wyo. LEXIS 108 (Wyo. 2008).

trial so they are in the courtroom only when called upon to testify and cannot coordinate their testimony with other witnesses. As a general rule, police officers and other government agents are considered officers of the court and are allowed to remain in the courtroom despite the fact that they will be called as witnesses. This is not an absolute rule, however.

After a witness has been sworn, the attorney representing the party calling him or her as a witness will conduct the questioning. This is direct examination of the witness. As a general rule, leading questions are not permitted on direct examination, although there are exceptions. For example, leading introductory questions, such as a witness's address, are allowed, and hostile witnesses may be asked leading questions. In addition, leading questions may be permitted on direct examination in order to correct an obviously erroneous statement, and children of tender years and others who have difficulty expressing themselves may, when necessary, be asked leading questions on direct examination.

Although it is preferable for witnesses to testify from memory in all situations, it is clear that witnesses do not always remember the facts after a substantial period of time has passed. Recognizing this human limitation, witnesses are allowed in some instances and under very controlled conditions to refresh their memories by referring to written statements. This is known as refreshing memory or, in some courts, "present memory revived."

When the witness has no present recollection of the events or has a deficient memory that does not allow the witness to testify properly and fully concerning what occurred at the time, and the information has been preserved, the writing may be admissible. Where the witness remembers that he or she recorded the facts concerning the action, the writing or memorandum of past recollection is admitted when the proponent has laid a proper foundation.

The right of cross-examination has for years been considered a constitutional right coexistent with the right of confrontation. The purpose of cross-examination is to give the opposing party an opportunity to challenge the credibility of statements given by the witness on direct examination. With some exceptions, cross-examination of the witness is limited to the scope of matters brought out on direct examination. On rare occasions, especially in cases involving sex offenses and small children, direct confrontation may be curtailed as long as the overall right of confrontation and its purposes have been met.

After a witness has been cross-examined, the party calling him or her may ask questions on redirect examination to explain matters brought out on cross-examination. Following this, the opposing party may then ask questions on recross-examination, but such questions are limited to new matters brought out on redirect examination.

Impeachment is the process of attempting to diminish the credibility of a witness by convincing the jury or court that the testimony may not be truthful or is unreliable. Common techniques in the impeachment process are to show bias, interest, or prejudice on the part of the witness, to introduce evidence of conviction of certain crimes, and to introduce evidence of prior inconsistent statements. In some instances, a confession may be used for impeachment purposes even though the *Miranda* warnings were not administered. However, if a confession was not made freely and voluntarily, it will not be admitted even for impeachment purposes due to questions concerning the truthfulness of the confession.

An impeached witness may be rehabilitated and evidence may be admitted to contradict the impeaching testimony.

Those involved in the criminal justice process are often confused and disappointed when they are not allowed to testify about what they think is pertinent, but the rules of evidence have created methods of achieving fundamental fairness while accommodating socially important goals. If the rules of evidence are fully understood and if justice personnel are familiar with the reasons for limiting the use of evidence, they will be more confident and better prepared for giving testimony.

Privileges 10

For more than three centuries it has now been recognized as a fundamental maxim that the public ... has a right to every man's evidence. When we come to examine the various claims of exemption, we start with the primary assumption that there is a general duty to give what testimony one is capable of giving, and that any exemptions which may exist are distinctly exceptional, being so many derogations from a positive general rule.

United States v. Bryan, 339 U.S. 323, 331 (1950)
(quoting 8 J. Wigmore, Evidence § 2192)

Chapter Outline

Section

10.1   Introduction

10.2   Reasons for Privileged Communications

10.3   Communications Between Husband and Wife

10.4   Communications Between Attorney and Client

10.5   Communications Between Physician and Patient

10.6   Communications to Clergy

10.7   Confidential Informant Privilege

10.8   State Secrets and Other Official Information

10.9   News Media-Informant Privilege

10.10   Summary

Key Terms and Concepts

assertion and waiver (of privilege)	privileged communications
duration (of privilege)	scope (of privilege)
exception	

§ 10.1 Introduction

Rule 501

General Rule

Except as otherwise required by the Constitution of the United States or provided by Act of Congress or in rules prescribed by the Supreme Court pursuant to statutory authority, the privilege of a witness, person, government, State, or political subdivision thereof shall be governed by the principles of the common law as they may be interpreted by the courts of the United States in the light of reason and experience. However, in civil actions and proceedings, with respect to an element of a claim or defense as to which State law supplies the rule of decision, the privilege of a witness, person, government, State, or political subdivision thereof shall be determined in accordance with State law.[1]

If the rules of evidence were constructed in such a way as to allow the introduction of virtually all evidence that would help prove or disprove a case, such practice might create other problems in society or infringe upon values that our culture holds dear. There are many instances in which humans make communications that they would expect or desire to be kept confidential or private or at least not have them forcibly disclosed within the context of a lawsuit. When a person communicates with a spouse, an attorney, a priest or other cleric, or a physician, that communication frequently involves sensitive information that is not intended for general publication and the relationship

---

[1]   FED. R. EVID. 501.

between those expecting confidentiality is enhanced by continued privacy concerning the communication.

A privilege has the effect of preserving the confidentiality of particular relationships by excluding from court highly believable and trustworthy evidence for social policy reasons even though such exclusion has the effect of clouding the truth. In many cases, courts refuse to admit otherwise relevant evidence due to the operation of legal privileges that promote particularly important relationships, interests, and rights. According to the Supreme Court, "[t]he lawyer-client privilege rests on the need for the advocate and counselor to know all that relates to the client's reasons for seeking representation if the professional mission is to be carried out."[2] The rule that protects the rights of persons in certain relationships to refuse to give information acquired as the result of the relationship and to refuse to disclose the identity of an informant in some instances is known in law as the testimonial privilege rule, or the privileged communications rule. However, most privileges come from a legislative enactment or have developed through case law. For example, there is no privilege under the First Amendment that would allow journalists to refuse to identify sources or that would permit a news reporter to refuse to divulge information given in confidence by a source[3] and where a journalist has a privilege it is usually the result of a legislative enactment.

In most instances in which the law recognizes a privilege, one person has communicated information to another person that was intended to be kept confidential by both parties and the privilege not to disclose generally serves an important social interest. For example, where a penitent confesses to a priest or rabbi as part of religious faith and practice and the information was intended to be kept private, society allows this confidentiality because it recognizes the benefit to society of religious teachings and practices. A society hostile to religion would reject this confidence and order the information to be disclosed in a court proceeding. Similarly, police are often permitted to decline a defense request to reveal the identity of secret informants. Society values the informant who is willing to assist law enforcement and, as an encouragement, permits the identity to remain secret to protect the informant and to encourage additional assistance in the future. In both of these examples, it is believed that the balance of benefits to society is on the positive side of the ledger and that to refuse to recognize such a privilege would not serve society as well.

The privileged communications rule includes information beyond items gathered from informant sources and may cover the identity of the person who gave the privileged information. It can be more accurately stated that there are really three categories of privileges: (1) those that protect privileged communications resulting from relationships, such as husband-wife and attorney-client; and (2) those relating to disclosing the identity of persons who made the communications, such as not revealing the identity of an informant, and

---

[2]   Trammel v. United States, 445 U.S. 40, 51 (1980). *See* case in Part II, Chapter 2.

[3]   Atlanta Journal-Constitution v. Jewell, 251 Ga. App. 808, 810, 555 S.E.2d 175, 179, 2001 Ga. App. LEXIS 1153 (2001).

(3) those that permit a defendant to not give the prosecutor constitutionally protected information and allows governments to keep from divulging secrets that are deemed essential or otherwise confidential. The privilege that exists between spouses actually involves two distinct privileges: one covering confidential communications[4] made to each other during the marriage and the other involving a privilege of the potential witness spouse not to testify against the other during the duration of the marriage. The second category permits the peace officer and the prosecutor to refuse to divulge the name of an informant and, in some jurisdictions, may allow news reporters the privilege of not revealing the identity of their confidential information sources.[5]

The rules regarding privileges have evolved over a long period through case law and legislative enactments.[6] Concern with privileges and their effects have energized critics who have been both numerous and vocal. Some authorities argue that the reasons for excluding valuable testimony because of these privilege rules are no longer valid and should be abandoned, or at least modified. As the late Chief Justice Burger once observed, "Whatever their origin these exceptions to the demand for everyman's evidence are not lightly created nor expansively construed, for they are in derogation of the search for truth."[7] Those who oppose the use of the privilege argue that prohibiting the use of some evidence because of certain relationships alters the normal mode of proof in a trial by denying the trier of fact some of the information that he or she otherwise would have been able to present to the court. These arguments have had some influence on judicial behavior and because these rules are either in derogation of the common law or are statutory enactments, there is a tendency on the part of the courts to construe the rules narrowly.[8]

As a general rule, most privileges that are based on confidences are narrowly construed,[9] a principle based on the fact that the use of privileges artificially restricts the admission of evidence while frequently frustrating the search for the truth. However, a contrary view exists that some privileges should be liberally construed because they have been founded on constitutional principles.[10] In a civil case involving potential criminal fraud in the

---

[4]   Communication includes speech and, in some jurisdictions, it includes conduct that one spouse performs in full view of the other while relying on the confidentiality of the relationship. When a husband killed a man in full view of his wife, the acts were not deemed to constitute confidential communication. *See* Roland v. State, 882 So. 2d 262, 265, 2004 Miss. App. LEXIS 911 (2004).

[5]   Persky v. Yeshiva University, 2002 U.S. Dist. LEXIS 23740 (S.D.N.Y. 2002); *and see* United States v. Hively, 202 F. Supp. 886, 889, 890 (E.D. Ark. 2002) for a brief discussion of the news reporters' privilege in federal courts.

[6]   For example, *see* 10 Del. C. § 4322 (2009), which allows reporters to refuse to reveal source identities and to decline to testify concerning the substantive content of the information derived from a confidential source.

[7]   United States v. Nixon, 418 U.S. 683, 94 S. Ct. 3090, 41 L. Ed. 2d 1039 (1974).

[8]   *See* Cavallaro v. United States, 153 F. Supp. 2d 52, 58, 2001 U.S. Dist. LEXIS 11232 (D. Mass. 2001).

[9]   United States v. Banks, 556 F.2d 967, 981, 2009 U.S. App. LEXIS 3696 (9th Cir. 2009).

[10] People v. Williams, 43 Cal. 4th 584, 613, 2008 Cal. LEXIS 4818 (Cal. 2008).

avoidance of corporate income taxes, the court ordered a former executive of a company to produce documents sought by the Internal Revenue Service.[11] According to the court, the documents had to be produced because the attorney-client privilege was narrowly construed and the executive did not carry the burden of proof that the privilege applied. A Washington court held that a conversation between a woman and her social agency counselor could be divulged by the counselor to the court when the substance of the counseling involved the woman's admissions of child neglect. Washington had a counselor-patient privilege, but that privilege did not survive when the court looked at the exceptions contained in another part of the Washington code.[12]

Under the common law, there was no accountant-client privilege, so where such a privilege exists, it does so based on statutory enactments. Similarly, there is not an accountant-client privilege under federal law,[13] except for the limited privilege granted under the Internal Revenue Code.[14] States that have an accountant-client privilege generally follow a statutory framework that allows a public accountant to refuse to divulge information in court that has been obtained by virtue of the employment relationship. Because statutory privileges are narrowly construed, the accountant-client privilege dictates that to be considered confidential and covered by a privilege, the communication must arise from actual accounting services and not have been generated from consulting or other related activities.[15]

The United States Supreme Court, when drafting the Rules of Evidence for Federal Courts and Magistrates in 1972, included comprehensive rules relating to privileges. The draft included guidelines relating to traditional privileges, such as the lawyer-client privilege, husband-wife privilege, and communications to clergy. In addition, these guidelines set limits on the use of evidence regarding the political vote, trade secrets, identity of informers, and state secrets.[16] When the draft of the Federal Rules of Evidence reached Congress, it ran into legislative opposition, with the result that Congress scrapped the proposed rules covering privileges and enacted Rule 501 in place of the proposed rules covering privileges. Congress determined that the federal case law respecting privileges was not to be frozen by detailed federal rules, but allowed to develop on a case-by-case basis. As a result, Congress never enacted the proposed comprehensive codifications and only a general provision regarding privileges remained in the version that was finally adopted by both houses of Congress.[17]

---

[11]   United States v. Trenk, 2009 U.S. Dist. LEXIS 15333 (D.N.J. 2009).

[12]   Hamilton v. Department of Social and Health Services, 109 Wash. App 718, 730, 37 P.3d 1227, 1233, 2001 Wash. App. LEXIS 2810 (2001).

[13]   United States v. Bisanti, 414 F.3d 168, 170, 2005 U.S. App. LEXIS 13575 (1st Cir. 2005).

[14]   *See* 26 U.S.C. § 7525, Confidentiality privileges relating to taxpayer communications.

[15]   PepsiCo, Inc. v. Baird, Kurtz & Dobson LLP, 305 F. 3d 813, 815, 2002 U.S. App. LEXIS 192 (8th Cir. 2002).

[16]   MOORE'S RULES PAMPHLET, FEDERAL RULES OF EVIDENCE, as effective July 1, 1975.

[17]   Trammel v. United States, 445 U.S. 40, 47, 1980 U.S. LEXIS 84 (1980). *See* case in Part II, Cases Relating to Chapter 2.

Notwithstanding the fact that Congress rejected the draft prepared by the Supreme Court and deleted the articles relating to privileges, the definitions and requirements developed in the document are well worth studying. Some of these definitions are used in this chapter.

In the sections that follow, the relationships recognized by law in which the exchange of confidential information is encouraged are discussed first. These relationships include: (1) attorney-client, (2) physician-patient, (3) husband-wife and (4) communications to clergy. A later section examines the law relating to privileges that protect the identity of informants and the news media-informant privilege.

§ 10.2 Reasons for Privileged Communications

The theoretical basis for privileges involving communication reflects concern for the protection of important personal relationships and the recognition of significant other legal rights and social interests that may be at stake. When the protection and importance of these relationships philosophically outweigh the need for the evidence, courts tend to uphold the privilege and exclude the evidence to protect perceived higher social values. Few privileges were recognized at common law, but a number of privileges have been created by statutory enactment. In general, a statute conferring a privilege should be strictly and narrowly construed,[18] a view recently cited with approval by the United States Supreme Court.[19]

The rationale for the privileged communication rules is that when people occupy certain confidential relations, the law, on public policy grounds, will not compel, or in some instances even allow, one of them to violate the confidence reposed in him or her by the other. This rule of privileged communications is not a rule of substantive law, but rather a rule of evidence that does not affect the general competency of a witness but merely renders him or her able to refuse to testify about particular matters covered by the privilege.

Traditionally, the courts recognize and protect the following relationships: (1) husband-wife, (2) attorney-client, (3) physician-patient, and (4) clergy-penitent. Some jurisdictions by statute recognize confidential communication privileges involving counselor-client, accountant-client, psychologist-client, and news reporter-source. In each instance there are specific rules regarding the scope of the privilege, who is considered a "holder" of the privilege, who is eligible to claim the privilege, and when, how, and in what context the privilege may be asserted. There are also some general requirements that apply in all

---

[18] *See* Mims v. Wright, 578 S.E.2d 606 (N.C. 2003), strictly construing doctor-patient privilege; *see* Perras v. Allstate Ins. Co. 2002 Conn. Super. LEXIS 3128 (2002), strict application of the attorney-client privilege.

[19] Pierce County v. Guillen, 537 U.S. 129, 123 S. Ct. 720, 730, 154 L. Ed. 2d 610, 625, 626, 2003 U.S. LEXIS 747 (2003).

instances. First, the exchange must be between two people whose relationship is recognized by law. Second, the communication must have been exchanged because of the confidential nature of the relationship. Third, the communication must be such that the interests of society will be benefited to a greater degree than the opposing party by keeping information secret rather than by revealing it.

A communication is not privileged merely because either party or all parties regard it as confidential. A confidential relationship that is recognized by the courts or by statute must exist and a communication intended to remain confidential must have occurred between the proper parties.

One other general principle is that when a third party who was not a member of the privileged relationship overhears the privileged communication, whether by accident or design, that person in most cases may testify about the substance of the communication. However, some jurisdictions allow the communication to remain privileged when the two parties reasonably believed that their communication was not likely to be heard by an eavesdropper.

In the sections that follow, the specific rules that apply to the respective privileged communications are explored.

§ 10.3　Communications Between Husband and Wife

Protection of confidential communications between spouses has origins in the common law and "is premised upon the belief that the marital union is sacred and that its intimacy and confidences deserve legal protection."[20] As an early Supreme Court case noted:

> This rule is founded upon the deepest and soundest principles of our nature. Principles which have grown out of those domestic relations, that constitute the basis of civil society, and which are essential to the enjoyment of that confidence which should subsist between those who are connected by the nearest and dearest relations of life. To break down or impair the great principles which protect the sanctities of husband and wife, would be to destroy the best solace of human existence.[21]

Common law rules that become obsolete in practice or for which a questionable basis emerges, are subject to judicial revision or rejection. For example, in the case of *Funk v. United States*,[22] the United States Supreme Court stated that a rule of evidence thought necessary at one time should yield

---

[20]　State v. Rollins, 2009 N.C. LEXIS 348 (N.C. 2009).

[21]　Stein v. Bowman, 38 U.S. (13 Pet.) 209, 223, 10 L. Ed. 129 (1839).

[22]　290 U.S. 371, 54 S. Ct. 212, 78 L. Ed. 369 (1933). *See* case in Part II, in Cases Relating to Chapter 1.

to the experience of a succeeding generation whenever experience has clearly demonstrated the fallacy of the proposition or where changed circumstances suggest an invalidation of the old rule. At no place is this more evident than in the law relating to the husband-wife testimonial privilege. In a 1980 case,[23] *Trammel v. United States*, the Supreme Court set aside rules for federal courts that had been established in the 1958 case of *Hawkins v. United States*.[24] As a result of *Trammel* and its influence on state jurisprudence, it is necessary to approach the husband-wife privilege from two perspectives.

A. Statement of the Rules

Rule 1. Marital communications are privileged, but only to the extent that the communications were made in the expectation of confidence.[25] This rule is followed in both federal and state courts and was not changed by the decision in *Trammel*, which applied only to federal courts.

Rule 2. A witness spouse cannot testify against a defendant spouse regarding any acts observed or regarding any nonconfidential communication that occurred before or during the marriage unless both spouses agree. Under this theory, both spouses hold the marital testimonial privilege and may assert it to prevent the witness spouse from giving testimony. This rule was established for federal courts in *Hawkins v. United States*,[26] but the *Trammel* case had the effect of reversing the *Hawkins* decision and held that only the witness spouse was a holder of the marital testimonial privilege with the right to refuse to testify against a defendant spouse in a federal court.[27] The *Hawkins* rule is still followed in some states, as demonstrated by a Minnesota statute that prohibits either spouse from being examined for or against the other in the absence of the other's consent.[28]

B. Scope of the Privilege

At common law, neither spouse possessed competency as a witness to give testimony, either for or against the other. This rule was based on the premise that husband and wife were one, and at common law, where one spouse was a party to a suit, whether civil or criminal, the other was not permitted to be a witness. This restrictive rule was gradually abolished by court decisions and statutes, and it was replaced by the rule that a spouse may testify for the other in a criminal proceeding, but in some instances a spouse may not testify against the other if either spouse objects.

---

[23]   Trammel v. United States, 445 U.S. 40, 100 S. Ct. 906, 63 L. Ed. 2d 145 (1980).

[24]   Hawkins v. United States, 358 U.S. 74, 79 S. Ct. 136, 3 L. Ed. 2d 125 (1958).

[25]   United States v. Dunbar, 553 F.3d 48, 58, 2009 U.S. App. LEXIS 1639 (1st Cir. 2009).

[26]   Hawkins v. United States, *supra* note 24.

[27]   *See* the footnotes by the court in the Trammel case cited *supra* note 23.

[28]   For example, MINN. STAT. § 595.02 (2008).

The *Trammel* case involved a husband who had been indicted on federal drug charges while his wife had been named in the indictment as an unindicted conspirator. The trial court ruled that confidential communications between Mr. Trammel and his wife were privileged and therefore inadmissible, but the wife was permitted to testify to any act she observed before or during the marriage and to any communication made in the presence of a third person. The Court in *Trammel* referred to studies which revealed that in 1958, when *Hawkins* was decided, 31 states allowed a defendant the privilege of preventing adverse spousal testimony, but the Court indicated that the number had declined to 24 in 1980. The Court then said, "Here we must decide whether the privilege against adverse spousal testimony promotes sufficiently important interests to outweigh the need for probative evidence in the administration of criminal justice."[29] With respect to nonconfidential communications within a marriage, the Supreme Court decided "that the existing rule should be modified so that in federal courts, the witness-spouse alone has a privilege to refuse to testify adversely; the witness may be neither compelled to testify nor foreclosed from testifying. This modification—vesting the privilege in the witness-spouse—furthers the important public interest in marital harmony without unduly burdening legitimate law enforcement needs."[30] *Trammel* affected only federal courts.

Prior to *Trammel*, in the case of *Blau v. United States*,[31] the Supreme Court reaffirmed the rule that in federal courts, confidential communications between husband and wife are privileged. The *Trammel* Court noted that the *Trammel* case did not change the *Blau* recognition of the marital confidential communication privilege in federal courts.[32] This meant that neither spouse could be required to testify concerning these communications, nor would the other be permitted to testify if the other objected. This case did not decide, however, the issue of whether the spouse may be permitted to testify to an act observed before or during the marriage, nor did it settle the issue of communications made in the presence of a third party. The lower court in *Trammel* agreed that confidential communications between husband and wife were privileged and therefore inadmissible, but the privilege permitted the wife to testify about any acts that she observed before and during the marriage, and about any communications made in the presence of a third person.

After discussing the arguments for and against permitting a spouse to testify about criminal acts observed during a marriage or non-confidential communications, the Court concluded:

> Accordingly, we conclude that the existing rule should be modified so that the witness spouse alone has the privilege to refuse to testify adversely: the witness may be neither compelled to testify nor foreclosed from testifying.

---

[29] Trammel v. United States, *supra* note 23.

[30] *Id.*

[31] Blau v. United States, 340 U.S. 332, 71 S. Ct. 301, 95 L. Ed. 306 (1950).

[32] *See* Trammel v. United States, note 5 of the Court's decision.

This modification—vesting the privilege in the witness spouse—furthers the important public interest in marital harmony without unduly burdening legitimate law enforcement needs.[33]

In some jurisdictions, written communications between spouses[34] and physical acts done in full view of the spouse may constitute confidential communications from which a testimonial privilege may arise. Private communications between spouses does not always occur behind closed doors and may be made openly when other persons are not able to hear or observe. In a murder prosecution, the trial court admitted conversations between the witness spouse and the defendant spouse in which the defendant spouse made incriminating confidential statements to the wife. In reversing the conviction, the Supreme Court of Kentucky noted that some of the conversations were completely private, one occurring in a hay barn away from other people. The court held that the trial court should not have allowed the wife to testify concerning those private conversations. The court also questioned the trial court ruling that permitted the testimony of the wife concerning her feeling a gun when she hugged her husband, because that communication could be considered conduct as well as privileged communication.[35]

To summarize, the general rule in both state and federal courts is that information privately disclosed between husband and wife in reliance on the confidential nature of the marital relationship is protected from compelled disclosure and both spouses are holders of this privilege. In most jurisdictions, the communications privilege protects confidential communications made between spouses while they are married and it survives the marriage."[36] Federal courts recognize two separate marital privileges: the marital confidential communications privilege and the marital testimonial privilege.[37] In federal courts and some state courts, the witness-spouse alone has the privilege to testify or refuse to testify adversely regarding criminal acts observed and nonconfidential communications occurring during the marriage. In other states, where the rule has not been changed by statute or court decision, an accused may object not only to a spouse testifying about confidential communications, but also to

---

[33] Trammel v. United States, *supra* note 23. *See also* United States v. Ramos-Osequera, 120 F.3d 1028 (9th Cir. 1997), in which the court held that the federal common law recognizes two different marital privileges: one bars testimony concerning statements privately and confidentially communicated between spouses and may be invoked by the testifying or non-testifying spouse; and the other permits a person to refuse to testify against his or her spouse about anything.

[34] United States v. Montgomery, 384 F. 3d 1050, 1056, 2004 U. S. App. LEXIS 19322 (2004).

[35] St. Clair v. Commonwealth, 174 S.W. 2d 474, 480, 2005 Ky. LEXIS 334 (2005). *See* case in Part II.

[36] Arizona v. Harrod, 200 Ariz. 309, 315, 26 P.3d 492, 498, 2001 Ariz. LEXIS 104 (2001), *cert. granted*, 536 U.S. 953, 122 S. Ct. 2653, 153 L. Ed. 2d 830, 2002 U.S. LEXIS 4892 (2002), *remanded for resentencing*, 65 P.3d 948, 2003 Ariz. LEXIS 31 (2003).

[37] United States v. Espino, 317 F.3d 788, 795, 2003 U.S. App. LEXIS 261 (8th Cir. 2003).

that spouse's testimony about any act observed before or during the marriage. However, with respect to the marital confidential communication privilege, generally both spouses are holders of this privilege and each may assert it independently of the other.

The part of the marital confidential communication privilege that concerns confidential communications during the marriage has periodically come under scrutiny. It has been argued that if the marriage is in "utter shambles," the force behind the rule no longer exists, and the spouse should be required to testify. In a federal prosecution on three counts of making false statements to a federally insured financial institution, the defendant contended that the trial court erred in allowing her estranged husband to testify concerning documents and conversations indicating falsity that he had acquired while visiting the former marital residence. During the visit, the estranged husband searched for papers related to his prior divorce from another woman, and inadvertently stumbled upon documents indicating that his wife had filed the materially false loan applications for which she was eventually convicted. After the husband observed the incriminating documents, he took his information to federal authorities and agreed to wear a concealed recording device to record any incriminating statements his wife might make. At an arranged meeting, the wife made several statements to the husband that indicated her consciousness of guilt in making the false statements. Over the objection of the wife, who alleged a violation of the marital confidential communication privilege, the trial court allowed the husband to testify to confidential matters he learned while in the wife's home and from meeting with her. The trial court held that the marital communication privilege should not be applied to communications made while the spouses, while still technically married, were living separate lives with no reasonable expectation of reconciliation or reunification as a happily married couple.[38]

However, current Arizona law holds that "[a] husband for or against his wife without her consent, nor a wife for or against her husband without his consent, as to events occurring during the marriage, nor can either, during the marriage or afterwards, without consent of the other, be examined as to any communication made by one to the other during the marriage."[39] Naturally these prohibitions against testimony do not apply in a criminal action or proceeding for a crime committed by one spouse against the other or against intimate family members or crimes like non-support or civil proceedings involving the marriage.[40] Arizona courts have interpreted the statute to forbid any testimony by a spouse concerning any confidential communication

---

[38]   United States v. Singleton, 260 F.3d 1295, 1297, 1298, 2001 U.S. App. LEXIS 17694 (11th Cir. 2001).

[39]   A.R.S. § 13-4062(1) Anti-marital fact privilege; other privileged communications (Matthew Bender 2008).

[40]   *Id.*

between them that occurred during the marriage, whether the marriage is intact at the time of the testimony or not, unless the other spouse gives consent to the testimony.[41] However, Arizona courts do not hold that the communication privilege protects nonconfidential communications or noncommunicative acts done when the other spouse may be in a position to observe. In one Arizona case involving a conspiracy to commit murder, the wife was properly permitted to testify about conduct of the defendant observed during the marriage when the acts were not intended as confidential communicative activities.[42] While the principle that the marital confidential communication privilege should not apply if a marriage is in utter shambles is probably still a minority view, the trend appears to be in that direction, especially in the federal courts.

An essential prerequisite for the assertion of the marital confidential communication privilege is the existence of a valid marriage at the time the spouse uttered the communication.[43] People who cohabitate and who do not qualify for common law marriage status, or who are of the same gender, are generally not considered married (although some exceptions exist) and cannot assert marital privileges.[44] The marriage is considered valid if there has been a formal ceremony as recognized by a state and the marriage has not been dissolved. If a couple or one member of a couple contends that the two have matured a common law marriage, the marriage must have been initiated in a state that recognized common law marriages and the burden to prove the existence of the marriage rests with the person making the allegation of marriage.[45] In the states that permit common law marriages to come into existence, certain requirements must be met. If those requirements are followed and the common law marriage is recognized in that state, a defendant in a criminal case could invoke either the marital communication privilege or the marital testimonial privilege in that state or any other.

In the absence of proof of a common law or formal marriage, no marital privilege attaches to any communication between a particular man and woman. When a valid common law marriage exists, other states are generally bound to recognize the marriage and treat it as equal to a marriage contracted in a traditional ceremony. For example, in Texas, where common law marriages are recognized, there was a common law marriage between the defendant and the witness, and the defendant could invoke the marital communication privilege.[46] The court decided that because the defendant and witness had lived together

---

[41]   State ex rel. Woods v. Cohen, 173 Ariz. 497, 501, 502, 844 P.2d 1147, 1151, 1152, 1992 Ariz. LEXIS 104 (1992).

[42]   Arizona v. Harrod, 200 Ariz. 309, 26 P.3d 492, 498, 499, 2001 Ariz. LEXIS 104 (2001).

[43]   United States v. Vo, 413 F.3d 1010. 1016, 2005 U.S. App. LEXIS 12695 (9th Cir. 2005).

[44]   *See* A.L.R. 4TH 422 (2006). Some states recognize same sex marriage, but these states remain in a distinct minority.

[45]   Perrotti v. Meredith, 2005 Pa. Super. 57, 868 A.2d 1240, 1243, 2005 Pa. Super. LEXIS 148 (2005).

[46]   People v. Badgett, 30 Cal. Rptr. 2d 152 (1994).

in Texas and held themselves out to the public as a married couple, and as the witness testified that she and the defendant agreed to live together as husband and wife and indicated on an employment application and tax records that she was married, and because the defendant and witness exchanged wedding rings, this was sufficient indication of a common law marriage and the defendant could invoke the marital communication privilege.

In another case, however, the common law marital relationship did not exist between the defendant and his girlfriend at the time the defendant made inculpatory statements regarding the murder of his wife, and there was no evidence that the defendant had divorced his wife or that his wife was dead.[47] Courts generally are under no obligation to inform a possible common law wife that she has a privilege not to testify because once a spouse takes the stand and offers testimony, the presumption arises that she has waived any marital privilege that she may have possessed.[48] One court refused to recognize a purported marriage because the "wife" of the defendant was still married to her first husband and could not be legally married to the defendant. The court held that there was no marital privilege of any type because there was nothing but a bigamous "marriage," which did not qualify as a legitimate marriage.[49]

Unless validly married under local law, marital confidential communication privileges generally do not extend to homosexuals in "spousal relationships."[50] This type of limitation on privileges of married couples may be affected by the Supreme Court's decision in *Lawrence v. Texas*, in which laws regulating private sexual activity between persons of the same sex were ruled to be unconstitutional.[51] However, litigation in California that recognized same-sex marriages[52] was called into question by a voter-initiated amendment to the California constitution that prohibited same-sex marriages. However, New York recently recognized that same-sex marriages created in other states would be recognized by New York[53] and spousal privileges probably come with this recognition, although no reported case yet exists.[54] Spousal privileges similar to traditional marriages or some similar legal theory may eventually

---

[47]   Duran v. State, 881 S.W.2d 569 (Tex. 1994).

[48]   Smith v. Georgia, 254 Ga. App. 107, 108, 561 S.E.2d 232, 233, 2002 Ga. App. LEXIS 274 (2002).

[49]   Arboleda v. Newland, Warden, 2003 U.S. Dist. LEXIS 513 (N.D. Cal. 2003).

[50]   Greenwald v. H & P 29th Street Associates, 659 N.Y.S.2d 473 (N.Y. 1997). *And see* Hernandez v. Robles, 2005 N.Y. Slip Op. 9436, 805 N.Y.S.2d 354, 2005 N.Y. App. Div. LEXIS 13892 (2005) determining that same-sex individuals were not eligible in New York to obtain marriage licenses.

[51]   *See* Lawrence v. Texas, 539 U.S. 558, 2003 U.S. LEXIS 5013 (2003).

[52]   In re Marriage Cases, 43 Cal. 4th 757, 2008 Cal. LEXIS 5247 (Cal. 2008).

[53]   See Lewis v. New York State Department of Civil Service, 2009 NY Slip Op 283, 2009 N.Y. App. LEXIS 415 (N.Y. 2009).

[54]   Research has not revealed any attempt to assert a spousal privilege in New York litigation since the recognition of out-of-state same-sex marriages.

be statutorily devised or created by case law that protects same-gender relationships in ways similar to current marriage practice, although some of the litigation indicates that the extension of this type of privilege may be a long way into the future.[55]

C. Exceptions

1. The privilege is generally limited to confidential communications

The marital privilege protects information privately disclosed between husband and wife that at the time was intended to be a confidential communication and can generally be asserted by either spouse.[56] Where no other people are able to hear a communication between spouses, the husband-wife confidential communication privilege should be recognized. In an Arkansas case, the husband and wife were in a car when the husband shot at people in a nearby car. While he paused, the wife asked him what he was doing and he told her that he was reloading to kill another person. The appellate court noted that the trial court committed error when it permitted the defendant's wife to testify concerning their roadside conversation. The court determined that a valid marital privilege existed that should have prevented the admission of the wife's testimony about his intent because the street discussion occurred in reliance on the confidential nature of their marital relationship.[57] The presence of unnecessary third parties prevents confidential communication between spouses, such as where a prisoner sends a letter to his wife.[58] One court admitted an incriminating message left by a defendant for his wife on an answering machine. Because the answering machine was not in the exclusive control of the wife and other people shared the machine, no confidential communication existed.[59] If other persons are present at the time of the communication, including immediate family members or children, no confidential communication occurs if the children are old enough to comprehend what the spouses are communicating. In a West Virginia case, the defendant had a conversation with his wife in an automobile where their eight-month-old infant was present. The conversation remained covered by the marital confidential communication privilege because the child was not a comprehending third party.[60]

---

[55] *See* Wilson v. Ake, 354 F. Supp. 2d 1298; 2005 U.S. Dist. LEXIS 755 (2005) and Li v. State, 338 Or. 376, 110 P.3d 91, 2005 Or. LEXIS 490 (2004).

[56] United States v. Montgomery, 384 F. 3d 1050, 1057, 2004 U.S. App. LEXIS 19322 (2004). The court noted (n.1) that 33 states and the District of Columbia allow either spouse to assert the confidential communication privilege.

[57] Walker v. State, 2005 Ark. App. LEXIS 471 (2005).

[58] United States v. Griffin, 440 F.3d 1138, 2006 U.S. App. LEXIS 6393 (9th Cir. 2006).

[59] Wong-Wing v. State, 156 Md. App. 597, 847 A.2d 1206, 2004 Md. App. LEXIS 65 (2004).

[60] West Virginia v. Bohon, 211 W. Va. 277, 279, 565 S.E.2d 399, 401, 2002 W. Va. LEXIS 51 (2002).

2. Communications overheard by third parties or made to third parties

Another exception to the marital privilege, concerns the testimony of a third party who was in a position to overhear communications between spouses. As a general rule, when a third party has overheard the conversation between the husband and wife, that person may testify about the communication, even where the spouses hoped that the conversation was private.[61] Another rationale for this exception is that by failing to take precautions to prevent others from hearing, the spouses are deemed to have waived the right to secrecy.[62] However, according to the Supreme Court of Mississippi and courts in other states, when a spouse who received or made a confidential communication to the other spouse communicates the message to a third party at a later time, the confidence may remain and the third party may not testify concerning the substance of the original confidential communication.[63]

In determining whether the marital confidential communication privilege should be recognized in a particular case, courts generally consider several factors that support the basis of the privilege. Some states that recognize this privilege apply it whenever it the facts meet the standards, while other states use a balancing test and do not always recognize the privilege. For example, under Tennessee law, before communications between husband and wife may be recognized as privileged in a criminal proceeding, a court must conduct an evaluation of the following statutory factors: "(A) the communications must originate in a confidence that they will not be disclosed; (B) the element of confidentiality is essential to the full and satisfactory maintenance of the relationship between the parties; (C) the relationship must be one which, in the opinion of the community, ought to be sedulously [diligently] fostered; and (D) the injury to the relation by disclosure of the communications outweighs the benefit gained for the correct disposal of litigation."[64] In applying such a test in a murder prosecution, a Tennessee appellate court upheld a trial court decision denying a husband's assertion of the marital confidential privilege. He made his incriminating statement in front of several witnesses, including his spouse. However, he was separated from his spouse while he lived with his girlfriend during weekdays. The appellate court noted that the statement failed to have been made in confidence with his spouse because there was no real confidential relationship with his wife. The court held that recognizing the existence of the privilege would

---

[61]   United States v. Espino, 317 F.3d 788, 795, 796, 2003 U.S. App. LEXIS 261 (8th Cir. 2002).

[62]   People v. Melski, 10 N.Y.2d 78, 176 N.E.2d 81 (1961); *see* People v. Gomez, 134 Cal. App. 3d 874, 185 Cal. Rptr. 155 (1982), which held that if the facts show that the communication was not intended to be kept confidential, the communication is not privileged.

[63]   In re Miss. Rules of Evidence, 2003 Miss. LEXIS 152 (2003), (2006). *See also* Comment to Miss. R. Evid. 504, (2006).

[64]   TENN. CODE. ANN. § 24-1-201(c)(2), Husband and Wife (2009). Tennessee allows both spouses to be holders of the confidential communication privilege and the testimonial privilege where there is a judicial finding that a privilege exists.

not foster his relationship with his wife and that disclosure outweighed any benefit gained from nondisclosure, so the court refused to hold that a confidential privilege existed.[65]

The privilege protecting confidential marital communication does not exist where the communication was not made to the spouse or was made in the presence of an unnecessary third party. In a Minnesota case, a husband returned to his marital home where his wife was present and she observed blood spatters on his clothes that came from the murder victim. The wife had overheard her husband plotting to rob the victim at an earlier time and heard the husband talking with his partner in crime subsequent to the killing. The wife's father overheard much of the same speech and observed the same conduct. According to the Supreme Court of Minnesota, because the communication did not originate in a confidential manner and an unnecessary third party (her father) easily overheard the angry husband's statements, both the wife and her father properly testified against the defendant.[66]

3. Prosecution against one spouse for acts against the other spouse or their child

It would be a miscarriage of justice and inconsistent with the rationale for the marital privilege for the rule to prevent one spouse from testifying against the other when the spouse was the victim of the aggressor spouse or their child[67] or a person living in their household.[68] This exception applies in prosecutions for child abuse, bigamy, adultery,[69] and cases involving criminal injury to the person or property of a family member.

In a ruling consistent with the exception concerning criminal acts committed against a household member, spouse, children, or their property, a Texas court agreed that a common-law wife could be permitted to testify against the spouse under the exception to the privilege where a member of the household has been injured.[70] In this Texas case, the defendant had been accused of beating his brother, who suffered from cerebral palsy, to death in a fit of rage. The brother of the defendant lived in the household with the defendant and his common-law wife. An Ohio court ruled that a husband charged with kidnapping and abduction, who bound his wife with duct tape after he had beaten her, had not been making confidential communications with her.

---

[65] *See* State v. Evans, 2006 Tenn. Crim. App. LEXIS 387 (2006). For another case where the court balanced the factors to deny the existence of a confidential communication privilege, *see* State v. Powers, 2002 Tenn. LEXIS 768 (2002), *cert. denied,* Powers v. Tennessee, 538 U.S. 1038, 2003 U.S. LEXIS 3797 (2003).

[66] State v. Palubicki, 700 N.W.2d 476, 484, 2005 Minn. LEXIS 418 (2005).

[67] Jackson v. State, 2005 Tex. App. LEXIS 3631 (2005); *and see* TEX. EVID. R. 504(a)(4)(C) (Matthew Bender 2009). There is no spousal privilege where there is an accusation that the defendant committed a crime against the spouse or minor child.

[68] KRE 504(c)(2) (Matthew Bender 2008).

[69] United States v. Taylor, 62 M.J. 636, 2006 CCA LEXIS 9 (2006).

[70] Killough v. State, 2008 Tex. App. LEXIS 1391, n.3 (Tex. 2008).

The couple had been celebrating their wedding anniversary but an argument ensued resulting in the violent encounter. The trial court required the wife to testify against the husband despite her effort to invoke the spousal testimonial privilege and rejected her argument that a confidential communication had been made because personal injury was not considered an essential element of kidnapping. The appellate court approved the admission of the wife's testimony, saying:

> This Court is not persuaded by appellant's argument. [Ohio law] in no way provides that the injury to the testifying spouse must be an element of the crime of which the defendant spouse is charged. It is irrelevant whether [the wife] suffered her injuries while she was actually restrained by appellant or whether she sustained injuries as a part of appellant's continuous course of conduct of which his restraint of [her] was a part.[71]

The marital privilege not to testify has a recognized exception when the criminal victim is the child of a defendant or witness spouse. In an Ohio case involving numerous rapes and sexual batteries by the husband on the couple's daughter, neither the marital confidential communication privilege nor the marital testimonial privilege applied because of the injury to the daughter; the trial court properly allowed the wife to testify against the husband. Under Ohio law, "Husband and wife are competent witnesses to testify in behalf of each other in all criminal prosecutions and to testify against each other in all actions, prosecutions, and proceedings for personal injury of either by the other, bigamy, or failure to provide for, neglect of, or cruelty to their children under 18 years of age or their physically or mentally handicapped child under 21 years of age."[72] Although the sexual abuse had been in private, the defendant confessed to his wife in the presence of his daughter-victim. The court's ruling, upheld on appeal, allowed the defendant's wife to testify because no marital privilege of any kind existed due to the crimes against a family member.[73]

Although a spouse may not be prohibited from testifying against the other spouse when the crime involves an alleged criminal act against the spouse, a Georgia court held that the wife of a defendant charged with kidnapping her had the right to invoke the marital testimonial privilege not to testify against her husband.[74]

Interestingly, some defendant spouses may prevent the adverse use of their spouse's voluntary statements when the statements have been offered prior to trial. In a case in which the wife made a tape-recorded statement to police that implicated her husband in criminal activity, the prosecution had been permitted to play the tape at trial. Over the husband's objection and the

[71]   State v. Purvis, 2006 Ohio 1555, 2006 Ohio App. LEXIS 1493 (2006).
[72]   ORC ANN. § 2945.42. Competency of witnesses, (Matthew Bender 2006).
[73]   State v. Wilson, 2006 Ohio 2000; 2006 Ohio App. LEXIS 1860 (2006).
[74]   Carter v. State, 275 Ga. App. 483, 486, 621 S.E.2d 503, 506, 2005 Ga. App. LEXIS 1003 (2005).

wife's refusal to testify about the alleged assault with intent to commit murder of a third party, the trial court allowed the wife's evidence to be recounted during the trial. The defendant raised a Sixth Amendment objection, contending that he was unable to confront cross-examine his wife at his trial because she refused to testify. The Supreme Court of the United States reversed the conviction and sent the case back to the trial court. The Court held that by playing the wife's tape-recorded statement at the trial, when the defense was unable to cross-examine the defendant's wife, violated the defendant's constitutional rights under the confrontation clause of the Sixth Amendment. According to the Court, the confrontation clause demanded that the testimonial evidence from the wife given to police had to be tested by the crucible of cross-examination. When testimonial evidence was at issue and where there was no prior opportunity to cross-examine the wife, the admission of her police-recorded statement constituted reversible error under the Sixth Amendment as applied to the states.[75]

4. Conspiracy

Where a husband and wife jointly have engaged in a criminal conspiracy, the defendant spouse cannot claim the marital testimonial privilege to prevent adverse testimony by the other spouse in a federal prosecution. In an Eighth Circuit case, the court allowed the testimony of a defendant's spouse in a prosecution for conspiracy to distribute methamphetamine. The defendant and his wife had engaged in drug trafficking but the prosecution offered her a possibility of a reduced sentence in her personal drug prosecution if she testified against her husband. In permitting the wife to testify, the trial court was careful to prevent any confidential communications that had occurred between her and her husband from being introduced but allowed the witness-wife to testify about their ongoing drug conspiracy and the defendant's actions, when it involved drug trafficking.[76]

A federal circuit court of appeals approved allowing a spouse who had conspired with her husband to testify against him by relying on the federal common law relating to marital privileges. The trial court rejected any role that the Nebraska state law of privilege might have because the trial involved a federal violation of conspiracy to distribute and possess methamphetamine. The trial court ruled that the federal common law interpreting marital privileges was the appropriate standard, and the case of *Trammel v. United States*[77] held that the privilege not to testify against a spouse-defendant resided with the other spouse. In this case, the wife had participated in a conspiracy with her husband and others, so there was no argument that a confidential communication privilege covered the wife's testimony and the holder of the federal testimonial

---

[75] *See* Crawford v. Washington, 541 U.S. 36, 2004 U.S. LEXIS 1838 (2004).

[76] United States v. Espino, 317 F.3d 788, 795, 796, 2003 U.S. App. LEXIS 261 (8th Cir. 2003).

[77] 445 U.S. 40, 47, 1980 U.S. LEXIS 84 (1980).

privilege is the witness-spouse who, in this case, could testify if she chose to do so, whether because of an agreement with the prosecution or otherwise.[78]

Minnesota has taken a completely different route concerning criminal conspiracies between spouses. According to Minnesota law, "A husband cannot be examined for or against his wife without her consent, nor a wife for or against her husband without his consent, nor can either, during the marriage or afterwards, without the consent of the other, be examined as to any communication made by one to the other during the marriage."[79] In offering an interpretation of the law, the state's top court held that a wife, over her husband's objection, should not be required to testify against her husband. In this case, the two spouses allegedly engaged in a conspiracy to commit a murder of a potential witness against them in a separate criminal proceeding. Minnesota requires the consent of the witness-spouse and of the defendant-spouse prior to offering any testimony concerning matters adverse to a defendant-spouse as long as the crime was not against the other, their children, or property.[80]

D. *Duration of the Privilege*

The Supreme Court opinion in *Trammel*[81] allowing the witness-spouse to decide whether to testify adversely makes the question of the duration of the marital testimonial privilege less important in federal trials. The majority of the states appear to have adopted the view that only the witness-spouse is a holder of the marital testimonial privilege. However, when the marital confidential communication privilege is implicated, the better view is that both marriage partners are holders and may assert the privilege in an appropriate setting. Generally, the privilege exists during the marriage and for an indefinite time after the marriage and may continue following the death of one of the marital partners.[82] In an Iowa case in which a defendant had been accused of having sex with an underage female, the Supreme Court reversed the conviction because the trial court had permitted his ex-wife to give testimony against the defendant. The applicable Iowa rule of evidence does not appear to require that a marital communication be accomplished in confidence. The ex-wife had erroneously been permitted to offer evidence that involved confidential communications with the defendant that covered incriminating matters with the underage female. Thus, in Iowa, the marital communication privilege, like that of many states, survives the termination of the marriage and may be asserted in subsequent criminal trials.[83]

---

[78]   United States v. Espino, 317 F.3d 788, 794, 2003 U.S. App. LEXIS 261 (8th Cir. 2003).

[79]   MINN. STAT. § 595.02 (1)(a) Testimony of Witnesses (2008).

[80]   Minnesota v. Gianakos, 644 N.W.2d 409, 418, 419, 2002 Minn. LEXIS 350 (2002). The defendant was later convicted in a related federal prosecution involving the same conduct. *See* United States v. Gianakos, 404 F.3d 1065 (2005), which was later reversed, 414 F.3d 912 (2005).

[81]   Trammel v. United States, *supra* note 23.

[82]   *See*, for example, IOWA CODE § 622.9 Communications between husband and wife (2008).

[83]   Iowa v. Anderson, 636 N.W.2d 26, 32, 33, 2001 Iowa Sup. LEXIS 217 (2001).

Although in most American jurisdictions, the marital privilege continues after divorce with respect to statements made in confidence between spouses during the existence of the marriage,[84] an argument could be made that the reason for the rule no longer applies after the divorce. When spouses are divorced at the time of the trial, allowing a willing former spouse to testify against the defendant spouse would not affect any present relationship. A commonsense approach allows a spouse or former spouse to testify about nonconfidential matters and also allows a defendant spouse to prohibit a spouse or former spouse from testifying against a defendant with respect to confidential matters discussed or communicated during the marriage.[85]

The protection offered by either spousal privilege does not extend to acts or utterances, whether confidential or not, made prior to the marriage or after divorce.[86] Moreover, the privilege does not apply when the defendant is merely living with the person who is called as a witness[87] unless there is a recognized common law marriage.[88] In a state that considers marriages between first cousins "void," that state generally will recognize marriages between first cousins as valid where the marriage occurred in a state that approves of first-cousin marriages,[89] a prerequisite for permitting an assertion of a marital privilege.

§ 10.4   Communications Between Attorney and Client

A. *Statement of the Rule*

Confidential communications made in the course of professional employment between an attorney or one reasonably believed to be an attorney and his or her client may not be divulged by the attorney without the consent of the client and neither the attorney nor the client can be compelled to testify regarding such communications. The purpose of the attorney-client confidential communication privilege is to encourage a full and open exchange of information between the attorney and the client, with both secure that the communication cannot be forcefully revealed.[90] This privilege has limitations and

---

[84] Commonwealth of Pennsylvania v. Weiss, 565 Pa. 504, 776 A.2d. 958, 2001 Pa. LEXIS 1574 (2001), in which the court held that disclosure of confidential communications made during a marriage is prohibited even following the dissolution of the marriage.

[85] Louisiana v. Nash, 821 So. 2d 678, 683, 684, 2002 La. App. LEXIS 1928 (2002).

[86] Pereira v. United States, 347 U.S. 1, 74 S. Ct. 358, 98 L. Ed. 435 (1954).

[87] Dermody v. State, 2002 Tex. App. LEXIS 6639 (2002); *see also* Arboleda v. Newland, Warden, 2003 U.S. Dist. LEXIS 513 (N.D. Cal. 2003).

[88] *See* Bevan v. Bevan, 2006 Ohio 2775, 2006 Ohio App. LEXIS 2605 (2006), for the essentials of common law marriage.

[89] Cook v. Cook, 209 Ariz. 487; 104 P.3d 857; 2005 Ariz. App. LEXIS 6 (2005).

[90] *See* United States v. Schussel, 291 Fed. Appx. 336, 2008 U.S. App. LEXIS 18836 (1st Cir. 2008).

is not absolute and only extends to confidential communications between the two individuals when made for the purpose of seeking legal advice and counsel. The privilege applies when a potential client initially consults an attorney, even though no professional relationship develops.

The privilege regarding confidential communications between client and attorney, as in the case of the marital communications privilege, was recognized at common law. As a general rule, the privilege applies only when statements are made to an attorney where there is an expectation that the information will remain confidential, but the privilege does not exist when a defendant spoke in such a loud voice that other people could hear him.[91] The purpose of the privilege is to facilitate full and complete communication between attorneys and their clients. Sound public policy recognized that the attorney's assistance could be effectively offered only when the client was free from the consequences of apprehension or discovery by reason of subsequent statements of the lawyer. In a case involving representation on a criminal or civil matter, the privilege prevents the attorney from being required to be an adverse witness. In fact, in the absence of the attorney-client privilege, the Sixth Amendment right to counsel would become a hollow shell. Although the privilege has the effect of preventing significant evidence from being offered in the search for the truth, good public policy holds that the interests protected by the privilege outweighs the desirability of placing all facts known to the attorney before the jury.

A Connecticut court, in an unreported case, accepted the government's argument that by filing a habeas corpus case alleging ineffective assistance of trial counsel, the defendant had waived his attorney-client privilege concerning documents desired by the state. Confidences are maintained until the interests of justice would be frustrated by the exercise of the privilege and then it must give way.[92]

In a 1981 case, the United States Supreme Court clarified the reason for the privilege and the extent of the privilege in federal courts.[93] According to the Court, the attorney-client privilege encourages "full and frank communication between attorneys and their clients and thereby promote[s] broader public interests in the observance of law and administration of justice."[94] The Court explained that the attorney-client privilege has been recognized in federal courts not only to protect professional advice given to those who can act upon it, but also the privilege gives information to a lawyer to enable him or her to give sound and informed advice. The protections extend only to communications with the attorney and not to facts known by the client so that the client need not disclose what the attorney was told but might have to reveal facts known to the client that are not otherwise privileged.

---

[91]   People v. Urbano, 128 Cal. App. 4th 396, 26 Cal. Rptr. 3d 871, 2005 Cal. App. LEXIS 572 (2005).

[92]   Breton v. Commissioner, 2006 Conn. Super. LEXIS 1240 (2006). Contra, People v. Madera, 112 P.2d 688, 2005 Colo. LEXIS 526 (2005).

[93]   Upjohn Co. v. United States, 449 U.S. 383, 101 S. Ct. 677, 66 L. Ed. 2d 584 (1981).

[94]   Id. at 389.

A party cannot conceal a fact under a claim of privilege merely by revealing it to his or her lawyer and a party who is testifying cannot refuse to answer questions concerning facts related to the case merely because he or she has at one time or another disclosed such facts to his or her lawyer. The witness may refuse to testify on other grounds but not merely because he or she has communicated the facts to his or her attorney.

B. *Scope of the Privilege*

The privilege is subject to statutory regulations and limitations based on court decisions. While it is desirable to protect communications between an attorney and his or her client, unless the facts demonstrate that such a relationship exists, the rule should not apply. As a general proposition, the burden to prove that an attorney-client relationship has developed rests with the defendant, who must show that an attorney has been hired, that the defendant was the client, that confidential communications involving the seeking or offering of legal advice were made between the two, and that no unnecessary third parties were present. In addition to client-attorney communication, the privilege generally covers other communications made by the client with people who are necessary to support the attorney in the rendition of legal services. These others include office personnel such as secretaries, law clerks, and investigators hired by the attorney. The privilege may also include a client's communications with a medical doctor or accountant employed by his attorney when made for the purpose of enabling the attorney to comprehend the client's fact situation in order to give appropriate legal advice.[95]

A classic comment from a landmark case illuminating the scope and attributes of the privilege is found in *United States v. United Shoe Machinery Corp.*[96] In that case, the Court commented:

> The privilege applies only if (1) the asserted holder of the privilege is or sought to become a client; (2) the person to whom the communication was made (a) is a member of the bar of a court, or his subordinate and (b) in connection with this communication is acting as a lawyer; (3) the communication relates to a fact of which the attorney was informed (a) by his client (b) without the presence of strangers (c) for the purpose of securing primarily either (i) an opinion on law or (ii) legal services or (iii) assistance in some legal proceeding, and not (d) for the purpose of committing a crime or tort; and (4) the privilege has been (a) claimed and (b) not waived by the client.

After referring to previous cases, a federal court reiterated that the attorney-client privilege is intended to be construed within the narrowest possible limits consistent with the logic of its principle. In one case, a defendant had been arrested and released and his attorney moved to withdraw from the case.

---

[95] In re Grand Jury Subpoenas, 2003 U.S. Dist. LEXIS 9022 (S.D.N.Y. 2003).
[96] 89 F. Supp. 357 (D. Mass. 1950); *see also* United States v. Schmidt, 360 F. Supp. 339 (M.D. Pa. 1973), for a discussion of the scope of the privilege.

The client failed to appear at the withdrawal hearing and was indicted for failure to appear. Over his objection, his former attorney testified that she had forwarded notice of the hearing date to the defendant. The court ruled that that she was not testifying in violation of the attorney-client privilege but was testifying concerning non-privileged information.[97]

As generally recognized, the privilege only applies when the person to whom the communication was made was a member of the bar or was reasonably believed to be a member of the bar, or his or her subordinate or agent. Included within the attorney-client privilege are statements made to an attorney's essential employee by a person seeking legal services from the attorney are covered by the privilege.[98] In most situations in which the presence of third parties is necessary, or at least useful to assisting attorney-client communication, the presence of those persons does not destroy the privilege.[99] When a potential homicide defendant asked his girlfriend-attorney questions about criminal problems, the attorney-client relationship may not exist, especially when the attorney was not a criminal attorney and her employment prohibited her from representing private clients. The attorney viewed the exchange as the usual boyfriend-girlfriend type of chatter even though it concerned a homicide, and did not consider it a request for legal advice.[100] However, the reasonable impressions and expectations of the potential client may hold more weight than the perceptions of the putative attorney.

The primary purpose of the privilege is to protect communications between attorney and client; however, the privilege is broad enough to also shield communications made by the client to an agent of the attorney, such as a scientific expert retained to aid in the preparation and presentation of the defense.[101] And information provided to an accountant by a client at the behest of his or her attorney for the purposes of interpretation and analysis is within the attorney-client privilege to the extent that it is provided in connection with the legal representation.[102] However, when the federal government wanted information from a taxpayer's accounting firm, the records were not privileged under the attorney-client rationale because the taxpayer, and not the attorney, had hired the accounting firm to provide accounting services that were not precisely related to the delivery of legal services.[103]

Although the attorney-client privilege has existed for several hundred years and is recognized in all courts, not all of the relationships are protected in

---

[97] State v. Kemper, 158 Ohio App. 3d 185, 187, 2004 Ohio 4050, 814 N.E.2d 540, 541, 2004 Ohio App. LEXIS 3677 (2004).

[98] American National Water Mattress Corp. v. Manville, 642 P.2d 1330 (Alaska 1982).

[99] Cavallaro v. United States, 284 F.3d 236, 246, 2002 U.S. App. LEXIS 5366 (1st Cir. 2002).

[100] Jones v. United States, 2003 D.C. App. LEXIS 434 (2003).

[101] State v. DeMarco, 275 N.J. Super 311, 646 A.2d 431 (1994).

[102] United States v. United Technologies Corp., 979 F. Supp. 108 (D. Conn. 1997).

[103] Cavallaro v. United States, 153 F. Supp. 2d 52, 57, 58, 2001 U.S. Dist. LEXIS 11232 (1st Cir. 2001).

all contexts. Some of the situations in which the confidential communication protection does not apply are discussed in the following sections.

C. Exceptions

1. Identity of client

The identity of the attorney's client has not been considered a privileged matter because it usually reveals little concerning the nature of the relationship or what has been discussed between the two individuals. As a general rule, the mere existence of an attorney-client relationship and the identity of the client is not a privileged communication, unless the identity of the client is the last piece of evidence needed to initiate a criminal prosecution or the disclosure would reveal a confidential communication.[104] The privilege pertains to the subject matter and not the fact of the employment as attorney, and as it presupposes the relationship of attorney and client, it does not attach to the creation of that relationship. Either the client or the attorney may be compelled to testify regarding his or her employment as an attorney, the fee or how it was paid, and certain services performed for the client but not concerning the substantive matters of the advice given. For example, a federal prosecutor wanted to discover the source of money that a suspected drug trafficker may have used to pay his defense counsel.[105] As a general rule the fee arrangement between an attorney and a client is not privileged. It is possible that such information might be protected if the person asserting the attorney-client privilege could demonstrate a strong chance that the fact of retention of an attorney or the way the fee was paid would implicate the client in the very criminal activity for which he is seeking legal advice. The fact that a defendant's family members might be fronting the defense money would not implicate either the defendant or the family in criminal matters and knowing the source of the money would not reveal any substantive matter concerning the receipt of legal advice. Therefore, the court ordered that the identity of the attorney's clients, their benefactors, and their fee arrangements be revealed because the attorney-client relationship had no application.[106]

Absent a unique situation or special circumstances, client identity and fee information are not privileged because neither the fact of employment nor the amount of the fee paid has any bearing on the matters discussed between the client and the attorney. Revealing this sort of information does not curtail or chill the communication between the necessary actors involved in the attorney-client relationship.[107] As a Maryland court noted, "[o]rdinarily fee arrangements are not within the scope of attorney-client privilege because revealing such information generally does not expose confidential communication between the attorney and client.[108]

---

[104]   Nester v. Jernigan, 908 So. 2d 145,149, 2005 Miss. LEXIS 467 (2005).
[105]   United States v. Cedeno, 496 F. Supp. 2d 562, 2007 U.S. Dist. LEXIS 49631 (E.D. Pa. 2007).
[106]   *Id.*
[107]   Sony v. Soundview, 2001 U.S. Dist. LEXIS 23220 (D. Conn. 2001).
[108]   Chesek v. Jones, 406 Md. 446, 463, 2008 Md. LEXIS 609 (Md. 2008).

Clarifying the rule for federal courts that the identity of the attorney's client is not subject to secrecy under the attorney-client privilege, as well commenting on the limitations on this exception, a federal district court noted that the identity of the client and the amount of the fee or the form of payment of the fee are not usually considered privileged.[109] The attorney's time records and billing statements are not considered covered by the attorney-client privilege, at least where the records and statements do not contain detailed accounts of the services performed.[110] With respect to confidentiality, in Massachusetts, the requirements dictate that a lawyer "should keep in confidence information relating to representation of a client except so far as disclosure is required or permitted by the Rules of Professional Conduct or other law."[111]

2. Advice in furtherance of crime

There is no privilege if either the attorney or the client has involved the other in a criminal endeavor or if the legal advice of the lawyer has been sought or obtained to facilitate or assist anyone in committing or planning a crime or committing a fraud.[112] In addition, there is no attorney-client privilege if the lawyer reasonably believes that a disclosure is required to prevent a criminal act that is likely to result in death or substantial harm to another person.[113] As one court noted, "Only when a client knowingly seeks legal counsel to further a continuing or future crime does the crime-fraud exception apply."[114] Under such circumstances, the attorney and the "client" may be forced to divulge any communication between them that relates to "covering up" an old crime or embarking on new criminal behavior. The privilege does not exist when the desired advice concerns future criminality, but the privilege will cover legal advice on resolving prior crimes within a lawful context. This exception to the attorney-client privilege prevents the attorney and/or client from giving or obtaining advice about how to commit a new crime or fraud.[115] Simply stated, communications between a client and his or her attorney seeking legal advice in order to initiate or accomplish an ongoing or future fraud do not carry any privilege under the attorney-client relationship.[116] The interests of public justice require that no shield be interposed to protect a person who takes

---

[109] Estate of Reiserer v. United States, 229 F.R.D. 172, 179, 2005 U.S. Dist. LEXIS 17597 (W.D. Wash. 2005).

[110] DiBella v. Hopkins, 403 F.3d 102, 120, 2005 U.S. App. LEXIS 5332 (2d Cir. 2005).

[111] Mass. R. Prof. Conduct, ALM Sup. Jud. Ct. Rule 3:07(3) (2009).

[112] For example, *see* CAL. EVID. CODE § 956 Crime or fraud (Matthew Bender 2008).

[113] CAL. EVID. CODE § 956.5 Disclosure necessary to prevent criminal act likely to result in death or bodily injury (Matthew Bender 2008).

[114] United States v. Doe, 429 F.3d 450; 2005 U.S. App. LEXIS 25256 (3d Cir. 2005).

[115] *See* Hawai'i v. Wong, 97 Haw. 512, 40 P.3d 914, 2002 Haw. LEXIS 100 (2002); *and see* LA. CODE EVID. ANN. Art. 506(C)(1)(b), in which attorney-client communications covering new crimes are not considered privileged.

[116] State v. Menard, 844 So. 2d 1117 (La. Dist. Ct. App. 2003).

counsel on how he or she can safely commit a new crime. This exception to the attorney-client privilege does not apply when a person has committed a crime, prior to consulting an attorney concerning what the client's legal rights may be and inquired how the crime may be lawfully adjusted. The crime-fraud exception prevents a privilege from being recognized when a "client" who, having committed a crime, seeks advice on how he or she can initiate or complete a "cover-up" of the offense. For example, when a prospective client asked the attorney to hide a murder weapon or otherwise aid in the disposition of a murder weapon, such conduct falls far outside of the attorney-client privilege.[117] In a similar fashion, the act of a jailed inmate, who called an attorney on a monitored line and spoke about whether he should trust a fellow inmate to arrange for a hit man to murder witnesses and maybe kill the prosecutor, fell into the crime-fraud exception to the attorney-client privilege. The acts contemplated need not be successful; the mere communication of criminal plans takes the communication outside the protections of the attorney-client privilege.[118]

Although the crime-fraud exception to the attorney-client privilege may have a narrow construction, in order to prevail on an allegation of crime-fraud, the burden of proving the exception rests with the party wishing to invade the attorney-client relationship. Where the prosecution wants to invoke the crime-fraud exception, it must make a prima facie demonstration that (1) the client was committing a fraud or crime and that (2) the communications between the attorney and the client were made in furtherance of the allege crime-fraud.[119] In a case in which the prosecution believed that the client was destroying e-mail communication necessary to a prosecution, the reviewing court found that the crime-fraud exception to the attorney-client privilege applied to the attorney's communication with his defendant regarding the types of e-mails the prosecution was seeking in a discovery request. The communication permitted the client to know which e-mails to destroy from the hard drive to keep them from being turned over to the government.[120]

3. Communications not intended to be confidential[121]

A communication is considered "confidential" if it is not intended to be disclosed to third parties other than those to whom its disclosure is necessary in rendering professional legal services to the client or to those persons reasonably necessary for the transmission of the communication. Communication will be remain confidential if an attorney or client needs to divulge information to an accountant, a private investigator, or similar person assisting the attorney in understanding or interpreting the facts. If the communication is not intended to

---

[117]   Mixon v. State, 179 S.W.3d 233, 235, 2005 Tex. App. LEXIS 9079 (2005).

[118]   United States v. Lentz, 419 F. Supp.2d 820, 829 (E.D. Va. 2005).

[119]   In re Grand Jury Proceedings, 445 F.3d 266, 274, 2006 U.S. App. LEXIS 10041 (2006).

[120]   *Id.* at 275.

[121]   *See* draft of FED. R. EVID. as submitted to Congress in 1972.

be confidential, then the rationale for the attorney-client privilege does not exist. It is clear that the attorney-client privilege restricts the full and free discovery of the truth and for that reason, the privilege is strictly construed and limited to situations in which the communication was intended to remain confidential.[122]

Where an unnecessary third party was present at the time the communications were made, the attorney-client privilege generally does not exist. Demonstrative of this principle is a Florida case in which a jailed defendant called his sister, who called his lawyer on a three-way telephone call. At the jail end of the conversation, an audible warning automatically notified the defendant that the conversation might be monitored and recorded. At trial, the court admitted into evidence a number of taped telephone conversations initiated by the defendant on the monitored line. One of the taped conversations that included incriminating information occurred among the defendant, the man who was his attorney at the time, and his sister on the three-way telephone conversation. The appellate court upheld the admission of the authenticated tape of the incriminating conversation as well as other taped conversations on the theory the attorney-client privilege only covers communications that are neither overheard by nor intended to be disclosed to third persons.[123]

4. Statements of the attorney relating to the client's mental or physical condition

The privilege does not extend to information received by the attorney that does not relate to communications, even though it was obtained while he or she was acting as an attorney. For example, testimony at the trial by the defendant's previous counsel from another proceeding concerning the defendant's mental competency does not violate the attorney-client privilege.[124] The court in *Clanton v. United States* stated:

> Here the attorney's testimony did not relate to private, confidential communications with his client during the time of communications prior to and at the entry of the pleas of guilty. He was qualified as a layman to express a view as to his client's mental competency.

However, an attorney has a duty of confidentiality to the client regardless of whether the information is available from other public or private sources. Such duty to preserve confidences extends beyond information that may be covered by a narrow interpretation of the attorney-client privilege.[125]

---

[122]   Ocean Mammal Inst. V. Gates, 2008 U.S. Dist. LEXIS 42068 (D.C. Haw. 2008). *See also* United States v. Lentz, 419 F. Supp. 2d 820, 826, 2005 U.S. Dist. LEXIS 41084 (E.D. Va. 2005).

[123]   State v. Black, 920 So. 2d 668, 670, 2006 Fla. App. LEXIS 48 (2006), *reh'g denied*, 2006 Fla. App. LEXIS 3673 (2006)

[124]   Clanton v. United States, 488 F.2d 1069 (5th Cir. 1974).

[125]   Sealed Party v. Sealed Party, 2006 U.S. Dist. LEXIS 28392 (2006).

5. Posthumous revelation exception

Does a compelling need for important evidence in criminal cases outweigh the confidentiality claims involving the attorney-client privilege? This issue received national attention when Whitewater special prosecutor Kenneth Starr asked a federal grand jury to issue subpoenas for handwritten notes made by the attorney who represented Deputy White House Counsel Vincent W. Foster Jr., who had committed suicide by the time the subpoenas were issued.

A federal grand jury issued subpoenas for the notes and litigation resulted when the district court refused to require that the attorney-client privilege be breached even following the client's death. The court of appeals reversed and held that the notes could be viewed by the grand jury, effectively holding that, in this case, the attorney-client privilege did not survive the death of the client.

The United States Supreme Court disagreed with the reasoning of the Court of Appeals, holding that the petitioner's notes were protected by the attorney-client privilege. The Supreme Court admonished that the relevant case law demonstrated that it has been overwhelmingly, if not universally, accepted for more than a century that the privilege survives the client's death in such a case.[126] After explaining that the Independent Counsel's arguments against the privilege's posthumous survival were invalid, the Supreme Court emphasized that "knowing that communications will remain confidential even after death serves a weighty interest in encouraging a client to communicate fully and frankly with counsel; posthumous disclosure of such communication may be as feared as disclosure during the client's lifetime."[127] "Balancing ex post the importance of the information against client interests, even limited to criminal cases, introduces substantial uncertainty into the privilege's application, and therefore must be rejected."[128]

In a more recent decision, an Ohio case involved the disappearance and probable death of a nine-year-old girl, in which authorities believed that a deceased woman had communicated information to her attorney. Her attorney refused to divulge what the client had communicated to her due to an Ohio law[129] that provided a durable attorney-client privilege after death that extended the privilege until consent to release the privilege had been given by a surviving spouse or personal representative. Numerous state and federal courts heard aspects of the case,[130] but the principle that an attorney-client privilege can survive the death of the client-holder of the privilege remained intact. The interests served by extending the attorney-client privilege beyond the life of the holder allows living holders of the privilege security in the knowledge that embarrassing or personal information shared with an attorney in the delivery of legal advice will remain private under most situations.

---

[126] Swidler & Berlin v. United States, 524 U.S. 399, 1998 U.S. LEXIS 4214 (1998).

[127] Id., Headnote.

[128] Id.

[129] OHIO REV. CODE § 2317.02 Privileged communications (2006).

[130] Ohio v. Doe, 433 F.3d 502, 2006 U.S. App. LEXIS 481 (6th Cir. 2006).

D. *Assertion and Waiver*

The burden rests with the party who asserts the attorney-client privilege to establish that the privilege existed in the first instance, and that there has been no waiver.[131] Where a court recognizes the existence of the privilege, the privilege prohibits disclosure of information that has been confidentially disclosed to an attorney. The information remains personal to the client or successor and must be asserted by the client-holder of the privilege and not by the attorney.[132] However, if the client is neither present nor available during the proceeding in which the attorney's testimony has been ordered, the attorney must honor the client's wishes and should assert the privilege on behalf of the client, but the attorney is not asserting on his or her own behalf.[133] In one case in which the parents of a minor child were present when the child talked to his attorney, a court of appeals held that the presence of the parents as third parties did not waive the attorney-client privilege because the parents were intent on keeping the conference confidential.[134]

Recent decisions have reaffirmed the rule that the waiver of the attorney-client privilege rests solely with the client, not the counsel. The attorney or agent may exercise that power only when acting with the client's authority.[135] Therefore, to allow the district attorney to invoke the attorney-client privilege that existed between a murder victim and his attorney is error.[136] However, while the attorney-client privilege belongs to the client and not the attorney, an attorney may and should assert it if done for the benefit of his or her client.[137]

A convicted defendant generally waives the attorney-client privilege when he or she raises a claim of ineffective assistance of counsel in an appellate setting or in a petition for a writ of habeas corpus. When a convict alleges that his trial attorney provided ineffective assistance of counsel in pursuing a particular defense strategy or in determining what witnesses to call or how to cross-examine, the person seeking habeas relief places at issue any attorney-client privilege that might apply to the substance of conversations that covered trial planning.[138] In a California case, a federal district court, entertaining an application for a writ

---

[131] United States v. Ary, 2005 U.S. Dist. LEXIS 21958 (D. Kan. 2005).

[132] For example, *see* CAL. EVID. CODE § 951 Client (2008) and HLC Properties, Ltd. v. Superior Court, 35 Cal. 4th 54, 62, 105 P.3d 560, 565, 2005 Cal. LEXIS 1607 (2005), where the court held that "the attorney-client privilege belongs only to the client, whether the client is a natural person, an unincorporated organization, or some other entity."

[133] Martin Marietta v. West Virginia, 227 F.R.D. 382, 2005 U.S. Dist. LEXIS 8379 (2005).

[134] Arizona v. Sucharew, 66 P. 2d 59, 65, 2003 Ariz. App. LEXIS 61 (2003).

[135] State v. Davis, 116 N.J. 341, 561 A.2d 1082 (1989).

[136] Smith v. State, 770 S.W.2d 70 (Tex. Ct. App. 1989).

[137] United States v. Loften, 518 F. Supp. 839 (S.D.N.Y. 1981).

[138] *See* In re Lott, 139 Fed. Appx. 658; 2005 U.S. App. LEXIS 12280 (2005). However, in later litigation, the Sixth Circuit Court of Appeals noted that "The Rules of Evidence make it abundantly clear that the attorney-client privilege stands in all federal judicial proceedings, which would include habeas proceedings where petitioners assert actual innocence." In re Lott, 424 F.3d 446, 452, 2005 U.S. App. LEXIS 19429, 2005 Fed. Appx. 383P (6th Cir. 2005).

of habeas corpus, entered an order prohibiting the state prosecutor from turning over to other prosecutors any evidence obtained by virtue of the defendant's waiver of the attorney-client privilege. The prosecution appealed the order, arguing that the defendant completely waived the attorney-client privilege and the district court had no authority to prevent the use of the nonprivileged materials to reprosecute the defendant. The Ninth Circuit affirmed the trial court order limiting the waiver to the habeas corpus case. In its opinion the court indicated that it affirmed the district court's order, adopting a narrow waiver rule. The Ninth Circuit held that the scope of the defendant's waiver extended only to the federal habeas petition, and that the privilege was not waived for other legal purposes. To have decided otherwise would have exposed a habeas corpus litigant to making a determination of whether to waive the privilege and have a chance at winning a habeas corpus claim but having all his formerly privileged information available to the state for a retrial, or foregoing any habeas corpus claim, secure that while he was serving time his confidences remained safe.[139] Thus, a waiver by filing a claim under habeas corpus does not necessarily waive the attorney-client privilege for a case under appellate consideration.

Once a client has effectively waived the attorney-client privilege, the attorney may testify regarding matters otherwise within the scope of the privilege; he or she has no standing to invoke the privilege if the client does not wish to do so.[140] However, an attorney, while testifying as a witness or otherwise, in the absence of a client's consent, may not disclose any privileged communication made to the client or received by the attorney.[141]

Unless a holder of the attorney-client privilege makes a positive effort to assert or claim the privilege, the benefits will be lost. Under the general rule, a failure to object constitutes waiver. For a holder of the privilege to avoid waiver, a claim of privilege must be promptly raised or the court will rule that the privilege has been waived. A holder waives the privilege when he or she places a confidential communication at issue that goes directly to a claim or defense, whether at trial or upon appeal.[142]

Voluntary testimony by the client, with neither compulsion nor complaint or upon the client's request, or by the attorney that discloses a portion of the confidential communication is a waiver as to the remainder of the particular communication. A holder waives the privilege by voluntarily divulging privileged information to a third party,[143] whether in court or otherwise. If a client alleges that his or her attorney's representation in a criminal case constituted ineffective assistance of counsel, the client has waived the attorney-client privilege to the extent of the allegation.[144]

---

[139] Bittaker v. Woodford, 331 F.3d 715, 2003 U.S. App. LEXIS 11298 (9th Cir. 2003).

[140] Barnes v. State, 460 So. 2d 126 (Miss. 1983).

[141] Arizona ex rel. Thomas v. Schneider, 130 P.3d 991, 994, 2006 Ariz. App. LEXIS 44 (2006).

[142] Jackson v. City of Chicago, 2005 U.S. Dist. LEXIS 32538 (N. D. Ill. 2005).

[143] United States v. Lentz, 419 F. Supp. 2d 820, 827, 2005 U.S. Dist. LEXIS 41084 (E.D. Va. 2005).

[144] LeCroy v. Secretary, Florida Dept. of Corrections, 421 F.3d 1237, 1253, 2005 U.S. App. LEXIS 18570 (11th Cir. 2005), n. 11.

§ 10.5 Communications Between Physician and Patient

A. Statement of the Rule

Unlike the attorney-client privilege and the husband-wife privilege, the physician-patient privilege did not exist at common law but instead is dictated by statute[145] or court decision.[146] Therefore, courts are generally not free to modify the statute's intent or to change its mandates,[147] but federal courts are permitted to define new privileges by interpreting common law principles in light of reason and experience.[148] The purpose of the statutes creating the physician-patient privilege is to encourage patients to reveal all relevant information to their physician without worrying that the information will later be disclosed. As the Supreme Court noted, "the physician must know all that a patient can articulate in order to identify and to treat disease; barriers to full disclosure would impair diagnosis and treatment."[149] While the statutes of the various states are inconsistent in defining which professional groups are covered by the physician-patient privilege, most modern statutes include psychologists and psychotherapists. Some statutes specifically include marriage counselors and social workers. Because state laws differ significantly, it is essential that the prosecutor or law enforcement official consult the statutes and analyze the cases interpreting the statutes. Of importance to prosecutors is the concept that where the patient's conduct creates an express or implied waiver, the medical information will usually be admissible because it is no longer privileged.[150] If the relationship is not specifically stated in the statute or covered by case law interpretation, the privilege will not be recognized.

California has a statute that provides that a patient has a privilege to refuse to disclose, and to prevent others from disclosing, any confidential communication made to a physician as long as the privilege is claimed by the patient privilege holder or a person authorized by the holder to claim the privilege. A person who was a physician[151] at the time of the confidential communication may claim the privilege for the life of the patient, unless released by the patient.[152]

---

[145]   Guerrier v. Florida, 811 So. 2d 852, 854, 2002 Fla. App. LEXIS 4087 (2002).

[146]   Jaffee v. Richmond, 518 U.S. 1, 15, 1996 U.S. LEXIS 3879 (1996). The Supreme Court recognized that a psychotherapist-patient privilege existed under Rule 501 for federal courts.

[147]   D'Amico v. Delliquardri, 114 Ohio App. 3d 579, 683 N.E.2d 814 (1996). *See also* State v. Hardin, 569 N.W.2d 517 (Iowa 1997).

[148]   *See* FED. R. EVID. 501, Notes of the Committee.

[149]   Trammel v. United States, 445 U.S. 40, 51, 1980 U.S. LEXIS 84 (1980).

[150]   State v. Bergmann, 2009 Iowa App. LEXIS 54 (Iowa 2009). *See* case in Part II.

[151]   A physician for purposes of California law is defined as a "person authorized, or reasonably believed by the patient to be authorized, to practice medicine in any state or nation." *See* CAL. EVID. CODE § (2008).

[152]   CAL. EVID. CODE § 994 Physician-patient privilege (Matthew Bender 2008).

At first impression, the California provision appears to offer complete coverage to confidential medical communications. However, § 998 of the California Evidence Code provides that "there is no privilege under this article in a criminal proceeding" for the doctor-patient privilege.[153] Similarly, there is no application of the medical privilege when the services of a physician were sought to enable a person to commit a tort (civil wrong) or to escape detection or apprehension following the commission of a tort or a crime.[154] When medical information that might prove embarrassing is weighed against the interests of justice and potential loss of freedom to a defendant, the confidential medical evidence will be admitted as a matter of public policy as expressed in California law.

The California psychotherapist-patient privilege law covers many more counselors by including physicians, psychiatrists, psychologists, licensed clinical social workers, school psychologists, licensed marriage and family therapists, and numerous other support workers in the mental health and counseling fields.[155] In a similar manner, Mississippi permits greater protection of the doctor-patient relationships because it holds that medical and even pharmacological records are privileged in criminal proceedings and cannot be divulged without the patient's consent.[156]

The Supreme Court of the United States has recognized a limited federal doctor-patient confidential communication privilege that protects the confidences of a patient and his or her psychotherapist or licensed clinical social worker pursuant to Federal Rule of Evidence 501. The case involved a police officer who had killed a fight participant and had subsequently sought mental health assistance to deal with the aftermath. The Committee Notes to Rule 501 of the Federal Rules of Evidence contemplated that federal courts would define new testimonial privileges consistent with developing federal common law, in accordance with new experiences and needs. In recognizing the new privilege, the Court observed that all 50 states had previously implemented laws to protect some sort of psychotherapist-patient privilege and that the need and rationale for such a privilege was the same as for the marital and attorney-client privileges.[157]

B. Scope of the Privilege

The privilege exists for the protection of the patient, not the physician, and for that reason the patient is considered the holder of the privilege and may assert this privilege.[158] However, although not a holder, a physician called to testify should alert the court that a medical privilege exists. The rationale

---

[153] CAL. EVID. CODE § 998 Criminal Proceeding (Matthew Bender 2008).

[154] CAL. EVID. CODE § 997 Crime or tort (Matthew Bender 2008).

[155] CAL. EVID. CODE § 1010 Psychotherapist (Matthew Bender 2008).

[156] Cox v. Mississippi, 2003 Miss. LEXIS 103 (2003)

[157] See Jaffee v. Richmond, 518 U.S. 1, 116 S. Ct. 1923 (1996).

[158] State v. Miles, 211 Ariz. 475; 123 P.3d 669, 673, 2005 Ariz. App. LEXIS 161 (2005).

for the rule is to shield the patient from disclosures that might be undesirable. There is no intent to protect third persons or other family members, although others may benefit incidentally. For the privilege to apply, the physician-patient relationship must have existed at the time that the physician acquired the information he or she is called upon to disclose. Interestingly, the federal courts do not recognize a physician-patient privilege, but federal courts do recognize a psychotherapist-patient privilege under federal common law.[159]

In an Oregon case, the court held that the doctor-patient privilege normally protected a juvenile's confidential information from revelation by her psychotherapist when the information was gained in the course of treatment and counseling. However, where a patient may have divulged confidential information relative to the patient's sexual abuse of another child, privilege law denies any privilege for communications between a psychotherapist and a patient. The statute makes no distinction based on the fact that the patient may be a minor and is also the person who allegedly perpetrated the abuse, rather than the victim. When a doctor/therapist receives information concerning child abuse, there may be an affirmative duty to report it and there is no privilege to withhold that information in some jurisdictions.[160]

Florida takes a blanket approach and holds that no provision exists under Florida law that would allow any breaching of the confidentiality accorded to doctor-patient confidences. In one case a defendant charged with attempted murder wanted to obtain all of the victim's psychiatric records from her psychiatrist, which he believed were necessary to assist in his defense. The court of appeal held that none of the records needed to be disclosed because Florida law failed to contain any statutory authority for revealing the privileged communication and did not offer any legal standard for determining whether or when to reveal confidential communications with a psychiatrist. According to the court of appeals, "there is neither an Evidence Code provision, nor an applicable constitutional principle, which allows the invasion of the victim's privileged communications with her psychotherapist."[161] Confidentiality under these circumstances may encourage people who need psychological assistance to contact medical resources, but it would also foreclose the discovery of important evidence to prevent a miscarriage of justice.

California distinguishes between the doctor-patient privilege, which may be asserted only in civil actions, and the psychotherapist-patient privilege, which sweeps with a much broader stroke and may be asserted in both civil and criminal cases. Under California law, a patient has the privilege to refuse to reveal (and to prevent the doctor from revealing) a confidential communication

---

[159]   Doe v. Oberweis Dairy, 2004 U.S. Dist. LEXIS 9204 (D. Ill. 2004) and Sterner v. DEA, 2005 U.S. Dist. LEXIS 18467 (2005).

[160]   State ex rel. Juvenile Department v. Michael Spencer, 198 Or. App. 599, 604 108 P.3d 1189, 1192, 2005 Or. App. LEXIS 346 (2005).

[161]   Florida v. Farmiglietti, 817 So. 2d 901, 907, 908, 2002 Fla. App. LEXIS 6199 (2002).

between the psychotherapist and the patient.[162] As a limitation on the privilege, a psychotherapist may have a duty to warn or disclose information when he or she reasonably believes that the patient or patients pose a credible and serious threat to another person or persons. As the California statute states, "There is no privilege under this article if the psychotherapist has reasonable cause to believe that the patient is in such mental or emotional condition as to be dangerous to himself or to the person or property of another and that disclosure of the communication is necessary to prevent the threatened danger."[163] Because there would be no privilege under these circumstances, appropriate action, such as notifying police and alerting possible victims, must be initiated if the psychotherapist becomes convinced during the course of treatment that the patient is a menace to himself or others.

C. Exceptions

While many states have created the doctor-patient privilege by statute, the exceptions that have been found necessary in order to obtain information required by the public interest or to avoid fraud are so numerous that the value of the privilege has been reduced in many jurisdictions.[164] In New York, among the exclusions from the statutory doctor-patient privilege, the following have been noted as not giving rise to any medical privilege and for which the doctor or other health worker may be required to testify: cases of communicable diseases, cases of child abuse, children under the age of 16 who have been crime victims, serious burns, and bullet and knife wounds.[165] California, for example, excludes cases in which the patient puts his or her condition in issue, all criminal proceedings (unless covered by the psychotherapist-patient privilege) will and similar contests, malpractice cases, and disciplinary proceedings, as well as certain other situations; thus, the exceptions leave virtually nothing covered by the privilege.

When a physician is required by state law to report to a law enforcement officer a gunshot wound, deadly weapon wounds, severe burns, or domestic violence, the physician may testify, without violating the physician-patient privilege, concerning the condition of the wounded person, the victim's personal information, and the description of the nature and location of such wound and how it occurred. Knowledge in these areas may be obtained by examination, observation, and treatment of the victim.[166]

---

[162] CAL. EVID. CODE § 1014, Psychotherapist—patient privilege (Matthew Bender 2008). The psychotherapist is considered a holder of the privilege unless released by the patient.

[163] CAL. EVID. CODE § 1024, Patient dangerous to self or others (Matthew Bender 2008).

[164] See ORC ANN. § 2921.22 (Matthew Bender 2009). Failure to report a crime or knowledge of a death or burn injury. All doctors and other people have duties to report the commission of known felonies unless covered by a privilege.

[165] See In re New York County, 98 N.Y.2d 525, 779 N.E.2d 173, 178, 749 N.Y.S.2d 462, 467, 2002 N.Y. LEXIS 3140 (2002).

[166] See ORC ANN. § 2151.421 (Matthew Bender 2009). Duty to report child abuse or neglect; investigation and follow-up procedures. See also ORC ANN. § 22317.02 Privileged communications (Matthew Bender 2009).

An example of a privilege with limited coverage is Florida, where the psychotherapist-patient privilege covers medical doctors and licensed psychologists but not other practitioners offering mental counseling and assistance. In one case involving the deaths of two children in a vehicle accident in which the wife had been driving, the prosecution sought information from her husband and her psychotherapist. Because both potential sources of information were covered by either a marital privilege or a psychotherapist privilege, the desired information could not initially be discovered. However, the prosecution added a count involving child abuse and neglect due to reckless driving. Under Florida law, this additional charge theoretically allowed the testimony of the psychotherapist and the defendant's husband despite confidential communications. The relevant statute contained an exception to confidential communications privileges when the communication involved a perpetrator or alleged perpetrator of known or suspected child abuse, abandonment, or neglect. The court approved properly limited questioning of both the husband and the psychotherapist concerning the child abuse theory based on the automobile wreck because of the exception in Florida law.[167]

Obtaining illicit drugs is not covered by the physician-patient privilege in most jurisdictions. In a Colorado case, a defendant had obtained numerous controlled substance prescriptions from different doctors. The policed arrested him after his doctor discovered that a local pharmacy had a "narcotics alert" on him due to the large number of pain prescriptions filled in a single month. A state statute criminalized the defendant's conduct of obtaining controlled substances illegally and an exception to the doctor-patient privilege allowed the doctor to testify as an exception to the privilege.[168]

The privilege may be justified only when disclosures are made in confidence. Therefore, when the communication is made in the presence of unnecessary third persons, some jurisdictions hold that the privilege is waived. For example, when the crime victim allowed her sister to be present in the emergency room along with a police officer, no doctor-patient privilege existed due to the presence of nonessential persons who overheard the medical information being divulged.[169] In a habeas corpus case, a federal appellate court accepted a state court determination that no physician-patient privilege existed where a patient made incriminating statements to hospital nurses in the presence of police officers. The Oklahoma statute covered nurses and other healthcare providers, but not when police officers, who were not necessary to diagnosis and treatment, were present.[170] New York holds an opposite position and upholds the privilege under similar circumstances if the police officer must be present according to law.[171]

---

[167] Hill v. State, 2003 Fla. App. LEXIS 8327 (2003).

[168] People v. Harte, 131 P.3d 1180, 2005 Colo. App. LEXIS 1861 (2005).

[169] State v. Gillespie, 710 N.W.2d 289, 298, 2006 Minn. App. LEXIS 24 (2006).

[170] Freeman v. Grubbs, 134 Fed. Appx. 233, 2005 U.S. App. LEXIS 10499 (10th Cir. 2005).

[171] People v. Jaffarian, 799 N.Y.S.2d 733, 735, 2005 N.Y. Misc. LEXIS 1640 (2005).

While statements made by a patient to a psychologist in the presence of unnecessary third persons are normally outside the protection of the physician-patient privilege, some jurisdictions permit the presence of third parties whose presence does not destroy a psychotherapist-patient privilege. For example, an Oklahoma statute permits the presence and participation of family members without destroying the physician and psychotherapist patient-doctor privilege.[172]

If a psychiatrist gives information to police regarding the identity of a suspect, the privilege does not apply. In an Arkansas case, the defendant's psychiatrist gave police officers sufficient information about the defendant to enable the officer to identify the defendant and to obtain a warrant to search the defendant's home. In this case, the court agreed that evidence developed as a result of the search was not excluded by the privilege.[173]

D. Assertion and Waiver

The physician-patient privilege belongs to the patient and the physician may be compelled to testify if the patient has waived the privilege.[174] State statutes creating a physician-patient privilege usually provide that if the patient voluntarily testifies about privileged matters, the physician may be compelled to testify on the same subject. In civil actions, the physician also may be compelled to testify by express consent of his or her patient or, if the patient is deceased, by the express consent of the surviving spouse, executor, or administrator of the estate of the deceased patient.[175] However, the physician may claim the privilege covering his or her patients' records in the absence of evidence that the patient for whom the doctor may serve as witness has waived his or her privilege.[176]

In making certain that the holder of the patient-physician privilege is the patient, the Supreme Court of Vermont stated "[w]hile the defendant [doctor] has the power to invoke the privilege, it is based on the presumption that he speaks for the patient. Once it is clear that he does not speak for the patient, his power to invoke the privilege ceases."[177]

In many jurisdictions, a defendant waives any claim of physician-patient confidentiality or privilege concerning information given to obtain an examination or treatment of mental conditions when the defendant asserts a defense

---

[172] *See* 12 OKLA. ST. § 2503, Physician and Psychotherapist-Patient Privilege (2009).

[173] Gruzen v. State, 267 Ark. 380, 591 S.W.2d 342 (1979), *cert. denied*, 449 U.S. 852, 101 S. Ct. 144, 66 L. Ed. 2d 64 (1980).

[174] *See* Wheeler v. Commissioner of Social Services, 662 N.Y.S.2d 550 (1997); *see also* ORC ANN. § 2317.02(B)(1) Privileged communications (Matthew Bender 2009). When the patient is clearly the holder of the privilege and the physician may be compelled to testify following waiver.

[175] ORC ANN. § 2317.02(B)(1)(a) and (b). Privileged communications (Matthew Bender 2009).

[176] People v. Bickham, 89 Ill. 2d 1, 431 N.E.2d 365 (1982).

[177] State v. Chenette, 560 A.2d 365 (Vt. 1989).

that he or she is not guilty by reason of insanity, or has a mental impairment that might affect culpability or makes an allegation that the defendant is not competent to stand trial.[178] Waiver may occur if the defense plans to introduce part of a doctor's report, and, as part of discovery, turns the report over to the prosecution. In a case involving attempted murder, the appellate court held that the trial court correctly ruled that the defendant waived his doctor-patient privilege because his public defender voluntarily turned over the toxicology reports to the prosecution, which bound the defendant.[179]

§ 10.6 Communications to Clergy

A. *Statement of the Rule*

The common law recognized no privilege for confidential communications or confessions to a religious advisor, and without state statutes providing for the privilege, it would not exist.[180] At present, all 50 states have enacted privilege statutes that cover confidential communications between religious leaders and followers[181] and have attempted to be inclusive in order to cover genuine religions and faiths. Representative of religious privilege statutes is a Colorado law, which states "[a] clergy member, minister, priest, or rabbi shall not be examined without both his or her consent and also the consent of the person making the confidential communication as to any confidential communication made to him or her in his or her professional capacity in the course of discipline expected by the religious body to which he or she belongs."[182] California defines a clergy member to mean a "priest, minister, religious practitioner, or similar functionary of a church or of a religious denomination or religious organization."[183]

In a New Jersey case, an appellate court held that the priest-penitent privilege could be invoked by either the cleric or the penitent.[184] In order to qualify under this religious privilege, the communication must have been in confidence to a cleric and in the cleric's role as a spiritual adviser. In a case in which the defendant allegedly had sexually abused his daughters and the pastor contacted the defendant in an effort to protect the children from further abuse, the defendant, in a manner of speaking, admitted to the abuse and spoke with the pastor one additional time concerning the sexual abuse. Although the

---

[178] *See*, for example, C.R.S. § 16-8-103.6 Waiver of Privilege (Colo. 2008).

[179] State v. Moses, 107 Haw. 282, 285, 112 P.3d 768, 772, 2005 Haw. App. LEXIS 174 (2005).

[180] State v. Morehous, 97 N.J.L. 285, 117 A. 296, 1922 N.J. LEXIS 186 (1922).

[181] *See* 73 N.Y.U. L. REV. 225, 231 (1998), n. 39, noting state statutes that provide for the privilege.

[182] C.R.S. 13-90-107 (1) (c) (2008).

[183] CAL. EVID. CODE § 1030 (2008).

[184] State v. J.G., 402 N.J. Super. 290, 293, 2008 N.J. Super. LEXIS 180 (N.J. 2008).

men spoke privately, at no time did the defendant request that the conversation remain confidential and there was not a particular religious slant to the communication. Under these circumstances there was no cleric-penitent privilege under New Jersey law and the pastor should have been permitted to offer his testimony concerning the defendant's admission or confession.[185]

The state statutes covering confidential communications made to and from clergy or similar religious advisors are rather varied and operate differently in their respective jurisdictions. For example, in Louisiana the code is very comprehensive and not only recognizes religious privileges, but also includes definitions. It provides:

> a person has a privilege to refuse to disclose and to prevent another person from disclosing a confidential communication by the person to a clergyman in his professional character as a spiritual advisor.[186]

The Louisiana legislature included definitions within the statutory formulation covering the priest-penitent privilege. The legislature noted that "A 'clergyman' is a minister, priest, rabbi, Christian Science practitioner, or other similar functionary of a religious organization or an individual believed so to be by the person consulting him."[187] "A communication is 'confidential' if it is made privately and not intended for further disclosure except to other persons present in furtherance of the purpose of the communication."[188] Under this statute, the privilege may be claimed by the person seeking spiritual advice, his or her legal representative, and may be claimed on behalf of the holder by the clergyperson, even after the person's death.[189]

The Michigan statute covering clergy-penitent communication is fairly concise but leaves some room for court interpretation. It provides:

> Any communications between . . . members of the clergy and the members of their respective churches, . . . are hereby declared to be privileged and confidential when those communications were necessary to enable . . . members of the clergy . . . to serve as such . . . member of the clergy.[190]

Only in the Court of Appeals for the Third Circuit has a federal priest-penitent privilege been recognized. The Court of Appeals determined that a federal clergy-communicant privilege exists and that this privilege protects the disclosure of communications from a communicant to a member of the clergy in his or her spiritual or professional capacity, by persons who seek spiritual counseling and who reasonably expect that their words will be kept in confidence.[191]

---

[185] *Id.* at 292.

[186] LA. C. E. Art. 5.11(B) (Matthew Bender 2008).

[187] LA. C. E. Art. 5.11(A)(1) (Matthew Bender 2008).

[188] LA. C. E. Art. 5.11(A)(2) (Matthew Bender 2008).

[189] LA. C.E. Art. 5.11(C) (Matthew Bender 2008).

[190] MICH. COMP. LAWS ANN. § 767.5 a.(2) (Matthew Bender 2008).

[191] In re Grand Jury Investigation, 918 F.2d 374 (3d Cir. 1990).

Similarly, under Washington's law regulating religious privileges, it states that "[a] member of the clergy, a Christian Science practitioner listed in the *Christian Science Journal*, or a priest shall not, without the consent of a person making the confession or sacred confidence, be examined as to any confession or sacred confidence made to him or her in his or her professional character, in the course of discipline enjoined by the church to which he or she belongs."[192] In a case in which a stepdaughter sought to obtain a church's report of disciplinary action against her sexually abusive stepfather in a tort action against the church and the stepfather, the appellate court upheld the defendant's assertion of the clergy-penitent privilege. The reviewing court noted that the church's disciplinary proceeding against the stepfather was conducted under church doctrine and the disciplinary counsel members were ordained clergy.[193]

B. *Scope of the Privilege*

In order for a communication of a church member to a clergy member to be privileged, the "communications between the penitent and clergy must be: (1) made to an ordained member of the clergy; (2) a confession . . . in the course of discipline enjoined by the church and (3) confidential"[194] and not be deemed to constitute casual communications. The privilege generally applies to a voluntary confession, as well as to one made under a mandate of the church, and to observations as well as to communications. A statute granting the privilege to a "clergyman or other minister of any religion" does not limit the privilege to priests or clergy of any one denomination.[195] The term "clergyman" as used in the draft of Federal Rule of Evidence 506 and in other statutes includes a minister, priest, rabbi, or other similar functionary of a religious organization.

Although the courts have been liberal in interpreting the definition of "clergyman" and other terms as used in the various statutes, the state of New York's cleric-congregant privilege did not encompass statements to an Alcoholics Anonymous gathering and its leader. While the group was acknowledged as a religious organization, the defendant's communication to the group fell outside the cleric-congregant privilege. The evidence divulged at the Alcoholics Anonymous meeting was properly used to convict the speaker of two homicides.[196]

C. *Exceptions*

In order for a communication to be privileged under most statutes, it must have been made to a clergy member in his or her professional capacity or

---

[192]　REV. CODE WASH. § 5.60.060(3) (Matthew Bender 2009).

[193]　Doe v. Church of Jesus Christ of Latter-Day Saints, 122 Wash. App. 556, 568, 90 P.3d 1147, 1154, 2004 Wash. App. LEXIS 1112 (2004).

[194]　State v. Martin, 137 Wash. 2d 774, 791, 975 P.2d 1020, 1029, 1999 Wash. LEXIS 287 (1999).

[195]　In re Swenson, 183 Minn. 602, 237 N.W. 589 (1931).

[196]　Cox v. Miller, 296 F.3d 89, 2002 U.S. App. LEXIS 14398 (2d Cir. 2002).

character. Statements made by priests suspected of child abuse taken by other church priests in the course of conducting "troubled-priest interventions" were not considered privileged because communications to and from the individual priests were routinely shared with third parties. Therefore, when a defendant priest spoke to other clergy members as a "friend" under an intervention program, no privilege resulted concerning the communication.[197]

For example, several individuals alleged in a lawsuit that a probationary Methodist clergy member had molested the individual plaintiffs. The churches involved resisted answering the interrogatories with which they had been served. The trial court had ordered the pretrial discovery of the various statements because it held that the clergy-penitent privilege did not apply under the circumstances. The appellate court reversed the trial court decision insofar as it rejected any application of the religious privilege because the appeals court determined that the trial court had used an incorrect legal standard in arriving at its decision. According to the appellate court, the lower court never determined whether the communications to the youth minister were "penitential communications." In suggesting the correct standard to be applied, the court suggested that:

> in order for a statement to be privileged, it must satisfy all of the conceptual requirements of a penitential communication: (1) it must be intended to be in confidence; (2) it must be made to a member of the clergy who in the course of his or her religious discipline or practice is authorized or accustomed to hear such communications; and (3) such member of the clergy must have a duty under the discipline or tenets of the church, religious denomination or organization to keep such communications secret.[198]

The court explained that the person making the statement to the religious leader may be of any faith because California law does not have any special requirement that the person making the communication have any connection to the church or to the clergy member to whom the communication has been addressed.[199]

When the communication is not made within the requisite nature of the confidential disclosure of a penitent seeking religious advice or consolation from a clergy member, a court should not recognize the privilege. No priest-penitent privilege existed where a defendant spoke to two preachers, whose wives were present, concerning his sexual activity with an underage female. The defendant made no effort to prevent the wives from hearing the preachers discuss his situation and the preachers did not, at the time, consider the communication and discussion as privileged.[200]

---

[197] Roman Catholic Archbishop of Los Angeles v. Superior Court, 131 Cal. App. 4th 417, 421, 32 Cal. Rptr. 3d 209, 2005 Cal. App. LEXIS 1164 (2005).

[198] Doe 2 v. Superior Court, 132 Cal. App. 4th 1504, 1516, 34 Cal. Rptr. 3d 458, 466, 2005 Cal. App. LEXIS 1537 (2005).

[199] *Id*. at 1517, 467.

[200] Rogers v. State, 2006 Miss. LEXIS 226 (2006).

D. Assertion and Waiver

The majority of the jurisdictions consider the clergy-penitent privilege to be for the benefit of the penitent. Therefore, the penitent may claim the privilege or waive the privilege as he or she sees fit. The general rule is that if the penitent waives the privilege, the clergy member may be required to testify about the communication.[201] On the other hand, in some jurisdictions, such as California, the clergy member is deemed to be a holder of the privilege on the theory that the state should neither force a member of the clergy to violate, nor punish him or her for refusing to violate, church doctrine where the church teaching requires clergy to maintain secrecy as to confidential statements made in the course of religious counseling.[202]

Evidence of statements made in confidence to a member of the clergy is subject to admission in court in certain situations under some statutes. For example, in Texas, communications that would normally covered by a priest-penitent or other privileges are not considered privileged when the case involves a sexual assault against a child.[203] Additionally, most jurisdictions hold that the privilege is waived if the holder of the privilege voluntarily discloses privileged material to non-ordained unnecessary third parties. In a Washington case it was not clear, but if the defendant authorized his attorney to allow the prosecutor to take a deposition about the case from his preacher, the reviewing court noted that such conduct would waive the priest-penitent privilege.[204]

§ 10.7   Confidential Informant Privilege

Because confidential informants have long proved essential to various types of law enforcement activities, a privilege has evolved for the protection of the identities of these informants. The rule against disclosure of their identities recognizes that the informants serve as an important resource in effective law enforcement. This privilege prompts citizen involvement in alerting police to wrongdoing with the general promise that the citizen's identity will remain undiscovered by criminal suspects. Some informants were merely observers, while other informants may have been materially involved in the crime to the point at which they may have to be witnesses in criminal trials. Dealing

---

[201] *See* REV. CODE WASH. § 5.60.060. Who are disqualified—Privileged communications (Matthew Bender 2009).

[202] CAL. EVID. CODE § 1034 (Matthew Bender 2008).

[203] *See* TEX. FAM. CODE § 261.202 (Matthew Bender 2009).Privileged Communication. "In a proceeding regarding the abuse or neglect of a child, evidence may not be excluded on the ground of privileged communication except in the case of communications between an attorney and client."

[204] State v. Glenn, 115 Wash. App. 540, 551, 62 P.3d 921, 927, 2003 Wash. App. LEXIS 161 (2003).

with two types of confidential informants has created confusion about the confidential informant privileges. Some clarity in this area may be obtained by approaching the topic from two perspectives. One approach is to consider the confidential informant who gives information from which the court can determine "probable cause" for securing an arrest or a search warrant. This is different from the informer who was an integral part of the illegal transaction, whose identity may be demanded by the defense, and who has been called a material witness.

United States Supreme Court decisions have made it clear that in most instances the state does not have to disclose the name of the informant who gave information upon which a court found probable cause for a search warrant. In *Illinois v. Gates*, the Supreme Court reemphasized that it is not necessary to disclose the identity of an informant who only gives information that helps establish probable cause.[205] In this case, police obtained a search warrant for a residence and an automobile based on an affidavit setting forth facts contained in a letter written to police by an undisclosed informant. Police and federal officers corroborated most of the facts contained in the letter. The *Gates* Court, in reaffirming that an informant's identity may be withheld, quoted an older case,[206] and stated that "the magistrate must be informed of some of the underlying circumstances from which the informant concluded that the narcotics were where he claimed they were, and some of the underlying circumstances from which the officer concluded that the informant, whose identity need not be disclosed . . . was 'credible' or his information 'reliable.' "[207] As a general rule, an informant who provides police with information that the police use to obtain a warrant or to foster an investigation may have his or her identity remain confidential. However, if the informant later testifies at trial, the identity must be disclosed to the defendant for Sixth Amendment confrontation reasons to facilitate cross-examination.

As developed from case law and practice, communications made by informants to public officers engaged in the discovery of crime may be privileged. As the Supreme Court noted in *Roviaro v. United States*:

> The purpose of the privilege is the furtherance and protection of the public interest in effective law enforcement. The privilege recognizes the obligation of citizens to communicate their knowledge of the commission of crimes to law-enforcement officials and, by preserving their anonymity, encourages them to perform that obligation.[208]

This privilege exists in order to conceal the identity of the informant, thereby allowing him or her to continue as a source of future information while

---

[205] Illinois v. Gates, 462 U.S. 213, 103 S. Ct. 2317, 76 L. Ed. 2d 527 (1983).
[206] Aguilar v. Texas, 378 U.S. 108, 114, 1964 U.S. LEXIS 994 (1964).
[207] *Gates* at 278.
[208] 353 U.S. 53, 59, 1957 U.S. LEXIS 1125 (1959).

protecting the confidential informant from reprisals based on the informant's cooperation with law enforcement. The public policy encouraging citizens to assist police in solving crimes outweighs the damage that may be done to any defendant's case unless the defendant's due process rights become compromised. Where the confidential informant's testimony is not relevant to the defendant's guilt or innocence, where the informant will not be a trial witness, and where the informant did not participate in the crime for which defendant has been charged, there is no requirement to reveal the identity of the informant. The policy of informant confidentiality has its limits where non-disclosure rule would frustrate a defendant from fairly presenting a defense. In such a case, the informant's identity may have to be divulged or the prosecution may have to dismiss the case. Where the disclosure is relevant and would be helpful to the defense or might be essential to a fair trial, the government's privilege must give way. In making a decision, trial courts must also consider whether revealing an informant's identity will endanger the informant.[209]

Whether the privilege must yield depends upon the facts and circumstances of the particular case based on the degree of the informant's involvement. The informant who merely observed criminal activity and informed police will rarely have his or her identity revealed while an informant who had an active and strong role in the crime may have his or her identity revealed as essential to a fair trial. Cases that fall between non-involvement and active participation in the crime prove to be the hardest to determine whether disclosure of identity should be revealed to a defendant.[210] But if the informer testifies for the state, the privilege may not be invoked and the identity must be revealed, consistent with the right of confrontation and cross-examination under the Sixth Amendment.

Several examples may help to clarify this exception. In an old, but important case decided by the Supreme Court, the justices ruled that the prosecutor was not privileged to withhold the name of the informant when the informant played a direct and prominent part at the crime scene as the sole participant with the accused, Roviaro, in the very offense for which the latter was being tried.[211] The informant had taken a material part in bringing about petitioner's possession of the drugs and he had been present with petitioner at the occurrence of the alleged crime and at the arrest.

In deciding whether to require an informant's identity to be revealed to the defendant, courts generally make a detailed inquiry into the facts. The primary issue concerns whether the informant really falls into the category of a material witness. If the witness has been an active and "hands on" participant in the offense, the prosecution will almost always have to reveal the identity of the witness because identity will be crucial to the development of

---

[209] United States v. Smith, 2005 U.S. Dist. LEXIS 3782 (E.D. Pa. 2005).

[210] United States v. Harrison, 2005 U.S. Dist. LEXIS 6195 (E.D. Pa. 2005).

[211] Roviaro v. United States, 353 U.S. 53, 77 S. Ct. 623, 1 L. Ed. 2d 639 (1957).

a defense. However, if the informant has been primarily an observer who conveyed information and did not actively participate in the offense, the witness probably will not be labeled an essential witness for the defense and will not be deemed a material witness. The usual burden rests with the defendant to demonstrate the materiality of the witness. He or she must provide more evidence than mere speculation that the witness possessed a greater degree of involvement.[212] Most courts conduct a rough balancing test, weighing the public's interest in obtaining necessary information against the individual defendant's right to prepare a defense without undue impediment. Once a court has made a decision not to require the identity of a confidential informant to be revealed, the decision is normally reviewed under an abuse of discretion standard, and infrequently will be reversed.

In order to obtain the identity of confidential informants, the criminal defendant bears the burden of demonstrating the need for disclosure. In one federal prosecution for distributing controlled substances, the defendant contended that he needed to know the identity of the confidential informant to whom he had allegedly sold drugs. Because the informant was the sole witness to the alleged transaction and the defendant alleged that he had no knowledge of the crime whatsoever, the identity of the informant was crucial to the construction of a defense. When the defendant's need was balanced against the government's desire to encourage future confidential informants and the chance of harm to the particular informant, the identity must be disclosed, according to the district court. In this case, the fact that the informant was a material witness to the alleged crime necessitated the release of his identity.[213]

Because the general rule holds that the identity of governmental informants may be privileged, the burden is on the party seeking to overcome the privilege claim to establish that the party's interests substantially outweigh any governmental secrecy interest.[214]

If a court decides that disclosure of the informant's identity has been shown to be essential to the defense when a failure to reveal the identity would harm the presentation of a defense, or that the informant was a participant in the crime charged, or that the informant's testimony may be crucial to determining guilt or innocence, the informant's identity must yield to the defendant's need for the evidence.[215] At this point, the government must choose between revealing the informant's name—thereby risking his or her safety and its own investigative efficacy—and forfeiting the informant's testimony. The privilege not to reveal the identity of confidential informants belongs to the governmental authority, whether state or federal, not to the informant, and thus only the prosecution has the power to waive the privilege.

---

[212] Carpenter v. Lock, 257 F.3d 775, 2001 U.S. App. LEXIS 15918 (8th Cir. 2001), *cert. denied*, 534 U.S. 1091, 122 S. Ct. 834, 151 L. Ed. 2d 714, 2002 U.S. LEXIS 394 (2002).

[213] United States v. Harrison, 2005 U.S. Dist. LEXIS 6195 (E.D. PA. 2005).

[214] State v. Williams, 925 So. 2d 567, 573, 2006 La. App. LEXIS 593 (2006).

[215] State v. Francis, 2003 Conn. Super. LEXIS 757 (2003).

§ 10.8 State Secrets and Other Official Information

Sovereign governments all need, have, and use information that would have negative effects if the data were openly revealed. Covert intelligence operations, state-of-the-art weapons systems, and diplomatic and military information can all be, at some levels, considered secret matters. In an early case, the executor of the estate of a United States spy sued to recover money allegedly owed under a contract to the estate due to the deceased's espionage work for President Lincoln against the Confederate States of America. The Court of Claims dismissed the case because it believed that the work under the contract was a secret service and that the facts surrounding the contract and its results were to be clandestinely secured and privately communicated. Public policy required that the case be dismissed. The Supreme Court affirmed, noting that, "[i]t may be stated as a general principle, that public policy forbids the maintenance of any suit in a court of justice, the trial of which would inevitably lead to the disclosure of matters which the law itself regards as confidential, and respecting which it will not allow the confidence to be violated."[216]

Recognizing the importance of governmental privilege to withhold sensitive information, the draft of Rule 509(b) of the Federal Rules of Evidence, provided that:

> The government has a privilege to refuse to give evidence and to prevent any person from giving evidence upon a showing of reasonable likelihood of danger that the evidence will disclose a secret of state or official information, as defined in this rule.[217]

The rule defined state secret as "a governmental secret relating to the national defense or the international relations of the United States." It defined official information as "information within the custody or control of a department or agency of the government, the disclosure of which is shown to be contrary to the public interest." While the privilege originally embraced only military secrets, courts now recognize that state secrets include all types of "information that would result in 'impairment of the nation's defense capabilities, disclosure of intelligence-gathering methods or capabilities, and disruption of diplomatic relations with foreign governments.' "[218]

This principle, which protects military and state secrets, was described as "well-established in the law of evidence" in the landmark case of *United States v. Reynolds*.[219] In this case, there were fatalities when a B-29 test aircraft

---

[216] Totten v. United States, 92 U.S. 105, 107, 1875 U.S. LEXIS 1732 (1875).

[217] The draft of the rule was prepared by the United States Supreme Court but never adopted by Congress.

[218] Molerio v. FBI, 242 U.S. App. D.C. 137, 749 F.2d 815, 820–21 (D.C. Cir. 1984) (quoting Ellsberg v. Mitchell, 228 U.S. App. D.C. 225, 709 F.2d 51, 57 (D.C. Cir. 1983)).

[219] 345 U.S. 1, 1953 U.S. LEXIS 2329 (1953).

crashed while on a secret test mission that included civilians. The surviving family members sued for damages under the Federal Tort Claims Act. As part of their proof, they wanted a copy of the accident investigation report, among other documents. The Air Force claimed a national secrets privilege that the courts ultimately upheld under a clearly deferential approach to the federal government's assertions. In adjudicating the claim of a state secrets privilege, the court held that:

> The privilege belongs to the Government and must be asserted by it; it can neither be claimed nor waived by a private party. It is not to be lightly invoked. There must be a formal claim of privilege, lodged by the head of the department which has control over the matter, after actual personal consideration by that officer. The court itself must determine whether the circumstances are appropriate for the claim of privilege, and yet do so without forcing a disclosure of the very thing the privilege is designed to protect.[220]

The plaintiff's claim of necessity was lessened when the Air Force offered to reveal the accident report and related information, but not the secret details of the equipment and the mission of the aircraft. The Supreme Court upheld the validity of the governmental secrets claim of privilege under these circumstances.[221]

The policy basis of the rule is the desirability of encouraging complete candor among executive department employees to discuss secret governmental operations with respect to their exchange of views within the executive branch of the federal government. Moreover, the state secrets privilege is consistent with the Freedom of Information Act.[222]

In order for the privilege to be allowed under the rule stated and under the general laws of evidence, the government must make a claim of a state secrets privilege and demonstrate a need for protecting the secret or other official information. The judge, in an in camera session, may require a showing of the entire text of the government's statements before granting the privilege. Then, if the privilege is successfully claimed by the government, the effect of such claim makes evidence unavailable as though the witness had died or claimed the privilege against self-incrimination.[223]

In pointing out the importance of the privilege, the United States Court of Appeals for the District of Columbia Circuit indicated that a ranking of the various privileges recognized in our courts would be a delicate undertaking at best, but that it is quite clear that the privilege to protect state secrets must head

---

[220] *Id.* at 7.

[221] United States v. Reynolds, 345 U.S. 1, 1953 U.S. LEXIS 2329 (1953).

[222] 5 U.S.C. § 552(a) and (b) (Matthew Bender 2009). The Freedom of Information Act (FOIA) and the Privacy Act contain exceptions for classified information. 5 U.S.C. § 552(b)(1) (FOIA); 5 U.S.C. § 552a(k) (Privacy Act).

[223] For a further discussion of the self-incrimination protection, *see* Chapter 16.

that list.[224] In another case, a Fifth Circuit Court of Appeals decision stated that "to the extent that the documents withheld are internal working papers in which opinions are expressed, policies are formulated, and actions are recommended, they are privileged."[225] However, the court went on to say that to the extent that the documents contain purely factual material in a form that can be separated without compromising the privileged portions of the document, the material is not privileged and is subject to discovery.

The state secrets privilege covers matters that, if revealed, might threaten military operations or diplomatic interests of the United States and are absolutely shielded from revelation. The privilege includes a prohibition on revelation of covert operations of intelligence agencies or their future operational plans. The privilege belongs to the federal government, which is the only entity permitted to assert or waive the privilege. The process to assert a state secrets claim begins with the agency or department that has responsibility for the area covered by the request. According to *United States v. Reynolds*:

> There must be a formal claim of [the state secrets] privilege, lodged by the head of the department which has control over the matter, after actual personal consideration by that officer. The court itself must determine whether the circumstances are appropriate for the claim of privilege, and yet do so without forcing a disclosure of the very thing the privilege is designed to protect.[226]

While there should be extreme deference given to the executive department that asserts a privilege, the difficult task is to determine whether the claimed privilege would harm the interests asserted without giving away the secret while at the same time protecting national security. The most strongly articulated need for the information will not, according to the Reynolds case, overcome a properly pled government claim of absolute privilege.

A claim of government secrets privilege arose when a covert Central Intelligence Agency Operations Officer sued the Central Intelligence Agency, its director, and 10 unnamed employees under Title VII of the Civil Rights Act that he had experienced unlawful discriminatory practices at the hands of CIA management and that job expectations of him were much higher than that for white CIA agents. The federal government moved to dismiss the case, citing the state secret privilege. The federal district court conducted a hearing to determine the validity of the government's state secrets contention. Following a thorough review of the merits of each side, the court determined that in order for the plaintiff properly to pursue the racial discrimination case, he would have to disclose the nature of his employment and the place of his employment, as well as similar information about fellow employees, including their

---

[224]　Halkin v. Helms, 598 F.2d 1 (D.C. Cir. 1978).

[225]　Branch v. Phillips Petroleum Co., 638 F.2d 873 (5th Cir. 1981).

[226]　*Reynolds*, 345 U.S. at 8.

duty stations. In fact, the names of most of his superiors were classified, which would have rendered proof of discrimination by comparing positions and duties a breach of national security. Because the court held that divulging government secrets would have been crucial to the deciding the core factual questions in the case, the state secrets doctrine compelled dismissal of the case.[227]

In another government secrets case that involved the Central Intelligence Agency, a married couple who had served as spies for the United States in their country of origin filed a suit that alleged the government had defaulted on its promises of financial assistance and support in exchange for their spying activities during the Cold War. The couple alleged that the CIA had eventually permitted them to reside in the United States, providing support for many years, but gradually reduced the support level as the couple's income rose. When the husband lost his job and was precluded from taking some jobs due to CIA requirements, they alleged that the government would no longer live up to its bargain to support them for life. Two lower courts allowed the suit to continue on the theory that the government secrets privilege did not apply, but the Supreme Court, citing the post-Civil War *Totten*[228] case, reversed on the theory that public policy prevents suits based on covert espionage agreements between the federal government and individuals.[229] Even if all the allegations were true, there is no remedy where state secrets would have to be revealed.

According to settled legal theory, when the federal government validly asserts the state secrets privilege to prevent the release of information during pretrial discovery or the release of any information that, if disclosed, would adversely affect national security, the privilege is absolute.[230] One government secrets case involved allegations that might form the plot of a thriller movie. In a suit against the Central Intelligence Agency (CIA) and its former director, George Tenet, among other defendants, plaintiff Khaled El-Masri, a German national of Lebanese descent, contended that he was abducted by Macedonian agents while attempting to cross the border between Serbia and Macedonia.[231] Following his abduction, El-Masri alleged that Macedonian authorities imprisoned him for 23 days in order to question him concerning his relationship with Al Qaeda. He contended that he was tortured prior to being flown to Kabul, Afghanistan, under CIA control. Prior to the flight to Kabul, he was sodomized, blindfolded, shackled, and drugged. El-Masri claims he was tortured in a small, cold cell under the control of the CIA. He alleged that he was held for four months, during which time he was interrogated about his alleged association with Mohammed Atta, one of the 9/11 terrorist pilots. During one of his hunger strikes, the CIA, he alleges, force-fed him with a tube in his throat.

---

[227]   Sterling v. Tenet, 416 F.3d 338, 341, 2005 U.S. App. LEXIS 15945 (4th Cir. 2005).

[228]   *See* Totten v. United States, 92 U.S. 105, 107, 1875 U.S. LEXIS 1732 (1875), in which secret spy contracts were deemed unenforceable based on state secrets and public policy.

[229]   Tenet v. Doe, 544 U.S. 1, 3, 2005 U.S. LEXIS 2202 (2005).

[230]   *See* Ellsberg v. Mitchell, 228 U.S. App. D.C. 225, 709 F.2d 51, 56 (D.C. Cir. 1983).

[231]   *See* El-Masri v. Tenet, et al., 2006 U.S. Dist. LEXIS 34577 (E.D. Va. 2006).

He claimed that when the CIA realized he was not the right person, the CIA eventually had him taken to Albania and released on the side of a road. All of this mistreatment and some injuries, El-Masri alleged, came at the hands of the CIA or its associates which prompted him to sue the head of the CIA, Director Tenet, and other unknown CIA agents under a variety of legal theories. He filed his suit in a federal district court that had jurisdiction for civil actions by non-citizens for torts committed in violation of the law of nations or in violation of a treaty of the United States. The United States government intervened in the suit and asserted a state secrets privilege and filed a motion to dismiss the suit. Once the federal government invoked the claim that the state secrets were endangered, the district court had to decide whether the proper official had invoked the privilege and then determine whether the government's assertion qualified as a state secret. According to the district court, the judiciary must not blindly accept the government's assertion at face value, but should independently determine whether the alleged government secrets claim deserves the protection of the privilege. Where the claim, if exposed, would harm the military or national defense, the claim will be accepted without requiring additional investigation. In this case, the government contended that damage to national security could result if the government or the defendants were required to participate in pretrial discovery to admit or deny El-Masri's allegations. Because there was no way to try this case without exposing state secrets, the claim had to be denied and the case dismissed.[232] The result may not deliver justice to the individual litigant, but the larger picture of governmental security will not be compromised by allowing government secrets to be divulged.

If a court recognizes the privilege in a particular case and the privilege serves to exclude evidence that may bear directly upon a substantive defense in a criminal case, it may be necessary to dismiss the case in the defendant's favor.[233]

When the federal government makes an allegation that evidence that a party wants to introduce, or discover, involves a sensitive state secret, the judge should consider whether the proper official invoked the privilege and whether the allegation could conceivably endanger a crucial government interest. Where the judge is convinced that the claim has been properly made and appears to be valid, the proceeding will have to be dismissed if the evidence was critical to the legal action contemplated. When a court holds that the government secrets privilege applies, it is absolute.

§ 10.9 News Media–Informant Privilege

In the absence of a statute or court ruling, a news gatherer possesses no privilege to refuse to divulge sources of information to courts, grand juries,

---

[232] *Id.*
[233] United States v. Andolschek, 142 F.2d 503 (2d Cir. 1944).

and other official governmental bodies. As part of their jobs, members of the print and broadcast media and Internet news outlets and bloggers often find themselves in situations that may inform them of facts and evidence that ordinary members of the public would not likely discover. Some of this data makes its way to newspapers, news magazines, or to the broadcast arena, but due to space and interest limitations, some of the news is never publicly disseminated. Internet bloggers, Twitterers, and posters of YouTube-type snippets are the newest arrivals to the news gathering-dissemination cycle, and they are likely to have a presence in news reporter-source litigation. Electronic communication through the Internet leaves a clear trail of file metadata that is often very traceable and legally discoverable and may indicate that other information may exist that has not been uploaded. Statutes have yet to address these new phenomena and may not cover them with any privilege where the shield statute is narrowly construed. News gatherers may find that not only may the judicial system be interested in their sources but police, legislative bodies, and private tort lawyers may develop an intense interest in a particular news source. The reason frequently offered to deny any news gatherer-source privilege concerns the superior interest that the public possesses in the proper administration of the law as opposed to private accommodations that have developed between newsgatherers and their sources.[234] Consistent with the general rule that a court is entitled to everyone's evidence, the traditional position held that news gatherers should offer their facts to a court as readily as any other citizen called to give evidence. An opposite position holds that if a news reporter were required to divulge every bit of confidential information known to him or her, including news sources, to the police, prosecutors, and the courts, their sources would be reluctant to give the information necessary for the public to become informed.[235] The First Amendment[236] as applied to the states and to the federal government arguably gives, or should give, some sort of privilege or shield to gather news without revealing all sources.

In recent years, all sorts of reporters, from the national newspapers and media outlets to reporters for small weekly newsletters, have litigated hundreds of cases confronting the issue of whether a reporter has the privilege to refuse to testify concerning information acquired in connection with that person's employment. There is no common law dealing with the news media-informant privilege and earlier cases clearly demonstrated that unless a statute creates a privilege, journalists are under the same duty as every other person to testify when properly called to court or to a grand jury.[237] In developing the law relating to the news media-informant privilege, journalists have refused to testify or otherwise reveal information on the grounds that the First Amendment

---

[234] *See* 99 A.L.R.3D 37 (Updated Oct. 2005).

[235] This is the same argument that allows police to shield some informants from disclosure of their identities.

[236] Congress shall make no law . . . abridging the freedom of speech, or of the press. . . ." Constitution of the United States, Amendment I.

[237] Clein v. State, 52 So. 2d 117 (Fla. 1951).

protects such communications and that statutes enacted by the various states enhanced this theoretical First Amendment protection.

The United States Supreme Court first confronted the constitutional issue of whether a reporter has a privilege to shield confidential sources in *Branzburg v. Hayes*.[238] In that case, for which Justice White authored a plurality opinion,[239] the Court acknowledged that news gathering qualified for some First Amendment protection, but found that the First Amendment does not guarantee the press a constitutional right of special access to information not generally available to the public. As Justice White wrote in *Branzburg*:

> we cannot seriously entertain the notion that the First Amendment protects a newsman's agreement to conceal the criminal conduct of his source, or evidence thereof, on the theory that it is better to write about crime than to do something about it. Insofar as any reporter in these cases undertook not to reveal or testify about the crime he witnessed, his claim of privilege under the First Amendment presents no substantial question.[240]

Reporters receive little protection under the federal Constitution and generally must respond to grand jury subpoenas as any other witness must do, and answer a United States Attorney's questions relevant to a federal criminal investigation.

Justice Douglas in the *Branzburg* case would have found an absolute immunity absent the reporter's personal involvement in the crime. Justice Stewart, writing for himself and two other justices, would have found a qualified privilege. Thus, four justices believed that there was no reporter's privilege, three believed in a qualified privilege, and one believed in an absolute privilege. Justice Powell authored the pivotal opinion, agreeing with the four justices, thereby making a majority, but he implied that there may be a form of privilege that should be considered on a case-by-case basis.

The justices of the Supreme Court disagreed at the time this case was decided, and the judges and justices of the federal courts and state courts continue to disagree on the issue. However, Justice White in the *Branzburg* decision invited Congress and the state legislatures to create statutory reporters' privileges.

Taking Justice White's invitation seriously, more than half of the states by statute or case law have provided newsgatherers either an absolute or qualified privilege from divulging information received in confidence.[241] These statutes have been labeled "shield laws." Congress has yet to enact a federal shield law, but efforts directed toward a federal law have been introduced in

---

[238] Branzburg v. Hayes, 408 U.S. 665, 1972 U.S. LEXIS 132 (1972).
[239] For a discussion of the opinions of the various judges in the case of *Branzburg v. Hayes, see* Liggett v. Superior Court, 260 Cal. Rptr. 161 (1989).
[240] *Branzburg*, 408 U.S. at 692.
[241] *See* 38 GONZ. L. REV. 445, 450, and n. 19.

Congress.[242] State laws differ in wording and have been interpreted differently by the respective state courts.

California's shield law was first enacted in 1935. This statute has undergone many amendments, and in 1980 the evidence code section relating to the News Gatherers Shield Law was incorporated into the California Constitution.[243] The California Evidence Code provision provides in pertinent part:

> A publisher, editor, reporter or other person connected with or employed under a newspaper . . . shall not be adjudged in contempt by a judicial, legislative, administrative body or any other body . . . for refusing to disclose the source of any information procured while so connected or employed . . . or refusing to disclose any unpublished information obtained or prepared in gathering, receiving, or processing information for communication to the public.[244]

> As used in this subsection, "unpublished information" includes information not disseminated to the public by the person from whom disclosure is sought, whether or not related information has been disseminated and includes, but is not limited to all notes, out takes, photographs, tapes, or other data of whatever sort not itself disseminated to the public through a medium of communication, whether or not published information based upon or related to such material has been disseminated.[245]

In a case involving online news magazines that had gathered and published information obtained from confidential sources to a mass online audience, the owner of the information wanted to find the magazine's sources. The topic of the story involved some stolen Apple Computer trade secrets to develop and release an electronic device that would assist in making live sound recordings on Apple computers. To find out who had stolen the trade secret material, Apple sued the web site to obtain the identity of the alleged criminal. Civil subpoenas were issued to force the web site to divulge its confidential sources. Although a trial court ordered the persons to comply with the subpoena and refused to grant a protective order, an appellate court held that any subpoenas demanding unpublished information from the online magazine's owners or employees would be unenforceable. According to the appeals court, any effort to enforce the subpoenas would run afoul of identical provisions of the California Constitution and the California Rules of Evidence protecting reporters from having to divulge their secret sources and unpublished confidential material.[246]

Even in states that have shield laws, there may be limitations on the application of the laws. If a reporter or a newspaper fails to assert that the

---

[242]   *See* 14 COMM. LAW CONSPECTUS 543.
[243]   CAL. CONST. art. I, § 2, cl. (b). Amended June 3, 1980.
[244]   CAL. EVID. CODE § 1070 (a) (Matthew Bender 2008).
[245]   CAL. EVID. CODE § 1070 (c) (Matthew Bender 2008).
[246]   O'Grady v. Superior Court, 2006 Cal. App. LEXIS 802 (2006).

interview in question was conducted under a cloak of confidentiality, a motion to reveal the reporter's notes, transcriptions, memoranda, or tape-recordings may be granted. In Pennsylvania, which has a shield law that allows news organizations and their staffs to protect confidential news sources from disclosure,[247] one case involved a newspaper reporter's article about a defendant charged with murder, in which the reporter interviewed the defendant. The reporter did not obtain the information from a confidential source and the defendant told only about his own version of the shooting without implicating any confidential source. The prosecutor had no other source from which to obtain the original raw interview data offered by the defendant and could not call the defendant to the witness stand to ask him. According to the trial court, because the newspaper reporter was not covered by the shield law and its privilege, the reporter was required to testify concerning the matters related to him by the defendant.[248]

While Pennsylvania law covers confidential sources, New Jersey's law is an example of a law that has greater coverage and offers significantly more protection to the news media[249] than that of Pennsylvania. The New Jersey shield law does not require that a confidential source have been the basis or genesis of a story as long as the individual reporter has been engaged in news gathering, procuring, transmitting, compiling, editing, or disseminating news material. Reporting that is contained within a book can also qualify under the shield law protecting sources in New Jersey. In a case in which a wealthy man alleged that he had been injured because his wealth was reported in a book written by the defendants as between 150 and 250 million and not anywhere near the billions he claimed. The plaintiff claimed that the erroneous reporting of his success harmed him in his business relations with other people who thought that he was not as credit worthy. Ultimately, the motion to compel the authors to reveal their confidential sources, who were former employees of the wealthy plaintiff, was defeated under the news person shield law in New Jersey.[250]

Maryland has taken an approach midway between Pennsylvania and New Jersey in developing a news gatherer shield that protects a news reporter from revealing stories or news or information procured by the reporter/news gatherer. However, Maryland may require disclosure of news sources when a court finds that the news or significant information is relevant to a major legal issue before any judicial, legislative, or administrative body, or anybody that has the power to issue subpoenas. A requirement to divulge news or data may be ordered when the news or information cannot be obtained from any other source when there is an overriding public interest in disclosure to the court

---

247   *See* 42 PA. C. S. § 5942 Confidential communications to news reporters (2008).

248   Commonwealth of Pennsylvania v. Tyson, 2002 Pa. Super. 168, 800 A.2d 327, 2002 Pa. Super. LEXIS 1071 (2002).

249   *See* N.J. STAT. § 2A:84A-21 Newspaperman's privilege (2009).

250   *See* Trump v. O'Brien, 403 N.J. Super 281, 2008 N.J. Super. LEXIS 217 (N.J. 2008).

or other public body. The source of the news remains protected from being divulged.[251] Maryland wants the source to remain private and not to become public while requiring that important information be made public.

Vermont has taken a different route from many jurisdictions and has opted to follow the strict view that the government is entitled to every person's evidence. While the state has no statute that protects the news media with a privilege not to disclose sources, reporters were believed to possess some protections. Following a celebration that turned into a riot at the University of Vermont, the police and prosecutor's office became aware that a television station had significant video footage taken at the crime scene. A local court issued a subpoena against the television station to produce the footage so that police could attempt to identify the individual vandals for prosecution. The trial court held that the reporters, even in the absence of statute, held a qualified privilege that could be overcome by the prosecution if it could demonstrate: (1) that the materials sought were material to a person's guilt or innocence and (2) that the identities of the vandals could be found from no other source. Relevancy was virtually a given, but because the government failed to demonstrate that alternative efforts would not produce the desired evidence, the trial court held that the television station and its reporters did not have to give their evidence to the prosecution. The Supreme Court of Vermont reversed the trial court in a resounding holding, saying:

> In the circumstances of this case, no privilege, qualified or otherwise, excuses [the station] from furnishing the videotape of the riot. Therefore, the State did not have to show that the materials were available from other sources. The facts here are essentially indistinguishable from those in *Branzburg v. Hayes*, 408 U.S. 665, 33 L. Ed. 2d 626, 92 S. Ct. 2646 (1972), in which the United States Supreme Court held that there is no constitutional privilege under the First Amendment that excuses reporters from appearing and testifying before grand juries investigating criminal conduct, even if the source of their information is confidential.[252]

The Supreme Court of Vermont based its decision on the view that every person's evidence should be available, especially where there is a possibility of criminal conduct. It noted that a grand jury had a duty to inquire everywhere except where a bona fide privilege existed. The Supreme Court of Vermont found no privilege in common law, applicable federal statutes, or the First Amendment, so it ordered the television station to give over its videotape.

While the news media-informant privilege of the journalist's privilege remains unsettled in many jurisdictions, some understanding can be gleaned from a review of two inconsistent recent cases. A federal court held that a

---

[251] MD. CODE ANN. § 9–112, Courts and Judicial Proceedings (Matthew Bender 2008).

[252] In re Inquest Subpoena (WCAX), 2005 Vt. 103, 890 A.2d 1240, 1241, 2005 Vt. LEXIS 244 (2005).

reporter did not have to reveal telephone numbers of sources who may have "leaked" information that the federal government was interested in particular Islamic charity organizations. The court noted that the reporters and their sources had placed reliance on their confidential relationships when nationally important matters were being investigated. The district court balanced the First Amendment rights given to a free press and the interests of the government under the situation and held that the balance tipped toward maintaining the secrecy of confidential news sources, even though there is no federal news gatherer-source privilege.[253] In a case that held public attention for a long time in which reporters were held in contempt of court for refusing to testify concerning their alleged confidential sources that related to the "leaking" of the identity of a CIA operative, Valerie Plame, reporters lost their legal arguments to establish a reporter's federal privilege. The case had political overtones and reached into the Office of the Vice President of the United States. The litigants contended that the First Amendment gave them a privilege not to reveal sources and confidential material and that they had a common law privilege, among other theories. The Court of Appeals for the District of Columbia circuit rejected their contentions completely and, relying on the Supreme Court's decision in *Branzburg v. Hayes*, upheld their contempt citations. As the Court of Appeals noted, "The Supreme Court in no uncertain terms rejected the existence of such a privilege. As we said at the outset of this discussion, the Supreme Court has already decided the First Amendment issue before us today."[254] With two differing decisions coming from federal courts in two different circuits, the Supreme Court of the United States may decide to resolve differences and reaffirm that there is no federal reporter confidential source privilege in the First Amendment or elsewhere.

§ 10.10 Summary

In arriving at the truth in a criminal trial, all evidence that helps prove or disprove an important point or issue should be admitted. However, our society holds that some relationships deserve protection and privileges that hide the truth have developed. In making the judgment that particular relationships should receive protection, the legislatures and courts have attempted to strike a fair balance between the need for evidence and the protection to be given to important relationships. In resolving these two considerations, courts and legislatures have developed rules limiting the admission of some types of evidence, while other jurisdictions prefer admission of evidence. In some situations, there are occasions when the protection of the relationship or right is considered more important than the need for the evidence, even when it may create an injustice to another person.

---

[253] New York Times v. Gonzales, 382 F. Supp. 2d 457, 2005 U.S. Dist. LEXIS 2642 (2005).

[254] In re Grand Jury Subpoena (Miller), 365 U.S. App. D.C. 13, 397 F.3d 964, 2005 U.S. App. LEXIS 2494 (2005).

An early privilege that developed over a period of many years is the husband-wife confidential communication privilege. The general rule relating to confidential communications between husband and wife is that testimony pertaining to confidential communications arising out of the marital relationship is forever privileged and a court will not require the conversations to be revealed unless both parties agree to do so. However, there are several exceptions to this rule where crimes have been committed against family members or their property or the case involves divorce or child custody. With respect to the marital testimonial privilege, the clear trend is to remove the defendant spouse as a holder and permit the potential witness-spouse to decide whether to testify against the other. This procedure makes sense if the relationship between the two spouses is such that there is no longer any harmony or interest in preserving the marriage. Under current interpretations, the marital testimonial privilege prevents a witness spouse from being forced to testify against the defendant spouse, but this privilege endures only as long as the marriage remains in existence.

A second common law privilege protects communications between attorney and client. Confidential communications made in the course of professional employment may not be divulged by the attorney without the client's consent. The privilege may not be claimed when the communication concerns the commission of a crime at some time in the future or how to cover up a prior crime. The client holds the privilege, and he or she may waive the privilege even if the attorney does not agree.

Although at common law there was no physician-patient privilege, most states have enacted statutes creating this testimonial privilege but many do not apply this privilege in criminal cases. Where statutes have been enacted, the privilege prohibits disclosure by the physician and allied support staff, when called to testify, of confidential communications made to him or her or information acquired by him or her, in the course of his or her professional attendance upon the patient. The privilege does not apply when a statute requires reports of gunshot wounds or wounds inflicted by deadly weapons. The privilege generally applies in civil cases when the disclosures were made in confidence, but some states allow medical privileges to be claimed in criminal cases. The patient must claim the privilege and only the patient may grant a waiver.

At common law, there was no privilege as to communications or confessions to a spiritual adviser but all 50 states now recognize the privilege. The clergy member, priest or rabbi may not disclose, over the objection of the party so confiding, the confessions or admissions made as a part of the practice of the particular church. In order for the communication to be privileged under the statutes, it must be made to the clergy member in a professional capacity. Generally, the privilege may be claimed only by the communicator, but the issue may be raised by the priest or rabbi.

One privilege that is of great concern to criminal justice personnel is the confidential informant privilege. It can be said that, as a general rule, the name of the informant does not have to be disclosed, especially if his or her information relates only to facts from which probable cause can be based. However, if the informant played an integral part in the illegal transaction and his or her disclosure is necessary and relevant to a fair defense, his or her identity may be required to be disclosed. Much discretion in this regard is in the hands of the judge when making a determination concerning whether an informant meets the requirements of a material witness.

Testimony relating to state secrets and other official information is sometimes privileged upon a showing of a reasonable likelihood of danger that the evidence will disclose state secrets or official information. Where this privilege is upheld, it is absolute.

The United States Supreme Court has determined that, in the absence of statutes, communications to a newspaper editor or reporter are not privileged in federal courts. In states recognizing the privilege, some courts apply a balancing test that focuses on the need for the information and potential availability from other sources. If collateral sources make the information available, the news media privilege will likely prevail. More than half of the states, by statute or otherwise, have enacted news media privilege laws that attempt to resolve conflicting interests.

Because of the common law privileges, as well as the statutory privileges, it is possible that much relevant evidence may be excluded from trials. However, there are many exceptions that permit much valuable evidence to be obtained, if criminal justice personnel are familiar with the rules and the exceptions.

Courts and legislatures frequently alter the confidential communication privilege rules in order to prevent abuse and to effectuate fair public policy. Changes in evidence rules and laws dictate that law enforcement officials consult the rules of evidence and state case law with a view to ascertaining changes that will affect the practice of criminal justice.

Opinions and Expert Testimony

11

Opinion evidence, to be of any value, should be based either upon admitted facts or upon facts, within the knowledge of the witness, disclosed in the record. Opinion evidence that does not appear to be based upon disclosed facts is of little or no value.

Balaban & Katz Corp. v. Commissioner of Internal Revenue,
30 F.2d 807 (7th Cir. 1929)

Chapter Outline

Section
11.1   Introduction
11.2   Definitions and Distinctions
11.3   Admissibility of Nonexpert Opinions
11.4   Subjects of Nonexpert Opinions
11.5   Opinions of Experts
11.6   Qualifications of an Expert
11.7   Selection of Expert Witness
11.8   Examination of Expert Witness
11.9   Cross-Examination of Expert Witness
11.10   Subjects of Expert Testimony
11.11   Experts from Crime Laboratories
11.12   Summary

§ 11.1   Introduction

All humans form opinions on a variety of subjects that are based on data and information presented to individuals. Opinions are really judgments, inferences, or conclusions that help people organize their lives and create priorities. A court is generally interested in the bare facts and unadorned data that humans use to create their opinions rather that the particular opinion formed based on those raw facts. Therefore, when a witness takes the stand, the testimony is normally restricted to the basic facts and actual circumstances within the personal knowledge and recollection of the witness, as distinguished from opinions, inferences, impressions, and conclusions that the facts may have generated in the mind of the same witness. Because opinions can be considered a type of conclusion and the purpose of the jury is to reach conclusions based on the facts presented, witnesses who are not considered experts are usually restricted from offering their opinions concerning what the evidence actually means.

However, the rule that excludes opinion evidence has exceptions that are based on reason and practical necessity. Frequently the only possible or practical method of getting proof of a fact in issue is by means of opinion evidence. If, from the nature of the subject matter, no better evidence can be obtained and opinion evidence will aid the members of the jury in their search for the truth, the judge in his or her discretion may admit the evidence even though it consists of an opinion. As one court noted, "[l]ay opinion is admitted when no particular or esoteric knowledge is required or when, as a practical matter, the subject of the testimony is too complex or subtle to enable the witness to accurately convey to the trier of fact his or her observations in any reasonable form other than an opinion. ...."[1] The law does not look with favor on opinion evidence because it invades the province of the fact finder, and, in theory, such evidence should not be admitted unless it is required to prevent a miscarriage of justice.

Over the years, courts and legislatures have approved dozens of exceptions to the opinion evidence rule—to the extent that some opinion evidence is admissible in almost every case. These rules of exception have developed in two areas: (1) opinions of nonexpert or lay witnesses and (2) opinions of expert witnesses. The rules of evidence treat lay witnesses differently from expert witnesses because lay witnesses are typically discouraged from offering opinions while expert witnesses generally are called to offer opinion evidence.

Occasionally criminal justice personnel testify as expert witnesses when they possess a particular expertise such as familiarity with drug transaction protocols, serial killer profiles, or fingerprint comparisons. However, in most instances criminal justice personnel testify as lay witnesses because they offer testimony covering facts within their personal knowledge, observation, or recollection. There is no bright line between lay and expert testimony because every person evaluates information based on individual experiences. Even a lay witness is capable of expressing opinions outside the normal knowledge held by most people without having to be qualified as an expert. When a juror may not fully understand the evidence or not be able to come to a conclusion concerning a fact at issue without the assistance of a person with specialized knowledge, that witness must then be qualified as an expert witness.[2]

The goals of this chapter focus on the general rules related to admissibility of lay opinion evidence and on the protocols required for the use of expert witnesses.[3] The chapter details some of the specific instances that are commonly presented in criminal justice situations and discusses some of the more common rules governing the admission of opinion evidence in criminal cases.

§ 11.2   Definitions and Distinctions

Before discussing the general rules and the exceptions related to opinion testimony of expert and nonexpert witnesses, some definitions are necessary to understand these rules.

A. Opinion Evidence

Opinion evidence is defined in *Black's Law Dictionary*[4] as a "witness's belief, thought, or inference, or conclusion concerning a fact or facts." The term

---

[1]   People v. Sneed, 2007 Cal. App. Unpub. LEXIS10270 (Cal. 2007).

[2]   Williams v. State, 2006 Tex. App. LEXIS 1687 (2006) quoting Osbourn v. State, 92 S.W.3d 531, 537 (Tex. Crim. App. 2002). *See* case in Part II.

[3]   *See* 2005 UTAH L. REV. 230 (2005) for a note that clarifies the distinction between lay and expert witnesses with respect to their proper subject matter.

[4]   BLACK'S LAW DICTIONARY (8th ed. 2004).

refers to opinions offered by witnesses while testifying in open court and is distinguished from extrajudicial opinions.

B. Expert Witness

An expert witness is particularly skilled, learned, or experienced in a particular art, science, trade, business, profession, or vocation, and has gained a thorough knowledge of a subject that is not possessed by the average layperson. *Black's Law Dictionary*[5] defines an expert witness as a "witness qualified by knowledge, skill, experience, training, or education to provide a scientific, technical, or other specialized opinion about the evidence or a fact issue." In one case, an expert witness was defined as one who has acquired the ability to deduce correct inferences from hypothetically stated facts or from facts involving scientific or technical knowledge.[6]

C. Nonexpert Witness

A nonexpert, or lay witness, is one who is not particularly skilled, learned, or experienced in the particular area that is at issue in the court, but who may have knowledge that an average person possesses about many of the things involved in everyday life. A person who is an expert in one field may be considered to be a lay witness when he or she takes the stand to testify about a field in which the witness can claim no expertise. The lay witness bases his or her conclusions on facts personally observed, while the expert witness, who must qualify as such by establishing that he or she has some special skill, knowledge, or experience, may base his or her opinions on facts of his or her own observation or on evidence presented by other witnesses. The lay witness may offer opinions concerning matters about which the average person forms opinions. For example, "[i]t is generally accepted that virtually any lay witness, including a police officer, may testify as to whether an individual appears intoxicated."[7] Similarly, a lay witness may offer testimony concerning the identity of a person.[8] The line between lay and expert testimony is not always easy to discern and the same witness may offer some evidence as a lay witness and also offer evidence as an expert.[9]

---

[5]   Black's Law Dictionary (8th ed. 2004).

[6]   City of Chicago v. Lehmann, 262 Ill. 468, 104 N.E. 829 (1914). "Expert witness" will be further defined in later sections of this chapter.

[7]   State v. Clark, 2007 Ohio 3777, 2007 Ohio App. LEXIS 3442 (Ohio 2007).

[8]   United States v. Beck, 418 F.3d 1008, 2005 U.S. App. LEXIS 16713 (9th Cir. 2005).

[9]   United States v. Ayala-Pizarro, 407 F.3d 25, 2005 U.S. LEXIS 8322 (1st Cir. 2005). *See* State v. Streckfuss, 171 N.C. App. 81; 2005 LEXIS 1190 (2005), in which a police officer was permitted to identify the smell of alcohol and give a lay opinion that the defendant driver was alcohol impaired.

§ 11.3 Admissibility of Nonexpert Opinions

Rule 701

Opinion Testimony by Lay Witnesses

If the witness is not testifying as an expert, the witness' testimony in the form of opinions or inferences is limited to those opinions or inferences which are (a) rationally based on the perception of the witness, and (b) helpful to a clear understanding of the witness' testimony or the determination of a fact in issue, and (c) not based on scientific, technical, or other specialized knowledge within the scope of Rule 702.[10]

Although subject to many exceptions, the general rule provides that "nonexpert" or lay witnesses must state facts or offer evidence based upon their personal knowledge and observations. With some exceptions, lay witnesses cannot give conclusions or opinions, but this rule is tempered by the fact that many items of evidence that could be considered opinions may not be viewed as such through the eyes of the law. For example, when a person testifies as to what he or she observes, hears, or smells, the testimony may be considered a statement of fact and not a conclusion or opinion—even though the statement is actually an opinion of what he or she saw, heard, or smelled.[11] Much effort has been expended to confine the testimony of witnesses to statements of what they saw, heard, or otherwise observed, as distinguished from inferences or opinions formed as a result of such observations. The legal distinction between opinion and fact has not been characterized as a bright line, but can be viewed as shades of gray. For example, one person may testify that the color of a swimming pool was blue while another might refer to the same pool as having an aqua color. Both persons probably view their respective characterizations of color as fact rather than realizing that each one has testified concerning their opinion of the color of the pool.

Despite occasional appellate disputes about whether it was proper for a lay witness to give an opinion[12] or whether the opinion offered by a particular witness should have been preceded by testimony establishing the witness's qualifications as an expert, the modern trend appears to allow more lay opinion to be introduced. As one court noted, "a lay witness can give opinion testimony if the witness' opinion is rationally based on such witness' perception and it is helpful in providing a clear understanding of the testimony of the witness or a determination of a fact at issue."[13] A trial court has broad discretion

---

[10] FED. R. EVID. 701.

[11] *See* Livingston v. Texas, 2006 Tex. App. LEXIS 2234 (2006), in which an appellate court upheld the trial court ruling that permitted a lay witness to testify concerning the identity of odors emanating from a boat that smelled "like cigarettes, stale beer, and sweaty sex."

[12] People v. Souva, 2005 Colorado App. LEXIS 1615 (2005).

[13] Ohio v. Zentner, 2003 Ohio App. LEXIS 2185 (2003).

on the admission of lay witness testimony and a judge's decision will only be disturbed on appeal for an abuse of discretion.[14] As one Texas court noted, "the opinions of lay witnesses, when competent, are admissible concerning estimates of age, size, weight, quantity, time, distance and speed of persons and things."[15] However, when a lay witness clearly crosses the line to offer testimony that requires special expertise, courts tend to prevent the lay witness from giving testimony that is beyond the competency of the witness.[16]

The lay witness may state a relevant opinion if it is: (1) based the original perception of the witness; (2) generally helpful to the finder of fact to obtain a clear understanding of the issues; and (3) not based on the types of evidence that are reserved for expert testimony.[17] The general rule is that as a condition of stating his or her opinion, the witness must state the facts on which such opinion is based, but if the basis is mentioned on direct examination, the witness will be required to offer it if asked on cross-examination. The enumeration of facts not only goes to show the competency of the witness, but also provides an opportunity to test the reasonableness of the inference, because a witness will not be permitted to state an opinion that is inconsistent with or finds no support in the facts.

The purpose of allowing a lay witness to testify concerning his or her opinion is to help the jury or fact finder obtain a clear understanding of the testimony or to help decide a fact at issue. However, opinion testimony may be admissible in some jurisdictions only after a showing that the witness's perceptions cannot adequately be conveyed except through opinions.[18] To allow opinion testimony absent a showing of the inadequacy of other means of expression may invade the province of the jury. This principle was succinctly explained by a Washington court, which held that a witness, whether lay or expert, may not offer an opinion concerning the defendant's guilt, whether by a direct statement or by inference, as such testimony is inherently prejudicial because it invaded the role reserved for the jury.[19] Courts generally hold that neither a lay nor an expert witness may testify as to the guilt of a defendant, even by inference, and such comments directly or indirectly are prohibited.[20] However, some courts allow lay witnesses to come dangerously close to offering an opinion concerning the ultimate issue. In a Texas case, the trial court properly permitted a lay witness to offer opinion evidence on the issue of whether a defendant properly used deadly force to protect another person,[21] an issue that went to the core of the case.

---

[14]   Colorado v. Caldwell, 43 P.3d 663, 667, 2001 Colo. App. LEXIS 1514 (2001).

[15]   Scott v. State, 2008 Tex. App. LEXIS 6172 (Tex. 2008).

[16]   See State v. Nobach, 2002 Mont. 91, 309 Mont. 342, 46 P.3d 618, 2002 Mont. LEXIS 189 (2002).

[17]   FED. R. EVID. 701.

[18]   Kight v. State, 512 So. 2d 922 (Fla. 1987).

[19]   State v. Thompson, 950 P.2d 977 (Wash. 1998).

[20]   Washington v. Olmedo, 112 Wash. App. 525, 531, 49 P.3d 960, 963, 2002 Wash. App. LEXIS 1705 (2002).

[21]   Garcia v. State, 2005 Tex. App. LEXIS 4424 (2005).

Even if the lay witness can describe some of the circumstances that led to an opinion, the witness may still give an opinion even when it is difficult to articulate all of the factors. For example, in a theft case in a retail store, a loss prevention security guard was permitted to offer lay opinion evidence concerning whether the defendant intended to deprive Wal-Mart of its property. While a lay witness cannot possess personal knowledge of what another person may be thinking, she may possess personal knowledge of facts from which an opinion regarding the mental state of another person may be drawn. The opinion offered by the lay witness in this theft case was based on her personal perceptions and observations and her opinion was rationally based on knowledge of the events observed.[22]

Apparently extending the use of opinion evidence by nonexpert witnesses, Federal Rule of Evidence 701(b) allows opinions or inferences if they are merely "helpful" to clarify the witness's testimony or to aid in the determination of a factual issue. With the addition of 701(c) in 2000, the lay witness may now offer an opinion as long as it is not based on scientific or specialized knowledge traditionally covered by expert testimony. For example, in a major drug trafficking case, a police officer was properly permitted to testify about his deciphering of a phone book, ledgers, and a date book to match customers with drug amounts purchased and money owed. The officer did some low-level deciphering of the books but did not embark on code breaking or sophisticated analysis to figure the meaning of the books. The court held that the testimony of the police officer constituted lay testimony for which no special foundation or expertise was necessary.[23] The 2000 amendment to Rule 701 may broaden the circumstances under which a lay witness may give an opinion or inference based upon personal observation,[24] but limits remain on the conclusions that lay witnesses may draw. In a state case, a police officer should not have been permitted to give an opinion concerning why people slide down in their car seats when they see police cars, because a jury is fully capable of forming its own conclusion.[25]

Referring to the proper standards for admissibility of lay opinion testimony, a federal court of appeals commented that lay opinion evidence should be admissible when the witness has had sufficient contact with the facts of the case that would render a lay opinion helpful to the judge or jury. In the case, a defendant's probation officer had been permitted to identify the defendant by looking at a still picture taken by a bank's surveillance system. The probation officer had previous significant contacts with the defendant that were considered sufficient to be able to recognize a picture of his client, the accused

---

[22] Hines v. State, 2006 Tex. App. LEXIS 3256 (2006).

[23] United States v. Cano, 289 F.3d 1354, 1361, 1362, 2002 U.S. App. LEXIS 8590 (11th Cir. 2002), *cert. denied*, 2003 U.S. LEXIS 433 (2003).

[24] FED. R. EVID. 701 had subsection (c) added in 2000 and became effective December 1, 2000.

[25] State v. Clark, 136 S.W. 3d 582, 2004 Mo. App. LEXIS 904 (2004).

bank robber. The Court of Appeals for the Ninth Circuit held that a lay witness probation officer's identification testimony was properly admissible within the meaning of Rule 701, where it was based upon personal observation and recollection of concrete facts.[26]

Although allowing some lay opinion evidence, Rule 701, however, does not allow the introduction of opinion evidence when the facts are clear and the jury can draw its own conclusion from the facts that have been presented. To allow lay opinion evidence under such circumstances would present the risk that the testimony might usurp the function of the jury.[27]

While Rule 701 placed some limits on the admissibility of opinion testimony by lay witnesses, the rule did not have the effect of prohibiting an undercover police officer from testifying concerning the identity of a defendant based on several telephone conversations and from knowledge of his voice gained from personal meetings. The court permitted the officer to offer the opinion that the defendant was the person with whom the officer spoke during the telephonic initiation of several drug transactions.[28]

It is obvious that significant evidence would be unavailable to the fact finders if all lay opinion evidence were excluded from criminal trials. Examples of proper subject matter for lay opinion testimony are discussed in § 11.4.

§ 11.4   Subjects of Nonexpert Opinions

A. Age

Lay witness opinion testimony is admissible when it is rationally based on personal knowledge and helpful to the trier of fact. It is a foregone conclusion that all humans evaluate other humans with respect to age for various reasons. Competent witnesses with firsthand knowledge will generally be permitted to offer an estimate or opinion as to the age of a person[29] and a witness may give his or her age, although the age of the witness was not personally known by the witness.[30] As one court noted, where age was concerned, it was "particularly appropriate for a lay witness to express an opinion on the subject."[31]

In criminal prosecutions involving possession of child pornography, the prosecution must demonstrate that some of the actors involved are less than 18 years of age. Because many of the films seized do not leave any way to find or discover the actors and their real ages as of the date of the video recording,

---

[26] United States v. Beck, 418 F.3d 1008; 2005 U.S. App. LEXIS 16713 (2005).

[27] United States v. Reneau, 390 F.3d 746, 2004 U.S. App. LEXIS 24837 (2d Cir. 2004), *cert. denied,* 544 U.S. 1007, 2005 U.S. LEXIS 3660 (2005).

[28] United States v. Bush, 405 F.3d 909, 2005 U.S. App. LEXIS 7114 (10th Cir. 2005).

[29] Asplundh Manufacturing Company v. Benton Harbor Engineering, 57 F.3d 1190, 1201, 1202 (3d Cir 1995).

[30] State v. Selmon, 2006 Ohio 65, 2006 Ohio App. LEXIS 50 (2006).

[31] United States v. Yazzie, 976 F.2d 1252, 1256 (9th Cir. 1992).

witnesses for the prosecution will have to offer evidence concerning age. In one child pornography prosecution, the federal government used lay witnesses to date the age of the actors involved over the objection of the defendant that expert witnesses were required to offer proof of age for underage victims. The court of appeals upheld the use of lay witnesses to prove the age of child victims on the theory that lay witnesses with some specialized knowledge could offer opinion evidence concerning the ages of the children in the film where the witnesses had served as postal inspectors and possessed years of training and experience in determining the ages of video actors.[32]

Necessity often requires that the opinion of the witness as to the age of a person be used because it is often impossible to testify to the exact age of another person. For example, a North Carolina court commented:

> The opinion of a lay witness concerning the age of an accused is admissible into evidence when the witness has had adequate opportunity to observe the accused.[33]

Thus, if the witness has had adequate opportunity to observe the accused and if it is impossible to determine the exact age of the person, then opinion evidence of the lay witness concerning age is admissible. If the exact age of an individual is available from documents or the individual in question, however, the use of that evidence is generally appropriate, sufficient,[34] and preferable to estimation of age by a lay or an expert witness.

B. *Appearance*

When individuals experience exciting events, become upset, have frightening experiences, or seem scared of another person or situation, an explanation of all the outward manifestations that give rise to the conclusion that a person has experienced excitement, fear, or another emotion are not easily described by another person. How one person's demeanor appears to another is a matter well within the human experience and would not ordinarily call for expert testimony. Assuming a witness meets the requirements of competency and has personally observed another person, a court normally should admit lay testimony concerning the appearance and demeanor of another. For example, in an assault case in which a man threatened his former girlfriend with a firearm, the trial court admitted testimony of a police officer that the victim appeared "fearful" and "excited" at the time he initially encountered her. The appellate court upheld the admission of the testimony describing the

---

[32] United States v. Davis, 41 Fed. Appx. 566, 571, 2002 U.S. App. LEXIS 15312 (3d Cir. 2002), and in another pornography case, the trial court properly permitted lay testimony concerning age. *See* United States v. Nelson, 38 Fed. Appx. 386, 392 (9th Cir. 2002).

[33] State v. Cobb, 295 N.C. 1, 243 S.E.2d 759 (1978).

[34] Commonwealth of Massachusetts v. Montalvo, 50 Mass. App. Ct. 85, 88, 735 N.E.2d 391, 394, 2000 Mass. App. LEXIS 763 (2000).

victim on the theory that lay testimony can be offered when it is based on the perception of the witness (the officer) and the testimony would be helpful to a clear understanding of the witness's testimony. The officer had firsthand perception and his statements were based on direct involvement and experience in the case.[35] In a case involving felony driving under the influence, an off-duty police officer had been drinking at a bar with three friends and became intoxicated. Prior to leaving the bar, a waitress noticed the off-duty police officer and concluded that he was "obviously intoxicated." A waitress in a bar would normally have observed the effects of alcohol on human behavior and have a foundation for her opinion. The trial judge allowed the waitress to offer her opinion or conclusion to the jury over the defendant's objection. According to the appellate court, because the waitress had firsthand knowledge that would be helpful to the jury and her opinion was rationally based on her perception, the trial court properly admitted her lay opinion under Mississippi's adaptation of Rule 701.[36]

In a different case, the trial court did not commit error when it allowed a detective's testimony in an assault case to describe the defendant's physical condition at the time of the incident, he had noticed the defendant was very muscular and had calloused knuckles. This testimony was relevant because it attempted to show, through appearance, that the defendant had the strength and ability to inflict the serious injuries sustained by the victim.[37]

C. *Conduct*

A lay witness may describe the acts, conduct, and demeanor of a person under investigation if necessary to enable the jury to draw a correct inference. In such a case the witness should be required—as far as is possible—to state the facts on which he or she based his or her opinions. In a prosecution for mail fraud and extorting campaign contributions by the city treasurer, prosecution witnesses, when describing the management style and conduct of the city treasurer, went too far when they testified that they had "no doubt" and had a "personal feeling" that the manager had ordered their supervisor to prevent recalcitrant contractors from receiving future business from the city. The opinion about the treasurer's inferred decisions offered by the lay witnesses was not grounded in any perception and constituted inadmissible speculation.[38]

However, lay opinion as to the mental state of another person may be admissible in some cases. One court properly permitted several law enforcement officers to testify that the defendant "tried to kill" one of the officers involved. The reviewing court held that the lay testimony of the officers "amounted to nothing more than shorthand statements of fact based on their knowledge and

---

[35]   Washington v. Bain, 2002 Wash. App. LEXIS 1863 (2002).

[36]   George v. Mississippi, 812 So. 2d 1103, 1105, 1106, 2001 Miss. App. LEXIS 436 (2001).

[37]   State v. Ames, 950 P.2d 514 (Wash. 1998).

[38]   United States v. Santos, 201 F.3d 953, 963, 963, 2000 U.S. App. LEXIS 649 (7th Cir. 2000).

observations." The testimony of the officers had the effect of explaining their perceptions and did not directly implicate the guilt or the mental state of the defendant,[39] although the testimony seemed to clearly reflect on the intended conduct of the defendant.

An appellate court approved allowing an eyewitness to a drug-related murder testify that the reason the defendant killed her sister was because her sister sold more drugs at her location than the defendant was selling at his drug point. The witness and the defendant were heavily involved in the drug trade and understood how it operated. Because the witness was subject to intense cross-examination, the trial court was within its discretion to allow the lay opinion concerning the reason for the murder.[40] When describing conduct, the better view would be to have the witness tell what he or she observed, saw, and heard, but the rules of evidence do not preclude the use of words of opinion-description when appropriate and when the opinion does not unnecessarily invade the province of the jury.

Testimony concerning observed conduct may prove crucial when investigating a suspected intoxicated automobile driver. In a Texas case, officers conducted field sobriety tests on a subject who was asked to do a one-leg stand test and a walk-and-turn test. The trial court permitted the officers involved to offer lay testimony concerning the tests and their observations of the subject's performance involving coordination, balance, and ability to follow instructions. The tests and their results were considered grounded in the common knowledge that persons who are impaired will not normally perform well on the tests and such observation of the test taking. The appellate court held that police officers could properly testify concerning the results of routine field tests for impairment.[41] In an Ohio case, police officers observed several subjects around a pickup truck and one man on the sidewalk leaning inside the vehicle. One officer testified that from the time of day, the location, the number of people around the vehicle, and considering the defendant's actions and hand movements, the officer believed that a drug transaction was taking place. The appellate court approved of the officers' testimony about the defendant's activities and agreed that they could properly offer their lay opinion that they believed a narcotics deal was being concluded.[42]

A Montana appellate court upheld a trial court decision that permitted police officers to offer lay opinions concerning whether the defendant possessed methamphetamine for the purposes of sale. According to the officers, based on their experience, the quantity of illegal drugs the defendant was carrying indicated possession with the intent to distribute. The officers testified concerning their training, experience, and knowledge of the manner that

[39] State v. McVay, 620 S.E.2d 883, 2005 N.C. App. LEXIS 2402 (2005).

[40] United States v. Vega-Figueroa, 234 F.3d 744, 755, 2000 U.S. App. LEXIS 32127 (1st Cir. 2000).

[41] Plouff v. State, 2006 Tex. App. LEXIS 2546 (2006).

[42] State v. Farrow, 2005 Ohio 3005, 2005 Ohio App. LEXIS 2799 (2005).

methamphetamine was typically distributed. The appellate court held that the testimony was rationally based on their perceptions and helped convey a clear understanding of the facts in the case.[43] In a Texas case, involving a similar rationale, the court upheld the admissibility of a detective's lay opinion that a quantity of methamphetamine was being held for purposes of sale because scales, packaging materials, and a large amount of money were present at the defendant's place of residence.[44]

While the recent trend has been to permit more lay opinion testimony, many courts still place some limitations on the use of lay opinion, especially where the testimony leans clearly toward being classified as expert testimony. In a Second Circuit case, where investigators listened to wiretaps of numerous suspects thought to be involved in the drug trade and offered their conclusions and opinions concerning the wiretap and other criminal activity to the court, such testimony was beyond the scope of lay testimony. The court rejected the prosecution's contention that the officer was offering testimony that would be helpful to the jury and concluded that the opinion offered usurped the role of the jury and should not have been admitted at trial.[45]

D. *Distance and Space*

In criminal cases it is often necessary to elicit testimony concerning location, distances, and space between objects. While it is preferable to introduce evidence to show exact distances, in some cases this is not practical, and opinion evidence becomes necessary. As a result, an ordinary witness may give his or her estimate of distances, provided that he or she is cognizant of the facts on which the estimate is based. The lay witnesses must have a sound foundation for offering an opinion concerning the speed of a vehicle. An appellate court approved a lower court's decision not to allow minor nondriver eyewitnesses, ages 10 and 13, respectively, to offer opinions about the actual speed of a truck immediately prior to a collision[46] but a federal district court allowed teenaged girls to give testimony concerning the speed of a vehicle even though they had little experience in driving motor vehicles.[47] In a more appropriate context involving the speed of a vehicle, courts have held that police officers, testifying as lay witnesses, may offer opinions concerning the speed of vehicles they have observed. In one case, an officer who had an unobstructed view saw and heard a defendant's truck proceeding up the street with its engine racing and noticed the bouncing of the vehicle due to speed. The court permitted the officer to give his opinion concerning whether the vehicle was being operated in

---

[43]　State v. Frasure, 323 Mont. 479, 100 P.3d 1013, 204 Mont. LEXIS 558 (2004).

[44]　Ortiz v. Texas, 2005 Tex. App. LEXIS 6721 (2005).

[45]　United States v. Reneau, 390 F.3d 746, 750, 2004 U.S. App. Lexis 24837 (2d Cir. 2004), *cert. denied,* 544 U.S. 1007, 2005 U.S. LEXIS 3660 (2005).

[46]　Marshall v. Williams, 153 N.C. 128, 134, 574 S.E.2d 1, 2002 N.C. App. LEXIS 1071 (2001).

[47]　Bradley v. O'Donoghue, 2005 U.S. Dist LEXIS 4716 (2005).

excess of the posted speed limit.[48] On the other hand, a victim-witness should not be permitted to give an estimate or opinion of the distance that a tractor-trailer truck pushed her car when she was not "sure" and did not "remember" how far the truck pushed her car.[49] In traffic enforcement cases, police are permitted to make an estimate that one vehicle was following another vehicle at too close of a distance and to base a traffic stop on such a conclusion.[50]

E. Time and Duration

Relying on this same rationale, courts have authorized witnesses to make estimates of elapsed time.[51] However, if the witness can give specifics from which the jury can make its own estimate of time, then the opinion evidence regarding the passage of time is inadmissible. In a case in which an alibi defense rested on proof of time, lay witnesses were permitted to offer opinions concerning when the defendant was present at particular locations, some of which supported his alibi with reference to time and some of which did not assist in his alibi defense.[52]

F. Intoxication and Drug Use

When a witness possesses an appropriate foundation to offer lay opinion evidence, the witness may state his or her conclusion without first detailing the facts on which he or she bases such opinion. The subject of the testimony must not encompass topics of a complex nature that would be appropriate only for expert witness testimony. Intoxication is such a matter and is so commonly encountered that almost anyone may discern it.[53] Therefore, a former police officer who observed the defendant speeding, hitting a vehicle, jumping a curb, rolling three times, getting out of the remains of the vehicle after an accident, having slurred speech, and stumbling around was permitted to offer his opinion that the defendant was intoxicated.[54] Because opinion evidence of intoxication is not restricted to expert testimony, a police officer may offer lay evidence that a person was impaired where sufficient basis for the opinion exists. In a driving while impaired prosecution, an officer concluded and was permitted to offer the opinion that the driver of a boat was operating the craft while under the influence of alcohol. The foundation or basis for the officer's opinion was the subject's poor performance on sobriety tests.[55] For any witness

---

[48]   State v. Barnhill, 166 N.C. 228, 601 N.E. 215. 204 N.C. App LEXIS 1607 (2004).

[49]   Heath v. Rush, 259 Ga. App. 887, 578 S.E.2d 564, 2003 Ga. App. LEXIS 287 (2003).

[50]   Ford v. State, 158 S.W.3d 488, 2005 Tex. Crim. App. LEXIS (2005).

[51]   Allison v. Wall, 121 Ga. 822, 49 S.E. 831 (1905).

[52]   Gonzalez v. Texas, 2000 Tex. App. LEXIS 3032 (2000).

[53]   Warren v. State, 164 Md. App. 153, 168, 882 A.2d 934, 943, 2005 Md. App. LEXIS 189 (2004).

[54]   Sloane v. State, 2004 Tex. App. LEXIS 6903 (2004).

[55]   Bowling v. State, 275 Ga. App. 45, 47, 619 S.E.2d 688, 689, 690, 2005 Ga. App. LEXIS 808 (2005). *See* case in Part II.

to offer an opinion concerning drug or alcohol use, the lay witness must show that he or she had a sufficient firsthand opportunity to observe the defendant while the proponent of the evidence must show that the witness possessed a foundation for the opinion.

While the arresting officer may not give a legal definition of driving while impaired, the officer may give his or her opinion that the defendant was a less safe driver as a result of alcohol consumption, based on the officer's experience with driving under the influence arrests and observations.[56] As a general rule, a police officer may not offer an opinion concerning whether an arrested driver was under the influence of controlled substances because that opinion must be offered by an expert. In a Texas case in which the officer testified that the driver appeared to be under the influence of alcohol or some controlled substance, the court of appeals reversed the driving under the influence conviction because the arresting officer gave no qualified evidence that the defendant was under the influence of a controlled substance and there was no other evidence that supported the conviction.[57]

A Montana court first explained the rule to be applied and then applied the rule relating to the admissibility of lay testimony when evidence of intoxication is offered. The court advised that the state complied with the foundational requirement of the evidence rule that requires testimony from personal knowledge and the evidence rule relating to opinion testimony by lay witnesses, and thus, admission of lay witness testimony pertaining to a witness's opinion as to whether the defendant was intoxicated on the night in question was not an abuse of discretion in a prosecution for driving while intoxicated. The court noted that the record made it clear that the witness's opinions as to the defendant's intoxication were rationally based on his perception and personal knowledge, and the state established that the witness knew the objective signs of intoxication, that he had a great deal of experience being around people who have been in varying states of intoxication, and that he had observed the defendant for quite some time before alerting police.[58]

In one case, the defendant was convicted of operating a motor vehicle while under the influence of intoxicants. On appeal, the defendant argued that the trial court erred in allowing a police officer to express an opinion concerning his intoxication. The court held that because the officer's perception was helpful in determining an issue in the case and the officer had a rational basis for his opinion based on significant experience with impaired drivers, he was properly allowed to testify, even though he was offering testimony as a lay witness.[59]

---

[56]   Hatcher v. State, 277 Ga. App. 611, 613, 627 S.E.2d 175, 177, 2006 Ga. App. LEXIS 164 (2005).

[57]   Kaleta v. State, 2003 Tex. App. LEXIS 2677 (2003).

[58]   State v. Carter, 948 P.2d 1173 (Mont. 1997).

[59]   Ohio v. Davis, 2002 Ohio App. LEXIS 7280 (2002).

As a result of appellate courts deciding a large number of criminal drug cases, the courts have developed a body of law concerning opinion evidence offered by law enforcement agents and other lay witnesses that has fairly specific application to drug testimony. Although police officers and other lay witnesses are not qualified to express an opinion about matters that are within the scope of the common knowledge and experience of the jury, or that are peculiarly within the specialized knowledge of experts, they are qualified to testify concerning matters related to controlled substances if the opinion testimony satisfies the criteria concerning firsthand knowledge and helpfulness to a clear understanding of the testimony or a fact in issue. Police training always includes experience with narcotics detection and identification that gives police officers a foundation for drug identification.

In a Texas case, a trial court permitted a police officer to testify that she smelled burned marijuana and found a baggie of marijuana inside an automobile that she had stopped for a traffic offense. She mentioned that she had training in the academy regarding what unburned marijuana looked like and had become familiar with the odor of burning marijuana during other training. The judge allowed the officer to testify as a lay witness with respect to the marijuana. Texas law permitted a lay witness to give testimony in the form of opinions where they were rationally based on the witness's perception and were helpful to a clear understanding of the witness's testimony or helped to determine a fact in issue. In affirming the conviction, the appellate court noted, "marihuana has a distinct appearance and odor that are familiar and easily recognizable to anyone who has encountered it. So [the officer]'s opinion that appellant possessed marihuana, based on the odor she smelled and the green, leafy substance she saw, was one that a reasonable person could draw from the circumstances. Her testimony regarding the identification of the marihuana was admissible as a lay opinion."[60]

Where the factual analysis appears more complicated, a court may reverse a conviction where police officer testimony was admitted as lay witness opinion but should have been admitted, if at all, as expert testimony. In a Maryland case, the appellate court held that police officers who had observed conduct that appeared to indicate the illicit sale of controlled substances were offering their opinions based on the officers' specialized knowledge, experience, and training in drug investigations. The officers were not merely identifying a drug from appearance, but were basing their opinion that narcotics sales had occurred based on their evaluation of various factors that would not have caused a lay witness to come to the same conclusion.[61] Following similar logic, a Colorado appellate court reversed a defendant's conviction for possessing pseudoephedrine with intent to manufacture a controlled substance. Police officers had been permitted to testify as lay witnesses that the defendant

---

[60]   Osbourn v. Texas, 92 S.W.3d 531, 537, 2002 Tex. Crim. App. LEXIS 236 (2002). *See* case in Part II.

[61]   Ragland v. State, 385 Md. 706, 870 A.2d 609, 2005 Md. LEXIS 119 (2005).

possessed not only precursor chemicals, but were permitted to explain to the jury how methamphetamine is manufactured and how the precursor chemicals were used. The officers' testimony would have been admissible as expert testimony had the prosecutor qualified the officers as experts, but the admission of the evidence as lay testimony constituted reversible error because the testimony may have substantially influenced the jury.[62]

In another example, one of the prosecution's lay witnesses was permitted identify a quantity of suspected drugs as cocaine due to his personal experience and knowledge of cocaine as well as from the circumstances of the transaction. The witness had consumed cocaine hundreds of times and snorted or smoked two to three grams per day for several years. Due to his personal involvement in cocaine use and his familiarity with the drug, the lay witness was properly permitted to identify the controlled substance that was the subject of the trial as cocaine. The court reasoned that the opinion of the lay witness was helpful to the trier of fact and the prosecutor offered a proper foundation to show that the witness was sufficiently familiar with cocaine to be able to identify it.[63] In a case that had an opposite result, the Supreme Court of Montana reversed the defendant's conviction for driving under the influence of drugs. After a defendant had taken prescription medications for his chronic pancreatitis and low blood pressure caused by atrial fibrillation, a police officer followed him and rescued him after his car left the road and rolled over on its top. When the traditional tests for alcohol intoxication did not indicate that alcohol had been a factor in the wreck, the officer concluded that the defendant was under the influence of drugs. The officer indicated that he noticed shallow breathing, slow responses to questions, and slurred speech, which led him to that conclusion. On appeal, Montana's top court reversed the conviction on the ground that, although the officer had familiarity and training to evaluate alcohol intoxication, he was not sufficiently trained to understand the pharmacological effects of particular drugs on motor skills or what levels would cause motor skill degradation such that an individual could not safely operate a vehicle. The court noted that the knowledge to make such determinations would require a qualified expert and that neither the officer nor the general public could make determinations as lay witnesses concerning whether drug intoxication caused the wreck and whether he was driving under the influence of drugs.[64]

G. Sanity or Mental Condition

While both expert and lay opinion may be admissible to assist the trier of fact in determining a person's mental condition or sanity, a jury may accept one version of the evidence over the other. In one case in which the defendant

---

[62]   People v. Veren, 2005 Colo. App. LEXIS 1957 (2005), *reh'g denied,* 2006 Colo. App. LEXIS 112 (2006).

[63]   State v. Maag, 2005 Ohio 3761, 2005 Ohio App. LEXIS 3461 (2005).

[64]   State v. Nobach, 2002 Mont. 91, 309 Mont. 342, 46 P.3d 618, 2002 Mont. LEXIS 189 (2002).

suffered from schizophrenia and killed the victim, he admitted the killing saying that he thought the victim turned into a witch and he was attempting to twist her head off. The defense and prosecution introduced evidence concerning his mental condition that included both lay and expert testimony. The defense experts testified that he was insane at the time of the killing while lay witnesses for the prosecution noted that his behavior seemed normal on the day of the crime prior to the killing. The jury ignored the expert testimony and, relying on the lay testimony, convicted the defendant. According to the appellate court, a jury remains free to disregard expert opinion in favor of lay evidence of the defendant's demeanor before and after the crime.[65]

A nonexpert witness, in response to purely hypothetical questions, may not give an opinion on the question of sanity. Subject to judicial approval, a witness may give testimony concerning another person's sanity when that witness clearly has demonstrated that he or she is acquainted with the person whose mental condition is at issue, and can detail facts and circumstances relating to his or her acquaintance and the conduct and conversation upon which his or her opinion is based.[66] Before a nonexpert witness is competent to testify as to the sanity, mental condition, or retardation of another person, the witness must demonstrate a foundational level of acquaintance involving close contact and duration as to indicate clearly that the testimony would be of value in determining the mental issue. In a North Carolina homicide case, the defendant, who was mentally retarded, shot and killed a co-worker who had been hazing him about his mental condition. The trial court permitted his former live-in girlfriend, with whom he had a child, to testify that the defendant was not retarded. The girlfriend had an intimate relationship with the defendant and had an opportunity to have observed the defendant in a variety of social contexts. She indicated that he performed the typical daily routine and, although he could be quiet sometimes, no one would think that anything was wrong.[67]

In the case above, where lay evidence of mental condition had been admitted, the North Carolina Court of Appeals suggested some specific conditions that must be applied in determining whether a lay witness may properly testify concerning a defendant's mental condition.[68] That court provided that the following factors are to be considered: (1) the witness's opinion must be rationally based on the personal perception of the lay witness; (2) the testimony must be helpful to the determination of a fact in issue; and (3) the subject of mental condition is an appropriate subject for lay opinion.

---

[65] Moler v. Indiana, 782 N.E.2d 454, 2003 Ind. App. LEXIS 119, *transfer denied,* 2003 Ind. LEXIS 119 (2003).

[66] Rupert v. People, 429 P.2d 276 (Colo. 1967); McCall v. State, 408 N.E.2d 1218 (Ind. 1980). *See also* United States v. Santos, 131 F.3d 16 (1st Cir. 1997).

[67] State v. McClain, 169 N.C. App. 657, 670, 610 S.E.2d 783, 792, 2005 N. C. App. LEXIS 804 (2005).

[68] *Id.*

There is no requirement as to the length of acquaintance. For example, the testimony of two police officers who were with the defendant for approximately ten and four hours respectively was not disqualified on the ground that the witnesses had insufficient opportunity to observe the defendant. The fact that the officers had not known the defendant for a longer period went to the weight of the testimony on the sanity question and not to its admissibility.[69]

H. Identification

Often the only adequate way that a person can be identified is by lay opinion. Therefore, the identification of a person need not be made in absolutely positive terms. A witness may testify that an accused "resembles" or "looks like" the person who committed the crime. He or she may testify that in his or her opinion the accused is the person who perpetrated the crime. Courts generally admit lay opinion concerning identity when a witness is sufficiently familiar with the person in question so that the lay witness is better suited to make the identification than the jury.[70] The sound of a person's voice also may be the basis of an opinion as to a person's identity.[71]

This rule also applies to the identity of things. A person who has tasted alcoholic beverages before may testify as to the nature and odor of a beverage. Police officers are generally permitted to testify concerning the smell of burned marijuana.[72] In a prosecution in which a man had been accused of manufacturing methamphetamine in his trailer home, police became suspicious when they served a warrant in an unrelated matter. Police detected the strong and distinctive chemical odor typical associated with methamphetamine manufacturing and procured a search warrant. The trial court permitted the officers involved to testify concerning the distinctive smell inside the trailer home because they had received training in recognizing methamphetamine manufacturing odors and were trained to recognize materials used in drug production.[73]

At trial, proper identification of the perpetrator often serves to resolve the primary issue because, in most cases, there is little doubt that a crime has occurred. In a case in which the defendant had been charged with robbery of a federally insured financial institution, he proposed to call an expert forensic anthropologist to refute expected identification testimony from the prosecution. Over the government's objection, the trial judge concluded that the proposed expert was qualified by training and education and would be permitted to offer testimony concerning ear morphology. The court permitted the anthropologist to testify that the defendant could not have been the bank robber because his earlobes were not attached to his neck while the pictures taken of the robber

---

[69]   Kaufman v. United States, 350 F.2d 408 (8th Cir. 1965).

[70]   United States v. Kornegay, 410 F.3d 89, 94, 2005 U.S. App. LEXIS 10707 (1st Cir. 2005).

[71]   *See* United States v. Norman, 415 F.3d 466, 2005 U.S. App. LEXIS 13149 (5th Cir. 2005).

[72]   *See* Ohio v. Bolling, 2001 Ohio App. LEXIS 3248 (2001).

[73]   State v. Lonsinger, 2005 Tenn. Crim. App. LEXIS 12 (2005).

indicated otherwise.[74] In another case in which the identity of the perpetrator proved to be the primary issue, the trial court permitted the victim's boyfriend to make an in-court identification of the defendant. In the crime, the victim's car had been taken in a carjacking when the perpetrator demanded the keys to the vehicle. The victim's boyfriend had a good opportunity to observe the perpetrator when he handed the vehicle keys to him and the boyfriend naturally had paid close attention to the person with the gun. The trial court allowed the victim's boyfriend to make an in-court identification that followed his identification of the defendant from a photographic array. Similarly, the trial court permitted the victim to make a separate identification because she had been present at the carjacking, had an excellent opportunity of view the perpetrator, and was only a few feet from the carjacker at the time the vehicle was taken. The appellate court approved the identification of the defendant by both the victim and her boyfriend because they had an excellent opportunity to view the perpetrator and the photographic arrays used in the case had not been unduly suggestive.[75]

When lay witnesses are able to make identifications based on their familiarity with characteristics of the defendant that are not immediately observable by the jury at the trial, the lay witness testimony is admissible. However, when the trier of fact is equally able to make an identification from the same evidence observed by a police officer, the lay testimony of an officer should not be admitted. In a Ninth Circuit case, a conviction for attempted murder was reversed when the trial court allowed an officer to identify the defendant as the person depicted on a videotape of the crime. The officer had seen the defendant at least two times and had spoken with him, but could not recall any specific occasion. In this situation, the judge or jury was equally as qualified as the officer to make the evaluation of whether the figure in the video was the defendant.[76]

I. Handwriting

Assuming a proper foundation, the opinion of a lay witness concerning the identity of an acquaintance's handwriting may be admissible. Although handwriting identification testimony involves a process of mental comparison, the lay witness is not permitted to fortify his or her opinion by making a physical comparison of the contested writing with genuine standards, for the reason that he or she has no more skill in making the comparison than do the jurors.[77]

---

[74]   United States v. McClintock, 2006 U.S. Dist. LEXIS 201 (E.D. Pa. 2006).

[75]   Graham v. State, 273 Ga. 187, 189, 614 S. E.2d 815, 818, 2005 Ga. App. LEXIS 442 (2005).

[76]   United States v. Kane, 146 Fed. Appx. 912, 2005 U.S. App. LEXIS 22877 (9th Cir. 2005).

[77]   *See* United States v. Saelee, 162 F. Supp. 2d 1097 (2001), in which the trial judge refused to allow a forensic document examiner testify as a layperson because the witness would not be offering testimony based on sensory perception.

In order for the lay witness to be permitted to identify a handwriting sample, a foundation must be established to show that the witness had an opportunity to become familiar with the handwriting. In a case involving signatures on a car dealership form in an embezzlement case, the victim was permitted to identify the defendant's signature. He had gained familiarity with the defendant's signature because he observed the genuine signature on various car dealership documents during the ordinary course of business. The reviewing court upheld the admission of the lay witness's identification of the signature because he had a basis or foundation for giving his opinion and the court believed that his opinion would be of assistance to the jury.[78] Proof that a witness has a foundation for identifying writing may be accomplished by showing that the witness corresponded with the writer, handled documents written by him or her, or by other means.

While lay witnesses, even with proof of a foundation, are not permitted to offer opinion evidence by comparing a known sample of a signature or more extensive writing, expert witnesses and jurors may be permitted to make such a comparison. In a California case involving insurance fraud, the defendant's genuine driver's license was offered in evidence, as was a fraudulent application for life insurance benefits. According to the prosecutor's theory of the case, both documents were signed by the defendant. The trial court permitted the jury, composed of laypersons, to compare the admittedly genuine signature with the questioned signature to determine whether the same person made both writings. According to the appellate court, the practice of allowing comparison of signatures was proper when done by a jury.[79]

In an action for misapplying and converting traveler's checks, the Eleventh Circuit Court of Appeals reasoned that the trial court did not err in admitting evidence of two coworkers' identifications of the defendant's handwriting on the converted checks.[80] In this case, both lay witnesses testified that they were familiar with the defendant's handwriting and that, in their opinion, it matched or was similar to the handwriting on the checks. The court explained that this testimony was valid under Federal Rules 701 and 901(b), which allow for the admission of nonexpert opinion as to the genuineness of handwriting based upon familiarity not acquired for the purpose of the litigation.

J. Speed

Most courts admit the testimony of a nonexpert witness relating to the speed of a motor vehicle, provided that the witness had sufficient opportunity to observe the vehicle in motion. Courts routinely allow lay witnesses to offer testimony concerning the speed of motor vehicles provided that the witness

---

[78]   Bell v. State, 910 So. 2d 640, 2005 Miss. App. LEXIS 159 (2005).

[79]   People v. Rodriguez, 133 Cal. App. 4th 545, 553, 553, 34 Cal. Rptr. 3d 886, 892, 2005 Cal. App. LEXIS 1628 (2005).

[80]   United States v. Barker, 735 F.2d 1280 (11th Cir. 1984).

has a basis for offering the opinion. A Georgia court upheld the speeding conviction of a juvenile and the admission in evidence of the officer's testimony that the officer observed the defendant speeding. The officer has been on routine patrol and observed the defendant's vehicle traveling at an excessive speed. The foundation for the officer's estimate of the vehicle's speed included eleven years as an officer, his experience in enforcing speed laws, his personal driving experience, and his experience in observing and estimating vehicle speed. As a general rule, the admissibility of an officer's estimate of vehicle speed is so strong that it allows a conviction for speeding, if no contested evidence has been admitted.[81] A California court upheld the admissibility of a police officer's estimate made from an aircraft that the defendant was speeding at 105 miles per hour despite the defendant's objection that the officer had not been trained to visually estimate vehicle speed on the public highway.[82] A trained runner may properly offer an estimate of the speed at which he normally runs where it is based on his experience running on a calibrated treadmill that measured miles per hour.[83] While lay witnesses generally are permitted to express opinion estimates of vehicle speed in terms such as "fast," "slow," "excessive," and the like, some opinions have been found to be conclusory in nature as well as lacking in evidentiary value.[84] The court in its discretion may disallow such opinion evidence.

In a case that was reviewed by a Florida appeals court, the judges advised that an estimate of the speed at which a conveyance or other object was moving at a given time is generally viewed as a matter of common observation rather than expert opinion, such that any person of ordinary ability and intelligence, having the opportunity of observation, is competent to testify to the rate of speed of such a moving object.[85] The court cautioned, however, that lay witness testimony regarding the speed of an object must be grounded in reliability and personal perception rather than speculation, and thus the lay witness's opportunity of observation is critical to the admissibility of testimony regarding speed. Applying this reasoning, the court held that a driver of an automobile who passed by the defendant prior to a fatal accident could give lay testimony in a vehicular homicide prosecution that the defendant was traveling 60 miles per hour in a 45 mile-per-hour zone, when the driver had ample time to observe the defendant and the testimony was not based on speculation but was based on observations at the time of the accident.

---

[81] In the Interest of B.D.S., 269 Ga. App. 89, 90, 91, 603 S.E.2d 488, 489, 2004 Ga. App. LEXIS 1084 (2004), *aff'd,* 273 Ga. App. 576, 615 S.E.2d 627, 2005 Ga. App. LEXIS 579 (2005).

[82] People v. Zunis, 134 Cal. App. 4th Supp. 1, 36 Cal. Rptr. 3d 489, 2005 Cal. App. 1873 (2005).

[83] Soto v. New York City Transit Authority, 2006 N.Y. LEXIS 518 (2006).

[84] Catina v. Maree, 498 Pa. 433, 447 A.2d 228 (1982).

[85] Lewek v. State, 702 So. 2d 527 (Fla. 1997).

§ 11.5   Opinions of Experts

Rule 702

Testimony by Experts

If scientific, technical, or other specialized knowledge will assist the trier of fact to understand the evidence or to determine a fact in issue, a witness qualified as an expert by knowledge, skill, experience, training, or education, may testify thereto in the form of an opinion or otherwise . . .[86]

In order to sustain proof beyond a reasonable doubt, many criminal case presentations require the use of expert witnesses and their special expertise. In the absence of the testimony of experts, it would be difficult for the prosecution to provide the jury with sufficient evidence to meet the burden of proof in cases in which the technical nature of the evidence exceeds the knowledge of the average person. Expert testimony may be admissible when the subject matter at issue involves concepts with which the average person is not sufficiently familiar or in cases in which the expert testimony would assist the jurors in understanding the issues or determining a fact at issue.[87] Over the years, laws relating to the use of expert opinion evidence have developed differently from those relating to the use of nonexpert opinion evidence. While the nonexpert, with some exceptions, may testify only if he or she has firsthand knowledge of the incident, the expert is generally permitted to give an opinion, even if he or she does not have firsthand knowledge. The expert may have analyzed the facts following the event and arrived at an opinion, may have conducted scientific experiments on some of the evidence and drawn a conclusion, or may have testified based on a hypothetical fact pattern offered by a party. An expert may consider reports and results of experiments conducted by other experts when such reliance is usual and customary in that field of expertise. Expert testimony may be presented by a qualified expert when the subject matter is such that the jury cannot necessarily be expected to understand without assistance, especially when the subject matter involves complex technical or scientific evidence. Testimony from a person who has special training, education, and knowledge is thought to assist the judge or jury in making proper decisions.

When the desirability of or need for expert testimony arises, generally the trial judge must make a decision concerning whether expert testimony will assist the trier of fact, regardless of whom the prosecutor or defense counsel proposes to call as the expert witness. In the District of Columbia, the courts hold that for expert testimony to be considered, the subject matter "must be so distinctively related to some science, profession, business or occupation as to be beyond the ken of the average layman" and the proposed expert "witness

---

[86]   Fed. R. Evid. 702.

[87]   State v. Nesbitt, 185 N.J. 504, 514, 888 A.2d 472, 478, 2006 N.J. LEXIS 7 (2006).

must have sufficient skill, knowledge, or experience in that field or calling to make it appear that his opinion" will assist the judge or jury, and that expert testimony cannot be admitted where the state of the knowledge does not permit a reasonable opinion to be offered, even by an expert.[88]

If expert testimony is proper and a witness qualified to offer an opinion is available, admissibility of expert testimony will be subject to additional judicial discretion and will focus on the expert personally. The Supreme Court of Nebraska noted that the trial court must evaluate the admissibility of expert testimony in a four-step process. The trial court must first decide whether a witness has the qualifications to testify as an expert through an evaluation of the proposed expert's knowledge, skill, training, and education. The trial judge must next determine whether the reasoning or methodology underpinning the expert testimony is valid and reliable. Then the judge must decide whether the methodology used by the expert was properly applied and that the appropriate protocols were followed and that any tests were performed properly. Finally, the court must evaluate whether the expert evidence and the opinions offered are more probative than unfairly prejudicial.[89]

When a prosecutor or a defense attorney wants to use an expert witness to present evidence, the trial judge has broad discretion in determining whether to admit the evidence. If a judge decides that expert testimony would be helpful and the subject matter is appropriate, a trial judge must still determine whether the proffered witness qualifies as an expert.[90] The judge initially decides whether the opinion evidence of the expert witness would aid the court or jury in reaching a conclusion and whether the particular witnesses offered as experts have the particular knowledge or experience that would make their opinions helpful to the court or jury. For example, the Tenth Circuit approved a trial court's determination that an agent could testify as an expert concerning the manner that drug kingpins use to avoid having their identities and drug activities becoming known to law enforcement. The trial court determined that the special agent was qualified as an expert and it believed that expert testimony would assist the jury in understanding a rather complex drug-selling operation[91] Taking a different opinion in a highly contested area of expertise, a district court permitted the use of an expert in the problems associated with eyewitness identification because the court believed that the expert's testimony could assist the jury in understanding the evidence or deciding a fact in issue.[92]

---

[88]   Hager v. United States, 856 A.2d 1143, 1148, 2004 D.C. App. LEXIS (2004), *cert. denied,* 2006 U.S. LEXIS 2452 (2006).

[89]   State v. Mason, 271 Neb. 16, 709 N.W.2d 638, 2006 Neb. LEXIS 23 (2006).

[90]   Burnett v. State, 815 N.E.2d 201, 205, 2004 Ind. App. LEXIS 1864 (2004), in which the court overruled a defense objection and permitted a police officer to testify as an expert in fingerprints and fingerprint identification. The court noted the officer's long career of study, field work, and training in the area of fingerprints.

[91]   United States v. Walker, 2006 U.S. App. LEXIS 11289 (10th Cir. 2006).

[92]   United States v. Sullivan, 246 F. Supp. 2d 696, 698, 2003 U.S. Dist. LEXIS 3015 (E.D. Ky. 2003).

Whether expert testimony shall be admitted has generally been left to the broad discretion of trial courts[93] and will not be overturned except upon proof of an abuse of judicial discretion.[94] When the court has properly admitted the opinion of an expert, the jury or the judge may consider the credentials of the expert in determining the weight to give to the expert's testimony.[95] Because the fact finder is permitted to determine the weight to accord expert testimony, it may accept it or reject it completely, or anywhere in between.

Other rules for the use of expert testimony have been handed down in various cases. In one case, a North Carolina court held that an expert's opinion may be based on hearsay statements or other reports that may not normally be admissible in evidence. An expert may base an opinion on tests performed and upon reports generated by other persons where such reliance is usual and customary in the field of expertise. The expert witness is usually permitted to disclose the basis for his or her opinion so that the finder of fact may assess the credibility and weight to be granted to the testimony.[96] Some courts have evaluated the admissibility of an expert's testimony on three factors: qualification, reliability, and fit."[97] The expert must have the special expertise required of any expert in the particular field; the expert must have utilized a proper method sufficient to assure reliability; and the expert must offer relevant testimony that is customarily used it the particular field of expertise.

Even though a witness qualifies as an expert, a trial court may refuse to permit the expert to offer testimony when such testimony fails to assist the finder of fact. For example, an expert's testimony will be excluded where there is a sufficient indication that his or her opinion is based on information that does not go beyond the experience and understanding of the average juror. In United States v. Carter, a bank robbery case, the defendant had been accused of robbing tellers at two separate federally insured banks. Because law enforcement officials offered a teller two separate photo arrays for identification purposes, Carter argued undue suggestiveness involving the identification process and asked to be permitted to use an expert witness who would explain the difficulties of making accurate eyewitness identifications. The trial court refused to permit expert testimony relative to eyewitness identification challenges. The appellate court upheld the trial court decision that expert testimony was not admissible due to the fact that expert testimony would not have aided the jury and might mislead them in their evaluations concerning identity of the robber. The appellate court noted that jurors understand that memory can be faulty, that stress on the eyewitness can cause problems in accuracy,

---

[93] State v. Vernes, 2006 Mont. 32, 331 Mont. 129, 132, 133, 130 P.3d. 169, 173, 2006 Mont. LEXIS 41 (2006).

[94] State v. Tolliver, 268 Neb 920, 921, 689 N.E.2d 567, 573, 2004 Neb. LEXIS 195 (2004).

[95] United States v. Rutland, 372 F.3d 543, 2004 U.S. App. LEXIS 12432 (3d Cir. 2004).

[96] State v. Lyles, 615 S.E.2d 890, 893, 894, 2005 N.C. App. LEXIS 1424 (2005).

[97] Elliot v. Kiesewetter, 112 Fed. Appx. 821, 824, 2004 U.S. 821, 2004 U.S. App. LEXIS 21628 (3d Cir. 2004).

that eyewitnesses vary in their degree of attention, and that there may be some problems in how police use identification procedures. An expert witness is not necessary to assist the jurors in coming to a conclusion concerning identity under the circumstances, according to the court of appeals.[98] Taking a different opinion in this often-contested area of expertise, a district court permitted the use of an expert in the problems associated with eyewitness identification because the court believed that the expert's testimony could assist the jury in understanding the evidence or deciding a fact in issue.[99]

An expert need not be a university-educated professional, such as a physician or scientist. He or she may be a plumber, carpenter, or police officer, if his or her technical expertise in his or her occupation would help the jury to understand a particular point in evidence. In addition, Federal Rule 702 has no provision that would rank academic training as being superior to demonstrated practical experience. An expert could be an immunized conspirator who understood drug dealing protocols or a law enforcement officer who has intimate knowledge about business practices of drug dealers or the mechanics of drug trafficking.[100] Any specialized knowledge that would not be generally held by the public at large may qualify a person as an expert in that field.

In state jurisdictions that have adopted a variation of the Federal Rules of Evidence, Rule 702 defines the conditions that must be present in order for an expert to testify. The rule states that if the testimony would "assist the trier of fact to understand the evidence or to determine a fact in issue," then an expert witness may testify. Because the expert may testify as to matters that are specialized as well as scientific or technical, the rule makes plain its intention to allow expert testimony on matters that are not necessarily beyond the understanding of laypersons. In interpreting this section, an appellate court approved the admission of the expert testimony of a 17-year veteran police officer, whose background included participation or leading a dozen gambling investigations. The court permitted the officer to describe generalized gambling operations and explain to the jury the gaming terminology used by the defendant because the officer was qualified by experience to understand the specific gambling operation involved. The subject matter involved was considered by the trial court to be beyond the understanding of lay jurors so expert testimony was admissible.[101]

In another case, the Seventh Circuit Court of Appeals approved the use of expert testimony in a case involving a violation of the Endangered Species Act[102] regarding whether exotic animal parts were derived from

---

[98] United States v. Carter, 410 F.3d 942, 949, 2005 U. S. App. LEXIS 10830 (7th Cir. 2006).

[99] United States v. Sullivan, 246 F. Supp. 2d 696, 698, 2003 U.S. Dist. LEXIS 3015 (E.D. Ky. 2003).

[100] United States v. Pomranky, 165 Fed. Appx. 259, 260, 2006 U.S. App. LEXIS 2490 (4th Cir. 2006).

[101] United States v. Anderson, 2006 U.S. App. LEXIS 11581 (8th Cir. 2006).

[102] 16 U.S.C.S. § 1531 et seq.

animals protected under the law.[103] In a prosecution for attempted and actual illegal distribution of Schedule III and IV drugs by a physician, the Eighth Circuit Court of Appeals held that the use of an expert witness physician who explained the protocols and standards of care for writing drug prescriptions was appropriate because the expert witness's testimony was helpful to the jury in understanding the case.[104]

§ 11.6   Qualifications of an Expert

A person who has acquired specialized knowledge of a particular subject matter over which he or she is to testify—either by academic study of the recognized authorities or by practical experience—and who can assist and guide the jury in resolving a problem or issue that the jury may not be able to determine because its knowledge is inadequate, may meet the qualifications as an expert witness.[105] A witness who, by education, training, and experience, has become an expert in any art, science, profession, or calling may be permitted to state his or her opinion as to a matter in which he or she is versed and that is material to the case, and he or she may also state the reasons for such opinion. Whether a witness qualifies as an expert rests within the sound discretion of the trial judge.[106] For example, a trial court erroneously characterized a volunteer acting chief's testimony concerning the cause of a fire as lay testimony rather that expert testimony. The witness had more than 30 years' experience investigating fires, had received training and education in causes of fires, had studied fire investigation according to national standards, and had taken approximately 40 classes offered by the state concerning fire investigation. The Supreme Court of Nebraska reversed a trial court determination that the volunteer fire fighter lacked sufficient knowledge, skill, and training and the fire fighter should have been allowed to testify as an expert in fire causation.[107] The gist of this case illustrates the principle that knowledge is the key to developing expertise and that knowledge can come from any source, even nontraditional learning situations or on-the-job training, and is not relegated to formalized university experiences culminating in a doctoral-level degree

An expert in a criminal case may offer an opinion based wholly upon personal knowledge of the facts disclosed in his or her testimony, or upon facts in evidence assumed in hypothetical questions, but the witness may not properly offer an opinion concerning the ultimate issue to be determined by the trier

---

[103] United States v. Kapp, 419 F.3d 666, 673, 2005 U.S. App. LEXIS 17606 (7th Cir. 2005).

[104] United States v. Katz, 2006 U.S. App. LEXIS 11462 (8th Cir. 2006).

[105] People v. Miller, 173 Ill. 2d 167, 670 N.E.2d 721 (1996); *see also* United States v. Sosa, U.S. Dist. LEXIS 2254 (2006), for a review of the foundational requirements for expert testimony.

[106] George v. Ellis, 2003 Pa. Super. 121, 820 A.2d 815, 2003 Pa. Super. LEXIS 441 (2003).

[107] Perry Lumber Company v. Durable Services, 271 Neb. 303, 310, 710 N.W.2d 854, 2006 LEXIS 47 (2006).

of fact because that opinion invades the function of the jury.[108] The Supreme Court of New Jersey reversed a conspiracy drug conviction in which the trial court permitted an expert witness to improperly give his opinion on the ultimate issue, the guilt of the defendant, when there was clearly a factual issue concerning whether the defendant was actually involved with the drug transaction. The testimony of the expert impermissibly invaded the role of the jury.[109]

However, some courts will permit expert witnesses to testify to ultimate issues and those decisions are not often reversed on this ground.[110] While there is no requirement that the expert express an opinion in terms of percentages or probability, many fields of expertise use mathematical models. Handwriting experts often express their opinions in probabilities, but there is no exclusion of evidence if an expert notes that a forged document "probably" was authored by the defendant, but such an answer could affect the weight of the testimony.[111]

One who has the necessary training, experience, and skill, and who has familiarized him- or herself with the necessary data, can form an expert opinion that is substantially superior to that of the average person and therefore useful to the jury. Expert witnesses may have some similarities in qualifications or possess different backgrounds and not have equal qualifications,[112] but as long as a proposed expert crosses the threshold of being an expert in the relevant field, the trial judge should permit the witness to testify. The duty of the jury is to determine the weight to give the testimony of each expert witness. Any difference or inconsistency between information that an expert possesses as the result of becoming an expert and information acquired from other sources for litigation purposes goes to the weight a jury may attach to the expert's testimony.[113] The absence of certificates, memberships, and the like does not in and of itself detract from the competency of an expert witness.[114] A court may not exclude expert testimony just because the expert lacks a degree or training that the district court thinks most appropriate.[115] The fact that the expert does not have a degree or license in his or her professed specialty goes to the weight of the testimony rather than to its admissibility.[116] The special knowledge necessary to qualify as an expert may be derived from experience as well as study.[117]

---

[108]   Missouri v. Churchill, 98 S.W. 3d 536, 2003 Mo. LEXIS 37 (2003).

[109]   State v. Boston, 380 N.J. Super 487, 493, 882 A.2d 987, 991, 2005 N.J. Super. LEXIS 292 (2005).

[110]   Jefferson v. Roe, 2002 U.S. Dist. LEXIS 6153 (N.D. Cal. 2002).

[111]   United States v. Mornan, 413 F.3d 372, 380, 2005 U.S. App. LEXIS 13043 (3d Cir. 2005).

[112]   Panitz v. Behrend, 2001 Pa. Super. 93, 771 A.2d 803, 2001 Pa. Super. LEXIS 372 (2001).

[113]   United States v. 60.14 Acres of Land, 362 F.2d 660 (3d Cir. 1966); Ziegler v. Crorfont, 516 P.2d 954 (Kan. 1973); Kline v. Lorillard, 878 F.2d 791 (4th Cir. 1989).

[114]   Tank v. Comm'r of Internal Revenue, 270 F.2d 477 (6th Cir. 1959); *see also* Moran v. Ford Motor Co., 476 F.2d 289 (8th Cir. 1973).

[115]   Waldorf v. Shuta, 916 F. Supp. 423 (D.N.J. 1996).

[116]   Dickerson v. Cushman, 909 F. Supp. 1467 (M.D. Ala. 1995).

[117]   Morrow v. State, 230 Ga. App. 137, 495 S.E.2d 609 (1998).

When a party offers a witness as an expert on a matter in issue, the judge must preliminarily determine whether the proposed expert's competency, with respect to a special skill or experience, will assist the trier of fact in reaching a determination. In the absence of an admission or a waiver by the adverse party, the judge must make a finding that the witness meets the qualifications of an expert in the particular field. When a party offers a witness as an expert, there is no presumption that the witness is competent to give an opinion; it is incumbent upon the party offering the witness to demonstrate that the witness has the necessary learning, knowledge, skill, or practical experience to enable him or her to give opinion testimony.

A Mississippi appellate court, noting the requirements for determining the admissibility of expert testimony, referred to a two-part test: (1) the witness must be qualified as an expert because of the knowledge, skill, experience, training, or education he or she possesses and (2) whether the witness's scientific, technical, or other specialized knowledge will assist the trier of fact.[118] Where a witness has been deemed to be "qualified" as an expert, testimony may be based on facts within the witness's personal knowledge, facts presented to the expert at trial, and/or facts presented out of court and not directly perceived where such facts are reasonably relied upon by other experts in the field.[119]

The weight and value of the testimony of an expert witness depends largely upon his or her qualifications as an expert, and these qualifications may be the subject of intensive inquiry by the opposing counsel.

§ 11.7   Selection of Expert Witness

Rule 706

Court Appointed Experts

(a) **Appointment.** The court may on its own motion or on the motion of any party enter an order to show cause why expert witnesses should not be appointed, and may request the parties to submit nominations. The court may appoint any expert witnesses agreed upon by the parties, and may appoint expert witnesses of its own selection. An expert witness shall not be appointed by the court unless the witness consents to act. A witness so appointed shall be informed of the witness' duties by the court in writing, a copy of which shall be filed with the clerk, or at a conference in which the parties shall have opportunity to participate. A witness so appointed shall advise the parties of the witness' findings, if any; the witness' deposition may be taken by any party; and the witness may be called to testify by the court or any party.

---

[118]   Mooneyham v. State, 915 So. 2d 1102, 1104, 2005 Miss. App. LEXIS 989 (2005).
[119]   FED. R. EVID. 703. *See also* United States v. Stone, 222 F.R.D. 334, 2004 U.S. Dist. LEXIS 12873 (E.D. Tenn. 2004).

The witness shall be subject to cross-examination by each party, including a party calling the witness.

(b) Compensation. Expert witnesses so appointed are entitled to reasonable compensation in whatever sum the court may allow. The compensation thus fixed is payable from funds which may be provided by law in criminal cases and civil actions and proceedings involving just compensation under the fifth amendment. In other civil actions and proceedings the compensation shall be paid by the parties in such proportion and at such time as the court directs, and thereafter charged in like manner as other costs.

(c) Disclosure of appointment. In the exercise of its discretion, the court may authorize disclosure to the jury of the fact that the court appointed the expert witness.

(d) Parties' experts of own selection. Nothing in this rule limits the parties in calling expert witnesses of their own selection.[120]

In an appropriate case, a judge may appoint an expert upon the judge's own motion, but usually the prosecutor, defense attorney, or both may request that experts be appointed by the court to evaluate evidence and testify in a case. To the extent possible, each party will attempt to suggest nominations of an expert who would testify most favorably for his or her side. In some state jurisdictions, and under Federal Rule 706, the judge may appoint expert witnesses based on agreement by the parties or the court may appoint witnesses based on the judge's preference, especially where there is disagreement. Any expert witness who receives an appointment will be informed of the expected duties by the judge in writing, and a copy of the letter of appointment will be filed with the clerk. Alternatively, the notice of appointment will be given to the parties at a conference in which the parties have the opportunity to participate. When an expert is appointed by the court, that expert must advise the parties of the expert's opinions and conclusions. The parties may take a deposition of the expert witness and the expert witness may be called to testify by any party or by the judge. Even though one party may have called the expert to the stand, the expert may be cross-examined by each party. In the interests of fairness and to eliminate bias, the judge, using discretion, may authorize disclosure to the jury that the expert was appointed by the judge and was not selected by a party.[121]

Rule 706 of the Federal Rules of Evidence continues the long-established practice of federal judges having authority to appoint expert witnesses. Section (c) of the rule authorizes federal courts and state courts that have adopted a version of the Federal Rules to disclose to the jury the fact that the court appointed the expert witness. Disclosure to the jury that the court appointed the expert witness should give the expert witness more credibility with the jury.

---

[120]   FED. R. EVID. 706.

[121]   *Id.*

Noting the provisions of Rule 706, one federal district court[122] commented that:

> The United States Court of Appeals for the Tenth Circuit has explained that "[a] court's authority to appoint an expert under Rule 706 is discretionary and we may only overturn the denial of such a motion for abuse of discretion. Under this standard, a trial court's decision will not be disturbed unless the appellate court has a definite and firm conviction that the lower court made a clear error of judgment or exceeded the bounds of permissible choice in the circumstances." *Cestnik v. Federal Bureau of Prisons*, 84 Fed. Appx. 51, 53, (10th Cir. 2003) citing *Duckett v. Mullin*, 306 F.3d 982, 999 (10th Cir. 2002).[123]

In a case in which the indigent litigant in a legal malpractice case requested the appointment of an expert witness to evaluate the standard of care for an attorney in an earlier criminal case, the district court exercised its discretion and refused to appoint an expert under Rule 706. As the court noted, "Because plaintiff's claims are straightforward, do not present any complex matters for determination, and are of the type of professional conduct that Kansas law permits to be evaluated by common knowledge without the use of expert testimony, the court concludes that it should not exercise its discretion to appoint an expert in this matter pursuant to Federal Rule of Evidence 706."[124]

§ 11.8   Examination of Expert Witness

> **Rule 703**
>
> **Bases of Opinion Testimony by Experts**
>
> The facts or data in the particular case upon which an expert bases an opinion or inference may be those perceived by or made known to the expert at or before the hearing. If of a type reasonably relied upon by experts in the particular field in forming opinions or inferences upon the subject, the facts or data need not be admissible in evidence in order for the opinion or inference to be admitted.[125]

> **Rule 704**
>
> **Opinion on Ultimate Issue**
>
> (a) Except as provided in subdivision (b), testimony in the form of an opinion or inference otherwise admissible is not objectionable because it embraces an ultimate issue to be decided by the trier of fact.

---

[122] Jama Investments v. Los Alamos, 2006 U. S. Dist. LEXIS 29554 (E.D.N.M. 2006).

[123] United States v. Michigan, 680 F. Supp. 928 (W.D. Mich. 1987).

[124] Ellibee v. Fox, 2006 U.S. Dist. LEXIS 13351 (D. Kan. 2006).

[125] FED. R. EVID. 703.

> (b) No expert witness testifying with respect to the mental state or condition of a defendant in a criminal case may state an opinion or inference as to whether the defendant did or did not have the mental state or condition constituting an element of the crime charged or of a defense thereto. Such ultimate issues are matters for the trier of fact alone.[126]

After the witness has qualified as an expert, he or she is first examined by the party who called the witness. There are two avenues through which expert evidence may be presented to the jury: (1) through testimony of the witness based on his or her personal knowledge and observation or from reports and results of tests performed by other experts when it is usual and customary to do so in the field of expertise,[127] and (2) through testimony of the witness when the expert witness is asked to assume that hypothetical facts (generally based on the case being tried) are true and to offer an opinion based on the hypothetical fact situation.[128] An expert witness may base his or her opinion partly upon personal knowledge of facts disclosed in his or her testimony and may be partially based on factual evidence assumed in a hypothetical question.[129] A hypothetical question need not include all of the facts in evidence, nor facts or theories advanced by opposing counsel. A trial judge may properly accept expert testimony predicated on facts that have been previously admitted in evidence as testimony by witnesses who themselves made relevant observations of primary facts. For example, a doctor called to testify may give his or her expert opinion as to whether facts already in evidence support an inference or causation or support a particular diagnosis or prognosis. Also, the expert witness may base his or her testimony on information from his or her knowledge of textbooks, treatises, articles, and other publications relevant to the particular field of expertise.

As a rule, expert testimony must be based on facts and evidence presented in the record or on hypothetical facts assumed to be true, but a hypothetical cannot be based on facts unsupported by any evidence.[130] The Federal Rules of Evidence provide, however, that if the external facts or data are of a type reasonably and customarily relied upon by experts in the particular field when forming opinions or inferences on the subject, the external facts or data need not be admissible in evidence.[131] In a bank fraud case involving check kiting, among other violations, a trial court permitted a federal law enforcement officer to give expert testimony based on his analysis of data that he had neither personally collected nor prepared. The federal officer had used information

---

[126] FED. R. EVID. 704.
[127] State v. Ayers, 2005 Tenn. Crim. App. LEXIS 1108 (2005).
[128] State v. Nesbitt, 185 N.J. 504, 511, 888 A.2d 472, 476, 2006 N.J. LEXIS 7 (2006).
[129] Lewis v. Virginia, 2004 Va. App. LEXIS 595 (2004).
[130] Wells v. State, 913 So. 2d 1053, 1057, 2005 Miss. App. LEXIS 434 (2005).
[131] FED. R. EVID. 703.

taken from bank records and analyzed the records using a computer program. The Court of Appeals for the Sixth Circuit upheld the admission of the opinion of the expert because the practice of permitting forensic financial examiners to analyze data collected by other persons prior to trial and to use the information to form an opinion was consistent with the Federal Rules of Evidence.[132] Similarly, a medical examiner may rely on a report prepared by a different medical examiner because reliance on the data prepared by other professionals was a common and standard protocol.[133]

In order to be admissible, the testimony of an expert witness must meet the other rules of evidence (i.e., the evidence must be relevant).[134] In accordance with the traditional teachings concerning the use of opinion testimony, various jurisdictions still hold to the common law rule that expert opinion testimony should not be admitted where such testimony would invade the province of the jury.[135] The common law rule held that experts may give opinions, but not opinions as to the "ultimate issue"; according to this reasoning, only the jury has that responsibility.[136] For example, Connecticut follows the rule that an expert witness may not give his or her opinion if it embraces an ultimate issue to be decided by the trier of fact.[137] The Federal Rules of Evidence have rejected the traditional view of opinion on the ultimate issue, according to the comments made by those who drafted it. Rule 704 of the Federal Rules of Evidence abolishes the "ultimate issue" rule except for opinions on mental states or conditions in criminal cases. In a federal prosecution for obtaining money through a fraudulent scheme, it was not reversible error to permit a handwriting expert for the government to offer an opinion that the signatures on financial documents were fraudulent, testimony that virtually went to the heart of the case and involved the ultimate issue.[138] Similarly, in a prosecution for drug possession with intent to distribute, a police officer with sufficient experience to be qualified as an expert on drug trafficking was permitted to offer his opinion that the defendant possessed the drugs because he expected to distribute them to other people. While this opinion was one that the jury would have to determine, it was permissible to allow the expert to express an opinion on this ultimate issue.[139]

---

[132] United States v. Abboud, 438 F.3d 554, 586, 2006 U.S. App. LEXIS 3797 (6th Cir. 2006).

[133] Sauerwin v. State, 2005 Ark. LEXIS 565 (2005).

[134] *See* Richman v. Sheahan, 415 F. Supp. 2d 929, 2006 U.S. Dist. LEXIS 6667 (N.D. Ill. 2006), in which trial court rejected police use of force expert from testifying concerning medical matters because evidence was not relevant. *See also* United States v. Monteiro, 407 F. Supp. 2d 351, 2006 U.S. Dist. LEXIS 227 (D. Mass. 2006), in which a trial court excluded expert testimony because the trial judge was not convinced of reliability of the particular theory, rendering the expert testimony irrelevant and inadmissible.

[135] State v. French, 2006 Haw. LEXIS 85 (2006).

[136] People v. Wilson, 25 Cal. 2d 341, 153 P.2d 720 (1944).

[137] State v. Finan, 275 Conn. 60, 63, 881 A.2d 187, 190, 2005 Conn. LEXIS 325 (2005). *Accord*, Smallwood v. Commonwealth, 2005 Va. App. LEXIS 196 (2005).

[138] United States v. Rutland, 372 F.3d 543, 545, 2004 U.S. App. LEXIS 12432 (3d Cir. 2004).

[139] State v. Walker, 2006 N.J. Super. LEXIS 145 (2006).

Notwithstanding the general rule that no witness, layperson, or expert is allowed to testify regarding his or her opinion about the guilt of the defendant, whether by direct statement or inference, some courts allow a witness to come fairly close to expressing an opinion concerning guilt. In a federal prosecution that involved a charge of possession with intent to distribute crack cocaine, a federal officer was permitted to testify as an expert concerning what quantities of crack cocaine would be possessed for personal use and "whether the quantity of the drugs, as well as the possession of a gun along with that quantity, indicated distribution."[140] Although the questions appeared to go to the ultimate issue of distribution, the actual question met the requirements of Rule 704(b) because it did not directly offer an opinion on the defendant's mental state or condition.

§ 11.9   Cross-Examination of Expert Witness

Rule 705

Disclosure of Facts or Data Underlying Expert Opinion

The expert may testify in terms of opinion or inference and give reasons therefore without first testifying to the underlying facts or data, unless the court requires otherwise. The expert may in any event be required to disclose the underlying facts or data on cross-examination.[141]

Following direct examination, an expert witness ordinarily faces a probing inquiry on cross-examination in an attempt to challenge the opinion, as well as the facts and data on which the expert's opinion is based. The rules governing the cross-examination of witnesses generally apply and the trial court has broad discretion in allowing cross-examination of expert witnesses both as to the manner and scope of cross-examination.[142] A California court stated that counsel may cross-examine an expert witness more extensively and searchingly than a lay witness, and the prosecution was entitled to attempt to discredit the expert's opinion.[143] The failure to allow cross-examination may constitute grounds for reversal if the error could have affected the outcome,[144] but a judge may impose reasonable limitations on cross-examination of an expert witness, especially when the facts underlying the expert's opinion are inadmissible for other legal reasons.[145]

---

[140]   Doe Boy v. United States, 2006 U.S. Dist LEXIS 13503 (D. Del. 2006).

[141]   FED. R. EVID. 705.

[142]   Dean v. State, 211 Iowa 143, 233 N.W. 36 (1930).

[143]   People v. Dennis, 71 Cal. Rptr. 2d 680, 950 P.2d 1035 (1998).

[144]   United States ex rel. Reed v. Gilmore, 1999 U.S. Dist. LEXIS 21525 (N.D. Ill. 1999).

[145]   Ward v. Dretke, 420 F.3d 479, 494, 2005 U.S. App. LEXIS 16596 (5th Cir. 2005).

On cross-examination, an expert witness may be interrogated concerning the basis for his or her opinion. Cross-examination may include an inquiry relative to the expert's knowledge of textbooks, treatises, articles, and other scholarly publications in the field; he or she may be confronted with excerpts from them and the expert may be asked whether he or she is familiar with them and whether he or she agrees with them. In a situation in which the expert refuses to acknowledge reliance on standard works in the field, the cross-examiner may lay the foundation that the treatise is authoritative and reliable using its own expert and impeach the opposing expert.[146] Rule 705 of the Federal Rules of Evidence allows an expert witness to testify on direct examination by offering opinions and conclusions without first having to disclose underlying facts on which the testimony is based. However, on cross-examination, where the basis for an expert's opinion has been challenged, an expert must explain how the expert developed his or her conclusions or opinions.[147]

In applying the Texas version of Rule 705, the courts allow a party to request a hearing outside of the presence of the jury, prior to allowing an expert to testify on direct examination. The purpose of this Rule 705 hearing is to allow the court to determine whether the expert witness's opinion has a sufficient basis for its admission. In one case involving severe injuries to a child, the defendant was permitted to extensively inquire concerning the qualifications of the emergency room doctor who treated the injuries and who was prepared to offer opinions regarding the trauma. Following the Rule 705 hearing, the court deemed that the doctor had a proper basis for his opinion and permitted the doctor to explain how such injuries could have been inflicted.[148] In Mississippi, Rule 705 operates similarly to the procedure in Texas, but it allows any party to request foundational data upon which an expert's opinion is expected to be based and such information is to be provided to the requesting opposing party prior to trial. Alternatively, the basis can be revealed on cross-examination by the party against whom the expert testimony is offered.[149] Whether the expert testifies in a federal or state court, the basis for the testimony can be revealed to the parties at trial or earlier so that the trier of fact may give proper weight to the evidence.

In an Ohio case involving cross-examination, one expert stated that he did not rely on any treatise as the basis of his opinion and did not believe that any were authoritative, while the opposing expert identified a couple of treatises as authoritative. When the doctor did not accept any treatise as authoritative, the trial court should have permitted the opposing party to attempt impeachment of the doctor by using excerpts from the treatises recognized as authoritative by the other expert. Under the staff notes to Rule 706, there is clear contemplation

[146] Armstrong v. Brown, 2002 Ohio App. LEXIS 6728 (2002), *appeal denied*, 98 Ohio St. 3d 1539, 2003 Ohio 1946, 786 N.E.2d 902, 2003 Ohio LEXIS 1076 (2003).

[147] United States v. Garcia, 2006 U.S. App. LEXIS 10555 (11th Cir. 2006).

[148] Montgomery v. State, 2006 Tex. App. LEXIS 3377 (2006).

[149] Lawrence v. State, 2005 Miss. App. LEXIS 552 (2005).

that when an expert refuses to recognize a treatise as authoritative, the opposing counsel may lay the foundation that the treatise is authoritative and pursue impeachment of the other expert by referring to the opposing view contained within the treatise.[150]

An expert witness who expresses an opinion that significantly relies on his or her readings of scholarly material may be cross-examined as to that opinion by reference to other reputable works in the field. However, the substance of the treatise or other scholarly writing may be used only to impeach the credibility of an expert witness if the witness has placed reliance on the treatise or has accepted the authoritative nature of the writing. The rationale for this rule is that such cross-examination tests the expert witness's credibility and reliability by inquiring into the extent of the expert's familiarity with the accepted authorities in his or her specialty and by asking the expert whether he or she agrees with the recognized authorities. The excerpts with which the witness is confronted on cross-examination do not, however, become affirmative evidence in the case.[151]

While the federal Constitution's Sixth Amendment confrontation clause guarantees the opportunity for confrontation and cross-examination of adverse witnesses, it does not guarantee that the cross-examination of expert witnesses will be effective or be as extensive as the defense might desire.[152] The problems and constitutional issues surrounding the admission of expert testimony typically concern the fact that an expert may testify to conclusions that may be based on the knowledge of other persons who never testify in the court. The essence of the argument concerns the fact that the person who conducted a test or wrote a treatise is in not in court when the information is mentioned by an expert witness and the outside writer or scientist cannot actually be cross-examined. In a North Carolina case in which a defendant had been accused of committing a variety of drug offenses involving opium and possession of prescription drugs, he complained that reversible error had been committed when the trial judge allowed the prosecution to introduce evidence of the chemical analysis of seized drug material. The analysis had been performed by an expert who never testified and the results were permitted to be introduced by a second expert who had not made the tests. The appellate court upheld the admission of the expert's opinion despite the defendant's argument that his Sixth Amendment right to confront and cross-examine adverse witnesses had been violated. The court noted that the results of outside tests or facts developed concerning information relied upon by an expert is not considered substantive evidence and does not violate the right of confrontation when used to show the basis for the expert's opinion. The court reasoned that it was the expert opinion itself that

---

[150] Armstrong v. Brown, 2002 Ohio App. LEXIS 6728 (2002), *appeal denied,* 98 Ohio St. 3d 1539, 2003 Ohio 1946, 786 N.E.2d 902, 2003 Ohio LEXIS 1076 (2003).

[151] Hinkle v. Cleveland Clinic, 159 Ohio App. 3d 351, 2004 Ohio 6853, 823 N.E.2d 945, 2004 Ohio App. LEXIS 6382 (2004).

[152] Delaware v. Fensterer, 474 U.S. 15, 106 S. Ct. 292 (1985).

must be regarded as the substantive evidence and the defendant is permitted to cross examine the testifying witness. Such a procedure is permissible when the tests are of the type reasonably relied upon by experts in the field and violate neither the hearsay rule nor the Sixth Amendment right of confrontation.[153]

The prosecution as well as the defense has the right of cross-examination of adverse witnesses. For example, in a Missouri murder case, the defense on appeal alleged that the prosecutor had engaged in inappropriate cross-examination when the prosecution interrogated the defendant's expert witness concerning whether her diagnosis had taken into consideration all of the facts, whether she had ever testified for the prosecution, whether she had actually reviewed all of the information provided to her, and whether she had adequately interviewed the defendant, among other grounds. The appellate court reviewed the record and held that the prosecutor had engaged in permissible cross-examination directed toward impeachment of an expert witness.[154]

§ 11.10   Subjects of Expert Testimony

While previous sections of this chapter discussed some of the general rules relating to expert witness testimony, the emphasis of this section relates to considerations of the proper subjects of expertise. There are numerous areas in which experts can meet the qualifications and assist the trier of fact in reaching logical conclusions; if fact, there is no closed list of subjects for which expert testimony might prove helpful. As new scientific and technology developments occur, additional fields of specialized knowledge that require expert testimony will be recognized by the courts. Expert testimony generally will be admissible as long as the testimony has a proper foundation, has been based on reliable principles, and the expert has applied the principles appropriately. Although it would be impossible to discuss all of the areas in which expert testimony would be admissible, especially in criminal cases, the subsections below discuss and illustrate some of the most common areas or subjects that will benefit from expert testimony.

A. Automobile Accidents

Expert testimony of police officers and others who may be qualified as accident reconstruction experts may be admissible at criminal or civil trials arising from motor vehicle accidents. In one Florida case, the court properly permitted one police officer, who was a qualified accident reconstruction expert, to give testimony of what he personally observed. In addition, the court permitted the expert to incorporate in his opinion information developed by

---

[153] State v. Delaney, 171 N.C. App. 141, 613 S.E.2d 699, 700, 701, 2005 N.C. App. LEXIS 1160 (2005). See also, State v. Bunn, 619 S.E.2d 918, 2005 N.C. App. LEXIS 2301 (2005).

[154] Missouri v. Dewey, 86 S.W.3d 434, 440, 2002 Mo. App. LEXIS 2055 (2002).

another officer who was deceased at the time of trial. Pursuant to the Florida version of Rule 705, the trial court permitted the officer-expert to give his opinion without offering prior disclosure of the underlying facts or data upon which he based his opinion. Experts are permitted to offer testimony based on inferences that have been drawn from facts supplied by other witnesses.[155] As a general rule, when an expert on direct examination does not specifically mention underlying data, he or she may be asked on cross-examination about the basic facts and data on which the opinion rests.[156] According to one treatise, "During cross-examination, the expert may be required to disclose all of the evidence relied upon regardless of whether it is otherwise admissible."[157] A Florida appellate court reversed a murder conviction where the trial court permitted the prosecution to introduce expert testimony that fiber evidence was found that pointed to the defendant being the driver of the vehicle involved in the death, a fact the defendant disputed. The trial court had rejected the defendant's attempt to introduce the expert opinion testimony of an accident reconstructionist and forensic scientist concerning how the accident happened, how the clothing fibers were released as a result of the wreck, and how they could be distributed as a result of the accident. The appellate court held that an understanding of how fibers are released from clothing, and the possible significance of the presence or absence of fibers in a particular part of an automobile after an accident were properly the subject of expert testimony. The trial court committed reversible error and abused its discretion in excluding the defendant's expert testimony.[158] In a different case involving a conviction of vehicular homicide, both the prosecution and the defense presented expert testimony concerning how the vehicle left the road. The defendant presented evidence by a mechanical engineer who analyzed skid marks, which supported the defendant's position that the wreck was an accident and that the death was not criminal. Using a more sophisticated approach, the prosecution offered an accident reconstruction expert who used a computer software program— PC-Crash. The prosecution's expert validated the program and testified that it had gained general acceptance in the expert accident reconstruction community. The appellate court upheld the conviction because, even though the two expert witnesses presented opposing conclusions, the jury could determine which version to believe.[159] In a vehicular homicide case in which the vehicle left the highway and broke apart, expert witnesses for the prosecution were permitted to offer expert opinions concerning the speed of the defendant's vehicle at the time of the accident. Their qualifications appeared to be proper

---

[155] *See* CHARLES W. EHRHARDT, FLORIDA EVIDENCE § 704.1 (2006 ed.).

[156] Carratelli v. Florida, 832 So. 2d 850, 861, 2002 Fla. App. LEXIS 17158 (2002).

[157] See Charles W. Ehrhardt, Florida Evidence § 704.1 (2002 ed.).

[158] Barfield v. State, 880 So. 2d 768, 770, 2004 Fla. App. LEXIS 8357 (2004), *reh'g denied*, 2004 Fla. App LEXIS 18629 (2004).

[159] *See* State v. Phillips, 123 Wash. App. 761, 98 P.3d 838, 2004 Wash. App. LEXIS 2296 (2004), *reh'g denied*, 2005 Wash. LEXIS 492 (2005).

and their methodology designed to evaluate a vehicle's speed at the time of the event proved appropriate to the task, including their evaluation of scuff marks and crossover marks on the pavement to help estimate vehicle speed.[160]

In many recent automobile collision cases in which the speed of a defendant's car may be at issue, newer technology, coupled with expert witnesses with cutting edge knowledge, proves decisive. In a Florida double manslaughter case, at issue was the speed of the defendant's Pontiac Trans Am at the time it hit the victims, who were in a car backing into a public street from a private driveway. The vehicle's "black box," or event data recorder, which also operated the defendant's air bag, recorded the speed at 114 m.p.h. in a 30 m.p.h. speed zone. According to the appellate court, using expert testimony was permissible to admit the speed of the vehicle based on the event data recorder because the state's expert testified concerning the reliability of the event data recorder and the fact that they are generally accepted in the accident reconstruction community.[161]

As a general rule, a court does not commit error when it permits a qualified expert witness to reconstruct a motor vehicle accident by basing his or her opinion on photographs, damage repair estimates, personal measurements at the accident scene, police reports, studies of victim injuries, and interviewing witnesses and participants. Where the expert's reconstruction will assist the trier of fact, the expert's testimony should be admitted.[162] In an action arising out of the death of an automobile driver in a head-on collision to which there were no eyewitnesses, testimony of a safety engineer, who saw one of the automobiles only after it had been brought into a salvage yard and altered, was admissible when, in his personal examination of the automobile in the salvage yard, he had considered pertinent to the subject of his investigation only the parts of the automobile that were photographed immediately after the collision.[163]

B. Airplane Crashes

Witnesses who have special training, education, or experience may qualify as experts in determining the cause of aircraft accidents.[164] For example, in an airplane crash where the plane had not flown in years, contained old fuel, and had been improperly certified as "airworthy," the inspector had a duty to conduct a more thorough inspection before certification. According to the experts, the crash was caused by engine failure which was, in turn, caused by poor and inadequate maintenance. The expert noted that the inspector did "not indicate that [he] completed the steps necessary to ensure the airworthiness of

---

[160] Maine v. Irving, 2003 Me. 31, 818 A 2d 204, 2003 Me. LEXIS 36 (2003).

[161] Matos v. State, 899 So. 2d 403, 405; 2005 Fla. App. LEXIS 4359 (2005).

[162] Hamilton v. Jones, 2005 Ark. App. LEXIS 92 (2005).

[163] Leeper v. Thornton, 344 P.2d 1101 (Okla. 1959)

[164] See In re Aircraft Accident at Little Rock, Arkansas, June 1, 1999, 231 F. Supp. 2d 852, 2002 U.S. Dist. LEXIS 22881 (E.D. Ark. 2002).

the fuel system including the carburetor or air intake filter." These conclusions involve evaluation of facts and circumstances that are beyond the knowledge of ordinary witnesses and require an expert to develop an opinion concerning the cause of this crash and apply to similar aircraft mishaps.[165] Naturally, expert testimony may be offered to demonstrate that one party was not negligent in an aircraft disaster. When a plaintiff alleged that the federal government had been negligent in offering some services to a pilot, including altimeter settings, alternative airports, and negligence in sending rescue equipment, an expert witness was properly permitted to offer admissible opinion evidence concerning whether the conduct of federal employees amounted to negligence.[166]

C. Physical and Mental Condition

A general practitioner may usually testify concerning matters within a medical specialty if his or her education or experience, or both, involve demonstrable knowledge of the subject. A skilled medical witness generally has no need to be duly licensed to practice medicine[167] and, in most cases, the expert does not have to be licensed in the particular jurisdiction. However, some jurisdictions require a better match between general knowledge and the specialty than merely possessing a medical degree or license. The general rule is that anyone who is shown to have special knowledge and skill in understanding human ailments may have the foundation to testify as an expert qualified to give an opinion on the particular question in issue. For example, medical doctors who are well-versed in the effects of insulin, hypoglycemia, and how intoxication might result when insulin protocols were not followed, may be permitted to offer testimony to help establish the defense of involuntary intoxication.[168]

While expert medical testimony may prove preferable, it is not always essential that an expert medical witness be a medical practitioner. Thus, non-medical witnesses who have had experience in electrical work may testify to the effects of electrical shock upon the human body. An expert witness in the field of toxicology was permitted to testify in a driving under the influence prosecution that the defendant was a user of marijuana based on the amount of marijuana metabolite found in his blood. She offered testimony concerning amounts of amphetamine, methamphetamine, and mirtazapine, a depressant, but she found no alcohol in the blood sample. Under questioning by the prosecutor, the expert was not able with certainty to say whether the defendant was under the influence or not based on her analysis of his blood chemistry. Even

---

[165]   Mills v. Oberg, 2005 Minn. App. LEXIS 106 (2005).

[166]   Bieberle v. United States, 255 F. Supp. 2d 1190, 1206, 1207, 2003 U.S. Dist. LEXIS 5427 (D. Kan. 2003).

[167]   *See* Tenet Healthcare Corp. v. Gilbert, 277 Ga. App. 895, 627 S.E.2d 821, 2006 Ga. App. LEXIS 167 (2006), in which an expert's affidavit had to be attached to a complaint to make the case actionable and the court held that the affidavit was sufficient even though the expert possessed no license to practice at the time of the complaint.

[168]   People v. Garcia, 113 P. 3d 775, 2005 Colo. LEXIS 562 (2005).

though the expert testified to medical evidence and she was not a medical doctor, her level of expertise was properly admitted in an effort to illuminate the condition of the defendant.[169]

An expert who gives testimony may carry more weight with a jury when explaining physical attributes or mental conditions. For example, a Tennessee court allowed a physician who was an expert in the area of pharmacology and toxicology to testify concerning the physiological effects of drinking ethylene glycol (automobile antifreeze). The court permitted the doctor to explain how ethylene glycol causes a patient's blood to become acidic while metabolizing into oxalic acid, which binds with calcium, causing kidney failure and death.[170] With the detail offered by the doctor, a trier of fact would most likely place great weight on the testimony. In a child molestation case in which an ordinary medical doctor took a history from the alleged victim and conducted a physical exam of the mouth and the child's privates, the court permitted the doctor to testify as an expert that the results of the overall exam indicated that, in the doctor's opinion, the child had been molested.[171] Evidence from this expert witness would be given much more weight by the trier of fact than would be given to a non-medical child counselor. However, a licensed physician's assistant, who treated the defendant in the hospital's emergency room on the night of the arrest, could be precluded from testifying as an expert about all the medical issues in the case, and his testimony could be limited to the examination and treatment of the defendant at the hospital.[172]

The trial court is given great discretion in deciding how testimony regarding a defendant's mental condition should be characterized following its admission. Some courts limit expert testimony relating to the conclusions drawn by an expert because of the danger that the expert's opinion might invade the province of the jury. Other jurisdictions do not exhibit a concern about whether an expert's conclusion might intrude into an area reserved for jury decision making. In a Florida case in which the defendant had murdered her mother, the trial court limited the testimony of a defense psychiatrist by preventing him from expressing an opinion concerning whether the defendant was "insane." The appellate court expressed the opinion that a medical expert can offer an opinion concerning whether a defendant is "insane" because expert witnesses in Florida are permitted to render an opinion concerning an ultimate issue in a case.[173] The federal rules under Rule 704 are slightly more restrictive that the Florida rules and allow an expert to offer an opinion or inference concerning the ultimate issue unless it relates to a mental state or condition of a criminal defendant.[174]

---

[169]   State v. Lee, 2005 Tenn. Crim. App. LEXIS 399 (2005).
[170]   Tennessee v. Combs, 2002 Tenn. Crim. App. LEXIS 799 (2002).
[171]   State v. Lente, 2005 NMCA 111, 119 P. 3d 737, 739, 740, 2005 N.M. LEXIS 105 (2005).
[172]   State v. Carlson, 559 N.W.2d 802 (N.D. 1996).
[173]   Reynolds v. Florida, 837 So. 2d 1044, 2002 Fla. App. LEXIS 19140 (2002).
[174]   *See* FED. R. EVID. 704.

In a California attempted murder case, the trial court held that expert testimony tending to prove or disprove whether the defendant harbored the necessary mental capacity to form the requisite criminal intent would not be admitted. The appellate court concurred because it believed that an expert would not be able to know what ability to form a specific intent was actually possessed by another human.[175] Finally, in a third case, the appellate court declared that the trial court erred in excluding an "expert opinion that the defendant was severely impaired in his ability to form an intent to kill and an intent to injure."[176]

If the members of the jury can readily observe the defendant's mental condition, expert testimony concerning the condition will be excluded.[177] In State v. Cortez, the reviewing court held that the trial court did not err in excluding the psychologist's testimony that the defendant was slow to answer, forgot easily, and did not express himself well, because these aspects of the accused's personality could be readily observed by the jurors when he testified at the trial.

D. Summaries

The Federal Rules of Criminal Procedure interface with the Federal Rules of Evidence when, as a precondition of admission of expert testimony, the criminal rules[178] require that both the prosecution and the defense prepare a written summary of any testimony that either side expects to have admitted under Federal Rule of Evidence 702, 703, or 705. As a general rule, the originals of the testimony summarized must be made available to the opposing party for examination in advance of trial or the expert's testimony may be excluded.[179] In an appeal from a federal conviction involving sexual abuse where the prosecution had not been completely forthcoming concerning the basis of its expert's opinion relative to the presence of semen, the trial court's decision to allow the expert to testify was upheld by the Eighth Circuit Court of Appeals. The trial court's admonition to the prosecution that it should be more forthcoming in the future with respect to pretrial summaries of expert testimony was noted with approval by the Court of Appeals.[180] Trial witnesses may also be permitted to offer summaries of testimony as an aid to the understanding of the jury. For example, summaries of various complex stock sale transactions may be properly admitted in cases involving income tax evasion. An internal revenue agent's summary of the prosecution's evidence was consistent with the Federal

---

[175] California v. Sanchez, 2002 Cal. App. Unpub. LEXIS 11068 (2002); *see* Steele v. State, 97 Wis. 2d 72, 294 N.W.2d 2 (1980).

[176] State v. Edmon, 28 Wash. App. 98, 621 P.2d 1310 (1981). *See also* Commonwealth v. Pallotta, 36 Mass. App. 669, 634 N.E.2d 915 (1994).

[177] State v. Cortez, 935 F.2d 135 (8th Cir. 1991).

[178] FED. R. CRIM PROC. 16.

[179] United States v. Roy, 2006 U. S. Dist. LEXIS 9583 (2006).

[180] United States v. Conroy, 424 F.3d 833, 838, 2005 U.S. App. LEXIS 21080 (2005).

Rules of Evidence where the testifying agent had specialized knowledge of the tax transactions at issue and was able to place the transactions in context. The summary witness need not necessarily be an expert witness, but in many cases summary witnesses do carry expert witness qualifications.[181]

E. Handwriting Comparisons

Analysis of handwriting consists of having an expert compare a known specimen of a person's handwriting to a questioned sample in order to determine whether the same person composed both documents. The scientific theory behind handwriting analysis is that each person's writing technique is different and unique from virtually everyone else.[182] Each time a handwriting expert testifies in court, he or she must demonstrate appropriate qualifications as an expert witness. Testimony that a certain person wrote an individual document is an opinion offered by the expert, but the handwriting analysis need not be absolutely certain as long as principles and proper methodology have been followed. To be qualified, he or she must have expert training and experience in handwriting analysis in general or must be intimately familiar with the handwriting of the individual in question. In a case involving the fraudulent recording of an easement, an expert handwriting witness testified that the signatures were not valid while intimate family members who had familiarity with their deceased relatives' signatures were permitted to testify that the signatures were not genuine and were forgeries.[183] In a criminal case, expert testimony proved crucial to the prosecution when expert witnesses concluded that a defendant in a drug case had signed a consent to search form.[184] A lay witness who has no familiarity with a person's handwriting is not qualified to offer an opinion. For example, a trial court committed error when the judge permitted a police officer to testify that the handwriting belonged to the defendant when the officer had no expertise and was not familiar with the defendant's handwriting prior to the trial.[185] However, a jury may be permitted to compare a known sample with a questioned sample of handwriting and come to a conclusion[186] even though the jury has no special expertise.

In contrast, comparison handwriting analysis is generally admissible in court when the evidence comes from a qualified expert. The purpose of allowing expert testimony is to assist the jury in deciding the questioned document and to draw the jury's attention to similarities between the known and the

---

[181] United States v. Pree, 408 F. 3d 855, 869, 2005 U.S. App. LEXIS 9222 (7th Cir. 2005). *See also* § 13.8 Summaries.

[182] United States v. Prime, 431 F.3d 1147, 1153, 2005 U.S. App. LEXIS 27276 (2005).

[183] The Berkshires, L.L.C. v. Sykes, 2005 UT App 536, 2005 Utah App. LEXIS 552 (Utah 2005).

[184] United States v. Ozuna, 561 F.3d 728, 2009 U.S. App. LEXIS 7034 (7th Cir. 2009).

[185] Ohio v. Brennan, 2002 Ohio App. LEXIS 5788 (2002).

[186] People v. Rodriguez, 133 Cal. App. 4th 545, 554, 34 Cal. Rptr. 3d 886, 892 2005 Cal. App. LEXIS 1628 (2005).

unknown writing sample.[187] When a qualified expert had years of experience in the field of handwriting analysis, he was permitted to offer his opinion that the defendant wrote the document in question[188] despite the fact that the jury would have to ultimately decide the same question.

Because handwriting identification cannot be based upon absolute scientific certainty, the opinion of an expert regarding handwriting must meet only the generally accepted standards adopted by questioned document examiners.[189] In a prosecution for mail and wire fraud, the defendant challenged the government's expert witness concerning her "methodology, the bases for her conclusions, and the degrees of certainty with which she was able to reach her conclusions."[190] She testified that her conclusions were within a reasonable degree of scientific certainty that the defendant wrote some of the questioned documents. Her conclusions were not stated in absolute terms but were within the parameters expected of an expert on handwriting comparisons and were, therefore, properly admitted by the trial court. The jury was permitted to accept or reject the expert's testimony.

In a case involving the fraudulent recording of an easement, an expert handwriting witness testified that the signatures were not valid while intimate family members who had familiarity with their deceased relatives' signatures were permitted to testify that the signatures were not genuine and were forgeries.[191] In a criminal case, expert testimony proved crucial to the prosecution when expert witnesses concluded that a defendant in a drug case had signed a consent-to-search form.[192]

The Supreme Court of the United States has emphasized that requiring a defendant to provide a handwriting sample for comparison purposes does not violate the privilege against self-incrimination.[193] According to the Court, the use of this type of evidence does not run counter to Fifth Amendment constitutional protections because the quality of the handwriting is used for the sole purpose of comparison with a document of uncertain authorship. A handwriting sample reveals the physical characteristics of writing style and does not require a defendant to give actual adverse testimony. "A mere handwriting exemplar, in contrast to the content of what is written, like the voice or body

---

[187] United States v. Smith, 153 Fed. Appx. 187, 2005 U.S. App. LEXIS 23798 (4th Cir. 2005) (forensic document examiner who helped develop standards for handwriting analysis was deemed to be qualified as an expert regarding forged instruments).

[188] *See* United States v. Brown, 152 Fed. Appx. 59, 2005 U.S. App. LEXIS 22703 (2d Cir. 2005).

[189] United States v. Herrera, 832 F.2d 833 (4th Cir. 1987).

[190] United States v. Mornan, 413 F.3d 372, 380, 2005 U.S. App. LEXIS 13043 (3d Cir. 2005).

[191] The Berkshires, L.L.C. v. Sykes, 2005 UT App 536, 2005 Utah App. LEXIS 552 (Utah 2005).

[192] United States v. Ozuna, 561 F.3d 728, 2009 U.S. App. LEXIS 7034 (7th Cir. 2009).

[193] Gilbert v. California, 388 U.S. 263, 265, 1967 U.S. LEXIS 1086 (1967); *see also* United States v. Dionisio, 410 U.S. 1 (1973), in which the court upheld a federal judge's order that required a suspect to give voice samples for grand jury consideration.

itself, is an identifying characteristic" that is outside the protection of the Fifth Amendment.[194]

Expert testimony may be admissible to determine authorship of a document based not upon handwriting analysis, but upon an evaluation of the style of word selection and textually unique qualities of a writing.[195] Some courts have admitted the testimony of forensic document examiners[196] who look for common artifacts, style, and linguistic markers in questioned documents, while other courts have been somewhat more reticent to take full advantage of this modern method of determining authorship of questioned documents.[197] In one federal case, the judge concluded that the principle of uniqueness of handwriting or hand printing failed to satisfy the requirements for reliability because there was no scientific proof that each person writes a document with characteristics unique to that person. However, the same judge allowed evidence of the mechanics of handwriting and comparisons of similarities or dissimilarities and other factors that would assist the jury in determining authorship of questioned documents.[198]

F. Typewriter Comparisons

In past years, experts who could qualify to make handwriting comparisons were more in demand than those who could give testimony regarding the source of typewritten documents. However, as the typewriter became more popular, experts who qualified to testify that typewritten documents were written on a specific typewriter were in demand. The need for experts in the typewriter comparison field, while once robust, has diminished in importance but has not completely evaporated. Because some traditional typewriters are still in use, this expertise retains some marginal utility in civil cases as well as in criminal prosecutions.[199] Today, with the more common use of various computer printers that print in a fairly uniform manner, discerning the source of a document has become somewhat more difficult.

Expert evidence is generally admissible to prove that a document was typed on a particular type of machine, such as an Underwood typewriter, even though the police never obtained the specific typewriter. In order to prove that

---

[194] Hiibel v. Sixth Judicial District Court of Nevada, 542 U.S. 177, 194, 2004 U.S. LEXIS 4385 (2004), quoting United States v. Wade, 388 U.S. 218, 223 (1967).

[195] *See* Sargur Srihari et al., *Individuality of Handwriting*, 47 J. FORENSIC SCI. 856 (2002).

[196] United States v. Gricco 2002 U.S. Dist. LEXIS 7564 (E.D. Pa. 2002).

[197] United States v. Lewis, 220 F. Supp. 2d 548, 2002 U.S. Dist. LEXIS 17062 (S.D. W.Va. 2002); United States v. Brewer, 2002 U.S. Dist. LEXIS 6689 (N.D. Ill. 2002); United States v. Saelee, 162 F. Supp. 2d 1097 (D. Alaska 2001); United States v. Fujii, 152 F. Supp. 2d 939 (N.D. Ill. 2000).

[198] *See* United States v. Hildalgo, 229 F. Supp. 2d 961, 2002 U.S. Dist. LEXIS 21633 (D. Ariz. 2002).

[199] Eta-Ndu v. Gonzales, 411 F.3d 977, 981, 982, 2005 U.S. App. LEXIS 12120 (8th Cir. 2005), in which forensic analysis of typewritten letters proved important in a deportation case.

a document was typed on a particular computer printer/typewriter using a specific daisywheel print wheel, courts frequently admit expert testimony.[200] In making comparisons, the expert usually points out the unique characteristics such as dirt particles changing the printed character, damage to a particular character, and any irregularities specifically unique to a particular print wheel. Sometimes a comparison of documents indicates that they were typed on the same machine even though they purportedly came from separate sources.[201] More modern methods of printing pose unique problems concerning identification, especially with recyclable inkjet print heads and refillable inks containing different chemical compositions from the original factory ink.

Determining the source of printed documents has taken a step forward because several manufacturers of color laser printers have designed hardware that prints the serial number and manufacturer's code in binary form on each sheet of paper printed by the machine. Documents printed by commercial printing companies will usually carry the same identification marks, as will color prints made from desktop laser printers.[202]

In some older cases, courts have allowed the opinion of an expert as to the identification of the operator of the typewriter. In doing so, the expert points out the individual style of the person typing the instrument, taking into consideration the force with which the typist struck particular keys. This identification is primarily predicated on the manner of punctuation, the length of the lines, the depth of the indentation, and other personal style characteristics.[203]

G. Polygraph Examination Results

For a variety of reasons, courts have not generally admitted the results of lie detector, or polygraph, tests because either the scientific principles behind such tests remain in question or the implementation of the testing continues to suffer from questionable reliability. One state court noted, "The general rule in Illinois is to preclude the introduction of evidence regarding polygraph examinations and their results because (1) the evidence is not sufficiently reliable, and (2) the results may be taken as determinative of guilt or innocence despite their lack of reliability."[204] The Fourth Circuit has a policy of banning the admission of polygraph evidence and it continues to refuse admission of test results because of precedent and questions concerning the reliability of the polygraph.[205] In some cases, courts will permit admission of polygraph

---

[200] United States v. Johns, 2000 U.S. App. LEXIS 542 (6th Cir. 2000).

[201] Caldron v. Ashcroft, 110 Fed. Appx. 789, 2004 U.S. App. LEXIS 19793 (9th Cir. 2004).

[202] *Investigating Machine Identification Code Technology in Color Laser Printers.* Electronic Frontier Foundation. 1 Jun 2009. Available at: http://www.eff.org/wp/investigating-machine-identification-code-technology-color-laser-printers.

[203] Thomas v. State, 197 Okla. 450, 172 P.2d 973 (1946).

[204] People v. Washington, 363 Ill. App. 3d 13, 842 N.E.2d 1193, 1199, 2006 Ill. App. LEXIS 24 (2006).

[205] United States v. Prince-Oyibo, 320 F.3d 494, 501, 2003 U.S. App. LEXIS 3568 (4th Cir. 2003) and United States v. Sprague, 134 Fed. Appx. 607, 2005 U.S. LEXIS 10127 (4th Cir. 2005).

tests if all parties consent,[206] but when there has been no written stipulation signed by all parties, courts almost uniformly deny the admission of polygraph results.[207] However, when a defendant agrees to take a polygraph test, to be bound by the results, and gives prior consent to the admission of the results, the polygraph operator may testify concerning his or her opinion of what the examination revealed. In a Georgia murder case, a female defendant agreed to take a polygraph and offered a written stipulation that the results could be admitted. The test results proved damaging to her defense and the Supreme Court of Georgia upheld the admission of the polygraph results under the circumstances.[208] California by statute bans the admission of polygraph evidence and the opinions of examiners from adult and juvenile proceedings, unless all parties stipulate to the admission of the results.[209]

While polygraph evidence generally is excludable absent agreement, the Supreme Court of Georgia held that there may be occasions in which a polygraph might be admissible in the penalty phase of a death penalty case. In one case, a defendant had passed a polygraph exam conducted a few days after the murder, but the polygraph evidence was not admitted at the guilt phase of the trial. The trial court refused to allow the convicted defendant to present the evidence during his portion of the sentencing. However, the state supreme court reversed the sentence, noting, "When the defendant seeks to introduce unstipulated polygraph test results as mitigation evidence, the trial court must exercise its discretion to determine whether those results are sufficiently reliable to be admitted."[210]

Polygraph examination results are admitted only after a proper foundation has been laid and the examiner's qualifications are established. In a Florida case, the reviewing court concluded that the claimant in a forfeiture proceeding failed to properly lay the foundation for the admission of polygraph examinations, in which the claimant sought only to admit the hard copy of the examination.[211] The court noted that there was no proffer to the court relating to the polygraph examiner's qualifications, or procedures and circumstances surrounding the admissions of the examinations.

While polygraph results are generally not admissible, statements made to polygraph operators that do not directly relate to or are not essential to the examination concerning the merits of a case or its important details may be admissible where they qualify as admissions or confessions.[212] Therefore,

---

[206]   *See* § 6.19 Polygraph Tests. *See also* § 15.5 for a general description of polygraph tests.

[207]   *See* Ohio v. DiBlasio, 2002 Ohio 2466, 2002 Ohio App. LEXIS 2691 (2002); *see also* J.R.T. II v. State, 783 N.E.2d 300, 2003 Ind. App. LEXIS 171 (2003).

[208]   Thornton v. State, 279 Ga. 676, 678, 620 S.E.2d 356, 360, 2005 Ga. App. LEXIS 634 (2005).

[209]   CAL. EVID. CODE § 351.1 (Matthew Bender 2006)

[210]   Height v. State, 278 Ga. 592, 594, 595, 604 S.E.2d 796; 2004 Ga. LEXIS 958 (2004). *Contra*, United States v. Roman, 368 F. Supp. 2d 119, 2005 U.S. Dist. LEXIS 7772 (2005).

[211]   United States v. One Parcel of Real Estate, 804 F. Supp. 319 (S.D. Fla. 1992).

[212]   *See* Esquibel v. Texas, 2005 Tex. App. LEXIS 6760 (2005).

voluntary statements that a polygraph subject makes before, during, or after the administration of a polygraph test may be admissible as long as the admission of the statements does not run afoul of other rules of evidence or any applicable constitutional provision.[213]

H. Neutron Activation Analysis

Although some courts have authorized expert witnesses to testify concerning the results of neutron activation analysis or gunpowder residue testing, some of these courts have expressed doubts concerning expert opinions. For example, in a Minnesota Supreme Court case, the neutron activation analysis was used to show that the defendant, who was accused of shooting a police officer, had fired a pistol shortly before his arrest. After the suspect was taken into custody, but prior to the time he was booked in the county jail, his hands were swabbed with a nitric acid solution. These swabs were sent to the Treasury Department laboratory in Washington for neutron activation analysis, a testing procedure that can determine the presence and amount of certain chemical elements that are normally present on the hand of a person who has recently fired a weapon. Although admitting the testimony of a representative of the Treasury Department, the court expressed concern about the sweeping and unqualified manner in which the expert testimony was offered.[214] The absence of test results may have adverse consequences for a defendant who does not cooperate with the police to a minimal degree. In a case in which a defendant refused to submit a sample for neutron activation testing, a trial court permitted the prosecution to comment, during closing arguments, on the refusal because there was no Fifth Amendment privilege to decline to allow a chemical sample to be taken from the defendant's hand.[215] On the other hand, when an arrestee demands to be subjected to a gunpowder residue test, the prosecution is generally under no obligation to conduct such a test and is certainly not under any duty to conduct a residue test to negate probable cause[216] or conduct a test when overwhelming evidence of guilt is present.[217]

Neutron activation analysis[218] was once used to determine whether a lead bullet came from a particular batch of lead melt from the lead manufacturer. If a crime scene bullet matched a bullet of similar composition in a cartridge found in the defendant's control, the inference would be that the cartridges containing the lead bullet came from the same source or box of ammunition. As science progressed, the theory that the lead in a particular melt was

---

[213] *See* State v. Damron, 151 S.W. 3d 510, 2004 Tenn. LEXIS 993 (2004).

[214] State v. Spencer, 216 N.W.2d 131 (Minn. 1974).

[215] Hubbert v. Mississippi, 759 So. 2d 504, 505, 506, 2000 Miss. App. LEXIS 196 (2000)

[216] Vazquez v. Rossnagle, 163 F. Supp. 2d 494, 2001 U.S. Dist. LEXIS 3974 (3d Cir. 2001).

[217] In re Crossley, 2003 Mich. App. LEXIS 327 (2003).

[218] The process requires access to a nuclear reactor where the lead sample is radiated to reveal the trace components contained within the lead.

homogenous received strong criticism and appears to be an unsupportable theory, even though neutron activation analysis can reveal the trace elements like silver, copper, antimony, or arsenic that are present in bullet lead.[219] It is doubtful if any trial court would admit such lead bullet evidence using neutron activation analysis at the present time.[220]

I. DNA Deoxyribonucleic Acid Identification

Scientific and technological advances in the past 25 years have made identification of suspects easier and more definite with the application of DNA typing. Deoxyribonucleic acid contains the pattern or unique hereditary "road-map" for all human beings and determines how humans develop, grow, and mature throughout life. The theory that everyone has unique DNA, except identical twins, has reached scientific certainty and the ability to translate the science from the laboratory to the courtroom has become routine. Suspects who have left samples of their DNA at the crime scene or on a victim may have their known DNA sample compared to recovered specimens. Where a person would never have had the opportunity to have lawfully been in a specific location to have left DNA evidence or would never have normally occupied a position to leave DNA evidence on or in a victim, the match that can be made may prove decisive in proving guilt. Similarly, wrongly convicted individuals may be able to prove that someone else was the criminal, and, in so doing, free themselves from illegal incarceration.

In recognition of the accuracy of DNA evidence, the Congress passed the DNA Analysis Backlog Elimination Act of 2000, which requires individuals who have been convicted of a qualifying federal offense, and who in prison, on parole or probation, or other supervised release, to provide DNA samples so that the federal government will be able to add the sample to the national DNA database of convicted felons.[221] One purpose of the database of DNA samples is to help clear older cases in which DNA evidence exists but has not yet been compared to known DNA samples, such as older rape cases in which rape kits have never been analyzed. Demonstrative of this practice, in a homicide case, a baseball cap worn by the shooter and recovered at the robbery scene, and a defendant's DNA taken from a recovered firearm matched a defendant's

---

[219] *See* Commonwealth v. Daye, 19 Mass L. Rep. 674, 2005 Mass. Super. LEXIS 368 (2005).

[220] The theoretical basis by which neutron activation analysis determines whether one lead specimen matched a different sample depends upon the homogenous nature of lead in the manufacturing process. Scientific research presently holds that lead samples are not homogenous, which dooms other scientific efforts to trace lead based on its composition. For a related discussion, *see* Clemmons v. State, 2006 Md. LEXIS 192 (2006). For one case that did permit bullet-lead analysis and was not reversed, *see* Smith v. Secretary, 2007 U.S. Dist. LEXIS 57703 (M.D. Fla. 2007).

[221] DNA Analysis Backlog Elimination Act of 2000, codified, as amended, at 18 U.S.C. § 3563 and 42 U.S.C.S. §§ 14132, 14135a, 14135e.

profile stored in a local CODIS DNA database.[222] The federal district court denied a motion to suppress the DNA evidence.

Although the scientific principle of DNA has been long accepted in American state and federal courts, alleged errors in statistical application and significance, the application of the science, the handling of DNA samples, issues involving alleged contamination,[223] hearsay allegations, and Sixth Amendment confrontation issues drive the litigation efforts of defendants to keep DNA evidence from being admitted at trial.

In an Ohio case in which the police collected the genetic material and transmitted the sample for testing to a crime lab, the trial court permitted the results to be introduced into court by an expert witness who had never observed the testing of the particular DNA sample. The trial expert witness used the report generated by the lab technician and offered his own conclusions linking the defendant to the crime. The intermediate reviewing court reversed the conviction based on the fact that the defendant was not able to cross-examine the lab technician.[224] On appeal, the Supreme Court of Ohio agreed with the trial court and held that the lab report was nontestimonial in nature and had been properly introduced.[225] Taking a similar view, a New York trial court admitted DNA evidence against a defendant where one sample had been taken in 1993, stored, and analyzed years later. The technician compared the stored DNA sample to a recent one taken from the defendant and reported a match. An expert witness in forensic biology and DNA typing testified that she supervised and reviewed the records of the DNA profile performed on the defendant's saliva at the medical examiner's office and she also reviewed and compared the DNA profile taken from the victim and testified that they all matched. The court found that the admission of the DNA evidence did not violate the defendant's right to confront witnesses and would not result in a reversal of the case on appeal.[226]

DNA analysis using the Restriction Fragment Length Polymorphism (RFLP) testing requires relatively large and non-degraded samples in order to obtain accurate results. The expert usually is able to testify using statistical probability to render an opinion concerning a DNA match. Newer methods, such as the Polymerase Chain Reaction (PCR) process of DNA testing, enable

---

[222] United States v. Davis, 602 F. Supp.2d 658, 2009 U.S. Dist. LEXIS 22514 (D. Maryland 2009). This case also contains an excellent description of the science supporting DNA analysis.

[223] *See* 3 CARDOZO PUB. L. POL'Y & ETHICS J. 847 (2006). *DNA in the Legal System: The Benefits Are Clear, The Problems Aren't Always.*

[224] State v. Crager, 164 Ohio App. 3d 816, 826, 827, 2005 Ohio 6868, 844 N. E. 2d 390, 398, 399, 2005 Ohio App. LEXIS 6188 (2005), *cert. granted,* 109 Ohio St. 3d 1421, 2006 Ohio 1967, 2006 Ohio LEXIS 1037 (2006).

[225] State v. Crager, 116 Ohio St. 3d 369, 2007 Ohio 6840, 2007 Ohio LEXIS 3355 (Ohio 2007).

[226] People v. Brown, 2005 N.Y. Slip Op. 25303, 9 Misc. 3d 420, 423, 801 N.Y.S.2d 709, 711, 2005 N.Y. Misc. LEXIS 1556 (2005).

scientists to amplify or copy DNA samples that are too small to subject to the RFLP process prior to amplification.[227] The expert who has conducted the testing, or the expert who will testify in court in reliance on the work of laboratory technicians, will testify concerning the collection of the evidence and its testing and will interpret the results in a form that will be useful for the trier of fact.

J. Fingerprint Identification

The basic theory that everyone has unique fingerprints and that fingerprints do not change with time or age allows identification between a known sample and an unknown impression. The standard methodology used in the United States, ACE-V, stands for analysis, comparison, evaluation, and verification.[228] From the first time it was admitted in court in 1911, these principles have generally been accepted by courts as offering a sound method of making reliable identifications.[229] By implementing these principles, law enforcement officers may make identifications using palm, toe, and heel prints, where suspects have generated print impressions. The police officer or evidence technician must testify concerning the recovery process that was used to obtain the visible impression or latent prints from a crime scene, but the analysis and interpretation of the results must generally be introduced in court by an expert. As required in other fields of expertise, the expert must establish an evidentiary foundation to show that by study, training, and experience he or she has attained sufficient expertise to offer opinion testimony. For example, in a burglary case, despite a defense objection, a judge accepted the prosecution's witness as an expert following her explanation concerning her qualifications. She testified:

> that her basic classroom work in "ridgeology" was done at the Hawai'i Criminal Justice Data Center in Honolulu, her advance classroom work was done with the Sacramento Police Department (SPD) in California, and she had a diploma or certificate for ridgeology from the SPD. [She] further testified that she did not receive any "FBI [United States Federal Bureau of Investigation] identification training," did not know if the SPD "had any kind of national accreditation," did not "have any kind of certification with any national or international group," and had not been assigned "any kind of error rate or proficiency" for her work in fingerprinting.[230]

---

[227] *See* United States v. Morrow, 374 F. Supp. 2d 51, 2005 U.S. Dist. LEXIS 8327 (D.D.C. 2005).

[228] Commonwealth v. Patterson, 445 Mass. 626, 628 n. 2, 840 N.E.2d 12, 14 n.2, 2005 Mass. LEXIS 765 (2005).

[229] Illinois v. Jennings, 252 Ill. 534, 96 N.E. 1077 (1911). More recently, the Court of Appeals upheld the validity of fingerprint identification in United States v. Crisp, 324 F.3d 261, 2003 U.S. App. LEXIS 6021 (4th Cir. 2003), *cert. denied*, 540 U.S. 888, 2003 U.S. LEXIS 6388 (2003). Utah recently upheld the principle of fingerprint identification validity in State v. Quintana 2004 Utah App. 418, 103 P.2d 168, 169, 2004 Utah App. LEXIS 459 (2004).

[230] State v. Medeiros, 206 Haw. App. LEXIS 185 (2006).

While a person must qualify as an expert at interpreting fingerprints in order to properly testify, police personnel or evidence technicians are assigned to collect and preserve fingerprint evidence. When properly obtained and preserved, other experts offer the evidence in court. The FBI and many large law enforcement agencies have experts trained in fingerprint analysis and schooled in courtroom presentation of that evidence. Some cases may present special challenges to obtaining usable fingerprint evidence. In a Virginia case, a police officer used a mixture of equal parts water, black fingerprint powder, and clear Ivory dish soap and applied it to the reverse side of a vehicle identification strip to reveal a defendant's fingerprints. The judge allowed the evidence to be introduced by a fingerprint analyst who testified that the specially revealed fingerprint matched the defendant's prints.[231]

To assist the jury in understanding fingerprint testimony, the expert normally will use enlarged photographs, PowerPoint presentations, or other means to show the points of similarity in the ridges and lines on which the expert has based his or her conclusion.

In a slightly different context, experts may be permitted to testify that footprints at the crime scene match or have a close resemblance to the shoes worn by the accused in a criminal case. For example, a trial court permitted a forensic technician to testify that shoe prints left in fireproofing dust from a safe cracked during a burglary matched the shoes worn by the defendant. The court observed that qualified expert testimony could be admitted because shoe print identification does not rest on arcane scientific principles, but on visual comparison of physical samples. An expert could recognize small anomalies in shoe design, wear, or physical traits characteristic of a particular shoe that might escape a non-expert. The judge ruled that such information could assist the jury and should be admitted.[232] In a Georgia rape and burglary case, the court admitted evidence of shoe impressions taken from the crime scene. A Georgia Bureau of Identification microanalyst conducted the comparisons between the impression and the actual shoes of the defendant and testified at trial that there was a good match between the wear pattern and tread design of defendant's shoe and the crime scene impressions.[233] However, some jurisdictions do not require an expert to make a shoe print comparison where a footprint has been photographed and compared to shoes a defendant was wearing at the time of apprehension. In one case, the trial court allowed photographs of the impressions and the actual shoes into evidence while allowing the jury to decide whether a match existed.[234]

K. Testimony Relating to Drug Operations

Drug manufacturing and distribution operations generally have significant similarities, such that law enforcement officials who have extensive experience

---

[231] Hasson v. Commonwealth, 2006 Va. App. LEXIS (2006).

[232] *See* Ratiff v. State, 110 P.3d 982, 2005 Alas. App. LEXIS 39 (2005).

[233] Thrasher v. Georgia, 2003 Ga. App. LEXIS 734 (2003).

[234] Redmond v. Mississippi, 815 So. 2d 1241, 1245, 2002 Miss. App. LEXIS 123 (2002).

in drug-related crime may be permitted to offer expert testimony concerning the modus operandi of drug traffickers. As a limitation, the expert must be careful to explain the usual pattern of drug operation within his or her area of expertise but not to carry the testimony so far as to offer a personal opinion concerning guilt[235] because that is beyond the area of expertise and intrudes on the province of the jury. Experts involved with investigating illegal drug use and sale can be permitted to respond to hypothetical situations posed by the prosecutor where the hypothetical closely mirrors the facts in the case. In a New Jersey case, an officer was asked to assume that a hypothetical was true and to offer an opinion concerning whether a person in the hypothetical would be possessing drugs for personal use or for sale. The Supreme Court of New Jersey approved allowing the officer to testify as an expert because the officer had extensive experience in investigation drug culture and sales protocols.[236] Expert witnesses may be authorized to testify regarding the identification, use, and value of narcotics, as well as the language used by narcotics dealers.[237] To qualify as an expert, the witness must show that his or her knowledge, skill, training, or experience allows the witness to help the fact finders understand and evaluate the significance of the evidence.[238] Qualified witnesses may be permitted to express their opinions concerning whether a given hypothetical fact pattern would indicate that a person who was engaged in drug transactions for personal use was involved in drug distribution.[239] In one case, the court found that there was no abuse of discretion in allowing a paid informant to testify as an expert witness about drug transactions when the evidence indicated that the informant had participated in more than 50 similar drug sales.[240]

A police officer may testify as an expert regarding drug-related practices if the evidence introduced indicates that the officer is qualified by experience, training, and education. For example, a reviewing court held that the trial court did not abuse its discretion in a drug-trafficking prosecution by admitting a police officer's expert testimony regarding countersurveillance techniques employed by a drug dealer to avoid detection.[241] To assist lay jurors, qualified law enforcement officers can testify concerning common practices of drug dealers, how sales occur, and that innocent adults are never permitted to be present at the scene of illegal drug sales.[242]

In a Pennsylvania case, defendants had been making telephone calls to each other in which they would use cryptic language. The question "What

---

[235] New Jersey v. Summers, 176 N.J. 306, 323, 324, 823 A.2d 15, 2003 N.J. LEXIS 567 (2003).

[236] New Jersey v. Nesbitt, 185 N.J. 504, 511, 888 A.2d 472, 478, 2006 N.J. LEXIS 7 (2006).

[237] United States v. Walker, 2006 U.S. App. LEXIS 11280 (6th Cir. 2006).

[238] United States v. Garcia, 2006 U.S. App. LEXIS 10955 (11th Cir. 2006).

[239] New Jersey v. Summers, 350 N.J. Super. 353, 365, 366, 795 A.2d 308, 2002 N.J. Super. LEXIS 195 (2002).

[240] United States v. Anderson, 813 F.2d 1450 (9th Cir. 1987).

[241] United States v. deSoto, 885 F.2d 354 (7th Cir. 1989). *See* case in Part II.

[242] United States v. Garcia, 439 F.3d 363, 366, 2006 U.S. App. LEXIS 5032 (7th Cir. 2006).

can you do for me?" is answered by, "Tomorrow." A second exchange queried, "Ain't nothing jumpin', " and received the reply, "Goddam boy, whatcha doin'?" The reply to this exchange was, "Just waiting around." The trial court ruling, affirmed on appeal, permitted an expert in drug sales to state that, in his opinion, this type of telephone exchange indicated that one person wanted to buy drugs and that the other person would sell but did not have any drugs to sell but was waiting for a new shipment.[243] In an older federal case, the court held that a detective could testify as an expert regarding the significance of extensive telephone traffic between the defendant and members of an alleged drug ring, because the evidence showed that the detective had specialized knowledge that would assist the trier of fact in understanding the evidence.[244] The court recognized that the detective had worked vice narcotics for seven years and tactical narcotics before that, participating in more than 200 street arrests and investigations.

L. *Other Subjects of Expert Testimony*

With the continued popularity of the Internet, the trading of child pornography has accelerated. In an effort to reduce the incidence of harm to children, state and federal prosecutors continue to bring many child pornography cases in which the age of the young subjects is an element to be proved. While lay opinion testimony can be admitted, expert testimony may assist the trier of fact in reaching a conclusion. In a California case in which the possession of child pornography was used to revoke probation, revocation required proof that a minor was involved in the depiction and the government had to prove that the probationer knew that the actors were under the age of 18. The trial court approved of the use of two experts who had special knowledge and were qualified to judge the age of persons depicted in the pornography. According to the trial court:

> Here the testimony of both [experts] was regarding developmental factors beyond the normal experience and knowledge of the average fact finder. The age of the actors was an element of the offense and the testimony of the experts was relevant to the conclusion.[245]

Expert testimony has not been limited to verbal evidence; computer generated animations have been permitted when created by crime scene reconstruction experts. The animations must be properly authenticated as depicting what they purport to depict by presenting a fair and accurate representation of

---

[243] Commonwealth v. Moss, 2004 Pa. Super 224, 852 A.2d 374, 2004 Pa. Super. LEXIS 1408 (2004).

[244] United States v. Brewer, 1 F.3d 1430 (4th Cir. 1993).

[245] California v. Kurey, 88 Cal. App. 4th 840, 846, 847, 106 Cal. Rptr. 2d 150, 2001 Cal. App. LEXIS 319 (2001). See also United States v. Hamilton, 413 F.3d 1138, 1143–1144, 2005 U.S. App. LEXIS 12790 (10th Cir. 2005).

the evidence. To be considered for admission, the probative value of computer generated animations must not outweigh any danger of unfair prejudice to the defendant. In a Pennsylvania case, the trial court permitted the prosecution's expert to offer a frame by frame image of how the expert believed that the killer committed the murder of his wife. In approving the admission of the evidence, the appellate court noted that the use of computer generated animations had to be weighed carefully because of the danger of prejudice. The animation was admissible because it assisted the expert in offering his opinion and served as a graphic representation that illustrated the previously formed opinion of the expert witness.[246]

Some of the many other subjects of expert testimony include modus operandi of offenders,[247] speed of vehicles,[248] cause of a fire,[249] cause of an explosion,[250] meaning of terms,[251] cause of death,[252] DNA profile identification,[253] blood alcohol content,[254] and shoe and tire imprint testimony.[255]

§ 11.11　Experts from Crime Laboratories

Because of the limitations placed on the use of confessions, more reliance is being placed upon the use of real evidence and other evidence obtained by laboratory technicians. With the addition of crime laboratories in all parts of the country, experts from these laboratories have become more readily available. These experts must qualify as do other experts, through experience, training, or knowledge before they can give opinions concerning the significance of laboratory tests and other scientific evidence and the evidence must be useful to the finder of fact. Expert testimony of this type is especially important in the field of ballistics—comparing cartridge cases and bullets found at the scene with those fired from a known weapon. For example, in a murder prosecution, the court permitted the commonwealth's laboratory expert to explain the methodology followed in using a comparison microscope to examine a known shotgun shell and compare it to a shell of unknown origin. The court allowed the ballistics expert to testify that the shell fired at the crime came from the defendant's shotgun because it contained the same markings as did the test-fired shell. The judge admitted the evidence linking the shell to the gun

---

[246]　Commonwealth v. Serge, 2006 Pa. LEXIS 561 (2006).

[247]　Johninson v. State, 878 S.W.2d 727 (Ark. 1994).

[248]　Matos v. State, 899 So. 2d 403, 2005 Fla. App. LEXIS 4359 (2005).

[249]　Commonwealth v. Lugo, 63 Mass. App. Ct. 204, 824 N.E.2d 481, 2005 Mass. App. LEXIS 296 (2005).

[250]　Bitler v. A.O. Smith, 400 F.3d 1227, 2004 U.S. LEXIS 28000 (10th Cir. 2004).

[251]　United States v. Walker, 2006 U.S. App. 11280 (10th Cir. 2006).

[252]　State v. Vining, 645 A.2d 20 (Me. 1994).

[253]　Brown v. State, 270 Ga. App. 176, 605 S.E.2d 885, 2004 Ga. App. LEXIS 1381 (2004).

[254]　State v. Taylor, 165 N.C. App. 750; 600 S.E.2d 483, 2004 N.C. App. LEXIS 1519 (2004).

[255]　Rodgers v. State, 2006 Tex. Crim. App. LEXIS (2006).

because ballistics was a proper subject for expert testimony.[256] No attempt will be made here to list all of the other areas in which a crime laboratory expert can testify, but these include tool mark comparisons and testimony concerning glass and glass fractures, enhancing latent fingerprint evidence with cyano-acrylate fuming, clothing, hairs, and fibers.

§ 11.12 Summary

Because most witnesses testify as lay witnesses, generally witnesses should confine their testimony to "who," "what," "where," and "when" types of answers and not "how" or "why" answers. Because humans typically form opinions in matters of everyday life, there is no absolute bar to admitting lay opinion evidence. The general rule excluding opinion evidence gives way in a variety of settings for lay witnesses and almost disappears when expert witnesses are concerned. The rule excluding lay opinion evidence is based on the principle that the witnesses are to furnish the facts and the jury has the responsibility of reaching conclusions based on these facts.

There are, however, necessary exceptions to the general rule limiting lay opinion testimony. These common-sense exceptions have been developed so that the jury will have better information and because the courts have recognized that it is often impossible to give facts to describe all situations. For example, it is difficult to give facts that explain a person's emotional state or to explain that a person was "nervous," "upset," or "acted suspiciously."

The rules relating to the exceptions to the opinion rule are discussed in two categories: those relating to nonexpert opinions and those relating to expert opinions. If the ordinary lay witness cannot adequately or accurately describe the facts so as to enable the jurors to draw an intelligent conclusion, the witness may be permitted to offer a lay opinion. For example, a lay witness, in the usual case and with certain limitations, may give opinion testimony as to age, smell, appearance, conduct, distance, mental condition, handwriting, identification, and speed of a vehicle.

Expert witness, when properly qualified, may offer opinions where the opinions will assist the trier of fact in situations where lay opinion would not be permitted. However, this exception possesses a different logical basis; therefore, the rules are different. This opinion testimony is allowed because the expert, due to training, experience, or knowledge, can give information on a specific subject that is substantially superior to the knowledge possessed by the average person. The opinion of the expert witness does not have to be, and usually is not, based on direct observation of prior incidents that brought about the trial. An expert's opinion may be based on scientific testing

---

[256] Commonwealth v. Whitacre, 2005 Pa. Super. 221, 878 A.2d 96, 100, 2005 Pa. Super. LEXIS 1500 (2005).

performed by the expert him- or herself, testing conducted by other experts, questions based on hypothetical assumed facts, or on facts presented by other witnesses in the trial.

Some examples of subjects of expert testimony are: (1) speed of automobile, (2) identification of vehicle from tire marks; (3) cause of death; (4) handwriting comparisons; (5) typewriter comparisons; (6) DNA identification; (7) fingerprint comparison identification and (8) firearms and ballistics identification.

Although sworn justice personnel will not normally present the case in court, because many officers will offer crucial portions of testimony, it is important to understand the lay opinion rule and the exceptions to it. While ordinary law enforcement personnel may actually qualify as expert witnesses due to specialized training and experience, most police officers will be testifying as lay witnesses in criminal trials where opinion evidence has limitations.

Hearsay Rule
and Exceptions

12

The determination that a statement is hearsay does not end the inquiry into admissibility; there must still be a further examination of the need for the statement at trial and the circumstantial guaranty of trustworthiness surrounding the making of the statement.

Zippo Mfg. Co. v. Rogers Imports, Inc.,
216 F. Supp. 670 (S.D.N.Y. 1963)

Chapter Outline

Section
12.1   Introduction
12.2   Definitions and Statement of the Hearsay Rule
12.3   History and Development of the Hearsay Rule
12.4   Exceptions to the Hearsay Rule—General
12.5   —Spontaneous and Excited Utterances
12.6   —Business and Public Records
12.7   —Family History and Records (Pedigree)
12.8   —Former Testimony
12.9   —Dying Declarations
12.10 —Declarations Against Interest
12.11 —Other Exceptions—Residual Exceptions
12.12 Nontestimonial Utterances
12.13 Summary

§ 12.1 Introduction

While virtually everyone has heard of the concept of hearsay evidence, whether from books, films, television shows, and newspapers, most people do not know how it operates in court and fewer still understand the rationale behind the hearsay rule. Even those who have some understanding of the rule are probably unaware that the exceptions to the hearsay rule allow may allow more evidence to be admitted than the rule excludes. When a court recognizes an exception and admits hearsay evidence, there are usually powerful reasons and other justifications for trusting the truthfulness of the evidence. If the hearsay rule were applied without exceptions, it would be very difficult in many criminal cases to present sufficient facts to prove guilt, and certainly much reliable evidence would be excluded from consideration.

As a practical matter, determining what kind of testimony can be considered hearsay provides the starting point for developing an understanding of this rule of exclusion. When an out-of-court statement is repeated in court by a person who overheard another person outside of court make a statement, the evidence that the witness utters in court may be excluded on the ground that it constitutes hearsay evidence. To be properly considered hearsay evidence, the substance of the out-of-court statement must have been offered in court to prove its truth. When an out-of-court statement is repeated in court and the purpose of offering the statement was merely to demonstrate that a particular person was physically present to be able to make the statement, the internal contents of the statement have not been offered for the proof of the truth contained within the words. In that situation, the out-of-court statement is not considered hearsay evidence. Courts tend to exclude hearsay evidence because subtle alterations in wording, demeanor, or inflection may change the meaning of spoken words. Every time a story is retold to a new person, the essence of the story alters slightly, with a detail added or unconsciously deleted, causing the meaning to shift. The general rule excluding hearsay statements is justified on these and other grounds. It is important to be aware of the historical justifications for the rule in order to understand the exceptions. If the reasons for the rule do not exist in a particular situation, then the evidence should be admitted to assist in determining the facts of the case. Some of the reasons for the exclusion of evidence under the hearsay rule are discussed in the following paragraphs.

1. "Traditionally, testimony that is given by a witness who relates not what he or she knows personally, but what others have said, and that is therefore dependent on the credibility of someone other than the witness."[1]

2. "Hearsay evidence is objectionable because the person who makes the offered statement is not under oath and is not subject to cross-examination."[2] Although the witness in court who has repeated what someone else has said will be under oath, the person who actually made the statement was not under oath so that hearsay statements generally lack trustworthiness.

3. The demeanor or conduct of the person who actually makes the statement cannot be observed by the judge and jury when the witness comes to court to tell what was stated outside the court. Evaluating demeanor proves important when judging credibility of witnesses and is an important aspect of the right of confrontation.[3]

4. There is a danger that the in-court witness who is reporting what was said by an out-of-court declarant may repeat the statement inaccurately. The proponent of the evidence "essentially asks the jury to assume that the out-of-court declarant was not lying or mistaken when the statement was made."[4]

5. One of the principal reasons for the hearsay rule is to exclude declarations whose veracity or truthfulness cannot be tested by cross-examination. Because the declarant's statement was made out of court, the declarant cannot be cross-examined and the adverse party against whom the evidence is offered is deprived of the opportunity to challenge his memory or sincerity.[5]

In explaining some of the reasons for excluding hearsay evidence from court, one reviewing court noted that "[h]earsay evidence is excluded because

---

[1]   BLACK'S LAW DICTIONARY (2004).

[2]   Missouri v. Mozee, 2003 Mo. App. LEXIS 940 (2003), quoting State v. Bowens, 964 S.W. 2d 232, 240, 1998 Mo. App. LEXIS 383 (1998).

[3]   *See* In re Kentron D., 101 Cal. App. 4th 1381, 125 Cal. Rptr. 2d 260, 2002 Cal. App. LEXIS 4629 (2002).

[4]   Armstead v. State, 255 Ga. App. 385, 389, 565 S.E.2d 579, 582, 2002 Ga. App. LEXIS 633 (2002).

[5]   Iowa v. Dullard, 2003 Iowa Sup. LEXIS 169 (2003).

the value of the statement rests on the credibility of the out-of-court asserter who is not subject to cross-examination and other safeguards of reliability."[6] Similarly, the Supreme Court of Connecticut offered related reasons for the hearsay rule when it stated:

> The declarant might be lying; he might have misperceived the events which he relates; he might have faulty memory; his words might be misunderstood or taken out of context by the listener. And the ways in which these dangers are minimized for in-court statements—the oath, the witness' awareness of the gravity of the proceedings, the jury's ability to observe the witness' demeanor, and, most importantly, the right of the opponent to cross-examine—are generally absent for things said out of court.[7]

Some forms of hearsay evidence prove more reliable than others and for that reason some hearsay will be admitted based on recognized and standardized hearsay exceptions. The courts, in seeking to allow as much evidence into court as possible while sifting out unreliable evidence, have developed many exceptions to the hearsay rule. For each exception, however, there is a clear justification designed to assure the trustworthiness of the evidence. In situations involving hearsay in which none of the well-known hearsay exceptions permits admission of the evidence, the federal rules allow a party to argue that the interests of justice would be promoted by admission of the hearsay evidence where there are guarantees that the evidence sought to be introduced would be trustworthy and probative on the point for which it is offered.[8]

While this chapter emphasizes many hearsay exceptions, some types of evidence that may be challenged as excludable hearsay have been discussed in other chapters of the book. For example, an out-of-court confession that is repeated by another person in a court is, technically, hearsay. However, this evidence is often admissible under one of the exceptions discussed in Chapter 16. The hearsay exception of "past recollection recorded" and its rationale were discussed in Chapter 9. Official records, ancient documents, and learned treatises are generally admissible as hearsay exceptions and will be considered in Chapter 13.

This chapter discusses and defines the hearsay rule of exclusion and introduces the important exceptions that permit hearsay evidence to be admitted in criminal courts. Among the exceptions treated within this chapter are declarations against interest, the business records exception, dying declarations, spontaneous and excited utterances, and family history.

---

6   State v. Taylor, 999 So. 2d 1262, 2009 La. App. Unpub. LEXIS 45 (La. 2009).
7   Connecticut v. Cruz, 260 Conn. 1, 792 A.2d 823, 2002 Conn. LEXIS 127 (2002).
8   *See* FED. R. EVID. 807.

§ 12.2 Definitions and Statement of the Hearsay Rule

Rule 801

Definitions

The following definitions apply under this article:

(a) Statement. A "statement" is (1) an oral or written assertion or (2) non-verbal conduct of a person, if it is intended by the person as an assertion.

(b) Declarant. A "declarant" is a person who makes a statement.

(c) Hearsay. "Hearsay" is a statement, other than one made by the declarant while testifying at the trial or hearing, offered in evidence to prove the truth of the matter asserted.

(d) Statements which are not hearsay. A statement is not hearsay if—

(1) Prior statement by witness.—The declarant testifies at the trial or hearing and is subject to cross-examination concerning the statement, and the statement is (A) inconsistent with the declarant's testimony, and was given under oath subject to the penalty of perjury at a trial, hearing, or other proceeding, or in a deposition, or (B) consistent with the declarant's testimony and is offered to rebut an express or implied charge against the declarant of recent fabrication or improper influence or motive, or (C) one of identification of a person made after perceiving the person; or

(2) Admission by party-opponent.—The statement is offered against a party and is (A) the party's own statement in either an individual or a representative capacity or (B) a statement of which the party has manifested an adoption or belief in its truth, or (C) a statement by a person authorized by the party to make a statement concerning the subject, or (D) a statement by the party's agent or servant concerning a matter within the scope of the agency or employment, made during the existence of the relationship, or (E) a statement by a co-conspirator of a party during the course and in furtherance of the conspiracy. The contents of the statement shall be considered but are not alone sufficient to establish the declarant's authority under subdivision (C), the agency or employment relationship and scope thereof under subdivision (D), or the existence of the conspiracy and the participation therein of the declarant and the party against whom the statement is offered under subdivision (E).[9]

During the course of both civil and criminal litigation, many courts have resolved and refined hearsay problems by explaining the concepts and defining hearsay and evaluating the admissibility of hearsay evidence. Although these explanations are worded differently, the general meaning of hearsay concepts emerges. Some of these definitions are included here as examples:

> Evidence of a statement which is made other than by the witness while testifying at a hearing, offered to prove the truth of the matter stated, is hearsay evidence and inadmissible, subject to certain statutory exceptions.[10]

---

[9] FED. R. EVID. 801.

[10] State v. Clark, 949 P.2d 1099 (Kan. 1997).

" 'Hearsay' is a statement, other than one made by the declarant while testifying at the trial or hearing, offered in evidence to prove the truth of the matter asserted."[11]

"Hearsay" is a statement, other than one made by the declarant while testifying at the trial or hearing, offered in evidence to prove the truth of the matter asserted.[12]

"Hearsay testimony" is an out-of-court statement offered to prove the truth of a matter asserted and is dependent on the credibility of the out-of-court declarant.[13]

The federal courts have interpreted and explained the Federal Rules of Evidence as litigants have raised legal questions and identified problems. For example, one court decided that evidence was "not hearsay" as defined in Rule 801(d)(1)(A) when a witness, although present and testifying at the trial, claimed no recollection of either the underlying events described in his prior grand jury testimony or of the giving of the testimony itself.[14] The trial court did not abuse its discretion in admitting the witness's grand jury testimony under Rule 801(d)(1)(A), which pertains to prior inconsistent statements. When prior inconsistent statements come within the rule, they are not considered hearsay and may be admitted as substantive evidence.

Under Rule 801(d)(1)(A), if an out-of-court statement is inconsistent with the declarant's trial testimony and was given under the penalty of perjury at a deposition, trial, hearing, or similar proceeding, the prior statement may be received as evidence and is not considered hearsay. For purposes of this rule, the word "inconsistent" does not include only statements diametrically opposed or logically incompatible, but also evasive answers, silence, changes in position, or in a reported change in memory.[15]

According to one court, the rationale for the admission of prior consistent statements as provided in Rule 801(d)(1)(B) is that the statements are considered relevant and necessary.[16] Where there is a charge of recent fabrication, a witness's prior deposition testimony is admissible to refute these charges of fabrication.[17] However, a sexual assault victim's videotaped statements were not admissible under this exception for prior statements by the witness when the victim was never subjected to cross-examination about the prior statements.[18]

---

[11]   Perkins v. State, 2009 Ala. Crim. App. LEXIS 12 (Ala. 2009).

[12]   IND. R. EVID. 801(c) (Matthew Bender 2009).

[13]   People v. Schoultz, 224 Ill. Dec. 885, 682 N.E.2d 446 (1997).

[14]   United States v. DiCaro, 772 F.2d 1314 (7th Cir. 1985).

[15]   United States v. Williams, 737 F.2d 594 (7th Cir. 1984). *See also* State v. Pusyka, 592 A.2d 850 (R.I. 1991), in which the court held that a witness's prior statement must be sufficiently inconsistent with the witness's in-court testimony to be admissible. This determination is within the sound discretion of the trial judge.

[16]   State v. Gardner, 490 N.W.2d 838 (Iowa 1992).

[17]   State v. Deases, 479 N.W.2d 597 (Iowa 1991).

[18]   State v. Palabay, 844 P.2d 1 (Wash. 1992).

The purpose of Rule 801(d)(1)(C) is to permit introduction of identifications made by a witness when the witness's memory was fresh and there was less opportunity for influence to be exerted upon him.[19]

The United States Supreme Court has determined that an out-of-court identification by the victim, naming the defendant as the assailant, was admissible as nonhearsay although the victim could not remember seeing the assailant.[20]

Section 801(d)(1)(B) of the Federal Rules of Evidence provides that a statement is not hearsay if consistent with the declarant's testimony and offered to rebut an express or implied charge against the declarant of recent fabrication or improper influence or motive. In a case that reached the United States Supreme Court, Tome v. United States, the interpretation of this provision was debated.[21] In Tome, the government initiated charges against the defendant involving the sexual abuse of his four-year-old daughter. The prosecution's theory was that the defendant committed the assaults while the child was with the defendant and disclosed the crime when she was spending vacation time with her mother. The defense argued that the allegations were concocted so that the mother would obtain custody and the child would not be returned to her father. After the alleged motive to fabricate arose, the child made out-of-court statements to witnesses. At the trial, the judge permitted the admission of the statements of some of these witness statements, despite the fact that they were introduced after charges of recent fabrication had been made. The United States Supreme Court reversed the conviction, deciding that Rule 801(d)(1)(B) permitted the introduction of a declarant's consistent out-of-court statements to rebut a charge of recent fabrication or improper influence, or motive only when those statements were made before the fabrication, influence, or motive arose.

Determining that the statements made by the child to other witnesses were made after the defendant's charge of fabrication, the Supreme Court remanded the case for further proceedings. The majority explained that to allow the out-of-court statements made after the in-court charge of fabrication would shift the emphasis of the trial to the out-of-court statements rather than the in-court statements.

Rule 801(d)(2)(E) of the Federal Rules, which has been made part of the rules of evidence in many states, provides that a statement is not hearsay if made by a conspirator during the course of and in furtherance of the conspiracy. Changes made to Federal Rule 801(d)(2)(E) in 1997 noted that the contents of a statement made by a conspirator are insufficient to establish that the conspirator can speak for the other conspirators. While an out-of-court statement made by a conspirator fits the traditional definition of hearsay, this rule of evidence simply declares that it shall not be deemed to be hearsay. In explaining the rule's purpose, a federal court noted that statements made by conspirators during the course of and in furtherance of a conspiracy do not fit

---

[19]   United States v. Marchand, 564 F.2d 983 (2d Cir. 1977).

[20]   United States v. Owens, 484 U.S. 554, 108 S. Ct. 838, 98 L. Ed. 2d 951 (1988).

[21]   Tome v. United States, 513 U.S. 150, 115 S. Ct. 696, 130 L. Ed. 2d 574 (1995).

within the definition of hearsay; rather, the court views these statements as party admissions.[22] A conspirator's statement is made in furtherance of the conspiracy (so as to be admissible as) when the statement is part of the information flow between the conspirators, intended to help each perform his or her role.[23] However, a mere conversation between the conspirators or merely narrative declarations among them would not constitute conversations made "in furtherance of a conspiracy" and would not be admissible under this provision.[24]

In case in which a doctor wanted to hire a hit man to kill his wife, the trial court refused to allow the doctor's son to testify, under Rule 801(d)(1)(B), that the doctor really only wanted the hit man to follow his wife and conduct some surveillance. The doctor told the son the surveillance story only after being arrested in the plot, and therefore he had a motive to fabricate despite his assertion to the contrary. Because the motive to fabricate arose before the statement to his son, the son could be prohibited from testifying about his father's statement because it would not meet Rule 801's requirements and would be considered inadmissible hearsay.[25]

Rule 802

Hearsay Rule

Hearsay is not admissible except as provided by these rules or by other rules prescribed by the Supreme Court pursuant to statutory authority or by Act of Congress.[26]

As defined in Rule 801 of the Federal Rules of Evidence, hearsay is "a statement other than one made by the declarant while testifying at the trial or hearing offered in evidence to prove the truth of the matter asserted."[27] Another definition is that hearsay evidence is evidence that derives its value not from the credit to be given to the witness upon the stand, but at least in part from the veracity and competency of another person who is not testifying. One court stated that "Hearsay is testimony of an out-of-court statement offered to establish the truth of the matter asserted therein and whose value thus depends upon the credibility of the out-of-court declarant."[28] For example, if a police officer were to testify concerning the meaning of numbers on a fast food receipt when the officer gathered his understanding of the significance of the numbers by speaking with an employee of the fast food establishment, the officer's testimony would

---

[22] United States v. Powell, 973 F.2d 885 (10th Cir. 1992), *cert. denied*, 507 U.S. 1161, 113 S. Ct. 1598, 123 L. Ed. 2d 161 (1992).
[23] United State v. Godinez, 110 F.3d 448 (7th Cir. 1997).
[24] United State v. Nazemian, 748 F.2d 552 (9th Cir. 1991).
[25] United States v. Drury, 2003 U.S. App. LEXIS 18152 (11th Cir. 2003).
[26] FED. R. EVID. 802.
[27] *Id.*
[28] Illinois v. Thompson, 327 Ill. App. 3d 1061, 765 N.E.2d 1203, 2002 Ill. App. LEXIS 162 (2002).

constitute hearsay evidence because it depends on the veracity and credibility of the fast food employee who was not in court or under oath.

While hearsay evidence may be excluded, out-of-court statements that are not offered for their substantive truth may be admissible because they do not meet the definition of hearsay. Where police arrested a suspected drug dealer after observing a sale, they found two cell phones during the post-arrest search of his person. When phones rang on two occasions, the officer answered the calls and had conversations with unknown persons who wanted to buy drugs. The trial court permitted the substance of the conversations to be admitted against the defendant because the statements were not offered to prove their substantive truth, only that other people thought they could buy drugs by phoning the defendant's cell phones. These phone conversations were circumstantial evidence that the defendant had the intent to distribute drugs.[29]

The term "statement," as used in the hearsay definition, consists of: (1) an oral or written assertion or (2) nonverbal conduct of a person, if it is intended by him or her as an assertion or is a substitute for speech. Therefore, a statement may be an actual verbal statement, a written statement, or nonverbal conduct, such as pointing, to identify a suspect in a lineup. The act of pointing to indicate a choice in a lineup context operates as a substitute for speech and when a police officer subsequently testifies in court about the out-of-court witness's indication, the officer has brought the out-of-court, nonverbal assertion into court as a hearsay statement. A "declarant," as used in the hearsay definition, is a person who makes a statement.

Admitting hearsay evidence generally involves having the out-of-court declarant's statement or evidence introduced in court with the result that the defendant cannot actually cross-examine that actual declarant. Cross-examination of the witness in court is certainly possible, but the person actually offering the evidence is not in court, a fact that creates constitutional issues that intermix with hearsay jurisprudence. In interpreting the Sixth Amendment right of confrontation and cross-examination, the Supreme Court overruled a case that allowed testimonial evidence without personal confrontation with the adverse witness. The older case, *Ohio v. Roberts*,[30] permitted the admission of prior testimony against the defendant when the witness was unavailable and when the prior testimony bore some "indicia of reliability." Unavailability was a fairly easy determination, but "indicia of reliability" seemed to invite judicial determination on uncertain terms. When the confrontation issue came to the Court in *Crawford v. Washington*,[31] the Court took the opportunity to overrule *Ohio v. Roberts* and to clearly enforce the original concept of the Sixth Amendment confrontation clause.

In *Crawford*, the defendant had been convicted of assaulting a man who attempted to rape his wife, using evidence given by the wife in a statement

---

[29]   Commonwealth v. Vasquez, 20 Mass. L. Rep. 319, 2005 Mass. Super. LEXIS 656 (Mass. 2005).
[30]   Ohio v. Roberts, 448 U.S. 56, 1980 U.S. LEXIS 140 (1980).
[31]   541 U.S. 36, 2004 U.S. LEXIS 1838 (2004).

to police. The defendant's wife invoked her marital testimonial privilege and did not testify against the defendant, with the result being that the trial judge allowed the wife's statement to the police to be used against the defendant. The judge followed the *Ohio v. Roberts* view and allowed the testimony because the judge viewed the defendant's wife as unavailable and considered the wife's out-of-court statement to be "reliable." The statement called into question the defendant's contention of self-defense. The Supreme Court reversed the decision of the Supreme Court of Washington that reinstated the trial court conviction and held that Crawford's Sixth Amendment right to confront and cross-examine adverse witnesses had been violated. The Court found a Sixth Amendment violation because, where testimonial evidence was at issue, the playing of the wife's testimony by audiotape prevented the defendant from confronting or conducting any cross-examination of the wife. The Court held that the Sixth Amendment demanded both unavailability and at least a prior opportunity to cross-examine the witness. In this case, the defendant had no opportunity to ever cross-examine his wife. The rule to be distilled from the *Crawford* case is that when testimonial evidence is involved, there must be a trial opportunity to cross-examine the witness or a proper earlier proceeding where the right of cross-examination existed and there must be proof of unavailability of the witness.[32] The case did not put an end to hearsay exceptions, but reinstated the right to confront and cross-examine witnesses where prior testimony is involved.

In a later Washington case,[33] the alleged victim in a domestic violence case made a 911 call to report an assault by her former boyfriend, who was under a no-contact order and who had just fled the victim's dwelling. The former girlfriend-victim did not testify against her attacker, but the trial court admitted an audiotape of the 911 call against the defendant, over his Sixth Amendment objection. The defendant appealed his resulting conviction through Washington courts with unsuccessful results. The Supreme Court of the United States affirmed after determining that the 911 call was not testimonial in nature and the use of the audiotape did not create a confrontation and cross-examination issue under the Sixth Amendment. The victim was speaking with an emergency operator while the events were in progress, describing current circumstances that necessitated a police response. As the Court noted in making a distinction between testimonial statements and nontestimonial statements, "Statements are nontestimonial when made in the course of police interrogation under circumstances objectively indicating that the primary purpose of the interrogation is to enable police assistance to meet an ongoing emergency. They are testimonial when the circumstances objectively indicate that there is no such ongoing emergency, and that the primary purpose of the interrogation is to establish or prove past events potentially relevant to later criminal prosecution."[34] The

---

[32]   *Id.*
[33]   Davis v. Washington, 547 U.S. 813, 2006 U.S. LEXIS 4886 (2006).
[34]   *Id.* at 822.

victim's statements were not testimonial because the statements were necessary to enable the police to resolve the ongoing emergency rather than to reconstruct what had happened in the past. Because the Court characterized the 911 call as nontestimonial, the Sixth Amendment was not implicated.

In *Hammon v. Indiana*,[35] a companion case to *Davis v. Washington*, police responded to a domestic disturbance at the home of a married couple. The wife told officers that nothing was wrong, but invited the police inside the home, where they separately questioned each spouse. The wife signed an affidavit indicating that she had been the victim of a battery at the hands of her husband. The wife did not appear to testify at the bench trial. Over the defendant-husband's Sixth Amendment cross-examination objection, the trial court admitted the affidavit and other information that the wife had given to one of the officers. The prosecution put the officer who had questioned the wife on the stand and asked him to testify to what the wife-victim told him and to authenticate her affidavit. In relevant parts, the Indiana court all affirmed the conviction. The Supreme Court found that the wife's statements to police were testimonial in nature and the admission of the wife's statements violated the defendant's Sixth Amendment right of confrontation and cross-examination. According to the *Hammon* Court, the officer's questions were directed at determining what had happened and was part of an investigation into alleged criminal conduct. The more formal features of the investigation and the affidavit strengthened the testimonial aspects of the testimony given by police and through the introduction of the affidavit at trial. The Court reversed the defendant's conviction and remanded the case.

Although the rule that hearsay evidence is inadmissible is generally true, significant hearsay evidence is admitted based on exceptions to the general rule of exclusion and despite Sixth Amendment confrontation and cross-examination issues. The exceptions to the hearsay rule are so numerous that the argument could be made that most hearsay evidence may be admissible while some hearsay evidence may be excluded. This chapter considers some of the well-recognized exceptions and the reasoning for those exceptions in the sections that follow.

§ 12.3   History and Development of the Hearsay Rule

In an article that appeared in the *Minnesota Law Review*, the authors included a thumbnail sketch of the history of the use of the hearsay rule.[36] This article included the following history:

> The hearsay rule was not the creation of some clever legal philosopher or rules-drafting committee. Rather, it was a byproduct of jury-based common law adjudication. It was molded and remolded over the course of more than

---

[35]   547 U.S. 813, 2006 U.S. LEXIS 4886 (2006). Companion case to *Davis v. Washington*.

[36]   Richard F. Rakos and Stephen Landsman, *The Hearsay Rule as the Focus of Empirical Investigation*, 76 MINN. L. REV. 655 (1992).

four centuries by lawyers pursuing the business of representing clients and by judges seeking to ensure proper verdicts. As a consequence of its incremental development, the rule, like so much in Anglo-American jurisprudence, does not have a single goal or express a single viewpoint. It reflects a variety of objectives sought at different times by participants in the courtroom contests.

Medieval English jury adjudication was, in essence, based upon hearsay. Juries in the thirteenth and fourteenth centuries decided cases on the basis of rumor, gossip, and community opinion to which they were exposed before the trial commenced. While reservations about hearsay were articulated as early as 1202, it was not until the latter half of the 1500s that serious concerns were voiced about its use in litigation.

The hearsay rule as we know it had its origin in England in the sixteenth century. Prior to that time, juries were permitted to obtain evidence by consulting persons who were not called as witnesses. Jurors did not decide the case on the basis of testimony given in open court, but were in fact chosen because they had some knowledge of the case.

In 1813, Chief Justice Marshall, in explaining the justification for the hearsay rule, stated, "Our lives, our liberty, and our property, are all concerned in the support of these rules, which have been matured by the wisdom of ages, and are now revered from their antiquity and the good sense in which they are founded. One of these rules is that hearsay evidence is by its own nature inadmissible." Justice Marshall went on to say that "[i]ts intrinsic weakness, its incompetency to satisfy the mind of the existence of the fact, and the frauds which might be practiced under its cover, combine to support the rule that hearsay evidence is totally inadmissible."[37]

As jurors began to be chosen only if they had no knowledge of the case that would influence their decision, the hearsay rule began to develop. By 1700, the rule prohibiting the admission of hearsay statements was formulated in criminal cases. Over the centuries, exceptions to the hearsay rule have developed because of the strict exclusionary nature of the rule.

§ 12.4   Exceptions to the Hearsay Rule – General

Although Chief Justice John Marshall argued that hearsay evidence should not be admitted in federal courts because of its intrinsic weakness and incompetency, and despite the fact that he concluded that "[t]his court is not inclined to extend the exceptions further than they have already been carried,"[38] state and federal courts have made exceptions and the exceptions have been extended over the years in all American courts.

---

[37]   Mima Queen and Child v. Hepburn, 7 U.S. (3 Cranch) 290 (1813). *See also* Donnelly v. United States, 288 U.S. 243, 33 S. Ct. 449, 57 L. Ed. 820 (1913) for a discussion of the history of the rules.

[38]   Mima Queen and Child v. Hepburn, *supra* note 31.

In Rules 803 and 804 of the Federal Rules of Evidence there are at least 28 specific exceptions, and Rule 807 contains one broad category of residual exceptions for situations not specifically covered by Rule 803 or Rule 804. Rule 807 provides for recognition of other exceptions when there are "equivalent circumstantial guarantees of trustworthiness."[39]

The reasons for the hearsay rule in the first instance are based on the facts that: (1) the declarant was not under oath to speak the truth; (2) the demeanor of the person who actually made the statement cannot be observed by the judge and jury; (3) there is danger that the statement may be repeated inaccurately; and (4) generally the declarant cannot be cross-examined despite the defendant's rights under the Sixth Amendment. The argument for admitting evidence under exceptions to the rule holds that if the purpose and rationale for excluding evidence under the hearsay rule do not exist in a specific case and if the interests of justice will be best served by admitting the statement into evidence, then the evidence should be admitted as an exception to the hearsay rule.

As a general rule, most hearsay exceptions have been categorized into fairly recognizable and repeating fact patterns addressed by the rules of evidence. Attorneys are able to intelligently argue the advantages and disadvantages of following a well-known exception by arguing the merits of the introduction of hearsay evidence. Thus, when hearsay statements fall within firmly rooted hearsay exceptions, or occur under circumstances with particularized guarantees of trustworthiness,[40] such statements are adequately reliable to be admissible in criminal cases.[41]

In the following sections, the text discusses some of the hearsay exceptions that are most frequently encountered by criminal justice personnel and explains the rationales for the exceptions.

§ 12.5 — Spontaneous and Excited Utterances

Rule 803

Hearsay Exceptions; Availability of Declarant Immaterial

* * *

The following are not excluded by the hearsay rule, even though the declarant is available as a witness:

* * *

---

[39]　FED. R. EVID. 807. The exceptions noted in Rules 803 and 804 are not included in this section. Rule 807 covers situations that are not specifically mentioned in Rules 803 and 804. These rules are included in the Appendix, and they should be reviewed before continuing.

[40]　*See* FED. R. EVID. 807.

[41]　United States v. Barrett, 8 F.3d 1296 (8th Cir. 1993); United States v. Matthews, 20 F.3d 358 (2d Cir. 1994).

> **(2) Excited utterance.** A statement relating to a startling event or condition made while the declarant was under the stress of excitement caused by the event or condition.[42]
>
>   * * *

Where hearsay evidence will be admitted as substantive evidence, as a general rule facts and circumstances that demonstrate the reliability and trustworthiness of the evidence must be present. Speech prompted in a declarant by an exciting event may be admissible as a hearsay exception if it qualifies as a spontaneous exclamation. The circumstances under which spontaneous declarations or excited utterances occur offer reasons to believe that a statement made under severe stress will be truthful. "Rule 803(2) allows the admission of excited utterances based on the theory that a person speaking about a startling event, while still under the stress of experiencing or observing that event, normally does not have either the capacity or the incentive to prevaricate."[43] The theory of this exception is that circumstances produce a condition of excitement that temporarily halts the capacity for reflection and produces utterances that are free of conscious and considered fabrication. Another way to indicate the spontaneity of such speech is to think of a stimulus that produces an instant human response without an opportunity for significant reflection. As one court properly described this hearsay exception, "An excited utterance is the event speaking and not the speaker."[44] "The crucial question, regardless of the time lapse, is whether, at the time the statement is made, the nervous excitement continues to dominate while the reflective processes remain in abeyance."[45] In order for a spontaneous or excited utterance to be admissible, a Wisconsin court noted that there must be: (a) proof of a startling event or experience, (b) the statement made by the declarant must relate to the startling event or situation, and (c) the statement must be made while the declarant is still under the stress or the excitement caused by the event or condition.[46] The court approved the admission of a victim's spontaneous statement offered to police after being hit in the head by a tire iron during a robbery perpetrated by the defendant. The victim knew the defendant, experienced the injury at the hands of the defendant, and gave his account concerning his injuries to the police within 10 minutes of being injured.[47] Following a similar rationale, a Washington court noted that for excited utterances to be admissible under the

---

[42]   FED. R. EVID. 803(2).

[43]   United States v. Brito, 427 F.3d 53, 61, 2005 U.S. App. LEXIS 22525 (1st Cir. 2006).

[44]   Pennsylvania v. Zukauskas, 501 Pa. 500, 503, 462 A.2d 236, 237, 1983 Pa. LEXIS 620 (1983).

[45]   Pennsylvania v. Keys, 2003 Pa. Super. 5, 814 A.2d 1256, 1258, 2003 Pa. Super. LEXIS 4 (2003).

[46]   State v. Mayo, 2006 Wis. App. 78, 713 N.W.2d 191, 2006 Wis. App. LEXIS 276 (Wis. 2006).

[47]   *Id.*

state's adaptation of the Federal Rules of Evidence, "A statement relating to 'a startling event or condition' made while the declarant was under the stress of excitement caused by the event or condition' is admissible as an excited utterance. ER 803(a)(2). An excited utterance has three closely related elements: First, a startling event or condition must have occurred. Second, the statement must have been made while the declarant was under the stress or excitement caused by the startling event or condition. Third, the statement must relate to the startling event or condition."[48] The statement in this case qualified as an excited utterance because the declarant had just been assaulted, had seen her vehicle destroyed, and seen a man's finger nearly bitten away from the hand. The declarant was under extreme stress and little time passed between the event and her statement to police officers.[49]

In another case, the victim was walking along a street and the defendant drove over to her in an attempt to pick her up. When she ultimately rebuffed his advances, he pulled his van ahead of her and was standing on the sidewalk when he grabbed her and tried to throw her into the van. The victim managed to get away and ran through traffic, pounding on cars trying to get help. The defendant stood nearby, pointed a gun at her, and threatened to shoot her. The victim managed to get to her house and call 911, but when police arrived she was hysterical and could not speak coherently. It took the officers 15 or 20 minutes to calm her down to the point where she could speak with them. Over the defendant's objection, the officers were permitted to render to the court what the hysterical victim had said to them while under the stress and the excitement following her assault. The reviewing court upheld the admission as an excited utterance, noting that there was a startling event, there was no time to contrive or misrepresent, and the statement was made while the victim was certainly under stress.[50]

Similar to the prior case, when police arrived in response to two 911 calls involving a domestic disturbance with a gun, the defendant's wife ran out of the home in a hurry shouting to police that "he's got a gun" and "he's going to kill me." The wife told the officers that her husband, at one point, had a gun to her head. During this time she appeared hysterical and in a state of panic. When the officers could not find the gun in the marital bedroom, they requested the wife's assistance in securing the firearm, but she was reluctant to help, appearing frantic and frightened to the officers. She told them that she did not want to go back in the house. Shortly after, the officers calmed her and took a detailed statement. At the defendant's federal trial for being a felon in possession of a firearm, the court admitted the spontaneous statements given by the wife upon the arrival of the police officers, over the defendant's objection. The Court of Appeals sustained the admission of the wife's excited utterance on the theory that the domestic disturbance constituted an exciting event, especially because

---

[48]   Washington v. Grzogorek, 2002 Wash. App. LEXIS 598 (2002).

[49]   *Id.*

[50]   Bell v. State, 847 So. 2d 558, 2003 Fla. App. LEXIS 8767 (Fla. 2003). *See* case in Part II.

the fight generated two 911 calls in rapid succession, the wife's statement was about the events in the home concerning the gun and the husband's threats, and she made them immediately after the events before she had a chance to calm herself or reflect on the events.[51]

In an Indiana case, police arrived at the scene of a reported criminal battery. The victim was crying and shaking, and her appearance and overall demeanor indicated that she was very upset. She was talking rapidly and showed signs of fresh physical injuries, including a bleeding cut above her eye. Her left eye was swollen and she was holding an ice pack to her eye. The attack had left marks on her neck that appeared to have been caused by someone grabbing her around the neck. Over the defendant's objection that the woman's story as told to an officer was not a spontaneous utterance, the trial court permitted the police officer to tell the court what the victim had told him at the scene concerning her injuries. The trial court noted that for a hearsay statement to be admitted as an excited utterance under Indiana's version of Rule 803(2), three elements must be shown: (1) a startling event occurs; (2) a statement is made by a declarant while under the stress of excitement caused by the event; and (3) the statement relates to the event. An Indiana appellate court held that the woman's statement to police met all the requirements and was properly admitted.[52]

The exciting event must affect the declarant with sufficient stress to remove or inhibit reflective ability. In sustaining a conviction for third-degree assault, the reviewing court approved the admission of a series of excited utterances made by the victim to a friend. The husband had been threatening his wife at their joint business when the wife phoned a friend for assistance in leaving the workplace, noting in a fearful voice that she was afraid her husband would hit her. A second call to the same friend requested that the friend rescue the wife immediately because her husband had beaten her and, when the rescuer arrived, the wife was crying and her face and arms were red. The wife did not testify at the trial, but the court permitted the wife's friend to relate virtually everything that the frightened and fearful wife told the rescuing friend about the ordeal at the time of the rescue. The Supreme Court of Colorado approved the admission of the rescuing friend's testimony because there was a startling event with the beating that created stress, the victim's spontaneous statement concerned the events and described them, and the wife related the story to her friend while still under the stress of the beating from her husband.[53]

As a general rule, to be admissible a spontaneous statement need not be completely spontaneous and may be made in response to a question by a police officer or other person.[54] The fact that the statement goes beyond a mere

51   United States v. Hadley, 431 F.3d 484, 496, 2005 U.S. App. LEXIS 26526 (6th Cir. 2005).

52   Cox v. State, 774 N.E.2d 1025, 2002 Ind. App. LEXIS 1533 (2002). *See* case in Part II.

53   Compan v. People, 121 P.3d 876, 882, 2005 Colo. LEXIS 873 (2005).

54   Washington v. Fikre, 2003 Wash. App. LEXIS 191 (2003); *see also* Massachusetts v. Ivy, 55 Mass. App. 851, 855, 774 N.E.2d 1100, 1104, 2002 Mass. App. LEXIS 1175 (2002).

description of the event may be considered in deciding whether the statement was sufficiently related to the event to be spontaneous, as required by the excited utterance exception to the hearsay rule, or whether the statement was a product of conscious reflection.[55]

The fact that the excited witness was a law enforcement agent does not exclude the admissibility of statements under the excited utterance exception to the hearsay rule.[56] A prostitute who had been kidnapped and held for six hours in the back of a van where she was forced to commit sexual acts with the strangers who had taken her made an excited utterance to several District of Columbia police officers. The woman gained her freedom following a shootout with the police officers after they overcame the resistance of the armed men. She had undergone a stressful kidnapping where the men threatened her with death if she did not have sex with them, forced her to drive the van while they committed at least two robberies, and was present in the van during the shootout. As the reviewing court noted, "Being inside a van that becomes the target of police gunfire certainly qualifies as a serious occurrence."[57] Her first words to an officer involved her rape allegations, even though those acts occurred earlier than the shootout. The trial court admitted her first statement made to police under the excited utterances exception to the hearsay rule on the theory that it was her first opportunity to comment about her ordeal, that there were sufficient events to cause stress, that she had not had an opportunity to fabricate, and that her remarks indicated the spontaneity of her speech. Her comment to another officer a few minutes later that she had been kidnapped and repeatedly raped were not inadmissible due to a lapse of time. The court held that the lapse of time is a factor to consider in determining spontaneity, but in this case, the lapse was rather short for both utterances to the police. Under the circumstances, the reviewing court affirmed the admission of the victim's excited utterances.

According to accepted practice, there is no definite time interval following an exciting event that will make the utterance either fall under the exception to the hearsay rule. The general rule is that an utterance following an exciting event must be made soon enough thereafter so that it can reasonably be considered a product of the stress of the excitement, rather than of reflection or deliberation. In a Massachusetts case, the reviewing court affirmed a conviction of digital rape when the victim awoke to find the defendant's finger inside her private area and his mouth on her breast. She became so upset that her frantic, screaming, and crying awakened everyone in the house and the victim made her statements describing the events while under the stress of the rape. In approving the admissibility of the victim's stressful utterances, the court noted that there was an exciting or startling event (awakening to digital rape)

---

[55]   United States v. More, 791 F.2d 566 (7th Cir. 1986).
[56]   Bryant v. United States, 859 A.2d 1093, 1106, 2004 D.C. App. LEXIS 526 (2004).
[57]   *Id.*

that caused a high degree of agitation in the declarant and that the statements were made while the victim was under the stress or influence of the exciting event (immediately) and before she had time to fabricate. The eyewitnesses universally described the victim as being upset to the point of being frantic. The trial court properly allowed witnesses to testify concerning the substance of what the victim stated following the rape.[58] A different court, in a case with some distinguishing facts, held that when a woman alleged that her husband had beaten her, dragged by the hair, and had held her captive overnight, such information did not fall under the excited utterance exception. The victim had walked eight or ten blocks to find a police officer after she escaped the next morning and told the officer her story. The appellate court reversed the trial court's admission of the officer's rendition of the beating because the court did not concur that the woman's story to the officer met the requirements for a spontaneous utterance. According to the appellate court, the utterances were offered as a narrative of overnight events and were not given as a reaction to a single startling episode and failed as an excited utterance. The reviewing court held that the admission of the statement denied the defendant the right to cross-examine the victim, who did not testify against the defendant.[59]

In making an evaluation concerning whether the elapsed time between the startling event and the declaration to another is too long that the statement is not an excited utterance, the trial court will focus on the declarant's state of mind at the time the alleged excited statement was made. To be deemed admissible, the stress and influence of the event must be present at the time that a declarant makes a statement to a third party. For example, in a case in which the defendant had been charged with lewd conduct with a minor under 16 years of age, the trial court permitted a sister of the victim to tell the court what the victim told her.[60] In a later conversation, the child told her mother substantially the same story. According to the evidence, the conduct occurred while the defendant was babysitting the victim when he placed his finger in her private area. The child stayed at the defendant's home that night, went to school the next day, and returned to stay at the defendant's house the next night. On the second day, the child's father picked her up and drove her to her mother's home. The child disclosed no details of the incident to anyone until the evening when her sister questioned her concerning whether something was wrong. At that time, the child told her sister about the illegal conduct, and subsequently she told her mother about the encounter with the defendant. Over an objection by the defendant's attorney, the judge permitted the sister and the mother of the victim to tell the jury what the victim told them on the theory that the excited utterance exception to the hearsay rule permitted admission of their testimony. In finding error in the admission of the child's story through the

---

[58]   Massachusetts v. Davis, 54 Mass. App. Ct. 756, 762, 767 N.E.2d 1110, 1116, 2002 Mass. App. LEXIS 674 (2002).
[59]   See Pennsylvania v. Keys, 2003 Pa. Super. 5, 814 A.2d 1256, 2003 Pa. Super. LEXIS 4 (2003).
[60]   State v. Field, 2006 Idaho App. LEXIS 44 (2006).

sister and mother, the reviewing court noted that an excited utterance requires that the declarant be under the stress of the event when making the statement. The court stated that:

> "[i]n considering whether a statement constitutes an excited utterance, the totality of the circumstances must be considered, including the nature of the startling condition or event, the amount of time that elapsed between the startling event and the statement, the age and condition of the declarant, the presence or absence of self-interest, and whether the statement was volunteered or made in response to a question."[61]

The reviewing court agreed with the prosecution that the event would be classified as startling or shocking, but that stress would, for the purposes of the excited utterance exception, last for hours but and not days, as was contended in this case. In finding that the declarant was not offering an excited utterance, the court stated that "at some point, the time span between a startling event and a subsequent statement simply becomes too great for the statement to be considered an excited utterance even when the declarant is a child."[62] If the situation indicates a lapse of time sufficient to manufacture or formulate a statement and if a statement lacks spontaneity, a trial court should not admit the alleged spontaneous statement.[63]

§ 12.6 — Business and Public Records

Rule 803

Hearsay Exceptions; Availability of Declarant Immaterial

* * *

The following are not excluded by the hearsay rule, even though the declarant is available as a witness:

* * *

(6) Records of regularly conducted activity. A memorandum, report, record, or data compilation, in any form, of acts, events, conditions, opinions, or diagnoses, made at or near the time by, or from information transmitted by, a person with knowledge, if kept in the course of a regularly conducted business activity, and if it was the regular practice of that business activity to make the memorandum, report, record, or data compilation, all as shown by the testimony of the custodian or other qualified witness, or by certification

---

[61]   *Id.*

[62]   *Id.*

[63]   North Carolina v. Riley, 54 N.C. App. 692, 695, 572 S.E.2d 857, 859, 2002 N.C. App. LEXIS 1531 (2002).

that complies with Rule 902(11), Rule 902(12), or a statute permitting certification, unless the source of information or the method or circumstances of preparation indicate lack of trustworthiness. The term "business" as used in this paragraph includes business, institution, association, profession, occupation, and calling of every kind, whether or not conducted for profit.

(7) Absence of entry in records kept in accordance with the provisions of paragraph (6). Evidence that a matter is not included in the memoranda, reports, records, or data compilations, in any form, kept in accordance with the provisions of paragraph (6), to prove the nonoccurrence or nonexistence of the matter, if the matter was of a kind of which a memorandum, report, record, or data compilation was regularly made and preserved, unless the sources of information or other circumstances indicate lack of trustworthiness.

(8) Public records and reports. Records, reports, statements, or data compilations, in any form, of public offices or agencies, setting forth (A) the activities of the office or agency, or (B) matters observed pursuant to duty imposed by law as to which matters there was a duty to report, excluding, however, in criminal cases matters observed by police officers and other law enforcement personnel, or (C) in civil actions and proceedings and against the Government in criminal cases, factual findings resulting from an investigation made pursuant to authority granted by law, unless the sources of information or other circumstances indicate lack of trustworthiness.[64]

* * *

Businesses, organizations, and government agencies collect and compile records generated during their ordinary and usual operations. Because businesses create these records with a view toward accuracy and with no motive to falsify, there is a presumption that they contain true and reliable information. Recognizing the accuracy principle, many states have adopted the Uniform Business Records Act, which facilitates the admission into evidence of records of regularly conducted operations of government and private entities. Demonstrative of the Uniform Business Records Act is the version adopted by the state of Washington, which provides that the "record of an act, condition or event, shall in so far as relevant, be competent evidence if the custodian or other qualified witness testifies to its identity and the mode of its preparation, and if it was made in the regular course of business, at or near the time of the act, condition or event, and if, in the opinion of the court, the sources of information, method and time of preparation were such as to justify its admission."[65]

---

[64]   Fed. R. Evid. 803. See also Fed. R. Evid. 803(9) and (10) in Appendix I.

[65]   Wash. Rev. Code § 5.45.020, Uniform Business Records As Evidence Act. (Matthew Bender 2006).

The purpose of the statute is to provide, as an exception to the hearsay rule, an acceptable substitute for the specific authentication of records kept in the ordinary course of business. The underlying rationale permitting this exception is that business records have the "earmark of reliability" or "probability of trustworthiness," because they reflect events occurring in the day-to-day operations of the enterprise, and business entities rely on their ordinary records in the conduct of business.

Under the Federal Rules of Evidence, the uniform law regarding records has been greatly expanded. According to these rules, various business and public records may be the source of evidence as exceptions to the hearsay rule. Some of these are records of regularly conducted activity, public records and reports, records of vital statistics, etc. Not only is information from the records admissible, but evidence also may be introduced to prove the absence of public records or entries or the absence of an entry in records of regularly conducted activities.[66]

All such records are admissible under this rule, but they are subject to exclusion if the sources of the information or other circumstances indicate a lack of trustworthiness. In interpreting the Arizona Rules of Evidence, one court approved the admission as business records of quality assurance records of calibrations for machines that detect alcohol intoxication. Where technicians had calibrated the Intoxilyzer 5000 and kept public records of the results for each machine, the records could be admitted as an exception to the hearsay rule under Rule 803(6). There is every reason to trust the results of the tests because no technician knows whether a given machine will be used and the technician has no motive to falsify or otherwise misstate the truth concerning which machines pass or failed the calibration tests.[67]

Although in a slightly different context, a secondary school might not seem like a business, but an Indiana court held that computer-stored school attendance records were admissible as a record of regularly conducted activity. The Indiana court noted that "data compilation, in any form" is a sufficiently broad category to include school records stored on a computer system.[68] An Arkansas court held that a state court did not commit error in a theft case by permitting the prosecution to introduce a state sales receipt that purported to establish the value of a stolen vehicle the defendant was alleged to have received. The vehicle was owned by the state and was sold at auction after recovery for fair market value. The office that oversaw Arkansas vehicles regularly kept appropriate records of sales of excess vehicles and had custody of the bill of sale that was properly introduced as a business record kept by a government agency in its regular course of business.[69]

---

[66]   FED. R. EVID. 803.

[67]   *See* Bohsancurt v. Eisenberg, 129 P.3d 471, 2006 Ariz. App. LEXIS 26 (2006).

[68]   J.L. v. Indiana, 789 N.E.2d 961, 963, 964, 2003 Ind. App. LEXIS 921 (2003).

[69]   Ervin v. State, 2006 Ark. App. LEXIS 95 (2006).

Business records that have been created with litigation in mind may potentially reflect some bias of the preparer and do not generally qualify for admission under the business records exception to the hearsay rule. In a New York prosecution for driving while impaired, the defendant had given a urine sample that was subsequently tested for drug metabolites. The doctor testified at the trial that he was a general supervisor at his lab and also indicated that his laboratory and other subordinate staff prepared reports in anticipation of litigation that were transmitted to the local prosecutor. The doctor testified that he had no personal knowledge concerning the tests performed on the sample from the urine container. The prosecutor attempted to get the litigation package that the lab had prepared into evidence and the trial judge rejected the 300-page litigation package. The case had to be dismissed because there was no admissible proof that the urine had prohibited substances contained within the sample and the business record prepared for litigation by the laboratory could not be introduced.[70] Similarly, in a Florida DUI case,[71] the defendant objected to a technician testifying to what tests were conducted on a blood sample and what results a colleague recorded in a report. The colleague had retired and the employee technician had not performed the lab work but reported the results obtained by the retired colleague. Another Florida court had determined that "a lab report prepared pursuant to police investigation and admitted to establish an element of a crime is testimonial hearsay even if it is admitted as a business record."[72] The reviewing court concluded that the hearsay evidence should not have been admitted because there was no proof that the retired employee who conducted the tests was unavailable.

Some types of business records that are routinely created as a usual business practice fail to qualify for admission under the business records exception, especially when they may include hearsay on hearsay. In a prosecution for spousal battery, the trial court permitted the admission of client intake data from a crisis intervention center log. The information included the specific reason the person needed shelter and detailed past crimes and stresses in the client's relationships. Employees routinely took information from women needing shelter from domestic problems and used the information in counseling the women during their stay. The custodian of the records explained the routine of collecting the information and how that data was stored. The appellate court agreed that the admission of the intake forms to prove the truth of the contents was erroneous because the form's contents were derived from hearsay statements that contained multiple layers of hearsay. The client's offering of facts for the form was the first layer of hearsay; the employee's recording of the facts constituted another layer; and the rendering of the form at the trial

---

[70] People v. Levy, 2008 NY Slip Op 51878U (N.Y. 2008).

[71] Sabota v. State, 2006 Fla. App. LEXIS 12505 (2006).

[72] Johnson v. State, 929 So. 2d 4, 7, 2005 Fla. App. LEXIS 20 (2005).

was a third layer. The trial court should have rejected the records because they failed to meet the business records hearsay exception.[73]

Although police reports containing statements concerning the cause of or responsibility for an accident are in a sense business or public records, they are often excluded because the person making the report is relying on what someone else told him or her and the record does not reflect what the officer personally observed from firsthand perception. For example, in a case in which a man was convicted of three counts of violating the animal control ordinance, the trial court refused to allow him to introduce police reports of incidents that he had reported to show that he and his neighbors had problems getting along.[74] Proof of the prior difficulties could show the motivation for the present complaints against him. The appellate court noted that "police reports showing prior incidents are generally, by themselves, inadmissible hearsay with no probative value" and that the narrative parts of a police report do not contain facts that should be admissible under the business records exception to the hearsay rule.[75] Police reports that contain admissible evidence personally observed by the officer, as well as inadmissible evidence obtained from other eyewitnesses and included within the report, can be received in evidence if the inadmissible portions are redacted from the report.[76] Some public record police reports may be admissible where they contain only firsthand information or have been prepared in the usual course of business. For example, when police had prepared typical repair and cost reports concerning damage done to a holding cell by a prisoner, the reports constituted a business record and could be admitted against a defendant because the report had been prepared in the ordinary course of the business of running a jail.[77]

In determining whether a proffered government document is either an investigative report or a compilation of factual findings that do not come within the public record exception of the hearsay rule, the court considers: (1) whether the document contains findings that address materially contested issues in the case; (2) whether the record or report contains factual findings; and (3) whether the report was prepared for advocacy purposes or in anticipation of litigation.[78]

Applying this test, an Indiana court agreed that a diagram of the scene of a single-vehicle accident in which the passenger died, which was prepared by the accident investigator for the state police, did not contain any interpretative factual findings, and thus was admissible under the public records exception to the hearsay rule in the prosecution of a motorist for operating the vehicle while

---

[73]   People v. Ayers, 125 Cal. App. 4th 988, 994, 23 Cal. Rptr. 3d 242, 245, 2005 Cal. App. LEXIS 50 (2005).

[74]   Pless v. State, 2006 Ga. App. LEXIS 523 (2006).

[75]   *Id.*

[76]   Pottorf v. Bray, 2003 Ohio 4255 (2003).

[77]   Williams v. State, 2003 Alaska App. LEXIS 136 (2003).

[78]   Shepherd v. State, 690 N.E.2d 318 (Ind. 1997).

intoxicated. The court explained that the diagram was merely a recording of physical conditions that were observed by the investigator, and the fact that the statute, which makes accident reports filed by persons involved in automobile accidents confidential, did not bar the admission of a Standard Crash Report filed by the officer who investigated the accident, because the statute contains an exception for such reports.

A police report may be admitted as an exception to the hearsay rule where the report is required to be recorded as part of a police department's regularly conducted activities. In Louisiana, a parish sheriff has a duty to seek out and obtain fingerprint evidence and record them as part of criminal investigations. In a case involving attempted armed robbery,[79] a defendant contended that the officer who lifted a latent fingerprint from the crime scene had to personally testify to that fact and that any other expert who so testified would be offering hearsay evidence. In rejecting the defendant's contention that the testifying officer would be offering hearsay, the reviewing court noted that the Supreme Court of Louisiana previously ruled that fingerprints on file with a police agency fall under the public documents exception to the hearsay rule and, in this case, the fingerprint evidence was properly introduced to show that the crime scene fingerprint matched the print of the defendant.

In some jurisdictions, police reports and other public records may be admissible as business or public records in civil cases, but inadmissible in criminal cases.[80] In a Texas case, a criminal defendant wanted the court to admit police records of other similar accidents that occurred on the same road following his vehicle accident. The defendant had been drinking alcohol and subsequently drove into a tree. The accident resulted in criminal charges. The defendant wanted to introduce evidence of other accidents on the wet highway that occurred the same night in order to mitigate his criminal responsibility. The trial court refused to admit any police reports of the other accidents because Texas law excluded police reports from admission in all criminal cases on the ground that such evidence constituted hearsay.[81] An autopsy report may meet the requirements of a business record exception to the hearsay rule but may be excluded on constitutional grounds. In an Alabama homicide case,[82] the defendant objected to the introduction of an autopsy report when it was introduced by a doctor who had not performed the autopsy, but had read the public records generated by the actual autopsy doctor. Under Alabama law, an autopsy report is generally admissible as a business records exception to the hearsay rule.[83] However,

---

[79]　State v. Arita, 900 So. 2d 37, 44, 2005 La. App. LEXIS 501 (2005).

[80]　*See* TEX. EVID. R. 803(8) Hearsay Exceptions; Availability of Declarant Immaterial (Matthew Bender 2009).

[81]　McCumber v. Texas, 202 Tex. App. LEXIS 7351 (2002). Police reports may be admissible at suppression hearings because the formal rules of evidence do not apply. *See* Caballero v. State, 2005 Tex. App. LEXIS 1865 (2005).

[82]　Smith v. State, 898 So. 2d 907, 2004 Ala. Crim. App. LEXIS 93 (2004).

[83]　*Id*. at 916.

the defendant made a Sixth Amendment right of confrontation argument that the actual declarant doctor giving the information was not present in court for cross-examination. In holding that the trial court committed error in admitting the autopsy report, the appellate court noted that the Sixth Amendment confrontation clause prevents a prosecutor from proving an essential element of the crime by hearsay evidence alone. According to the reviewing court, if the prosecution had only to introduce an autopsy report and shift the burden to the defendant to refute the hearsay facts contained within, the report would not be consistent with due process of law. So while an autopsy report might be admissible as a business record exception in a civil case, the effect of the Sixth Amendment prevents the admission of an autopsy report in criminal cases when it is not offered by the doctor who performed the procedure.

It is well-known that business and public records are commonly entered and stored on computer systems and that police departments are moving toward generating fewer paper records. Computer records stored on servers or personal computers are unavailable and useless except by accessing the data on a display or printing the data on paper. In admitting computer-generated printouts, which reflect the records stored on the computer, courts are actually following the best evidence rule. This is not departing from the business records hearsay rule, because the data contained must meet any hearsay hurdles that are presented, as well as meeting the requirements of authentication of a writing. In a Virginia case[84] in which the defendants were observed committing theft from a retail store, the trial court admitted a computer-generated inventory report as an exception to the hearsay rule under the business records theory. In the past, Virginia courts have admitted business records into evidence even though the witness did not prepare them, because their trustworthiness or reliability is guaranteed by the regularity of preparation and the records are used by the business in transacting business. As the reviewing court noted, "[t]he evidence proved that Rite-Aid maintained a computerized inventory in the regular course of its business, and regularly used the Telethon device to determine the status of its inventory."[85] Following the observed theft, a loss prevention officer used a hand-held scanner to take inventory of the remaining products on the shelf to determine what items had been stolen and the computer system generated a report that was admitted into evidence.

Computer-generated maps may fall under the definition of business records stored on electronic computing equipment and should admissible in evidence if they are relevant and material, without the necessity of identifying, locating, and producing as witnesses the individuals who made the entries in the regular course of business. In a prosecution for manufacturing crack cocaine within 1,500 feet of a school zone, the trial court allowed the introduction into evidence of a computer-generated map of the jurisdiction purporting to

---

[84]   McDowell v. Commonwealth, 48 Va. App. 104, 628 S.E.2d 542, 2006 Va. App. LEXIS 229 (2006).

[85]   *Id.*

demonstrate that a school existed within 1,500 feet of the crack laboratory. To be admissible as a business record, the evidence must have been made in the regular course of business, that it was the regular course of business to produce this record (a map), and that it must have been prepared at the time described in the report. In this case, the custodian of the map data personally prepared the map from computer-stored data, had sufficient knowledge of the methods used to generate city maps, and was well acquainted with the technology used to produce city maps. Thus, the trial court held that the city map produced by the witness in the usual course of business could be admitted as a hearsay exception under the business records exception to help prove that the crack lab was within 1,500 feet of a school.[86]

The absence of a business record when it normally would have been recorded may constitute negative evidence of an event or evidence that the event most likely did not happen. The foundational showing that the business or entity normally recorded and kept such records and that a due diligence search has not revealed the entry where it would normally have been entered allows the custodian of the records to note the nonexistence of the data.[87]

§ 12.7　　—Family History and Records (Pedigree)

Rule 803

Hearsay Exceptions; Availability of Declarant Immaterial

The following are not excluded by the hearsay rule, even though the declarant is available as a witness:

* * *

(11) Records of religious organizations. Statements of births, marriages, divorces, deaths, legitimacy, ancestry, relationship by blood or marriage, or other similar facts of personal or family history, contained in a regularly kept record of a religious organization.

(12) Marriage, baptismal, and similar certificates. Statements of fact contained in a certificate that the maker performed a marriage or other ceremony or administered a sacrament, made by a clergyman, public official, or other person authorized by the rules or practices of a religious organization or by law to perform the act certified, and purporting to have been issued at the time of the act or within a reasonable time thereafter.

(13) Family records. Statements of fact concerning personal or family history contained in family Bibles, genealogies, charts, engravings on rings, inscriptions on family portraits, engravings on urns, crypts, or tombstones, or the like.

---

[86]　*See* Connecticut v. Polanco, 69 Conn. App. 169, 797 A.2d 523, 2002 Conn. App. LEXIS 187 (2002).

[87]　Washington v. Knott, 2002 Wash. App. LEXIS 392 (2002).

> **(19) Reputation** among members of a person's family by blood, adoption, or marriage, or among a person's associates, or in the community, concerning a person's birth, adoption, marriage, divorce, death, legitimacy, relationship by blood, adoption, or marriage, ancestry, or other similar fact of personal or family.[88]
>
> * * *

Evidence of one's family information that occurred or existed prior to the declarant's birth by its nature involves hearsay. No person has an actual awareness of his or her date of birth except through hearsay information, and most family history falls into the same category. Almost all evidence relating to pedigree, genealogy, and family history consists of hearsay but usually will be admissible as an exception to the general rule excluding hearsay evidence. The family history exception to the hearsay rule is based in part on the inherent trustworthiness of a declaration by a family member regarding matters of family history and on the usual unavailability of other evidence. For example, in one case in which the defendant had been charged with incest and the rape of his daughter, the prosecution sought to prove that the victim was actually his daughter. The defendant had accepted the girl as his daughter; the mother testified that the defendant was the biological father of the victim; the victim called the defendant "Daddy;" and the entire family had accepted the girl as his daughter. In addition, a civil court entered a judgment of paternity against the defendant finding that the victim was his child. According to the trial court, the hearsay exception under the Louisiana equivalent of Federal Rule 803(19) governing reputation concerning family history and family relationship proved that the defendant was the father of the victim sufficient to support a conviction of aggravated incest.[89]

The family history exception does not extend to every facet of a defendant's life or his family history in a way that would allow every piece of exculpatory evidence to be admitted. In a death penalty case, in an effort to have the jury spare the life of her son, the mother of the defendant gave a videotaped interview covering many facts of the family in Cuba, her son's lack of problems with the law, and some additional inculpatory family history evidence. The defendant appealed the exclusion by the trial court of portions of the audio of the video as well the transcript of the same information. According to the defendant, the video contained sound information that should have been admitted under the family history exception of Rule 804. The court noted that the unavailability of the witness (she could not travel from Cuba) was clear, but the exception to the hearsay rule for family matters did not extend so far

---

[88]   FED. R. EVID. 803.

[89]   Louisiana v. Scott, 823 So. 2d 960, 968, 2002 La. App. LEXIS 93 (2002), *remedial writ denied*, 843 So. 2d 1122, 2003 La. LEXIS 1653 (2003).

as to cover testimony about the mother's own medical problems, appellant's difficulties with the Texas Youth Commission, the defendant's desire to leave Cuba, his clean record in Cuba, and child abuse inflicted upon appellant by his stepfather. The Texas Court of Criminal Appeals affirmed the conviction and death sentence.[90]

Oral declarations by a family member regarding matters of family history are admissible as an exception to the hearsay rule, while other evidence of family history may be admissible where the information has been recorded in a manner that suggests reliability. Oral declarations of the names of uncles, aunts, and cousins and their point of origin in Eastern Europe may be accepted as family history sufficient to make a claim to an intestate relative's estate.[91] Virtually no family would record a birth record in a family bible if the birth never occurred, a factor that gives reliability to family histories contained within religious books. Family records contained within the family bible are admissible when a proper showing is made as to the authority or authenticity of entries of the family record, especially when better evidence is not available. Such matters as births, deaths, and marriages are competent as evidence.

Some jurisdictions permit the entry of family history when it has been entered in a family Bible even where the persons who know the history remain alive. In a polygamy investigation, there was some belief that proof of the multiple marriages and sexual activity with underage wives resulting in live births would be found in a family Bible. The result of a search warrant revealed a bible with missing pages that were alleged to contain the intimate and illegal family history. The focus of the prosecution changed to tampering with evidence with the Bible being admitted in evidence against the defendant.[92] In some instances, the absence from the jurisdiction of the person who made the statements or the entries in the Bible, or insanity or illness hindering his or her presence at the trial is enough to make the evidence admissible. In some jurisdictions, entries in family Bibles are declared admissible by statute,[93] while some states recognize the hearsay exception for family records that have been included in family Bibles.[94]

Federal Rule of Evidence 803(11) provides that regularly kept records of a religious organization may be consulted in order to find family information, and if this information meets the legal requirements, it should be admissible as an exception to the hearsay rule. Although many people do not have close ties to organized religion, many people are intimately involved with their religion in situations in which careful records of church membership, birth, baptism, bar

---

[90]   *See* Valle v. Texas, 109 S.W.3d 500, 2003 Tex. Crim. App. LEXIS 143 (2003).

[91]   *See* In re Estate of Doris Rosen, Deceased, 2003 Pa. Super. 96, 819 A.2d 585, 2003 Pa. Super. LEXIS 364 (2003).

[92]   State v. Sliwinski, 2004 Mont. 1221, 2004 Mont. Dist. LEXIS 2119 (2004).

[93]   FED. R. EVID. 803.

[94]   Estate of Earl Wallace, Deceased, 2004 Phila. Ct. Com. Pl. LEXIS 134 (Pa. 2004).

mitzvah, and wedding information are generated. Because there is every desire to record this information in an accurate manner and no reason to erroneously enter the information, there is a presumption that the records are accurate. In interpreting this rule, one federal court explained that the exception is limited to personal information and does not authorize evidence of statements of monetary contributions to a church, because these do not fall within the religious records exception to the hearsay rule.[95]

Under Federal Rule of Evidence 803(19) and its state equivalents, family relationships that exist by blood, adoption, or marriage may be proved by persons who have intimate knowledge of the family or by associates of family members concerning family history. For example, a father or mother could give the date of birth of their respective parents, even though they could not possibly know this information from firsthand knowledge. And a father could testify to the birth date of his son or daughter, even thought the father was not present at the birth or even in the geographical area of the birth. In a case in which a defendant was accused of harboring an illegal alien, among other crimes, a trial court permitted the illegal alien's aunt to testify that he was from El Salvador and was not a United States citizen.[96] People who do not have a close association with the family or group are not permitted to offer this sort of hearsay in court. For example, in a prosecution for aggravating driving under the influence of an intoxicant while a person under 15 years of age was in the vehicle,[97] the trial court permitted the arresting officer to relate to the court the fact that he had heard the putative father of the 15-year-old state that the boy passenger was only 13. While the investigation was ongoing, a different adult male came to take charge of the child and noted to the officer that the boy was his 13-year-old son. Police proved unable to locate the boy or his father prior to trial, so the trial judge permitted the police officer to state the age of the child, an element of the aggravating driving under the influence charge. At trial, the defendant entered a hearsay objection that the trial court rejected. The appellate court determined that the trial court committed reversible error in allowing the officer to give an age to the boy by stating that he looked young and that the putative father had stated to the officer that the boy was 13. The officer who testified had no personal knowledge concerning the age of the child, had not been a member of the family community, and was a stranger to the child and his father. Because the family history related to an element of the crime, the appellate court reversed the conviction.

---

[95] Hall v. C.I.R., 729 F.2d 632 (9th Cir. 1984).

[96] United States v. Garcia-Flores, 136 Fed. Appx. 685; 2005 U.S. App. LEXIS 12732 (5th Cir. 2005).

[97] State v. May, 210 Ariz. 452, 455, 112 P.3d 39, 42, 2005 Ariz. App. LEXIS 73 (2005).

§ 12.8　—Former Testimony

Rule 804

Hearsay Exceptions; Declarant Unavailable

* * *

(b) Hearsay exceptions.—The following are not excluded by the hearsay rule if the declarant is unavailable as a witness:

(1) Former testimony. Testimony given as a witness at another hearing of the same or a different proceeding, or in a deposition taken in compliance with law in the course of the same or another proceeding, if the party against whom the testimony is now offered, or, in a civil action or proceeding, a predecessor in interest, had an opportunity and similar motive to develop the testimony by direct, cross, or redirect examination.[98]

* * *

Every criminal defendant has a Sixth Amendment right to confront and cross-examine adverse witnesses and not having the opportunity to confront a witness will likely lead to the reversal of a conviction. Therefore, when evidence is introduced against a defendant in a manner that has the effect of preventing meaningful cross-examination, the trial judge should exclude the evidence. A literal construction of the Sixth Amendment would prevent virtually all hearsay evidence from being considered for admission, and have the effect of making trials difficult. Where a substitute for cross-examination exists or where the defendant originally had motive, opportunity, and incentive to conduct cross-examination at a prior proceeding between the same parties, the evidence may be admitted even though it constitutes hearsay testimony. This exception does not require that the defendant have conducted cross-examination of the witness at the earlier proceeding, only that the defendant had the opportunity. As a general rule, to have an opportunity to use testimony given in a prior proceeding, the parties to the lawsuit must be identical, the now-absent witness must have been under oath in the first proceeding, the absent witness must now be unavailable for testimony, and the lawsuit must cover the same issues covered in the first proceeding. Under Rule 804, the declarant must be unavailable for testimony where unavailability may involve an assertion of a constitutional or other privilege, when the witness is beyond the power of the court to command attendance, or when the witness simply refuses to testify through no fault of the offering party, or when the witness testifies to a lack of memory, or when the witness is dead. If a hearsay exception absolutely conflicts with the Sixth

---

[98]　Fed. R. Evid. 804.

Amendment provision that states: "in all criminal prosecutions, the accused shall enjoy the right to be confronted with the witnesses against him," the evidence will not be admissible.

In a case in which the witness had disappeared after the first trial and prior to the second trial, the defendant objected, complaining that his rights under the Sixth Amendment to confront and cross-examine adverse witnesses and Federal Rule of Evidence 804(b)(1) were violated.[99] The defendant objected to the prosecution using the transcript of the witness from the first trial. In order for the prior testimony to be used at a second trial, the party against whom the evidence is to be admitted must have had an opportunity and similar motive to conduct cross-examination at the first proceeding. Reviewing courts have looked at transcripts of the original cross-examination to determine whether the trial counsel had a full opportunity to probe and expose the witness's testimony and undermine its credibility where appropriate. In holding that the former testimony could be constitutionally used against the defendant at his second trial on the same issue, the Court of Appeals concluded:

> that this prior cross-examination sufficiently allowed the jury at the second trial to evaluate the truth of [the missing witness'] testimony, and that [the defendant] had a similar motive in both trials. This conclusion is further strengthened by the facts that evidence of [the missing witness'] flight was put before the jury in the second trial, defense counsel emphasized the flight in his summation, and the district court specifically referred to it in the charge to the jury. Therefore, the admission of [the missing witness'] prior testimony at [the defendant's] second trial did not violate [the defendant's] right to confrontation under the Sixth Amendment nor was it contrary to Federal Rule of Evidence 804(b)(1).[100]

In affirming the conviction, the Court of Appeals was satisfied that the defendant had sufficient reason conduct appropriate cross-examination of the missing prosecution witness at the prior trial and that it would not be unfair to allow evidence of what the witness said at the first trial into evidence at the second trial.

In one case, the defense wanted to use former testimony in favor of a defendant.[101] The trial issue involved missing witnesses who testified at a grand jury proceeding and then disappeared. The prosecution successfully contended that it did not have the same incentive, motive, and intent to examine the witnesses at the grand jury stage of the criminal process as it would have at a trial. The defendant wanted the grand jury testimony of the two missing witnesses to be admitted at trial because their evidence would deflect the responsibility for the crime from the defendant and place it on a third party. The parties were

---

[99] United States v. Garcia, 117 Fed. Appx. 162, 2004 U.S. App. LEXIS 25480 (2d Cir. 2004).

[100] *Id.* at 164.

[101] United States v. Carson, 455 F.3d 336, 2006 U.S. App. LEXIS 18361 (D.C. Cir. 2006).

in agreement that the witnesses were missing and unavailable, but the quality and thrust of the questions asked of the missing grand jury witness was simply different than if the prosecution were to have cross-examined them at trial. The Court of Appeals agreed with the federal prosecutor and upheld the refusal to admit the evidence.[102] Not argued in the case was the concept that the government did not ever cross-examine the witnesses because they were called to the grand jury by the prosecution as grand jury witnesses and the prior grand jury proceeding was not an adversarial one.

Some jurisdictions and legal authorities assert that former testimony is actually not hearsay, because it was given under oath and subject to cross-examination. The Federal Rules of Evidence and derivative state adopters recognize former testimony as hearsay, but hold that it is admissible under an exception to the hearsay rule. Under either approach, when a witness for the prosecution or defense is unavailable and cannot be produced at the present trial or, being present, refuses to testify, courts will generally admit the recorded testimony of such witness from a prior criminal proceeding where it meets the other qualifications for this hearsay exception. A witness who is expected to assert some constitutional or statutory privilege is not considered to be unavailable until the witness is placed on the witness stand and formally asserts a privilege not to testify or simply refuses to testify even though no legal basis exists for the refusal.[103]

In admitting reported testimony, a Tennessee reviewing court approved the admission into evidence of prior testimony from a witness who had testified at the preliminary hearing but was deceased at the time of the trial.[104] The court noted that two issues were involved—the right of confrontation and whether a hearsay exception applied. The court noted that the defendant had ample opportunity and motive to conduct effective cross-examination of the witness at the preliminary hearing and that a preliminary hearing is precisely what the rules of evidence contemplate when Rule 804 mentions former testimony.

In an Arkansas criminal case[105] in which there was a companion civil case that had been filed, an attorney for the civil plaintiff deposed a witness in the homosexual rape case and the witness died prior to the date of the criminal trial. The judge permitted the evidence from the deceased witness to be admitted into evidence because the declarant was deceased and the court found that the defendant's civil attorney had an opportunity that he did not exercise to cross-examine the now-dead witness. Additionally, the defendant's criminal attorney could have deposed the adverse witness but chose not to do so. In upholding the admission into evidence of the earlier deposition testimony, the reviewing court noted that the civil trial and criminal trial involved the same

---

[102] *Id.*

[103] *See* Edmonds v. State, 2006 Miss. App. LEXIS 311 (Miss. 2006).

[104] State v. Bowman, 2009 Tenn. Crim. App. LEXIS 35 (Tenn. 2009).

[105] Simmons v. State, 2006 Ark. App. LEXIS 276 (2006).

facts and same participants, giving the defendant's civil attorney proper motive and incentive to cross-examine at the earlier proceeding. An important concept that the appellate court may have missed is that the parties were different in the civil trial from the criminal trial because the plaintiff in the civil trial was the injured party and the plaintiff in the criminal trial was the prosecution.

In summary, when a party wants to admit into evidence earlier testimony offered at prior proceedings, there should be an identity of parties, and identity of issues between the prior proceeding and the present one. There must have been ample motive, incentive, and opportunity for the adverse party to have developed sufficient cross-examination of a witness who must have been under oath for the former testimony exception to be permitted. Where all the statutory and legal issues are met involving former testimony, "[o]nly the absence of an opportunity for the trier to observe the witness's demeanor detracts from the ideal conditions for giving testimony."[106]

§ 12.9   – Dying Declarations

Rule 803

Hearsay Exceptions; Declarant Unavailable

* * *

(b) Hearsay exceptions.—The following are not excluded by the hearsay rule if the declarant is unavailable as a witness:

* * *

(2) Statement under belief of impending death. In a prosecution for homicide or in a civil action or proceeding, a statement made by a declarant while believing that the declarant's death was imminent, concerning the cause or circumstances of what the declarant believed to be impending death.[107]

To qualify as a dying declaration, the victim must have made a statement concerning the cause and circumstances of his or her own impending death by homicide and the statement must have been made with a clear understanding that death was imminent. The victim must have given up all hope of recovery or living any appreciable length of time. Dying declarations in homicide cases have from ancient times been admitted in evidence either: (1) because of solemnity—the solemnity of the occasion and the fear that one would not want to meet one's maker with a lie on one's lips, or (2) because of necessity—because the victim of the homicide cannot testify, it is necessary to protect the

---

[106] 5-804 WEINSTEIN'S FEDERAL EVIDENCE § 804.04. Chapter 804 Hearsay Exceptions; Declarant Unavailable (Matthew Bender 2009).

[107] FED. R. EVID. 804.

public against homicidal criminals and prevent a miscarriage of justice. Under the common law, the person making the dying declaration must actually die,[108] but the federal courts do not require death in order for the declaration to be admissible. Consistent with the position of many states, a Tennessee appellate court noted the five requirements for the admissibility of a dying declaration:

> (1) The declarant must be dead at the time of the trial; (2) the statement is admissible only in the prosecution of a criminal homicide; (3) the declarant must be the victim of the homicide; (4) the statement must concern the cause or the circumstances of the death; and (5) the declarant must have made the statement under the belief that death was imminent.[109]

From the legal perspective, the dying declaration has the same effect and carries the same presumptive weight as if it were testimony given under oath, although a jury is free to give any weight it might desire to such evidence.

In order for a judge to admit a dying declaration, the declarant's statement must describe the circumstances and events immediately surrounding or leading up to the defendant's conduct that caused death of the declarant. Under current hearsay and Sixth Amendment standards, a dying declaration has a better chance of admission when the declarant makes a spontaneous statement rather than answering questions from a police officer.[110] To meet a defendant's objection to the admission of a dying declaration under the Sixth Amendment, the Commonwealth of Virginia takes the position that a defendant forfeits the right of confrontation and cross-examination when there is proof by a preponderance of the evidence that the defendant's act has caused the absence of the dying declarant.[111] Similarly, in Texas, one court permitted a dying declaration to be admitted against the a defendant who was on trial for killing the dying declarant.[112] The person making a dying declaration generally does not have to unequivocally and unambiguously state that the victim knows death is imminent but the awareness of impending death may be inferred from the character of the wounds, the language used by the declarant, from the facts and surrounding circumstances, or from what has been told to the victim by medical personnel. The expectation of imminent demise may be shown by the circumstances of his or her condition or by his or her acts, such as sending for a minister or rabbi before making the declaration or requesting last rites from a minister or priest.

---

[108] If the person survived, the individual could personally testify or the statement might be admissible as an excited utterance.

[109] State v. Mayes, 2004 Tenn. Crim. App. LEXIS 9 (2004) and State v. Lewis, 2006 Tenn. Crim. App. LEXIS 237 (2006).

[110] See Crawford v. Washington, 541 U.S. 36, 2004 U.S. LEXIS 1838 (2004).

[111] Commonwealth v. Morgan, 69 Va. Cir. 228, 232, 2005 Va. Cir. LEXIS 189 (Va. 2005).

[112] Gonzalez v. State, 195 S.W.3d 114, 2006 Tex. Crim. App. LEXIS 1129 (Tex. 2006). *See* case in Part II.

In an old case, *Mattox v. United States*, the Supreme Court of the United States succinctly stated conditions under which the dying declaration exception to the hearsay rule applied in federal criminal trials and set forth the justification for the rule:[113]

> Dying declarations are admissible in a trial for murder, as to the fact of the homicide and the person by whom it was committed, in favor of the defendant as well as against him. . . . But it must be shown by the party offering them in evidence that they were made under a sense of impending death. This may be made to appear from what the injured person said; or from the nature and extent of the wounds inflicted, being obviously such that he must have felt or known that he could not survive; as well as from his conduct at the time and the communications, if any, made to him by medical advisors, if assented to or understandingly acquiesced in by him. The length of the time elapsing between the making of the declaration and the death is one of the elements to be considered . . .

Approving the admission of the dying declarations in the case, the Court commented further:

> The admission of the testimony is justified on the ground of necessity, and in view of the consideration that certain expectation of almost immediate death will remove all temptation to falsehood and enforce as strict adherence to the truth as the obligation of an oath could impose. But the evidence must be received with the utmost caution, and, if the circumstances do not satisfactorily disclose that the awful and solemn situation in which he is placed is realized by the dying man because of the hope of recovery, it ought to be rejected.

Under the modern Federal Rules of Evidence, the dying declarant need not actually die, but many states still hold that or the dying declaration is not admissible unless the declarant has died. Even with the guidelines established by federal and state statutes and the Supreme Court of the United States and state supreme courts, lower courts are required to apply the test to specific cases. For example, are the victim's statements admitted as dying declarations if they are elicited by questions? Must the victim affirmatively state that he or she is dying? Is the length of time the declarant lives after making a dying declaration material? Must the person actually die?

In a New York murder prosecution,[114] the trial court admitted a series of comments and responses to questions as a dying declaration. The decedent's wife heard gunshots and found her husband on the sidewalk bleeding from two shots in his back. He told her that "it hurt" and to call an ambulance. He subsequently told her that "I'm dying" as the police arrived. Police asked his

---

[113] Mattox v. United States, 146 U.S. 140, 13 S. Ct. 50, 36 L. Ed. 917 (1892).

[114] People v. Durio, 7 Misc. 3d 729, 731, 794 N.Y.S.2d 863, 685, 2005 N.Y. Misc. LEXIS 398 (N.Y. 2005).

wife to inquire of the decedent as to who shot him because the victim spoke only Spanish. He replied by giving the defendant's name, who he identified by using a nickname. He died a few hours later. At trial, the dying declaration was admitted against the defendant. Years later, on the strength of *Crawford v. Washington*,[115] the defendant contended that the statements should not have been used as a dying declaration because the statements were "testimonial in nature" and he was not be able to exercise his Sixth Amendment right to confront and cross-examine the dead declarant. The New York court that reviewed the defendant's motion to vacate his homicide conviction noted that dying declarations constitute an exception to the ban on testimonial evidence that cannot be subjected to cross-examination. The court mentioned that the Supreme Court of the United States recently referred to dying declarations and noted that many dying declarations may not be testimonial in nature but that even those that were could be admitted.[116]

An Illinois court, in deciding whether a dying declarant possessed a belief that imminent death was a virtual certainty, held that a trial court could have inferred that the decedent knew death was approaching when he knew that he had been shot twice, he mentioned that he could not move his legs, he was gasping for air, he appeared to be in pain, and he told a friend that he was dying. At the hospital the dying victim told a doctor that he was not doing well and the doctor agreed with him that he was in "bad shape." At the hospital, the victim gave police a description of the defendant. The victim had been in an altercation the evening prior to the shooting with the defendant after the defendant forced the victim's girlfriend to have sex with him. The defendant was alleged to have shot the victim as the victim answered his front door. The reviewing court agreed with the trial court that the victim's statements were properly admitted as a dying declaration because the victim's words pertained to the cause or circumstances of the victim's receipt of final injuries, the victim knew he was dying, and the victim possessed the mental faculties to offer an accurate statement or statements concerning how his injuries were received.[117]

When an injured person does not believe that he or she is going to die or the proof may be uncertain that the victim has that belief, the statement may be admissible as an excited utterance. In a Texas case, in the victim was found by friends in a parking lot suffering from a tremendous beating that included a broken neck. In the parking lot, six witnesses heard the victim say in response to a question that the defendant had done this to him. The appellate court approved the admission into evidence of the victim statement as an excited

---

[115] 541 U.S. 36, 2004 U.S. LEXIS 1838 (2004). *See* the material on this case in § 12.8—Former Testimony. The Supreme Court of California held that *Crawford v. Washington* and its Sixth Amendment concerns did not apply to dying declarations. *See* People v. Monterroso, 34 Cal. 743, 22 Cal. Rptr. 3d 1, 101 P.3d 956 (2004).

[116] *Id.*

[117] People v. Gilmore, 356 Ill. App. 3d 1023, 1031, 828 N.E.2d 293, 301, 2005 Ill. App. LEXIS 314 (2005).

utterance or as a dying declaration. It was clear that the victim had suffered an exciting traumatic event and other evidence indicated that he knew he was in precarious shape. When the victim was about to be removed from a ventilator, he indicated to others that the defendant had given him his final injuries and it was clear to the victim that he would not live very long once removed from the ventilator.[118]

As a matter of logic, a dying declaration must be made between the infliction of the fatal injury and the death of the declarant. For admission as a dying declaration, the length of time a declarant lives after making a dying declaration is immaterial in determining whether the statement qualifies a dying declaration for purposes of the hearsay exception. In a California case, the dying declarant was well aware of his impending death and despite the fact that he lived 11 more days was not material to the determination of whether the statement was admissible as a dying declaration.[119]

While the typical dying declaration is usually offered orally and later reduced to a writing, a dying declaration may be either written or oral but must relate to final injuries suffered by the declarant prior to his or her death and may never explain the death of a third party. Due to the typical police response to reported homicides, in many instances the dying statements are made to law enforcement officers and emergency medical responders. Law enforcement officers are generally trained to recognize that while a statement by a declarant may not qualify as a dying declaration, it may be admissible under the hearsay exception known as the excited utterance exception. Police officers should take care to record the substance of a statement and the circumstances under which it was uttered as soon as possible in order to clearly convey the final statements regarding a victim's final injuries. Cross-examination by defense attorneys should also be anticipated at the time the dying declaration is offered in court by the police officer or other third party so that the witness will be prepared to give accurate testimony about what he or she heard.

§ 12.10   — Declarations Against Interest

Rule 804

Hearsay Exceptions; Declarant Unavailable

* * *

(b) Hearsay exceptions.—The following are not excluded by the hearsay rule if the declarant is unavailable as a witness:

* * *

---

[118] Sadlier v. State, 2009 Tex. App. LEXIS 2962 (Tex. 2009). *See* case in Part II.
[119] People v. Monterroso, 34 Cal. 4th 743, 763, 101 P.3d 956, 971, 22 Cal. Rptr. 3d 1, 18, 2004 Cal. LEXIS 11763 (2004).

(3) Statement against interest. A statement which was at the time of its making so far contrary to the declarant's pecuniary or proprietary interest, or so far tended to subject the declarant to civil or criminal liability, or to render invalid a claim by the declarant against another, that a reasonable person in the declarant's position would not have made the statement unless believing it to be true. A statement tending to expose the declarant to criminal liability and offered to exculpate the accused is not admissible unless corroborating circumstances clearly indicate the trustworthiness of the statement.[120]

A. Declarations Against Pecuniary Interests

Any time a person makes an oral or written statement that could have the effect of harming his or her pecuniary or monetary interests, such statement may qualify as an exception to the hearsay rule. Because most individuals are somewhat self-serving, when people make declarations against pecuniary interests that are out of line with typical statements, they are probably being truthful. A statement qualifying as a declaration against interest may be admissible as an exception to the hearsay rule because declarations against interest have been found to offer a high probability of truthfulness. Admission into evidence has become acceptable out of necessity, because most individuals decline to repeat such statements while under oath in a court of law because admitting a declaration against interest may have an adverse result. The legal theory holds that a person does not make statements against his or her own pecuniary interest unless the statements generally are true and have thus considered such statements trustworthy, even though there may be no opportunity to confront or to cross-examine the witness.

A declaration against interest by a person who is not a party nor in privity with a party to an action is admissible in evidence when: (1) the person making such declaration is either dead or unavailable as a witness due to sickness, insanity, or absence from the jurisdiction; (2) the declarant had peculiar means of knowing the facts that he or she stated; (3) the declaration was against his or her pecuniary or proprietary interest; and (4) he or she had no probable motive to falsify the facts stated.[121] Applying the declaration against interest theory, an Arkansas court revoked a prior judgment ordering a trustee to pay child support to a child beneficiary's custodian.[122] The trustee refused to comply with the court's original order when the trustee gained knowledge that the custodian-father and the non-custodial mother appeared to have colluded to defraud the court and the trust. The mother, who could not be found for the hearing, told the trustee that she and the custodian father had concocted a scheme to get $2,000 per month from the trustee for the benefit of the child and that the

---

[120]   FED. R. EVID. 804.
[121]   Gichner v. Antonio Troiano Tile Co., 410 F.2d 238 (D.C. Cir. 1969).
[122]   Osborne v. Salmon, 2006 Ark. App. LEXIS 266 (2006).

mother and father were planning on splitting the $2,000 each month. At the time of the court's hearing, the mother was absent and the statement clearly was against her pecuniary interest because if the trustee acted properly knowing the truth about the fraud, her share of the monthly child support would not likely be paid. She must have known that the statement was against her pecuniary interest when it was made and her absence permitted the hearsay use of her statement. As the appellate court noted in approving the trial court admission of the mother's declaration against interest, "Here, Ms. Salmon was unavailable because no one knew her location and attempts to find her had proved unavailing. Ark. R. Evid. 804(a)(4). Moreover, Ms. Salmon's statements that she had colluded with Mr. Osborne (the father) were admissible because such statements were declarations against the pecuniary interest of her estate.[123]

A hearsay statement may qualify as a declaration against interest if the statement, at the time of its original utterance, was contrary to the declarant's pecuniary, proprietary, or social interest, or tended to subject the declarant to civil or criminal liability, or to render invalid the declarant's claim against another, so that a reasonable person in the declarant's position would not have uttered the statement unless that person believed the statement to be true.[124] A statement may qualify as a declaration against the interest when the statement threatens loss of employment or reduces chances for future employment. For example, a hearsay statement made by the lessee's employee to a fire investigator that he and others were smoking on the leased premises a few hours before the fire started was against the employee's pecuniary and proprietary interests, and because the statement also concerned a subject of which the employee was personally cognizant and there was no conceivable motive to falsify, the statement was admitted as a declaration against the interest of the employee. The court in that case agreed, however, that the statement would not be admitted unless the employee was unavailable to testify at the trial.[125]

In a Texas case, the trial court first acknowledged the rule relating to declarations against interest and reviewed the admissibility requirements, including the fact that the statement must have adverse consequences to the one making the statement. When police executed a search warrant of a residence where the defendant was present, the police discovered a quantity of cocaine in the presence of the defendant and a friend. Several days later, after posting bail for an associate, the defendant stated to his girlfriend that he knew the cocaine belonged to the friend who had been present during the search because the defendant admitted selling the cocaine to the same friend. In approving the admission of the declaration made to his girlfriend, the reviewing court noted that: "The voluntary statement, although made several days after the arrest, was not the

---

[123] *Id.*

[124] New Jersey v. Brown, 170 N.J. 138, 148, 784 A.2d 1244, 1251, 2001 N.J. LEXIS 1409 (2001).

[125] Gichner v. Antonio Troiano Tile Co., *supra* note 125.

product of coercion or questioning. . . . McElroy's incriminating statements were made to his live-in girlfriend, and thus, he had no reason to believe that statements made to her would be used against him."[126] In this case, the original declarant, the defendant, was unwilling to repeat his statement on the witness stand and therefore was "unavailable" to testify within the meaning of the statute governing the inadmissibility of declarations against interest.

B. *Statements Against Penal Interests—Confessions and Admissions*

Included within the general exception introduced above is the hearsay exception concerning admissions and confessions. A confession, as it is used in criminal law, consists of a suspect admitting responsibility for all the elements of the crime or crimes, and constitutes a complete acknowledgment of guilt by one who has committed a crime or crimes. The confession is the admission of the criminal act itself, not an admission of a fact or circumstances from which guilt may be inferred. An admission, as distinguished from a confession, consists of the suspect admitting to some involvement or having responsibility for some elements of a crime or admitting to facts that, when linked to other facts, may show guilt. However, the statement falls short of a complete confession for the criminal act itself. An admission may consist of a partial confession, but the admission fails to take complete responsibility for committing incriminating acts or conduct that equals guilt. In a Tennessee murder case, police videotaped a voluntary statement of the eventual defendant, in which she admitted being at the scene of the homicide, but denying any involvement. This kind of statement qualifies as an admission, but not a full confession, because it only placed her at the crime scene, and nothing more.[127]

In a Michigan case, a man was robbed at gunpoint while using a public phone. The two assailants went through the victim's pockets and took his watch and pager but were upset when he did not have anything else of value. At that moment, one of the felons shot the victim in the back. Police officers encountered the defendants within a few minutes after the incident because they appeared to be acting in a suspicious fashion. At this moment a radio broadcast alerted police of the robbery and shooting and when one of the officers asked to have the robbers' descriptions repeated, the defendant blurted out, "I did it—I'm the shooter!" According to the Supreme Court of Michigan, the defendant's statement was properly introduced against the defendants as a declaration against penal interest because at that time the defendant knew that it was not in his best interests to admit to a robbery and a shooting.[128]

---

[126]   Risher v. Texas, 85 S.W.3d 839, 842, 2002 Tex. App. LEXIS 6086 (2002).

[127]   State v. Lewis, 2006 Tenn. Crim. App. LEXIS 237 (2006).

[128]   *See* State v. Washington, 664 N.W.2d 203, 2003 Mich. LEXIS1465 (Mich. 2003). *See* case in Part II.

Consistent with the Maryland practice, under the Federal Rules of Evidence the statement against interest exception includes statements that are against penal interest as well as those against pecuniary and proprietary interests.[129] In a federal prosecution, the defendant had been caught with a firearm under the seat of the car in which he was a passenger and suffered a federal conviction for being a felon in possession of a firearm.[130] One of the points of his appeal involved the fact that the trial court refused to allow his girlfriend to testify that a third-party friend of the defendant admitted to her that the gun belonged to the third party and that the third party admitted placing it under the car seat in which the defendant was riding at the time of his arrest. The appellate court noted that the declaration against interest (penal) was subject to two conditions. The first condition required that the person making the declaration be unavailable for testimony, a fact clearly present in this case because the third party asserted the Fifth Amendment privilege against self-incrimination at the trial. The second requirement for admission failed because the trial court did not find corroborating circumstances that could indicate the trustworthiness of the declaration against interest and the trustworthiness of the declarant. The girlfriend would like to see her boyfriend before he finished a prison term, so there was a motive for her to be less than honest. The third party had denied that he ever admitted to having the gun to his own parole officer. Under the circumstances, the reviewing court agreed with the trial court that the declaration against interest failed the tests of admissibility under the rules of evidence.[131]

When declarants make out-of-court confessions that could subject them to criminal prosecution and who are not defendants in a case, the confessions qualify as hearsay evidence and may be admitted as declarations against the interests of the people making the declarations. Such evidence may be admissible as an exception to the hearsay rule when the evidence meets the requirements of the declaration against interest.[132] The reason for admitting the confession as an exception to the hearsay rule is that a reasonable person in such a position would not have made the incriminating statement constituting a confession unless he believed it to be true, and if the confession is not true, the defendant is free to explain why he or she made a false confession. Confessions are made for a variety of reasons and may involve efforts to protect other people or by an attack of conscience and honesty, and for other unknown reasons.

In interpreting Federal Rule 804(b)(3), Statement against interest, the District of Columbia Court of Appeals observed that the Rule requires a three-step process to determine whether an admissible statement against penal interest

---

[129] FED. R. EVID. 804(b)(3).

[130] United States v. Johnson, 121 Fed. Appx. 912, 2005 U.S. App. LEXIS 2533 (2d Cir. 2005).

[131] *Id.*

[132] *See* Chapter 16 for a discussion of the constitutional issues concerning confessions and admissions. *See also* Kansas Annotated Statutes, K.S.A. § 60-460(j) Hearsay evidence excluded; exceptions. (2006).

has been made.[133] The court should consider whether the alleged declarant actually made a statement, determine whether the declarant actually is unavailable for testimony, and evaluate whether there are corroborating circumstances that support the trustworthiness of the statement. Of course, the statement must have had the tendency to subject the declarant to some sort of criminal penalty and the declarant must have been aware of that fact. There must be some proof that the declarant understood that the statement was against his or her penal interest at the time it was made. Corroboration need not be as strong as having a second person overhear the declarant; it just must appear that under the circumstances, the statement meets a threshold of believability or plausibility sufficient to admit the statement.[134]

In a case in which the declarant had a motive to falsify a declaration against interest, the trial court properly refused to admit the hearsay statement. During a murder prosecution, the defendant attempted to have the court admit the declaration against penal interest made by his father for jury consideration. In addition to the usual considerations concerning admissibility, the court evaluated whether the out-of-court declaration of the father would have been influenced by any motive to falsify. The father's statement did not fully incriminate him, but it was designed to remove suspicion from his son. According to the court, there were inconsistencies in the father's statement that created a credibility question concerning the trustworthiness of his statement. In addition, the father knew that police were looking for his son in connection with the killing, and the court expressed concern that the father's statement was not credible. The effort by the father to accept complete responsibility for attacks on three people half his age whom he did not know, and who were seriously wounded or killed, proved implausible to the court. After considering the appeal, the reviewing court upheld the convictions and agreed that the trial court was correct in refusing to admit the father's alleged declaration against penal interest.[135]

Before leaving the declaration against interest exception to the hearsay rule, a couple of caveats should be noted. First, the federal rule, as well as most state rules, requires corroboration of both the declarant's trustworthiness as well as the statement's trustworthiness. The party who seeks to introduce the unavailable witness's statement against penal interest has a duty to introduce sufficient proof that a rational juror could believe in its truth. In order to determine whether a declarant's statement is sufficiently trustworthy, a judge should focus on whether there are corroborating circumstances that clearly demonstrate the trustworthiness of the declarant's statement.[136] In other words, the proponent must demonstrate sufficient corroboration of the statement in context with other facts in the case in order for the declaration to be admissible.

133   Ingram v. United States, 885 A.2d 257, 264, 2005 D.C. App. LEXIS 533 (2005).
134   *Id.*
135   *See* Stewart v. Maryland, 151 Md. App. 425, 827 A.2d 850, 2003 Md. App. LEXIS 75 (2003).
136   United States v. Franklin, 415 F.3d 537, 547, 2005 U.S. App. LEXIS 14540 (5th Cir. 2005).

Moreover, there is no declaration against penal interest if the declarant has not mentioned facts that, if true, would most assuredly implicate the declarant in crime. Early stage criminal planning or merely thinking about a crime is not a crime in itself. In a Michigan case, the court held that a declarant's statements implicating the defendant in a scheme to burn down the defendant's house were not against the declarant's penal interest as required for admission under the hearsay exception. Because the arson had not yet taken place and significant steps toward completion had not taken place, the statements only demonstrated an intent to commit a crime in the future.[137]

§ 12.11   — Other Exceptions — Residual Exceptions

Rule 807

Residual Exception

A statement not specifically covered by Rule 803 or 804 but having equivalent circumstantial guarantees of trustworthiness, is not excluded by the hearsay rule, if the court determines that (A) the statement is offered as evidence of a material fact; (B) the statement is more probative on the point for which it is offered than any other evidence which the proponent can procure through reasonable efforts; and (C) the general purposes of these rules and the interests of justice will best be served by admission of the statement into evidence. However, a statement may not be admitted under this exception unless the proponent of it makes known to the adverse party sufficiently in advance of the trial or hearing to provide the adverse party with a fair opportunity to prepare to meet it, the proponent's intention to offer the statement and the particulars of it, including the name and address of the declarant.[138]

While there are other specific exceptions, including those listed in Federal Rules 803 and 804, that cover the typical hearsay exceptions, Rule 807 regulates the admission into evidence of hearsay evidence that is not regulated by other rules governing hearsay. The rules have made it clear that merely because some of the exceptions are listed, such listing does not close the door to the use of other non-typical hearsay evidence as exceptions to the hearsay rule. It would be presumptuous to assume that all possible desirable exceptions to the hearsay rule have been catalogued or that accused individuals might never create any new situations in which there is reason to trust hearsay evidence will never arise. Therefore, Rule 807 specifically provides for other exceptions when certain conditions are met.[139]

---

[137] People v. Brownridge, 225 Mich. App. 291, 570 N.W.2d 672 (1997).

[138] FED. R. EVID. 807.

[139] The provisions of former Rule 803 (24) and former Rule 804(b)(5) have effectively been transferred to Rule 807 effective December 1, 1997 and remain in the latest 2008 version of the federal rules.

In order to admit a statement under Rule 807, one court noted that:

> [T]here must be a showing that (1) the statement has equivalent circumstan-
> tial guarantees of trustworthiness to the other hearsay exceptions; (2) the
> statement is offered as evidence of a material fact; (3) the statement is more
> probative on the point for which it is offered than any other evidence which
> the proponent can procure through reasonable efforts; (4) the general pur-
> poses of the rules and the interests of justice will best be served by its admis-
> sion; and (5) adequate notice must be given to the opposing party.[140]

To summarize, admissibility under Rule 807 must overcome five hurdles,
including trustworthiness, materiality, probative importance, the interests of
justice, and timely notice to the opposing party. In fact, the Second Circuit
noted that the residual exception of Rule 807 is to be used "very rarely, and
only in exceptional circumstances."[141]

Interpreting the rule authorizing evidence to be admitted under the exceptions of Rule 807, one commentator noted that they exist to provide some flexibility for the courts to deal with unique situations; they preserve the integrity
of the specifically listed exceptions under Rules 803 and 804; and ultimately
facilitate the basic goal of the Federals of evidence which is to determine the
truth and fairly adjudicate controversies that come before the courts.[142] Courts
in a variety of jurisdictions have repeatedly indicated that the residual hearsay
exception under rule 807 should be used only rarely and for especially exceptional circumstances.[143]

In a case in which the defendant attempted to introduce hearsay evidence
under Rule 807, the trial judge denied his efforts.[144] In the case, the defendant, who served in the military in Iraq, had been accused of selling military
body armor on E-bay. Among other offenses, he had been charged with mail
fraud and unauthorized sale of government property. During the investigation, a Defense Department employee interviewed the defendant in Iraq in the
presence of two superior noncommissioned officers when the defendant, in
response to a question, denied selling government body armor on E-bay. At
the trial, the prosecution put one of the noncommissioned officers on the stand
and he testified that he had been present when the defendant denied selling the
armor. On cross-examination of the witness, when the witness admitted that he
could not remember every detail of the meeting, the defense attorney sought
to refresh the witness's memory by using a report of the meeting that had
been prepared by the Defense Department employee. When the prosecution

---

140 United States v. Peneaux, 432 F.3d 882, 891, 2005 U.S. App. LEXIS 28877 (8th Cir. 2005).
141 McGory v. City of New York, 2002 U.S. Dist. LEXIS 20177 (S.D.N.Y. 2002), quoting
     Parsons v. Honeywell, 929 F.2d 901, 907 (2d Cir. 1991).
142 Weinstein's Federal Evidence § 807.02 (Matthew Bender 2009).
143 United States v. Wilson, 281 Fed. Appx. 96, 2008 LEXIS 12302 (3rd Cir. 2008).
144 United States v. Avery, 2005 U.S. Dist. LEXIS 15979 (E.D. Pa. 2005).

objected, the judge had the witness silently read the report to himself. The report contained the defendant's assertion that he purchased boots and body armor from a man in North Carolina. Defense counsel attempted to further cross-examine the witness with the Defense Department report in an effort to rebut the prosecutor's theory that the defendant had stolen the armor from the federal government. When the prosecutor complained that the report was hearsay evidence, the judge agreed and would not allow the statement to be used as evidence. The defendant's counsel sought to have the statement admitted under the residual exception covered by Rule 807. The trial court refused on the ground that to be admissible under Rule 807, a statement must meet five requirements: trustworthiness, materiality, probative importance, interests of justice and notice to the opposing party. According to the trial court,

> The trustworthiness of [the] statement is compromised, however, by the fact that his statement concerned events that took place, at the very at least, ten months earlier, and while he was deployed in Iraq. Moreover, [the declarant's] statement is contained in an interview report that he did not himself prepare, and there is no indication that the information he provided during the interview was made under oath and subject to the penalty of perjury.[145]

The court rejected the efforts of the defendant to have the statement-report admitted as an exception to the hearsay rule under Rule 807 because its trustworthiness could not be substantiated.

In applying Rule 807, a federal district court properly excluded an investigator's report from evidence when the report was designed to help the remaining defendant.[146] One conspirator pleaded guilty to robbery charges and testified against the other conspirator in the robbery of an armored truck driver. An investigator for the defendant had conversations with a third Brinks employee, which could have been used to impeach the government's conspirator witnesses who had already pled guilty. The conversations that the investigator wanted to relate to the jury were hearsay, but the defendant did not effectively show why the words spoken to the defendant's investigator would have any independent indicia of reliability or trustworthiness. There was no proof that the statements had been made under oath, and no proof that they were videotaped or voluntarily made. The reviewing court upheld the trial court's determination that the hearsay evidence should not having been admitted under Rule 807.

In a landmark case, *Crawford v. Washington*,[147] the Supreme Court of the United States dealt a harsh blow to prosecution efforts to successfully get evidence admitted under Rule 807 and related state evidence rules. In the *Crawford* case, a trial court convicted the defendant of assault of a man who had tried to rape the defendant's wife. At trial, the court permitted his wife's recorded out-of-court statement given to police to be admitted against him.

---

[145]   *Id.*
[146]   United States v. Rodriguez, 2009 U.S. App. LEXIS 4506 (9th Cir. 2009).
[147]   Crawford v. Washington, 541 U.S. 36, 52, 2004 U.S. LEXIS 1838 (2004).

The defendant's wife did not testify at trial after defendant invoked his state marital privilege to prevent her testimony, but the prosecution used her out-of-court recorded statements as substantive evidence against him. Because his wife did not testify, he was effectively prevented from confronting and cross-examining her. The Supreme Court reversed the assault conviction with the view that allowing the wife's statement against him that contained testimonial evidence, the trial court prevented the defendant's exercise of his Sixth Amendment right to confront and cross-examine an adverse witness. Only in exceptional situations will testimonial evidence be admitted when confrontation and cross-examination are impossible. In the *Crawford* case, the court noted that statements taken by police during investigations are generally considered testimonial in nature and can be excluded on Sixth Amendment grounds.[148]

Even before the *Crawford* case, courts hesitated to admit evidence under the residual exception unless all of the conditions were met. In a federal case that involved the admission of evidence under Rule 807, the defendant had been charged and convicted of kidnapping resulting in death based upon the disappearance of his ex-wife.[149] He filed a motion for a new trial based partly on the fact that the jury had seen and considered some evidence that the judge had not formally admitted into evidence and the defendant argued that it could not have been admitted even under the residual exception of Rule 807. The evidence that is contested by the defendant consisted of two day planner books that belonged to the defendant's ex-wife in which she penned some of her thoughts as an unhappy wife prior to the divorce. According to the trial court, the day planners were intentionally supplied to the jury by the government. The inadmissible evidence included notes within the day planners in which the deceased ex-wife mentioned harassing or threatening telephone calls by the defendant, referred to a protective order that she had sought at an earlier time, and included her cryptic notations about conversations she had with the defendant's daughter. The day planners also contained telephone numbers for a police detective who worked with protective orders and the number for a domestic violence support group. The trial judge found that the evidence contained in the day planners was virtually all hearsay and some of it had multiple layers of hearsay to which the defendant could obtain no cross-examination even if they had been admitted by the judge. There were also "moving and powerful" notes in the planners in the decedent's own handwriting. As the judge noted, "[t]his evidence, although compelling, bears no indicia of reliability because these statements do not fall within any of the twenty-three recognized exceptions to the hearsay rule, nor do they indicate any particularized guarantees of trustworthiness."[150] According to the judge's reasoning, the fact that the jury saw and evaluated unadmitted hearsay evidence constituted a violation of the defendant's right to confrontation. In resolving whether the evidence could

---

[148]   *Id.*

[149]   United States v. Lentz, 2004 U.S. Dist. LEXIS 29650 (E.D. Va. 2004).

[150]   *Id.*

have been admitted, the judge considered that the decedent was unavailable, that there were no circumstantial guarantees of trustworthiness, that the evidence might relate to a material fact, whether the evidence was probative, whether admission would serve justice, and whether the opposing side had received notice. The court evaluated and rejected the government's contention that the day planner evidence could be admitted under the residual exception of Rule 807 and reversed the conviction.

In a different situation, a trial judge allowed evidence under the residual exception of Rule 807 when one minor was accused of the aggravated sexual battery of another minor.[151] At a bench trial, the judged adjudicated the alleged juvenile aggressor, a minor, as a juvenile delinquent. The evidence against the defendant consisted of some testimony from the minor victim and evidence presented by a forensic examiner who had questioned the victim. The forensic examiner followed proper interrogation protocols in interviewing the minor victim. As is required under Rule 807, the government gave the defendant notice that the forensic examiner would be called as a prosecution witness. Over the defendant's objection, the forensic questioner answered some foundational questions and explained the techniques used in talking to the juvenile victim. Over the juvenile defendant's objections on Rule 807 and Sixth Amendment confrontation grounds, the court allowed the forensic examiner to tell the court what the girl-victim told the forensic examiner concerning when the events occurred and how the defendant's and the victim's private areas had been joined together, among other relevant facts. Specifically, the court considered that the forensic examiner's evidence was material to the case, and, because the victim's testimony was unclear on some matters in court that she had freely mentioned out of court, the forensic examiner's testimony was the most probative available. The court found the examiner's testimony trustworthy when considered with other evidence in the case and proper notice had been given to the defendant. Admitting the evidence under the residual exception to the hearsay rule appeared to serve the interests of justice, so the court affirmed the juvenile adjudication.

If the reasons for excluding hearsay evidence are not strong and the interests of justice would best be served by admission of a hearsay statement into evidence, the proponent must assert logical rationales that support admitting the evidence under the residual exception theory to the hearsay rule. Admitting evidence under the residual exception rule had a chance of court approval where there are special cases involving unique circumstances.

§ 12.12 Nontestimonial Utterances

The previous sections discussed the hearsay rule and demonstrated some of the well-known exceptions that allow admission of evidence in contravention

---

[151] United States v. W.B., 452 F.3d 1002, 2006 U.S. App. LEXIS 17378 (8th Cir. 2006).

of the general rule. Courts recognize the legal principle that states that if an out-of-court statement is offered to show what was said, rather than for the truth of the matter stated, the out-of-court statements are not considered hearsay.[152] Demonstrative of this principle is a situation in which an officer believed that stolen property had been hidden in a wooded area, but he was not certain. When he asked the defendant's son where the stolen goods were located, the son pointed to the woods behind a motel, but did not speak. The trial court allowed the officer to testify concerning the one-sided conversation he had with the defendant's son over the defense objection that the evidence constituted inadmissible hearsay. The boy's gesture, or verbal act, conveyed information but the gesture was not used to prove the truth of the matters visually asserted by the boy. His gesture was admitted to show why the officer walked into the wooded area where he found the stolen goods. The court of appeals held that the testimony of the officer explaining the boy's gesture, did not qualify as hearsay because it was not offered for its truth.[153]

A Virginia court advised that whether an out-of-court statement or act constituted hearsay depended on the purpose for which the statement was offered at trial; a statement that was offered for proof of its truth qualified as hearsay, but a statement or act that has been offered to the purpose of explaining or throwing light on the conduct of an individual to whom the statement was directed is not considered hearsay.[154] Where a witness testified that she called police after observing a larcenist leaving her store and mentioned that the reason the man piqued her interest was because another store employee gave her a detailed description of the repeat larcenist. The statement describing the appearance of the repeat larcenist was not offered for proof of its truth; it was offered only to explain why the witness scrutinized the behavior of the particularly described customer.[155] However, "a nod of the head in response to a question calling for a "yes" or "no" answer, or a gesture pointing to a particular person when asked to identify a perpetrator, are examples of assertive conduct"[156] that qualifies as hearsay evidence.

A Florida trial court committed reversible error resulting in the wrongful conviction of a defendant for grand theft of a motor vehicle. The defendant's position was that another person told the defendant that the other person was the owner of the van and that the defendant had permission to drive it. If this were true, the defendant's necessary state of mind for larceny would have been lacking. The testimony was not hearsay and should not have been excluded because the defendant did not offer it for the truth of the matter asserted within

---

[152]   Cormier v. State, 955 S.W.2d 161 (Tex. 1997).

[153]   Saunders v. Commonwealth, 2003 Va. App. LEXIS 394 (2003).

[154]   Farrar v. Commonwealth, 2006 Va. App. LEXIS 301 (2006).

[155]   *Id.*

[156]   People v. Jurado, 38 Cal. 4th 72, 129, 131 P.3d 400, 438, 41 Cal. Rptr. 3d 319, 365, 2006 Cal. LEXIS 4391 (2006).

the statement. The defendant's purpose in offering the evidence was to show that because he heard the statement by the alleged owner, the defendant possessed a good faith belief that the other person owned the van, and that he had lawful permission to drive it.[157]

"A verbal act is an utterance of an operative fact that gives rise to legal consequences."[158] The hearsay rule does not apply to verbal acts when the evidence has not been offered for its truth. In one case, a defendant contended on appeal that his counsel failed to object to inadmissible hearsay offered by the prosecution. A police officer testified that he asked the defendant for permission to search his apartment and the officer stated that the defendant answered in the affirmative. The defendant's statement could be called a verbal act "because the statement [was] admitted merely to show that it was actually made, not to prove the truth of what was asserted."[159] The trial court held, and the appellate court agreed, that no hearsay evidence had been permitted in that context because the officer was not offering the defendant's positive answer for its truth, only to indicate that the defendant had made a statement that would indicate to the officer that he had the legal authority to make a lawful entry and search of the apartment.[160]

Under what is sometimes referred to as the verbal act doctrine, a statement that accompanies conduct is admissible because it gives legal significance to the act. The Florida Supreme Court explained a verbal act as:

> an utterance of an operative fact that gives rise to legal consequences. Verbal acts, also known as statements of legal consequence, are not hearsay, because the statement is admitted merely to show that it was actually made, not to prove the truth of what was asserted in it.[161]

The Florida court noted that in order for verbal acts to be admissible, the conduct that is explained by the words must be independently material or important to the issue at hand, the conduct that occurs must be equivocal, and the words uttered must assist in giving legal context or significance to the conduct, and the words must be spoken with the conduct.[162] Where the evidence is offered only to show that words were spoken and not for proof of the truth of what was said, the evidence is not hearsay. For example, in a case in which a trial court convicted the defendant of the sale and delivery of cannabis and possession of cannabis, the case depended upon the testimony of a confidential informant.[163] The trial court refused to allow a separate witness to offer the

---

[157] Alfaro v. Florida, 837 So. 2d 429, 2002 Fla. App. LEXIS 13992 (2002).

[158] 5-801 WEINSTEIN'S FEDERAL EVIDENCE § 801.11[3] Verbal Acts (Matthew Bender 2009).

[159] *Id.*

[160] Dragani v. Bryant, 2005 U.S. Dist. LEXIS 38057, n. 7 (M.D. Fla. 2005).

[161] Banks v. Florida, 790 So. 2d 1094, 2001 Fla. LEXIS 1411 (2001).

[162] *Id.*

[163] Burkey v. State, 922 So. 2d 1033, 1035, 2006 Fla. App. LEXIS 2772 (2006).

defendant's response to a question from the confidential informant. One of the witnesses who had been present at the crime scene was prepared to tell the court that when the defendant had been asked to sell marijuana by the prosecution's confidential informant, the defendant told her, "I don't do that kind of stuff."[164] The trial court rejected allowing the witness to tell what the defendant answered to the confidential informant on the ground that it was hearsay. The appellate court held that the trial court should have allowed the witness to state what the defendant had said in response to an offer to commit a crime from the confidential informant. The statement was a verbal act of the defendant that was not hearsay and it should have been admitted just to show that he made the statement. The fact that the defendant would refuse an offer to commit drug selling is material for his defense that he was not involved in the drug sale that occurred within the home. In a different case, a "waitress" at a bar/club came over to where an undercover officer was sitting and rubbed her buttocks on his lap as an invitation to a free lap dance and said that the fun did not have to end there, that there was a private room. The undercover officer paid $50 to the proprietor and the "waitress" said the $50 would pay for oral sex but that a tip would be nice. The appellate court held that the words of the "waitress" were verbal acts because the statements were made merely to demonstrate that the operative words were uttered and not to prove their substantive truth. In this case, the words explain why the undercover officer wanted to go to the private room. The nonverbal conduct of the "waitress" was equivocal, the words spoken were important to understanding the situation, and the words accompanied her conduct and were admissible under the verbal act doctrine.[165]

§ 12.13　Summary

The general rule is that once evidence is identified as hearsay it should not be admissible in court because of the concern that hearsay evidence may not be reliable or truthful and may not have been given under oath. Hearsay evidence is defined as oral testimony or written evidence presented in court from a statement uttered or written out of court, when the statement is offered in court to prove the truth of matters asserted therein. Thus, evidence that relies on the credibility of the out-of-court declarant will be classified as hearsay and excluded. Although this general rule is universally applied and based on sound reasoning, there are many exceptions. If evidence meets the requirements of a recognized exception or the residual exception, it may be admissible, even though it is classified as hearsay.

Examples of exceptions to the hearsay rule include spontaneous and excited utterances, some business and public records, family history and

---

[164]　*Id.*

[165]　Pronesti v. Florida, 847 So. 2d 1165, 1166, 2003 Fla. App. LEXIS 9472 (2003).

records, former testimony, dying declarations, declarations against interest, and exceptions under the residual exception rule. Under each of the traditional hearsay exceptions evidence may be admitted for substantive proof; however, it must meet the specific requirements that have been established for the particular exception because these requirements help assure trustworthiness.

The Sixth Amendment to the U.S. Constitution guarantees defendants the right to confront and cross-examine the witnesses against them. When out-of-court hearsay statements are admitted as evidence in court, the defendant may not have the opportunity to cross-examine or even confront the adverse declarant whose evidence is introduced by the one who overheard the declarant speak. Since the Supreme Court recently held that testimonial evidence normally requires that actual confrontation and cross-examination must be permitted, some hearsay exceptions have come under more intense scrutiny by trial courts.[166] While preserving of the rights of confrontation for defendants, the interests of justice require that a balance exist between the rights of defendants and the necessities of justice and fairness for society.

The hearsay rule does not exclude evidence when the out-of-court statements are offered solely as evidence that a statement was made, and not for the substantive content of the statement. Witnesses to out-of-court statements who repeat them in court, not for the substantive truth of the statement, but to indicate the person's physical or mental condition, will be permitted to offer evidence.

From the foregoing discussion, it is clear that although some hearsay evidence is not admissible in court, there are many exceptions to the hearsay rule. The exceptions to the rule may result in most evidence classified as hearsay being admitted and very little evidence being excluded, but where courts admit hearsay evidence, the requirements of the exceptions assure truthfulness. In order to offer the greatest level of admissible evidence to the prosecutor, good practice dictates that criminal justice personnel be familiar not only with the rules that exclude hearsay evidence, but also with the hearsay exceptions and their individual requirements, which permit the admission of hearsay evidence in court.

---

[166] *See* Crawford v. Washington, 541 U.S. 36, 2004 U.S. LEXIS 1838 (2004).

Evidence via Documents and Real Evidence

Documentary Evidence   13

Before any writing will be admitted in evidence, it must be authenticated in some manner, i.e., its genuineness or execution must be proved. Even a competent public record or document must be properly identified, verified or authenticated by some recognized method before it may be introduced in evidence.

City of Randleman v. Hinshaw,
2 N.C. App. 381, 163 S.E.2d 95 (1968)

Chapter Outline

Section
13.1   Introduction
13.2   Authentication
13.3   Self-Authentication
13.4   Methods of Authentication
13.5   Specific Examples of Documentary Evidence
13.6   Best Evidence Rule
13.7   Secondary Evidence
13.8   Summaries
13.9   Learned Treatises
13.10   Summary

§ 13.1   Introduction

Evidence that courts admit at trial can be arranged in three general categories: (1) oral testimony that witnesses offer from the witness stand in open court, (2) documentary evidence introduced by witnesses, and (3) real evidence that has tangible essence, which is offered and authenticated by witnesses who make its introduction possible. While the discussion in previous chapters related primarily to oral evidence, this chapter focuses on the broad category of documentary evidence. This type of evidence encompasses evidence beyond what the term "documentary evidence" would normally bring to mind. Documentary evidence includes evidence furnished by written instruments, inscriptions, and documents of all kinds. The term is broad enough to encompass every form of writing and applies to both public and private documents. Under the Federal Rules of Evidence, a writing or recording has been defined as including "letters, words, or numbers, or their equivalent, set down by handwriting, typewriting, printing, Photostatting, photographing, magnetic impulse, mechanical or electronic recording, or other form of data compilation."[1] Originally, a document provided a way of storing information in a fairly permanent manner, but that concept has grown to include movies, phonograph records, video- and audiotapes, computers and their mass storage devices, and photographs. Because the general rules of admissibility apply to all types of evidence, documentary evidence must meet these usual requirements. In addition, there are certain rules that apply uniquely to documentary evidence. These rules are discussed in this chapter. In Chapter 14 the rules relating to the introduction of real evidence will be discussed and explained.

---

[1]   Fed. R. Evid. 1001(1).

Under the law of evidence, the word *document* is a term of art and has a rather broad definition that encompasses many items that are not ordinarily considered documents. A document may be defined as any message that has been expressed, described, inscribed, embedded, saved, or recorded in or upon any substance by means of letters, figures, or marks, and intended to be used for the purpose of recording that matter. Examples of private documents are photographs, computer data, videotape data, films, deeds, wills, agreements, and personal and commercial contracts. Birth records, death records, marriage records, registrations of various kinds, some police records, and licensing records are examples of public documents.

To be admitted into evidence, documentary evidence must meet the same rules of evidence as oral testimony concerning relevancy and materiality. In addition, the party that introduces a document must lay a foundation for the introduction of the documentary evidence to demonstrate that it is genuine and that the document is what it purports to be. As a threshold matter, the proponent must bring sufficient evidence to authenticate, verify, or identify the document offered. Meeting the requirements for authentication and the best evidence rule are two tests that relate primarily to documentary evidence. The following sections of this chapter address the general rules relating to these tests and their requirements, and demonstrate the principles by offering some specific examples.

§ 13.2 Authentication

Rule 901

Requirement of Authentication or Identification

(a) General provision

The requirement of authentication or identification as a condition precedent to admissibility is satisfied by evidence sufficient to support a finding that the matter in question is what its proponent claims.

(b) Illustrations

By way of illustration only, and not by way of limitation, the following are examples of authentication or identification conforming with the requirements of this rule:

(1) Testimony of witness with knowledge

Testimony that a matter is what it is claimed to be.

(2) Nonexpert opinion on handwriting

Nonexpert opinion as to the genuineness of handwriting, based upon familiarity not acquired for purposes of the litigation.

(3) Comparison by trier or expert witness

Comparison by the trier of fact or by expert witnesses with specimens which have been authenticated.

(4) Distinctive characteristics and the like

Appearance, contents, substance, internal patterns, or other distinctive characteristics, taken in conjunction with circumstances.

(5) Voice identification

Identification of a voice, whether heard firsthand or through mechanical or electronic transmission or recording, by opinion based upon hearing the voice at any time under circumstances connecting it with the alleged speaker.

(6) Telephone conversations

Telephone conversations, by evidence that a call was made to the number assigned at the time by the telephone company to a particular person or business, if (A) in the case of a person, circumstances, including self-identification, show the person answering to be the one called, or (B) in the case of a business, the call was made to a place of business and the conversation related to business reasonably transacted over the telephone.

(7) Public records or reports

Evidence that a writing authorized by law to be recorded or filed and in fact recorded or filed in a public office, or a purported public record, report, statement, or data compilation, in any form, is from the public office where items of this nature are kept.

(8) Ancient documents or data compilation

Evidence that a document or data compilation, in any form, (A) is in such condition as to create no suspicion concerning its authenticity, (B) was in a place where it, if authentic, would likely be, and (C) has been in existence 20 years or more at the time it is offered.

(9) Process or system

Evidence describing a process or system used to produce a result and showing that the process or system produces an accurate result.

(10) Methods provided by statute or rule

Any method of authentication or identification provided by Act of Congress or by other rules prescribed by the Supreme Court pursuant to statutory authority.[2]

A writing that lacks any provable connection to a case has no ability to influence any of the elements that must be proved or disproved in a criminal case and is not admissible. As a fundamental rule of evidence, no writing, as broadly defined, may be admitted into evidence without some proof that it is genuine or authentic and that it is what it purports to be. As one early writer stated, "A writing, of itself, is evidence of nothing, and therefore is not, unless accompanied by proof of some sort, admissible in evidence."[3] Another court recently noted that "[a]uthentication requirements are satisfied if the trial

---

[2]   FED. R. EVID. 901.

[3]   Stamper v. Griffin, 20 Ga. 312 (1856).

court, in its discretion, concludes that the evidence presented is genuine and, in reasonable probability, has not been tampered with or altered in any significant manner."[4] The requirement of authentication does not demand that the proponent of a document conclusively prove that the document or article is genuine, but only that the document or article has enough evidence presented by the proponent that supports the finding that the item is what its proponent claims it to be.[5] According to the rationale behind this rule, absent a showing that the evidence is what the proponent alleges, it has no logical or legal relevance. The required proof may be contained within the document itself, in that the document may become, by authority of statute or otherwise, "self-authenticating." Otherwise, outside proof is required to lay a foundation for admission of the documentary evidence. Authentication merely means that there must be preliminary proof of genuineness, authenticity, or identity of the document sufficient to prove that the evidence is what its proponent purports the evidence to be.

Under Rule 901(a), authentication or identification is a condition precedent to admissibility and is designed to ensure that a piece of evidence is what it purports to be. Therefore, a proponent need only introduce evidence that would allow a reasonable judge to conclude that the document or article is the genuine item and that it is what it appears to be. Another way of phrasing the requirement of authentication is to have the proponent "present foundational evidence that is sufficient to constitute a rational basis for a jury to decide that the primary evidence is what its proponent claims it to be."[6]

While authentication is necessary for admission of documentary evidence, the proponent may use a variety of evidence to demonstrate its genuine quality, including direct or circumstantial evidence.[7] For example, in an arranged drug purchase, police gave their confidential operative marked money and a hidden cassette recorder prior to the informant making a drug purchase. The informant was outside of the view of the officer at some times, but returned with the recording of the transaction and the purchased drugs. The confidential informant testified under oath that the tape-recording was a genuine and accurate recording of the drug transaction and the officer testified that the recorder had been in the police vault since it was originally returned. The reviewing court upheld the admission of the sound recording because it had been properly authenticated as a writing under the state's version of Rule 901 by the officer and the informant.[8]

---

[4]   Bobo v. State, 102 Ark. 329, 334, 2008 Ark. App. LEXIS 427 (Ark. 2008).

[5]   State v. Anglemyer, 269 Neb. 237, 243, 691 N.W.2d 153, 160, 2005 Neb. LEXIS 35 (2005).

[6]   Ohio v. Payton, 2002 Ohio App. LEXIS 496 (2002).

[7]   State v. Carpenter, 275 Conn. 785, 856, 882 A.2d 604, 648, 2005 Conn. LEXIS 396 (2005).

[8]   Wilkerson v. State, 2005 Ark. App. LEXIS 12 (Ark. 2005). *See* case in Part II.

Depending on the character of the document that a proponent seeks to have introduced into evidence, the requirements vary concerning authentication. The proponent of documentary evidence usually offers sworn testimony by a witness concerning the source and genuineness of the writing. Having the witness identify the writing and swear to its authenticity while under oath will typically suffice to authenticate a writing. In some instances, however, such specific testimony is not required. For example, a trial court accepted a copy of a different court's record of a defendant's prior convictions when the document had the authentication seal of the court affixed to the documents and the signatory of the authentication notation certified that each document was a true copy of the ones in the official records. The appellate court held that the documents were properly authenticated.[9] In a Tennessee case, the reviewing court held that an abstract of a driving record that contained a certification of authenticity, but bore no seal of the office or official, was not self-authenticating and therefore should not have been admitted.[10] Formal proof of authenticity will not be necessary if the parties to the case agree to stipulate to the authenticity of a particular writing.

In an effort to promote judicial economy, statutes have been designed to do away with the formal authentication requirements when such requirements obviously serve little purpose. Even when such statutes are in effect, the opposing party is not foreclosed from disputing authenticity by introducing evidence that the documents fail to meet the requirements or are not authentic. Rule 901(b) of the Federal Rules of Evidence lists ten examples of authentication or identification that conform to the rule. Some of these deal with real evidence, which is discussed in the next chapter, while some refer to documentary or oral evidence.

In authenticating written documents under Rule 901(b)(2), state courts have universally agreed that a nonexpert witness may properly identify a signature or handwriting if the witness is sufficiently familiar with the writing of another person so that the testimony would aid the jury. The witness may have become familiar with a person's handwriting by observing him or her write on previous occasions, whether the observations were made from a social setting, interactions at work, or through personal correspondence. However, knowledge of another person's writing may be acquired by any means, as long as it is not obtained especially for the trial.[11] Courts have not set a minimum number of occasions or encounters with examples for familiarity to be sufficient for authentication purposes. However, evidence must be introduced to show that the witness possessed sufficient familiarity with the handwriting. In a Texas case, the trial judge permitted a detective who worked at the jail where a defendant was housed to authenticate a letter purportedly written by the defendant. It was not clear if the detective knew the defendant. As part of

---

9   Conley v. Commonwealth, 2005 Va. App. LEXIS 516 (2005).

10   State v. Troutman, 2008 Tenn. Crim. App. LEXIS 899 (Tenn. 2008).

11   *See* FED. R. EVID. 901(b)(2).

the detective's duties, he read all incoming and outgoing prisoner mail and had become familiar with the defendant's name, writing style, and his unique prison identification number and could recognize the defendant's handwriting. The reviewing court held that the defendant's letter had been properly authenticated by the detective.[12]

Rule 901(b)(7) provides that the requirement of authentication of a public record or report, as a condition precedent to admissibility, is satisfied if evidence is introduced to show that the writing was authorized by law to be recorded or filed in a public office. Under this section, the proponent of the evidence need only demonstrate that the office from which the party obtained the records served as the legal custodian of the records or served as the official repository. The public records need not be in any particular form in order to be deemed authentic, and minor irregularities in appearance should not preclude admittance if the record is authentic.

When old documents must be authenticated, challenges arise because the people who could authenticate older documents may not remember the documents in question and persons who could authenticate a document may be deceased or, if living, may have memory problems. The authentication rules have been relaxed concerning the authentication of older or ancient documents. Rule 901(b)(8) of the Federal Rules of Evidence liberalizes the common law "ancient document" rule. The federal rule provides that a document may be admitted when requirements pertaining to age, non-suspicious condition, and appropriate custody are satisfied. Under this rule, a document must be demonstrated to be at least 20 years old before it may be authenticated as an ancient document. Many states that have state variations of the Federal Rules have used the same requirements for ancient document authentication, including the 20-year period necessary to qualify as an ancient document,[13] but some states adhere to the 30-year requirement.[14]

In states following the 30-year provision, the rules dictate that the document "must on its face be free from suspicion and must come from proper custody."[15] The requirement that the document be free from suspicion does not concern the content of the document, but rather whether the document is genuine. Questions as to the document's content and completeness bear on the weight to be given to the evidence and do not affect the threshold issue of authenticity.

In interpreting the "ancient document" authentication rule, a trial court in Hawai'i properly permitted a lease for land that had been executed in 1872 to be admitted in a trial court in a dispute over title to land on Maui. The opponent contended that the internal language of the document failed to mention a

---

[12]   Galbraith v. State, 2008 Texas App. LEXIS 8433 (Tex. 2008).

[13]   *See*, for example, WIS. STAT. § 909.015 (2008).

[14]   TENN. R. EVID. 803(16) Statements in Ancient Documents Affecting an Interest in Property (2009).

[15]   29A AM. JUR. 2D *Evidence* § 1204 (2008).

particular parcel of land and that the ancient document dealing with the disputed land was not relevant. The Intermediate Court of Appeals of Hawai'i disagreed and held that under the ancient document rules of Rule 901, the document had been properly authenticated.[16] Most assuredly, no one who was a party to the original lease was alive to help otherwise authenticate the document.

Rule 901(b)(9) provides that evidence describing a process or system used to produce a result and showing that the process or system produced an accurate result satisfies the authentication requirement. Examples of evidence that has been held admissible under this subsection are X-rays, computer output, electrocardiograms, surveys and polls, and statistical samples. Typically evidence produced by a process or system is presented to the jury or the judge by means of expert testimony, and usually the witness who conveys the substance of the evidence also lays the necessary foundation.

When computer records and evidence were rare and were not usually introduced as evidence, courts were reluctant to apply this exception to computer printouts.[17] As the business use of computers has become necessary and commercial transactions are virtually always recorded in computer databases, courts have been forced to determine when and under what circumstances computer-generated data should be authenticated. Federal Rule of Evidence 901(B)(9) offers an example of authentication identification conforming to the requirements of this rule. This section states that evidence describing a process or system used to produce a result and showing that the process or system produces an accurate result conforms to the authentication requirements of the rule.

More recently, courts have admitted computer printouts in accordance with this provision. In a state prosecution in which an automatic teller machine technician had been accused of illegally removing money from the machine, electronically and automatically generated evidence stored on a computer was admitted against him. The trial court rejected his lack of authentication argument. The trial court admitted the computer-generated records as having met the minimum standards for authentication, especially because the records were based on automatic data inputs and were not dependent on human interaction. The appellate court noted that computer business records have a level of trustworthiness that the individually prepared records lack.[18]

Recognizing that evidence generated or gathered by means of a process or system is often highly technical and complex in nature, some courts appear to require a higher level of authentication for computer-generated records when they are offered for admission into evidence. In a case involving convictions for fraud on a financial institution and identity deception, the prosecution had introduced an affidavit titled "Certificate of Authentication and Reliability"

---

[16] Makila Land Co. v. Kapu, 2006 Haw. App. LEXIS 181 (2006).

[17] United States v. Fendley, 522 F.2d 181 (5th Cir. 1975).

[18] State v. Huehn, 53 P.3d 733, 737, 2002 Colo. App. LEXIS 21 (2002). *See* case in Part II.

that accompanied 13 pages of computer printouts that purported to be from the defrauded company's computer system. The affidavit was designed to identify the printout data as being genuine. The affidavit was signed and dated October 23, but the computer printouts were not created until October 24. In reversing the conviction, the appellate court noted that because the affidavit was predated, and for other reasons, the computer printouts were not properly authenticated and should not have been admitted in evidence.[19]

§ 13.3 Self-Authentication

Rule 902

Self-Authentication

Extrinsic evidence of authenticity as a condition precedent to admissibility is not required with respect to the following:

(1) Domestic public documents under seal. A document bearing a seal purporting to be that of the United States, or of any State, district, Commonwealth, territory, or insular possession thereof, or the Panama Canal Zone, or the Trust Territory of the Pacific Islands, or of a political subdivision, department, officer, or agency thereof, and a signature purporting to be an attestation or execution.

(2) Domestic public documents not under seal. A document purporting to bear the signature in the official capacity of an officer or employee of any entity included in paragraph (1) hereof, having no seal, if a public officer having a seal and having official duties in the district or political subdivision of the officer or employee certifies under seal that the signer has the official capacity and that the signature is genuine.

(3) Foreign public documents. A document purporting to be executed or attested in an official capacity by a person authorized by the laws of a foreign country to make the execution or attestation, and accompanied by a final certification as to the genuineness of the signature and official position (A) of the executing or attesting person, or (B) of any foreign official whose certificate of genuineness of signature and official position relates to the execution or attestation or is in a chain of certificates of genuineness of signature and official position relating to the execution or attestation. A final certification may be made by a secretary of an embassy or legation, consul general, consul, vice consul, or consular agent of the United States, or a diplomatic or consular official of the foreign country assigned or accredited to the United States. If reasonable opportunity has been given to all parties to investigate the authenticity and accuracy of official documents, the court may, for good cause shown, order that they be treated as presumptively authentic without final certification or permit them to be evidenced by an attested summary with or without final certification.

---

[19]   Speybroeck v. State, 875 N.E.2d 813, 820, 2007 Ind. App. LEXIS 2408 (Ind. 2007).

(4) Certified copies of public records. A copy of an official record or report or entry therein, or of a document authorized by law to be recorded or filed and actually recorded or filed in a public office, including data compilations in any form, certified as correct by the custodian or other person authorized to make the certification, by certificate complying with paragraph (1), (2), or (3) of this rule, or complying with any Act of Congress or rule prescribed by the Supreme Court pursuant to statutory authority.

(5) Official publications. Books, pamphlets, or other publications purporting to be issued by public authority.

(6) Newspapers and periodicals. Printed materials purporting to be newspapers or periodicals.

(7) Trade inscriptions and the like. Inscriptions, signs, tags, or labels purporting to have been affixed in the course of business and indicating ownership, control, or origin.

(8) Acknowledged documents. Documents accompanied by a certificate of acknowledgment executed in the manner provided by law by a notary public or other officer authorized by law to take acknowledgments.

(9) Commercial paper and related documents. Commercial paper, signatures thereon, and documents relating thereto to the extent provided by general commercial law.

(10) Presumptions under Acts of Congress. Any signature, document, or other matter declared by Act of Congress to be presumptively or prima facie genuine or authentic.

(11) Certified domestic records of regularly conducted activity. The original or a duplicate of a domestic record of regularly conducted activity that would be admissible under Rule 803(6) if accompanied by a written declaration of its custodian or other qualified person, in a manner complying with any Act of Congress or rule prescribed by the Supreme Court pursuant to statutory authority, certifying that the record:

(A) was made at or near the time of the occurrence of the matters set forth by, or from information transmitted by, a person with knowledge of those matters;

(B) was kept in the course of the regularly conducted activity; and

(C) was made by the regularly conducted activity as a regular practice.

A party intending to offer a record into evidence under this paragraph must provide written notice of that intention to all adverse parties, and must make the record and declaration available for inspection sufficiently in advance of their offer into evidence to provide an adverse party with a fair opportunity to challenge them.

(12) Certified foreign records of regularly conducted activity. In a civil case, the original or a duplicate of a foreign record of regularly conducted activity that would be admissible under Rule 803(6) if accompanied by a written declaration by its custodian or other qualified person certifying that the record:

(A) was made at or near the time of the occurrence of the matters set forth by, or from information transmitted by, a person with knowledge of those matters;

(B) was kept in the course of the regularly conducted activity; and

(C) was made by the regularly conducted activity as a regular practice.

The declaration must be signed in a manner that, if falsely made, would subject the maker to criminal penalty under the laws of the country where the declaration is signed. A party intending to offer a record into evidence under this paragraph must provide written notice of that intention to all adverse parties, and must make the record and declaration available for inspection sufficiently in advance of their offer into evidence to provide an adverse party with a fair opportunity to challenge them.[20]

Courts have developed a substantial body of decisional law governing instances in which authenticity may be viewed as sufficiently established without extrinsic evidence. In addition, updates to modern evidence codes have provided somewhat simpler methods of authenticating documents. However, under older case law and pursuant to older rules of evidence, there were only a few self-authenticating documents, such as ancient documents, documents bearing a certificate of acknowledgment, and replies to letters.[21] However, to save the time of the court, the number of types of documents that are self-authenticating has grown. For example, the Federal Rules of Evidence now lists 12 types or categories of writings that are presently considered self-authenticating. Rule 902 of the Federal Rules of Evidence provides that extrinsic evidence of authenticity as a condition precedent to admissibility is not required with respect to the following: (1) domestic public documents under seal; (2) domestic public documents not under seal but certified by the appropriate public officer in charge of them; (3) foreign public documents accompanied by certification as to genuineness of signature and official position of executing or attesting person; (4) copies of public or official records certified by the custodian of the original record; (5) official publications issued by public authority; (6) newspapers and periodicals; (7) trade inscriptions and labels; (8) documents acknowledged by a notary public or other officer authorized by law to take acknowledgments; (9) commercial paper and related documents; (10) documents declared by Congress to be presumptively authentic, (11) certified foreign records of regularly conducted activity, and (12) certified domestic records of regularly conducted activity.[22]

In a prosecution involving the trespass by civilians on a United States military base without permission, the trial court admitted a document that certified that the individual trespasser's name was not on a government list of persons permitted to enter the base. The Certificate of Non-Existence of Record (CNER) signed by the lieutenant commander of the base stated that a diligent search of the records did not reveal the defendant's name. In rejecting the defendant's argument that the document had not been properly authenticated,

---

[20] FED. R. EVID. 902.

[21] TRACY, HANDBOOK OF THE LAW OF EVIDENCE (1952).

[22] *See, generally,* FED. R. EVID. 902.

the court, under Rule 902(1), held that the CNER admitted by the district court clearly exhibited the raised seal of the United States Department of the Navy and carried the signature of the lieutenant commander who certified and swore that the contents of the letter were true. Consistent with the Federal Rule 902, the seal of any executing officer or custodian will generally suffice to authenticate a document under Rule 902(1).[23]

Rule 902(3) governs the authentication and admissibility of foreign public documents in federal courts. As a matter of practice, a federal appeals court noted that there are two requirements for the authentication of foreign public documents.[24] First, some proof must be introduced that the document is what it purports to be, executed by a proper official in his official capacity and, second, there must be some indication that the public official of the foreign government vouching for the document is who he or she purports to be. In a Department of Homeland Security-initiated prosecution involving a defendant who allegedly engaged in sexual activities with underage children, where a United States citizen was alleged to have had traveled to a foreign country to engage in such activity, proof of the age of the victim was part of the prosecution's case. First, in order to be admissible in court, a foreign public document, such as a birth certificate, had to appear to be genuine on its face. In this case, the defendant complained about its authenticity. Secondarily, the rules dictate that one of a specified group of foreign officials has to issue a final certification attesting to the genuine quality of the signature and title of the person executing the original document. In this case, the reviewing court held that the birth certificate appeared to be genuine and properly issued and was properly deemed as authenticated by the trial court.

Where a public record may be self-authenticating, it must be presented in proper order with appropriate seals or signatures in order to meet the requirements of Rule 902(4). In a tax suit, the trial court had admitted tax documents introduced by a city and a school district in an effort to collect back property taxes. The tax documents contained an affidavit and were notarized by a tax assessor as being true copies of the original delinquent tax statements. The documents were not considered records under seal and had not been signed by someone authorized within the school district or city under seal who could attest to the signor's authority. The reviewing court reversed the trial court's finding of authentication on the ground that because the tax documents "did not bear a seal or contain a certification under seal from a public officer, the tax statements were not self-authenticating as certified public records"[25] under the Texas version of Rule 901(4).

---

[23] United States v. Ventura-Melendez, 275 F.3d 9, 14, 2001 U.S. App. LEXIS 26901 (1st Cir. 2001).

[24] United States v. Deverso, 518 F.3d 1250, 1256, 2008 U.S. App. LEXIS 4629 (11th Cir. 2008).

[25] Al-Nayem v. Irving Independent School District, 159 S.W.3d 762, 764, 2005 Tex. App. LEXIS 1919 (2005).

In a criminal case in which the court admitted copies of the defendant's juvenile adjudications that were certified copies and were given under the hand and seal of the office of the juvenile court clerk, the defendant contended that the documents were not properly presented to be self-authenticating public documents under seal. Even if there were some slight irregularities in the seal of one of the documents, the reviewing court concluded that the proof met the minimum requirements for authentication and were properly admitted against the defendant at his sentencing hearing.[26] But a Texas Youth Commission self-authenticating business record packet that also included juvenile court records could not authenticate the court records because uncertified court records cannot be self-authenticating.[27] A different court held that a copy of a driving record obtained from a state's official repository of records constituted an official public record under Rule 902(4) that the court deemed to be self-authenticating when accompanied by a notarized certification of the correctness of the record executed by a clerk in the state license bureau.[28]

In a drug conspiracy trial in which the defendants generated hotel, motel, private mailbox rental receipts, and other records made by businesses with which they transacted business, the business records were properly considered to be self-authenticating under Rule 902(11). The prosecution complied with the federal rule requirement that the opposing party give sufficient notice to the other party prior to the time of introduction of the records to avoid unfair surprise. The prosecution and the defense may authenticate a business record through a written declaration by a qualified custodian that the record met the necessary foundational requirements that the business made the record at or near the time of the transaction, proof that the business generated the record in the usual course of business, and proof that the business kept the record in the usual course of business. Because the prosecution followed the evidentiary requirements, the Seventh Circuit Court of Appeals rejected the defendant's argument that authentication of the business records had not been properly established and approved the introduction of the self-authenticating business records because they had been certified by their respective custodians as accurate renditions of the records generated by their respective business organizations.[29]

Under Federal Rule 902 and similar state rules of evidence, extrinsic evidence is not required for documents within the self-authenticating group, and such documents are admissible without further authentication. The opposing party may introduce evidence that disputes a judge's preliminary ruling on authentication and may attempt to have perfectly authenticated documentary

---

[26]   Hull v. State, 172 S.W.3d 186, 189, 2005 Tex. App. LEXIS 6502 (2005).

[27]   Rangel v. State, 2009 Tex. App. LEXIS 1555 (Tex. 2009).

[28]   United States v. Mirelez, 59 Fed. Appx. 286, 2003 U.S. App. LEXIS 2162 (10th Cir. 2003).

[29]   United States v. Bledsoe, 70 Fed. Appx. 370, 2003 U.S. App. LEXIS 13312 (7th Cir. 2003). *See also* FED. R. EVID. 902 (11) in Appendix I.

evidence rejected based on arguments that the authenticated documents possess insufficient relevancy to the case.

§ 13.4   Methods of Authentication

Because all writings must be authenticated to be admissible as evidence, when written documents are not self-authenticating, the proponent of a writing must offer a sufficient evidentiary foundation to support its admission. Generally, one of four methods may be followed in offering sufficient proof of authenticity: (1) proof of signing, (2) proof of signature, (3) comparison of signatures, and (4) circumstantial evidence.[30] Requirements include proof of the genuineness and proper execution of the document, and that the document correctly states what the party claims. However, there is no requirement to authenticate a writing that will not be introduced in evidence.

The most common method of authentication of a written document is offering proof of signing. It is common for the authenticating witness to testify that he or she saw the person sign the document in question. The next most common method of authentication is proof of the signature. If the witness did not see the person sign, but is familiar with and can identify the signature, this is sufficient authentication. Such evidence is as competent and valid as the testimony of the writers themselves and is not to be considered secondary evidence.[31] Some written documents may be self-authenticating under Rule 901(7) covering trade inscriptions, sign, and tags. In an Indiana prosecution for possession of methamphetamine precursor chemicals, the trial court approved the admission of several boxes that originally contained pseudoephedrine hydrochloride, a chemical used in the manufacture of methamphetamine. The original packaging contained printed data that told the weight of the drugs within the box and the state offered the labels under the Indiana rule of evidence that allow self-authentication for "inscriptions, signs, tags, or labels purporting to have been affixed in the course of business and indicating ownership, control, or origin."[32]

A tape-recording or a 911 call recording constitutes a writing and must be authenticated in order to be introduced at trial. In a Michigan case, the defendant alleged that a voice recording had not been properly authenticated, a view that the reviewing court instantly rejected. A surviving victim in a murder case, had testified that the audiotape voice belonged to him.[33] In a different case involving a burglary charge, the defendant wanted to introduce a recording of a 911 call made by a resident in the apartment building that he was alleged to have burglarized. The trial court refused to admit two unau-

---

[30]   TRACY, HANDBOOK OF THE LAW OF EVIDENCE (1952).

[31]   United States v. Moreno, 68 U.S. 400 (1863).

[32]   Reemer v. State, 835 N.E.2d 1005, 1007, 2005 Ind. LEXIS 955, n.4 (Ind. 2005).

[33]   People v. Hammock, 2008 Mich. App. LEXIS 1983 (Mich. 2008). Unpublished opinion.

thenticated recordings of 911 calls that detailed what had the defendant had been observed doing. The defendant had not called any witness to prove who made the 911 calls and the defense had previously passed on an opportunity to ask a witness if she was the one who made the emergency calls. Because there was no proof of authentication of the 911 calls, the trial court properly excluded them.[34]

In a Tennessee case, the defendant, who was in custody, used a monitored jail phone to make outside phone calls that were monitored and recorded. The defendant worked the phone to arrange the absences of prosecution witnesses from his criminal trial. The jail phone system made recordings of outgoing calls and the numbers to which they were connected, a fact known to all the persons in custody. An individual in charge of the jail made a compact disc from the defendant's conversations that had been stored on a jail computer's hard drive that was integrated with the telephone monitoring system. At trial, a detective testified that he recognized several voices on the compact disc because he had been involved in speaking with them during the course of the investigation and the investigation included speaking with the defendant. The defendant appealed his conviction partly based on the alleged lack of authentication of a compact disc of his own voice. The reviewing court rejected his argument concerning lack of authentication because the detective had a basis for his opinion concerning identity of the voices. Tennessee evidence law allowed authentication where the opinion of identifying person has been "based upon hearing the voice at any time under circumstances connecting it with the alleged speaker."[35]

With respect to a written document, if a witness who can state that he or she witnessed the signing of the document, that testimony would authenticate the document. When an eyewitness is not available, an expert may authenticate a document by comparing signatures following an examination. In one case, a defendant had been convicted of attempted carjacking based partly on notes he allegedly wrote to friends from jail indicating that he wanted the friend to "take out" two of the victims in the case. One former friend testified that he received a letter purportedly from the defendant and that he was familiar with the defendant's handwriting because he had watched him write rap songs several times. The Supreme Court of Delaware held that this evidence was sufficient proof of authentication even though there was additional evidence that the distinctive content of the letters indicated that the author was the defendant.[36] In determining admissibility of questioned documents, trial judges have considerable discretion in determining what evidence is admissible for proving the authenticity of a questioned document.

To have a witness authenticate a writing, there must be a foundation presented to show the reasons the witness has familiarity with a signature or

---

[34] State v. Peay, 96 Conn. App. 421, 435, 900 A.2d 577, 2006 Conn. App. LEXIS 326 (2006).

[35] State v. Farrar, 2008 Tenn. Crim. App. LEXIS 825 (Tenn. 2008).

[36] Smith v. Delaware, 2006 Del. LEXIS 340 (2006).

writing. The procedure generally followed in qualifying a witness to identify a writing, a signature, or a tape recording is to place the witness on the stand and ask the witness foundational questions that will assure the jury and the judge that the witness is familiar with the writing and demonstrates how the witness gained the familiarity. The witness may be asked, "Will you state whether you are acquainted with the handwriting of the writer?" If the witness answers in the affirmative, the witness will then be asked to look at the letter or signature and tell whether it is the handwriting of the writer. In addition, the witness may be asked questions that could confirm whether he or she is or is not qualified. For example, he or she may be asked whether he or she has had an exchange of correspondence with the person, whether he or she has seen writing that the person has admitted to be his or her own, or whether the witness has become familiar with the person's writing by doing business with him or her on a day-to-day basis.[37]

Videotape and DVD recordings must be authenticated prior to being introduced into evidence and authentication follows procedures familiar in other contexts. Generally, authentication requires that the proponent of the evidence to document who operated the recorder that videotaped the event and when and where the taping occurred. In a Georgia prosecution for being a felon in possession of firearms, the defendant and his brother were in the back of a police cruiser and engaged in a conversation that was videotaped by a cruiser-cam that included audio. This tape had been received from an unnamed and unknown officer from a different jurisdiction. Because the non-defendant brother testified for the prosecution and identified his voice and the voices of others and admitted that the tape accurately reflected the conversation with his brother, the reviewing court held that the videotape had been properly authenticated as genuine, even though there was a break in the chain of custody.[38]

§ 13.5 Specific Examples of Documentary Evidence

Social and business interactions in the modern world produce a variety of evidentiary items that are classified as "writings" but do not fall into the category of paper documents, as traditionally understood. From electronic checks, computer data, web pages and their accompanying metadata, cell phone data, to actual paper documents, these "writings" preserve and explain much of human activity. Although human memories will eventually fade, documents created in the course of human events remain to assist in the reconstruction of the recent past. When the activities involve crimes, these documents may help prove or disprove elements in criminal cases. Even though the primary amount of evidence introduced into courts consists of oral evidence, documentary evidence plays an important part in recreating the full picture for the finder of fact. Documentary

---

[37] W.T. Rawleigh Co. v. Overstreet, 71 Ga. App. 873, 32 S.E.2d 574 (1944).

[38] Smallwood v. State, 296 Ga. App. 16, 2009 Ga. App. LEXIS 115 (Ga. 2009).

evidence includes written proof of laws; judicial records and proceedings; public records; private documents such as business records, account books, corporate records, letters, telegrams, and other correspondence; books; church records; hospital records; hotel registers; and many others. In each instance, the general rules of evidence, as well as the authentication requirements discussed in this chapter, must be considered when arguing for or against admission. Court decisions and statutes in various states must be consulted for more precise rules concerning the introduction of documentary evidence.

In order to develop an understanding of some of the rules relating to documentary evidence, examples of specific types of such evidence are included here. These examples have been selected as those most likely to be encountered by criminal justice personnel[39] and are not exclusive to problems related to the admission of documentary evidence.

A. *Public Records and Documents*

Writings that have been deposited in public offices or were created by those public offices are generally easier to authenticate than some private writings. In many cases, because a public official is under a duty to keep records or make reports of acts or transactions occurring in the course of his or her official duty, records or reports so made by or under the supervision of the public official are admissible as prima facie evidence of facts stated.[40] A public officer may be a county recorder, coroner, tax assessor, member of a board of elections, or a law enforcement official.

Even though a document has been labeled as a "public document" or "public record" does not make the document admissible in court. A publicly recorded document may include opinion, conclusions, and hearsay evidence and, although properly authenticated, it may be excluded on relevancy grounds. The fact that a document contains opinions and conclusions may create particular problems for the admission of some police records because hearsay evidence commonly is included in police reports.

In a variety of situations, police officers and law enforcement personnel may have a duty record or may create records of transactions that occur in the usual course of their work. The official records and writings made by such officers, or under their supervision, are of a public nature and are ordinarily admissible in evidence as proof of their contents, even though not proved by the person who actually made the entries. The extraordinary degree of confidence reposed in such documents is founded principally upon the fact that they have been made by authorized, accredited officers and deputies appointed for that purpose. In one Ohio case, a trial court refused to allow a police officer, who was the custodian of records for the police agency, to testify that a certificate showing that a public record revealed that a police officer had been

---

[39] *See* Chapter 14 for a discussion of the use of photographs, diagrams, maps, and models.
[40] People v. Hudson, 655 N.Y.S.2d 219 (1997).

certified to operate a machine that checked blood-alcohol content. The officer had been prepared to testify that the certificate was a true copy of the original. The appellate court reversed the suppression of the certificate and noted that certified copies of public records do not generally require extrinsic evidence of authenticity because they are deemed to be self-authenticating.[41]

Following this rationale, in a Texas prosecution, in order to obtain a sentence enhancement, the prosecutor needed to prove prior criminal acts of a defendant whose convictions were from a foreign American state. In a Texas prosecution involving sentence enhancements due to prior felony convictions, the trial court accepted a New Mexico Corrections Department certification that the penitentiary packet sent to a Texas court was authentic. There was also an attestation by the New Mexico Secretary of State that the person signing the penitentiary packet certification was actually the records supervisor for the State Corrections Department. Two sets of photographs and fingerprints were included in the prison packet, all certified by the district clerk of the appropriate county court as being genuine. According to the reviewing court, even though the attestation of the Secretary of State that bears her signature failed to carry a seal, the documents were considered self-authenticating and were properly admitted against the defendant.[42]

When properly authenticated and relevant, police training and policy manuals may be admissible under the public document provisions of statutes. In a murder prosecution resulting in a conviction for the manslaughter of a police officer, the police department manual was admissible to demonstrate that the victim, an off-duty police officer who had been shot during a robbery attempt, was under a duty to apprehend felons at all times.[43] A Mississippi court held that certificates attesting to proper calibration of Intoxilyzer machines were considered public records for which authentication existed as a matter of law. The government only needed to demonstrate that the certificates had been prepared by the state agency pursuant to statute under authority granted to the department of public safety and had to comply with the requirements of that law in order to be considered authenticated for evidentiary purposes.[44]

Many public records, including death certificates and autopsy reports, contain undisputed facts that have occurred; they are generally considered public documents that may be admissible as self-authenticating. Admitting court records of prior convictions for violating domestic relations no-contact orders was proper even if the records did not have the seal of the court as required. The appellate court noted that there was no abuse of discretion in admitting the certified records and there was evidence the court found the records sufficiently authenticated.[45]

---

[41]   Ohio v. Mustafa, 2001 Ohio App. LEXIS 5661 (2001).

[42]   Williams v. State, 2008 Tex. App. LEXIS 2241 (Tex. 2008).

[43]   Michell v. State, 689 So. 2d 1118 (Fla. 1997).

[44]   Pulliam v. Mississippi, 2003 Miss. App. LEXIS 299 (2003).

[45]   State v. Lux, 2005 Wash. App. LEXIS 980 (2005).

In a different case[46] involving a prosecution for unlawful imprisonment, the prosecution wanted the defendant to be required to register under the Sexual Offender Registration Act because the victim was under 17 years of age at the time of the crime. The court rejected the offer of proof of the birth certificate and passport from the Dominican Republic because both documents were in Spanish, there was no certified transcript of the documents, and the Dominican Republic had never signed an international convention that would have assisted in a finding of self-authentication. Due to the failure to authenticate the birth certificate, the defendant had no duty to register as a sex offender.

While most public records and documents are generally admissible without extrinsic evidence of authenticity, most comply with the requirements as set out in state and federal rules of evidence. The statutes for the respective states must be examined to determine whether there are any additional conditions that must be met to assure admissibility, such as giving reasonable notice of intent to use the evidence or by delivering a copy to the adverse party in a reasonable time before the trial.[47]

B. Private Writings

Written documents classified as "private writings" encompass a wide variety of documents. They include personal correspondence, e-mail, text messages, blog and other Internet postings, many business records, and individual business contracts. Credit card receipts, ATM receipts, telephone bills, as well as cash register tapes from retail stores qualify as private writings. In order for a private writing to be admissible in court, it must be proven to be genuine and also that it is what it appears to be. The genuineness may be proven by the testimony of anyone who saw the writing executed, by indirect or circumstantial evidence, or from testimony that an automated process generated the writing. However, if circumstantial evidence is used to establish the authenticity of a document, it must be of such force and character that the person's authorship or the identity of the person responsible for the creation of the writing can be legitimately deduced from its contents or from attendant circumstances.

Circumstantial evidence in one murder case authenticated a letter written by the defendant to his brother in which the defendant admitted to being the person who shot the deceased.[48] The letter named the judge hearing the murder case; named and discussed a friend, who had turned state's witness; mentioned two witnesses who could identify the defendant; and was signed using the defendant's name and jail address. It was dated and postmarked on days the defendant was in custody. With all of this evidence, the trial judge properly

---

[46]   *See* People v. Vazquez, 2006 NY Slip Op 26225 (N.Y. 2006). *See also* United States v. Torres-Reyes, 46 Fed. Appx. 925 (2002).

[47]   *See* FED. R. EVID. 1005 for an example of other requirements that may assist in admission of evidence. Meeting the hearsay rules also may influence the admission of evidence under Rule 902.

[48]   State v. Townshend, 2005 Ohio 6945, 2005 Ohio App. LEXIS 6239 (2005).

ruled that the letter had been sufficiently authenticated to be admissible against the defendant.

Expert and lay witnesses may testify to their opinions respecting authorship or genuineness of writings provided they are properly qualified and the proponent has offered a proper foundation. An Ohio court noted, "[t]estimony by a non-expert witness who is familiar with the alleged author's handwriting can authenticate a document.[49] The proponent of the document usually establishes that the witness gained the necessary familiarity with the handwriting by observing the person write or by receiving letters or other written material from the purported author. In this case, the grandmother had a familiarity with the granddaughter's handwriting from prior exchanges of letters and testified that both the letter and the signature were written by her granddaughter. According to the reviewing court, the letters were properly authenticated.[50] If a party offers an expert witness to authenticate a document, the expert must be qualified as having expertise with handwriting prior to offering opinions concerning the known sample and the questioned sample of writing.

Authenticating e-mails, letters, and text messages may be done in a variety of ways. In a Pennsylvania case,[51] two juveniles engaged in a dispute about ownership of a DVD and one juvenile severely injured the other in an unprovoked attack. The trial court permitted the state to introduce a computerized instant text message allegedly sent by the defendant to the victim that contained threats of physical injury. The messages were authenticated by the accused juvenile's consistent use of an instant message name, by the mention of an alleged stolen DVD, and by the fact that the juvenile's threatening behavior contained in the instant message actually occurred in front of witnesses. According to the reviewing court, the instant messages were properly authenticated as having come from the defendant. Alternatively, the accused juvenile's Internet service provider could have provided data that authenticated the messages, their times, and origination points.

Documents on private computers can be properly authenticated by following one of several techniques. In one case[52] in which a father allegedly sexually abused his own daughter, the court allowed the prosecution to introduce two letters that police found on the defendant's computer hard drive. The evidence of authentication showed that each person in the household had an individual computer and they did not use another family member's computer. Properly trained police examined the hard drive of the defendant's computer, finding two relevant letters that indicated the time and date of creation and copying

---

[49]   State v. Hupp, 2009 Ohio 1912, 2009 Ohio App. LEXIS 1622 (Ohio 2009). FED. R. EVID. 901(b)(2). This federal rule specifies that the familiarity not be acquired for purposes of the litigation when a lay witness provides the authentication.

[50]   *Id.*

[51]   In the Interest of F.P., 2005 Pa. Super. 220, 878 A.2d 91, 93, 2005 Pa. Super. LEXIS 1499 (2005).

[52]   State v. John L., 85 Conn. App. 291, 299, 856 A.2d 1032, 1038, 2004 Conn. App. LEXIS 407 (Conn. 2004).

to floppy disks and telephone records from the home when the defendant was alone indicated that he was the one home when the computer letters were written. The subject of the computer letters involved details related to the sexual assaults of his daughter. The appellate court concluded that there was no error in admitting the text of the letters against the defendant because they had been properly authenticated.

Private letters, e-mails, and text messages may be authenticated by the use of the "reply-letter doctrine" where a letter or other correspondence mailed or sent to another provokes a response that is genuine on its face and is responsive to the original letter. When these facts have been proved, the received letter is deemed to be authenticated and is generally admissible without any further proof.[53]

Business records that are generated in the ordinary and usual course of business may be authenticated and introduced in court. In one case[54] in which the defendant was alleged to have violated a restraining order of "no contact" by calling the victim's cell phone and regular phone, an employee of the cell phone provider was permitted to lay a foundation for introducing evidence of the times that the defendant violated the order by making reference to computer-generated calling records of the phone calls between the defendant's phone and the phones of the victim. The regularly and automatically generated phone records also may be considered as self-authenticating because they are records of regularly conducted business operations.[55]

§ 13.6 Best Evidence Rule

Rule 1002

Requirement of Original

To prove the content of a writing, recording, or photograph, the original writing, recording, or photograph is required, except as otherwise provided in these rules or by Act of Congress.[56]

Where the substantive contents of a writing, as broadly defined, are at issue, the writing must be authenticated before such evidence will be admitted for proof of its contents. Authentication may not suffice to permit documentary evidence to be admitted in court unless it meets the other rule peculiar to documentary evidence, the best evidence rule. In order for the best evidence rule to apply, the internal content of the writing must be at issue.[57] As the rule has commonly, but imperfectly, been stated, the best evidence that is obtainable

---

[53]   *See* Varkonyi v. State, 276 S.W.3d 27, 2008 Tex. App. LEXIS 3353 (Tex. 2008).
[54]   Smith v. State, 839 N.E.2d 780, 785, 2005 Ind. App. LEXIS 2442 (2005).
[55]   *Id.*
[56]   FED. R. EVID. 1002.
[57]   Hasson v. Commonwealth, 2006 Va. App. LEXIS 225 (Va. 2006).

under the circumstances of the case must be presented to prove any disputed fact. The label "best evidence" is not exactly correct because, although the rule "expresses a preference for the original of documentary evidence when the contents of the documentary evidence are sought to be proved,"[58] it does not always require the production of the original. Where proof is to be made of a fact that is recorded in a writing, the best evidence and probably the most accurate rendition of the contents of the writing involves the production of the original document. Any proof of a lower degree is secondary evidence that will only be received as proof when nonproduction of the original writing is properly excused, usually through no fault of the party offering the secondary evidence. A Florida reviewing court noted that when the best evidence rule requires the original or a qualified substitute, a court should accept no secondary evidence if the secondary evidence serves merely as a substitute for the original.[59] The best evidence rule rests upon the principle that if original evidence is available, the original must be produced to assure the court that there has been no alteration of the information contained within the writing.

The justices of the Ninth Circuit Court of Appeals, in discussing the application of the best evidence rule, included this comment:

> The best evidence rule embodied in Rules 1001–1008 represents a codification of a long-standing common law doctrine. Dating back to 1700, the rule requires not, as the name implies, the best evidence in every case, but rather the production of an original document instead of a copy. Many commentators refer to the rule not as the best evidence rule but as the original document rule.[60]

Drafters of the Federal Rules of Evidence included this note regarding the best evidence rule:

> Traditionally the rule requiring the original centered upon the accumulations of data and expressions affecting legal relations set forth in words and

---

[58]   Village Discount v. Department of Employment Security, 384 Ill. App.3d 522, 2008 Ill. App. LEXIS 757 (Ill. 2008).

[59]   McKeehan v. State, 838 So. 2d 1257, 1259, 2003 Fla. App. LEXIS 3367 (2003). *See* case in Part II. *But see* Commonwealth v. Leneski, 66 Mass. App. Ct. 291, 294, 846 N.E.2d 1195, 1198, 2006 Mass. App. LEXIS 525 (2006), in which the court noted that the best evidence rule does not apply in that jurisdiction to photographs, videotapes, or films. In referring to the best evidence rule in Ohio, one court noted that "This rule has been generally abrogated, though, by Evid. R. 1003, which states: '[a] duplicate is admissible to the same extent as an original unless (1) a genuine question is raised as to the authenticity of the original or (2) in the circumstances it would be unfair to admit the duplicate in lieu of the original.'" *See* State v. Dobrovich, 2005 Ohio 1441, 2005 Ohio App. LEXIS 1405 (2005). Virginia takes a different view and one that is similar to that of Massachusetts and does not apply the best evidence rule to anything but a traditional writing; video tapes are not considered writings and are not covered by the best evidence rule. *See* Brown v. Commonwealth, 2009 Va. App. LEXIS 226 (Va. 2009).

[60]   Siler v. Lucasfilm, Ltd., 979 F.2d 1504 (9th Cir. 1986).

figures. This meant that the rule was one essentially relating to writings. Present day techniques have expanded methods of storing data, yet the essential form which the information ultimately assumes for useable purposes is words and figures. Hence the considerations underlying the Rule dictate its expansion to include computers, photographic systems and other modern developments.[61]

The real purpose of, and reasons for, the best evidence rule were well stated by Dean Wigmore:[62]

> (1) As between a supposed literal copy and the original, the copy is always liable to errors on the part of the copyist, whether by willfulness or by inadvertence; this contingency wholly disappears when the original is produced. Moreover, the original may contain, and the copy will lack, such features of handwriting, paper, and the like, as may afford the opponent valuable means of learning legitimate objections to the significance of the document. (2) As between oral testimony, based on recollection, and the original, the added risk, almost the certainty, exists, of errors of recollection due to the difficulty of carrying in the memory literally the tenor of the document.

The focus of the best evidence rule concerns only the substantive content of a writing and does not regulate other evidence, especially evidence that exists independently of the writing. Therefore, testimony as to other facts about a writing, such as its existence, its contents, who created it, the date of creation, or how or why it was created, may be admissible. Thus, in a case in which the defendant had been accused of being involved in a murder and he signed a waiver of rights form and made a statement indicating his involvement that was recorded on audiotape, the tape could have been admissible. However, the police lost the audiotape and were permitted to offer their testimony concerning their memory of what the defendant had stated on the tape. The best evidence rule was not implicated here because the officers had independent recollection of what the defendant had stated and the loss of the tape-recording did not prevent the officer from testifying from memory.[63]

"The [best evidence] rule is inapplicable when content is not at issue."[64] When a document actually exists and when witnesses possess the same knowledge that was incorporated into the writing, witnesses may testify independently of the introduction of the document as long as they do so from personal knowledge. In a trial for felony theft of pistols, the trial court allowed one of the prosecution witnesses to testify about the substantive contents of a confession made by the defendant. The defendant had previously orally offered his

---

[61]   These original drafters' comments were included with Rule 1001 of the Federal Rules of Evidence.

[62]   IV WIGMORE, EVIDENCE § 1179 (3d ed. 1940). *See also* United States v. Holton, 116 F.3d 1536 (D.C. Cir. 1997).

[63]   Brown v. State, 2007 Ala. Crim. App. LEXIS 111 (Ala. 2007).

[64]   6 JACK B. WEINSTEIN ET AL., WEINSTEIN'S FEDERAL EVIDENCE § 1002.05[1] (2d ed. 2002).

confession to a detective who tape-recorded the confession, but neither the taped confession nor a writing was ever introduced at the defendant's trial. The trial court decision held that the best evidence rule was not implicated because the detective gave the testimony concerning the confession from the witness stand from his own memory and did not rely upon the writing/tape recording. The Supreme Court of Arkansas agreed on the theory that because the prosecution did not introduce a writing of the confession, the best evidence rule did not apply.[65]

On some occasions, the best evidence rule will apply and the original or a duplicate original and other secondary evidence may be admitted. In one North Carolina case, the police videotaped a defendant's admissions of responsibility in a rape case and introduced an audio copy, made from the videotape and a transcript of the conversation, into evidence. The defendant's contention that this practice constituted plain error under the best evidence rule was dismissed. As the reviewing court noted, "[a]lthough the audio recording was the 'best evidence' of defendant's interview, the admission of the transcript did not prejudice defendant. The transcript only reiterated the evidence presented through the audio recording."[66]

§ 13.7   Secondary Evidence

Rule 1003

Admissibility of Duplicates

A duplicate is admissible to the same extent as an original unless (1) a genuine question is raised as to the authenticity of the original or (2) in the circumstances, it would be unfair to admit the duplicate in lieu of the original.[67]

A duplicate of a writing, or as it is often called, a duplicate original, as defined in Rule 1001(4), "is a counterpart produced by the same impression as the original or from the same matrix, or by means of photography, including enlargements and miniatures, or by mechanical or electronic re-recording, by chemical reproduction, or by other equivalent techniques that accurately reproduce the original." If the original has been lost or destroyed through inadvertent conduct of the proponent of the evidence, secondary evidence may be admitted where the loss or destruction of the original was not the fault of the proponent and where there is no reason to doubt the accuracy of the secondary

---

[65]   Gamble v. Arkansas, 351 Ark. 541, 550, 95 S.W.3d 755, 761, 2003 Ark. LEXIS 44 (2003).

[66]   State v. Fernandez, 2008 N.C. App. LEXIS 1828 (N.C. 2008).

[67]   *See* FED. R. EVID. 1003.

evidence or duplicate original.[68] In a ruling in a case from Mississippi, a trial court admitted a duplicate, though slightly edited, videotape of the criminal drug sale. The defendant allegedly sold marijuana to an informant while the act was videotaped. The original tape contained evidence of other crimes, so the prosecution had the other crimes edited out of the version shown to the jury over the defendant's best evidence rule objection. The eyewitness-informant testified that the edited videotape recording accurately depicted the original version. The appellate court affirmed the admissibility of the edited tape by noting that Mississippi Rule of Evidence 1003 provides that "a duplicate is admissible to the same extent as an original unless (1) a genuine question is raised as to the authenticity of the original or (2) in the circumstances it would be unfair to admit the duplicate in lieu of the original."[69] The rationale for Rule 1003 is that when the only concern is with introducing the words or other contents before the court with accuracy and precision, a counterpart serves equally as well as the original if the counterpart or duplicate original is the product of a method that ensures accuracy and authenticity.[70]

Applying this rationale to the California version of Rule 1003, a court permitted the admission of a printout of an e-mail that one witness had sent to another who forwarded the e-mail to a police officer. The printout of the e-mail on the police officer's computer was permitted to be introduced into evidence. The sender of the e-mail indicated from the witness stand that she had no present memory of writing it, but the original recipient testified concerning her receipt of the message and authenticated the source of the e-mail. The reviewing court held that it was sufficiently authenticated by its original recipient admitting to using e-mail to communicate with the other and there was no dispute concerning the terms of the writing and it had properly been admitted as secondary evidence.[71] In a Georgia case, a trial court permitted the prosecution to introduce a copy of the original printout from an Intoxilyzer blood-alcohol test over the defendant's objection that the best evidence rule required the original printout or an excuse for its nonproduction. In reviewing the case, the appellate court observed that the prosecution made no effort to explain why the original was missing or how it became lost or destroyed and so secondary evidence (the copy) was not admissible. The appellate court reversed the driving under the influence of alcohol conviction on the ground that the best evidence rule had been violated and there was no other evidence on the record against the defendant.[72]

---

[68] United States v. Codrington, 2008 U.S. Dist. LEXIS 35859 (E.D.N.Y. 2008). Fifteen seconds missing from surveillance tape does not make duplicate original inadmissible.

[69] Griffin v. State, 918 So. 2d 882, 884, 2006 Miss. App. LEXIS 12 (Miss. 2006).

[70] Notes of the Advisory Committee on the Proposed Rules.

[71] People v. Whicker, 2007 Cal. App. Unpub. LEXIS 5197 (Cal. 2007). Unpublished opinion.

[72] Lumley v. State, 2006 Ga. LEXIS 755 (Ga. 2006).

Rule 1004

Admissibility of Other Evidence of Contents

The original is not required, and other evidence of the contents of a writing, recording, or photograph is admissible if—

(1) Originals lost or destroyed. All originals are lost or have been destroyed, unless the proponent lost or destroyed them in bad faith; or

(2) Original not obtainable. No original can be obtained by any available judicial process or procedure; or

(3) Original in possession of opponent. At a time when an original was under the control of the party against whom offered, that party was put on notice, by the pleadings or otherwise, that the contents would be a subject of proof at the hearing, and that party does not produce the original at the hearing; or

(4) Collateral matters. The writing, recording, or photograph is not closely related to a controlling issue.[73]

As a concession to necessity, in situations when the original writing has been lost or destroyed, secondary evidence of its contents may become admissible when absence of the original has not occurred through the culpable fault of the offering party. The party desiring to offer secondary evidence may be required to show that a reasonable search has been made for the lost writing in the place where it was last known to have been, and the offering party should inquire of persons most likely to have custody or who might have some knowledge of its whereabouts. Rule 1004 of the Federal Rules of Evidence provides that the original is not required and secondary evidence of the contents of a writing (or recording or photograph) is admissible if: (1) originals are lost or destroyed (not in bad faith); (2) the original is not obtainable; (3) the original is in the possession of an opponent; or (4) the writing, recording, or photograph is not related to the controlling issue.

In an unpublished opinion, an Arkansas appellate court ruled that the original surveillance tape from a convenience store should have been introduced in court against a defendant accused of shoplifting. The clerk-witness did not observe the theft directly, but immediately played the surveillance tape that revealed the theft by the defendant. The defendant objected to the clerk-witness testifying concerning what the videotape recording showed, contending that the clerk-witness had no personal knowledge and that the videotape was the original copy that had to be produced because its contents were at issue in the case. The court of appeals reversed the conviction on the ground that the original writing (the videotape) must be admitted, rather than secondary evidence,

---

[73] FED. R. EVID. 1004.

because the original had not been lost or destroyed and the prosecution had not accounted for its absence.[74]

Where the original and duplicate original copies have all been destroyed prior to trial, a judge has discretion to allow secondary evidence of what the original videotape contained. In an unpublished Minnesota case,[75] an original videotape was copied and made available to the police, the prosecution, and the defense and all parties had a chance to view it. For unexplained reasons, the case took a significant time to come to trial, with the result that all parties had destroyed all versions of the videotape through inadvertence or through planned recycling. The defendant made no allegation that the videotape was lost through the prosecutor's fault, fraud, or bad faith. The trial court held that under Rule 1004, allowing other evidence of the contents, there was no abuse of judicial discretion to permit a police officer to explain some of what he had observed on the videotape as secondary evidence.

The state of Nevada, as well as many other states, has codified the common law best evidence rule.[76] Nevada's statute is identical to Rule 1004 of the Federal Rules of Evidence. In *Tomlinson v. State*, a defendant who had been convicted of robbery argued that all four of the requirements established in the state statute should be met before other secondary evidence could be admissible.[77] The Supreme Court of Nevada, however, agreed with the state that only one of the four requirements is necessary for the nonoriginal evidence to be admissible.

While all states allow the admission of secondary evidence, the proponent of the evidence must lay a foundation that explains why the original evidence disappeared and support the admission of secondary evidence. The party must satisfy the judge that the original evidence has been lost, destroyed, or is otherwise unavailable through no fault of the moving party and that one of the reasons contained in Rule 1004 applies. In a Texas case,[78] the police or the judiciary lost the last page of an affidavit for a search warrant at some point after the warrant had been served. An unsworn but true copy of the last page of the affidavit was offered as secondary evidence of the terms of the original writing. The secondary evidence did not have the magistrate's signature or the affiant officer's signature but was admitted into evidence. The appellate court approved the admission of secondary evidence of the affidavit because there was no proof of bad faith as the reason for the loss or destruction of the original

---

[74]   Bradley v. State, 2003 Ark. App. LEXIS 756 (2003). *See also* People v. Jimenez, 796 N.Y.S.2d 232; 2005 N.Y. Misc. LEXIS 1114 (2005).

[75]   *See* State v. Mack, 2006 Minn. App. Unpub. LEXIS 53 (2006). *Contra,* Brown v. Commonwealth, 2009 Va. App. LEXIS 226 (Va. 2009), where the court noted that the best evidence rule was not to be applied to video tape evidence because Virginia only recognized the concept as having application to traditional written instruments.

[76]   NEV. REV. STAT. ANN. § 52.255 (Matthew Bender 2009).

[77]   Tomlinson v. State, 878 P.2d 311 (Nev. 1994).

[78]   McCormick v. State, 2006 Tex. App. LEXIS 1619 (2006).

writing and the reviewing court did not address the issue of prosecutorial or police negligence in mishandling the affidavit page.

When the original writing cannot be located and appropriate justifications have been proffered, proper secondary evidence may be admissible. A common misconception concerns the type of secondary evidence that should be admitted in place of the original. Although some support for the next best evidence may be found in some cases, generally any type of secondary evidence may be admitted as long as it meets the authentication and relevancy tests.

Modern developments with the use of desktop computers and the use of network server computers have created additional challenges concerning what really constitutes the original, the duplicate original, and what serves as secondary evidence. In at least one case, data and records stored on magnetic and optical media have been held to fall within the bounds of "best evidence" because they represent a "writing." Printouts or computer screen output are the best evidence because of the impossibility in practice of reading the original, which is a piece of magnetic disc, a compact disc, or videodisc.[79]

The rules relating to best and secondary evidence generally apply to recordings and photographs as well as documents. For example, in a case originating in a domestic dispute, police were allowed to read the transcript of an audiotape containing details of the dispute that the complaining witness had given to police officers. The officer used a duplicate of the original recording and read the transcript of that recording to the jury over the objection of the defendant based on the best evidence rule. The prosecution presented no evidence as to when, where, how, or by whom the original audiotape was made. According to the reviewing court, the trial court abused its discretion when these admitted the audiotape and the transcript because a proponent of secondary evidence must first authenticate the original writing and establish that the proffered evidence is secondary evidence of the original.[80]

The proven fact that a person recorded a conversation does not automatically implicate the best evidence rule or serve to exclude oral testimony concerning the issue. The best evidence rule does not require that a party prove the loss of a recording before offering testimony about the conversation.[81] In a North Carolina case, police videotaped the defendant's confession and had a transcript prepared. At the trial, an audiotape of the confession and a printed transcript were introduced over the defendant's objection. According to the reviewing court, "the admission of the transcript did not prejudice defendant. The transcript only reiterated the evidence presented through the audio recording."[82] As would be required in all such

---

[79]   FED. R. EVID. 1004 and 1001(4).

[80]   People v. Dicharry, 2007 Cal. App. Unpub. LEXIS 5538 (Cal. 2007). Unpublished opinion.

[81]   United States v. Rose, 590 F.2d 232 (7th Cir. 1978), *cert. denied*, 442 U.S. 929 (1979).

[82]   State v. Fernandez, 2008 N.C. LEXIS 1828 (N.C. 2008).

cases, the proponent offering the transcript would have to lay a foundation demonstrating the accuracy of the transcript.

When a fact may be subject to proof in more than one manner, the proponent may choose the method that best suits the party. In the course of introducing evidence sufficient to demonstrate that a defendant had committed a robbery, the prosecutor had a police officer introduce photographs of the actual currency seized from the defendant. Over an objection that the money was a writing and the originals should have been introduced, the defendant contended that the admission of the money violated the best evidence rule and secondary evidence of the money should not have been permitted. In approving the trial court's admission of the photographs, the appellate court noted that a witness can testify concerning tangible objects (such as money) without introducing the actual objects and without violating the best evidence rule.[83] Another way of considering a case like this is to note that, other than the fact that the writing on the currency denoted its value, it was the fact that money was taken in a robbery, and not precisely how much, that was important.

§ 13.8 Summaries

> **Rule 1006**
>
> **Summaries**
>
> The contents of voluminous writings, recordings, or photographs which cannot conveniently be examined in court may be presented in the form of a chart, summary, or calculation. The originals, or duplicates, shall be made available for examination or copying, or both, by other parties at a reasonable time and place. The court may order that they be produced in court.[84]

The evidentiary rule allowing the use of summaries is consistent with the common law and permits the use of summaries of evidence when that method may be the only practical way to present the evidence to a court.[85] The admissibility of summary evidence is a matter that rests within the sound discretion of the trial court, but standards have evolved to guide courts in exercising their discretion. As a general rule, a proper foundation must be offered with regard to the admissibility of the originals. The Sixth Circuit holds that there are five requirements for admission of a summary under Rule 1006.

> [T]he Rule imposes five requirements for the admission of summary evidence: (1) the underlying documents are so voluminous that they cannot be conveniently examined in court; (2) the proponent of the summary must

---

[83] Wingfield v. State, 2005 Ark. 574 (2006).

[84] FED. R. EVID. 1006.

[85] Washington v. Dudley, 2003 Wash. App. LEXIS 1551 (2003).

have made the documents available for examination or copying at a reasonable time and place; (3) the underlying documents must be admissible in evidence; (4) the summary must be accurate and nonprejudicial; and (5) the summary must be properly introduced through the testimony of a witness who supervised its preparation.[86]

Failure to meet these or similar requirements in other jurisdictions may result in summary evidence being refused by the trial judge or a reversal on appeal.

According to one New Jersey court, there are three kinds of evidentiary summaries that are often admitted in court. The first can be called a primary evidence summary and is used to condense large amounts of material that could not otherwise be grasped by a court or jury. The second type of summary involves a pedagogical device summary, which serves as a demonstrative aid to present or clarify drawings, charts, calculations, or models, and can simplify evidence already admitted in a case. The final type can be called a secondary evidence summary because it is a combination of the first two types of summaries. This summary assists the jury in accurately understanding complex evidence that they would otherwise have difficulty placing in context or understanding its importance.[87]

The purpose of using a summary or a chart is to assist the jury in understanding the evidence. A college student might read a summary of a Shakespeare play as a way to better understand what the playwright intended. Similarly, political science and scientific journals tend to have an abstract of each article that serves the purpose of educating the reader concerning what the article contains. The purpose of a summary or a chart under Rule 1006 is to assist in educating the jury and allowing it to comprehend and place in context a large body of evidence that has been presented. A summary that has been prepared for a jury must be fair and accurate and be presented in a correct and non-misleading manner.[88] In the interests of fairness, the summaries should be supplied to the opposing party at a reasonable time prior to courtroom use so that the party has time to check to see if the summaries or charts are accurate.[89]

The preparation and submission to the jury of summaries prepared by an expert is almost indispensable to the understanding of a long and complicated set of facts. When summaries are used and physically given to the jury, the court must ascertain with certainty that they are based upon, and fairly represent, competent evidence already before the jury. Such summaries, if given to the jury, must be accompanied by appropriate instructions concerning their

---

[86]   United States v. Moon, 513 F.3d 527, 2008 U.S. App. LEXIS 879 (6th Cir. 2008), quoting United States v. Jamieson, 427 F.3d 394, 409, 2005 U.S. App. LEXIS 23337 (6th Cir. 2005).

[87]   *See* Heinzerling v. Goldfarb, 359 N.J. Super. 1, 8, 818 A. 2d 345, 349, 2002 N.J. Super. LEXIS 531 (2002).

[88]   United States v. Wainwright, 351 F.3d 816, 2003 U.S. App. LEXIS 24731 (8th Cir. 2003).

[89]   United States v. Dukes, 242 Fed. Appx. 37, 2007 U.S. App. LEXIS 15961 (4th Cir. 2007).

nature and use. The jury should be advised that the summaries do not, in and of themselves, constitute evidence in the case, but only purport to summarize the documentary and detailed evidence already admitted; that the jury should examine the basis upon which the summaries rest and be satisfied that they accurately reflect other evidence in the case; and that, if the jury is not so satisfied, the summaries should be disregarded. In addition, broad cross-examination should be permitted upon the summaries to afford a thorough test of their accuracy.

Summaries may used to assist the jury in understanding large amounts of information or to place large amounts of data in perspective, but the summaries are generally not considered evidence unless specifically admitted.[90] In a case in which the defendant had been charged with transporting fraudulently obtained merchandise across state lines, the prosecution presented summaries of some of the evidence. According to the government, the defendant would add himself as an authorized user to store credit cards and charge goods that he sold in interstate commerce. During the prosecution's case-in-chief, the government introduced more than 220 exhibits, including receipts for bogus credit card purchases, fraudulent additions to credit card account applications, and related evidence that it condensed into several summaries for use during trial as a way to place the evidence in context. On appeal, the defendant argued that the government failed to offer an adequate foundation for the summaries because it failed to allow the defendant to view the underlying records prior to trial. The Seventh Circuit rejected the defendant's contentions, noting that there was nothing in the record that indicated that the defense had not been permitted to view and inspect the underlying data and the defendant failed to object at trial. The court found no error in the use of summaries under the circumstances.[91]

Courts "cannot rationally expect an average jury to compile summaries and to create sophisticated flow charts to reveal patterns that provide important inferences about the defendant's guilt."[92] It does not have to be demonstrably impossible to examine all of the underlying records before a summary chart may be utilized under Rule 1006, but only that in-court examinations would be an inconvenience.

In interpreting Rule 1006, the Fifth Circuit Court of Appeals approved the use of summary charts in a case involving mail fraud in conjunction with perjury in receiving workers' compensation. The defendant was collecting disability payments for a back injury while he worked as a pilot for several charter airline companies. The government presented summaries in the form of a timeline chart comparing the dates that the defendant worked and payments received, to the dates of fraudulent forms filed with the government to continue his disability benefits. The defendant claimed that the trial court erred

---

[90]   United States v. Green, 428 F.3d 1131, 1134, 2005 U.S. App. LEXIS 24583 (8th Cir. 2005).

[91]   United States v. Murry, 395 F.3d 712, 717, 2005 U.S. App. LEXIS 8 (7th Cir. 2005).

[92]   United States v. Buck, 324 F.3d 786, 791, 2003 U.S. App. LEXIS 4820 (5th Cir. 2003).

when it admitted the timeline summary chart along with a government witness who explained the summary chart. The reviewing court noted that summary evidence is admissible based on the court's discretion and past practice permits a summary witness in a limited way to explain voluminous records. The court rejected the defendant's complaints because pursuant to the defendant's trial objection, the chart was never admitted into evidence and the court did not allow the summary chart to go to the jury room. In affirming the conviction, the Court of Appeals found no error in the use of the summary under Rule 1006.[93] However, when summary charts are erroneously admitted in a manner that substantially affects the legal rights of a defendant, such admission may result in a reversal of a trial jury decision and the awarding of a new trial.[94]

Obviously, the admission of summary exhibits must be conditioned on the requirement that the items of evidence upon which they rest must be admissible. For example, in a federal case[95] involving conspiracy to import and harbor illegal aliens, the defendant contended that the summary spreadsheet exhibit offered by the prosecution, which tracked the status of illegal aliens working on the farms of defendant's clients, was unnecessary because the data was not voluminous, his counsel had not been permitted a chance to examine the underlying documents, and the items of evidence on which the summary spreadsheet was based involved inadmissible hearsay. The reviewing court rejected the defendant's arguments and noted, "[t]he spreadsheet was introduced to establish the alienage of the workers. As the government demonstrates, however, even without the admission of the summary exhibit, the evidence of the alienage of the persons involved was uncontested."[96] Even if there was any error, which the court did not find, any error was harmless.

Even when the underlying documents have not been introduced under Rule 1006, the charts or summaries are admissible. In a federal embezzlement case involving employees of a labor union, the reviewing court rejected the defendant's contention that charts were not permissible when the opposing party had not actually introduced them, but had offered certifications for the underlying documents. As the court noted, "the point of Rule 1006 is to avoid introducing all the documents."[97]

While Rule 1006 allows the use of summaries when all of the conditions are met, a court should exclude summaries when the proponent of the summary fails to meet the requirements or where hearsay evidence has been included as one of the bases of the summary. In a prosecution for selling cocaine base, the trial court permitted the federal government to introduce summaries of the numbers of defendant's cell phone calls, and to whom they were made, when

---

[93] United States v. Harms, 442 F.3d 367, 375, 2006 U.S. App. LEXIS 6622 (5th Cir. 2006).

[94] United States v. Hart, 295 F.3d 451, 2002 U.S. App. LEXIS 11246 (2002).

[95] United States v. Matousek, 131 Fed. Appx. 641, 2005 U.S. App. LEXIS 9063 (10th Cir. 2005).

[96] *Id.*

[97] United States v. Hemphill, 514 F.3d 1350, 2008 U.S. App. LEXIS 2786 (D.C. Cir. 2008).

the evidence that supported the summaries was never authenticated. In addition, some of the evidence was hearsay; the government failed to make the cell phone records available for examination and copying; and the government failed to give written notice to the defendant that it was going to use cell phone records in a summary. The reviewing court noted that the summaries should not have been admitted because the summaries did not meet the requirements for admission. However, in affirming the conviction, the court viewed the other evidence as sufficiently strong that the admission of the summaries constituted harmless error.[98]

A federal district court, following the directive of the Sixth Circuit, suggested that when summaries or charts are used under Rule 1006, they should be accompanied by a limiting instruction that informs the jury of the purpose of the summary or the chart and that the summary or chart does not constitute evidence.[99] In a different case, the appellate court grudgingly allowed a verdict to stand where the prosecution had permitted one of its own witnesses to summarize trial testimony just before the government rested its case. The Court of Appeals noted that under Rule 1006 there is no provision that addresses summary witnesses who summarize trial testimony, but some courts have permitted summary testimony in a limited capacity. The court took the position that while the use of summary evidence often serves an important purpose, one of the purposes of Rule 1006 is to not permit the prosecution to repeat its entire case-in-chief shortly before jury deliberations and prior to final arguments.[100]

§ 13.9 Learned Treatises

Medical books or treatises, even though properly identified and authenticated and shown to be recognized as standard authorities on the subjects to which they relate, are not generally admissible in evidence due to their hearsay status. According to the common law rule, proponents of evidence are not permitted to use learned treatise passages as substantive proof of their contents.[101] For example, according to Pennsylvania case law, "learned writings which are offered to prove the truth of the matters therein are hearsay and may not properly be admitted into evidence for consideration by the jury."[102] Similarly, in Ohio, a learned treatise may be part of the basis for an expert opinion and can be used to impeach a witness, but it cannot be used for substantive evidence.[103]

---

[98] United States v. Laguerre, 119 Fed. Appx. 458, 2005 U.S. App. LEXIS 213 (4th Cir. 2005).

[99] O'Brien v. Ed Donnelly Enterprises, 2007 U.S. Dist. LEXIS 92973 (S.D. Ohio 2007).

[100] United States v. Fullwood, 342 F.3d 409, 2003 U.S. App. LEXIS 16309 (5th Cir. 2003), *cert. denied*, 540 U.S. 1111 (2004).

[101] Aldridge v. Edmunds, 561 Pa. 323, 331, 750 A.2d 292, 296, 2000 Pa. LEXIS 1059 (2000).

[102] Calandra v. St. Agnes Med. Ctr., 2005 Phila. Ct. Com. Pl. LEXIS 254 (2005).

[103] *See* Beard v. Meridia Huron Hospital, 106 Ohio St. 3d 237, 239, 2005 Ohio 4787, 834 N.E.2d 323, 326, 2005 Ohio LEXIS 2077 (2005).

However, the federal courts do not exclude learned treatises from use as substantive evidence to the extent that an expert witness relies upon the treatise, as long as the treatise is established as a reliable authority by admission by that witness or another witness or by the use of judicial notice.[104]

A few states have adopted the rule that a published treatise, periodical, or pamphlet on a subject of history, science, or art may be admitted in evidence in some limited types of cases to prove the truth of a matter stated therein if the judge takes judicial notice or an expert witness in the subject area testifies that the writer of the treatise, periodical, or pamphlet is a recognized authority on the subject. Under a Massachusetts statute,[105] as a prerequisite to the admission of a medical treatise as evidence in medical malpractice actions, the proponent of such evidence must demonstrate for the trial judge that the offered treatise statements are relevant and that the writer of such statements is recognized in his profession or calling as an expert on the subject.[106]

§ 13.10 Summary

In addition to oral testimony, documentary evidence may be used in court to assist the jury and judge in determining the ultimate facts. Documentary evidence includes all kinds of documents, records, and writings. The concept of a writing proves to be an expansive idea and many jurisdictions include computer data wherever and however stored, movies, videotapes, digital video disc and compact disc storage, as well as almost anything that contains data under the definition of a writing. To be admissible, documentary evidence must meet the same requirements of relevancy, competency, and materiality, as does oral evidence, and must meet other requirements specifically related to writings. As a prerequisite to admission, documentary evidence must also be authenticated by one of several processes. As a rule, competent evidence must be introduced to show that the writing is what it purports to be.

In the interests of judicial economy, courts have recognized practical and simplified methods of authentication that are to be used in specific instances. Domestic public documents under seal are often deemed to be self-authenticating, while documents that have been certified as accurate copies of documents on file by the official custodian are similarly considered to be self-authenticating. Official publications by government agencies, including statutes and official regulations, may be self-authenticating because the concept of authentication is only a threshold consideration that the document is what it purports to be. Given that authentication is a rather low standard, the opposing party may introduce evidence that disputes the judge's initial determination

---

[104] *See* FED. R. EVID. 803(18).

[105] ALM GL ch. 233 § 79C (Matthew Bender 2009).

[106] Lasalvia v. Johnson, 15 Mass. 622, 2003 Mass. Super. LEXIS 9 (2003).

that a document has been authenticated and the ultimate decision concerning whether the document has evidentiary value belongs to the finder of fact.

Although these are not necessarily exclusive, there are four general methods of authenticating a document: (1) proof of signing; (2) proof of signature; (3) comparison of signatures, usually by an expert; and (4) circumstantial evidence. The degree of proof varies with the type of document. As a general rule, public records and documents are admissible into evidence as exceptions to the hearsay rule without the same degree of authenticity as is required for private writings. This is allowed because of the extraordinary degree of confidence reposed in documents drafted by authorized and accredited officers or required by law to be filed publicly. This same degree of confidence is not placed in private writings, and such writings must be proven by slightly more exacting standards to be genuine before they are admissible as evidence.

To prevent the admission of forgeries, fabrications, and false writings, the best evidence rule accepts the principle of law that there is a decided preference for the original document where the contents of the writing are at issue. Although the rule permits several types of secondary evidence to be considered acceptable to the courts, many jurisdictions recognize several significant exceptions to producing the original. When the original cannot be obtained through any judicial process or has been lost or destroyed through no fault of the proponent, courts will frequently accept secondary evidence. The historical basis for this rule assumes that a copy is more likely to have errors and that a typewritten or computer-generated copy and will lack such features as handwriting and original paper impressions and could be more easily manipulated. Without individual characteristics of the original, an opponent has few means to detect alteration or fraud on secondary evidence. Currently, most modern writings are produced in ways that allow many duplicate originals that have not been produced by the human hand and are indistinguishable from each other. For this reason, many of the rationales for requiring the original are no longer valid, and exceptions have been included in statutes and codes, consistent with the interests of justice.

Real Evidence 14

Stains of blood, found upon the person or clothing of the party accused, have always been recognized among the ordinary indicia of homicide. The practice of identifying them by circumstantial evidence and by the inspection of witnesses and jurors has the sanction of immemorial usage in all criminal tribunals. ... the degree of force to which it is entitled may depend upon a variety of circumstances to be considered and weighed by the jury in each particular case; but its competency is too well settled to be questioned in a court of law.

People v. Gonzalez, 35 N.Y. 49 (1866)

Chapter Outline

Section
14.1   Introduction
14.2   Admissibility Requirements
14.3   Exhibition of Person
14.4   Articles Connected with the Crime
14.5   View of the Scene
14.6   Photographs
14.7   Motion Pictures and Videotapes
14.8   X-rays
14.9   Sound Recordings
14.10 Diagrams, Maps, and Models
14.11 Courtroom Demonstrations and Experiments
14.12 Preservation and Disclosure of Evidence Favorable to the Defense
14.13 Summary

§ 14.1 Introduction

Real evidence is *evidence that is addressed directly to the senses such as by sight, hearing, or taste, and it is without the intervention of witnesses.* This type of evidence has a physical and tangible existence as compared to oral testimony alone. Real evidence has often been referred to by the terms, "demonstrative" or "physical" evidence. Some authorities distinguish between demonstrative and real evidence by defining real evidence as that which involves the introduction of an object that had a direct part in the incident, such as the exhibition of injured parts of the body or an actual gun or knife used in a crime. On the other hand, demonstrative evidence involves the production in court of such things as models made for the trial, maps, photographs taken for use in litigation, X-rays, films, and weapons that are used only for demonstrative purposes and were not actually used in the crime. The term "demonstrative real evidence" generally refers to a physical object that had no historical connection to the crime, but will be used to show how a similar item was actually used in the crime or how a similar object reacted to events or forces that occurred during the crime.[1] Demonstrative items of evidence possess no probative value themselves[2] but serve merely as visual aids to assist the triers of fact in understanding the verbal testimony of a witness.[3] When demonstrative evidence is admitted, the decision is based on judicial discretion and is reviewable under the standard of abuse of discretion.[4] For example, in a murder prosecution in which a man had been killed while in his girlfriend's

---

[1]   Torres v. Texas, 2003 Tex. App. LEXIS 6580 (2003).
[2]   *Id.*
[3]   32 C.J.S. *Evidence* § 602 (1996).
[4]   Washington v. Fairbanks, 2003 Wash. App. LEXIS 2050 (2003).

bed, the trial court permitted the government to bring a mannequin head to help the jury understand the testimony of the medical examiner. To further the jury understanding, the court permitted a wooden dowel to be inserted in the mannequin's head to demonstrate the trajectory of the bullet. The medical examiner authenticated the head and dowel representing the trajectory as accurately depicting the original crime scene. The Supreme Court of Georgia approved of using this demonstrative real evidence because the mannequin head served to illustrate the medical examiner's testimony.[5] In this and the following chapter, real evidence includes both types.

In admitting real evidence, courts must carefully weigh the probative value against the risk of unfair prejudice because real evidence is generally considered an especially persuasive class of evidence. In a Texas case, the court permitted the prosecution to dress a dummy in the bloody clothes of the deceased over the objection of the defendant that the danger of unfair prejudice outweighed any probative value of the dummy. Demonstrative real evidence must accurately depict what it purports to depict, and in this case the dummy appeared much smaller than the size of the deceased. Even though the defense unsuccessfully contended that having the dummy in court in the defendant's bloody clothes would prejudice the defendant, it failed to mention the size discrepancy. The reviewing court upheld the original trial court ruling.[6]

Court decisions have emphasized the necessity of developing more sophisticated methods of obtaining and utilizing real evidence in criminal cases. Because of the constitutional limitations placed upon the use of confessions, more emphasis is placed upon the use of real evidence. For example, in the case of *Schmerber v. California*,[7] the United States Supreme Court held that the Fifth Amendment self-incrimination protection applied to evidence of a testimonial or communicative nature, but not to real evidence. In that case the Court stated:

> On the other hand, both federal and state courts have usually held that it [the Fifth Amendment] offers no protection against compulsion to submit to fingerprinting, photographing, or measurements, to write or speak for identification, to appear in court, to stand, to assume a stance, to walk, or to make a particular gesture.

The Court also noted that:

> Compulsion which makes a suspect or accused the source of real or physical evidence does not violate it [the Fifth Amendment].

---

[5]   Moss v. Georgia, 274 Ga. 740, 559 S.E.2d 433, 2002 Ga. LEXIS 48 (2002).

[6]   Runnels v. State, 193 S.W.3d 105, 107, 2006 Tex. App. LEXIS 17 (Tex. 2006). The trial court might not have admitted the dummy if the defense had objected to its use because it did not properly depict the size of the victim.

[7]   384 U.S. 757, 86 S. Ct. 1826, 16 L. Ed. 2d 908 (1966). *See* case in Part II. *See* Chapter 16 for discussion of constitutional safeguards that regulate the admissibility of evidence.

In rendering the *Schmerber* decision, the Court upheld the collection of real evidence derived from the suspect personally and indicated that the evidence could be used against that same defendant. Similarly, DNA samples can be compelled and forcefully taken without violating a person's Fifth Amendment privilege against self-incrimination because the evidence is neither testimonial nor communicative in nature.[8]

The sections that follow discuss the tests for general admissibility relating to real evidence and offer some examples of the types of real evidence of particular concern to criminal justice personnel. In Chapter 15, emphasis is placed on the use of results of experiments and tests conducted in and out of court.

§ 14.2 Admissibility Requirements

To be admissible, real evidence must generally meet the same requirements of relevancy, competency, and materiality as documentary evidence and oral testimony. In addition, a foundation proving authenticity must be laid before real evidence is admissible. Generally, the foundation is laid by an attorney calling a witness and asking questions relating to the real evidence to be introduced. To provide a proper foundation, the real evidence offered must be identified as being the same evidence or object involved in the alleged crime and it must be shown that the object has not undergone any important or material change.[9] In many instances criminal justice personnel are most familiar with the evidence and can most correctly connect the evidence with the crime and the accused by using several authentication techniques. Occasionally, a defendant may be willing to stipulate facts that support admission of adverse evidence.[10] Finally, the prosecuting attorney may call upon the victim to take the stand to establish the identity and relevance of the real evidence.

As a general rule for real evidence to be admissible at trial, the proponent must show that it is sufficiently connected with case through the defendant, the victim, or the crime.[11] The state must demonstrate a reasonable probability that tampering, substitution, or alteration of the evidence did not occur. Trial courts may assume and appellate courts will concur, "absent a showing of bad faith or ill will, that the officials charged with custody of the evidence properly discharged their duties and did not tamper with the evidence."[12]

The party offering an item in evidence bears the burden of presenting evidence sufficient to support a finding that the matter in question is what the party claims, and in satisfying its burden the party may authenticate the

---

[8] Smith v. State, 2009 WY 2, 2009 Wyo. LEXIS 2 (Wyo. 2009).

[9] State v. McClure, 2006 N.C. App. LEXIS 47 (N.C. 2006).

[10] *See* People v. Garth, 353 Ill. App. 3d 108, 817 N.E.2d 1085, 2004 Ill. App. LEXIS 1192 (2004).

[11] People v. Hogan, 114 P.3d 42, 51, 2004 Colo. App. LEXIS 2001 (Colo. 2004), *reh'g denied*, 2005 Colo. LEXIS 597 (Colo. 2005).

[12] State v. Goff, 191 S.W.3d 113, 116, 2006 Mo. App. LEXIS 712 (2006).

item either by having a witness visually identify the item as the one that was involved in the crime or by establishing a chain of custody that indirectly establishes the identity and integrity of the evidence by tracing its continuous location. During a trial, a decision concerning whether an item of evidence has been sufficiently authenticated for admission rests with the trial judge, whose decision is subject to review on the basis of an abuse of discretion standard.[13] Once the proponent of the real evidence has laid a minimally sufficient foundation, "a lack of positive identification or a defect in the chain of custody goes to the weight of the evidence rather than the admissibility."[14]

Four general rules regarding the admissibility of real evidence are often applied. They are: (1) establishment of a chain or continuity of custody; (2) necessity; (3) relationship to crime; and (4) proper identification.

A. Establishment of a Chain or Continuity of Custody

In establishing a chain of custody, the proponent of the evidence must demonstrate where the evidence has been stored or housed since the evidence originally came into the possession of the police or the evidence may be excluded from use at trial.[15] Chain of custody applies to defendants as well, but normally the issue is one for the prosecution because it will be introducing most of the real evidence. The necessity of proving chain of custody exists because many people may handle the evidence from the time of its original collection. Proof of where the evidence has been minimizes the chances that someone tampered with the evidence, substituted evidence, lost and replaced it, or otherwise allowed it to be altered in some manner.[16] A failure to make a chain of custody objection at the time the evidence is introduced generally waives any chain of custody argument.[17] Proving the chain of custody assures authenticity of the evidence, and without authentication the evidence would be inadmissible. While it is preferable to introduce evidence to show that the chain of custody was not broken at any time, in offering proof of the chain of custody, the prosecution need not eliminate each and every possibility of tampering with the evidence. As one court noted, "Minor uncertainties in the proof of chain of custody are matters to be argued by counsel and weighed by the jury, but they do not render the evidence inadmissible as a matter of law."[18] In one case in which the officer testified about collecting contraband, the officer stated that it was in the same condition except for some changes that occurred during chemical testing. The chemist in the case indicated similar guarantees of control and custody and the judge held that the drug evidence could be admitted

---

[13] People v. Lee, 2005 Mich. App. LEXIS 3186 (2005).

[14] State v. Housley, 922 So.2d 659, 665, 2006 La. App. LEXIS 116 (2006).

[15] State v. Cowans, 336 Ill. App. 3d 173, 782 N.E.2d 779, 2002 Ill. App. LEXIS 1170 (2002), *appeal denied*, 2003 Ill. LEXIS 649 (2003). *See* case in Part II.

[16] Tennessee v. Woods, 2001 Tenn. Crim. App. LEXIS 797 (2001).

[17] Miller v. State, 2004 Tex. App. LEXIS 11547 (Tex. 2004).

[18] Green v. State, 2006 Ark. LEXIS 167 (Ark. 2006).

due to proof of the chain of custody.[19] In proving sufficient chain of custody, the prosecutor is not "required to foreclose every possibility of tampering; it need only show reasonable assurance of the identity of the evidence."[20]

In the case of *New York v. Lanza*,[21] the appellate court reviewed the standards for chain of custody and held that, under the circumstances of the case, the chain had been properly proven. In *Lanza*, the defendant sold crack cocaine to an undercover police officer on two occasions. Each time, the undercover officer acquired the drug and handed the substance to another officer, who placed the suspected drug in a plastic evidence bag, labeled the bag, and locked it in a special police drug locker. Subsequently, the sample was removed and transported in two separate containers to the crime lab where he watched an evidence receiving technician weigh each bag, mark them, and place them in a safe storage area within a different plastic bag. At trial, a chemist identified a certified copy of the crime lab record for the two, bagged items of suspected crack cocaine. The court noted the procedure followed by the chemist, in which:

> she retrieved the two bags from the vault and placed them in a locked box to which only she had access. Approximately two weeks later, she removed the bags from the locked box, opened them and took a small amount of material from each for testing. We conclude that this evidence, including the certified Crime Lab record, was sufficient to establish a complete chain of custody (citations omitted). In addition, defendant does not dispute that the substance contained in the two exhibits admitted at trial was the substance sold by him, as demonstrated by the undisputed testimony of the undercover officer and Kane, and the forensic chemist testified that those two exhibits were the ones from which she obtained the substance for testing.[22]

According to the appellate court in *Lanza*, the chain of custody had been clearly shown at the trial proceeding by appropriate evidence. In this case, the prosecution proved that the defendant possessed crack cocaine and sold it to the undercover officer, who had it properly analyzed, and the lab expert properly explained the identity of the controlled substance. Chain of custody need not be perfect in every respect; it is sufficient that once the prosecution introduces evidence that strongly suggests the presence of virtually every link in the chain, any gaps go to the weight rather than to the admissibility of the evidence.[23]

When the chain of custody covers an extended period, but the chain has been sufficiently proved to be unbroken, the evidence should be admitted.

---

[19] In the Matter of Kassan D., 287 A.D.2d 564, 565, 566, 731 N.Y.S.2d 487, 2001 N.Y. App. Div. LEXIS 9594 (2001).

[20] Franklin v. State, 2006 Ga. App. LEXIS 1111 (2006).

[21] New York v. Lanza, 299 A.D.2d 649, 650, 749 N.Y.S.2d 618, 620, 2002 N.Y. App. Div. LEXIS 10780 (2002).

[22] *Id.*

[23] Troxell v. Indiana, 778 N.E.2d 811, 814, 2002 Ind. LEXIS 888 (2002), *and see* Hawkins v. Arkansas, 105 S.W.3d 397, 2003 Ark. App. LEXIS 334 (2003).

In 1994, the brother of a female marijuana dealer found that someone had killed her by cutting her throat. Police found blood on a washcloth on the back fence that contained blood. They properly tagged it and sent it to an Atlanta lab. At the time, the amount of DNA that was collected was insufficient for testing, so the samples were stored properly in a secured cold room until 2001, when the science had advanced to permit new testing that disclosed that the defendant's and the victim's DNA were present in the washcloth sample.[24] At the defendant's murder trial, police officers, crime scene technicians, lab officials who conducted the DNA testing, and other individuals who had been involved in the case testified concerning the chain of custody of the blood samples from the time of the original collection to the introduction of the results at trial. The defendant objected to the introduction of the DNA evidence based on alleged, but not clearly specified, problems with the chain of custody of the blood sample. The trial judge admitted the evidence because he found that a proper chain of custody had been proven even though a significant period had elapsed between the crime and the trial. In upholding the murder conviction, the appellate court observed that as long as the blood samples had been handled in a routine manner and there was no reason to raise a suspicion that the blood-based results were not from the original blood sample, a sufficient chain of custody was properly proven.[25] The length and duration of the chain of custody, where properly demonstrated, will not prevent the introduction of evidence when the custody of the evidence has been unbroken.

However, the failure to follow proper chain-of-custody procedures or a failure to allege and prove them in court will have serious consequences for the prosecution. For example, an Illinois appeals court reversed a probation revocation based on the defendant's delivery of a controlled substance within 1,000 feet of a church where a defendant had sold crack cocaine to an undercover police agent. The officer stated that when he received the crack he inventoried the item, but offered absolutely no other evidence concerning chain of custody. Following his probation revocation based on the crack cocaine sale, the defendant appealed on the lack of chain of custody proof. In analyzing the requirements for the chain of custody, the appellate court noted that:

> When contraband is sought to be introduced, it is the State's burden to establish "a chain of custody of sufficient completeness to render it improbable that the [evidence] has been tampered with, exchanged, or contaminated." The State must show that the police took reasonable protective measures to ensure that the substance taken from the defendant was the same as the substance tested by the forensic chemist. This requires proof of delivery, presence, and safekeeping. Unless the defendant produces evidence of actual tampering, substitution, or contamination, the State is only required

---

[24]   Schmerber v. California, 384 U.S. 757, 1966 U.S. LEXIS 1129 (1966) held that the use of a defendant's own blood does not violate the Fifth Amendment privilege against self-incrimination. *See* case in Part II.

[25]   Paschal v. State, 280 Ga. 430, 432, 628 S.E.2d 586, 589, 2006 Ga. LEXIS 202 (2006).

to establish that reasonable protective measures were employed to protect the evidence from the time that it was seized and that it is improbable that the evidence was altered.[26]

In this case, because the prosecution failed to present any evidence concerning the handling and safekeeping of the evidence between the time the state received the crack from the defendant and the delivery of some substance to the state forensic scientist, proof of the chain of custody failed. Because the state either failed to follow the proper procedures or failed to prove that it followed them, the appellate court reversed the case.[27]

Notwithstanding the fact that the courts have been reluctant to prohibit the use of evidence even if there has been a gap in the chain of custody, it is quite clear that unless the prosecution can to show that the item has not been contaminated or has not been subjected to tampering, it will not be admitted. Evidence may be admitted with slight deficiencies in the chain of custody, but a court or jury will give less weight to such evidence.

B. Necessity

Because of the weight that may be placed upon the use of real evidence, courts have reasoned that it should not be admitted unless a valid reason for its admission is offered. While real evidence does not require absolutely perfect links in the chain of custody to qualify for admission in evidence,[28] the admission or exclusion of real evidence rests largely within the sound discretion of the trial judge.[29] In some instances, the party offering a demonstration of the real evidence is required to give good reason for its acceptance into evidence. As one court stated, the evidence should be admitted when it is both relevant and highly probative, better evidence cannot reasonably be anticipated, and the dangers are small in comparison to the advantages.[30]

While the admission of certain evidence is not improper merely because it may tend to influence the emotions, it should be excluded when it appears to be designed to appeal to the emotional and sympathetic tendencies of a judge or jury. In a trial for having her husband murdered, the court initially excluded a sexually suggestive photograph of the defendant, found in the possession of the defendant's paramour, as being unfairly prejudicial and cumulative.[31] The jury might become motivated for unfair reasons. The trial court later reversed its ruling and admitted the explicit photo after the defendant testified that she had not

---

[26] Illinois v. Moore, 335 Ill. App. 3d 616, 781 N.E.2d 493, 2002 Ill. App. LEXIS 1058 (2002).

[27] *Id.*

[28] People v. Conner, 2005 Mich. App. LEXIS 653 (2005).

[29] *See* Washington v. Delgado, 2003 Wash. App. LEXIS 87 (2003), which held that a judge in his or her discretion may admit or exclude real evidence in the form of photographs.

[30] Commonwealth v. Inhabitants of Holliston, 107 Mass. 232 (1871).

[31] United States v. Brudette, 86 Fed. Appx. 121, 2004 U.S. App. LEXIS 804 (6th Cir. 2004).

had a consensual sexual relationship with the government witness who hired the hit man to kill her husband. Once her testimony was on the record as denying her relationship with her lover, the photograph became more relevant and less prejudicial to explain her relationship with her paramour, who hired the hit man.

When photographs of a murder victim serve only to inflame the passion of the jury, their prejudicial effect outweighs their probative value and admission is improper. However, to win an argument that the photographs of a deceased murder victim are too gruesome to admit into evidence, a strong case of unfair prejudice must be demonstrated. In a Florida case where the bodies were taken apart with a chain saw, the trial court admitted the photographs for particular purposes and the Supreme Court of Florida did not see fit to reverse the case based on the use of some rough photographs.[32]

C. Relationship to Crime

Evidence may be excluded at the discretion of the judge when facts that the prosecution seeks to prove are only remotely connected to the issues. In other words, the evidence that a party seeks to have admitted must tend to prove or disprove a fact at issue in the case and when the effects of an item of evidence are marginal, it should be excluded. In addition, if the evidence would be likely to mislead or confuse the jury, a judge may refuse to allow the evidence.[33] In a drug sale case in which the defendant wanted the jury to view the scene, the judge refused to allow a jury view of the crime scene because the physical area in which the alleged drug sale occurred had changed significantly since the time of the defendant's arrest.[34]

In cases in which the prosecution wants to introduce a physical object (such as a weapon) connected with the commission of a crime, it may properly be admitted into evidence only after it has been satisfactorily identified and shown to have a sufficient connection to the crime charged. In a case involving a series of car thefts in which firearms were used, a witness positively identified a distinctive gun used by the defendants, connecting the gun and the defendants and assuring its admissibility.[35] If there is insufficient evidence to show that the article is connected with the crime, it should not be admitted. For example, in a child sexual misconduct case, the prosecution had a plastic bag containing hair taken from the defendant's possession marked as an exhibit, but it never introduced the bag of hair into evidence.[36] The prosecution had planned to ask the defendant about the hair if he took the witness stand, but the opportunity never arose. A reviewing court concluded that the bag of hair did not make any fact that was

---

[32] Doorbal v. State, 983 So.2d 464, 2008 Fla. LEXIS 215 (Fla. 2008).

[33] 32 C.J.S. *Evidence* § 602.

[34] Sherman v. Arkansas, 2005 Ark. App. LEXIS 141 (2005).

[35] Attaway v. Georgia, 259 Ga. App. 822, 826, 827, 578 S.E.2d 529, 533, 2003 Ga. App. LEXIS 270 (2003).

[36] State v. Jacobson, 87 Conn. App. 440, 450, 866 A.2d 678, 687, 2005 Conn. App. LEXIS 64 (2005).

of consequence to the case more or less probable than it would have been without it. The reviewing court concluded the hair was improperly introduced because it may have encouraged jury speculation, but the appellate court thought that the hair evidence constituted harmless error and did not reverse the convictions.

Although the burden is on the party introducing the evidence to show that it complies with the requirements, in most instances the court will admit real evidence if it has any logical bearing upon the case. The judge has the discretion as to whether the evidence is related to the crime, and his or her decision is not subject to review unless there has been a clear abuse of this discretion.

D. *Proper Identification*

When the prosecution wants to introduce an object, article, tool, weapon, or similar tangible item in evidence to prove a fact to which it is connected from a previous time or event, the item is not competent evidence unless it is first identified as being the same object that was originally recovered and is shown to be in substantially the same condition as it was during the time or event to which it is claimed to be related.[37] A Texas court noted that in identifying evidence, "[t]he chain of custody is conclusively proven if an officer is able to identify that he or she seized the item of physical evidence, put an identification mark on it, placed it in the property room, and then retrieved the item being offered on the day of trial."[38] The requirement that physical objects be identified or authenticated as genuine serves to prevent the introduction of false evidence or evidence that has been subjected to tampering. In a case in which the defendant had been accused of having a firearm under a disability, he contended that the prosecution had not properly authenticated or identified the gun in court as the one originally taken from the defendant. The evidence showed that one officer recovered the gun and his radio transmissions gave verification, while another officer accepted the gun and logged it into the property room using a voucher and the gun's serial number. The officer at trial testified that the serial number of the gun at trial matched the recorded number on the property room voucher. The trial court held that the gun in court had been sufficiently identified as the actual gun taken from the defendant and denied the motion to set aside the guilty verdict.[39] The identification requirement prevents the chance of incorrect evidence being introduced against a defendant.

---

[37] Gutman v. Industrial Comm., 71 Ohio App. 383, 50 N.E.2d 187 (1942); *see also* State v. Campbell, 103 Wash. 2d 1, 691 P.2d 929, cert. denied, 471 U.S. 1094, 105 S. Ct. 2169, 85 L. Ed. 2d 526 (1984), which held that before a physical object connected with the commission of a crime may properly be admitted into evidence, it must be satisfactorily identified and shown to be in substantially the same condition as it was when the crime was committed. The factors to be considered include the nature of the article, circumstances surrounding its preservation and custody, and the likelihood of intermeddlers tampering with it.

[38] Bridges v. State, 2005 Tex. App. LEXIS 10389 (Tex. 2005).

[39] United States v. Stukes, 2004 U.S. Dist. LEXIS 21486 (S.D.N.Y. 2004), *aff'd*, 2006 U.S. App. LEXIS (2d Cir. 2006).

Generally, physical evidence is properly admitted if it is readily identifiable by some unique feature or other identifying mark.[40] When a real or physical object is offered as evidence in a criminal prosecution, an adequate foundation for admission requires testimony that the one is the same object that was involved in the alleged incident, and the condition of the object is substantially unchanged.[41]

The state met the identification requirement in a Michigan case in which the 7–11 store pre-positioned a $2 bill that had a recorded serial number in the cash register.[42] This $2 bill was to be given out to robbers and, following a robbery, an arrested defendant possessed a $2 bill with the same pre-recorded serial number, which was recovered by police. The serial number sufficiently identified the $2 bill as having been taken in a robbery and it was properly admitted into evidence at the defendant's robbery trial.

Articles are sometimes admitted into evidence even though a slight alteration or change has occurred, e.g., a court admitted the serrated blade of a knife discovered at a murder scene after a fire when a surviving victim stated that the defendant had cut his throat with a complete knife[43] and two mangled bullets recovered from a wall that a ballistics expert stated were fired from the same gun.[44]

§ 14.3 Exhibition of Person

When the prosecution of the defendant is based on physical harm to the victim, it would seem that the best evidence of such harm would be the exhibition of the person of the victim to the jury. Such a witness would be more valuable in determining what happened than would oral testimony, photographs, or even X-rays, in some instances. Courts as a rule will allow the display of injuries to the jury—often in spite of the fact that the injury is gruesome.

The trial judge has a great deal of discretion in determining whether the physical display of the injury is so inflammatory as to unduly influence the jury. Such decisions are seldom overruled, unless there is a clear abuse of discretion. However, if the judge determines that the display of the person and the injury is so inflammatory that it may prejudice the jury, the judge may refuse to allow the display of a crime-related injury. In a California case, a judge permitted the jury to view a videotape of a man who was in a hospital after being attacked with a hammer by the defendant. He was in poor condition after the attack and was so elderly that he died prior to the defendant's trial. There were questions concerning the reliability of the witness's statement, but

---

[40] United States v. Abreu, 952 F.2d 1458 (1st Cir.), *cert. denied*, 503 U.S. 994, 112 S. Ct. 1695, 118 L. Ed. 2d 406 (1992).

[41] United States v. Miller, 994 F.2d 441 (8th Cir. 1993).

[42] People v. Grandberry, 2005 Mich. App. LEXIS 2099 (2005).

[43] Commonwealth v. Edwards, 2006 Pa. LEXIS 1529 (2006).

[44] Grayson v. King, 2006 U.S. App. LEXIS 21215 (11th Cir. 2006).

the judge allowed the jury to observe the man and hear his story on videotape, which had been recorded after the attack.[45]

Although the judge in his or her discretion may permit the witness to be exhibited at the trial in a criminal case in order to determine the extent of injury, the judge runs the risk of committing reversible error if he or she compelled a defendant to appear at a trial in handcuffs or shackles. In one case, upheld on appeal, the trial court required the defendant to wear wrist restraints at trial because the defendant refused to take his medication, refused to change out of prison clothes, and there was evidence that he might be trying to escape and hurt people.[46] Where a defendant consented to being shackled out of the jury's sight as a condition of serving as his own attorney, no constitutional due process violation occurred.[47] If a prosecutor is able to develop, on the record, facts that indicate a particularized need for restraints, restraints may not constitute a violation of due process.[48] In the penalty phase of a state death penalty case, the trial court ordered that the defendant be shackled with visible leg irons, handcuffs, and a belly chain without taking any evidence or showing special circumstances that might have suggested that restraint was actually needed. The Supreme Court of the United States reversed the death penalty, noting that the restraints almost certainly affected the jury's perception of the defendant's character.[49] Although a court may not compel a defendant to wear jail or prison clothes during the defendant's jury trial, a failure to object to being tried in custodial clothing is sufficient to negate an actionable constitutional violation.[50]

§ 14.4 Articles Connected with the Crime

Real evidence that includes weapons, tools, devices, and instruments that an accused person has employed in committing the alleged crime are admissible in evidence provided that the prosecutor can properly connect each item of evidence to the defendant and to the crime. An item of real evidence must be authenticated as the thing the proponent represents it to be. If the object is one a witness can particularly identify from memory of its appearance or attributes, it will be sufficiently authenticated. Alternatively, an item of evidence may be authenticated by creating a chain of custody that is largely intact.[51]

---

[45] *See* California v. Tatum, 108 Cal. App. 4th 288, 133 Cal. Rptr. 2d 267, 2003 Cal. App. LEXIS 629 (2003).

[46] United States v. Montgomery, 152 Fed. Appx. 822, 826, 2005 U.S. App. LEXIS 21893 (11th Cir. 2005).

[47] Overton v. Mathes, 425 F.3d 518, 520, 2005 U.S. App. LEXIS 21885 (8th Cir. 2005).

[48] United States v. Salehi, 2006 U.S. App. LEXIS 16285 (3d Cir. 2006).

[49] Deck v. Missouri, 544 U.S. 622, 628, 2005 U.S. LEXIS 4180 (2005).

[50] Tolliver v. Greiner, 2005 U.S. Dist. LEXIS 32402 (N.D.N.Y. 2005). *See also* United States v. Salehi, 2006 U.S. App. LEXIS 16285 (3d Cir. 2006).

[51] Commonwealth v. Herring, 66 Mass. App. Ct. 360, 365, 2006 Mass. App. LEXIS 569 (Mass. 2006).

Federal Rule of Evidence 901(a) notes that "authentication or identification as a condition precedent to admissibility is satisfied by evidence sufficient to support a finding that the matter in question is what its proponent claims." Examples of types of articles that have been acquired by investigators and submitted for consideration are discussed in the paragraphs that follow.

A. Weapons

Weapons admitted in criminal cases must be authenticated and must have sufficient relevancy to the case to be properly admitted. In a case in which the prosecution failed to establish that a firearm had been used in an assault, no sufficient connection existed to allow the weapon into evidence. However, the trial court permitted a police officer to explain how, during the defendant's arrest, the officer discovered a handgun on the defendant's person. The court, in the absence of an objection, allowed the officer to describe the non-crime-related pistol and its holster in great detail and admitted the pistol into evidence. The appellate court noted that the admission of the second weapon that had no connection to the case was error, but the court considered the error to be harmless under the circumstances.[52]

In order to prove a defendant guilty of a homicide committed with a stolen firearm, the prosecutor presented evidence from police officers concerning the location from which a gun had been recovered. The firearm was of the correct caliber; it was near the location of the homicide; and contained six fired shell casings. The connection of the gun to the case was completed when the owner of the gun identified it as having been the one stolen from him a few days earlier. The trial court held that the gun could be admitted in court as real evidence.[53]

In a case from the District of Columbia, a defendant contended that the prosecution failed to authenticate a firearm that the defendant allegedly had possessed while under a disability. The gun that the defendant threw away during a chase was tagged, bagged, and sealed, along with 11 cartridges. At the trial, it was discovered that the bag had been opened and two rounds of ammunition were missing, but the gun was present. There was no explanation why the bag had become unsealed, but a police officer testified that the gun appeared to be the one he had recovered after the defendant threw it away and he recalled the make, model, and color of the gun he originally seized. He testified that the serial number on the gun matched the serial number that he recorded at the time he seized the gun. The reviewing court upheld the admission into evidence of the gun and ammunition, because the prosecution only had to prove that as a matter of reasonable probability, there was no misidentification of the gun in order to properly authenticate it using the chain of custody theory.[54]

---

[52]   Davis v. Arkansas, 2003 Ark. App. LEXIS 386 (2003).

[53]   Andrews v. Texas, 78 S.W.3d 13, 18, 2002 Tex. App. LEXIS 1056 (2002).

[54]   United States v. Goddard, 2006 U.S. App. LEXIS 6970 (D.C. Cir. 2006).

A weapon that appears to have virtually no connection with a homicide can be excluded from evidence when it lacks relevance to the facts of a case. Under the circumstances, a judge may refuse to permit it to be authenticated and introduced into evidence. In a Mississippi homicide case, police arrested the defendant, who was wearing bloody clothes and sleeping on top of a .32 pistol and a .380 handgun. At the trial, the defendant wanted to introduce evidence that he also possessed the .380 handgun at the time of his arrest.[55] The deceased had been fatally shot with the .32 caliber pistol possessed by the defendant, but there was never any evidence that the .380 handgun had been present at the murder scene. In arguments to the trial judge, the defendant's counsel contended that the .380 had been at the murder scene, but neither party introduced any actual evidence that the .380 handgun had any role in the homicide. The Supreme Court of Mississippi upheld the trial judge's exclusion of the extra firearm, noting that the judge did not abuse his discretion. In this case, it might be argued that the defendant wanted to "muddy the waters" in an effort to create some confusion on the part of the jury.

For many types of weapons, proof of a chain of custody will not be the only method of proving a sufficient connection to a particular crime. All modern firearms must have serial numbers stamped on the frame of the weapon, so that a firearm identified at the crime scene by a serial number may be authenticated at trial by reference to the same number. Even when the serial number has not been used, the failure to establish a chain of custody is not essential if the weapon introduced is clearly identified by one or more witnesses or through expert ballistics evidence. Demonstrative of these principles for authentication, in an Arkansas aggravated robbery case, a witness identified a .22 Ruger pistol that the prosecution introduced by its appearance as the gun that the witness had given the defendant.[56] The witness testified that the serial number on the .22 Ruger was the identical number that had been on the pistol the witness had transferred to the defendant. In this case, the witness was able to identify the gun by its overall appearance as well as by its serial number, sufficiently authenticating the gun for use as evidence against a suspected armed robber. In one case, Delaware courts permitted the authentication of a firearm by accepting proof that the gun was likely the one associated with the crime, coupled with evidence that the same gun was connected to the defendant and the commission of the crime. According to the reviewing court, the firearm was properly authenticated and admitted against the defendant.[57]

In addition to firearms, other weapons used to commit crimes may be introduced into evidence if properly identified. For example, a knife was properly introduced when its authenticity was established by the testimony of a police officer who took the knife from the defendant and provided proof of chain of custody until its introduction at the defendant's trial.[58]

---

[55]　Flora v. State, 925 So. 2d 797, 813, 2006 Miss. LEXIS 49 (2006).

[56]　Looney v. State, 2005 Ark. LEXIS 326 (Ark. 2005).

[57]　Pierce v. State, 937 A.2d 140, 2007 Del. LEXIS 497 (Del. 2007).

[58]　Maranda v. State, 253 S.W.3d 762, 2007 Tex. App. LEXIS 9285 (Tex. 2007).

B. Instruments Used in the Crime

Instruments associated with crimes, such as burglary tools, screwdrivers, explosives, lock picks, and other implements adapted to crime, especially burglary, are admissible if reasonably identified, although more weight will be given to the evidence if identification is certain. If the witness is uncertain concerning the identification of an item of real evidence, the witness's uncertainty goes only to the weight of the physical evidence and not to its admissibility.[59]

In a Hawai'i case, an apartment manager observed a subject with a bicycle and a backpack attempting to gain entry into the apartment's parking garage by prying on the steel-framed locked door.[60] When asked why he did not use a key, the subject noted that he did not have a key. Upon additional inquiry, the manager realized the subject was an interloper who had a rope, a cord, and a chisel in his hand. A shoving match between the two men followed, in which the backpack fell to the ground, revealing screwdrivers, pliers, and a pair of scissors. The defendant argued on appeal that physical evidence did not support the proof of possession of burglar tools and that the eyewitness did not give believable testimony. The reviewing court rejected the defendant-appellant's contention because it thought that reasonable minds could find guilt beyond a reasonable doubt based on the manager's testimony concerning the real evidence.

In a prosecution for having or making burglary tools and second-degree burglary, a defendant had been found inside a fenced compound where recreational vehicles had been stored and where she had no permission to enter. In her possession were tools commonly used and possessed by burglars—a flashlight and a drill. The burglary had taken place at night in the area where she was found and some of the items stolen from the property had been physically disassembled or detached from some of the structures. Despite the defendant's claim that she was using the tools for disassembling her own property, the trial verdict, upheld on appeal, was that she was guilty of possession of burglary tools.[61]

Evidence that has a strained chain of custody or may be difficult to identify may be admitted against a defendant when it meets the threshold of authenticity. In a commercial burglary of a bar, a bar owner caught the defendant, who he recognized, inside the building with a crowbar while standing near a lottery vending machine.[62] As the defendant with the crowbar approached the bar owner, the bar owner shot the defendant in the leg. The defendant dropped the crowbar and made a successful initial escape, but police eventually arrested him. The bar owner produced the crowbar at the request of the prosecutor about a week prior to the trial. The defendant objected to the introduction of the crowbar because the prosecution never properly offered a foundation for the crowbar as being

---

[59]   *See* Commonwealth v. Crork, 2009 Pa Super 24, 2009 Pa. Super LEXIS 31 (Pa. 2009).

[60]   State v. Tetu, 2005 Haw. App. LEXIS 435 (Haw. 2005).

[61]   Washington v. Baker, 2002 Wash. App. LEXIS 2998 (2002).

[62]   State v. Boydston, 2006 Mo. App. LEXIS 1246 (2006).

the one that the burglar dropped after being shot. The reviewing court rejected the defendant's arguments, noting that a specific objection had not been tendered at trial and the court did not find plain error in the admission of the crowbar that the bar owner claimed to have taken from the real burglar.

C. Clothing

Clothing that a witness identifies as having been worn by the accused or the victim during the commission of the crime may be submitted to the jury for inspection. For example, in one case, clothing that had been taken in a robbery from a retail store was admitted against an accused robber.[63] Police recovered the stolen clothing from a garbage bag that was discovered in the defendant's bedroom closet. The defendant's accomplices in the robbery testified about how they had packaged the stolen goods and delivered them to the defendant. The testimony sufficiently connected the stolen goods to the possession of the defendant at his place of residence and the clothing was in substantially the same condition when presented at trial as it was at the time police recovered it. As a general rule, any deficiency in the chain of custody with respect to an item of evidence affects the weight of the evidence, but not its admissibility.

In a capital murder case, the prosecution introduced some bloody clothing that the murder victim had been wearing at the time of her death.[64] The evidence disclosed that a crime scene technician collected the bloody clothing from the morgue from the gurney on which the deceased's body had been processed, placed it in a secured box, and properly stored the clothing in the police property room. At the trial, the same evidence technician opened the box, outside the presence of the jury, and labeled each item. The judge admitted the clothes into evidence because the prosecution had established a proper chain of custody for admission into evidence. The reviewing court approved the admission of the bloody clothes as it noted that it was a well-established principle that clothing that was demonstrated to have been worn by the victim at the time a crime was committed is considered to be admissible evidence.

Police may seize clothing and other tangible personal articles belonging to an arrestee following a lawful arrest and may hold the clothing as evidence without violating the arrestee's Fourth Amendment right to be free from unlawful searches and seizures. Similarly, when police encountered a person who seemed to have been a crime victim at a hospital emergency room and observed evidence in plain view, they may lawfully seize it. In an Illinois case, police had been called to an emergency room because a patient had a gunshot wound, where they observed and seized the defendant's bloody pants and shoes.[65] After additional investigation, police sent the articles of clothing

---

[63] People v. Green, 2006 N.Y. Slip Op. 6014, 818 N.Y.S.2d 862, 2006 N.Y. App. Div. LEXIS 9719 (N.Y. 2006).

[64] State v. Chapman, 359 N.C. 328, 352, 611 S.E.2d 794, 814, 2005 N.C. LEXIS 361 (2005).

[65] People v. Hillsman, 362 Ill. App. 3d 623, 626, 839 N.E.2d 1116, 1120, 2005 Ill. App. LEXIS 1209 (2005).

for DNA testing that disclosed that some of the blood on the items of clothing belonged to a homicide victim as well as to the defendant. The defendant attempted to have the evidence suppressed, but the trial court refused. The real evidence, consisting of the clothing, shoes, and the DNA evidence, was properly introduced because a patient at an emergency room has no expectation of privacy and the real evidence was in plain view of the officers. In a different case, a Washington trial court noted in a case in which a defendant alleged that he had an expectation of privacy in his shoes held by the police, "The United States Supreme Court has held, under the Fourth Amendment, that a defendant has no reasonable expectation of privacy in property jail personnel seize from a defendant upon arrival after a lawful arrest."[66] Therefore, when the police possessed the defendant's shoes following an arrest for rape, they could properly maintain the chain of custody and use the shoes for identification purposes and to obtain a shoeprint to assist in the rape prosecution without violating any of the defendant's constitutional rights. In a similar situation, police arrested a man for the murder of his ex-wife. Because he seemed unconcerned about the shooting death of his ex-wife and because police were aware of his rocky relationship with her, they developed probable cause for his arrest. Following the arrest, police tested his clothing for evidence of gunshot residue. The tests revealed the presence of chemicals indicating that the wearer of the clothing had recently fired a gun. On appeal, the reviewing court approved of the warrantless seizure and scientific testing of the clothing as evidence and held that the evidence had been properly admitted by the trial court.[67]

A Texas appeals court did not disturb a trial court holding admitting the underwear that the defendant had been wearing on the night that a child in his exclusive care had been raped.[68] From a single stain on defendant's underwear, experts determined that the stain tested positive for blood from the infant victim and semen from the defendant. The trial court also admitted a washcloth used at an emergency room that had been used to wipe the infant's private area that contained presence of semen. Because the real evidence in the case appeared to meet all the requirements of authentication by chain of custody, the appeals court affirmed the conviction for aggravated sexual assault on a child.

D. Bloodstains

The practice of identifying blood and criminals by circumstantial evidence and by the inspection of witnesses and jurors has had the sanction of immemorial usage in criminal tribunals.[69] With the development of twentieth-century blood testing, science generated new data on types and subtypes of blood, yielding additional information from blood analysis. Most recently, the

---

[66] Washington v. Cheatam, 112 Wash. App. 778, 785, 51 P.3d 138, 143, 2002 Wash. App. LEXIS 1832 (2002).

[67] Colorado v. Rogers, 68 P.3d 486, 2002 Colo. App. LEXIS 1627 (2002).

[68] Smith v. State, 2004 Tex. App. LEXIS 11851 (2004).

[69] People v. Gonzales, 35 N.Y. 49 (1866).

use of deoxyribonucleic acid (DNA) as a method of identifying the source of blood left at crime scenes opened new avenues of identification of criminals, as well as screening the innocent away from prosecution. The testing has also evolved to the point at which extremely small samples of blood may be used to reveal DNA information that previously would not have been available. Blood is only one type of body fluid that contains DNA for which law enforcement officers may find use.

The discovery of the presence of blood on the person or clothing of the accused party or the victim has been recognized as being among the ordinary indicia of homicide and lesser criminal injury. Blood-related evidence left by the perpetrator at the scene of the crime, whether that of the defendant or the victim, tends to prove who has been present and may indicate by its patterns what occurred and how long ago the acts took place. Blood evidence may be visible to law enforcement officers or may require enhancement by chemicals introduced at the scene. Police and evidence technicians have used Luminol[70] as a screening test to detect latent evidence of blood since 1955, when it was first used in the investigation of a crime scene and introduced in court.[71] Even a recent challenge to the use of Luminol was deflected by a court, noting that the science in this area is not new and has been universally accepted as a presumptive test for blood.[72]

The use of blood-obtained information and bloodstain evidence will generally require expert collection, expert evaluation, and expert testimony.[73] In one murder case, the victim had been killed by an unknown assailant, but blood testing provided a way to determine the identity of the perpetrator. The body of a young woman was found by her sister in their home. A medical examiner determined, based on an examination of the body at the scene and an autopsy, that the deceased had been beaten and stabbed multiple times with a screwdriver. In addition, the doctor determined that she had been sexually assaulted. Evidence in the form of bloodstained clothes and a partial Walkman headset were found at the defendant's home. The headset part matched one part found under the body of the deceased. A Walkman and blood-stained underwear were found in the defendant's bedroom. The prosecution introduced DNA evidence obtained from blood at the crime scene. The DNA evidence demonstrated that the DNA profile of blood samples taken from the defendant's screwdriver and personal property found at his home matched the victim's DNA profile and that semen samples taken from the victim's body matched the defendant's DNA profile. With such overwhelming evidence arrayed against him, the defendant contended that the DNA testing process had not been shown to meet the

---

[70] A chemical compound that reacts with blood and semen and chemically changes to give off light.

[71] People v. Wooten, 283 A.D.2d 931, 933, 725 N.Y.S.2d 767, 770, 2001 N.Y. App. Div. LEXIS 4659 (N.Y. 2001).

[72] People v. Cumbee, 851 N.E.2d 934, 948, 2006 Ill. App. LEXIS 578 (2006).

[73] People v. Driver, 62 Ill. App. 3d 847, 379 N.E.2d 840 (1978).

general acceptance of the general scientific acceptance standard and should not have been admitted. The reviewing court rejected the recent approach taken by the Supreme Court of the United States and held that newer DNA testing must meet the general scientific acceptance standard that had been in effect for many years. The murder conviction was remanded for a hearing to decide whether the newest DNA testing was sufficiently reliable to be admitted in the state court system of Minnesota.[74] Following remand, the court determined that the testing met the general scientific acceptance standard followed by Minnesota.[75]

As a general rule, scientific evidence involving blood grouping and DNA analysis will be admissible once courts determine that the newest advances meet the requirements of relevancy and reliability. If the prosecution needs to explain bloodstain patterns as a way to prove how a crime occurred, expert witnesses will be essential. The prosecution is required to show that evidence concerning the impact of bloodstain evidence is based upon a well-recognized scientific principle or technique that has gained general acceptance in the particular field to which it belongs.[76] In a Tennessee murder case, expert witnesses were permitted to offer opinions using blood spatter analysis to explain that the victim was wearing only a bra when she was fatally assaulted with rocks and that bloodstains on the victim's arms indicated that her arms were raised during part of the assault.[77]

Evaluating blood splatter patterns that remain at crime scenes helps to corroborate truthful oral evidence or challenge witness statements that may be false, misleading, or erroneous. Blood spatter analysis involves mechanical scrutiny based on the physics of fluid flow and an evaluation of impact angles at which the spatters hit other objects rather than only concerning microscopic scientific analysis. For example, a significant number of state jurisdictions have held that blood spatter analysis is reliable and may be admitted where the witness qualifies as an expert through training, education, and experience. Blood splatter analysis has been recognized as known and accepted scientific discipline by many courts because of its logical and scientific basis.[78] In a Virginia case involving expert testimony covering blood splash patterns, the high court accepted the principles on which bloodstain pattern interpretation has been based and noted that expert testimony is recognized to explain the pattern of bloodstains. The court observed that:

> many of the specific physical elements of blood spatter analysis are capable of being tested using the laws of physics and chemistry, and by employing principles of gravity, inertia, and viscosity. In accordance with other

---

[74]   *See* Minnesota v. Roman Nose, 649 N.W.2d 815, 2002 Minn. LEXIS 554 (2002).

[75]   Minnesota v. Roman Nose, 667 N.W.2d 386, 2003 Minn. LEXIS 513 (2003).

[76]   *See* Frye v. United States, 54 App. D.C. 46, 293 F. 1013 (1923), which followed the general scientific acceptance approach and many state jurisdictions followed the logic. When the Supreme Court decided *Daubert v. Merrell Dow Pharmaceuticals*, 509 U.S. 579 (1993), it ruled that Federal Rule of Evidence 702 had superseded the Frye standard for federal courts.

[77]   State v. Gilley 2008 Tenn. Crim. App. LEXIS 660 (Tenn. 2008).

[78]   Hudson v. State, 95 Ark. 85, 102, 146 S.W.3d 380, 390, 2004 Ark. App. LEXIS 124 (2004). *See also* State v. Torres, 137 N.M. 607, 113 P.3d 877; 2005 N.M. App. LEXIS 56 (2005).

jurisdictions, we adhere to the view that this form of scientific analysis can form a basis for admissible proof upon an appropriate foundation.[79]

The Virginia court held that a trial court committed no error when it permitted a blood pattern analyst to offer testimony that the victim had not been standing, when the defendant said that he shot her as she was standing and attacking him. The blood pattern expert assisted in refuting the defendant's claim of self-defense and helped prove that the victim was sitting when murdered.[80]

E. Narcotics and Narcotics Paraphernalia

Drug-related crimes involving major trafficking, possession with intent to sell, and simple possession have increased in the past 20 years to such an extent that a large percentage of local, state, and federal agents' time is devoted to investigating such crimes and testifying against the accused persons. Naturally, the high level of litigation that surrounds drug prosecutions generates a significant number of court decisions in which defendants test the rules for admission and exclusion of drug-related evidence. As a general rule, courts require a more conclusively established chain of custody for proof of authentication where interchangeable items like drugs or blood are involved,[81] a factor that may help some drug defendants.

While prosecutors can expect that narcotics evidence will be challenged by defendants when the government attempts to introduce narcotics or other controlled substances as evidence, state evidence codes and case law developed that require precise and documented steps to assure admissibility. Failure to comply with the rigorous procedures may result in evidence not being admitted. While the reviewing courts have generally approved the admissibility of narcotics in trial courts, there is a fine line between what is admissible and what is inadmissible.

In order to introduce seized drugs as evidence, federal and state courts require that the prosecutor prove a proper chain of custody as a prerequisite to admission in evidence. In one Illinois case, the defendant objected that the prosecution had offered inadequate proof of the chain of custody of drugs that allegedly had been in the defendant's possession and had been seized by a drug task force.[82] The trial court admitted the cocaine and the lab tests, but the appellate court had some concerns that the chain of custody had weak links or gaps in its proof. There was no evidence concerning what the seizing officer did with the plastic bag that he took from the defendant and proof was missing that police placed the seized bag in another sealed container and no proof that it was dated or initialed by the seizing officers. The reviewing court had

---

[79]   Smith v. Commonwealth, 265 Va. 250, 576 S.E.2d 465, 2003 Va. LEXIS 36 (2003).

[80]   *Id.*

[81]   Thompson v. State, 2006 Ark. App. LEXIS 364 (2006).

[82]   People v. Echavarria, 362 Ill. App.3d 599, 607, 840 N.E.2d 815, 823, 2005 Ill. App. LEXIS 1284 (2005).

concerns that "[n]o evidence showed how a bag taken from defendant ended up in a sealed evidence bag. No evidence showed this bag is different in any way from other bags of controlled substances that may have been handled by the task force, or transported to the lab, or stored. No evidence showed the bag presented as exhibit No. 1 is the same one recovered from defendant"[83] by one of the officers. However, the reviewing court upheld the authentication of the cocaine under the chain of custody theory because the court noted that the prosecution need not prove every single link in the chain of custody and the defendant failed to introduce any evidence that cast strong doubt on the chain of custody or proved some level of tampering.

However, in a Georgia case, an appellate court reversed a drug possession conviction based on incompetency of counsel who failed to contest the chain of custody of the drugs. Police testified that the drugs were placed in the property room but did not indicate that they were properly marked for storage as evidence. Drug testing was performed, but there was no indication of the source of the drugs that were tested or that they were from the defendant. The court of appeals reversed the conviction because it believed that the chain of custody must be more closely proved in cases of fungible materials, like drugs, and there was not a reasonable certainty that the evidence seized was the evidence introduced against the defendant.[84]

Generally, courts have authorized the introduction of not only narcotics seized from the defendants or from their residences, but also related objects such as drug paraphernalia, containers used for packaging, records, pagers, and other "tools of the trade." Some examples will highlight the types of evidence that have been introduced and the conditions surrounding the introduction of the evidence.

In an Ohio case involving possession of nine ounces of cocaine, the trial court rejected the defendant's motion to exclude some items seized from his person and his home.[85] The items allowed to be introduced at trial included guns, ammunition, a bulletproof vest, cash, and creatine found during the consent search of his home. The appellate court held that there was no error admitting these items into evidence because:

> several witnesses testified that creatine is a "cutting agent" used to dilute cocaine and increase its sales value. Moreover, there was testimony that guns and large amounts of cash are tools of the drug dealers' trade. On this uncontroverted testimony, we cannot say that the items which were admitted were irrelevant or unfairly prejudicial.[86]

Similarly, in a Tennessee case involving drug-related evidence, a trial court admitted three aerosol cans that originally contained engine starting fluid,

---

[83]   *Id.* at 608.

[84]   Wilson v. State, 271 Ga. App. 359, 362, 609 S.E.2d 703, 706, 2005 Ga. App. LEXIS 41 (2005).

[85]   State v. Graves, 2003 Ohio 2359, 2003 Ohio App. LEXIS 2190 (Ohio 2003).

[86]   *Id.*

one component of which was ether, used in manufacturing methamphetamine. Police initially stopped the defendant's vehicle because he had been reported to have recently purchased large quantities of Sudafed, an over-the-counter decongestant that can be used as a precursor chemical in the production of methamphetamine. A problem with admission of the three starter fluid cans occurred when one deputy sheriff checked two cans from the property room and used them to clean the carburetor on his personal boat motor. Because the original officer identified the three starting fluid cans at trial as being the ones he seized from the defendant, the appellate court did not find error in the chain of custody and stated, "The identification or chain of custody is sufficient if the facts establish a reasonable assurance of the identity of the evidence and its integrity."[87]

F. Other Types of Evidence

Other articles connected with a crime are also admissible if they meet the general tests. For example, in a Missouri homicide case in which the deceased had been the victim of a hit-and-run accident, police ascertained the type of vehicle from the debris at the scene of the impact and discovered the color from paint samples left on the body of the deceased. They eventually discovered the defendant's vehicle complete with front-end damage and paint scrapes and paint shards resting on the driveway. The police seized the paint shards and other evidence and eventually, through expert testimony, entered them into evidence in the murder prosecution. The trial court rejected the defendant's constitutional challenges to the collection of the evidence and the court of appeals affirmed the method of collection and the admission into evidence of the paint chips.[88]

In a sexual assault case in which there was insufficient violence to produce either the victim's blood or the defendant's blood, medical and evidence technicians obtained evidence from the victim to place in a rape kit that included saliva, blood, clothing, fingernail scrapings, and a hair sample.[89] The defendant objected to the introduction of various types of evidence derived from the rape kit that helped the prosecution convict him. His major contentions involved arguments that the chain of custody of the rape kit was not sufficiently proven, that the exhibits had not been properly preserved and that there was no proof that the exhibits contained the same specimen and evidence originally taken from the complainant. The reviewing court rejected the defendant's arguments because there was proof that the doctor took the personal material from the victim, transferred them to another health worker who sealed the envelopes and transferred them a police officer, who added his name to the chain of custody. The officer delivered the samples to the police department's secure property

---

[87] State v. Long, 2005 Tenn. Crim. App. LEXIS 199 (2005).

[88] Missouri v. Pacheco, 101 S.W.3d 913, 2003 Mo. App. LEXIS 543 (2003).

[89] Vinson v. State, 2006 Tex. App. LEXIS 1634 (2006).

room. Later, an investigator for the district attorney's office took possession and delivered the rape kit to the testing laboratory. At no point did any custodian note that any tampering appeared visible. Evidence technicians followed a similar path and procedure in collecting buccal saliva swabs from the defendant. According to the appellate court, the prosecutor demonstrated "a complete chain of custody from the first step, the collection of evidence from the complainant and appellant, to the final step, turning the evidence over to the Identigene laboratory. As there was no evidence of tampering, any gaps alleged by appellant went to the weight of the evidence, not its admissibility."[90] The trial court committed no error in admitting the results of the rape kit into evidence.

In an unpublished California arson case, a court convicted a grandmother and her grandson of committing arson of their residential home and insurance fraud.[91] Firefighters responded to a report of the fire and discovered several old burn areas on floors and an active fire in a linen closet that they later concluded had been intentionally set. When other evidence aroused additional suspicion of firefighters that the fire might have been intentionally set, they procured a criminal search warrant. In executing the warrant, investigators

> found bills indicating [defendant] was past due on her mortgage and a credit card account. They also found receipts from Wal-Mart for the recent purchase of storage containers and garbage cans. In a motor home on the property, investigators found storage containers matching the type on the receipts. They also found several cats in small cages, clothing, food, and a computer. Further, they located receipts for three storage units at a self-storage facility. A search of these units revealed clothing, furniture, and household furnishings in good condition. Some items in the units were contained in storage bins matching the type on the receipts.[92]

The trial court permitted the evidence of pre-fire planning and other real evidence to be introduced against both defendants and a jury rendered a guilty verdict on all counts. The court of appeals upheld the convictions, noting that any rational trier of fact could have found that all the essential elements of the crimes had been proven beyond a reasonable doubt.

§ 14.5 View of the Scene

In almost all jurisdictions, the trial court has the discretion to determine whether to allow a jury view of the scene of the alleged crime, and the trial court's decision will only be reversed on appeal based on a showing of an abuse of the judge's discretion.[93] Generally, the defendant and legal counsel

---

[90] *Id.*

[91] People v. Mead, 2006 Cal. App. Unpub. LEXIS 3150 (2006).

[92] *Id.*

[93] People v. Alston, 24 A.D.3d 391, 806 N.Y.S.2d 208, 209, 2005 N.Y. App. Div. LEXIS 14894 (2005).

must be permitted to accompany the jury to a view of the scene, and a failure to permit their presence may be reversible error.[94] The trial judge may act on a motion by either party or may order the jurors to be escorted to a place where a material fact occurred or an offense was committed, without a motion of either party. In deciding whether to allow a view of the scene, a judge may:

> consider the totality of the circumstances of the case, including, but not limited to, the timing of the request for the jury view, the difficulty and expense of arranging it, the importance of the information to be gained by it, the extent to which that information has been or could be secured from more convenient sources (e.g., photographs, videotapes, maps, or diagrams), and the extent to which the place or object to be viewed may have changed in appearance since the controversy began.[95]

The purpose of a view of the scene is to allow visual observation by the jury of the premises or place in question so that the jury may see places or objects that are relevant to the case and thus to provide them with a mental picture of the locality.[96] As another court phrased it, "The purpose of a jury site visit is to help the jury understand existing evidence, not to take new evidence."[97] There exists a conflict in law as to whether a view constitutes independent evidence; however, the resulting difference in opinion has little operational effect because the jury has the power to give a view of the scene whatever weight it chooses.

The procedure for viewing the premises varies from state to state, and the manner of viewing the scene is often regulated by statute or rule of the court. Good practice dictates that the trial judge accompany the members of the jury to the viewing, although it may not constitute reversible error if the judge does not view the scene.[98] In conducting a view of the scene, "the jury must be kept together throughout under the supervision of an appropriate public servant or servants appointed by the court, and the court itself must be present throughout. The prosecutor, the defendant and counsel for the defendant may as a matter of right be present throughout, but such right may be waived."[99] As a general rule, the parties and their counsel are allowed to be present; however, they are not permitted to discuss their case with members of the jury and jurors are not allowed to discuss the case among themselves. For example, Kansas criminal procedure holds that while conducting a view of the scene, generally

---

[94]   *See* People v. Garcia, 36 Cal. 4th 777, 115 P.3d 1191, 31 Cal. Rptr. 3d 541, 2005 Cal. LEXIS 8226 (Cal. 2005). *But see* State v. Engelhardt, 280 Kan. 113, 123, 119 P.3d 1148, 1159, 2005 Kan. LEXIS 462 (Kan. 2005), holding that a defendant may have no right to be present at a jury view of the scene.

[95]   Andika v. State, 2005 Tex. App. LEXIS 4862 (2005).

[96]   *See* NY CLS CPL § 270.50 Trial jury; viewing of premises (Matthew Bender 2009).

[97]   State v. Dalluge, 2005 Wash. App. LEXIS 450 (2005).

[98]   State v. Campbell, 2006 Tenn. Crim. App. LEXIS 584 (2006).

[99]   NY CLS CPL § 270.50 Trial jury; viewing of premises (Matthew Bender 2009).

"no person other than the officer and the person appointed to show them the place shall speak to them on any subject connected with the trial."[100]

In criminal cases, most states permit the accused to be present; in others, allowing the accused to be present is within the discretion of the judge. For example, in one state, "[t]he accused has the right to attend such view by the jury, but may waive this right."[101] While most jurisdictions do not permit jurors to ask questions at the scene, there are situations in which a judge may permit juror questions. Inevitably, what the jurors see at a view of the scene will be used in reaching a verdict; therefore, viewing the scene must be carefully planned and the activities at the scene must be kept under close supervision. A defendant may base an appeal on crime scene views if prejudice to the case resulted from the viewing.[102]

§ 14.6   Photographs

As mentioned in previous sections, it is often possible to exhibit the person of the victim to the jury or judge, to introduce articles connected with the crime, or to have the jury view the scene of the crime. In other instances, it is impracticable to bring all of the tangible evidence before the court. On the other hand, it is often impossible to define tangible evidence and properly convey its importance by words alone. Photographs, if properly taken and explained, bring this type of evidence into court in a more convenient fashion. Photographs frequently convey information to the court and jury more accurately than words. Although photos are merely graphic representations of the oral testimony of witnesses, they often have far greater value than words and may pose a risk of unfair prejudice because of the chance that jurors may be swayed by emotion or vindictiveness.

When a party desires to introduce photographs that have relevance to the case, the trial judge has discretion to admit or refuse the photo evidence based on the judge's evaluation of whether the photographs pose a danger of unfair prejudice or whether the probative value outweighs any potential for prejudice. Evidence (including photographs) can be excluded where there is a danger of creating a "confusion of the issues, or misleading the jury, or by considerations of undue delay, waste of time, or needless presentation of cumulative evidence."[103] Precisely how this calculation is made varies with the case, the need for the evidence, and the perception of the judge. In considering the admissibility of photographs, the Supreme Court of Arkansas suggested that:

> When photographs are helpful to explain testimony, they are ordinarily admissible. Further, the mere fact that a photograph is inflammatory or is

---

[100]   K.S.A. § 22-3418 View of place of crime (2008).

[101]   Ohio Rev. Code Ann. 2945.16 (Matthew Bender 2009).

[102]   State v. Matthis, 970 So. 2d 505, 2007 La. LEXIS 2389 (La. 2007).

[103]   Fed. R. Evid. 403.

cumulative is not, standing alone, sufficient reason to exclude it. Even the most gruesome photographs may be admissible if they assist the trier of fact in any of the following ways: by shedding light on some issue, by proving a necessary element of the case, by enabling a witness to testify more effectively, by corroborating testimony, or by enabling jurors to better understand the testimony. Other acceptable purposes are to show the condition of the victims' bodies, the probable type or location of the injuries, and the position in which the bodies were discovered. Absent an abuse of discretion, this court will not reverse a trial court for admitting photographs into evidence.[104]

This passage offers some standards to judge whether to admit a photograph and does not simply mean that any and all photographs should be admitted into evidence. To be properly considered for admission, the trial judge must evaluate the probative value and consider the prejudicial effect in the exercise of judicial discretion.

Unless photographs were part of the crime such as would be the case in child pornography or extortion by use of a photograph, photographs are generally inadmissible as original or substantive evidence. However, as demonstrative real evidence, photographs should be admissible where they help the witness explain testimony or assist the jury in understanding the testimony of a witness. As one court noted, "Even the most gruesome photographs may be admissible if they assist the trier of fact by shedding light on some issue, proving a necessary element of the case, enabling a witness to testify more effectively, corroborating testimony, or enabling jurors to better understand the testimony."[105] The same court upheld the admission of photographs of the victim's dead body at the crime scene and two photographs taken during the victim's autopsy. The reviewing court agreed with the admissibility of the photos because the pictures at the crime scene were useful to show how the crime scene appeared and the others demonstrated the nature of the victim's wounds.[106]

The proponent of photographic evidence must supply the court with a proper foundation prior to admission into evidence. Federal Rule of Evidence 901 requires authentication or identification that an item of evidence is what its proponent claims. In the case of a photograph, the person who took the photo presumably could offer evidence concerning where, when, how, and under what circumstances he or she took the photo. A photo may be authenticated by anyone who has sufficient knowledge to prove that the contents of a photo depict what it purports to depict. For example, in a stabbing case, the defendant objected to the admission of photographs by a police officer who did not take the picture, but was able to state that he was present and observed the stab wounds and the wounds were accurately depicted in the photographs at issue.[107]

---

[104]   Davis v. State, 350 Ark. 22, 35, 84 S.W.3d 427, 435, 2002 Ark. LEXIS 446 (2002).

[105]   Holloway v. State, 2005 Ark. LEXIS 497 (Ark. 2005).

[106]   *Id.*

[107]   State v. High Elk, 330 Mont. 259, 265, 127 P.3d 432, 436, 2006 Mont. LEXIS 6 (2006).

Additionally, the prosecutor obtained the officer's testimony that he observed the victim's wounds when he first arrived at the crime location and when medical personnel treated the victim, both at the crime scene and at the hospital. The reviewing court rejected the defendant's arguments concerning lack of proper foundation and noted that the admission of photographic evidence lies within the sound discretion of the trial court. To be admissible, a photograph must first be made a part of a qualified person's testimony. Someone, often a law enforcement officer, must serve as its testimonial sponsor; in other words, it must be verified. A photograph may not be received by itself, but must be brought to court by a witness and authenticated as genuine and correctly representing what it purports to represent.[108]

A trial court has broad discretion to determine the admissibility of photographs and videotapes by weighing the probative value of such evidence against its unfair prejudicial effect.[109] For example, autopsy photographs may be admissible when they help explain the other evidence in the case. In a case in which a defendant was accused of strangling the victim and then setting fire to her apartment in an effort to cover up his crime, the judge allowed some gruesome photographs of the victim's body into evidence.[110] The defendant argued that no one was disputing the victim's death and the photos failed to show any injury to the throat of the victim. The prosecution contended that the autopsy photos helped to demonstrate the pathologist's testimony that the deceased was dead prior to the fire because the photographs showed that her back, which was next to the floor, was not as badly burned as the rest of her body and they also indicated her prior death because if she had been attempting to escape the fire, her body would have been more evenly burned. The reviewing court upheld the admission of the somewhat gruesome photographs of the deceased murder victim noting that "If a photograph illustrates or makes clear some controverted issue in a homicide case, a proper foundation having been laid, it may be received, even if gruesome."[111]

In addition to being properly verified or identified, photographic evidence will not be admitted unless it is relevant and necessary. Photographs are generally admissible to prove facts at issue in a criminal case, if they have a tendency to prove or disprove some disputed point or if the photographs offer corroboration of other evidence. Even photographs that might inflame the passions of the jury may be admissible where there is a need for the evidence and the prejudicial value is not outrageously high. In one case in which the court admitted extensive autopsy photographs that the defendant argued were unfairly prejudicial, the appellate court approved the introduction of the

---

[108] 3 WIGMORE, EVIDENCE § 794 (3d ed. 1970); *see also* Phillips v. State, 550 N.E.2d 1290 (Ind. 1990), which held that photographs are generally admissible if they depict an object or scene that a witness would be permitted to describe in his or her testimony.

[109] State v. Davlin, 272 Neb. 139, 158, 719 N.W.2d 243, 2006 Neb. LEXIS 123 (2006).

[110] *Id.*

[111] *Id.*

photographs because there were significant reasons to allow their use.[112] There was sufficient evidence in the case to prove that the defendant murdered the victim during a kidnapping and robbery spree, despite the defendant's claim of ineffective assistance of counsel based on not objecting to the introduction of the photographs. The photographs the court allowed included standard pictures taken from above the autopsy gurney, pictures of the victim's defensive wounds to her left hand, and a close-up picture of an abdominal injury. In addition, the court admitted pictures that showed internal parts of the victim's skull that depicted extensive hemorrhaging from a blunt force wound to the head. The reviewing court stated that the pictures would have been admissible even if the defendant's attorney had lodged an objection with the court.[113] Autopsy photographs that may be cumulative are not always excluded.

A defendant cannot prevent the prosecution from using photographs by conceding or admitting that a deceased died from a gunshot wound, or from a beating, or from specific injuries. It has often been stated that the is no rule that requires a prosecutor to try a case based on stipulations,[114] so by removing some issues from the contest, a defendant cannot defeat the use of photographs by the prosecution. Even after an offer of a stipulation, the prosecution may introduce photographs because they help present the true story of a case and may be helpful to a jury in rendering a verdict or a sentence and therefore remain relevant.[115]

In allowing admission of a photograph that arguably possessed strong prejudicial value, a federal trial court did not commit error when it permitted the prosecution to introduce a photograph of the defendant wearing jail clothes.[116] The prosecution contended that the defendant had killed a fellow American Indian but the defendant claimed self-defense, stating that the victim threw a punch, clipping him in the chin. Following the defendant's arrest, the government took his picture to help refute the self-defense argument because the picture demonstrated that the defendant was uninjured on the day of the killing. The trial court gave a limiting instruction to the jury concerning the jail clothing that the jury was not to infer guilt from the dress of the defendant in the picture. The Court of Appeals for the Eighth Circuit refused to disturb the conviction and held that the photograph, though somewhat prejudicial, had been properly admitted.

In several cases the question has arisen as to whether it is necessary to follow the rules relating to the chain of custody as discussed in § 14.2. Still photographs and video movies are treated differently from instrumentalities of the crime or fungible drugs that do not necessarily have unique qualities. In a

---

[112] Eggers v. State, 914 So. 2d 883, 914, 2004 Ala. Crim. App. LEXIS 266 (2004).

[113] Id.

[114] Green v. Commonwealth, 197 S.W.3d 76, 2006 Ky. LEXIS 140 (Ky. 2006), quoting Payne v. Commonwealth, 623 S.W.2d 867, 877 (Ky. 1981).

[115] Green v. Commonwealth, 197 S.W.3d 76, 2006 Ky. LEXIS 140 (Ky. 2006).

[116] United States v. Two Crow, 178 Fed. Appx. 610, 2006 U.S. App. LEXIS 11165 (8th Cir. 2006).

prosecution in which a security camera captured the crime and getaway, the prosecution played the video for the jury and made a few still photos from the video that were introduced over the defendant's objection on chain of custody grounds. The video and the still photographs did not require any proof of chain of custody because witnesses authenticated the pictures by testifying to their genuine quality.[117] The fact that it is not necessary to establish the chain of custody of a photograph, however, does not mean that it may be used without authentication. Evidence must be introduced to demonstrate that the photograph constitutes a genuine representation of the object or scene depicted.

Not all photographs are admissible, even when a proper foundation is laid. If, in obtaining a photograph, the state violates the Constitution the defendant has constitutional grounds to object to its admissibility. In the case of *California v. Ciraolo*, police officers took an airplane flight over the defendant's backyard and photographed marijuana under cultivation.[118] The United States Supreme Court held that the photographs were lawfully taken from a public vantage point and no constitutional violation occurred. However, when officers use infrared photography without a warrant to scan a home or apartment for extra heat escaping from the building that might indicate marijuana production, the image produced can be suppressed from admission in court due to the Fourth Amendment violation.[119]

A. Posed Photographs

Some courts will allow the introduction into evidence of staged or posed photographs of attempted reproductions of crime scenes showing posed persons, dummies, or other objects. However, one court held that posed photographs of trial witnesses that were prepared for the sole purpose of allowing the jury to take them to the jury room to associate a name with a witness's face constituted error.[120] If based on facts admitted in the case, staged photographs can illustrate one party's theory of what occurred in the case at the time of the crime. In most jurisdictions where this question has arisen, the courts have held such photographs admissible when a proper foundation has been laid by preliminary testimony showing that the pictures are faithful representations of what actually took place. An Ohio court upheld a posed photo of a defendant handcuffed on his stomach with money and crack cocaine placed on his back by police. The Ohio Court of Appeals noted that "[w]e agree with appellant that the photographs had limited probative value but we do not find them misleading or prejudicial as argued by the appellant."[121] A Georgia trial court permitted the prosecution to introduce two staged photographs that had

[117] State v. Thomas, 158 S.W.3d 361, 2005 Tenn. LEXIS 135 (Tenn. 2005).

[118] California v. Ciraolo, 476 U.S. 267, 106 S. Ct. 1809, 90 L. Ed. 2d 210 (1986).

[119] State v. Detroy, 102 Haw. 13, 72 P.3d 485, 2003 Haw. LEXIS 314 (Haw. 2003). *See also* Kyllo v. United States, 533 U.S. 27, 2001 U.S. LEXIS 4487 (2001).

[120] State v. Chomnarith, 654 N.W.2d 660, 666, 2003 Minn. LEXIS 2 (Minn. 2003).

[121] State v. Owings, 2006 Ohio 4281 (Ohio 2006).

been designed to demonstrate the trajectory of a fatal bullet.[122] In that case, the Supreme Court of Georgia approved of the prosecutor's use of the staged photographs to test and determine whether a person could shoot through the roof of an automobile while sitting in the passenger seat. In a different case, the Supreme Court of Georgia approved the use of a staged photograph of a police officer holding a particular stance to demonstrate the trajectory of a fatal bullet. According to the court, there was no abuse of discretion by the trial court.[123] In recent years, posed photographs have seen diminished use in criminal trials, probably because of computer-generated animations and some reluctance of courts to admit posed photographs.

B. *Gruesome Photographs*

As a general rule, trial courts are rarely reversed based on abuse of discretion in the admission of photographs that might be classified as gruesome or inflammatory. There is the requirement that the probative value of the photographs outweigh the risk of unfair prejudice, but that measuring concept remains a rather subjective device so that appellate courts often choose to defer to the trial court judgment. An Arkansas court noted:

> Even the most gruesome photographs may be admissible if they assist the trier of fact by shedding light on some issue, by proving a necessary element of the case, by enabling a witness to testify more effectively, by corroborating testimony, or by enabling jurors to better understand the testimony. Other acceptable purposes are to show the condition of the victim's body, the probable type or location of the injuries, and the position in which the body was discovered.[124]

On the other hand, a different court held that photographs that are gruesome or inflammatory and lack any evidentiary purpose should be excluded.[125] After making this general observation, a Mississippi court noted that when deciding on the admissibility of gruesome photographs, the trial judge must consider: (1) whether the proof is absolute or in doubt as to the identity of the guilty party; (2) whether the photographs are necessary evidence or simply a ploy on the part of the prosecutor to arouse passion and prejudice in the jury. A New York appellate court approved the admission of photographs of a deceased victim as well as photographs of the crime scene because the trial court found the photographs were relevant to various trial issues and helped corroborate the testimony of a surviving victim.[126]

While many defendants base their appeals partially on alleged error in the admission of prejudicial photographs, few are ever successful on this ground.

---

[122] Grier v. Georgia, 273 Ga. 363, 541 S.E.2d 369, 2001 Ga. LEXIS 56 (2001).
[123] Rowe v. State, 276 Ga. 800, 582 S.E.2d 119, 2003 Ga. LEXIS 549 (2003).
[124] Garcia v. State, 2005 Ark. LEXIS 559 (Ark. 2005).
[125] Underwood v. State, 708 So. 2d 18 (Miss. 1998). *See* case in Part II.
[126] New York v. Byrd, 303 A.D. 2d 184, 756 N.Y.S.2d 190, 2003 N.Y. App. Div. LEXIS 2223 (2003).

The line between photographs that are inadmissible because they unduly arouse passion or prejudice and those that have sufficient probative value remains a gray area rather than a bright line. For example, a Michigan court allowed the admission of a black-and-white photograph of the female decedent's body lying naked on her back with her arms crossed, revealing a stab wound to her neck.[127] In a Kansas case involving a rough photo, the court held that a photograph of the victim's naked body on the autopsy table with the internal organs protruding from each end and the skin in a decomposed state with portions hanging on the table, was properly admitted, despite its gruesome nature, because its probative nature showed the condition in which the body was found, the manner in which the defendant disposed of the body, and premeditation. If photographs of this type do not result in reversal, it is difficult to predict which types of photographs will find favor with reviewing courts. Another court explained that photographs have evidentiary value in homicide cases, even if gruesome, when they assist in describing the circumstances of a killing, describe the location where the body was found, and describe the cause of death, and supplement or explain the clarity of witness testimony.[128]

In Virgin Islands case, where the federal district court sits as an appellate court for the local trial court, the district court upheld the admission in evidence of pictures of a severely decomposed corpse from various angles that showed a mummified section of the body that had been exposed to the sun and a hole near the right armpit that was a stab wound.[129] The reviewing court noted, "[t]he relevance of the photographs to the fact of death and the condition and location of the body as it was discovered, which were relevant to the manner and probable time of death, all militated in favor of admission of the evidence."[130]

The general rule that can be discerned from the case law suggests that if photographs are relevant to a fact in issue and are not so inflammatory or prejudicial as to outweigh their probative value, the mere fact that they are somewhat inflammatory or gruesome does not bar their admission. If, however, the photographs have the potential to distort the deliberative process and unfairly skew the trial's outcome, their prejudicial effect outweighs their probative value and admission is improper.

C. Time of Taking

In authenticating photographs for admission in criminal cases, the photograph must accurately depict what it purports to depict so that the picture is not misleading either because too much time has passed between the event in question and the time the photograph was taken because the picture may not accurately capture the situation as it existed on the relevant date. To be

---

[127]   People v. Benore, 2005 Mich. App. LEXIS 2718 (2005).

[128]   McIntosh v. State, 917 So. 2d 78, 84, 2005 Miss. LEXIS 754 (Miss. 2005).

[129]   Krepps v. Government of the Virgin Islands, 2006 U.S. Dist. LEXIS 24904 (D.V.I. 2006).

[130]   *Id.*

admissible, a photograph must be sufficiently identified as a true and accurate representation of what it is supposed to represent. Therefore, if the time between the incident and the taking of the photograph is so great as to make it unlikely that the photograph actually portrays the situation as it existed at the time of the incident, such a photograph cannot be authenticated as accurately portraying the reality of the original event or scene and should not be admissible. For example, if a body had been discovered in the spring before ground cover became extensive, admission of a late summer photograph of the same scene with lush foliage would potentially be very misleading.

In a murder case involving a six-month-old infant, the Supreme Court of Mississippi upheld the admission of a photograph of the baby, taken when the child was alive dressed in a Christmas outfit, for the purpose of proving identity. The court noted that the photo was not offered for the purposes of inflaming the jury but fell within accepted case law allowing photographs of victims for identity purposes.[131]

Demonstrative of the principle that pictures must be taken at the appropriate time, in a homicide case, officers took still pictures of scratches on the defendant's neck, and took still and video pictures of the home where the death occurred. Later, police took pictures of the defendant's injured hand for future use during the trial. The taking of the still and video pictures had the effect of "freezing" the crime scene for future reference, when, without the contemporaneous pictures, the crime scene could not have been reconstructed.[132] So long as the photographs accurately depict what they purport to show and are not otherwise misleading, most courts will admit the photographs.

D. Color Photographs

Color photographs, color slides, PowerPoint presentations, and other methods of displaying photographs are admissible in evidence subject to the same limitations and restrictions placed on black-and-white photographs. Even though color photographs are often more lifelike and consequently may be more gruesome and revolting, the fact that a picture is in color constitutes a factor in determining whether it can be admitted.[133] In an aggravated assault case in which the prosecution used several enlarged color pictures of the victim's injuries, the defendant contended that the trial court committed reversible error in admitting the pictures.[134] The reviewing court rejected the contention because showing the nature and extent of the victim's injuries was relevant to proving the prosecution's case. The court noted that they were unpleasant to observe, but the probative value outweighed any prejudice. Because color photographs are subject to color distortion, however, it is more difficult to take photographs that

---

[131] Havard v. State, 928 So. 2d 771, 2006 Miss. LEXIS 90 (Miss. 2006). *See also* Lamar v. Georgia, 256 Ga. App. 567, 571, 568 S.E.2d 837, 2002 Ga. App. LEXIS 957 (2002).

[132] Gracia v. State, 2006 Tex. Crim. App. LEXIS 1284 (2006).

[133] Wilson v. State, 2009 Texas App. LEXIS 2954 (Tex. 2009).

[134] State v. Dunfee, 327 Mont. 335, 340, 114 P.3d 217, 221, 2005 Mont. LEXIS 225 (2005).

show the actual colors as they existed at the scene, and the proponent is often subject to a strong cross-examination on the subject of distortion.

In a murder trial, where a sober driver led police officers on a high-speed chase in which one of the officers was killed, the defendant objected to the admission of color photographs from different angles taken of the deceased officer's body in the emergency room.[135] Because the defendant did not dispute that the officer died in a car accident, he contended that the gruesome pictures were introduced to prejudice the jury. The reviewing court disagreed, noting that the pictures had a legitimate purpose, that a stipulation does not relieve the government from proving all essential elements of the case, and that a government witness can use photographs to tell a more complete story.

E. Enlargements and Aerial Photographs

Photographs that have been enlarged in the same aspect ratio generally will be admitted if a smaller print or a photo on a computer screen would have been admissible. Although a defendant will typically object to the use of an enlarged picture on the grounds that the larger picture may cause unfair prejudice, courts routinely admit enlarged pictures because they help the jury better understand the evidence. In a North Carolina murder case in which the deceased had been killed by a firearm and injured with a knife, the court permitted, over the defendant's objection, the prosecution to show enlarged autopsy photographs projected on a large courtroom screen. The court reasoned that the enlarged photos would help the jury understand the extent of the injuries received by the deceased. The photos showed two knife wounds to the deceased and the fatal gunshot wound. In upholding the use of the enlarged autopsy photos, the appellate court stated that the probative value outweighed any danger of unfair prejudice and then noted, "[t]he photographs were not used in a repetitive manner and it was not excessive to project them onto a screen for the purpose of making them more easily viewed."[136] Enlarged photographs are frequently used in cases involving the comparison of handwriting or to show the place of an accident or the scene of a crime.

There seems to be no distinction between aerial and other types of photographs insofar as their admissibility is concerned, but authentication may be an issue. In a case in which a defendant had been charged with dealing drugs within 1,000 feet of a church, an aerial photograph was authenticated and used to prove that the defendant's drug business had transpired within the 1,000-foot prohibited area.[137] In another case, the prosecution used an aerial photograph to show how far a defendant moved a victim to support a charge of kidnapping.[138]

---

[135] State v. Betha, 167 N.C. App. 215, 223, 605 S.E.2d 173, 179, 2004 N.C. App. LEXIS 2150 (2004).

[136] State v. Snider, 168 N.C. App. 701, 706, 609 S.E.2d 231, 235, 2005 N.C. App. LEXIS 395 (2005).

[137] Illinois v. Sparks, 335 Ill. App. 3d 249, 253, 780 N.E.2d 781, 784, 2002 Ill. App. LEXIS 1132 (2002).

[138] People v. Dominguez, 39 Cal. 4th 1141, 1153, 47 Cal. Rptr. 3d 575, 2006 Cal. LEXIS 9977 (Cal. 2006).

The admission of aerial photographs is not uncommon and they are usually admitted into evidence for the purpose of giving the jury an accurate view of an object or geographic scene that is relevant to a fact in issue; however, they may be excluded from evidence at the discretion of the court when the court has previously admitted other evidence covering the same issues.[139]

§ 14.7 Motion Pictures and Videotapes

Motion pictures, videotape recordings, DVD or CD video recordings, and accurate copies are admissible in evidence "once a proper foundation has been laid if the [recording] is a true, authentic, and accurate representation of the event taped without distortions or deletions."[140] The proponent of admission of a videotape recording or of a traditional movie film must lay a foundation that demonstrates that the film or video properly depicts what it purports to depict. The questions concerning authenticity are similar to those involved when laying the foundation for admission of a still photograph. The party desiring to introduce recorded motion pictures must establish that the contents of the motion pictures are relevant to an issue and that they accurately demonstrate what they purport to show. The authentication process also must demonstrate that the pictures are accurate, genuine, and that no tampering has occurred. In some cases, the admissibility of motion pictures depends upon testimony by the operator of the camera that the film or video accurately portrays what he or she observed at the time and place of the action in question. Although modern evidence rules permit the admission of film, DVD, or still photos taken in sequence that some banks use, by permitting authentication by a person who can identify the contents of the recording,[141] some jurisdictions require a more formal presentation of a foundation. In one case involving forgery, an Indiana court noted the method of proving a foundation for film cameras requires that "there should be evidence as to how and when the camera was loaded, how frequently the camera was activated, when the photographs were taken, and the processing and chain of custody of the film after its removal from the camera."[142] In this forgery case, the bank camera recorded transactions and it included one from the defendant teller forging a withdrawal record from a customer's account. The appellate court approved the admission of the bank surveillance tape showing the defendant's crime because the bank manager removed the videotape and a police officer checked it to identify the proper date of the tape. The officer watched that same videotape to match transaction

---

[139] *See* United States v. Chiquito, 175 Fed. Appx. 215, 2006 U.S. App. LEXIS 8724 (10th Cir. 2006) and Helmig v. Kemna, 2006 U.S. App. LEXIS 22564 (8th Cir. 2006).

[140] Parkinson v. Kelly, 2006 U.S. Dist. LEXIS 54661 (N.D.N.Y. 2006).

[141] *See* FED. R. EVID. 901. Requirement of Authentication or Foundation.

[142] McHenry v. State, 820 N.E.2d 124, 128, 2005 Ind. LEXIS 4 (Ind. 2005), quoting Edwards v. State, 762 N.E.2d 128, 136, 2002 Ind. App. LEXIS 50 (2002).

numbers to customer accounts with representations that were depicted on the video. In addition, the custodian of the bank's records signed an affidavit that the surveillance taping was a regularly conducted business activity of the bank and that the custodian had verified the trustworthiness of the tape. This evidence proved to sufficiently lay the foundation for the video evidence.[143]

In determining whether photos and related matter should be admitted into evidence, a Georgia statute provides:

> Subject to any other valid objection, photographs, motion pictures, video-
> tapes, and audio recordings produced at a time when the device producing
> the items was not being operated by an individual person or was not under
> the personal control or in the presence of an individual operator shall be
> admissible in evidence when the court determines, based on competent evi-
> dence presented to the court, that such items tend to show reliably the fact
> or facts for which the items are offered, provided that prior to the admission
> of such evidence the date and time of such photograph, motion picture, or
> videotape recording shall be contained on such evidence and such date and
> time shall be shown to have been made contemporaneously with the events
> depicted in the photograph, videotape, or motion picture.[144]

In applying the statute, a Georgia appellate court approved the introduction of a videotape made by three teenagers while engaging in sexual acts in a motel room. One victim proved to be somewhat unconscious during the taping, and was unavailable to authenticate the tape from personal knowledge, but she was able review the tape and to identify herself as appearing on the tape. The mother of another child identified her daughter engaging in sexual activities on the video-tape. In a pretrial statement, the juvenile defendant admitted to activities that were depicted on the tape. According to the reviewing court, "[v]iewing the circum-stances under which the videotape was discovered and considering its contents, the trial court did not abuse its discretion in ruling that there was sufficient compe-tent evidence that it reliably showed the facts for which it was offered so that it was admissible in evidence to be given whatever weight the jury chose to accord it."[145]

With respect to authentication and introduction of videotapes made by an automatic surveillance system, an Ohio court admitted a surveillance tape that had been edited by police, but that was considered to be an accurate and true recording of what transpired.[146] In the case, police alleged that the defendant and others severely beat the victim in full view of a digital video security recorder. The owner of the apartment complex, who was licensed to install security cameras, testified that he installed the system at issue. The two cameras used in this case snapped images that are identified and stored on an 80-gigabyte

[143] McHenry v. State, 820 N.E.2d 124, 128, 2005 Ind. LEXIS 4 (Ind. 2005). See case in Part II.
[144] O.C.G.A. § 24-4-48 (c) Admissibility of photographs, motion pictures, videotapes, and audio recordings (2006).
[145] Wilson v. State, 279 Ga. App. 459, 631 S.E.2d 391, 2006 Ga. App. LEXIS 483 (2006).
[146] State v. Arafat, 2006 Ohio 1722, 2006 Ohio App. LEXIS 15 (Ohio 2006).

hard drive. Each image contained the date and time of day that the system recorded it. Police made four compact disc copies of the photo images from the hard drive and an officer who was a forensic video analyst used a process called "padding" to make a virtual movie of the events. In using "padding," the forensic analyst slows down the fast motion generated by the video images taken at set intervals and weaves the images into a final product that approximates real-time viewing. Duplicate images were used to make the appearance of a seamless movie that was transferred to videotape and a DVD. The victim proved to be little help in authenticating the pictures and the movie constructed from the stills. Using the knowledge of the officers concerning the physical layout of the crime scene, the information from the man who installed the system, and the recording of the defendant entering and leaving the apartment and pulling the victim from the bushes after having severely beaten him, police officers were able to help authenticate the result. The appellate court approved the admission of the reconstructed real time movie as accurately displaying the actual events as they really occurred. Under the "silent witness" method of authentication, the evidence speaks for itself and constitutes substantive evidence that is admissible despite not having a sponsoring witness.

With respect to authentication of videotapes made by automatic processes, an Illinois court adopted the "silent witness" theory of authentication for films, pictures, and videotape recordings. A drug sting had been arranged by Illinois police officers, where police installed a camera and video recorder within a confidential informant's vehicle. The camera automatically recorded videotape evidence of a defendant selling drugs to the confidential informant. When the prosecutor introduced the videotape evidence against the drug dealer, he objected, citing improper authentication of the video, because the confidential informant did not testify. As the defendant alleged, no person who had knowledge testified concerning authentication. The appellate court held that the "silent witness" theory may be used to admit photographic evidence in situations in which the trial judge determines that the videotape is reliable after carefully considering the evidence establishing the time and date of the taping or the time of the making of the photographic evidence. The judge must consider whether there was any evidence of editing or tampering and must be sure that the operating condition ensured accuracy and reliability of the video or motion picture. In the Illinois case, the appellate court held that the judge had not abused discretion in admitting the videotape against the defendants because the officers were able to assist in authentication along with the "silent witness." Therefore, the court upheld the convictions.[147]

In a capital murder prosecution, a Michigan trial court permitted a security videotape to be admitted on behalf of the prosecution that showed the victim going into the defendant's apartment, after which she was never seen alive.[148]

---

[147] 336 Ill. App. 3d 893, 899, 784 N.E.2d 410, 415, 2003 Ill. App. LEXIS 111 (2003).
[148] People v. Rocafort, 2005 Mich. App. LEXIS 3274 (2005), appeal denied, 475 Mich. 870, 714 N.W.2d 322, 2006 Mich. LEXIS 1151 (Mich. 2006).

The defendant contended that a proper foundation had not been shown sufficient to authenticate the tape as genuine due to a lack of testimony concerning the acceptability of the recording methods. Michigan Rule of Evidence 901 accepts that authentication is satisfied when there has been evidence introduced sufficient to support the finding that the matter in question is what it purports to be. In this case, security technicians testified that the security tape system had been installed properly and was in good working order on the date in question. Other witnesses who were seen in the tape testified that the tape accurately recorded their activities on the day in question. Because the reviewing court held the opinion that the proper foundation had been laid to introduce the videotape, the trial court did not abuse its discretion in admitting the video.

Newer cases may involve computer-generated animations (CGA) that incorporate the opinions of several expert witnesses in a manner that appears as a recreation of a how a crime happened. The use of CGAs in criminal cases requires that the jury be informed that the animation constitutes only a demonstrative exhibit or an illustration that will be used to demonstrate the prosecution's theory of a case that is based on interpretation of actual evidence in the case. In one Pennsylvania case that involved a police officer as a defendant in a homicide prosecution, the trial court permitted the commonwealth to show the jury a CGA that incorporated the expert opinion of a forensic pathologist and a crime scene reconstructionist that was based on the forensic and physical evidence found at the actual crime scene.[149] Following the police officer's conviction of the murder of his wife, he appealed, contending that the CGA was unfairly prejudicial, lacked authentication, presented cumulative evidence, and should not have been admitted. The Supreme Court of Pennsylvania concluded that the admission or exclusion of computer-generated animations should be governed by the concepts of authentication and relevancy, by weighing the chance for unfair prejudicial value against the probative effect of the evidence. The top Pennsylvania court noted that some concerns prior to the admission decision carry more weight and deserve closer scrutiny than when a court faces the admission or exclusion of more traditional evidence. The Supreme Court affirmed the police officer's conviction for first-degree murder because, among other issues, the admission of the CGA did not create unfair prejudice to his case and provided relevant evidence. The Court of Criminal Appeals of Oklahoma reversed a murder conviction in which a computer-generated animation attempted to demonstrate how the defendant killed her fiancé with a firearm.[150] The court overturned the conviction because the CGA failed to accurately and properly demonstrate what actually occurred. Insufficient data existed to tell which positions each person occupied during the event and there was no data to explain the trajectory of the bullet. Essentially, the CGA filled in the gaps of evidence with what amounted to speculation. The prejudicial effect clearly outweighed any probative value offered by the animation.

---

[149]   Commonwealth v. Serge, 896 A.2d 1170, 1178, 2006 Pa. LEXIS 561 (Pa. 2006).

[150]   *See* Dunkle v. State, 2006 Okla. Crim. 29, 139 P.3d 228, 2006 Okla. Crim. App. LEXIS 29 (2006).

Traditional motion pictures, videotape recordings, DVD recordings, and virtual movies constructed by the use of "padding" must be authenticated as accurately portraying what they purport to depict, as a threshold for admission into evidence. Video evidence and computer-generated animation must be relevant to a fact that is at issue in the case and the prejudicial value cannot outweigh the probative value in order for a judge to allow the video evidence as proof in a case.

§ 14.8   X-rays

For purposes of admission, X-ray evidence generally is treated like other photographs,[151] although some slightly different admission problems may arise. The purpose of an X-ray "picture" is to reveal inner portions of the body that cannot be seen by the naked eye by passing X-ray radiation through the human body to place an image on film that is sensitive to radiation produced by X-rays. Because no person ever really sees the body part depicted on X-ray film, it cannot be verified in the same manner as an ordinary photograph—that is, by testimony that it is a correct representation of the object that it purports to depict.

In a recent decision involving the potential termination of a parent's rights due to extreme child abuse, the mother contended that X-ray images taken at a hospital should not have been admitted to show broken bones of her child because the government had not authenticated them properly. The X-rays were taken at a children's hospital that used film-less images that were viewed on computer monitors. The evaluating doctor testified that he is a specialist in the area of interpretation of pediatric imaging studies. He also testified that he was the radiologist who evaluated the child's X-ray images and that the images were appropriate for use. The doctor helped authenticate the X-rays by testifying that the images taken had the child's name and the date of the X-ray on them.[152] In this case, the radiologist who worked at the hospital that took the images, printed the X-ray image from a computer program that allowed but did not require slight alterations of the image. The radiologist testified that the computer program could alter the contrast, brightness, and could crop the edges of the X-ray but could not otherwise manipulate the X-ray image. The Supreme Court of Texas held that the trial court properly admitted the X-ray image stored on the computer and did not abuse its discretion.[153]

Some jurisdictions hold that an X-ray has been sufficiently authenticated if the evidence shows that the X-ray was taken by a qualified expert who is familiar with X-ray techniques and procedures, and that the X-ray is a true depiction of what it purports to represent. The foundation for an X-ray picture may be established when the physician or radiologist under whose supervision and control the picture was taken interprets it in court for the jury.

---

[151] FED. R. EVID. 1001(2).

[152] In the Interest of J.P.B., 2005 Texas App LEXIS 1159 (Tex. 2005).

[153] In the Interest of J.P.B, 180 S.W.3d 570, 575, 2005 Tex. LEXIS 912 (Tex. 2005).

Professional medical witnesses may illustrate X-rays through a view screen, PowerPoint display or other projection device available in a courtroom. Using X-rays in a different manner, a computer tomography imaging system (CAT scan) provides excellent images of living tissue, bone, and blood structures and the resulting images can be admitted into evidence upon a proper foundation. Magnetic resonance imaging (MRI) offers better views of living tissue and experts frequently testify once the doctor or other professional has provided a proper foundation. Similar issues of authentication arise with MRI and CAT data that accompany traditional X-ray evidence.

§ 14.9 Sound Recordings

Public sound recordings generally present few constitutional issues due to a lack of any Fourth Amendment or statutory expectation of privacy that exists when speaking in public[154] and sounds or speech voluntarily uttered generally do not implicate Fifth Amendment self-incrimination allegations. Surreptitious recordings may present both constitutional issues as well as concerns relating to authentication of the voices that may be present on a wiretap recording. Recording conversations with prior notice to at least one party,[155] such as recording a prisoner's non-lawyer phone calls, does not transgress state or federal law and the recording may be admissible against a prisoner.[156] Federal law and many state statutes regulate wiretapping and surreptitious recording of conversations, but provide for methods to properly record and to admit the fruits of a wiretap.[157] Through these laws and through constitutional protections, privacy rights are generally protected despite the advances in the ability of law enforcement agents and private citizens to record almost anything at anytime. Despite defense bar concerns that extensive law enforcement use of recording devices raises serious constitutional questions, sound recordings are frequently admitted into evidence.[158]

Recordings of 911 emergency telephone calls provide an excellent source of evidence that may be admissible at criminal trials.[159] In one case in which

---

[154] *See* Commonwealth v. Rivera, 445 Mass. 119, 833 N.E.2d 1113; 2005 Mass. LEXIS 491 (2005), in which a convenience store robbery suspect failed in his argument to suppress video and audio of his conduct and words during a murder.

[155] Some states require consent of both parties to a conversation.

[156] *See* Sanchez v. State, 2005 Tex. App. LEXIS 5084 (2005).

[157] *See* OHIO REV. CODE ANN. 2933.52 Interception of wire, oral or electronic communications (Matthew Bender 2009).

[158] Seymour v. State, 949 P.2d 881 (Wyo. 1997). In this case, the court noted that admission of tape-recordings is especially appropriate when the witness who heard the statements also testifies and the report gives an independent support to his testimony.

[159] *See* Crawford v. Washington, 541 U.S. 36, 2004 U.S. LEXIS 1838 (2004), where out of court evidence that is determined to be testimonial in nature cannot be admitted because of Sixth Amendment confrontation concerns.

an intruder had murdered a woman's husband, neighbors began placing 911 calls that were later introduced against the accused murderer.[160] He contended that the calls had not been properly authenticated because the 911 operator should have testified and the 911 log book should have been introduced to authenticate the calls properly. The trial court permitted one of the 911 callers to testify that she had recently listened to the tape and that the recording was an accurate account of her call to the 911 operator. She identified her own voice and testified that she made a 911 call on the night of the killing. In approving the authentication process used for the 911 calls, the Alabama court noted that generally there were two methods of authenticating sound recordings. One, used in this case, requires that a competent witness testify that the sound or other medium accurately and reliably represents what she or he sensed at the time in question. Under this theory the witness must testify that the witness had sufficient personal knowledge of the scene or events pictured or recorded that the item of evidence accurately and reliably represents the actual sounds or scene.[161] The other method, called the "silent witness" foundation, requires:

1. a showing that the device or process or mechanism that produced the item being offered as evidence was capable of recording what a witness would have seen or heard had a witness been present at the scene or event recorded,

2. a showing that the operator of the device or process or mechanism was competent,

3. establishment of the authenticity and correctness of the resulting recording, photograph, videotape, etc.,

4. a showing that no changes, additions, or deletions have been made,

5. a showing of the manner in which the recording, photograph, videotape, etc., was preserved,

6. identification of the speakers, or persons pictured, and

7. for criminal cases only, a showing that any statement made in the recording, tape, etc., was voluntarily made without any kind of coercion or improper inducement.[162]

Authentication for 911 tapes may in actual practice be an easier task than authenticating recordings involving surreptitious audiotaping or wiretapping, where acquiring evidence to authenticate an unknown voice may prove difficult. The fact that the proponent of an audio recording has sufficiently authenticated it does not mean that the substantive content will be admissible; the concept of authentication is a preliminary hurdle that must be overcome prior to considerations of admission of the internal content.

---

[160] Calhoun v. State, 932 So. 2d 923, 2005 Ala. Crim. App. LEXIS 101 (2005), *cert. denied*, 2006 U.S. LEXIS 5233 (2006).

[161] *Id.* at 954.

[162] *Id.*

Authenticating audiotapes and voices may pose problems when the law enforcement official has minimally dealt with criminal targets personally and talked on telephones sporadically when some conversations were taped and others were not recorded. In a drug investigation operation, a detective dealt frequently with a man named J.R., and for a large part of the investigation, did not know his true identity.[163] On several occasions, the detective met with the defendant, but did not know that he was really J.R. because the conversations were cryptic and short. Over the course of the investigation, the detective spoke with the defendant three times in person and began to believe that the defendant was J.R. The trial court permitted the detective to authenticate an incriminating audiotape of the defendant's voice as being the voice of J.R. and to state that the voiced belonged to the same person. The defendant voiced an objection that although the detective had 10 substantive conversations with J.R., the detective had insufficient understanding of the defendant's voice to authenticate that voice as the voice of J.R. The trial court rejected the defendant's argument that the authentication had to be done by precisely following the suggestions of Federal Rule of Evidence 901, while noting that voice identification only had to rise to a level involving minimal familiarity in order to be considered as proper identification of a voice or tape-recording. In affirming the trial court's finding of sufficient authentication, the Court of Appeals for the Tenth Circuit noted, "[o]nce minimal familiarity is satisfied, it is for the jury to assess any issues regarding the extent of the witness's familiarity with the voice."[164]

In determining whether to admit an audiotape recording, the judge must consider whether the probative value of the audiotape outweighs the danger of unfair prejudice to the defendant. In a federal kidnapping case in which the victim died, the trial court properly admitted an audiotape where, in remarking about the death of the victim, the defendant stated, "I feel bad about it but I'm not gonna let it ruin my life, you know what I mean. I didn't know her that well. . . . I hate to be so cold and heartless about it but who gives a shit, it happens every day."[165] The court concluded that the statement was relevant because the defendant was discussing the maid of honor at his wedding who was his child's babysitter and that it was not unfairly prejudicial to allow the audiotape to be played for the jury.

An audiotape, of which portions are inaudible, may be admitted into evidence, assuming relevancy and a proper foundation. Despite any defendant's contention, the mere fact that some portions of a tape recording are inaudible does not, by itself, require exclusion of the tape in criminal prosecutions.[166] In a case in which the defendants were accused of a strong-arm robbery, the 911 call made by the hysterical female occupant of an apartment was largely unintelligible after the defendants forcefully entered the apartment. The hysteria

---

[163]   United States v. Bush, 405 F.3d 909, 2005 U.S. App. LEXIS 7114 (10th Cir. 2005).

[164]   *Id.* at 919.

[165]   United States v. Gianakos, 415 F.3d 912, 925, 2005 U.S. App. LEXIS 15236 (8th Cir. 2005).

[166]   Benavides v. State, 808 N.E.2d 708, 710, 2004 Ind. App. LEXIS 901 (2004).

continued until long after the defendants left the scene of the crime. According to the reviewing court, the probative value of the audiotape consisted of what the caller stated before she became hysterical and the later hysteria was probative that the intruders had no permission to enter the apartment. In another case, a police officer wore a wire to record the defendant who offered the officer $20,000 to kill her husband before her divorce was final, but portions of the recording could not be fully understood. In admitting the audiotape, the court correctly concluded that the probative value far exceeded any potential for unfair prejudice and noted that the inaudible sections affected the weight of the evidence.[167]

The use of recording devices to overhear conversations beyond the area in which they might normally be heard does not in itself require the evidence to be suppressed. Section 2511 of the United States Code states in detail the procedures that must be followed when using electronic surveillance devices to overhear and record conversations. Informants and undercover law enforcement agents may use hidden recorders or wear wire transmitters to tape or record a conversation and the same agents can invite unsuspecting criminals into bugged locations controlled by police without violating 18 U.S.C. § 2515. In federal courts, as long as one party to the conversation consented to the electronic recording of the conversations, they will not be excluded unless other rules of evidence prevent admission.[168]

If one party does not agree to the recording of a conversation, the procedures specified in the statute must be followed to the letter if the recording is to be free from challenge on constitutional grounds.[169] Federal law prohibits the use of illegally seized audio information in court. For example:

> § 2515. Prohibition of use as evidence of intercepted wire or oral communications
>
> Whenever any wire or oral communication has been intercepted, no part of the contents of such communication and no evidence derived therefrom may be received in evidence in any trial, hearing, or other proceeding in or before any court, grand jury, department, officer, agency, regulatory body, legislative committee, or other authority of the United States, a State, or a political subdivision thereof if the disclosure of that information would be in violation of this chapter [18 U.S.C. § 2515.].[170]

Noncompliance with the statute renders otherwise excellent evidence inadmissible in court.

Related to sound recordings are text messages, as well as e-mail correspondence that may be sent and received on cell phones, personal digital

---

[167] State v. Jackson, 2005 Tenn. Crim. App. LEXIS 193 (2005).
[168] *See* 18 U.S.C. § 2510 *et seq.* (2009).
[169] *See* 18 U.S.C. § 2515 (2009).
[170] *Id.*

assistants, and other devices. Criminals have embraced the new technology in an effort to make their operations more difficult to detect and to provide better communication to facilitate criminal activities, especially drug transactions. Generally, courts have determined that the Federal Wiretap Act, 18 U.S.C. §§ 2510 *et seq.*, governs only the "acquisition of the contents of electronic communications that occur contemporaneously with their transmission,"[171] and the Act does not regulate data that is acquired from electronic storage by information service providers. To obtain text messages and other stored electronic data, Title II of the Electronic Communications Privacy Act of 1986, 18 U.S.C. § 2701 *et seq.*, federal officials must apply for a warrant based on probable cause that is consistent with the Federal Rules of Criminal Procedure. The warrant requires that the provider or storing entity to disclose the contents of wire or electronic communication that the holder has in storage to the federal government. Congress made this type of information easier to obtain than information gathered by following the Federal Wiretap Act, whereby, for stored information, the government need not explain why the evidence could not be obtained by any other method, prior to being able to procure a warrant.[172]

§ 14.10 Diagrams, Maps, and Models

The propriety of permitting a witness to explain his or her testimony by visual illustration is now firmly established; however, unless the illustration is essential to an understanding of the testimony, it is largely cumulative in effect, and the admission or exclusion rests within the discretion of the trial judge. A prosecutor could use a map to help a witness illustrate his or her testimony and it could either be used only as a exhibit or the proponent could move for it to be admitted into evidence. In a murder case, the court permitted the prosecution to use a map that was not drawn to scale as an exhibit but the witness described it as essentially accurate. The trial court later admitted the map into evidence over the defendant's objection. The fact that the map was not a genuine map and was not to scale went to its weight and did not affect admissibility.[173]

Authenticated maps may be admissible to demonstrate drug-free zones around schools and other locations. In New Jersey, state law permits municipalities to produce maps for the purpose of depicting the 1,000-foot boundary around school properties or the 500-foot area near public housing that is drug-free. In one case, a prosecutor used a genuine municipal map but did not introduce the municipal ordinance that approved the map into evidence.[174] The

---

[171]   United States v. Jones, 2006 U.S. Dist. LEXIS 56473 (D.D.C. 2006), citing United States v. Steiger, 318 F.3d 1039, 1048–49 (11th Cir. 2003).

[172]   *Id.*

[173]   Calhoun v. State, 932 So. 2d 923, 951, 2005 Ala. Crim. App. LEXIS 101 (2005).

[174]   State v. Trotman, 366 N.J. Super. 226, 234, 840 A.2d 952; 2004 N.J. Super. LEXIS 52 (N.J. 2004).

reviewing court held that any map could be used to demonstrate the drug-free area if it was properly admitted under the rules of evidence. The officer who testified against the defendant was familiar with the area and the area maps in general and he testified that the sale of drugs was within the drug-free area. Another public official, who was a director of the public housing authority, authenticated the map as being genuine. He demonstrated his familiarity with the drug-free area and noted that a sale at a particular point would be within the 500-foot area. The reviewing court held that the map was properly introduced as evidence and upheld the conviction.[175]

Charts may be used to show relationships and organizational structure if properly introduced and used for a limited purpose. Generally, charts should show factual data and not advocate one position or another. In an employment discrimination case, the plaintiff's attorney proffered charts that the judge viewed as advocacy charts and did not reflect what the plaintiff's attorney personally knew, but revealed what she advocated.[176] Federal courts may admit charts, summaries, or calculations at the discretion of the court under Federal Rule of Evidence 1006. The trial judge refused to admit her charts because they indicated how the attorney believed that other documents in the case should be interpreted.

Models, when properly identified and authenticated, may be used for illustration purposes if the evidence offered as a result of the use of a model is relevant and material to the ultimate fact to be demonstrated.[177] Neither an exact model nor a full-size model is required if the original is substantially represented so the model will not prove misleading to the jury or judge. If a replica of the original is used, the jury should be instructed that the object is not the one used in the crime and that it is to be considered as evidence that demonstrates or illustrates the object used in the crime. In a Virginia murder prosecution involving the Virginia, Maryland, and District of Columbia sniper shootings of 2002, the prosecution used a model of the trunk of the car from which the commonwealth alleged the shooting took place. The defendant objected that the model was "not complete" and "was out of context." The appellate court upheld the trial judge's decision to allow the model of the car trunk to be used as demonstrative evidence because it sufficiently represented the original Caprice trunk in most important aspects.[178]

Plastic models of the human skeleton and of the heart, brain, kidney, or other organs—when criminal injury to one of them is involved—are frequently used to illustrate the testimony of a coroner or other medical expert.

---

[175] *Id.*

[176] Hutchins v. UPS, 2006 U.S. App. LEXIS 19885 (3d Cir. 2006).

[177] State v. Mitchel, 56 Wash. App. 610, 784 P.2d 568 (1990). *See also* Taylor v. State, 640 So. 2d 1227 (Fla. 1994), in which the court noted that demonstration exhibits may be used at the trial as an aid to the jury's understanding, but only if the exhibits constitute an accurate and reasonable reproduction of the object involved.

[178] Muhammad v. Commonwealth, 611 S.E.2d 537, 576, 2005 Va. LEXIS 39 (Va. 2005).

§ 14.11 Courtroom Demonstrations and Experiments

While it is usually more convenient to videotape or photograph demonstrations or experiments that are performed outside of court, in some instances courtroom demonstrations are logically permitted because they more convincingly depict the situation to the jury. In order for a courtroom demonstration to be admissible as evidence, the party wishing to conduct the demonstration must convince the trial judge that the demonstration will be relevant and will be conducted under conditions that are substantially the same as the actual event to which it relates.[179] As a general rule, virtually all of the same foundational and legal requirements and elements affecting the admissibility and use of demonstrative evidence apply to courtroom experiments and demonstrations.

An experiment or demonstration may be permitted by the judge where it clearly resembles the actual event and is not unfairly prejudicial while still offering relevant evidence connected to the issues in the case. In a case involving fraud in the federal agricultural support program, the court permitted the defendant to demonstrate how the moisture content of corn could be measured and later raised by misting it and then subjecting it to a Dickey John machine for a re-read of the moisture content. The person conducting the experiment was qualified because he used the Dickey John machine to measure the moisture content of corn that he actually purchased. The Court of Appeals upheld the use of the demonstration in the courtroom because it found the judge had not abused his discretion.[180]

To be legally relevant, demonstration or experiment must meet the test of "similarity of conditions," but it is not necessary that the conditions be exactly the same, because this would generally be difficult or impossible. In a Massachusetts drug case in which a police officer used a telescope to observe drug transactions at night illuminated by streetlights and business signs, the officer radioed other officers to make drug arrests.[181] The trial court permitted the officer to position the actual telescope for jurors to look from the courthouse to a distance approximating the distance used in the defendant's drug bust. Even though the jurors looked out during the daylight hours from a different vantage point at a different distance, the trial judge allowed the demonstration to proceed. He offered a cautionary note to the jury that the conditions were somewhat different. The appellate court approved the use of the demonstration as not abusing judicial discretion and because the defendant's trial objection only concerned the lighting differences.

---

[179] United States v. Williams, 2006 U.S. App. LEXIS 21337 (4th Cir. 2006).

[180] United States v. Howard, 51 Fed. Appx. 118, 2002 U.S. App. LEXIS 23711 (4th Cir. 2002).

[181] Commonwealth v. Perryman, 55 Mass. App. Ct. 187, 193, 770 N.E.2d 1, 6, 2002 Mass. App. LEXIS 8 (Mass. 2002).

§ 14.12　Preservation and Disclosure of Evidence Favorable to the Defense

In the classic case of *Brady v. Maryland*, the United States Supreme Court decided that a defendant has a due process right to request and obtain from the prosecution evidence that is either material to the guilt or innocence of the defendant or relevant to punishment to be imposed.[182] The *Brady* material that must be disclosed includes impeachment evidence that could be useful to a defendant.[183] In the Brady case, the prosecution knew of an extrajudicial confession to murder by Brady's accomplice and Brady was never informed. The rationale of disclosure supports the view that fundamental fairness requires that the government not affirmatively hide evidence known to it that could be helpful to the rendering of actual justice. The *Brady* Court cautioned that failure to disclose such evidence following a defense request denies due process—irrespective of the good or bad faith of the prosecutor.

According to the Supreme Court in *United States v. Agurs*, the prosecution has a duty to disclose evidence that might be exculpatory for the defendant, even if the defendant does not request discovery of exculpatory evidence. Fundamental fairness requires that the prosecution seek justice and not be interested in winning the case at the cost of injustice.[184] However, the Court at the same time rejected the argument that a "prosecutor has a constitutional duty routinely to deliver his entire file to the defense counsel,"[185] even though some prosecutors do have a completely open file policy toward defendants.

In *Moore v. Illinois*, the Court observed that:

> We know of no constitutional requirement that the prosecution make a complete and detailed accounting to the defense of all police investigatory work on a case.[186]

To prove a *Brady* violation, the Supreme Court noted in *Strickler v. Greene* that the defendant must demonstrate that: "The evidence at issue must be favorable to the accused, either because it is exculpatory, or because it is impeaching; that evidence must have been suppressed by the state, either willfully or inadvertently; and prejudice must have ensued."[187] The Supreme Court of the United States held that Greene proved everything necessary to show that a *Brady* violation existed, except that he was not prejudiced because the case against the defendant was so strong that the outcome would not have changed.[188]

---

[182]　Brady v. Maryland, 373 U.S. 83, 1963 U.S. LEXIS 1615 (1963).

[183]　United States v. Bagley, 473 U.S. 667, 677, 1985 U.S. LEXIS 130 (1985).

[184]　United State v. Agurs, 427 U.S. 97, 1976 U.S. LEXIS 72 (1976).

[185]　*Id*. at 111.

[186]　Moore v. Illinois, 408 U.S. 786, 92 S. Ct. 2562, 33 L. Ed. 2d 706 (1972).

[187]　Strickler v. Greene, 527 U.S. 263, 282, 1999 U.S. LEXIS 4191 (1999).

[188]　*Id*. at 296.

The Court explained that the police officers were acting "in good faith and in accord with their normal practice" and did not destroy the breath samples in a calculated effort to circumvent the due process requirement. Therefore, the conviction was affirmed.

In 2006, the Supreme Court considered a *Brady* discovery case from West Virginia that involved evidence known to a police officer but not known to the prosecution. The conviction involved a sexual assault conviction in which the defendant maintained his innocence consistently. Following the trial and conviction, a defense investigator discovered that two of the victims had written a graphically explicit note that taunted the defendant for being played for a fool and one "victim" thanked him for oral sex. The letter squarely supported the defendant consent theory of the encounter and, if believed, could have changed the outcome of the case. A state trooper had seen the note, declined to take possession of it, and suggested that it be destroyed. Evidence favorable to the accused under *Brady* appeared to have been suppressed. The Supreme Court sent the case back for a determination of whether the exculpatory note required reversal of the conviction based on the *Brady* principles of discovery.[189]

From these cases emerges the rule that due process requires disclosure, upon the defendant's request, of evidence favorable to the defendant, but unless a criminal defendant can show bad faith on the part of the police, failure to preserve potentially useful evidence does not constitute a denial of due process of law. When the interests of justice clearly require it, the police and prosecutor have an obligation to preserve the evidence. If the evidence is destroyed through bad faith, a due process protection has occurred that may constitute reversible error.

§ 14.13   Summary

In addition to the use of oral testimony and documentary evidence, real evidence may be introduced to help the jury or other factfinders in determining what happened in a particular case. Real evidence may involve the actual objects from the crime or crime scene or they may be called demonstrative real evidence when they consist of duplicate items such as guns or knives or when the evidence was constructed for trial, such as models. The use of real evidence to assist the court and jury in determining the guilt or innocence of the accused in criminal cases has had the sanction of immemorial usage. In many instances, real evidence is more persuasive and aids the jury more in reaching a decision than does the testimony of the witness. The courts, recognizing the desirability of obtaining all the facts, have actually encouraged the use of real evidence.

With the use of real evidence, care must be taken to offer probative evidence that does not pose a risk of unfair prejudice. This may be a special

---

[189]   Youngblood v. West Virginia, 547 U.S. 867, 2006 U.S. LEXIS 4884 (2006).

concern when using demonstrative real evidence. To avoid unfair prejudice, certain rules have been established and must be followed if such evidence is to be admitted. For example, the prosecution must show that there is a connection between the instrument or article introduced and the accused, that the article is relevant to the particular case, and that the object is substantially in the same condition as it was when it was used in connection with the crime—or the change in condition, if any, is explained. Also, the prosecution must show a chain or continuity of custody concerning the article to be introduced, but a break in the chain may go more toward weight than admissibility. Alternatively, the proponent may properly identify the evidence by identifying a unique mark or serial number.

There are various types of real evidence that have been held admissible, and for each type, certain conditions must be met. In some instances, the exhibition of the person of the witness may be the best way to explain an injury. In this event, the judge in his discretion may allow such exhibition even though it may be somewhat gruesome.

Articles connected with the crime, such as weapons or clothing, may be introduced as real evidence if the prosecution can show that there was or is a connection between the properly authenticated article and the accused. Also, the judge may allow the jury to visit and view the scene of the incident if, in his or her discretion, this will help the jury in determining the facts of the case.

If it is not practicable to let the jury view the scene or to bring all of the evidence into court, photographs are admissible as a form of real evidence. Before a photograph may be introduced, a foundation must be laid; i.e., a competent witness who has personal knowledge of the area or thing photographed must testify that the picture is an accurate representation of the object or person depicted. In addition to still photographs, motion pictures, DVDs, X-rays, CT scans, MRI scans, and sound recordings may be introduced. As in the case of photographs, a foundation must be laid before such evidence is admitted into court.

With the use of demonstrative real evidence it is possible for witnesses to more effectively explain the events that occurred by using guns, knives, diagrams, maps, charts, and models. When references are made to such a diagram, map, or model, a witness must testify that it is a correct portrayal of the situation or thing represented.

Due process requires disclosure, upon the defendant's request, of evidence favorable to the defense and the prosecution has a duty to disclose exculpatory evidence even without a request. Evidence known to police or prosecutors, even where known only to one and not the other, is deemed to be known by the government for disclosure purposes.

Results of Examinations and Tests

15

It is now well established that a witness who qualifies as an expert in the science of ballistics, may identify a gun from which a particular bullet was fired by comparing the markings on that bullet with those on a test bullet fired by the witness through the suspect gun.

Roberts v. Florida, 164 So. 2d 817 (Fla. 1964)

Chapter Outline

Section

15.1   Introduction

15.2   Examination of the Person

15.3   Intoxication Tests

15.4   Blood Grouping Tests and Blood Comparisons

15.5   Polygraph Examinations

15.6   "Truth Serum" Results

15.7   Fingerprint Comparisons

15.8   Ballistics Experiments

15.9   Speed Detection Readings

15.10   Neutron Activation Analysis

15.11   Deoxyribonucleic Acid (DNA) Tests

15.12   Other Examinations and Tests

15.13   Summary

Key Terms and Concepts

ballistics experiments	implied consent
Breathalyzer test	radar
DNA	scientific evidence
horizontal gaze nystagmus test	admissibility test

---

§ 15.1 Introduction

In Chapter 14, the general rules concerning the collection, protection, and introduction of real evidence were considered. Evidence is characterized as real evidence if it is the result of experiments and tests either in or out of court, even though in many cases the evidence is of little value unless it is accompanied by oral testimony.

Although a comparatively small part of the evidence produced at trial in the usual criminal case results from out-of-court tests and examinations, such evidence is often very convincing and is certainly important in helping the factfinders to determine what actually occurred. Convictions for drug possession and related activities are often decided on the results of tests administered out of court. Prosecutions are initiated following out-of-court tests—such as having a drug detection dog sniff a car and obtaining a positive result,[1] testing residue found in trash pulls that reveal the presence of illegal drugs,[2] and testing powders found in a prison cell that indicate the presence of drug contraband.[3] Juries and judges rely on the admission of these drug tests in deciding whether to convict because most tests prove to be quite convincing. Prosecutors use scientific testing results to prove that a vehicle driver has been driving under the influence of alcohol. Similarly, DNA testing in rape cases carries significant weight with factfinders in many cases, especially where a stranger has been charged with adult sexual assault or the test indicates illegal contact between relatives.[4]

---

[1] Illinois v Caballes, 543 U.S. 405, 2005 U.S. LEXIS 769 (2005).

[2] *See* United States v. Faust, 456 F.3d 1342, 2006 U.S. App. LEXIS 18366 (11th Cir. 2006).

[3] *See* Garcia v. Martinez, 2006 U.S. App. LEXIS 24199 (7th Cir. 2006).

[4] McGregor v. State, 2004 Tex. App. LEXIS 3365 (2004).

While evidence concerning the results of examinations and tests has a great impact in criminal cases, such evidence is admissible only when it clears several evidence hurdles. First, forensic evidence must meet the same tests as most other evidence, such as the tests of relevancy, materiality, and competency. Before such evidence is admitted, a foundation must be laid. For example, in a Georgia case, the foundation for admission of the results of scientific tests of a seized sample requires that care be taken that the correct sample is tested.

> Evidence such as suspected cocaine, seized from a crime scene, is typically placed in a sealable evidence bag that can be marked with the date, time, location, suspect, arresting officer, and other particulars. The evidence should be promptly delivered to a safe, suitable storage site that provides "reason-able assurance" that the evidence will not be tampered with or corrupted. Evidence may be sent by certified mail, return receipt requested, to a crime lab and sent to the prosecutor in the same manner. The mail receipts, once identified by the witness, are admissible to help prove the chain of custody. ... For fungible evidence that has been tested, it generally is sufficient to provide the testimony of the police officer who seized and transported the evidence, according to the department's routine, and the lab technician who tested the evidence and recorded the results according to the crime lab's routine.[5]

If a sample is not labeled properly, a significant break in the chain of custody has occurred and a trial court may rule that the proper foundation has not been made for the introduction of the results of the scientific testing.[6]

If the courts have not previously accepted the results of a novel scientific test or a test that has not reached general scientific acceptance, the party seeking to introduce the evidence must demonstrate that the new or different test or experiment meets the test required for introduction in that particular jurisdiction.[7]

For many years, state and federal courts followed the *Frye* standard, which courts used for evaluating the admissibility of scientific tests and experiments. The test gradually gained national acceptability following the decision in *Frye v. United States*.[8] In that case, the court stated:

> Just when a scientific principle or discovery crosses these lines between the experimental and the demonstratable stages is difficult to define. Somewhere in this twilight zone the evidential force of the principle must be recognized, and while courts will go a long way in admitting expert testimony deduced from a well-recognized scientific principle or discovery, the thing from which the deduction is made must be sufficiently established to have gained general acceptance from the particular field in which it belongs.[9]

---

[5]   Wilson v. State, 271 Ga. App. 359, 362, 609 S.E.2d 703, 706, 2005 Ga. App. LEXIS 41 (2005).
[6]   *Id.*
[7]   Kanani v. Phillips, 2004 U.S. Dist. LEXIS 20444 (S.D.N.Y. 2004).
[8]   293 F. 1013 (D.C. Cir. 1923).
[9]   *Id.* at 1014.

In the ensuing years, the majority of state and federal jurisdictions adopted the Frye "general acceptance" test, discussing, defining, and attempting to refine it, as new and more complex forms of novel evidence have surfaced in the legal arena.[10] Many states have not adopted the different test for scientific evidence admissibility required in the federal courts by the Supreme Court decision in *Daubert v. Merrell Dow* and have retained the *Frye* standard. Among these states are Alabama and Florida, where the arguably slightly more rigorous *Frye* standard remains good law and is applied to the full range of scientific testing when court admissibility is desired.[11]

In the case of *Daubert v. Merrell Dow Pharmaceuticals, Inc.*, the United States Supreme Court held that the Federal Rules of Evidence supersede the *Frye* test for cases involving federal law.[12] The Court held that the admissibility of expert opinion testimony concerning novel scientific evidence no longer is limited solely to knowledge or evidence "generally accepted" as reliable in the relevant scientific community. The Court did not, however, sanction the wholesale abandonment of standards for admission of expert opinion or knowledge, but stated:

> that the *Frye* test was displaced by the Rules of Evidence does not mean, however, that the Rules themselves place no limits on the admissibility of purportedly scientific evidence. Nor is the trial judge disabled from screening such evidence. To the contrary, under the Rules the trial judge must ensure that any and all scientific testimony or evidence admitted is not only relevant but reliable.

The Court in *Daubert* held that Rule 702 is the "primary locus" of a trial judge's screening of purportedly scientific evidence for relevancy and reliability under Rule 104a for federal trials.[13] The *Daubert* Court stated, " 'General acceptance' is not a necessary precondition to the admissibility of scientific evidence under the Federal Rules of Evidence, but the Rules of Evidence—especially Rule 702—do assign to the trial judge the task of ensuring that an expert's testimony both rests on a reliable foundation and is relevant to the task at hand. Pertinent evidence based on scientifically valid principles will satisfy those demands."[14] The concept of requiring proof of a scientific foundation guarantees that admissible evidence will have a firm grounding in scientific methods and practices.

---

[10]   United States v. Martinez, 3 F.3d 1191 (8th Cir. 1993). *See also Fifty Years of* Frye *in Alabama: The Continuing Debate over Adopting the Test Established in* Daubert v. Merrell Dow Pharmaceuticals, 35 CUMB. L. REV. 231 (2004/2005).

[11]   *See* Arnold v. Florida, 807 So. 2d 136, 2002 Fla. App. LEXIS 743 (2002) and Slay v. Keller Industries, 823 So. 2d 623; 2001 Ala. LEXIS 439 (Ala. 2002).

[12]   Daubert v. Merrell Dow Pharmaceuticals, 509 U.S. 579, 1993 U.S. LEXIS 4408 (1993).

[13]   Rule 702 provides that "if scientific, technical or other specialized knowledge will assist the trier of fact to understand the evidence or to determine a fact in issue, a witness qualified an expert by knowledge, skill, experience, training, or education may testify thereto."

[14]   *Daubert* at 597.

The *Daubert* Court established the following nonexclusive list of non-exclusive factors to guide lower federal courts in assessing the reliability of scientific evidence:

1. Whether a scientific theory or technique can be (or has been) tested;
2. Whether the theory or technique has been subjected to peer review and publication;
3. The known or potential rate of error and the existence and maintenance of standards controlling the technique's operation;
4. Whether the technique is generally accepted or has widespread acceptance.[15]

The *Daubert* Court emphasized that the inquiry in determining the reliability of scientific evidence is a flexible one, focusing on the principles and methodology proffered as evidence rather than the conclusions they generate. The *Daubert* principles are to be read in conjunction with Rule 702, which permits expert scientific witness where their testimony "will assist the trier of fact to understand the evidence or to determine a fact in issue." In addition, the evidence must be based on reliable principles and scientific methods and the expert witness must be shown to have applied the scientific principles properly.[16] Under *Daubert*, scientific evidence brought to court by expert witnesses must be both relevant and reliable and meet the other standards in order to be properly admitted in evidence.[17]

A Colorado appeals court referred to both the *Frye* test and the Federal Rules of Evidence as links to the *Daubert* case and stated the applicable law in these terms:

> Under the *Frye* test, novel scientific evidence is not admissible unless its proponent shows that the theory supporting the proffered conclusion exists and is generally accepted in the scientific community, the techniques that are generally accepted in the scientific community exist and are capable of producing reliable results, and accepted scientific techniques were performed.[18]

The Colorado court noted that the *Daubert* test superseded the *Frye* test for federal trials.

> Under the federal counterpart of CRE 702, the admissibility of scientific evidence, "novel" or otherwise, now rests on several considerations, including: (1) whether the theory or technique is or can be tested; (2) whether a theory or technique has been subjected to peer review and publication; (3) whether a technique has a known or potential rate of error; (4) whether

---

[15]   *Daubert* at 593.
[16]   Smith v. Cangieter, 2006 U.S. App. LEXIS 23085 (8th Cir. 2006).
[17]   United States v. McGinnis, 2006 U.S. App. LEXIS 24451 (5th Cir. 2006), quoting Pipitone v. Biomatrix, Inc., 288 F.3d 239, 244–45 (5th Cir. 2002).
[18]   People v. Brooks, 950 P.2d 649, 652, 1997 Colo. App. LEXIS 183 (1997).

a technique's operation is controlled by existing and maintained standards; and (5) whether the theory or technique is generally accepted in the scientific community.[19]

According to the Colorado court, where scientific expertise was not helpful or where the evidence could be presented by laypersons or non-scientific experts, any test for admissibility of scientific evidence did not apply. The Colorado court noted:

> If the proffered evidence does not depend upon any scientific device, method, or process, neither the *Frye* nor the *Daubert* test for admissibility applies.[20]

The proponent of the scientific evidence has the burden of proving its relevancy as well as its scientific reliability, both of which are deemed proven where a particular court has previously approved the use of a particular scientific test.[21]

Once a test for admissibility of scientific evidence has been approved in a substantial number of courts, the trial judge may judicially notice (without receiving evidence) that the procedure has been established with verifiable certainty, or that it rests on the laws of nature.[22]

§ 15.2　Examination of the Person

Examination of the body of the defendant in a criminal case in a reasonable manner is not considered violative of his or her constitutional right of privacy or his or her privilege against self-incrimination. Both federal and state courts have usually held that the privilege against self-incrimination as protected by the Fifth Amendment to the United States Constitution offers no protection against being compelled to submit to fingerprinting, photographing, or measurements; to write or speak for identification; to appear in court; to stand; to assume a stance; to walk; or to make a particular gesture.[23] The courts have allowed procedures that involve minor interferences—for purposes of identification—with the person of individuals charged with crimes. Numerous cases uphold reasonable out-of-court identification procedures against claims of violation of the Fifth Amendment; for example, requiring the prisoner to try on a blouse that fit him;[24] requiring the accused to submit to

---

[19]　*Id.*

[20]　*Id.*

[21]　United States v. Dien Vy Phung, 127 Fed. Appx. 594, 2005 U.S. App. LEXIS 6146 (3d Cir. 2005).

[22]　Gentry v. State, 443 S.E.2d 667 (Ga. Ct. App. 1994).

[23]　Schmerber v. California, 384 U.S. 757, 86 S. Ct. 1826, 16 L. Ed. 2d 908 (1966). *See* case in Part II at cases relating to Chapter 14. See also Chapter 16 for additional discussion of the privilege against self-incrimination.

[24]　Holt v. United States, 218 U.S. 245, 31 S. Ct. 2, 54 L. Ed. 1021 (1910); State v. Lerner, 308 A.2d 324 (R.I. 1973).

a lineup;[25] ordering an accused to give a voice sample at trial for identification purposes;[26] examination of a defendant's body for traces of blood;[27] ordering a subject to give his name,[28] examination of the body for marks and bruises;[29] and requiring the defendant to remove items of clothing or to assume poses.[30] Similarly, taking saliva samples from a convicted defendant does not violate the Fifth Amendment,[31] and requiring a person convicted of theft to give a saliva sample as a condition of federal probation violates no constitutional provision.[32]

In both homicide and wrongful death cases, the results of an autopsy of the body of the deceased by a trained pathologist can be introduced as evidence in a court. The pathologist may offer testimony concerning the condition of the body, the cause of death, and the injuries sustained. Examination of the body generally includes photographs that the doctor may have taken during an autopsy. Crime scene pictures taken by the medical examiner may be introduced to illustrate the injuries sustained by a deceased and to support an expert opinion on the cause of death. The medical examiner's report is admissible as to his or her anatomical findings, anatomical diagnosis, and cause of death.

§ 15.3 Intoxication Tests

Intoxication may be scientifically determined by testing the subject's blood, breath, urine, or saliva. Evidence resulting from such out-of-court tests is usually admissible. Types of tests and limitations on the use of such evidence are discussed in the following paragraphs.

A. Blood Tests

Statutes in the several states have amended their driving while intoxicated statutes to hold that a driver is considered to be in violation of the law when the blood-alcohol content is .08 percent or higher. Many states formerly did not recognize intoxication until it reached .15 percent blood-alcohol content. Demonstrative of this change in state law is the Alaska statute.

> Sec. 28.35.030. Operating a vehicle, aircraft or watercraft while under the influence of an alcoholic beverage, inhalant, or controlled substance

---

[25]   United States v. Gaines, 2006 U.S. App. LEXIS 22584 (7th Cir. 2006).

[26]   Hubanks v. Frank, 392 F.3d 926, 932, 2004 U.S. App. LEXIS 26791 (7th Cir. 2004).

[27]   McFarland v. United States, 150 F.2d 593 (D.C. Cir. 1945); Brattain v. Herron, 309 N.E.2d 150 (Ind. 1974).

[28]   *See* Hiibel v. Sixth Judicial District Court, 542 U.S. 177, 2004 U.S. LEXIS 4385 (2004) and United States v. Doe, 128 Fed. Appx. 179, 2005 U.S. App. LEXIS 5707 (2d Cir. 2005).

[29]   Leeper v. Texas, 139 U.S. 462 (1891).

[30]   Gilbert v. United States, 366 F.2d 923 (9th Cir. 1966); United States v. Robertson, 19 F.3d 1318 (10th Cir. 1994).

[31]   Wilson v. Wilkinson, 2009 U.S. Dist. LEXIS 31895 (S.D. Ohio 2009).

[32]   *See* United States v. Hand, 2006 U.S. App. LEXIS 17715 (11th Cir. 2006).

(a) A person commits the crime of driving while under the influence of an alcoholic beverage, inhalant, or controlled substance if the person operates or drives a motor vehicle or operates an aircraft or a watercraft

  (1) while under the influence of an alcoholic beverage, intoxicating liquor, inhalant, or any controlled substance, singly or in combination; or

  (2) and if, as determined by a chemical test taken within four hours after the alleged operating or driving, there is 0.08 percent or more by weight of alcohol in the person's blood or 80 milligrams or more of alcohol per 100 milliliters of blood, or if there is 0.08 grams or more of alcohol per 210 liters of the person's breath.[33]

A driver may be proven to violate the Alaska law by objective evidence that the driver was under the influence of an intoxicant by proving behavior consistent with impairment, even at levels below .08. This provision becomes particularly useful when a problem exists in a blood or breath test and the results are excluded from evidence. Alaska law and its jury instructions require that the .08 blood-alcohol content be proven to have existed at the time the person operated the motor vehicle and not at a later time.[34]

A number of cases involving blood tests and constitutional issues spawned by the collection of blood and introduction into evidence of blood results have reached the Supreme Court of the United States. Litigants complained of search-and-seizure and self-incrimination violations. Over last 50 years, most of the important constitutional issues have been decided with the result that legal issues involving driving while intoxicated cases have been determined and can be considered settled law.

In *Breithaupt v. Abram*,[35] police officers caused blood to be drawn from the driver of an automobile involved in an accident, and medical staff conducted a blood-alcohol test. The Court found that there was ample justification for the conclusion that the driver was under the influence of alcohol. The Court determined that because a physician drew the blood in a medically acceptable manner in a hospital environment, there was no violation of the driver's constitutional rights, even though the driver was unconscious at the time the blood was drawn and had no opportunity to object to the procedure. The Court affirmed the conviction resulting from the use of the test, holding that under the circumstances, the withdrawal did not offend fundamental concepts of due process under the Fourteenth Amendment.

In a landmark case, *Schmerber v. California*,[36] the Supreme Court held that the extraction and testing of blood samples from the accused while he was in

[33] ALASKA STAT. § 28.35.030. Operating a vehicle, aircraft or watercraft while under the influence of an alcoholic beverage, inhalant, or controlled substance (Matthew Bender 2009).

[34] Peters v. State, 2007 Alas. App. LEXIS 158 (Alas. 2007).

[35] 352 U.S. 432, 77 S. Ct. 408, 1 L. Ed. 2d 448 (1957).

[36] 384 U.S. 757, 1966 U.S. LEXIS 1129 (1966). *See* case in Part II at cases relating to Chapter 14. *See also* Winston v. Lee, 470 U.S. 753, 105 S. Ct. 1611, 84 L. Ed. 2d 662 (1985), in which reference was made to the balancing test approved in the *Schmerber* case.

the hospital after being arrested for driving under the influence of intoxicating liquor had been conducted in a reasonable manner and did not violate his rights under the Fourth Amendment to be free from unreasonable searches. The Court also decided that the physician's withdrawal of a blood sample at the direction of a police officer and the admission of the blood analysis against Schmerber did not deny him due process of law. Neither was the evidence excludable on the theory that it violated the defendant's Fifth Amendment privilege against self-incrimination, which states that a person should not be compelled in a criminal case to be a witness against himself. The Court held that the blood evidence was not of a testimonial nature, but was more of a scientific fact.

Proving impairment may be made by proof of objective conduct by the driver or by a finding of a prohibited level of alcohol in the driver's blood. In 2006, a Missouri court of appeals held that proof that a driver had a .08 percent or greater blood-alcohol content was sufficient for a license revocation. Under Missouri law, the driver may request a trial to litigate whether the blood-alcohol content was actually at, above, or below the .08 percent. Proof of a valid probable cause arrest and proof of a greater than .08 percent blood-alcohol content creates the presumption that the driver was intoxicated. In order to avoid a conviction, the driver has an opportunity to introduce evidence that the blood-alcohol content was less than .08 percent.[37]

B. Breath Tests

A doctor, chemist, or medical technician with the proper equipment can determine the level of alcohol in the blood from a blood sample. Due to the inconvenience and cost of obtaining and analyzing a blood sample, other means have been invented to determine blood-alcohol content without actually taking blood. The law enforcement use of breath samples has become common and has the advantage of being more convenient and less painful. In developing probable cause for arrest, many jurisdictions use a non-admissible preliminary blood-alcohol test that a motorist generally may refuse without consequence.[38] The breath test that police use that is more accurate than the preliminary portable roadside models and is admissible if conducted according to the manufacturer's instructions. The admissible breath test has the advantage of being administered by a law enforcement officer, while generally a physician or nurse is needed when blood is to be drawn.

In the use of devices such as "Breathalyzers," "Intoxilyzers," "Alcosensor IV," and other "alcometers," the blood-alcohol content is determined by a formula applied to a test of the breath of the subject, who is required to blow deep lung or alveolar air into a collection device. Different detectors operate

---

[37]   *See* Kaufman v. Director of Revenue, 193 S.W.3d 300, 2006 Mo. App. LEXIS 215 (2006).

[38]   *See* Wis. Stat. § 343.303 Preliminary breath screening test.(2006). *But see* Blank v. State, 2006 Alaska App. LEXIS 144 (2006), where the preliminary test refers only to the time of administration and not to a diagnostic test to determine probable cause.

on separate scientific theories. For example, the modern Breathalyzer brand alcohol detectors have the subject breathe into the device. The breath thus captured is allowed to expel itself through a tube containing a mixture of sulphuric acid, potassium dichromate, silver nitrate, and water. The sulphuric acid removes the alcohol from the air and forms a liquid solution and the alcohol reacts with the potassium dichromate to create a color change in the solution that can be compared to a control solution. This change of color is directly related to the amount of alcohol in the breath sample that the Breathalyzer operator can determine by manipulating the machine's controls.[39]

The major emphasis on apprehending, punishing, and deterring the drinking driver has led to novel methods of attacking the problem. While the traditional driving while intoxicated or driving under the influence of alcohol prosecution continues to be addressed criminally, some states have devised alternative methods to remove drinking drivers from the road. For example, Illinois provides that a person suspected of driving under the influence may be asked to take a preliminary breath test, which the driver may refuse. The results of the preliminary blood test are not admissible against the driver in a driving while intoxicated prosecution. If the officer has probable cause to arrest even in the absence of the preliminary breath test, the officer may arrest and request that the motorist take the admissible breath test. If the motorist refuses to take the admissible blood-alcohol test, under state law, the driver's license is administratively suspended for a minimum of 12 months[40] and may still be prosecuted for driving under the influence. If the driver consents and takes the test with the results indicating a prohibited blood-alcohol level, that test may be admitted against the arrestee in court.[41]

Before evidence regarding breath test results is admissible in a criminal prosecution, the party offering the evidence must establish a proper foundation for the machine and that it was operated properly.[42] The standards for each machine are somewhat different and states have protocols to assure that breath analysis machines are working properly. For example, in establishing a proper foundation for breath evidence, a Georgia appellate court approved the admissibility of breath tests conducted with the Intoxilyzer 5000 by an officer who had completed a training course covering that specific model machine and held a proper and current state permit to operate the machine.[43] A copy of the state permit was introduced in the court and a separate certificate showed that the

---

[39]   See Craig Freudenrigh, *How Breathalyzers Work.* May 2009. Available at: http://electronics. howstuffworks.com/gadgets/automotive/breathalyzer3.htm. *See also Breathalyzer Accuracy in Actual Enforcement Practice*, 32 J. FORENSIC SCI. 1235 (1987), in which it was found that the blood-alcohol concentration tended to be underestimated by the Breathalyzer.

[40]   *See* 625 ILCS 5/6-208.1 Period of statutory summary alcohol, other drug, or intoxicating compound related suspension (Matthew Bender 2009).

[41]   *See* People v. Lynn, 388 Ill. App.3d 272, 2009 Ill. App. LEXIS 82 (Ill. 2009).

[42]   *See* O.C.G.A. § 40-60392 Chemical tests for alcohol or drugs in blood (2009). *See also* Goethe v. State, 294 Ga. App. 232, 234, 2008 Ga. App. LEXIS 1157 (Ga. 2008).

[43]   Lancaster v. State, 294 Ga. App. 12, 17, 2008 Ga. App. LEXIS 1094 (Ga. 2008).

Intoxilyzer 5000 has been tested and found to be in good working order before and after the officer used the machine to test the defendant's breath. Additional foundational evidence indicated that the machine passed its own diagnostic self-test and appeared to be in good working order and had no parts missing when the machine was used on the defendant. According to the appellate court a proper foundation had clearly been laid for the introduction of the evidence of intoxication.

In a different case, a defendant questioned the foundational requirements for admission of evidence produced by the Intoxilyzer 5000. Then in current use within the state, the machine had been deemed to meet the state's requirements for accuracy as long as a state chemist certified that the machine was operating properly 30 days before and 30 days after the machine was used to test a subject. In Delaware, the results of the tests are admissible under the state's evidence code regulating business records hearsay exceptions. To be admissible, "the evidence admitted must be: (1) prepared in the regular course of business; (2) made at or near the time of the event; (3) trustworthy; and (4) testified to by custodian of the record or other qualified person."[44] The officer must demonstrate that he or she possessed knowledge of how to properly operate the Intoxilyzer; the officer was familiar with the calibration process, and knew how the certification sheets were maintained by the police agency.[45] These steps are designed to provide accurate information on the blood-alcohol level and to protect persons who are tested from having inaccurate information used against them.

In many jurisdictions, the test that has been designated the Preliminary Breath Test (PBT) has been considered sufficiently reliable to test for the presence of alcohol consumption but is not usually admitted in court as substantive evidence.[46] However, the PBT can be used by a police officer as a screening tool to help determine whether a person has consumed alcohol and may assist in making the decision concerning whether probable cause exists.[47] The court held in this case that these tests, if positive, create a rebuttable presumption that the defendant has engaged in the prohibited activity. With respect to the preliminary breath test, at least one state will admit the PBT as trial evidence if an arrest followed and the traditional admissible test for blood-alcohol content indicated intoxication.[48] Most jurisdictions will allow evidence of a refusal to take either a PBT[49] or the traditional intoxication tests following an arrest.

There is no deprivation of constitutional rights involving search and seizure or the privilege against self-incrimination when a person, charged with the

---

[44] State v. Boyer, 2006 Del. C.P. LEXIS 67 (Del. 2006).

[45] *Id.*

[46] State v. Whitney, 889 N.E.2d 823, 2008 Ind. App. LEXIS 1344 (Ind. 2008). *See also* People v. Bock, 357 Ill. App. 3d 160, 168, 827 N.E.2d 1089, 1095, 2005 Ill. App. LEXIS 386 (2005).

[47] *Id.*

[48] *See* State v. Pollman, 286 Kan. 881, 2008 Kan. LEXIS 450 (Kan. 2008).

[49] State v. Logan-Price, 197 P.3d 904, 2008 Kan. App. Unpub. LEXIS 976 (Kan. 2008).

offense of operating a motor vehicle while under the influence of intoxicating liquor, voluntarily submits to a test to determine blood-alcohol level. States use the concept of implied consent to permit the collection of blood, breath, or urine samples for analysis. Statutes typically note that if a person has been driving on the roads within a jurisdiction and probable cause exists to believe that the person has operated or been in control of a motor vehicle while in violation of the statutes prohibiting impaired driving or other triggering conditions, the act of driving indicates that the driver has given prior consent to search him- or herself for alcohol impairment or drug use by operation of law.[50]

C. Urine Tests

Although the analysis of urine to infer blood-alcohol content has some advantages, it also has disadvantages. One is that concentration of alcohol or drugs in the urine lags behind alcohol concentration in the blood, so that an impaired person's urine might not indicate the level of impairment. Demonstrative of this principle is a Kentucky case that showed the defendant's urine contained bare traces of drugs while a blood test indicated an absence of drugs.[51] Further, the test results are rendered unreliable by the fact that dilution is greater or lesser according to the amount of urine in the bladder, and the person conducting the test has no way of knowing this information. Expert testimony in one case indicated that the first urine sample is not reliable for alcohol content and the second sample is the one to be used for testing purposes.[52] As contrasted with blood collection, obtaining a urine sample can be compromised by psychological stress or, in one case, physical problems. In an Ohio case, a breath machine indicated that suspect had a .07 percent blood-alcohol content, so the officer wanted a urine sample.[53] The man proved unable to provide a sample due to an enlarged prostate. On appeal, the court reversed the administrative revocation of his driving privileges because the man did not refuse to provide a sample; he was unable to produce one.

One advantage of urine testing for drugs is that while the percentage for alcohol is usually required and is reported by standard blood-alcohol tests, the amount of legal or illegal drugs that affects motor control is not typically reported.[54] The lab reports the presence of the metabolites produced by various drugs, but not the amount, and mere presence of the metabolites does not prove or disprove impairment. Because courts generally admit the fact of the presence of other drugs, this evidence helps the prosecution because a jury can give these drug tests any weight that a jury deems appropriate.

---

[50]   *See* IOWA CODE § 321J.6 Implied consent to test (2005). *See also* ALA. CODE § 32-5-192 Consent to testing; suspension of license; hearing (2006).

[51]   Thompson v. Commonwealth, 177 S.W.3d 782, 783, 2005 Ky. LEXIS 370 (Ky. 2005). *See also* State v. Smith, 2006 Tenn. Crim. App. LEXIS 145 (2006).

[52]   State v. Watson, 2007 Ohio 2804, 2007 Ohio App. LEXIS 2565 (Ohio 2007).

[53]   State v. Norman, 2006 Ohio 3362, 2006 Ohio App. LEXIS 3254 (2006).

[54]   State v. Tripathi, 226 Or. App. 552, 555, 2009 Or. App. LEXIS 147 (Or. 2009).

D. *Horizontal Gaze Nystagmus Tests*

With the development of the Horizontal Gaze Nystagmus Test (HGN), police officers have one more field diagnostic test available to assist them in the determination of whether probable cause to arrest exists in a particular case. The basis of the test is the inability of the eyes to maintain visual fixation as they are turned to the side following consumption of alcohol. This test was described by the Supreme Court of New Hampshire in 2006 in these terms:

> In summary, it is a standardized field sobriety test designed to detect nystagmus, i.e., an involuntary, rapid, back-and-forth jerking of the eyes. The administering police officer positions a stimulus, such as a pen, penlight, or finger, approximately twelve to fifteen inches in front of the suspect's eyes and gradually moves the stimulus laterally towards the suspect's ear. The officer observes the suspect's eyeballs to detect the following three signs, which could indicate intoxication: (1) the inability of the eye to smoothly track the stimulus; (2) the presence of nystagmus at the eye's maximum horizontal deviation; and (3) the point at which nystagmus, if present, begins as the stimulus is moved. The officer tests each eye and gives the suspect a point for each sign observed; therefore, a total of six points is possible.[55]

Nystagmus is a well-known physiological phenomenon caused by, among other things, ingestion of alcohol. The courts in virtually all American jurisdictions have recognized that the horizontal gaze nystagmus (HGN) test is based on scientific principles and, when properly performed, produces reliable and admissible evidence. Because the horizontal gaze nystagmus test is based on science, the HGN testing must be performed by an expert trained in its use and interpretation. A Florida appellate court reversed a driving under the influence of alcohol conviction because the officer had not been qualified as an expert when he testified in court and other evidence in the case was not sufficiently strong to make the error harmless.[56]

Therefore, as a general rule, an officer who has been properly trained in the use of the horizontal gaze nystagmus test and properly qualified in court is permitted to testify to a subject's performance and whether the test indicated intoxication. Although some evidence exists to demonstrate that a police office can estimate the blood-alcohol content from a subject's performance, a Georgia court excluded a defense expert's testimony that would have offered an estimated blood-alcohol reading. The court noted "[i]t may be an open question, however, whether the HGN test has reached a state of verifiable certainty in the scientific community as a basis for determining the numerical level of a driver's blood-alcohol level."[57] A Maryland court

---

[55]   State v. Cochrane, 897 A.2d 952, 955, 2006 N.H. LEXIS 48 (N.H. 2006).

[56]   Robinson v. State, 982 So. 2d 1260, 2008 Fla. App. LEXIS 8099 (Fla. 2008).

[57]   Webb v. State, 277 Ga. App. 355, 359, 626 S.E.2d 545, 549, 2006 Ga. App. LEXIS 85 (2006).

was more certain and held that the HGN test could not be used to estimate a specific blood-alcohol content.[58]

E. Implied Consent Statutes

Many states have enacted statutes that provide that a driver, whether licensed locally, unlicensed, or licensed in another state, is deemed to have given his consent, by the individual's act of driving in the state, to submit to an alcohol test if probable cause exists to believe that he or she is driving while intoxicated; if he or she refuses to take the test, his or her license may be suspended. For example, California law provides:

> A person who drives a motor vehicle is deemed to have given his or her consent to chemical testing of his or her blood or breath for the purpose of determining the alcoholic content of his or her blood, if lawfully arrested for an offense [specified in the law].[59]

California also provides that a failure to take or complete the required chemical testing will result in a fine, possible imprisonment, and a one-year suspension of driving privileges.[60]

The state of Alaska gives added incentive to arrested drivers to comply with the state's implied consent statute.[61] Any Alaska driver who refuses to take a blood-alcohol test when properly requested to do so commits a separate crime. The state must prove that the defendant was under arrest for driving while under the influence, that the arrestee knew that he had a legal duty to take the test, and that he or she refused to take an appropriate blood-alcohol test. Refusal has serious consequences, especially with a driver who has prior under the influence driving convictions. In one case the refusal constituted a felony and the prior driving convictions made the driving under the influence charge a separate, but second, felony.[62]

In most jurisdictions, a driver who is advised of his or her rights under a state's implied consent law and declines to submit to a chemical test to determine his or her blood-alcohol content is deemed to have refused the test. As a general rule, an administrative suspension, either immediate or within a few days, will be imposed on the refusing driver.[63] According to a Pennsylvania law,[64] the suspension of a driver's license will follow a refusal to submit to

---

[58]   State v. Blackwell, 2009 Md. LEXIS 62 (Md. 2009).

[59]   CAL. VEH. CODE § 23612 (2009).

[60]   Id.

[61]   ALASKA STAT. § 28.35.030. Operating a vehicle, aircraft or watercraft while under the influence of an alcoholic beverage, inhalant, or controlled substance (Matthew Bender 2009).

[62]   Mattox v. State, 191 P.3d 148, 2008 Alaska App. LEXIS 86 (Alas. 2008).

[63]   See FLA. STAT. § 322.2615. Suspension of license; right to review (Matthew Bender 2009).

[64]   See 75 PA. C.S. § 1547 Chemical testing to determine amount of alcohol or controlled substance (2008).

a breath, urine, or blood test. The officer must have reasonable grounds for arrest and the driver must have been arrested, and have refused to take the test suggested by the police officer. The administrative suspension lasts for 12 months. The fact of refusal is statutorily deemed to be admissible in any civil or criminal proceeding, a fact that might support both a civil and a criminal penalty.

Drivers who had lost driving privileges believed that the implied consent laws violated their federal constitutional rights and one impaired driver managed to have the Supreme Court review his constitutional arguments. In *South Dakota v. Neville*, the Court examined not only the implied consent statutes, but also the constitutionality of prosecutors using closing arguments to comment on the failure of defendants to take a blood-alcohol test.[65] In this case, the defendant was arrested for driving while intoxicated. The arresting officer asked him to submit to a blood-alcohol test and warned him that he would lose his license administratively if he refused. The South Dakota trial court granted a motion to suppress all evidence, and the South Dakota Supreme Court affirmed on the ground that the statute, which allowed the introduction of evidence of refusal to take the blood-alcohol test, violated the Fifth Amendment privilege against self-incrimination as applied to the states. The prosecution asked for a review by the United States Supreme Court.

First, the United States Supreme Court pointed out the reason for the implied consent law: that, as part of the program to deter drinkers from driving, South Dakota made it easier for law enforcement officials to obtain evidence from the drinking driver. The United States Supreme Court held that the Fifth Amendment's self-incrimination clause was not implicated because the results of blood-alcohol tests were not testimonial in nature so it was permissible to introduce evidence of a refusal to take a blood-alcohol test and for a prosecutor to comment on that failure.

As to the constitutionality of commenting on the failure to take the test, the Court stated that it was not fundamentally unfair, or in violation of due process, to use a defendant's refusal to take a blood-alcohol test as evidence of guilt, even though the police failed to warn him that the refusal could be used against him at trial. In making this decision, the Court explained, "the offer of taking the blood-alcohol test is clearly legitimate, and the action becomes no less legitimate when the state offers a second option of refusing the test, with the attendant penalties for making that choice." Summarizing the opinion, the Court concluded "that a refusal to take a blood-alcohol test, after a police officer has lawfully requested it, is not an act coerced by the officer, and thus is not protected by the privilege against self-incrimination."[66]

---

[65]   South Dakota v. Neville, 459 U.S. 553, 1983 U.S. LEXIS 129 (1983).

[66]   *Id.*, at 564.

§ 15.4   Blood Grouping Tests and Blood Comparisons

In the days prior to DNA testing and prior to the time that DNA testing became highly sophisticated and regularly admitted as evidence, general blood grouping tests often served a very useful identification purpose in criminal prosecutions for rape,[67] assault and battery,[68] or nonsupport. In a rape and murder case, the defendant argued on appeal that the trial court erred in admitting evidence of a serologist that the defendant was one of 35 percent of the male population who are Type O secretors.[69] The evidence was offered to show that the defendant could have had been the male who had sexual contact with the victim. The reviewing court agreed that this was not improper evidence, because it only indicated that the defendant fell into the suspect percentage of the population who could have been the perpetrator. This appellate court ordered exclusion of the evidence upon retrial because the risk of unfair prejudice outweighed the probative value of the evidence.

Some other examples of the use of blood comparisons in criminal cases indicate the importance of this type of test. In a prosecution for kidnapping and for engaging in lewd and lascivious conduct with a child, blood grouping evidence taken from the victim's clothing indicated a high probability that it came from the defendant. According to expert testimony that helped convict the defendant, the defendant's blood met the factors contained within the sample tested because the blood "had to have come from either an ABO Type B secretor or a nonsecretor who is PGM two plus."[70] DNA testing of semen from the victim's shirt matched the defendant's DNA profile.[71] In another case, the trial court admitted results from electrophoretic typing of aged, dried bloodstains from the defendant's tennis shoes over his objections that the electrophoretic testing did not have scientific acceptance.[72] Electrophoresis results in revealing the type of individual blood protein and enzyme patterns found in a blood sample by a method that separates electrically charged molecules but does not evaluate DNA. The reviewing court noted that "electrophoresis is generally accepted in the scientific community and, once a scientific procedure such as electrophoretic testing of bloodstains has become generally accepted, mere variations in technique or procedure go to the weight of the evidence, not its admissibility."[73]

---

[67]   Shanks v. State, 185 Md. 437, 45 A.2d 85 (1945).

[68]   Commonwealth v. Statti, 16 Pa. Super. 577, 73 A.2d 688 (1950).

[69]   State v. Duncan, 698 S.W.2d 63 (Tenn. 1985).

[70]   California v. Funston, 2002 Cal. App. Unpub. LEXIS 3513 (2002).

[71]   Id.

[72]   People v. Cook, 40 Cal. 4th 1334, 2007 Cal. LEXIS 5070 (Cal. 2007).

[73]   Id., 1345.

Some older pre-DNA testing cases are still moving through the criminal justice system where convictions were obtained based on older blood grouping methodology. A California capital case is demonstrative of prosecutions involving older blood identification science that are continuing to be litigated.[74] In this case, police discovered the eight-year-old female child's body inside the defendant's apartment inside his suitcase. Ordinarily this type of evidence might prove to be devastating to a defendant, but police and the prosecutor's office pursued blood-grouping tests that were commonly available in 1994. Using older technology, one of the criminalists typed the victim's blood as ABO type A and another criminalist identified the defendant's blood as ABO type B. In the defendant's apartment, police found the sheet in which the victim had been wrapped and found bloodstains of ABO type AB, semen, and amylase, a component of saliva. A forensic serologist testified at trial that the sample, ABO type AB, could be a mixture of the defendant's blood and the victim's blood or it could have come from an unknown third person. Police found stained tissue paper in defendant's wastebasket that, upon analysis, revealed that the tissue paper exhibited semen stains consistent with the defendant and high amylase activity consistent with saliva from the victim. Expert testimony indicated that the stains were consistent with the result of oral copulation. The blood evidence alone might have been sufficient to convict, but with that evidence being less than certainly conclusive on the issue of identity at that time in history, the evidence mentioned and other extensive evidence resulted in a guilty verdict and a death sentence.

Older science that provided much-needed evidence of identification has largely been supplanted by DNA testing because the DNA testing proves much more definitive in making identifications and is able to discriminate among different donors of blood and body material when human material becomes commingled.

§ 15.5 Polygraph Examinations[75]

The polygraph, also known as the lie detector, is an electronic device that, when properly connected to the human body, graphically records changes in blood pressure, heart rate, and respiration. These basic features may be supplemented with a unit for recording what is known as the galvanic skin reflex, based on changes in the activity of the sweat pores in a subject's hands, and

---

[74]   People v. Panah, 35 Cal. 4th 395, 414, 107 P.3d 790, 803, 25 Cal. Rptr. 3d 672, 689, 2005 Cal. LEXIS 2712 (Cal. 2005).

[75]   *See* Chapter 6, *supra*, for discussion of admissibility of polygraph results on stipulation. *See also The Re-Lie-ability of Polygraph Evidence: An Evaluation of Whether Texas's Per Se Rule Against the Admissibility of Polygraph Evidence is Violative of the Texas Rules of Evidence*, 58 BAYLOR L. REV. 265 (2006).

another unit for recording muscular movements and pressures. A galvanometer used alone is totally inadequate for lie detection.

As an investigative technique, the use of the polygraph is based on the assumption that lying leads to conflict; that conflict causes fear and anxiety; that this mental state is the direct cause of measurable physiological changes that can be accurately recorded; and that the polygraph operator, by a study of these reactions, can tell whether the subject is being deceptive or truthful. The polygraph presents problems concerning reliability, scientific acceptability, consistency, and accuracy among examiners, and operation of the polygraph still cannot answer the questions that it purports to answer without engaging detractors who present good arguments against admissibility. An early blow to the admissibility of polygraph evidence occurred in a famous case, *Frye v. United States*, where the court of appeals held that polygraph evidence was not admissible because the field of polygraph testing had not been "sufficiently established to have gained general acceptance in the particular field in which it belongs."[76] According to the Supreme Court of New Mexico, as of 2004, 27 states apply a per se rule of exclusion to the admission of polygraph evidence.[77] As the court noted, "These per se states ban polygraph evidence, including test results, offers to take the test, as well as refusals to take the test, for a variety of reasons. These courts found that the polygraph has not been proven valid or reliable or that it has not been generally accepted in the scientific community."[78] Echoing the view that polygraph evidence lacks reliability, one law review commentator compared the use of the polygraph to find the truth to the task of pinning the tail on a donkey at a child's birthday party.[79]

Taking a different view, the Supreme Court of New Mexico considered the admission of polygraph evidence and, in principle, approved the admission of polygraph evidence in the courts of the state.[80] The court reviewed the theory of the polygraph.

> The polygraph instrument records "physiological responses that are believed to be stronger during acts of deception than at other times." These physiological responses include cardiovascular activity, electrodermal activity (electrical conductance at the skin surface), and respiratory activity. In general, a polygraph examination consists of "a series of yes/no questions to which the examinee responds while connected to sensors that transmit data on these physiological phenomena by wire to the instrument, which uses analog or digital technology to record the data." "The record of physiological

---

[76] 293 F. 1013, 1014, 1923 U.S. App. LEXIS 1712 (D.C. Cir. 1923).

[77] Lee v. Martinez, 136 N.M. 166, 96 P.3d 291, 2004 N.M. LEXIS 378 (N.M. 2004).

[78] *Id.* at 185.

[79] *Playing "Pin the Tail on the Truth" in the Eleventh Circuit: Why Polygraph Evidence Should Be Excluded in Federal Courts*, 30 STETSON L. REV. 2000.

[80] Lee v. Martinez, 136 N.M. 166, 2004 NMSC 27, 96 P.3d 291, 2004 N.M. LEXIS 378 (N.M. 2004).

responses during the polygraph test is known as the polygraph chart." The polygraph examination is based on the theory that "a deceptive response to a question causes a reaction—such as fear of detection or psychological arousal—that changes respiration rate, heart rate, blood pressure, or skin conductance relative to what they were before the question was asked." [Internal citations omitted.][81]

The Supreme Court reviewed the three general types of polygraph examination techniques and eventually focused on the second theory for use in New Mexico courts.

Three different polygraph questioning techniques have been developed. First, in the "relevant/irrelevant" technique, the examinee is asked two different types of questions—"the relevant questions are typically very specific and concern an event under investigation"; whereas, "the irrelevant questions may be completely unrelated to the event and may offer little temptation to deceive." A deceptive person is expected to have a stronger physiological response to the relevant questions than to the irrelevant questions. Second, in the "control question technique" or "comparison question technique," instead of coupling the relevant questions with irrelevant questions, the irrelevant questions are replaced with control questions "intended to generate physiological reactions even in nondeceptive examinees." An example of a control question might be, "Have you ever lied to a friend?" Truthful examinees are expected to experience stronger physiological responses to the control questions; whereas, deceptive examinees are expected to experience stronger physiological responses to the relevant questions. Third, in the "guilty knowledge polygraph test," the examinee is asked a number of "questions about details of an event under investigation that are known only to investigators and those with direct knowledge of the event." Examinees are expected to experience the greatest physiological responses to those questions that accurately describe the event. [Internal citations omitted.][82]

Under the New Mexico rules regulating the admission of evidence, the judge must assure that any and all scientific evidence or results meets the tests of reliability and relevancy. The trial judge must also determine whether the scientific methodology is really based on science and whether that science will support conclusions based on probability rather than mere guess or conjecture.

In making this determination, we consider: "(1) whether a theory or technique can be (and has been) tested; (2) whether the theory or technique has been subjected to peer review and publication; (3) the known potential rate of error in using a particular scientific technique and the existence

[81]   *Id*. at 170.

[82]   *Id*.

and maintenance of standards controlling the technique's operation; and (4) whether the theory or technique has been generally accepted in the particular scientific field." [Internal citations omitted.][83]

The court reviewed some of the reasons for admitting this sort of testimony and noted that the research that has been conducted shows that the basic science demonstrated support for the theories on which the polygraph examination is based. The court considered the perceived rate of error related to polygraph examinations and evaluated the fact that a number of polygraph validation studies had been conducted with adequate results. Additionally, the court surveyed some of the peer-reviewed scholarly publications that addressed polygraph issues and testing, some of which cautioned that polygraph studies have not reached the high level of research desired in scientific inquiry, but it noted that some studies have appeared in high-quality research journals. Professional standards have been developed by the leading professional association, the American Polygraph Association, which, when followed, should produce reliable evidence, according to the court. The court concluded that the control question polygraph examination technique proved to be appropriate to admit if general standards for admission of evidence were followed.[84]

An interesting factor to which the Supreme Court of New Mexico referred was the fact that the very groups and individuals wanting to keep polygraph evidence from admission in New Mexico courts were those who used polygraph examination results in their own governmental pursuits. "Often the same government officials who vigorously oppose the admission of exculpatory polygraphs of the accused find polygraph testing to be reliable enough to use in their own decisionmaking. Federal and state governments rely upon the results of polygraph examinations for a variety of law enforcement purposes, even in jurisdictions where polygraph evidence is inadmissible."[85] The court mentioned that polygraph results have been used to determine probable cause, whether to prosecute, whether to arrest, and judges have considered the results in deciding whether to issue an arrest warrant. In order for polygraph results to be admitted, each trial judge must evaluate the situation and make an individual determination based on the facts of each case, but the clear thrust of this case was to permit, and not to absolutely prohibit, the admission of polygraph evidence that has been conducted by licensed examiners who have followed the standards of the professional associations and meet the criteria established by the Supreme Court of New Mexico.

In a recent case, the Supreme Court of New Mexico upheld the use of a polygraph examination that had been administered to one of the defendant's relatives.[86] The top Mexico court indicated that polygraph evidence was

---

[83] *Id.* at 173.

[84] *Id.* at 171.

[85] *Id.* at 181.

[86] State v. Holly, 2009 NMSC 4, 2009 N.M. LEXIS 3 (N.M. 2009).

generally admissible and would be disturbed only for an abuse of discretion by the trial judge. According to the court, any doubt concerning the admissibility of scientific evidence should be resolved in favor of admitting the evidence. The defendant's remedies include aggressive cross-examination, the presentation of rebuttal evidence and final arguments to the jury. In this case, defendant had ample opportunity to cross-examine the state's polygraph examiner and to inquire about the validity of his conclusions. In fact, in rebuttal, the defendant introduced evidence from his own polygraph examiner in an effort to show that the method of scoring the state's polygraph test was erroneous.

Prior to the *Lee* decision above, the Supreme Court of the United States had an opportunity to liberalize the admission of polygraph evidence in federal courts, but determined not to go in that direction. The case decided in 1998 involved an appeal from the Court of Appeals for the Armed Forces in which an airman had been accused of ingesting methamphetamine and he contended that he absolutely had not taken any drugs.[87] In the case, *United States v. Scheffer*, the trial court refused to admit polygraph evidence based on a unique military rule of evidence. Military Rule of Evidence 707 provides, among other things, that "[n]otwithstanding any other provision of law, the results of a polygraph examination, the opinion of a polygraph examiner, or any reference to an offer to take, failure to take, or taking of a polygraph examination, shall not be admitted into evidence."[88] The evidence available resulted in a conviction at court-martial. On appeal, the Court of Appeals reversed the conviction, noting that in that case, the per se exclusion of the polygraph evidence violated the Sixth Amendment right to put on a defense. The Supreme Court considered the case and rejected the Sixth Amendment argument while stating:

> Rule 707 serves several legitimate interests in the criminal trial process. These interests include ensuring that only reliable evidence is introduced at trial, preserving the jury's role in determining credibility, and avoiding litigation that is collateral to the primary purpose of the trial. The rule is neither arbitrary nor disproportionate in promoting these ends. Nor does it implicate a sufficiently weighty interest of the defendant to raise a constitutional concern under our precedents.[89]

The Supreme Court mentioned that the defendant was not categorically prohibited from introducing a defense because he could introduce any factual evidence he possessed and nothing prohibited him from taking the witness stand in his own defense. Writing for the majority, Justice Thomas noted, "[t]he contentions of respondent and the dissent notwithstanding, there is simply no consensus that polygraph evidence is reliable."[90] From the perspective of the Supreme Court, it appears that a general approval for the admission of

---

[87] United States v. Scheffer, 523 U.S. 303, 1998 U.S. LEXIS 2303 (1998).

[88] *Id.* at 306–307.

[89] *Id.* at 309.

[90] *Id.*

polygraph evidence in federal courts may be a long time coming, if ever. The *Scheffer* Court upheld Military Rule 707, totally excluding polygraph evidence in military trials, but the case does not prohibit a federal district judge from using discretion to allow polygraph evidence. It simply means that there is no constitutional right to have the evidence admitted.

According to one law review article, when the Supreme Court heard arguments in the *Scheffer* case, "twenty-two states allowed for the admission of polygraph evidence to some degree, and twenty-seven states plus the District of Columbia did not allow for polygraph evidence in criminal trials."[91] The author noted that in 2000, only two federal circuits, the Fourth Circuit and the District of Columbia Circuit, continued to hold that polygraph evidence was per se inadmissible.[92] With customary inertia, jurisdictions that refuse to allow any polygraph evidence tend to continue on the same path, while jurisdictions that permit polygraph under some circumstances tend to remain open to polygraph evidence on a case-by-case basis.

In conformity with the practice that most state courts tend to exclude polygraph evidence, an Idaho trial court refused to permit a defendant to introduce polygraph evidence in a murder prosecution in the absence of a stipulation by the parties. The trial judge reasoned that the polygraph evidence did not help the jury but substituted decisions that the jury should be making. The Supreme Court of Idaho indicated that it supported the trial judge's decision by citing *United States v. Scheffer*, which held that, in non-military trials, admission of polygraph evidence was up to the trial judge's discretion.[93] When the case reached the federal district court in a petition for a writ of habeas corpus, the district court failed to find that the exclusion of polygraph evidence was cause for an unconstitutional conviction despite the defendant's allegation that the exclusion violated his Sixth Amendment right to put on a defense. The federal district court found that there was nothing that was contrary to established law that lawfully prevented the state trial judge from excluding polygraph evidence. As the district court noted, "[p]etitioner has not shown that the Idaho Supreme Court's decision affirming the trial court's refusal to admit Petitioner's own polygraph test is contrary to, or an unreasonable application of, United States Supreme Court precedent."[94]

A substantial minority of courts admit polygraph evidence upon stipulation of the parties subject to judicial discretion. For the most part, this result has been achieved by court decision, although statutory provisions may achieve the same result. A few courts recognize a trial court's discretion to

---

[91] *See* Dorian D. Peters, *Per Se Prohibitions of the Admission of Polygraph Evidence as Upheld in* Scheffer *are Both Violative of the Constitution and the Federal Rules of Evidence as Applied by* Daubert, 27 AM. J. CRIM. L. 249 (2000).

[92] *Id.*

[93] *See* State v. Trevino, 132 Idaho 888, 980 P.2d 552, 1999 Idaho LEXIS 54 (1999).

[94] Trevino v. Hardison, 2006 U.S. Dist. LEXIS 27294 (D. Idaho 2006).

admit polygraph evidence even in the absence of stipulation. The Seventh Circuit Court of Appeals has adopted this approach.

There are generally three identifiable approaches to the admissibility of polygraph evidence. The first holds that the evidence is inadmissible per se, the second approach allows the evidence upon the stipulation of all the parties, subject to the judicial discretion, and the third approach permits polygraph evidence in the absence of stipulation when certain circumstances exist such as impeachment or corroboration. The approaches in the various jurisdictions are discussed below with the caveat that the decisions of each jurisdiction must be examined to determine the law applicable in that jurisdiction.

1. Some states take the position that polygraph evidence is inadmissible per se and under all circumstances. Whether to impeach, corroborate, or use as substantive evidence, the results of a polygraph test cannot be used in court.[95] Evidence is not admissible by either party either as substantive evidence or as relating to the credibility of the witness. Demonstrative of this principle, the Intermediate Court of Appeals of Hawai'i noted that polygraph examination results are not admissible in the state's courts.[96] In this case, the trial court's refusal to grant a continuance in a prostitution case to permit the defendant to find a witness who would have testified to the results of the defendant's polygraph test did not constitute reversible error.

2. Any reference to polygraph evidence is excluded unless both parties stipulate to the evidence's admissibility. For example, in California courts, according to statute, results of a polygraph exam or any reference to taking an examination or an offer to take an examination cannot be admitted in any criminal court, unless all parties stipulate to the admission of polygraph results.[97] Similarly, in Ohio courts, polygraph "results are admissible only if both the prosecution and defense jointly stipulate that an accused will take a polygraph test and that the results will be admissible."[98]

3. Polygraph evidence is admissible in the absence of a stipulation when certain circumstances exist; for example, for impeachment where the defendant opened the door or corroboration or to determine whether a defendant's prior confession had been voluntarily offered. An appellate court approved the mention by correctional officers during the penalty stage that the defendant knew how to beat a polygraph. Allowing the officer to mention the polygraph was appropriate because the defendant had "opened the door" when he had earlier testified that he passed the polygraph.[99]

---

[95] A.C.A. § 12-12-704 Results inadmissible (Ark. 2006). *But see* Rollins v. State, 2005 Ark. LEXIS 293 (Ark. 2005), in which stipulations by both parties have been admitted.

[96] State v. Cho, 2009 Haw. App. LEXIS 98 (Haw. 2009).

[97] *See* Cal. Evid. Code § 351.1 Exclusion of results of polygraph examination (2008).

[98] State v. Dunlap, 2007 Ohio 1624 (Ohio 2007).

[99] *See* Hinton v. State, 2006 Ala. Crim. App. LEXIS 72 (2006).

In jurisdictions in which the results of polygraph examinations are inadmissible in court, police still use the polygraph during investigations and as a tool to encourage admissions and confessions. Even though the results may be useless in court, statements made before, during, and after an examination may be admissible. In a Tennessee, where polygraph results are inadmissible, a suspect in a child rape case agreed to take a polygraph test concerning the facts.[100] After the examiner finished asking questions, he told the subject that he had observed deception on a few questions and stated to the subject that the child contended that she had been forced to engage in sexual intercourse. The subject noted to the examiner, "she was not forced." At the trial the court permitted the polygraph examiner to tell the court that the defendant stated that in reference to the sexual activity, that "she was not forced." The defendant appealed and offered the argument that "Tennessee courts have held repeatedly that polygraph test results, testimony concerning such results, and testimony concerning a defendant's willingness or refusal to submit to a polygraph test are inadmissible."[101] The reviewing court held that the evidence had been properly introduced against the defendant because, according to the general rule followed in a majority of jurisdictions in the United States, the introduction of voluntary statements made during a polygraph examination are admissible because the reliability of a voluntary statement does not depend on the accuracy or reliability of the polygraph.

Even if the state court has held that polygraph results are generally inadmissible, even for impeachment purposes, absent a stipulation of the parties, the prosecutor's failure to disclose to the defense that a key government witness had failed a polygraph test may be a due process violation.[102] In Bartholomew v. Wood, the defendant claimed that the state denied him due process by failing to disclose that a crucial witness on the issue of premeditation had failed a polygraph test. The Ninth Circuit Court of Appeals agreed with the defendant that failure to disclose to the defendant that the witness had failed the test was a due process violation of the kind condemned in *Brady v. Maryland.*[103]

Evidence or mention of the fact that the defendant or a witness either took or refused to take or passed a lie detector examination is generally not admissible and could create reversible error if mentioned by a witness.[104] As a Michigan court stated that, "[a] "reference to a polygraph examination is generally considered plain error, but does not always require reversal."[105] There is a difference in directly soliciting a witness to mention polygraph evidence and

---

[100]   State v. Damron, 151 S.W.3d 510, 515, 2004 Tenn. LEXIS 993 (Tenn. 2004).

[101]   *Id.* at 516.

[102]   Bartholomew v. Wood, 34 F.3d 870 (9th Cir. 1994).

[103]   Brady v. Maryland, 373 U.S. 83, 83 S. Ct. 1174, 10 L. Ed. 2d 215 (1963). *See* § 4.9 for a discussion of the *Brady* rule

[104]   *See* CAL. EVID. CODE § 351.1 Exclusion of results of polygraph examination (2006). *See also* People v. May, 2008 Cal. App. Unpub. LEXIS 7458 (Cal. 2008).

[105]   People v. Johnson, 2007 Mich. App. LEXIS 2858 (Mich. 2007).

an inadvertent mention by a witness who answers a question while casually mentioning polygraph evidence. A cautionary instruction may suffice to reduce any damage.

The polygraph examiner should receive his or her training in the lie detector technique under the guidance of an experienced examiner with a sufficient volume of actual cases to permit the trainee to make frequent observations of lie detector tests and to conduct tests him- or herself under the instructor's personal supervision. In addition, the trainee should read and take courses in the pertinent areas of psychology and physiology and should examine and interpret a considerable number of lie detector test records in verified cases.[106] Some states now require licensing of polygraph operators. To practice in Illinois, the law requires that the examiner possess a state license. To qualify, an Illinois polygraph examiner must: have good moral character, have passed the state examination, have at least a baccalaureate degree, and have completed six months of study in detection of deception.[107]

From the foregoing, it is apparent that the laws relating to the use of polygraph evidence in court are still changing. Some courts now hold that the polygraph has attained a degree of validity and reliability, and that such evidence may be admitted. Future cases and legislation will determine whether this recognition will be approved by the courts.

§ 15.6 "Truth Serum" Results

The term "truth serum" has no precise medical or scientific meaning.[108] To refer to sodium amytal or sodium pentothal as "truth serum" is a misnomer, as they have no propensity or chemical effect to cause a person "to speak the truth." These drugs do not induce a state of mind in which a person tells the truth, but instead causes the subject to speak more freely than he or she otherwise might. The use of sodium amytal can produce any one of four results: truth, falsehood, fantasy, or response to suggestion.[109] One court refused to allow expert witnesses to use sodium amytal-influenced answers to

---

[106] Inbau, F.E. and J.E. Reid, *The Lie-Detector Technique: A Reliable and Valuable Investigative Aid*, 50 A.B.A.J. 470 (May 1964).

[107] 225 ILCS 430/11 Qualifications for licensure as an examiner (Ill. 2009). *See also* § 26 V.S.A. § 2904 Qualifications for license (Vt. 2009).

[108] *See* Townsend v. Sain, 372 U.S. 293, 83 S. Ct. 745, 768, 9 L. Ed. 2d 770 (1963) (Stewart, J., dissenting).

[109] Freeman v. New York Central R. Co., 174 N.E.2d 550 (Ohio Ct. App. 1960), a civil action in which the plaintiff told his psychiatrist that he was unable to recall the events leading up to his accident, and asked the doctor to try to restore his memory. The doctor administered a treatment of sodium amytal, which placed the plaintiff in a hypnotic or semiconscious state during which the doctor conversed with the plaintiff and made a record of the questions and answers. At the trial, the plaintiff's testimony was based upon his medically refreshed memory. The court did not expressly decide on the propriety of this method of refreshing one's memory.

questions posed to a defendant because all the experts in the case agreed that sodium amytal interviews are not scientifically reliable for ascertaining truth.[110] Constitutionally, any substance that might be administered as a way of recovering or discerning the truth will require the consent of the defendant and, as a result, if any truth serum drug is to be administered, it is the defense rather than the prosecution that has an opportunity to consider this avenue.

An admission or a confession induced by the administration of drugs is constitutionally inadmissible where it was not the product of a rational free will and intellect.[111] In a prosecution for murder in which police questioned the defendant at the hospital after he had been shot by police three times, he had been recovering from surgery hours earlier, he was on significant amounts of pain medication, he had not eaten for several days, he was in the intensive care unit, he had tubes in his nose and mouth, and he was suicidal. The interrogation conducted by police under these circumstances did not produce a free and voluntary confession. The defendant's answers to police questions were delusional and a doctor testified that he was not sane or competent to waive any rights. Officers noted that he waived his *Miranda* rights so they continued to question him because he was responsive. The answers were mostly unintelligible. Other medications were withheld from the defendant that led the federal district court to conclude that withholding medication must be considered coercive. The drugs given the defendant may have had "truth serum" properties, but the federal district court granted the writ of habeas corpus because of the dangers of interrogating a person in the drugged state in which the police found the defendant.

Although excessive alcohol causes people to talk and say things that ordinarily would not be said when sober, the mere fact that a subject is intoxicated, without more, does not make a waiver of rights improper or interrogation constitutionally suspect. In an Ohio case, a court of appeals upheld a conviction when the defendant made an allegation that he was too drunk to understand *Miranda* warnings.[112] The court reviewed the defendant's tape-recorded words that he understood his rights and that he had read them and held that the effects of alcohol did not render the statement invalid or coerced.

In a case involving drug use prior to a confession, a federal court of appeals refused to disturb a verdict of murder and a sentence of death in an Alabama case where the defendant alleged that his confession had been involuntarily taken.[113] He contended that he was under the influence of marijuana and alcohol and suffering a withdrawal from alcohol at the time he made incriminating comments to police. During a post-conviction hearing, medical experts in psychiatry, forensic psychiatry, and drug abuse testified that the defendant would have been in a mixed state of marijuana and alcohol intoxication and

---

[110]   State v. Pitts, 116 N.J. 580, 625, 562 A.2d 1320, 1345, 1989 N.J. LEXIS 73 (N.J. 1989).

[111]   Hanna v. Price, 2005 U.S. Dist. LEXIS 30380 (W.D. Mich. 2005).

[112]   State v. Hill, 2006 Ohio 1408 (2006).

[113]   Parker v. Allen, 2009 U.S. App. LEXIS 8275 (11th Cir. 2009).

may have understood the basic questions being asked of him, but would have been in a situation that made it more difficult for him to control impulses. One expert indicated that the drugs used by the defendant would have acted like a truth serum and would have reduced his control over his volitional and willful processes. The state court rejected the argument that the confession was involuntarily taken and held that even if the medical testimony had been offered at the suppression hearing, the result would have been no different. The court of appeals upheld the state court's factual determination because it was not objectively unreasonable, and refused to issue a writ of habeas corpus.

In a California double murder case, the defendant offered a confession shortly after the killings.[114] The actual defense centered around his sexual and psychological abuse as a child, as well as being a victim of adult trauma. Ten months after his confession, the defendant underwent interrogation by his doctor while under the influence of sodium amytal, a short-acting barbiturate drug that has some truth-serum properties. The purpose in administering sodium amytal was to refresh the defendant's memory of the events in question. At the time the doctor began working with the defendant, the defendant could not remember what he did to one of the deceased individuals from the time he shot her until he saw her dead in a pool of blood. According to the reviewing court opinion, "Dr. Glaser believed defendant's psychological profile was most consistent with the phenomenon of 'dissociative states' in which a person is not fully in control of his or her thoughts, feelings, or behavior. Individuals with dissociative disorders are aware of the occurrence of lost periods of time or memory lapses."[115] The defendant testified at the trial based on his viewing of the videotapes taken when his doctor questioned him while the defendant was under the influence of sodium amytal. The doctor testified on behalf of the defendant and offered the opinion, based on his examination of the defendant and on his questioning him under the influence of the truth serum, that the defendant had not planned or premeditated the killing of one of the prostitutes or weighed the consequences due to his mental problems. The efforts by the doctor to use the truth serum to refresh the defendant's memory failed to convince the jury that he should be found not guilty of killing the two women. The use of the truth serum, sodium amytal, due to the defendant's alleged lack of memory, may not have influenced the jury because he made confessions after his arrest at a time when his memory did not seem impaired. After careful review, the Supreme Court of California upheld the defendant's capital convictions and death sentences.

The use of a truth serum or truth-inducing drug by the prosecution on a defendant has doubtful utility because of questions involving self-incrimination, voluntariness, and the overall issue of relevance. From the defense perspective, the use of so-called truth serums have generally not produced an outcome in the defendant's favor, whether at trial stage or during post-trial appellate proceedings.

---

[114] People v. Rogers, 39 Cal. 4th 826, 2006 Cal. LEXIS 9862 (Cal. 2006).

[115] *Id*. at 843.

§ 15.7   Fingerprint Comparisons

The first use of fingerprints as a means of identification seems to have originated in Assryia and they have been preserved in clay tablets in the British Museum. Fingerprints were used by the British as early as 1858 in Bengal to curb check forgeries by natives.[116] The courts take judicial notice of the fact that fingerprint identification is one of the surest methods of identification and that no two persons have identical fingerprints. The primary purpose of fingerprinting is the positive identification of an accused. Another purpose of fingerprinting is evidentiary, e.g., to compare the fingerprints of the defendant with fingerprints left at the scene of the crime or on an object connected to the crime. The evidentiary purpose may or may not be present in a given case.

According to Supreme Court interpretations of the Fifth Amendment, the taking and using of fingerprint evidence does not violate the Fifth Amendment privilege against compelled testimonial self-incrimination. Furthermore, warrantless fingerprinting of individuals who have been validly arrested or formally charged with a crime does not constitute an unreasonable search and seizure within the meaning of the Fourth Amendment.[117]

In a criminal case, to compare two or more samples of fingerprint evidence with a view to making an identification or an exclusion, the person must qualify as an expert to the satisfaction of the trial court. In response to a defendant's challenge that a police officer was not qualified as an expert and should not have been permitted to offer evidence, the evidence showed that the officer was able to explain the traditional rules for fingerprint identification, which included the number of matching points required to offer a positive identification. The trial judge made additional inquiries into his expertise and ultimately determined that the officer was sufficiently qualified to offer testimony.[118] In a different case, a woman who had been doing fingerprint identification for 24 years, who had compared more than three million fingerprints, and who had never misidentified a fingerprint match was qualified as an expert and was qualified to testify concerning fingerprint identification.[119] Whether a witness has the requisite qualifications of a fingerprint expert is a question within the discretion of the trial court.

---

[116] Moon v. State, 22 Ariz. 418, 424, 198 P. 288 (Ariz. 1921), quoting People v. Sallow, 100 Misc. 447, N.Y. Misc. LEXIS 809 (N.Y. 1917).

[117] United States v. Laub Baking Co., 283 F. Supp. 217 (N.D. Ohio 1968); Schmerber v. California, 384 U.S. 757, 86 S. Ct. 1826, 16 L. Ed. 2d 908 (1967); see KANOVITZ & KANOVITZ, CONSTITUTIONAL LAW (11th ed. 2008) and WALKER AND HEMMENS, LEGAL GUIDE FOR POLICE (8th ed. 2008). See also United States v. Snow, 82 F.3d 935 (10th Cir. 1996), in which the court held that asking a subject to sign a fingerprint identification card does not violate the Fifth Amendment privilege against self-incrimination and a suspect is not required to be Mirandized before signing the card, because there is no constitutional right not to be fingerprinted.

[118] State v. Lewis, 990 So. 2d 109, 116, 2008 La. App. LEXIS 1120 (La. 2008), *writ denied,* 2009 La. LEXIS 379 (La. 2009).

[119] United States v. Cruz, 2006 U.S. App. LEXIS 18353 (10th Cir. 2006).

Evidence of palmprints left at the scene of a crime is admissible under the same standards and is just as reliable and accurate as fingerprints. In one case, the trial court permitted a latent print expert to testify that a bloody palmprint that the expert detected on the murder weapon compared favorably with a known sample of the defendant's palmprint and could have been made only when the blood on the handgun was wet.[120] In a different murder case, the trial court admitted evidence of bare footprints that matched the defendant's bare footprint, some of which were mingled with the blood of the deceased.[121] Some footprints may be latent and require the skills of a latent print specialist, while some are quite visible and photography will properly preserve them as evidence.

A court that orders a defendant to submit a fingerprint or palmprint after he or she has been indicted has not interfered with a defendant's rights under the Fourth Amendment or the Fifth Amendment. In a case involving illegal aliens who had been indicted for possession of a firearm by a felon and an indictment for possession of a firearm by an illegal alien, the prosecution moved that the defendants submit handprints for comparison purposes.[122] The defendants argued against having to produce a handprint, alleging that their rights to be free from unreasonable searches and seizures would be violated if they were forced to submit handprint samples. In rejecting the defendants' Fourth Amendment contention, the trial judge noted that prior cases held that there was no expectation of privacy in the quality of one's voice and a grand jury could order that a sample be given for consideration. This principle that privacy does not extend to personal characteristics held open to the public applied to photographs, measurements, and fingerprints. The judge rejected the defendants' arguments that the forced production of a palmprint violated their right not to incriminate themselves under the Fifth Amendment. Compelling a suspect to offer real or physical evidence to the prosecution fails to violate the Fifth Amendment because the self-incrimination clause only protects against compelling verbal testimony or testimonial communications. Accordingly, the trial judge ordered the defendants to submit a sample of their handprints.

A search warrant is not necessary to take the fingerprints or palmprint of a person lawfully in custody. The fact that the person is under arrest permits the taking of a print as an incident of a lawful arrest and removes any Fourth Amendment search and seizure issue[123] but a search warrant or consent would be necessary for a person not in custody.

Although the police or evidence technicians may collect fingerprint evidence at the crime scene that an expert may use to make comparisons at trial, the government is under no duty to gather fingerprint evidence and has

---

[120]   People v. Valdez, 32 Cal. 4th 73, 84, 82 P.3d 296, 308, 8 Cal. Rptr. 3d 271, 2004 Cal. LEXIS 4 (Cal 2004).

[121]   State v. Robinson, 2003 Iowa App. LEXIS 550 (Iowa 2003).

[122]   United States v. Meza-Rodrigues, 2006 U.S. Dist. LEXIS 58619 (W.D. Mich. 2006).

[123]   United States v. Johnson, 445 F.3d 793, 2006 U.S. App. LEXIS 85, n.1 (5th Cir. 2006).

"no duty to conduct fingerprint tests."[124] Even if the defendant argues that the police destroyed evidence, this alone may not create reversible error. In a case in which no evidence of the defendant's fingerprints was obtained from materials that constituted a methamphetamine lab, there was no duty on behalf of law enforcement to attempt to find fingerprints that they did not know existed or that they did not believe were necessary.[125] In this particular case the police called the hazardous materials team to dispose of hazardous waste at the meth lab and did not attempt to collect fingerprint evidence. The court noted that when police have not collected fingerprint evidence and have not conducted any analysis, there is no duty to preserve what amounts to nonexistent evidence.

In the case of *United States v. Sanchez-Garcia*, the use of fingerprint evidence played a strong role in justifying an enhanced drug offense sentence.[126] Due to an informant's tip, police suspected that the subject had been and was dealing and smuggling drugs as well as being an illegal alien. Following a lawful traffic stop that revealed that the subject's name did not match his identification, police received permission to search the subject's car and apartment. A records check of the name offered by the subject returned a complete set of fingerprints, a list of his aliases, and a photograph. A consent-based search of the subject's residence revealed illegal drugs and a firearm with a latent fingerprint. Comparisons of that fingerprint with a fingerprint database revealed that the subject's print matched the fingerprint of an illegal alien who had prior drug offenses and who had been lawfully deported. Ultimately, the jury trial resulted in the defendant being convicted of a variety of drug- and weapons-related offenses. In order to enhance the penalties, the prosecution used photographs of one of the defendant's alias identities and compared that photo to his presence in court. Additionally, the court considered the testimony at trial that the defendant was the individual with a different name who had previously been convicted of drug-related offenses and concluded that the fingerprint evidence demonstrated that the alias identity and the defendant in court were the same person beyond a reasonable doubt. The reviewing court agreed that the trial judge acted properly when she imposed a heightened sentence because the current drug crimes were committed after a previous felony drug conviction.

Fingerprint evidence that has been validly collected and appropriately preserved may be introduced against a defendant to prove guilt and to enhance a sentence based on certification of prior criminal activity. In such case the fingerprint evidence is used to make certain that the prior offenses actually were committed by the defendant. Comparisons of fingerprint samples require the use of expert witnesses who have to be qualified as such in order to testify in a court of law.

---

[124]   Smith v. United States, 966 A.2d 367, 2009 D.C. App. LEXIS 35 (D.C. App. 2009).

[125]   State v. Best, 2008 Tenn. App. LEXIS 744 (Tenn. 2008).

[126]   United States v. Sanchez-Garcia, 402 F.3d 175; 2005 U.S. App. LEXIS 4568 (8th Cir. 2006).

§ 15.8　Ballistics Experiments

The art and science of forensic ballistics concerns the techniques used to determine whether a particular projectile was fired from a particular firearm. It involves, among other factors, the analysis of the size or caliber of the projectile and of the weapon and marks made on the projectile and may include consideration of the cartridge and its toolmarkings. The application of this technology may be able to determine the brand or class of firearm by analyzing the remains of a projectile and comparing it to known firearm classes and subclasses.[127] The field of ballistics may involve test firings of recovered weapons to produce a sample projectile that can be the basis for comparison with a crime scene projectile. Rifle barrels produce markings on each projectile as the bullet twists through the barrel during the firing sequence, but these markings made by all guns will change over the life of the firearm depending on firearm care, how many rounds have been fired, and the type of projectile fired. These markings, called striations, often aid or enable the forensic examiner to determine which particular gun or brand of gun fired the questioned projectile. In addition to striation marks on a bullet, firearms leave marks on brass shells that are ejected from many guns by automatic extractors and even revolvers may sometime leave telltale signs and scratches on the cartridges used in the gun. An expert in ballistics may be permitted to offer testimony to show that the bullet that killed a person was fired from a weapon possessed by the defendant. Before a witness may testify in regard to the identification of firearms and bullets, the attorney for one of the parties must qualify the person as an expert by demonstrating the background, experience, and education of the proposed expert to give such scientific and opinion testimony. If the proponent of the expert demonstrated that the witness had specialized training and experience as an employee of a crime laboratory or can be qualified as an independent expert in forensic ballistics, the court will allow the witness to testify as an expert.

For example, in appealing convictions for murder and narcotics trafficking, one defendant questioned the validity of the field of forensic ballistics, but the trial court rejected the challenge and noted that under Rule 702, dealing with expert testimony, the field of ballistics possesses demonstrated reliability for its techniques.[128] In this case, to qualify as an expert the prosecution had the proposed expert explain her qualifications. The expert had served as a firearms examiner in a county crime lab for 12 years, had received hands-on training from her section supervisor, attended seminars on firearms identification, was a member of a nationally recognized firearms and toolmark identification organization, had published in the field, given numerous presentations, and

---

[127]　A projectile's class characteristics include caliber and the number of the land and groove impressions.

[128]　United States v. Williams, 506 F.3d 151, 2007 U.S. App. LEXIS 24726 (2d Cir. 2007), *cert. denied*, 2008 U.S. LEXIS 2859 (2008).

had examined approximately 2,800 different types of firearms and provided expert testimony in a trial setting between 20 and 30 times. The trial court properly determined that she was qualified as an expert witness in the field of forensic ballistics and appropriately offered testimony in the murder and narcotics trafficking case.[129]

A ballistics expert may testify that the firing-pin marking on cartridge shells remaining in a revolver or on spent cartridges found in a defendant's possession corresponds to the marking on a test shell fired from the defendant's revolver.[130] Ballistics evidence may be able to prove that particular bullets came from the same firearm[131] due to microscopic markings placed on a bullet by the effect of the rifling lands and grooves as it twists down the barrel[132] or due to unique markings made on spent cartridges ejected from the gun.[133] Likewise, a ballistics expert witness who is also trained in toolmark analysis[134] may testify that an empty shotgun shell found at the scene of a homicide had been fired from the defendant's shotgun or may testify that a bullet did not come from a defendant's gun or indicate that the toolmarks are not conclusive for any purpose either to include or exclude.[135] The brand of a firearm can often be identified, or sometimes excluded, by careful observation of the lands and grooves.[136] In some situations, ballistics experts will be permitted to offer expert opinion concerning the probable trajectory of a bullet fired from a firearm based on forensic evidence in a particular case.[137]

Gunpowder burn patterns on clothing or bare skin can be used by a qualified expert in some cases to determine whether a gun was fired at a close range or from a distance.[138] The burn pattern can also determine whether a wound was an entry or an exit wound.[139] With respect to powder burns, an expert in firearms, toolmarks, and gunshot residue could identify gunshot residue in a pair of underwear to indicate that a gun had been fired within an inch of the person wearing them.[140] Powder burns may indicate who recently fired the gun.[141] Experts can evaluate the presence of stippling, small abrasions on skin that are

---

[129] *Id.*

[130] Sanchez v. State, 2005 Tex. App. LEXIS 5084 n.2 (2005).

[131] State v. Burnes, 997 So. 2d 906, 2008 La. App. Unpub. LEXIS 715 (La. 2008).

[132] Hinton v. State, 2006 Ala. Crim. App. LEXIS 72 (2006).

[133] United States v. Hicks, 389 F.3d 514, 523, 2004 U.S. App. LEXIS 22688 (5th Cir. 2004).

[134] United States v. Green, 405 F. Supp. 2d 104, 118, 2005 U.S. Dist. LEXIS 34273 n.26 (D. Mass. 2005).

[135] United States v. Williams, 506 F3d 151, 159, 159, 007 U.S. App. LEXIS 24726 (2d Cir. 2007).

[136] *See* Maine v. Cookson, 2002 Me. Super. LEXIS 256 (2002) for discussion of the merits and techniques of ballistics.

[137] Ronquillo v. Washington, 2001 Wash. App. LEXIS 2615 (2001).

[138] State v. Reardon, 2009 N.C. App. LEXIS 306 (N.C. 2009).

[139] State v. Austin, 2005 Tenn. Crim. App. LEXIS 815 (2005).

[140] State v. Foulk, 2009 Tenn. Crim. App. LEXIS 16 (Tenn. 2009).

[141] State v. Georgekopoulos, 2005 Ohio 5106, 2005 Ohio App. LEXIS 4624 (2005).

made by powder and other particles that travel with a bullet when it strikes skin, to determine a gun's distance from the wound at the time it was fired.[142]

In order for an expert to give opinion testimony concerning ballistics test results, the opinion must be based upon facts within the knowledge of the expert, or the expert may give an opinion based upon a hypothetical question that is itself based on facts already in evidence. This does not necessarily mean that real evidence itself must be admitted. For example, in the case of Hinton v. State, test bullets fired by the state's ballistics expert were compared with the bullets recovered from the crime scene. Even though the test bullets were not admitted into evidence, the reviewing court found that the decision of the lower court was not error because the experts used the test bullets only in analyzing the pieces of evidence that they were asked to examine.[143]

§ 15.9   Speed Detection Readings

The principle of Radio Detection and Ranging (RADAR) applies exact laws of science and nature in the measurement of distance and speed. The radar speed-detecting devices commonly used in traffic control operate on what is known as the Doppler effect and utilize a continuous beam of micro-waves emitted at a fixed frequency. The Doppler effect can be experienced by noticing the sound of a train horn when it is approaching and listening for the sound change as the train and its horn pass the observer. The frequency shift in the sound of the horn is an example of the Doppler effect. The operation depends upon the physical law that when such waves are intercepted by a moving object, the frequency changes in such a ratio to the speed of the intercepted object that, by measuring the change of the frequency, the speed may be determined.[144] The scientific principle is so universally accepted that courts routinely take judicial notice of the reliability of the principles upon which radar is based.[145] Where difficulty in enforcing speed laws with radar units arises, defendants normally attack the operational techniques of the officers using the equipment or the calibration and maintenance of the machines, because the principles are not easily refuted.

In operation, traffic enforcement police use a vehicle in which the radar speed detection system has been installed in such a way as to beam radio waves toward the motoring public. Modern radar devices are designed to be calibrated at set intervals of time to assure that the units are operating properly. When a moving vehicle enters the radar unit's broadcast radio beam, the returned radio wave has a frequency shift that registers with the radar unit,

---

[142]   Ayala v. Quarterman, 2009 U.S. Dist. LEXIS 13019 (S.D. Tex. 2009).
[143]   *See* Hinton v. State, 2006 Ala. Crim. App. LEXIS 72 (2006).
[144]   Kopper, *The Scientific Reliability of Radar Speedmeters*, 33 N.C.L. REV. 343 (1955).
[145]   Cleveland Heights v. Katz, 2001 Ohio App. LEXIS 5394 (2001). *See* case in Part II.

where the speed of the vehicle is instantly computed. The office may initiate a stop or radio to another officer to make the traffic stop.

For many years, the public, especially those who have been ticketed, have been aware of the widespread use of radio, microwaves, and other electronic devices in detecting the speed of motor vehicles and other moving objects. While the intricacies of such devices are not fully understood by all drivers, their general accuracy and effectiveness had few scientific or legal challenges once courts in the several states accepted the basic scientific principles. Once the principles of radar as applied to speed detection gained general legal acceptance, courts then took judicial notice of the scientific principles and did not require expert testimony on the principles before admitting evidence produced by radar units. In most jurisdictions, to establish the foundation for admission of radar-produced speed evidence, there must be expert testimony or judicial notice of the construction and accuracy of the device, evidence that the device is in good working order, and evidence that the officer using the device is qualified by training and experience.[146]

In laying a proper foundation for admission of radar-produced evidence, the officer must explain his or her training, the calibration of the machine, and that it was used properly during the event being litigated. In one Nebraska case, the officer explained that he had used the same type of radar unit since becoming a trooper, he was certified to use the particular type of radar, and his training certificate was up to date.[147] The officer testified to the use of tuning forks to assure proper operation of the radar unit and that the radar unit itself had a current certificate of calibration. At the start of each shift, the officer presses a switch on the unit to conduct a self-test and the unit runs a self-test every 10 minutes while in operation. The unit indicated that it was functioning properly by a four-count beep. He also noted that a technician checks the accuracy of the tuning forks once a year and that the radar units are checked for accuracy by the technician on a yearly basis. The reviewing court held that the prosecution had established a sufficient foundation for admitting the evidence of speed produced by the Stalker Dual SL radar unit.

Although radar speed detection remains one of law enforcement's tools for regulating the speed of motorists, laser detection has become a strong companion tool for police officers. Laser detection of speed poses different challenges from the use of radar, and the theoretical accuracy may make this system a superior law enforcement tool. Before any new scientific tool may be used, the proponent must prove that it accurately does what it says it will do. Initially, a foundation concerning the principles of laser speed detection had to be introduced by experts, then as the science and its application became known, judicial notice of the principles behind the use of lasers in speed detection gained acceptance, and some jurisdictions, like Georgia, specify by statute the types of speed detection devices that are permissible to use and those that will be admitted in court. In the case of laser detection, the courts

---

[146] *See* City of Cleveland v. Tisdale, 2008 Ohio 2807, 2008 Ohio App. LEXIS 2372 (Ohio 2008).

[147] State v. Huff, 2004 Neb. App. LEXIS 117 (2004).

initially had to be convinced by expert testimony that the principles were scientifically sound and that the device that purported to apply the science did so regularly and routinely.

The Intermediate Court of Appeals of Hawai'i upheld the use of laser speed detection where the prosecution did not produce any expert witnesses to testify concerning how the laser speed detection system operates.[148] The defendant appealed her speeding conviction, contending that the trial court erred in admitting evidence of her speed obtained by a laser unit when the prosecution offered no expert testimony relative to the principles behind laser speed detection. The reviewing court noted that expert testimony may be required when a scientific technique is new and creates an issue of first impression for a court. The court observed that once a scientific principle or process has been fully vetted and established, expert testimony is no longer necessary because a court may take judicial notice of the validity of the principle. The defendant argued that no reviewing court "in Hawai'i has recognized widespread acceptance of the reliability or accuracy of laser technology as a means of measuring speed"[149] and that courts in other jurisdictions have held that using laser-based speed detection units had failed to reach sufficient scientific acceptance to be introduced in the absence of expert testimony. The Intermediate Court of Appeals of Hawai'i rejected the defendant's arguments that expert witnesses were required. The court noted that: (1) the science of laser speed detection is based on well-understood principles; (2) the accuracy and reliability of laser speed-detection devices for monitoring traffic speed have been approved in other jurisdictions (Maryland, Minnesota, and New Jersey as well as a municipal court in the state of Ohio); and (3) the laser device used in this case met all the requirements of the Hawai'i Supreme Court for accuracy. The officer in the case testified:

> that he performed the required functionality tests on the laser gun prior to beginning his patrol, and that the readings indicated that the device was functioning properly. He also testified that he possessed a valid certification for operating the laser gun and that he had twenty years' experience in performing traffic enforcement duties.[150]

The Intermediate Court noted that it joined other jurisdictions that have taken judicial notice of the scientific acceptance of the accuracy and reliability of the modern laser units for measuring the speed of motor vehicles.

To facilitate police use of laser equipment, some states have passed statutes that permit police use and court admissibility of laser-generated information concerning speed.[151] Georgia's legislature passed a statute that operates like

---

[148]   State v. Stoa, 2006 Haw. App. LEXIS 397 (2006).

[149]   *Id.*

[150]   *Id.*

[151]   Odum v. Georgia, 255 Ga. App. 70, 564 S.E.2d 490, 2002 Ga. App. LEXIS 478 (2002). The trial court admitted laser-generated evidence of speed upon proof that the officer and officer's use of the device met state standards.

a rule of evidence and, subject to some conditions, permits evidence of laser-detected speed to be admitted in court. The law provides:

> § 40-14-17. Laser devices; reliability and admissibility of evidence
>
> Evidence of speed based on a speed detection device using the speed timing principle of laser, which is of a model that has been approved by the Department of Public Safety shall be considered scientifically acceptable and reliable as a speed detection device and shall be admissible for all purposes in any court, judicial, or administrative proceedings in this state. A certified copy of the Department of Public Safety list of approved models of such laser devices shall be self-authenticating and shall be admissible for all purposes in any court, judicial, or administrative proceedings in this state.[152]

When a law enforcement officer operates the approved laser speed detection unit according to the manufacturer's instructions and uses a Georgia-approved laser speed detection device that has been properly calibrated according to the manufacturer's specifications, the evidence should be admissible. Similar procedures permit admissibility of the evidence in other jurisdictions. When a Georgia prosecutor failed to introduce the required list of approved laser speed detection models, a proper foundation for laser-generated speed evidence was lacking and the result of the laser unit was not admissible in evidence.[153]

In one case, a defendant who had been convicted of speeding appealed based on the alleged inaccuracy of an LTI 20/20 laser speed measuring system used to clock the speed of his car.[154] Although there was no evidence offered in the trial court concerning the scientific accuracy of the LTI 20/20, the reviewing court held that the trial court properly took judicial notice that another trial court found that the device was scientifically accurate because the other trial court actually heard testimony from a qualified expert witness where the expert explained how the LTI 20/20 worked and concluded that it offered reliable data concerning speed of vehicles. Five months before stopping the defendant, the police officer had been recertified to use the LTI 20/20 and his state certification was demonstrated to be current. Under the circumstances, the defendant's conviction was upheld; the device was accurate, was working properly, and was being operated by a certified police officer.

There are some different methods of detecting speed of motor vehicles that involve global positioning satellites and computers that are nested in modern motor vehicles. For example, onboard computers of currently manufactured motor vehicle record the last few seconds of the vehicle's speed and stores the data,

---

[152] O.C.G.A. § 40-14-17 (Ga. 2009).
[153] In the Interest of J. D. S., a child, 273 Ga. App. 576, 615 S.E.2d 627, 2005 Ga. App. LEXIS 579 (2005).
[154] State v. Kim, 2008 Ohio 6928 (Ohio 2008).

purges that data, and then stores the most recent date and repeats the process. Recently manufactured motor vehicles often contain an onboard diagnostics computer system, OBD II, that captures various information about the performance of the individual motor vehicle, such as whether seat belts were fastened, when brakes were last applied, when the air bag deployed, and the speed of the motor vehicle. In General Motors cars since 1990, an SDM, or sensing diagnostic module, records, among other parameters, the:

> acceleration or deceleration and makes decisions every 10 milliseconds whether or not to deploy the passive restraint system in the vehicle. The system also stores vehicle data such as vehicle speed, engine RPM, throttle percentage and brake data, change in velocity or delta V and seat belt usage, all in one second increments for a period of five seconds.[155]

In a Massachusetts case involving the death of a passenger in an automobile, police believed that the automobile had been going too fast for the slushy road conditions immediately prior to leaving the road and colliding with a large tree.[156] In order to determine the speed of the automobile immediately prior to the impact, police obtained a warrant to download data from the SDM, the electronic data recorder in the Chevrolet Tahoe. The police officer, an expert in accident reconstruction, obtained data from the SDM that indicated the motor vehicle was traveling at 58 miles per hour five seconds before the crash and 40 miles per hour one second prior to impact. This information, along with other information generated by the officer, was admitted against the defendant and resulted in a conviction for motor vehicle homicide.

Similarly, data from a General Motors event data recorder, the sensing and diagnostic module, recorded a defendant's Firebird excessively speeding in a 30 m.p.h. zone.[157] The Florida trial court admitted the computer-generated speed evidence in a double manslaughter case involving the deaths of two 16-year-old girls whom the defendant killed while he was driving down a residential street at 114 miles per hour. An expert witness testified that the data from computer event data recorders are used by the auto industry to design automobiles, in crash testing analysis, and in the medical fields and in biomechanics. The prosecutor introduced evidence that insurance companies and accident crash investigators rely on this type of collected data because it is believed to be accurate and reliable. For these reasons, the Florida reviewing court upheld the admissibility of the data collected from the motor vehicle computer.

---

[155] People v. Christmann, 3 Misc. 3d 309, 311, 776 N.Y.S.2d 437, 439, 2004 N.Y. Misc. LEXIS 45 (N.Y. 2004).

[156] *See* Commonwealth v. Zimmermann, 70 Mass. App. Ct. 357, 2007 Mass. App. LEXIS 1050 (Mass. 2007).

[157] Matos v. State, 899 So. 2d 403, 405–406, 2005 Fla. App. LEXIS 4359 (2005).

§ 15.10   Neutron Activation Analysis

Neutron activation analysis is a process by which the chemical composition of materials can be determined, but it has been eclipsed by some newer technologies. The admission of the results of this process was approved in a federal case that involved sending a package bomb through the mail.[158] In this case, the court approved the explanation of the process, which appeared in *American Jurisprudence's* "Proof of Facts," stating:

But we feel that the following description is the most understandable and succinct explanation which we have found available.

American Jurisprudence's "Proof of Facts" describes the process thus:

One of the newest and most promising techniques of forensic science is neutron activation analysis. The ability of this nuclear method to detect traces of elements in minute samples enables it to solve many problems of identification that have heretofore been considered hopeless. ... The process is essentially one whereby the material to be analyzed is first made radioactive—i.e., it is "charged" so that it will give off or emit radiation in the form of gamma rays. This radioactive sample is then exposed to a scintillation crystal; and every time a gamma ray from the radioactive material interacts with the crystal, it emits a flash of light, which is converted into an electrical pulse whose voltage is proportional to the energy of the gamma rays. An electronic device called a multi-channel differential analyzer then sorts the electrical impulses into different energy groups and adds up the pulses in each group. The result is a graph shown on an oscilloscope screen. The graph contains information related to the kind and amount of elements in the radioactive sample and can be transcribed immediately or stored on magnetic tape or punched paper tapes for future reference.

Virtually no sample of material is too small to be analyzed by activation analysis. A single hair, a shred of marijuana, or a fleck of automobile paint no longer than the period at the end of this sentence can be analyzed and correctly identified. Furthermore, activation analysis' high sensitivity allows quantitative measurement of elements in the parts per million and parts per billion range. For instance, if one thimbleful of arsenic poison were diluted in ten tankcars of water, the exact amount of arsenic present could be determined by activation analysis. In most cases, the analysis is also nondestructive, so that material evidence may be preserved for presentation in court or saved for analysis by another method.

A Pennsylvania case illustrates the use of neutron activation testing to match a bullet fragment with other bullets taken from a case of cartridges from defendant's apartment.[159] The gun used in the homicide was never recovered.

---

[158]   United States v. Stifel, 433 F.2d 431 (6th Cir. 1970).
[159]   Commonwealth v. Kretchmar, 2009 Pa. Super. 63, 2009 Pa. Super. LEXIS 79 (Pa. 2009).

Comparative Bullet Lead Analysis (CBLA) using neutron activation analysis demonstrated that that the bullets recovered from the victim's body "matched" in trace metal content, those in the box of ammunition recovered from defendant's apartment. In November 2007 the FBI offered a press release that also indicated its concerns with the concept of CBLA and indicated that it would work with the defense bar to rectify any injustices that had occurred.[160] The reviewing court duly noted that there were in existence arguments that comparative bullet lead analysis was not the exact science that some had contended, but it decided to affirm the defendant's conviction despite the fact that the case was primarily a circumstantial evidence case and more questions on CBLA had been raised.

Some crime scenes may not prove conducive to either neutron activation analysis or to a related test, atomic-absorption analysis, especially where numerous potential defendants have been present at the crime scene and have similar contaminants on their persons. Therefore, the limits of the testing process indicate that it will not solve all gun-firing crime issues, but in a variety of contexts, neutron activation analysis will be able to indicate who has fired a weapon if the testing is conducted promptly.

Although the neutron activation analysis does not conclusively establish whether the subject has recently fired a gun, because the component chemicals could have had a different origin than firing a firearm or handling a gun, the test results are generally admissible in evidence despite this inherent inconclusiveness. The evidence is admissible as relevant because it shows a probability that the suspect did or did not fire a gun; its probative value is for the jury to determine.

A newer technology than neutron activation analysis that offers some promise is called inductively coupled plasma-optical emission spectroscopy (ICP).[161] The process is able to distinguish discrete components of different products, such as lead. The goal of distinguishing different components of lead would, in theory, allow scientists to compare lead from one batch of lead bullets to see if it matched other bullets possessed by a defendant. Comparative bullet lead analysis would permit a recovered bullet's chemical composition to be compared with remaining bullets contained in a defendant's remaining cartridges. Ultimately, the FBI abandoned the process because the science did not allow the reliable chemical bullet matching that had originally been anticipated.[162]

---

[160] *See* the FBI Press Release of 17 November 2007 that questions the reliability of comparisons of lead. Available at: http://www.fbi.gov/pressrel/pressrel07/bulletlead111707.htm.

[161] "In 1993, the technique of FBI choice was changed to inductively coupled plasma, atomic emission spectroscopy (ICP)." *See* State v. Behn, 375 N.J. Super. 409, 426, 868 A.2d 329, 341, 2005 N.J. Super. LEXIS 73 (N.J. 2005).

[162] *See* Clemmons v. State, 392 Md. 339, 896 A.2d 1059, 2006 Md. LEXIS 192 n.8 (Md. 2006). *See also* Commonwealth v. Daye, 19 Mass. L. Rep. 674, 2005 Mass. Super. LEXIS 368 (Mass. 2005). *See also* http://www.cbsnews.com/stories/2007/11/16/60minutes/main3512453.shtml for a *60 Minutes* exposé on lead bullet analysis.

§ 15.11 Deoxyribonucleic Acid (DNA) Tests

Researchers have made a significant breakthrough in using the deoxyribonucleic acid (DNA) code present in human cells, blood, and other body fluids to link evidence, such as bloodstains or semen specimens, to a specific individual, while excluding all others. According to an article that appeared in a National Institute of Justice publication dated October 1987, DNA patterns are so different between people who are not identical twins so as to provide virtually definite identification. In recent years, smaller and smaller samples of fluids containing DNA have been required because the science has advanced in the area of amplification of samples to usable levels.

A California case demonstrates the significant advances that have occurred in the years since the DNA testing revolution changed criminal investigations forever. In this case, a woman was raped by someone she knew. The rapist injured the woman sufficiently that her DNA and the attacker's DNA became mixed together so that the rape testing kit contained multisource DNA. Blood samples were taken from the victim and from the attacker and, along with DNA samples collected from a sexual assault kit, were sent to a DNA laboratory.

As the court explained the theory of DNA testing:

> Deoxyribonucleic acid is material present in each cell of the human body that determines an individual's characteristics. Virtually all deoxyribonucleic acid is the same from one human to another. However, a small percentage of the deoxyribonucleic acid is different in each individual. Cellmark Diagnostics tests deoxyribonucleic acid by comparing an unknown sample from a crime scene to that from known individuals. The tests serve to either include or exclude an individual as a possible source of the biological sample. As will be explained in more detail below, the polymerase chain reaction is a technique that has been used in the field of molecular biology since the 1980s to copy small specific regions of deoxyribonucleic acid. The deoxyribonucleic acid is isolated into a form that can be copied. Then copies of that deoxyribonucleic acid sequence are copied. Finally, the actual deoxyribonucleic acid types are examined and compared to other samples to determine whether they could be included or excluded as a donor source for the sample.[163]

The evidence demonstrated that the lab followed extremely strict protocols to avoid contamination of samples or inaccurate results. The results demonstrated that the nonsperm DNA fraction had a primary source that was female and was consistent with the profile from the victim, while the sample

---

[163] California v Smith, 107 Cal. App. 4th 646, 131 Cal. Rptr. 2d 230, 2003 Cal. App. LEXIS 475 (2003), *petition for review denied*, 2003 Cal. LEXIS 3547 (2003). For additional enlightenment, this case has a scientifically interesting account of DNA information contained within the opinion.

of DNA taken from the sperm faction indicated the source was from a male. In addition, the interpretation of the results demonstrated that the defendant was the source of the male fraction taken from the victim using the sexual assault kit.

In a hearing consolidated from several California cases with similar issues, a judge made a determination that the science has progressed to the point that DNA at a crime scene can properly be compared with samples donated by suspects and victims to see if a match can be declared and such results would be admissible. The evidence discussed included STR (short tandem repeat) testing and PCR (polymerase chain reaction) testing and found that both theories had scientific validity for the purposes in question. The court ruled that DNA testing, based on analysis and separation of mixed samples, was generally accepted in the scientific community and the results could be admitted against the defendant in the rape case.[164]

With the general admissibility of DNA evidence permitted under the *Daubert* or the *Frye* standards for admission of scientific evidence, the battle for prosecutors and for the defense bar moved from challenging the concept to challenging the methodology and admissibility of the newest advances in DNA testing. For example, in a quadruple murder case involving four rapes and strangulations, the defendant mounted an attack on the admissibility of the DNA evidence that the defense expected would be offered by the prosecution.[165] He challenged the testing laboratory's methodology in dealing with mixed DNA samples and alleged that the lab violated generally accepted protocols. The defendant alleged that the laboratory failed to perform its tests properly and to report them accurately. In addition, the defendant contended that the lab failed to adhere to the conservative protocols of the DNA test kit manufacturer. In the math area of DNA testing, he contended that the use of the product rule to make frequency calculations for mixed samples was faulty. Finally, the defendant contended that the database used by the lab proved inadequate for frequency calculations. The Supreme Judicial Court of Massachusetts serially addressed each of the defendant's contentions and upheld the trial court's rejection of all of his arguments. The posture of this type of case demonstrates that defendants are contesting the application of the science of DNA testing rather than arguing about the basic validity of the concept that each person (except identical twins) carries a unique DNA profile.

As courts approved the admission of DNA results and approved different types of testing procedures, the prosecution and defense bars have embraced the use of DNA evidence where appropriate. The defense bar adopted the concept of DNA testing for the purpose of establishing actual innocence in older death penalty cases in which a convicted defendant alleged that the

---

[164] *Id.*

[165] Commonwealth v. Gaynor, 443 Mass. 245, 263, 820 N.E.2d 233, 249, 2005 Mass. LEXIS 7 (Mass. 2005). *See* case in Part II.

wrong person had been convicted. DNA testing has resulted in some people being removed from death row by excluding them as the source of DNA at homicide scenes. In a Tennessee case, a jury convicted a defendant of the murder of another man's wife.[166] At the trial, an FBI serologist testified that a secretor belonging to the ABO blood group was the one who deposited the semen on the victim's nightgown and on her underwear. The evidence showed that the defendant was a member of that blood grouping. Although the government neither alleged nor proved any sexual offense, the prosecution argued that implication during the closing argument. The defendant had blood on his jeans that did not belong to him and that was consistent with the blood type of the deceased victim. With newer refinements to the testing process, DNA evidence demonstrated that the semen came from the deceased woman's husband and not the defendant. Also, at some point, the deceased woman's husband had made a drunken confession to her murder. When presented with the new DNA results, a federal district court held a hearing but ruled that all claims had been procedurally defaulted and that the defendant had failed to demonstrate actual innocence. The Court of Appeals affirmed the federal district court's decision. The Supreme Court of the United States reversed the defendant's conviction and remanded the case on the strength of the new DNA test results.[167]

As the science of DNA testing has become more accepted and admissible, other legal challenges involve proper collection, storing, and preventing contamination of samples[168] rather than arguing against the science. Proper handling of deoxyribonucleic acid (DNA) samples in conformity with established procedures is essential before DNA evidence can be considered reliable.[169] Convicted defendants have demanded that older evidence be tested to exclude them from guilt by attempting to force the prosecution to conduct DNA tests on evidence that neither the police nor the prosecution had reason or desire to test.[170]

A collateral issue concerning the collection and use of DNA data arises when former convicts, probationers, and parolees are ordered to submit a DNA sample to be added to state and local DNA databanks or the federal databank, the Combined DNA Index System of the Federal Bureau of Investigation (CODIS). Most jurisdictions require persons convicted of felonies or sex-

---

[166] *See* House v. Bell, 547 U.S. 518, 2006 U.S. LEXIS 4675 (2006). *See also* 44 AM. CRIM. L. REV. 1069, *Every Juror Wants a Story: Narrative Relevance, Third Party Guilt and the Right to Present a Defense* (2007).

[167] *Id.*

[168] United States v. Morrow, 374 F. Supp. 42, 46 (D.D.C. 2005).

[169] Commonwealth v. Blasioli, 685 A.2d 151 (Pa. 1996).

[170] *See* United States v. Fasono, 2008 U.S. Dist. LEXIS 64055 (S.D. Miss. 2008), in which appellant wanted various personal articles tested to see if another person's DNA and not the defendant's might have been present.

ual offenses to submit a DNA sample for inclusion in national and state databanks.

In a case from the District of Columbia, government agents ordered that a probationer give a DNA sample for inclusion in the CODIS databank.[171] The authority for the order came from a federal statute stating that officials "shall collect a DNA sample from each individual under the supervision of the Agency who is on supervised release, parole, or probation who is, or has been, convicted of a qualifying District of Columbia offense . . ." Under the DNA Analysis Backlog Elimination Act of 2000, persons with former convictions were required to give DNA samples. When his probation was about to be revoked for failure to give his sample, the probationer sued in federal court alleging that his constitutional rights would be violated by requiring him to give a sample. Over his argument dealing with the Fourth Amendment search and seizure provision and the Fourteenth Amendment's due process clause, the trial court ruled in favor of the federal government. The court noted that probationers have a reduced expectation of privacy and that future searches of the database would not be a search of the probationer. Because DNA profiles can be collected from probationers, such evidence can also be collected from parolees because they are similarly situated for Fourth Amendment purposes.

The Combined DNA Index System may assist wrongly convicted defendants in proving their allegations of actual innocence. In the face of the FBI's refusal to run a DNA database search of this system to assist an inmate who alleged that he had wrongly been convicted, a federal district court in Illinois concluded that the FBI had acted arbitrarily and ordered it to run the DNA comparison on behalf of the convicted defendant.[172]

§ 15.12   Other Examinations and Tests

As other techniques and procedures have met the requirements for admission by way of expert testimony, courts have recognized the new tests and have admitted evidence based on those tests. For example, in a New Jersey case, the trial court permitted an expert witness to testify that the bullets taken from the crime scene were tested using the Plasma Atomic Emission Spectroscopy testing process along with bullets from live cartridges possessed by the defendant and their lead composition was the same. The plasma atomic emission spectroscopy testing method determines what trace elements are contained in a lead sample and compares that result to another sample bullet. If they are of the same composition, the conclusion is that they came from the same original source. On a petition for habeas corpus, the federal district court held that the

---

[171] Johnson v. Quander, 370 U.S. App. D.C. 167, 440 F.3d 489, 499, 2006 U.S. App. LEXIS 6601 (D.C. Cir. 2006). *Accord*, United States v. Sczubelek, 402 F.3d 175, 2005 U.S. App. LEXIS 4568 (3d Cir. 2006).

[172] Rivera v. Mueller, 596 F. Supp. 2d 1163, 2009 U.S. Dist. LEXIS 9308 (N.D. Ill. 2009).

admission of the expert testimony did not violate any federal constitutional right.[173] The process of using plasma atomic emission spectroscopy probably analyzes the trace metals in lead properly but there has been some concern in other jurisdictions and among some experts that the original sources of lead for bullets fails to have the consistency of composition that is required for this type of bullet matching to be valid.[174]

A Florida trial court admitted expert testimony in a homicide case that used plasma atomic emission spectroscopy analysis to demonstrate that the lead in a bullet fragment taken from the victim matched other lead bullets that were linked to the defendant.[175] The state's witness testified as an expert in neutron activation analysis and inductively coupled plasma atomic emissions spectrometry and indicated that his conclusions were correct. The defense offered rebuttal expert witnesses who testified somewhat differently but did not dispute the scientific concept behind plasma atomic omission spectroscopy. The Supreme Court of Florida upheld the admission of the expert testimony and the conviction,[176] and a federal district court denied a writ of habeas corpus.[177]

In contrast to the above cases, comparative bullet lead analysis originally had been admitted against a defendant to help prove that the bullets recovered from the homicide matched the lead in other bullets remaining in his gun's unfired cartridges, and the reviewing court reversed.[178] Using inductively coupled plasma-optical emission spectroscopy as a successor to neutron activation analysis might reveal the constituents of a lead bullet, but that information may still remain irrelevant. To make valid comparisons of lead in different bullets and establish that they came from a common source would require that the common source be a completely homogenous source of lead. The best testimony indicated that within each run of lead used to make bullets, significant differences exist in the constituent trace metals. The reviewing court held that the use of any of the different methods of conducting comparative bullet lead analysis should not have been admitted because, under the *Frye* test for admission of scientific evidence, several fundamental assumptions were not generally accepted by the relevant scientific community.[179]

---

[173] *See* Noel v. Hendricks, 2006 U.S. Dist. LEXIS 41374 (D.N.J. 2006).

[174] *See* Clemmons v. State, 392 Md. 339, 896 A.2d 1059, 2006 Md. LEXIS 192 n.8 (Md. 2006). *See also* State v. Behn, 375 N.J. Super. 409, 868 A.2d 329, 2005 N.J. Super. LEXIS 73 (N.J. 2005).

[175] Smith v. Secretary, Department of Corrections, 2007 U.S. Dist. LEXIS 57703 (M.D. Fla. 2007).

[176] Smith v. State, 931 So. 2d 790, 2006 Fla. LEXIS 388 (Fla. 2006).

[177] Smith v. Secretary, Department of Corrections, 2007 U.S. Dist. LEXIS 57703 (M.D. Fla. 2007).

[178] *See* Clemmons v. State, 392 Md. 339, 896 A.2d 1059, 2006 Md. LEXIS 192 n.8 (Md. 2006). *See also* Commonwealth v. Daye, 19 Mass. L. Rep. 674, 2005 Mass. Super. LEXIS 368 (Mass. 2005).

[179] *Id.*

Whether plasma atomic emission spectroscopy analysis will eventually meet general scientific acceptability and be generally admissible in most of the nation's state courts remains to be seen. As mentioned in § 15.11, the Federal Bureau of Investigation Laboratory used this method of bullet analysis until its discontinuation.

In another court, in discussing a scientific procedure used to analyze cement dust, the reliability the Fourier Transform Infrared Spectrophotometer (FTIR) analysis procedure was questioned by the defendant. The issue concerned whether the Fourier Transform Infrared Spectrophotometer (FTIR) analysis was based upon scientific principles that are generally accepted as reliable within the relevant scientific community. The process at issue used advanced materials science analysis to compare safe cement linings that deposited its dust on a safecracker's tools, clothing, and other articles personal to the alleged safecracker. The trial court found that this scientific test of cement residue was admissible in criminal proceedings.[180] The use of the Fourier Transform Infrared Spectrophotometer has not been litigated in the reported cases since 1997. In this case, the expert testimony evidence tended to prove that cement dust samples taken from the crime scene, from the remains of the victims' safe, and from the defendant's tools, were all consistent with safe lining cement, which could have come from the victim's safe, was sufficiently reliable to be admissible in a burglary prosecution.

§ 15.13 Summary

Real evidence is often not admitted directly into court but is used for experiments and tests conducted out of court. General rules have been established regarding the admissibility of testimony concerning the results of experiments and tests, and the use of evidence such as charts and graphs resulting from experiments and tests. In recent years, the trend has been for the courts to allow and encourage the use of such evidence, and this has been held to be consistent with the rights of the accused.

As a general rule, examination of the body for evidence such as marks and bruises, and the taking of samples (such as saliva, urine, and blood) from the body do not violate the privilege against self-incrimination. Such evidence is admissible if proper standards concerning the testing of this type of evidence are met. Also, the common practice of determining blood-alcohol content by testing the suspect's blood, breath, or urine has been approved when law enforcement officials meet the conditions dictated by the Constitution, by the courts, and by legislative bodies.

Blood grouping test results provide useful information, but are increasingly being replaced by DNA testing, which is both more reliable and very precise. Blood-based evidence is generally used for purposes of identifica-

---

[180] People v. Roraback, 666 N.Y.S.2d 397 (1997).

tion when that element is at issue in criminal prosecutions involving rape, assault, homicide, and in civil and criminal paternity actions. For the results of blood-based testing to be admissible, it must be demonstrated that a qualified person conducted the test, that the qualified technician observed proper protocols during the testing procedure, and that the testing methods revealed no discrepancies in the results.

Courts are divided concerning the admissibility of polygraph evidence with a strong bias in favor of exclusion. Three approaches have been taken by various federal and state courts: (1) the traditional approach of per se inadmissibility; (2) polygraph evidence is admissible only when both parties so stipulate; and (3) polygraph evidence is admissible even in the absence of stipulation when special circumstances exist.

The reasoning that has been applied in the use of the polygraph is similar to that of most courts in finding that so-called "truth serum" tests are not admissible for or against the defendant in a criminal case because of the lack of scientific certainty about the results. However, the courts take an entirely different view as to fingerprint comparisons. The results of fingerprint comparisons made out of court may be introduced to compare the fingerprints of the defendant with fingerprints left at the scene of the crime. This procedure has become so well recognized that the courts will take judicial notice of the fact that fingerprint identification is one of the most accurate methods of personal identification.

The science of forensic ballistics is also a well-recognized subject of expert testimony. The courts will generally allow such expert testimony to show, for example, that the bullet that entered the body was fired from a weapon belonging to the defendant in the case. Before such evidence is admissible, the introducing party must show that approved procedures were followed and that the person testifying is qualified as an expert in the field.

The use of speed detection devices using the principle of radar are universally approved, and testimony concerning the readings on such devices is generally accepted in evidence. However, test results are not admissible in court unless there is proof that the equipment was properly calibrated and the witness is qualified to testify concerning the meaning of such tests. Many jurisdictions have approved the use of laser-based speed detection, as long as police use approved laser units and follow proper protocols provided by the manufacturer.

Neutron activation analysis provided strong evidence to detect trace compounds but has fallen into disuse in criminal cases in recent times. Evidence concerning the results of such analysis will face challenges where lead bullet identification is concerned.

Scientific research has resulted in the development of forensic DNA analysis as a scientific technique that reveals distinctive patterns in human genetic material in blood and some body fluids, hair, and tissue. Courts routinely admit the results of this "DNA fingerprint" test to prove identity and to exclude suspects because this science has general acceptance by the experts in the field. Generally, proof that the experts have properly applied the technology assures admission into evidence.

Because criminal justice personnel conduct many of the out-of-court examinations and tests, it is essential that such personnel be aware of the value of such evidence and be familiar with the requirements designed to protect the rights of those who are accused of crime.

Exclusion of Evidence on Constitutional Grounds

Evidence Unconstitutionally Obtained

16

Today we once again examine Wolf's constitutional documentation of the right of privacy free from unreasonable state intrusions, and, after its dozen years on our books, are led by it to close the only courtroom door remaining open to evidence secured by official lawlessness in flagrant abuse of that basic right, reserved to all persons as a specific guarantee against that very same unlawful conduct. We hold that all evidence obtained by searches and seizures in violation of the Constitution is, by that same authority, inadmissible in a state court.

Mapp v. Ohio, 367 U.S. 643, 81 S. Ct. 1684,
6 L. Ed. 2d 1081 (1961)

Chapter Outline

Section
16.1   Introduction
16.2   Development of the Exclusionary Rule
16.3   Search and Seizure Exclusions
16.4   Exclusion of Evidence Obtained by Illegal Wiretapping
        or Eavesdropping
16.5   Exclusion of Confessions Obtained in Violation
        of Constitutional Provisions
16.6   Self-Incrimination and Related Protections
16.7   Due Process Exclusions
16.8   Right to Counsel as It Relates to the Exclusion of Evidence
16.9   Summary

§ 16.1   Introduction

In a democracy where the rule of law is of paramount importance, the government must follow the law so that fundamental fairness and predictability of behaviors serve as the norm for both the government and its citizens. Fair dealing is a rough equivalent to due process, which everyone should be able to expect and all are entitled to receive from government. On the rare occasion when a local, state, or the federal government fails to follow the policy of due process and fairness, a remedy should be readily accessible for the constitutional violation. In the discussion of the rules of evidence in Chapter 2, the text indicated that some judicially created rules exclude evidence that has been obtained in violation of the rights protected by the Constitution. This is not because the evidence is not relevant or material; it is to remove any incentive for future improper governmental behavior so that the executive branch law enforcers observe the rule the next time the situation arises. In fact, in many instances, the evidence obtained in violation of the constitutional provisions is highly relevant and material and would be admissible under the traditional rules of evidence. The courts have reasoned that even though the evidence is otherwise admissible and would help prove or disprove a fact at issue, illegally obtained evidence should not be admitted because authorizing the use of illegally obtained evidence would encourage violation of citizens' rights as enumerated in the Constitution and give a judicial stamp of approval for future law enforcement violations of the Constitution.

Although the exclusionary rules relating to the various types of evidence have been extended greatly in recent years, much doubt remains as to what evidence will be excluded and what will be admissible. Under recent United States Supreme Court decisions, evidence is primarily excluded when the seizure of evidence violates the rights protected by the Fourth, Fifth, or Sixth Amendments to the Constitution. The general rules concerning search and seizure, self-incrimination, right to counsel, and other constitutional provisions cannot be discussed comprehensively due to space limitations. However, rules relating to the admission or exclusion of the evidence obtained by conduct that infringes on these rights will be discussed briefly.[1]

§ 16.2　Development of the Exclusionary Rule

Comparatively speaking, the search and seizure exclusionary rule is of recent origin. This rule provides very succinctly that when evidence has been illegally obtained, or obtained in violation of the Constitution, it will be excluded from use in court.

First, it should be pointed out that this exclusionary rule is not universally applied. Today in England and in most other countries that follow Anglo-Saxon legal tradition evidence is admitted even if obtained illegally. The principle that evidence should not be excluded merely because the constable has blundered in obtaining evidence was followed in about one-half of the states as late as 1961. This rule, also known as the common law "English Rule," was justified by an English judge, who explained:[2]

> I think it would be a dangerous obstacle to the administration of justice if we were to hold that because evidence was obtained by illegal means, it could not be used against the party charged with an offense. It therefore seems to me that the interests of the state must excuse the seizure of documents, which seizure would otherwise be unlawful, if it appears in fact that such documents were evidence of a crime committed by anyone.

Although the exclusionary rule as it relates to searches in violation of the Constitution was mentioned as far back as 1886 by the United States Supreme Court, it was not until 1914 that the Supreme Court, in the case of *Weeks v. United States*,[3] made the exclusionary rule applicable in federal courts in this country. The Supreme Court held that, in a federal prosecution, the Fourth Amendment barred the use of evidence secured through an illegal search and seizure.

The reason for adopting the exclusionary rule is that the rule (according to the court) is the only way for the judiciary to ensure that police and prosecutors will not violate or encourage violation of the rights protected by the Constitution and its amendments. If courts allowed illegally seized evidence to

---

[1]　For a more comprehensive discussion of the constitutional limitations, *see* KANOVITZ & KANOVITZ, CONSTITUTIONAL LAW (11th ed. 2008) and WALKER AND HEMMENS, LEGAL GUIDE FOR POLICE (8th ed. 2008).

[2]　Elias v. Pasmore, 2 K.B. 65 (1934).

[3]　232 U.S. 383, 34 S. Ct. 341, 58 L. Ed. 652 (1914).

be introduced for jury consideration, the courts could be considered tainted by the illegality that they would be condoning. The situation becomes more clear when one lawbreaker, the criminal, is prosecuted by evidence obtained by another lawbreaker, the police officer, who obtained evidence illegally. While the English courts argue that the remedy is action against the officer who violates these provisions, the courts in this country emphasize that only by excluding the evidence can these privileges be sufficiently protected. By removing illegally seized evidence from admissibility, the incentive for law enforcement agents to violate the law or constitution is substantially diminished. A civil action for damages against the offending officer by the injured party may be a possibility under state law or pursuant to a federal *Bivens* action, which may allow a civil suit against federal officers.[4]

"The ordinary remedy in a criminal case for violation of the Fourth Amendment is suppression of any evidence obtained by the illegal police conduct."[5] Exclusion of evidence serves as a judicially created sanction that indirectly enforces the Fourth Amendment by removing any reward for its violation.[6] The primary purpose of the exclusionary rule is to remove the incentive for police to disregard the provisions of the Fourth Amendment.[7] When the illegally seized evidence is excluded, the prosecutor may have no prosecutable case that remains, the degree of seriousness of the case may be reduced, or the case may have sufficient legal evidence remaining to enable a successful prosecution.

Although the exclusionary rule based on illegal searches and seizures has been applied in federal courts since 1914,[8] it was not until 1961 that the Supreme Court determined that the Fourth Amendment and the exclusionary rule were applicable against the states in search and seizure cases.[9] A reason for the extension of the exclusionary rule to the states has to do with the doctrine of selective incorporation of many of the rights contained in the Bill of Rights into the due process clause of the Fourteenth Amendment.

Partially on the basis of the Fourth Amendment and the exclusionary rule, and consistent with statutory requirements, wiretapping and eavesdropping evidence is often excluded if government conduct has failed to meet legal dictates. However, if the wire or telephone intercept meets the requirements of state and federal wiretap laws, evidence obtained by wiretapping and eavesdropping is admissible.[10] Following the events of September 11, 2001, Congress

---

[4]   Bivens v. Six Unknown Named Agents of Federal Bureau of Narcotics, 403 U.S. 388, 1971 U.S. LEXIS 23 (1971)

[5]   United States v. Olivares-Rangel, 2006 U.S. App. LEXIS 20595 (10th Cir. 2006).

[6]   State v. Klosterman, 114 Ohio App. 3d 327, 683 N.E.2d 100 (1996).

[7]   Hudson v. Michigan, 547 U.S. 586, 2006 U.S. LEXIS 4677 (2006).

[8]   Weeks v. United States, 232 U.S. 383, 1914 U.S. LEXIS 1368 (1914).

[9]   Mapp v. Ohio, 367 U.S. 643, 81 S. Ct. 1684, 6 L. Ed. 2d 1081 (1961).

[10]   *See* United States v. Moore, 452 F.3d. 382, 2006 U.S. App. LEXIS 14152 (5th Cir. 2006), for a case in which wiretapping in a federal prison did not require suppression of evidence seized since it complied with the Federal Wiretap Act.

strengthened the ability of the federal government to conduct wiretaps under the Foreign Intelligence Surveillance Act (FISA) to allow enhanced electronic intelligence gathering that might affect the United States.[11] The target of the surveillance must be a foreign power or an agent for a foreign power and where a criminal prosecution results, there is not a provision for exclusion of evidence under FISA. Individual civil suits attacking the FISA provisions have generally not seen success in either getting the eavesdropping to cease or in getting cases to trial where damages or other remedies have been sought.[12]

The United States Supreme Court has determined that involuntary confessions and statements taken in violation of the *Miranda* warnings may not be admitted in court. Coerced confessions violate the concept of due process and the Fifth Amendment protections against self-incrimination and coerced statements call into question the reliability and truthfulness of a confession. Statements taken in violation of *Miranda* may be reliable but are excluded under public policy decisions made by the Supreme Court. More recently, the courts have applied exclusionary reasoning to exclude evidence obtained in violation of the right to counsel provisions of the Sixth Amendment to the Constitution.

Before leaving the general discussion of the exclusionary rule, it is important to emphasize that the rule applies not only to evidence obtained directly as a result of unlawful action by enforcement personnel, but also to "derivative evidence." Whenever an original search proved to be unlawful, but the results pointed toward other evidence that would only have been discovered because of the original illegality, that other evidence is also excluded[13] in order to ensure that the prosecution is not put in a better position that it would have been if no illegality had transpired.[14] However, if the prosecution can show that the evidence ultimately or inevitably would have been discovered by lawful means,[15] the exclusionary rule serves no deterrent purpose and does not apply.[16] The degree of application of these rules of exclusion is discussed in the following sections.

§ 16.3   Search and Seizure Exclusions

The Fourth Amendment to the Constitution provides:

The right of the people to be secure in their persons, houses, papers, and effects, against unreasonable searches and seizures, shall not be violated,

---

[11]   50 U.S.C. § 1801.

[12]   *See* ACLU v. National Security Agency, 493 F.3d 644, 2007 U.S. App. LEXIS 16149 (6th Cir. 2007).

[13]   Wong Sun v. United States, 371 U.S. 471 (1963).

[14]   State v. Seager, 571 N.W.2d 204 (Iowa 1997). *See also* United States v. Watson, 118 F.3d 1315 (9th Cir. 1997).

[15]   *See* Murray v. United States, 487 U.S. 533 (1988) and Nix v. Williams, 467 U.S. 431 (1984).

[16]   State v. Ballon, 703 So. 2d 130 (La. 1997).

and no Warrants shall issue, but upon probable cause, supported by Oath or affirmation, and particularly describing the place to be searched, and the persons or things to be seized.[17]

The amendment that is now known as the Fourth Amendment was part of the first 10 amendments that were proposed as a means of inducing the necessary number of states to ratify the proposed Constitution of the United States. The first 10 amendments became known as the Bill of Rights and were designed to place limitations on the national government. At this point in history, the Fourth Amendment and the other amendments in the Bill of Rights did not apply to state officials, but were added to prohibit the officials of a strong central government from abridging the rights of the citizens of the various states.

Initially, in the case of *Weeks v. United States*,[18] the Supreme Court of the United States devised the exclusionary rule to help enforce the Fourth Amendment by excluding evidence from federal courts when federal officials had obtained evidence through illegal searches. In a later reconsideration of the coverage of the Fourth Amendment, the Supreme Court in *Mapp v. Ohio* (1961) extended the rule to cover state and local courts because the Court believed that the rule was needed to enforce the due process clause of the Fourteenth Amendment.[19] By making the exclusionary rule applicable to the states, the Court made it necessary for state prosecutors and judges to consider and follow the decisions of the Supreme Court of the United States for minimum federal constitutional search and seizure standards.

In the *Mapp* case, the Supreme Court indicated that the decision closed the last door to the use of illegally seized evidence. However, in 1984, the Supreme Court adopted the good faith exception to the exclusionary rule. In the case of *United States v. Leon*, police officers acting in good faith executed a search warrant instructing them to search residences for controlled substances.[20] Although it was later determined that the search warrant was invalid due to lack of probable cause, the evidence seized pursuant to the warrant could be admitted in court. The *Leon* Court made this comment:

> We conclude that the marginal or nonexistent benefits produced by suppressing evidence obtained in objectively reasonable reliance on a subsequently invalidated search warrant cannot justify the substantial costs of exclusion.

The Supreme Court acknowledged that the exclusionary rule had been modified, but included this warning:

> We do not suggest, however, that exclusion is always inappropriate in cases where an officer has obtained a warrant and abided by its terms. ...

---

[17]   U.S. CONST. amend. IV.
[18]   232 U.S. 383, 1914 U.S. LEXIS 1368 (1914).
[19]   367 U.S. 643, 1961 U.S. LEXIS 812 (1961).
[20]   468 U.S. 897, 104 S. Ct. 3405, 1984 U.S. LEXIS 153 (1984). *See* case in Part II.

Nevertheless, the officer's reliance on the magistrate's probable cause determination and on the technical sufficiency of the warrant he issues must be objectively reasonable . . . and it is clear that in some circumstances the officer will have no reasonable grounds for believing that the warrant was properly issued.

The original intent of the Fourth Amendment's exclusionary rule was to deter illegal police conduct. When the wrong did not come from the police but came from a judge, the police could not have been deterred by using a facially valid search warrant. When, under particular circumstances, there was no deterrent effect on the police, there is no rationale for applying the exclusionary rule.

In *Massachusetts v. Shepherd*, which was decided on the same day as *Leon*, the Supreme Court upheld a search for real evidence when the search was executed in good faith by the officers.[21] The Court determined that the evidence should be admitted even though a reviewing court later found that the description in the search warrant did not meet constitutional standards and the error had been made by the judge.

In both the *Leon* and *Shepherd* cases, police officers executed what they reasonably believed to be valid warrants. Soon after these cases were decided, the question arose as to whether the "good faith" rationale would be applied to situations in which officers acted without a warrant. In the case of *Illinois v. Krull*, officers acting pursuant to a statute, warrantlessly inspected an automobile wrecking yard and discovered several stolen cars.[22] The state statute, similar to those in many other states, regulated the business of buying and selling motor vehicles, parts, and scrap metal. The day after the warrantless search, a federal court ruled that such a statute was unconstitutional, and at the trial a motion was made to exclude the evidence obtained by the officers, even though the officers acted in good faith under the statute. On review, the United States Supreme Court reversed the lower court decision and decided that the evidence should have been admitted, as the application of the exclusionary rule in these circumstances would have little deterrent effect on police conduct because police cannot foretell which laws might be later ruled unconstitutional. In fact, the police made no error; the Illinois legislature erred in passing the unconstitutional statute. In both *Leon* and *Shepherd* the basic deterrent effect would not operate to affect judicial behavior because the intent of the exclusionary rule was to modify police behavior. As Justice O'Connor once stated, "Where the rule's deterrent effect is likely to be marginal, or where its application offends other values central to our system of constitutional governance or the judicial process, we have declined to extend the rule to that context."[23]

---

[21] Massachusetts v. Shepherd, 468 U.S. 897, 104 S. Ct. 3424, 82 L. Ed. 2d 677 (1984).

[22] Illinois v. Krull, 475 U.S. 868, 107 S. Ct. 1160, 94 L. Ed. 2d 364 (1987). *See Kanovitz & Kanovitz, Constitutional Law* (11th ed. 2008) for a more thorough discussion of the search and seizure requirements.

[23] Duckworth v. Eagan, 492 U.S. 195, 208 (1989).

Although the court in the *Krull* case did not extend the "good faith" exception to a considerable extent, it did clarify the reasoning concerning the exclusionary rule with these comments:

> Application of the Exclusionary Rule "is neither intended nor able to cure the invasion of the defendant's rights which he has already suffered". . . . Rather, the rule "operates as a judicially created remedy designed to safeguard Fourth Amendment rights generally through its deterrent effect, rather than as a personal constitutional right of the party aggrieved". . . . As with any remedial device, application of the exclusionary rule properly has been restricted to those situations in which its remedial purpose is effectively advanced.

These cases indicate a trend by the Supreme Court to apply less technical rules in search and seizure cases. However, the exclusionary rule still applies in a majority of cases when evidence has been obtained illegally. Therefore, it is essential that the rules concerning the constitutionality of searches be followed.

Stops and brief searches on less than probable cause may create constitutional issues when police were looking for drugs rather than impaired drivers. In *Indianapolis v. Edmond*, the defendant had been stopped based on absolutely no suspicion at a citywide checkpoint in an effort to locate drivers with illegal substances. The court held that while brief stops to detect drunk drivers was a reasonable approach under the Fourth Amendment,[24] stopping people for general crime control on absolutely no suspicion could not be squared with the Constitution.[25] However, for a specific important purpose, such as a roadblock designed to obtain more information about a recent hit-and-run offense and not to investigate any particular driver, a checkpoint can be reasonable under the Fourth Amendment.[26] Police contact with motorists consisted of an information request and they gave each motorist an informational flyer.

When police proceed without probable cause or a warrant, there may be some limitations. Clearly, entering a private residence in the absence of a warrant, exigent circumstances, or probable cause may run afoul of the doctrine of the *Mapp* case, but the thermal imaging of a dwelling involves no physical intrusion. However, evidence obtained from heat scans of residential buildings should not be used as part of probable cause to obtain a warrant. In *Kyllo v. United States*, the Court held that using a thermal-imaging device to take a scan of the heat signature from a residence that indicated the possibility that there was marijuana growing inside constituted a Fourth Amendment search for which a warrant or a substitute was constitutionally required.[27]

---

[24]   *See* Michigan v. Sitz, 496 U.S. 444 (1990).
[25]   Indianapolis v. Edmond, 531 U.S. 32 (2000).
[26]   *See* Illinois v. Lidster, 540 U.S. 419, 2004 U.S. LEXIS 656 (2004).
[27]   Kyllo v. United States, 533 U.S. 27 (2001).

Exigent or emergency circumstances permit police to enter a home or other location without a warrant to save a life or to prevent serious bodily injury. In a Utah case, police responded to a call about a loud party at 3:00 A.M. to find juveniles drinking alcoholic beverages in the yard and a fight going on inside the home among four adults and a juvenile.[28] Officers observed the fight and blood from outside and announced their presence, but no one responded to the officers. The police entered the kitchen fight area and arrested various adults for contributing to the delinquency of a minor. The Supreme Court of the United States held that the situation fell into the exigent or emergency circumstances category of an exception to the warrant requirement, where police may enter a home when they have an objectively reasonable basis to believe a person may be seriously injured or is threatened with death or serious bodily injury. Evidence so acquired is admissible and is not excluded by the *Mapp* doctrine.

Other exceptions to the exclusionary rule include the independent source rule, in which evidence is admitted when the Fourth Amendment has been violated but there is a separate avenue by which the evidence could be legally obtained.[29] In one case, officers illegally entered a building to determine whether the evidence remained inside, but they included only good, untainted evidence on an affidavit for a search warrant. The illegal entry did not taint the warrant because there was a good independent source for probable cause.[30]

Unlawfully obtained evidence may be admitted when it would have been inevitably discovered by lawful means within a reasonable time[31] under the rule of inevitable discovery. In this case, an officer violated the principles of *Miranda* to obtain the location of a murder victim, but the evidence of the body was not excluded because the police were searching in the area and would inevitably have found the body lawfully within a reasonable time.[32] When the illegality is separated or attenuated from the illegal collection of evidence by time and distance, the evidence is not excluded.[33] In this case, the defendants went to police to confess and make a deal several days after an alleged illegal search of their homes. The confession evidence was separated by an independent act of free will and by time and distance, and would not be excluded on Fourth Amendment grounds.

One type of search, which is universally recognized as legal, is a search with a warrant. Both the United States Constitution and the constitutions of the various states describe the circumstances under which search warrants may be issued.

In order for a search warrant to be valid, it must meet certain requirements. Some of the requirements are enumerated in the Constitution. Others

---

[28]   Brigham City v. Stuart, 547 U.S. 398, 2006 U.S. LEXIS 4155 (2006).
[29]   Murray v. United States, 468 U.S. 796 (1984).
[30]   *Id.*
[31]   Nix v. Williams, 467 U.S. 431, 1984 U.S. LEXIS 101 (1984).
[32]   Nix v. Williams, 467 U.S. 431, 1984 U.S. LEXIS 101(1984).
[33]   *See* Wong Sun v. United States, 371 U.S. 471, 1963 U.S. LEXIS 2431 (1963).

have been added by legislation or court interpretation. In order for a search warrant to be enforceable, the following requirements must be met:

1. The warrant must be issued on probable cause.
2. The warrant must be supported by oath or affirmation.
3. The proper judicial official must issue the warrant.
4. The place to be searched and the things to be seized must be particularly described.[34]

The United States Supreme Court, as well as other courts, has encouraged the use of a search warrant in making a search. In 1983, the Court, in reinforcing this preference and in indicating a trend to approve less technical procedures, modified the probable cause requirements for a search warrant. In previous cases, the Court had approved the use of undisclosed informants in determining probable cause and had established what was known as the "two-pronged" test.[35] Under this test, the judge must be given facts from an informant that equal probable cause and the judge must have clear reasons why the informant is to be believed. This standard for testing the credibility of an informant's tip upon which a magistrate is asked to rely was: (1) that the magistrate must be given some of the underlying circumstances from which the affiant concluded that the informant was credible or that his or her information was reliable; and (2) that the magistrate must be given some of the underlying circumstances from which the informant reached the conclusion conveyed in the tip.

In a reconsideration of the use of informants to help establish probable cause, in *Illinois v. Gates* the Supreme Court abandoned the two-pronged test in which probable cause must be based on informant information and established the "totality of circumstances" test.[36] While agreeing with the Illinois Supreme Court that an informant's veracity, reliability, and basis of knowledge were all highly relevant in determining whether an informant's report equals probable cause, the Court indicated that the totality of circumstances approach was far more consistent with the Court's prior treatment of probable cause. Under this test, the issuing judicial official must make a practical, commonsense decision, given all the circumstances set forth in the affidavit, that there is a fair probability that contraband or evidence of a crime will be found in a particular place. State courts are free to require a higher standard for informant-based probable cause under state laws or constitutions.[37]

---

[34] *See* WALKER AND HEMMENS, LEGAL GUIDE FOR POLICE: CONSTITUTIONAL ISSUES (8th ed. 2008) and the Fourth Amendment.

[35] Aguilar v. Texas, 378 U.S. 108, 84 S. Ct. 1509, 12 L. Ed. 2d 723 (1964).

[36] 462 U.S. 213, 103 S. Ct. 2317, 76 L. Ed. 2d 527 (1983). *See also* People v. Jack, 70 Cal. Rptr. 2d 676 (1997).

[37] *See* People v. Tarver, 292 A.D.2d 110, 741 N.Y.S.2d 130, 2002 N.Y. App. Div. LEXIS 3631 (N.Y. 2002) and People v. Williams, 284 A.D.2d 564, 726 N.Y.S.2d 740, 2001 N.Y. App. Div. LEXIS 11474, n.1 (N.Y. 2001).

Even though a warrant has been issued correctly, the evidence can be made inadmissible by improper execution of the warrant. In executing the warrant, the officer must follow these guidelines:

1. The warrant must be executed by the officer named or the officer must come within the class designated.
2. The warrant must be executed within certain time limitations.
3. Only necessary force may be used in executing the warrant.
4. Prior notice and demand shall usually precede forcible entry.
5. Only the property described may to be seized under the warrant.

One of the requirements of the Fourth Amendment is that searches and seizures must be reasonable in the way they are executed. One of the common law hallmarks indicating reasonableness was the concept that the officers should knock and announce before resorting to breaking into a house. The knock-and-announce rule serves to protect the privacy of the individual, avoids needless destruction of property, and reduces confusion, shielding police and occupiers from attack by each other. Notwithstanding the statutes and case law requiring prior notice and demand, the courts have recognized an exception for exigent circumstances, such as immediate physical danger, flight, or clear potential for destruction of evidence. In the case of *Wilson v. Arkansas*, the United States Supreme Court noted that "this Court has little doubt that the Amendments' framers thought that whether the officers announced their presence and authority before entering a dwelling was among the factors to be considered in assessing a search's reasonableness."[38] The court recognized, however, that there are exceptions to the rule, "including the threat of physical harm to the police, the fact that an officer is pursuing a recently escaped arrestee, and the existence of reason to believe that evidence would likely be destroyed if advance notice were given may establish the reasonableness of unannounced entry."

The Court retreated from a preference for the knock-and-announce requirement when faced with a clearly guilty defendant who wanted evidence suppressed based on an imperfect knock and announce by police. In this case,[39] under the authority of a search warrant, the police announced their presence and entered, all within the space of three to five seconds. The defendant's door was unlocked at the time the police entered to find narcotics and illegal guns. The prosecution conceded that the police had violated the *Wilson v. Arkansas* rule, but contended that suppression of the evidence was not the appropriate remedy. The Supreme Court noted, "[t]he common-law principle that law enforcement officers must announce their presence and provide residents an opportunity to open the door is an ancient one,"[40] but the Court was not inclined to suppress

---

[38]   Wilson v. Arkansas, 514 U.S. 927, 115 S. Ct. 1914, 131 L. Ed. 2d 976 (1995).

[39]   Hudson v. Michigan, 547 U.S. 586, 2006 U.S. LEXIS 4677 (2006).

[40]   *Id.*

the evidence just because there was a Fourth Amendment violation. It noted that the knock and announce rule did not protect the citizen from keeping the government from seeing evidence described in a warrant. The deterrence effect on police must outweigh the substantial social costs of suppression and the Court believed that the deterrent effect was small and every litigant would be contesting the failure to knock and announce if the result of a win would be suppression of all the evidence. What the Court stated in *Wilson v. Arkansas* had been difficult to apply in practice and the Court no longer requires that police knock and announce. The present rule seems to suggest that knock and announce may be proper but that if police fail to knock and announce, they run little risk of having the evidence suppressed from use by the prosecutor.

Although preference is given to the search warrant as a means of making a search, and the search warrant is the only such means mentioned in the Constitution as proper, Supreme Court jurisprudence has recognized the necessity of conducting some searches without warrants, especially in emergency situations[41] or when the officer might be facing an unclear danger.[42] Case law illuminates and illustrates the typical exceptions to the general necessity of a warrant. In each instance, an exception applies only when certain requirements are met. The paragraphs that follow discuss the most important examples of these exceptions.

A. *Search Incident to a Lawful Arrest*

The right to make a search incident to a lawful arrest has been recognized by all courts, including the United States Supreme Court,[43] but does require an actual lawful arrest prior to conducting a valid search.[44] In addition to a valid arrest, the search incident to arrest requires that the search be made contemporaneously with the arrest, or immediately after, and that the search be reasonable in scope. Naturally, the arrest must be made in good faith that arrest probable cause exists.[45] If police make an arrest based on an erroneous entry into a database that discloses an active warrant and discover criminal evidence as a result of the search incident to later arrest, the evidence will not be excluded because excluding the evidence would not alter police practice in the future.[46] An arrest

---

[41]   *See* Warden v. Hayden, 387 U.S. 294 (1967) and New York v. Quarles, 467 U.S. 649 (1984).

[42]   *See* United States v. Arellano-Ochoa, 2006 U.S. App. LEXIS 22466 (9th Cir. 2006), in which the court permitted a warrantless entry where an officer could not see through the screen of a house trailer door under circumstances in which the officer might have been dealing with an armed drug trafficker.

[43]   Chimel v. California, 395 U.S. 752, 89 S. Ct. 2034, 23 L. Ed. 2d 685 (1969).

[44]   *See* Knowles v. Iowa, 525 U.S. 113, 1998 U.S. LEXIS 8068 (1998).

[45]   Arizona v. Evans, 514 U.S. 1, 1995 U.S. LEXIS 1806 (1995). *See also* United States v. Miller, 382 F. Supp. 2d 350 (N.D. N.Y. 2005).

[46]   Herring v. United States, _____ U.S. _____, 2009 U.S. LEXIS 581 (2009). An arrest is not illegal even where police acted based on outdated information contained with a computer system. The evidence seized will not be excluded from trial or other use.

is lawful even if the law of the jurisdiction does not permit the arrest as long as police have probable cause to believe the individual has committed a crime and police do not otherwise violate the Fourth Amendment.[47] Under these circumstances, police can conduct a search incident to the lawful arrest and evidence is not excluded under the Fourth Amendment.

While the United States Supreme Court has left no doubt that a search of the person incident to a lawful arrest may occur slightly before the actual arrest if the arrest occurs contemporaneously with the search, it is preferable to conduct a search incident to an arrest following the arrest.[48] In the case of *Smith v. Ohio*, the United States Supreme Court was asked to answer the single question of "whether a warrantless search, which provides probable cause for an arrest, can nonetheless be justified as an incident of that arrest."[49] In this case, the defendant, when asked by an officer to "come here a minute," threw onto the hood of his car a paper grocery sack that he was carrying. The officer, before making the arrest, pushed the defendant's hand away and opened the bag, which contained drug paraphernalia.

The search was illegal because the defendant was not arrested until after the contraband was discovered. Therefore, the contraband could not serve as a part of the justification for a lawful arrest and could not support a lawful search incident to an arrest. The Court reversed the conviction and concluded that:

> The exception for searches incident to arrest permits the police to search a lawfully arrested person and areas within his immediate control . . . it does not permit police to search any citizen without a warrant or probable cause so long as an arrest immediately follows.

Because a search incident to a lawful arrest is intended to protect the searching officer and to prevent the destruction of evidence, the scope of the area of the search is limited generally to the lunge area where a weapon could be obtained or evidence destroyed. In the case of *Chimel v. California*, the area of search was defined as "the area within his immediate control—construing that phrase to mean the area from which he might gain possession of a weapon or destructible evidence."[50]

However, in applying the *Chimel* rule when the search is made of a residence incident to a lawful arrest, police may not search the interior of the arrestee's home when the arrest occurred on the sidewalk outside of the home. In one case, the search of the arrestee's home was unreasonable because it was not conducted incident to his arrest and was not confined to a cursory

---

[47]   Virginia v. Moore, _____ U.S. _____, _____, 2008 U.S. LEXIS 3674 (2008).

[48]   Rawlings v. Kentucky, 448 U.S. 98, 111, 1980 U.S. LEXIS 142 (1980). *Accord,* United States v. Montgomery, 377 F. 3d 582, 2004 U. S. App. LEXIS 15438 (6th Cir. 2004).

[49]   Smith v. Ohio, 494 U.S. 541, 110 S. Ct. 1288, 108 L. Ed. 2d. 464 (1990).

[50]   Chimel v. California, 395 U.S. 762, 89 S. Ct. 2034, 23 L. Ed. 2d 685 (1969); *see also* United States v. Robinson, 414 U.S. 218 (1973), which held that the authority to search incident to a lawful arrest includes the right to search the person arrested for evidence not related to the crime.

inspection. The Fourth Amendment allows a sweep if the officers lawfully enter an arrestee's home but where the officers have no right to enter, there can be no lawful sweep.[51] If an arrest is made in one part of the house, the Fourth Amendment permits a properly limited protective sweep in conjunction with the in-home arrest when the searching officers possess a reasonable belief, based on specific and articulable facts, that the area to be swept harbors an individual posing a danger to those on the arrest scene. However, the fact that an arrest is made in the living room does not justify a full search of the whole house without a warrant unless there is consent by one who has authority to consent.[52] In making a sweep to make sure that no one is on the premises who could launch an immediate attack, police may look anywhere in a home that a person might be hiding. There must be articulable facts along with rational inferences would warrant a prudent officer in believing that the sweep area harbors an individual who poses a danger.[53]

In a 2009 case, *Arizona v. Gant*,[54] the Supreme Court overruled some earlier cases that had permitted a search of the interior of a motor vehicle following a lawful arrest of a driver or passenger. In *Gant*, the driver had been arrested for driving under a suspended license and he and some other people who were his friends had been handcuffed and secured in patrol cars when the vehicle search occurred. There was no chance at any of the individuals could gain access to the motor vehicle in a way that might endanger the officers or destroy evidence. Under the new Fourth amendment interpretation of a search incident to a lawful arrest involving a motor vehicle, the police may search a vehicle's interior only if there is reason to believe that the arrestee might access the vehicle at the time of the search or if the police believe that the vehicle contains evidence of the offense for which the driver or occupant has been arrested. In this particular case, there was no expectation that evidence of the crime of driving under a suspended license would be found and there was no chance that the arrested individuals could gain access to the motor vehicle and therefore the search of its interior was unreasonable.

In summarizing the scope of a "sweep search," a federal appeals court indicated that a "sweep search" is narrowly confined to a cursory visual inspection of places in a building where a person might be hiding.[55] The court continued by noting that officers are permitted to take reasonable steps to ensure their safety, and may, without probable cause or reasonable suspicion, look in closets or other spaces immediately adjoining the places of arrest from which an attack could be immediately launched. A protective sweep became an unreasonable

---

[51]   *See* United States v. Rios-Ramirez, 2004 U.S. Dist. LEXIS 26573 (D.P.R. 2004).

[52]   Maryland v. Buie, 494 U.S. 325, 110 S. Ct. 1093, 108 L. Ed. 2d 276 (1990).

[53]   *Id.*

[54]   Arizona v. Gant, 556 U.S. _____, 2009 U.S. LEXIS 3120 (2009). *See* case in Part II.

[55]   United States v. Barnett, 989 F.2d 546 (1st Cir.), *cert. denied,* 510 U.S. 850, 114 S. Ct. 148, 126 L. Ed. 2d 110 (1993). See also United States v. Hutchings, 127 F.3d 1255 (10th Cir. 1997).

search when officers conducted a sweep of an apartment where they could see all the rooms of the apartment from the foyer and the defendant was not the target of the officer's attentions. The defendant was not under arrest and the bedroom where the illegal drugs were discovered was not within the lunge area of the defendant. From the view that the officers originally had in the foyer, there was no need for a protective sweep and the drugs were suppressed as fruits of an illegal "sweep search."[56]

B. Search After a Waiver of Constitutional Right

In accordance with the general principles that allow a person to waive his or her constitutional rights, the rights protected by the Fourth Amendment to the Constitution and state provisions concerning search and seizure may be waived. In order for this exception to the warrant rule to apply, the prosecution must show that the consent was voluntarily and freely given, and that the person who gave the consent had the capacity and authority to consent. The general rule is that the consent of one who has dominion and control over the premises or effects is the proper person and may give valid consent against the absent nonconsenting person with whom the authority is shared,[57] unless the nonconsenting person is present and refuses to grant consent.[58] In one case, a couple shared dominion and control over the marital residence and a domestic dispute brought the police. The wife alleged that the defendant had drugs within the home and consented to a police search of the marital home. The husband refused to grant consent to search and the Supreme Court held that one spouse had no recognized authority in law or in social practice to prevail over the other spouse who was present and refused consent to search. The police had no better claim to reasonably enter the marital premises than any other person when joint consent was not available.[59] Apparent shared authority over real or personal property will permit one of the persons to give lawful consent to search where police act in a reasonable manner and the other person with authority is not present[60] or if present, offers no objection. In a Second Circuit case, the court affirmed the validity of a consent search where a live-in girlfriend granted federal officers consent to search of the shared bedroom while the arrested defendant made no objection.[61] The test for a waiver of consent encompasses the totality of the circumstances—in which the age, education, legal education, if any, coerciveness of the atmosphere, whether the person

---

[56]   United States v. Ali, 2006 U.S. Dist. LEXIS 21543 (E.D.N.Y. 2006).

[57]   United States v. Matlock, 415 U.S. 164, 94 S. Ct. 988, 39 L. Ed. 2d 242 (1974). *See* KANOVITZ & KANOVITZ, CONSTITUTIONAL LAW (11th ed. 2008) for a discussion of the authority of a spouse, a minor child, and a parent to consent to a search.

[58]   Georgia v. Randolph, 547 U.S. 103, 2006 U.S. LEXIS 2498 (2006).

[59]   *Id.*

[60]   Illinois v. Rodriguez, 497 U.S. 177 (1990).

[61]   United States v. Lopez, 547 F.3d 397, 2008 U.S. App. LEXIS 23303 (2dCir. 2008).

was under arrest or threatened with arrest, and whether the person knew of the right to refuse without facing adverse consequences—are considered.[62]

In considering the waiver of constitutional rights, the police and the courts must carefully observe any limitations placed upon the consent. A general consent to search for drugs in a vehicle generally extends to any part of the vehicle where the drugs might reasonably be hidden[63] in the absence of some limitation by the consenting party.[64] There is some authority stating that a person may revoke the consent during the process of the search.[65] If the consent is revoked, evidence obtained from a continuing search is not admissible unless justified on other grounds.

To be constitutionally adequate, the consent must be given without force, duress, or compulsion of any kind.[66] Where the government agent used subtle coercion, the consent may be ruled as inadequate and involuntary. In a case in which an officer used pressure to gain consent to search a car, the consent was not valid.[67] The government has the burden of proving that the consent was truly voluntary, unfettered by coercion, whether express or implied.[68] However, the Fourth Amendment does not require that a lawfully seized detainee be affirmatively advised that he or she is "free to go" before his or her consent to search will be recognized as voluntary.[69]

Some situations exist when the consent to search may not be completely voluntarily given but evidence seized remains admissible. In the context of probation or parole, a convict may be forced to agree to a reduction or waiver of some Fourth Amendment rights as a condition of release. In one California case,[70] as a condition of release, the parolee was forced to agree in writing to allow a search and seizure of his person, property, place of residence, and any other location where he might have an expectation of privacy, to search anytime, with or without a warrant, by any probation officer or law enforcement officer. A police officer conducted a warrantless search of the parolee's person and found methamphetamine, which was a violation of his parole. The convict argued that the Fourth Amendment could not be construed to force him to give up his rights in exchange for conditional freedom. The Supreme Court held that a condition of release can constitutionally diminish a parolee's expectation of privacy to permit a suspicionless search and the evidence discovered is not subject to exclusion from court.

---

[62] *See* Schneckloth v. Bustamonte, 412 U.S. 218 (1973).

[63] Florida v. Jimeno, 500 U.S. 248, 1991 U.S. LEXIS 2910 (1991).

[64] United States v. Gregoire, 425 F.3d 872, 880, 2005 U.S. App. LEXIS 21398 (10th Cir. 2005).

[65] *Id.* at 881. *See also* United States v. Flores-Ocampo, 173 Fed. Appx. 688, 691, 2006 U.S. App. LEXIS 8367 (10th Cir. 2006), in which a general consent to search a car included gas tank and sun roof area.

[66] Schneckloth v. Bustamonte, 412 U.S. 218 (1973).

[67] Ohio v. Robinette, 519 U.S. 33 (1996).

[68] Commonwealth v. Rogers, 444 Mass. 234, 344, 827 N.E.2d 669, 677, 2005 Mass. LEXIS 216 (Mass. 2005).

[69] Ohio v. Robinette, 517 U.S. 33, 177 S. Ct. 417, 136 L. Ed. 2d 347 (1996).

[70] Samson v. California, 547 U.S. 843, 2006 U.S. LEXIS 4885 (2006).

The court looks at the totality of circumstances to determine whether a consent to search has been voluntary in fact,[71] and if consent is not sufficiently an act of the free will to purge the primary taint of the illegal search warrant, then the results of the search must to be suppressed as "fruit of poisonous tree."[72]

C. Search of a Vehicle That Is Moving or about to Be Moved

Recognizing a difference between the search of a dwelling house, for which a warrant can be readily obtained, and the search of an automobile, ship, wagon, airplane, or other movable object, for which securing a warrant may not be practical because of the mobility of the vehicle, courts have determined that some vehicles may be searched without a warrant as long as probable cause exists.[73] Two requirements that must be met in order for a search of this type to be valid are: (1) the officer must have probable cause that would justify the issuance of a search warrant if the facts were presented to a judge and (2) the vehicle must be readily movable. In such a case, the decision concerning whether to seize the vehicle while a warrant is obtained or conduct an immediate warrantless search is left to the determination of the officer involved. According to the Supreme Court, either course of action is reasonable.

While a person who owns or leases a motor vehicle generally has an expectation of privacy in that automobile, that person could argue that the exclusionary rule should permit suppression of evidence. The Supreme Court has ruled that a police stop of a motor vehicle results in the seizure of every occupant in the vehicle.[74] Therefore, any occupant has the right to challenge the legality of the stop of the vehicle and may be able to suppress evidence subsequently seized if a court determines that the stop was not justified.

In determining the extent of an automobile search, the United States Supreme Court reconsidered some prior case law governing the scope of the search under the moving vehicle doctrine and held that police acting under the automobile exception to the Fourth Amendment warrant requirement may search every part of the vehicle, including closed containers in the trunk, that

---

[71] *See* United States v. Drayton, 536 U.S. 194, 2002 U.S. LEXIS 4420 (2002), in which officers were "working the buses" and obtained consent to search luggage from interstate bus passengers.

[72] United States v. Cowdin, 984 F. Supp. 1374 (D. Kan. 1997). In this case, a revolver obtained as a result of a search without voluntary consent was held inadmissible. *See also* Wong Sun v. United States, 371 U.S. 471 (1963).

[73] Chambers v. Maroney, 339 U.S. 42, 90 S. Ct. 1975, 26 L. Ed. 2d 419 (1970). The genesis for this theory seems to have been Carroll v. United States, 267 U.S. 132, 1925 U.S. LEXIS 361 (1925), in which police conducted a warrantless search of a moving automobile that had been stopped where there was probable cause to search. See also Wyoming v. Houghton, 526 U.S. 295 (1999), in which the United States Supreme Court, after referring to United States v. Ross, held that police officers with probable cause to search a car may inspect passengers' belongings found in the car that are capable of concealing the object of the search.

[74] *See* Brendlin v. California, 551 U.S. 249, 2007 U.S. LEXIS 7897 (2007).

might conceal the contraband for which the police have probable cause.[75] However, officers may not search the trunk of a vehicle where there is no probable cause to believe that seizable property is contained within.[76] Under the stop-and-frisk standard, officers may briefly stop, ask questions, and request consent to search when there is a reasonable basis to suspect that criminal activity might be afoot.[77] When subjects fit a drug courier profile, police may stop and talk to occupants of automobiles.[78]

The scope of the search under the moving vehicle doctrine depends upon the object of the search and the places in which there is probable cause to believe the object may be found.[79] Where there is probable cause to search an entire car, it would be permissible to search a woman's purse found within the car.[80] For example, if probable cause exists to believe that a container placed in the trunk of an automobile contains contraband,[81] the vehicle search theory permits an immediate warrantless seizure and search of the container[82] but would not necessarily justify a search of the entire car. A search of other parts of the car might be justified under the search incidental to a lawful arrest theory, the vehicle inventory search theory, or if consent is given by the person in possession of the automobile.

As a general rule, the movable vehicle doctrine, which authorizes the search of a vehicle that is in movable condition, applies to automobiles, boats, and airplanes if the criteria are met. A federal court of appeals reversed a trial court holding that a particular moveable vehicle could be searched without a warrant.[83] Police searched the subject's home pursuant to a warrant and also searched a Suburban SUV for which probable cause existed. Police searched a Cadillac owned by the subject that was parked in the apartment complex lot, by relying on the fact that there had been an allegation that drugs had been stored in the Suburban SUV. In rejecting the legality of the search of the Cadillac, the appellate court noted that the vehicle exception did not apply to the movable Cadillac and observed:

> The Cadillac was not subject to a valid warrantless search under the auto-mobile exception since Appellees had no probable cause to believe that marijuana would be found in the Cadillac. See *United States v. Hogan* (determining that the seizure of a vehicle was invalid for lack of probable cause because all of the evidence indicated that drugs would be found in the defendant's home or in a different vehicle, and none of the evidence indicated

---

[75]   United States v. Ross, 456 U.S. 798, 1982 U.S. LEXIS 18 (1982).
[76]   United States v. Jackson, 367 U.S. App. D.C. 320, 415 F.3d 88, 92, 2005 U.S. App. LEXIS 14951 (D.C. Cir. 2005).
[77]   *See* Alabama v. White, 496 U.S. 325 (1990).
[78]   Orlenas v. United States, 517 U.S. 690 (1996).
[79]   United States v. Gastfiaburo, 16 F.3d 582 (4th Cir. 1994).
[80]   Wyoming v. Houghton, 526 U.S. 295 (1999).
[81]   California v. Acevedo, 500 U.S. 565 (1991).
[82]   *Id.*
[83]   Mack v. City of Abilene, 461 F.3d 547, 553 (5th Cir. 2006).

that drugs would be found in the particular vehicle that was seized). Here, the informant reported to Appellees [police] only that Appellant sometimes kept marijuana in his Suburban, not the Cadillac. Furthermore, upon looking into the vehicle, Appellees do not claim they saw or smelled something that might lead to probable cause. Therefore, no search of the Cadillac was allowed under the automobile exception.

The exception to the warrant requirement under the movable vehicle doctrine allows warrantless searches of motor vehicles, provided probable cause to search exists at the moment the search begins. Where a driver has been removed from a vehicle and secured away from the vehicle, the vehicle may be searched when there is reason to believe that seizable property may be within the vehicle that relates to the reason for the arrest. No search of the vehicle may occur where no evidence relating to the reason for the arrest is expected.[84]

Some vehicle stops may be initiated on less than probable cause[85] and some cursory searches may mature into full probable cause vehicle searches. In one case, border patrol officials determined that a vehicle had tripped a sensor on a road typically used by drug smugglers. As a federal official interdicted the minivan, he noticed that the occupants did not want to look at him and the children had their legs up on some cargo on the backseat floorboards. Probable cause to search did not exist, but the officer followed the *Terry* stop-and-frisk protocol as applied to motor vehicles to make a stop and brief inquiry. Following the stop, the story offered by the driver of the heavily loaded minivan did not make sense, and eventually probable cause developed, allowing a warrantless search that revealed that the driver was smuggling recreational drugs.[86] Various factors considered on an individual basis may not lead to a reasonable basis to suspect criminal activity under the stop-and-frisk standard or to probable cause for a search or arrest, but when considered under a totality of the circumstances, the stop-and-frisk standard may mature or probable cause for a vehicle search may be present.[87]

D. *The Seizure of Evidence When No Search Is Required (Plain View)*

The plain view doctrine allows seizures of objects that either offend the law by their mere presence or are objects that, under the circumstances, appear to constitute criminal evidence. In an earlier case, *Coolidge v. New Hampshire*, the Court seemed to require that seizures under the plain view doctrine must have been discovered inadvertently from a vantage point where the police officer had the legal right to be.[88] In one sense, the plain view doctrine does not involve

---

[84] *See* Arizona v. Gant, _____ U.S. _____, 2009 U.S. LEXIS 3120 (2009). *See* case in Part II.
[85] Alabama v. White, 496 U.S. 325, 1990 U.S. LEXIS 3053 (1990).
[86] United States v. Arvizu, 534 U.S. 266, 2002 U.S. LEXIS 490 (2002).
[87] *Id.*
[88] 403 U.S. 443, 469, 1971 U.S. LEXIS 25 (1971).

a search; the law enforcement officer merely observes the seizable object in full view without any need to conduct a search. The officer must legally be in the place from which the clear view was available. For example, in one case, a police officer was lawfully inside an apartment investigating a gunshot when he observed expensive electronic equipment that looked out-of-place in the shabby apartment. He moved one item to secure a serial number from the rear of the unit. This was held to be a search and could not be justified under the plain view doctrine.[89] In a typical situation, the officer is merely on the premises and, unexpectedly, the officer observes an object that seems to indicate that a crime has been committed. The plain view doctrine comes into play when an officer on a domestic call observes white powder and a scale or when a parole officer, when meeting with the parolee, observes a gun on a bed.

The gloss of inadvertence as a requirement of the plain view doctrine ended when the Supreme Court decided *Horton v. California*.[90] In that case, the police executed a warrant at Horton's home for proceeds from an armed robbery. The warrant mentioned some objects but did not describe a gun that the officers expected to find and did find. The *Horton* Court held that inadvertence was not a necessary condition under this warrant exception. The Court considered the gun to have been lawfully seized, even though its presence was expected. The United States Supreme Court reiterated that the warrantless seizure of an object in plain view is valid if the following conditions are met: (1) the officer did not violate the Fourth Amendment in entering the place where the object was seen; (2) the object's incriminating character was immediately apparent, and (3) the officer had lawful access to the object itself. The *Horton* Court added that the concept of inadvertency as part of this warrant exception was never an essential part of the holding in *Coolidge v. New Hampshire* even though most plain view doctrine seizures occur due to the unexpected finding of contraband. "The normal Fourth Amendment rule is that items discovered in plain view are admissible if the officers were legitimately on the premises"[91] as long as there was probable cause to seize the evidence at the time it was encountered.

In a Colorado case that involved the plain view doctrine,[92] officers observed a syringe containing a clear liquid in a partially opened bedside table in a motel room. The police used a tactic known as a "knock and talk" in which they approach the door of a place of interest and ask the occupant if they might talk to the person inside the building. The defendant permitted four officers to enter her motel room to talk to her, resulting in the plain view sighting and seizure of the syringe and drugs. The trial court refused to suppress the drug evidence that resulted in the defendant's conviction. The reviewing court held that the officers were in the motel room lawfully due to the defendant's consent

---

89 *See* Arizona v. Hicks, 480 U.S. 321, 1987 U.S. LEXIS 1056 (1987).
90 496 U.S. 128, 141, 1990 U.S. LEXIS 2937 (1990). *See* case in Part II.
91 Georgia v. Randolph, 547 U.S. 103, 137, 2006 U.S. LEXIS 2498 (2006). *See* case in Part II.
92 People v. Bostic, 2006 Colo. App. LEXIS 622 (2006).

and they observed the syringe by looking around the room without conducting a search.

Officers may not lawfully use the plain view doctrine where they have no lawful access to a defendant's premises. In a Georgia case, officers procured the consent of a landlord to enter a defendant's rented trailer. As the officer opened the door, he observed growing marijuana plants. Using the evidence gathered under the plain view doctrine, the officer procured a search warrant and later seized the plants. The Court of Appeals held that the plain view doctrine did not produce good evidence because the officer had no legal right to enter the trailer home where the right was based on the landlady's "consent" and, therefore, the officer was not lawfully on the premises.[93]

Generally, state and federal courts have agreed that the use of an officer's flashlight to illuminate a darkened area in an automobile does not constitute a search, and thus triggers no Fourth Amendment protection.[94] One court reasoned that an officer who peers into the interior of a vehicle during a traffic stop, and who uses a flashlight for illumination and safety, commits no Fourth Amendment wrong.[95]

E. Seizure of Evidence from Premises Not Protected by the Fourth Amendment (Open Fields)

In 1984, the United States Supreme Court confirmed the rule that only "houses, papers, and effects" are protected by the Constitution and that a search of open fields does not violate the Fourth Amendment.[96] The closing paragraph of the Supreme Court opinion in this case summarizes the decision with these words:

> We conclude that the open fields doctrine, as enunciated in Hester, is consistent with the plain language of the Fourth Amendment and its historical purposes.

While the Constitution protects houses, including the curtilage,[97] evidence obtained from outside the curtilage is admissible even if entry amounts to a trespass in the civil or criminal sense. In the case of *United States v. Dunn*, the United States Supreme Court suggested some guidelines that could be applied in determining whether an area is within the curtilage for Fourth Amendment

---

[93] Looney v. State, 293 Ga. App. 639, 2008 Ga. App. LEXIS 1039 (Ga. 2008).

[94] People v. Brown, 2006 Cal. App. Unpub. LEXIS 4196 (2006).

[95] State v. Young, 895 So. 2d 753, 757, 2005 La. App. LEXIS 536 (2005).

[96] Oliver v. United States, 466 U.S. 170, 104 S. Ct. 1735, 80 L. Ed. 2d 214 (1984), reaffirming Hester v. United States, 265 U.S. 57 (1924).

[97] BLACK'S LAW DICTIONARY (2004) defines curtilage as "[t]he land or yard adjoining a house, usu. within an enclosure." Commonly the curtilage is the area around an individual home that might be reasonably fenced if a fence were installed.

purposes.[98] The *Dunn* Court enumerated four factors to be considered in determining extent-of-curtilage questions:

1. The proximity of the area to the home;
2. Whether the area is within an enclosure surrounding the home;
3. The nature and uses to which the area is put; and
4. The steps taken by the resident to protect the area from observation by passersby.

Applying these criteria, the Court ruled that a barn, located 50 yards from the house, behind several animal fences, and not within the area enclosed by a fence surrounding the house, was not within the curtilage of the home. Additionally, the government had evidence that the barn was not being used for intimate family purposes.

In a federal case out of Virginia, the prosecutor charged a landowner with taking or possessing migratory birds without a permit in violation of federal law.[99] The property owner had placed traps that snared the migratory birds, which the defendant later killed. Evidence in the case came from a surveillance camera placed on the private property by Commonwealth game officials, who had entered the property without a warrant to install the camera. The cameras were a mile or more from the defendant's home and were clearly outside the curtilage. The Court of Appeals held that the occupier of the land had no expectation of privacy in the open fields and that the use of concealed cameras was not significantly different from observations that government agents that might make if they walked on the defendant's land.

Although occurring close to the home, some human conduct indicates that individuals may no longer assert or expect privacy when placing refuse for collection at curb of their homes. Placing an end to significant inconsistent state and federal court decisions, the United States Supreme Court concluded that the Fourth Amendment does not prohibit the warrantless seizure of garbage and trash left for collection outside of the curtilage.[100] In a California case, the defendant had indicated that he wanted to make no additional use of the trash and that he had abandoned it by placing it at the curb and beyond the curtilage of his home. When the police arranged to have private trash haulers collect the evidence from the trash at the curb in front of the defendant's home, they committed no Fourth Amendment wrong and the evidence of drug possession and use was properly admitted against the resident defendant.

---

[98] United States v. Dunn, 480 U.S. 294, 107 S. Ct. 1134, 94 L. Ed. 2d 326 (1987). *See also* State v. Moley, 490 N.W.2d 764 (Wis. 1992).

[99] United States v. Vankesteren, 2009 U.S. App. LEXIS (4th Cir. 2009).

[100] California v. Greenwood, 486 U.S. 35, 1988 U.S. LEXIS 2279 (1988). *See* the case for a review of lower court decisions.

F. Search by a Private Individual

The Fourth Amendment provisions apply to government officials, not to private individuals who are not acting as agents of the government or with participation or knowledge of any government official. In the case of *United States v. Jacobsen* in 1984, the Supreme Court held that employees of a private carrier who examined a package did not violate the Fourth Amendment; therefore, the evidence obtained in the examination was admissible.[101]

This exception to the warrant requirement applies to private conduct when there is either no official governmental involvement or only minimal entanglement. In order to show that private activity in conducting searches has so much government connection that it cannot be deemed private, "two elements must be shown in order to treat ostensibly private action as a state-sponsored search: (1) the police must have instigated, encouraged, or participated in the search; and (2) the private individual must have engaged in the search with the intent of assisting the police."[102] Private conduct that did not implicate the Fourth Amendment was held to exist when hotel employees smelled burning marijuana and reported it to supervisory staff, who contacted the local police. The police requested that the trash from each room be kept separate and labeled. After police inspected the trash, they obtained a search warrant, using the evidence from the trash pulls. The defendant contended that the hotel employees were acting as police agents but the reviewing court noted that the hotel employees were asked by the police only to label and not commingle the trash from the respective rooms. In addition, private individuals working at the hotel first contacted the police and not the other way around. The court held that the evidence obtained had been properly admitted because only private conduct had been involved in obtaining the evidence.[103] However, if the government initiated the searching process, the activity would probably be considered to be governmental conduct and the Fourth Amendment would apply.

If a private individual, without the prior knowledge of a law enforcement agent, makes a private search of another person's personal computer and anonymously sends the information to a local police agency, the search of the hard drive will not be considered a search by a government agency and will not be suppressible under the Fourth Amendment.[104] In similar case, a private individual obtained a videotape that depicted his girlfriend's father engaged in sexual activities with underage females. The private search of the videotape by the individual who seized it and who was not operating under police direction did not offend the principles of the Fourth Amendment and the evidence was properly admitted against the defendant who appeared in the video.[105]

---

[101]   466 U.S. 109, 104 S. Ct. 1652, 80 L. Ed. 2d 85 (1984).

[102]   United States v. Bruce, 396 F.3d 697, 705, 2005 U.S. App. LEXIS 1712 (6th Cir. 2005).

[103]   *Id.*

[104]   United States v. Kline, 112 Fed. Appx. 562, 2004 U.S. App. LEXIS 20759 (9th Cir. 2004), *cert. denied,* 544 U.S. 950, 2005 U.S. LEXIS 2818 (2005).

[105]   State v. Robinson, 653 S.E.2d 889, 2007 N.C. App. LEXIS 2556 (N.C. 2007).

In an early case concerning the status of public school officials, the United States Supreme Court held that teachers and administrators are considered government officials for Fourth Amendment purposes. The Court justified the search of students when there are reasonable grounds for suspecting that the search would turn up evidence that either the law or a rule of the school had been violated.[106] With parental consent, public schoolchildren can be tested for drugs as a condition of participating in extracurricular sports or related academic activities, even in the absence of any individualized suspicion.[107] As a general rule, these results are not used for purposes of criminal prosecution. Even though the Fourth Amendment applies, these searches are considered "reasonable" because the tests cannot be performed unless parents consent and because the purpose of the testing was to reduce drug use by public school students. Private schools are not covered by Fourth Amendment principles and may require students to submit to drug testing consistent with school policy and parental consent.

Probation officers are also considered government officials for Fourth Amendment purposes. As one court recognized, "[i]t is well-settled that conditions that allow probation officers to conduct visits to and searches of the residences of probationers are valid under the Fourth Amendment."[108] In order to be reasonable, the entry must be authorized by law, a regulation, or an agreed-upon condition of probation. The reason may be routine or may involve suspicion or probable cause to believe that the probationer has violated some condition of probation.[109]

In some jurisdictions, a private police officer may carry sufficient authority of the state so that the officer must comply with the Fourth Amendment. In a Michigan casino, private security officers employed by the casino had the power from the state to detain errant patrons as well as full arrest powers. When a dispute involving the Fourth Amendment arose, the trial court held that, as a matter of law, the security officer was a state actor subject to the restraints of the Fourth Amendment.[110]

G. Search after Lawful Impoundment

Inventory searches have been approved when objects or vehicles come into the control of police, but inventory searches are improper and will not produce admissible evidence unless the police department has a policy regulating such searches.[111] The general rule is that "[e]vidence discovered during an

---

[106]   New Jersey v. T.L.O., 469 U.S. 325, 105 S. Ct. 733, 83 L. Ed. 2d 720 (1985).

[107]   Board of Education v. Earls, 536 U.S. 822, 2002 U.S. LEXIS 4882 (2002).

[108]   Cass v. County of Suffolk, 2005 U.S. Dist. LEXIS 8623 (E.D.N.Y. 2005).

[109]   *Id.*

[110]   Romanski v. Detroit Entertainment, L.L.C., 428 F.3d 629, 635, 2005 U.S. App. LEXIS 23336 (6th Cir. 2005).

[111]   Florida v. Wells, 495 U.S. 1 (1990). *See also* State v. Hensley, 2005 Minn. App. LEXIS 233 (2005), in which an inventory search did not produce admissible evidence because the sheriff's department had no inventory policy.

inventory search conducted pursuant to standardized procedures is admissible, unless the police acted in bad faith or for the sole purpose of investigation."[112] Often the police have the duty and responsibility to impound a car that has been abandoned, is blocking traffic, is illegally parked, or has been left without a driver after the driver has been arrested. In such instances, the officer is usually required, either by law or departmental regulations, to search the vehicle and make a list of its contents before impounding it. Provided that the police department has and follows an inventory policy routinely and not just when police think something incriminating might be discovered, evidence seized during an inventory search will be admissible against the occupier of the vehicle.[113] The issues of the reasonableness of inventory seizures reached the United States Supreme Court in the case of *Colorado v. Bertine* in 1987.[114] In approving the opening of closed containers found in a van that was lawfully impounded, the Court held that important government interests were served by inventory searches. An inventory search protects the citizen from loss of property by police or their agents while it protects the police from false claims of loss. In addition, an inventory search prevents police from harboring a vehicle that might contain harmful cargo, contraband, or dangerous items and it prevents vandalism to the vehicle. Two caveats apply here:

1. The police must follow standard procedures in carrying out the search, and
2. The police must perform the inventory search for the purpose of actually obtaining an inventory and not for the sole purpose of conducting a criminal investigation.[115]

In following a departmental inventory search policy, police may look for incriminating items that might be present as long as their sole purpose is not to investigate a crime.[116] Therefore, police may not use the inventory search theory as a justification for supporting a search that was simply a search for incriminating evidence.

H. Stop-and-Frisk Search

To complete the discussion concerning the admissibility of search and seizure evidence, the stop-and-frisk limited search must be mentioned. In 1968, the United States Supreme Court authorized the admission of evidence

---

[112] United States v. Thompson, 2006 U.S. App. LEXIS 12734 (3d Cir. 2006).
[113] South Dakota v. Opperman, 328 U.S. 364, 96 S. Ct. 3092, 49 L. Ed. 2d 1000 (1976); Arkansas v. Sullivan, 532 U.S. 769, 2001 U.S. LEXIS 4118 (2001), in which the court approved an inventory search following the driver's arrest.
[114] Colorado v. Bertine, 479 U.S. 367, 107 S. Ct. 738, 93 L. Ed. 2d 739 (1987). *See also* Florida v. Wells, 495 U.S. 1, 110 S. Ct. 1632, 109 L. Ed. 2d 1 (1990), in which the United States Supreme Court discussed the necessity of having a departmental policy regarding inventory searches, and United States v. McKnight, 17 F.3d 1139 (8th Cir. 1994).
[115] State v. Hensley, 2005 Minn. App. Lexis 233 (2005).
[116] United States v. Kennedy, 427 F.3d 1136, 1143, 2005 U.S. App. LEXIS 23962 (8th Cir. 2005).

obtained by a police officer who articulated his reasons for "frisking" a person that he suspected was "casing a job."[117] The Court explained the limitation of such a seizure in this language:

> The sole justification of the search in the present situation is the protection of the police officer and others nearby, and it must, therefore, be confined in scope to an intrusion reasonably designed to discover guns, knives, clubs, or other hidden instruments for the assault of the police officer.

The frisk that is authorized by the *Terry v. Ohio* case is limited to a frisk for weapons when an officer has reasonable suspicion that the person with whom he is dealing may be armed and dangerous. When there is no reasonable suspicion that a subject may be armed and dangerous, a frisk does not appear to be warranted. When an officer who has made a valid *Terry* stop has reasonable suspicion that the person with whom he or she is dealing may be armed, the officer may frisk the outer garments of the detainee to search for weapon-like lumps. Applying the *Terry* reasoning, the Supreme Court upheld the investigatory stop of a motorist and the search of a paper bag located in his car.[118] The Court reasoned that the protective search of the driver and of the passenger compartment was reasonable under the principles articulated in *Terry*. The pat-down may be conducted where the facts would allow a reasonable officer to conclude that the person may be armed or have arms close at hand and may pose a serious and present danger to the safety of the officer. The Supreme Court held that if a *Terry* detainee refuses to identify him- or herself, and where state law permits, the detainee may be arrested and subjected to a search incident to a lawful arrest.[119] In that case, a police officer received a phone call reporting that a man was engaged in an assault on a woman inside a red and silver pick-up truck on a particular road. When he arrived, the male subject was not cooperative, said that he had done nothing wrong, and refused to produce any identification or orally identify himself. The officer arrested the driver for refusing to produce identification. According to the Court, the arrest was proper and any evidence obtained in a search incident to an arrest would be admissible against the motorist.

The *Terry* rule was also applied in holding that law enforcement agents may temporarily detain luggage on reasonable suspicion amounting to less than probable cause that the luggage contains narcotics.[120] The Supreme Court noted that if an officer's observation leads him or her reasonably to suspect that a traveler may be carrying luggage that contains narcotics, the officer may detain the luggage briefly to investigate the circumstances that aroused his or her suspicion, provided that the investigative detention is properly limited in

---

[117]　Terry v. Ohio, 392 U.S. 1, 88 S. Ct. 1868, 20 L. Ed. 2d 720 (1968).

[118]　Michigan v. Long, 463 U.S. 1032, 103 S. Ct. 3469, 77 L. Ed. 2d 1201 (1983); *and see* California v. Acevedo, 500 U.S. 565 (1991).

[119]　*See* Hiibel v. Sixth Judicial District Court, 542 U.S. 960, 2004 U.S. LEXIS 4385 (2004).

[120]　United States v. Place, 462 U.S. 696, 103 S. Ct. 2637, 77 L. Ed. 2d 110 (1983).

scope. In this case, the 90-minute time span between the luggage seizure and its exposure to a search by a trained narcotics detection dog was unreasonable under the circumstances; therefore, the court suppressed the evidence.

In the *Terry* case, the United States Supreme Court approved the practice of frisking suspects on less than probable cause when there were reasonable grounds to believe that criminal activity might be afoot. The court noted, however, that the frisk had to be confined in scope to an intrusion reasonably designed to discover guns, clubs, knives, or other hidden instruments for the assault of the police officer. Several years after that decision was handed down by the Supreme Court, the question the Supreme Court was asked to answer was whether, while in the process of searching for a weapon on a person, officers could seize other articles that were not dangerous if the other articles came into plain view or under the "plain feel" doctrine as a result of the frisk for weapons.[121]

In the case of *Minnesota v. Dickerson*, the officer, upon observing the suspect's seemingly evasive actions when approached by police officers and the fact that he had just left a building known for narcotics trafficking, decided to investigate further and ordered the suspect to submit to a pat-down search because a drug trafficker might be armed. The officer who conducted the search testified that he felt a small lump in the suspect's jacket, and believed it to be a lump of crack cocaine after rolling it between his thumb and fingers. The search revealed a small bag of cocaine. According to the Court, the rolling of the crack between the thumb and index finger constituted a search beyond the scope of a frisk and the rock of cocaine should not have been admitted at his trial.[122] In a different case,[123] an officer who had responded to another officer's traffic stop observed a man across the street watching the event. As the officer walked over to the traffic stop, the man across the street turned away and put his hand in his mouth. Two officers walked over to the subject to frisk him when one officer observed drugs in the subject's mouth. Under the circumstances, there was no reason for a stop or a frisk because the subject's behavior did not appear to be criminal and the trial court properly suppressed the evidence from trial.

From the foregoing, it is obvious that some evidence, such as the rock of cocaine in the *Dickerson* case, obtained in an illegal search is logically relevant and material to a case, and would be admissible under the rules of evidence if no other considerations were involved. For constitutional reasons and consistent with court-generated rules designed to enforce constitutional provisions some evidence cannot be admitted. Evidence will be excluded if the search is illegal or if the search does not come within one of the recognized exceptions.

---

[121]   Minnesota v. Dickerson, 508 U.S. 366, 1993 U.S. LEXIS 4018 (1993).

[122]   *Id.*

[123]   State v. Bennett, 2008 Ohio 3969, 2008 Ohio App. LEXIS 3349 (2008). People v. Sanders, 2006 Mich. App. LEXIS 2 (2006).

§ 16.4   Exclusion of Evidence Obtained by Illegal Wiretapping or Eavesdropping

At one time, the United States Supreme Court refused to include wiretapping within the scope of the Fourth Amendment. In the case of *Olmstead v. United States*,[124] after reviewing the historical context in which the Fourth Amendment was adopted, the Court concluded that the proscription was limited to search and seizure of material things, and did not apply to evidence procured by the sense of hearing. However, in a later decision, *Nardone v. United States*,[125] the Supreme Court held that although wiretapping did not violate the Constitution, it did violate the Federal Communications Act of 1934, and the Court ruled that evidence obtained by officers who violated the provisions of this Act was inadmissible in federal court. This rule was not originally applied to the state courts, but many states adopted the rule, either by legislation or by court interpretation. In a landmark decision in 1967, *Katz v. United States*,[126] the Supreme Court rejected the contention that surveillance without trespass and without the seizure of material fell outside the purview of the Constitution. This and other decisions make it clear that wiretapping and electronic or mechanical eavesdropping are within the protection of the Fourth Amendment.

After several efforts, Congress in 1968 finally enacted a comprehensive scheme designed to regulate eavesdropping and wiretapping on a uniform nationwide basis.[127] This law, as amended, must be studied thoroughly in order to understand the requirements for wiretapping or eavesdropping. Broadly speaking, the interception of wire or oral communications is illegal unless conducted in conformity with statutory procedures. To be admissible, evidence obtained by wiretapping or eavesdropping must comply with the standards established by federal law as interpreted by the courts.

Title 18 United States Code §§ 3121–3126 sets forth the procedures for wiretapping and eavesdropping. Section 2511 prohibits the interception and disclosure of wire, oral, or electronic communications except when in compliance with a detailed statutory procedure. Section 2516 lists the procedures by which an investigative agency may apply for an order authorizing the interception of a wire or oral communication. In effect, this portion of the statute authorizes designated federal and state officers to apply for a court order, similar to a search warrant, to intercept wire or oral communications when the crimes charged are specifically enumerated.

In addition, some evidence obtained by means of wiretapping and eavesdropping is admissible if one party to the conversation consents. Section 2511(2)(c) authorizes federal law enforcement officers to intercept wire, oral,

---

[124]   277 U.S. 438, 48 S. Ct. 564, 72 L. Ed. 944 (1928).

[125]   302 U.S. 379, 58 S. Ct. 275, 82 L. Ed. 314 (1937).

[126]   389 U.S. 347, 88 S. Ct. 507, 19 L. Ed. 2d 576 (1967).

[127]   *See* Chapter 119 of the Omnibus Crime Control Act of 1968, 18 U.S.C. § 2510 (amended in 1986 by Pub. L. No. 99–508, and codified at 18 U.S.C. § 2510 *et seq.*)

or electronic communications with the consent of one party without a court order unless a state statute prohibits such interception.

While federal law and some state laws include an exception that allows interception of communications if one party consents, the consent must be voluntary.[128] It is not voluntary if it is coerced by either explicit or implicit means or by an implied threat or covert force. Where federal prisoners are permitted to make telephone calls, the prisoner must consent to having the calls recorded or telephone privileges will not be extended. In one case, the prisoner continued to run a heroin importation ring using a prison phone following his imprisonment for prior crimes.[129] The phone calls that the prisoner made were monitored with his consent and some of the tapes of the calls were used at his subsequent trial for conspiracy to distribute heroin. The trial court and the court of appeals rejected his contention that the government taping violated § 2515 of the Federal Wiretap Act[130] and the phone evidence should have been excluded from his trial. The defendant offered the theory that consent was not sufficient to allow admission and the conversations should have been excluded because they were not collected in the ordinary course of law enforcement. According to the Court of Appeals for the Fifth Circuit, consent by one party is all that is required to render a telephone recording admissible in a federal court.

Cases interpreting and explaining the provisions of the federal law have been voluminous. When law enforcement officers circumvent the requirements of the wiretap authorization statute, courts must suppress evidence obtained from the illegal wiretap. For example, in a drug conspiracy case, a state judge had issued a wiretap order for the defendants' digital beepers, which required the police to record and store the data recovered on tape or another storage device. The police did not follow the court order, and recorded the data recovered in handwriting. Due to the disregard of the judge's order, the evidence was suppressed. The federal government wanted to try the defendants for the same act under federal law and the defendants contended that the evidence should be suppressed because 18 U.S.C. § 2510 contains virtually identical language to the state statute violated by state officers and suppression is a remedy when the government violates the law. The federal district judge suppressed the evidence because the government failed to follow the judicial order and if the evidence were allowed it could encourage law enforcement officials to sidestep other requirements in electronic eavesdropping.[131]

While states may enact wiretap and eavesdrop statutes that are more restrictive than the federal statutes, they may not enforce statutes that are less restrictive. But if the federal government's wiretap procedure complied with

---

[128] United States v. Antoon, 933 F.2d 200 (3d Cir.), *cert. denied*, 502 U.S. 907, 112 S. Ct. 300, 116 L. Ed. 2d 243 (1991).

[129] United States v. Moore, 452 F.3d 382; 2006 U.S. App. LEXIS 14152 (5th Cir. 2006).

[130] 18 U.S.C. § 2515.

[131] United States v. Amanuel, 418 F. Supp. 2d 244; 2005 U.S. Dist. LEXIS 30108 (W.D.N.Y. 2005), Adhered to, On reconsideration by United States v. Amanuel, 418 F. Supp. 2d 244, 2006 U.S. Dist. LEXIS 3890 (W.D.N.Y. 2006).

the federal law, evidence obtained thereby is admissible in federal courts, even if those procedures violated the state law.[132]

Detecting and recording phone numbers and other data associated with phone communications originally were viewed as not violating any expectation of privacy possessed by users of telecommunication facilities[133] and law enforcement agencies were free to collect such data. Recognizing that collecting the information might constitute a violation of privacy, Congress addressed the pen register and the trap-and-trace device issue to prohibit the warrantless use of such devices, subject to limited exceptions.[134] Later, Congress modified 18 U.S.C. § 3121 as part of the USA PATRIOT Act by expanding the coverage of pen registers and similar devices by redefining a pen register. Under the revised statute, "the term 'pen register' means a device or process which records or decodes dialing, routing, addressing, or signaling information transmitted by an instrument or facility from which a wire or electronic communication is transmitted, provided, however, that such information shall not include the contents of any communication."[135] Presently, pen registers and trap-and-trace devices must be used with court orders where the goal is to obtain cell phone numbers, web addresses, e-mail addresses, and similar noncontent data. The statute defined a trap-and-trace device as "a device or process which captures the incoming electronic or other impulses which identify the originating number or other dialing, routing, addressing, and signaling information reasonably likely to identify the source of a wire or electronic communication," but the captured information may not contain the contents of any communication.[136] One limitation that may exist concerns cell phone tower usage, which could reveal where the person making or taking the call was located. In a federal case, the government sought such evidence but was rebuffed in a federal district court in 2005.[137]

Global positioning satellite (GPS) tracking devices may require probable cause in some federal jurisdictions while in others, a reduced level of reasonable suspicion may suffice. In a Wisconsin drug prosecution, officers warrantlessly attached a GPS tracking device to the defendant's automobile to record where it traveled and periodically retrieved it to download the information. The Court of Appeals rejected the defendant's contention that his car had been illegally seized and it noted that the Supreme Court has held that tracking a vehicle is not a search. The reviewing court upheld the trial court's decision to admit the evidence obtained as a result of the GPS device as well as the derivative evidence discovered.[138] At this point, the Supreme Court has not ruled on the level of proof required and has not determined whether a prior warrant

---

[132]   United States v. Padilla-Pena, 129 F.3d 457 (8th Cir. 1997).

[133]   Smith v. Maryland, 442 U.S. 375 (1979).

[134]   18 U.S.C. § 3121.

[135]   18 U.S.C. § 3127.

[136]   *Id.*

[137]   In re Application of the United States of America for an Order Authorizing the Installation and Use of a Pen Register, 402 F. Supp. 2d 597 (D. Md. 2005).

[138]   United States v. Garcia, 474 F.3d 994, 2007 U.S. App. LEXIS 2272 (7thCir. 2007).

based on probable cause will be required when it settles the divergent views of the various federal circuits concerning GPS and other tracking devices.

Because the state laws are still inconsistent, one must look to the statutes and decisions of the various states as well as the federal statutes to determine whether wiretapping, eavesdropping are permissible in a particular state and if permitted, under what circumstances. Federal law remains in a state of flux because of the tension between the need for national security and the desire to protect civil liberties. If the evidence is obtained in violation of federal or state laws or decisions, it usually may not be admitted into court.[139]

§ 16.5 Exclusion of Confessions Obtained in Violation of Constitutional Provisions

Although a confession or an admission of guilt would seem to be the best kind of relevant evidence, in many instances evidence of a confession is not admissible because the officer obtaining the confession violated certain constitutional provisions. In making a determination of whether a confession has been voluntarily taken consistent with the Fifth Amendment, the ultimate question to be answered is "whether, under the totality of the circumstances, the challenged confession was obtained in a manner compatible with the requirements of the Constitution."[140] A confession that has been secured following a violation of the Fourth Amendment generally cannot be used against the person due to the Fourth Amendment exclusionary rule unless the confession can be shown to be an act of free will sufficient to purge the taint of the original illegality.[141]

It is essential that both federal and state laws be examined when considering the admissibility rules. Although the federal courts have established minimum standards to be applied, states may employ more stringent standards concerning the admissibility of confessions than the due process requirements pronounced in federal cases, but less stringent state standards are prohibited.[142]

A. The Free and Voluntary Rule

At early common law, courts permitted the use of admissions or confessions as evidence of guilt despite the fact that they were products of force or

---

[139] For further discussions of the use of wiretap and eavesdrop evidence see KANOVITZ & KANOVITZ, CONSTITUTIONAL LAW (11th ed. 2008). *See also* WALKER AND HEMMENS, LEGAL GUIDE FOR POLICE: CONSTITUTIONAL ISSUES (8th ed. 2008).

[140] Miller v. Fenton, 474 U.S. 104, 112, 1985 U.S. LEXIS 144 (1985).

[141] Kaupp v. Texas, 538 U.S. 626, 632, 2003 U.S. LEXIS 3670 (2003). An illegal arrest without probable cause quickly followed by a confession will ordinarily result in the confession being suppressed under the Fourth Amendment.

[142] Griffin v. State, 230 Ga. App. 318, 496 S.E.2d 480 (1998).

duress. The rule allowing the admissibility of such evidence was abandoned because it was found by experience that persons accused of a crime would admit to committing the crime in order to avoid torture. As a result, the courts developed what came to be known as the "free and voluntary" rule.

The free and voluntary rule states that the confession of a person accused of crime is admissible against the accused only if freely and voluntarily made, without fear, duress, or compulsion in its inducement. Excluding coerced confessions made logical sense because involuntary confessions might not be reliable and courts insisted on the requirement of voluntariness because the Fifth Amendment requirement that no person shall be compelled in a criminal case to be a witness against himself seemed to dictate the rejection of coerced confessions.[143] When a defendant raises the issue concerning voluntariness of a confession, the burden to prove whether the confession was voluntarily and freely given rests upon the prosecution.[144] A determination of voluntariness of a confession requires that the trial court consider various factors, including the defendant's age, intelligence, and level of education. The court must factor into the decision the length of the defendant's detention and the length and nature of the interrogation, whether the police advised the defendant of constitutional rights, and whether the defendant had been subject to any physical coercion.[145]

Although the "free and voluntary rule" was formulated more than a century ago, the courts continue to define the rule. In 1991, the Supreme Court upheld the Supreme Court of Arizona's reversal of a murder conviction of a man who had been coerced into a confession. A fellow inmate, who was working for the government inside the prison, offered protection from harm from other inmates if the defendant confessed to the government's inmate agent. The Supreme Court of Arizona held that the first confession had been involuntarily given under coercion.[146] In 1993, a federal court stated that in evaluating the voluntariness of a confession, the court looks to the totality of the circumstances in which the confession was given to determine whether the government agent's conduct was such as to overbear the defendant's will to resist and to bring about confessions not freely self-determined.[147]

The test for the voluntariness of a confession is whether, under the totality of circumstances, the statement was made freely, without compulsion or inducement, with consideration given to the characteristics of the accused and the details of the interrogation. Under the totality of the circumstances, the "[f]actors to be considered include: the defendant's age, intelligence, background, experience, mental capacity, education and physical condition at the

---

[143] Bram v. United States, 168 U.S. 532, 18 S. Ct. 187, 42 L. Ed. 568 (1897).

[144] United States v. Jett, 2006 U.S. Dist. LEXIS 27829 (N.D. Ind. 2006), citing Lego v. Twomey, 404 U.S. 477, 489, 1972 U.S. LEXIS 100 (1972).

[145] United States v. Lopez, 437 F.3d 1059, 1063, 2006 U.S. App. LEXIS 4052 (2006).

[146] Arizona v. Fulminante, 499 U.S. 279 (1991).

[147] United States v. Kaba, 999 F.2d 47 (2d Cir.), *cert. denied*, 510 U.S. 1002, 114 S. Ct. 577, 126 L. Ed. 2d 476 (1993).

time of questioning, the legality and duration of the detention, the duration of the questioning, and any physical or mental abuse by the police, including any threats or promises. No single factor is dispositive."[148]

The United States Supreme Court in 1985 reaffirmed its authority to review state cases in which the confession was admitted as part of the evidence. The Court noted that the voluntariness of a confession is a matter that is subject to review by federal courts.[149] Although in this case the New Jersey Supreme Court had determined that the petitioner's confession was voluntary, the United States Supreme Court announced that it was not bound by a state court finding as to voluntariness.

Regardless of which historical approach is most persuasive, a confession obtained by force or duress, or by promises of reward, whether the confession is a judicial confession or an extrajudicial confession, should not be admitted.[150] The issue to be determined in each case is whether the defendant's will was overborne at the time that the defendant made the confession.[151] For example, a defendant's will was overborne when officers falsely told him that a gunpowder residue test was positive and that they had six eyewitnesses when they had only two. The officers told the defendant that if he cooperated he could get six years instead of 60, the difference between murder and a mistake. The appellate court upheld the trial court decision that suppressed the two confessions in the case because the misrepresentations of the evidence, together with the promise of leniency, were powerful enough to make the confessions involuntary.[152] However, in the event that a confession has been erroneously admitted, any conviction resulting from the admission of an improper confession should be tested by the harmless error standard.

Judges in various courts have often disagreed as to the amount of evidence required to determine whether a confession is voluntary. When an allegation has been made and some evidence demonstrated, the prosecution has the burden of proof to demonstrate that the confession was given freely and voluntarily. In *Lego v. Twomey*,[153] the judge in the lower court had not found the

---

[148] Bridges v. Chambers, 447 F.3d 994, 997, 2006 U.S. App. LEXIS 11763 (7th Cir. 2006), quoting People v. Bridges, 2003 Ill. App. LEXIS 888).

[149] Miller v. Fenton, 474 U.S. 104, 106 S. Ct. 445, 88 L. Ed. 2d 405 (1985).

[150] The United States Supreme Court in the case of Arizona v. Fulminante, 499 U.S. 279, 113 L. Ed. 2d 302, 111 S. Ct. 1246 (1991) ruled that defendants whose coerced confessions were improperly used as evidence are not always entitled to a new trial. The use of such confessions may be considered "harmless error" if other trial evidence was sufficient to convict the defendant. In this case, the Supreme Court affirmed the decision of the Arizona Supreme Court that the harmless error analysis could not be used to save the conviction because a second confession that would have been admissible was tainted by the first one that was deemed illegally taken. The Court remanded the case for a new trial without the use of the first confession.

[151] United States v. Yukins, 444 F.3d 713, 719, 2006 U.S. App. LEXIS 8160 (6th Cir. 2006).

[152] *See* United States v. Lopez, 437 F.3d 1059, 2006 U.S. App. LEXIS 4052 (10th Cir. 2006).

[153] Lego v. Twomey, 404 U.S. 477, 92 S. Ct. 619, 30 L. Ed. 2d 618 (1972).

confession voluntary "beyond a reasonable doubt" and the defendant argued that this made the admission of the confession erroneous. The Supreme Court disagreed, however. The Court explained that the defendant is presumed innocent, and that the burden falls on the prosecution to prove guilt beyond a reasonable doubt; however, the Court continued, "[t]his is not the same burden that applies in determining the admissibility of a confession." The Court agreed that the prosecution must prove the confession to be free and voluntary by a preponderance of the evidence, but that it was not required to prove the confession to be free and voluntary "beyond a reasonable doubt."

B. The Delay in Arraignment Rule

Under *Riverside v. McLaughlin*, when police make a warrantless arrest, the arrestee must be taken before a judicial official for a determination of probable cause within 48 hours. If a warrant has been the basis for arrest or if the arrest followed an indictment by a grand jury, a second determination of probable cause is not necessary. When a person has been arrested without any judicial involvement or grand jury action, it becomes imperative that a judicial official make a decision regarding whether probable cause exists within the allotted time.[154] In *Corley v. United States*,[155] federal officials arrested the defendant but did not present him to a judicial official for almost 30 hours during which he made inculpatory statements. Federal Rule of Criminal Procedure 5 requires that any arrestee be taken to a judicial official within a reasonable time. Federal prosecutors contended that the defendant's confession should be admissible since it was voluntarily given by traditional measures. The government cited a section of federal law that seemed to indicate admissibility but the Supreme Court ruled that the confession was not admissible based on Federal Rule 5 and the *McNabb-Mallory* rule. Older case law gave rise to the concept that an unreasonable delay required the suppression of a confession and the Supreme Court felt that Rule 5 read in conjunction with the *McNabb-Mallory* rule required that the confession had to be excluded.

C. The Miranda Rule

The restrictions concerning the use of unwarned confessions and admissions as evidence were broadened in 1966. The confessions in *Miranda v. Arizona* and its three companion cases were declared inadmissible by the Supreme Court because the suspects were not given the constitutionally required warnings prior to being interrogated. The Supreme Court held that for a confession or an inculpatory statement to be deemed admissible, the person who has been taken into custody or otherwise deprived of his or her freedom of action in any significant way must be warned before questioning that: (1) the individual has a right to remain silent; (2) if the subject does make a

---

[154] Riverside v. McLaughlin, 500 U.S. 44 (1991).
[155] Corley v. United States, 129 S. Ct. 1558, 2009 U.S. LEXIS 2512 (2009).

statement, anything he or she says can and will be used against him or her in court; (3) the individual has the right to have an attorney present or to consult with an attorney; and (4) if he or she cannot afford an attorney, one will be appointed prior to any questioning if he or she so desires.[156]

Although the earlier cases interpreting the requirements of *Miranda* held that the warning must be given in the exact terms as stated in the case, the Supreme Court has retreated from that position in recent cases. In the case of *Duckworth v. Eagan*, the United States Supreme Court found that the warning need not be given in the exact terms as stated in *Miranda*, but that the warning must reasonably convey to a suspect his or her rights as required by *Miranda*.[157] To produce admissible evidence, the warnings must be given, even where the person in custody states that he "knows" the warnings, otherwise the oral evidence obtained will generally be suppressed for use in proving guilt.[158]

The *Miranda* warnings are not required unless the individual has been placed in custody and the police anticipate interrogating the subject. The ultimate inquiry in determining whether a suspect is in custody for *Miranda* purposes is simply whether there is a formal arrest or restraint of the freedom of movement of the degree associated with a formal arrest. In determining whether the suspect was in custody for *Miranda* purposes, the courts should inquire how a reasonable person in the suspect's position would have understood his or her situation.[159] In *Thompson v. Keohane*, the police interrogated the defendant for a period of time and allowed him to leave the police station after he admitted killing his ex-wife. Following his allegation that he had been in custody for *Miranda* purposes, the Supreme Court sent the case back for a decision concerning custody[160] and the Ninth Circuit found that Keohane was not in custody and *Miranda* warnings were not necessary.[161] In another case, the police wanted to talk to a suspect in an axe murder who willingly rode with police to the stationhouse. She voluntarily entered the police station and was told that she was free to leave at any time and that she was not under arrest during the officer's polite interrogation. The reviewing court concluded that the interrogation only became custodial after the suspect confessed to her participation.[162] Only then would the *Miranda* warnings have been required.

The fact of custody and the desire to interrogate dictate that the initial warnings be given but the subject must understand that the right to cease talking or to consult an attorney may be exercised at any time during questioning. If the accused indicates in an unambiguous manner that he or she wants

---

[156]   Miranda v. Arizona, 384 U.S. 436, 16 L. Ed. 2d 694, 86 S. Ct. 1602 (1966).

[157]   492 U.S. 195, 109 S. Ct. 2875, 106 L. Ed. 2d 166 (1989).

[158]   United States v. Patane, 542 U.S. 630, 639, 2004 U.S. LEXIS 4577 (2004).

[159]   United States v. Hicks, 967 F. Supp. 242 (E.D. Mich. 1997).

[160]   Thompson v. Keohane, 516 U.S. 99 (1995).

[161]   Thompson v. Keohane, 1998 U.S. App. LEXIS 9432 (9th Cir. 1998).

[162]   Slwooko v. State, 2006 Alaska App. LEXIS 114 (2006).

to speak with an attorney, interrogation must cease immediately and not be attempted later.[163]

Also, at any stage of the questioning, the person in custody may waive his or her rights and make a statement. There has been some question as to what constitutes a waiver and whether an express waiver is an essential requirement or whether the facts taken as a whole indicate that the waiver has been made. When an arrestee responds to additional police-initiated interrogation following an initial request for counsel, there has been no valid waiver.[164] The burden is on the prosecution to show that the defendant has waived his or her rights to silence and to an attorney. If an accused, after invoking his right to counsel under *Miranda*, does not begin new discussions with law enforcement agents, any later statement procured by law enforcement efforts is not admissible for proof of guilt. In one case, an inmate who was in Florida custody wanted an attorney and Florida officers had ceased attempts at interrogation. Ohio police officers violated the principles of *Miranda* when they arrived at the Florida lockup and began a new interrogation. The Ohio officers knew the suspect had requested an attorney and chose to interrogate him anyway. Because the Ohio officers took the statements in violation of *Miranda* and because the Ohio prosecutors could not show a waiver by the defendant, the evidence should not have been used against him.[165] If an arrestee clearly initiates new contact and wants to talk, the conduct indicates a waiver of *Miranda*. In a case in which the subject wants to talk and answer questions, but refuses to sign or make a written statement, the oral statements constituted admissible evidence.

Despite the rules that restrict how confessions and inculpatory statements may be obtained, confessions continue to be an useful investigative tool and provide evidence that a prosecutor can use during the government's case-in-chief. In fact, the Supreme Court in the *Miranda* case stated that confessions remained a proper element in law enforcement and that any statement given freely and voluntarily without any compelling influence was admissible in evidence.[166] In a subsequent case, the Court held that a person may volunteer any statement, even one prompted by mental problems, and the statement will not be excluded on *Miranda* grounds as long as the police did not coerce the subject.[167] In this case, when a person with mental problems approached a police officer to confess to a homicide, the officer properly listened to the confession and it was not considered to have been involuntarily taken under *Miranda*. The Court held that "coercive police activity is a necessary predicate to the finding that a confession is not 'voluntary' within the meaning of the Due Process Clause of the Fourteenth Amendment."[168] Therefore, it is clear

---

[163]   Edwards v. Arizona, 451 U.S. 477 (1981).

[164]   *Id.*

[165]   Van Hook v. Anderson, 444 F.3d 830, 834, 2006 U.S. App. LEXIS 9628 (6th Cir. 2006).

[166]   Miranda v. Arizona, 384 U.S. 436, 1966 U.S. LEXIS 2817 (1966).

[167]   Colorado v. Connelly, 479 U.S. 157, 1986 U.S. LEXIS 23 (1986).

[168]   *Id.* at 167.

that confessions continue to be admitted into evidence, and the skilled and informed investigator can obtain confessions or statements and still comply with the requirements established by the courts. Even if police fail to meet the strict requirements of *Miranda*, as long as the confession is voluntarily given, the evidence may be admitted for impeachment purposes where a defendant takes the stand and offers testimony contradictory to an otherwise inadmissible *Miranda* statement.[169]

In the case of *Harris v. New York*, the defendant was charged with selling heroin, and at the trial he took the stand in his own defense. The prosecution did not offer an admission/confession made by the defendant during its case-in-chief because it had been taken in violation of the principles of *Miranda*. After the defendant testified by telling a story that was in direct conflict with his voluntary statement taken in violation of *Miranda*, the prosecution offered the original confession to impeach the testimony of the defendant. Although the United States Supreme Court allowed the admission of the confession even though *Miranda* warnings had not been given, the Court held that a confession may be used for impeachment purposes if it has been freely and voluntarily made. In so doing, the Court reasoned that:

> Having voluntarily taken the stand, petitioner was under an obligation to speak truthfully and accurately, and the prosecution did no more than utilize the traditional truth-testing devices of the adversary process.

In a more recent application of the *Harris* principle, a defendant contended that his confession should not have been admissible as impeachment evidence. Police had an informant placed in the defendant's cell after the right to counsel had attached and the informant engaged the defendant in a conversation in which the accused admitted his guilt to robbing and shooting the victim. After the defendant took the witness stand and blamed the shooting and crime on another person, the government called the informant who offered the defendant's confession as impeachment evidence. The Supreme Court approved the admission of the evidence by the jailhouse informant on the theory that the interests safeguarded by excluding tainted evidence for impeachment purposes are outweighed by a need to reduce the opportunities for perjury and to assure the integrity of the trial process.[170]

Alternatively, if a confession has been coerced and was not voluntarily made even though *Miranda* warnings were given, the confession is not admissible in evidence even for impeachment purposes.[171]

In 1984, the Supreme Court decided a case involving an emergency situation in which a suspect's incriminating answer to a police officer's question

---

[169] Harris v. New York, 401 U.S. 222, 91 S. Ct. 643, 28 L. Ed. 2d 1 (1971); Oregon v. Hass, 420 U.S. 714, 91 S. Ct. 1215, 43 L. Ed. 2d 570 (1975).

[170] Kansas v. Ventris, _____ U.S. _____, 2009 U.S. LEXIS 3299 (2009).

[171] Mincey v. Arizona, 437 U.S. 385, 98 S. Ct. 2408, 57 L. Ed. 2d 290 (1978).

was admitted even though the *Miranda* warnings were not administered prior to the suspect's emergency interrogation. The Supreme Court recognized a "narrow exception" to the *Miranda* rule, which stated that statements elicited from an arrestee, as well as real evidence obtained from exploiting such statements, may be admitted against the arrestee-defendant even if the officers failed to recite the *Miranda* warnings before asking the questions, as long as the officer's safety or the safety of others appeared to be in jeopardy.[172] In recognizing a "public safety" exception to the *Miranda* rule, the Court concluded that if the officer or the public may be in life-threatening danger, the threat to the public safety outweighs the need for the rule protecting the Fifth Amendment privilege against self-incrimination, and evidence resulting from questions not preceded by *Miranda* warnings is admissible under these limited circumstances. In a newer case, police questioned a domestic dispute subject concerning guns in plain view on a living room couch after having gained custody of the subject in a bedroom.[173] The officer asked, "What are those doing there?" and the subject admitted that he was trying to hide them because he knew the police were coming. The subject had a prior felony conviction and was not lawfully permitted to have the firearms. Under the circumstances, the subject's answer to the officer's pre-*Miranda* question constituted admissible evidence against him due to the emergency in getting control of the domestic dispute situation.

Following the original *Miranda* decision, the Congress demonstrated its disagreement with the ruling by passing the Omnibus Crime Control and Safe Streets Act of 1968, which contained a provision intended to reverse the effects of the *Miranda* decision in federal courts. The applicable part of this Act is 18 U.S.C. § 3501(c), which reads as follows:

> In any criminal prosecution by the United States or by the District of Columbia, a confession made or given by a person who is a defendant therein, while such person was under arrest or other detention in the custody of any law enforcement officer or law enforcement agency, shall not be inadmissible solely because of delay in bringing such person before a commissioner or other officer empowered to commit persons charged with offenses against the laws of the United States or of the District of Columbia if such confession is found by the trial judge to have been made voluntarily . . .[174]

The clear intention of the statute was to undermine the *Miranda* warnings by statutorily overruling the Supreme Court. Congress may change laws that

---

[172] New York v. Quarles, 467 U.S. 649, 104 S. Ct. 2626, 81 L. Ed. 2d 550 (1984).

[173] *See* United States v. Martinez, 406 F.3d 1160, 1163, 2005 U.S. App. LEXIS 8624 (9th Cir. 2002).

[174] A delay in bringing an arrestee before a judge or magistrate may cause a detainee to file a civil suit, but generally, it does not seem to have resulted in the dismissal of a criminal case. See Turner v. City of Taylor, 412 F.3d 629, 2005 U.S. App. LEXIS 11233 (6th Cir. 2005) and Bryant v. City of New York, 404 F.3d 128, 2005 U.S. App. LEXIS 5376 (2d Cir. 2005).

it has passed and nullify Supreme Court decisions that have interpreted those laws, but it has no power to overrule Supreme Court decisions when the Court has interpreted a provision of the Constitution of the United States. In the case of *Dickerson v. United States*, the Supreme Court found that § 3501 was an unconstitutional exercise by Congress of its powers because the Court held that the *Miranda* decision and its accompanying warnings were of constitutional dimension.[175] That is to say, the Court held that the *Miranda* warnings were required by the Constitution and that Congress had no power to attempt to change a decision of constitutional dimensions. In the *Dickerson* case, the defendant, a bank robber, had been arrested by federal agents and interrogated voluntarily without being given his *Miranda* warnings. By all objective measures, the interrogation and incriminating statements were given in a completely voluntary manner; the only problem with their use was the *Miranda* decision. The trial court suppressed the statement but the Court of Appeals for the Fourth Circuit, by reversing and remanding the case, noted that the requirements of § 3501 had been met and that the confession was voluntarily made. After granting certiorari, the Supreme Court reversed the Fourth Circuit, holding that *Miranda* warnings were required by the Constitution and that any voluntariness standard suggested by the statute would not square with the *Miranda* decision and the federal constitution.[176] The attempt by Congress to overturn the *Miranda* decision failed and the accused robber's confession could not be used in court.

It is apparent from this discussion concerning confessions and other statements that although courts have established strict rules concerning how to evaluate their admissibility, confessions and admissions constitute admissible evidence and continue to be valuable tools in the prosecution of criminal activity. Generally, voluntary statements obtained in accordance with the requirements of the Fifth Amendment, *Miranda*, and other rules established by the Supreme Court will be admissible evidence.

§ 16.6 Self-Incrimination and Related Protections

Often evidence is challenged because the officer, in obtaining the evidence, violated the Fifth Amendment privilege against self-incrimination. The pertinent section concerning self-incrimination provides that: "No person . . . shall be compelled in any criminal case to be a witness against himself." This provision, like the Fourth Amendment search and seizure provision, was included as a part of the Bill of Rights and became a part of the Constitution in 1791. The Fifth Amendment restrictions were not made applicable to the states until 1964 when the Supreme Court held that the due process clause of

---

[175] Dickerson v. United States, 530 U.S. 428, 440, 2000 U.S. LEXIS 4305 (2000).
[176] *Id.*

the Fourteenth Amendment included protections against self-incrimination.[177] The United States Supreme Court, in the case of *Malloy v. Hogan*, stated in its decision:

> We hold today that the Fifth Amendment's exception from compulsory self-incrimination is also protected by the Fourteenth Amendment against abridgement by the states.

This means that the Fifth Amendment standards to be applied in the states are the same standards as determined by the Supreme Court for federal courts and not the standards that were developed by state courts. After many conflicting decisions, the Supreme Court in the case of *Schmerber v. California*[178] clearly limited the application of the privilege against self-incrimination to evidence that can be categorized as "testimonial" in nature.

> We hold that the privilege protects the accused only from being compelled to testify against himself, or otherwise provide the state with evidence of a testimonial or communicative nature, and that the withdrawal of blood and use of the analysis in question in this case did not involve compulsion to these ends.

Following this interpretation, obtaining physical evidence from a defendant's person, such as evidence from a lineup, taking blood or DNA samples, and taking handwriting samples, does not constitute testimonial self-incrimination. As the *Schmerber* Court noted, the Fifth Amendment as applied to the states "offers no protection against compulsion to submit to fingerprinting, photographing, or measurements, to write or speak for identification, to appear in court, to stand, to assume a stance, to walk, or to make a particular gesture."[179] On the other hand, if an accused was forced to take a lie detector test or was coerced to give other evidence of a testimonial or communicative nature, such as being required to produce a response to a subpoena that has hallmarks of being testimonial in nature,[180] the Fifth Amendment's self-incrimination provisions can be violated, and evidence so obtained may be ruled as inadmissible.

As a general rule, when a defendant invokes a constitutional right, the claim of right cannot be used as a sword against the defendant by commenting on it or highlighting its invocation. However, when there is no constitutional right to withhold evidence under the Fifth Amendment, a prosecutor may properly mention the fact to the jury during closing arguments. In the case of *South Dakota v. Neville*, the United States Supreme Court approved the

---

[177]   Malloy v. Hogan, 378 U.S. 1, 84 S. Ct. 1489, 12 L. Ed. 2d 653 (1964).

[178]   384 U.S. 757, 86 S. Ct. 1826, 16 L. Ed. 2d 908 (1966). *See* case in Part II in Cases Relating to Chapter 14.

[179]   *Id.* at 764.

[180]   United States v. Ponds, 454 F.3d 313, 319, 2006 U.S. App. LEXIS 17718 (D.C. Cir. 2006).

admission of evidence that the defendant refused to submit to a blood-alcohol test.[181] Summarizing its opinion, the Court stated:

> We hold, therefore, that a refusal to take a blood alcohol test, after a police officer has lawfully requested it, is not an act coerced by the officer, and thus is not protected by the privilege against self-incrimination.

The Fifth Amendment self-incrimination provision neither prohibits the compelled display of identifiable physical characteristics such as tattoos, bodily scars, or deformities that help identify a person, nor does it protect against having to provide saliva and hair samples to a grand jury.[182] Echoing the *Schmerber* case, the Supreme Court of New Hampshire held in a sexual assault case that neither the state constitution nor the federal Fifth Amendment were violated by requiring a defendant to provide DNA samples that were introduced with blood evidence against him, because the evidence was non-testimonial in nature.[183] Requiring a handwriting sample from a defendant does not violate the Fifth Amendment or a similar state provision because the sample is an identifying physical fact and nothing more.[184]

While it is not generally a violation of the Fifth Amendment self-incrimination provision to require a suspect to give handwriting specimens or voice exemplars for identification purposes and it is not a violation for a prosecutor to comment on the failure to provide such sample, but it constitutes a violation of the Fifth Amendment for a prosecutor to comment to the jury on the failure of the accused to testify.[185]

In Arizona, when reasonable suspicion exists that an individual may be driving impaired, there is no right to refuse to take field sobriety tests and the tests do not violate the privilege against self-incrimination. Therefore, a driver who refuses to allow a search to determine whether he or she is impaired may be mentioned to the jury by police witnesses and used in closing arguments.[186] Following a similar logic, requiring an arrestee to comply with an officer's request for a urine sample did not violate his Fifth Amendment privilege against self-incrimination, inasmuch as a sample was not evidence of a testimonial or communicative nature.[187] Likewise, where a defendant refused to give a urine sample in a drug possession case, the prosecution may comment on the defendant's refusal and the jury may give it whatever weight it chooses to give.[188]

---

[181]   South Dakota v. Neville, 459 U.S. 553, 103 S. Ct. 916, 75 L. Ed. 2d 748 (1983).

[182]   *See* People v. Watson, 214 Ill. 2d 271, 825 N.E.2d 257, 2005 Ill. LEXIS 2 (Ill. 2005).

[183]   State v. Hearns, 151 N.H. 226, 855 A.2d 549, 2004 N.H. LEXIS 129 (N.H. 2004).

[184]   State v. Wiggins, 2004 Del. Super. LEXIS 64 (Del. 2004). The Delaware courts have interpreted the Delaware Constitution of 1897, art. I, § 7, dealing with self-incrimination to be coextensive with the federal Fifth Amendment.

[185]   Griffin v. California, 380 U.S. 609, 85 S. Ct. 1229, 14 L. Ed. 2d 106 (1965).

[186]   State ex rel. Verburg v. Jones, 211 Ariz. 413, 121 P.3d 1283, 1285, 2005 Ariz. App. LEXIS 148 (2005).

[187]   United States v. Edmo, 140 F.3d 1289 (9th Cir. 1998).

[188]   State v. Mattson, 2005 S.D. 71, 698 N.W.2d 538, 552, 2005 S.D. LEXIS 73 (S.D. 2005).

All defendants have the privilege against self-incrimination based on state constitutions or on the federal Fifth Amendment, but it can successfully be asserted only when the evidence would be considered testimonial in nature. Evidence that involves physical attributes, personal characteristics, and scientific data about the defendant may implicate Fourth Amendment search and seizures issues, but rarely involve a violation of the Fifth Amendment.

§ 16.7   Due Process Exclusions

Closely related to the self-incrimination protections are the limitations that the due process clause of the Fourteenth Amendment imposes on the conduct of criminal proceedings of the states. If investigators, in obtaining evidence, violate the due process clause of the Fifth Amendment (in federal cases) or of the Fourteenth Amendment (in state cases), evidence obtained thereby will not be admissible. The reasoning here, as in other instances involving constitutional violations, is that to allow the admission of such evidence would encourage conduct that is prohibited by the Constitution.

Although the courts have refused to define specifically what is included in the due process protection, police and law enforcement actions that violate concepts of "fundamental fairness" generally violate the concept of due process.

For example, evidence obtained as a result of an improper lineup or photographic array is inadmissible. If a lineup or other confrontation for identification is held in such a way as to be unduly suggestive, i.e., to suggest to the witnesses who make the identification which person in the lineup is the suspect, then the in-court identification would be contaminated.[189] For example, where the suspect wore dreadlocks, it did not violate due process when no more than two other men in the lineup appeared in dreadlocks.[190] The argument can be made that when photographs are shown to victims for identification purposes in such a way as to be unduly suggestive, the procedure denies due process to the suspect. Therefore, evidence obtained in this way may be inadmissible on due process grounds, but the Supreme Court has recognized that the due process clause does not always require a blanket rule of exclusion, suppressing testimony following an impermissibly suggestive identification procedure.[191] However, the taking of blood, breath, saliva or urine samples—if done properly—does not violate the due process clause, and such evidence is admissible if other conditions are met.[192]

To summarize, if evidence is obtained by federal agents in violation of the due process clause of the Fifth Amendment, or by state agents in violation

---

[189] Foster v. California, 394 U.S. 440, 89 S. Ct. 1127, 22 L. Ed. 2d 402 (1969).

[190] Dobson v. Walker, 150 Fed. Appx. 49, 50, 2005 U.S. App. LEXIS 21294 (2d Cir. 2005).

[191] Amador v. Dretke, 2005 U.S. Dist. LEXIS 6072 (W.D. Tex. 2005), *aff'd sub nom.*, Amador v. Quarterman, 2006 U.S. App. LEXIS 19301 (5th Cir. 2006).

[192] Davis v. District of Columbia, 247 A.2d 417 (D.C. Ct. App. 1968).

of the due process clause of the Fourteenth Amendment, courts will generally exclude such evidence when used for proof of guilt.

§ 16.8 Right to Counsel as It Relates to the Exclusion of Evidence

One of the protections of the Bill of Rights that has been very broadly interpreted in recent years is the section of the Sixth Amendment that provides: "In all criminal prosecutions, the accused shall enjoy the right ... to have the assistance of counsel for his defense." In early decisions, this right was made available to the accused only at the trial if a defendant could afford an attorney but later was extended to require that free lawyers be appointed to defend indigents who were charged with felonies[193] and later, the Supreme Court held that the right to counsel extended to anyone who faced any incarceration if convicted.[194] Subsequently, the Supreme Court determined that the Sixth Amendment right to the assistance of counsel applied during the early stages of criminal investigations when a focus on individual suspects occurred and that, where this right had been violated and produced incriminating evidence, that evidence had to be excluded from trial.

As a means of enforcing the right to counsel provisions, a confession or statement obtained when the right to counsel is not protected will be excluded from evidence. For example, in *Escobedo v. Illinois*, the defendant moved to suppress the use of incriminating statements taken after he had requested counsel and had been refused. In this pre-*Miranda* right to counsel case, the Supreme Court held that the Sixth Amendment right to counsel attaches once the police have narrowed their inquiry to a specific subject, have taken the subject into custody, the subject has requested the assistance of an attorney, and police have embarked on efforts to question and elicit incriminating statements. Because Escobedo had been denied his right to the assistance of counsel, his convictions were reversed and the case remanded.[195]

Although in the *Escobedo* case the accused requested counsel, the Supreme Court in *Miranda*[196] stated that such a request was unnecessary because police must inform the person in custody of constitutional rights. Under the *Miranda* ruling, if the suspect is in custody when the police desire to conduct interrogation, the burden is placed on the police to inform the suspect of his or

---

[193] Gideon v. Wainwright, 372 U.S. 335, 1963 U.S. LEXIS 1942 (1963).

[194] *See* Argersinger v. Hamlin, 407 U.S. 25 (1972). The Supreme Court recently ruled that an indigent has a right to counsel where the defendant appears in front of a magistrate judge to learn of the charges against him. The initiation of adversarial judicial proceedings causes the right to counsel to attach. *See* Rothgery v. Gillespie County, _____ U.S. _____, 2008 U.S. LEXIS 5057 (2008).

[195] *See* Escobedo v. Illinois, 378 U.S. 478, 1964 U.S. LEXIS 827 (1964).

[196] Miranda v. Arizona, 384 U.S. 436, 1966 U.S. LEXIS 2817 (1966).

her constitutional rights and to refrain from asking any questions unless the accused knowingly waives his or her right to counsel.

From these and other cases, it is obvious that if custody exists and the accused requests counsel prior to or during the interrogation and counsel is not allowed, any statements obtained will not be admissible for proof of guilt. The *Miranda* Court reasoned that there are compelling pressures that exist in any custodial police interrogation and in order to help a suspect "to combat these pressures and to permit a full opportunity to exercise the privilege against self-incrimination, the accused must be adequately and effectively appraised of his rights and the exercise of those rights must be fully honored."[197] Under the *Miranda* reasoning, if police take a suspect into custody and question him or her with a view to obtaining incriminating statements, the police must advise him or her of his or her right to counsel and to silence or any evidence obtained will be excluded from trial to prove guilt.

The suspect may waive the right to counsel provided the waiver is made voluntarily, knowingly, and intelligently. However, the Supreme Court in *Edwards v. Arizona* determined that if the accused has clearly requested the assistance of counsel, interrogation must cease until counsel has been made available to the accused or until the accused initiates additional communication.[198] Although the Court in *Edwards* did not define "initiation of further communications," the Court in a later case determined that the question from the suspect, "Well, what is going to happen to me now?" really amounted to an attempt by the defendant to initiate further questioning, and that ensuing statements given by the defendant, even after he was warned further of his rights, were admissible.[199]

The rationale that was framed in *Edwards v. Arizona* was applied when the Supreme Court decided that if police initiate an interrogation after a defendant's assertion of his or her right to counsel at the arraignment or similar proceedings, a waiver of that right after police-initiated interrogation is invalid unless counsel is present. Once a suspect has been arraigned and has requested counsel at the arraignment or preliminary hearing, a police officer may not initiate questioning. The suspect may initiate additional communication with the police, but the burden is on the prosecution to show that the suspect did, in fact, initiate further questioning.[200] In *Michigan v. Jackson*, the arrestee initially requested the appointment of counsel, but before the attorney had a chance to meet with the arrestee, police had initiated interrogation and obtained a confession. The Supreme Court agreed with the state supreme court that the defendant's conviction must be reversed. According to the Supreme Court

---

[197]   *Id.* at 467.

[198]   Edwards v. Arizona, 451 U.S. 477, 101 S. Ct. 1880, 68 L. Ed. 2d 378 (1981).

[199]   Oregon v Bradshaw, 463 U.S. 1039, 103 S. Ct. 2830, 77 L. Ed. 2d 405 (1983).

[200]   Michigan v. Jackson, 475 U.S. 625, 1986 U.S. LEXIS 91 (1986). *See also* Poynter v. Murray, 964 F.2d 1404 (4th Cir.), *cert. denied,* 506 U.S. 958, 113 S. Ct. 419, 121 L. Ed. 2d 342 (1992).

of the United States, "[i]f police initiate an interrogation after a defendant's assertion of his right to counsel at an arraignment or similar proceeding, as in these cases, any waiver of that right for that police-initiated interrogation is invalid."[201] The prosecution does not get a chance to argue otherwise, even if the waiver might have honestly been a valid waiver.

In determining whether events subsequent to the accused's exercise of the right to be silent or have counsel present during a custodial interrogation constitute a waiver of the previously asserted right, the court must first determine whether the accused actually invoked the right, and, if so, the court must then determine whether the accused initiated further discussion with the police and knowingly and intelligently waived the previously asserted rights.[202]

Statements that might not be admissible under the *Edwards* case or the *Michigan v. Jackson* case may be used for impeachment purposes to cast doubt on a defendant's false or inconsistent testimony if a defendant takes the witness stand and offers testimony that is materially different from what the defendant stated to investigators during the illegal interrogation.[203] The court explained that while the Sixth Amendment prohibits the use of evidence obtained after the defendant has invoked his or her Sixth Amendment right to counsel for his or her case-in-chief, this shield should not be perverted into a license defensive perjury, free from the risk of confrontation with prior inconsistent utterances.

Another case that has had influence on the admissibility of evidence when the right to counsel is at issue is *United States v. Wade*.[204] This case concerned the right to counsel during a police lineup. In *Wade*, the Supreme Court stated that both the defendant Wade and his counsel should have been notified of the impending post-indictment lineup and that counsel's presence should have been a requisite to the conduct of the lineup, absent an intelligent waiver. The Court asserted that the best method of enforcing this right to counsel at the lineup is to prohibit in-court identification by witnesses if the court finds that the pretrial confrontation or lineup tainted the in-court identification. In other words, the Court reasoned that the post-indictment in-person lineup was a critical stage of the proceedings and that counsel should be present—unless the right is waived—if the identifying witness is to testify in court. In justifying this stand, the Court stated:

> Since it appears that there is a grave potential for prejudice, intentional or not, in the pretrial lineup, which may not be capable of reconstruction at trial, and since presence of counsel itself can often avert prejudice and assure a meaningful confrontation at trial, there can be little doubt that for Wade the post-indictment lineup was a critical stage of the prosecution.

If the accused's attorney is present or if the accused intelligently waives the right to an attorney, then a witness who made an identification of the

---

[201]   *Id.* at 636.

[202]   State v. Lane, 262 Kan. 373, 940 P.2d 422 (1997).

[203]   Michigan v. Harvey, 494 U.S. 344, 110 S. Ct. 1176, 108 L. Ed. 2d 293 (1990).

[204]   388 U.S. 218, 87 S. Ct. 1926, 18 L. Ed. 2d 1149 (1967).

accused at the lineup may be called upon in court to identify the accused in court. However, if the attorney was not present at a post-information or post-indictment lineup and the defendant did not waive the right to counsel, the witness may not be permitted to make an in-court identification of the defendant. If the prosecution can establish that an in-court identification will not be based on or tainted by the uncounseled lineup and will be based on a crime scene identification by clear and convincing proof, the identification evidence can be admitted.[205] In such circumstances, the in-court identification may be admissible even though counsel was not present at the pretrial confrontation.

In *Kirby v. Illinois*, the United States Supreme Court refused to extend the right to counsel for a face-to-face confrontation between an arrestee and a victim where neither an indictment had been returned nor an information had been filed.[206] Police had arrested the subject for a different crime and allowed the victim of a robbery to make an in-person one-on-one identification. Under such circumstances, no attorney need be present for the arrestee and any identification will not be excluded on grounds that a violation of the right to counsel has occurred. Subjecting a person to an in-person lineup does not involve a deprivation of the privilege against self-incrimination and the Court further explained that counsel is not required at a pre-arrest, pre-indictment identification confrontation. The Court distinguished this one-on-one identification of *Kirby v. Illinois* situation from the *Wade* post-indictment confrontation for identification, holding that a post-indictment lineup or confrontation for identification is a critical stage, and the right to counsel attaches if the witness is to identify the accused at trial. However, the pre-arrest, pre-indictment, pre-information confrontation is not a critical stage for Sixth Amendment purposes, and identification evidence may be offered at trial even if counsel was not present at the lineup or showup.

Case law in some states helps clarify when the right to counsel attaches in state prosecutions. For example, in New York, a suspect does not have a right to counsel when police conduct a pre-arraignment lineup[207] where there has been no indictment. And in Michigan, the right to counsel for in-person lineups does not attach until adversarial judicial proceedings have been initiated.[208] In an additional limitation of the right to counsel at identification procedures, the Supreme Court held that "the Sixth Amendment does not require that defense counsel be present when a witness views police or prosecution photographic arrays[,]"[209] although a state would be free to require them. Due process

---

[205]   Moore v. Illinois, 434 U.S. 220, 225, 1977 U.S. LEXIS 163 (1977).

[206]   406 U.S. 682, 92 S. Ct. 1877, 32 L. Ed. 2d 411 (1972).

[207]   People v. Woolcock, 2005 NY Slip Op 25045 (N.Y. 2005).

[208]   People v. Harris, 2005 Mich. App. LEXIS 3264 (2005). Michigan grants the right to counsel for corporeal identifications only at or after the initiation of adversarial judicial proceedings and there is no right to counsel at photographic arrays. *See* People v. Hickman, 470 Mich. 602, 684 N.W.2d 267, 2004 Mich. LEXIS 1544 (Mich. 2004).

[209]   United States v. Ash, 413 U.S. 300, 1973 U.S. LEXIS 45 (1973).

requirements still dictate that a photographic array or photo lineup cannot be unduly suggestive if police want to have the evidence admitted at a defendant's trial.

§ 16.9 Summary

Although the traditional common law doctrine is that evidence is admissible if relevant even though obtained illegally, much evidence is not admissible if a federal or state constitutional provision has been violated. Exclusionary rules have developed over time and have been made applicable both to federal and state courts on a piecemeal basis.

Under the present rules as established by the United States Supreme Court and lower courts, most evidence obtained by search and seizure in violation of the Constitution is inadmissible in both federal and state courts. The cases must be examined thoroughly to determine what is considered an illegal search and under what circumstances the exclusionary rules apply.

Although wiretap evidence at first was not considered to be within the protection of the constitutional provisions, recent cases have held that wiretapping and eavesdropping fall within the protection of the Fourth Amendment as well as state and federal law. Under the Omnibus Crime Control Act of 1968, certain wiretap and eavesdrop evidence is admissible if the statutory requirements are met or if one party to the conversation consents. Evidence obtained in violation of the statute will not be admitted into court. The Patriot Act expanded the definition of a pen register so that newer methods of transmitting data and communication may be covered when the executive branch obtains a warrant.

As a means of ensuring that confessions will be obtained freely and voluntarily, courts have established rules that prohibit the admissibility of confessions obtained in violation of established standards. Although evidence continues to be challenged with arguments that the admission of physical facts or scientific evidence results in a violation of the Fifth Amendment self-incrimination privilege, this protection has been interpreted to apply only to evidence of a testimonial or a communicative nature. Evidence that is of a testimonial or communicative nature is inadmissible unless this protection is waived.

Evidence acquired in violation of the due process clauses of the Fifth and Fourteenth Amendments is also inadmissible. While most due process arguments for excluding evidence fall under specific provisions of the Bill of Rights, some evidence is subject to exclusion under due process standards. Court opinions must be studied to determine what activities constitute a violation, keeping in mind that some states offer greater protection under due process than is required by the federal constitution.

Evidence is also excluded if the right to counsel provisions of the Sixth Amendment are violated. Again, it is essential that cases be studied carefully to determine the various courts' interpretations concerning what is a violation of the Sixth Amendment.

Although courts exclude certain evidence to enforce constitutional provisions that have been violated, criminal justice personnel should not take a negative attitude, because these limitations uphold the rule of law. Proper investigation that follows constitutional requirements and interpretations will result in both protecting the rights of the individual and successful prosecutions of wrongdoers with admissible evidence.

Part II
Judicial Decisions
Relating To Part I

Part II: Table of Cases

Cases Relating to Chapter 1
History and Development of Rules of Evidence
    Funk v. United States, 290 U.S. 371 (1933) 693

Cases Relating to Chapter 2
Approach to the Study of Criminal Evidence
    State v. Craft, 274 Ga. App. 410 (2005)
    Trammel v. United States, 445 U.S. 40 (1980)
    State v. Anthony, 218 Ariz. 439 (2008) 699

Cases Relating to Chapter 3
Burden of Proof
    In re Winship, 397 U.S. 358 (1970)
    Victor v. Nebraska, 511 U.S. 1 (1994)
    State v. Eichelberger, 2005 Wash. App. LEXIS 2429 (2005)
    Martin v. Ohio, 480 U.S. 228 (1987) 709

Cases Relating to Chapter 4
Proof via Evidence
    Maddox v. Montgomery, 718 F.2d 1033 (11th Cir. 1983)
    Brown v. State, 897 A.2d 748 (Del. 2006)
    State v. Jordan, 2002 Ohio 1418 (Ohio App. 2002) 719

Cases Relating to Chapter 5
Judicial Notice
    State v. Vejvoda, 231 Neb. 668, 438 N.W.2d 461 (1989)
    Robinson v. State, 260 Ga. App. 186 (2003)
    State v. Richardson, 811 So. 2d 154 (La. App. 2002)
    State v. Smith, 2006 Del. C.P. LEXIS 34 (2006)...................................727

Cases Relating to Chapter 6
Presumptions, Inferences and Stipulations
   State v. Jackson, 112 Wash. 2d 867, 774 P.2d 1211 (1989)
   State v. Purcell, 325 Ill. App. 3d 551, 758 N.E.2d 895 (2001)
   Bozeman v. State, 931 So. 2d 1006 (Fla. App. 2006)............................739

Cases Relating to Chapter 7
Relevancy and Materiality
   Commonwealth v. Prashaw, 57 Mass. App. 19, 781 N.E.2d 19 (2003)
   Jackson v. United States, 856 A.2d 1111 (D.C. App. 2004)..................749

Cases Relating to Chapter 8
Competency of Evidence and Witnesses
   United States v. Phibbs, 999 F.2d 1053 (6th Cir. 1993)
   State v. Wells, 2003 Ohio 3162 (Ohio App. 2003)................................757

Cases Relating to Chapter 9
Examination of Witnesses
   United States v. Drummond, 69 Fed. Appx. 580 (2003)
   People v. Melendez, 102 P.3d 315 (Colo. 2004)
   State v. Sands, 2008 Ohio 6981 (Ohio App. 2008)................................763

Cases Relating to Chapter 10
Privileges
   St. Clair v. Commonwealth, 174 S.W.3d 474,
      2005 Ky. LEXIS 334 (2005)
   State v. Bergmann, 2009 Iowa App. LEXIS 54 (2009)
   New York City Health v. Morgenthau, 98 N.Y.2d 525,
   779 N.E.2d 173 (2002) 773

Cases Relating to Chapter 11
Opinions and Expert Testimony
   Bowling v. State, 275 Ga. App. 45, 619 S.E.2d 688 (2005)
   Osbourn v. State, 92 S.W.3d 531 (Tex. Crim. App. 2002)
   United States v. Delatorre, 309 Fed. Appx. 366 (11th Cir. 2009)..........783

Cases Relating to Chapter 12
Hearsay Rule and Exceptions
   Bell v. Florida, 847 So. 2d 558 (Fla. App. 2003)
   Gonzalez v. State, 195 S.W.3d 114 (Tex. Crim. App. 2006)
   Cox v. State, 774 N.E.2d 1025 (Ind. App. 2002)

Sadler v. State, 2009 Tex. App. LEXIS 2962(2009)
State v. Washington, 664 N.W.2d 203 (Mich. 2003) 793

Cases Relating to Chapter 13
Documentary Evidence
    Wilkerson v. State, 2005 Ark. App. LEXIS 12 (2005)
    State v. Huehn, 53 P.3d 733 (Colo. App. 2002)
    McKeehan v. State, 838 So. 2d 1257 (Fla. App. 2003) 805

Cases Relating to Chapter 14
Real Evidence
    Schmerber v. California, 384 U.S. 757 (1966)
    State v. Cowans, 782 N.E.2d 779, 2002 Ill. App. LEXIS 1170,
        appeal denied by People v. Cowans, 2003 Ill. LEXIS 649 (2003)
    Underwood v. State, 708 So. 2d 18 (Miss. 1998)
    McHenry v. State, 820 N.E.2d 124 (Ind. 2005) 813

Cases Relating to Chapter 15
Results of Examinations and Tests
    Commonwealth v. Gaynor, 443 Mass. 245, 820 N.E.2d 233 (2005)
    People v. Wilkinson, 33 Cal. 4th 821, 2004 Cal. LEXIS 6833(2004)
    City of Cleveland Heights v. Katz, 2002 Ohio 4241
    (Ohio App. 2001) 829

Cases Relating to Chapter 16
Evidence Unconstitutionally Obtained
    United States v. Leon, 468 U.S. 897 (1984)
    Arizona v. Gant, ___ U.S. ___, 2009 U.S. LEXIS 3120 (2009)
    Georgia v. Randolph, 547 U.S. 103 (2006)
    Horton v. California, 496 U.S. 128 (1990) 843

Cases Relating to Chapter 1

History and Development of Rules of Evidence

FUNK
v.
UNITED STATES

Supreme Court of the United States
290 U.S. 371, 54 S. Ct. 212 (1933)

JUSTICE SUTHERLAND delivered the opinion of the Court.

The sole inquiry to be made in this case is whether in a federal court the wife of the defendant on trial for a criminal offense is a competent witness in his behalf. Her competency to testify against him is not involved.

The petitioner was twice tried and convicted in a federal district court upon an indictment for conspiracy to violate the prohibition law. His conviction on the first trial was reversed by the circuit court of appeals upon a ground not material here. 46 F.2d 417. Upon the second trial, as upon the first, defendant called his wife to testify in his behalf. At both trials she was excluded upon the ground of incompetency. The circuit court of appeals sustained this ruling upon the first appeal, and also upon the appeal which followed the second trial. 66 F.2d 70. We granted certiorari, limited to the question as to what law is applicable to the determination of the competency of the wife of the petitioner as a witness.

Both the petitioner and the government, in presenting the case here, put their chief reliance on prior decisions of this court. The government relies on *United States v. Reid*, 12 How. 361; *Logan v. United States*, 144 U.S. 263; *Hendrix v. United States*, 219 U.S. 79; and *Jin Fuey Moy v. United States*, 254 U.S. 189. Petitioner contends that these cases, if not directly contrary to the decisions in *Benson v. United States*, 146 U.S. 325, and *Rosen v. United States*, 245 U.S. 467, are so in principle. We shall first briefly review these cases, with the exception of the *Hendrix* case and the *Jin Fuey Moy* case, which we leave for consideration until a later point in this opinion.

In the *Reid* case, two persons had been jointly indicted for a murder committed upon the high seas. They were tried separately, and it was held that one of them was not a competent witness in behalf of the other who was first tried. The trial was had in Virginia; and by a statute of that state passed in 1849, if applicable in a federal court, the evidence would have been competent. Section 34 of the Judiciary Act of 1789 declares that the laws of the several states, except where the Constitution, treaties or statutes of the United States otherwise provide, shall be regarded as rules of decision in trials at common law in the courts of the United States in cases where they apply; but the court said that this referred only to civil cases and did not apply in the trial of criminal offenses against the United States. It was conceded that there was no act of Congress prescribing in express words the rule by which the federal courts would be governed in the admission of testimony in criminal cases. "But," the court said (p. 363), "we think it may be found with sufficient certainty, not indeed in direct terms, but by necessary implication, in the acts of 1789 and 1790, establishing the courts of the United States, and providing for the punishment of certain offences."

The court pointed out that the Judiciary Act regulated certain proceedings to be had prior to impaneling the jury, but contained no express provision concerning the mode of conducting the trial after the jury was sworn, and prescribed no rule in respect of the testimony to be taken. Obviously however, it was said, some certain and established rule upon the subject was necessary to enable the courts to administer the criminal jurisprudence of the United States, and Congress must have intended to refer them to some known and established rule "which was supposed to be so familiar and well understood in the trial by jury that legislation upon the subject would be deemed superfluous. This is necessarily to be implied from what these acts of Congress omit, as well as from what they contain." (p. 365.) The court concluded that this could not be the common law as it existed at the time of the emigration of the colonists, or the rule which then prevailed in England, and [therefore] the only known rule which could be supposed to have been in the mind of Congress was that which was in force in the respective states when the federal courts were established by the Judiciary Act of 1789. Applying this rule, it was decided that the witness was incompetent.

In the *Logan* case it was held that the competency of a witness to testify in a federal court sitting in one state, was not affected by his conviction and sentence for felony in another state; and that the competency of another witness was not affected by his conviction of felony in a Texas state court, where the witness had since been pardoned. The indictment was for an offense committed in Texas and there tried. The decision was based not upon any statute of the United States, but upon the ground that the subject "is governed by the common law, which, as has been seen, was the law of Texas . . . at the time of the admission of Texas into the Union as a State." (p. 303.)

We next consider the two cases upon which petitioner relies. In the *Benson* case two persons were jointly indicted for murder. On motion of the government there was a severance, and Benson was first tried. His codefendant was called as a witness on behalf of the government. The *Reid* case had been cited as practically decisive of the question. But the court, after pointing out what it conceived to be distinguishing features in that case, said (p. 335), "We do not feel ourselves, therefore, precluded by that case from examining this question in the light of general authority and sound reason."

The alleged incompetency of the codefendant was rested upon two reasons, first, that he was interested, and second, that he was a party to the record, the basis for the exclusion at common law being fear of perjury. "Nor," the court said, "were those named the only grounds of exclusion from the witness stand; conviction of crime, want of religious belief, and other matters were held sufficient. Indeed, the theory of the common law was to admit to the witness stand only those presumably honest, appreciating the sanctity of an oath, unaffected as a party by the result, and free from any of the temptations of interest. The courts were afraid to trust the intelligence of jurors. But the last fifty years have wrought a great change in these respects, and to-day the tendency is to enlarge the domain of competency and to submit to the jury for their consideration as to the credibility of the witness those matters which heretofore were ruled sufficient to justify his exclusion. This change has been wrought partially by legislation and partially by judicial construction." Attention then is called to the fact that Congress in 1864 had enacted that no witness should be excluded from testifying in any civil action, with certain exceptions, because he was a party to or interested in the issue tried; and that in 1878 (c. 37, 20 Stat. 30) Congress made the defendant in any criminal case a competent witness at his own request. The opinion then continues (p. 337):

> Legislation of similar import prevails in most of the States. The spirit of this legislation has controlled the decisions of the courts, and steadily, one by one, the merely technical barriers which excluded witnesses from the stand have been removed, till now it is generally, though perhaps not universally, true that no one is excluded therefrom unless the lips of the originally adverse party are closed by death, or unless some one of those peculiarly confidential relations, like that of husband and wife, forbids the breaking of silence.

. . . If interest and being party to the record do not exclude a defendant on trial from the witness stand, upon what reasoning can a codefendant, not on trial, be adjudged incompetent?

That case was decided December 5, 1892. Twenty-five years later this court had before it for consideration the case of *Rosen v. United States, supra.* Rosen had been tried and convicted in a federal district court for conspiracy. A person jointly indicted with Rosen, who had been convicted upon his plea of guilty, was called as a witness by the government and allowed to testify over Rosen's objection. This court sustained the competency of the witness. After saying that while the decision in the *Reid* case had not been specifically overruled, its authority was seriously shaken by the decisions in both the *Logan* and *Benson* cases, the court proceeded to dispose of the question, as it had been disposed of in the *Benson case*, "in the light of general authority and sound reason."

"In the almost twenty [twenty-five] years," the court said [pp. 471, 472], "which have elapsed since the decision of the Benson Case, the disposition of courts and of legislative bodies to remove disabilities from witnesses has continued, as that decision shows it had been going forward before, under dominance of the conviction of our time that the truth is more likely to be arrived at by hearing the testimony of all persons of competent understanding who may seem to have knowledge of the facts involved in a case, leaving the credit and weight of such testimony to be determined by the jury or by the court, rather than by rejecting witnesses as incompetent, with the result that this principle has come to be widely, almost universally, accepted in this country and in Great Britain.

"Since the decision in the *Benson* Case we have significant evidence of the trend of congressional opinion upon this subject in the removal of the disability of witnesses convicted of perjury, Rev. Stats., § 5392, by the enactment of the Federal Criminal Code in 1909 with this provision omitted and § 5392 repealed. This is significant, because the disability to testify, of persons convicted of perjury, survived in some jurisdictions much longer than many of the other common-law disabilities, for the reason that the offense concerns directly the giving of testimony in a court of justice, and conviction of it was accepted as showing a greater disregard for the truth than it was thought should be implied from a conviction of other crime.

"Satisfied as we are that the legislation and the very great weight of judicial authority which have developed in support of this modern rule, especially as applied to the competency of witnesses convicted of crime, proceed upon sound principle, we conclude that the dead hand of the common-law rule of 1789 should no longer be applied to such cases as we have here, and that the ruling of the lower courts on this first claim of error should be approved."

It is well to pause at this point to state a little more concisely what was held in these cases. It will be noted, in the first place, that the decision in the Reid case was not based upon any express statutory provision. The court found from what the congressional legislation omitted to say, as well as from what it actually said, that in establishing the federal courts in 1789 some definite rule in respect to the testimony to be taken in criminal cases must have been in the mind of Congress; and the rule which the court thought was in the mind of that body was that of the common law as it existed in the thirteen original states in 1789. The *Logan* case in part rejected that view and held that the controlling rule was that of the common law in force at the time of the admission of the state in which the particular trial was had. Taking the two cases together, it is plain enough that the ultimate doctrine announced is that in the taking of testimony in criminal cases, the federal courts are bound by the rules of the common law as they existed at a definitely specified time in the respective states, unless Congress has otherwise provided.

With the conclusion that the controlling rule is that of the common law, the *Benson* case and the *Rosen* case do not conflict; but both cases reject the notion, which the two earlier ones seem to accept, that the courts, in the face of greatly changed conditions, are still chained to the ancient formulae and are powerless to declare and enforce modifications deemed to have been wrought in the common law itself by force of these changed conditions. Thus, as we have seen, the court in the *Benson* case pointed to the tendency during the preceding years to enlarge the domain of competency, significantly saying that the changes had been wrought not only by legislation but also "partially by judicial construction"; and that it was the spirit (not the letter, be it observed) of this legislation which had controlled the decisions of the courts and steadily removed the merely technical barriers in respect of incompetency, until generally no one was excluded from giving testimony, except under certain peculiar conditions which are set forth. It seems difficult to escape the conclusion that the specific ground upon which the court there rested its determination as to the competency of a codefendant was that, since the defendant had been rendered competent, the competency of the codefendant followed as a natural consequence.

This view of the matter is made more positive by the decision in the *Rosen* case. The question of the testimonial competency of a person jointly indicted with the defendant was disposed of, as the question had been in the Benson case, "in the light of general authority and sound reason." The conclusion which the court reached was based not upon any definite act of legislation, but upon the trend of congressional opinion and of legislation (that is to say of legislation generally), and upon the great weight of judicial authority which, since the earlier decisions, had developed in support of a more modern rule. In both cases the court necessarily proceeded upon the theory that the resultant modification which these important considerations had wrought in the rules of the old common law was within the power of the courts to declare and make operative.

That the present case falls within the principles of the *Benson* and *Rosen* cases, and especially of the latter, we think does not reasonably admit of doubt.

The rules of the common law which disqualified as witnesses persons having an interest, long since, in the main, have been abolished both in England and in this country; and what was once regarded as a sufficient ground for excluding the testimony of such persons altogether has come to be uniformly and more sensibly regarded as affecting the credit of the witness only. Whatever was the danger that an interested witness would not speak the truth—and the danger never was as great as claimed—its effect has been minimized almost to the vanishing point by the test of cross-examination, the increased intelligence of jurors, and perhaps other circumstances. The modern rule which has removed the disqualification from persons accused of crime gradually came into force after the middle of the last century, and is today universally accepted. The exclusion of the husband or wife is said by this court to be based upon his or her interest in the event. *Jin Fuey Moy v. United States, supra.* And whether by this is meant a practical interest in the result of the prosecution or merely a sentimental interest because of the marital relationship, makes little difference. In either case, a refusal to permit the wife upon the ground of interest to testify in behalf of her husband, while permitting him, who has the greater interest, to testify for himself, presents a manifest incongruity.

Nor can the exclusion of the wife's testimony, in the face of the broad and liberal extension of the rules in respect of the competency of witnesses generally, be any longer justified, if it ever was justified, on any ground of public policy. It has been said that to admit such testimony is against public policy because it would endanger the harmony and confidence of marital relations, and, moreover, would subject the witness to the temptation to commit perjury. Modern legislation, in making either spouse competent to testify in behalf of the other in criminal cases, has definitely rejected these notions, and in the light of such legislation and of modern thought they seem to be altogether fanciful. The public policy of one generation may not, under changed conditions, be the public policy of another. *Patton v. United States*, 281 U.S. 276, 306.

The fundamental basis upon which all rules of evidence must rest—if they are to rest upon reason—is their adaptation to the successful development of the truth. And since experience is of all teachers the most dependable, and since experience also is a continuous process, it follows that a rule of evidence at one time thought necessary to the ascertainment of truth should yield to the experience of a succeeding generation whenever that experience has clearly demonstrated the fallacy or unwisdom of the old rule.

It may be said that the court should continue to enforce the old rule, however contrary to modern experience and thought, and however opposed, in principle, to the general current of legislation and of judicial opinion, it may have become, leaving to Congress the responsibility of changing it. Of course, Congress has that power; but if Congress fail to act, as it has failed in respect of the matter now under review, and the court be called upon to decide the question, is it not the duty of the court, if it possess the power, to decide it in accordance with present day standards of wisdom and justice rather than in accordance with some outworn and antiquated rule of the past? That this court has the power to do so is necessarily implicit in the opinions delivered in deciding the *Benson* and *Rosen* cases. And that implication, we think, rests upon substantial ground. The rule of the common law which denies the competency of one spouse to testify in behalf of the other in a criminal prosecution has not been modified by congressional legislation; nor has Congress directed the federal courts to follow state law upon that subject, as it has in respect of some other subjects. That this court and the other federal courts, in this situation and by right of their own powers, may decline to enforce the ancient rule of the common law under conditions as they now exist we think is not fairly open to doubt.

In *Hurtado v. California*, 110 U.S. 516, 530, this court, after suggesting that it was better not to go too far back into antiquity for the best securities of our liberties, said:

It is more consonant to the true philosophy of our historical legal institutions to say that the spirit of personal liberty and individual right, which they embodied, was preserved and developed by a progressive growth and wise adaptation to new circumstances and situations of the forms and processes found fit to give, from time to time, new expression and greater effect to modern ideas of self-government.

This flexibility and capacity for growth and adaptation is the peculiar boast and excellence of the common law. . . . and as it was the characteristic principle of the common law to draw its inspiration from every fountain of justice, we are not to assume that the sources of its supply have been exhausted. On the contrary, we should expect that the new and various experiences of our own situation and system will mould and shape it into new and not less useful forms.

Compare *Holden v. Hardy*, 169 U.S. 366, 385–387.

To concede this capacity for growth and change in the common law by drawing "its inspiration from every fountain of justice," and at the same time to say that the courts of this country are forever bound to perpetuate such of its rules as, by every reasonable test, are found to be neither wise nor just, because we have once adopted them as suited to our situation and institutions at a particular time, is to deny to the common law in the place of its adoption a "flexibility and capacity for growth and adaptation" which was "the peculiar boast and excellence" of the system in the place of its origin.

The final question to which we are thus brought is not that of the power of the federal courts to amend or repeal any given rule or principle of the common law, for they neither have nor claim that power, but it is the question of the power of these courts, in the complete absence of congressional legislation on the subject, to declare and effectuate, upon common law principles, what is the present rule upon a given subject in the light of fundamentally altered conditions, without regard to what has previously been declared and practiced. It has been said so often as to have become axiomatic that the common law is not immutable but flexible, and by its own principles adapts itself to varying conditions. In *Ketelsen v. Stilz*, 184 Ind. 702; 111 N. E. 423, the supreme court of that state, after pointing out that the common law of England was based upon usages, customs and institutions of the English people as declared from time to time by the courts, said (p. 707):

> The rules so deduced from this system, however, were continually changing and expanding with the progress of society in the application of this system to more diversified circumstances and under more advanced periods. The common law by its own principles adapted itself to varying conditions and modified its own rules so as to serve the ends of justice as prompted by a course of reasoning which was guided by these generally accepted truths. One of its oldest maxims was that where the reason of a rule ceased, the rule also ceased, and it logically followed that when it occurred to the courts that a particular rule had never been founded upon reason, and that no reason existed in support thereof, that rule likewise ceased, and perhaps another sprang up in its place which was based upon reason and justice as then conceived. No rule of the common law could survive the reason on which it was founded. It needed no statute to change it but abrogated itself.

That court then refers to the settled doctrine that an adoption of the common law in general terms does not require, without regard to local circumstances, an unqualified application of all its rules; that the rules, as declared by the English courts at one period or another, have been controlling in this country only so far as they were suited to and in harmony with the genius, spirit and objects of American institutions; and that the rules of the common law considered proper in the eighteenth century are not necessarily so considered in the twentieth. "Since courts have had an existence in America," that court said (p. 708), "they have never hesitated to take upon themselves the responsibility of saying what are the proper rules of the common law."

And the Virginia Supreme Court of Appeals, in *Hanriot v. Sherwood*, 82 Va. 1, 15, after pointing to the fact that the common law of England is the law of that commonwealth except so far as it has been altered by statute, or so far as its principles are inapplicable to the state of the country, and that the rules of the common law had undergone modification in the courts of England, notes with obvious approval that "the rules of evidence have been in the courts of this country undergoing such modification and changes, according to the circumstances of the country and the manner and genius of the people."

The supreme court of Connecticut, in *Beardsley v. Hartford*, 50 Conn. 529, 541–542, after quoting the maxim of the common law, *cessante ratione legis, cessat ipsa lex*, said:

> This means that no law can survive the reasons on which it is founded. It needs no statute to change it; it abrogates itself. If the reasons on which a law rests are overborne by opposing reasons, which in the progress of society gain a controlling force, the old law, though still good as an abstract principle, and good in its application to some circumstances, must cease to apply as a controlling principle to the new circumstances.

The same thought is expressed in *People v. Randolph*, 2 Park. Cr. Rep. (N. Y.) 174, 177:

> Its rules [the rules of the common law] are modified upon its own principles and not in violation of them. Those rules being founded in reason, one of its oldest maxims is, that where the reason of the rule ceases the rule also ceases.

* * *

Judgment reversed.

MR. JUSTICE CARDOZO concurs in the result.

MR. JUSTICE McREYNOLDS and MR. JUSTICE BUTLER are of opinion that the judgment of the court below is right and should be affirmed.

Cases Relating to Chapter 2

Approach to the Study of Criminal Evidence

CRAFT

v.

STATE

Court of Appeals of Georgia

274 Ga. App. 410, 2005 Ga. App. LEXIS 778 (2005).

Opinion by Phipps, Judge.

Rodney Craft was tried by a jury and convicted of two counts of child molestation. He was sentenced to forty years, ten in confinement and thirty on probation. On appeal, he claims that the trial court erred in its questioning of two witnesses and in refusing to allow his trial counsel to introduce evidence of the victims' academic records. Craft also charges his trial counsel with ineffective assistance. We conclude that the trial court violated OCGA 17-8-57 by its questioning of one witness. We further conclude that the statutory violation, coupled with the trial court's failure to allow Craft a thorough and sifting cross-examination, constituted plain error. Therefore, we reverse. Because the evidence was sufficient to support the verdict under the standard of *Jackson v. Virginia*, the case can be retried.

The evidence showed that C.W. and T.J., both 15 years old, were walking to school in Columbus on August 26, 2002. As they walked by Craft's house, Craft said to C.W., "Hey, look over here." C. W. looked in that direction and saw Craft standing naked at his door, masturbating. C.W. told T.J. to look, and T.J. also saw Craft naked and masturbating. They ran the rest of the way to school and reported

the incident to the assistant principal, Senobia Moore. After investigation by Columbus police officers, Craft was arrested.

Craft claims that the trial court erred by asking Moore questions about the character of the victims in such a manner as to cause the jury to believe that the court had formed or expressed an opinion about the veracity of the victims, in violation of OCGA 17-8-57.

The following exchange is at issue:

THE COURT: Ms. Moore, I just have a couple of questions for you. Do you know what kind of students these two girls are?

THE WITNESS: Yes. They are very good students. Actually, one is a cheerleader and they are very mannerable, very poli[t]e young ladies. And, again, knowing that they are not ones that are real wild and real, you know, loud in the halls and everything, the way that I saw them that day, you know, caused my attention to go to them.

THE COURT: Are the cheerleaders at [your school] required to make a certain grade-point average?

THE WITNESS: Yes, well, we follow the State, the code that goes with athletes, and if you—

THE COURT: So that's the same requirement?

THE WITNESS: Yes, it is. And if you fail two classes, you cannot participate. So it's the fail-no-participate rule. However, our students are still monitored. All of our athletes are monitored; and if their grades begin to fall low, they can be pulled from a game or pulled from participating for a period of time.

THE COURT: Based on the individual school policy?

THE WITNESS: Yes.

"The credibility and standing of the witness is an issuable fact in every case — a most material fact. Therefore, anything which tends to uphold, to support, to disparage, or to lower the character and the resulting credibility of the witness is vitally connected with the facts of the case." 8 This case was based almost entirely on the testimony of the victims. As a result, their credibility was the most important issue in the case.

Focused on what it calls the court's "leeway" in posing questions during a criminal trial, the dissent misses the point. We do not challenge the trial court's right to "occasional and cautious" questioning of witnesses to develop the truth of a case. Instead, we hold that the specific questioning in this case constituted a violation of OCGA 17-8-57. Contrary to the dissent's argument, we are not breaking new ground or establishing a new rule in holding that a trial court violates OCGA 17-8-57 when it intimates its opinion as to the credibility of a witness — an issue within the sole province of the jury. We are merely applying existing case law to the specific facts of this case — a task performed daily by judges at the trial and appellate levels.

We do not conclude that the trial court's improper questioning, standing alone, constituted plain error. Instead, we consider the issue of plain error in connection with Craft's next claim.

After the court asked Moore questions about the victims' school performance, Craft sought to question her about their academic history and disciplinary history. Craft asked Moore what kind of student C.W. was, Moore admitted that even polite students get into minor trouble and, at Craft's request, Moore explained "administrative detention." The state objected to the line of questioning

at that point. Craft's counsel responded that he had documents that contradicted some of Moore's testimony about the victims' school performance and conduct. The court refused to allow Craft to pursue the matter further, stating "you're not going to make these victims look bad." Although this statement was made during a bench conference, it demonstrated that the trial court had reached the conclusion that the state had already proven that the girls were victims. Further, that conclusion likely formed the basis for the trial court's decision to shut down Craft's cross-examination. Craft claims that the trial court's refusal to allow further cross-examination constituted an abuse of the court's discretion.

As noted previously, the testimony elicited by the trial court bolstered the credibility of the victims, which had not previously been challenged. After opening the door to this line of questioning and allowing Moore to testify that the victims were very good students who were well-behaved, the trial court refused to allow Craft to rebut this testimony. Craft had documents showing that C.W. had been disciplined for disrespect and had been placed in administrative detention on two occasions, along with one showing that T.J. had been cited for screaming in the hallway and subjected to in-school suspension. Other documents showed that both victims had failed at least two classes.

The dissent argues that it was sufficient to allow Craft to ask four questions that "inferred to the jury that the two students fell short of perfection." But the limited questioning allowed by the court clearly was not adequate to rebut the critical testimony the court had elicited and did not provide Craft the thorough and sifting cross-examination to which he was entitled.

The right of cross examination is a substantial right, the preservation of which is essential to the proper administration of justice and extends to all matters within the knowledge of the witness, the disclosure of which is material to the controversy. This right should not be abridged.

Here, not only did the court refuse to allow Craft further questioning of the witness; it refused to allow Craft to introduce the documentary evidence that would have specifically rebutted Moore's testimony regarding the behavior and academic standing of the victims.

We disagree with the dissent's implication that the focus should be on the number of questions asked by the trial court instead of the impact of those questions on the judicial proceedings. The dissent also seems to misunderstand our ultimate conclusion — when the trial court's improper questioning was compounded with the court's refusal to allow Craft to rebut the testimony the court had elicited, it "seriously affected the fairness, integrity, and public reputation" of the judicial proceedings.

Because it is possible that the situation could occur on retrial, we address Craft's claim that the trial court erred when it asked T.J. the following:

THE COURT: Did you have any trouble seeing through the screen door on any of the occasions that you saw him standing behind the screen door?

THE WITNESS: No, ma'am.

THE COURT: Could you be mistaken about what he was doing?

THE WITNESS: No, ma'am.

THE COURT: On any of the times that you saw him?

THE WITNESS: No, ma'am.

Craft argues that the questioning bolstered T.J.'s credibility and revealed a clear bias toward the prosecution, in violation of OCGA 17-8-57.

During direct examination by the state, T. J. testified that she had seen Craft in his boxer shorts on August 19, while she was walking to school. She testified that when she saw him on August 26, he was standing behind a screen door and a light was on behind him. On cross-examination, Craft's counsel asked T.J. numerous questions about what she could and could not see through Craft's screen door.

Because Craft raised no objection to the questioning, he waived his right to assert the issue on appeal. Even if Craft had objected,

we find that no error occurred because the trial court merely sought to clarify T.J.'s testimony. The trial court may propound questions to any witness to develop the truth of the case.

Craft's remaining claims are moot.

Judgment reversed. Barnes, J., concurs. Ruffin, C. J., and Blackburn, P. J., concur specially. Andrews, P. J., Johnson, P. J., and Mikell, J., dissent

TRAMMEL
v.
UNITED STATES

Supreme Court of the United States
445 U.S. 40, 100 S. Ct. 906, 63 L. Ed. 2d 186 (1980)

MR. CHIEF JUSTICE BURGER delivered the opinion of the Court.

We granted certiorari to consider whether an accused may invoke the privilege against adverse spousal testimony so as to exclude the voluntary testimony of his wife. 440 U.S. 934 (1979). This calls for a re-examination of *Hawkins v. United States*, 358 U.S. 74 (1958).

I.

On March 10, 1976, petitioner Otis Trammel was indicted with two others, Edwin Lee Roberts and Joseph Freeman, for importing heroin into the United States from Thailand and the Philippine Islands and for conspiracy to import heroin in violation of 21 U. S. C.§§ 952 (a), 962 (a), and 963. The indictment also named six unindicted co-conspirators, including petitioner's wife Elizabeth Ann Trammel.

According to the indictment, petitioner and his wife flew from the Philippines to California in August 1975, carrying with them a quantity of heroin. Freeman and Roberts assisted them in its distribution. Elizabeth Trammel then ounsello to Thailand where she purchased another supply of the drug. On November 3, 1975, with four ounces of heroin on her person, she boarded a plane for the United States. During a routine customs search in Hawaii, she was searched, the heroin was discovered, and she was arrested. After discussions with Drug Enforcement Administration agents, she agreed to cooperate with the Government.

Prior to trial on this indictment, petitioner moved to sever his case from that of Roberts and Freeman. He advised the court that the Government intended to call his wife as an adverse witness and asserted his claim to a privilege to prevent her from testifying against him. At a hearing on the motion, Mrs. Trammel was called as a Government witness under a grant of use immunity. She testified that she and petitioner were married in May 1975 and that they remained married. She explained that her cooperation with the Government was based on assurances that she would be given lenient treatment. She then described, in considerable detail, her role and that of her husband in the heroin distribution conspiracy.

After hearing this testimony, the District Court ruled that Mrs. Trammel could testify in support of the Government's case to any act she observed during the marriage and to any communication "made in the presence of a third person"; however, confidential communications between petitioner and his wife were held to be privileged and inadmissible. The motion to sever was denied.

At trial, Elizabeth Trammel testified within the limits of the court's pretrial ruling; her testimony, as the Government concedes, constituted virtually its entire case against petitioner. He was found guilty on both the substantive and conspiracy charges and sentenced to an indeterminate term of years pursuant to the Federal Youth Corrections Act, 18 U. S. C. § 5010 (b).

In the Court of Appeals petitioner's only claim of error was that the admission of the adverse testimony of his wife, over his objection, contravened this Court's teaching in *Hawkins v. United States, supra*, and therefore constituted reversible error. The Court of Appeals rejected this contention. It concluded that *Hawkins* did not prohibit "the voluntary testimony of a spouse who appears

as an unindicted co-conspirator under grant of immunity from the Government in return for her testimony." 583 F.2d 1166, 1168 (CA10 1978).

II.

The privilege claimed by petitioner has ancient roots. Writing in 1628, Lord Coke observed that "it hath been resolved by the Justices that a wife cannot be produced either against or for her husband." 1 E. Coke, A Commentarie upon Littleton 6b (1628). See, generally, 8 J. Wigmore, Evidence § 2227 (McNaughton rev. 1961). This spousal disqualification sprang from two canons of medieval jurisprudence: first, the rule that an accused was not permitted to testify in his own behalf because of his interest in the proceeding; second, the concept that husband and wife were one, and that since the woman had no recognized separate legal existence, the husband was that one. From those two now long-abandoned doctrines, it followed that what was inadmissible from the lips of the defendant-husband was also inadmissible from his wife.

Despite its medieval origins, this rule of spousal disqualification remained intact in most common-law jurisdictions well into the 19th century. See id., § 2333. It was applied by this Court in *Stein v. Bowman*, 13 Pet. 209, 220-223 (1839), in *Graves v. United States*, 150 U.S. 118 (1893), and again in *Jin Fuey Moy v. United States*, 254 U.S. 189, 195 (1920), where it was deemed so well established a proposition as to "hardly [require] mention." Indeed, it was not until 1933, in *Funk v. United States*, 290 U.S. 371, that this Court abolished the testimonial disqualification in the federal courts, so as to permit the spouse of a defendant to testify in the defendant's behalf. Funk, however, left undisturbed the rule that either spouse could prevent the other from giving adverse testimony. Id., at 373. The rule thus evolved into one of privilege rather than one of absolute disqualification. See J. Maguire, Evidence, Common Sense and Common Law 78–92 (1947).

The modern justification for this privilege against adverse spousal testimony is its perceived role in fostering the harmony and sanctity of the marriage relationship.

Notwithstanding this benign purpose, the rule was sharply criticized. Professor Wigmore termed it "the merest anachronism in legal theory and an indefensible obstruction to truth in practice." 8 Wigmore § 2228, at 221. The Committee on Improvements in the Law of Evidence of the American Bar Association called for its abolition. 63 American Bar Association Reports 594-595 (1938). In its place, Wigmore and others suggested a privilege protecting only private marital communications, ounsell on the privilege between priest and penitent, attorney and client, and physician and patient. See 8 Wigmore § 2332 et seq.

These criticisms influenced the American Law Institute, which, in its 1942 Model Code of Evidence, advocated a privilege for marital confidences, but expressly rejected a rule vesting in the defendant the right to exclude all adverse testimony of his spouse. See American Law Institute, Model Code of Evidence, Rule 215 (1942). In 1953 the Uniform Rules of Evidence, drafted by the National Conference of Commissioners on Uniform State Laws, followed a similar course; it limited the privilege to confidential communications and "[abolished] the rule, still existing in some states, and largely a sentimental relic, of not requiring one spouse to testify against the other in a criminal action." See Rule 23 (2) and comments. Several state legislatures enacted similarly patterned provisions into law.

In *Hawkins v. United States*, 358 U.S. 74 (1958), this Court considered the continued vitality of the privilege against adverse spousal testimony in the federal courts. There the District Court had permitted petitioner's wife, over his objection, to testify against him. With one questioning concurring opinion, the Court held the wife's testimony inadmissible; it took note of the critical comments that the common-law rule had engendered, but chose not to abandon it. Also rejected was the Government's suggestion that the Court modify the privilege by vesting it in the witness-spouse, with freedom to testify or not independent of the defendant's control. The Court viewed this proposed modification as antithetical to the widespread belief, evidenced in the rules then in effect in a majority of the

States and in England, "that the law should not force or encourage testimony which might alienate husband and wife, or further inflame existing domestic differences." Id., at 79.

Hawkins, then, left the federal privilege for adverse spousal testimony where it found it, continuing "a rule which bars the testimony of one spouse against the other unless both consent." Id., at 78. Accord, *Wyatt v. United States*, 362 U.S. 525, 528 (1960). However, in so doing, the Court made clear that its decision was not meant to "foreclose whatever changes in the rule may eventually be dictated by 'reason and experience.'" 358 U.S., at 79.

III.

A.

The Federal Rules of Evidence acknowledge the authority of the federal courts to continue the evolutionary development of testimonial privileges in federal criminal trials "governed by the principles of the common law as they may be interpreted . . . in the light of reason and experience." Fed. Rule Evid. 501.

* * *

Although Rule 501 confirms the authority of the federal courts to reconsider the continued validity of the *Hawkins* rule, the long history of the privilege suggests that it ought not to be casually cast aside. That the privilege is one affecting marriage, home, and family relationships—already subject to much erosion in our day—also counsels caution. At the same time, we cannot escape the reality that the law on occasion adheres to doctrinal concepts long after the reasons which gave them birth have disappeared and after experience suggests the need for change. This was recognized in *Funk* where the Court "[declined] to enforce . . . ancient [rules] of the common law under conditions as they now exist." 290 U.S., at 382. For, as Mr. Justice Black admonished in another setting, "[when] precedent and precedent alone is all the argument that can be made to support a court-fashioned rule, it is time for the rule's creator to destroy it." *Francis v. Southern Pacific Co.*, 333 U.S. 445, 471 (1948) (dissenting opinion).

B.

Since 1958, when *Hawkins* was decided, support for the privilege against adverse spousal testimony has been eroded further. Thirty-one jurisdictions, including Alaska and Hawaii, then allowed an accused a privilege to prevent adverse spousal testimony. 358 U.S., at 81, n. 3 (STEWART, J., concurring). The number has now declined to 24.[1] In 1974, the National Conference on Uniform State Laws revised its Uniform Rules of Evidence, but again rejected the *Hawkins* rule in favor of a limited privilege for confidential communications. See Uniform Rules of Evidence, Rule 504. That proposed rule has been enacted in Arkansas, North Dakota, and Oklahoma—each of which in 1958 permitted an accused to exclude adverse spousal testimony.[2] The trend in state law toward divesting the accused of the privilege to bar adverse spousal testimony has special relevance because the laws of marriage and domestic relations are concerns traditionally reserved to the states. See *Sosna v. Iowa*, 419 U.S. 393, 404 (1975). Scholarly criticism of the *Hawkins* rule has also continued unabated.

Support for the common-law rule has also diminished in England. In 1972, a study group there proposed giving the privilege to the witness-spouse, on the ground that "if [the wife] is willing to give evidence . . . the law would be showing excessive concern for the preservation of marital harmony if it were to say that she must not do so." Criminal Law Revision Committee, Eleventh Report, Evidence (General) 93.

C.

Testimonial exclusionary rules and privileges contravene the fundamental principle that "the public . . . has a right to every man's evidence." *United States v. Bryan*, 339 U.S. 323, 331 (1950). As such, they must be strictly construed and accepted "only to the very limited extent that permitting a refusal to testify or excluding relevant evidence has a public good transcending the normally predominant principle of utilizing all rational means for ascertaining truth." *Elkins v. United States*, 364 U.S. 206, 234 (1960) (Frankfurter, J.,

dissenting). Accord, *United States v. Nixon*, 418 U.S. 683, 709-710 (1974). Here we must decide whether the privilege against adverse spousal testimony promotes sufficiently important interests to outweigh the need for probative evidence in the administration of criminal justice.

It is essential to remember that the *Hawkins* privilege is not needed to protect information privately disclosed between husband and wife in the confidence of the marital relationship—once described by this Court as "the best solace of human existence." *Stein v. Bowman*, 13 Pet., at 223. Those confidences are privileged under the independent rule protecting confidential marital communications. *Blau v. United States*, 340 U.S. 332 (1951); see n. 5, *supra*. The *Hawkins* privilege is invoked, not to exclude private marital communications, but rather to exclude evidence of criminal acts and of communications made in the presence of third persons.

No other testimonial privilege sweeps so broadly. The privileges between priest and penitent, attorney and client, and physician and patient limit protection to private communications. These privileges are rooted in the imperative need for confidence and trust. The priest-penitent privilege recognizes the human need to disclose to a spiritual counsellor, in total and absolute confidence, what are believed to be flawed acts or thoughts and to receive priestly consolation and guidance in return. The lawyer-client privilege rests on the need for the advocate and counsellor to know all that relates to the client's reasons for seeking representation if the professional mission is to be carried out. Similarly, the physician must know all that a patient can articulate in order to identify and to treat disease; barriers to full disclosure would impair diagnosis and treatment.

The *Hawkins* rule stands in marked contrast to these three privileges. Its protection is not limited to confidential communications; rather it permits an accused to exclude all adverse spousal testimony. As Jeremy Bentham observed more than a century and a half ago, such a privilege goes far beyond making "every man's house his castle," and permits a person to convert his house into "a den of thieves." 5 Rationale of Judicial Evidence 340

(1827). It "secures, to every man, one safe and unquestionable and ever ready accomplice for every imaginable crime." Id., at 338.

The ancient foundations for so sweeping a privilege have long since disappeared. Nowhere in the common-law world—indeed in any modern society—is a woman regarded as chattel or demeaned by denial of a separate legal identity and the dignity associated with recognition as a whole human being. Chip by chip, over the years those archaic notions have been cast aside so that "[no] longer is the female destined solely for the home and the rearing of the family, and only the male for the marketplace and the world of ideas." *Stanton v. Stanton*, 421 U.S. 7, 14-15 (1975).

The contemporary justification for affording an accused such a privilege is also unpersuasive. When one spouse is willing to testify against the other in a criminal proceeding—whatever the motivation—their relationship is almost certainly in disrepair; there is probably little in the way of marital harmony for the privilege to preserve. In these circumstances, a rule of evidence that permits an accused to prevent adverse spousal testimony seems far more likely to frustrate justice than to foster family peace. Indeed, there is reason to believe that vesting the privilege in the accused could actually undermine the marital relationship. For example, in a case such as this, the Government is unlikely to offer a wife immunity and lenient treatment if it knows that her husband can prevent her from giving adverse testimony. If the Government is dissuaded from making such an offer, the privilege can have the untoward effect of permitting one spouse to escape justice at the expense of the other. It hardly seems conducive to the preservation of the marital relation to place a wife in jeopardy solely by virtue of her husband's control over her testimony.

IV.

Our consideration of the foundations for the privilege and its history satisfy us that "reason and experience" no longer justify so sweeping a rule as that found acceptable by the Court in Hawkins. Accordingly, we conclude that the existing rule should be modified so that the witness-spouse alone has a privilege to refuse to testify adversely; the witness may be neither compelled to testify nor foreclosed from testifying. This modification—vesting the privilege in the witness-spouse—furthers the important public interest in marital harmony without unduly burdening legitimate law enforcement needs.

Here, petitioner's spouse chose to testify against him. That she did so after a grant of immunity and assurances of lenient treatment does not render her testimony involuntary. *Cf. Bordenkircher v. Hayes*, 434 U.S. 357 (1978). Accordingly, the District Court and the Court of Appeals were correct in rejecting petitioner's claim of privilege, and the judgment of the Court of Appeals is

Affirmed.

STATE
v.
ANTHONY

Supreme Court of Arizona
218 Ariz. 439
2008 Ariz.. LEXIS 123 (2008)

En Banc

HURWITZ, Justice

On July 7, 2001, Donna Jean Anthony and her two children failed to arrive in Ohio as planned for a family visit. David Lamar Anthony, Donna's husband, was later charged with murdering the three. Anthony was convicted of three counts of first-degree murder after a jury trial in Maricopa County Superior Court; three death sentences were imposed.

This is an automatic appeal pursuant to Arizona Rule of Criminal Procedure 31.2(b) from the convictions and sentences. We have jurisdiction under Article 6, Section 5(3) of the Arizona Constitution and A.R.S. 13-4031 (2001).

I.

At the time of trial, the bodies of the victims had not been recovered. Anthony did not admit to the crimes and there were no witnesses to the murders. The State's case was therefore built on circumstantial evidence. We begin by summarizing that evidence.

A.

Anthony and Donna were married in 1997. Donna had two minor children from a previous marriage — Danielle Romero, born in 1987, and Richard Romero, born in 1988 — both of whom lived with the Anthonys. The Anthony marriage was troubled almost from the outset. Donna and Anthony frequently argued and the evidence suggests that Anthony was unfaithful. Donna apparently did not trust Anthony in financial matters. In late 2000, the family home was refinanced. Donna instructed the mortgage officer not to release the loan proceeds, approximately $ 105,000, to Anthony. She deposited the check into her personal savings account at Bank One, which Anthony could not access.

B.

[On June 25, 2001, Donna purchased plane tickets for herself and her children to visit her family in Columbus, Ohio. Three days later somebody changed the PIN on her bank card and later moved the mortgage money from her account to the defendant's account. On July 6, 2001, her credit card was used at a gasoline station at a time when she would have been finishing up her second shift. Donna and the children were never seen again and they never boarded the scheduled flight to Columbus, Ohio on 7 July. Defendant contracted to purchase a new truck in late June, but delayed taking delivery until July. He contracted for a carpet cleaning service to clean the home on July 9.]

C.

Anthony was questioned several times by MCSO officers in connection with the family's disappearance. He told detectives that Donna and the children had left for the airport between 5:00 and 5:30 a.m. on July 7. He said Donna customarily carried large amounts of cash and sometimes wore expensive jewelry; he suggested that she may have put herself in danger by driving through the wrong neighborhood. He also speculated that

Donna may have driven to the airport, but then decided to drive to Las Vegas. Anthony claimed that "they" had transferred the funds from Donna's account into the joint account; $40,000 was to be used for the new truck and the balance to settle a pending lawsuit with neighbors. He denied any marital problems.

* * *

In the master bedroom, small drops of blood (totaling about the volume of one sugar cube) were found on the wall behind the bed. DNA testing identified some of the blood as Donna's. The DNA of a second person was also found; Anthony could not be excluded as the possible contributor. Carpeting to the right of the bed also tested positive for blood.

In the home office, three spots on the carpeting several inches in diameter tested positive for blood. The concrete slab underneath the carpet had a visible stain that tested positive for blood. The blood on the concrete slab was Danielle's.

In Richard's [the son's] room, the side of the mattress, the side of the box springs, a body pillow, and a wall tested positive for blood. The blood on the mattress and on the body pillow was Richard's. Blood from an unidentified person was also found on the side of the mattress; Donna and Danielle could not be excluded as contributors. In the hallway outside the children's rooms, four spots on the wall tested positive for blood. One of the stains contained Richard's DNA, as well as DNA that was consistent with either Donna or Danielle.

A hamper in the children's bathroom tested positive for blood. Blood was found on the coat closet door, on the threshold of the door leading from the kitchen to the backyard, on the exterior wall just outside the door between the kitchen and the backyard, on the back patio, and on a wooden picnic bench on the patio. Several spots in the garage tested positive for blood.

The State's expert testified that the volume of blood discovered in the house was too small to prove either that the victims had died or the cause of any death.

* * *

Anthony was indicted for the first-degree murders of Donna, Danielle, and Richard on August 10, 2001; the State subsequently filed a notice of intent to seek the death penalty. The jury found Anthony guilty on all three counts on April 1, 2002. Penalty proceedings began before a new jury on February 18, 2004. 4 On March 2, 2004, that jury found three aggravating circumstances: A.R.S. 13-703(F)(5) (pecuniary gain), -(F)(8) (multiple homicides), and -(F)(9) (victim under the age of fifteen). On March 10, after the penalty phase, the jury returned death verdicts for each murder.

* * *

[DNA examination taken from blood samples from the teenage daughter's bedroom indicated positive for three contributors. It also tested positive for aspermatic semen, the type left by a person with a vastectomy, which the defendant had undergone. Because of this evidence, the state contended that the defendant had molested the teenaged stepdaughter, Danielle, in a sexual manner and that was the reason and the motive for the murders. Following the pretrial hearing, the trial court agreed to admit the blood and DNA evidence as circumstantial evidence that something sexual happened in the bedroom. The prosecution introduced evidence that condoms were found in the septic tank and that the teenaged honor did not like her stepfather. Additional evidence was introduced that indicated the defendant had placed his hands on the teenaged daughter's chest as well as are crotch at different times. During closing arguments, the prosecutor argued the molestation theory and that the defendant had murdered her and the others to cover up hid sexual crimes].

Anthony argues that the superior court erred in allowing the State to argue that he molested Danielle. A defendant's prior bad acts are not admissible "to show action in conformity therewith," but can be used to prove "motive, opportunity, intent, preparation, plan, knowledge, identity, or absence of mistake or accident." Ariz. R. Evid. 404(b). Although the jury must ultimately determine whether the other act is proved,

"before admitting evidence of prior bad acts, trial judges must find that there is clear and convincing proof both as to the commission of the other bad act and that the defendant committed the act." *State v. Terrazas*, 189 Ariz. 580, 582, 944 P.2d 1194, 1196 (1997). Even if the trial judge concludes that the prior act is shown by clear and convincing evidence, the judge must also (1) find that the act is offered for a proper purpose under Rule 404(b); (2) find that the prior act is relevant to prove that purpose; (3) find that any probative value is not substantially outweighed by unfair prejudice; and (4) give upon request an appropriate limiting instruction. Id. at 583, 944 P.2d at 1197.

D.

The trial court concluded that there was "circumstantial evidence that something sexual happened" and that there was a possible "inference to be drawn" of "untoward" activity. The appropriate question under Terrazas [a prior case], however, is whether there was clear and convincing evidence that Anthony molested Danielle. The trial court erred by applying the wrong legal standard to its evaluation of the prior bad acts evidence. *State v. Vigil*, 195 Ariz. 189, 192, P 16, 986 P.2d 222, 225 (App. 1999).

Analyzing the DNA evidence under the Terrazas clear and convincing evidence standard, we conclude that the allegation that Anthony molested Danielle should have been excluded. Three DNA profiles were in the tested portion of the mattress: Danielle's and possibly those of Anthony and Donna. The State's expert could not opine that the blood found was in fact Danielle's, only that she was the primary DNA contributor. The expert also could not opine that Anthony in fact contributed any DNA to the sample; he testified instead only that Anthony could not be excluded. Nor could the expert conclude that the semen was Anthony's, only that it was aspermatic.

It is reasonable to assume that the aspermatic semen was Anthony's. It is also reasonable to assume that the blood was Danielle's. But even making these assumptions, the forensic evidence at most established that, at some point or points in time, Anthony's semen, Danielle's blood, and the DNA of a third person, perhaps Donna, were left on the mattress. There was no evidence as to when the three individuals left the DNA, let alone whether any two of them left DNA at the same time.

This evidence fell far short of proving either that Danielle was molested or that Anthony had done so. It is clear that Anthony and Danielle were not the only prior users of the mattress; the tested sample also contained DNA of a third contributor, perhaps Donna [the deceased wife]. It is difficult to understand how all three DNA contributions could have been made simultaneously; at least two of three DNA contributors were almost surely on the mattress at different times. This evidence, even taking all inferences in the light most favorable to the State, simply does not establish that Danielle and Anthony were simultaneous occupants of the bed, much less that he molested her.

[The reviewing court noted that the trial court considered only the mattress stain evidence in allowing the allegation of sexual molestation of the teenaged daughter into evidence. The court also noted that it could not conclude that there was sufficient evidence for jury to believe by clear convincing evidence that the defendant had ever molested the stepdaughter and the testimony that some people saw a defendant allegedly touching the teenaged daughter at a basketball game was not very probative of a sexual relationship with the stepdaughter. In this particular case, it might appear that any probative effect that the blood evidence might have toward proving a sexual molestation of the stepdaughter would clearly be outweighed the nature of unfair prejudice to the defendant's case. The defendant was suffered undue prejudice when the jury considered unreliable evidence in coming to a conclusion in this case. In applying the harmless error test the court was *unable* to conclude beyond reasonable doubt that the improperly admitted evidence, dealing with child sexual molestation, did not affect the verdict and therefore the court reversed the conviction and remanded for a new trial.]

Cases Relating to Chapter 3

Burden of Proof

IN RE WINSHIP

Supreme Court of the United States
397 U.S. 358, 90 S. Ct. 1068,
25 L. Ed. 2d 368 (1970)

MR. JUSTICE BRENNAN delivered the opinion of the Court.

Constitutional questions decided by this Court concerning the juvenile process have centered on the adjudicatory stage at "which a determination is made as to whether a juvenile is a 'delinquent' as a result of alleged misconduct on his part, with the consequence that he may be committed to a state institution." *In re Gault*, 387 U.S. 1, 13 (1967). *Gault* decided that, although the Fourteenth Amendment does not require that the hearing at this stage conform with all the requirements of a criminal trial or even of the usual administrative proceeding, the Due Process Clause does require application during the adjudicatory hearing of "'the essentials of due process and fair treatment.'" Id., at 30. This case presents the single, narrow question whether proof beyond a reasonable doubt is among the "essentials of due process and fair treatment" required during the adjudicatory stage when a juvenile is charged with an act which would constitute a crime if committed by an adult.

Section 712 of the New York Family Court Act defines a juvenile delinquent as "a person over seven and less than sixteen years of age who does any act which, if done by an adult, would constitute a crime." During a 1967 adjudicatory hearing, conducted pursuant to

§ 742 of the Act, a judge in New York Family Court found that appellant, then a 12-year-old boy, had entered a locker and stolen $112 from a woman's pocketbook. The petition which charged appellant with delinquency alleged that his act, "if done by an adult, would constitute the crime or crimes of Larceny." The judge acknowledged that the proof might not establish guilt beyond a reasonable doubt, but rejected appellant's contention that such proof was required by the Fourteenth Amendment. The judge relied instead on § 744 (b) of the New York Family Court Act which provides that "any determination at the conclusion of [an adjudicatory] hearing that a [juvenile] did an act or acts must be based on a preponderance of the evidence." During a subsequent dispositional hearing, appellant was ordered placed in a training school for an initial period of 18 months, subject to annual extensions of his commitment until his 18th birthday— six years in appellant's case. The Appellate Division of the New York Supreme Court, First Judicial Department, affirmed without opinion. The New York Court of Appeals then affirmed by a four-to-three vote, expressly sustaining the constitutionality of § 744 (b). We noted probable jurisdiction. We reverse.

I.

The requirement that guilt of a criminal charge be established by proof beyond a reasonable doubt dates at least from our early years as a Nation. The "demand for a higher degree of persuasion in criminal cases was recurrently expressed from ancient times, [though] its crystallization into the formula 'beyond a reasonable doubt' seems to have occurred as late as 1798. It is now accepted in common law jurisdictions as the measure of persuasion by which the prosecution must convince the trier of all the essential elements of guilt." C. McCORMICK, EVIDENCE § 321, pp. 681–682 (1954); see also 9 J. WIGMORE, EVIDENCE § 2497 (3d ed. 1940). Although virtually unanimous adherence to the reasonable-doubt standard in common-law jurisdictions may not conclusively establish it as a requirement of due process, such adherence does "reflect a profound judgment about the way in which law should be enforced and justice administered." *Duncan v. Louisiana*, 391 U.S. 145, 155 (1968).

Expressions in many opinions of this Court indicate that it has long been assumed that proof of a criminal charge beyond a reasonable doubt is constitutionally required. [Citations omitted.] Mr. Justice Frankfurter stated that "it is the duty of the Government to establish . . . guilt beyond a reasonable doubt. This notion—basic in our law and rightly one of the boasts of a free society—is a requirement and a safeguard of due process of law in the historic, procedural content of 'due process.'" *Leland v. Oregon, supra*, at 802–803 (dissenting opinion). In a similar vein, the Court said in *Brinegar v. United States, supra*, at 174, that "guilt in a criminal case must be proved beyond a reasonable doubt and by evidence confined to that which long experience in the common-law tradition, to some extent embodied in the Constitution, has crystallized into rules of evidence consistent with that standard. These rules are historically grounded rights of our system, developed to safeguard men from dubious and unjust convictions, with resulting forfeitures of life, liberty and property." *Davis v. United States, supra*, at 488, stated that the requirement is implicit in "constitutions . . . [which] recognize the fundamental principles that are deemed essential for the protection of life and liberty." In Davis a murder conviction was reversed because the trial judge instructed the jury that it was their duty to convict when the evidence was equally balanced regarding the sanity of the accused. This Court said: "On the contrary, he is entitled to an acquittal of the specific

crime charged if upon all the evidence there is reasonable doubt whether he was capable in law of committing crime. . . . No man should be deprived of his life under the forms of law unless the jurors who try him are able, upon their consciences, to say that the evidence before them . . . is sufficient to show beyond a reasonable doubt the existence of every fact necessary to constitute the crime charged." Id., at 484, 493.

The reasonable-doubt standard plays a vital role in the American scheme of criminal procedure. It is a prime instrument for reducing the risk of convictions resting on factual error. The standard provides concrete substance for the presumption of innocence—that bedrock "axiomatic and elementary" principle whose "enforcement lies at the foundation of the administration of our criminal law." *Coffin v. United States, supra*, at 453. As the dissenters in the New York Court of Appeals observed, and we agree, "a person accused of a crime . . . would be at a severe disadvantage, a disadvantage amounting to a lack of fundamental fairness, if he could be adjudged guilty and imprisoned for years on the strength of the same evidence as would suffice in a civil case." 24 N.Y.2d, at 205, 247 N.E.2d, at 259.

The requirement of proof beyond a reasonable doubt has this vital role in our criminal procedure for cogent reasons. The accused during a criminal prosecution has at stake interests of immense importance, both because of the possibility that he may lose his liberty upon conviction and because of the certainty that he would be stigmatized by the conviction. Accordingly, a society that values the good name and freedom of every individual should not condemn a man for commission of a crime when there is reasonable doubt about his guilt. As we said in *Speiser v. Randall, supra*, at 525–526: "There is always in litigation a margin of error, representing error in factfinding, which both parties must take into account. Where one party has at stake an interest of transcending value—as a criminal defendant his liberty—this margin of error is reduced as to him by the process of placing on the other party the burden of . . . persuading the factfinder at the conclusion of the trial of his guilt beyond a reasonable doubt. Due process commands that no man shall lose his liberty unless the Government has borne the burden of . . . convincing the factfinder of his guilt." To this end, the reasonable-doubt standard is indispensable, for it "impresses on the trier of fact the necessity of reaching a subjective state of certitude of the facts in issue." Dorsen & Rezneck, *In Re Gault and the Future of Juvenile Law*, 1 FAMILY LAW QUARTERLY, No. 4, pp. 1, 26 (1967).

Moreover, use of the reasonable-doubt standard is indispensable to command the respect and confidence of the community in applications of the criminal law. It is critical that the moral force of the criminal law not be diluted by a standard of proof that leaves people in doubt whether innocent men are being condemned. It is also important in our free society that every individual going about his ordinary affairs have confidence that his government cannot adjudge him guilty of a criminal offense without convincing a proper factfinder of his guilt with utmost certainty.

Lest there remain any doubt about the constitutional stature of the reasonable-doubt standard, we explicitly hold that the Due Process Clause protects the accused against conviction except upon proof beyond a reasonable doubt of every fact necessary to constitute the crime with which he is charged.

II.

We turn to the question whether juveniles, like adults, are constitutionally entitled to proof beyond a reasonable doubt when they are charged with violation of a criminal law. The same considerations that demand extreme caution in factfinding to protect the innocent adult apply as well to the innocent child. We do not find convincing the contrary arguments of the New York Court of Appeals. *Gault* rendered untenable much of the reasoning relied upon by that court to sustain the constitutionality of § 744 (b). The Court of Appeals indicated that a delinquency adjudication "is not a 'conviction' (§ 781); that it affects no right or privilege, including the right to hold public office or to obtain a license (§ 782); and a cloak of protective confidentiality is thrown around all the proceedings (§§ 783–784)." 24 N.Y.2d, at 200, 247 N.E.2d, at 255–256. The court said further: "The delinquency status is not made

a crime; and the proceedings are not criminal. There is, hence, no deprivation of due process in the statutory provision [challenged by appellant] . . . ." 24 N.Y.2d, at 203, 247 N.E.2d, at 257. In effect the Court of Appeals distinguished the proceedings in question here from a criminal prosecution by use of what *Gault* called the " 'civil' label-of-convenience which has been attached to juvenile proceedings." 387 U.S., at 50. But *Gault* expressly rejected that distinction as a reason for holding the Due Process Clause inapplicable to a juvenile proceeding. 387 U.S., at 50–51. The Court of Appeals also attempted to justify the preponderance standard on the related ground that juvenile proceedings are designed "not to punish, but to save the child." 24 N.Y.2d, at 197, 247 N.E.2d, at 254. Again, however, *Gault* expressly rejected this justification. 387 U.S., at 27. We made clear in that decision that civil labels and good intentions do not themselves obviate the need for criminal due process safeguards in juvenile courts, for "[a] proceeding where the issue is whether the child will be found to be 'delinquent' and subjected to the loss of his liberty for years is comparable in seriousness to a felony prosecution." Id., at 36.

Nor do we perceive any merit in the argument that to afford juveniles the protection of proof beyond a reasonable doubt would risk destruction of beneficial aspects of the juvenile process. Use of the reasonable-doubt standard during the adjudicatory hearing will not disturb New York's policies that a finding that a child has violated a criminal law does not constitute a criminal conviction, that such a finding does not deprive the child of his civil rights, and that juvenile proceedings are confidential. Nor will there be any effect on the informality, flexibility, or speed of the hearing at which the factfinding takes place. And the opportunity during the post-adjudicatory or dispositional hearing for a wide-ranging review of the child's social history and for his individualized treatment will remain unimpaired. Similarly, there will be no effect on the procedures distinctive to juvenile proceedings that are employed prior to the adjudicatory hearing.

The Court of Appeals observed that "a child's best interest is not necessarily, or even probably, promoted if he wins in the particular inquiry which may bring him to the juvenile court." 24 N.Y.2d, at 199, 247 N.E.2d, at 255. It is true, of course, that the juvenile may be engaging in a general course of conduct inimical to his welfare that calls for judicial intervention. But that intervention cannot take the form of subjecting the child to the stigma of a finding that he violated a criminal law and to the possibility of institutional confinement on proof insufficient to convict him were he an adult.

We conclude, as we concluded regarding the essential due process safeguards applied in *Gault*, that the observance of the standard of proof beyond a reasonable doubt "will not compel the States to abandon or displace any of the substantive benefits of the juvenile process." *Gault, supra*, at 21.

* * *

III.

In sum, the constitutional safeguard of proof beyond a reasonable doubt is as much required during the adjudicatory stage of a delinquency proceeding as are those constitutional safeguards applied in Gault—notice of charges, right to counsel, the rights of confrontation and examination, and the privilege against self-incrimination. We therefore hold, in agreement with Chief Judge Fuld in dissent in the Court of Appeals, "that, where a 12-year-old child is charged with an act of stealing which renders him liable to confinement for as long as six years, then, as a matter of due process . . . the case against him must be proved beyond a reasonable doubt." 24 N.Y.2d, at 207, 247 N.E.2d, at 260.

Reversed.

VICTOR
v.
NEBRASKA

Supreme Court of the United States
511 U.S. 1, 114 S. Ct. 1239,
127 L. Ed. 2d 583 (1994)

SYLLABUS:

The government must prove beyond a reasonable doubt every element of a charged offense. In re Winship, 397 U.S. 358. In upholding the first degree murder convictions and death sentences of petitioners Sandoval and Victor, the Supreme Courts of California and Nebraska, respectively, rejected contentions that due process was violated by the pattern jury instructions defining "reasonable doubt" that were given in both cases.

Held: Taken as a whole, the instructions in question correctly conveyed the concept of reasonable doubt, and there is no reasonable likelihood that the jurors understood the instructions to allow convictions based on proof insufficient to meet the Winship standard. Pp. 1–20.

(a) The Constitution does not dictate that any particular form of words be used in advising the jury of the government's burden of proof, so long as "taken as a whole, the instructions correctly convey the concept of reasonable doubt," *Holland v. United States*, 348 U.S. 121, 140. In invalidating a charge declaring, among other things, that a reasonable doubt "must be such . . . as would give rise to a grave uncertainty," "is an actual substantial doubt," and requires "a moral certainty," the Court, in *Cage v. Louisiana*, 498 U.S. 39, 40, observed that a reasonable juror could have interpreted the instruction to allow a finding of guilt based on a degree of proof below that which is constitutionally required. However, in *Estelle v. McGuire*, 502 U.S. __, __, and n. 4, the Court made clear that the proper inquiry is not whether the instruction "could have" been applied unconstitutionally, but whether there is a reasonable likelihood that the jury did so apply it. Pp. 1–3.

(b) The instructions given in Sandoval's case defined reasonable doubt as, among other things, "not a mere possible doubt," but one "depending on moral evidence," such that the jurors could not say they felt an abiding conviction, "to a moral certainty,"of the truth of the charge. Pp. 3–6.

(c) Sandoval's objection to the charge's use of the 19th century phrases "moral evidence" and "moral certainty" is rejected. Although the former phrase is not a mainstay of the modern lexicon, its meaning today is consistent with its original meaning: evidence based on the general observation of people, rather than on what is demonstrable. Its use here is unproblematic because the instructions given correctly pointed the jurors' attention to the facts of the case before them, not (as Sandoval contends) the ethics or morality of his criminal acts. For example, in the instruction declaring that "everything relating to human affairs, and depending on moral evidence, is open to some possible or imaginary doubt," moral evidence can only mean empirical evidence offered to prove matters relating to human affairs—the proof introduced at trial. Similarly, whereas "moral certainty," standing alone, might not be recognized by modern jurors as a synonym for "proof beyond a reasonable doubt," its use in conjunction with the abiding conviction language must be viewed as having impressed upon the jury the need to reach the subjective state of near certitude of guilt, see *Jackson v. Virginia*, 443 U.S. 307, 315, and thus as not having invited conviction on less than the constitutionally required proof. Moreover, in contrast to the situation in Cage, there is no reasonable likelihood that the jury here would have understood moral certainty to be disassociated from the evidence in the case, since the instruction explicitly told the jurors, among other things, that their conclusion had to be based upon such evidence. Accordingly, although this Court does not condone the use of the antiquated "moral certainty" phrase, its use in the context of the instructions as a whole cannot be said to have rendered those instructions unconstitutional. Pp. 6–14.

(d) Sandoval's objection to the portion of the charge declaring that a reasonable doubt is "not a mere possible doubt" is also rejected. That the instruction properly uses "possible" in the sense of fanciful is made clear by the fact that it also notes that everything "is open to some possible or imaginary doubt." P. 14.

(e) The instructions given in Victor's case defined reasonable doubt as, among other things, a doubt that will not permit an abiding conviction, "to a moral certainty," of the accused's guilt, and an "actual and substantial doubt" that is not excluded by the "strong probabilities of the case." Pp. 14–16.

(f) Victor's primary argument—that equating a reasonable doubt with a "substantial doubt" overstated the degree of doubt necessary for acquittal—is rejected. Any ambiguity is removed by reading the phrase in question in context: The *Victor* charge immediately distinguished an "actual and substantial doubt" from one "arising from mere possibility, from bare imagination, or from fanciful conjecture," and thereby informed the jury that a reasonable doubt is something more than a speculative one, which is an unexceptionable proposition. *Cage, supra*, at 41, distinguished. Moreover, the instruction defined a reasonable doubt alternatively as a doubt that would cause a reasonable person to hesitate to act, a formulation which this Court has repeatedly approved and which gives a common-sense benchmark for just how substantial a reasonable doubt must be. Pp. 16–18.

(g) The inclusion of the "moral certainty" phrase in the Victor charge did not render the instruction unconstitutional. In contrast to the situation in Cage, a sufficient context to lend meaning to the phrase was provided by the rest of the *Victor* charge, which equated a doubt sufficient to preclude moral certainty with a doubt that would cause a reasonable person to hesitate to act, and told the jurors that they must have an abiding conviction of Victor's guilt, must be convinced of such guilt "after full, fair, and impartial consideration of all the evidence," should be governed solely by that evidence in determining factual issues, and should not indulge in speculation, conjectures, or unsupported inferences. Pp. 18–19.

(h) The reference to "strong probabilities" in the *Victor* charge does not unconstitutionally understate the government's burden, since the charge also informs the jury that the probabilities must be strong enough to prove guilt beyond a reasonable doubt. *See Dunbar v. United States*, 156 U.S. 185, 199. P. 19.

No. 92-8894, 242 Neb. 306, 494 N.W.2d 565, and No. 92-9049, 4 Cal. 4th 155, modified, 4 Cal. 4th 928a, 841 P.2d 862, affirmed.

STATE
v.
EICHELBERGER

Court of Appeals of Washington, Division One
2005 Wash. App. LEXIS 2429 (2005)

APPELWICK, J.—Donald Eichelberger was convicted of two counts of trafficking in stolen property in the second degree after he found a suitcase full of compact discs. One count was charged for selling 35 of the CDs the day he found them, and the other count for attempting to sell additional CDs two days later. Eichelberger argues that his conviction for two counts violated his protection against double jeopardy because he committed only one unit of crime, that the State failed to meet its burden of proof beyond a reasonable doubt, and that the trial court erred in determining his offender score because it included a point based on a fact that should have been presented to the jury and found beyond a reasonable doubt. Finding no error, we affirm.

FACTS

Donald Eichelberger was walking through the University District of Seattle in the late afternoon of May 20, 2003. He spotted a black suitcase lying on the ground, in an alley close to a dumpster. There were no people or vehicles around. Eichelberger opened the suitcase and saw that it contained many CDs. He did not inspect the CDs, and from the way they were arranged in the suitcase he could see only the spines of the CDs. Having been a University of Washington student himself, Eichelberger knew that students often move out of their residences and leave behind items that they no longer consider valuable, but that others might. He thought that the former owner of the suitcase had abandoned it and that he was thus entitled to take it. Eichelberger did not notice any identifying information on the CDs or the suitcase, did not attempt to ascertain who owned the CDs, and did not notify the police. Instead, Eichelberger took the bus to CD Trader, a used CD store in Queen Anne where he had previously sold CDs. He sold 35 of the CDs that day for $92. The record contains conflicting evidence about whether Eichelberger left because he was short on time and decided to return later to sell the remaining CDs, or whether he left because the clerk asked him to return later in the week to sell the remaining CDs.

It turns out that many of the CDs had been stolen from Stuart Sanderson during a burglary on May 20. Sanderson had affixed a sticker on many of his CDs that included his name and driver's license number. Sanderson

filed a police report after the theft. The police investigation turned up no fingerprints at his home. On May 21, Sanderson called several used CD stores to see if his CDs had turned up. The manager at CD Trader informed Sanderson that several CDs with his sticker on them had been sold to the store the previous day. Sanderson went to the store and identified all 35 of the CDs Eichelberger had sold to CD Trader as his CDs. The manager took the CDs out of inventory and eventually turned them over to the police. Eichelberger returned to CD Trader on May 22 to sell more of the CDs. The manager recognized Eichelberger's name and came up with a ruse to keep Eichelberger in the store while he called the police. The police arrived and arrested Eichelberger. He was charged with two counts of trafficking in stolen property in the second degree. The State had no evidence to link Eichelberger to the burglary of Sanderson's home, and the court specifically instructed the jury not to make any such inference from the evidence or allow it to influence their verdict. The jury convicted Eichelberger on both counts. . . .

ANALYSIS

I. Eichelberger's Two Convictions Did Not Violate His Protection Against Double Jeopardy.

* * *

We hold that the State was entitled to charge Eichelberger with two counts of trafficking in stolen property in the second degree, and that there was no double jeopardy violation.

II. Eichelberger's Convictions Were Supported By Sufficient Evidence

The test for sufficiency is whether, viewing the evidence in a light most favorable to the State, any rational trier of fact could have found each essential element of the charge beyond a reasonable doubt. State v. Salinas, 119 Wn.2d 192, 201, 829 P.2d 1068 (1992). "A claim of insufficiency admits the truth of the State's evidence and all inferences that reasonably can be drawn therefrom." A reviewing court neither weighs the evidence nor needs to be convinced that it established guilt beyond a reasonable doubt. A trier of fact may properly render a guilty verdict based on circumstantial evidence alone, even if the evidence is also consistent with the hypothesis of innocence. A conviction will not be overturned unless there is no substantial evidence to support it. [Some citations omitted].

To find Eichelberger guilty of trafficking in stolen property in the second degree, the jury had to be satisfied beyond a reasonable doubt that he recklessly trafficked in stolen property. A person "acts recklessly when he knows of and disregards a substantial risk that a wrongful act may occur and his disregard of such substantial risk is a gross deviation from conduct that a reasonable man would exercise in the same situation." RCW 9A.08.010(1)(c). Reckless conduct therefore includes both a subjective and an objective component. State v. R.H.S., 94 Wn. App. 844, 847, 974 P.2d 1253 (1999). A trier of fact is permitted to find actual subjective knowledge if there is sufficient information that would lead a reasonable person to believe that a fact exists. RCW 9A.08.010(1)(b)(ii); R.H.S., 94 Wn App. at 847.

The evidence here was that Eichelberger came upon a suitcase. He opened the suitcase and saw that it contained CDs. When he saw the CDs, he thought that he would cash them in for money. His next act was to wheel the suitcase down the street, get on the bus, and go to Queen Anne to sell the CDs to CD Trader. He did not notify the police and did not check the CDs to see if they had anyone's name on them. He did not attempt to find out if they actually belonged to someone and were lost. Many of the CDs were labeled with the owner's name and driver's license number, which would have allowed a reasonable person to easily ascertain whether they were actually abandoned, or whether they were in fact lost or stolen.

Taking all inferences in the light most favorable to the state, the evidence was sufficient to permit the jury to find actual subjective knowledge. A reasonable person faced with similar circumstances would know that there was a substantial risk that the CDs were stolen or lost, and would take some steps to determine who the owner was prior to selling the CDs. Thus, the jury was entitled to find

that Eichelberger had subjective knowledge of and disregarded the substantial risk that a wrongful act would occur when he converted the CDs to his own use. And, as the court instructed the jury when it asked for the definition of gross deviation, "[t]he law provides no precise definitions of these terms. The jury should rely on their understanding of the common meaning of 'gross deviation.'"

Eichelberger presents plausible explanations for the appearance of the suitcase other than that it was lost or stolen property, and testified that he thought the suitcase was abandoned. But the test is whether there was sufficient evidence to support the jury's verdict, not whether the jury could have reached a different result. We conclude that sufficient evidence supported the jury's verdict.

III. The Trial Court Did Not Err in Calculating Eichelberger's Offender Score

* * *

We affirm.

MARTIN
v.
OHIO

Supreme Court of the United States
480 U.S. 228, 107 S. Ct. 1098,
94 L. Ed. 2d 267 (1987)

JUSTICE WHITE delivered the opinion of the Court.

The Ohio Code provides that "[every] person accused of an offense is presumed innocent until proven guilty beyond a reasonable doubt, and the burden of proof for all elements of the offense is upon the prosecution. The burden of going forward with the evidence of an affirmative defense, and the burden of proof by a preponderance of the evidence, for an affirmative defense, is upon the accused." Ohio Rev. Code Ann. § 2901.05(A)(1982). An affirmative defense is one involving "an excuse or justification peculiarly within the knowledge of the accused, on which he can fairly be required to adduce supporting evidence." Ohio Rev.

Code Ann. § 2901.05(C)(2)(1982). The Ohio courts have "long determined that self-defense is an affirmative defense," 21 Ohio St. 3d 91, 93, 488 N.E.2d 166, 168 (1986), and that the defendant has the burden of proving it as required by § 2901.05(A).

As defined by the trial court in its instructions in this case, the elements of self-defense that the defendant must prove are that (1) the defendant was not at fault in creating the situation giving rise to the argument; (2) the defendant had an honest belief that she was in imminent danger of death or great bodily harm, and that her only means of escape from such danger was in the use of such force; and (3) the defendant did not violate any duty to retreat or avoid danger. App. 19. The question before us is whether the Due Process Clause of the Fourteenth Amendment forbids placing the burden of proving self-defense on the defendant when she is charged by the State of Ohio with committing the crime of aggravated murder, which, as relevant to this case, is defined by the Revised Code of Ohio as "purposely, and with prior calculation and design, [causing] the death of another." Ohio Rev. Code Ann. § 2903.01 (1982).

The facts of the case, taken from the opinions of the courts below, may be succinctly stated. On July 21, 1983, petitioner Earline Martin and her husband, Walter Martin, argued over grocery money. Petitioner claimed that her husband struck her in the head during the argument. Petitioner's version of what then transpired was that she went upstairs, put on a robe, and later came back down with her husband's gun which she intended to dispose of. Her husband saw something in her hand and questioned her about it. He came at her, and she lost her head and fired the gun at him. Five or six shots were fired, three of them striking and killing Mr. Martin. She was charged with and tried for aggravated murder. She pleaded self-defense and testified in her own defense. The judge charged the jury with respect to the elements of the crime and of self-defense and rejected petitioner's Due Process Clause challenge to the charge placing on her the burden of proving self-defense. The jury found her guilty.

Both the Ohio Court of Appeals and the Supreme Court of Ohio affirmed the conviction. Both rejected the constitutional challenge to the instruction requiring petitioner to prove self-defense. The latter court, relying upon our opinion in *Patterson v. New York*, 432 U.S. 197 (1977), concluded that the State was required to prove the three elements of aggravated murder but that Patterson did not require it to disprove self-defense, which is a separate issue that did not require Mrs. Martin to disprove any element of the offense with which she was charged. The court said, "the state proved beyond a reasonable doubt that appellant purposely, and with prior calculation and design, caused the death of her husband. Appellant did not dispute the existence of these elements, but rather sought to justify her actions on grounds she acted in self defense." 21 Ohio St. 3d, at 94, 488 N.E.2d, at 168. There was thus no infirmity in her conviction. We granted certiorari, 475 U.S. 1119 (1986), and affirm the decision of the Supreme Court of Ohio.

In re Winship, 397 U.S. 358, 364 (1970), declared that the Due Process Clause "protects the accused against conviction except upon proof beyond a reasonable doubt of every fact necessary to constitute the crime with which he is charged." A few years later, we held that *Winship's* mandate was fully satisfied where the State of New York had proved beyond reasonable doubt each of the elements of murder, but placed on the defendant the burden of proving the affirmative defense of extreme emotional disturbance, which, if proved, would have reduced the crime from murder to manslaughter. *Patterson v. New York, supra*. We there emphasized the preeminent role of the States in preventing and dealing with crime and the reluctance of the Court to disturb a State's decision with respect to the definition of criminal conduct and the procedures by which the criminal laws are to be enforced in the courts, including the burden of producing evidence and allocating the burden of persuasion. 432 U.S., at 201–202. New York had the authority to define murder as the intentional killing of another person. It had chosen, however, to reduce the crime to manslaughter if the defendant proved by a preponderance of the evidence that he had acted under the influence of extreme emotional distress. To convict of murder, the jury was required to find beyond a reasonable doubt, based on all the evidence, including that related to the defendant's mental state at the time of the crime, each of the elements of murder and also to conclude that the defendant had not proved his affirmative defense. The jury convicted Patterson, and we held there was no violation of the Fourteenth Amendment as construed in *Winship*.

* * *

As in *Patterson*, the jury was here instructed that to convict it must find, in light of all the evidence, that each of the elements of the crime of aggravated murder has been proved by the State beyond reasonable doubt, and that the burden of proof with respect to these elements did not shift. To find guilt, the jury had to be convinced that none of the evidence, whether offered by the State or by Martin in connection with her plea of self-defense, raised a reasonable doubt that Martin had killed her husband, that she had the specific purpose and intent to cause his death, or that she had done so with prior calculation and design. It was also told, however, that it could acquit if it found by a preponderance of the evidence that Martin had not precipitated the confrontation, that she had an honest belief that she was in imminent danger of death or great bodily harm, and that she had satisfied any duty to retreat or avoid danger. The jury convicted Martin.

We agree with the State and its Supreme Court that this conviction did not violate the Due Process Clause. The State did not exceed its authority in defining the crime of murder as purposely causing the death of another with prior calculation or design. It did not seek to shift to Martin the burden of proving any of those elements, and the jury's verdict reflects that none of her self-defense evidence raised a reasonable doubt about the State's proof that she purposefully killed with prior calculation and design. She nevertheless had the opportunity under state law and the instructions given to justify the killing and show herself to be blameless by proving that she acted in self-defense. The jury thought she had failed to do so, and Ohio is as entitled to punish Martin as one guilty of murder as New York was to punish Patterson.

It would be quite different if the jury had been instructed that self-defense evidence could not be considered in determining whether there was a reasonable doubt about the State's case, i.e., that self-defense evidence must be put aside for all purposes unless it satisfied the preponderance standard. Such an instruction would relieve the State of its burden and plainly run afoul of Winship's mandate. 397 U.S., at 364. The instructions in this case could be clearer in this respect, but when read as a whole, we think they are adequate to convey to the jury that all of the evidence, including the evidence going to self-defense, must be considered in deciding whether there was a reasonable doubt about the sufficiency of the State's proof of the elements of the crime.

We are thus not moved by assertions that the elements of aggravated murder and self-defense overlap in the sense that evidence to prove the latter will often tend to negate the former. It may be that most encounters in which self-defense is claimed arise suddenly and involve no prior plan or specific purpose to take life. In those cases, evidence offered to support the defense may negate a purposeful killing by prior calculation and design, but Ohio does not shift to the defendant the burden of disproving any element of the state's case. When the prosecution has made out a prima facie case and survives a motion to acquit, the jury may nevertheless not convict if the evidence offered by the defendant raises any reasonable doubt about the existence of any fact necessary for the finding of guilt. Evidence creating a reasonable doubt could easily fall far short of proving self-defense by a preponderance of the evidence. Of course, if such doubt is not raised in the jury's mind and each juror is convinced that the defendant purposely and with prior calculation and design took life, the killing will still be excused if the elements of the defense are satisfactorily established. We note here, but need not rely on, the observation of the Supreme Court of Ohio that "[appellant] did not dispute the existence of [the elements of aggravated murder], but rather sought to justify her actions on grounds she acted in self-defense." 21 Ohio St. 3d, at 94, 488 N.E.2d, at 168.

Petitioner submits that there can be no conviction under Ohio law unless the defendant's conduct is unlawful, and that because self-defense renders lawful what would otherwise be a crime, unlawfulness is an element of the offense that the state must prove by disproving self-defense. This argument founders on state law, for it has been rejected by the Ohio Supreme Court and by the Court of Appeals for the Sixth Circuit. *White v. Arn*, 788 F.2d 338, 346–347 (1986); *State v. Morris*, 8 Ohio App. 3d 12, 18–19, 455 N.E.2d 1352, 1359–1360 (1982). It is true that unlawfulness is essential for conviction, but the Ohio courts hold that the unlawfulness in cases like this is the conduct satisfying the elements of aggravated murder—an interpretation of state law that we are not in a position to dispute. The same is true of the claim that it is necessary to prove a "criminal" intent to convict for serious crimes, which cannot occur if self-defense is shown: the necessary mental state for aggravated murder under Ohio law is the specific purpose to take life pursuant to prior calculation and design. *See White v. Arn, supra*, at 346.

As we noted in *Patterson*, the common-law rule was that affirmative defenses, including self-defense, were matters for the defendant to prove. "This was the rule when the Fifth Amendment was adopted, and it was the American rule when the Fourteenth Amendment was ratified." 432 U.S., at 202. . . . We are aware that all but two of the States, Ohio and South Carolina, have abandoned the common-law rule and require the prosecution to prove the absence of self-defense when it is properly raised by the defendant. But the question remains whether those States are in violation of the Constitution; and, as we observed in Patterson, that question is not answered by cataloging the practices of other States. We are no more convinced that the Ohio practice of requiring self-defense to be proved by the defendant is unconstitutional than we are that the Constitution requires the prosecution to prove the sanity of a defendant who pleads not guilty by reason of insanity. We have had the opportunity to depart from *Leland v. Oregon*, 343 U.S. 790 (1952), but have refused to do so. *Rivera v. Delaware*, 429 U.S. 877 (1976). These cases were important to the *Patterson* decision and they, along with *Patterson*, are authority for our decision today.

The judgment of the Ohio Supreme Court is accordingly Affirmed.

Cases Relating to Chapter 4

Proof via Evidence

MADDOX
v.
MONTGOMERY

United States Court of Appeals, Eleventh Circuit 718 F.2d 1033 (11th Cir. 1983)

Fay, Vance and Kravitch, Circuit Judges.

PER CURIAM

Appellant Jimmy Maddox was convicted of rape in a Georgia state court and sentenced to life imprisonment. At the trial, appellant and the alleged victim, Kathy Elder, gave radically different accounts of the events in question. Elder testified that on a number of occasions prior to the alleged rape, appellant had approached her purportedly seeking to sell her an insurance policy. On the morning in question, while Elder was dressing her two sons, appellant appeared at her apartment and again asked whether she wanted the insurance. After explaining that she had discovered that she could get insurance at work, Elder went into the bedroom to retrieve coats for the boys. Elder testified that appellant followed her into the room and forcibly raped her on the bed. Another witness for the prosecution, Debbie Phillips, testified that she had once taken out insurance with appellant, but had dropped it after he had come to her home on a Saturday night. Appellant testified that he and Elder had had voluntary sexual relations on several occasions prior to the alleged rape and that Elder had consented to their sexual relations on the morning in question.

Having unsuccessfully pursued his direct appeal and the state post-conviction remedy,

appellant filed a federal habeas corpus petition alleging prosecutorial suppression of exculpatory evidence in violation of the doctrine of *Brady v. Maryland*, 373 U.S. 83, 83 S. Ct. 1194, 10 L. Ed. 2d 215 (1963). Specifically, appellant asserted that his right to due process was violated by the state's failure to disclose (1) a photograph taken by the police shortly after the alleged rape showing Elder's bed neatly made, (2) the results of a police examination of the bedspread which revealed no blood, semen or other fluid, and (3) a written statement by another witness, Brenda Phelps, that Debbie Phillips had stated that she dropped her insurance with appellant for financial reasons. Appellant appeals the denial of habeas relief. We affirm.

There are four types of situations in which the *Brady* doctrine applies: (1) the prosecutor has not disclosed information despite a specific defense request; (2) the prosecutor has not disclosed information despite a general defense request for all exculpatory information or without any defense request at all; (3) the prosecutor knows or should know that the conviction is based on false evidence; (4) the prosecutor fails to disclose purely impeaching evidence not concerning a substantive issue, in the absence of a specific defense request. *United States v. Anderson*, 574 F.2d 1347, 1353 (5th Cir. 1978). Inasmuch as appellant filed no pretrial request—specific or general—for exculpatory information, the present case falls within the second category with respect to the photograph of the bed and the results of the police examination of the bedspread and within the fourth category with respect to Phelps' statement.

In order to prevail on a *Brady* claim, one must establish the materiality of the exculpatory information suppressed by the prosecution. *United States v. Kopituk*, 690 F.2d 1289, 1339 (11th Cir.1982), *cert. denied*, 461 U.S. 928, 103 S. Ct. 2089, 77 L. Ed. 2d 300 (1983); *Anderson*, 574 F.2d at 1353. The applicable threshold of materiality, however, varies depending on the type of situation. Where, as here, the state failed to disclose substantive evidence favorable to the defendant for which there was no specific request, the standard set forth in *United States v. Agurs*, 427 U.S. 97, 96 S. Ct. 2392, 49 L. Ed. 2d 342 (1976), governs. In *Agurs*, the Supreme Court stated that such a failure to disclose violates due process only "if the omitted evidence creates a reasonable doubt that did not otherwise exist." Id. at 112, 96 S. Ct. at 2401; accord *United States v. Kubiak*, 704 F.2d 1545, 1551 (11th Cir.1983). In *Cannon v. Alabama*, 558 F.2d 1211 (5th Cir. 1977), *cert. denied*, 434 U.S. 1087, 98 S. Ct. 1281, 55 L. Ed. 2d 792 (1978), the former Fifth Circuit explained: Applying this standard requires an analysis of the evidence adduced at trial and of the probable impact of the undisclosed information. In this context, we cannot merely consider the evidence in the light most favorable to the government but must instead evaluate all the evidence as it would bear on the deliberations of a factfinder. Id. at 1213–14.

With regard to the photograph of the bed, we agree with the district court that "the undisclosed photograph does not create a reasonable doubt as to [appellant's] guilt that did not otherwise exist," Order, p. 8, and thus is not material under *Agurs*. Similarly, the results of the police examination of the bedspread do not give rise to a reasonable doubt and again are immaterial under *Agurs*. Although both pieces of evidence, if admitted at trial, might conceivably have affected the jury's verdict, the constitutional threshold of materiality is higher. *See Agurs*, 427 U.S. at 108–09, 96 S. Ct. at 2400. Insofar as this information is merely consistent with appellant's version of the incident and scarcely contradicts the alleged victim's testimony, and in view of the substantial inculpatory evidence in the record, the evidence at issue is not sufficiently material to render the state's failure to disclose unconstitutional.

The standard of materiality in a case, such as this one, involving the prosecution's suppression of impeaching evidence absent a specific request was recently discussed in *United States v. Blasco*, 702 F.2d 1315 (11th Cir.), cert. denied, 464 U.S. 914, 104 S. Ct. 275, 78 L. Ed. 2d 256 (1983). There this Court noted, "if the suppressed evidence is purely impeaching evidence and no defense request has been made, the suppressed evidence is material only if its introduction probably would have resulted in acquittal." Id. at 1328; accord *Anderson*, 574 F.2d at 1354. Given the relatively minor role of Phillips' testimony and the limited impact that Phelps' statement would likely have had on the jury's assessment of Phillips' credibility, appellant is unable to demonstrate that the undisclosed evidence probably would have resulted in an acquittal. Accordingly, the evidence is immaterial under *Blasco*, and its suppression did not violate appellant's due process right.

For the foregoing reasons, the district court's dismissal of appellant's habeas petition is AFFIRMED.

BROWN
v.
STATE

Supreme Court of Delaware
897 A.2d 748, 2006 Del. LEXIS 163 (2006)

Before STEELE, Chief Justice, HOLLAND and JACOBS, Justices.

HOLLAND, Justice:

The defendant-appellant, Jeron Brown, appeals from his convictions of Burglary in the Second Degree, Theft, two counts of Receiving Stolen Property, and Criminal Mischief. In this appeal, Brown alleges that the Superior Court erred by: first, denying his motion to suppress evidence obtained during a search incident to his arrest because the police did not have probable cause to arrest him; second, denying his request for a mistrial after the State disclosed potentially exculpatory evidence during the trial; and third, failing to provide, *sua sponte*, a missing evidence jury instruction because a witness was unavailable to testify at trial. We conclude that there was no reversible error. Therefore, the judgments of the Superior Court must be affirmed.

Facts

On January 20, 2004, the Del-Mar Appliance store and two private residences in Dover, Delaware, were burglarized. After the third burglary, the police reviewed a video surveillance tape from a local 7–11 store that showed an African American male and female attempting to sell items to the store clerk. Anwar Al-Rasul, the third burglary victim, had earlier identified the items on the tape as items that were stolen from his home. Later that day, the police received a tip from Mr. Al-Rasul's wife that an African American man would soon attempt to sell items similar to those stolen from her home at a nearby store, named the Closet.

The police set up surveillance outside the Closet. Jeron Brown approached the store carrying a duffel bag and wearing a jacket similar to the jacket worn by the man whose image was captured in the 7–11 video surveillance tape. Brown was also the same race, height, and build of the man shown in the tape. Brown entered the Closet and left shortly thereafter.

As he exited the store, the police approached Brown and immediately handcuffed him. The officers asked Brown if they could pat him down. They also asked Brown if they could search his jacket and duffel bag. Brown consented to both requests. Mr. Al-Rasul identified the items found by the police in Brown's jacket and duffel bag as his stolen property. The police then obtained a search warrant for Brown's residence, where they searched and seized more stolen property.

Probable Cause Established

[The appellate court agreed that probable cause was properly established.]

Mistrial Properly Denied

On the morning of the third day of Brown's trial, his defense counsel moved for a mistrial because alleged *Brady* material [a request to be notified concerning exculpatory evidence in the hands of the prosecution] was not disclosed by the prosecution until the preceding Friday, following two days of Brown's trial. The alleged *Brady* material at issue was a laptop computer stolen during the January 20, 2004 burglary of the Del-Mar Appliance store in Dover. The stolen laptop computer was recovered by the Delaware Probation Department from an individual named Moustapha Bobbo. After a probation officer took the laptop from Bobbo, it was turned over to Detective Virdin of the Dover Police Department. Detective Virdin then returned the computer to its rightful owner, Bruce Nygard.

Brown contends that, because the State did not inform him of information regarding Nygard's recovered laptop computer and because the computer was found in the possession of Bobbo, not Brown, this prevented Brown from introducing witnesses at trial to trace the whereabouts of the computer after it was stolen from the Del-Mar Appliance store. In denying the mistrial motion, the trial judge noted that Brown's contention concerning the laptop computer related to only one of his three pending burglary charges.

The State tried to mitigate any potential prejudice to Brown by the late disclosure of the information regarding the laptop computer. The State was able to locate both Moustapha Bobbo and Antonio Medina, another witness who had some information as to how the laptop computer came to be in the possession of Bobbo. Both Bobbo and Medina appeared at Brown's trial and testified as defense witnesses.

The Superior Court has a variety of remedies available for a discovery violation under Superior Court Criminal Rule 16(d)(2). As this Court has noted, "In determining the question of whether sanctions should be imposed, the trial court should weigh all relevant factors, such as the reason for the State's delay and the extent of prejudice to the defendant." As we pointed out in *Doran*, "Superior Court Criminal Rule 16 sets forth four alternative sanctions: 1) order prompt compliance with the discovery rule; 2) 'grant a continuance;' 3) 'prohibit the party from introducing in evidence material not disclosed;' or 4) such other order the Court 'deems just under the circumstances.'"

Whether a mistrial should be declared is a matter entrusted to the trial judge's discretion. The trial judge is in the best position to assess the risk of any prejudice resulting from trial events. n16 "A trial judge should grant a mistrial only where there is 'manifest necessity' or the 'ends of public justice would be otherwise defeated.'" The remedy of a mistrial is "mandated only when there are 'no meaningful and practical alternatives' to that remedy."

In this case, the practical alternative to granting a mistrial was to permit Brown to present the testimony of both Moustapha Bobbo and Antonio Medina regarding the stolen laptop computer. Both could testify that Jeron Brown had no ostensible connection with that particular item of stolen property before its seizure by a probation officer and ultimate return to the true owner. In fact, Brown presented testimony to that effect by both of those witnesses.

Brown argues on appeal that, had he known about this information at an earlier date, his trial examinations of Medina and Bobbo would have been different. He fails to explain, however, how their examinations would have been different and how the difference(s), if any, would have mattered. The record reflects that there was no abuse of discretion in the trial judge's refusal to grant Brown's motion for a mistrial.

No Plain Error

Finally, Brown contends that the trial judge, *sua sponte*, should have given a missing evidence instruction pursuant to *Deberry v. State*. Brown's request for the *Deberry* missing evidence jury instruction did not involve the physical evidence at issue (the laptop computer), but, rather, related to a missing witness, Laura Johansen, who was not available to testify at Brown's trial. Johansen was the person who gave the stolen laptop computer to Bobbo and presumably could have testified that she purchased the laptop computer from someone other than Brown.

Brown made no request at trial for a *Deberry* missing evidence jury instruction. Therefore, that claim has been waived by Brown and may now be reviewed on appeal only for plain error. To be plain, the alleged

error must affect substantial rights, generally meaning that it must have affected the outcome of Brown's trial. In demonstrating that a forfeited error is prejudicial, the burden of persuasion is on Brown.

Brown was found in possession of a digital camera and camera printer taken from the Del-Mar Appliance store when he was arrested by the police. The digital camera and printer that the police discovered in Brown's possession linked him to the stolen property from the Del-Mar appliance burglary. Accordingly, there was an independent evidentiary basis for the jury to conclude that Brown was guilty of receiving that other stolen property.

Brown was not convicted of the Del-Mar Appliance store burglary. He was convicted only of receiving stolen property resulting from that burglary, property that included the digital camera and the printer. Consequently, Brown cannot demonstrate plain error, because even if Johanson had appeared at trial and testified that she purchased the stolen laptop computer from someone other than Brown, the ultimate result at trial would have been the same.

Conclusion

The judgments of the Superior Court are affirmed.

STATE
v.
JORDAN

COURT OF APPEALS OF OHIO, THIRD APPELLATE DISTRICT

2002 Ohio 1418, 2002 Ohio App. LEXIS 1469 (2002)

HADLEY, J. The defendant/appellant, Neil L. Jordan ("the appellant"), appeals his conviction by the Seneca County Municipal Court, finding him guilty of three counts of vehicular manslaughter, in violation of R.C. 2903.06(A)(4). Based on the following, we reverse the judgment of the trial court.

Mr. Jordan was returning home from a basketball game on January 21, 2001 when, at approximately 8:30 p.m., his auto collided with another at the intersection of U.S. Route 224 and Hopewell Township Road 113 in Hopewell Township, Seneca County, Ohio. As a result of that accident, Lisa M. Johnson and Daniel P. Shaver, the occupants of the other auto, were killed. The eight to twelve week old fetus that Ms. Johnson was carrying also perished.

The appellant was charged with three counts of vehicular manslaughter. The state alleged that he violated R.C. 4511.43(A), in that he failed to stop at the point nearest the intersecting roadway where he had clear view of approaching traffic on the intersecting roadway before entering it, and that he consequently caused the deaths of Lisa M. Johnson, Daniel P. Shaver, and the unlawful termination of Ms. Johnson's pregnancy, in violation of R.C. 2903.06(A)(4). The appellant was found guilty of all three counts by a jury. He was sentenced to 45 days in jail on each count, to be served consecutively, and fined $375.00, plus costs.

The appellant now appeals his convictions, raising three assignments of error for our review.

ASSIGNMENT OF ERROR NO. I

As a matter of law, the trial judge committed error prejudicial to the defendant-appellant by denying his motion for judgment of acquittal at the conclusion of the State's case, at the conclusion of all of the evidence, and after the return of the verdict, since the State failed to provide any evidence (direct, circumstantial, or otherwise) that the defendant-appellant failed to stop in violation of Revised Code § 4511.43(A).

* * *

The appellant asserts in his first assignment of error that the trial court erred in failing to grant his motions for judgment of acquittal at various stages of his trial because, he alleges, the state failed to prove a material element of the charges against him. We agree with the appellant.

Crim.R. 29 prohibits a court from entering an order of judgment of acquittal if the evidence is such that reasonable minds can reach different conclusions as to whether each material element of a crime has been proved beyond a reasonable doubt. Furthermore, in reviewing a ruling on a Crim.R. 29 motion for judgment of acquittal, a reviewing court must construe the evidence in a light most favorable to the prosecution. Thus, we must determine if, construing the evidence in the light most favorable to the state, evidence was presented before the trial court which would allow reasonable minds to reach different conclusions as to whether the state proved all the material elements of vehicular manslaughter beyond a reasonable doubt.

The portion of R.C. 2903.06 under which the appellant was charged reads, in relevant part:

(A) No person, while operating or participating in the operation of a motor vehicle, motorcycle, snowmobile, locomotive, watercraft, or aircraft, shall cause the death of another or the unlawful termination of another's pregnancy in any of the following ways:

* * *

(4) As the proximate result of committing a violation of any provision of any section contained in Title XLV of the Revised Code that is a minor misdemeanor or of a municipal ordinance that, regardless of the penalty set by ordinance for the violation, is substantially equivalent to any provision of any section contained in Title XLV of the Revised Code that is a minor misdemeanor.

The underlying minor misdemeanor the appellant was found to have violated is R.C. 4511.43(A), which states:

Except when directed to proceed by a law enforcement officer, every driver of a vehicle or trackless trolley approaching a stop sign shall stop at a clearly marked stop line, but if none, before entering the crosswalk on the near side of the intersection, or, if none, then at the point nearest the intersecting roadway where the driver has a view of approaching traffic on the intersecting roadway before entering it. After having stopped, the driver shall yield the right-of-way to any vehicle in the intersection or approaching on another roadway so closely as to constitute an immediate hazard during the time the driver is moving across or within the intersection or junction of roadways.

The appellant argues that the state presented no evidence that he failed to stop in violation of R.C. 4511.43(A). Rather, he argues, in order for the jury to find that he failed to stop, it had to draw an inference from another inference.

It is impermissible for a trier of fact to draw "an inference based * * * entirely upon another inference, unsupported by any additional fact or another inference from other facts[.]" If, however, the second inference is based in part upon another inference and in part upon facts, it is a parallel inference and, if reasonable, is permissible. Likewise, a trier of fact may draw multiple inferences from the same set of facts.

There was no direct evidence presented at the trial regarding whether the appellant failed to stop at the stop sign. What follows is a summary of the relevant evidence that was presented:

1. Pictures and descriptive testimony of the crash scene, including evidence that the victims' car was wrapped around a telephone pole and torn almost in half;

2. Testimony regarding the position of the stop sign;

3. Testimony about the point nearest the intersecting roadway where the appellant had a clear view of approaching traffic on the intersecting roadway, which was identified as the point where the fog line on U.S. 224 would traverse 113 if projected into the intersection, and testimony as to the distance between that point and the point of impact;

4. Testimony that the appellant's car was traveling southbound at the time of the accident and the victims' car was traveling westbound;

5. Testimony that the cars traveled in a basically southerly direction after the initial impact;

6. Testimony that no evasive action was taken by either driver prior to impact;

7. Testimony that the final resting point of both cars was the southwest corner of the intersection of U.S. 224 and Township Road 113;

8. And testimony regarding the injuries to and causes of death of the victims.

We agree with the appellant that the only way the jury could have concluded that he failed to stop in accordance with [state law] R.C. 4511.43(A) was to first infer from the evidence that his vehicle was traveling at a high rate of speed at the time of impact. Any further inference beyond this must have been supported by additional facts. The record reveals no other evidence to support an inference that the appellant failed to stop, nor do the facts that were presented independently support it. Thus, the inference that the appellant failed to stop could only be based on an inference that his vehicle was traveling at a high rate of speed, which amounts to an impermissible inference built upon another inference. Thus, we find that the appellant's Crim. R. 29 motion should have been granted because reasonable minds could only find that the State failed to prove beyond a reasonable doubt that the appellant violated R.C. 4511.43(A).

The crucial flaw in the state's case was the lack of expert testimony and scientific evidence, which, if properly presented, would have assisted the jury in understanding the significance of the state's demonstrative evidence. The limited accident reconstruction testimony in this case, in conjunction with photographs and diagrams, established the extent of damage to the vehicles, points of impact, and relative positions of the vehicles following the collision. While this evidence is significant, in order to use it as the cornerstone of their case, the state needed to establish that based on the evidence: 1) the appellant's vehicle must have been traveling at a minimum speed and 2) this speed was greater than the appellant's vehicle could have achieved in any acceleration from a proper stop at either the stop sign or the fog line.

No scientific evidence or expert opinion was placed before the jury to assist them in establishing the speed of appellant's vehicle at the point of impact with the other car. In addition, no scientific evidence or expert opinion was placed before the jury to properly assist them in ascertaining the acceleration capability of appellant's vehicle from either the fog line (approximately three feet from the point of impact) or the stop sign (some 24–27 feet from the point of impact), to the point of impact. In fact there was brief testimony from the state's expert that the acceleration capability of appellant's vehicle to the point of impact might have been anywhere from zero to thirty miles per hour or possibly even zero to sixty miles per hour from a stop at the fog line.

As a result, from the crash scene evidence alone, the jury in this case was permitted to determine for itself, without any expert or other supporting testimony: 1) that the appellant had to be traveling at a certain minimum speed sufficient to create the existing crash scene and 2) that this speed exceeded the capability of appellant's car to accelerate from a lawful stop at the stop sign or

the fog line—in order to then determine that appellant did not stop at either location prior to the collision.

In addition to requiring an improper stacking of inferences, the impact-speed and acceleration determinations described above are beyond the knowledge or experience of lay persons and therefore constitute determinations which are not permissible for a jury to make from crash scene evidence alone, without the assistance of expert testimony.

Because we find for the appellant on this assignment of error, we need not address his second or third assignments of error.

Accordingly, the appellant's first assignment of error is well taken and hereby affirmed.

Having found error prejudicial to the appellant herein, in the particulars assigned and argued, we reverse the judgment of the trial court and remand the matter for further proceedings consistent with this opinion.

Judgment Reversed.

SHAW, P.J., and WALTERS, J., concur.

Cases Relating to Chapter 5

Judicial Notice

STATE
v.
VEJVODA

231 Neb. 668, 438 N.W.2d 461 (1989)

Hastings, C.J., Boslaugh, White, Caporale, Shanahan, and Fahrnbruch, J.J. White, J., dissenting.

SHANAHAN, OPINION:

In a bench trial in the county court for Hall County, Mark Vejvoda was convicted of drunk driving and received an enhanced sentence as the result of his second conviction for drunk driving. See Neb. Rev. Stat. § 39-669.07 (Reissue 1988). On appeal, the district court affirmed Vejvoda's conviction and sentence. Vejvoda contends that the evidence is insufficient to sustain his conviction for drunk driving and that the State failed to prove that Hall County was the venue for his trial because the court improperly took judicial notice that locations mentioned in Vejvoda's trial were within Hall County.

VEJVODA'S TRIAL

Officer Elmer Edwards of the Grand Island Police Department was the sole witness at Vejvoda's trial. Edwards testified that on May 1, 1987, at 2:14 A.M., he was in the vicinity of 7th and Vine Streets and noticed a vehicle proceeding west on 7th Street, "weaving back and forth across the entire width of the street." Edwards had observed the vehicle for "2½ to 3 blocks," when the car commenced a right turn from 7th Street onto Oak

Street and "ran over the curb section located at the . . . northeast corner of the intersection." In pursuit, Edwards followed the car northbound on Oak Street to 8th Street, where Edwards stopped the pursued vehicle.

On confronting the car's driver, whom Edwards eventually identified as Vejvoda, Edwards observed that Vejvoda's eyes were bloodshot and watery, and a strong odor of alcohol emanated from Vejvoda's car. According to Edwards, Vejvoda's reactions were "slow and sluggish" while he fumbled to produce a driver's license. Edwards then asked Vejvoda to step out of his car for field sobriety tests. Vejvoda was "swaying and wobbling" and had difficulty maintaining his balance during the field sobriety tests. In Edwards' opinion, Vejvoda was under the influence of alcohol when stopped by the officer, who later arrested Vejvoda for drunk driving. In all his testimony concerning his observations, pursuit, and stop of the vehicle, Edwards never mentioned the city or county where the events occurred. Defense counsel did not cross-examine Edwards, and the prosecution rested.

After Vejvoda offered no evidence, the prosecutor apparently realized that Edwards had not testified that the events involving Vejvoda occurred in Hall County. When the prosecutor asked leave to recall Edwards for testimony concerning the location of events, the court responded, "The Court will take judicial notice of the fact that all of the addresses and areas described are those— are those within the city limits of the city of Grand Island which lies wholly within Hall County." Vejvoda objected to the court's "taking judicial notice after the . . . State has rested." In closing argument, Vejvoda argued, among other things, that the State had failed to prove proper venue. The court then found Vejvoda guilty of drunk driving. Vejvoda contends, first, that there is insufficient evidence to sustain his conviction for drunk driving, and, second, the court improperly took judicial notice of facts establishing the site of the events on which his conviction is based. In essence, Vejvoda's venue claim is an assertion that the court improperly took judicial notice that Grand Island in Hall County was the site of the events in question and, as the result of the improper judicial notice, determined that venue was evidentially established as Hall County.

* * *

GUARANTEE OF VENUE

The venue problem in this appeal could have been easily avoided by the court's merely granting the State's motion to withdraw its rest and present evidence on venue. "Even in criminal prosecutions the withdrawal of a rest in a trial on the merits is within the discretion of the trial court." *State v. Putnam*, 178 Neb. 445, 448–49, 133 N.W.2d 605, 608 (1965). Unfortunately, however, instead of allowing the State to recall Edwards to answer a single, simple question identifying venue, the court chose to try to remedy the evidential situation and created the venue problem presented in Vejvoda's appeal.

* * *

Vejvoda's right to be tried in the county in which the criminal offense is alleged to have been committed is secured by statute rather than by the Nebraska Constitution. Neb. Rev. Stat. § 29-1301 (Reissue 1985) provides that "[a]ll criminal cases shall be tried in the county where the offense was committed . . . unless it shall appear to the court by affidavits that a fair and impartial trial cannot be had therein." While proper venue in a criminal case may be established by circumstantial evidence, we have held that the State must prove proper venue beyond a reasonable doubt. *Union P. R. Co. v. State*, 88 Neb. 547,

130 N.W. 277 (1911); *Keeler v. State*, 73 Neb. 441, 103 N.W. 64 (1905). It is clear from Nebraska decisions that a defendant may waive the statutorily designated venue for the trial of a criminal case in accordance with § 29-1301 concerning a change of venue. See *Kennison v. State*, 83 Neb. 391, 119 N.W. 768 (1909). Whether venue is an element of the substantive offense charged against an accused is apparently an unresolved issue in Nebraska. See, however, *State v. Harris*, 48 Wash. App. 279, 281–82, 738 P.2d 1059, 1061 (1987): "As a general rule, proof of venue is necessary in a criminal prosecution. [Citations omitted.] However, venue is not an element of the crime [citations omitted], and it need not be proved beyond a reasonable doubt [citation omitted]." See, further, *State v. Graycek*, 335 N.W.2d 572, 574 (S.D. 1983): "Venue, not being an integral part of a criminal offense, does not affect the question of the guilt or innocence of the accused [and may be proved] by a preponderance of the evidence . . . ." Cf., *State v. Barnes*, 7 Ohio App. 3d 83, 84, 454 N.E.2d 572, 574 (1982): "Venue with respect to the situs of a crime is ordinarily considered an element of the offense which must be proved along with the other elements"; State v. Hester, 145 Ariz. 574, 703 P.2d 518 (1985) (venue is an essential element).

* * *

PROOF OF VENUE

The venue of an offense may be proven like any other fact in a criminal case. It need not be established by positive testimony, nor in the words of the information; but if from the facts appearing in evidence the only rational conclusion which can be drawn is that the offense was committed in the county alleged, it is sufficient. [Citations omitted.]

The only testimony regarding venue was that of Edwards, a Grand Island police officer, who observed Vejvoda's car at "7th and Vine Streets" and later apprehended Vejvoda on a street called "Oak." Edwards never identified the city or county where he observed and apprehended Vejvoda. As this court noted in *State v. Bouwens*, 167 Neb. 244, 247, 92 N.W.2d 564, 566 (1958), the fact that a defendant was arrested by policemen of a particular city "is not proof that the offense was committed within the jurisdiction . . . of the city. . . ." When the judicial notice in question is disregarded, the evidence offered in Vejvoda's case fails to establish that either a Vine Street or an Oak Street exists in Grand Island or Hall County. A defendant's arrest by a law enforcement officer of a particular political subdivision does not identify or establish the political subdivision as the proper venue in a criminal case. *State v. Bouwens, supra.* Therefore, without the court's judicial notice that events concerning Vejvoda occurred in Grand Island within Hall County, the evidence fails to establish venue.

In this appeal, the State does not challenge the current Nebraska rule that a waiver does not result from a defendant's inaction on a venue question in a criminal case, nor does the State take issue with the necessity of evidence beyond a reasonable doubt regarding proof of venue.

JUDICIAL NOTICE

Neb. Evid. R. 201(2), Neb. Rev. Stat. § 27-201(2) (Reissue 1985), pertains to judicial notice of adjudicative facts and states: "A judicially noticed fact must be one not subject to reasonable dispute in that it is either (a) generally known within the territorial jurisdiction of the trial court or (b) capable of accurate and ready determination by resort to sources whose accuracy cannot reasonably be questioned."

A fact is adjudicative if the fact affects the determination of a controverted issue in litigation, or, as one author has characterized adjudicative facts:

When a court or an agency finds facts concerning the immediate parties—who did what, where, when, how, and with what motive or intent—the court or agency is performing an adjudicative function, and the facts so determined are conveniently called adjudicative facts. . . .

Stated in other terms, the adjudicative facts are those to which the law is applied in the process of adjudication. They are the facts that normally go to the jury in a jury case.

They relate to the parties, their activities, their properties, their businesses. Davis, *Judicial Notice*, 55 COLUM. L. REV. 945, 952 (1955).

* * *

When neither of the alternative tests prescribed in Neb. Evid. R. 201(2) is satisfied, judicial notice of an adjudicative fact is improper. See *Cardio-Medical Assoc. v. Crozer-Chester Med. Ctr.*, 721 F.2d 68 (3d Cir. 1983). See, also, 1 J. WEINSTEIN & M. BERGER, *supra.*

A judge or court may take judicial notice, whether requested or not. Neb. Evid. R. 201(3). Judicial notice of an adjudicative fact may be taken at any stage of the proceedings. Neb. Evid. R. 201(6).

JUDICIAL NOTICE: A SPECIES OF EVIDENCE

Judicial notice of an adjudicative fact is a species of evidence, which, if relevant as an ultimate fact or a fact from which an ultimate fact may be inferred, is received without adherence to the Nebraska Evidence Rules otherwise applicable to admissibility of evidence and establishes a fact without formal evidentiary proof. Judicial notice "means that the court will admit into evidence and consider, without proof of the facts, matters of common and general knowledge"; "Judicial notice is an evidentiary concept which operates to admit matters into evidence without formal proof. . . ." Although Neb. Evid. R. 201 does not expressly require relevance for judicial notice, an irrelevant fact cannot be validly classified as an "adjudicative fact," the only type of fact noticeable under Neb. Evid. R. 201. [Paragraph citations omitted.].

JUDICIAL NOTICE v. A JUDGE'S PERSONAL KNOWLEDGE

Judicial notice, however, is not the same as extrajudicial or personal knowledge of a judge. "What a judge knows and what facts a judge may judicially notice are not identical data banks. . . . [A]ctual private knowledge by the judge is no sufficient ground for taking judicial notice of a fact as a basis for a finding or a final judgment. . . ." McCORMICK ON EVIDENCE § 329 at 922–23 (E. Cleary 3d ed. 1984). As Wigmore observes:

> There is a real but elusive line between the judge's personal knowledge as a private man and these matters of which he takes judicial notice as a judge. The latter does not necessarily include the former; as a judge, indeed, he may have to ignore what he knows as a man and contrariwise. . . .

* * *

JUDICIAL NOTICE IN CRIMINAL CASES

In function and effect, judicial notice in a civil action is fundamentally different from judicial notice in a criminal case. "In a civil action or proceeding, the judge shall instruct the jury to accept as conclusive any fact judicially noticed. In a criminal case, the judge shall instruct the jury that it may, but is not required to, accept as conclusive any fact judicially noticed." Neb. Evid. R. 201(7). In a civil action, the adjudicative fact judicially noticed is conclusively established and binds the jury, whereas in a criminal case a jury ultimately has the freedom to find that an adjudicative fact has not been established notwithstanding judicial notice by the trial court. If the conclusive effect of judicial notice in a civil action were transposed to the trial of a criminal case, judicial notice might supply proof of an element in the charge against an accused and thereby have the practical effect of a directed verdict on the issue of the defendant's guilt. The actual danger of judicial notice as a directed verdict against an accused was carefully considered in *State v. Lawrence*, 120 Utah 323, 234 P.2d 600 (1951), which involved a conviction of grand larceny, that is, theft of property with value in excess of $50. As recounted by the court in Lawrence:

> At the conclusion of the evidence, the defendant's counsel moved the court for a directed verdict on the ground that there had been no evidence of value of the stolen car. The State's attorney might properly and with little difficulty have moved to re-open and supply the missing evidence.

He did not do so but instead argued that judicial notice could be taken of the value of the car. The court denied defendant's motion and included in its instructions to the jury the following:

> . . . .

> In this case you will take the value of this property as being in excess of $50.00 and therefore the defendant, if he is guilty at all, is guilty of grand larceny." 120 Utah at 326, 234 P.2d at 601.

In that setting, the Lawrence court directed its attention to the prosecution's argument that the court could take judicial notice of the automobile's value and instruct the jury accordingly. Rejecting the State's argument, the court concluded:

> It is to be admitted that upon the surface there doesn't appear to be much logic to the thought that a jury would not be bound to find that the car involved here (1947 Ford 2-Door Sedan) is worth more than $50. However, under our jury system, it is traditional that in criminal cases juries can, and sometimes do, make findings which are not based on logic, nor even common sense. No matter how positive the evidence of a man's guilt may be, the jury may find him not guilty and no court has any power to do anything about it. Notwithstanding the occasional incongruous result, this system of submitting all of the facts in criminal cases to the jury and letting them be the exclusive judges thereof has lasted for some little time now and with a fair degree of success. If the result in individual cases at times seems illogical, we can be consoled by the words of Mr. Justice Holmes, that in some areas of the law, "a page of history is worth a volume of logic." We, who live with it, have a fervent devotion to the jury system, in spite of its faults. We would not like to see it destroyed nor whittled away. If a court can take one important element of an offense from the jury and determine the facts for them because such fact seems plain enough to him, then which element cannot be similarly taken away, and where would the process stop?

120 Utah at 330–31, 234 P.2d at 603. The court then reversed Lawrence's conviction and ordered a new trial.

In *U.S. v. Mentz*, 840 F.2d 315 (6th Cir. 1988), the government prosecuted Mentz in a jury trial on charges of bank robbery. To convict Mentz, the government had to prove that Mentz robbed a financial institution insured by the Federal Deposit Insurance Corporation. See 18 U.S.C. § 2113(a) and (f) (1982). When Mentz moved for dismissal of the charges at the close of the government's case, claiming that evidence failed to establish that the banks were FDIC-insured at the time of the robberies, the court overruled Mentz' motion and, although there was no evidence of FDIC insurance, instructed the jury that each of the banks, which Mentz was accused of robbing, was "insured by the Federal Deposit Insurance Corporation at the time of the offense alleged in the indictment." (Emphasis omitted.) 840 F.2d at 318–19. In reversing Mentz' conviction, the court stated:

Regardless of how overwhelming the evidence may be, the Constitution delegates to the jury, not to the trial judge, the important task of deciding guilt or innocence. "[The jury's] overriding responsibility is to stand between the accused and a potentially arbitrary or abusive Government that is in command of the criminal sanction. For this reason, a trial judge is prohibited from entering a judgment of conviction or directing the jury to come forward with such a verdict, regardless of how overwhelming the evidence may point in that direction. The trial judge is thereby barred from attempting to override or interfere with the jurors' independent judgment in a manner contrary to the interests of the accused." *United States v. Martin Linen Supply Co.* [citation omitted]. 840 F.2d at 319.

The *Mentz* court continued:

We agree with Mentz that the trial judge invaded the jury's province by instructing that body, in clear and unequivocal language, that the banks were FDIC insured at the time the robberies occurred. His conclusive statement left no room for the jury

to believe otherwise. The judge improperly cast himself in the role of trier of fact, and directed a verdict on an essential element of the bank robbery charge. His instructions had the effect of relieving the government of its burden of proving, beyond the jury's reasonable doubt, that the accused committed the crimes charged. . . .

* * *

The court in *Mentz* then noted: "Since the government's evidence on this issue consisted mainly of witness testimony, the trial judge replaced the jury by reaching a conclusion based on assessing the credibility of witnesses and weighing the probative value of the evidence." 840 F.2d at 320 n.8.

Specifically referring to judicial notice under Fed. R. Evid. 201(g), the counterpart to Neb. Evid. R. 201(7), the court concluded in *Mentz*:

A court may take judicial notice of adjudicative facts in a criminal case, whether requested or not. Rule 201(c), (f), Fed. R.Evid. When the court does so, however, there will normally be a record of this. "Care should be taken by the court to identify the fact it is noticing, and its justification for doing so." *Colonial Leasing Company of New England v. Logistics Control Group International*, 762 F.2d 454, 459 (5th Cir. 1985). This facilitates intelligent appellate review, and is particularly necessary when the fact noticed is an essential element of the crime charged. . . .

* * *

A trial court commits constitutional error when it takes judicial notice of facts constituting an essential element of the crime charged, but fails to instruct the jury according to Rule 201(g). The court's decision to accept the element as established conflicts with the bedrock principle that the government must prove, beyond the jury's reasonable doubt, every essential element of the crime. [Citation omitted.]

Even assuming the district court in this case judicially noticed the insurance coverage by the FDIC, it was obligated to inform the jury that it could disregard the facts noticed. The court's failure to make such a statement permitted the jury to convict Mentz without ever examining the evidence concerning an element of the crime charged, and thus violated his Sixth Amendment right to a jury trial. 840 F.2d at 322–23.

* * *

JUDICIAL NOTICE IN VEJVODA'S CASE

Under the Nebraska Evidence Rules, the trial court's sua sponte judicial notice was permissible at the point in Vejvoda's trial where adduction of evidence had been concluded and the case was ready for submission to the factfinding process. See Neb. Evid. R. 201(4): "A judge or court shall take judicial notice if requested by a party and supplied with the necessary information." See, also, Neb. Evid. R. 201(6): "Judicial notice may be taken at any stage of the proceeding."

However, from the record in Vejvoda's case, one cannot conclude that the location of the municipal microcosm known as Vine Street or 8th and Oak Streets was known throughout the length and breadth of Hall County and, therefore, a fact "known within the territorial jurisdiction of the trial court." Neb. Evid. R. 201(2)(a). Consequently, we must focus on the alternative expressed in Neb. Evid. R. 201(2)(b), that is, whether the location of Vine and Oak Streets in Grand Island and the site of Vejvoda's arrest are adjudicative facts "capable of accurate and ready determination by resort to sources whose accuracy cannot reasonably be questioned."

For resolution of Vejvoda's claim regarding the impropriety of the trial court's judicial notice, we must first identify and characterize the scope of the trial court's "judicial notice," which actually has two components: (1) Vine, Oak, 7th, and 8th Streets exist in Grand Island, which is located in Hall County, and (2) Vejvoda's drunk driving occurred at 8th and Oak in Grand Island. Thus, existence of Grand Island streets is inferentially correlated with Edwards' testimony, producing a conclusion judicially noticed by the trial court, namely, the judicially noticed streets

are the same streets mentioned in Edwards' testimony, and, therefore, Vejvoda was arrested in Grand Island.

An inference may be entirely reasonable, yet nevertheless an improper subject for judicial notice[.] [Neb. Evid. R. 201] puts judges and attorneys on notice that underlying assumptions must be analyzed to ascertain whether their validity can be verified and placed beyond practical dispute. Attorneys must be alert to instances . . . where a court's statement, although plausible on the surface, may be based on unverified [and unverifiable] hypotheses. 1 J. WEINSTEIN & M. BERGER, WEINSTEIN'S EVIDENCE para. 201[03] at 201–34 (1988).

When a fact is not generally known within the territorial jurisdiction of the trial court, judicial notice may be taken only if an adjudicative fact can be verified by "sources whose accuracy cannot reasonably be questioned." Neb. Evid. R. 201(2)(b). The inference that Vejvoda was arrested in Grand Island is not "capable of accurate and ready determination by resort to sources whose accuracy cannot reasonably be questioned." Neb. Evid. R. 201(2)(b). We cannot imagine any unimpeachable source or sources which quickly and accurately verify the trial court's inferential determination that Vejvoda's drunk driving occurred in Grand Island. While a map of Grand Island would verify existence of Vine and Oak Streets within the city, a Grand Island map would not indisputably establish that Vejvoda was driving in that city.

As a matter of judicial notice, the trial court's conclusion that Vejvoda's drunk driving occurred in Grand Island is verifiable only by the cumbersome process of examining all locations outside Grand Island, which might match Edwards' description of a site with "Vine" and "Oak" streets, and then eliminating those locations which are inconsistent with Edwards' testimony about the direction traveled by Vejvoda's vehicle, for example, Vejvoda's car traveled west on 7th Street, turned right from 7th Street onto Oak Street, and stopped at 8th and Oak Streets. In the foregoing process of comparison and elimination, a court would have to consult not only a map of Grand Island, but also maps of cities and towns outside Grand Island and Hall County which have streets designated "Vine," "Oak," "7th," and "8th." Although a court might, after a laborious comparison of virtually innumerable city maps, confirm Edwards' identification of "Vine" and "Oak" as the streets traveled by Vejvoda within Grand Island, such an unavoidably burdensome procedure is not only impracticable but contrary to Neb. Evid. R. 201(2)(b), which specifies that a judicially noticed adjudicative fact must be "capable of . . . ready determination."

A court may take judicial notice concerning the location of streets in a particular political subdivision within the court's jurisdiction. [Citations omitted.] In the trial of a criminal case, whether a political subdivision has a street identified by a particular name used in evidence is an adjudicative fact for judicial notice, but whether the street location mentioned in testimony is actually within the political subdivision is a matter of reasonable inference by the fact finder. *United States v. Mendell*, 447 F.2d 639 (7th Cir. 1971).

In Vejvoda's case, the trial court could properly take judicial notice that Grand Island, which is wholly within Hall County, has streets named "Vine" and "Oak." Furthermore, by simply referring to a map of Grand Island, the court could properly take judicial notice that the intersection of 7th and Vine Streets is within two blocks of the intersection of 8th and Oak Streets. At that point the site of the offense was an issue submissible to the trier of fact.

Although the location of streets within Grand Island is readily verifiable by reference to a city map, a source capable of ready verification and a cartographic source of information which cannot reasonably be questioned, the county court took another and impermissible step by judicially noticing the inference that Vejvoda was driving in Grand Island. The court's locational inference necessary for venue was not an adjudicative fact "capable of accurate and ready determination by resort to sources whose accuracy cannot reasonably be questioned." The county court erred in taking judicial notice of the inference that Vejvoda was driving in Grand Island and, therefore, that Vejvoda's drunk driving occurred in Grand Island. If Vejvoda had been convicted in a jury trial, we would reverse Vejvoda's conviction on

account of the trial court's invasion of the factfinding process within a jury's province in the trial of a criminal case. However, as mentioned, Vejvoda's case was tried to the court. Although Vejvoda's arrest by Edwards, a Grand Island police officer, does not establish venue, Edwards' official affiliation as a Grand Island police officer was a circumstance bearing on the issue of venue. When combined with other evidence, namely, the trial court's judicial notice of "Vine" and "Oak" as streets in Grand Island, Edwards' testimony supplied a sufficient evidentiary basis for a fact finder's determination that Vejvoda's drunk driving occurred in Grand Island, Hall County, Nebraska. "Harmless error exists in a jury trial of a criminal case when there is some incorrect conduct by the trial court which, on review of the entire record, did not materially influence the jury in a verdict adverse to a substantial right of the defendant." *State v. Watkins*, 227 Neb. 677, 686, 419 N.W.2d 660, 666 (1988). The preceding principle applicable in a jury trial of a criminal case is equally applicable to a judgment embodying factfinding in the bench trial of a criminal case.

Therefore, the trial court's error in judicially noticing the inferential location of Vejvoda's conduct, namely, drunk driving, is harmless error beyond a reasonable doubt. Vejvoda's conviction is affirmed.

Affirmed.

ROBINSON
v.
STATE

Court of Appeals of Georgia, Second Division

260 Ga. App. 186, 2003 Ga. App. LEXIS 366 (2003)

JUDGES: MIKELL, Judge. Johnson, P. J., and Eldridge, J., concur.

OPINION: MIKELL, Judge.

On December 15, 2001, Christina Robinson was charged with driving under the influence of alcohol. A bench trial was conducted on March 28, 2002, in the City of Jonesboro Municipal Court. The court convicted Robinson of DUI and sentenced her to one day in jail, a $963 fine, and sixty hours of community service. The Superior Court of Clayton County affirmed the conviction. Robinson appeals, arguing that her conviction cannot stand because the state failed to prove venue beyond a reasonable doubt. We agree and reverse the conviction.

Our Supreme Court has mandated that "venue is more than a mere procedural nicety; it is a [Georgia] constitutional requirement that all criminal cases be conducted in the county in which the crimes are alleged to have occurred. *Graham v. State*, 275 Ga. 290, 292 (2) (565 S.E.2d 467) (2002). In *Jones v. State*, 272 Ga. 900 (537 S.E.2d 80) (2000), the Supreme Court held that the state's failure to prove venue beyond a reasonable doubt warranted reversal of a defendant's felony murder conviction. Id. at 904 (3). The Court reasoned that:

Our Georgia Constitution requires that venue in all criminal cases must be laid in the county in which the crime was allegedly committed. Ga. Const. (1983), Art. VI, Sec. II, Par. VI; O.C.G.A. § 17-2-2. Venue is a jurisdictional fact, and is an essential element in proving that one is guilty of the crime charged. Like every other material allegation in the indictment, venue must be proved by the prosecution beyond a reasonable doubt. Proof of venue is a part of the State's case, and the State's failure to prove venue beyond a reasonable doubt renders the verdict contrary to law, without a sufficient evidentiary basis, and warrants reversal.

(Punctuation and footnotes omitted.) Id. at 901–902 (2). Accord *Walker v. State*, 258 Ga. App. 354 (2) (574 S.E.2d 317) (2002) (even when evidence demonstrated that the crimes were committed in the City of Atlanta, convictions must be reversed because the state failed to prove the county in which venue was proper).

We note that this Court is bound by decisions of the Supreme Court; therefore, we are without authority to overlook the requirement that venue be expressly proven, even in a case such as this where the City of Jonesboro is entirely within Clayton County. "The application of the doctrine of stare decisis is essential to the performance of a well-ordered system of jurisprudence." *Etkind v. Suarez*, 271 Ga. 352, 357 (5) (519 S.E.2d 210) (1999), citing *Cobb v. State*, 187 Ga. 448, 452 (200 SE 796) (1939).

The only evidence of venue presented in the case sub judice was the testimony of Sergeant Pat Cauchy of the City of Jonesboro Police Department that he observed Robinson driving within the city limits of Jonesboro. "By long-standing precedent, proving that a crime took place within a city without also proving that the city is entirely within a county does not establish venue." (Footnote omitted.) *Graham, supra* at 293 (2). Our research reveals no authority for the presumption that the trial court, acting as the finder of fact in a bench trial, took judicial notice of venue, nor is there any indication in the record that such judicial notice was taken in this case. Accordingly, because the state did not establish the county in which the crime was committed, we reverse Robinson's conviction. We note that retrial would not be barred by the Double Jeopardy Clause. See *Jones, supra* at 905 (4).

Judgment reversed. Johnson, P. J., and Eldridge, J., concur.

STATE
v.
SMITH

Court of Common Pleas of Delaware, Sussex

2006 Del. C.P. LEXIS 34 (2006)

Rosemary Betts Beauregard

DECISION ON STATE'S APPEAL

Pending before this Court is an appeal by the State of Delaware ("State") from a decision by the Justice of the Peace Court ("J.P. Court") suppressing evidence in favor of the defendant, Mack K. Smith ("Defendant") because it found that the arresting officer did not have probable cause to arrest. This Court set a schedule for briefing on the State's appeal. After reviewing the briefs provided, the Court finds and determines as follows outlined below.

PROCEDURAL BACKGROUND

The Defendant was arrested for committing a violation of 21Del. C. § 4177(a), Driving Under the Influence ("DUI"), and for committing a violation of 21 Del. C. § 4169, Speeding, on November 27, 2004. The State filed the Information in J.P. Court. Thereafter, the court scheduled the motion to suppress and trial for hearing on April 20, 2005. At the hearing, the court granted the Defendant's motion to suppress, and the State certified that the evidence was essential to the prosecution of the case, in accordance with 10 Del. C. § 9902(b). However, the court did not dismiss the case at the conclusion of the hearing. Instead, upon further inquiry by the State via letter on May 6, 2005, the court properly dismissed the case on May 24, 2005. The State timely filed its appeal pursuant to 10 Del. C. § 9902(c) on June 3, 2005.

STATEMENT OF FACTS

Trooper Mark Little ("Officer") stopped the Defendant on State Route 26 ("SR 26"), west of Dagsboro, Delaware, at 2:52 p.m. on November 27, 2004. The Officer testified that SR 26 has portions that curve and wind and portions that are straight. The Officer stated that he observed and stopped the vehicle as it traveled on a long, straight stretch of the roadway in the opposite direction that the Officer was traveling. Just prior to stopping the Defendant, the Officer observed his vehicle passing several other vehicles. According to the Officer's radar, the Defendant's vehicle was speeding, thus, the Officer stopped the Defendant, who appropriately pulled his vehicle over to the shoulder of the roadway. Upon approaching the vehicle and informing the Defendant that he had stopped him for speeding, the Officer observed that the Defendant had rosy cheeks, bloodshot eyes and that he omitted a moderate odor of alcohol, however, the Defendant spoke well and he appeared to have no trouble producing his license and registration. The Defendant admitted to the Officer that he had been speeding and that he had consumed approximately two beers earlier in the day.

Upon making his observations, the Officer administered a number of routine field sobriety tests to determine whether the Defendant was driving under the influence. First, the Officer administered the alphabet test, wherein the Defendant did not begin or end at the instructed letters and he recited other letters out of order. Second, the Officer asked the Defendant to count backwards from 100 to 85. The Defendant failed to stop at the appropriate number. Next, the Officer had the Defendant perform a finger dexterity test, which the Defendant successfully completed. Thereafter, the Officer asked the Defendant to exit his vehicle, which he did without any visible problem.

Once the Defendant was out of his vehicle, the Officer administered the horizontal gaze nystagmus test ("HGN"), a test on which he had received training during his education with the police academy in 1995, and as a field officer. Additionally, in 2001, the Officer became a certified HGN instructor, which enabled him to assist in instruction at the academy and a special event devised to educate certain members of the legal community. At the hearing, the Officer testified as to how the HGN test is administered, signals that the administrator looks for while conducting the test, and what factors other than alcohol consumption might create nystagmus in the subject, including strobe lights, rotating lights and rapidly moving traffic within close proximity. Furthermore, the Officer testified that when he performed the HGN test on the Defendant, he observed six out of six clues. On cross examination, the Officer admitted that while looking for nystagmus at maximum deviation, which was the second part of the three part test, he only caused the Defendant's eye to be held at the maximum deviation position for two to three seconds, rather than four seconds, which is required by the NHTSA manual. Additionally, the Officer acknowledged that the NHTSA manual states that the HGN test is only validated when it is administered in the prescribed fashion. The Officer also stated that strobe lights, rotating lights and some moving traffic in close proximity where all present when he administered the test.

After conducting the HGN test, the Officer then administered the walk and turn test. Although it is preferred that the test be conducted on a painted line, the Officer had the Defendant complete the test on the side of the road for safety reasons. Thus, the test was administered in an area, which the Officer described as grassy, with a slight slope designed for drainage purposes. According to the Officer, the slight grade did not affect the results of the test. The Officer described the weather as "windy and clear" at the time of the stop. While the Officer explained the test to the Defendant, he observed that the Defendant was unable to maintain his balance while standing with one foot in front of the other. When the Defendant completed the walk and turn test, the Officer perceived that the Defendant took ten steps instead of nine, and he took one large step instead of a series of small steps to make the turn, as instructed. The Defendant accurately took a second series of nine steps back to his original starting point.

Next, the Officer administered the one leg stand test. At that time, the Defendant informed the Officer that one of his feet was weaker than the other. Thus, the Officer suggested that he complete the test using his stronger foot for balance. The Officer observed that the Defendant raised his arms for balance, swayed, and put his foot down at different points throughout the test. Lastly, the Officer administered a portable breath test ("PBT") on the Defendant. Although the J.P. Court permitted such evidence, the State never established the results of that test.

After the court admitted the foregoing evidence, it ruled that the Officer lacked probable cause to arrest. In its decision, the court relied heavily on its personal knowledge of the roadway where a number of the field sobriety tests were administered to find that the area was not an acceptable place to administer the tests.

DISCUSSION

An appeal by the State pursuant to 10 Del. C. § 9902(c) shall be heard on the record. CCP Crim. R. 39(f). When addressing appeals from the J.P. Court this Court sits as an intermediate appellate court. The function of the Court in this capacity is to 'correct errors of law and to review the factual findings of the court below to determine if they are sufficiently supported by the record and are the product of an orderly and logical deductive process.' *State v. Richards*, 1998 WL 732960,

*1 (Del. Super.)(citing *Baker v. Connell*, 488 A.2d 1303 (Del. 1985). Therefore, the Court must apply a *de novo* standard of review to the lower court's legal determinations and a clearly erroneous standard to findings of fact. *State v. Arnold*, 2001 WL 985101, *2 (Del. Super.).

The State argues that the J.P. Court inappropriately relied on information outside of the record, and applied the wrong legal standard in its decision on the Defendant's motion to suppress. Accordingly, the first question presented is whether the J.P. Court erred when it considered facts that were not in evidence. The second question at issue is whether the J.P. Court erred when it decided that the Officer did not have probable cause to arrest the Defendant.

The J.P. Court Inappropriately Relied on Facts Not in Evidence

The transcript reflects that as the J.P. Court considered the evidence admitted for purposes of establishing probable cause, the court enlarged the record with its own personal knowledge. The sole witness at the hearing, the Officer who administered the tests, provided that the testing area was grassy, with a slight grade, but hard, not muddy and not rocky. However, upon ruling on the motion, the Court interjected its own knowledge of the area and disregarded the Officer's testimony. Specifically, when determining the probative value of the walk and turn test and the one leg stand test, the court spoke as to its personal knowledge of the roadway. The court noted that the tests were improper because they were conducted,

"on the side of a road, on a road that I know, and everyone else in Sussex County, knows it is not only a grass shoulder road but a very tapered grass shoulder road into a heavy ditch in low lying swamp ground. We know what that road is. We know why they call it a Nine Foot Road. It was a miraculous piece of construction when they put that concrete road on that piece of road on 26 because it is a low lying piece of swamp that was drained off to put into agriculture. I mean I know all these things. And this is not the place to do that test."

Because the facts depended on by the J.P. Court were not admitted into evidence, the question arises whether reliance on those facts constituted error. The Delaware Rules of Evidence provide that courts are permitted to take judicial notice of an adjudicative fact. D.R.E. 202. However, courts may only take judicial notice of a fact that is not subject to reasonable dispute in that it either is generally known within the territorial jurisdiction of the court, or it is capable of accurate and ready determination in sources whose accuracy cannot reasonably be questioned. D.R.E. 202(b). The doctrine of judicial notice should be applied with due care because if there is even a mere possibility of dispute as to whether the fact asserted is accurate, or of common knowledge, judicial notice is inappropriate and evidence is required to establish the fact. *Fawcett v. State*, 697 A.2d 385, 388 (Del. 1997).

Although the court stated that "everyone in Sussex County, knows [the area] is not only a grass shoulder road but a very tapered grass shoulder road into a heavy ditch in low lying swamp ground," the Officer's contrary testimony wherein he described the testing area as grassy, with a slight grade, but hard, not muddy and not rocky indicates that the conditions of that area at the time of administration were indeed subject to reasonable dispute. The court did not indicate that it determined the Officer was untrustworthy. Rather, the court relied solely on its own opinion of the conditions that may or may not have been present in the testing area to discredit the tests. The court's opinion is therefore not an adjudicative fact. Accordingly, I find that the J.P. Court committed plain error when it relied on evidence that was outside of the record in its decision finding that the Officer did not have probable cause to arrest the Defendant.

Probable Cause Existed

The State argues that the court improperly "diluted each [of the Officer's probable cause] observation[s] with hypothetically innocent explanations and then rejected them," without considering the Officer's observations under the totality of the circumstances.

* * *

[The Court reviewed the facts supporting a finding of probable cause.]

In conclusion, the Officer made the following observations of the Defendant (1) blood shot eyes, (2) rosy cheeks, (3) moderate odor of alcohol, (4) admission of consuming alcohol, (5) failure to follow instruction and properly perform the alphabet, counting and walk and turn tests, (6) trouble maintaining balance on the walk and turn and one leg stand tests, (7) several clues present upon application of the HGN test and (8) Speeding. Case law suggests that such factors are adequate to establish probable case.

* * *

CONCLUSION

This Court concludes that the J.P. Court inappropriately relied on facts not in evidence. Furthermore, this Court finds that the Officer had probable cause to believe that the Defendant had been driving under the influence when he arrested the Defendant. Thus, the Court hereby reverses the J.P. Court's decision on the Defendant's motion to suppress and remands the case for further proceeding consistent with this Order.

IT IS SO ORDERED, this 6th day of June 2006.

The Honorable Rosemary Betts Beauregard

Cases Relating to Chapter 6

Presumptions, Inferences, and Stipulations

STATE
v.
JACKSON

112 Wash. 2d 867, 774 P.2d 1211 (1989)

En Banc. Callow, C.J. Utter, Dolliver, Dore, Pearson, and Andersen, J.J., concur. Smith, J., concurs in the result only; Durham and Brachtenbach, JJ., dissent by separate opinion.

CALLOW, OPINION:

The defendant, Destin L. Jackson, was convicted of attempted second degree burglary. He contends the trial court erred in giving an inference of intent instruction.

The issues presented are:

1. In an attempted burglary case, is it error to instruct the jury that it may infer the defendant acted with intent to commit a crime within the building from the fact that the defendant may have attempted entrance into the building?

* * *

3. Does federal due process require the State to plead the nature of the crime a defendant intended to commit inside the building he tried to enter? See and compare *State v. Bergeron*, 105 Wn.2d 1, 711 P.2d 1000 (1985), overruling *State v. Johnson*, 100 Wn.2d 607, 674 P.2d 145 (1983).

We hold the trial court cannot instruct the jury, where the charge is attempted burglary, that it may infer the defendant acted with intent to commit a crime within a building, where the evidence is that the defendant may

have attempted entrance into a building, but there exist other equally reasonable conclusions which follow from the circumstances.

On the evening of February 2, 1986, a Seattle police officer received a dispatch call to proceed to Neals Tailoring and Beverage Shop. As the officer was coming around a corner he saw the defendant kicking the front door of the shop. The defendant was taking short running kicks at the door and bouncing off. The kicks were aimed at the window area of the door. Once the defendant spotted the officer, he proceeded to briskly walk away. The officer placed the defendant under arrest. The officer testified that no one else was in the vicinity and that the defendant was constantly in his sight. When the door was examined it was found that about 10 inches of Plexiglas had been pushed inward and part of the wood stock around the Plexiglas was broken out of its frame. Footprints existed on the Plexiglas and they appeared to match the shoes of the defendant. The Plexiglas was not taken into custody, even though the right edge had been pushed inward, as it still prevented entry into the business. The molding which holds the glass in the door was broken on the inside, and there was wood on the floor. The pressure from the outside tore the molding off on the inside.

The defendant was charged with attempted second degree burglary. At trial, the defendant denied kicking the door. He claimed he noticed the broken door as he was walking by the shop and was arrested as he continued on his way.

At the conclusion of the State's case, the defendant moved for a dismissal asserting:

This may get to attempting malicious mischief, but to stack inferences of intent as to what was intended in terms of kicking or knocking out the door, then another inference if he intended to break in, he intended to commit a crime is beyond the limits of reasonable inferences. One inference is not enough. There is evidence to support one inference that he intended to break in, but you are asking, or the State would be asking, your honor, for the jury to do is to stack inferences. First of all, you have to infer he intended to break in based on his conduct. If you believe that once—that he did it, then that he intended to commit a crime. Stacking inferences is something that is beyond a prima facie case. Therefore, the case should proceed only on attempted criminal trespass or malicious mischief.

The trial court denied the motion. At the conclusion of the trial, the court heard exceptions to the proposed instructions to the jury.

[Defense Counsel] The defense would except to your Honor's failure to give the lesser included. The defense would suggest that the attempt statute is so broad. When you get down to what is alleged, namely, Destin Jackson broke the door in an attempt to get in that, indeed, legally and factually you would have to commit malicious mischief, or attempted burglary, which in a manner which has been charged in this case. For that reason, I would except to your Honor's failure to give that lesser included instruction. . . .

[Defense Counsel] In addition, the defense would except to your Honor's giving the inference Instruction No. 10. Factually, the cases do not support that inference. The instruction reads, "A person who remains unlawfully in a building with intent to commit a crime." However, the record does not support the allegation Mr. Jackson even if you assume it was Mr. Jackson who entered or remained unlawfully, he is charged with attempting to do so. Again, in the motion to dismiss at the end of the State's case, you are asking the jury first to infer what his intent is, then asking them to infer what his intent was assuming the inference, that is inappropriate. It is clear on the face of the instruction it doesn't

apply here because no injury was or entry was actually made. That is the reason this instruction is inappropriate and the defense would except to it being given.

. . . [Defense Counsel] Your Honor, in terms of our record, then having changed that, the defense would still suggest it is inappropriate because it stacks inferences. It requires the jury to make one conclusion, then, based on that conclusion, suggests they make another inference. It is a permissive inference as outlined here, but it is a comment on the evidence, if you find this then you can find that, then move on from there. The defense believes it is stacking inferences and would rely on that as previously explained.

Over the defendant's objection the court gave the following jury instruction:

A person who *attempts to* enter or remain unlawfully in a building may be inferred to have acted with intent to commit a crime against a person or property therein unless such entering or remaining shall be explained by evidence satisfactory to the jury to have been made without such criminal intent. This inference is not binding upon you and it is for you to determine what weight, if any, such inference is to be given.

(Italics ours.) WPIC 60.05 does not include the italicized words "attempts to". The defendant objected to the trial court's failure to give a lesser included instruction. (See WPIC 4.11.) However, the defendant did not propose an instruction setting out the crime, nor did he except to the instruction which defined burglary. These issues were not raised in the petition for review; only the objection to the inference of intent instruction and whether there is evidence of an actual entry are raised before us. The jury found the defendant guilty as charged.

In ruling on the motion for new trial the trial court stated in part:

The Court: [C]ounsel reminded me that there was a motion for a new trial brought by the defense in regard to an instruction, . . . which I gave to the jury, in regard to the inference of intent to commit a crime therein, this being an attempted burglary in the second degree in which the jury found defendant was guilty of the crime of attempted burglary in the second degree.

The trial court denied the motion for new trial, the defendant appealed and we granted a petition for review after the Court of Appeals affirmed his conviction.

I.

Quaere: What Is the Function of an Inference and When Is an Inference Permissible?

" ' "Presumptions" . . . "may be looked on as the bats of the law, flitting in the twilight but disappearing in the sunshine of actual facts." . . .' " *Bradley v. S.L. Savidge, Inc.* 13 Wn.2d 28, 123 P.2d 780 (1942) (citing *Beeman v. Puget Sound Traction, Light & Power Co.*, 79 Wash. 137, 139, 139 P. 1087 (1914) (quoting *Paul v. United Rys. Co.*, 152 Mo. App. 577, 134 S.W. 3 (1911))).

The basic notions upon which presumptions are grounded are simple. When fact A (the basic fact) is proved at a trial the courts will by rule assume that fact B (the presumed fact) exists for certain purposes and with certain limitations. This specific assumption or inference by application of a general rule is a presumption. 5 K. TEGLAND, WASH PRAC., EVIDENCE A4 65, at 127 (2d ed. 1982).

Most presumptions have come into existence primarily because the judges have believed that proof of fact B renders the inference of the existence of fact A so probable that it is sensible and timesaving to assume the truth of the fact A until the adversary disproves it. E. CLEARY, MCCORMICK ON EVIDENCE A4 343, at 969 (3d ed. 1984).

We follow *Bradley v. S.L. Savidge, Inc.*, *supra,* in quoting the definition of presumption as defined in *Heidelbach v. Campbell*, 95 Wash. 661, 668, 164 P. 247 (1917):

A presumption is an inference, affirmative or disaffirmative, of the truth of a proposition of fact which is drawn by a process of reasoning from some one or more matters of known fact. The presumption arises from a want of knowledge of the truth of the proposition. It is in the nature of evidence, and if it be known whether the given proposition is true or false, there can be no presumption because the fact is established which the presumption tends to prove or disprove.

Presumptions are one thing; inferences another. Presumptions are assumptions of fact which the law requires to be made from another fact or group of facts; inferences are logical deductions or conclusions from an established fact. Presumptions deal with legal processes, whereas inferences deal with mental processes. *Lappin v. Lucurell*, 13 Wn. App. 277, 284, 534 P.2d 1038, 94 A.L.R.3d 594 (1975). "An inference is simply a logical deduction or conclusion which the law allows, but does not require, following the establishment of the basic facts." 5 K. Tegland, at 127–28.

RCW 9A.52.040 creates an "inference of intent" as applied to burglary and trespass as follows:

In any prosecution for burglary, any person who enters or remains unlawfully in a building may be inferred to have acted with intent to commit a crime against a person or property therein, unless such entering or remaining shall be explained by evidence satisfactory to the trier of fact to have been made without such criminal intent.

RCW 9A.52.040 is reflected in WPIC 60.05 to read:

A person who enters or remains unlawfully in a building may be inferred to have acted with intent to commit a crime against a person or property therein [unless such entering or remaining shall be explained by evidence satisfactory to the jury to have been made without such criminal intent]. This inference is not binding upon you and it is for you to determine what weight, if any, such inference is to be given.

Both RCW 9A.52.040 and WPIC 60.05 permit the inference of one fact from another as a presumption. Burglary consists of two elements; entry or unlawfully remaining upon another's premises, and intent. RCW 9A.52.030. RCW 9A.52.040 provides that a burglary may be inferred (intent exists) if one either unlawfully remains upon another's premises or an entry occurs. "Inferences and presumptions are a staple of our adversary system of factfinding. It is often necessary for the trier of fact to determine the existence of an element of the crime—that is, an 'ultimate' or 'elemental' fact—from the existence of one or more 'evidentiary' or 'basic' facts." *County Court of Ulster Cy. v. Allen*, 442 U.S. 140, 156, 60 L. Ed. 2d 777, 99 S. Ct. 2213 (1979). "The most common evidentiary device is the entirely permissive inference or presumption, which allows—but does not require—the trier of fact to infer the elemental fact from proof by the prosecutor of the basic one and which places no burden of any kind on the defendant." *Ulster Cy. Court*, at 157.

WPIC 60.05 provides for a permissive inference or presumption, which allows the trier of fact to either infer the elemental fact from proof by the prosecutor, or reject the inference. WPIC 60.05 does not apply to those attempting to enter or remain unlawfully "unless it can at least be said with substantial assurance that the presumed fact is more likely than not to flow from the proved fact on which it is made to depend." [Citation omitted.]

For a trier of fact to draw inferences from proven circumstances, the inferences must be "rationally related" to the proven facts. *State v. Jeffries*, 105 Wn.2d 398, 442, 717 P.2d 722, *cert. denied*, 479 U.S. 922 (1986). A rational connection must exist between the initial fact proven and the further fact presumed. "The jury is permitted to infer from one fact the existence of another essential to guilt, if reason and experience support the inference." *Tot v. United States*, 319 U.S. 463, 467, 87 L. Ed. 1519, 63 S. Ct. 1241 (1943).

For a criminal statutory presumption to meet the test of constitutionality the presumed fact must follow beyond a reasonable doubt from the proven fact. [Citation omitted.]

WPIC 60.05 may be given as a proper instruction in a burglary case. However, where the State pleads and proves only attempted burglary, as here, this instruction

is improper. In *State v. Bergeron, supra*, the defendant signed a statement wherein he admitted that when he threw a rock through a window he intended to enter the premises. In *Bergeron* we reasoned that while intent may be inferred from all the facts and circumstances surrounding the commission of an act, intent may not be inferred "from conduct that is patently equivocal." In order to give an instruction that an inference of an intent to commit a crime existed in a burglary case, there must be evidence of entering or remaining unlawfully in a building. The instruction on intent cannot be given without evidence to support it and that must place the defendant within a building. *State v. Ogden*, 21 Wn. App. 44, 49, 584 P.2d 957 (1978).

A presumption is only permissible when no more than one conclusion can be drawn from any set of circumstances. An inference should not arise where there exist other reasonable conclusions that would follow from the circumstances. Here the inferences are twofold: (1) attempted burglary or (2) vandalism or malicious destruction. Therefore, an inference cannot follow that there was intent to commit a crime within the building just by the defendants' shattering of the window in the door. This evidence is consistent with two different interpretations; one indicating attempted burglary, a felony; and the other malicious mischief, a misdemeanor.

II.

Quaere: Could the Giving of the Instruction Be Considered Harmless Error?

"A 'harmless error' is one which is "trivial, or formal, or merely academic, and was not prejudicial to the substantial rights of the party assigning it, and in no way affected the final outcome of the case."" *State v. Pam*, 98 Wn.2d 748, 754, 659 P.2d 454 (1983) (quoting *State v. Wanrow*, 88 Wn.2d 221, 237, 559 P.2d 548 (1977)). Here, the giving of the instruction could not be harmless error since it tended to prove an element of the commission of a crime. The instruction coming from the trial judge indicated that the defendant had entered the building and did so with the intent to commit a crime against the property therein. We do not need to determine whether the "overwhelming evidence" test would be applicable since we are convinced the inference of intent instruction was not harmless. See *State v. Guloy*, 104 Wn.2d 412, 426, 705 P.2d 1182 (1985).

III.

* * *

IV.

Quaere: Must the State Specify the Crime a Defendant Intended To Commit Upon Entry Into Property?

We have held that our burglary statutes simply require an intent to commit a crime against a person or property inside the burglarized premises. As stated in *State v. Bergeron*, 105 Wn.2d 1, 4, 711 P.2d 1000 (1985):

The intent to commit a specific named crime inside the burglarized premises is not an "element" of the crime of burglary in the State of Washington. . . . The intent required by our burglary statutes is simply the intent to commit any crime against a person or property inside the burglarized premises.

We adhere to the decision in *Bergeron*. The conviction of attempted second degree burglary is reversed and the cause is remanded for a new trial.

STATE
v.
PURCELL

APPELLATE COURT OF ILLINOIS, SECOND DISTRICT

325 Ill. App. 3d 551, 758 N.E.2d 895, 2001 Ill. App. LEXIS 837 (2001)

JUDGES: JUSTICE GEIGER delivered the opinion of the court. HUTCHINSON, P.J., and McLAREN, J., concur.

The defendant, Willard Purcell, has filed the instant appeal pursuant to Supreme Court Rule 604(c) (188 Ill. 2d R. 604(c)), seeking review of the September 10, 2001, order of the

circuit court of Winnebago County denying bail. On appeal, the defendant argues (1) that section 110-4(b) of the Code of Criminal Procedure of 1963 (the Code) (725 ILCS 5/110-4(b) (West 2000)) is unconstitutional; and (2) that the trial court erred in denying his request for pretrial bail.

On August 2001, the defendant was arrested and indicted on four counts of first-degree murder (720 ILCS 5/9-1(a)(2) (a)(3), (b)(19) (West 2000)). The defendant was alleged to have killed his wife, Barbara Purcell, by striking her repeatedly in the head with a blunt object. If convicted of the charged offense, the defendant may receive a sentence of life imprisonment. 730 ILCS 5/5-8-1(a)(1)(b) (West 2000).

Following his arrest, the defendant filed a motion requesting bail. The defendant also filed a motion seeking a determination that section 110-4 of the Code (725 ILCS 5/110-4 (West 2000)) is unconstitutional. Section 110-4(a) provides that a defendant may not obtain bail where "the proof is evident or the presumption great" that the defendant committed a capital offense or an offense for which he may be sentenced to life imprisonment. 725 ILCS 5/110-4(a) (West 2000). Section 110-4(b) places the burden of demonstrating that the proof of guilt is not evident and the presumption of guilt not great upon the individual seeking release on bail. 725 ILCS 5/110-4(b) (West 2000). In his motion before the trial court, the defendant argued that subsection (b) violates the presumption of innocence accorded to criminal defendants while awaiting trial. See *Stack v. Boyle*, 342 U.S. 1, 96 L. Ed. 3, 72 S. Ct. 1 (1951).

On August 15, 2001, the trial court denied the defendant's motion to declare section 110-4(b) of the Code unconstitutional. Then, on September 10, 2001, following a hearing, the trial court denied the defendant's motion for pretrial bail. The trial court found that the defendant did not meet his burden of demonstrating that the proof of his guilt was not evident and that the presumption of his guilt was not great. The defendant then filed the instant appeal pursuant to Supreme Court Rule 604(c).

We will first address the defendant's constitutional argument. The right of an accused to obtain pretrial bail is governed by article I, section 9, of the Illinois Constitution of 1970. Ill. Const. 1970, art. I, A4 9. That section provides:

> "All persons shall be bailable by sufficient sureties, except the following offenses where the proof is evident or the presumption great: capital offenses and offenses for which a sentence of life imprisonment may be imposed as a consequence of conviction ∗∗∗." III. Const. 1970, art. I, A4 9.

Section 110-4 of the Code is a codification of this constitutional provision. That section provides:

> "(a) All persons shall be bailable before conviction, except the following offenses where the proof is evident or the presumption great that the defendant is guilty of the offense: capital offenses and offenses for which a sentence of life imprisonment may be imposed as a consequence of conviction ∗∗∗.

> (b) A person seeking release on bail who is charged with a capital offense or an offense for which a sentence of life imprisonment may be imposed shall not be bailable until a hearing is held wherein such person has the burden of demonstrating that the proof of his guilt is not evident and the presumption is not great." 725 ILCS 5/110-4 (West 2000).

Subsection (b) goes beyond the language of article I, section 9, and was added to clarify the issues of proof that might arise during bail proceedings. 725 ILCS Ann. 5/110-4, Committee Comments 1963, at 48 (Smith-Hurd 1992). The language contained in this subsection was taken from section 68(2) of the Code of Criminal Procedure promulgated by the American Law Institute in 1930. ALI Code of Criminal Procedure A4 68(2) (1930). Under this provision, the burden falls upon the defendant seeking pretrial bail to establish that the proof of his guilt is not substantial.

As the defendant correctly notes, the due process clauses of both the United States and the Illinois Constitutions guarantee the accused that he will not be convicted on proof less than reasonable doubt of every fact necessary to constitute the crime with which he is charged. U.S. Const., amend. XIV; Ill. Const. 1970, art. I, A4 2; *Sullivan v. Louisiana*, 508 U.S. 275, 277–78, 124 L. Ed. 2d 182, 187–88, 113 S. Ct. 2078, 2080 (1993). The complement to this guarantee is that the State bears the burden of proof and that the accused is presumed innocent. *People v. Devine*, 295 Ill. App. 3d 537, 544, 229 Ill. Dec. 796, 692 N.E.2d 785 (1998). The presumption of innocence attaches to the accused from the onset of the proceedings and is one of the underpinnings of an accused's right to bail. See *Stack*, 342 U.S. at 4, 96 L. Ed. at 6, 72 S. Ct. at 3. The traditional right to freedom before conviction permits the unhampered preparation of a defense and serves to prevent the infliction of punishment prior to conviction. *Stack*, 342 U.S. at 4, 96 L. Ed. at 6, 72 S. Ct. at 3.

The question of whether section 110-4(b) infringes upon an accused's presumption of innocence has not previously been addressed by an Illinois court. However, Illinois' constitutional bail provision is not unique; the constitutions of most states contain similar provisions guaranteeing bail to the accused, except in cases punishable by death or life imprisonment where the proof is evident or the presumption great. As a result, there are a number of reported cases nationwide in which courts have considered the question of whether the State or the accused bears the burden during a bail hearing for an offense for which death or life imprisonment may be imposed, to show, or to disprove, that the proof is evident or the presumption great. See H. Hirschberg, *Annotation, Upon Whom Rests Burden of Proof, Where Bail is Sought Before Judgment But After Indictment in Capital Case, as to Whether Proof is Evident or the Presumption Great*, 89 A.L.R.2d 355 (1963). The decisions in these cases have been conflicting, some holding that the State has the burden, and others holding that the burden falls on the accused.

In those cases placing the burden upon the State to prove that the accused's guilt is evident or that the presumption of such guilt is great, the courts have relied upon the presumption of innocence. See *Orona v. District Court*, 184 Colo. 55, 518 P.2d

839 (1974); *In re Steigler*, 250 A.2d 379 (Del. 1969); *State v. Arthur*, 390 So. 2d 717 (Fla. 1980); *Young v. Russell*, 332 S.W.2d 629 (Ky. 1960); *Application of Wheeler*, 81 Nev. 495, 406 P.2d 713 (1965); *Fountaine v. Mullen*, 117 R.I. 262, 366 A.2d 1138 (1976). These courts have explained that the presumption of innocence precludes any inference that the accused committed the charged offense. Finding that an indictment has no evidentiary value, these courts have held that the indictment does not raise a presumption, prima facie or otherwise, that the accused is guilty. See, e.g., *Arthur*, 390 So. 2d at 719–20. Additionally, in placing the burden of proof on the State, these courts have explained that the right to bail is constitutionally guaranteed, subject only to exceptions for certain designated offenses. These courts hold that the State has the burden to show the existence of one of the exceptions and prove that the defendant is not entitled to bail. See *Beck v. State*, 648 S.W.2d 7 (Tex. Crim. App. 1983).

For example, in *Arthur*, the Florida Supreme Court held that the presumption of innocence protected the accused for all purposes while awaiting trial and that it was the State's burden to prove the facts which removed the accused's entitlement to bail. *Arthur*, 390 So. 2d at 719–20. The court explained that, under the State's constitution, bail could only be denied when the accused was charged with a crime punishable by death of life imprisonment and that the proof of guilt was evident or the presumption great. The court therefore held that the indictment or information, standing alone, could not serve as proof or a presumption of guilt. *Arthur*, 390 So. 2d at 719. Rather, the court held that the State was required to come forward with an independent showing that the proof of guilt was evident or the presumption of guilt great. *Arthur*, 390 So. 2d at 720. The court also noted that, as a matter of convenience, fairness, and practicality, it was preferable that the State carry the burden of proof, as it was presumably in a better position to present to the court the evidence upon which it intended to rely. *Arthur*, 390 So. 2d at 720.

In Wheeler, the Nevada Supreme Court similarly concluded that the State bears the burden to show that the accused should not be admitted bail. Wheeler, 81 Nev. at 499,

406 P.2d at 716. The Nevada constitution provides that "all persons shall be bailable by sufficient sureties; unless for Capital Offenses when the proof is evident, or the presumption great." Nev. Const., art. 1, A4 7. Construing this language, the court concluded that all offenses are bailable, including capital offenses, as a matter of right. However, the court noted that the right to bail in a capital case could be limited upon a showing that the proof of guilt is evident or the presumption great. *Wheeler*, 81 Nev. at 499, 406 P.2d at 715. Explaining that the accused is presumed innocent of the charged offense until proven guilty, the court held that the burden rests on the State to show that the right to bail is limited rather than absolute. *Wheeler*, 81 Nev. at 499, 406 P.2d at 716.

In *Steigler*, the Delaware Supreme Court considered the effect of a statute similar to section 110-4(b) of the Code. *Steigler*, 250 A.2d at 382. That statute placed the burden upon the accused seeking pretrial bail in a capital case to demonstrate that "there is good ground to doubt the truth of the accusation." *Steigler*, 250 A.2d at 382. Although the court did not hold the statute unconstitutional, it nonetheless found that the burden of going forward with evidence at a bail hearing could not be placed upon the accused. The court explained:

"Delaware seemingly [is] among the states holding that the indictment raises a prima facie presumption of proof positive or presumption great. We think, however, the rule, if indeed it has been the rule of this State, offends against a basic concept of our criminal law—the presumption of innocence until found guilty after trial. There is something inherently contradictory in maintaining the presumption of innocence until final conviction and, at the same time, presuming probable guilt from the fact of indictment when the accused seeks to exercise his constitutional right to bail.

The right to bail is constitutionally conferred in all offenses with one exception—a capital offense where the proof is positive or the presumption great. Since the general rule is admission to bail, the State, if it seeks to invoke the exception to the rule, must bear the burden of going forward with the evidence to produce facts to warrant the invocation of the exception." *Steigler*, 250 A.2d at 382–83.

The court therefore held that the State must go forward with evidence tending to show "proof positive or presumption great." The court explained that, once this has been done, the State has sufficiently laid the basis for the application of the exception to the constitutional right to bail and the burden of proof then falls upon the accused to demonstrate the contrary. *Steigler*, 250 A.2d at 383.

Other jurisdictions have held that the burden to show that the proof of guilt is not evident or the presumption of guilt not great falls upon the accused seeking bail. The courts in these jurisdictions have found that the indictment raises a prima facie presumption of guilt that the accused must overcome by sufficient rebuttal evidence. See *Partlow v. State*, 453 N.E.2d 259 (Ind. 1983); *State v. Green*, 275 So. 2d 184 (La. 1973); *Fischer v. Ball*, 212 Md. 517, 129 A.2d 822 (1957). This presumption is held to create an inference of guilt for all purposes except the actual trial. As already noted, this was the view taken by the American Law Institute in its 1930 Code of Criminal Procedure. ALI Code of Criminal Procedure A4 68(2) (1930).

For example, in *Green*, the Louisiana Supreme Court held that a state statute that placed the burden of proof on the accused seeking to obtain pretrial bail in capital cases did not violate the presumption of innocence or the due process clause of the fourteenth amendment to the United States Constitution. *Green*, 275 So. 2d at 186. The statute provided that "after indictment [the burden of proof] is on the defendant to show that the proof is not evident nor the presumption great that he is guilty of the capital offense." *Green*, 275 So. 2d at 185, citing La. Code Crim. Proc. art. 313. The court explained:

"The presumption of innocence is a guide to the jury. If it were absolute and operative at every stage of a prosecution, the defendant could never be jailed until conviction. It does not prevent arrest. There is little relationship between the right to bail

and the presumption of innocence. The presumption of innocence is operative and protects against conviction, not against arrest (which is taking into custody). We find no merit in defendant's argument that La.C.Cr.P. art. 313 is unconstitutional." *Green*, 275 So. 2d at 186.

In *Fischer*, a Maryland court also concluded that the finding of the indictment created, at the very least, a prima facie presumption of guilt. *Fischer*, 212 Md. at 523–24, 129 A.2d at 826. The court held that the State had the right to rely on this presumption during a hearing to determine pretrial bond. Thus, the court held that, when the accused seeks to remain at liberty on bail, the burden is upon him to rebut the presumption by introducing evidence that the proof of guilt is not positive and the presumption not great. *Fischer*, 212 Md. at 523–24, 129 A.2d at 826. Accord *Partlow v. State*, 453 N.E.2d 259 (Ind. 1983); *State v. Monroe*, 397 So. 2d 1258 (La. 1981).

After careful consideration of the foregoing authorities, we conclude that the correct approach is taken by those jurisdictions that place the burden upon the State to prove that the proof of the accused's guilt is evident and the presumption great. We believe that such an approach is required by the due process guarantees of both the United States and Illinois Constitutions. As noted above, the United States Supreme Court has held that the presumption of innocence applies during bail proceedings and is a primary underpinning of allowing pretrial bail. See *Stack*, 342 U.S. at 4, 96 L. Ed. at 6, 72 S. Ct. at 3. Accordingly, we must disagree with those jurisdictions that have held the presumption of innocence is not operative until the time of trial.

Because the presumption of innocence is operative during pretrial bail proceedings, we fail to see how an accused can be constitutionally required to prove that the evidence of his guilt is not great. Such a burden plainly flies in the face of the presumption of innocence and impermissibly shifts the evidentiary burden from the State to the accused. See *Arthur*, 390 So. 2d at 720. The presumption of innocence guarantees that the accused has no obligation to come forward with any evidence concerning the proof, or lack thereof, of any of the elements of the charged offense. Rather, as both the federal and state constitutions protect the right to bail, we believe that the State must have the burden of demonstrating that the defendant should be deprived of such a right.

Additionally, we note that principles of basic fairness also require that the burden of proof fall upon the State. See *Arthur*, 390 So. 2d at 720. As a practical matter, the accused is not in a good position to gather and present evidence during a bail hearing, as the criminal proceeding has been only recently initiated and the accused is in jail. The State, on the other hand, has ready access to the evidence of the alleged offense and is in a better position to present such evidence during a bail hearing. Indeed, in most cases, the State already will have presented evidence in order to secure an indictment from the grand jury.

* * *

We therefore hold that, in those cases where bail may be denied, the burden falls upon the State to show that the defendant is not entitled to bail because the proof of his guilt is evident and the presumption great. Accordingly, we find that section 110-4(b) of the Code is unconstitutional.

We further hold that invalidity of subsection (b) is not fatal to the remainder of the statute. This court has an obligation to uphold legislative enactments whenever reasonably possible, and we may excuse an offending provision of a statute and preserve the remainder provided the remainder is complete in and of itself and is capable of being executed wholly independently of the severed portion. *People v. Sanders*, 182 Ill. 2d 524, 534, 231 Ill. Dec. 573, 696 N.E.2d 1144 (1998).

* * *

For the foregoing reasons, we vacate the trial court's September 10, 2001, order, and we remand the cause for a new hearing upon the defendant's motion for pretrial bail conducted in conformity with the views expressed herein.

Order vacated; cause remanded.

HUTCHINSON, P.J., and McLAREN, J., concur.

BOZEMAN
v.
STATE

Court of Appeal of Florida, Fourth District
931 So. 2d 1006, 2006 Fla. App. LEXIS 8986 (2006)

Taylor, J. Gunther, J., concurs. Farmer, J., dissents with opinion.

Taylor, J.

Appellant Oliver Bozeman was tried by jury and convicted of grand theft of an automobile. He appeals, arguing that the trial court erred in instructing the jury on the inference to be drawn from possession of recently stolen property. He argues that the evidence was insufficient to show the exclusive possession required for the instruction. We disagree and affirm appellant's conviction.

While on routine patrol in Lauderdale Lakes shortly after midnight, Deputy William Leffew observed a 1990 Mazda pushing a 1967 Chevrolet Malibu. The deputy stopped the two vehicles. Appellant was driving the Mazda. His brother, Antoine McIntyre, was in the front passenger seat. Appellant was using the Mazda to push the Chevrolet Malibu. The Malibu had been stolen from a residence earlier that evening. Joe Bolling was in the driver's seat of the stolen Malibu. The Malibu's headlights were not on and the engine was not running. There was no vehicle tag on the Malibu. Inside, the vehicle's steering wheel column was damaged and there was no key in the ignition. The Malibu's driver side window was shattered and broken glass was on that side of the floorboard. When stopped, appellant told the deputy that McIntyre had purchased the Malibu and that he was merely helping him transport it to McIntyre's house. All three men were arrested at the scene for theft of the Chevrolet Malibu.

Co-defendant Bolling pled guilty to grand theft and possession of burglary tools. When he was sentenced, he told the judge that appellant had nothing to do with the crime. Bolling also testified at appellant's trial. He said that he and McIntyre elicited appellant's help in moving the car without telling appellant that the car was stolen.

During the jury charge conference, defense counsel argued that the standard instruction allowing the jury to infer that the defendant knew that the property was stolen based on his possession of the recently stolen property should not be given because it did not apply. The trial court disagreed and instructed the jury, as follows:

Proof of possession of recently stolen property, unless satisfactorily explained, gives rise to an inference that the person in possession of the property knew or should have known that the property had been stolen.

Fla. Std. Jury Instr. (Crim.) 14.1 at 270.

The jury found appellant guilty of grand theft. He was sentenced to ten years in prison as a habitual felony offender. On appeal, he challenges the above instruction and his sentence.

Appellant argues that the trial court erred in instructing the jury on the inference arising from possession of recently stolen property because the evidence did not demonstrate that appellant possessed the stolen vehicle or that he possessed the vehicle to the extent that he exercised any dominion and control over it.

A defendant to have a jury determine whether he has the requisite predicate convictions for a habitual felony offender sentence"), and *Washington v. State*, 895 So. 2d 1141, 1143 (Fla. 4th DCA 2005) (holding that "shotgun" notice of intent to seek habitual offender sentence is valid).

At trial, appellant's defense to the grand theft charge was that he did not know that the car was stolen. The jury instruction at issue isl a standard jury instruction in theft cases that permits the prosecution to prove by inference that a defendant knew or should have known that property in his possession was stolen. *See Scobee v. State*, 488 So. 2d 595, 598 (Fla. 1st DCA 1986). However, before the prosecution can receive the benefit of this jury instruction, it must first produce evidence that the defendant possessed the property. [Citation omitted.] The state must demonstrate that the possession was personal, i.e., involved a distinct and conscious assertion of possession by the accused, and that the possession was exclusive. [Citations omitted].

As the first district explained in *Scobee*:

The "exclusive" requirement does not mean that defendant's possession must be separate from the possession of all other persons. The joint possession of two or more persons acting in concert is "exclusive" as to any one of them.

Scobee, 488 So. 2d at 598; *see also Walker v. State*, 896 So. 2d 712, 720 n.5 (Fla. 2005) (approving *Scobee's* analysis of the "exclusive" requirement in joint possession cases).

In *People v. White*, 99 Ill. App. 2d 270, 240 N.E.2d 342 (Ill. App. 1968), officers observed the defendant pushing a recently stolen automobile into an alley at 3:00 a.m., and another person sitting at the wheel of the vehicle. When the officers approached, the man at the steering wheel fled. The court stated that the evidence established that "the car was in the joint possession of the defendant and his partner." *Id.* at 343. In finding the facts sufficient to raise a presumption of guilt and warrant a conviction for theft, the court explained that "[a]lthough the defendant was not inside the vehicle, he was exerting control over it by pushing in into the alley." *Id.*

Similarly, in this case, the evidence showed that appellant exercised dominion and control over the Malibu by pushing it while Bolling controlled the car's steering and braking. Without appellant's actions, the car could not have been moved. The two men jointly controlled the car and jointly possessed it. Because this was the sort of possession necessary to support the instruction on inference of knowledge, the trial court did not abuse its discretion in giving this instruction to the jury. It was up to the jury to weigh appellant's explanation for possessing the car and decide whether to accept the correctness of the inference. *See Scobee*, 488 So. 2d at 599.

* * *

Affirmed.

Gunther, J., concurs.
Farmer, J., dissents with opinion.
Farmer, J., dissenting.

* * *

I cannot agree that there is any evidence that this defendant had possession of a stolen automobile when he was simply pushing it with his vehicle.

Cases Relating to Chapter 7

Relevancy and Materiality

COMMONWEALTH

v.

PRASHAW

Appeals Court of Massachusetts

57 Mass. App. Ct. 19, 781 N.E.2d 19,
2003 Mass. App. LEXIS 5 (2003)

JUDGES: Present: Lenk, Mason, & Berry, JJ.

BERRY, J. In this appeal, the defendant challenges the admission in evidence of photographs depicting her naked in various sexually provocative positions. Balancing the minimal probative value of the pictures with respect to the nonsex-related offenses being tried against the marked prejudice, we conclude that this is one of those exceptional cases where the bounds of the usual grant of wide discretion to a trial judge concerning the admission of photographic evidence were exceeded. Accordingly, we reverse the judgments of conviction.

1. Background facts. On December 26, 1999, a fire broke out in the house in which the defendant and her husband resided. During a "cause-and-origin" survey of the house after the blaze, an investigator saw in plain view in an upstairs bedroom a twelve-gauge shotgun standing in a corner against the wall, and marijuana "roaches" in an ashtray. The shotgun was immediately confiscated. Based on these sightings, the police applied for a warrant to search the house.

The defendant's husband was present in the house both when the fire started and during the fire investigation. The defendant was not at home and had left the house a few days before Christmas following an altercation with her husband during which he beat her and hit her face (this abuse was of a continuing pattern over many years, including past incidents of domestic violence requiring hospital treatment). Following this incident of violence, the defendant sought shelter at her mother's house in New York State. On the day after Christmas, she returned home, only to see the house smouldering from the fire and firefighters and police on the scene.

The defendant entered the house, spoke to an officer, gathered some belongings, and described the assault that had led to her fleeing from the house. The defendant's face had not healed and still bore a bruise from that assault. One of the officers escorted the defendant to the police station, where she applied for, and was granted, a protective order under G.L.C. 209A. Thereafter, she returned to the house, even though she had been previously told by an officer that she could not enter because the police were seeking a search warrant. There were curious aspects surrounding the circumstances of the defendant's return and her explanation of the reasons why she came back to the house. The details do not matter, but of moment is that, when she returned, there was a man with her (whom the officers throughout the trial only described as a black man) and that she had a plan to reenter the house with this man, notwithstanding the police directive not to do so.

While waiting for the search warrant application to be processed, the police had cordoned off the house and stationed an officer as sentry in an unmarked cruiser in front of the house. It was during this time that the defendant and the unidentified man returned to the burned-out house. The man entered the house through the back. When the entry was discovered, another officer was dispatched to the scene to investigate the break-in. A witness, a neighbor, identified the defendant, who was standing nearby, as having "had something to do with this" break-in. The officer approached the defendant, handcuffed her, and conducted a patfrisk. A "crack" cocaine pipe containing cocaine residue was found in her pocket. The defendant was arrested. The man who had entered the house had been arrested by the officer stationed in front of the house.

Thereafter, two search warrants—one for the house and one for a Toyota Four-Runner sport utility vehicle—were executed. Seized from the Toyota were a knife with a seven-inch blade, a small quantity of marijuana, and rolling papers. Seized from the upstairs bedroom were marijuana roaches, a small amount of marijuana in a plastic bag, two bottles that had been crafted into crack cocaine pipes, aluminum foil with marijuana residue, a nonworking postal scale, another scale, the defendant's driver's license and firearm identification card, a joint tax return, and eighteen Polaroid photographs. The photographs depicted the defendant in various sexually explicit poses. In another upstairs room, in a gun cabinet, the police seized two packages of fireworks.

2. The introduction of the photographs. The Commonwealth indicated prior to trial that it would seek to admit all eighteen photographs. In response, the defendant filed a motion in limine. Following a hearing, the trial judge excluded all but three photographs. Although the Commonwealth sought to introduce the three photographs as exhibits, after an unrecorded sidebar conference, only two of the photographs were marked as exhibits and admitted in evidence for the jury's deliberations. In each of the two photographs, the defendant is naked, posing with an object in her hands and displaying the object vis-a-vis her body in a sexually provocative way. The objects being held appear blurry in the pictures. When confronted with the photographs during cross-examination, the defendant described the objects as a cigarette lighter and a billy club;

the Commonwealth inferred from its scrutiny that the objects were a handgun and a shotgun. However, as to the latter, the Commonwealth concedes that, even assuming that the object is a shotgun, it is not the same shotgun that was standing in the bedroom and which was the subject of the unlawful storage charge.

The overarching principle is that "the admissibility of photographic evidence is left to the discretion of the trial judge, and [an appellate court] will overturn the judge's decision only where a defendant is able to bear the heavy burden of demonstrating an abuse of that discretion." *Commonwealth v. Waters*, 399 Mass. 708, 715, 506 N.E.2d 859 (1987). Such judicial discretion has a wide berth, as the trial judge is best positioned to determine evidentiary value and to balance the probative value and relevancy against prejudicial effect. However, notwithstanding this wide latitude, there still are "rare instances in which the probative value of the evidence is overwhelmed by its inflammatory potential." *Commonwealth v. Repoza*, 382 Mass. 119, 128, 414 N.E.2d 591 (1980). In this case, we determine "whether sexually explicit photographs . . . '[were] so inflammatory as to outweigh their probative value.'" *Commonwealth v. Halsey*, 41 Mass. App. Ct. 200, 203, 669 N.E.2d 774 (1996), quoting from *Commonwealth v. Hrycenko*, 31 Mass. App. Ct. 425, 431, 578 N.E.2d 809 (1991). The defendant objected to the admission of the photographs, and, thereby, preserved the issue for appeal. Accordingly, we seek to determine whether there was prejudicial error. We conclude that the answer to that question is in the affirmative. In the balance to be struck, the extraordinary prejudice far overbore the minimal probativeness.

A. Probative value. We begin with an assessment of the evidentiary probativeness of the photographs. As noted, the objects being held by the defendant in the photographs are murky, but, even if viewed by the Commonwealth's lights, and even assuming such additional candle power would have led the beholder to perceive a shotgun of some sort being held in one photograph, it is not, as the Commonwealth concedes, the shotgun identified in the improper storage charge. The Commonwealth, therefore, concedes that neither photograph was relevant to the wrongful storage of a firearm charge and concedes error in admission on that basis. Instead, the Commonwealth argues on appeal, as the sole basis for admission, that the photographs were probative of the defendant's control of the upstairs bedroom where the marijuana, scales, and crack pipes were found.

We note at the outset that there was no dispute that the room was the defendant's bedroom and, in effect, belonged to her. As the prosecutor put it in the closing: "This, ladies and gentlemen, is her room; and there's no question about that. And these things were found in her closet; there's no questions about that, in her bureau, throughout her things; there's no question about the possession, ladies and gentlemen, no question." Precisely so, the defendant's general control over, and association with, the bedroom was well-established by abundant evidence—wholly apart from the photographs. This other evidence included the defendant's clothing, both stored in bureaus and strewn about the bedroom, as well as her driver's license, firearm identification card, and tax return, all of which were found within the bedroom. *See Commonwealth v. Rarick*, 23 Mass. App. Ct. 912, 912–913, 499 N.E.2d 1233 (1986) (personal effects belonging to the defendant linked her to contraband found in proximity to those effects even though multiple persons shared the dwelling). The strength of this other connective evidence substantially diminished the probative need for introduction of the sexually explicit pictures on the issue of general control of the bedroom, which was not even being disputed. Put another way, that this was the defendant's bedroom was fairly obvious, and the photographs added little but prejudice.

The principal issue with respect to control was limited to the defendant's absence from the house for the five days she stayed with her mother. Given this sojourn, there was a question, it appears from the evidence, as to whether someone else may have used the bedroom for some sort of partying and drinking spree. Indeed, that someone else was in the bedroom during this period might have been inferred from an empty bottle of whiskey and a pizza box which, according to the defendant, were not there before she left for New York, and the fact that, before she left, the photographs were kept in her locked closet. This

and other evidence suggest that the defendant did not have control of the room during her absence and that the defendant's estranged, alcoholic husband may well have gone on a drinking binge in that room.

Given this lapse in the defendant's control, the probative value of the photographs, if any, is to be analyzed with respect to this five-day period. Any such probative link between the photographs and this period of time was extremely weak. There was no evidence, and the four corners of the photographs do not manifest, that the pictures were taken within the five-day time frame. Nor was there any evidence that the photographs were taken in the bedroom area where either the drugs or paraphernalia were found or in the corner of the room where the shotgun was standing. Further undercutting the Commonwealth's contention that the photographs showed the defendant's association with, and control over, the bedroom is a handwritten notation, "George's house," on the face of one of the photographs, which suggests that the pictures were taken someplace else. In fact, there was no substantive evidence whatsoever linking the photographs to control of the bedroom by the defendant during her five-day absence. Rather than such authentication, the photographs were simply dropped in evidence as items seized in the search and were not further authenticated by time, place, or manner during the course of trial. "To be admissible in evidence, a photograph must be shown to be accurate and bear enough similarity to circumstances at the time in dispute to be relevant and helpful to the jury in its deliberations." *Henderson v. D'Annolfo*, 15 Mass. App. Ct. 413, 428, 446 N.E.2d 103 (1983). Thus, on a sliding scale, the probative value of the photographs was minimal. We next consider the prejudice.

B. Prejudicial effect. In this case, the prejudicial effect was depicting the defendant as "a lewd [woman] and to lead the jury to believe that a [woman] of [her] character would be likely to commit the crimes charged." *Commonwealth v. Ellis*, 321 Mass. 669, 670, 75 N.E.2d 241 (1947). It does not take much imagination to conjure that the purpose and effect of the introduction of the pictures was so that the jury, appalled by the defendant's posing in such a manner, might be swayed to perceive the defendant as not of good moral character and more likely to have committed criminal offenses. Such a prejudicial effect, inherent in sexually explicit depictions, was amplified in this case because the trial did not involve a sex-related offense. Moreover, although only two photographs were published to the jury, one of the officers testified that there were eighteen such Polaroid photographs seized. See, e.g., *Commonwealth v. Allen*, 377 Mass. 674, 680, 387 N.E.2d 553 (1979) (photograph of the victim's bloody crotch, which was due to natural decomposition, possessed "great potential for inciting jury speculation about possible sexual overtones to the crime" in a murder trial); *Commonwealth v. Darby*, 37 Mass. App. Ct. 650, 654, 642 N.E.2d 303 (1994) (photograph of the male defendant in a sexually turgid state was unduly prejudicial where impotence or sexual dysfunction was not "directly or inferentially" relevant to the case). As a last resort, the Commonwealth suggests harmless error should cause us to affirm the convictions, but we are unable to say the photographs did not unduly and unfairly influence the jury, or had just a slight effect. In sum, the risk was great that the sexually suggestive pictures, which had little to do with the case at hand, unduly swayed the jury. For these reasons, we conclude that it was error to admit the photographs.

* * *

The judgments of convictions on all the complaints tried are reversed and the verdicts are set aside. The denial of the motion to suppress is affirmed.

So ordered.

JACKSON
v.
UNITED STATES

District of Columbia Court of Appeals
856 A.2d 1111, 2004 D.C. App. LEXIS 413 (2004)

Before STEADMAN and SCHWELB, Associate Judges, and NEBEKER, Senior Judge.

STEADMAN, Associate Judge: Appellant and his co-defendant were selling music compact discs ("CDs") from a table they had set up on the sidewalk near Union Station. The CDs were "counterfeit"; that is, they were manufactured without the authorization of the copyright owner. Appellant was convicted at a bench trial of attempted deceptive labeling of a sound recording, in violation of D.C. Code §§ 22-103 (attempt) and -3814.1 (deceptive labeling) (1996).

The only issue on appeal is whether the trial court erred in admitting, in the government's case in chief, evidence of prior criminal conduct in violation of the strictures of the case law emanating from *Drew v. United States*, 118 U.S. App. D.C. 11, 331 F.2d 85 (1964). Specifically, evidence was introduced that five weeks prior to the date of the offense for which he was on trial, appellant had been arrested, also in the vicinity of Union Station, when he was also vending counterfeit CDs and was warned at that time that he was selling counterfeit CDs. (The actual arrest in that prior case was for vending without a license.) The government takes the position that the evidence went to the issue of appellant's knowledge that the CDs were counterfeit at the time of the offense for which he was on trial. Appellant argues that his knowledge was not then a materially contested issue, and his defense, in fact, was that he was not selling the CDs at all but rather just happened to be passing by at the time. The introduction of the evidence, he asserts, thus violated the prohibition that he reads into *Thompson v. United States*, 546 A.2d 414 (D.C. 1988), against the introduction of *Drew* evidence which bore only upon issues not genuinely in dispute. We conclude that this is far too broad a reading of *Thompson* and affirm the conviction.

I.

The principal government witness in its case in chief was Officer Tracey Hanbury. He testified that he saw two men selling compact discs from a table they had set up on the sidewalk near Union Station. He saw both men sell CDs to customers. When he confronted the two individuals, he realized they were the same two men whom he had arrested some five weeks previously after witnessing them selling CDs outside Union Station. Although the prior arrest was for vending without a license, Officer Hanbury had advised appellant that the CDs he was selling were counterfeit.

Officer Hanbury further testified that the CDs he observed in appellant's possession at the time of the second arrest were "obviously counterfeits." He noted: "The front of the CD [was] just a thin piece of paper . . . that was copied on the CD and ... was cut with a pair of scissors where some of them don't have perfectly straight lines ... They were also wrapped in saran wrap type wrapping and that wasn't consistent with what you would see in a music CD store."

The government presented an expert witness, Phillip Brooks, who testified that counterfeit CDs often have "poor shrink wrappings . . . poorly folded corners . . . while a legitimate compact disc is characterized by tight corners, [and] tightly sealed." He further explained that "the insert card on a counterfeit disc will be a thin piece of paper . . . of poor quality," while the insert cards on a legitimate compact disc "are one of the more expensive aspects of the disc." He also said that the playing side of a counterfeit compact disc "will be greenish or bluish in tint which indicates it's a CD recordable," while "the legitimate compact disc will be silver and . . . legitimate record companies do not manufacture their compact disc on CD recordables."Mr. Brooks identified as counterfeits a random selection of discs from the box of 62 CDs seized from appellant.

Testifying in his own defense, appellant said he had come to Union Station for a dinner and movie with his common-law wife. After he parked his car and was walking toward the entrance, a police car came speeding towards him, two officers jumped out and escorted appellant over to the co-defendant and placed them under arrest. Appellant testified he was not selling any CDs and didn't receive any money from any customers. Appellant stated that he had never sold CDs in the District, but had other people sell CDs for him. Appellant acknowledged that he had been previously arrested and was then informed that the CDs being sold at his vending table were counterfeit but he said that at the time he had no idea

that they were counterfeit. Once he found this out, he stopped carrying CDs at his vending table. Appellant's co-defendant testified that all of the property on the table belonged to him and that he had not given appellant any money that evening and, in fact, the co-defendant had not made a single sale all evening.

In rebuttal, the government called Officer Aisha Jackson, who testified that on several previous occasions she had "shut down" appellant for selling CDs without a vending license in the vicinity of Union Station. She accompanied Officer Hanbury at the time of the prior arrest when the warning was given to appellant that the CDs that he was selling were counterfeit. On that occasion, appellant acknowledged that the CDs were his and stated, "Yeah, these are mine, everybody is doing it."

II.

"If evidence of prior bad acts that are criminal in nature and independent of the crime charged is offered to prove predisposition to commit the charged crime, it is inadmissible. . . . 'It is a principle of long standing in our law that evidence of one crime is inadmissible to prove disposition to commit crime, from which the jury may infer that the defendant committed the crime charged. Since the likelihood that juries will make such an improper inference is high, courts presume prejudice and exclude evidence of other crimes unless that evidence can be admitted for some substantial, legitimate purpose.'" *Johnson v. United States*, 683 A.2d 1087, 1092 (D.C. 1996) (en banc) (quoting *Drew, supra*, 331 F.2d at 89–90) (other citations omitted), *cert. denied*, 520 U.S. 1148, 137 L. Ed. 2d 484, 117 S. Ct. 1323 (1997). This presumption of prejudice may be overcome if "the [other crimes] evidence [is] offered for a substantial, legitimate purpose," n4 and "the court. . . considers the relative probative value of the evidence and the danger of unfair prejudice that it poses, and concludes that the balance favors admission." *Id*. at 1092–93 (citations omitted). Moreover, *Drew* does not apply at all where "such evidence (1) is direct and substantial proof of the charged crime, (2) is closely intertwined with the evidence of the charged crime, or (3) is necessary to place the charged crime in an understandable context." *Id.* at 1098.

The government first contends that *Drew* is inapplicable to the disputed evidence because the circumstances surrounding appellant's prior arrest provided "direct and substantial proof" of a constituent element of the crime charged, by demonstrating his knowledge of the counterfeit nature of the CDs at issue. The government's argument, that a factor in a previous crime which tends to make more probable an element of the current crime charged is therefore direct and substantial proof of the current crime charged, if too broadly read could threaten to swallow up the very protection that *Drew* endeavors to provide. *Drew* places upon other crime evidence a presumption of prejudice not because such evidence is "irrelevant; on the contrary, it is said to weigh too much with the jury and to ... overpersuade them...." *Thompson, supra,* 546 A.2d at 418 (quoting *Michelson v. United States,* 335 U.S. 469, 475–76, 93 L. Ed. 168, 69 S. Ct. 213 (1948)). The difficulty is that *Drew* evidence often itself operates as "direct and substantial proof" of an element of a charged crime, such as with, for example, the intent and identity exceptions. It is no easy task to articulate the line that divides evidence subject to *Drew* from evidence not subject to *Drew* on the ground that the latter is "direct and substantial proof" of the offense.

A substantial portion of our cases declaring other crimes evidence to be "direct and substantial proof" of the crime charged involve the admission of evidence of prior possession of a weapon, which was also used in the charged crime. [Citations omitted.] We have held such determinations to be "consistent with the principle that 'an accused person's prior possession of the physical means of committing the crime is some evidence of the probability of his guilt, and is therefore admissible.'" [Citations omitted.]

* * *

III.

The government argues, and we agree, that applying *Drew,* the evidence in question

was properly admitted to prove appellant's knowledge that the CDs were counterfeit.

We have not previously expressly recognized "knowledge" as a legitimate purpose for which other crimes evidence may be offered and, thereby, escape *Drew's* prohibition. In *Johnson,* we enumerated substantial and legitimate purposes warranting admission of other crimes evidence, which "included, but [were] *not limited* to . . . (1) motive; (2) intent; (3) absence of mistake or accident; (4) common scheme or plan; [and] (5) identity." *Johnson, supra,* 683 A.2d at 1092 (emphasis added). Furthermore, we have identified as "consistent with District of Columbia law" the following language from Federal Rule of Evidence 404(b): "Evidence of other crimes, wrongs, or acts is not admissible to prove the character of a person in order to show action in conformity therewith. It may, however, be admissible for other purposes, such as proof of motive, opportunity, intent, preparation, plan, *knowledge,* identity, or absence of mistake or accident." *Id.* at 1100 n.17 (emphasis added). Knowledge is widely accepted as a non-propensity purpose for which other crimes evidence may be admitted. [Citations omitted.] Thus, we now explicitly hold that other crimes or bad acts evidence may be offered for the purpose of demonstrating "knowledge" and, absent a finding that the prejudicial effect of the evidence substantially outweighs its probative value, evidence offered for such purpose will overcome *Drew's* presumption of inadmissibility.

Given our adoption of this further exception to *Drew,* we must evaluate whether the evidence of appellant's previous arrest for the purpose of showing his knowledge was properly admitted. "A decision on the admissibility of evidence, of course, is committed to the sound discretion of the trial court." *Sanders, supra,* 809 A.2d at 590 (citation omitted). Moreover, "the evaluation and weighing of evidence for relevance and potential prejudice is quintessentially a discretionary function of the trial court, and we owe a great degree of deference to its decision." *Johnson, supra,* 683 A.2d at 1095.

Appellant was convicted of attempted deceptive labeling. "A person commits the offense of deceptive labeling if, for commercial advantage or private financial gain, that person *knowingly* advertises, offers for sale, resale, or rental, or sells, resells, rents, distributes, or transports, or possesses for such purposes, a sound recording or audiovisual work, the label, cover, or jacket of which does not clearly and conspicuously disclose the true name and address of the manufacturer thereof." D.C. Code § 22-3814.1(b) (emphasis added). Thus, to secure a conviction for deceptive labeling, the government was required to prove that appellant knew that "the label, cover, or jacket of [the CDs in question]... [did] not clearly and conspicuously disclose the true name and address of the manufacturer thereof." Such knowledge would be implicit if appellant knew the CDs were counterfeit, and therefore could not reflect the true name of the manufacturer. Testimony that appellant had been previously warned that the CDs he was selling were counterfeit went to the issue of whether he knew the CDs at issue were counterfeit. Although the government presented no direct evidence that the appearance of the CDs at issue was the same as the CDs about which appellant was warned, a fair inference to that effect could be made from the expert's general description of counterfeit CDs and the testimony of Officer Hanbury, the same individual who had previously warned

the appellant about counterfeit CDs, that he immediately recognized that the CDs at issue were counterfeit. Thus, the trial court did not abuse its discretion in admitting evidence that appellant had previously sold counterfeit CDs because the evidence was not admitted to establish appellant's criminal propensity but to demonstrate appellant's knowledge as to the counterfeit nature of the discs, an essential element of the crime charged.

* * *

IV.

* * *

V.

The trial court did not err in permitting, in the government's case in chief, the introduction of other crime evidence for the purpose of demonstrating appellant's knowledge of the counterfeit nature of the CDs, even where he had not at that time disputed, nor did he later dispute, that issue. Accordingly, the judgment appealed from is hereby

Affirmed.

Cases Relating to Chapter 8

Competency of Evidence and Witnesses

UNITED STATES
v.
PHIBBS

United States Court of Appeals,
Sixth Circuit
999 F.2d 1053 (1993)

Before: GUY and SUHRHEINRICH, Circuit Judges; and DOWD, District Judge.

RALPH B. GUY, JR., Circuit Judge.

Defendants, Raymond Huckelby, Diane Whited, Robert Phibbs, Victor Rojas, and Robert Murr appeal their convictions arising from their participation in a cocaine distribution ring operating in Tennessee and Kentucky. In addition, Phibbs and Rojas challenge the appropriateness of their sentences.

* * *

E. Competency of Jerry Parks and Tommy McKeehan

Whited claims that witnesses Jerry Parks and Tommy McKeehan were incompetent to give testimony on grounds of mental incapacity. In the case of Parks, he had previously been found incompetent to stand trial, had a history of auditory delusions, and had spent time in mental health facilities. As for McKeehan, Whited cites an affidavit filed with the district court by his treating psychiatrist that he could not assist his counsel in an upcoming trial because he suffered from "confusion, agitation, paranoia and hallucinations." This affidavit was dated four days prior to McKeehan having entered into a plea agreement with the government. Because of such information, Whited contends that, at the very least, it was error for the court not to conduct a preliminary examination of Parks' and McKeehan's competency as witnesses.

Under Rule 601 of the Federal Rules of Evidence (General Rule of Competency), "every person is competent to be a witness except as otherwise provided in these rules." The Advisory Committee Notes to Rule 601 explain that "this general ground-clearing eliminates all grounds of incompetency not specifically recognized in the rules of this Article." Accordingly, "no mental or moral qualifications for testifying as a witness" are specified. Id. This is because "standards of mental capacity have proved elusive in actual application." Id.

Thus, the Federal Rules of Evidence strongly disfavor barring witnesses on competency grounds due to mental incapacity. As we wrote in *United States v. Ramirez*, 871 F.2d 582, 584 (6th Cir.), cert. denied, 493 U.S. 841, 107 L. Ed. 2d 88, 110 S. Ct. 127 (1989):

> What must be remembered, and is often confused, is that "competency" is a matter of status not ability. Thus, the only two groups of persons specifically rendered incompetent as witnesses by the Federal Rules of Evidence are judges (Rule 605) and jurors (Rule 606). The authority of the court to control the admissibility of the testimony of persons so impaired in some manner that they cannot give meaningful testimony is to be found outside of Rule 601. For example, the judge always has the authority under Rule 403 to balance

the probative value of testimony against its prejudicial effect. Similarly, under Rule 603, the inability of a witness to take or comprehend an oath or affirmation will allow the judge to exclude that person's testimony. An argument can also be constructed that a person might be impaired to the point that he would not be able to satisfy the "personal knowledge" requirement of Rule 602. Again though, it is important to remember that such decisions by a trial judge to either admit or exclude testimony will only be reversed for a clear abuse of discretion.

(Footnote omitted.)

The district court did not rule on Parks' competency before he took the stand; later, in considering a motion for judgment of acquittal, the court indicated that Parks and McKeehan "were not crazy witnesses." Likewise, it addressed the question of McKeehan's mental capacity during a bench conference held after he had begun to testify. The court stated that it had "observed Mr. McKeehan, and he appears to the Court to be sober, cogent. He appears to the Court to know exactly where he is and what he is doing. His testimony has been direct, and his testimony has not been confused." When pressed concerning the psychiatrist's affidavit that McKeehan could not help in his own defense, the court opined that "he sure has made a remarkable recovery . . . [His condition is] fodder for cross-examination, and it would appear that either the psychiatrist made an inaccurate diagnosis September the 5th or the witness has made a remarkable recovery. And the Court observes that—repeats that he does not appear to be confused today."

At a hearing on defendants' post-trial motions, the district court supplemented its findings regarding Parks' and McKeehan's competency, and the need for a special examination of their mental faculties. The court noted that

one of the reasons I overlooked stating as to my belief that an independent evaluation at this time would be a waste of time is that—is that such a finding, even if they found that they were incompetent here in

April of 1992, would not be dispositive as to their competence or mental state when they testified in September of 1991 at the trial of this case or at the hearings that we held in August.

. . . .

Similarly, even if I had such an opinion from a psychiatrist or psychologist or whoever that gave us an independent opinion that these people were— Mr. Parks and McKeehan were total screwballs, I would—I would find those opinions to have little probative value and of little weight, and I would not—I would not accept them as being—as being conclusive on the matter. And I would not let such opinions override my own judgment after having seen—personally witnessed their performance in court.

Hence, the district court did not find that Parks and McKeehan were incapable of understanding their oath and obligation to testify truthfully. Nor did the court find, based on its observations, that their mental abilities were so limited that they did not have sufficient capacity to perceive events, to remember them, and to describe them for the benefit of the trier of fact. See Fed. R. Evid. 602. The court was not required, as Whited would have it, to conduct a special examination into their competency. If either Parks' or McKeehan's behavior raised concerns stemming from Rule 602 or 603, it could have excluded their testimony (or portions thereof) without any examination whatsoever. Furthermore, the court had the additional authority, pursuant to Rule 403, to exclude their testimony in light of their past or present mental state. The court chose not to take any of these measures in the circumstances. Instead, it permitted defense counsel to use the psychiatric records of Parks and McKeehan, as well as other indicia of their mental capacity, to vigorously attack their credibility.

After carefully reviewing the record, we conclude that the district court did not abuse its discretion in doing so. As long as a witness appreciates his duty to tell the truth, and is minimally capable of observing, recalling, and communicating events, his testimony should come in for whatever it is worth. It is then up to the opposing party to dispute the witness' powers of apprehension, which well may be impaired by mental illness or other factors. As we are persuaded that Parks and McKeehan were at least minimally capable of offering reliable evidence, the possible weaknesses in their testimony went to its credibility, and so were to be assessed by the jury. *See United States v. Moreno*, 899 F.2d 465, 469 (6th Cir. 1990).

Whited also argues that defendants should have been allowed to introduce the psychiatric records of Parks and McKeehan as substantive evidence. They were ruled inadmissible hearsay by the district court. Whited alleges, however, that they were not put forward for the truth of the matters asserted within, but to show how manipulative Parks and McKeehan could be if they were not, in fact, mentally unbalanced. Such use of the records during cross-examination to challenge Parks' and McKeehan's credibility was appropriate. However, we believe that they would have constituted hearsay if employed as part of a substantive defense. They would have to have been offered to show that the psychiatrists making the records actually concluded that Parks and McKeehan were mentally ill. Otherwise, Parks' and McKeehan's deception would have no basis in fact. Consequently, the district court did not err in declining to admit the psychiatric records.

* * *

AFFIRMED.

State
v.
Wells

COURT OF APPEALS OF OHIO, NINTH APPELLATE DISTRICT, SUMMIT COUNTY

2003 Ohio 3162, 2003 Ohio App. LEXIS 2840 (2003)

JUDGES: LYNN C. SLABY. SLABY, P. J. CONCURS. BATCHELDER, J. CONCURS. CARR, J. DISSENTS.

This cause was heard upon the record in the trial court. Each error assigned has been reviewed and the following disposition is made:

Per curiam.

Appellant, Jerome Wells, appeals from his conviction in the Summit County Court of Common Pleas of one count of gross sexual imposition. This Court reverses and remands for a new trial.

Wells was indicted on one count of rape, in violation of R.C. 2907.02(A)(1)(b). He allegedly engaged in sexual conduct with a child under thirteen years of age on or about December 9, 2001. The alleged victim of his crime, T.V., was five years old at the time the case proceeded to trial during May 2002. Prior to trial, because T.V. was less than ten years old, a hearing was held to determine whether she was competent to testify. Following an examination by the trial judge, the prosecutor and defense counsel, the trial court determined that T.V. was competent to testify.

Following a jury trial, Wells was convicted of the lesser included offense of gross sexual imposition. Wells appeals and raises five assignments of error.

FIRST ASSIGNMENT OF ERROR

"THE TRIAL COURT ERRED AND ABUSED ITS DISCRETION BY FINDING A FIVE (5) YEAR OLD CHILD COMPETENT TO TESTIFY PURSUANT TO EVID.R. 601 WHERE SHE CLEARLY WAS INCAPABLE OF RECEIVING JUST IMPRESSIONS OF FACTS AND DID NOT COMPREHEND THE CONCEPT OF A LIE OR ITS CONSEQUENCES."

Wells contends that the trial court erred in determining that five-year-old T.V., the alleged victim, was competent to testify because she was not capable of receiving just impressions of fact and did not understand the concept of a lie or the consequences of lying. Evid.R. 601(A) provides:

"Every person is competent to be a witness except * * * children under ten years of age, who appear incapable of receiving just impressions of the facts and transactions respecting which they are examined, or of relating them truly."

The burden falls on the proponent of the witness to establish that the witness exhibits "certain indicia of competency." *State v. Clark* (1994), 71 Ohio St.3d 466, 469, 1994 Ohio 43, 644 N.E.2d 331. In *State v. Frazier* (1991), 61 Ohio St.3d 247, 574 N.E.2d 483, syllabus, the Supreme Court of Ohio set forth five factors that the trial court "must take into consideration" when determining whether a child under the age of ten is competent to testify:

"(1) the child's ability to receive accurate impressions of fact or to observe acts about which he or she will testify, (2) the child's ability to recollect those impressions or observations, (3) the child's ability to communicate what was observed, (4) the child's understanding of truth and falsity and (5) the child's appreciation of his or her responsibility to be truthful."

These factors "are aimed at protecting the accused by ascertaining that a child witness is trustworthy." *State v. Ulch* (Apr. 19, 2002), 6th Dist. No. L-00-1355, 2002 Ohio App. LEXIS 1866.

At the hearing to determine whether T.V. was competent to testify in this case, the State failed to meet its burden of presenting sufficient evidence of T.V.'s competency. Specifically, there was not a sufficient inquiry into the fourth or fifth Frazier competency factors: the child's understanding of truth and falsity and the child's appreciation of his or her responsibility to be truthful. "[A] child may be competent to testify even though the child *** initially does not recognize the concept of truth, so long as the voir dire continues on to demonstrate that the child *** generally *** understands the concept of truthfulness." *State v. Brooks* (Oct. 26, 2001), 2nd Dist. No. 18502, 2001 Ohio 1650, quoting *State v. Boyd* (Oct. 31, 1997), 2d Dist. No. 97 CA 1, 1997 Ohio App. LEXIS 4748.

In this case, however, after T.V. initially demonstrated that she did not understand the concepts of truth and falsity, the further voir dire on this issue was not sufficient to demonstrate that T.V. did, in fact, generally understand the concept of truthfulness or that

she appreciated her responsibility to tell the truth. The trial court errs in finding a child witness competent without sufficient evidence before it to consider each of the five Frazier factors. *See State v. Wilson* (Feb. 18, 2000), 4th Dist. No. 99CA672, 2000 Ohio App. LEXIS 677. Because there was not an adequate demonstration on the fourth and fifth *Frazier* factors, the trial court erred in finding T.V. competent to testify.

It has been held that such a deficiency in the hearing on the child's competency can be cured if the child's subsequent testimony at trial demonstrates that the trial court was justified in finding the child competent to testify. See *State v. Wilson*, citing *State v. Lewis* (1982), 4 Ohio App.3d 275, 4 Ohio B. 494, 448 N.E.2d 487. At the time T.V. testified at trial, however, the State failed to elicit any further testimony regarding her understanding of the concept of truthfulness. Consequently, the error could not have been cured by her later testimony.

Because there was insufficient evidence before the trial court to demonstrate that T.V. had an understanding of the concepts of truth and falsity or that she appreciated her responsibility to be truthful, the trial court exceeded the scope of its discretion by finding that she was competent to testify. *See Frazier*, 61 Ohio St.3d at 247, syllabus. The first assignment of error is sustained and the judgment is reversed and remanded for a retrial.

The remaining assignments of error have been rendered moot and will not be reached. See App.R. 12(A)(1)(c). The judgment of the trial court is reversed and the cause is remanded for a new trial.

Judgment reversed and the cause remanded.

CONCUR: BATCHELDER, J.

Although I agree with the reasoning of the principal opinion, I write separately to emphasize the lack of the evidence before the trial court regarding T.V.'s competency to testify. There was almost no evidence on the fourth *Frazier* factor, "the child's understanding of truth and falsity" and there was a complete lack of evidence on the fifth factor, "the child's appreciation of his or her responsibility to be truthful." *See Frazier*, 61 Ohio St.3d at 247, syllabus. As indicated above, the trial judge had an mandatory obligation to consider all five factors. See id.

At the competency hearing, the testimony elicited by the prosecutor from T.V. regarding her understanding of truth and falsity and her appreciation of her responsibility to be truthful was the following:

"Q. Okay. [T,] do you know what it means to have to tell the truth?

"A. (Witness shook head.)

"Q. Okay. You are shaking your head. Which do you mean? If you tell the truth, what do you have to do? Let me ask you a different way. You are wearing a jump suit today, aren't you?

"A. (Witness nodded.)

"Q. Is that a yes?

"A. Yes.

"Q. Okay. If I said your jump suit was green, is that right?

"A. (Witness shook head.) No.

"Q. No? What color is your jump suit?

"A. Pink.

"Q. It is pink. You are right, it is pink.

"A. Pink and white.

"Q. Pink and white, you are right. Yes, it is. And who is this right here?

"A. My bear.

"Q. That's a bear. If I told you that this was a kitty cat; is that right?

"A. No.

"Q. No, it is not right, is it. Did you talk with me about having to come to the courtroom today?

"A. Yes.

"Q. Okay. And did I tell you that you would have to tell the truth when you came here?

"A. Yes.

"Q. Okay. And did your mom tell you that, too?

"A. Yes.

"Q. Okay. Did we tell you that that means that you have to tell us what happened and you can't make it up?

"A. Yes.

"Q. Yes, okay."

After T.V. indicated that she did not understand what it meant to have to tell the truth, the prosecutor did not ask any follow-up questions on that specific issue. Instead, the prosecutor asked T.V. questions about what is "right" and

"not right," never linking those two concepts to truth and/or falsity. Equating right and not right with truth and falsity is not necessarily something that a five-year-old child is able to do and, absent some demonstration to that effect, the trial court had no reason to presume that this child was able to do so. Further questioning of T.V. failed to even suggest that this child had such an understanding. Although, at the conclusion of the prosecutor's questioning, T.V. agreed that she had been told to tell "the truth" when she came to court, there had been no demonstration that she understood what "the truth" was.

Defense counsel's subsequent questioning of the child only served to demonstrate that the child remained confused:

"Q. [T,] do you remember when [the prosecutor] asked you if you understood what telling the truth was?

"A. Yes.

"Q. Did you shake your head back and forth like a no?

"A. (Witness nodded.)

"Q. You did shake your head back and forth from side to side?

"A. Yes.

"Q. [T.,] do you know what a lie is?

"A. No.

"Q. No? Is that what you are saying?

"A. (Witness nodded.)"

T.V. again indicated a lack of understanding of the concepts of truth and falsity. After these responses by T.V. to direct questions on the issue, there was no follow-up questioning by defense counsel or anyone else to demonstrate that the child was not, in fact, completely confused about the issue.

The trial judge concluded with the following line of questioning:

"Q: [T.,] I am going to ask you a question right now. What you said to me and to [the prosecutor] so far today, have you been telling the truth? She asked you about what the truth is. You have told the truth in this court to this Judge?

"A: Yes.

"Q: Everything you said now is the truth?

"A: (Witness nodded.)

"Q: Is there any question about that in your mind as to whether it is true or not?

"A: Yes.

"Q: There is a question?

"[Prosecutor]: I don't think she understood the question, Judge.

"Q: Okay. You told the truth as far as what happened?

"A. Yes.

"Q: All the questions you answered are—were the truth, right?

"A: Yes.

"Q: And you know what it is to tell the truth, you already answered that.

"A: Yes.

"Q: It is something that really happened, right?

"A: Yes.

"Q: Not something you make up, right?

"A: Yes.

"Q: So you are going to keep telling the truth now from here on, and what you are going to say is what really happened, right?

"A: Yes."

T.V.'s answers to the trial judge's questions might seem appropriate, if viewed in isolation.

Given the confusion that T.V. had already demonstrated, however, her answers to the judge's questions failed to demonstrate that she did, in fact, have a general understanding of the concepts of truth and falsity.

Moreover, even if the judge's questioning somehow cured the shortcomings of the confused testimony elicited from T.V. on the fourth *Frazier* factor, there was absolutely no testimony elicited from T.V. on the fifth mandatory *Frazier* factor, an appreciation of her responsibility to be truthful.

The trial judge had the discretion to find the child competent to testify only upon a consideration of all five of the *Frazier* factors. Because there was not adequate evidence before the trial court on all five factors, I agree with the principal opinion that the trial judge exceeded the scope of his discretion by finding that this child was competent to testify and I would reverse the judgment of the trial court on that basis.

Cases Relating to Chapter 9

Examination of Witnesses

UNITED STATES
v.
DRUMMOND

UNITED STATES COURT OF APPEAL, THIRD CIRCUIT

69 Fed. Appx. 580, 2003 U.S. App. LEXIS 14819 (2003)

OPINION: OPINION OF THE COURT

ROSENN, Circuit Judge:

This case raises the issue of whether the District Court committed reversible error when it denied the motion in limine of defendant, Alvin Drummond, to compel the Government's case agent to testify first at trial. The purpose of the motion was to prevent the possibility that the case agent might endeavor, when called as a witness, to conform his testimony to that of the preceding Government witness.

On reviewing the matter de novo, we hold that, under the circumstances of this case, the harm to the Government's case that would have resulted from granting Drummond's motion far outweighs any possible harm to Drummond from denying the motion. The District Court did not abuse its discretion in denying the motion. We affirm. Drummond timely appealed.

I.

A jury convicted Drummond on two counts of cocaine distribution. The trial court sentenced him to a 327-month prison term.

Before his trial began, he filed a Motion in Limine requesting that the Court order the Government to call its case agent, Detective Ronald Marzec, as its first witness at trial. The District Court denied the motion, holding that, under Federal Rule of Evidence 615, it was outside its authority to control the sequence of the Government's witnesses.

At trial, the Government first called Detective Marvin Charles Mailey, Jr., who testified that, while he was working undercover, Drummond sold him cocaine. Mailey testified to his close contact with Drummond, and unequivocally identified him as the person who sold him cocaine on multiple occasions. Agent Marzec then testified that he witnessed some of the drug-sales transactions between Drummond and Mailey from a distance, sometimes aided by binoculars. Marzec verified that the person present at these transactions was Drummond and, in that respect, his testimony was consistent with Mailey's. Drummond's defense was primarily based on a challenge to the prosecution's identification of Drummond. Drummond's witnesses testified, inter alia, that Drummond had brothers who closely resembled him, and that he often loaned one of his cars—the car in which Mailey and Marzec testified some of the drug sales had occurred in—to others.

Drummond now challenges the District Court's denial of his motion to compel Marzec to testify first.

II.

Our review here is plenary. The District Court is alleged to have misinterpreted the

Rules of Evidence. This is a question of whether it correctly understood the scope of its authority under the Rules. We review the District Court's refusal to require the case agent to testify first for abuse of discretion.

The District Court erred in its exclusive reliance on Rule 615. Rule 615 provides that a court shall order the sequestration of witnesses, upon the request of a party. However, Rule 615 does not permit the exclusion from trial of "an officer or employee of a party which is not a natural person designated as its representative by its attorney." Fed. R. Evid. 615(2). We have held that a case agent for the Government falls within this exemption, and ordinarily cannot be sequestered pursuant to Rule 615. *United States v. Gonzalez*, 918 F.2d 1129, 1138 (3d Cir. 1990). Thus, Marzec, as the case agent, could not have been validly sequestered under this Rule. The District Court apparently believed that Rule 615 somehow protected the Government against judicial intervention in its sequence of trial witnesses.

However, Rule 611(a) does not exempt case agents. It merely provides: "The court shall exercise reasonable control over the mode and order of interrogating witnesses and presenting evidence so as to (1) make the interrogation and presentation effective for the ascertainment of the truth, (2) avoid needless consumption of time, and (3) protect witnesses from harassment or undue embarrassment." Fed. R. Evid. 611(a). There is no obvious reason why the Rule 615 case agent exemption, designed to allow a representative of the Government to be in the courtroom at all times, would have any relevance to Rule 611.

Accordingly, other courts of appeals have held that case agents, ineligible for sequestration under Rule 615, might nonetheless be forced to testify first at trial, to avoid giving the prosecution unfair advantage. *See United States v. Parodi*, 703 F.2d 768, 774 (4th Cir. 1983). (permission for the investigating officer to remain in court at trial under Rule 615 may be conditioned on requirement that the officer be forced to testify first); *In Re United States*, 584 F.2d 666, 667 (5th Cir. 1978) ("The District Court may, in the exercise of its discretion under [Rule 611(a), conclude that the government should be required to present [its

case agent's] testimony at an early stage of the government's case."). Thus, the District Court's sole reliance on Rule 615 was error; the language of the Rules of Evidence and the persuasive holdings of our sister courts suggest that Rule 611(a) was applicable.

Drummond next urges that, in determining the standard under which a district court should evaluate a request to have the case agent testify first, we should adopt a rule promulgated by the Court of Appeals for the Fourth Circuit. Under its rule, a Government case agent "should ordinarily be called first so as to avoid giving the prosecution unfair advantage or the appearance that the prosecution is being favored." *United States v. Frazier*, 417 F.2d 1138, 1139 (4th Cir. 1969). That court went on to state that "this should be the order of presentation unless, in the judge's considered opinion, it would unduly break the continuity and seriously impair the coherence of the Government's proof." Id. At the opposite interpretive pole is the Court of Appeals for the First Circuit. In *United States v. Machor*, 879 F.2d 945, 954 (1st Cir. 1989), the court held that "good reason should exist before the court intervenes [as to the sequence of witnesses] in what is essentially a matter of trial strategy."

Drummond insists that regardless of the standard we choose, we must set forth some interpretive benchmark as to Rule 611 motions or any other motion regarding the sequencing of case agent witnesses. Because this court has not previously ruled on this issue, he asserts that we must remand to the District Court so that it can apply whatever standard we announce. However, Drummond was not entitled to have Marzec testify first. The Government has an interest in the order of its presentation, cf. (sequencing of witnesses is "essentially a matter of trial strategy"), and here the chief witness was Mailey. It would have been confusing to the jury and harmful to the Government case to force it to have its secondary witness testify first.

Furthermore, in Gonzalez, we observed that there was no prejudice in declining to sequester a case agent, because "[the defendant's] argument that [two Government] agents could coordinate their testimony does not pose a likelihood of prejudice since they had ample time before trial to do that, were they so inclined." 918 F.2d at 1138. Here, the two witnesses were both law enforcement officers, who had worked closely together throughout the investigation, and Drummond gave no other reason for his motion than to prevent deliberate conformity of testimony. If the witnesses were so inclined, and we have confidence that they were not, the two easily could have discussed their testimony before trial.

Therefore, the Government's interests in the orderly presentation of its case far outweighs the negligible possibility of prejudice to Drummond. Although this might be a more difficult issue if Marzec's testimony were not clearly subsidiary to Mailey's, or if there were non-Government witnesses involved for whom pre-trial coordination of testimony would be more difficult, in this case there was no justification for ordering Marzec to testify first. Moreover, Rule 611 only calls for an ordering of witnesses to maximize the "ascertainment of the truth." While there may be instances where the defense is hamstrung by its inability to sequester a case agent, and where it may be justified in requesting that the case agent to testify first, such a measure is not warranted here and would not further the trial's truth-seeking function. The judgment of conviction and sentence is affirmed.

Max Rosenn, Circuit Judge

PEOPLE
v.
MELENDEZ

Supreme Court of Colorado
102 P.3d 315, 2004 Colo. LEXIS 1006 (2004).

JUSTICE HOBBS delivered the Opinion of the Court.

EN BANC

We granted certiorari under C.A.R. 49 to review the court of appeals' decision in People v. Melendez, 80 P.3d 883 (Colo. App. 2003). The trial court precluded the testimony of a defense witness who allegedly violated a sequestration order. Because the record does not demonstrate an adequate inquiry by the trial court into whether the sequestration violation actually occurred and because preclusion of the witness's testimony was not harmless error, we affirm the judgment of the court of appeals.

I.

A jury convicted Jorge Melendez of multiple counts of sexual assault in the first and second degrees, aggravated incest, sexual assault on a child, sexual assault on a child-pattern of abuse, and sexual assault on a child under fifteen by one in a position of trust.

Melendez's former step-daughter, a seven-year-old girl, reported to her grandparents that he had sexually assaulted her on several occasions when he was married to her mother. Melendez defended on the basis that the child fabricated the allegations due to emotional problems with her mother, Melendez, and the divorce.

The trial court issued a sequestration order barring witnesses from the courtroom while other witnesses were testifying at trial, but made an exception for Detective Kenneth Brecko, a prosecution advisory witness.

The prosecution proceeded with testimony by Jodi Curtin, the child advocacy center interviewer who had interviewed the child after the police began investigating the allegations. The prosecution showed a video-tape of Curtin's interview with the child to the jury. Curtin testified about her observations of the child's behavior during the interview, emphasizing a change in her demeanor when the alleged assaults were mentioned. On cross examination, defense counsel asked Curtin whether false allegations are more common in "high conflict" situations and she answered that they may be. She also said false accusations can occur in interviews but not often, in her experience.

After Curtin's testimony, Brecko, the detective assigned to the Melendez case, testified about general procedures used in investigating sexual assault cases.

* * *

[T]he defense presented testimony from its expert witness, Dr. Spiegle. Spiegle criticized the manner in which Curtin conducted her interview, opining that she had used inappropriately suggestive and leading questions with the child, which may have affected the reliability of the child's answers. He also testified about a study showing that some twenty-three percent of sexual assault allegations by children in the Denver area in a particular time period proved to be false. Spiegle also testified about his evaluation of the child's behavior as seen on the videotaped interview. His view was that various pre-allegation events in her life may have impacted her emotional wellbeing and behavior.

Following Spiegle's testimony, the defense called the director of the child advocacy center where Curtin worked, followed by the officer who had responded to the neglect call. This testimony concluded at the end of the business day.

The defense planned to call Robert Curry the next day. Curry, a friend of Melendez, would have testified to his observations of the child's relationship with Melendez, as well as her behavior with her mother. The trial court precluded Curry from testifying.

The trial court based its preclusion order solely on the prosecution's assertion that Brecko had reported seeing Curry in the courtroom during portions of Curtin's testimony and during bench discussions after the recess.

Defense counsel responded that he was not aware of Curry's presence in the courtroom. He argued that Curry's testimony would not have been tainted by any of Curtin's testimony that he may have overheard, because Curry was planning to testify to completely different matters. Defense counsel made the following offer of proof regarding Curry's testimony:

> Judge, the expected nature of the testimony of Mr. Curry would essentially be that he has observed Mr. Melendez with the alleged victim in this case. He has seen him with the mother in this case. He has seen interactions between parent/child, Mr. Melendez and child. This is essentially the scope of his testimony.

Counsel also asserted that "having [Curry] stricken as a defense witness I believe is a really severe sanction in this case. I think that the Court could inquire or admonish or ask questions of Mr. Curry but not allowing him

to testify I think would be a severe prejudice to the defendant."

The prosecutor answered that Curtin testified about the child's behavior and the kinds of behavioral changes to be expected after sexual assaults. The prosecutor argued that this testimony could taint Curry's testimony because it suggested ways to show that the child was emotionally disturbed before she made her allegations. The prosecutor also noted that Brecko had subsequently told her that he had seen Curry talking to the defendant during a break and it sounded as if they were discussing the case. The trial court delayed ruling on the issue until the following morning.

The next day, defense counsel and the prosecutor made essentially the same arguments. The court precluded Curry's testimony, ruling that,

> considering argument of both the defense and the prosecution, noting the length of time the defendant (sic) was in the courtroom, paying particular attention that the witness was in the courtroom during the testimony of Ms. Curtin, the Court is going to not allow the witness to be called for the defense.

The trial court did not ask any questions of Brecko, Curry, or Melendez concerning the alleged sequestration violation.

Defense counsel rested his case after Melendez testified. The jury convicted Melendez on several counts.

On appeal, Melendez argued, inter alia, that the trial court abused its discretion by precluding Curry's testimony and that the error was not harmless. We agree and affirm the court of appeals' judgment.

II.

Because the record does not demonstrate an adequate inquiry by the trial court into whether the sequestration violation actually occurred, and because preclusion of the witness's testimony was not harmless error, we affirm the judgment of the court of appeals.

A. Standard of Review

In proper circumstances, the trial court may sequester witnesses, find that a witness has violated the sequestration order, and impose sanctions for the sequestration violation. *See People v. Wood*, 743 P.2d 422, 429–30 (Colo. 1987); *People v. P.R.G.*, 729 P.2d 380, 382 (Colo. App. 1986). We review the trial court's determinations for abuse of discretion. *People v. Stewart*, 55 P.3d 107, 122 (Colo. 2002). If an abuse of discretion occurred, we must then determine whether the error is reversible. *See Salcedo v. People*, 999 P.2d 833, 841 (Colo. 2000).

B. Sequestration Order Violations

Trial courts shall impose sequestration orders on witnesses at the request of either party. *Martin v. Porak*, 638 P.2d 853, 854 (Colo. App. 1981); CRE 615. The court may order witnesses to remain outside the courtroom and not discuss the case with each other. *People v. Brinson*, 739 P.2d 897, 899 (Colo. App. 1987).

* * *

Before it considers sanctions for a sequestration violation, the trial court must first determine that a violation has actually occurred and prejudice will result from unrestricted admission of the testimony. *See Wood*, 743 P.2d at 429–30.

Sanctions for violations of sequestration orders fall into three general categories: (1) citing the witness for contempt; (2) permitting counsel or the court to comment to the jury on the witness's noncompliance as a reflection on his or her credibility; and (3) precluding the witness's testimony. *P.R.G.*, 729 P.2d at 382; *see also* J. WEINSTEIN & M. BERGER, 4 WEINSTEIN'S FEDERAL EVIDENCE § 615.07[2] (2d ed. 2004). Additionally, mistrial is a possible but rarely justified sanction. *P.R.G.*, 729 P.2d at 382.

Disqualifying witness testimony is a severe sanction to be imposed only after careful consideration.

* * *

We have allowed prosecution witnesses to testify despite the allegation of a sequestration violation. *See Wood*, 743 P.2d at 429 (finding no prejudice to defendant requiring exclusion of witness for sequestration violation); cf. *People v. Gomez*, 632 P.2d

586, 594 (Colo. 1981) (approving trial court's limitation on scope of testimony by witness who violated sequestration order).

We have not had occasion for over one hundred years to consider the implications of precluding a defense witness from testifying due to a sequestration violation. *See Vickers v. People*, 31 Colo. 491, 73 P. 845 (Colo. 1903).

Sanctioning a defense witness for violating a sequestration order implicates important rights of the criminal defendant. *See Washington v. Texas*, 388 U.S. 14, 19, 18 L. Ed. 2d 1019, 87 S. Ct. 1920 (1967) ("The right to offer the testimony of witnesses . . . is in plain terms the right to present a defense, the right to present the defendant's version of the facts as well as the prosecution's to the [fact finder] so it may decide where the truth lies."); *People v. Chastain*, 733 P.2d 1206, 1212 (Colo. 1987) (noting that a defendant's right to offer testimony at trial is a "fundamental element of due process of law") (internal citations omitted).

While fundamental, the right to present defense evidence is not absolute. A defendant must "make some plausible showing of how [the] testimony would have been both material and favorable to his defense."

* * *

Nevertheless, cumulative evidence that may corroborate the defendant's own statement should ordinarily be admitted. *See People v. Green*, 38 Colo. App. 165, 553 P.2d 839, 840 (Colo. App. 1976) ("It is manifest that [evidence which is cumulative to some degree] should not be prohibited when it is sought to be introduced to corroborate [the defendant's] statement, which . . . may be, and often is, looked upon by the jury with some degree of suspicion.") (internal quotations omitted); *Towner v. State*, 685 P.2d 45, 50 (Wyo. 1984) (the only evidence offered to corroborate defendant's testimony was admissible even though duplicative to defendant's own statement).

C. Trial Court's Duty of Inquiry

The trial court has a duty of diligent inquiry into allegations of a sequestration violation. The trial court must first determine whether the violation actually occurred and, if so, whether prejudice will result from allowing the testimony.

* * *

In 1986, the Colorado Court of Appeals . . . set forth three principal factors for trial court consideration in determining a sanction. *P.R.G.,* 729 P.2d at 382. First, the trial court must consider the involvement, or lack thereof, of a party or counsel in the violation of the order by the witness. Id. Second, the trial court should consider the witness's actions and state of mind in his or her violation of the sequestration order, and whether the violation was inadvertent or deliberate. Id. Finally, the trial court should consider the subject matter of the violation in conjunction with the substance of the disobedient witness's testimony and if the testimony is unrelated in substance to the violation of the sequestration order, the court enjoys wide discretion in its ability to allow the witness to testify. Id. We agree, but modify the first factor to require evidence of the party's or counsel's consent, connivance, procurement, or knowledge regarding the violation before a sanction can be imposed against that party. We base adoption of these factors, as modified, on our review of the case law.

* * *

D.   Application to This Case

In the case before us, the trial court did not make an adequate inquiry into whether the sequestration violation actually occurred. It simply accepted the prosecution's assertions. The record contains no verification that Curry was actually in the courtroom, let alone any facts regarding the length of his presence or what he heard. Similarly, the record is devoid of any indication that the trial court considered the factors applicable to the choice of appropriate sanction.

* * *

E. Not Harmless Error

The defendant objected to the preclusion of Curry's testimony. Defense counsel argued to the court that: 1) an inquiry could be made

to determine the severity of the violation; 2) other sanctions might be imposed, such as admonishment; and 3) that exclusion of Curry would be prejudicial to his client.

We do not require that parties use "talismanic language" to preserve particular arguments for appeal, but the trial court must be presented with an adequate opportunity to make findings of fact and conclusions of law on any issue before we will review it. [Citations omitted.]

Here, defense counsel offered the trial court an adequate opportunity to commence a sufficient inquiry into the violation and the possible prejudice resulting from its exclusion order. Curry's was the only evidence offered to corroborate the defendant's own testimony, as well as the only evidence offered that would link the expert's testimony about factors leading to false allegations with the case at hand. Our review of the record reveals that Curry's evidence would have materially assisted Melendez's case.

A defendant has a fundamental constitutional right to present his or her version of the facts and favorable evidence. See Washington, 388 U.S. at 19. Here, a constitutional error was properly preserved for appeal, and the constitutional harmless error standard applies. See *Blecha v. People*, 962 P.2d 931, 942 (Colo. 1998). We cannot say beyond a reasonable doubt that the exclusion of Curry's testimony did not contribute to the guilty verdict.

III.

Accordingly, we affirm the court of appeals' judgment. [Reversing the convictions.]

STATE
v.
SANDS

Court of Appeals, Eleventh Appellate District
2008 Ohio 6981, 2008 Ohio App. LEXIS 5610 (2008)

MARY JANE TRAPP, J.

Appellant, Joseph A. Sands, appeals from the Lake County Court of Common Pleas judgment of his conviction and sentence for engaging in a pattern of corrupt activity and attempting to commit murder and aggravated arson with public officials as his targets.

As Francis Bacon said, "Revenge is a kind of wild justice, which the more man's nature runs to the more ought law to weed it out." A Lake County jury listened to the revengeful voice of a calculating man outline a chilling plot with his girlfriend and friend to kill a mayor, a prosecutor, and a judge; all because he was aggrieved by prosecutions for various misdemeanor offenses.

Unbeknownst to Mr. Sands, in an effort to stop the plot and weed out the conspirators, Mr. Sands' friend, Mr. Green, became a confidential informant. Over a period of five days he recorded Mr. Sands' detailed plans for the acquisition of materials for the construction of pipe bombs which were to be used to fire bomb officials' homes. The plot had progressed to the point where a dry run for the bombing of the mayor's home was undertaken. When Mr. Green expressed some concern as to any children who would surely be in the mayor's home, Mr. Sands matter-of-factly replied, "[his] kid is going to die with him."

The plot was foiled, the conspirators prosecuted, and the rule of law, not the street, prevailed in the jury's verdict. We affirm the jury's verdict for the reasons that follow.

Substantive and Procedural History

On April 1, 2006, Jason Green contacted Madison Township Detective Mark Parisi and requested that they meet outside of his hometown, North Perry Village. At the meeting, Mr. Green informed him that his friend, Mr. Sands, and Mr. Sands' girlfriend, Dawn Holin, were conspiring to kill four local officials. The intended targets were Painesville Municipal Court Judge Michael Cicconetti, North Perry Police Chief Denise Mercsak, North Perry Mayor Tom Williams, and North Perry Prosecutor Joseph Gurley.

* * *

Both Mr. Green and Mr. Sands had an embattled history over the years with the North Perry Village Police and Mayor Williams, and both believed they were being unfairly harassed. There were incidents and altercations where the police would be

called to Mr. Sands' automotive repair shop, JB Performance, which he owned with his girlfriend and co-conspirator, Ms. Holin. Mr. Green also had a lengthy criminal history, and faced various charges in the past few years for theft, menacing, animal cruelty, and littering, to name a few among the many.

* * *

After hearing Mr. Sands lay out this chilling plot, Mr. Green went to the police. Since both Mr. Green and Mr. Sands had been voluntary informants for Detective Parisi in the past, Mr. Green felt he could trust the detective with this information. Mr. Green told the detective that Mr. Sands wanted to kill the victims by building homemade pipe bombs that were going to be loaded with shrapnel and ether, as well as possibly, homemade napalm. The plan was to kill Mayor Williams in the first few weeks of April by throwing a pipe bomb through the bay window of his home. The next target was to be Prosecutor Gurley. Then, after Mr. Sands was sentenced for failing to file his taxes on April 20, they would move on to the judge. By killing Mayor Williams and Prosecutor Gurley, Mr. Sands hoped to intimidate Judge Cicconetti to impose a lesser sentence. [Police set up Mr. Green with recording devices to record his conversations with Mr. Sands.]

* * *

Mr. Sands devised all facets of the plan. His firebombing target was Mayor Williams. He was adamant that Mr. Green would drive, so he could run and throw the bomb into Mayor Williams' home. At the request of the police, Mr. Green suggested involving a third party, but Mr. Sands did not want anyone else involved. Mr. Sands also developed their alibi that they had gotten drunk and the three just stayed at the Sands/Holins' home. Since their history with the village was notorious, Mr. Sands knew they would be under suspicion. Because of that they would hit Prosecutor Gurley a month after Mayor Williams, and then they would possibly have to wait as long as a year to shoot Judge Cicconetti.

Between April 4 and April 9 of 2006, Mr. Green continued to record conversations with Mr. Sands, recording approximately seven conversations. . . .

* * *

By Friday, April 7, the three had everything they would need with the exception of the wick to light the pipe bomb. To purchase this, Mr. Sands wanted Mr. Green to accompany him to a store some sixty miles away in Ashland, Ohio, called Fin, Fur, & Feather. Like the pipe, he did not want to make the purchase in the local area, where everyone seemed to know each other. Ms. Holin provided them with directions. Unbeknownst to Mr. Sands, ATF, the police, and the FBI were following them, with a plan to arrest the pair upon purchase. On the way to Ashland, Mr. Sands told Mr. Green they could not use the pipe they purchased because it was too identifiable. The police could easily discover that Mr. Green had purchased the pipe, thus, Mr. Sands suggested getting some pipe from his brother-in-law.

At the store, . . . both were arrested and placed in separate vehicles. Mr. Green did not know in advance of the plans for arrest.

At the time of arrest, Mr. Sands consented to a search of his home and business, which produced all of the equipment needed to make a pipe bomb.

* * *

Mr. Sands was subsequently charged with [a variety felonies, including several conspiracy counts, and engaging in a pattern of corrupt activity.]

Mr. Sands, in his defense, testified that the plan was Mr. Green's idea and he was merely a cohort. He was, in fact, trying to "control" Mr. Green to prevent him from carrying out the plan.

After an almost two week trial, the jury found Mr. Sands guilty on six counts of the indictment, finding him guilty of engaging in a pattern of corrupt activity, three counts of conspiracy to commit aggravated murder as they related to Judge Cicconetti, Mayor Williams, and Prosecutor Gurley; as well as two counts of conspiracy to commit aggravated arson as they related to Mayor Williams and his property. . . . [Defendant received a twenty year prison sentence.]

Mr. Sands now timely appeals, raising seven assignments of error:

* * *

[Error # 4.] The Trial Court erred in admitting other acts evidence denying Appellant a fair trial.

Evidence of Other Acts

In his fourth assignment of error, Mr. Sands contends that the trial court abused its discretion in permitting the state to cross-examine him [to impeach him] on other acts [prior criminal activities] that he introduced by way of his direct examination. Specifically, Mr. Sands argues that the trial court erred in allowing the state to question him on an incident in which he forced his thirteen-year old son to file a false police report. Because of the ensuing charge [related to the false police report], Mr. Sands worked as a confidential informant with Mr. Green on a drug case [to get the charge related to the false police report dropped]. We find this argument to be without merit.

"The determination to admit or exclude evidence is within the sound discretion of the trial court and will not be reversed by an appellate court absent a showing of an abuse of discretion." *Vinson* at P48, citing *State v. Sledge*, 11th Dist. No. 2001-T-0123, 2003 Ohio 4100, P20, citing *State v. Rootes* (Mar. 23, 2001), 11th Dist. No. 2000-P-0003, 2001 Ohio App. LEXIS 1391, 45, citing *Renfro v. Black* (1990), 52 Ohio St.3d 27, 32, 556 N.E.2d 150. Abuse of discretion connotes more than error of law or of judgment; it implies that the court's attitude is unreasonable, arbitrary, or unconscionable. [Citation omitted.]

Mr. Sands argues that the essence of the "false charge" testimony implied he was dishonest; thus this was so prejudicial it denied him a fair trial. A review of the record, however, reveals otherwise. The court allowed a limited cross-examination after his counsel objected, specifically because Mr. Sands testified on direct examination that he and Mr. Green were informants for the police in the drug case. Mr. Sands' defense was that Mr. Green was the mastermind behind this conspiracy and that he was set up. Thus, he opened the door as to this line of questioning. The trial court then gave a limiting instruction to the jury before deliberations cautioning that such testimony [about the false police report] could be used only to determine Mr. Sands' credibility.

Evid.R. 401 defines "relevant evidence" as "evidence having any tendency to make the existence of any fact that is of consequence to the determination of the action more probable or less probable than it would be without the evidence."

Furthermore, evidence that is relevant is generally admissible, subject to certain exclusions, and irrelevant evidence is generally inadmissible. [Citation omitted.]

Moreover, Evid.R. 403(A) governs one of the circumstances under which the exclusion of relevant evidence is made mandatory. Id, citing *State v. Hamilton*, 11th Dist. No. 2000-L-003, 2002 Ohio 1681, P81. "The rule states that the trial court is required to exclude otherwise relevant evidence in cases where the probative value of the evidence is 'substantially outweighed by the danger of unfair prejudice, of confusion of the issues, or of misleading the jury.'" Id., quoting *State v. Totarella*, 11th Dist. No. 2002-L-147, 2004 Ohio 1175, P34; *State v. Entze*, 11th Dist. No. 2003-P-0018, 2004 Ohio 5321, P28.

Pursuant to Evid.R. 609 impeachment by evidence of a conviction of a prior crime may be used to attack the credibility of a witness when:

"(A)(3) Notwithstanding Evid.R. 403(A), but subject to Evid.R. 403(B), evidence that any witness, including an accused, has been convicted of a crime is admissible if the crime involved dishonesty or false statement, regardless of the punishment and whether based upon state or federal statute or local ordinance." (Emphasis added.)

Furthermore, "[a]ny time an accused testifies, the accused's prior conviction is admissible, unless the probative value of the evidence is outweighed by its prejudicial effect." *Cortner, supra*, citing *State v. Lane* (1997), 118 Ohio App.3d 230, 234, 692 N.E.2d 634. Thus, "Evid.R. 609(A)(2) specifically permits the State the ability to conduct a limited cross-examination for the purposes of impeachment." Id., citing *State v. Bryan*, 101 Ohio St.3d 272, 2004 Ohio 971, P132, 804 N.E.2d 433; *State v. Green* (1993), 66 Ohio St.3d 141, 147, 1993 Ohio 26, 609 N.E.2d 1253, *see, also, State v. Slagle* (1992), 65 Ohio St.3d 597, 605, 605 N.E.2d 916, citing Evid.R. 611(B) ("As a general rule cross-examination is 'permitted on all relevant matters and matters affecting credibility.'") "The extent of cross-examination allowed is within the discretion of the trial court, and will not be overturned absent an abuse of that discretion." Id., citing *State v. Acre* (1983), 6 Ohio St.3d 140, 145, 6 Ohio B. 197, 451 N.E.2d 802.

The state was allowed to cross-examine Mr. Sands on this issue because he testified as to it on direct. This relevant testimony certainly goes to the issue of Mr. Sands' credibility because he claimed Mr. Green was the mastermind in this current plot, and that they had been "snitches" in the past. As to the past incident, however, the state's cross-examination elicited only that Mr. Sands had been facing charges at that time, that Mr. Green had arranged for them to be confidential informants in an effort to help the police and Mr. Sands, and that in exchange, the charges against Mr. Sands were dropped.

Even if we did find this testimony was allowed in error, which we do not, the error would be harmless as "there is no reasonable possibility that exclusion of the evidence would have affected the result of this trial." [Citations omitted.]

This testimony was not so prejudicial as to confuse the jurors. Furthermore, Mr. Sands himself opened the door to this testimony. We do not find an abuse of discretion in permitting this limited cross-examination, or the trial court's giving a limiting instruction as to its use before jury deliberations began.

Mr. Sands' fourth assignment of error is without merit.

* * *

The judgment of the Lake County Court of Common Pleas is affirmed.

Cases Relating to Chapter 10

Privileges

ST. CLAIR

v.

COMMONWEALTH

Supreme Court of Kentucky
174 S.W.3d 474, 2005
Ky. LEXIS 334 (2005)

OPINION OF THE COURT BY CHIEF
JUSTICE LAMBERT
REVERSING AND REMANDING

FACTS

Appellant, Michael D. St. Clair, was convicted
of two counts of receiving stolen property
over $ 100, criminal attempt to commit mur-
der, second-degree arson, and capital kidnapping. He was sentenced to death for the
kidnapping of Frank Brady, during which
Brady was murdered. Appellant waived his
right to jury sentencing on the non-capital
charges, and agreed to a sentence of twenty
years for attempted murder, twenty years
for second-degree arson, and five years on
each count of receiving stolen property over
$ 100, for a total of fifty years. Appellant now
appeals to this Court as a matter of right.

This is not the first time this particular
defendant is before this Court. In February of
1992, a Bullitt County Grand Jury indicted
Appellant for the Capital Murder of Frank
Brady. He was tried and convicted in August,
and sentenced to death in September of 1998.
This Court in a recent decision, St. Clair v.
Commonwealth, (hereinafter "St. Clair I"),
reversed and remanded for a new penalty
phase hearing on Appellant's death sentence.

Prior to trial in Hardin County, this Court
rendered St. Clair v. Roark, (St. Clair II), in
which St. Clair's petition for extraordinary
relief to prevent his prosecution for capital
kidnapping in Hardin County was denied. In
large part a complete recitation of the facts is
contained in St. Clair I and St. Clair II, and
is relied upon to illustrate the facts relevant
to this appeal.

According to the evidence, Appellant
escaped from Oklahoma authorities in
September of 1991 while awaiting final sentencing for two Oklahoma murder convictions. St. Clair and Dennis Gene Reese stole
a pickup truck from a jail employee and fled
from the jail in Durant, Oklahoma. The pickup
truck eventually ran out of gas and Reese and
St. Clair stole another pickup truck, a handgun, and some ammunition from the home of
Vernon Stephens and headed for the suburbs
of Dallas, Texas. St. Clair's wife at the time,
Bylynn St. Clair n4 ("Bylynn"), met with her
husband and Reese in Texas, and provided
them with money, clothing, and other items.
Reese was arrested several months later in Las
Vegas, Nevada, and confessed to his involvement in the Kentucky events detailed below.

According to Reese, after escaping from
jail in Oklahoma, he and St. Clair traveled
to Colorado where they kidnapped Timothy
Keeling and stole Keeling's pickup truck.
Keeling was later murdered in New Mexico.
St. Clair and Reese proceeded to drive
Keeling's truck to New Orleans, Louisiana,
then through Arkansas and Tennessee before
arriving at a rest stop in southern Hardin
County, Kentucky. While in Hardin County,
they decided to steal Frank Brady's late

model pickup truck. They kidnapped Brady and drove him from Hardin County to Bullitt County where St. Clair shot and killed Brady. St. Clair and Reese then returned to Hardin County and set fire to Keeling's truck.

Witnesses to the arson gave the Kentucky State Police a description of the Brady truck seen near the location where Keeling's truck was on fire. Based on that description, Trooper Herbert Bennett stopped Reese and St. Clair while they were still driving Brady's truck through Hardin County. St. Clair fired two shots at Trooper Bennett, one of which penetrated the radiator of the police cruiser. A high-speed chase followed, but Reese and St. Clair escaped when Bennett's cruiser became disabled. Reese was arrested two weeks later in Las Vegas and waived extradition to Kentucky. St. Clair was arrested about two months later in Hugo, Oklahoma.

On December 20, 1991, St. Clair was indicted for two counts of receiving stolen property, criminal attempt to commit murder, and second-degree arson. On January 17, 1992, the Hardin County Grand Jury indicted St. Clair for capital kidnapping. On June 19, 1998, the Commonwealth filed its Notice of Intent to Seek Death Penalty. St. Clair was convicted in February of 2001 of the Capital Kidnapping of Frank Brady, and he was sentenced to death. Additional facts will be presented as necessary. St. Clair argues that his wife Bylynn was improperly allowed to testify to four privileged conversations, and that those conversations should have been excluded by his assertion of the marital privilege under KRE 504. When the statements were made, St. Clair and Bylynn were married.

I. Marital Privilege

The first contested statement given by Bylynn was that when she met St. Clair in Texas before St. Clair reached Kentucky, she hugged him and felt something hard on his belt. Over St. Clair's objection, she testified that when she asked if he had a gun, she testified that he, St. Clair, told her he took a gun off that old man whose house he had broken into (the home of Vernon Stephens in Oklahoma).

Bylynn's second statement concerned her meeting St. Clair in Oklahoma at Frost's Farm in December of 1991, the night before he was arrested. It was there that St. Clair stated to Bylynn that St. Clair and Reese had to leave their belongings and that they burned a truck. St. Clair told Bylynn that he returned to Oklahoma by riding with truck drivers. St. Clair objected and moved for a mistrial on the grounds that this latter statement had not been included in the Commonwealth's notice, and that it was privileged under the marital privilege.

Bylynn's third statement at trial concerned a telephone conversation between her and St. Clair. She testified that St. Clair called her from Louisiana and that Reese was in the bathroom while he was calling. The Commonwealth then elicited that St. Clair told Bylynn that he had to leave some of his things behind in the truck, and that he said something about being in Louisiana. St. Clair objected on the grounds that he was not provided notice of the Commonwealth's intention to introduce evidence relating to his travel to Louisiana, and that it was not an unexpected answer since the Commonwealth asked her if St. Clair had ever said anything about being in Louisiana. The Commonwealth responded that this testimony was not new information since Bylynn had testified to it at the Bullitt County trial.

Bylynn's fourth statement is that St. Clair told her that he was in Louisiana, and that he had told her he had been in Oklahoma for a few weeks before he saw her in December at a friend's house in Durant County, Oklahoma. She stated that he had told her that the Oklahoma State Bureau of Investigation (OSBI) had searched the place, but that he was hiding under some hay and they never saw him. The Commonwealth then asked Bylynn how long St. Clair had told her he had been in Oklahoma and the date of the conversation when he did so. She responded that it was December 17, 1991, the day before his arrest. This testimony was elicited to contradict Reese's anticipated testimony that St. Clair had arrived at his farm on October 1, 1991.

St. Clair objected to the testimony, and the trial court overruled the objection on the grounds that the Commonwealth could cross-examine Bylynn about any subject to which she had previously testified. St. Clair now argues that the introduction of this testimony violated due process, his right to a fair trial and that Bylynn's testimony was admitted in violation of the marital privilege. St. Clair also argues that at the time of trial, KRS 421.210(1) was applicable and allowed one spouse to prohibit the other from testifying to communications made during their marriage, which are confidential in nature. Finally, St. Clair argues that Bylynn's statements that incriminated St. Clair were also inadmissible since they violated RCr 7.24(1).

The Commonwealth contends that the marital privilege does not apply in this case for two reasons. First, the Commonwealth argues that Bylynn and St. Clair were involved in joint criminal activity under KRE 504(c)(1). It posits that no privilege is applicable since the communications testified to occurred during St. Clair's escape from the Bryan County Jail in Oklahoma and that Bylynn provided him with items which he later used to kidnap and kill Brady. Second, the Commonwealth argues that these communications were not confidential because they were made in the presence of Reese.

KRE 504 contains a spousal testimonial privilege, KRE 504(a), a confidential marital communications privilege, KRE 504(b), and exceptions to those privileges in KRE 504(c). Both privileges are designed to protect and enhance the marital relationship at the expense of otherwise useful evidence. KRE 504(c)(1) codifies preexisting law, KRS 421.210(1). KRE 504 provides:

(a) Spousal testimony. The spouse of a party has a privilege to refuse to testify against the party as to events occurring after the date of their marriage. A party has a privilege to prevent his or her spouse from testifying against the party as to events occurring after the date of their marriage.

(b) Marital communications. An individual has a privilege to refuse to testify and to prevent another from testifying to any confidential communication made by the individual to his or her spouse during their marriage. The privilege may be asserted only by the individual holding the privilege or by the holder's guardian, conservator, or personal representative. A communication is confidential if it is made privately by an individual to his or her spouse and is not intended for disclosure to any other person.

(c) Exceptions. There is no privilege under this rule:

(1) In any criminal proceeding in which sufficient evidence is introduced to support a finding that the spouses conspired or acted jointly in the commission of the crime charged;

(2) * * *

(3) In any proceeding in which the spouses are adverse parties.

KRE 504(a) and (b) changed the spousal privilege from KRS 421.210(1) in two significant respects. First, the testimonial privilege in KRE 504(a) was expanded to enable a party spouse to preclude a witness spouse from testifying against him. Second, the marital communications privilege in KRE 504(b) was narrowed by defining the term "confidential" to require that the communication was not intended for disclosure to any other person, i.e., there must have been a positive expectation of confidentiality.

The issue we must first address is whether subsection (c)(1) applies in this situation. We begin our analysis by examining the plain language of KRE 504(c)(1). The plain language of the exception states that there must be "sufficient evidence" to "support a finding that the spouse conspired or acted jointly in the commission of the crime charged." Plainly, this exception to the privilege applies only if each spouse has contributed to or participated in the crime charged. In Gill v. Commonwealth, this Court discussed the application of the marital communications privilege and its exceptions as they existed under KRS 421.210(1). In Gill, testimony of one spouse was held not privileged where both spouses were accused of being *particeps criminis* with the wife having been indicted for the same crime that her husband had been convicted of committing.

In this case, Bylynn facilitated St. Clair's flight after his prison escape, but there was no evidence that Bylynn conspired or acted jointly in the commission of the crimes with which St. Clair was charged (two counts of receiving stolen property over $ 100, criminal attempt to commit murder, second-degree arson, or capital kidnapping).

This Court has reviewed the record extensively. Statements two and three were undoubtedly made outside the presence of Reese or any other person. Bylynn acknowledged on the stand that statement two occurred in private when she and St. Clair were in a barn loft. She also confirmed that statement three occurred during a phone conversation with St. Clair while Reese was out of the room. As stated in KRE 504(b), "[a] communication is confidential if it is made privately by an individual to his or her spouse and is not intended for disclosure to any other person." St. Clair was running from the authorities, and confided certain information to his wife. His statements implicated him in various crimes, and their sensitive nature combined with the circumstances of their disclosure rendered them confidential. For these reasons statements two and three fall within the ambit of a confidential communication, and should have been excluded by virtue of the marital privilege.

Upon review, there is some doubt as to the confidential nature of statements one and four. Statement one took place at a fair, and apparently was made in full view of the public eye. Moreover, based on the testimony of Bylynn, it is unclear whether St. Clair was alone or with Reese at the time of this statement. However, confidential statements need not be given behind closed doors to retain their confidential character. A hushed or whispered statement from one spouse to another may be considered confidential depending on the circumstances of its disclosure. In this case, the record is insufficient to make a definitive determination as to the confidential nature of statement one. Therefore, upon remand the trial judge should hear additional evidence regarding the circumstances of statement one and make a factual finding.

Whether statement four was confidential is equally unclear. At trial, Bylynn seemed to relate the statement four disclosure to the same telephone conversation in which the statement three disclosure was made. If this is the case, statement four would enjoy the same privileged status as statement three.

However, review of the record leaves the Court with enough doubt to require a hearing on the statement four issue.

Accordingly, statements two and three were privileged and should have been excluded at trial. As to statements one and four, a hearing should be held on remand to determine their status.

The admission of the privileged statements was prejudicial because the Commonwealth used this testimony to corroborate Reese's testimony that St. Clair was the ringleader and the shooter. Bylynn was a critical witness as her testimony repeated the details of the jail escape and that St. Clair had stolen the alleged murder weapon. It revealed that she felt a gun on Appellant's person when she met him in Dallas, and her testimony contradicted St. Clair's defense that he had never been in Kentucky because he told her he had burned a truck in Kentucky. Bylynn's testimony was crucial because it contained the only admission by St. Clair of guilt, and one of a few pieces of evidence that placed St. Clair in Kentucky at the time of the kidnapping and murder. Consequently, the admission of Bylynn's testimony was prejudicial error and retrial is required.

II. Jury Instructions

III. Various Other Claims

For the forgoing reasons, we reverse and remand.

DISSENTING OPINION BY JUSTICE WINTERSHEIMER

I must respectfully dissent from the majority opinion because there was no error on the part of the trial judge in permitting the testimony of the ex-wife concerning communications between the accused and her during his escape and other patently criminal activities. The majority opinion construes the marital privilege too broadly.

The marital communications privilege does not apply in this situation because the communications involved aiding St. Clair in patently criminal activity and because the communications sought to be privileged were likely intended to be shared with a third party. Furthermore, the wife's testimony has substantial probative value thereby outweighing the minimal prejudicial effect.

Thus, the majority has interpreted the confidential marital communications privilege too broadly. Privileges are to be interpreted narrowly. [Citation omitted.] Porter, supra, states that "privileges must be strictly construed and accepted only to the very limited extent that permitting a refusal to testify or excluding relevant evidence has a public good transcending the normally predominate principle of utilizing all rational means for ascertaining truth." 986 F.2d at 1019 *citing Trammel v. United States*, 445 U.S. 40, 50, 100 S. Ct. 906, 63 L. Ed. 2d 186 (1980); *United States v. Nixon*, 418 U.S. 683, 709–10, 94 S. Ct. 3090, 41 L. Ed. 2d 1039 (1974).

In concluding that statements two and three were confidential, the majority opinion fails to analyze whether the information shared between St. Clair and his wife were "not intended for disclosure to any other person." KRE 504(b). Because St. Clair and Reese escaped and stole a pickup truck together, it is reasonable to infer that they made plans on securing the means to continue their escape. For instance, communications to the wife concerning the need for clothing, money, and other items would be expected to be non confidential because St. Clair would tell Reese from where aid to their escape would come. Accordingly, statements from St. Clair to his wife concerning his and Reese's location, future location, and plans would also fail the "not intended for disclosure to another person" test because Bylynn was a source of aid to them.

KRE 504(c)(1) states that the privilege is excepted "in any criminal proceeding in which sufficient evidence is introduced to support a finding that the spouses conspired or acted jointly in the commission of the crime charged." The majority interprets this to mean that Bylynn must have directly aided in receiving stolen property, criminal attempt to commit murder, or second-degree arson. It is arguable whether aiding and abetting the escape results in conspiring for the purposes of rendering the privilege. *Gill v. Commonwealth*, 374 S.W.2d 848 (Ky. 1964) states, "when husband and wife are co-conspirators, or when the evidence justifies such a conclusion, a declaration of the husband or wife at the time of the act in

question is not privileged". Certainly, under the situation described in these facts, the wife became some part of the criminal activities by her assistance. Furthermore, this analysis is more consistent with the 6th Circuit's interpretation of the joint participation exception to the confidential marital communications privilege. *See United States v. Sims*, 755 F.2d 1239 (6th Cir. 1985) (Exception to privilege for confidential marital communications arising out of joint criminal activity exists for conversations that pertain to patently illegal activity.). Even though this part of the analysis may be a close call in this case, the communications were not confidential.

The majority opinion states that the evidence of the wife's testimony would be prejudicial. This analysis is incorrect under KRE 403. KRE 403 disallows evidence whose prejudicial value outweighs the probative value. Because her testimony corroborated some other evidence, and especially because her testimony was the critical key to place St. Clair in Kentucky at the time of the criminal commissions, it has significant probative value. Accordingly, the trial judge did not err in admitting the testimony after disallowing the confidential marital communications privilege to apply.

Therefore, there was no confidential marital communications privilege here. The trial judge properly instructed the jury. I would affirm the conviction in all respects.

Graves and Scott, JJ., join this dissent.

STATE
v.
BERGMANN

2009 Iowa App. LEXIS 54 (2009)

POTTERFIELD, J.

I. Background Facts and Proceedings

On January 11, 2006, Rodney Bergmann was found unconscious in his vehicle, which was in gear with the engine running. Bergmann was roused and taken by ambulance to the hospital. A phlebotomist at the hospital drew Bergmann's blood, which showed a blood alcohol level of .216. [This blood test was separate from another test of Bergmann's blood and urine that was performed pursuant to Iowa Code chapter 321J. The results of that test were suppressed because the specimens were improperly obtained.] Bergmann's attorney sent a letter to Black Hawk County Deputy Sheriff William Locke that contained the medical records for treatment Bergmann received at the hospital. The Black Hawk County Attorney filed a trial information on February 13, 2006, charging Bergmann with operating while intoxicated in violation of Iowa Code section 321J.2 (2005).

Bergmann told rescuers that he took fentanyl for a back injury, and fentanyl was found in his vehicle. A treating nurse noted that Bergmann had refilled a prescription for fentanyl earlier that day. Bergmann asserted that the fentanyl was the cause of his condition and that ingestion of Nyquil caused his elevated blood alcohol level.

The State filed a motion to adjudicate law points seeking to use the analysis of Bergmann's blood that was performed at the hospital as was revealed in the medical records he provided. Bergmann resisted, stating these records were protected by the physician-patient privilege. [Bergmann did not execute a release of information.] The district court found that the records were admissible because Bergmann destroyed the confidentiality between him and his physician when he released his medical records to the sheriff.

On July 3, 2007, the State applied for and received, ex parte, a county attorney's subpoena duces tecum commanding hospital personnel to provide the identity and address of the person who had tested Bergmann's blood. The subpoena also ordered the production of related information, which the county attorney obtained orally from the hospital personnel. The court order required the prosecutor to serve defense counsel with the application and order by fax the same day. The State argued the subpoena was necessary so that it could list the individual's name and address in the minutes of testimony as required by the Iowa Rules of Criminal Procedure.

On July 19, 2007, Bergmann filed a motion to quash the information obtained by the subpoena as it was protected by the physician-patient privilege. 3 On July 24, 2007, the district court overruled Bergmann's motion to quash, finding that Bergmann had waived the physician-patient privilege.

Bergmann was convicted by a jury on July 27, 2007. He appeals, arguing the district court erred by: (1) finding that his medical records were admissible and issuing a subpoena; and (2) overruling his motion to quash.

II. Standard of Review

We review the district court's ruling for a correction of errors of law. *State v. Henneberry*, 558 N.W.2d 708, 709 (Iowa 1997).

III. Admissibility of Medical Records

Bergmann provided the State with medical documents to support his claim that he suffered from a fentanyl overdose. Those documents included the lab report revealing his blood alcohol content. Bergmann argues that, absent his release of additional records, the State should have access to only those medical records that he provided and nothing more.

A doctor is prohibited from disclosing a patient's confidential communications without the patient's consent. Iowa Code 622.10. Unless the physician-patient privilege is waived, the hospital should not provide the State with medical information, including the blood alcohol test results. The patient can waive this privilege by disclosure or consent to disclosure. *State v. Demaray*, 704 N.W.2d 60, 65 (Iowa 2005). In this case, Bergmann disclosed medical information to the State. "[V]oluntary disclosure of the content of a privileged communication constitutes waiver as to all other communications on the same subject." *Miller v. Continental Ins. Co.*, 392 N.W.2d 500, 504–05 (Iowa 1986). Bergmann cannot waive the physician-patient privilege as to information that benefits his case and invoke the privilege against harmful information. Id. at 505. He can choose to invoke or waive the physician-patient privilege, but his decision is final and applies to all communication on that subject. Id. When Bergmann disclosed his medical records to the State, he waived his physician-patient privilege as to his treatment on that occasion.

The district court did not err in overruling Bergmann's motion to quash.

AFFIRMED.

NEW YORK CITY HEALTH
v.
MORGENTHAU

COURT OF APPEALS OF NEW YORK

98 N.Y.2d 525, 779 N.E.2d 173, 749 N.Y.S.2d 462, 2002 N.Y. LEXIS 3140 (2002)

JUDGES: Opinion by Judge Rosenblatt. Chief Judge Kaye and Judges Smith, Levine, Ciparick, Wesley and Graffeo concur.

OPINIONBY: ROSENBLATT

Hospitals may assert a physician-patient privilege under CPLR 4504 (a) to maintain the confidentiality of patient medical records. The case before us involves the extent to which grand juries may, compatibly with CPLR 4504 (a), acquire medical records for the purpose of identifying criminal assailants.

On May 25, 1998, an unidentified assailant stabbed a man to death in Manhattan. Police could determine only that the assailant was a Caucasian male in his 30s or early 40s and that he may have been bleeding when he fled the scene. Over 2 1/2 years later, still unable to identify him, the District Attorney of New York County conjectured that the assailant may have sought medical treatment at a local hospital shortly after the homicide. In early 2001, the District Attorney served grand jury subpoenas duces tecum on 23 hospitals, including four facilities operated by the New York City Health and Hospitals Corporation (HHC). Those subpoenas sought:

"any and all records pertaining to any male Caucasian patient between the ages of 30 to 45 years, who was treated or who sought treatment on May 25th, 1998 through May 26th, 1998 for a laceration, puncture wound or slash, or other injury caused by or possibly caused by a cutting instrument and/or sharp object, said injury being plainly observable to a lay person without expert or professional knowledge; said records including but not limited to said patient's name, date of birth, address, telephone number, social security number and other identifying information, except any and all information acquired by a physician, registered nurse or licensed practical nurse in attending said patient in a professional capacity and which was necessary to enable said doctor and/or nurse to act in that capacity."

Citing CPLR 4504 (a), n1 HHC invoked the physician-patient privilege and refused to turn over emergency room triage logs potentially responsive to these subpoenas, claiming that compliance would necessarily breach patient confidentiality in violation of the statute. After the District Attorney moved to hold HHC in contempt, HHC cross-moved for an order quashing the subpoenas. Supreme Court denied both motions but ordered HHC to submit the records for in camera inspection. The Appellate Division unanimously reversed and granted the motion to quash, holding that compliance with the subpoenas would violate the physician-patient privilege because "the assessment of the nature and cause of the injuries triggering production of the relevant documents involves an inherently medical evaluation" (287 AD2d 287, 288, 731 N.Y.S.2d 17 [2001]). This Court granted the District Attorney leave to appeal, and we now affirm.

Our analysis begins with the history and purpose of the physician-patient privilege. Common law did not recognize any confidentiality in communications between patients and medical professionals. New York was the first state to enact a physician-patient privilege statute (see 2 Rev Stat of NY, part III, ch VII, tit III, § 73 [1st ed 1829]; see also Dillenbeck v Hess, 73 NY2d 278, 284, 536 N.E.2d 1126, 539 N.Y.S.2d 707 [1989]; FISCH, NEW YORK EVIDENCE § 541, at 356 [2d ed 1977]). The modern codification of the privilege, CPLR 4504 (a), serves three core policy objectives implicated on this appeal (see generally PRINCE, RICHARDSON ON EVIDENCE §§5-301, 5-302, at 246-249 [Farrell 11th ed]). First, the physician-patient privilege seeks to maximize unfettered patient communication with medical professionals, so that any potential embarrassment arising from public disclosure will not "deter people from seeking medical help and securing adequate diagnosis and treatment" (*Dillenbeck* at 285, quoting *Williams v Roosevelt Hosp.*, 66 N.Y.2d 391, 395, 497 N.Y.S.2d 348, 488 N.E.2d 94 [1985]; *see also Matter of Grand Jury Proceedings [Doe]*, 56 N.Y.2d 348, 352, 437 N.E.2d 1118, 452 N.Y.S.2d 361 [1982]). Second, the privilege encourages medical professionals to be candid in recording confidential information in patient medical records, and thereby averts a choice "between their legal duty to testify and their professional obligation to honor their patients' confidences" (*Dillenbeck* at 285, citing FISCH § 541; see also Revisers' Reports and Notes, 3 Rev Stat of NY, at 737 [2d ed 1836]). Third, the privilege protects patients' reasonable privacy expectations against disclosure of sensitive personal information (*see* MARTIN, CAPRA & ROSSI, NEW YORK EVIDENCE HANDBOOK § 5.3.1, at 367 [1997]; *Developments in the Law—Privileged Communications, Medical and Counseling Privileges*, 98 HARV L REV 1530, 1544–1548 [1985]).

Though in derogation of the common law, the physician-patient privilege is to be given a "broad and liberal construction to carry out its policy" (*Matter of Grand Jury Investigation of Onondaga County*, 59 NY2d 130, 134, 450 N.E.2d 678, 463 N.Y.S.2d 758 [1983]; *Matter of City Council of the City of N.Y. v Goldwater*, 284 NY 296, 300, 31 N.E.2d 31 [1940]).

On this appeal, the District Attorney contends that enforcement of the subpoenas would not offend these policies or violate CPLR 4504 (a). The prosecutor argues that the subpoenas do not seek information acquired by means of medical diagnosis, treatment or expertise, and should be enforced because they purport to seek records only of injuries "plainly observable to a lay person without expert or professional knowledge." We disagree.

The physician-patient privilege generally does not extend to information obtained outside the realms of medical diagnosis and treatment. Indeed, because the policies underlying the physician-patient privilege implicate confidential patient relationships with

medical professionals as medical professionals, we have generally limited the privilege to information acquired by the medical professional "through the application of professional skill or knowledge" (*Dillenbeck*, 73 N.Y.2d at 284 n 4). Accordingly, notwithstanding CPLR 4504 (a), medical professionals have been authorized to disclose observations of a heroin packet falling from a patient's sock (*see People v Capra*, 17 NY2d 670, 216 N.E.2d 610, 269 N.Y.S.2d 451 [1966]), injuries on a patient's cheek and lip (see *People v Giordano*, 274 A.D.2d 748, 711 N.Y.S.2d 557 [2000]), and a patient's slurred speech and alcohol-laced breath incident to intoxication (*see People v Hedges*, 98 A.D.2d 950, 470 N.Y.S.2d 61 [1983]). Likewise, photographs of methadone-treatment patients taken to prevent unauthorized individuals from obtaining the drug (*see People v Newman*, 32 NY2d 379, 384, 298 N.E.2d 651, 345 N.Y.S.2d 502 [1973], cert denied 414 U.S. 1163, 39 L. Ed. 2d 116, 94 S. Ct. 927 [1974]) and the names and addresses of a medical professional's patients (*see In Matter of Albert Lindley Lee Mem. Hosp.*, 115 F. Supp. 643 [ND NY 1953], *affd* 209 F.2d 122 [2d Cir], cert denied sub nom. *Cincotta v United States*, 347 U.S. 960, 98 L. Ed. 1104, 74 S. Ct. 709 [1954]) are outside the ambit of CPLR 4504 (a) and must be surrendered pursuant to a valid subpoena.

We conclude, however, that Onondaga County controls this appeal and directs that the challenged subpoenas be quashed. In Onondaga County, as in the instant case, the victim was stabbed to death under circumstances that led investigators to conclude that the assailant may have left the scene bleeding. Endeavoring to identify the assailant, the District Attorney of Onondaga County issued a grand jury subpoena on a hospital, seeking "all medical records pertaining to treatment of any person with stab wounds or other wounds caused by a knife" *(Onondaga County*, 59 N.Y.2d at 133). In quashing the subpoena, the Court held that compliance might have "required the hospital to which it is addressed to divulge information protected by the physician-patient privilege" (59 N.Y.2d at 132). The Court concluded that under those circumstances, it was "not … possible to comply with a demand for names and addresses of all persons treated for a knife wound without disclosing privileged information concerning diagnosis and treatment" (59 N.Y.2d. at 135).

We perceive no difference of any actual substance between the subpoena quashed in Onondaga County and the ones challenged here. The records potentially responsive to the HHC subpoenas are precisely the same as those sought in Onondaga County. Though the District Attorney crafted the instant subpoenas with Onondaga County in mind by broadening their scope (to include most bleeding wounds rather than only knife wounds) and narrowing their reach (to include only wounds "plainly observable to a lay person"), the subpoenas still run afoul of Onondaga County.

Here, much as in Onondaga County, the challenged subpoenas define the class of records sought by the "cause or potential cause" of injury. Thus, the subpoenas inevitably call for a medical determination as to causation "through the application of professional skill or knowledge" (*Dillenbeck*, 73 N.Y.2d at 284 n 4). It is precisely this intrusion into the physician-patient relationship that CPLR 4504 (a) seeks to prevent. The inherently medical nature of this judgment is not obviated by attempting to qualify it in terms of what a layperson might plainly observe.

By merely reviewing hospital records after patients obtain emergency medical treatment, hospitals cannot reasonably determine whether particular injuries and their causes would have been obvious to a layperson. Medical records are not organized on the basis of what laypersons—as opposed to medical professionals—might discern. Even if a particular medical record does state the cause of injury, the record may not indicate reliably how the hospital ascertained the cause. Medical professionals may have learned the cause from the patient, or discovered it based on their medical expertise. Hospitals should not face contempt proceedings merely because they cannot distinguish the indistinguishable.

This result is further justified by the policy objectives of the physician-patient privilege and the broad construction of CPLR 4504 (a) required to achieve them. Patients should not fear that merely by obtaining emergency medical care they may lose the confidentiality of their medical records and their physicians' medical determinations. A contrary result would discourage critical emergency care, intrude on patients' confidential medical relationships and undermine patients' reasonable expectations of privacy.

Finally, we note that none of the Legislature's many statutory exceptions to the physician-patient privilege apply here. For example, notwithstanding CPLR 4504 (a), Public Health Law § 2101 (1) obliges physicians to disclose immediately any case of communicable disease (*see Thomas v Morris*, 286 NY 266, 268–270, 36 N.E.2d 141 [1941]), and Social Services Law § 413 (1) requires all medical professionals to report actual or suspected cases of child abuse (*see People v Trester*, 190 Misc 2d 46, 48, 737 N.Y.S.2d 522 [2002]). CPLR 4504 (b) exempts from the privilege "information indicating that a patient who is under the age of sixteen years has been the victim of a crime." Likewise, Penal Law § 265.26 requires hospitals and medical professionals to report to law enforcement authorities certain cases of serious burns (*see Rea v Pardo*, 132 A.D.2d 442, 446, 522 N.Y.S.2d 393 [1987]), and Penal Law § 265.25 obliges hospitals and medical professionals to report every case of a bullet wound, gunshot wound, powder burn and "every case of a wound which is likely to or may result in death and is actually or apparently inflicted by a knife, icepick or other sharp or pointed instrument" (emphasis added; see also Onondaga County, 59 N.Y.2d at 133, 135–136; DONNINO, PRACTICE COMMENTARIES, MCKINNEY'S CONS LAWS OF NY, Book 39, Penal Law §§ 265.25, 265.26, at 220, 222).

Inasmuch as the Legislature enacted an exception to CPLR 4504 (a) directing the reporting of potentially life-threatening stab wounds (see Penal Law § 265.25), we reaffirm our conclusion that the Legislature intended CPLR 4504 (a) to protect against disclosure those medical records of patients whose stab wounds are less severe (see *Onondaga County*, 59 N.Y.2d at 136). Thus, because none of the Legislature's other exceptions to the privilege apply, the records the District Attorney seeks remain privileged under CPLR 4504 (a), and the subpoenas seeking their disclosure must be quashed.

Accordingly, the order of the Appellate Division should be affirmed, without costs.

Chief Judge Kaye and Judges Smith, Levine, Ciparick, Wesley and Graffeo concur.

Order affirmed, without costs.

Cases Relating to Chapter 11

Opinions and Expert Testimony

BOWLING
v.
STATE

Court of Appeals of Georgia
**275 Ga. App. 45, 2005 Ga. App. LEXIS
808 (2005)**

Writ of certiorari denied, 2006 Ga. LEXIS
51 (Ga. 2006)

Johnson, Presiding Judge. Ruffin, C. J.,
and Barnes, J., concur.

Johnson, Presiding Judge.

A jury found Daniel Bowling guilty of
operating a boat while under the influence
of alcohol to the extent it was less safe for
him to do so. He appeals from his conviction, claiming the evidence was insufficient
to show that he was a less safe driver, or that
he was less safe as a result of being under the
influence of alcohol. We disagree and affirm
his conviction.

On appeal the evidence is viewed in a
light most favorable to the verdict, and an
appellant no longer enjoys a presumption of
innocence; moreover, this Court determines
evidence sufficiency and does not weigh the
evidence or determine the credibility of witnesses. The jury's verdict must be upheld if
any rational trier of fact could have found the
essential elements of the crime beyond a reasonable doubt.

Viewing the evidence in the proper
light, it shows that an officer with the
Georgia Department of Natural Resources was
patrolling Lake Lanier when he observed a
boat traveling at night without a stern light. The
officer pulled alongside the vessel and told
the driver, Bowling, that he was stopping the
boat because of the light violation. The officer proceeded to conduct a safety inspection,
and asked Bowling to produce a lifejacket for
each person on board, a "throwable" lifesaving device, a fire extinguisher, and the boat's
registration. Bowling had difficulty trying
to find some of the items, and was unable
to produce the registration or a throwable
lifesaving device. The officer testified that
Bowling seemed confused while looking
for the items. Bowling said he thought the
registration card was in the glove compartment, but instead of looking there, he looked
around the driver's seat for the card. The
officer testified that Bowling asked to use the
officer's flashlight, even though Bowling had
just looked straight at the floor where there
was a large spotlight. The officer noticed an
empty wine glass on the floorboard of the
boat, and detected an odor of alcohol coming
from the boat. He asked Bowling if he had
been drinking. Bowling said he had not.

Based on his observations, as well as
Bowling's mannerisms and demeanor, the
officer asked Bowling to perform field sobriety tests to determine if he was under the
influence of alcohol.

With Bowling in his own boat and the officer in the patrol boat, the officer administered
the horizontal gaze nystagmus (HGN) test,
testing for involuntary jerking of the eyes.
Bowling was unable to perform the test properly because he kept moving his head after
being told not to do so. The officer testified

that Bowling exhibited all six "clues" on the HGN test, though he did not explain for the jury what that meant in terms of intoxication.

The officer asked Bowling to step over into the patrol boat. He noted that Bowling stumbled badly when doing so. The officer noticed an odor of alcohol coming from Bowling's person. When the officer asked Bowling to recite the alphabet without singing, Bowling started reciting it, then stopped, started over, repeated letters, laughed and sang part of the test. He omitted several letters. Bowling was unable to do a finger dexterity exercise or a hand pat exercise as instructed. Bowling refused to submit to an alco-sensor test.

The officer placed Bowling under arrest for boating under the influence, and then read the implied consent notice. Bowling became hostile and demanded to be returned to his boat. Instead, the officer took Bowling to the police station. Once there, Bowling refused to take a breath test. According to the officer, Bowling displayed mood swings throughout the incident, going from belligerent and irritated to calm. When the officer was asked at trial where he believed the odor of alcohol was coming from, he stated that there was a strong odor of alcohol coming from the boat, and a moderate odor of alcohol coming from Bowling. *When asked whether he determined that Bowling "was under the influence to the extent that [it] was less safe to operate that vessel," the officer testified that he concluded after conducting field sobriety tests that Bowling "was a less safe boat operator."* [Emphasis added.]

Bowling contends that the evidence was insufficient to prove beyond a reasonable doubt that he was a less safe driver, or that he was a less safe driver due to the presence of alcohol. He urges that the officer could not recall whether the life jackets and fire extinguisher were eventually found, did not know whether the boat's spotlight worked (which would explain why Bowling asked for a flashlight), and admitted that some operators cannot locate registration documents. He argues further that there was no evidence that he was operating the boat in an unsafe manner, that the hand pat and finger dexterity tests are not part of standard field sobriety exercises, that argumentativeness does not necessarily prove

that someone is under the influence of alcohol, that the officer failed to give his opinion of what the six clues of the HGN test indicate about a person's level of intoxication, that a counting test was performed correctly, and that the officer gave inconsistent statements regarding the source and strength of the alcohol odor. Reversal is not required.

In order to obtain a conviction for driving under the influence of alcohol to the extent it is less safe to drive, the state must prove that the defendant had impaired driving ability as a result of drinking alcohol. A trier of fact can find that a driver was "less safe" based on circumstantial evidence, such as where the driver exhibited signs of intoxication. Field sobriety tests are not designed to detect the mere presence of alcohol, but to produce information regarding whether alcohol is present at an impairing level such that the driver is less safe.

Bowling's refusal to submit to chemical tests of his breath is circumstantial evidence of intoxication. And, a jury could have found from Bowling's performances on several of the sobriety tests that he was not as alert or physically capable and was a less safe driver than he would have been had he not consumed alcohol. Moreover, there was evidence that the smell of alcohol emanated from Bowling's person, that he stumbled badly while trying to board the patrol boat, that an empty wine glass lay on the floorboard, and that Bowling was confused. There was also opinion testimony from the officer that Bowling was under the influence to the extent he was a less safe boat operator. This testimony followed a series of questions regarding the officer's detection of the odor of alcohol emanating from the boat and from Bowling's person. A police officer may offer opinion evidence that a person was a less safe driver. We add that, contrary to Bowling's position, the state was not required to prove that he committed an unsafe act in order to show it was "less safe" for him to operate the vessel.

A rational trier of fact could have found from evidence of alcohol on the boat, the odor of alcohol emanating from Bowling's person, Bowling's refusal to submit to chemical tests of his breath, his demeanor and conduct, and his performance on several sobriety tests, that he was impaired and that the impairment was a result of alcohol consumption. The evidence was sufficient for a rational trier of fact to find Bowling guilty beyond a reasonable doubt of operating a boat while under the influence of alcohol to the extent it was less safe for him to do so.

Judgment affirmed. Ruffin, C. J., and Barnes, J., concur.

OSBOURN
v.
STATE

COURT OF CRIMINAL APPEALS OF TEXAS

92 S.W.3d 531, 2002 Tex. Crim. App. LEXIS 236 (2002)

JUDGES: Meyers, J., delivered the unanimous opinion of the Court.

OPINION BY: Meyers

Appellant was convicted in a bench trial of possession of marihuana, a usable amount of less than two ounces. Punishment was assessed at twenty days' confinement in the county jail. The Court of Appeals affirmed the trial court's conviction. We granted review to decide whether the Court of Appeals erred when it held that the arresting officer's identification of marihuana was admissible as a lay opinion under Texas Rule of Evidence 701. We will affirm.

Appellant was the passenger in a vehicle that was stopped by Officer Nicole Saval. During the traffic stop, Saval smelled alcohol and the odor of burning marihuana emanating from the vehicle and suspected that the driver of the vehicle was under the influence. While Saval questioned appellant, another officer performed a field sobriety test on the driver who was subsequently arrested. Saval asked appellant if she and the driver had been smoking marihuana. Appellant first denied that she had been smoking marihuana and claimed that the odor was cigarettes. After Saval explained to appellant that cigarette smoke does not smell like marihuana smoke,

appellant admitted that she and the driver had been smoking marihuana. Appellant then told the officer that there was more marihuana in the vehicle, which Saval found in a clear plastic bag between the two front seats.

Saval documented her identification of the marihuana in the offense report that was given to appellant before trial. After receiving the offense report, appellant requested and the court ordered the State to provide notice of its intent to offer expert testimony pursuant to Article 39.14(b) of the Texas Code of Criminal Procedure. The State did not respond to the order.

At trial, Saval testified about her police academy training. She stated that the trainees were shown what different drugs looked like and were able to smell marihuana both before and after it was burned. She stated that although she was not a drug recognition expert and was not certified as one, based on her training at the academy and her experience on the police force, she was able to identify what marihuana looks and smells like.

During Saval's testimony, appellant objected claiming that the State was attempting to qualify Saval as an expert without providing notice. The State responded that Saval was not being offered as an expert under Rule 702, rather as an individual who can identify what marihuana looks and smells like. The court withheld ruling on the admissibility and allowed the testimony to continue. At the end of the trial, the court concluded that the officer was testifying as an expert due to her specialized knowledge, however, the testimony was admissible because the offense report was adequate notice.

On appeal, appellant claimed that the testimony of the officer was improperly admitted due to the State's failure to provide notice of intent to offer expert testimony. Appellant also claimed that without this testimony, the evidence was legally insufficient to support a conviction.

The Court of Appeals concluded that the testimony was admissible as lay opinion testimony under Rule of Evidence 701. *Osbourn v. State*, 59 S.W.3d 809, 815 (Tex. App.- Austin 2001). Because Saval's testimony was personal knowledge that was rationally based on her perceptions, inferences, and impressions, the Court of Appeals held that she was not testifying as an expert.

Id. at 814. Because the trial court found the evidence admissible under the alternative theory that Saval was testifying as an expert, the Court of Appeals also addressed the issue of notice. The court found that because the offense report was made available to appellant prior to the request for notice, appellant could anticipate the content of the testimony of the arresting officer. Since appellant was not surprised by the testimony and the State's actions did not constitute bad faith, the Court of Appeals reviewed the trial court's admission of the testimony for abuse of discretion. Id. at 816. Finding no abuse, the court declined to disturb the trial court's ruling.

Appellant advances two grounds for review but in view of our disposition of the case only ground two will require discussion. The issue raised by the determinative ground of error is whether the Court of Appeals erred when it held that a police officer's identification of marihuana is admissible as a lay opinion under Texas Rule of Evidence 701.

Appellant argues that the Court of Appeals erred when it held that the officer's testimony regarding the identification of marihuana was admissible under Rule of Evidence 701. Because Saval's opinion was based on the training she received at the police academy and the experience she gained during her three years as a police officer, appellant contends that she was an expert witness under Rule 702. Appellant claims that only a witness who testifies based on personal knowledge, rather than experience and training, can identify marihuana as a lay witness under Rule 701.

The State counters appellant's assertion by claiming that expert testimony is not necessary to identify marihuana because appellant herself identified the substance as marihuana. Additionally, the fact that all police officers have training and experience does not necessarily make them expert witnesses. The State contends that since Saval personally observed the marihuana, she was not testifying as an expert.

Both lay and expert witnesses can offer opinion testimony. Rule 701 covers the more-traditional witness—one who "witnessed" or participated in the events about which he or she is testifying—while Rule 702 allows for a witness who was brought in as an expert to testify. A witness can testify in the form of

an opinion under Rule 701 if the opinions or inferences are (a) rationally based on his or her perceptions and (b) helpful to the clear understanding of the testimony or the determination of a fact in issue. *Fairow v. State*, 943 S.W.2d 895, 898 (Tex. Crim. App. 1997). Perceptions refer to a witness's interpretation of information acquired through his or her own senses or experiences at the time of the event (i.e., things the witness saw, heard, smelled, touched, felt, or tasted). Since Rule 701 requires the testimony to be based on the witness's perception, it is necessary that the witness personally observed or experienced the events about which he or she is testifying. Id. at 898. Thus, the witness's testimony can include opinions, beliefs, or inferences as long as they are drawn from his or her own experiences or observations. This also incorporates the personal knowledge requirement of Rule 602 which states that a witness may not testify to a matter unless he or she has personal knowledge of the matter. *Bigby v. State*, 892 S.W.2d 864, 889 (Tex. Crim. App.1994). There is, however, a provision in Rule 602 for opinion testimony by expert witnesses which allows a person testifying as an expert under Rule 702 to base his or her opinion on facts and data that are of a type reasonably relied upon by experts in the field. TEX. R. CRIM. EVID. 703. Thus, expert testimony serves the purpose of allowing certain types of relevant, helpful testimony by a witness who does not possess personal knowledge of the events about which he or she is testifying.

When a witness who is capable of being qualified as an expert testifies regarding events which he or she personally perceived, the evidence may be admissible as both Rule 701 opinion testimony and Rule 702 expert testimony. A person with specialized knowledge may testify about his or her own observations under Rule 701 and may also testify about the theories, facts and data used in his or her area of expertise under Rule 702. Texas Rules of Evidence Manual art. VII-6–7 (6th ed. 2002) states that: "A witness may qualify to give testimony both under Rule 702-because of his or her superior experiential capacity-and under Rule 701, if the witness's testimony and opinion are based upon firsthand knowledge." This court has never addressed the issue of whether someone with training and experience can testify as a lay witness but the Courts of Appeals have admitted such testimony as both lay and expert opinion. *See e.g., Harnett v. State*, 38 S.W.3d 650, 659 (Tex. App.-Austin 2000, pet. ref'd) (a social worker was permitted to testify under Rule 701 based on her personal observations of the appellant and under Rule 702 based on her training and experience); *Thomas v. State*, 916 S.W.2d 578, 581 (Tex. App.-San Antonio 1996, no pet.) (police officer qualified as both lay opinion and expert witness to testify regarding the operation of a "crack" house); *Ventroy v. State*, 917 S.W.2d 419, 422 (Tex. App.-San Antonio 1996, pet. ref'd) (police officer was permitted to testify under Rules 701 and 702 based on his experience and personal knowledge about the scene of an accident); *Yohey v. State*, 801 S.W.2d 232, 243 (Tex. App.-San Antonio 1990, pet. ref'd) (police officer's testimony regarding time of death was admissible under both Rule 701 and 702); *Austin v. State*, 794 S.W.2d 408, 409–411, (Tex. App.-Austin 1990, pet. ref'd) (police officer testified under Rules 701 and 702 that, based on his experience and observation, "Swedish Deep Muscle Rub" was a term for prostitution). Thus, although police officers have training and experience, they are not precluded from offering lay testimony regarding events which they have personally observed. See e.g., *Reece v. State*, 878 S.W.2d 320, 325 (Tex. App.-Houston [1 dist.] 1994, no pet.) (police officer testified that, in his opinion, based on his experience, the actions he observed were consistent with someone selling drugs); State v. Welton, 774 S.W.2d 341, 343 (Tex. App.-Austin 1989, pet. ref'd) (police officer permitted to testify as non-expert opinion witness regarding intoxication based in part on smelling the odor of alcohol).

The ninth circuit has addressed the issue of whether a police officer with experience and training can testify as a lay witness. In *United States v. Von Willie*, 59 F.3d 922, 929 (9th Cir. 1995) the ninth circuit allowed a police officer who searched appellant's residence to testify as a lay witness about the nexus between drug trafficking and the possession of the type of weapons found during the search. The court stated that "these observations are common

enough and require such a limited amount of expertise, if any, that they can, indeed, be deemed lay witness opinion." Id. At 929. Thus, although the police officer testified based on his experience, his testimony was admitted as a lay opinion under Rule 701 because it was rationally based on his perceptions during the search and was helpful to the determination of a fact in issue. Id. at 929. However, not all observations by witnesses with experience and training can be admitted as lay opinion testimony. This Court, in *Emerson v. State*, 880 S.W.2d 759, 763 (Tex. Crim. App. 1994) declined to admit as a lay opinion an officer's testimony regarding appellant's intoxication. Because the officer's opinion was based on his observations while administering the horizontal gaze nystagmus (HGN) test, this Court held that the testimony could only be admissible as expert testimony under Rule 702. Id. at 763. Although the officer personally perceived the appellant's eye movements during the HGN test, we held that his observations were not considered mere lay opinion because the test is based on a scientific theory. Id. at 763.

A distinct line cannot be drawn between lay opinion and expert testimony because all perceptions are evaluated based on experiences. However, as a general rule, observations which do not require significant expertise to interpret and which are not based on a scientific theory can be admitted as lay opinions if the requirements of Rule 701 are met. This is true even when the witness has experience or training. Additionally, even events not normally encountered by most people in everyday life do not necessarily require the testimony of an expert. The personal experience and knowledge of a lay witness may establish that he or she is capable, without qualification as an expert, of expressing an opinion on a subject outside the realm of common knowledge. *United States v. James Earl Paiva*, 892 F.2d 148, 157 (1st Cir. 1989). It is only when the fact-finder may not fully understand the evidence or be able to determine the fact in issue without the assistance of someone with specialized knowledge that a witness must be qualified as an expert.

It does not take an expert to identify the smell of marihuana smoke. Testimony as to the identity of an odor is admissible in some instances even though the person testifying is not an expert. *Chess v. State*, 172 Tex. Crim. 412, 357 S.W.2d 386, 387–388 (1962). While smelling the odor of marihuana smoke may not be an event normally encountered in daily life, it requires limited, if any, expertise to identify. *See e.g., Kemner v. State*, 589 S.W.2d 403 (Tex. Crim. App. 1979) (airline employee recognized odor of marihuana emanating from appellant's suitcase and informed DEA); *Chaires v. State*, 480 S.W.2d 196 (Tex. Crim. App. 1972) (airline baggage agent smelled odor of marihuana in appellant's suitcase, opened the suitcase and identified the grassy substance it contained as marihuana); *Hattersley v. State*, 487 S.W.2d 354 (Tex. Crim. App. 1972) (airline employee determined by sight and smell that appellant's suitcase contained marihuana); *Sorensen v. State*, 478 S.W.2d 532 (Tex. Crim. App. 1972) (appellantmother testified that she recognized the odor of marihuana when she found it in her son's room); *Mumphrey v. State*, 774 S.W.2d 75 (Tex. App.-Beaumont 1989, pet. ref'd) (13 year old rape victim testified that she smelled the odor of marihuana on the clothes of appellant). Although it cannot be presumed that everyone is capable of identifying marihuana by smell, a witness who is familiar with the odor of marihuana smoke through past experiences can testify as a lay witness that he or she was able to recognize the odor.

The admissibility of evidence is within the discretion of the trial court and will not be reversed absent an abuse of discretion. *Powell v. State*, 63 S.W.3d 435, 438 (Tex. Crim. App. 200; *Harnett*, 38 S.W.3d at 657; *Ventroy*, 917 S.W.2d at 422. If there is evidence supporting the trial court's decision to admit evidence, there is no abuse and the appellate court must defer to that decision. *Powell*, 63 S.W.3d at 438; *Fairow*, 943 S.W.2d at 901. Even when the trial judge gives the wrong reason for his decision, Salas v. State, 629 S.W.2d 796, 799 (Tex. Crim. App. 1981), if the decision is correct on any theory of law applicable to the case it will be sustained. *Romero v. State*, 800 S.W.2d 539, 543 (Tex. Crim. App. 1990); Moreno v. State, 170 Tex. Crim. 410, 411, 341 S.W.2d 455, 456 (Tex. Crim. App. 1961); *Calloway v. State*, 743 S.W.2d 645, 651–652 (Tex. Crim. App. 1988). This is especially true with regard to the admission of evidence. *Dugard v. State*, 688 S.W.2d 524 (Tex. Crim. App. 1985), overruled by *Williams v. State*, 780 S.W.2d 802 (Tex. Crim. App. 1989); *Sewell v. State* 629 S.W.2d 42, 45 (Tex. Crim. App. 1982). Taking this into account, we will now determine whether the Court of Appeals erred in upholding the trial court's admission of Saval's testimony.

Using the standard set out above, Saval's observation that the odor she smelled was marihuana did not require significant expertise to interpret. And, her observations were not interpreted based on a scientific theory. Thus, if her testimony meets the requirements of Rule 701, it is admissible as a lay opinion. Rule 701 allows a lay witness to give testimony in the form of opinions or inferences that are rationally based on the witness' perception and helpful to a clear understanding of the witness' testimony or the determination of a fact in issue. Thus, if the witness perceived events and formed an opinion that a reasonable person could draw from the facts, then the first part of the rule is met. If the opinion is also helpful for the trier of fact to understand the witness's testimony or aids in the determination of a fact in issue, then the opinion is admissible under Rule 701. Here, Saval participated in the events about which she testified and her opinion was based on what she perceived at the scene of the traffic stop. That is, she smelled an odor that she recognized as marihuana smoke. And, the testimony was helpful to the determination of a fact in issue (i.e., whether appellant was in possession of marihuana). Her belief or inference that the substance was marihuana was based on identifiable facts that were within her personal knowledge such as the green, leafy appearance and the distinct odor. Unlike other drugs that may require chemical analysis, marihuana has a distinct appearance and odor that are familiar and easily recognizable to anyone who has encountered it. So Saval's opinion that appellant possessed marihuana, based on the odor she smelled and the green, leafy substance she saw, was one that a reasonable person could draw from the circumstances. Her testimony regarding the identification of the marihuana was admissible as a lay opinion under Rule 701.

The record also indicates that appellant objected to Saval's testimony on the basis that her opinion was based on her training and experience as a police officer, making her a Rule 702 expert witness. There are certain fields where a witness may qualify as an expert based upon experience and training, however, use of the terms "training" and "experience" do not automatically make someone an expert. All opinions are formed by evaluating facts based on life experiences including education, background, training, occupation, etc. While Saval may have had the potential to be qualified as an expert because she possessed knowledge, skill, experience and education, she was not testifying as an expert when she identified the marihuana. Rather, she was testifying based on her firsthand sensory experiences. Saval herself smelled the odor that she perceived to be burnt marihuana. The fact that she had smelled marihuana before in the course of her employment as a police officer does not necessarily make her an expert. And, again, even if she was an expert, that would not preclude her from offering a lay opinion about something she personally perceived.

Although the trial court admitted Saval's testimony under a different theory, because evidence supports admission of the testimony under Rule 701, the trial court did not abuse its discretion. Consequently, the Court of Appeals correctly upheld the trial court's admission of the testimony. The judgment of the Court of Appeals is affirmed.

Meyers, J.

UNITED STATES
v.
DeLATORRE

United States Court of Appeals, Eleventh Circuit

309 Fed. Appx. 366, 2009 U.S. App. LEXIS 2183 (2009)

[Only the part of the case that relates to opinion and expert testimony is included here.]

PER CURIAM:
Alberto Naranjo Delatorre appeals his convictions for conspiracy to possess with intent to distribute at least five kilograms of cocaine and aiding and abetting possession with intent to distribute at least five kilograms of cocaine. He asserts that there was insufficient evidence for the jury to convict him on either count and that the district court abused its discretion by permitting an expert witness to testify to matters outside the scope of her expertise. After reviewing the record and the parties' briefs, we AFFIRM his convictions.

* * *

At trial, multiple witnesses testified regarding the allegations against Delatorre. Ron Skipper, a Drug Enforcement Agency ("DEA") agent, discussed Delatorre's actions on 27 February 2006. On that date, Skipper was conducting surveillance on a house in Duluth, Georgia that he had reason to believe would be the site of drug transaction. R10 at 30–33. According to Skipper, Villanueva-Naranjo arrived at the house in a green Infiniti car, parked in the driveway, and went inside the building. Id. at 35–36. About one minute later, Delatorre came out of the front door to the house, entered the Infiniti, and backed out of the driveway. Id. at 36–37. Around the same time, a black Ford Focus driven by Villanueva-Naranjo emerged from the garage and backed out of the driveway. Id. at 37–38. Delatorre then parked the Infiniti, approached the Ford, spoke briefly to Villanueva-Naranjo, returned to the Infiniti, and drove off, with the Ford following behind him. Id. at 39. Skipper tailed the two cars. At one point, when the cars had pulled up side-by-side, he observed Delatorre and Villanueva-Naranjo speaking to each other. Id. at 41. Shortly thereafter, Georgia law enforcement conducted a traffic stop on the Ford, based on a request by the DEA, and discovered over sixteen kilograms of cocaine hidden inside the side panels of that car. Id. at 45, 48, 54. A different witness, DEA agent Robert Murphy, testified that he saw Delatorre drive past the traffic stop twice, slowing down on the second occasion to look at the scene.

Jay Mortenson, another DEA agent, testified regarding the 21 April 2006 execution of a search warrant for a house in Lawrenceville, Georgia. Id. at 223, 225, 228. In the course of this search, Mortenson encountered Delatorre, for whom he had two arrest warrants. Id. at 229, 236–37. The agents conducting the search found four cellular telephones in the master bedroom as well as a notebook containing names and telephone numbers and more than $ 16,000 in cash. Id. at 239–43, 247. The assigned phone number for one of the telephones matched a number that was the subject of a DEA investigation. Id. at 241–42. In addition, a separate witness, Maria Cervantes-Suarez, who had lived in the house for two years, testified that Delatorre was a resident of the house and slept in the master bedroom.

Anthony Hall, a former drug dealer, also testified at trial. Id. at 397–98. Hall stated that sixteen kilograms of cocaine would be an amount commensurate with distribution rather than personal use. Id. at 407. He also noted that, when he was a drug dealer, he frequently changed cellular phones to avoid wiretapping and employed coded language when requesting drugs, such as "girls" for cocaine, "paper" for money, and "work" for any type of drug. Id. at 409–12. In addition to these more general topics, Hall also discussed his interactions with Delatorre and Villanueva-Naranjo. Hall first met Villanueva-Naranjo, whom he knew as "Polo," through a mutual acquaintance, Lee Braggs. Villanueva-Naranjo supplied Braggs and Hall with marijuana and cocaine, the latter ranging from two to five kilograms.

* * *

The government also called Spring Williams, who was the DEA case agent for Delatorre's case, as an expert witness on the organization and structure of Mexican drug-trafficking organizations. Delatorre conducted a voir dire examination of Williams, after which he decided not to object to her opinions, and the court deemed her to be a qualified expert in the aforementioned areas. Id. at 572–74. As part of Williams's testimony, she noted her belief that, based on her training and experience, the house in Duluth was a "stash house"—a storing place for drugs in which people might live but without the normal array of furnishings. Id. at 579–80. She also discussed her familiarity with the lingo of the drug trade, including the use of

particular code words in both oral conversations and drug ledgers. Id. at 588–90. Relying on this knowledge, she stated the notebook found at the Lawrenceville house was a drug ledger because of the language used in it. Id. at 590–92.

Williams also discussed a wiretapping investigation the DEA conducted for a different case, in which they had recorded various telephone calls involving Delatorre, including one made to "Bucio," a large-scale Atlanta drug distributor. Id. at 608–09. In these telephone calls, she explained, Delatorre used coded words to identify himself as a source of drugs and discussed purchasing and supplying drugs. Id. at 616–618. Williams also testified about a number of other calls which had been wiretapped either for this investigation or another case, in many of which Delatorre was making coded statements regarding the buying, selling, and shipping of drugs. After the completion of Williams's testimony, Delatorre moved for a directed verdict on both counts of the indictment. Id. at 754. The court found that the government had presented sufficient evidence in support of its allegations and thus denied the motion. Id. at 755. Delatorre now appeals this decision as well as his convictions.

II. DISCUSSION

Delatorre raises three issues on appeal. . . . Second, he asserts that the district court erred in allowing Williams to testify as an expert witness about matters beyond the scope of her expertise.

* * *

B. Agent Williams's Testimony

Delatorre argues that the district court erred by permitting Williams to testify as an expert regarding matters outside the scope of his expertise. In particular, he takes issue with Williams's testimony regarding the proper interpretation of language in the wiretapped conversations and notebooks, which she asserted were coded drug references. Delatorre notes that since Williams was not an expert in Mexican drug traffickers, she should not have been allowed to testify regarding the meaning of certain terms allegedly used by such individuals. The government's failure to provide someone involved in the conspiracy who could independently corroborate Williams's interpretations, he asserts, effectively usurped the jury's ability to evaluate accurately and fully the evidence. In addition, Delatorre contends that the probative value of this evidence was outweighed by its prejudicial value and thus should have been inadmissible under Federal Rule of Evidence 403.

We review a district court's decisions regarding the admissibility of expert testimony and the reliability of expert opinions for abuse of discretion *See United States v. Frazier*, 387 F.3d 1244, 1258 (11th Cir. 2004) (en banc). The Federal Rules of Evidence permit expert witnesses to testify about any form of "specialized knowledge [that] will assist the trier of fact to understand the evidence or to determine a fact in issue" so long as they are "qualified as an expert by knowledge, skill, experience, training, or education." Fed. R. Evid. 702. The testimony is admissible if it is "based upon sufficient facts or data" and "is the product of reliable principles and methods" that the witness has applied reliably to the facts of the particular case. Id. If we find that the district court improperly allowed evidence to be introduced, we then look at whether the error would be harmless in light of the non-problematic evidence produced. *See United States v. Carrazana*, 921 F.2d 1557, 1568 (11th Cir. 1991) (noting that, even if drug lingo testimony was excluded, there was ample evidence in record to support defendant's drug conspiracy conviction).

Drug enforcement agents can provide expert testimony regarding drug dealing operations because of their ability "to help a jury understand the significance of certain conduct or methods of operation unique to the drug distribution business." *United States v. Garcia*, 447 F.3d 1327, 1335 (11th Cir. 2006) (quotation marks and citation omitted). For much the same reason, we have found that a district

court's admission of expert testimony of policemen interpreting drug codes, slang, and other jargon does not violate Rule 702. See id. Delatorre correctly notes, however, that the officers whom we previously have permitted to testify as experts regarding drug jargon appear to have been more well-versed in the particular drug trafficking schemes at issue than Williams was here. See, e.g., id. (Mexican drug trafficking case in which officer took part in over 50 drug investigations, the majority of which involved Mexican drug traffickers); *Carrazana*, 921 F.2d at 1567 (officer in Cuban drug case was "a native Spanish speaker with an understanding of slang peculiar to the Cuban dialect"). Nevertheless, we find that Williams's knowledge of and expertise in dealing with drug trafficking schemes was sufficient experience to allow her to testify as an expert about matters relating to such organizations, including drug jargon. See *Garcia*, 447 F.3d at 1335 (noting that officer's past involvement with drug investigations and familiarity "with the coded language that some drug trafficking organizations use" was sufficient to make him "an experienced narcotics agent") (quotation marks omitted).

Delatorre's Rule 403 argument also fails. Evidence regarding coded drug language can be highly probative because of the often secretive nature of discussions involving drug dealers. See id. This probative value generally is sufficient to outweigh any potential prejudice, and we see no reason to view the value of Williams's testimony any differently. See id.

Accordingly, we find that the district court did not abuse its discretion in permitting Williams to testify about drug jargon based on her own experience, especially since the jury could take into account her expertise in that area. In addition, the government presented ample independent evidence concerning Delatorre's involvement in the drug conspiracy. Any error in admitting expert witness testimony therefore would be harmless.

[The convictions were affirmed.]

Cases Relating to Chapter 12

Hearsay Rule and Exceptions

BELL

v

STATE

COURT OF APPEAL OF FLORIDA, THIRD DISTRICT

847 So. 2d 558, 2003 Fla. App. LEXIS 8767 (2003)

COPE, J.

Gary Paul Bell appeals his conviction and sentence for attempted kidnapping. We affirm.

Defendant-appellant Bell argues that the trial court should have excluded as hearsay the officer's testimony regarding the victim's account of the crime. The trial court admitted the testimony under the hearsay exception for excited utterances.

The victim testified that she was walking along the street during the daytime when the defendant twice drove up to her in his van and offered to give her a ride to her destination. She refused. When the victim next saw the defendant he was standing on the sidewalk with his van parked nearby. He grabbed her around the neck, held a gun to her head, and attempted to force her into the van. She broke free, ran into traffic, pounded on cars, and asked for help in getting away. The defendant, standing nearby, pointed his gun and threatened to shoot her.

The victim returned to her house and called the police. They found the victim to be hysterical and very fearful that the defendant may have followed her home. The victim was so upset that she could not speak. It took the officers fifteen or twenty minutes to calm the victim down to the point where she could give them a statement.

The hearsay exception for excited utterances applies to "[a] statement or excited utterance relating to a startling event or condition made while the declarant was under the stress of excitement caused by the event or condition." § 90.803(2), Fla. Stat. (2001).

The Florida Supreme Court has said:

The essential elements necessary to fall within the excited utterance exception are that (1) there must be an event startling enough to cause nervous excitement; (2) the statement must have been made before there was time to contrive or misrepresent; and (3) the statement must be made while the person is under the stress of excitement caused by the event.

The spontaneous statement exception and the excited utterance exception often overlap. However, as noted by Professor Ehrhardt:

The two exceptions differ mainly in the amount of time that may lapse between the event and the statement describing the event. Under Section 90.803(2) it is not necessary that there be contemporaneity between the event and the statement. As long as the excited state of mind is present when the statement is made, the statement is admissible if it meets the other requirements of Section 90.803(2). This excited state may exist a substantial length of time after the event. Factors that the trial judge can consider in determining whether the necessary state of stress or excitement is present are the age of the declarant, the physical and mental condition of the declarant, the characteristics of the event and the subject matter of the statements.

Whether the necessary state of mind is present is a preliminary fact for the court to determine pursuant to Section 90.104. (citation omitted).

The defendant argues that the victim's statements in this case fail the excited utterance test because there was a time delay of approximately 50 minutes between the time of the incident and the time the victim became calm enough to speak. According to the defendant, this was sufficient time for the victim to contrive or misrepresent.

As the Jano decision indicates, however, points two and three of the test are interwoven. The theory of this hearsay exception is that so long as the declarant remains under the stress of excitement caused by the event, the declarant is unlikely to contrive or misrepresent.

In this case the investigating officer described the victim as hysterical when he first reached the house. She kept going to the window and looking outside to be sure that the defendant was not there. She was so upset she could not speak at all. The trial court permissibly concluded that the victim remained sufficiently under the stress of excitement of the event to make this an excited utterance for purposes of the hearsay exception. Henyard v. State, 689 So. 2d 239, 251 (Fla. 1996). Even if there were any error here, and we do not think there is any, we fail to see any harm as the victim herself testified and was subject to defense cross-examination on all of this.

* * *

Affirmed.

GONZALEZ
v.
STATE

Court of Criminal Appeals of Texas
195 S.W.3d 114, 2006 Tex. Crim. App. LEXIS 1129 (2006)

COCHRAN

The question presented in this case of first impression is whether appellant forfeited, by his own misconduct of fatally shooting Maria Herrera during a robbery or the burglary of her home, his right to confront Maria in court about hearsay statements she made before she died. We find that he did, and we therefore affirm the judgment of the court of appeals which held the same.

I.

San Antonio police officers, responding to 911 calls, arrived at Maria and Baldomero Herrera's home shortly after 6:00 P.M. on May 3, 2002, and found that both of them had been shot. Maria lay near the front door. She was in shock, scared and bleeding, but she was still conscious and asking for help. Baldomero was sprawled unconscious in an easy chair. When officers asked her what had happened, Maria excitedly said that she and her husband had been shot by "a Latin male, blondish colored hair, and he was about 18 years old." She said "the person that did it is related to the people that live across the street in the rock house." Maria kept repeating that he had colored or bleached hair. She stated "that the guy that shot her took her truck" and "she had recognized him from—from the house across the street that had a rock wall in front of it." Maria said it was "just one person." Baldomero died at their home; Maria died at the hospital a few hours later.

Officers found the license plate number of the Herreras' new white Nissan truck and broadcast it over the police radio. There was only one house with a rock face across the street; appellant's grandmother lived there. Appellant's aunt had left him there earlier in the day. His hair was spiky and blonde on top.

* * *

While appellant was at Sylvia's apartment, a police officer on routine patrol, who had heard the broadcast about the Herreras' stolen truck, saw it parked at [appellant's cousin's] apartment complex. He radioed for assistance, and undercover officers in unmarked cars soon arrived and set up surveillance. Around 7:45 p.m., undercover officers noticed a "bleach blonde Latin," later identified as appellant, and another male walk out to the truck, then they both went back inside. At 9:20 p.m., three people, including appellant, came out of the apartment.

Appellant got into the Herreras' Nissan; the other two people got into the Ford truck. The Nissan then followed the Ford out of the apartment complex. When the SWAT officers followed behind him, appellant raced off in the stolen truck, leading officers on a sometimes high-speed chase that lasted about 15 minutes. Eventually, appellant drove down a one-way street and was blocked in by police cars. Appellant refused to get out of the truck, so he was pulled out, handcuffed, and searched. Officers found a black address book, containing Baldomero's credit cards, in his pocket. Appellant was taken to jail and his clothes, a white shirt, jeans and tennis shoes, were collected. Maria's blood was found on the tennis shoes.

The medical examiner testified that Baldomero died from a single gunshot wound to the chest; Maria, who had been shot from three to five times, died from a gunshot wound to the abdomen.

Appellant was charged with capital murder. In a motion *in limine*, and again at trial, appellant objected to the admission of Maria's statements to the police officers as hearsay and as violating his confrontation rights. The trial court held a hearing outside the presence of the jury to determine if Maria's statements to three different officers were admissible. The State argued that Maria's statements, though hearsay, were admissible under the excited utterance and dying declaration exceptions. Appellant argued that the statements were not dying declarations; he pointed to the officers' testimony that Maria was not aware of the gravity of her condition. He also argued that her statements were not excited utterances because they were not spontaneous; instead, they were answers to police questions. The trial judge doubted that the statements were dying declarations, but he admitted them "mainly under the excited utterance" exception, noting that they also fell under the hearsay exceptions for present-sense impression and then-existing physical condition. The jury convicted appellant of capital murder and sentenced him to life imprisonment.

One of appellant's claims on appeal was that the admission of Maria's out-of-court "testimonial" statements violated his right to confrontation under *Crawford v. Washington*,

which the Supreme Court had delivered during the pendency of his appeal. The court of appeals held that Maria's statements were excited utterances and decided that it need not resolve whether they were also testimonial because appellant had forfeited his right to confrontation under the doctrine of forfeiture by wrongdoing. Noting that the Supreme Court had stated in *Crawford* that it would continue to recognize the doctrine of forfeiture by wrongdoing, which "extinguishes confrontation claims on essentially equitable grounds," the court of appeals held that "Gonzalez is precluded from objecting to the introduction of Maria's statements on Confrontation Clause grounds because it was his own criminal conduct (in this case, murder) that rendered Maria unavailable for cross-examination."

II.

In all criminal prosecutions, the accused has a Sixth Amendment right to be confronted with the witnesses against him. Even when hearsay offered against a defendant is admissible under evidentiary rules, that evidence may implicate the Confrontation Clause of the Sixth Amendment if the defendant is not afforded the opportunity to confront the out-of-court declarant. In *Crawford v. Washington,* the Supreme Court held that "where testimonial statements are at issue, the only indicium of reliability sufficient to satisfy constitutional demands is the one the Constitution actually prescribes: Confrontation." Nevertheless, the Supreme Court recognized that equitable exceptions to the Confrontation Clause may still apply, and it specifically mentioned the doctrine of forfeiture by wrongdoing which "extinguishes confrontation claims on essentially equitable grounds" as one that it accepts.

The doctrine of forfeiture by wrongdoing has been a part of the common law since at least 1666. In early English cases, the doctrine allowed a witness's deposition testimony to be admitted instead of live testimony if the defendant caused the witness's absence from trial. The doctrine is based on the principle that "any tampering with a witness should once for all estop the tamperer from making any objection based on the results of his own chicanery." In other words, the rule is based on "common honesty" and the maxim that "no one shall be permitted to take advantage of his own wrong."

* * *

In 1997, the "forfeiture by wrongdoing" doctrine was codified in the Federal Rules of Evidence as a hearsay exception. By that time every circuit that had addressed the issue had recognized the doctrine of forfeiture by misconduct. The doctrine was added to Rule 804 to clarify that a party forfeits the right to object, on hearsay grounds, to the admission of a declarant's prior statement when that party's deliberate wrongdoing procured the unavailability of the declarant as a witness. As the advisory committee note explained:

> The most obvious situation for employing this exception is where a criminal defendant kills a witness, or has him killed, to prevent him from testifying; by engaging in this conduct, the defendant has forfeited the right to object on hearsay grounds to any of the victim's statements. The Rule was derived from cases that have held that a criminal defendant forfeits his right to confrontation if he causes or acquiesces in the witness' unavailability. If the defendant's conduct is such as to cause a forfeiture of the constitutional objection, it should *a fortiori* be enough to cause a forfeiture of the parallel hearsay objection.

Before the Rule 804(b)(6) hearsay exception can apply, the offering party must show that the opposing party committed the wrongdoing with the intent to prevent the declarant's testimony:

> Under the Rule, it must be shown that the party against whom the evidence is offered acted with intent to procure the unavailability of the declarant as a witness. If the defendant kills a declarant simply because he didn't like him, or because he was burned in a drug deal by him, then the defendant has not forfeited his right to object to the declarant's hearsay statement. It follows that the defendant in a murder case cannot be held to have forfeited his objection to hearsay statements made by the victim. The defendant might have

murdered the victim, but he undoubtedly didn't murder the victim to prevent him from testifying in the murder trial.

Some version of the forfeiture doctrine has been adopted in various state courts. While courts have widely accepted the doctrine of forfeiture by wrongdoing to reject both hearsay objections and confrontation claims, the test for determining whether there is a forfeiture has varied. Courts have agreed that forfeiture requires (1) the declarant's unavailability, (2) as a result of the defendant's act of misconduct. Courts have disagreed on whether the defendant must intend that his act of misconduct silence the witness. Courts also have disagreed on whether evidence inadmissible under Federal Rule 804(b)(6) (*i.e.* when the predicate wrongdoing is the same crime for which the defendant is being tried) might nonetheless be admissible over a confrontation clause objection under the forfeiture doctrine.

This debate has taken on new life since the *Crawford* decision. Several courts have used the language in *Crawford* to apply the forfeiture doctrine expansively— when the wrong doing is the same crime for which the defendant is being tried and without regard to whether the defendant intended to silence the witness. Other courts have held that the forfeiture doctrine does not apply in those situations because (1) the defendant's wrongdoing only indirectly "procured" the witness's absence; (2) the wrongful act was not done with the intent to prevent the witness from testifying; or (3) it is the same wrongful act for which the defendant is on trial.

In *United States v. Mayhew*, the district court cited to the amicus brief filed by a group of law school professors in *Crawford* to apply the forfeiture doctrine even though the defendant was on trial for the very act of murder that caused the declarant's unavailability. In their brief, the professors did not mention the role of the wrongdoer's intent. They simply stated,

> If the trial court determines as a threshold matter that the reason the victim cannot testify at trial is that the accused murdered her, then the accused should be deemed to have forfeited the confrontation right, even though

the act with which the accused is charged is the same as the one by which he allegedly rendered the witness unavailable.

* * *

In the present case, the San Antonio Court of Appeals cited state-court decisions that have held the same, including the Kansas Supreme Court in *State v. Meeks* as well as Colorado and California appellate courts in *State v. Moore,* and *People v. Giles.* Some post-*Crawford* decisions have declined to apply the forfeiture doctrine when the defendant's actions did not directly cause the witness's absence or were not intended to make his testimony unavailable. For example, in *People v. Melchor*, the evidence showed that the defendant had intentionally absconded and engaged in an elaborate scheme to avoid the law for ten years, during which time the sole eyewitness to the shooting, Ortiz, died from a drug overdose. The forfeiture doctrine did not apply because there was no causal link between the defendant's misconduct and the witness's unavailability.

In sum, the majority of post-*Crawford* cases have applied the forfeiture by wrongdoing doctrine when the trial court makes a preliminary finding under Rule 104(a) that the defendant's act of misconduct caused the witness's unavailability, although some have also required that the defendant acted with the intent to prevent the witness's testimony.

III.

The determination of whether the forfeiture doctrine applies in the present case appears, at first glance, to depend upon an interpretation of the scope of the "forfeiture by wrongdoing" doctrine. We have been favored with thorough briefing by both the State and appellant. The State cites to the language in *Crawford* and in the law professors' amicus brief, and argues that the court of appeals correctly applied the forfeiture doctrine because forfeiture by wrongdoing, as an equitable doctrine, does not require the prosecution to establish the defendant's motive. Appellant, on the other hand, asserts that the doctrine cannot apply unless the State shows that the defendant engaged in the wrongdoing for

the purpose of preventing the witness from testifying at a future trial. Appellant notes that pre-*Crawford*, the doctrine was generally applied only in the context of witness tampering, and that the Supreme Courts in Pennsylvania, Alaska, and New York had expressly held that the doctrine does not apply where the defendant murders the declarant for personal reasons rather than to prevent the declarant from testifying. Appellant faults post-*Crawford* cases applying the doctrine as the court of appeals did in this case for fastening on language in *Crawford* and [another case], without sufficient analysis of the history and intent of the rule.

We need not settle that dispute in this case. An examination of the entire record clearly supports the inference that appellant shot the Herreras to silence them. They knew him. They lived across the street from his grandmother and were friends with her and other members of her family. Appellant entered the Herreras' home without a disguise and with a very distinguishing characteristic— his dark hair dyed blonde. Indeed, there was no sign of forced entry, so he was either welcomed or walked through an unlocked door. Appellant entered the Herreras' home armed. And he shot to kill. Baldomero, who had not even gotten up from his easy chair, was shot through the heart. Maria was also shot in the chest—and when she did not die appellant shot her again and again. Both were shot from beyond two feet. Both were left for dead.

A logical inference is that appellant killed the Herreras because he wanted to steal their truck and their money, and he didn't want any witnesses to his crime—especially witnesses that knew him, and knew where to find him. This case is factually different from the post-*Crawford* cases that the court of appeals relied on. Those cases involved passion or revenge killings—killings for personal reasons. There was no evidence in this case that appellant had any personal grudge against the Herreras; the evidence strongly supports the inference that appellant committed burglary or robbery for financial gain and then murdered the two witnesses who could identify him.

We agree with those post-*Crawford* cases and the *Crawford* amicus brief that the doctrine of forfeiture by wrongdoing may apply even though the act with which the accused is charged is the same as the one by which he allegedly rendered the witness unavailable. The trial court in this case did not make a preliminary ruling on whether appellant killed Maria, at least in part, to prevent her from testifying against him because this case was tried before *Crawford* was decided. Nonetheless, an evidentiary ruling, such as the one admitting Maria's out-of-court statements, will be upheld on appeal if it is correct on any theory of law that finds support in the record. We agree with the court of appeals that the record provides ample support for the admission of Maria's out-of-court statements, despite appellant's Confrontation Clause objection, because appellant forfeited his right to confront Maria by his own wrongful act. The evidence strongly suggests that the procurement of Maria's absence was motivated, at least in part, by appellant's desire to permanently silence her and prevent her from identifying him. We express no opinion on the court of appeals's broader holding that the procurement of a witness's absence need not be motivated by a desire to silence the declarant for the forfeiture by wrongdoing doctrine to apply.

We affirm the judgment of the court of appeals.

Johnson, J., *filed a concurring opinion*.

I concur in the judgment of the Court. First, I think that Mrs. Herrera's statements were admissible as a dying declaration. Despite the police officers' assertions that she was not aware of the gravity of her situation, no one seems to have inquired of her what her perception of her injuries was. Certainly she was aware that she had been shot multiple times, including a gunshot wound to the abdomen. Under such circumstances, it is probable that she understood quite clearly the gravity of her situation. The *Crawford* Court conceded that dying declarations may, by historical imperative, be admissible, despite the lack of an opportunity to cross-examine.

There is also the argument that Mrs. Herrera's statements were not testimonial. Depending on the circumstances, a police officer asking, "What happened?" may or may not be interrogation. Even if her statements were testimonial and the trial court erred in admitting them, I would find the error harmless. The Herreras' truck was missing, a fact easily ascertained from sources other than

Mrs. Herrera's statements. The license plate number was also easily ascertainable by law officers. A bulletin about the missing truck was broadcast to police officers. An officer on routine patrol saw the truck and called for assistance. After a chase, officers stopped the truck and arrested appellant, the driver, who had Mr. Herrera's credit cards in his pocket and Mrs. Herrera's blood on his shoes. With such evidence, Mrs. Herrera's statements were superfluous.

I do not think that this is the right case in which to consider expanding the concept of forfeiture by wrongdoing. The basis for such an expansion seems to be based on federal Rule of Evidence 804(b)(4), which by its very terms does not apply in this case. In addition, there is a logical disconnect in saying that a defendant killed a person to prevent them from testifying at the defendant's trial for killing that person; if the defendant did not kill the person, there would be no murder trial and hence no need to suppress damaging testimony, so killing the person creates the reason for killing the person. Such reasoning is circular and should not be incorporated into the law.

Cox
v.
State

COURT OF APPEALS OF INDIANA, SECOND DISTRICT

774 N.E.2d 1025, 2002 Ind. App. LEXIS 1533 (2002)

JUDGES: ROBB, Judge. RILEY, J., and MATTINGLY-MAY, J., concur.

James Cox was convicted following a bench trial of domestic battery, a Class A misdemeanor. Cox appeals his conviction. We affirm.

Issues

Cox raises two issues for our review, which we restate as follows:

1. Whether the trial court properly admitted hearsay testimony under the excited utterance hearsay exception; and

2. Whether the State presented sufficient evidence to support his conviction.

Facts and Procedural History

Deputy Sheriff Daniel Herrick responded to a radio dispatch of a reported battery on October 12, 2001. When he arrived at the scene, he observed Cox standing in front of an apartment building talking to another police officer. Deputy Herrick found Denise Hogan inside the apartment building a few minutes later. He noticed that she was crying and shaking and appeared to be very upset. He also noticed that she was talking very quickly and showed signs of a fresh injury. Hogan had a cut above her eye which was bleeding, her left eye was swollen and she was holding an ice pack to her eye. Additionally, she had marks on her neck that appeared to have been caused by someone grabbing her on her neck.

Hogan told Deputy Herrick how she sustained the injuries and that it was Cox who injured her. At trial, Deputy Herrick testified to the statements Hogan made to him. Cox objected, asserting that Herrick's testimony was hearsay. The State responded that the statements were being offered under the "excited utterance" exception. The trial court allowed the testimony.

Following the trial, the trial court found Cox guilty of domestic battery. This appeal ensued.

Discussion and Decision

I. Admission of Testimony

A. Standard of Review

Our standard of review in this area is well settled. The admission of evidence is within the sound discretion of the trial court, and the decision whether to admit evidence will not be reversed absent a showing of manifest abuse of the trial court's discretion resulting in the denial of a fair trial. *Prewitt v. State*, 761 N.E.2d 862, 869 (Ind. Ct. App. 2002). An abuse of discretion involves a decision that is clearly against the logic and effect of the facts and circumstances before the court. Id. In determining the admissibility of evidence, the reviewing court will only consider the evidence in favor of the trial court's

ruling and any unrefuted evidence in the defendant's favor. Id.

B. Admission of Deputy Herrick's Testimony

Hearsay is a statement made out-of-court that is offered into evidence to prove the fact or facts asserted in the statement itself. Ind. Evidence Rule 801(c); *Craig v. State*, 630 N.E.2d 207, 209 (Ind. 1994). In the present case, the contested portions of Deputy Herrick's testimony constitute hearsay. Hogan made the statements out-of-court and Deputy Herrick repeated the statements at trial, for the purpose of proving the facts asserted in the out-of-court statements, namely that Cox struck and choked Hogan. Such hearsay is not admissible at trial unless it fits within some exception to the hearsay rule. *Craig*, 630 N.E.2d at 207.

Cox contends that the hearsay testimony of Deputy Herrick is inadmissible because it does not fit into any hearsay exception and because Hogan did not appear for trial. Alternatively, he contends that, if the testimony falls under the excited utterance exception, then the State failed to lay a proper foundation for the evidence. We disagree.

The excited utterance exception is found in Evidence Rule 803(2). The rule provides that:

The following are not excluded from the hearsay rule, even though the declarant is available as a witness.

* * *

(2) A statement relating to a startling event or condition made while the declarant was under the stress of excitement caused by the event or condition.

For a hearsay statement to be admitted as an excited utterance under Evidence Rule 803(2), three elements must be shown: (1) a startling event occurs; (2) a statement is made by a declarant while under the stress of excitement caused by the event; and (3) the statement relates to the event. *Jenkins v. State*, 725 N.E.2d 66, 68 (Ind. 2000). This is not a mechanical test; it turns on whether the statement was inherently reliable because the witness was under the stress of an event and unlikely to make deliberate falsifications. Id. Additionally, while the time period between the startling event and a subsequent statement is, of course, one factor to consider in determining whether the statement was an excited utterance, no precise length of time is required. *Simmons v. State*, 760 N.E.2d 1154, 1161 (Ind. Ct. App. 2002).

Cox argues that Hogan's absence makes her statement inadmissible hearsay. However, the language of Rule 803 makes it clear that the exceptions listed are not excluded from the hearsay rule, "even though the declarant is available as a witness." Evid. R. 803. Therefore, Rule 803 lists exceptions which are not hearsay regardless of whether the declarant is available. The fact that Hogan did not appear for trial has no effect on Deputy Herrick's testimony. Hogan's statements to Deputy Herrick fit squarely within the excited utterance exception and were admissible at trial.

Cox also argues that the State failed to lay a proper foundation for the excited utterance exception. We disagree.

We have recently held that a victim's statement made to a police officer after a battery constituted an excited utterance. *Gordon v. State*, 743 N.E.2d 376, 378 (Ind. Ct. App. 2001). In Gordon, a police officer was dispatched to an apartment complex where he found a woman who was shaking and had redness about her neck. The woman told the officer that her boyfriend had struck her. Because the woman did not testify at trial, Gordon argued that the police officer's testimony was inadmissible hearsay. This court examined the circumstances surrounding the statements made by the victim and held that it was reasonable to infer that the woman was upset because of a startling event and that the event was the physical altercation she described to the officer. Id.

As in Gordon, we find that Hogan's statements to Deputy Herrick satisfy the conditions for excited utterances. The record reflects that Hogan placed a 911 call at 2:21 a.m., that Deputy Herrick was dispatched to the scene at approximately 2:33 a.m., and that he arrived there within minutes of receiving the dispatch. n1 Deputy Herrick testified that Hogan was crying and shaking and appeared to be upset when he spoke with her. It is clear that Hogan was still upset by a startling event, which she had reported in the 911 call only

minutes before; it is also reasonable to infer that the startling event that caused her visible distress was the physical altercation with Cox that she described to Deputy Herrick.

Cox also contends that the State failed to lay a proper foundation for the excited utterance exception because he asserts that Hogan was capable of thoughtful reflection when she made the statements to Deputy Herrick. In support of this, Cox compares Hogan's voice on the 911 call with Deputy Herrick's testimony regarding Hogan's emotional state when he interviewed her. Specifically, Cox seems to be arguing that Deputy Herrick testified that Hogan was calm when he interviewed her. However, our review of the record reveals that Deputy Herrick testified that Hogan was upset and crying. The trial court did not abuse its discretion in finding that the State had laid a proper foundation through Deputy Herrick's testimony regarding Hogan's emotional state.

* * *

Our supreme court examined the requirements for a statement to be considered an excited utterance and found the victim's statement met these requirements. 694 N.E. 2d at 1140–41. The main question was whether the victim's statement met the requirements for an excited utterance because the victim was answering questions from the officer rather than making his own statements. 694 N.E. 2d at 1141. The court noted that the officer did not suggest who the shooter was and there was no evidence that someone had coerced the victim to falsely name Montgomery. Id. Therefore, the court held that the hearsay testimony was properly admitted under the excited utterance exception.

We are presented with facts similar to Montgomery in the present case. Deputy Herrick was the first person at the scene to talk with Hogan. He asked her questions and she identified Cox as the person who had hit her. Cox has presented no evidence that Deputy Herrick suggested Cox's name to Hogan or that someone had coerced Hogan to Identify Cox as her assailant. Therefore, because Hogan's statements to Deputy Herrick satisfy the requirements for excited utterances and Cox has presented no evidence of coercion, the trial court did not abuse its discretion in admitting Deputy Herrick's testimony under the excited utterance hearsay exception.

* * *

Conclusion

The trial court did not abuse its discretion in admitting Deputy Herrick's testimony under the excited utterance hearsay exception. Additionally, there was sufficient evidence to support Cox's conviction. Therefore, Cox's conviction is affirmed.

SADLER
v.
STATE

COURT OF APPEAL OF TEXAS

2009 Tex. App. LEXIS 2962 (2009)

OPINION BY: Felipe Reyna.
MEMORANDUM OPINION
A jury convicted Michael Shawn Sadler of murder and assessed his punishment at thirty years' imprisonment. Sadler argues on appeal that the court erred by: (1) admitting evidence of an extraneous offense; (2) permitting the State to impeach his fiance on a collateral issue; (3) admitting various hearsay statements which did not qualify under exceptions for excited utterances, statements made for purposes of medical diagnosis or treatment, or dying declarations; (4) admitting a videotaped interview of the victim in violation of Sadler's right of confrontation; and (5) admitting a prior written statement which was not inconsistent with his testimony. We will affirm.

Sadler, Luis Castillo, and others were attending a gathering on a Saturday night at the apartment of Rachel Byrd. At some point, an argument arose between Sadler and Castillo which involved some pushing and shoving. The party ended around 1:30 or 2:00 in the morning. When Sadler left, he called Byrd and told her that Castillo was injured and lying in the parking lot. Byrd and Larry Whatley went out and found Castillo lying on the ground, injured badly, and unable to

move his arms or legs. Castillo told them that Sadler had assaulted him. He did not want to seek medical attention so they carried him into Byrd's apartment.

Around 8:00 or 8:30 that morning, Byrd called for an ambulance, and Castillo was taken to the local hospital in Clifton. Because of the extent of his injuries, he was later transported to Scott & White Hospital in Temple. The treating physician at Scott & White testified that Castillo essentially suffered a broken neck. He was placed on a ventilator within a few hours after his arrival at Scott & White.

Clifton Police Chief Rex Childress received a call from Scott & White on Wednesday advising that Castillo was about to be taken off the ventilator at his own request and that he may not survive for long afterward. Childress went to the hospital to conduct a videotaped interview that afternoon. During the interview, Castillo indicated that Sadler had assaulted him.

With limited treatment options available, Castillo was taken off the ventilator. He died about two weeks after the assault.

* * *

Dying Declaration

Sadler argues in his fourth point that the court abused its discretion by admitting the testimony of Beki Bollinger under the dying declarations exception to the hearsay rule. Specifically, Sadler contends that Bollinger's testimony is not admissible under this exception because there is nothing to suggest that Castillo believed his death was imminent when he talked to her.

Bollinger was Castillo's employer. She came to see him at Scott & White on Monday morning. Over objection, Bollinger testified that, when she asked Castillo who had assaulted him, she read his lips to indicate that "Michael" had done it. 5 See TEX. R. EVID. 801(a) (defining in part a "statement" for purposes of the hearsay rule as "nonverbal conduct of a person, if it is intended by the person as a substitute for verbal expression"). Bollinger continued to talk with Castillo about the assault.

After Luis had been read his last rites, and made the decision to have the ventilator taken off of him and he knew that it was a possibility he was going to pass I was standing by his side and [at] that moment he could speak. And I asked him, "Luis, why did Michael do this to you?"

Over Sadler's objection, Bollinger was permitted to tell the jury Castillo's answer, which was, "Michael probably gottie too much mad."

A statement meets the dying declaration exception to the hearsay rule if the declarant is unavailable at the time of trial and the statement is "[a] statement made by a declarant while believing that the declarant's death was imminent, concerning the cause or circumstances of what the declarant believed to be impending death." . . . A declarant's belief that death was imminent "may be inferred from the circumstances of the case, such as the nature of the injury, medical opinions stated to him, or his conduct."

Martinez v. State, 17 S.W.3d 677, 689 (Tex. Crim. App. 2000) (quoting TEX. R. EVID. 804(b)(2); *Thomas v. State*, 699 S.W.2d 845, 853 (Tex. Crim. App. 1985)) (citations omitted).

Here, Castillo was unavailable at trial because of his death. It is undisputed that his injuries were severe and his prognosis was grim. Given the extent of his injuries, Bollinger's impression that he knew there was a possibility he would die after being removed from the ventilator, and the giving of last rites, we cannot say that the court abused its discretion by admitting Bollinger's testimony under the dying declarations exception to the hearsay rule. See id.; *Medrano v. State*, 701 S.W.2d 337, 339 (Tex. App.—El Paso 1985, pet. ref'd). Sadler's fourth point is overruled.

* * *

We affirm the judgment.

STATE
v.
WASHINGTON

SUPREME COURT OF MICHIGAN

**664 N.W.2d 203; 2003 Mich.
LEXIS 1465 (2003)**

JUDGES: Chief Justice Maura D. Corrigan, Justices Michael F. Cavanagh, Elizabeth A. Weaver, Marilyn Kelly, Clifford W. Taylor, Robert P. Young, Jr., Stephen J. Markman. KELLY, J. (dissenting).

OPINION: PER CURIAM

Defendant was convicted of armed robbery and assault with intent to do great bodily harm less than murder. The Court of Appeals reversed the convictions because the accomplice's statement, in which the accomplice identified himself as the shooter, was improperly admitted against defendant. 251 Mich. App. 520; 650 N.W.2d 708 (2002). It also found that the trial court abused its discretion in denying defense counsel the opportunity to conduct voir dire of a juror in mid-trial. We reverse the judgment of the Court of Appeals and reinstate the verdict.

I

On May 8, 1998, two men robbed James Turner while he was using a public pay phone at a Detroit gas station. One of the men pulled a gun, pointed it at Turner's head, and demanded money. The other went through Turner's pockets and took his watch and pager. When Turner told his assailants that he didn't have anything else of value, he was shot in the back.

A few minutes later, two police officers saw a car containing defendant and Daniel Mathis drive into an alley behind a gas station that was approximately a mile from the scene of the robbery. The officers decided to investigate because the area was known for drug sales and prostitution. Defendant was uncooperative with the officers and, following a scuffle, he was handcuffed pending further investigation. As the officers returned to talk to Mathis, who had remained in the car, the report of the Turner robbery and a description of his assailants were broadcast over the police radio. When one of the officers asked to have the description repeated, Mathis blurted out, "I did it—I'm the shooter." Turner identified defendant in a lineup as one of his assailants. He failed to identify Mathis.

Defendant and Mathis were charged with armed robbery, MCL 750.529, and assault with intent to murder, MCL 750.83. They were tried separately. On the morning of defendant's trial, the issue whether Mathis's statement was admissible was raised. Without elaboration, the trial court decided that the statement would be allowed into evidence. Defendant was convicted of armed robbery and assault with intent to do great bodily harm less than murder, MCL 750.84.

The Court of Appeals reversed defendant's convictions. It concluded that Mathis's statement was improperly admitted as a statement against penal interest because it was not reliable. According to assertions made by defense counsel, Mathis was mentally ill. n1 In addition, the panel found that the trial court should have allowed defense counsel to question a juror in mid-trial.

II

The decision to admit evidence is reviewed for an abuse of discretion. *People v Starr*, 457 Mich. 490, 494; 577 N.W.2d 673 (1998). When the decision regarding the admission of evidence involves a preliminary question of law, such as whether a statute or rule of evidence precludes admissibility of the evidence, the issue is reviewed de novo. *People v Lukity*, 460 Mich. 484, 488; 596 N.W.2d 607 (1999).

III

Declarations against penal interest constitute an exception to the general proscription against hearsay provided by MRE 802. MRE 804(b)(3), in pertinent part, defines a declaration against penal interest as

[a] statement which was at the time of its making ... so far tended to subject the declarant to civil or criminal liability ... that a reasonable person in the declarant's position would not have made the statement unless believing it to be true. A statement tending to expose the declarant to criminal liability and offered to exculpate the accused is not admissible unless corroborating circumstances clearly indicate the trustworthiness of the statement.

The exception is based on the assumption that people do not generally make statements about themselves that are damaging unless they are true. *People v Poole*, 444 Mich. 151, 161; 506 N.W.2d 505 (1993), citing the comment of the Advisory Committee on Federal Rules of Evidence relating to FRE 804(b)(3). Mathis's statement is against his penal interest and, therefore, is admissible.

The inquiry, however, does not stop there because the Confrontation Clauses of the federal and state constitutions are implicated. US Const, Am VI; Const 1963, art 1, § 20. The admission of Mathis's statement as substantive evidence does not violate the Confrontation Clause if the prosecution can establish that Mathis was unavailable as a witness and that his statement bore adequate indicia of reliability. Alternatively, the Confrontation Clause is not violated if the statement fell within a firmly rooted hearsay exception. Poole, supra at 163.

Some jurisdictions have held that the hearsay exception for statements against penal interest is a firmly rooted hearsay exception. *See, e.g., United States v McKeeve*, 131 F.3d 1, 9 (CA 1, 1997), *People v Wilson*, 17 Cal App 4th 271, 278; 21 Cal.Rptr.2d 420 (1993), and *State v Tucker*, 109 Ore. App. 519, 526; 820 P.2d 834 (1991). However, we need not decide that issue because Mathis had been charged with the crimes and was considered unavailable because it was expected that he would assert his Fifth Amendment right not to testify. Additionally, Mathis's statement bears adequate indicia of reliability.

In *Poole*, supra at 165, we instructed:

In evaluating whether a statement against penal interest that inculpates a person in addition to the declarant bears sufficient indicia of reliability to allow it to be admitted as substantive evidence against the other person, courts must evaluate the circumstances surrounding the making of the statement as well as its content.

The presence of the following factors would favor admission of such a statement: whether the statement was (1) voluntarily given, (2) made contemporaneously with the events referenced, (3) made to family, friends, colleagues, or confederates—that is, to someone to whom the declarant would likely speak the truth, and (4) uttered spontaneously at the initiation of the declarant and without prompting or inquiry by the listener.

On the other hand, the presence of the following factors would favor a finding of inadmissibility: whether the statement (1) was made to law enforcement officers or at the prompting or inquiry of the listener, (2) minimizes the role or responsibility of the declarant or shifts blame to the accomplice, (3) was made to avenge the declarant or to curry favor, and (4) whether the declarant had a motive to lie or distort the truth.

Courts should also consider any other circumstance bearing on the reliability of the statement at issue. See, generally, *United States v Layton*, 855 F.2d 1388, 1404–1406 (CA 9, 1988). While the foregoing factors are not exclusive, and the presence or absence of a particular factor is not decisive, the totality of the circumstances must indicate that the statement is sufficiently reliable to allow its admission as substantive evidence although the defendant is unable to cross-examine the declarant.

When those precepts are applied to the facts at bar, we find that Mathis's statement to the police officers bears sufficient indicia of reliability to satisfy Confrontation Clause concerns and to allow its admission as substantive evidence at trial. The statement was voluntarily given and made contemporaneously with the events referenced. It was uttered spontaneously by Mathis and without prompting or inquiry by the officers. In fact, the officers had just heard of the robbery when Mathis made the statement. Mathis did not minimize his role in the crimes, admitting that he shot the victim, and he had no motive to lie or distort the truth. In addition, there is nothing in the statement indicating that the declarant was attempting to curry favor at the time he made the statement.

We agree with the dissenting judge of the Court of Appeals that there was no record evidence establishing that Mathis "suffered from mental illness." The unsubstantiated assertions of defense counsel are not substantive evidence and cannot be used to undermine the indicia of reliability contained in the accomplice's statement.

IV

* * *

V

We conclude that the accomplice's statement contains sufficient "particularized guarantees of trustworthiness," considering the totality of the circumstances surrounding its utterance, to justify its admission. Poole, supra at 164.

* * * Accordingly, we reverse the judgment of the Court of Appeals and reinstate the judgment of the circuit court. MCR 7.302(F)(1).

Cases Relating to Chapter 13

Documentary Evidence

WILKERSON
v.
STATE

**Court of Appeals of Arkansas,
Division Two
2005 Ark. App. LEXIS 12 (2005)**

ROBERT J. GLADWIN, Judge. HART and BAKER, JJ., agree.

ROBERT J. GLADWIN, Judge

Appellant Jeffery Scott Wilkerson seeks the reversal of his conviction for delivering a Schedule VI controlled substance—marijuana. On appeal, appellant argues that the trial court erred: (1) by denying his motion for a directed verdict because there was insufficient evidence to support the conviction; (2) in admitting into evidence a tape recording between a confidential informant and appellant that was not properly authenticated; (3) in failing to suppress evidence where the application for search warrant failed to set forth particular facts bearing on the informant's reliability; (4) by denying his motion to suppress where the search warrant did not indicate that it was based upon either recorded testimony or sworn affidavits. We affirm.

Lonnie Cogburn testified that while he was working as a confidential informant for Officer Chris Martin, he contacted appellant in an effort to purchase marijuana. Officer Martin equipped Cogburn with a micro-cassette recorder and gave him a twenty-dollar bill and a ten-dollar bill as buy money, both of which were photocopied by the police for verification purposes. On or about January

15, 2003, Cogburn met appellant on the road and asked him about the drugs, at which time appellant handed him the marijuana through the car window in exchange for the thirty dollars. Cogburn then returned to Officer Martin and gave him the quarter-bag of marijuana and the micro-cassette recorder and tape.

On or about January 23, 2003, appellant was charged with the delivery of a Schedule VI controlled substance, a Class C felony, pursuant to Ark. Code Ann. § 5-64-401(a)(1)(iv) for allegedly delivering to a confidential informant, directly supervised by an officer with the 18th West Judicial District Drug Task Force, marijuana, the aggregate weight of which, including adulterants or dilutents, was less than one ounce. A trial was held on September 2, 2003, and appellant was convicted by a Montgomery County jury, sentenced to six years in the Arkansas Department of Correction, and ordered to pay a $ 5000 fine. This appeal followed.

Denial of motion for directed verdict

The standard of review in cases challenging the sufficiency of the evidence is well established. We treat a motion for a directed verdict as a challenge to the sufficiency of the evidence. . . .

Arkansas Code Annotated section 5-64-401 provides that it is unlawful for any person to deliver a controlled substance. "Delivery" is defined as the actual, constructive, or attempted transfer of a controlled substance or counterfeit substance in exchange for money or anything of value. *See* Ark. Code Ann. § 5-64-101(f). There was testimony from Cogburn, the confidential informant who supposedly bought the marijuana, describing the details of the "buy" from appellant. There was also a tape recording of the transaction; however, no written transcript of the tape is available to confirm its corroboration of Cogburn's testimony. There was also evidence that the specific twenty-dollar bill and ten-dollar bill that were given to Cogburn as buy money were found in appellant's wallet at the time of his arrest, as verified by the photocopies previously made by the police and by testimony from Officer Martin. Resolution of conflicts in testimony and assessment of witness credibility is for the fact-finder. *Slater v. State*, 76 Ark. App. 365, 65 S.W.3d 481 (2002). There was substantial evidence to support appellant's conviction for delivery of a controlled substance.

Admitting into evidence a tape recording between the a confidential informant and appellant that allegedly was not properly authenticated

Appellant alleges that the micro-cassette recording purporting to corroborate Cogburn's description of the drug buy was erroneously allowed into evidence without proper authentication under Rule 901 of the Arkansas Rules of Evidence. Rule 901(a) specifically states that the requirement of authentication or identification as a condition precedent to admissibility is satisfied by evidence sufficient to support a finding that the matter in question is what its proponent claims. Appellant argues that prior to the admission of the recording, none of the parties speaking on the recording testified that it was a true and accurate depiction of the conversation, and he further contends that Officer Martin was not present when that conversation took place.

Officer Martin testified that after Cogburn left with the thirty dollars and the micro-cassette recorder, there were numerous times during the course of the drug buy that Cogburn was out of his sight. Appellant attempts to distinguish the facts of this case from those in *Smithey v. State*, 269 Ark. 538, 602 S.W.2d 676 (Ark. App. 1980), where the Arkansas Supreme Court found proper authentication where the officer involved testified that he saw the informant talking with the defendant while the officer listened to the conversation electronically and watched a videotape of the

parties. In the instant case, Cogburn was the only witness for the State who was present when the recording was made, and he testified that he had never listened to it.

Additionally, Officer Martin testified that he had limited knowledge about the recording, in that he only knew what the recording itself told him about the interaction between Cogburn and appellant. Appellant maintains that this scenario is markedly different from the facts in *Walker v. State*, 13 Ark. App. 124, 680 S.W.2d 915 (1984), where the supreme court found that where one of the undercover officers who was present when the tapes were recorded testified as to their accuracy and authenticity, the officer's testimony was sufficient to authenticate the recordings.

Officer Martin testified that he gave Cogburn the micro-cassette recorder and then followed him around "as best as [he] could" until Cogburn returned with the recorder and the marijuana he purchased from appellant. Officer Martin explained that there were times Cogburn was out of his sight because he could not follow Cogburn too closely, considering that everyone knew the vehicle he drove and that he did not want to put either Cogburn or himself in danger. Officer Martin stated that after receiving the tape and recorder back from Cogburn, he took it to the police department and logged it into the evidence vault. He testified that the transaction lasted only seconds and that he had listened to the tape many times since receiving it from Cogburn. The State reiterates that the tape recording is corroborated by Cogburn's testimony regarding the transaction. The State argues that the authentication requirement of Rule 901(a) is satisfied where a trial judge, in his discretion, is satisfied that the physical evidence presented is genuine and in reasonable probability has not been tampered with. *Guydon v. State*, 344 Ark. 251, 39 S.W.3d 767 (2001).

In evidentiary determinations, a trial court has wide discretion, and we will not reverse a trial court's ruling on the admission of the evidence absent an abuse of discretion. *See Davis v. State*, 350 Ark. 22, 86 S.W.3d 872 (2002). Further, we do not reverse a trial court's evidentiary decision absent a showing of prejudice. *Id.* The tape was properly introduced, and the content of the recording goes to the weight of the evidence rather than to its admissibility. There is also substantial evidence of appellant's guilt, including Cogburn's eyewitness account of the buy, as well as the "buy money" being recovered from appellant's wallet upon his arrest. The tape recording of the drug buy is cumulative, and any error occasioned by the trial court's admission of the recording was rendered harmless beyond a reasonable doubt by the admission of the other evidence. *See Jackson v. State*, __ Ark. __, __ S.W.3d __, 2004 Ark. LEXIS 638 (Nov. 4, 2004).

* * *

[The defendant's other arguments possessed insufficient merit to obtain a reversal of his conviction.]

Affirmed.
HART and BAKER, JJ., agree.

STATE
v.
HUEHN

COURT OF APPEALS OF COLORADO, DIVISION FIVE

53 P.3d 733, 2002 Colo. App. LEXIS 21 (2002)

JUDGES: Opinion by JUDGE VOGT Kapelke and Erickson, JJ., concur.

Defendant, Daniel Huehn, appeals the judgment of conviction entered on a jury verdict finding him guilty of theft. We affirm.

On December 24, 1998, technicians responding to a call to service a Key Bank automated teller machine (ATM) discovered that the safe at the bottom of the machine was unlocked and the money cassettes normally found there were missing. The cassettes had been in the safe when the ATM was serviced on the morning of December 23, and customers had withdrawn money from the machine throughout that day. Computer records showed that the safe had been opened at approximately 9:30 p.m. on December 23, although there had been no call for service at that hour.

Defendant, one of the ATM technicians who had access to this machine, admitted in a written statement to his employer that he had opened the safe sometime between 8:30 and 9:30 p.m. on December 23 while at the site on a call regarding another ATM. He claimed, however, that the cassettes were still in the safe at that time.

I.

Defendant first contends that the trial court abused its discretion in admitting into evidence certain computer-generated records that were not sufficiently authenticated. We disagree.

The exhibits at issue are computer records reflecting customer transactions and technician servicing at the ATM on December 23 and 24, 1998. Four of the exhibits were records generated for Key Bank by Money Access Services (MAC), with whom Key Bank had contracted to process its ATM transactions. Defendant objected to admission of these records on the grounds that there was an insufficient foundation for their admission as business records under CRE 803(6) and the records were not authenticated in accordance with CRE 901(b)(9). The trial court overruled the objections and admitted the exhibits.

Although he did not object on this basis at trial, defendant also contends on appeal that Exhibit 14, a portion of a status tape that recorded the openings and closings of the ATM vault on a hard drive inside the machine, should have been excluded for lack of authentication.

A.

As an initial matter, we reject defendant's contention that, because computer-generated evidence is "a species of scientific evidence," the prosecution had to make the showing required under *Frye v. United States*, 54 App. D.C. 46, 293 F. 1013 (D.C. Cir. 1923), or *Daubert v. Merrell Dow Pharmaceuticals, Inc.*, 509 U.S. 579, 113 S. Ct. 2786, 125 L. Ed. 2d 469 (1993), before the evidence could be admitted. *See People v. Shreck*, 22 P.3d 68 (Colo. 2001)(CRE 702, rather than *Frye*, governs admissibility of scientific evidence).

In support of his contention, defendant cites R. Bailin et. al., Colorado Evidentiary Foundations (Miche 1997). However, that authority itself recognizes that, while presentation of scientific evidence usually requires proof of the validity of the underlying theory and the reliability of the instrument, "computers are so widely accepted and used that the proponent of computer evidence need not prove those two elements of the foundation." Colorado Evidentiary Foundations, supra, ch. 4(C)(2), at 52; *see also Brooks v. People*, 975 P.2d 1105, 1112 n.7 (Colo. 1999)(rejecting view that "whenever one can find 'science' by scratching beneath the surface of expert testimony, the validation rules governing scientific evidence would have to apply").

The trial court in this case properly focused its inquiry on whether a sufficient foundation had been laid to warrant admission of the proffered records under the applicable rules of evidence.

B.

The admissibility of a computer printout is governed by the rules of relevancy, authentication, and hearsay. *Benham v. Pryke*, 703 P.2d 644 (Colo. App. 1985), rev'd on other grounds, 744 P.2d 67 (Colo. 1987). The relevancy of the computer records in this case is not disputed.

The requirement of authentication as a condition precedent to admissibility is satisfied by evidence sufficient to support a finding that the matter in question is what its proponent claims. CRE 901(a). Whether a proper foundation has been established is a matter within the sound discretion of the trial court, whose decision will not be disturbed absent a clear abuse of that discretion. *People v. Slusher*, 844 P.2d 1222 (Colo. App. 1992).

* * *

C.

Here, Key Bank's ATM accounting supervisor testified that transactions at the bank's ATMs are electronically communicated to, and recorded by, MAC, which handles the processing of the transactions. MAC's computer-generated reports for each ATM are transmitted daily to Key Bank, stored for three months in Key Bank's computer, then transferred to fiche. The witness testified that Key Bank received and stored the records in the ordinary course of its business, and he identified the exhibits at issue as accurate copies of Key Bank's fiche record of activity at the ATM on the relevant dates.

A representative of the company that serviced Key Bank's ATMs testified similarly that the status tapes for the ATMs are kept inside the ATMs on the hard drive and automatically record each opening and closing of the safe.

It was undisputed that the entries on all the exhibits were made within a reasonable time of the transactions involved.

Defendant contends that this testimony was insufficient to satisfy the requirements for admitting computer records under CRE 803(6) because (1) the first four exhibits were MAC records but were not introduced by anyone from MAC, and (2) the prosecution did not show that the computer input procedures were accurate by complying with the authentication procedure in CRE 901(b)(9). We reject both contentions.

1.

The fact that the records created by MAC were introduced through the Key Bank officer, whose department received and kept the records, did not preclude their admission under CRE 803(6). *See Hauser v. Rose Health Care Systems*, 857 P.2d 524 (Colo. App. 1993)(documents created by one business but regularly received, maintained, and relied upon by another may be admitted as business records of the latter); *Teac Corp. v. Bauer*, 678 P.2d 3 (Colo. App. 1984) (records prepared by another source that are adopted and integrated in regular course of established business procedures into records sought to be introduced are admissible under CRE 803(6), even if identity of person whose first-hand knowledge was the basis of a particular entry is not established).

2.

Defendant also argues that, to establish the accuracy of the input procedures, the prosecution was required to proceed in accordance with CRE 901(b)(9), which permits authentication by "evidence describing a process or system used to produce a result and showing that the process or system produces an accurate result." This showing was not made, he contends, because the Key Bank foundation witness admitted on cross-examination that he did not know how or when the MAC computer had been programmed, whether it had been repaired, or whether procedures were used to ensure the accuracy of the program. Nor did the authentication witness for Exhibit 14, the status list, testify that the system that generated the list produced an accurate result.

Defendant acknowledges that Colorado cases have not previously required compliance with CRE 901(b)(9) as a condition of admitting computer-generated business records. However, he cites Colorado Evidentiary Foundations, supra, for the proposition that Colorado courts have been "lax" in applying the authentication requirement to computer records, admitting them with "minimal analysis of authenticity issues," and he argues that we should require such further authentication in this case. We decline to do so.

First, although CRE 901(b)(9) may be used to authenticate computer records, there is no requirement, either in the rule itself or in Colorado case law construing the rule, that computer records be authenticated only in this way.

Second, computer business records have a greater level of trustworthiness than an individually generated computer document such as that at issue in People v. Slusher, supra, relied on by defendant, in which a division of this court upheld the exclusion of a purported lease agreement that was apparently created by the defendant on his computer.

Finally, courts have generally declined to require testimony regarding the functioning and accuracy of the computer process where, as here, the records at issue are bank records reflecting data entered automatically rather than manually. See United States v. Moore, 923 F.2d 910 (1st Cir. 1991) (testimony by bank's loan officer was sufficient to authenticate computer-generated loan histories); State v. Veres, 7 Ariz. App. 117, 436 P.2d 629 (Ariz. Ct. App. 1968) (fact that bank's

foundation witness was unfamiliar with operation of encoding machine that generated bank records did not preclude their admission as business records), overruled by State v. Osborn, 107 Ariz. 295, 486 P.2d 777 (Ariz. 1971); People v. Lugashi, 205 Cal. App. 3d 632, 252 Cal. Rptr. 434 (Cal. Ct. App. 1988) (where computer record consists of retrieval of automatic inputs rather than computations based on manual entries, testimony on acceptability, accuracy, maintenance, and reliability of computer hardware and software need not be produced for purposes of admitting record into evidence).

In People v. Lugashi, microfiche copies of computer tapes containing credit card account information were introduced in a prosecution for grand theft. In rejecting an authentication argument similar to that made here, the Lugashi court observed that bank statements prepared in the regular course of banking business, in accordance with banking regulations, are in a different category than ordinary business and financial records of a private enterprise. The court also noted that the "bulk of other jurisdictions" had similarly declined to require more extensive authentication of such records. People v. Lugashi, supra, 252 Cal. Rptr. at 442 (collecting cases).

We agree with the rationale of those decisions upholding the admission of computer-generated bank records without the additional authentication urged by defendant, and accordingly conclude that the trial court did not abuse its discretion in declining to exclude the computer records in this case based on lack of authentication.

II.

Defendant next contends that admission of an incomplete copy of the status tape that recorded openings and closings of the ATM safe violated the best evidence rule. We disagree.

Under CRE 1002 and 1003, the so-called "best evidence rules," an original is generally required to prove the contents of a writing, but a duplicate is admissible to the same extent as an original unless (1) a genuine question is raised as to the authenticity of the original, or (2) under the circumstances, it would be unfair to admit the duplicate in lieu of the original.

CRE 1004(1) further provides that an original is not required if it has been lost or destroyed, unless it was lost or destroyed in bad faith.

Determining the admissibility of evidence offered in lieu of an original writing under these rules is within the trial court's discretion, and that court's determination will not be disturbed absent clear evidence of mistake amounting to an error of law. *United Cable Television of Jeffco, Inc. v. Montgomery LC, Inc.*, 942 P.2d 1230 (Colo. App. 1996).

Mere speculation or supposition that an original document may have contained information that the duplicate did not, or vice versa, does not amount to a showing that it would be unfair to admit the duplicate and thus does not preclude admission of the duplicate under CRE 1003. *Equico Lessors, Inc. v. Tak's Automotive Service*, 680 P.2d 854 (Colo. App. 1984).

The prosecution's foundation witness for Exhibit 14 identified it as a copy of a portion of the status tape that was kept inside the ATM on the hard drive. The tape was retrieved by a technician who took it off the machine in the presence of the witness. The witness then took the original tape roll and photocopied the portions offered into evidence. At the time of trial, he did not know where the original tape was.

Defendant objected to admission of the copy on the basis that it was incomplete and portions of some entries were cut off at the bottom of the page. He argued that the original tape was required. The trial court disagreed, noting that the critical portion, showing entry into the safe at 9:30 p.m. on December 23, was not cut off.

Admission of the duplicate was not an abuse of discretion. The foundation witness testified that the location of the original tape was unknown, and there was nothing to indicate that the original had been lost or destroyed in bad faith. For the reasons set forth in Part I, above, there is no genuine question as to the authenticity of the original tape. Finally, defendant has not shown that it was unfair to admit the duplicate in lieu of the original. He argues that a cut-off entry at the bottom of the first page of the exhibit might have shown a door opening at 6:56 p.m. on December 23, thereby establishing that the theft could have occurred then. This

argument is not only speculative, *see Equico Lessors, Inc. v. Tak's Automotive Service, supra*, but also contradicts defendant's own written statement that the cassettes were in the safe when he opened it between 8:30 and 9:30 p.m. on December 23.

* * *

The judgment is affirmed

McKEEHAN
v.
STATE

COURT OF APPEAL OF FLORIDA, FIFTH DISTRICT

838 So. 2d 1257, 2003 Fla. App. LEXIS 3367 (2003)

JUDGES: MONACO, J. THOMPSON, C.J., and SAWAYA, J., concur.

The defendant, Ronald McKeehan, was found guilty after jury trial of robbery with a firearm, grand theft, aggravated assault with a firearm, and kidnapping with intent to commit a felony. All of these crimes were purportedly committed at a Sleep Inn Motel in Orlando. McKeehan asserts that the trial court committed error by allowing the State to prove the contents of a videotape with oral testimony, rather than with the tape itself.

During the course of the trial, the State introduced collateral crime evidence of a robbery of an Extended Stay America Hotel that was close to the site of the Sleep Inn that occurred a few days before the crimes related to the present case. A clerk who worked at the Extended Stay Hotel testified and identified McKeehan as the perpetrator of the robbery there. The State then called an investigator with the sheriff's office who investigated both robberies. He testified that he had seen a surveillance videotape of the Extended Stay robbery. When the prosecutor asked him if he saw the defendant on the tape, the defense objected, citing the best evidence rule, and pointed out that the State should be required to introduce the tape. The objection, however, was overruled, and the investigator was permitted to testify that the defendant was shown on the videotape.

During jury deliberations, the jury asked the court by written inquiry two questions concerning the evidence. First, the jury asked why the videotape had not been introduced into evidence. The jury also asked if it was permitted to consider the investigator's testimony concerning his observation of the defendant on the tape "as evidence." The trial judge explained to the jury that he could not answer why the videotape had not been introduced, but that the jury was permitted to consider the testimony of the investigator with regard to the tape.

The best evidence rule is set forth in section 90.952, Florida Statutes (2002), as follows:

Except as otherwise provided by statute, an original writing, recording, or photograph is required in order to prove the contents of the writing, recording, or photograph.

Section 90.954, Florida Statutes, amplifies the preceding statute by providing that:

The original of a writing, recording, or photograph is not required, except as provided in s. 90.953 [concerning duplicates], and other evidence of its contents is admissible when:

(1) All originals are lost or destroyed, unless the proponent lost or destroyed them in bad faith.

(2) An original cannot be obtained in this state by any judicial process or procedure.

(3) An original was under the control of the party against whom offered at a time when that party was put on notice by the pleadings or by written notice from the adverse party that the contents of such original would be subject to proof at the hearing, and such original is not produced at the hearing.

(4) The writing, recording, or photograph is not related to a controlling issue.

The best evidence rule, as codified by statute, requires that if the original evidence or a statutorily authorized alternative is available, no evidence should be received which is merely "substitutionary in nature." *Liddon*

v. Bd. of Pub. Instruction for Jackson County, 128 Fla. 838, 175 So. 806, 808 (Fla. 1937); *Sun Bank of St. Lucie County v. Oliver*, 403 So. 2d 583, 584 (Fla. 4th DCA 1981). Thus, evidence which indicates that a more original source of information is available should be excluded. Id. In short, unless otherwise excused by the evidence code, the original must be produced unless it is shown to be unavailable for a reason other than the serious fault of the proponent. See *Williams v. State*, 386 So. 2d 538, 540 (Fla. 1980); *Firestone Serv. Stores, Inc. of Gainesville v. Wynn*, 131 Fla. 94, 179 So. 175 (Fla. 1938).

This rule is predicated on the principle that if the original evidence is available, that evidence should be presented to ensure accurate transmittal of the critical facts contained within it. *See Williams*; *State v. Eubanks*, 609 So. 2d 107 (Fla. 4th DCA 1992). Thus, in Williams it was found to be error for the trial court to permit introduction of oral evidence of what the victim of an attempted murder wrote (which implicated the defendant in the crime), while at a hospital awaiting treatment. The supreme court noted that no effort had been made by the state to explain the absence of the original writing.

The same is true in the instant case concerning the videotape of the Extended Stay Hotel robbery. The State sought to prove the contents of the videotape not by introduction of the tape, but by oral testimony of its contents without ever establishing the videotape's unavailability. Accordingly, the admission of the testimony violated the best evidence rule.

A violation of the best evidence rule may, however, constitute harmless error. In *Williams*, the supreme court affirmed despite the error, explaining:

Rather than contesting the accuracy of the terms contained in Ms. Marshall's note, appellant's objection was directed to the reliability of the out-of-court identification, an issue not addressed by the best evidence rule. Moreover, counsel had ample opportunity to discredit the identification by cross-examining Ms. Marshall about the events at the hospital. Given this posture, we do not believe that the trial court's technical error injuriously affected the substantial rights of appellant. § 59.041, Fla. Stat. (1975). 386 So. 2d at 540 (footnote omitted).

Under a harmless error analysis, the state must show beyond a reasonable doubt that the error complained of did not contribute to the verdict, or, stated alternatively, that there is no reasonable possibility that the error contributed to the conviction. *State v. DiGuilio*, 491 So. 2d 1129, 1136 (Fla. 1986); *Stires v. State*, 824 So. 2d 943 (Fla. 5th DCA 2002). Application of the rule "requires an examination of the entire record by the appellate court including a close examination of the permissible evidence on which the jury could have legitimately relied and, in addition, an even closer examination of the impermissible evidence which might have possibly influenced the jury verdict." *DiGuilio*, 491 So. 2d at 1135. [**7] As our supreme court has noted, harmless error analysis focuses on the effect of the error on the trier of fact." *Goodwin v. State*, 751 So. 2d 537, 542 (Fla. 1999) (quoting *State v. Lee*, 531 So. 2d 133, 137 (Fla. 1988)).

The question, therefore, is not whether the evidence against the defendant was overwhelming. *Lee*, 531 So. 2d at 136–37; *Jones v. State*, 754 So. 2d 792 (Fla. 1st DCA 2000). A reviewing court "must resist the temptation to make its own determination of whether a guilty verdict could be sustained by excluding the impermissible evidence and examining only the permissible evidence." *Goodwin*, 751 So. 2d at 542.

In the instant case, the pivotal issue at trial concerned identification of the perpetrator of the Sleep Inn robbery. The sole evidence directly tying the defendant to the Sleep Inn robbery was the desk clerk's eyewitness testimony. The State attempted to bolster the desk clerk's identification with Williams rule evidence linking the defendant to another recent and very similar hotel robbery in the same vicinity. The victim of the second robbery identified McKeehan as the perpetrator of that crime.

The State then presented an investigator's identification of the defendant from the videotape. As this identification confirmed the identification of the defendant made by the victim, it might appear to amount to the erroneous admission of cumulative evidence that would constitute harmless error. [Citations omitted.]

In the present case, however, the jury's inquiry of the court relating, first, to the absence of the videotape, and then to the investigator's identification testimony based on his examination of the tape, makes it quite evident that the jury seriously considered that particular testimony in reaching its verdict. Moreover, the use by the State in this case of evidence less than the original, when there was no demonstration that the original was unavailable, authorizes an inference that the proponent's position would have been defeated if the best evidence had been furnished. *Liddon*, 175 So. at 808. Under the circumstances, therefore, we cannot say that there is no reasonable possibility that the inadmissible testimony contributed to the conviction. *DiGuilio*, 491 So. 2d at 1135. Given the questions from the jury, in fact, it is far more likely that the erroneously admitted testimony had an influence on the jury verdict. Accordingly, we reverse the convictions and order a new trial.

REVERSED and REMANDED.

THOMPSON, C.J., and SAWAYA, J., concur.

Cases Relating to Chapter 14

Real Evidence

SCHMERBER
v.
CALIFORNIA

**Supreme Court of the
United States
384 U.S. 757, 86 S. Ct. 1826,
16 L. Ed. 2d 908 (1966)**

MR. JUSTICE BRENNAN delivered the opinion of the Court.

Petitioner was convicted in Los Angeles Municipal Court of the criminal offense of driving an automobile while under the influence of intoxicating liquor. He had been arrested at a hospital while receiving treatment for injuries suffered in an accident involving the automobile that he had apparently been driving. At the direction of a police officer, a physician at the hospital then withdrew a blood sample from petitioner's body. The chemical analysis of this sample revealed a percent by weight of alcohol in his blood at the time of the offense which indicated intoxication, and the report of this analysis was admitted in evidence at the trial. Petitioner objected to receipt of this evidence of the analysis on the ground that the blood had been withdrawn despite his refusal, on the advice of his counsel, to consent to the test. He contended that in that circumstance the withdrawal of the blood and the admission of the analysis in evidence denied him due process of law under the Fourteenth Amendment, as well as specific guarantees of the Bill of Rights secured against the States by that Amendment; his privilege against self-incrimination under the Fifth Amendment; his right to counsel under the Sixth Amendment;

and his right not to be subjected to unreasonable searches and seizures in violation of the Fourth Amendment. The Appellate Department of the California Superior Court rejected these contentions and affirmed the conviction. In view of constitutional decisions since we last considered these issues in *Breithaupt v. Abram*, 352 U.S. 432—see *Escobedo v. Illinois*, 378 U.S. 478; *Malloy v. Hogan*, 378 U.S. 1, and *Mapp v. Ohio*, 367 U.S. 643—we granted certiorari. 382 U.S. 971. We affirm.

I.

The Due Process Clause Claim

Breithaupt was also a case in which police officers caused blood to be withdrawn from the driver of an automobile involved in an accident, and in which there was ample justification for the officer's conclusion that the driver was under the influence of alcohol. There, as here, the extraction was made by a physician in a simple, medically acceptable manner in a hospital environment. There, however, the driver was unconscious at the time the blood was withdrawn and hence had no opportunity to object to the procedure. We affirmed the conviction there resulting from the use of the test in evidence, holding that under such circumstances the withdrawal did not offend "that 'sense of justice' of which we spoke in *Rochin v. California*, 342 U.S. 165." 352 U.S., at 435. *Breithaupt* thus requires the rejection of petitioner's due process argument, and nothing in the circumstances of this case or in supervening events persuades us that this aspect of *Breithaupt* should be overruled.

II.

The Privilege Against Self-Incrimination Claim

Breithaupt summarily rejected an argument that the withdrawal of blood and the admission of the analysis report involved in that state case violated the Fifth Amendment privilege of any person not to "be compelled in any criminal case to be a witness against himself," citing *Twining v. New Jersey*, 211 U.S. 78. But that case, holding that the protections of the Fourteenth Amendment do not embrace this Fifth Amendment privilege, has been succeeded by *Malloy v. Hogan*, 378 U.S. 1, 8. We there held that "the Fourteenth Amendment secures against state invasion the same privilege that the Fifth Amendment guarantees against federal infringement—the right of a person to remain silent unless he chooses to speak in the unfettered exercise of his own will, and to suffer no penalty . . . for such silence." We therefore must now decide whether the withdrawal of the blood and admission in evidence of the analysis involved in this case violated petitioner's privilege. We hold that the privilege protects an accused only from being compelled to testify against himself, or otherwise provide the State with evidence of a testimonial or communicative nature, and that the withdrawal of blood and use of the analysis in question in this case did not involve compulsion to these ends.

It could not be denied that in requiring petitioner to submit to the withdrawal and chemical analysis of his blood the State compelled him to submit to an attempt to discover evidence that might be used to prosecute him for a criminal offense. He submitted only after the police officer rejected his objection and directed the physician to proceed. The officer's direction to the physician to administer the test over petitioner's objection constituted compulsion for the purposes of the privilege. The critical question, then, is whether petitioner was thus compelled "to be a witness against himself."

If the scope of the privilege coincided with the complex of values it helps to protect, we might be obliged to conclude that the privilege was violated. In *Miranda v. Arizona, ante*, at 460, the Court said of the interests protected by the privilege: "All these policies

point to one overriding thought: the constitutional foundation underlying the privilege is the respect a government—state or federal—must accord to the dignity and integrity of its citizens. To maintain a 'fair state-individual balance,' to require the government 'to shoulder the entire load' . . . to respect the inviolability of the human personality, our accusatory system of criminal justice demands that the government seeking to punish an individual produce the evidence against him by its own independent labors, rather than by the cruel, simple expedient of compelling it from his own mouth." The withdrawal of blood necessarily involves puncturing the skin for extraction, and the percent by weight of alcohol in that blood, as established by chemical analysis, is evidence of criminal guilt. Compelled submission fails on one view to respect the "inviolability of the human personality." Moreover, since it enables the State to rely on evidence forced from the accused, the compulsion violates at least one meaning of the requirement that the State procure the evidence against an accused "by its own independent labors."

As the passage in *Miranda* implicitly recognizes, however, the privilege has never been given the full scope which the values it helps to protect suggest. History and a long line of authorities in lower courts have consistently limited its protection to situations in which the State seeks to submerge those values by obtaining the evidence against an accused through "the cruel, simple expedient of compelling it from his own mouth. . . . In sum, the privilege is fulfilled only when the person is guaranteed the right 'to remain silent unless he chooses to speak in the unfettered exercise of his own will.'" Ibid. The leading case in this Court is *Holt v. United States*, 218 U.S. 245. There the question was whether evidence was admissible that the accused, prior to trial and over his protest, put on a blouse that fitted him. It was contended that compelling the accused to submit to the demand that he model the blouse violated the privilege. Mr. Justice Holmes, speaking for the Court, rejected the argument as "based upon an extravagant extension of the Fifth Amendment," and went on to say: "The prohibition of compelling a man in a criminal court to be witness against himself is a prohibition of the use of physical or moral compulsion to extort communications from him, not an exclusion of his body as evidence when it may be material. The objection in principle would forbid a jury to look at a prisoner and compare his features with a photograph in proof." 218 U.S., at 252–253.

It is clear that the protection of the privilege reaches an accused's communications, whatever form they might take, and the compulsion of responses which are also communications, for example, compliance with a subpoena to produce one's papers. *Boyd v. United States*, 116 U.S. 616. On the other hand, both federal and state courts have usually held that it offers no protection against compulsion to submit to fingerprinting, photographing, or measurements, to write or speak for identification, to appear in court, to stand, to assume a stance, to walk, or to make a particular gesture. The distinction which has emerged, often expressed in different ways, is that the privilege is a bar against compelling "communications" or "testimony," but that compulsion which makes a suspect or accused the source of "real or physical evidence" does not violate it.

Although we agree that this distinction is a helpful framework for analysis, we are not to be understood to agree with past applications in all instances. There will be many cases in which such a distinction is not readily drawn. Some tests seemingly directed to obtain "physical evidence," for example, lie detector tests measuring changes in body function during interrogation, may actually be directed to eliciting responses which are essentially testimonial. To compel a person to submit to testing in which an effort will be made to determine his guilt or innocence on the basis of physiological responses, whether willed or not, is to evoke the spirit and history of the Fifth Amendment. Such situations call to mind the principle that the protection of the privilege "is as broad as the mischief against which it seeks to guard," *Counselman v. Hitchcock*, 142 U.S. 547, 562.

In the present case, however, no such problem of application is presented. Not even a shadow of testimonial compulsion upon or enforced communication by the accused was involved either in the extraction or in the chemical analysis. Petitioner's testimonial capacities were in no way implicated; indeed, his participation, except as a donor, was irrele-

vant to the results of the test, which depend on chemical analysis and on that alone. Since the blood test evidence, although an incriminating product of compulsion, was neither petitioner's testimony nor evidence relating to some communicative act or writing by the petitioner, it was not inadmissible on privilege grounds.

* * *

Affirmed. MR. JUSTICE HARLAN, whom MR. JUSTICE STEWART joins, concurring.

In joining the Court's opinion I desire to add the following comment. While agreeing with the Court that the taking of this blood test involved no testimonial compulsion, I would go further and hold that apart from this consideration the case in no way implicates the Fifth Amendment. Cf. my dissenting opinion and that of MR. JUSTICE WHITE in *Miranda v. Arizona, ante*, pp. 504, 526.

MR. CHIEF JUSTICE WARREN, dissenting.

While there are other important constitutional issues in this case, I believe it is sufficient for me to reiterate my dissenting opinion in *Breithaupt v. Abram*, 352 U.S. 432, 440, as the basis on which to reverse this conviction.

MR. JUSTICE BLACK with whom MR. JUSTICE DOUGLAS joins, dissenting.

I would reverse petitioner's conviction. I agree with the Court that the Fourteenth Amendment made applicable to the States the Fifth Amendment's provision that "No person . . . shall be compelled in any criminal case to be a witness against himself. . . ." But I disagree with the Court's holding that California did not violate petitioner's constitutional right against self-incrimination when it compelled him, against his will, to allow a doctor to puncture his blood vessels in order to extract a sample of blood and analyze it for alcoholic content, and then used that analysis as evidence to convict petitioner of a crime.

* * *

MR. JUSTICE DOUGLAS, dissenting.

I adhere to the views of THE CHIEF JUSTICE in his dissent in *Breithaupt v. Abram*,

352 U.S. 432, 440, and to the views I stated in my dissent in that case (id., 442) and add only a word.

We are dealing with the right of privacy which, since the Breithaupt case, we have held to be within the penumbra of some specific guarantees of the Bill of Rights. *Griswold v. Connecticut*, 381 U.S. 479. Thus, the Fifth Amendment marks "a zone of privacy" which the Government may not force a person to surrender. Id., 484. Likewise the Fourth Amendment recognizes that right when it guarantees the right of the people to be secure "in their persons." Ibid. No clearer invasion of this right of privacy can be imagined than forcible bloodletting of the kind involved here.

MR. JUSTICE FORTAS, dissenting.

I would reverse. In my view, petitioner's privilege against self-incrimination applies. I would add that, under the Due Process Clause, the State, in its role as prosecutor, has no right to extract blood from an accused or anyone else, over his protest. As prosecutor, the State has no right to commit any kind of violence upon the person, or to utilize the results of such a tort, and the extraction of blood, over protest, is an act of violence. Cf. CHIEF JUSTICE WARREN's dissenting opinion in *Breithaupt v. Abram*, 352 U.S. 432, 440.

STATE
v.
COWANS

APPELLATE COURT OF ILLINOIS, FIRST DISTRICT, SIXTH DIVISION

336 Ill. App. 3d 173, 782 N.E.2d 779, 2002 Ill. App. LEXIS 1170
Appeal denied by People v. Cowans, 2003 Ill. LEXIS 649

(Ill., Apr. 2, 2003)

JUDGES: JUSTICE O'MARA FROSSARD delivered the opinion of the court. O'BRIEN, P.J., and GALLAGHER, J., concur.

Following a bench trial defendant was found guilty of one count of possession of a controlled substance with intent to deliver. The trial court sentenced defendant to seven years in the Illinois Department of Corrections. On appeal, defendant challenges the sufficiency of the evidence and contends the stipulated facts, together with the entire trial record, fail to establish a complete chain of custody for the controlled substance.

BACKGROUND

The State called Officer McCarthy as a witness and introduced additional evidence through two stipulations. McCarthy testified that around 9:45 p.m. on January 22, 2000, near 4936 West Huron Street, he observed defendant with the aid of binoculars. During a five-minute surveillance McCarthy saw four individuals approach defendant, engage in a brief conversation, and give defendant money. Defendant placed the money in his pants pocket and gave a small object to each individual. When McCarthy was about 15 feet away, defendant looked in his direction and threw a number of small plastic bags to the ground. McCarthy recovered from the ground nine small plastic bags containing what he suspected to be cocaine. Defendant was arrested. McCarthy searched defendant and recovered $ 190 from his pants pocket. McCarthy testified that he later inventoried the nine small plastic bags under inventory number 2295494 and the money under inventory number 2295495. The Nash School was located about one block away.

The State offered two stipulations agreed to by defense counsel. By way of stipulation it was agreed that if Investigator Tansy were to testify he would state that he measured the distance from 4936 West Huron Street to the Nash School and found it was 742 feet. It was further stipulated that if forensic scientist Maureen Dully were to testify she would state that she received nine items under inventory number 2295494 and tested five of the nine items, which she found contained 1.2 grams of cocaine.

Defendant and Lonniece Young-Frazier testified in the defense case. Frazier testified that she knows defendant, but does not know him personally. On January 22, 2000, between 9 p.m. and 10 p.m., she was a passenger in a car in front of 4935 West Huron Street. She saw the defendant walking westbound on the north side of Huron Street when two uniformed officers, a male and female, approached him. Defendant put his hands up in the air. Frazier testified that she did not see defendant drop anything on the ground and did not see anyone passing objects for money. She testified that the officers searched defendant, handcuffed him, and placed him in the police car. Frazier testified that the male officer had a flashlight and was looking on the ground all over the area, including under porches two or three houses away.

Defendant testified that he was walking home from the store after playing the lottery. He was on the north side of Huron Street. Officer McCarthy and a female police officer pulled up in a marked squad car. Defendant denied he had anything in his hands or dropped anything; he denied selling drugs or possessing any drugs. Defendant stated that McCarthy searched him, found money, and told the female officer that defendant must be doing something. Defendant was handcuffed and placed in the squad car. McCarthy searched the area with a flashlight. Defendant testified that when McCarthy got into the car he showed defendant a plastic pouch and then drove to the police station.

ANALYSIS

Defendant stipulated to certain facts at trial. Generally, a defendant is precluded from attacking any facts previously agreed to in a stipulation. Defendant does not attack the specific facts agreed to in the stipulation. Defendant, relying on *In re R.F.*, 298 Ill. App. 3d 13, 16, 232 Ill. Dec. 519, 698 N.E.2d 610 (1998), challenges the sufficiency of the evidence and argues that the stipulated facts, together with the entire trial record, fail to establish a sufficiently complete chain of custody.

When a defendant challenges the sufficiency of the evidence, the relevant inquiry is whether, after viewing the evidence in the light most favorable to the prosecution, any rational trier of fact could have found the essential elements of the crime beyond a reasonable doubt. [Citations omitted.] A challenge to the sufficiency of the evidence is not subject to the waiver rule and may be raised

for the first time on direct appeal. *People v. Enoch*, 122 Ill. 2d 176, 119 Ill. Dec. 265, 522 N.E.2d 1124 (1988).

Before real evidence may be admitted at trial, the State must provide an adequate foundation either by way of live testimony or stipulation which establishes that the item sought to be introduced is the actual item involved in the alleged offense and that its condition is substantially unchanged. *People v. Cole*, 29 Ill. App. 3d 369, 375, 329 N.E.2d 880 (1975). Where an item possesses unique and readily identifiable characteristics and its substance is relatively impervious to change, testimony at trial that the item sought to be admitted in evidence is the same one recovered and in substantially the same condition as when recovered is sufficient to establish an adequate foundation. *People v. Gilbert*, 58 Ill. App. 3d 387, 15 Ill. Dec. 956, 374 N.E.2d 739 (1978). If the item is not readily identifiable or if it is susceptible to alteration by tampering or contamination, its chain of custody must be established by the State with sufficient completeness to render it improbable that the original item has either been exchanged, contaminated, or subjected to tampering. *People v. Winters*, 97 Ill. App. 3d 288, 289, 52 Ill. Dec. 763, 422 N.E.2d 972 (1981).

The character of the item determines which method for laying an adequate foundation must be used. [Citation omitted.] Based on the character of the evidence in this case, the chain of custody must be established by the State with sufficient completeness to render it improbable that the original item has either been exchanged, contaminated, or subjected to tampering. Thus, the State was required to establish a chain of custody to demonstrate the connection between the items recovered from the ground by Officer McCarthy after discarded by defendant and the items tested by forensic scientist Maureen Dully.

Regarding that connection, the record contained the testimony of Officer McCarthy and the stipulated testimony of forensic scientist Maureen Dully. The testimony of Officer McCarthy on direct examination by the State regarding recovering and handling the controlled substance was as follows:

"Q. What happened as you were approaching the defendant?

A. He looked in my direction, and he threw to the ground numerous plastic bags. I recovered these bags and found them to be nine clear, plastic bags each containing white, rocky substance that I believed to be crack cocaine.

***

Q. Officer, did you later inventory the U.S. currency and the suspect rock cocaine?
A. Yes.
Q. And did you inventory the nine, clear baggies containing the suspect rock cocaine under inventory number 2295494?
A. Yes."

On cross-examination McCarthy testified as follows:

"Q. And you were 15 feet away from him, and that's when he threw these things down on the ground?
A. I said approximately 15 feet.
Q. And could you see then what those things were?
A. I could tell they were, at least, clear, plastic bags.
Q. Were they tinted at all?
A. Yes.
Q. What color tint?
A. Green."

The agreed stipulation between the State and defense regarding the testimony of forensic scientist Duffy was as follows:

"[711 LAW CLERK FOR THE STATE]: Also, that if Maureen Dully, a forensic scientist employed by the Illinois State Police Division of Forensic Services were to be called, she would testify that on February 7, 2000, she received the following inventory number, 2295494, which contained nine items, and that she tested five of those nine items and that she has determined that—with a reasonable degree of scientific certainty that the five tested items tested positive for 1.2 grams of cocaine. So stipulated?

[DEFENSE ATTORNEY]: Yes."

The testimony of Officer McCarthy and the stipulation regarding the testimony of forensic scientist Dully was in total the evidence produced by the State regarding chain of custody.

In order to prove its case, the State is required to prove a connection between the defendant and the illegal contraband. In doing so the State is required to establish a proper chain of custody. A sufficient chain of custody does not require that every person involved in the chain testify, nor must the State exclude all possibilities that the evidence may have been subject to tampering. *Winters*, 97 Ill. App. 3d at 295. The State must demonstrate that the evidence has not been changed in any important respect. *People v. Hominick*, 177 Ill. App. 3d 18, 29, 126 Ill. Dec. 422, 531 N.E.2d 1049 (1988). The State is required to establish that it took reasonable protective measures since the substance was seized. *People v. Hermann*, 180 Ill. App. 3d 939, 944, 129 Ill. Dec. 656, 536 N.E.2d 706 (1988). The purpose of the protective measures is to ensure that the substance taken from the defendant was the same as the substance tested by the forensic chemist. *People v. Ryan*, 129 Ill. App. 3d 915, 919, 85 Ill. Dec. 93, 473 N.E.2d 461 (1984).

We are mindful that unless the defendant produces actual evidence of tampering, substitution, or contamination, the State need only establish a probability that tampering, substitution or contamination did not occur, and any deficiencies go to the weight rather than the admissibility of the evidence. *Hominick*, 177 Ill. App. 3d at 29. In the instant case, defendant did not produce actual evidence of tampering, substitution, or contamination. Therefore, the State is only required to establish a probability that reasonable protective measures were employed to protect the evidence from the time it was seized and that it was improbable the evidence was altered. *People v. Bynum*, 257 Ill. App. 3d 502, 510, 196 Ill. Dec. 179, 629 N.E.2d 724 (1994). To establish a sufficiently complete chain of custody, the State is required to prove delivery, presence, and safekeeping of the evidence. *People v. Gibson*, 287 Ill. App. 3d 878, 882, 223 Ill. Dec. 234, 679 N.E.2d 419 (1997).

The State, relying on *People v. Irpino*, 122 Ill. App. 3d 767, 78 Ill. Dec. 165, 461

N.E.2d 999 (1984), contends that the chain of custody was sufficiently established in this case because the "testimony clearly demonstrated that the evidence seized 'matched' the evidence subjected to chemical analysis." We recognize that if one link in the chain is missing, but there is evidence describing the condition of the evidence when delivered which matches the description of the evidence when examined, the evidence can be sufficient to establish chain of custody. *Irpino*, 122 Ill. App. 3d at 775.

Officer McCarthy testified he recovered from the ground nine small plastic bags with a green tint that contained suspected crack cocaine after being discarded by the defendant. The record reflects by way of stipulation that the forensic scientist received nine items and tested the contents of five items, which she found to contain 1.2 grams of cocaine. The officer's description includes details about the color, shape and packaging of the items, but not the weight. The forensic scientist's stipulation contains no corresponding details about the color, shape and packaging of the items. The forensic scientist's stipulation includes a weight estimate, but in no way further describes the items.

Here, the only common features in the testimony describing the condition of the evidence when seized and the description of the evidence when tested are the number of items and the inventory number. The stipulation of the testimony provided by the forensic scientist did not include whether the items she received were in plastic bags or whether the bags were colored or clear. The stipulation of the testimony provided by the forensic scientist did not include any description as to size, shape, or color of the items received. Officer McCarthy described the evidence as a white, rocky substance. However, there was no corresponding or "matching" description provided by the forensic scientist in the stipulation as to the shape and color of the substance. While there was evidence that the nine plastic bags retrieved from the ground by Officer McCarthy were distinctive in color, that distinctive color was not included in the description of the items tested by the forensic scientist provided by

the State's stipulation. Rather, the stipulation referenced the evidence by use of the generic term "items." The "items" received by forensic scientist Duffy were given no further description in the stipulation.

As noted, where there is evidence describing the condition of the evidence when seized, which matches the description of the evidence when examined, the evidence can be sufficient to establish chain of custody. Irpino, 122 Ill. App. 3d at 775. For the reasons previously discussed, we cannot conclude that the record reflects the condition of the evidence when seized sufficiently matches the description of the evidence when tested. This gap in the chain of custody is not resolved by the record.

Moreover, the record reflects several additional missing links in the chain of custody regarding proof of handling, delivery, presence, and safekeeping of the evidence. To establish a sufficiently complete chain of custody, the State is required to prove delivery, presence, and safekeeping of the evidence. Gibson, 287 Ill. App. 3d at 882. The record reflects no reasonable protective techniques regarding custody, handling, delivery, presence, and safekeeping of the alleged contraband. The State presented no evidence of what procedures, if any, were used in the handling and safekeeping of the evidence between Officer McCarthy's recovery of the plastic bags and the receipt of the evidence by forensic scientist Dully 16 days later. The record contains no evidence either by live testimony or stipulation as to what Officer McCarthy did with the plastic bags he retrieved from the ground after defendant allegedly discarded them, other than the fact that McCarthy inventoried those items under an inventory number. There is no evidence that the plastic bags recovered from the ground from Officer McCarthy were placed in any closed or sealed container or envelope or were initialed or dated by Officer McCarthy; no evidence as to what condition the items were kept in during the 16 days that passed before forensic scientist Dully received them; no evidence that the items received at the crime laboratory were received sealed; and no evidence of the whereabouts of the plastic bags for the 16 days that passed from the time Officer McCarthy recovered the plastic bags on January 22, 2000, and February 7, 2000, when forensic scientist Duffy received the items.

Regarding chain of custody, the State relies on *People v. Leemon*, 66 Ill. 2d 170, 172, 5 Ill. Dec. 250, 361 N.E.2d 573 (1977), and argues "the court held in *Leemon* that the police officer's testimony identifying the bag he recovered from the defendant, together with a stipulation between the parties that the contents of the bag were LSD, made a sufficient showing of continuity of possession of custody." In *Leemon*, Officer Edwards described the bag of LSD he purchased from defendant which he had marked with the date and his initials. That plastic bag containing LSD was received in evidence. Unlike *Leemon*, the record in this case contains no testimony by Officer McCarthy during trial identifying the baggies he recovered from the defendant, either in the form of live testimony or by way of stipulation. There is no evidence that Officer McCarthy marked the baggies with the date and his initials. In *Leemon*, the plastic bag containing LSD recovered by the police officer from the defendant was received in evidence. Unlike *Leemon*, in the instant case the baggies containing the controlled substance recovered by Officer McCarthy were not offered into evidence by the State or received into evidence by the court either through live testimony or by way of stipulation. The controlled substance in this case was never given an exhibit number. Here, the State not only failed to provide an adequate foundation to introduce the contraband into evidence, but it never sought to introduce into evidence the controlled substance either by live testimony or stipulation.

As previously noted, the State must provide an adequate foundation demonstrating the item sought to be offered into evidence is the actual item involved in the alleged offense and its condition is substantially unchanged. McCarthy never identified the narcotics as those retrieved after being discarded by defendant nor did the State establish that fact by way of stipulation. McCarthy never testified that, at the time of trial, the controlled substance was in substantially the same condition as when he inventoried it, nor did the State establish that fact by way of stipulation. The record reflects no evidence by way of

live testimony or stipulation that the items recovered by McCarthy were substantially unchanged from the time of the offense to the time of trial. The record contains no evidence either by live testimony or stipulation that Officer McCarthy would identify the items tested by Dully and would testify that these items were in the same or substantially the same condition as when he recovered these items from the ground after they were allegedly discarded by defendant on January 22, 2000. These gaps in the chain of custody are not resolved by the record.

There are additional gaps in the chain of custody. There is no evidence either by way of direct testimony or stipulation regarding delivery of the items to the crime laboratory. The stipulation indicates the items were received on February 7, 2000. However, there is no evidence in the record as to where those "items" were for 16 days from January 22, 2000, until February 7, 2000. There is no testimony, live or stipulated, describing the condition of the items when delivered to the crime laboratory. There is no evidence the items were delivered in a closed or sealed container. There is no evidence of any protective measures the State took from the point the substance was recovered by Officer McCarthy until the point the items were received 16 days later at the crime laboratory by forensic scientist Duffy.

Reversal for evidentiary insufficiency is required when the State fails to prove its case. As recently noted in *People v. Moore*, "When the issue is one which concerns the sufficiency of the evidence, we are required to reverse outright, whereas the erroneous admission of evidence is a procedural error which allows us to remand for a new trial." *People v. Moore*, 335 Ill. App. 3d 616, 781 N.E.2d 493, 2002 Ill. App. LEXIS 1058, (November 15, 2002), citing *People v. Olivera*, 164 Ill. 2d 382, 393, 207 Ill. Dec. 433, 647 N.E.2d 926 (1995). In this case, defendant challenges the sufficiency of the evidence. There is no issue regarding the erroneous admission of the controlled substance, because the State never sought to admit the controlled substance either by live testimony or stipulation.

Moreover, in this case there is no challenge to the stipulated facts and no contention that the stipulations were misstated. *See People v. Maurice*, 31 Ill. 2d 456, 457–59, 202 N.E.2d 480 (1964) (where stipulation was misstated, court concluded admission of heroin into evidence without sufficient chain of custody required reversal and remand for new trial). Rather, in the instant case, the defendant challenges the sufficiency of the evidence and argues that the stipulated facts, considered together with the entire trial record, fail to establish a sufficiently complete chain of custody. *See In re R.F.,* 298 Ill. App. 3d at 15 (insufficient foundation provided by State for admission of controlled substance required outright reversal).

CONCLUSION

The evidence was insufficient to sustain defendant's conviction because the State failed to establish a sufficient chain of custody for the controlled substance. The State failed to demonstrate that the police took reasonable protective measures to ensure that the substance recovered by Officer McCarthy from the ground after abandoned by defendant was the same or substantially the same as the items tested by forensic chemist Dully. There was no evidence regarding the handling and safekeeping of the controlled substance from the point in time when Officer McCarthy recovered the evidence until the point in time when forensic scientist Dully received the evidence 16 days later.

Other than the testimony of Officer McCarthy that he inventoried the evidence under inventory number 2295494, the only other evidence offered to prove the chain of custody was the stipulation, which merely established that Duffy tested five of nine "items" assigned to inventory number 2295494, which tested positive for 1.2 grams of cocaine. The State failed to establish a sufficiently complete chain of custody by proof of delivery, presence and safekeeping of the controlled substance. The State failed to establish a probability that reasonable measures were used to protect the evidence from the time that it was seized and that it was improbable the evidence was altered.

For the reasons previously discussed, we find the evidence was insufficient to prove defendant guilty beyond a reasonable doubt.

Reversed.

O'BRIEN, P.J., and GALLAGHER, J., concur.

UNDERWOOD
v.
STATE

Supreme Court of Mississippi
708 So. 2d 18 (1998)

En Banc.

SULLIVAN, Presiding Justice, for the Court:

PART ONE: GUILT PHASE

1. Justin Underwood was indicted for capital murder by the grand jury for Madison County during the March Term of 1994. The indictment charged that Underwood had murdered Virginia Ann Harris on or about February 15, 1994, by shooting her with a pistol, during the course of kidnapping, in violation of Miss. Code Ann. § 97-3-19(2)(e). Underwood pleaded not guilty and proceeded to trial on May 22, 1995, in the Circuit Court of Madison County. The jury returned a verdict of guilty on the charge of capital murder on May 24. The sentencing phase of the trial was held on the following day, and the jury found that Underwood should be sentenced to death. Circuit Judge John B. Toney entered the final judgment of conviction and sentence on May 25, and ordered that Underwood be put to death by lethal injection on July 7, 1995. Following denial of his motion for judgment notwithstanding the verdict, or in the alternative for a new trial, Underwood perfected his appeal to this Court.

STATEMENT OF THE FACTS

2. On February 15, 1994, Lindsay Harris spoke with his wife, Virginia Ann Harris, before leaving their home in Flora to travel to his produce business at the Farmer's Market in Jackson. Mrs. Harris asked her husband to eat dinner in Jackson on his way home from work, because she planned to do some shopping in Jackson that day. Mr. Harris

agreed, told his wife goodbye, and left for work at about 6:00 A.M. He worked from 6:30 A.M. until closing time at 4:00 P.M., when he loaded a delivery order in his truck and left for Flora at about 4:30 P.M.

3. When Mr. Harris arrived at his house, he saw his wife's car, a blue Lincoln Towncar, in the garage, but when he entered the home and called her name, there was no answer. He noticed that the lights and television were on in the den, and the curtains were drawn. Walking back to their bedroom, Mr. Harris saw that Mrs. Harris's makeup drawer was pulled open, the lights were on, and a makeup bottle was left upside down on the counter. Mr. Harris and his son Kyle both testified that it was unlike Mrs. Harris to leave the house in such a condition.

4. At about 5:00 P.M., Mr. Harris changed clothes and left to go feed his cattle. When he returned, Mrs. Harris still wasn't home. He showered and dressed for bed, and by 8:00 P.M. he was extremely worried about his wife. He started calling family and friends, but no one knew where she was. At midnight Mr. Harris called the police and reported Mrs. Harris as a missing person. At 12:30 or 1:00 A.M., Officer Ogden Wilson arrived at the Harris home and filled out a missing person report, which he forwarded to the sheriff's department.

5. At 1:30 A.M. Mr. Harris called his son Kyle and told him that Mrs. Harris was still missing. Kyle came over immediately, and the two conducted a search of the house and yard. On their way back into the house through the garage, Kyle noticed that the keys to Mrs. Harris's Lincoln were in the ignition. They also discovered Mrs. Harris's purse on the floor of the front passenger side of the car, which was not Mrs. Harris's custom. Kyle testified that his mother normally kept her purse on the seat beside her. There was no money in the purse, which was unusual for Mrs. Harris, who usually carried at least $40 with her at all times. The only unlocked car door was the driver's door, indicating that only one person had exited the car, because when the ignition was turned, all of the doors automatically locked. The front seat of the car was pushed back to its furthermost position, which was also out of character for Mrs. Harris. Mr. Harris testified that he

was 5'9", and his feet didn't touch the pedals in Mrs. Harris's car with the seat that far back. Charles Scarborough, Master Sergeant Trooper with the Mississippi Highway Patrol, testified that he was 5'11" and would not be comfortable with the seat in that position. Mr. Harris also testified that he believed the Lincoln was parked in the garage differently than Mrs. Harris usually parked it. Nothing was missing from the house, other than possibly some cash from Mrs. Harris's purse. At this point, Mr. Harris and Kyle agreed that Mrs. Harris must have been kidnapped.

6. At 6:00 A.M. on February 16, the highway patrol, police, and sheriff's department were contacted, and detectives began arriving at the Harris home to take over the investigation. Sergeant Scarborough lifted fingerprints and fibers from Mrs. Harris's Lincoln and took pictures of the car. Only two latent prints of value were lifted from the car, and neither were matched with anyone, including the defendant, Justin Underwood. The fibers taken from Mrs. Harris's car similarly were not linked to anyone, including Underwood. Sergeant Judy Tucker with the Mississippi Highway Patrol Investigation Bureau was called to head up the investigation. Mr. Harris described to Sergeant Tucker the state of the house as he found it on the evening of February 15. He also showed her Mrs. Harris's pill box with two of five pills missing from her February 15 doses, her diet log book showing that she had consumed only two glasses of water on the morning of February 15, and a shopping list left on the kitchen counter of items that Mrs. Harris planned to buy in Jackson on February 15. Based upon the state of the house when Mr. Harris arrived home on February 15, Sergeant Tucker determined that Mrs. Harris had not left the house of her own free will.

7. Sergeant Tucker contacted her supervisors for further instructions, and a search of the area was organized, including an aerial search. The investigators discovered that Mrs. Harris had missed her 11:15 appointment at Jenny Craig Weight Loss Centre and her afternoon nail appointment at Mona's Nails in Jackson. Mona's had called the Harris home at 2:30 P.M. on February 15 with no response. With the help of Mrs. Harris's daughter-in-law, Lynette Harris, they deter-

mined that Mrs. Harris's red house shoes, blue robe, and a wide black belt were missing.

8. Around 4:40 P.M. in the afternoon on February 16, Webb Bozeman informed authorities that two of his employees had seen Mrs. Harris's car backed into a cattle gap on his property on old Highway 49, approximately 1.5 miles from the Harris home, between 9:00 and 10:00 A.M. on February 15. Testimony at trial placed Underwood's car, or one very similar to it, in a driveway near the Harris home on February 15 at approximately 10:00 or 10:30 A.M. Based upon the tip from Mr. Bozeman's employees, Sergeant Tucker and other law enforcement officers went to the cattle gap and began searching. At about 5:10, Officer Donny Spell found a black belt in a fire lane on the Bozeman property near Bozeman Lake. Continuing on around the lake shore, at about 5:20, Sergeant Tucker discovered Mrs. Harris's body, clothed in a blue pleated shirt, black knit pants, and red house shoes. Clumps of grass and weeds were clutched in her hands. Mrs. Harris only had foundation makeup on the right side of her face. At trial, Mr. Harris testified that in more than forty years of marriage, his wife had never left the house without having makeup on or without being properly dressed. After contacting the crime scene unit, Sergeant Tucker accompanied Dudley Bozeman to notify Mr. Harris and his family.

9. Mrs. Harris had been shot four times. Two of the bullets did not exit Mrs. Harris's body, and these were sent to the Mississippi Crime Lab for testing following the autopsy. One bullet traveled from her back through her right lung, diaphragm, and liver. A second bullet struck the right side of her back and penetrated her right lung. Dr. Steven Hayne, who performed the autopsy, testified that either of these first two gunshot wounds would have individually caused death due to extensive internal bleeding. A third bullet struck Mrs. Harris's left ear, went through the ear, struck and went through the left side of her neck, and struck her front right shoulder. Dr. Hayne testified that this gunshot would not have caused death by itself. The fourth bullet entered the front of Mrs. Harris's left arm and exited the inner arm. This gunshot wound was also nonlethal. All four of the gunshot wounds were distant, meaning

that the shots were fired more than 1 to 2 feet away, and they occurred at or about the same time. The angles of the gunshot wounds were consistent with Mrs. Harris being on her knees and the shooter standing behind her. Dr. Hayne testified that the manner of Mrs. Harris's death was homicide, and that it would have taken a minimum of fifteen to twenty minutes for Mrs. Harris to die from her wounds.

10. When Mrs. Harris's body was discovered, rigor mortis had set in, indicating that Mrs. Harris had been dead for at least two hours, but no more than forty eight hours. Fly larvae, or maggots, were in both of Mrs. Harris's ears, indicating that she had been dead for at least twelve to twenty four hours. Based upon Sergeant Tucker's testimony that the body was discovered at about 5:20 P.M. on February 16, and Mr. Harris's testimony that he saw his wife alive at about 6:00 A.M. on February 15, this evidence would place the time of death between approximately 6:00 A.M. on February 15, and 5:20 A.M. on February 16. One of the Harris's neighbors, Bill Richardson, testified that he heard three gunshots near Bozeman Lake around 10:15 or 10:20 A.M. on February 15.

11. In late January or February of 1994, Charlie Palmer, Justin Underwood's uncle, discovered that some items were missing from his home, including his pistol and some tools. Mr. Palmer spoke with Chief Deputy Hubert Roberts of the Madison County Sheriff's Department about the stolen items, but did not file an official report, because he thought that his ex-wife might have used the spare keys to enter his home. Mr. Palmer decided to check his nephew's home to find out if Underwood had taken the items. Underwood let his uncle search his car, a light yellow Oldsmobile Cutlass, in which Mr. Palmer found his tools and his pistol. On March 7 or 8, Mr. Palmer went to see Deputy Roberts again, and this time Deputy Roberts filled out a report on the items that Mr. Palmer had discovered were missing over the last month. Included in this report was the RG blue steel .32 caliber revolver, serial number 0207090, that Mr. Palmer had recovered. Although Mr. Palmer was somewhat confused about exactly when he noticed that his pistol was missing, he was certain that it was missing before March 7 or 8, when he

gave this report to Deputy Roberts. The statement says that the pistol was missing in late January or early February.

12. When Mr. Palmer gave his statement to Deputy Roberts, he also turned over the pistol and the box of .32 caliber revolver bullets that he used with the gun to the deputy. Deputy Roberts then wrote down the gun's serial number and gave the pistol and bullets to Sergeant Tucker on March 8. No attempts were made to lift fingerprints from the gun, because it had already been handled by Charlie Palmer and Deputy Roberts before he handed it over to Sergeant Tucker. However, Steve Byrd, a forensic scientist specializing in firearms examinations at the crime lab, concluded from his examination that the bullets taken from Mrs. Harris's body were fired from Charlie Palmer's pistol. His conclusion was corroborated by the findings of a second analyst who initialed Byrd's report.

13. On March 9, Deputy Roberts arrested Underwood for the burglary of Charlie Palmer's residence. Later that afternoon, Underwood gave his statement to Terry Barfield, an investigator with the Madison County Sheriff's Office, and W.H. Hathcock with the Mississippi Highway Patrol. In his statement, Underwood admitted to breaking into Charlie Palmer's home on February 5 and taking items, including the pistol that Charlie Palmer retrieved from Underwood's car on March 7.

14. The next day, March 10, Underwood gave another statement to Officer Barfield and Investigator Larry Saxton in which he admitted to killing Mrs. Harris by shooting her at Bozeman Lake. However, he stated that Mrs. Harris had asked him to kill her because her husband had given her AIDS. Both parties stipulated at trial that Mrs. Harris never had AIDS or HIV. Evidence was presented at trial showing that Mrs. Harris was taking amitriptyline, a medication commonly prescribed for depression. However, Mrs. Harris had undergone a radical mastectomy, so it wouldn't be unusual for her doctor to prescribe an antidepressant. Dr. George Allard, Mrs. Harris's primary care physician testified that amitriptyline could also be prescribed for an intestinal tract problem, which would be consistent with Mrs. Harris's medical history.

15. According to Underwood's March 10 statement made to Officers Barfield and Saxton, Mrs. Harris saw Underwood drive by on February 15 and waved for him to come to her house. Mrs. Harris knew Underwood, because he had done some yard work for her. When he came into the house, Underwood said that Mrs. Harris asked if he had a gun, so he went and got it out of his car, and she offered him money to kill her. Underwood stated that she drove them to the cattle gap, where they got out of the car and walked to the lake, stopping periodically for Mrs. Harris to catch her breath. He said that Mrs. Harris got down on her knees and started praying, so Underwood got down on his knees, and then Mrs. Harris said, "Do it." Underwood got up, closed his eyes, and shot the pistol six times. The pistol was the same one that he had taken from Charlie Palmer's house. Then he left Mrs. Harris lying on the ground, drove her car back to her house, and left in his own car.

16. After presenting the foregoing evidence, the State rested its case. The defense rested without calling any witnesses. Following closing arguments and jury instructions, the jury convicted Underwood of capital murder. At the close of the sentencing phase, the jury found that Underwood should be sentenced to death.

* * *

V.

THE PREJUDICIAL EFFECT OF THE INTRODUCTION OF THE VIDEO TAPE OF THE CRIME SCENE DEPICTING THE VICTIM'S BODY OUTWEIGHED THE TAPE'S PROBATIVE VALUE.

VI.

THE PREJUDICIAL EFFECT OF THE INTRODUCTION OF NUMEROUS GRUESOME PHOTOGRAPHS OUTWEIGHED THEIR PROBATIVE VALUE AND CONSTITUTES REVERSIBLE ERROR BY THE LOWER COURT.

44. Underwood's next two assignments of error are directed toward the trial court's allowing photographs and a video tape of

Mrs. Harris's body at the crime scene and photographs of the body prior to the autopsy to be shown to the jury. "Although relevant, evidence may be excluded if its probative value is substantially outweighed by the danger of unfair prejudice, confusion of the issues, or misleading the jury, or by considerations of undue delay, waste of time, or needless presentation of cumulative evidence." Miss. R. Evid. 403. Underwood argues that the photographs and video tape created unfair prejudice in the minds of the jury that outweighed any probative value.

A general rule of this court leaves the admission of photographs into evidence to the sound discretion of the trial judge. Her decision is upheld unless there has been an abuse of that discretion. Stringer v. State, 548 So.2d 125, 134 (Miss. 1989). " '[P]hotographs which are gruesome or inflammatory and lack an evidentiary purpose are always inadmissible as evidence.' " McNeal v. State, 551 So.2d 151, 159 (Miss. 1989) quoting McFee v. State, 511 So.2d 130, 135 (Miss. 1987). Mackbee v. State, 575 So.2d 16, 31 (Miss. 1990).

When deciding on the admissibility of gruesome photos, trial judges must consider: "(1) whether the proof is absolute or in doubt as to identity of the guilty party, [and] (2) whether the photos are necessary evidence or simply a ploy on the part of the prosecutor to arouse the passion and prejudice of the jury." Holland v. State, 587 So.2d 848, 864 (Miss.1991) (quoting McNeal, 551 So.2d at 159).

[T]he lower court's judgment will not be reversed on the ground that photographs are gruesome and prejudicial, unless the lower court has abused its discretion.

Moreover, in a slaying such as the instant case, in which the only eyewitness was the defendant, and it was argued that the slaying was something other than murder, the relevancy of photographs showing the scene and victim is increased. Griffin v. State, 557 So.2d 542, 549–50 (Miss. 1990) (internal citations omitted). "The same standards applicable to determining the admissibility of photographs are applicable to video tapes." Blue v. State, 674 So.2d 1184, 1210 (Miss. 1996) (citing Holland, 587 So.2d at 864).

45. Over Underwood's objection, Judge Toney allowed the prosecution to enter five pictures of Mrs. Harris's body into evidence. State's Exhibit 5 is an 8×10 color photograph of Mrs. Harris's body as found by the lakeshore. It shows the body face down on the ground, wearing a blue shirt, black pants and belt, and red house shoes. There are patches of blood visible on the blue shirt. State's Exhibits 10, 11, and 12 are all 8x10 color photographs of the body just before the autopsy, showing the gunshot wounds. Little or no blood is evident in any of the autopsy photographs. Exhibit 10 shows Mrs. Harris's back with the two gunshot wounds, Exhibit 11 depicts the two arm wounds, and Exhibit 12 is a photograph of the gunshot wound to Mrs. Harris's neck and to the shoulder. State's Exhibit 17 is a 3×4 color photograph taken at the autopsy of Mrs. Harris's hand showing abrasions on her palm and fingers. These pictures are not particularly gruesome or inflammatory so as to shock or prejudice the jury in this case. The photographs were all relevant to show the victim's injuries and to help the jury visualize the crime and crime scene, corroborating the testimony of the investigators and partially corroborating Underwood's confession. Photographs showing Mrs. Harris's body wearing the red house shoes and the scratches on her hands from clutching weeds and grass were relevant to support the prosecution's theory of kidnapping, to refute any theory of assisted suicide, and to corroborate Dr. Hayne's testimony that Mrs. Harris did not die immediately. The trial court did not abuse its discretion in allowing these photographs to be admitted into evidence.

46. Also over Underwood's objection, Judge Toney allowed the prosecution to play a video tape for the jury of Mrs. Harris's body as it was found by investigators. After hearing the arguments from counsel, the judge determined that the jury would not be allowed to take the tape into deliberations, because he instructed the prosecutor to stop the tape before the body was turned over. The portion of the video tape shown to the jury depicts little more than State's Exhibit 5, the photograph of Mrs. Harris's body at the crime scene. The only additional footage is a shot of Mrs. Harris's ear, revealing that maggots had infested her ear. Judge Toney allowed

the prosecution to show the tape through a closeup of the ear, because that evidence was used to help establish the time of death. Out of precaution, however, Judge Toney ruled that the remainder of the video tape, showing the investigators' further examination of the body after turning it over, would not be shown to the jury.

47. Underwood specifically points to this Court's decision in McNeal, supra, to support his argument that the video depicting maggots in Mrs. Harris's ear was inflammatory and lacked any evidentiary purpose. In McNeal, we held that the admission of closeup color photographs of the victim's decomposed, maggot-infested skull was an abuse of discretion. *McNeal*, 551 So.2d at 159. However, the Court described those photographs as "some of the most gruesome photographs ever presented to this Court." Id. Here, the short segment of video tape showing the inside of Mrs. Harris's ear is not exceptionally gruesome, particularly since there is no visual evidence of decomposition. Furthermore, unlike the photographs in *McNeal*, the video of the maggots in Mrs. Harris's ear is relevant, because the evidence was used to establish the time of death. Judge Toney properly reviewed this evidence under Rule 403, and did not abuse his discretion in allowing the jury to view that portion of the prosecution's video tape.

* * *

Conviction of murder affirmed.
[Parts of case omitted]

McHENRY
v.
STATE

Supreme Court of Indiana
820 N.E.2d 124, 2005 Ind.
LEXIS 4 (2005)

Dickson, Justice. Shepard, C.J., and Sullivan, Boehm, and Rucker, JJ., concur.

Dickson, Justice.

Following a jury trial, the defendant, Mirtha McHenry, a bank teller, was convicted of forgery, a class C felony, and theft, a class D felony, as a result of her actions relating to an unauthorized withdrawal of $6,500 from the account of a bank customer. Concluding that the evidence was insufficient to establish her guilt of either crime, the Court of Appeals reversed the convictions and remanded with instructions that she be discharged.

We grant transfer and affirm the trial court.

In her appeal from the convictions, the defendant alleges three grounds for reversal: (1) insufficient evidence; (2) refusal to strike two jurors for cause; and (3) erroneous admission of surveillance videotape.

1. Sufficiency of Evidence

The defendant contends that neither of her convictions were supported by sufficient evidence. Upon a challenge to the sufficiency of evidence to support a conviction, a reviewing court does not reweigh the evidence or judge the credibility of the witnesses, and respects "the jury's exclusive province to weigh conflicting evidence." We have often emphasized that appellate courts must consider only the probative evidence and reasonable inferences supporting the verdict. Expressed another way, we have stated that appellate courts must affirm "if the probative evidence and reasonable inferences drawn from the evidence could have allowed a reasonable trier of fact to find the defendant guilty beyond a reasonable doubt."

Evidence at her jury trial established that the defendant, a bank teller, withdrew $6,500 from the account of Charles Landes. The defendant testified that someone had come to her wanting to make this withdrawal, that she had filled in the withdrawal slip, and that she had the customer sign it and gave him the money. Upon receiving his bank statement and discovering a $6,500 withdrawal from his account, Landes immediately reported the error to the bank and signed an affidavit of forgery stating that the signature on the withdrawal slip was not his and that he did not receive any of the proceeds. The withdrawal slip was time-stamped 4:44 p.m. The bank's videotape showed no one at the defendant's teller window when the transaction occurred.

Bank records also disclosed that the defendant had accessed and viewed this customer's account records twice during the two weeks before the withdrawal.

Although reciting that "in reviewing the sufficiency of the evidence, we will not reweigh the evidence or judge the credibility of witnesses," the Court of Appeals reversed the convictions, speculating that the withdrawal slip "*may have been* received earlier and only stamped at 4:44 p.m." and that the defendant's prior inquiries into the customer's account balance "*may have been* precipitated by a phone call request."

In reversing the jury's verdict, the Court of Appeals failed to restrict its consideration to only the evidence and reasonable inferences favorable to the trial court's verdict, but instead reweighed the evidence, improperly substituting its own judgment for that of the jury. While the jury could have drawn the same inferences as the Court of Appeals, they did not. They returned a unanimous verdict of guilt on each count.

The defendant urges that the State failed to present evidence that she intended to defraud the customer or the bank or that she took the money. The State responds (and the defendant concedes) that intent to defraud may be proven by circumstantial evidence, and the State argues that the defendant acknowledged accessing the customer's account and performing the transaction that removed $6,500 from the account—money that the customer did not receive. And the videotape enabled the jury to infer that there was no customer at the defendant's teller window when the withdrawal was made.

Finding that the probative evidence and reasonable inferences drawn from the evidence could have allowed a reasonable trier of fact to find the defendant guilty beyond a reasonable doubt, we conclude that the evidence was sufficient to support the judgment.

2. Failure to Exclude Jurors for Cause

* * *

3. Surveillance Videotape

The defendant also contends that the trial court committed reversible error in admitting

the bank's surveillance video. The video shows that no person was at the defendant's teller window at the time she entered the questioned transaction. The defendant objection at trial was that the videotape was not a business record and that there was an inadequate foundation, the particulars of which were not specified. On appeal, the defendant does not present argument as to the business record issue but rather argues generally that because the state did not present information to support the reliability of the surveillance tape other than the affidavit of a records custodian, it failed to lay a proper foundation for the admission of the video.

The parties agree that under a "silent witness" theory, videotapes may be admitted as substantive evidence, but "there must be a strong showing of authenticity and competency" and that when automatic cameras are involved, "there should be evidence as to how and when the camera was loaded, how frequently the camera was activated, when the photographs were taken, and the processing and changing of custody of the film after its removal from the camera."

The State argues that witness testimony established the videotape's authenticity. The bank manager removed the videotape, and a police detective checked it to assure that it was the tape covering the date in question. The detective then watched the tape to match the transactions and customers' account numbers with the representations on the videotape. In addition, the bank's custodian of records verified by affidavit that the tape was a regularly conducted activity of the bank and that she had examined the records to verify its trustworthiness.

Rulings on the admission of evidence are subject to appellate review for abuse of discretion. We are not persuaded that the trial court abused its discretion in admitting the videotape.

Conclusion

We grant transfer and affirm the judgment of the trial court. [Reversed the Court of Appeals.]

Shepard, C.J., and Sullivan, Boehm, and Rucker, JJ., concur.

Cases Relating to Chapter 15

Results of Examinations and Results

COMMONWEALTH
v.
GAYNOR

Supreme Judicial Court
of Massachusetts
443 Mass. 245, 2005 Mass. LEXIS 7 (2005)

Judges Present: Marshall, C.J., Greaney, Spina, & Sosman JJ.

SPINA, J. The defendant was convicted of the aggravated rape and murder of four women in Springfield between November 1, 1997, and March 11, 1998. The jury returned verdicts under all three theories of murder in the first degree in each case. On appeal, the defendant asserts error in certain pretrial rulings, including . . . rulings that deoxyribonucleic acid (DNA) evidence taken from mixed DNA samples was sufficiently reliable to be admitted in evidence, and that the database on which Cellmark Diagnostics based its frequency calculations was adequate. . . . Finally, the defendant asks us to grant him a new trial under G. L. c. 278, § 33E. We affirm the convictions and decline to grant relief under § 33E.

1. *Facts.* The jury could have found the following facts.

a. *Victim no. 1.* The victim put her children to bed at 10 P.M. on October 31, 1997. Sometime between midnight and 12:30 A.M., the first-floor tenant at 866 Worthington Street in Springfield heard a "scream of pain" followed by a "thud" from the victim's second-floor apartment. The victim's son discovered her body on the living room couch after he awoke at 7 A.M.. on November 1. Her naked body was covered by a blanket and a towel had been placed over her head. Her hands were bound behind her back.

An autopsy revealed that death was caused by asphyxia due to manual strangulation. The victim's blood tested positive for metabolites of cocaine and alcohol. Her anus was widely dilated, consistent with penetration.

The defendant's thumb print was identified on a broken ashtray found in the living room, and his palm print was identified on a hair gel container, also in the living room. Fecal matter was found on a sock and inside the rim of a small vase recovered from the victim's living room. The defendant told his brother that he had had anal intercourse with women he met in the Worthington-Federal Streets section of Springfield, an area known for prostitutes and "crack" cocaine. The defendant's brother had driven him several times in October and November, 1997, to the neighborhood where the victim lived.

Several items collected from the scene and all biological evidence recovered from the first victim's body, as well as blood samples given by the defendant were sent to Cellmark for DNA analysis. Cellmark performed two series of polymerase chain reaction (PCR) tests on DNA samples taken from items submitted in all four cases. The first series of tests were performed at nine genetic loci: DQ Alpha, five polymarker (PM) loci, and three (TPOX, THO1, and CSF) short tandem repeat (STR) loci. In some instances testing was done at a tenth locus, identified as D1S80. Some of these tests were witnessed by a defense expert. A second series of PCR tests was done on some samples at thirteen core STR loci (including the three STR loci where testing previously had been done) designated for inclusion in the national database that contains DNA profiles of convicted felons, known as the combined DNA index system, or CODIS. See G. L. c. 22E, § 1 (definitions). A defense expert was present during the second series of tests. DNA samples from seven other suspects were examined and all seven were excluded as contributors in each case.

* * *

[Three other murder victims presented similar DNA evidence from murder scenes.]

* * *

5. *Admissibility of DNA evidence.* The defendant filed a pretrial motion in which he requested a *"Daubert-Lanigan* hearing" with respect to the admissibility of DNA evidence the Commonwealth was expected to offer in all four cases. *See Daubert v. Merrell Dow Pharmaceuticals, Inc.,* 509 U.S. 579, 125 L. Ed. 2d 469, 113 S. Ct. 2786 (1993); *Commonwealth v. Lanigan,* 419 Mass. 15, 641 N.E.2d 1342 (1994). Hearings were conducted as to both the first and second series of tests, and the defendant now appeals from rulings that (1) Cellmark's methodology in dealing with mixtures and technical artifacts is generally accepted within the scientific community; (2) Cellmark both performed its tests properly and reported the results accurately; (3) Cellmark's election not to stay within conservative recommendations of test kit manufacturers regarding the minimum quantity of DNA tested did not invalidate the studies; (4) the use of the product rule to make frequency calculations for identifiable primary contributors in a mixed DNA sample is acceptable; and (5) the database used by Cellmark to make frequency calculations is adequate and common within the field.

a. *Mixtures and artifacts.* The defendant first claims that the evidence does not support the judge's conclusion that Cellmark can reli-

ably distinguish technical artifacts from true alleles, or primary from secondary contributors in mixed samples of DNA. He does not challenge the scientific validity of PCR testing. We previously have held that PCR-based DNA analysis, both generally and at the DQ Alpha locus, the PM loci, and the D1S80 locus, is a scientifically valid methodology for developing DNA profile evidence. *See Commonwealth v. Vao Sok,* 425 Mass. 787, 799, 801–802, 683 N.E.2d 671 (1997). We reached the same conclusion with respect to PCR testing at STR loci identified as CSF1P0, TPOX, and TH01. *Commonwealth v. Rosier,* 425 Mass. 807, 812–813, 685 N.E.2d 739 (1997). The defendant does not challenge the scientific validity of PCR testing at the other STR loci designated under CODIS. His challenge focuses on the second, or reliability prong of the *Daubert-Lanigan* inquiry.

A determination of the reliability of the testing process entails a fact-based inquiry, including questions of credibility. *See Commonwealth v. Vao Sok, supra* at 797, 798. The analysis calls on a judge to determine whether testing was properly performed, *Commonwealth v. McNickles,* 434 Mass. 839, 850, 753 N.E.2d 131 (2001), and whether an expert's conclusions based on clinical experience and observations were sufficiently reliable. *Canavan's Case,* 432 Mass. 304, 313, 733 N.E.2d 1042 (2000). The judge's decision under the reliability prong is reviewed under the abuse of discretion standard. Id. at 312.

Testimony indicated that it is not unusual to find mixtures of DNA (a sample containing DNA from two or more persons) in cases of sexual assault. The presence of a mixture of DNA can create difficulties in interpreting test results. For example, where DNA from two contributors is present in a mixture in relatively equal amounts, the dots or bands (depending on the particular test) produced by the two samples during the testing process will display comparable intensity (darkness). In such cases the Cellmark analyst will report the existence of a combination without attempting to interpret the results.

Similar interpretive challenges arise from the presence of technical artifacts: mistakes in the PCR amplification process that replicates a defined segment of DNA through the use of enzymes. Artifacts typically give faint readings. When a test result suggests either an artifact or a secondary contributor and the difference in intensity between readings is slight, the Cellmark analyst will not attempt to distinguish them but will report the result as not interpretable.

Where DNA from two contributors is present in a mixture in unequal amounts, readings produced by the larger sample will be darker than those of the smaller sample, roughly in direct proportion to the difference between the amounts of the samples. Where the differences are such that intensity readings from the greater sample are dark and those from the lesser sample are faint, the Cellmark analyst may conclude that the darker reading is produced by a primary contributor and report her conclusion in the same way she reports a single source sample, conformably with the recommendation of the National Resource Council (NRC), The Evaluation of Forensic DNA Evidence (1996) at 129. We have treated the reports of the NRC as authoritative works for purposes of determining generally accepted standards within the scientific community for (a) the validity of the underlying scientific theory, or (b) the reliability of the underlying process for developing forensic DNA evidence. *See Commonwealth v. Rosier, supra* at 815; *Commonwealth v. Vao Sok, supra* at 801.

Here, only test results based on a single source of DNA, or, where there appeared to be a mixture, only test results that yielded strong evidence (dark bands or dots) of a primary contributor were used. Consequently, a weak reading of a secondary contributor or technical artifact had no effect on Cellmark's ability to report the result of the primary contributor and calculate a statistic of the probability of a random match to the defendant's DNA profile. The judge's findings that Cellmark's methodology in reporting tests of a mixed sample with an identifiable primary contributor in the same way it reports tests of a single source sample conforms to the recommendation of the NRC, and that Cellmark's methodology in dealing with the presence of mixtures or technical artifacts is generally accepted within the scientific community, were made with record support and well within his discretion.

b. *Conduct of tests.* The defendant suggests other known conditions that could affect the accuracy and reliability of test results, including contamination, loci dropout, allele dropout, differential amplification, stochastic effect, spikes, and peak imbalances. We need not engage in a lengthy discussion about these conditions. For purposes of this appeal, it is sufficient to note that Cellmark analysts considered each of these issues and factored them into their test results. The judge accepted the testimony of Dr. Robin Cotton, Cellmark's forensic laboratory director, with respect to the many controls and safeguards that Cellmark uses to adjust for these challenges, including threshold control dots to detect minimum sample size at the DQ Alpha locus, the use of two different manufacturers' test kits that test DNA at four of the same loci for CODIS testing, controls to ensure against contamination at the PM and D1S80 loci, and others. The judge found that Cellmark follows the standards adopted by the DNA advisory board, a group of individuals authorized by Congress to advise the Federal Bureau of Investigation on DNA testing, and the guidelines published by the Technical Working Group for DNA Analysis Methods (TWGDAM) in 1995, except in cases where those guidelines have been superseded by the DNA advisory board standards. The judge did not abuse his discretion in ruling that the test results were sufficiently reliable to be put before the jury and that the questions raised by the defendant were more appropriately addressed to the weight of the evidence. *See Commonwealth v. McNickles*, 434 Mass. 839, 850–854, 753 N.E.2d 131 (2001).

c. *Manufacturer's recommendations.* There is no merit to the defendant's contention that Cellmark's failure to comply with the minimum standards for DNA sample sizes set by the test kit manufacturers invalidated the test results. The user's manuals for the Profiler Plus and Cofiler kits, both manufactured by PerkinElmer, Inc., recommended that they not be used with less than one to 2.5 nanograms (one-billionth of a gram) of questioned DNA, but many of the tests were conducted with less than the recommended amounts. The judge found that the manufacturers' recommendations were just that, recommendations. They were intended to ensure optimal results. He found, with record support, that Cellmark had conducted validation studies that supported the reliability of testing based on amounts smaller than recommended by the manufacturers, amounts as small as one-half nanogram. Cellmark had also conducted validation studies indicating that analysts could reliably interpret computerized test results (the second series of tests performed under CODIS) based on readings as low as forty relative fluorescent units (RFUs) rather than the conservative level of 150 RFUs recommended by the manufacturers, and the judge found that Cellmark's readings were reliable. There was no abuse of discretion.

The defendant's expert, Dr. Donald E. Riley, ultimately conceded Cellmark's conclusions (that test results matched the defendant's profile) were supported by the data and that the defendant's and the victims' identified alleles matched those identified by Cellmark's testing. The judge observed that "[a]ll that Dr. Riley can really say is that there is a 'potential' for this system of analysis to miss alleles and distort results. I recognize that the potential for error exists in *any* scientific testing, but I am satisfied that Cellmark has done all that is reasonably possible to eliminate that potential" (emphasis in original). He correctly noted that the issues raised by the defendant went to the weight of the evidence, not its admissibility.

d. *Use of the product rule.* The defendant argues that the judge erred by accepting the proposition that if an analyst can distinguish between a primary contributor and a secondary contributor in a mixed DNA sample, the analyst may properly treat the primary contributor as a single source for statistical purposes. His argument, essentially, is that the "product rule," which has been held to be a scientifically acceptable method for calculating frequency profiles based on results of PCR testing of single source samples, see Commonwealth v. Rosier, supra at 816–817, produces unreliable results in mixed samples; and that a "likelihood ratio," which has been held to be a scientifically acceptable method of calculating frequency profiles based on results of testing of mixed samples, should have been used. See *Commonwealth v. McNickles, supra* at 845–848.

Likelihood ratio analysis is appropriate for test results of mixed samples when the primary and secondary contributors cannot

be distinguished. Id. at 846. It need not be applied when a primary contributor can be identified. Contrary to the defendant's view, the use of the product rule is scientifically acceptable where the analyst can distinguish between a primary and a secondary contributor in a mixed sample, and thereafter treat the primary contributor as a single source for statistical purposes. See NRC, Evaluation of Forensic DNA Evidence (1996), Executive Summary Recommendation 4.1 at 5; *State v. Roman Nose*, 667 N.W.2d 386, 398 (Minn. 2003). In any event, at trial, Dr. Christopher Basten, the Commonwealth's statistician in the field of population genetics, recalculated the profile frequencies using likelihood ratios and reached results comparable to those obtained under the product rule.

e. *Cellmark's database.* Finally, the defendant contends that the judge erred in ruling that Cellmark's database was adequate, that the absence of data on African-Americans from Springfield in Cellmark's database was not a matter of concern, and that the results of Cellmark's profile frequency calculations through use of the product rule were reliable and accurate.

The product rule refers to the product, or multiplication, of the frequencies (probabilities) with which each allele in a tested sample of DNA occurs in the population included in the database. The resulting number is the probability of someone's having the same characteristics as the sample tested. *See Commonwealth v. Curnin*, 409 Mass. 218, 224, 565 N.E.2d 440 (1991). The product rule is based on two assumptions about the nature of genetic variants in the population. Those assumptions are known as the condition of Hardy-Weinberg equilibrium, and the condition of linkage equilibrium. Hardy-Weinberg equilibrium is a condition that is achieved when there is no particular relationship between the occurrence of alleles within a single genetic marker. That is, when a person's parents meet randomly in the general population. Linkage equilibrium is a condition that is achieved when there is no particular relationship between genes. That is, when genes are inherited independently, and not linked to other genes. See id. at 225 n.11; NRC, Evaluation of Forensic DNA Evidence (1996) at 90–91, 106–107.

Dr. Basten testified that he had conducted a study of fifty databases, including Cellmark's, to determine whether the frequencies of alleles at particular loci varied between databases or between racial groups within the databases for the population of the United States. He had presented the details and the results of his study at two scientific conventions. Dr. Basten concluded that there was consistency of allelic frequency between the various databases and within the various racial groups, but that allelic frequency varied between racial groups. He also concluded that the size of Cellmark's database, 103 persons, is adequate and common within the field, and that a database larger than Cellmark's would produce no significant difference in result. He explained that the reliability of profiling depends more on the number of alleles in the database than the number of persons in the database. Dr. Basten discounted the absence of data on any African-American from Springfield in Cellmark's database because his study of the fifty databases indicated that the African-American population is fairly homogeneous across the United States. He endorsed Cellmark's use of the product rule in making its profile frequency calculations, and verified Cellmark's test results through the use of the theta factor, a statistical adjustment recommended by the NRC when dealing with possible subgroups, or small isolated populations. See NRC, Evaluation of Forensic DNA Evidence (1996) at 29–30. Dr. Basten employed the more conservative of the two theta factors recommended by the NRC. Verification also was made through the use of "confidence intervals." See Commonwealth v. Rosier, supra at 814 n.14.

The judge found that Dr. Basten's use of the conservative theta factor and confidence intervals were an "appropriate corrective measure" to account for any possible substructure with the African-American community in Springfield. He acted within his discretion in ruling that Cellmark's database was adequate and that the use of the product rule produced reliable results. *See Commonwealth v. Rosier, supra* at 813–814.

* * *

Relief under G. L. c. 278, § 33E. We have reviewed the transcript, the record, and the briefs, and conclude that there is no reason to reduce the verdicts or grant a new trial pursuant to our power under G. L. c. 278, § 33E.

Judgments affirmed.

PEOPLE
v.
WILKINSON

Supreme Court of California
33 Cal. 4ᵗʰ 821, 2004Cal. LEXIS 6833
(2004)

DISPOSITION: Judgment of the Court of Appeal reversed.

GEORGE, C.J.—Defendant Jaleh Wilkinson was convicted at trial of the offenses of battery on a custodial officer, driving a vehicle under the influence of alcohol, and failing to stop at the scene of an accident. The Court of Appeal reversed defendant's convictions on two unrelated grounds, concluding that (1) the statutory scheme pertaining to battery on a custodial officer violates equal protection principles because the statutes allow battery on a custodial officer without injury to be punished more severely than battery on a custodial officer with injury, and (2) the trial court erred in denying defendant a hearing, pursuant to the *Kelly/Frye* doctrine (*People v. Kelly* (1976) 17 Cal.3d 24 [130 Cal. Rptr. 144, 549 P.2d 1240]; *Frye v. United States* (D.C. Cir. 1923) 54 App. D.C. 46 [293 F. 1013]), regarding the admissibility of polygraph evidence to support defendant's claim that her commission of the charged offenses resulted from her unknowing and involuntary ingestion of drugs. We granted review to consider the Court of Appeal's resolution of both issues.

For the reasons discussed below, we conclude that (1) . . . , (2) in light of the categorical prohibition on the admission of polygraph evidence in Evidence Code section 351.1, the trial court did not err in declining to hold a *Kelly/Frye* hearing regarding the evidence proffered by defendant. Accordingly, we shall reverse the judgment of the Court of Appeal.

* * *

A.

With regard to the second issue before us [whether the trial court should have held hearings concerning the admissibility of polygraph results], the Attorney General contends the Court of Appeal erred by remanding for a *Kelly/Frye* hearing [concerning the admissibility of scientific evidence], because Evidence Code section 351.1 establishes a categorical prohibition on the admission of polygraph evidence in criminal cases absent a stipulation. Subdivision (a) of section 351.1, which was enacted in 1983, provides: "Notwithstanding any other provision of law, the results of a polygraph examination, the opinion of a polygraph examiner, or any reference to an offer to take, failure to take, or taking of a polygraph examination, shall not be admitted into evidence in any criminal proceeding, including pretrial and post conviction motions and hearings, or in any trial or hearing of a juvenile for a criminal offense, whether heard in juvenile or adult court, unless all parties stipulate to the admission of such results."

* * *

On appeal, defendant contended that, notwithstanding the apparent categorical prohibition of Evidence Code section 351.1, she was entitled to a *Kelly/Frye* hearing to determine the admissibility of her proposed polygraph evidence under the reasoning of this court's decisions in *People v. Jackson* (1996) 13 Cal.4th 1164 [56 Cal. Rptr. 2d 49, 920 P.2d 1254] (Jackson), and *People v. Fudge* (1994) 7 Cal.4th 1075 [31 Cal. Rptr. 2d 321, 875 P.2d 36] (Fudge) (discussed post). The Court of Appeal agreed with defendant that she had "made a sufficient offer of proof to entitle her to a [*Kelly/Frye*] hearing" under the reasoning of Jackson and Fudge, observing that "we do not see what more such an offer would need to meet the threshold required to convene such a hearing." The court, concluding that the denial of a *Kelly/Frye* hearing prejudiced defendant, remanded the case to the trial court with directions to conduct such a hearing and to set aside defendant's convictions in the event the trial court "concludes the polygraph evidence is admissible."

B.

Prior to the enactment of Evidence Code section 351.1, the admission of polygraph evidence in California was governed by the test of *Frye v. United States, supra,* 293 F. 1013. Under that test, one who seeks the admission of evidence based upon a new scientific technique must make "a preliminary showing of general acceptance of the new technique in the relevant scientific community." (*Kelly, supra,* 17 Cal.3d at p. 30; see id. at p. 32 ["reaffirm[ing] our allegiance" to the *Frye* "'general acceptance'" test for new scientific techniques]; *see also People v. Leahy* (1994) 8 Cal.4th 587, 593–604 [34 Cal. Rptr. 2d 663, 882 P.2d 321] [retaining the *Kelly/Frye* test as the applicable California standard and declining to adopt the new federal standard set forth in *Daubert v. Merrell Dow Pharmaceuticals, Inc.* (1993) 509 U.S. 579. Relying upon *Frye* and its progeny, a long line of California decisions has held or recognized that the results of a polygraph examination are inadmissible at trial absent a stipulation by the parties. See *People v. Carter* (1957) 48 Cal.2d 737, 752 ["Lie detector tests do not as yet have enough reliability to justify the admission of expert testimony based on their results.]

* * *

The legal landscape in California changed with the Court of Appeal's opinion in *Witherspoon v. Superior Court* (1982) 133 Cal. App. 3d 24 [183 Cal. Rptr. 615] (*Witherspoon*). The majority in *Witherspoon* criticized the judicial rule that consistently excludes polygraph evidence as "an almost 'knee jerk' response" "based more on considerations of policy rather than any demonstrated lack of reliability or acceptance of the test" considerations that the majority felt "are more properly matters for legislative rather than judicial determination." (Id. at 29, 31.) The majority, not finding any provision in the Evidence Code expressly barring the admission of polygraph evidence, concluded the defendant was entitled to a hearing to determine the admissibility of the evidence, suggesting that the polygraph evidence should be admitted so long as the evidence was relevant (Evid. Code, 210), its probative value was not substantially outweighed by the probability of undue prejudice (id., 352), and the defendant could satisfy the requirements for the admission of expert testimony (id., 801 [expert opinion testimony]; see also id., 720 [qualification of expert witness]; id., 405 [determination of preliminary fact]). (*Witherspoon, supra*, at pp. 30–35.)

"It was in reaction to Witherspoon that the Legislature enacted Evidence Code section 351.1." (*People v. Kegler* (1987) 197 Cal. App. 3d 72, 85 [242 Cal. Rptr. 897] (Kegler); *In re Kathleen W.* (1987) 190 Cal. App. 3d 68, 72 [235 Cal. Rptr. 205].) The Assembly Committee on Criminal Law and Public Safety's analysis of the bill that became section 351.1 expressly stated the bill was "'intended to overrule [*Witherspoon*] and to create an exception to the truth-in-evidence section of Proposition 8 that bars exclusion of any relevant evidence.' (Assembly Com. on Crim. Law and Pub. Safety, staff comments on Sen. Bill. No. 266 as amended Mar. 16, 1983 (1983–1984 Reg. Sess.), for hg. on June 8, 1983, p. 2.)" (*Kegler, supra*, 197 Cal. App. 3d at p. 84.) Legislative history materials expressed concerns that (1) the Witherspoon procedure would "'substantially increase trial time by requiring courts to litigate collateral issues regarding the reliability of the particular test and qualifications of the specific polygraph examiner in every case,'" (2) polygraph testing procedures lack standardization and cannot be tested for accuracy, and (3) jurors would "'assign too much credence to the results of a polygraph examination.'" (*Kegler, supra*, 197 Cal. App. 3d at p. 89.)

As past decisions make clear, the *Kelly/Frye* test constitutes a judicially created rule relating to the admissibility of certain types of evidence and, as such, a rule that is subject to legislative revision. . . . By enacting Evidence Code section 351.1, the Legislature abrogated the *Kelly/Frye* rule with respect to the admission of polygraph evidence in criminal cases. As noted, the Legislature enacted section 351.1 to overrule the then recently decided appellate court decision in *Witherspoon, supra*, 133 Cal. App. 3d 24, which had criticized the routine application of the *Frye* test to exclude polygraph evidence and had suggested that such evidence

could be admitted if the proponent made a showing of admissibility under certain provisions of the Evidence Code. Thus, in adopting Evidence Code section 351.1, the Legislature effectively codified the rule set forth in the pre-*Witherspoon* California cases involving polygraph evidence, namely that such evidence is categorically inadmissible in the absence of the stipulation of all parties.

This understanding of Evidence Code section 351.1 is consistent with numerous cases that subsequently have interpreted the statute to exclude polygraph evidence categorically in criminal cases, absent the stipulation of the parties. (*See In re Aontae D.* (1994) 25 Cal.App.4th 167, 173 [30 Cal. Rptr. 2d 176]; *Kegler, supra*, 197 Cal. App. 3d at p. 84; *In re Kathleen W., supra*, 190 Cal. App. 3d at p. 72.) Defendant concedes that this is the import of section 351.1, but she argues she nonetheless was entitled to a *Kelly/Frye* hearing under this court's precedents, in particular the decisions in *Jackson, supra*, 13 Cal.4th 1164, and *Fudge, supra*, 7 Cal.4th 1075 [31 Cal.Rptr.2d 321, 875 P.2d 36]. Insofar as section 351.1's categorical exclusion is applied to deprive her of the opportunity to demonstrate the current reliability of proffered polygraph evidence under the *Kelly/Frye* standard, defendant claims the statute infringes upon her right to present a defense at trial, in violation of the federal Constitution. 9

C.

We first address defendant's claim that she was entitled to a *Kelly/Frye* hearing [concerning the admissibility of scientific evidence, the polygraph in this case] notwithstanding Evidence Code section 351.1. We begin with a review of the relevant portions of the decisions in *Jackson*, supra, 13 Cal.4th 1164, and *Fudge, supra*, 7 Cal.4th 1075, upon which defendant relies. In Jackson, the defendant, at the guilt phase of a capital trial, sought to present evidence that he had "passed" a polygraph test and had stated truthfully in the polygraph session that he had not killed the victim. (*Jackson, supra*, 13 Cal.4th at p. 1212.) The defendant in *Jackson* contended he was entitled to a *Kelly/Frye* hearing notwithstanding section 351.1, arguing that the statute's exclusion of such "reliable exculpatory evidence" denied him his right to due process of law under the federal Constitution. (*Jackson, supra,* 13 Cal.4th at p. 1212.) We rejected this claim, reasoning: "Even if defendant's argument were true in the abstract, he has failed to make the proper offer of proof under *Kelly/Frye* that the polygraph is now viewed in the scientific community as a reliable technique. ' ". . . Having failed to make the proper offer of proof, defendant is in no position to assign error in the trial court's ruling." ' " (Ibid., quoting *Fudge, supra,* 7 Cal.4th at p. 1122.)

In *Fudge,* the defendant attempted to present evidence at the penalty phase of a capital trial that he had "passed" a polygraph examination, arguing that Evidence Code section 351.1 unconstitutionally deprived him of his right to present "relevant mitigating evidence." [Fudge ultimately lost his argument.] (*Fudge, supra,* 7 Cal.4th at pp. 1121, 1122.)

* * *

As the foregoing decisions demonstrate, defendant is correct in observing that, even after the enactment of Evidence Code section 351.1, we have required, as a prerequisite to preserving the claim for appeal, that a challenge to the constitutionality of this statute include an offer of proof that the proffered polygraph evidence is generally accepted under the *Kelly/Frye* standard. . . .

The Court of Appeal correctly concluded in the present case that defendant had preserved her constitutional challenge to section 351.1 by making her offer of proof regarding the reliability of polygraph evidence under *Kelly/ Frye.* The court, however, went further and remanded the case to the trial court to conduct a *Kelly/Frye* hearing, directing the trial court to set aside the judgment if that court found the polygraph evidence to be "admissible" under the *Kelly/Frye* standard, that is, if defendant demonstrated at the hearing that the polygraph technique employed was generally accepted in the scientific community.

Although our past cases have determined that an offer of proof regarding the reliability of polygraph evidence is a prerequisite for raising a constitutional challenge against Evidence Code section 351.1's categorical exclusion, we never have held that such

proof is sufficient by itself to make out such a claim, that is, we never have suggested that evidence that satisfies the *Kelly/Frye* test must, as a constitutional matter, be admitted in evidence notwithstanding the statutory provision barring such admission. Indeed, in our recent decision in *People v. Burgener, supra,* 29 Cal.4th 833, we cautioned: "Before a criminal defendant can establish a federal due process right to use the results of a polygraph examination, it is necessary (although perhaps not sufficient) to offer proof that the technique has become generally accepted in the scientific community." (Id. at p. 871, italics added.) Thus, the Court of Appeal erred by remanding the case for a *Kelly/Frye* hearing without specifically addressing the question whether section 351.1's categorical exclusion of polygraph evidence would be unconstitutional in the event defendant is able to satisfy the *Kelly/Frye* test. Because defendant has preserved her federal constitutional challenge to section 351.1, we now address that issue.

D.

The Attorney General contends that under the reasoning of *United States v. Scheffer, supra,* 523 U.S. 303, the categorical exclusion of polygraph evidence mandated by Evidence Code section 351.1 does not violate the federal Constitution. In that case, the United States Supreme Court rejected a constitutional challenge to Military Rules of Evidence, rule 707(a), which bans polygraph evidence in military trials. The defendant, an airman who faced a military court-martial for alleged drug use, sought the admission of evidence that he had "passed" a polygraph examination, in order to bolster his testimony that he innocently had ingested the drugs. In a portion of the opinion authored by Justice Thomas and joined by seven other justices, the high court noted that "there is simply no consensus that polygraph evidence is reliable," observing that this lack of consensus is "reflected in the disagreement among state and federal courts concerning both the admissibility and the reliability of polygraph evidence." (*United States v. Scheffer, supra,* 523 U.S. at pp. 309–311 (lead opn. of Thomas, J.).) In light of this circumstance, the court concluded that the per se exclusion of polygraph evidence "is a rational and proportional means of advancing the legitimate interest in barring unreliable evidence" and that "[i]ndividual jurisdictions therefore may reasonably reach differing conclusions as to whether polygraph evidence should be admitted. We cannot say, then, that presented with such widespread uncertainty, the President acted arbitrarily or disproportionately in promulgating a per se rule excluding all polygraph evidence." (Id. at p. 312.)

Justice Kennedy, in a concurring opinion joined by three other justices, 12 commented that the "continuing, good-faith disagreement among experts and courts on the subject of polygraph reliability counsels against our invalidating a per se exclusion of polygraph results," and "[g]iven the ongoing debate about polygraphs, I agree the rule of exclusion is not so arbitrary or disproportionate that it is unconstitutional." (*United States v. Scheffer, supra*, 523 U.S. at p. 318 (conc. opn. of Kennedy, J.).) Justice Kennedy, however, expressed doubt "that the rule of per se exclusion is wise, and some later case might present a more compelling case for introduction of the testimony than this one does." (Ibid.)

We recently applied *Scheffer* in *Maury, supra*, 30 Cal.4th 342, in which the defendant sought the admission of evidence that he had " 'passed' " a polygraph examination, in order to bolster his claim that someone else had killed the victim. (Id. at p. 413.) We concluded that in light of *Scheffer*, "[e]xcluding such evidence does not violate defendant's constitutional right to present a defense." (Ibid.) . . .

We reach the same conclusion here. *Scheffer* noted that "the scientific community remains extremely polarized about the reliability of polygraph techniques." (*United States v. Scheffer, supra*, 523 U.S. at p. 309 (lead opn. of Thomas, J.).) With respect to the reliability of the "control question technique" employed in the present case, *Scheffer* observed that studies ran the gamut from showing an 87 percent accuracy rate to a rate " 'little better than could be obtained by the toss of a coin,' that is, 50 percent." (Id. at p. 310.) This disagreement in the scientific community in turn has been reflected

"in the disagreement among state and federal courts concerning both the admissibility and the reliability of polygraph evidence." (Id. at pp. 310–311.)

Defendant cannot persuasively contend that between the time of the *Scheffer* decision and defendant's trial, a span of two and one-half years, the deep division in the scientific and legal communities regarding the reliability of polygraph evidence, as recognized by *Scheffer*, had given way to a general acceptance that would render the categorical exclusion of polygraph evidence "so arbitrary or disproportionate that it is unconstitutional." (*United States v. Scheffer, supra*, 523 U.S. at p. 318 (conc. opn. of Kennedy, J.).) Indeed, defense counsel conceded at oral argument that the disagreement within the scientific community regarding the reliability of polygraph evidence had not been significantly altered in that time period. Further, defendant's offer of proof in the trial court regarding the reliability of polygraph evidence consisted of a publication of the APA that outlined the studies and briefing presented in the *Scheffer* case—materials which the United States Supreme Court expressly considered and cited in *Scheffer* in concluding there existed no scientific consensus on the reliability of polygraph evidence in general and the control question technique in particular. Likewise, the legal authorities cited by defendant in the trial court as indicative of a "major reevaluation of the admissibility of polygraph evidence by the federal courts" all predate the *Scheffer* decision and, in any event, did not consider the constitutionality of a categorical exclusion of polygraph evidence. . . . In light of the continuing division of opinion regarding the reliability of polygraph evidence, as recognized by *Scheffer*, the California Legislature has not acted "arbitrarily or disproportionately in promulgating [and retaining] a per se rule excluding all polygraph evidence." (*Scheffer, supra*, 523 U.S. at p. 312 (lead opn. of Thomas, J.); *see In re Aontae D., supra*, 25 Cal.App.4th at p. 177 [exclusion of polygraph evidence under Evidence Code section 351.1 does not deny due process]; *Kegler, supra*, 197 Cal. App. 3d at p. 89 [same].)

* * *

IV.

The judgment of the Court of Appeal is reversed. [The trial court's determination that it did not need to consider whether polygraph evidence should have been admissible was upheld and defendants have no right to introduce polygraph evidence in California, absent stipulation and court consent.]

Baxter, J., Werdegar, J., Chin, J., Brown, J. and Moreno, J., concurred.

CITY OF CLEVELAND HEIGHTS
v.
KATZ

COURT OF APPEALS OF OHIO, EIGHTH APPELLATE DISTRICT, CUYAHOGA COUNTY

2002 Ohio 4241, 2001 Ohio App. LEXIS 5394 (2001)

TIMOTHY E. McMONAGLE, P.J.:

Defendant-appellant, Daniel Katz, appeals the judgment of the Cleveland Heights Municipal Court, entered after a bench trial, finding him guilty of speeding, in violation of Section 333.03 of the Codified Ordinances of Cleveland Heights, and fining him $55.

Cleveland Heights Police Officer Don Roach testified at appellant's trial that at approximately 8:37 p.m. on February 7, 2001, he was parked in a police cruiser in the median at the intersection of Fairmount and Arlington Boulevards in Cleveland Heights. Roach was facing west, monitoring the speed of eastbound vehicles on Fairmount with a radar device. Roach testified that he observed appellant's SUV pulling away from a huge group of cars and approaching him at a pretty good rate. According to Roach, he locked in the radar device on appellant's SUV and then heard a high-pitched tone, which confirmed his visual sighting of appellant's high speed. The reading on the radar unit indicated that appellant was traveling 47 miles per hour in a zone marked 35 miles per hour. Roach testified that appellant's speed was unreasonable for the conditions.

Roach testified that he had received specialized training, including 8 hours of specialized training at the police academy and 40 hours of on-the-road training, regarding operation of the model 96-11 KR-10 radar unit he was using on September 7, 2001. Roach also testified that his main function as a police officer since his graduation from the police academy twelve years prior had been operating radar equipment.

Roach testified that he performed a light test, an internal calibration test and an external calibration test on the radar unit prior to using it on September 7, 2001. The light test involved pressing a special button on the unit to make sure that all the lights on the unit were working properly. According to Roach, the internal calibration test involved pressing another designated button on the unit to elicit a preset reading of 32 miles per hour. Roach then used two tuning forks to test the external calibration of the unit. According to Roach, one fork is set at 35 miles per hour and the other is set at 65 miles per hour. When he tapped the forks against a non-metallic object and then placed them in front of the radar unit, they gave readings of 35 miles per hour and 65 miles per hour respectively. Roach testified that the three tests he performed indicated that the radar unit was working properly on September 7, 2001.

Scott Whitmer, a communications and radar technician for the City of Cleveland Heights Police Department, also testified at appellant's trial.

Whitmer testified that one of his job responsibilities was to test the calibration of the radar units used by City of Cleveland Heights police officers, including the unit used by Roach on February 7, 2001. Whitmer testified further that he had received extensive training regarding testing and calibrating radar devices from Simco Electronics, the manufacturer of the devices, and through his service in the United States Air Force.

Whitmer testified that he tests and calibrates all of the radar devices once a year, using three pieces of equipment specifically designed for testing radar equipment.

Whitmer testified that on September 20 and 21, 2000, he calibrated the radar device used by Roach according to the manufacturer's instructions and when the machinery left our precinct, it was working true and accurate. Whitmer testified further that he had no records reflecting that any repairs had been completed on the unit after that time.

The trial court admitted four records created by Whitmer concerning his tests on the unit: 1) an inventory sheet reflecting the model and serial numbers of the unit and its associated tuning forks; 2) a certificate reflecting that Whitmer calibrated the unit on September 21, 2000 at 35 miles per hour, 50 miles per hour and 65 miles per hour; 3) a certificate of accuracy reflecting that one tuning fork associated with the unit was properly calibrated at 35 miles per hour; and 4) a certificate of accuracy reflecting that the other tuning fork associated with the unit was properly calibrated at 65 miles per hour.

Whitmer also testified that the equipment he used to test Roach's radar unit was shipped to Simco Electronics in August 2000 for testing and calibrating.

According to Whitmer, Simco subsequently returned the equipment with certificates of calibration indicating that the test equipment was properly calibrated.

Defense counsel objected to the admission of the certificates of calibration, however, arguing that they were not authenticated. Defense counsel argued further that without the certificates or any testimony by a representative of Simco Electronics that the testing equipment had been properly calibrated, there was no way of knowing whether the equipment used by Whitmer to test the radar device used by Roach was properly calibrated and, therefore, no way of knowing whether the radar device used by Roach to determine that appellant was speeding was accurate. Accordingly, defense counsel asserted that Officer Roach's testimony regarding appellant's speed, as determined by the radar device, was not admissible for consideration by the trier of fact.

In a journal entry filed on April 4, 2001, the trial court ruled that Officer Roach's testimony regarding the radar reading was admissible, finding that the level of proof proposed by appellant, i.e., that evidence of a radar reading is not admissible absent evidence that the equipment used to calibrate the radar device has itself been properly calibrated, was not necessary to the radar reading.

In light of Officer Roach's testimony, the trial court found that appellant was traveling at 47 miles per hour in a zone marked 35 miles per hour and that the speed was unreasonable for the conditions. On April 9, 2001, the trial court fined appellant $ 55 plus costs but stayed the sentence pending appeal.

Appellant raises two assignments of error for our review:

> THE CONVICTION AGAINST DANIEL KATZ SHOULD BE REVERSED SINCE THERE WAS INSUFFICIENT TESTIMONY AS TO THE PROPER CALIBRATION OF OFFICER DONALD ROACH'S RADAR EQUIPMENT.

> II. THE CONVICTION AGAINST DANIEL KATZ SHOULD BE REVERSED WHERE THE TRIAL COURT DECISION WAS AGAINST THE MANIFEST WEIGHT OF THE EVIDENCE.

In his first assignment of error, appellant asserts that the trial court erred in admitting Officer Roach's testimony regarding his speed because there was insufficient testimony regarding the calibration of Officer Roach's radar equipment.

A court may take judicial notice of the technical theory of operation and the scientific reliability of stationary radar devices. *East Cleveland v. Ferell* (1958), 168 Ohio St. 298, 154 N.E.2d 630; *Cleveland Heights v. Bartell*, 1987 Ohio App. LEXIS 7152, (Feb. 19, 1987), Cuyahoga App. No. 51719, unreported. Although not raised in his brief on appeal, at oral argument appellant asserted that the trial court improperly took judicial notice of the scientific reliability of the KR-10 stationary radar device used by Officer Roach. Appellant did not raise this issue in the trial court, however, and therefore has waived it on appeal.

In *Cleveland Heights v. Bartell* (1987), Cuyahoga App. No. 51719, unreported, the trial court took judicial notice of the scientific reliability of the KR-10 radar unit and this court upheld that finding. Contrary to appellant's argument, our holding did not preclude appellant from further challenging the unit's reliability at trial. If appellant had wanted to challenge the reliability of the KR-10 unit at trial, he could have subpoenaed representatives from the manufacturer of the device and questioned them regarding its reliability. As counsel admitted in oral argument, however, appellant did not do so, and accordingly, there is no evidence in the record to indicate the unit is not reliable. Therefore, the trial court did not err in taking judicial notice of the scientific reliability of the KR-10 radar unit, in reliance on Bartell.

Once judicial notice of the operation and reliability of a radar device is taken, the court must further determine 1) that the radar device was in good operating condition and properly calibrated at the time of use; 2) that the operator of the radar device was properly qualified to use the device; and 3) that the police officer properly operated and read the radar device. Id.

Although appellant concedes that a court may take judicial notice of the reliability and operation of a radar device, as the trial court did here, appellant asks this Court to find that the City failed to prove that the radar device at issue was calibrated properly because 1) Officer Roach should have performed more than three tests on his unit to ascertain its accuracy; and 2) the City did not produce evidence that the equipment used by Whitmer to calibrate the unit and its associated tuning forks was itself properly calibrated.

Appellant argues that the trial court should have required evidence that more than three tests had been performed on Officer Roach's radar unit before concluding that it was properly calibrated because there are limitations to the three tests performed by Officer Roach. Appellant asserts that the light test performed by Roach was insufficient because it merely determined that the light fixtures inside the radar unit were functioning properly. He also asserts that tuning forks may get dented or bent and, if used on a radar unit that is out of calibration, could possibly indicate accuracy when, in fact, the unit is out of calibration.

We refuse to speculate, however, about possible problems with the tests. This court has previously held that as few as two tests (an internal calibration test and an external calibration test) are sufficient to demonstrate that a radar unit is properly calibrated. *Lyndhurst v. Danvers*, 1988 Ohio App. LEXIS 4621, (Nov. 23, 1988), Cuyahoga App. No. 55537, unreported; *Cleveland Heights v. Bartell, supra*. Moreover, appellant offered

no evidence whatsoever that any of the three tests performed by Officer Roach on February 7, 2001 were flawed or produced inaccurate results. Accordingly, there was no reason for the trial court to require evidence of more tests before concluding that Roach's radar unit was accurate.

Appellant also contends that there was insufficient evidence that Roach's radar unit was properly calibrated at the time of use because the City failed to show that Simco Electronics properly calibrated the equipment used by Whitmer to subsequently test and calibrate the unit. Appellant asserts that Whitmer's calibrations of Roach's radar unit were accurate only if the test equipment used to perform the calibrations was itself properly calibrated. Therefore, appellant contends, without testimony from a representative of the manufacturer that the test equipment was properly calibrated, there was no evidence that the radar device used by Roach was functioning properly and, accordingly, Roach's testimony regarding appellant's speed was inadmissible.

* * *

The circumstances of this case demonstrate that it was not necessary for the City to prove that the test equipment used by Whitmer to calibrate Roach's radar unit was itself properly calibrated. First, appellant presented no evidence whatsoever that the testing equipment was not in proper working order. Accordingly, as in Ellison, supra, there was no need for the City to produce evidence that the testing equipment was properly calibrated.

Moreover, although no one from Simco Electronics testified regarding the accuracy of the testing equipment, Scott Whitmer testified that the testing equipment was sent to Simco in August 2000 to be tested and calibrated and was subsequently returned with certificates of calibration indicating that the test equipment was properly calibrated. Therefore, contrary to appellant's assertion, there was, in fact, evidence that the testing equipment was in proper working order.

Appellant contends that his argument that the City must demonstrate that the testing equipment was itself properly calibrated has been suggested and followed by the Ohio Supreme Court in *State v. Bonar* (1973), 40 Ohio App. 2d 360, 319 N.E.2d 388. Appellant's reliance on *Bonar*, however, is misplaced. First, *Bonar* was decided by the Seventh Appellate District Court of Appeals, not the Supreme Court of Ohio.

Moreover, *Bonar* clearly does not support appellant's argument. In *Bonar*, the defendant was convicted of operating a motor vehicle at a speed of 75 miles per hour in a 60 miles per hour zone. The defendant appealed his conviction, arguing that the State had put on no evidence to indicate that the radar unit that had clocked his speed was functioning properly. The Seventh Appellate District Court of Appeals reversed the defendant's conviction, finding that there was . . . no testimony as to whether the radar measuring equipment was properly installed, set up or operating correctly. Accordingly, the Seventh District held that the trial court should have granted the defendant's motion for a directed verdict.

The Seventh Appellate District did not hold, as appellant contends, that in any case involving a radar detector, the State must prove that the equipment used to calibrate the radar detector has itself been properly calibrated. Rather, the Bonar court held that the State must demonstrate, as it did here, that the unit was properly set up, tested and functioning properly.

* * *

Here, in addition to the light test and internal calibration tests, Officer Roach used two individually-calibrated tuning forks to test the external calibration of his radar unit. If in Bechtel the use of two tuning forks was sufficient to demonstrate the accuracy of a radar device, we see no reason in this case to require further proof that the equipment used to calibrate the radar device and tuning forks was itself properly calibrated, especially where there was no evidence that the testing equipment was not functioning properly.

Appellant's first assignment of error is therefore overruled.

In his second assignment of error, appellant contends that because the City failed to prove that the testing equipment used to calibrate Roach's radar unit was itself properly calibrated, it failed to demonstrate the accuracy of Roach's unit and, therefore, Roach's testimony regarding appellant's speed as determined by the radar device was not admissible at trial. Appellant further contends that without Roach's testimony there was no competent evidence produced at trial to establish that he was speeding and, therefore, his conviction was against the manifest weight of the evidence. We disagree.

As set forth in our discussion regarding appellant's first assignment of error, the City was not required to prove that the equipment used to calibrate Officer Roach's radar unit was itself properly calibrated. Rather, Officer Roach's testimony regarding appellant's speed as determined by the radar unit was admissible if the City demonstrated that the radar device was in good operating condition and properly calibrated at the time of use, the operator of the device was properly trained and qualified to use it and did, in fact, properly operate the radar device. *See State v. Bechtel, supra.*

Scott Whitmer testified for the City that Roach's unit had been tested and calibrated on September 20 and 21, 2000 and no repairs were made to the unit after that time. Officer Roach testified that he performed three tests on the unit on February 7, 2001 prior to apprehending appellant and all three tests indicated that the unit was operating properly. He testified further that he had been specially trained in operating the radar device used to determine appellant's speed on February 7, 2001 and that he was properly operating the device at the time of appellant's speeding violation.

This testimony laid a sufficient foundation to establish the accuracy of Roach's radar unit and, therefore, Roach's testimony regarding appellant's speed as established through the radar unit was properly admissible.

In light of this testimony, the trial court did not err in finding appellant guilty of speeding.

Appellant's second assignment of error is therefore overruled.

*** The defendant's conviction having been affirmed, any bail pending appeal is terminated. Case remanded to the trial court for execution of sentence.

Cases Relating to Chapter 16

Evidence Unconstitutionally Obtained

UNITED STATES
v.
LEON

Supreme Court of the United States
468 U.S. 897, 104 S. Ct. 3405, 82 L. Ed. 2d 677 (1984)

JUSTICE WHITE delivered the opinion of the Court.

This case presents the question whether the Fourth Amendment exclusionary rule should be modified so as not to bar the use in the prosecution's case in chief of evidence obtained by officers acting in reasonable reliance on a search warrant issued by a detached and neutral magistrate but ultimately found to be unsupported by probable cause. To resolve this question, we must consider once again the tension between the sometimes competing goals of, on the one hand, deterring official misconduct and removing inducements to unreasonable invasions of privacy and, on the other, establishing procedures under which criminal defendants are "acquitted or convicted on the basis of all the evidence which exposes the truth." Alderman v. United States, 394 U.S. 165, 175 (1969).

I.

In August 1981, a confidential informant of unproven reliability informed an officer of the Burbank Police Department that two persons known to him as "Armando" and "Patsy" were selling large quantities of cocaine and methaqualone from their residence at 620 Price Drive in Burbank, Cal. The informant also indicated that he had witnessed a sale of methaqualone by "Patsy" at the residence approximately five months earlier and had observed at that time a shoe-box containing a large amount of cash that belonged to "Patsy." He further declared that "Armando" and "Patsy" generally kept only small quantities of drugs at their residence and stored the remainder at another location in Burbank.

On the basis of this information, the Burbank police initiated an extensive investigation focusing first on the Price Drive residence and later on two other residences as well. Cars parked at the Price Drive residence were determined to belong to respondents Armando Sanchez, who had previously been arrested for possession of marihuana, and Patsy Stewart, who had no criminal record. During the course of the investigation, officers observed an automobile belonging to respondent Ricardo Del Castillo, who had previously been arrested for possession of 50 pounds of marihuana, arrive at the Price Drive residence. The driver of that car entered the house, exited shortly thereafter carrying a small paper sack, and drove away. A check of Del Castillo's probation records led the officers to respondent Alberto Leon, whose telephone number Del Castillo had listed as his employer's. Leon had been arrested in 1980 on drug charges, and a companion had informed the police at that time that Leon was heavily involved in the importation of drugs into this country. Before the current investigation began, the Burbank officers had learned that an informant had told a Glendale police officer that Leon stored a large quantity of methaqualone at his residence in Glendale. During the course of this investigation, the Burbank officers learned that Leon was living at 716 South Sunset Canyon in Burbank.

Subsequently, the officers observed several persons, at least one of whom had prior drug involvement, arriving at the Price Drive residence and leaving with small packages; observed a variety of other material activity at the two residences as well as at a condominium at 7902 Via Magdalena; and witnessed a variety of relevant activity involving respondents' automobiles. The officers also observed respondents Sanchez and Stewart board separate flights for Miami. The pair later returned to Los Angeles together, consented to a search of their luggage that revealed only a small amount of marihuana, and left the airport. Based on these and other observations summarized in the affidavit, App. 34, Officer Cyril Rombach of the Burbank Police Department, an experienced and well-trained narcotics investigator, prepared an application for a warrant to search 620 Price Drive, 716 South Sunset Canyon, 7902 Via Magdalena, and automobiles registered to each of the respondents for an extensive list of items believed to be related to respondents' drug-trafficking activities. Officer Rombach's extensive application was reviewed by several Deputy District Attorneys.

A facially valid search warrant was issued in September 1981 by a State Superior Court Judge. The ensuing searches produced large quantities of drugs at the Via Magdalena and Sunset Canyon addresses and a small quantity at the Price Drive residence. Other evidence was discovered at each of the residences and in Stewart's and Del Castillo's automobiles. Respondents were indicted by a grand jury in the District Court for the Central District of California and charged with conspiracy to possess and distribute cocaine and a variety of substantive counts.

The respondents then filed motions to suppress the evidence seized pursuant to the warrant. The District Court held an evidentiary hearing and, while recognizing that the case was a close one, see id., at 131, granted the motions to suppress in part. It concluded

that the affidavit was insufficient to establish probable cause, but did not suppress all of the evidence as to all of the respondents because none of the respondents had standing to challenge all of the searches. In response to a request from the Government, the court made clear that Officer Rombach had acted in good faith, but it rejected the Government's suggestion that the Fourth Amendment exclusionary rule should not apply where evidence is seized in reasonable, good-faith reliance on a search warrant.

The District Court denied the Government's motion for reconsideration, id., at 147, and a divided panel of the Court of Appeals for the Ninth Circuit affirmed, judgt. order reported at 701 F.2d 187 (1983). The Court of Appeals first concluded that Officer Rombach's affidavit could not establish probable cause to search the Price Drive residence. To the extent that the affidavit set forth facts demonstrating the basis of the informant's knowledge of criminal activity, the information included was fatally stale. The affidavit, moreover, failed to establish the informant's credibility. Accordingly, the Court of Appeals concluded that the information provided by the informant was inadequate under both prongs of the two-part test established in *Aguilar v. Texas*, 378 U.S. 108 (1964), and *Spinelli v. United States*, 393 U.S. 410 (1969). The officers' independent investigation neither cured the staleness nor corroborated the details of the informant's declarations. The Court of Appeals then considered whether the affidavit formed a proper basis for the search of the Sunset Canyon residence. In its view, the affidavit included no facts indicating the basis for the informants' statements concerning respondent Leon's criminal activities and was devoid of information establishing the informants' reliability. Because these deficiencies had not been cured by the police investigation, the District Court properly suppressed the fruits of the search. The Court of Appeals refused the Government's invitation to recognize a good-faith exception to the Fourth Amendment exclusionary rule. App. to Pet. for Cert. 4a.

The Government's petition for certiorari expressly declined to seek review of the lower courts' determinations that the search warrant was unsupported by probable cause and presented only the question "[whether] the Fourth Amendment exclusionary rule should be modified so as not to bar the admission of evidence seized in reasonable, good-faith reliance on a search warrant that is subsequently held to be defective." We granted certiorari to consider the propriety of such a modification. 463 U.S. 1206 (1983). Although it undoubtedly is within our power to consider the question whether probable cause existed under the "totality of the circumstances" test announced last Term in *Illinois v. Gates*, 462 U.S. 213 (1983), that question has not been briefed or argued; and it is also within our authority, which we choose to exercise, to take the case as it comes to us, accepting the Court of Appeals' conclusion that probable cause was lacking under the prevailing legal standards. See this Court's Rule 21.1(a).

We have concluded that, in the Fourth Amendment context, the exclusionary rule can be modified somewhat without jeopardizing its ability to perform its intended functions. Accordingly, we reverse the judgment of the Court of Appeals.

II.

Language in opinions of this Court and of individual Justices has sometimes implied that the exclusionary rule is a necessary corollary of the Fourth Amendment, *Mapp v. Ohio*, 367 U.S. 643, 651, 655–657 (1961); *Olmstead v. United States*, 277 U.S. 438, 462–463 (1928), or that the rule is required by the conjunction of the Fourth and Fifth Amendments. *Mapp v. Ohio, supra*, at 661–662 (Black, J., concurring); *Agnello v. United States*, 269 U.S. 20, 33–34 (1925). These implications need not detain us long. The Fifth Amendment theory has not withstood critical analysis or the test of time, *see Andresen v. Maryland*, 427 U.S. 463 (1976), and the Fourth Amendment "has never been interpreted to proscribe the introduction of illegally seized evidence in all proceedings or against all persons." *Stone v. Powell*, 428 U.S. 465, 486 (1976).

A.

The Fourth Amendment contains no provision expressly precluding the use of evidence obtained in violation of its commands, and an examination of its origin and purposes makes clear that the use of fruits of a past unlawful search or seizure "[works] no new Fourth Amendment wrong." *United States v. Calandra*, 414 U.S. 338, 354 (1974). The wrong condemned by the Amendment is "fully accomplished" by the unlawful search or seizure itself, ibid., and the exclusionary rule is neither intended nor able to "cure the invasion of the defendant's rights which he has already suffered." *Stone v. Powell, supra*, at 540 (WHITE, J., dissenting). The rule thus operates as "a judicially created remedy designed to safeguard Fourth Amendment rights generally through its deterrent effect, rather than a personal constitutional right of the party aggrieved." *United States v. Calandra, supra*, at 348.

Whether the exclusionary sanction is appropriately imposed in a particular case, our decisions make clear, is "an issue separate from the question whether the Fourth Amendment rights of the party seeking to invoke the rule were violated by police conduct." *Illinois v. Gates, supra*, at 223. Only the former question is currently before us, and it must be resolved by weighing the costs and benefits of preventing the use in the prosecution's case in chief of inherently trustworthy tangible evidence obtained in reliance on a search warrant issued by a detached and neutral magistrate that ultimately is found to be defective.

The substantial social costs exacted by the exclusionary rule for the vindication of Fourth Amendment rights have long been a source of concern. "Our cases have consistently recognized that unbending application of the exclusionary sanction to enforce ideals of governmental rectitude would impede unacceptably the truth-finding functions of judge and jury." *United States v. Payner*, 447 U.S. 727, 734 (1980). An objectionable collateral consequence of this interference with the criminal justice system's truth-finding function is that some guilty defendants may go free or receive reduced sentences as a result of favorable plea bargains. Particularly when law enforcement officers have acted in objective good faith or their transgressions have been minor, the magnitude of the benefit conferred on such guilty defendants offends basic concepts of the criminal justice system. *Stone v. Powell*, 428 U.S., at 490. Indiscriminate application of the exclusionary rule, therefore, may well "[generate] disrespect for the law and administration of justice." Id., at 491. Accordingly, "[as] with any remedial device, the application of the rule has been restricted to those areas where its remedial objectives are thought most efficaciously served." *United States v. Calandra, supra*, at 348; *see Stone v. Powell, supra*, at 486–487; *United States v. Janis*, 428 U.S. 433, 447 (1976).

B.

Close attention to those remedial objectives has characterized our recent decisions concerning the scope of the Fourth Amendment exclusionary rule. The Court has, to be sure, not seriously questioned, "in the absence of a more efficacious sanction, the continued application of the rule to suppress evidence from the [prosecution's] case where a Fourth Amendment violation has been substantial and deliberate. . . ." *Franks v. Delaware*, 438 U.S. 154, 171 (1978); *Stone v. Powell, supra*, at 492. Nevertheless, the balancing approach that has evolved in various contexts— including criminal trials—"forcefully [suggests] that the exclusionary rule be more generally modified to permit the introduction of evidence obtained in the reasonable good-faith belief that a search or seizure was in accord with the Fourth Amendment." *Illinois v. Gates*, 462 U.S., at 255 (WHITE, J., concurring in judgment).

In *Stone v. Powell, supra*, the Court emphasized the costs of the exclusionary rule, expressed its view that limiting the circumstances under which Fourth Amendment claims could be raised in federal habeas corpus proceedings would not reduce the rule's deterrent effect, id., at 489–495, and held that a state prisoner who has been afforded a full and fair opportunity to litigate a Fourth Amendment claim may not obtain federal habeas relief on the ground that unlawfully obtained evidence had been introduced at his trial. Cf. *Rose v. Mitchell*, 443 U.S. 545, 560–563 (1979). Proposed extensions of the exclusionary rule to proceedings other than the criminal trial itself have been evaluated and rejected under the same analytic

approach. In *United States v. Calandra*, for example, we declined to allow grand jury witnesses to refuse to answer questions based on evidence obtained from an unlawful search or seizure since "[any] incremental deterrent effect which might be achieved by extending the rule to grand jury proceedings is uncertain at best." 414 U.S., at 348. Similarly, in *United States v. Janis*, supra, we permitted the use in federal civil proceedings of evidence illegally seized by state officials since the likelihood of deterring police misconduct through such an extension of the exclusionary rule was insufficient to outweigh its substantial social costs. In so doing, we declared that, "[if] . . . the exclusionary rule does not result in appreciable deterrence, then, clearly, its use in the instant situation is unwarranted." Id., at 454.

As cases considering the use of unlawfully obtained evidence in criminal trials themselves make clear, it does not follow from the emphasis on the exclusionary rule's deterrent value that "anything which deters illegal searches is thereby commanded by the Fourth Amendment." *Alderman v. United States*, 394 U.S., at 174. In determining whether persons aggrieved solely by the introduction of damaging evidence unlawfully obtained from their co-conspirators or codefendants could seek suppression, for example, we found that the additional benefits of such an extension of the exclusionary rule would not outweigh its costs. Id., at 174–175. Standing to invoke the rule has thus been limited to cases in which the prosecution seeks to use the fruits of an illegal search or seizure against the victim of police misconduct. *Rakas v. Illinois*, 439 U.S. 128 (1978); *Brown v. United States*, 411 U.S. 223 (1973); *Wong Sun v. United States*, 371 U.S. 471, 491–492 (1963). Cf. *United States v. Payner*, 447 U.S. 727 (1980).

Even defendants with standing to challenge the introduction in their criminal trials of unlawfully obtained evidence cannot prevent every conceivable use of such evidence. Evidence obtained in violation of the Fourth Amendment and inadmissible in the prosecution's case in chief may be used to impeach a defendant's direct testimony. *Walder v. United States*, 347 U.S. 62 (1954). *See also Oregon v. Hass*, 420 U.S. 714 (1975); *Harris v. New York*, 401 U.S. 222 (1971). A similar assessment of the "incremental furthering" of the ends of the exclusionary rule led us to conclude in *United States v. Havens*, 446 U.S. 620, 627 (1980), that evidence inadmissible in the prosecution's case in chief or otherwise as substantive evidence of guilt may be used to impeach statements made by a defendant in response to "proper cross-examination reasonably suggested by the defendant's direct examination." Id., at 627–628.

When considering the use of evidence obtained in violation of the Fourth Amendment in the prosecution's case in chief, moreover, we have declined to adopt a per se or "but for" rule that would render inadmissible any evidence that came to light through a chain of causation that began with an illegal arrest. *Brown v. Illinois*, 422 U.S. 590 (1975); *Wong Sun v. United States, supra*, at 487–488. We also have held that a witness' testimony may be admitted even when his identity was discovered in an unconstitutional search. *United States v. Ceccolini*, 435 U.S. 268 (1978). The perception underlying these decisions—that the connection between police misconduct and evidence of crime may be sufficiently attenuated to permit the use of that evidence at trial—is a product of considerations relating to the exclusionary rule and the constitutional principles it is designed to protect. *Dunaway v. New York*, 442 U.S. 200, 217–218 (1979); *United States v. Ceccolini, supra*, at 279. In short, the "dissipation of the taint" concept that the Court has applied in deciding whether exclusion is appropriate in a particular case "attempts to mark the point at which the detrimental consequences of illegal police action become so attenuated that the deterrent effect of the exclusionary rule no longer justifies its cost." *Brown v. Illinois, supra*, at 609 (POWELL, J., concurring in part). Not surprisingly in view of this purpose, an assessment of the flagrancy of the police misconduct constitutes an important step in the calculus. *Dunaway v. New York, supra*, at 218; *Brown v. Illinois, supra*, at 603–604.

The same attention to the purposes underlying the exclusionary rule also has characterized decisions not involving the scope of the rule itself. We have not required suppression of the fruits of a search incident to an arrest made in good-faith reliance on a substantive criminal statute that subsequently is declared unconstitutional. *Michigan v. DeFillippo*, 443

U.S. 31 (1979). Similarly, although the Court has been unwilling to conclude that new Fourth Amendment principles are always to have only prospective effect, *United States v. Johnson*, 457 U.S. 537, 560 (1982), no Fourth Amendment decision marking a "clear break with the past" has been applied retroactively. *See United States v. Peltier*, 422 U.S. 531 (1975); *Desist v. United States*, 394 U.S. 244 (1969); *Linkletter v. Walker*, 381 U.S. 618 (1965). The propriety of retroactive application of a newly announced Fourth Amendment principle, moreover, has been assessed largely in terms of the contribution retroactivity might make to the deterrence of police misconduct. *United States v. Johnson, supra*, at 560–561; *United States v. Peltier, supra*, at 536–539, 542.

As yet, we have not recognized any form of good-faith exception to the Fourth Amendment exclusionary rule. But the balancing approach that has evolved during the years of experience with the rule provides strong support for the modification currently urged upon us. As we discuss below, our evaluation of the costs and benefits of suppressing reliable physical evidence seized by officers reasonably relying on a warrant issued by a detached and neutral magistrate leads to the conclusion that such evidence should be admissible in the prosecution's case in chief.

III.

A.

Because a search warrant "provides the detached scrutiny of a neutral magistrate, which is a more reliable safeguard against improper searches than the hurried judgment of a law enforcement officer 'engaged in the often competitive enterprise of ferreting out crime,'" *United States v. Chadwick*, 433 U.S. 1, 9 (1977) (quoting Johnson v. United States, 333 U.S. 10, 14 (1948)), we have expressed a strong preference for warrants and declared that "in a doubtful or marginal case a search under a warrant may be sustainable where without one it would fall." *United States v. Ventresca*, 380 U.S. 102, 106 (1965). *See Aguilar v. Texas*, 378 U.S., at 111. Reasonable minds frequently may differ on the question whether a particular affidavit establishes probable cause, and we have thus concluded that the preference for warrants is most appropriately effectuated by according "great deference" to a magistrate's determination. *Spinelli v. United States*, 393 U.S., at 419. *See Illinois v. Gates*, 462 U.S., at 236; *United States v. Ventresca, supra*, at 108–109.

Deference to the magistrate, however, is not boundless. It is clear, first, that the deference accorded to a magistrate's finding of probable cause does not preclude inquiry into the knowing or reckless falsity of the affidavit on which that determination was based. *Franks v. Delaware*, 438 U.S. 154 (1978). Second, the courts must also insist that the magistrate purport to "perform his 'neutral and detached' function and not serve merely as a rubber stamp for the police." *Aguilar v. Texas, supra*, at 111. *See Illinois v. Gates*, supra, at 239. A magistrate failing to "manifest that neutrality and detachment demanded of a judicial officer when presented with a warrant application" and who acts instead as "an adjunct law enforcement officer" cannot provide valid authorization for an otherwise unconstitutional search. *Lo-Ji Sales, Inc. v. New York*, 442 U.S. 319, 326–327 (1979).

Third, reviewing courts will not defer to a warrant based on an affidavit that does not "provide the magistrate with a substantial basis for determining the existence of probable cause." *Illinois v. Gates*, 462 U.S., at 239. "Sufficient information must be presented to the magistrate to allow that official to determine probable cause; his action cannot be a mere ratification of the bare conclusions of others." Ibid. *See Aguilar v. Texas, supra*, at 114–115; *Giordenello v. United States*, 357 U.S. 480 (1958); *Nathanson v. United States*, 290 U.S. 41 (1933). Even if the warrant application was supported by more than a "bare bones" affidavit, a reviewing court may properly conclude that, notwithstanding the deference that magistrates deserve, the warrant was invalid because the magistrate's probable-cause determination reflected an improper analysis of the totality of the circumstances, *Illinois v. Gates, supra*, at 238–239, or because the form of the warrant was improper in some respect.

Only in the first of these three situations, however, has the Court set forth a rationale for suppressing evidence obtained pursuant

to a search warrant; in the other areas, it has simply excluded such evidence without considering whether Fourth Amendment interests will be advanced. To the extent that proponents of exclusion rely on its behavioral effects on judges and magistrates in these areas, their reliance is misplaced. First, the exclusionary rule is designed to deter police misconduct rather than to punish the errors of judges and magistrates. Second, there exists no evidence suggesting that judges and magistrates are inclined to ignore or subvert the Fourth Amendment or that lawlessness among these actors requires application of the extreme sanction of exclusion.

Third, and most important, we discern no basis, and are offered none, for believing that exclusion of evidence seized pursuant to a warrant will have a significant deterrent effect on the issuing judge or magistrate. Many of the factors that indicate that the exclusionary rule cannot provide an effective "special" or "general" deterrent for individual offending law enforcement officers apply as well to judges or magistrates. And, to the extent that the rule is thought to operate as a "systemic" deterrent on a wider audience, it clearly can have no such effect on individuals empowered to issue search warrants. Judges and magistrates are not adjuncts to the law enforcement team; as neutral judicial officers, they have no stake in the outcome of particular criminal prosecutions. The threat of exclusion thus cannot be expected significantly to deter them. Imposition of the exclusionary sanction is not necessary meaningfully to inform judicial officers of their errors, and we cannot conclude that admitting evidence obtained pursuant to a warrant while at the same time declaring that the warrant was somehow defective will in any way reduce judicial officers' professional incentives to comply with the Fourth Amendment, encourage them to repeat their mistakes, or lead to the granting of all colorable warrant requests.

B.

If exclusion of evidence obtained pursuant to a subsequently invalidated warrant is to have any deterrent effect, therefore, it must alter the behavior of individual law enforcement officers or the policies of their departments.

One could argue that applying the exclusionary rule in cases where the police failed to demonstrate probable cause in the warrant application deters future inadequate presentations or "magistrate shopping" and thus promotes the ends of the Fourth Amendment. Suppressing evidence obtained pursuant to a technically defective warrant supported by probable cause also might encourage officers to scrutinize more closely the form of the warrant and to point out suspected judicial errors. We find such arguments speculative and conclude that suppression of evidence obtained pursuant to a warrant should be ordered only on a case-by-case basis and only in those unusual cases in which exclusion will further the purposes of the exclusionary rule.

We have frequently questioned whether the exclusionary rule can have any deterrent effect when the offending officers acted in the objectively reasonable belief that their conduct did not violate the Fourth Amendment. "No empirical researcher, proponent or opponent of the rule, has yet been able to establish with any assurance whether the rule has a deterrent effect. . . ." *United States v. Janis*, 428 U.S., at 452, n. 22. But even assuming that the rule effectively deters some police misconduct and provides incentives for the law enforcement profession as a whole to conduct itself in accord with the Fourth Amendment, it cannot be expected, and should not be applied, to deter objectively reasonable law enforcement activity.

As we observed in *Michigan v. Tucker*, 417 U.S. 433, 447 (1974), and reiterated in *United States v. Peltier*, 422 U.S., at 539:

"The deterrent purpose of the exclusionary rule necessarily assumes that the police have engaged in willful, or at the very least negligent, conduct which has deprived the defendant of some right. By refusing to admit evidence gained as a result of such conduct, the courts hope to instill in those particular investigating officers, or in their future counterparts, a greater degree of care toward the rights of an accused. Where the official action was pursued in complete good faith, however, the deterrence rationale loses much of its force."

The Peltier Court continued, id., at 542:

"If the purpose of the exclusionary rule is to deter unlawful police conduct, then evidence obtained from a search should be suppressed only if it can be said that the law enforcement officer had knowledge, or may properly be charged with knowledge, that the search was unconstitutional under the Fourth Amendment." See also *Illinois v. Gates*, 462 U.S., at 260–261 (WHITE, J., concurring in judgment); United States v. Janis, supra, at 459; *Brown v. Illinois*, 422 U.S., at 610–611 (POWELL, J., concurring in part).

In short, where the officer's conduct is objectively reasonable, "excluding the evidence will not further the ends of the exclusionary rule in any appreciable way; for it is painfully apparent that . . . the officer is acting as a reasonable officer would and should act in similar circumstances. Excluding the evidence can in no way affect his future conduct unless it is to make him less willing to do his duty." *Stone v. Powell*, 428 U.S., at 539–540 (WHITE, J., dissenting).

This is particularly true, we believe, when an officer acting with objective good faith has obtained a search warrant from a judge or magistrate and acted within its scope. In most such cases, there is no police illegality and thus nothing to deter. It is the magistrate's responsibility to determine whether the officer's allegations establish probable cause and, if so, to issue a warrant comporting in form with the requirements of the Fourth Amendment. In the ordinary case, an officer cannot be expected to question the magistrate's probable-cause determination or his judgment that the form of the warrant is technically sufficient. "[Once] the warrant issues, there is literally nothing more the policeman can do in seeking to comply with the law." Id., at 498 (BURGER, C. J., concurring). Penalizing the officer for the magistrate's error, rather than his own, cannot logically contribute to the deterrence of Fourth Amendment violations.

C.

We conclude that the marginal or nonexistent benefits produced by suppressing evidence obtained in objectively reasonable reliance on a subsequently invalidated search warrant cannot justify the substantial costs of exclusion. We do not suggest, however, that exclusion is always inappropriate in cases where an officer has obtained a warrant and abided by its terms. "[Searches] pursuant to a warrant will rarely require any deep inquiry into reasonableness," *Illinois v. Gates*, 462 U.S., at 267 (WHITE, J., concurring in judgment), for "a warrant issued by a magistrate normally suffices to establish" that a law enforcement officer has "acted in good faith in conducting the search." *United States v. Ross*, 456 U.S. 798, 823, n. 32 (1982). Nevertheless, the officer's reliance on the magistrate's probable-cause determination and on the technical sufficiency of the warrant he issues must be objectively reasonable, cf. *Harlow v. Fitzgerald*, 457 U.S. 800, 815–819 (1982), and it is clear that in some circumstances the officer will have no reasonable grounds for believing that the warrant was properly issued.

Suppression therefore remains an appropriate remedy if the magistrate or judge in issuing a warrant was misled by information in an affidavit that the affiant knew was false or would have known was false except for his reckless disregard of the truth. *Franks v. Delaware*, 438 U.S. 154 (1978). The exception we recognize today will also not apply in cases where the issuing magistrate wholly abandoned his judicial role in the manner condemned in *Lo-Ji Sales, Inc. v. New York*, 442 U.S. 319 (1979); in such circumstances, no reasonably well trained officer should rely on the warrant. Nor would an officer manifest objective good faith in relying on a warrant based on an affidavit "so lacking in indicia of probable cause as to render official belief in its existence entirely unreasonable." *Brown v. Illinois*, 422 U.S., at 610–611 (POWELL, J., concurring in part); see Illinois v. Gates, supra, at 263–264 (WHITE, J., concurring in judgment). Finally, depending on the circumstances of the particular case, a warrant may be so facially deficient—i.e., in failing to particularize the place to be searched or the things to be seized—that the executing officers cannot reasonably presume it to be valid. Cf. *Massachusetts v. Sheppard*, post, at 988–991.

In so limiting the suppression remedy, we leave untouched the probable-cause standard and the various requirements for a valid warrant. Other objections to the modification of the Fourth Amendment exclusionary rule we consider to be insubstantial. The good-faith exception for searches conducted pursuant to warrants is not intended to signal our unwillingness strictly to enforce the requirements of the Fourth Amendment, and we do not believe that it will have this effect. As we have already suggested, the good-faith exception, turning as it does on objective reasonableness, should not be difficult to apply in practice. When officers have acted pursuant to a warrant, the prosecution should ordinarily be able to establish objective good faith without a substantial expenditure of judicial time.

Nor are we persuaded that application of a good-faith exception to searches conducted pursuant to warrants will preclude review of the constitutionality of the search or seizure, deny needed guidance from the courts, or freeze Fourth Amendment law in its present state. There is no need for courts to adopt the inflexible practice of always deciding whether the officers' conduct manifested objective good faith before turning to the question whether the Fourth Amendment has been violated. Defendants seeking suppression of the fruits of allegedly unconstitutional searches or seizures undoubtedly raise live controversies which Art. III empowers federal courts to adjudicate. As cases addressing questions of good-faith immunity under 42 U. S. C. § 1983, compare *O'Connor v. Donaldson*, 422 U.S. 563 (1975), with *Procunier v. Navarette*, 434 U.S. 555, 566, n. 14 (1978), and cases involving the harmless-error doctrine, compare *Milton v. Wainwright*, 407 U.S. 371, 372 (1972), with *Coleman v. Alabama*, 399 U.S. 1 (1970), make clear, courts have considerable discretion in conforming their decisionmaking processes to the exigencies of particular cases.

If the resolution of a particular Fourth Amendment question is necessary to guide future action by law enforcement officers and magistrates, nothing will prevent reviewing courts from deciding that question before turning to the good-faith issue. Indeed, it frequently will be difficult to determine whether the officers acted reasonably without resolving the Fourth Amendment issue.

Even if the Fourth Amendment question is not one of broad import, reviewing courts could decide in particular cases that magistrates under their supervision need to be informed of their errors and so evaluate the officers' good faith only after finding a violation. In other circumstances, those courts could reject suppression motions posing no important Fourth Amendment questions by turning immediately to a consideration of the officers' good faith. We have no reason to believe that our Fourth Amendment jurisprudence would suffer by allowing reviewing courts to exercise an informed discretion in making this choice.

IV.

When the principles we have enunciated today are applied to the facts of this case, it is apparent that the judgment of the Court of Appeals cannot stand. The Court of Appeals applied the prevailing legal standards to Officer Rombach's warrant application and concluded that the application could not support the magistrate's probable-cause determination. In so doing, the court clearly informed the magistrate that he had erred in issuing the challenged warrant. This aspect of the court's judgment is not under attack in this proceeding.

Having determined that the warrant should not have issued, the Court of Appeals understandably declined to adopt a modification of the Fourth Amendment exclusionary rule that this Court had not previously sanctioned. Although the modification finds strong support in our previous cases, the Court of Appeals' commendable self-restraint is not to be criticized. We have now reexamined the purposes of the exclusionary rule and the propriety of its application in cases where officers have relied on a subsequently invalidated search warrant. Our conclusion is that the rule's purposes will only rarely be served by applying it in such circumstances.

In the absence of an allegation that the magistrate abandoned his detached and neutral role, suppression is appropriate only if the officers were dishonest or reckless in preparing their affidavit or could not have harbored an objectively reasonable belief in the existence of probable cause. Only respondent Leon has contended that no reasonably well trained police officer could have believed that there existed probable cause to search his house; significantly, the other respondents advance no comparable argument. Officer Rombach's application for a warrant clearly was supported by much more than a "bare bones" affidavit. The affidavit related the results of an extensive investigation and, as the opinions of the divided panel of the Court of Appeals make clear, provided evidence sufficient to create disagreement among thoughtful and competent judges as to the existence of probable cause. Under these circumstances, the officers' reliance on the magistrate's determination of probable cause was objectively reasonable, and application of the extreme sanction of exclusion is inappropriate.

Accordingly, the judgment of the Court of Appeals is

Reversed.

* * *

ARIZONA
v.
GANT

Supreme Court of the United States
_____ U.S. _____, 2009 U.S. LEXIS 3120. (2009)

JUSTICE STEVENS delivered the opinion of the Court.

After Rodney Gant was arrested for driving with a suspended license, handcuffed, and locked in the back of a patrol car, police officers searched his car and discovered cocaine in the pocket of a jacket on the backseat. Because Gant could not have accessed his car to retrieve weapons or evidence at the time of the search, the Arizona Supreme Court held that the search-incident-to-arrest exception to the Fourth Amendment's warrant requirement, as defined in *Chimel v. California*, 395 U.S. 752, 89 S. Ct. 2034, 23 L. Ed. 2d 685 (1969), and applied to vehicle searches in *New York v. Belton*, 453 U.S. 454, 101 S.

Ct. 2860, 69 L. Ed. 2d 768 (1981), did not justify the search in this case. We agree with that conclusion.

Under *Chimel*, police may search incident to arrest only the space within an arrestee's "'immediate control,'" meaning "the area from within which he might gain possession of a weapon or destructible evidence." 395 U.S., at 763, 89 S. Ct. 2034, 23 L. Ed. 2d 685. The safety and evidentiary justifications underlying *Chimel*'s reaching-distance rule determine *Belton*'s scope. Accordingly, we hold that *Belton* does not authorize a vehicle search incident to a recent occupant's arrest after the arrestee has been secured and cannot access the interior of the vehicle. Consistent with the holding in *Thornton v. United States*, 541 U.S. 615, 124 S. Ct. 2127, 158 L. Ed. 2d 905 (2004), and following the suggestion in JUSTICE SCALIA's opinion concurring in the judgment in that case, id., at 632, 124 S. Ct. 2127, 158 L. Ed. 2d 905, we also conclude that circumstances unique to the automobile context justify a search incident to arrest when it is reasonable to believe that evidence of the offense of arrest might be found in the vehicle.

I.

On August 25, 1999, acting on an anonymous tip that the residence at 2524 North Walnut Avenue was being used to sell drugs, Tucson police officers Griffith and Reed knocked on the front door and asked to speak to the owner. Gant answered the door and, after identifying himself, stated that he expected the owner to return later. The officers left the residence and conducted a records check, which revealed that Gant's driver's license had been suspended and there was an outstanding warrant for his arrest for driving with a suspended license.

[When the officers next encountered Gant, he was observed parking his car near the North Walnut Avenue address. Gant had walked about 10 or 12 feet away from his car, when the officers identified him and arrested him for driving with a suspended license. Because several other arrestees from the drug selling house on North Walnut were already in the police cruisers, one officer called for backup. When the additional officers arrived,

they placed Gant in the back of a cruiser after handcuffing him. They then proceeded to search his motor vehicle under the doctrine of "search instant to a lawful arrest." The police found a gun and cocaine in a jacket pocket within the car. Gant was charged with possession of a narcotic drug for sale and possession of drug paraphernalia. Gant filed a motion to suppress the evidence taken from the car on the theory that the police could not have reasonably believed that Gant could have any access to gun or cocaine since he was handcuffed in a cruiser and secondarily, police could not have discovered any evidence inside the automobile to support the driving under a suspension charge. The trial court denied his motion to suppress the evidence and he was convicted. After complicated state court proceedings, the Supreme Court of Arizona ruled that the search of his car was unreasonable as incident to a lawful arrest. The Supreme Court granted certiorari.]

II.

Consistent with our precedent, our analysis begins, as it should in every case addressing the reasonableness of a warrantless search, with the basic rule that "searches conducted outside the judicial process, without prior approval by judge or magistrate, are per se unreasonable under the Fourth Amendment— subject only to a few specifically established and well-delineated exceptions." *Katz v. United States*, 389 U.S. 347, 357, 88 S. Ct. 507, 19 L. Ed. 2d 576 (1967)(footnote omitted). Among the exceptions to the warrant requirement is a search incident to a lawful arrest. *See Weeks v. United States*, 232 U.S. 383, 392, 34 S. Ct. 341, 58 L. Ed. 652, T.D. 1964 (1914). The exception derives from interests in officer safety and evidence preservation that are typically implicated in arrest situations. *See United States v. Robinson*, 414 U.S. 218, 230–234, 94 S. Ct. 467, 38 L. Ed. 2d 427 (1973); *Chimel*, 395 U.S., at 763, 89 S. Ct. 2034, 23 L. Ed. 2d 685.

In *Chimel*, we held that a search incident to arrest may only include "the arrestee's person and the area 'within his immediate control' – construing that phrase to mean the area from within which he might gain possession of a weapon or destructible evidence." Ibid. That limitation, which continues to define the boundaries of the exception, ensures that the scope of a search incident to arrest is commensurate with its purposes of protecting arresting officers and safeguarding any evidence of the offense of arrest that an arrestee might conceal or destroy. See ibid. (noting that searches incident to arrest are reasonable "in order to remove any weapons [the arrestee] might seek to use" and "in order to prevent [the] concealment or destruction" of evidence (emphasis added)). If there is no possibility that an arrestee could reach into the area that law enforcement officers seek to search, both justifications for the search-incident-to-arrest exception are absent and the rule does not apply. E.g., Preston v. United States, 376 U.S. 364, 367–368, 84 S. Ct. 881, 11 L. Ed. 2d 777 (1964).

In *Belton*, we considered *Chimel's* application to the automobile context. A lone police officer in that case stopped a speeding car in which Belton was one of four occupants. While asking for the driver's license and registration, the officer smelled burnt marijuana and observed an envelope on the car floor marked "Supergold"—a name he associated with marijuana. Thus having probable cause to believe the occupants had committed a drug offense, the officer ordered them out of the vehicle, placed them under arrest, and patted them down. Without handcuffing the arrestees, 1 the officer " 'split them up into four separate areas of the Thruway . . . so they would not be in physical touching area of each other' " and searched the vehicle, including the pocket of a jacket on the backseat, in which he found cocaine. 453 U.S., at 456, 101 S. Ct. 2860, 69 L. Ed. 2d 768.

* * *

[In *Belton*,] we held that when an officer lawfully arrests "the occupant of an automobile, he may, as a contemporaneous incident of that arrest, search the passenger compartment of the automobile" and any containers therein. Belton, 453 U.S., at 460, 101 S. Ct. 2860, 69 L. Ed. 2d 768 (footnote omitted). That holding was based in large part on our assumption "that articles inside the relatively narrow compass of the passenger

compartment of an automobile are in fact generally, even if not inevitably, within 'the area into which an arrestee might reach.' " Ibid.

* * *

III.

Despite the textual and evidentiary support for the Arizona Supreme Court's reading of *Belton*, our opinion has been widely understood to allow a vehicle search incident to the arrest of a recent occupant even if there is no possibility the arrestee could gain access to the vehicle at the time of the search. This reading may be attributable to Justice Brennan's dissent in *Belton*, in which he characterized the Court's holding as resting on the "fiction . . . that the interior of a car is always within the immediate control of an arrestee who has recently been in the car." 453 U.S., at 466, 101 S. Ct. 2860, 69 L. Ed. 2d 768. Under the majority's approach, he argued, "the result would presumably be the same even if [the officer] had handcuffed Belton and his companions in the patrol car" before conducting the search. Id., at 468, 101 S. Ct. 2860, 69 L. Ed. 2d 768.

* * *

Although it does not follow from *Chimel*, we also conclude that circumstances unique to the vehicle context justify a search incident to a lawful arrest when it is "reasonable to believe evidence relevant to the crime of arrest might be found in the vehicle." Thornton, 541 U.S., at 632, 124 S. Ct. 2127, 158 L. Ed. 2d 905 (SCALIA, J., concurring in judgment). In many cases, as when a recent occupant is arrested for a traffic violation, there will be no reasonable basis to believe the vehicle contains relevant evidence. *See, e.g., Atwater v. Lago Vista*, 532 U.S. 318, 324, 121 S. Ct. 1536, 149 L. Ed. 2d 549 (2001); *Knowles v. Iowa*, 525 U.S. 113, 118, 119 S. Ct. 484, 142 L. Ed. 2d 492 (1998). But in others, including *Belton* and *Thornton*, the offense of arrest will supply a basis for searching the passenger compartment of an arrestee's vehicle and any containers therein.

Neither the possibility of access nor the likelihood of discovering offense-related evidence authorized the search in this case. Unlike in *Belton*, which involved a single officer confronted with four unsecured arrestees, the five officers in this case outnumbered the three arrestees, all of whom had been handcuffed and secured in separate patrol cars before the officers searched Gant's car. Under those circumstances, Gant clearly was not within reaching distance of his car at the time of the search. An evidentiary basis for the search was also lacking in this case. Whereas Belton and Thornton were arrested for drug offenses, Gant was arrested for driving with a suspended license—an offense for which police could not expect to find evidence in the passenger compartment of Gant's car. Cf. *Knowles*, 525 U.S., at 118, 119 S. Ct. 484, 142 L. Ed. 2d 492. Because police could not reasonably have believed either that Gant could have accessed his car at the time of the search or that evidence of the offense for which he was arrested might have been found therein, the search in this case was unreasonable.

* * *

VI.

Police may search a vehicle incident to a recent occupant's arrest only if the arrestee is within reaching distance of the passenger compartment at the time of the search or it is reasonable to believe the vehicle contains evidence of the offense of arrest. When these justifications are absent, a search of an arrestee's vehicle will be unreasonable unless police obtain a warrant or show that another exception to the warrant requirement applies. The Arizona Supreme Court correctly held that this case involved an unreasonable search. Accordingly, the judgment of the State Supreme Court is affirmed.

It is so ordered.

GEORGIA
v.
RANDOLPH

SUPREME COURT OF THE UNITED STATES

126 S. Ct. 1515, 164 L. Ed. 2d 208. 2006
U.S. LEXIS 2498 (2006)

Justice Souter delivered the opinion of the Court.

The Fourth Amendment recognizes a valid warrantless entry and search of premises when police obtain the voluntary consent of an occupant who shares, or is reasonably believed to share, authority over the area in common with a co-occupant who later objects to the use of evidence so obtained. *Illinois v. Rodriguez*, 497 U.S. 177, 110 S. Ct. 2793, 111 L. Ed. 2d 148 (1990); *United States v. Matlock*, 415 U.S. 164, 94 S. Ct. 988, 39 L. Ed. 2d 242 (1974). The question here is whether such an evidentiary seizure is likewise lawful with the permission of one occupant when the other, who later seeks to suppress the evidence, is present at the scene and expressly refuses to consent. We hold that, in the circumstances here at issue, a physically present co-occupant's stated refusal to permit entry prevails, rendering the warrantless search unreasonable and invalid as to him.

I.

Respondent Scott Randolph and his wife, Janet, separated in late May 2001, when she left the marital residence in Americus, Georgia, and went to stay with her parents in Canada, taking their son and some belongings. In July, she returned to the Americus house with the child, though the record does not reveal whether her object was reconciliation or retrieval of remaining possessions.

On the morning of July 6, she complained to the police that after a domestic dispute her husband took their son away, and when officers reached the house she told them that her husband was a cocaine user whose habit had caused financial troubles. She mentioned the marital problems and said that she and their son had only recently returned after a stay of several weeks with her parents. Shortly after the police arrived, Scott Randolph returned and explained that he had removed the child to a neighbor's house out of concern that his wife might take the boy out of the country again; he denied cocaine use, and countered that it was in fact his wife who abused drugs and alcohol.

One of the officers, Sergeant Murray, went with Janet Randolph to reclaim the child, and when they returned she not only renewed her complaints about her husband's drug use, but also volunteered that there were "'items of drug evidence'" in the house. Brief for Petitioner 3. Sergeant Murray asked Scott Randolph for permission to search the house, which he unequivocally refused.

The sergeant turned to Janet Randolph for consent to search, which she readily gave. She led the officer upstairs to a bedroom that she identified as Scott's, where the sergeant noticed a section of a drinking straw with a powdery residue he suspected was cocaine. He then left the house to get an evidence bag from his car and to call the district attorney's office, which instructed him to stop the search and apply for a warrant. When Sergeant Murray returned to the house, Janet Randolph withdrew her consent. The police took the straw to the police station, along with the Randolphs. After getting a search warrant, they returned to the house and seized further evidence of drug use, on the basis of which Scott Randolph was indicted for possession of cocaine.

He moved to suppress the evidence, as products of a warrantless search of his house unauthorized by his wife's consent over his express refusal. The trial court denied the motion, ruling that Janet Randolph had common authority to consent to the search.

The Court of Appeals of Georgia reversed, 264 Ga. App. 396, 590 S. E. 2d 834 (2003), and was itself sustained by the State Supreme Court, principally on the ground that "the consent to conduct a warrantless search of a residence given by one occupant is not valid in the face of the refusal of another occupant who is physically present at the scene to permit a warrantless search." 278 Ga. 614, 604 S. E. 2d 835, 836 (2004). The Supreme Court of Georgia acknowledged this Court's holding in *Matlock,* 415 U.S. 164, 94 S. Ct. 988, 39 L. Ed. 2d 242, that "the consent of one who possesses common authority over premises or effects is valid as against the absent, nonconsenting person with whom that authority is shared," id., at 170, 94 S. Ct. 988, 39 L. Ed. 2d 242, and found *Matlock* distinguishable just because Scott Randolph was not "absent" from the colloquy on which the police relied for consent to make the search. The State Supreme Court

stressed that the officers in *Matlock* had not been "faced with the physical presence of joint occupants, with one consenting to the search and the other objecting." 278 Ga., at 615, 604 S. E. 2d, at 837. It held that an individual who chooses to live with another assumes a risk no greater than "'an inability to control access to the premises during [his] absence,'" ibid. (quoting 3 W. LaFave, SEARCH AND SEIZURE § 8.3(d), p 731 (3d ed. 1996) (hereinafter LaFave)), and does not contemplate that his objection to a request to search commonly shared premises, if made, will be overlooked.

We granted certiorari to resolve a split of authority on whether one occupant may give law enforcement effective consent to search shared premises, as against a co-tenant who is present and states a refusal to permit the search. 544 U.S. 973, 544 U.S. 973, 125 S. Ct. 1840, 161 L. Ed. 2d 722 (2005). We now affirm.

* * *

II.

To the Fourth Amendment rule ordinarily prohibiting the warrantless entry of a person's house as unreasonable per se, *Payton v. New York,* 445 U.S. 573, 586 (1980); *Coolidge v. New Hampshire,* 403 U.S. 443, 454–455 (1971), one "jealously and carefully drawn" exception, *Jones v. United States,* 357 U.S. 493, 499 (1958), recognizes the validity of searches with the voluntary consent of an individual possessing authority, *Rodriguez,* 497 U.S., at 181. That person might be the householder against whom evidence is sought, *Schneckloth v. Bustamonte,* 412 U.S. 218, 222 (1973), or a fellow occupant who shares common authority over property, when the suspect is absent, [*United States v.*] *Matlock, supra,* at 170, and the exception for consent extends even to entries and searches with the permission of a co-occupant whom the police reasonably, but erroneously, believe to possess shared authority as an occupant, *Rodriguez, supra,* at 186. None of our co-occupant consent-to-search cases, however, has presented the further fact of a second occupant physically present and refusing permission to search, and later moving to suppress evidence so obtained. The significance of such a refusal turns on the underpinnings of the co-occupant consent rule, as recognized since *Matlock*.

A.

The defendant in that case was arrested in the yard of a house where he lived with a Mrs. Graff and several of her relatives, and was detained in a squad car parked nearby. When the police went to the door, Mrs. Graff admitted them and consented to a search of the house. In resolving the defendant's objection to use of the evidence taken in the warrantless search, we said that "the consent of one who possesses common authority over premises or effects is valid as against the absent, non-consenting person with whom that authority is shared." Id., at 170. Consistent with our prior understanding that Fourth Amendment rights are not limited by the law of property, we explained that the third party's "common authority" is not synonymous with a technical property interest:

"The authority which justified the third-party consent does not rest upon the law of property, with its attendant historical and legal refinement, but rests rather on mutual use of the property by persons generally having joint access or control for most purposes, so that it is reasonable to recognize that any of the co-inhabitants has the right to permit the inspection in his own right and that the others have assumed the risk that one of their number might permit the common area to be searched." 415 U.S., at 171, n. 7 (citations omitted).

* * *

The constant element in assessing Fourth Amendment reasonableness in the consent cases, then, is the great significance given to widely shared social expectations, which are naturally enough influenced by the law of property, but not controlled by its rules. Matlock accordingly not only holds that a solitary co-inhabitant may sometimes consent to a search of shared premises, but stands for the proposition that the reasonableness of

such a search is in significant part a function of commonly held understanding about the authority that co-inhabitants may exercise in ways that affect each other's interests.

B.

Matlock's example of common understanding is readily apparent. When someone comes to the door of a domestic dwelling with a baby at her hip, as Mrs. Graff did, she shows that she belongs there, and that fact standing alone is enough to tell a law enforcement officer or any other visitor that if she occupies the place along with others, she probably lives there subject to the assumption tenants usually make about their common authority when they share quarters. They understand that any one of them may admit visitors, with the consequence that a guest obnoxious to one may nevertheless be admitted in his absence by another.

* * *

C.

Although we have not dealt directly with the reasonableness of police entry in reliance on consent by one occupant subject to immediate challenge by another, we took a step toward the issue in an earlier case dealing with the Fourth Amendment rights of a social guest arrested at premises the police entered without a warrant or the benefit of any exception to the warrant requirement. *Minnesota v. Olson*, 495 U.S. 91 (1990), held that overnight houseguests have a legitimate expectation of privacy in their temporary quarters because "it is unlikely that [the host] will admit someone who wants to see or meet with the guest over the objection of the guest," id., at 99. If that customary expectation of courtesy or deference is a foundation of Fourth Amendment rights of a houseguest, it presumably should follow that an inhabitant of shared premises may claim at least as much, and it turns out that the co-inhabitant naturally has an even stronger claim.

To begin with, it is fair to say that a caller standing at the door of shared premises would have no confidence that one occupant's invitation was a sufficiently good reason to enter when a fellow tenant stood there saying, "stay out." Without some very good reason, no sensible person would go inside under those conditions. Fear for the safety of the occupant issuing the invitation, or of someone else inside, would be thought to justify entry, but the justification then would be the personal risk, the threats to life or limb, not the disputed invitation.

* * *

D.

Since the co-tenant wishing to open the door to a third party has no recognized authority in law or social practice to prevail over a present and objecting co-tenant, his disputed invitation, without more, gives a police officer no better claim to reasonableness in entering than the officer would have in the absence of any consent at all. Accordingly, in the balancing of competing individual and governmental interests entailed by the bar to unreasonable searches, the cooperative occupant's invitation adds nothing to the government's side to counter the force of an objecting individual's claim to security against the government's intrusion into his dwelling place. Since we hold to the "centuries-old principle of respect for the privacy of the home," Wilson v. Layne, 526 U.S. 603, 610 (1999), "it is beyond dispute that the home is entitled to special protection as the center of the private lives of our people," Minnesota v. Carter, 525 U.S. 83, 99 (1998) (KENNEDY, J., concurring). We have, after all, lived our whole national history with an understanding of "the ancient adage that a man's home is his castle [to the point that the poorest man may in his cottage bid defiance to all the forces of the Crown," Miller v. United States, 357 U.S. 301, 307 (1958) (internal quotation marks omitted).

Disputed permission is thus no match for this central value of the Fourth Amendment, and the State's other countervailing claims do not add up to outweigh it.

* * *

E.

There are two loose ends, the first being the explanation given in Matlock for the constitutional sufficiency of a co-tenant's consent to enter and search: it "rests . . . on mutual use of the property by persons generally having joint access or control for most purposes, so that it is reasonable to recognize that any of the co-inhabitants has the right to permit the inspection in his own right. . . ." 415 U.S., at 171, n. 7. If Matlock's co-tenant is giving permission "in his own right," how can his "own right" be eliminated by another tenant's objection? The answer appears in the very footnote from which the quoted statement is taken: the "right" to admit the police to which Matlock refers is not an enduring and enforceable ownership right as understood by the private law of property, but is instead the authority recognized by customary social usage as having a substantial bearing on Fourth Amendment reasonableness in specific circumstances. Thus, to ask whether the consenting tenant has the right to admit the police when a physically present fellow tenant objects is not to question whether some property right may be divested by the mere objection of another. It is, rather, the question whether customary social understanding accords the consenting tenant authority powerful enough to prevail over the co-tenant's objection. The Matlock Court did not purport to answer this question, a point made clear by another statement: the Court described the co-tenant's consent as good against "the absent, nonconsenting" resident. Id., at 170.

The second loose end is the significance of Matlock and Rodriguez after today's decision. Although the Matlock defendant was not present with the opportunity to object, he was in a squad car not far away; the Rodriguez defendant was actually asleep in the apartment, and the police might have roused him with a knock on the door before they entered with only the consent of an apparent co-tenant. If those cases are not to be undercut by today's holding, we have to admit that we are drawing a fine line; if a potential defendant with self-interest in objecting is in fact at the door and objects, the co-tenant's permission does not suffice for a reasonable search, whereas the potential objector, nearby but not invited to take part in the threshold colloquy, loses out.

This is the line we draw, and we think the formalism is justified. So long as there is no evidence that the police have removed the potentially objecting tenant from the entrance for the sake of avoiding a possible objection, there is practical value in the simple clarity of complementary rules, one recognizing the co-tenant's permission when there is no fellow occupant on hand, the other according dispositive weight to the fellow occupant's contrary indication when he expresses it.

* * *

III.

This case invites a straightforward application of the rule that a physically present inhabitant's express refusal of consent to a police search is dispositive as to him, regardless of the consent of a fellow occupant. Scott Randolph's refusal is clear, and nothing in the record justifies the search on grounds independent of Janet Randolph's consent. The State does not argue that she gave any indication to the police of a need for protection inside the house that might have justified entry into the portion of the premises where the police found the powdery straw (which, if lawfully seized, could have been used when attempting to establish probable cause for the warrant issued later). Nor does the State claim that the entry and search should be upheld under the rubric of exigent circumstances, owing to some apprehension by the police officers that Scott Randolph would destroy evidence of drug use before any warrant could be obtained.

The judgment of the Supreme Court of Georgia is therefore affirmed.

It is so ordered.

Justice Alito took no part in the consideration or decision of this case.

HORTON
v.
CALIFORNIA

Supreme Court of the United States
496 U.S. 128, 10 S. Ct. 2301, 110 L. Ed. 2d 112 (1990)

SYLLABUS:

A California policeman determined that there was probable cause to search petitioner

Horton's home for the proceeds of a robbery and the robbers' weapons. His search warrant affidavit referred to police reports that described both the weapons and the proceeds, but the warrant issued by the Magistrate only authorized a search for the proceeds. Upon executing the warrant, the officer did not find the stolen property but did find the weapons in plain view and seized them. The trial court refused to suppress the seized evidence, and Horton was convicted of armed robbery. The California Court of Appeals affirmed. Since the officer had testified that while he was searching Horton's home for the stolen property he was also interested in finding other evidence connecting Horton to the robbery, the seized evidence was not discovered "inadvertently." However, in rejecting Horton's argument that *Coolidge v. New Hampshire*, 403 U.S. 443, therefore required suppression of that evidence, the Court of Appeal relied on a State Supreme Court decision holding that *Coolidge's* discussion of the inadvertence limitation on the "plain view" doctrine was not binding because it was contained in a four-Justice plurality opinion. Held: The Fourth Amendment does not prohibit the warrantless seizure of evidence in plain view even though the discovery of the evidence was not inadvertent. Although inadvertence is a characteristic of most legitimate plain view seizures, it is not a necessary condition. Pp. 4–13.

(a) *Coolidge* is a binding precedent. However, the second of the *Coolidge* plurality's two limitations on the plain view doctrine—that the discovery of evidence in plain view must be inadvertent, id., at 469—was not essential to the Court's rejection of the State's plain view argument in that case. Rather, the first limitation—that plain view alone is never enough to justify a warrantless seizure, id., at 468—adequately supports the Court's holding that gunpowder found in vacuum sweepings from one of the automobiles seized in plain view on the defendant's driveway in the course of his arrest could not be introduced against him because the warrantless seizures violated the Fourth Amendment. In order for a warrantless seizure of an object in plain view to be valid, two conditions must be satisfied in addition to the essential predicate that the officer did not violate the Fourth Amendment in arriving at the place from which the object could be plainly viewed. First, the object's incriminating character must be "immediately apparent," id., at 466. Although the cars in *Coolidge* were obviously in plain view, their probative value remained uncertain until after their interiors were swept and examined microscopically. Second, the officer must have a lawful right of access to the object itself. Justice Harlan, who concurred in the *Coolidge* judgment but did not join the plurality's plain view discussion, may well have rested his vote on the fact that the cars' seizure was accomplished by means of a warrantless trespass on the defendant's property. Pp. 4–8.

(b) There are two flaws in the *Coolidge* plurality's conclusion that the inadvertence requirement was necessary to avoid a violation of the Fourth Amendment's mandate that a valid warrant "'particularly describe . . . [the] . . . things to be seized,"' id., at 469–471. First, evenhanded law enforcement is best achieved by applying objective standards of conduct, rather than standards that depend upon the officer's subjective state of mind. The fact that an officer is interested in an item and fully expects to find it should not invalidate its seizure if the search is confined

in area and duration by a warrant's terms or by a valid exception to the warrant requirement. Second, the suggestion that the inadvertence requirement is necessary to prevent the police from conducting general searches, or from converting specific warrants into general warrants, is not persuasive because that interest is already served by the requirements that an unparticularized warrant not be issued and that a warrantless search be circumscribed by the exigencies which justify its initiation. Here, the search's scope was not enlarged by the warrant's omission of reference to the weapons; indeed, no search for the weapons could have taken place if the named items had been found or surrendered at the outset. The prohibition against general searches and warrants is based on privacy concerns, which are not implicated when an officer with a lawful right of access to an item in plain view seizes it without a warrant. Pp. 8–13. JUDGES: Stevens, J., delivered the opinion of the Court, in which Rehnquist, C. J., and White, Blackmun, O'Connor, Scalia, and Kennedy, JJ. joined. Brennan, J., filed a dissenting opinion, in which Marshall, J., joined.

Glossary

Adjudicative facts Facts that concern the immediate parties and are determinative oɩ the outcome of the case.

Affirmation A solemn declaration without oath. The privilege of affirming in judicial proceedings is now generally extended to all persons who object to taking an oath.

Affirmative defense A response to a claim for relief that states information not otherwise before the court, e.g., a plea of self-defense, defense of another, or an insanity defense. (2) A justification or avoidance.

Alibi A defense resorted to where the party accused, in order to prove that he or she could not have committed the crime with which he or she is charged, offers evidence that he or she was in a different place at the time the offense was committed.

Authentication An attestation made by a proper officer, by which he or she certifies that a record is in due form of law, and that the person who certifies it is the officer appointed so to do. In the admission of evidence, evidence that proves the item is what it purports to be or proves that the item is the genuine article.

Ballistics experiments The science of gun examination, frequently used in criminal cases, especially cases of homicide, to determine the firing capacity of a weapon, its fireability, and whether a given bullet was fired from a particular gun.

Best evidence rule Also called the original document rule. The proof that provides the greatest certainty of the fact to be proven; the most reliable evidence. Under the best evidence rule, which is ordinarily applied to documents and writings sought to be proven, usually the highest degree of proof, i.e., the original document, must be presented if it is available.

Beyond a reasonable doubt Fully satisfied, entirely convinced, satisfied to a moral certainty.

Breathalyzer test Test to determine alcohol content of blood in one arrested for operating a motor vehicle under the influence of alcohol. The results of such tests, if properly administered, constitute admissible evidence.

Burden of going forward Refers to the obligation resting upon a party to produce prima facie evidence on a particular issue.

Burden of persuasion Refers to the burden of persuading the factfinder of the truth of the evidence produced by one side or the other.

Burden of proof   The duty of proving facts disputed on the trial of a case by the proper weight of the evidence.

Chain of custody   In evidence, one who offers real evidence (such as narcotics in the trial of a drug case) must account for the custody of the evidence from the moment when it reaches his or her custody until the moment when it is offered in evidence, and such evidence goes to the weight, not the admissibility, of the evidence.

Circumstantial evidence   Evidence of one fact from which a second fact is reasonably inferred, although not directly proven. It is often introduced when direct evidence is not available.

Clear and convincing evidence   A flexible term concerning the degree of proof required for certain issues in some civil cases. It is less than the degree required in criminal cases, but more than required in the ordinary civil action.

Competency   The legal fitness or capacity of a witness to testify on the trial of a case that requires an oath, original perception, recollection, and an ability to communicate. (2) Freedom from mental illness or defect because of which a person is unable to understand in a reasonable manner the nature and consequences of a transaction, or he or she is unable to act in a reasonable manner in relation to the transaction. The quality of evidence offered, that makes it proper to be received.

Competent evidence   The quality of evidence offered that makes it proper to be received.

Corroborative evidence   Additional testimony to reinforce a point that was previously the subject of proof.

Cross-examination   The questioning of a witness by the party opposed to the party who called the witness for direct examination. This usually occurs after the direct examination but on occasion may be otherwise allowed.

Cumulative evidence   Testimony that is offered to prove what has already been proven by other evidence.

Delay in arraignment rule   This rule provides that if there has been a delay in bringing the accused person before a magistrate, and if a confession has been obtained during this unnecessary delay, the confession may not be admitted, even though voluntarily made.

Direct evidence   Testimony or other proof that expressly or straightforwardly proves the existence of a fact; opposite of circumstantial evidence.

Direct examination   The initial questioning of a witness by the party who calls him or her.

DNA Deoxyribonucleic acid   A long, threadlike chain of molecules found in the nucleus of virtually every cell of the body. The DNA chains are tightly coiled into bodies called chromosomes of which humans have 23. No two individuals (except for identical twins) have identical DNA. Within a given person, however, DNA does not vary from cell to cell.

Documentary evidence   Evidence that is furnished by written documents, records, and computer-generated reports.

Due process   A flexible term for the compliance with the fundamental rules for fair and orderly legal proceedings, e.g., the right to be informed of the nature and cause of the accusation, to be confronted with the witnesses against you, to have compulsory process for obtaining witnesses in your favor, to have the assistance of counsel for your defense, and to have a fair and impartial jury. (2) Legal proceedings that observe the rules designed for the protection and enforcement of individual rights and liberties.

Dying declaration   Hearsay evidence of what a person said when he or she was aware that his or her death was imminent that must relate to the way the declarant received final injuries. Under particular circumstances and in certain cases, it is competent evidence in some courts. (2) In a prosecution for homicide or in a civil action or proceeding, a statement made by a declarant while believing that his or her death was imminent, concerning the cause or circumstances of what he or she believed to be his or her impending death. It is not excluded by the hearsay rule if the declarant is unavailable as a witness. Fed. R. Evid. 804(b)(2).

Eavesdropping   Knowingly and without authority entering into a private place with the intent to surreptitiously listen to a private conversation or to observe the personal conduct of any other person or persons therein conducted by personal listening or electronic collection of sounds.

Evidence   Proof, either written or unwritten, of allegations at issue between parties.

Evidence-in-chief   Proof upon which a party primarily relies in order to support a claim or defense.

Exception   A form of objection to a ruling or order of a trial court, which has as its purpose the preservation of the point at issue for adjudication on appeal. Under modern rules of civil procedure, formal exceptions to court rulings or orders are unnecessary.

Exclusionary rule   This rule requires that when evidence has been obtained in violation of the privileges guaranteed by the United States Constitution, the evidence must be excluded at the trial. Evidence that is obtained by an unreasonable search and seizure is excluded from evidence under the Fourth Amendment to the U.S. Constitution, and this rule applies to the states.

Exculpatory circumstances   Exonerative facts; excusing evidence; facts tending to clear from a charge of fault or guilt.

Expert witness   A person who has acquired by special study, practice, and experience, peculiar skill and knowledge in relation to some particular science, art, or trade.

(2) A witness who, because of such special knowledge, is called to testify or give his or her opinion in cases depending on questions peculiar to such science, art, or trade.

Federal Rules of Evidence   Rules governing the admissibility of evidence at trials in federal courts and before United States Magistrate judges.

Former testimony   Testimony given by a witness at another hearing of the same or a different proceeding, or in a deposition taken in compliance with law in the course of the same or another proceeding, if the party against whom the testimony is now offered, or in a civil action or proceeding, a predecessor in interest, had an opportunity and similar motive to develop the testimony by direct, cross, or redirect examination. It is not excluded by the hearsay rule if the declarant is unavailable as a witness. Fed. R. Evid. 804(b)(1).

Free and voluntary rule   The confession of a person accused of crime is admissible against the accused only if freely and voluntarily made, without fear, duress, or compulsion in its inducement and with full knowledge of the nature and consequences of the confession.

Hearsay evidence   Statements offered by a witness, based upon what someone else has told him or her, and not upon personal knowledge or observation. Usually, such evidence is inadmissible, but exceptions are made, e.g., in questions of pedigree, custom, reputation, dying declarations, and statements made against the interest of the declarant. (2) A statement, other than one made by the declarant while testifying at the trial or hearing, offered in evidence to prove the truth of the matter asserted. Fed. R. Evid. 801(c).

Hearsay rule   Rule prohibiting the admission of hearsay evidence—evidence of a statement that was made other than by a witness while testifying at the hearing and that is offered to prove the truth of the matter stated.

Horizontal gaze nystagmus test   Horizontal gaze nystagmus is the inability of the eyes to maintain visual fixation as they are turned to the side. Nystagmus is a physiological phenomenon that is caused by, among other things, the ingestion of alcohol and is used to determine whether a person is intoxicated.

Hostile witness   A person who is called to give evidence and is unfriendly or inimical to the party whose attorney called him and is really allied with the opposing party. Such a person is subject to cross-examination by the party calling him or her.

Impeachment of witness   To prove that a witness has a bad reputation for truth and veracity and is therefore unworthy of belief.

Implied consent   Various state laws that provide that any person who operates a motorized vehicle in the state is deemed to have given his or her consent to a chemical test, e.g., of his or her blood, breath, urine or saliva, for the purpose of determining the alcoholic content of his or her blood, if committed while driving, or in any physical control of, a motor vehicle in the state while under the influence of intoxicating beverages.

Impoundment   Seizing and taking into custody of the law or a court, such as the police duty and responsibility to impound an automobile that has been abandoned, is illegally parked, or has been left without a driver when the driver has been arrested.

Incriminating circumstances   Facts or circumstances, collateral to the fact of the commission of a crime, that tend to show either that such a crime has been committed and/or that some particular person committed it.

Inference   A rational conclusion deduced from facts proved.

Judicial notice   The acceptance by the court of certain notorious facts without proof. (2) A judicially noticed adjudicative fact must be one not subject to reasonable dispute in that it is either (a) generally known within the territorial jurisdiction of the trial court, or (b) capable of accurate and ready determination by resort to sources whose accuracy cannot reasonably be questioned. Fed. R. Evid. 201(b).

Lay witness   Any witness that is not an expert. A lay witness simply must have the general capacity to testify, record, recollect, narrate, attest to, and affirm certain conditions and facts. Additionally, he or she must have the requisite level of mental capacity and emotional competency to outline in some logical and sensible sequence the facts, conditions, and events before the trier.

Leading question   An inquiry of a witness that by its form suggests the answer that the attorney would prefer. A question in which the substance of the correct answer is embedded within the question and suggests the answer. The type of question that is generally permissible on cross-examination.

Legal evidence   General term meaning all admissible evidence, both oral and documentary, that is of such a character that tends reasonably and substantially to prove the point, not to raise a mere suspicion or conjecture.

Material evidence   Evidence that goes to the substantial matters in dispute or has a legitimate and effective influence or bearing on the decision of the case. Evidence that may tend to prove or disprove a fact that is at issue in a case.

Materiality   Importance; relevance; capable of properly influencing the result of a lawsuit.

Motive   The purpose underlying a defendant's conduct; the reason a person forms a criminal intent prior to engaging in a criminal act.

Negative evidence   Testimony that an alleged fact does not exist; an absence of evidence.

Neutron activation analysis   A testing procedure that determines the presence and amount of certain trace chemical elements.

Oath　Various solemn affirmations, declarations or promises, made under a sense of responsibility to God, for the truth of what is stated or the faithful performance of what is undertaken.

Objection　A resistance or protest on legal grounds, e.g., to the admissibility of evidence, or to the entry of an order or judgment.

Opinion evidence　An inference or a conclusion, formed or entertained by a witness, as opposed to facts directly seen, heard, or perceived by him. Usually, a person's opinions are not competent testimony in a case unless the person has qualified as an expert witness.

Past recollection recorded　A memorandum or record concerning a matter about which a witness once had knowledge but now has insufficient recollection to enable him or her to testify fully and accurately, shown to have been made or adopted by the witness when the matter was fresh in his or her memory and to reflect that knowledge correctly, is not excluded by the hearsay rule, even though the declarant is available as a witness. If admitted, the memorandum or record may be read into evidence but may not itself be received as an exhibit unless offered by an adverse party. Fed. R. Evid. 803(5).

Pecuniary interest　A direct interest related to money in an action or case as would, for example, require a judge to disqualify him- or herself from sitting on a case if he or she owned stock in a corporate party.

Penal interest　Pertaining to or respecting punishment. A statement that tends to incriminate the speaker in a crime.

Plain view doctrine　A rule of law creating an exception to the requirement that police officers have a search warrant, when the police, while conducting themselves lawfully, e.g., while patrolling the streets or executing a search warrant for something else, observe incriminating evidence, and it is immediately apparent to the police that they have evidence of a crime. In such a situation, the evidence may be seized without a warrant if the officer physically occupies the place where the contraband is situated.

Polygraph examination　An electromechanical instrument that simultaneously records certain physiological changes in the human body, which are believed to be involuntarily caused by an examinee's conscious attempts to deceive an interrogator while responding to a carefully prepared set of questions.

Preponderance of the evidence　The greater weight of the evidence, in merit and in worth. (2) Sufficient evidence to overcome doubt or speculation. (3) Any evidence whose weight is greater than 50 percent.

Present memory revived　The act of a witness who consults his or her documents, memoranda, or books, to clarify his or her recollection the details of past events or transactions, concerning which he or she is testifying. The witness testifies from present memory.

Presumption   A conclusion or inference drawn from the proven existence of some fact or group of facts. A jury is not bound by a presumption and may reject the presumed fact.

Presumption of fact   Not the subject of a fixed rule, but merely natural presumptions, such as appear from common experience, that arise from particular circumstances of any case.

Presumption of law   An inference or deduction that, in the absence of direct evidence on the subject, the law requires to be drawn from the existence of certain established facts in civil case but a deduction that cannot be enforced in criminal cases.

Prima facie evidence   Proof of a fact or collection of facts that creates a presumption of the existence of other facts, or from which some conclusion may be legally drawn, but which presumption or conclusion may be discredited or overcome by other relevant proof.

Prior inconsistent statement   In evidence, prior statements made by the witness that contradict statements made on the witness stand may be introduced to impeach the witness after a foundation has been laid concerning where and when the inconsistent statement was uttered and an opportunity given to the witness to affirm or deny whether such prior statements were made.

Privileged communications   Statements made by one person to another when there is a necessary relation of trust and confidence between them, which the person receiving them cannot be legally compelled to disclose, e.g., the statements made by a husband to his wife, or a client to his or her attorney.

Proof   Establishing the truth of an allegation by evidence. (2) The evidence itself. The person claiming the affirmative of an allegation ordinarily has the necessity of proving it. (3) The affidavits made to support a claim or statement of fact, which is doubted or disputed or of which a person acting in a representative capacity requires evidence under oath.

Radar   Radio Detection and Ranging. Used in law enforcement to measure distance and speed of motor vehicles.

Real evidence   Evidence that has physical essence; evidence provided by the physical items themselves as opposed to descriptions of the evidence.

Rebuttal   Proof that is given by one party in a lawsuit to explain or disprove evidence produced by the other party.

Recross-examination   An examination of a witness by a cross-examiner subsequent to a redirect examination of the witness.

Redirect examination   An examination of a witness by the direct examiner following the cross-examination.

Rejoinder   The opportunity to introduce evidence contrary to that introduced by the prosecution during the rebuttal.

Relevancy   The connection between a fact tendered in evidence and the issue to be proved.

Relevant evidence   Evidence having any tendency to make the existence of any fact that is of consequence to the determination of the action more probable or less probable than it would be without the evidence. Fed. R. Evid. 401.

Search incident to arrest   A warrantless search that occurs following a lawful arrest. It includes a search of the person of the arrestee and the surrounding area under the potential dominion and control of the arrestee. Probable cause for a search is not required.

Scientific evidence admissibility test   Admissibility of scientific evidence rests on several considerations: whether a scientific theory or technique can or has been tested; whether the theory or technique has been subjected to peer review and publication; the known or potential rate of error and the existence and maintenance of standards controlling the technique's operation; whether the technique is generally accepted. A proponent of the scientific evidence has the burden of proving its relevancy as well as the scientific reliability by clear and convincing evidence.

Secondary evidence   Evidence that is inferior to primary or best evidence. It becomes admissible when the primary or best evidence of the fact in question has been lost, destroyed, or is inaccessible through no fault of the offering party.

Self-authentication   Instrument or document in which authenticity is taken as sufficiently established for purposes of admissibility without extrinsic evidence to that effect. Statutes frequently provide that certain classes of writings will be received in evidence "without further proof." Bank videotapes can be self-authenticating by their content and time and date stamp.

Self-defense   The protection of one's person and property from injury. A person may defend himself when attacked, repel force by force, and even commit homicide in resisting an attempted felony involving a risk of death or serious injury, e.g., murder, rape, robbery, burglary, and the like.

Self-incrimination   An act or declaration either as testimony at trial or prior to trial by which one implicates oneself in a crime.

Sequestration   Separating or setting apart; excluding witnesses from the courtroom except when testifying, to prevent one witness from being influenced deliberately or subconsciously by hearing what another witness says.

Spontaneous utterance   A statement relating to a startling event or condition made while the declarant was under the stress of excitement cause by the event or condition.

It is not excluded from evidence as hearsay, even though the declarant is available as a witness. Fed. R. Evid. 803(2).

Stipulation An agreement; a bargain, proviso, or condition, e.g., an agreement between opposing litigants that certain facts are true and are not in dispute. It is binding without consideration if it complies with an applicable statute or rule of court.

Sufficiency of the evidence In a criminal case, whether the evidence is such that a jury could logically have found that a defendant was guilty beyond a reasonable doubt or that an affirmative defense was properly proven.

Summaries The contents of voluminous writings, recordings, computer-generated data or photographs that cannot be conveniently examined in court may be presented in the form of a chart, summary, or calculation. The originals, or duplicates, shall be made available for examination or copying, or both, by other parties at a reasonable time and place. The court may order that they be produced in court. Fed. R. Evid. 1006.

Ultimate issue The questions that must finally be answered, such as the defendant's guilt in a criminal action.

Unfair prejudice A prejudgment, or bias, that interferes with a person's impartiality and sense of justice.

Uniform Rules of Evidence Prepared by the National Conference of Commissioners on Uniform State Laws, these are patterned after the Federal Rules and have consistent numbering with the Federal Rules. They are designed for adoption by legislatures of the states.

Waiver A positive act by which a legal right is relinquished.

Weight of evidence The balance or preponderance of evidence; the inclination of the greater amount of evidence, offered in trial, to support one side of the issue rather than the other.

Wiretapping A form of electronic eavesdropping in which, upon a court order, law enforcement officials surreptitiously listen to land and cell phone conversations, e-mail, text messages, and similar communications.

APPENDIX I

FEDERAL RULES OF EVIDENCE

As amended and effective through December 1, 2008
The Committee on the Judiciary
House of Representatives

ARTICLE I
GENERAL PROVISIONS

RULE 101. Scope
RULE 102. Purpose and Construction
RULE 103. Rulings on Evidence
   (a)   Effect of erroneous ruling
   (b)   Record of offer and ruling
   (c)   Hearing of jury
   (d)   Plain error
RULE 104. Preliminary Questions
   (a)   Questions of admissibility generally
   (b)   Relevancy conditioned on fact
   (c)   Hearing of jury
   (d)   Testimony by accused
   (e)   Weight and credibility
RULE 105. Limited Admissibility
RULE 106. Remainder of or Related Writings or Recorded Statements

ARTICLE II
JUDICIAL NOTICE

RULE 201. Judicial Notice of Adjudicative Facts
   (a)   Scope of rule
   (b)   Kinds of facts
   (c)   When discretionary
   (d)   When mandatory
   (e)   Opportunity to be heard
   (f)   Time of taking notice
   (g)   Instructing jury

ARTICLE III
PRESUMPTIONS IN CIVIL ACTIONS AND PROCEEDINGS

RULE 301. Presumptions in General in Civil Actions and Proceedings
RULE 302. Applicability of State Law in Civil Actions and Proceedings

ARTICLE IV
RELEVANCY AND ITS LIMITS

RULE 401. Definition of "Relevant Evidence"
RULE 402. Relevant Evidence Generally Admissible; Irrelevant Evidence Inadmissible
RULE 403. Exclusion of Relevant Evidence on Grounds of Prejudice, Confusion, or Waste of Time
RULE 404. Character Evidence not admissible to Prove Conduct; Exceptions; Other Crimes
   (a)   Character evidence generally
   (b)   Other crimes, wrongs, or acts
RULE 405. Methods of Proving Character
   (a)   Reputation or Opinion
   (b)   Specific Instances of Conduct
RULE 406. Habit; Routine Practice
RULE 407. Subsequent Remedial Measures
RULE 408. Compromise and Offers to Compromise
   (a)   Prohibited uses
   (b)   Premitted uses
RULE 409. Payment of Medical and Similar Expenses
RULE 410. Inadmissibility of Pleas, Plea Discussions, and Related Statements
RULE 411. Liability Insurance
RULE 412. Sex Offense Cases; Relevance of Alleged Victim's Past Sexual Behavior or Alleged Sexual Predisposition
   (a)   Evidence generally inadmissible
   (b)   Exceptions
   (c)   Procedure to determine admissibility
RULE 413. Evidence of Similar Crimes in Sexual Assault Cases
RULE 414. Evidence of Similar Sex Crimes in Child Molestation Cases
RULE 415. Evidence of Similar Acts in Civil Cases Concerning Sexual Assault or Child Molestation

ARTICLE V
PRIVILEGES

RULE 501. General rule
RULE 502. Attorney-Client Privilege and Work Product; Limitations on Waiver

ARTICLE VI
WITNESSES

RULE 601. General Rule of Competency
RULE 602. Lack of Personal Knowledge

RULE 603. Oath or Affirmation
RULE 604. Interpreters
RULE 605. Competency of Judge as Witness
RULE 606. Competency of Juror as Witness
    (a)   At the trial
    (b)   Inquiry into validity of verdict
           or indictment
RULE 607. Who May Impeach
RULE 608. Evidence of Character and Conduct of Witness
    (a)   Opinion and reputation evidence of character
    (b)   Specific instances of conduct
RULE 609. Impeachment by Evidence of Conviction of Crime
    (a)   General rule
    (b)   Time limit
    (c)   Effect of pardon, annulment, or certificate of rehabilitation
    (d)   Juvenile adjudications
    (e)   Pendency of appeal
RULE 610. Religious Beliefs or Opinions
RULE 611. Mode and Order of Interrogation and Presentation
    (a)   Control by court
    (b)   Scope of cross-examinations
    (c)   Leading questions
RULE 612. Writing Used to Refresh Memory
RULE 613. Prior Statements of Witnesses
    (a)   Examining witness concerning prior statement
    (b)   Extrinsic evidence of prior inconsistent statement of witness
RULE 614. Calling and Interrogation of Witness by Court
    (a)   Calling by court
    (b)   Interrogations by court
    (c)   Objections
RULE 615. Exclusions of Witnesses

ARTICLE VII
OPINIONS AND EXPERT
TESTIMONY

RULE 701. Opinion Testimony by Lay Witnesses
RULE 702. Testimony by Experts
RULE 703. Bases of Opinion Testimony by Experts
RULE 704. Opinion on Ultimate Issue
RULE 705. Disclosure of Facts or Data Underlying Expert Opinion
RULE 706. Court Appointed Experts
    (a)   Appointment
    (b)   Compensation
    (c)   Disclosure of appointment
    (d)   Parties' experts of own selection

ARTICLE VIII HEARSAY

RULE 801. Definitions
    (a)   Statement
    (b)   Declarant
    (c)   Hearsay
    (d)   Statements which are not hearsay
RULE 802. Hearsay Rule
RULE 803. Hearsay Exceptions; Availability of Declarant Immaterial
RULE 804. Hearsay Exceptions; Declarant Unavailable
    (a)   Definition of Unavailability
    (b)   Hearsay Exceptions
RULE 805. Hearsay Within Hearsay
RULE 806. Attacking and Supporting Credibility of Declarant
RULE 807. Residual Exception

ARTICLE IX
AUTHENTICATION AND
IDENTIFICATION

RULE 901. Requirement of Authentication or Identification
    (a)   General provision
    (b)   Illustrations
RULE 902. Self-authentication
RULE 903. Subscribing Witness' Testimony Unnecessary

ARTICLE X
CONTENTS OF WRITINGS,
RECORDINGS, AND PHOTOGRAPHS

RULE 1001. Definitions
RULE 1002. Requirement of Original
RULE 1003. Admissibility of Duplicates
RULE 1004. Admissibility of Other Evidence of Contents
RULE 1005. Public Records
RULE 1006. Summaries
RULE 1007. Testimony or Written Admission of a Party
RULE 1008. Functions of Court and Jury

ARTICLE XI
MISCELLANEOUS RULES

RULE 1101. Applicability of Rules
    (a)   Courts and judges
    (b)   Proceedings generally
    (c)   Rule of privilege
    (d)   Rules inapplicable
    (e)   Rules applicable in part
RULE 1102. Amendments
RULE 1103. Title

FEDERAL RULES OF EVIDENCE

Effective July 1, 1975, as amended to December 1, 2006

ARTICLE I: GENERAL PROVISIONS

RULE 101. Scope

These rules govern proceedings in the courts of the United States and before United States bankruptcy judges and United States magistrate judges, to the extent and with the exceptions stated in rule 1101.

(Amended, eff. Dec. 1993).

RULE 102. Purpose and Construction

These rules shall be construed to secure fairness in administration, elimination of unjustifiable expense and delay, and promotion of growth and development of the law of evidence to the end that the truth may be ascertained and proceedings justly determined.

RULE 103. Rulings on Evidence

(a) Effect of erroneous ruling. Error may not be predicated upon a ruling which admits or excludes evidence unless a substantial right of the party is affected, and

> **(1) Objection.** In case the ruling is one admitting evidence, a timely objection or motion to strike appears of record stating the specific ground of objection, if the specific ground was not apparent from the context; or

> **(2) Offer of proof.** In case the ruling is one excluding evidence, the substance of the evidence was made known to the court by offer or was apparent from the context within which questions were asked.

Once the court makes a definitive ruling on the record admitting or excluding evidence, either at or before trial, a party need not renew an objection or offer of proof to preserve a claim of error for appeal.

(b) Record of offer and ruling. The court may add any other or further statement which shows the character of the evidence, the form in which it was offered, the objection made, and the ruling thereon. It may direct the making of an offer in question and answer form.

(c) Hearing of jury. In jury cases, proceedings shall be conducted, to the extent practicable, so as to prevent inadmissible evidence from being suggested to the jury by any means, such as making statements or offers of proof or asking questions in the hearing of the jury.

(d) Plain error. Nothing in this rule precludes taking notice of plain errors affecting substantial rights although they were not brought to the attention of the court.

(As amended Apr. 17, 2000, eff. Dec. 1 2000.)

RULE 104. Preliminary Questions

(a) Questions of admissibility generally. Preliminary questions concerning the qualification of a person to be a witness, the existence of a privilege, or the admissibility of evidence shall be determined by the court, subject to the provisions of subdivision (b). In making its determination it is not bound by the rules of evidence except those with respect to privileges.

(b) Relevancy conditioned on fact. When the relevancy evidence depends upon the fulfillment of a condition of fact, the court shall admit it upon, or subject to, the introduction of evidence sufficient to support a finding of the fulfillment of the condition.

(c) Hearing of jury. Hearings on the admissibility of confessions shall in all cases be conducted out of the hearing of the jury. Hearings on other preliminary matters shall be so conducted when the interests of justice require, or when an accused is a witness and so requests.

(d) Testimony by accused. The accused does not, by testifying upon a preliminary matter, become subject to cross-examination as to other issues in the case.

(e) Weight and credibility. This rule does not limit the right of a party to introduce before the jury evidence relevant to weight or credibility.

(Amended, eff. 10-1-87)

RULE 105. Limited Admissibility

When evidence which is admissible as to one party or for one purpose but not admissible as to another party or for another purpose is admitted, the court, upon request, shall restrict the evidence to its proper scope and instruct the jury accordingly.

106. Remainder of or Related Writings or Recorded Statements

When a writing or recorded statement or part thereof is introduced by a party, an adverse party may require the introduction at that time of any other party or any other writing or recorded statement which ought in fairness to be considered contemporaneously with it.

(Amended, eff. 10-1-87)

ARTICLE II. JUDICIAL NOTICE

RULE 201. Judicial Notice of Adjudicative Facts

(a) Scope of rule. This rule governs only judicial notice of adjudicative facts.

(b) Kinds of facts. A judicially noticed fact must be one not subject to reasonable dispute in that it is either (1) generally known within the territorial jurisdiction of the trial court or (2) capable of accurate and ready determination by resort to sources whose accuracy cannot readily be questioned.

(c) When discretionary. A court may take judicial notice, whether requested or not.

(d) When mandatory. A court shall take judicial notice if requested by a party and supplied with the necessary information.

(e) Opportunity to be heard. A party is entitled upon timely request to an opportunity to be heard as to the propriety of taking judicial notice and the tenor of the matter noticed. In the absence of prior notification, the request may be made after judicial notice has been taken.

(f) Time of taking notice. Judicial notice may be taken at any stage of the proceeding.

(g) Instructing jury. In a civil action or proceeding, the court shall instruct the jury to accept as conclusive any fact judicially noticed. In a criminal case, the court shall instruct the jury that it may, but is not required to, accept as conclusive any fact judicially noticed.

ARTICLE III. PRESUMPTIONS IN CIVIL ACTIONS AND PROCEEDINGS

RULE 301. Presumptions in General in Civil Actions and Proceedings

In all civil actions and proceedings not otherwise provided for by Act of Congress or by these rules, a presumption imposes on the party against whom it is directed the burden of going forward with evidence to rebut or meet the presumption, but does not shift to such party the burden of proof in the sense of the risk of nonpersuasion, which remains throughout the trial upon the party on whom it was originally cast.

RULE 302. Applicability of State Law in Civil Actions and Proceedings

In civil actions and proceedings, the effect of a presumption respecting a fact which is an element of a claim or defense as to which State law supplies the rule of decision is determined in accordance with State law.

ARTICLE IV. RELEVANCY AND ITS LIMITS

RULE 401. Definition of "Relevant Evidence"

"Relevant evidence" means evidence having any tendency to make the existence of any fact that is of consequence to the determination of the action more probable or less probable than it would be without the evidence.

RULE 402. Relevant Evidence Generally Admissible; Irrelevant Evidence Inadmissible

All relevant evidence is admissible, except as otherwise provided by the Constitution of the United States, by Act of Congress, by these rules, or by other rules prescribed by the Supreme Court pursuant to statutory authority. Evidence which is not relevant is not admissible.

RULE 403. Exclusion of Relevant Evidence on Grounds of Prejudice, Confusion, or Waste of Time

Although relevant evidence may be excluded if its probative value is substantially outweighed by the danger of unfair prejudice, confusion of the issues, or misleading the jury, or by considerations of undue delay, waste of time, or needless presentation of cumulative service.

RULE 404. Character Evidence not Admissible to Prove Conduct; Exceptions; Other Crimes

(a) Character evidence generally. Evidence of a person's character or trait of character is not admissible for the purpose of proving action in conforming therewith on a particular occasion, except:

(1) **Character of accused.** In a criminal case, evidence of a pertinent trait of character offered by an accused, or by the prosecution to rebut the same, or if evidence of a trait of character of the alleged victim of the crime is offered by an accused and admitted under Rule 404 (a)(2), evidence of the same trait of character of the accused offered by the prosecution;

(2) **Character of victim.** In a criminal case, and subject to the limitations imposed by Rule 412, evidence of a pertinent trait of character of the alleged victim of the crime offered by an accused, or by the prosecution to rebut the same, or evidence of a character trait of peacefulness of the victim offered by the prosecution in a homicide case to rebut evidence that the victim was the first aggressor;

(3) **Character of witness.** Evidence of the character of witness, as provided in Rules 607, 608 and 609.

(b) Other crimes, wrongs, or acts. Evidence of other crimes, wrongs, or acts is not admissible to prove the character of a person in order to show action in conformity therewith. It may, however, be admissible for other purposes, such as proof of motive, opportunity, intent, preparation, plan, knowledge, identity, or absence of mistake or accident, provided that upon request by the accused, the prosecution in a criminal case shall provide reasonable notice in advance of trial, or during trial if the court excuses pretrial notice on good cause shown, of the general nature of any such evidence it intends to introduce at trial.

(Amended, eff. Dec. 1991; Apr 17, 2000, eff. Dec. 1 2000; eff. 12-1-06)

RULE 405. Methods of Proving Character

(a) Reputation or opinion. In all cases in which evidence of character or trait of character of a person is admissible, proof may be made by testimony as to reputation or by testimony in the form of an opinion. On cross-examination, inquiry is allowable into relevant instances of conduct.

(b) Specific instances of conduct. In cases in which character or a trait of character of a person is an essential element of a charge, claim, or defense, proof may also be made of specific instances of that person's conduct.

(Amended, eff. 10-1-87)

RULE 406. Habit; Routine Practice

Evidence of the habit of a person or of the routine practices of an organization, whether corroborated or not and regardless of the presence of eyewitnesses, is relevant to prove that the conduct of the person or organization on a particular occasion was in conformity with the habit or routine practice.

RULE 407. Subsequent Remedial Measures

When, after an injury or harm allegedly caused by an event, measures are taken that, if taken previously, would have made the injury or harm less likely to occur, evidence of the subsequent measures is not admissible to prove negligence, culpable conduct, a defect in a product, a defect in a product's design, or a need for a warning or instruction. This rule does not require the exclusion of evidence of subsequent measures when offered for another purpose, such as proving ownership, control, or feasibility of precautionary measures, if controverted, or impeachment.

(As amended, Apr. 11, 1997, eff. Dec. 1, 1997.)

RULE 408. Compromise and Offers to Compromise

(a) Prohibited uses. Evidence of the following is not admissible on behalf of any party, when offered to prove liability for, invalidity of, or amount of a claim that was disputed as to validity or amount, or to impeach through a prior inconsistent statement or contradiction:

(1) furnishing or offering or promising to furnish or offering or promising to accept a valuable consideration in compromising or attempting to compromise the claim; and

(2) conduct or statements made in compromise negotiations regaring the claim, except when offered in a criminal case and the negotiations related to a claim by a public office or agency in the exercise of regulatory, investigative, or enforcement authority.

(b) Permitted uses. This rule does not require exclusion if the evidence is offered for purposes not prohibited by subdivision (a). Examples of permissible purposes include proving a witness' bias or prejudice; negating a contention of undue delay and proving an effort to obstruct a criminal investigation or prosecution. (Eff. 12-1-06)

RULE 409. Payment of Medical and Similar Expenses

Evidence of furnishing or offering or promising to pay medical, hospital, or similar expenses occasioned by an injury is not admissible to prove liability for the injury.

RULE 410. Inadmissibility of Pleas, Plea Discussions, and Related Statements

Except as otherwise provided in this rule, evidence of the following is not, in any civil or criminal proceeding, admissible against the defendant who made the plea or was a participant in the plea discussions:

(1) a plea of guilty which was later withdrawn;

(2) a plea of nolo contendere;

(3) any statement made in the course of any proceedings under Rule 11 of the Federal Rules of Criminal Procedure or comparable state procedure regarding either of the foregoing pleas; or

(4) any statement made in the course of plea discussions with an attorney for the prosecuting authority which do not result in a plea of guilty or which result in a plea of guilty later withdrawn.

However, such a statement is admissible (i) in any proceeding wherein another statement made in the course of the same plea or plea discussions has been introduced and the statement ought in fairness be considered contemporaneously with it, or (ii) in a criminal proceeding for perjury or false statement if the statement was made by the defendant under oath, on the record and in the presence of counsel.

(Amended, 12-12-75; 4-30-79, eff. 12-1-80)

RULE 411. Liability Insurance

Evidence that a person was or was not insured against liability is not admissible upon the issue whether the person acted negligently or otherwise wrongfully. This rule does not require the exclusion of evidence of insurance against liability when offered for another purpose, such as proof of agency, ownership, or control, or bias or prejudice of witness.

(Amended, eff. 10-1-87)

RULE 412. Sex Offense Cases; Relevance of Alleged Victim's Past Sexual Behavior or Alleged Sexual Predisposition

(a) Evidence generally inadmissible. The following evidence is not admissible in any civil or criminal proceeding involving alleged sexual misconduct except as provided in subdivisions (b) and (c):

(1) Evidence offered to prove that any alleged victim engaged in other sexual behavior.

(2) Evidence offered to prove any alleged victim's sexual predisposition.

(b) Exceptions.

(1) In a criminal case, the following evidence is admissible, if otherwise admissible under these rules:

(A) evidence of specific instances of sexual behavior by the alleged victim offered to prove that a person other than the accused was the source of semen, injury, or other physical evidence;

(B) evidence of specific instances of sexual behavior by the alleged victim with respect to the person accused of the sexual misconduct offered by the accused to prove consent or by the prosecution; and

(C) evidence the exclusion of which would violate the constitutional rights of the defendant.

(2) In a civil case, evidence offered to prove the sexual behavior or sexual predisposition of any alleged victim is admissible if it is otherwise admissible under these rules and its probative value substantially outweighs the danger of harm to any victim and of unfair prejudice to any party. Evidence of an alleged victim's reputation is admissible only if it has been placed in controversy by the alleged victim.

(c) Procedure to determine admissibility.

(1) A party intending to offer evidence under subdivision (b) must—

(A) file a written motion at least 14 days before trial specifically describing the evidence and stating the purpose for which it is offered unless the court, for good cause requires a different time for filing or permits filing during trial; and

(B) serve the motion on all parties and notify the alleged victim or, when appropriate, the alleged victim's guardian or representative.

(2) Before admitting evidence under this rule the court must conduct a hearing in camera and afford the victim and parties a right to attend and be heard. The motion, related papers, and the record of the hearing must be sealed and remain under seal unless the court orders otherwise.

(As added Oct. 28, 1978, eff. Nov. 28, 1978' amended Nov. 18, 1988; Apr. 29, 1994, eff. Dec. 1 1994; Sept. 13, 1994, eff. Dec. 1, 1994.)

RULE 413. Evidence of Similar Crimes in Sexual Assault Cases

(a) In a criminal case in which the defendant is accused of an offense of sexual assault, evidence of the defendant's commission of another offense or offenses of sexual assault is admissible, and may be considered for its bearing on any matter to which it is relevant.

(b) In a case in which the Government intends to offer evidence under this rule, the attorney for the Government shall disclose the evidence to the defendant, including statements of witnesses or a summary of the substance of any testimony that is expected to be offered, at least fifteen days before the scheduled date of trial or at such later time as the court may allow for good cause.

(c) This rule shall not be construed to limit the admission or consideration of evidence under any other rule.

(d) For purposes of this rule and Rule 415, "offense of sexual assault" means a crime under Federal law or the law of a State (as defined in section 513 of title 18, United States Code) that involved—

(1) any conduct proscribed by chapter 109A of title 18, United States Code;

(2) contact, without consent, between any part of the defendant's body or an object and the genitals or anus of another person;

(3) contact, without consent, between the genitals or anus of the defendant and any part of another person's body;

(4) deriving sexual pleasure or gratification from the infliction of death, bodily injury, or physical pain on another person; or

(5) an attempt or conspiracy to engage in conduct described in paragraphs (1)–(4).

RULE 414. Evidence of Similar Crimes in Child Molestation Cases

(a) In a criminal case in which the defendant is accused of an offense of child molestation, evidence of the defendant's commission of another offense or offenses of child molestation is admissible, and may be considered for its bearing on any matter to which it is relevant.

(b) In a case in which the Government intends to offer evidence under this rule, the attorney for the Government shall disclose the evidence to the defendant, including statements of witnesses or a summary of the substance of any testimony that is expected to be offered, at least fifteen days before the scheduled date of trial or at such later time as the court may allow for good cause.

(c) This rule shall not be construed to limit the admission or consideration of evidence under any other rule.

(d) For purposes of this rule and Rule 415, "child" means a person below the age of fourteen, and "offense of child molestation" means a crime under Federal law or the law of a State (as defined in section 513 of title 18, United States Code) that involved—

(1) any conduct proscribed by chapter 109A of title 18, United States Code, that was committed in relation to a child;

(2) any conduct proscribed by chapter 110 of title 18, United States Code;

(3) contact between any part of the defendant's body or an object and the genitals or anus of a child;

(4) contact between the genitals or anus of the defendant and any part of the body of a child;

(5) deriving sexual pleasure or gratification from the infliction of death, bodily injury, or physical pain on a child; or

(6) an attempt or conspiracy to engage in conduct described in paragraphs (1)–(5).

(Added Sept. 13, 1994, eff. July 9, 1995.)

RULE 415. Evidence of Similar Acts in Civil Cases Concerning Sexual Assault or Child Molestation

(a) In a civil case in which a claim for damages or other relief is predicated on a party's alleged commission of conduct constituting an offense of sexual assault or child molestation, evidence of that party's commission of another offense or offenses of sexual assault or child molestation is admissible and may be considered as provided in Rule 413 and Rule 414 of these rules.

(b) A party who intends to offer evidence under this Rule shall disclose the evidence to the party against whom it will be offered, including statements of witnesses or a summary of the substance of any testimony that is expected to be offered, at least fifteen days before the scheduled date of trial or at such later time as the court may allow for good cause.

(c) This rule shall not be construed to limit the admission or consideration of evidence under any other rule.

(Added Sept. 13, 1994, eff. July 9, 1995.)

ARTICLE V. PRIVILEGES

RULE 501. General Rule

Except as otherwise required by the Constitution of the United States or provided by Act of Congress or in rules prescribed by the Supreme Court pursuant to statutory authority, the privilege of a witness, person, government, State, or political subdivision thereof shall be governed by the principles of the common law as they may be interpreted by the courts of the United States in the light of reason and experience. However, in civil actions and proceedings, with respect to an element of a claim or defense as to which State law supplies the rule of decision, the privilege of a witness, person, government, State, or political subdivision thereof shall be determined in accordance with State law.

RULE 502. Attorney-Client Privilege and Work Product; Limitations on Waiver

The following provisions apply, in the circumstances set out, to disclosure of a communication or information covered by the attorney-client privilege or work-product protection.

(a) Disclosure made in a Federal proceeding or to a Federal office or agency; scope of a waiver.—When the disclosure is made in a Federal proceeding or to a Federal office or agency and waives the attorney-client privilege or work-product rotection, the waiver extends to an undisclosed communication or information in a Federal or State proceeding only if:

(1) the waiver is intentional;

(2) the disclosed and undisclosed communications or information concern the same subject matter; and

(3) they ought in fairness to be considered together.

(b) Inadvertent disclosure.—When made in a Federal proceeding or to a Federal office or agency, the disclosure does not operate as a waiver in a Federal or State proceeding if:

(1) the disclosure is inadvertent;

(2) the holder of the privilege or protection took reasonable steps to prevent disclosure; and

(3) the holder promptly took reasonable steps to rectify the error, including (if applicable) following Federal Rule of Civil Procedure 26(b)(5)(B).

(c) Disclosure made in a State proceeding.—When the disclosure is made in a State proceeding and is not the subject of a State-court order concerning waiver, the disclosure does not operate as a waiver in a Federal proceeding if the disclosure:

(1) would not be a waiver under this rule if it had been made in a Federal proceeding; or

(2) is not a waiver under the law of the State where the disclosure occured.

(d) Controlling effect of a court order.— A Federal court may order that the privilege or protection is not waived by disclosure connected with the litigation pending before the court—in which event the disclosure is also not a waiver in any other

Federal or State proceeding.

(e) Controlling effect of a party agreement.—An agreement on the effect of disclosure in a Federal proceeding is binding only on the parties to the agreement, unless it is incorporated into a court order.

(f) Controlling effect of this rule.— Notwithstanding Rules 101 and 1101, this rule applies to State proceedings and to Federal court-annexed and Federal court-mandated arbitration proceedings, in the circumstances set out in the rule. And notwithstanding Rule 501, this rule applies even if State law provides the rule of decision.

(g) Definitions.—In this rule:

(1) "attorney-client privilege" means the protection that applicable law provides for confidential attorney-client communications; and

(2) "work-product protection" means the protection that applicable law provides for tangible material (or its intangible equivalent) prepared in anticipation of litigation or for trial.

(As added Sept. 19, 2008.)

ARTICLE VI. WITNESS

RULE 601. General Rule of Competency

Every person is competent to be a witness except as otherwise provided in these rules. However, in civil actions and proceedings, with respect to an element of a claim or defense as to which State law supplies the rule of decision, the competency of a witness shall be determined in accordance with State law.

RULE 602. Lack of Personal Knowledge

A witness may not testify to a matter unless evidence is introduced sufficient to support a finding that the witness has personal knowledge of the matter. Evidence to prove personal knowledge may, but need not, consist of the witness' own testimony. This rule is subject to the provisions of rule 703, relating to opinion testimony by expert witnesses.

(Amended, eff. 10-1-87; 11-1-88)

RULE 603. Oath or Affirmation

Before testifying, every witness shall be required to declare that the witness will testify truthfully, by oath or affirmation administered in a form calculated to awaken the witness' conscience and impress the witness' mind with the duty to do so.

(Amended, eff. 10-1-87)

RULE 604. Interpreters

An interpreter is subject to the provisions of these rules relating to qualification as an expert and the administration of an oath or affirmation to make a true translation.

(Amended, eff. 10-1-87)

RULE 605. Competency of Judge as Witness

The judge presiding at the trial may not testify in that trial as a witness. No objection need be made in order to preserve the point.

RULE 606. Competency of Juror as Witness

(a) At the trial. A member of the jury may not testify as a witness before that jury in the trial of the case in which the juror is sitting. If the juror is called so to testify, the opposing party shall be afforded an opportunity to object out of the presence of the jury.

(b) Inquiry into validity of verdict or indictment. Upon an inquiry into the validity of a verdict or indictment, a juror may not testify as to any matter or statement occurring during the course of the jury's deliberations or the effect of anything upon that or any other juror's mind or emotions as influencing the juror to assent to or dissent from the verdict or indictment or concerning the juror's mental processes in connection therewith. But a juror may testify about (1) whether extraneous prejudicial information was improperly brought to the jury's attention, (2) whether any outside influence was improperly brought to bear upon any juror or whether there was a mistake in entering the verdict onto the verdict form. A juror's affidavit or evidence of any statement by the juror may not be received on a matter about which the juror would be precluded from testifying.

(Amended, eff. 12-12-75; 10-1-87; eff. 12-1-06)

RULE 607. Who May Impeach

The credibility of a witness may be attacked by any party, including the party calling the witness.

(Amended, eff. 10-1-87)

RULE 608. Evidence of Character and Conduct of Witness

(a) Opinion and reputation evidence of character. The credibility of a witness may be attacked or supported by evidence in the form of opinion or reputation, but subject to these limitations: (1) the evidence may refer only to character for truthfulness or untruthfulness, and (2) evidence of truthful character is admissible only after the character of the witness for truthfulness has been attacked by opinion or reputation evidence or otherwise.

(b) Specific instances of conduct. Specific instances of the conduct of a witness, for the purpose of attacking or supporting the witness' credibility, other than conviction of crime as provided in rule 609, may not be proved by extrinsic evidence. They may, however, in the discretion of the court, if probative of truthfulness or untruthfulness, be inquired into on cross-examination of the witness (1) concerning the witness' character for truthfulness or untruthfulness, or (2) concerning the character for truthfulness or untruthfulness of another witness as to which character the witness being cross-examined has testified.

The giving of testimony, whether by an accused or by any other witness, does not operate as a waiver of the accused's or the witness' privilege against self-incrimination when examined with respect to matters which relate only to character for truthfulness.

(Amended, eff. 3-27-03; 12-1-03)

RULE 609. Impeachment by Evidence of Conviction of Crime

(a) General rule. For the purpose of attacking the character for truthfulness of a witness, (1) evidence that a witness other than an accused has been convicted of a crime shall be admitted, subject to Rule 403, if the crime was punishable by death or imprisonment in excess of one year under the law under which the witness was convicted, and evidence that an accused has been convicted of such a crime shall be admitted if the court determines that the probative value of admitting this evidence outweighs its prejudicial effect to the accused; and (2) evidence that any witness has been convicted of a crime shall be admitted regardless of the punishment, if it can be determined that establishing the elements of the crime required proof of admission of an act of dishonesty or false statement by the witness.

(b) Time limit. Evidence of a conviction under this rule is not admissible if a period of more than ten years has elapsed since the date of the conviction or of the release of the witness from the confinement imposed for that conviction, whichever is the later date, unless the court determined, in the interests of justice, that the probative value of the conviction supported by specific facts and circumstances substantially outweighs its prejudicial effect.

However, evidence of a conviction more than 10 years old as calculated herein, is not admissible unless the proponent gives to the adverse party sufficient advance written notice of intent to use such evidence to provide the adverse party with a fair opportunity to contest the use of such evidence.

(c) Effect of pardon, annulment, or certificate of rehabilitation. Evidence of a conviction is not admissible under this rule if (1) the conviction has been the subject of a pardon, annulment, certificate of rehabilitation, or other equivalent procedure based on a finding of the rehabilitation of the person convicted, and that person has not been convicted of a subsequent crime which was punishable by death or imprisonment in excess of one year, or (2) the conviction has been the subject of a pardon, annulment or other equivalent procedure based on a finding of innocence.

(d) Juvenile adjudications. Evidence of juvenile adjudications is generally not admissible under this rule. The court may, however, in a criminal case allow evidence of a juvenile adjudication of a witness other than the accused if conviction of the offense would be admissible to attack the credibility of an adult and the court is satisfied that admission in evidence is necessary for a fair determination of the issue of guilt or innocence.

(e) Pendency of appeal. The pendency of an appeal therefrom does not render evidence of a conviction inadmissible. Evidence of the pendency of an appeal is admissible.

(Eff. 12-1-06)

RULE 610. Religious Beliefs or Opinions

Evidence of the beliefs or opinions of a witness on matters of religion is not admissible for the purpose of showing that by reason of their nature the witness' credibility is impaired or enhanced.

(Amended, eff. 10-1-87)

RULE 611. Mode and Order of Interrogation and Presentation

(a) Control by court. The Court shall exercise reasonable control over the mode and order of interrogating witnesses and presenting evidence so as to (1) make the interrogation and presentation effective for the ascertainment of the truth, (2) avoid needless consumption of time and, (3) protect witnesses from harassment or undue embarrassment.

(b) Scope of cross-examination. Cross-examination should be limited to the subject matter of the direct examination and matters affecting the credibility of the witness. The court may, in the exercise of discretion, permit inquiry into additional matters as if on direct examination.

(c) Leading questions. Leading questions should not be used on the direct examination of a witness except as may be necessary to develop the witness' testimony. Ordinarily leading questions should be permitted on cross-examination. When a party calls a hostile witness, an adverse party, or a witness identified with an adverse party, interrogation may be by leading questions.

(Amended, eff. 10-1-87)

RULE 612. Writing Used to Refresh Memory

Except as otherwise provided in criminal proceedings by section 3500 of title 18, United States Code, if a witness uses a writing to refresh memory for the purpose of testifying, either—

(1) while testifying, or

(2) before testifying, if the court in its discretion determines it is necessary in the interests of justice,

an adverse party is entitled to have the writing produced at the hearing, to inspect it, to cross-examine the witness thereon, and to introduce in evidence those portions which relate to the testimony of the witness. If it is claimed that the writing contains matters not related to the subject matter of the testimony the court shall examine the writing in camera, excise any portions not so related, and order delivery of the remainder to the party entitled thereto. Any portion withheld over objections shall be preserved and made available to the appellate court in the event of an appeal. If a writing is not produced or delivered pursuant to order under this rule, the court shall make any order justice requires, except that in criminal cases when the prosecution elects not to comply, the order shall be one striking the testimony or, if the court in its discretion determines that the interests of justice so require, declaring a mistrial.

(Amended, eff. 10-1-87)

RULE 613. Prior Statements of Witnesses

(a) Examining witness concerning prior statement. In examining a witness concerning a prior statement made by the witness, whether written or not, the statement need not be shown nor its contents disclosed to the witness at that time, but on request the same shall be shown or disclosed to opposing counsel.

(b) Extrinsic evidence of prior inconsistent statement of witness. Extrinsic evidence of a prior inconsistent statement by a witness is not admissible unless the witness is afforded an opportunity to explain or deny the same and the opposite party is afforded an opportunity to interrogate the witness thereon, or the interests of justice otherwise require. This provision does not apply to admissions of a party-opponent as defined in rule 801(d)(2).

(Amended, eff. 10-1-87; 11-1-88)

RULE 614. Calling and Interrogation of Witnesses by Court

(a) Calling by court. The court may, on its own motion or at the suggestion of a party, call witnesses, and all parties are entitled to cross-examine witnesses thus called.

(b) Interrogations by court. The court may interrogate witnesses, whether called by itself or by a party.

(c) Objections. Objections to the calling of witnesses by the court or to interrogation by it may be made at the time or at the next available opportunity when the jury is not present.

At the request of a party the court shall order witnesses excluded so that they cannot hear the testimony of other witnesses, and it may make the order of its own motion. This rule does not authorize exclusion of (1) a party who is a natural person, or (2) an officer or employee of a party which is not a natural person designated as its representative by its attorney, or (3) a person whose presence is shown by a party to be essential to the presentation of the party's cause, or (4) a person authorized by statute to be present.

RULE 615. Exclusion of Witnesses

At the request of a party the court shall order witnesses excluded so that they cannot hear the testimony of other witnesses, and it may make the order of its own motion. This rule does not authorize exclusion of (1) a party who is a natural person, or (2) an officer or employee of a party which is not a natural person designated as its representative by its attorney, or (3) a person whose presence is shown by a party to be essential to the presentation of the party's cause, or (4) a person authorized by statute to be present.

(Amended, eff. 4-24-98; 12-1-98)

ARTICLE VII. OPINIONS AND EXPERT TESTIMONY

RULE 701. Opinion Testimony by Lay Witnesses

If the witness is not testifying as an expert, the witness' testimony in the form of opinions or inferences is limited to those opinions or inferences which are (a) rationally based on the perception of the witness and (b) helpful to a clear understanding of the witness' testimony or the determination of a fact in issue, and (c) not based on scientific, technical, or other specialized knowledge within the scope of Rule 702.

(Amended, eff. 10-1-87; Apr. 17, 2000, eff. Dec. 1, 2000.)

RULE 702. Testimony by Experts

If scientific, technical, or other specialized knowledge can assist the trier of fact to understand the evidence or to determine a fact in issue, a witness qualified as an expert by knowledge, skill, experience, training, or education, may testify thereto in the form of an opinion or otherwise, if (1) the testimony is based upon sufficient facts or data, (2) the testimony is the product of reliable principles and methods, and (3) the witness has applied the principles and methods reliably to the facts of the case.

(As amended, Apr. 17, 2000, eff. Dec. 1, 2000.)

RULE 703. Bases of Opinion Testimony by Experts

The facts or data in the particular case upon which an expert bases an opinion or inference may be those perceived by or made known to the expert at or before the hearing. If of a type reasonably relied upon by experts in the particular field in forming opinions or inferences upon the subject, the facts or data need not be admissible in evidence in order for the opinion or inference to be admitted. Facts or data that are otherwise inadmissible shall not be disclosed to the jury by the proponent of the opinion or the inference unless the court determines that their probative value in assisting the jury to evaluate the expert's opinion substantially outweighs their prejudicial effect.

(Amended, eff. 10-1-87; As amended, Apr. 17, 2000, eff. Dec. 1, 2000.)

RULE 704. Opinion on Ultimate Issue

(a) Except as provided in subdivision (b), testimony in the form of an opinion or inference otherwise admissible is not objectionable because it embraces an ultimate issue to be decided by the trier of fact.

(b) No expert witness testifying with respect to the mental state or condition of a defendant in a criminal case may state an opinion or inference as to whether the defendant did or did not have the mental state or condition constituting an element of the crime charged or of a defense thereto. Such ultimate issues are matters for the trier of fact alone.

(Amended, eff. 10-12-84)

RULE 705. Disclosure of Facts or Data Underlying Expert Opinion

The expert may testify in terms of opinion or inference and give reasons therefor without first testifying to the underlying facts or data, unless the court requires otherwise. The expert may in any event be required to disclose the underlying facts or data on cross-examination.

(Amended, eff. 12-1-93)

RULE 706. Court Appointed Experts

(a) Appointment. The court may on its own motion or on the motion of any party enter an order to show cause why expert witnesses should not be appointed, and may request the parties to submit nominations. The court may appoint any expert witnesses agreed upon by the parties, and may appoint expert witnesses of its own selection. An expert witness shall not be appointed by the court unless the witness consents to act. A witness so appointed shall be informed of the witness' duties by the court in writing, a copy of which shall be filed with the clerk, or at a conference in which the parties shall have opportunity to participate. A witness so appointed shall advise the parties of the witness' findings, if any; the witness' deposition may be taken by any party; and the witness may be called to testify by the court or any party. The witness shall be subject to cross-examination by each party, including a party calling the witness.

(b) Compensation. Expert witnesses so appointed are entitled to reasonable compensation in whatever sum the court may allow. The compensation thus fixed is payable from funds which may be provided by law in criminal cases and civil actions and proceedings involving just compensation under the fifth amendment. In other civil actions and proceedings the compensation shall be paid by the parties in such proportion and at such time as the court directs, and thereafter charged in like manner as other costs.

(c) Disclosure of appointment. In the exercise of its discretion, the court may authorize disclosure to the jury of the fact that the court appointed the expert witness.

(d) Parties' experts of own selection. Nothing in this rule limits the parties in calling expert witnesses of their own selection.

(Amended, eff. 10-1-87)

ARTICLE VIII. HEARSAY

RULE 801. Definitions

The following definitions apply under this article:

(a) Statement. A "statement" is (1) an oral or written assertion or (2) non-verbal conduct of a person, if it is intended by the person as an assertion.

(b) Declarant. A "declarant" is a person who makes a statement.

(c) Hearsay. "Hearsay" is a statement, other than one made by the declarant while testifying at the trial or hearing, offered in evidence to prove the truth of the matter asserted.

(d) Statements which are not hearsay. A statement is not hearsay if—

(1) Prior statement by witness. The declarant testifies at trial or hearing and is subject to cross-examination concerning the statement, and the statement is (A) inconsistent with the declarant's testimony, and was given under oath subject to the penalty of perjury at a trial hearing, or other proceeding, or in a deposition, or (B) consistent with the declarant's testimony and is offered to rebut an express or implied charge against the declarant of recent fabrication or improper influence or motive, or (C) one of identification of a person made after perceiving the person; or

(2) Admission by party-opponent. The statement is offered against a party and is (A) the party's own statement, in either an individual or a representative capacity or (B) a statement of which the party has manifested an adoption or belief in its truth, or (C) a statement by a person authorized by the party to make a statement concerning the subject, or (D) a statement by the party's agent or servant concerning a matter within the scope of the agency or employment, made during the existence of the relationship, or (E) a statement by a coconspirator of a party during the course and in furtherance of the conspiracy. The contents of the statement shall be considered but are not alone sufficient to establish the declarant's authority under subdivision (C), the agency or employment relationship and scope thereof under subdivision (D), or the existence of the conspiracy and the party against whom the statement is offered under subdivision (E).

(Amended, eff. 10-31-75; 10-1-87; Apr. 11, 1997, eff. Dec. 1, 1997.)

RULE 802. Hearsay Rule

Hearsay is not admissible except as provided by these rules or by other rules prescribed by the Supreme Court pursuant to statutory authority or by Act of Congress.

RULE 803. Hearsay Exceptions; Availability of Declarant Immaterial

The following are not excluded by the hearsay rule, even though the declarant is available as a witness:

(1) Present sense impression. A statement describing or explaining an event or condition made while the declarant was perceiving the event or condition, or immediately thereafter.

(2) Excited utterance. A statement relating to a startling event or condition made while the declarant was under the stress of excitement caused by the event or condition.

(3) Then existing, mental, emotional, or physical condition. Statement of the declarant's then existing state of mind, emotion, sensation, or physical condition (such as intent, plan, motive, design, mental feeling, pain, and bodily health), but not including a statement of memory or belief to prove the fact remembered or believed unless it relates to the execution, revocation, identification, or terms of declarant's will.

(4) Statements for purposes of medical diagnosis or treatment. Statements made for purposes of medical diagnosis or treatment and describing medical history, or past or present symptoms, pain, or sensations, or the inception or general character of the cause or external source thereof insofar as reasonably pertinent to diagnosis or treatment.

(5) Recorded recollection. A memorandum or record concerning a matter about which a witness once had knowledge but now has insufficient recollection to enable the witness to testify fully and accurately, shown to have been made or adopted by the witness when the matter was fresh in the witness' memory and to reflect that knowledge correctly. If admitted, the memorandum or record may be read into evidence but may not itself be received as an exhibit unless offered by an adverse party.

(6) Records of regularly conducted activity. A memorandum, report, record, or data compilation, in any form, of acts, events, conditions, opinions, or diagnoses, made at or near the time by, or from information transmitted by, a person with knowledge, if kept in the course of a regularly conducted business activity, and if it was the regular practice of that business activity to make the memorandum, report, record, or data compilation, all as shown by the testimony of the custodian or other qualified witness, or by certification that complies with Rule 902 (11), Rule 902 (12), or a statute permitting certification, unless the source of information or the method or circumstances of preparation indicate lack of trustworthiness. The term "business" as used in this paragraph includes business, institution, association, profession, occupation, and calling of every kind, whether or not conducted for profit.

(7) Absence of entry in records kept in accordance with the provisions of paragraph (6). Evidence that a matter is not included in the memoranda, reports, records, or data compilations, in any form, kept in accordance with the provisions of paragraph (6) to prove nonoccurrence or nonexistence

of the matter, if the matter was of a kind of which a memorandum, report, record, or data compilation was regularly made and preserved, unless the sources of information or other circumstances indicate lack of trustworthiness.

(8) Public records and reports. Records, reports, statements, or data compilations, in any form, of public offices or agencies, setting forth (A) the activities of the office or agency, or (B) matters observed pursuant to duty imposed by law as to which matters there was a duty to report, excluding, however, in criminal cases matters observed by police officers and other law enforcement personnel, or (C) in civil actions and proceedings and against the government in criminal cases, factual findings resulting from an investigation made pursuant to authority granted by law, unless the sources of information or other circumstances indicate lack of trustworthiness.

(9) Records of vital statistics. Records or data compilations, in any form, of births, fetal deaths, deaths, or marriages, if the report thereof was made to a public office pursuant to requirements of law.

(10) Absence of public record or entry. To prove the absence of a record, report, statement, or data compilation, in any form, or the nonoccurrence or nonexistence of a matter of which a record, report, statement, or data compilation, in any form, was regularly made and preserved by a public office or agency, evidence in the form of a certification in accordance with Rule 902, or testimony, that diligent search failed to disclose the record, report, statement, or data compilation, or entry.

(11) Records of religious organizations. Statements of births, marriages, divorces, deaths, legitimacy, ancestry, relationship by blood or marriage, or other similar facts of personal or family history, contained in a regularly kept record of a religious organization.

(12) Marriage, baptismal, and similar certificates. Statements of fact contained in a certificate that the maker performed a marriage or other ceremony or administered a sacrament, made by a clergyman, public official, or other person authorized by the rules or practices of a religious organization or by law to perform the act certified, and purporting to have been issued at the time of the act or within a reasonable time thereafter.

(13) Family records. Statements of fact concerning personal or family history contained in family Bibles, genealogies, charts, engravings on rings, inscriptions on family portraits, engravings on urns, crypts, or tombstones, or the like.

(14) Records of documents affecting an interest in property. The record of a document purporting to establish or affect an interest in property, as proof of the content of the original document and its execution and delivery by each person by whom it purports to have been executed, if the record is a record of a public office and an applicable statute authorizes the recording of documents of that kind in that office.

(15) Statements in documents affecting an interest in property. A statement contained in a document purporting to establish or affect an interest in property if the matter stated was relevant to the purpose of the document, unless dealings made with the property since the document was made have been inconsistent with the truth of the statement or the purport of the document.

(16) Statements in ancient documents. Statements in a document in existence twenty years or more the authenticity of which is established.

(17) Market reports, commercial publications. Market quotations, tabulations, lists, directories, or other published compilations, generally used and relied upon by the public or by persons in particular occupations.

(18) Learned Treatises. To the extent called to the attention of an expert witness upon cross-examination or relied upon by the expert witness in direct examination, statements contained in published treatises, periodicals, or pamphlets on a subject of history, medicine, or other science or art, established as a reliable authority by the testimony or admission of the witness or by other expert testimony or by judicial notice. If admitted, the statements may be read into evidence but may not be received as exhibits.

(19) Reputation concerning personal or family history. Reputation among members of a person's family by blood, adoption, or marriage or among a person's associates, or in the community, concerning a person's birth, adoption, marriage, divorce, death, legitimacy, relationship by blood, adoption, or marriage, ancestry, or other similar fact of personal or family history.

(20) Reputation concerning boundaries or general history. Reputation in a community, arising before the controversy, as to boundaries of or customs affecting lands in the community, and reputation as to events of general history important to the community or State or nation in which located.

(21) Reputation as to character. Reputation of a person's character among associates or in the community.

(22) Judgment of previous conviction. Evidence of a final judgment, entered after a trial or upon a plea of guilty (but not upon a plea of nolo contendere), adjudging a person guilty of a crime punishable by death or imprisonment in excess of one year, to prove any fact essential to sustain the judgment, but not including, when offered by the Government in a criminal prosecution for purposes other than impeachment, judgments against persons other than the accused. The pendency of an appeal may be shown but does not affect admissibility.

(23) Judgment as to personal, family, or general history, or boundaries. Judgments as proof of matters of personal family, or general history, or boundaries, essential to the judgment, if the same would be provable by evidence of reputation.

(24) [Other exceptions.] [Transferred to Rule 807]

(Amended, eff. 12-12-75; 10-1-87; Apr. 11, 1997, eff. Dec. 1, 1997; Apr. 17, 2000, eff. Dec. 1, 2000)

RULE 804. Hearsay Exceptions: Declarant Unavailable

(a) Definition of unavailability. "Unavailability as a witness" includes situations in which the declarant—

(1) is exempted by ruling of the court on the ground of privilege from testifying concerning the subject matter of the declarant's statement; or

(2) persists in refusing to testify concerning the subject matter of the declarant's statement despite an order of the court to do so; or

(3) testifies to a lack of memory of the subject matter of the declarant's statement; or

(4) is unable to be present or to testify at the hearing because of death or then existing physical or mental illness or infirmity; or

(5) is absent from the hearing and the proponent of a statement has been unable to procure the declarant's attendance (or in the case of a hearsay exception under subdivision (b)(2), (3), or (4), the declarant's attendance or testimony) by process or other reasonable means.

A declarant is not unavailable as a witness if exemption, refusal, claim of lack of memory, inability, or absence is due to the procurement or wrongdoing of the proponent of a statement for the purpose of preventing the witness from attending or testifying.

(b) Hearsay exceptions.

The following are not excluded by the hearsay rule if the declarant is unavailable as a witness:

(1) Former testimony. Testimony given as a witness at another hearing of the same or a different proceeding, or in a deposition taken in compliance with law in the course of the same or another proceeding, if the party against whom the testimony is now offered, or, in a civil action or proceeding, a predecessor in interest, had an opportunity and similar motive to develop the testimony by direct, cross, or redirect examination.

(2) Statement under belief of impending death. In a prosecution for homicide or in a civil action or proceeding, a statement made by a declarant while believing that the declarant's death was imminent, concerning the cause or circumstances of what the declarant believed to be impending death.

(3) Statement against interest. A statement which was at the time of its making so far contrary to the declarant's pecuniary or proprietary interest, or so far tended to subject the declarant to civil or criminal liability, or to render invalid a claim by the declarant against another, that a reasonable person in the declarant's position would not have made the statement unless believing it to be true. A statement tending to expose the declarant to criminal liability and offered to exculpate the accused is not admissible unless corroborating circumstances clearly indicate the trustworthiness of the statement.

(4) Statement of personal or family history. (A) A statement concerning the declarant's own birth, adoption, marriage, divorce, legitimacy, relationship by blood, adoption, or marriage, ancestry, or other similar fact of personal or family history, even though declarant had no means of acquiring personal knowledge of the matter stated; or (B) a statement concerning the foregoing matters, and death also, of another person, if the declarant was related to the other by blood, adoption, or marriage or was so intimately associated with the other's family as to be likely to have accurate information concerning the matter declared.

(5) [Other exceptions.] [Transferred to Rule 807]

(6) Forfeiture by wrongdoing. A statement offered against a party that has engaged or acquiesced in wrongdoing that was intended to, and did, procure the unavailability of the declarant as a witness.

(As amended Dec. 12, 1975; Mar. 2, 1987, eff. Oct. 1, 1987; Nov. 18, 1988; Apr. 11, 1997, eff. Dec. 1, 1997.)

RULE 805. Hearsay Within Hearsay

Hearsay included within hearsay is not excluded under the hearsay rule if each part of the combined statements conforms with an exception to the hearsay rule provided in these rules.

RULE 806. Attacking and Supporting Credibility of Declarant

When a hearsay statement, or a statement defined in Rule 801(d)(2)(C), (D), or (E) , has been admitted in evidence, the credibility of the declarant may be attacked, and if attacked may be supported, by any evidence which would be admissible for those purposes if declarant had testified as a witness. Evidence of a statement or conduct by the declarant at any time, inconsistent with the declarant's hearsay statement, is not subject to any requirement that the declarant may have been afforded an opportunity to deny or explain. If the party against whom a hearsay statement has been admitted calls the declarant as a witness, the party is entitled to examine the declarant on the statement as if under cross-examination.

(Jan. 2, 1975, P.L. 93-595, A4 1, 88 Stat. 1943; Mar. 2, 1987, eff. Oct. 1, 1987; Apr. 11, 1997, eff. Dec. 1, 1997.)

RULE 807. Residual Exceptions

A statement not specifically covered by Rule 803 or Rule 804 but having equivalent circumstantial guarantees of trustworthiness, is not excluded by the hearsay rule, if the court determines that (A) the statement is offered as evidence of a material fact; (B) the statement is more probative on the point for which it is offered than any other evidence which the proponent can procure through reasonable efforts; and (C) the general purposes of these rules and the interests of justice will best be served by admission of the statement into evidence. However, a statement may not be admitted under this exception unless the proponent of it makes known to the adverse party sufficiently in advance of the trial or hearing to provide the adverse party with a fair opportunity to prepare to meet it, the proponent's intention to offer the statement and the particulars of it, including the name and address of the declarant.

(Added Apr. 11, 1997, eff. Dec. 1, 1997.)

ARTICLE IX. AUTHENTICATION AND IDENTIFICATION

RULE 901. Requirement of Authentication or Identification

(a) General provision. The requirement of authentication or identification as a condition precedent to admissibility is satisfied by evidence sufficient to support a finding that the matter in question is what its proponent claims.

(b) Illustrations. By way of illustration only, and not by way of limitation, the following are examples of authentication or identification conforming with the requirements of this rule:

(1) Testimony of witness with knowledge. Testimony that a matter is what it is claimed to be.

(2) Nonexpert opinion on handwriting. Nonexpert opinion as to the genuineness of handwriting, based upon familiarity not acquired for purposes of the litigation.

(3) Comparison by trier or expert witness. Comparison by the trier of fact or by expert witnesses with specimens which have been authenticated.

(4) Distinctive characteristics and the like. Appearance, contents, substance, internal patterns, or other distinctive characteristics, taken in conjunction with circumstances.

(5) Voice Identification. Identification of a voice, whether heard firsthand or through mechanical or electronic transmission or recording, by opinion based upon hearing the voice at any time under circumstances connecting it with the alleged speaker.

(6) Telephone conversations. Telephone conversations, by evidence that a call was made to the number assigned at the time by the telephone company to a particular person or business, if (A) in the case of a person, circumstances, including self-identification, show the person answering to be the one called, or (B) in the case of a business, the call was made to a place of business and the conversation related to business reasonably transacted over the telephone.

(7) Public records or reports. Evidence that a writing authorized by law to be recorded or filed and in fact recorded or filed in a public office, or a purported public record, report, statement, or data compilation, in any form, is from the public office where items of this nature are kept.

(8) Ancient documents or data compilation. Evidence that a document or data compilation, in any form, (A) is in such condition as to create no suspicion concerning its authenticity, (B) was in a place where it, if authentic, would likely be, and (C) has been in existence twenty years or more at the time it is offered.

(9) Process or system. Evidence describing a process or system used to produce a result and showing that the process or system produces an accurate result.

(10) Methods provided by statute or rule. Any method of authentication or identification provided by Act of Congress or by other rules prescribed by the Supreme Court pursuant to statutory authority.

RULE 902. Self-authentication

Extrinsic evidence of authenticity as a condition precedent to admissibility is not required with respect to the following:

(1) Domestic public documents under seal. A document bearing a seal purporting to be that of the United States, or of any State, district, Commonwealth, territory, or insular possession thereof, or the Panama Canal Zone, or the Trust Territory of the Pacific Islands, or of a political subdivision, department, officer or agency thereof, and a signature purporting to be an attestation or execution.

(2) Domestic public documents not under seal. A document purporting to bear the signature in the official capacity of an officer or employee of any entity included in paragraph (1) hereof, having no seal, if a public officer having a seal and having official duties in the district or political subdivision of the officer or employee certifies under seal that the signer has the official capacity and that the signature is genuine.

(3) Foreign public documents. A document purporting to be executed or attested in an official capacity by a person authorized by the laws of a foreign country to make the execution or attestation, and accompanied by a final certification as to the genuineness of the signature and official position (A) of the executing or attesting person, or (B) of any foreign official whose certificate of genuineness of signature and official position relates to the execution or attestation or is in a chain of certificates of genuineness of signature and official position relating to the execution or attestation. A final certification may be made by a secretary of an embassy or legation, consul general, consul, vice consul, or consular agent of the United States, or a diplomatic or consular official of the foreign country assigned or accredited to the United States. If reasonable opportunity has been given to all parties to investigate the authenticity and accuracy of official documents, the court may, for good cause shown, order that they be treated as presumptively authentic without final certification or permit them to be evidenced by an attested summary with or without final certification.

(4) Certified copies of public records. A copy of an official record or report or entry therein; or of a document authorized by law to be recorded or filed and actually recorded and filed a public office, including data compilations in any form, certified as correct by the custodian or other person authorized to make the certification, by certificate complying with paragraph (1), (2), or (3) of this rule or complying with any Act of Congress or rule prescribed by the Supreme Court pursuant to statutory authority.

(5) Official publications. Books, pamphlets, or other publications purporting to be issued by public authority.

(6) Newspapers and periodicals. Printed material purporting to be newspapers or periodicals.

(7) Trade inscriptions and the like. Inscriptions, signs, tags, or labels purporting to have been affixed the course of business and indicating ownership, control, or origin.

(8) Acknowledged documents. Documents accompanied by a certificate of acknowledgment executed in the manner provided by a law by a notary public or other officer authorized by law to take acknowledgments.

(9) Commercial paper and related documents. Commercial paper, signatures thereon, and documents relating thereto to the extent provided by general commercial law.

(10) Presumptions under Acts of Congress. Any signature, document, or other matter declared by Act of Congress to be presumptively or prima facie genuine or authentic.

(11) Certified domestic records of regularly conducted activity. The original or a duplicate of a domestic record of regularly conducted activity that would be admissible under Rule 803(6)if accompanied by a written declaration of its custodian or other qualified person, in a manner complying with any Act of Congress or rule prescribed by the Supreme Court pursuant to statutory authority, certifying that the record:

(A) was made at or near the time of the occurrence of the matters set forth by, or from information transmitted by, a person with knowledge of those matters;

(B) was kept in the course of the regularly conducted activity; and

(C) was made by the regularly conducted activity as a regular practice.

A party intending to offer a record into evidence under this paragraph must provide written notice of that intention to all adverse parties, and must make the record and declaration available for inspection sufficiently in advance of their offer into evidence to provide an adverse party with a fair opportunity to challenge them.

(12) Certified foreign records of regularly conducted activity. In a civil case, the original or a duplicate of a foreign record of regularly conducted activity that would be admissible under Rule 803(6) if accompanied by a written declaration by its custodian or other qualified person certifying that the record:

(A) was made at or near the time of the occurrence of the matters set forth by, or from information transmitted by, a person with knowledge of those matters;

(B) was kept in the course of the regularly conducted activity; and

(C) was made by the regularly conducted activity as a regular practice.

The declaration must be signed in a manner that, if falsely made, would subject the maker to criminal penalty under the laws of the country where the declaration is signed. A party intending to offer a record into evidence under this paragraph must provide written notice of that intention to all adverse parties, and must make the record and declaration available for inspection sufficiently in advance of their offer into evidence to provide an adverse party with a fair opportunity to challenge them.

(Amended, eff. 10-1-87; Apr. 25, 1988, eff. Nov. 1, 1988; Apr. 7, 2000, eff. Dec. 1, 2000.)

RULE 903. Subscribing Witness' Testimony Unnecessary.

The testimony of a subscribing witness is not necessary to authenticate a writing unless required by the laws of the jurisdiction whose laws govern the validity of the writing.

ARTICLE X. CONTENTS OF WRITINGS, RECORDINGS, AND PHOTOGRAPHS

RULE 1001. Definitions

For purposes of this article the following definitions are applicable.

(1) Writings and recordings. "Writings" and "recordings" consist of letters, words, or numbers, or their equivalent, set down by handwriting, type-writing, printing, Photostatting, photographing, magnetic impulse, mechanical or electronic recording, or other forms of data compilation.

(2) Photographs. "Photographs" include still pictures, X-ray films, video tapes, and motion pictures.

(3) Original. An "original" of a writing or recording is the writing or recording itself or any counterpart intended to have the same effect by a person executing or issuing it. An "original" of a photograph included the negative or any print therefrom. If data are stored in a computer or similar device, any printout or other output readable by sight, shown to reflect the data accurately, is an "original."

(4) Duplicate. A "duplicate" is a counterpart produced by the same impression as the original, or from the same matrix, or by means of photography, including enlargements and miniatures, or by mechanical or electronic re-recording, or by chemical reproduction, or by other equivalent techniques which accurately reproduces the original.

RULE 1002. Requirement of Original

To prove the content of a writing, recording or photograph, the original writing, recording, or photograph is required, except as otherwise provided in these rules or by Act of Congress.

RULE 1003. Admissibility of Duplicates

A duplicate is admissible to the same extent as an original unless (1) a genuine question is raised as to the authenticity of the original or (2) in the circumstances it would be unfair to admit the duplicate in lieu of the original.

RULE 1004. Admissibility of Other Evidence of Contents

The original is not required, and other evidence of the contents of a writing, recording, or photograph is admissible if—

(1) Originals have been lost or destroyed. All originals are lost or have been destroyed, unless the proponent lost or destroyed them in bad faith; or

(2) Original not obtainable. No original can be obtained by any available judicial process or procedure; or

(3) Original in possession of opponent. At time when an original was under the control of the party against whom offered, that party was put on notice, by the pleadings or otherwise, that the contents would be a subject of proof at the hearing, and that party does not produce the original at the hearing; or

(4) Collateral matters. The writing, recording, or photograph is not closely related to a controlling issue.

(Amended, eff. 10-1-87)

RULE 1005. Public Records

The contents of an official record, or of a document authorized to be recorded or filed and actually recorded or filed, including data compilations in any form, if otherwise admissible, may be proved by copy, certified as correct in accordance with Rule 902 or testified to be correct by a witness who has compared it with the original. If a copy which complies with the foregoing cannot be obtained by the exercise of reasonable diligence, then other evidence of the contents may be given.

RULE 1006. Summaries

The contents of voluminous writings, recordings, or photographs which cannot conveniently be examined in court may be presented in the form of a chart, summary, or calculation. The originals, or duplicates, shall be made available for examination or copying, or both, by other parties at reasonable time and place. The court may order that they be produced in court.

RULE 1007. Testimony or Written Admission of a Party

Contents of writings, recordings, or photographs may be proved by the testimony or deposition of the party against whom offered or by that party's written admission, without accounting for the nonproduction of the original.

(Amended, eff. 10-1-87)

RULE 1008. Functions of Court and Jury

When the admissibility of other evidence of contents of writings, recordings, or photographs under these rules depends upon the fulfillment of a condition of fact, the question whether the condition has been fulfilled is ordinarily for the court to determine in accordance with the provisions of Rule 104. However, when an issue is raised (a) whether the asserted writing ever existed, or (b) whether another writing, recording, or photograph produced at the trial is the original, or (c) whether other evidence of contents correctly reflects the contents, the issue is for trier of fact to determine as in the case of other issues of fact.

ARTICLE XI. MISCELLANEOUS RULES

RULE 1101. Applicability of Rules

(a) Courts and judges. These rules apply to the United States district courts, the District Court of Guam, the District Court of the Virgin Islands, the District Court for the Northern Mariana Islands, the United States Courts of Appeals, the United States Claims Court, and to United States bankruptcy judges and United States magistrate judges, in the actions, cases, and proceedings and to the extent hereinafter set forth. The terms "judge" and "court" in these rules include United States bankruptcy judges and United States magistrate judges.

(b) Proceedings generally. These rules apply generally to civil actions and proceedings, including admiralty and maritime cases, to criminal cases and proceedings, to contempt proceedings except those in which the court may act similarly, and to proceedings and cases under title 11, United States Code.

(c) Rule of privilege. The rule with respect to privileges applies at all stages of all actions, cases, and proceedings.

(d) Rules inapplicable. The rules (other than with respect to privileges) do not apply in the following situations:

(1) Preliminary question of fact. The determination of questions of fact preliminary to admissibility of evidence when the issue is to be determined by the court under Rule 104.

(2) Grand jury. Proceedings before grand juries.

(3) Miscellaneous proceedings. Proceedings for extradition or rendition; preliminary examinations in criminal cases; sentencing, or granting or revoking probation; issuance of warrants for arrest, criminal summonses, and search warrants; and proceedings with respect to release on bail or otherwise.

(e) Rules applicable in part. In the following proceedings these rules apply to the extent that matters of evidence are not provided for in statutes which govern procedure therein or in other rules prescribed by the Supreme Court pursuant to statutory authority: the trial of misdemeanors and other petty offenses before United States magistrate judges; review of agency actions when the facts are subject to trial de novo under section 706(2)(F) of title 5, United States Code; review of orders of the Secretary of Agriculture under section 2 of the Act entitled "An Act to authorize association of producers of agricultural products" approved February 18, 1922 (7 U.S.C. 292), and under sections 6 and 7(c) of the Perishable Agricultural Commodities Act, 1930 (7 U.S.C. 499f, 499g(c); naturalization and revocation of naturalization under sections 310–318 of the Immigration and Nationality Act (8 U.S.C. 1421–1429); prize proceedings in admiralty under sections 7651–7681 of title 10, United States Code; review of orders of the Secretary of the Interior under section 2 of the Act entitled "An Act authorizing associations of producers of aquatic products" approved June 25, 1934 (15 U.S.C. 522); review of orders of petroleum control boards under section 5 of

the Act entitled "An Act to regulate interstate and foreign commerce in petroleum and its products by prohibiting the shipment in such commerce of petroleum and its products produced in violation of State law, and for other purposes," approved February 22, 1935 (15 U.S.C. 715d); actions for fines, penalties, or forfeitures under part V of title IV of the Tariff Act of 1930 (19 U.S.C. 1581–1624), or under the Anti-Smuggling Act (19 U.S.C. 1701–1711); criminal libel for condemnation, exclusion of imports, or other proceedings under the Federal Food, Drug, and Cosmetic Act (21 U.S.C. 301–392); disputes between seamen under sections 4079, 4080, and 4081 of the Revised Statutes (22 U.S.C. 256–258); habeas corpus under sections 2241–2254 of title 28, United States Code; motions to vacate, set aside or correct sentence under section 2255 of title 28, United States Code; actions for penalties for refusal to transport destitute seamen under section 4578 of the Revised Statutes (46 U.S.C. 679); actions against the United States under the Act entitled "An Act authorizing suits against the United States in admiralty for damage caused by and salvage service rendered to public vessels belonging to the United States, and for other purposes," approved March 3, 1925 (46 U.S.C. 781–790), as implemented by section 7730 of title 10, United States Code.

(Amended, eff. 12-1-93)

RULE 1102. Amendments

Amendments to the Federal Rules of Evidence may be made as provided in section 2072 of title 28 of the United States Code.

(As amended, Apr. 30. 1991, eff. Dec. 1, 1991.)

RULE 1103. Title

These rules may be known and cited as the Federal Rules of Evidence.

APPENDIX II
Table of Jurisdictions in which Uniform Rules of Evidence Have Been Adopted — 2009[1]

Jurisdiction	Laws	Effective Date	Statutory Citation
Alaska	Sup.Ct.Order 364	8-1-1979	A.R.E. Rules 101 to 1101.
Arizona		9-1-1977	17A A.R.S. Rules of Evid., Rules 101 to 1103.
Arkansas	1975, No. 1143	7-1-1976	A.C.A. A4 16-41-101
Colorado		1-1-1980	West's C.R.S.A., Title 13 App., Evid. 101-1102.
Delaware		7-1-1980	D.R.E. 101 to 1103.
Florida	1976, c. 76–237	7-1-1977	West's F.S.A. A4A4 90.101 to 90.958.
Hawai'i	1980, c. 164	1-1-1981	HRS A4A4 626-1 (Hawaii Rules of
Evidence, Rules			100 to 1102) to 626-3.
Idaho		7-1-1985	Rules of Evidence, Rules 101 to 1103.
Indiana	Sup.Ct.Order 8-24-1993	1-1-1994	Rules of Evidence, Rules 101 to 1101.
Iowa		7-1-1983	Iowa R.Evid., Rules 101 to 1103.
Kentucky	1990, c. 88 Sup.Ct. Order	7-1-1992	KRE 101 to 1104
Louisiana	1988 Act 515	1-1-1989	LSA Evid.Code, arts. 101 to 1103.
Maine		2-2-1976	Rules of Evidence, Rules 101 to 1102.
Michigan		3-1-1978	Rules of Evidence, Rules 101 to 1102.
Minnesota		7-1-1977	50 M.S.A.Evid. Rules 101 to 1101.
Mississippi	Sup.Ct.Order 9-24-1985	1-1-1986	M.R.E. 101 to 1103.
Montana	1976, En. Sup.Ct. Ord. 12729	7-1-1977	Rules of Evidence, Rules 100 to 1008.
Nebraska	1975, L.B. 279	8-24-1975	R.R.S.1943, A4A4 27-101 to 27-1103.
Nevada	1971, c. 775		N.R.S. A4 47.929 et seq.
New Hampshire	7-1-1985		Rules of Evidence, Rules 100 to 1103.
New Jersey			New Jersey Rules of Evidence Rules 101-1103.
New Mexico	1973, S.C.Order	7-1-1973	N.M.R.Evid., Rules 101 to 1102.
North Carolina	1983, c. 701	7-1-1984	G.S. A4 8C-1, Rules 101 to 1102.
North Dakota		2-15-1977	NDR Evid.Rules 101 to 1103.
Ohio		7-1-1980	Rules of Evidence, Rules 101 to 1103.
Oklahoma	1978, c. 285	10-1-1978	12 Okl.St.Ann. A4A4 2101 to 3103.
Oregon	1981, c. 892	1-1-1982	ORS 40.010 to 40.585.
Rhode Island		1986*	Rules of Evidence, Rules 100 to 1008.
South Carolina		9-3-1995	South Carolina Rules of Evidence
South Dakota			SDCL 19-9-1 to 19-18-8.
Tennessee		1-1-1990	Rules of Evidence, Rules 101 to 1008.
Texas		9-1-1983	Rules of Civil Evidence, Rules 101 to 1008.
		9-1-1986	Rules of Criminal Evidence, Rules 101 to 1101.
Utah		9-1-1983	Rules of Evidence, Rules 101 to 1103.
Vermont		4-1-1983	Titled: Vermont Court Rules, Rules 101 to 1103.
Washington		4-2-1979	Rules of Evidence, Rules 101 to 1103.
West Virginia		2-1-1985	W.V.R.E., Rules 101 to 1102.
Wisconsin	Sup.Ct.Order, 59 W.(2d), page R9	1-1-1974	W.S.A. 901.01 to 911.02.
Wyoming		1-1-1978	Rules of Evidence, Rules 101 to 1104.

[1] Legal Information Institute, http://www.law.cornell.edu/uniform/evidence.html (6-03-2009).

APPENDIX III
TABLE OF CONTENTS
UNIFORM RULES OF EVIDENCE
(Last Revised or Amended in 2005)[1]

Article I

GENERAL PROVISIONS

Rule
101.   Definitions.
102.   Scope, Purpose and Construction.
103.   Rulings on Evidence.
104.   Preliminary Questions.
105.   Limited Admissibility.
106   Remainder of, or Related, Record.

Article II

JUDICIAL NOTICE

201.   Judicial Notice of Adjudicative Facts.

Article III

PRESUMPTIONS

301.   Definitions.
302.   Effect of Presumptions in Civil Cases.
303.   Scope and Effect of Presumptions in Criminal Cases.

Article IV

RELEVANCY AND ITS LIMITS

401.   Definition of "Relevant Evidence."
402.   Relevant Evidence Generally Admissible; Irrelevant Evidence Inadmissible.
403.   Exclusion of Relevant Evidence on Grounds of Prejudice, Confusion, or Waste of Time.
404.   Character Evidence Not Admissible to Prove Conduct, Exceptions; Other Crimes.
405.   Methods of Proving Character.
406.   Habit; Routine Practice.
407.   Subsequent Remedial Measures.
408.   Compromise and Offers to Compromise.
409.   Payment of Medical and Similar Expenses.
410.   Inadmissibility of Pleas, Plea Discussions, and Related Statements.

---

[1] Full text of the Uniform Rules of Evidence with 2005 amendments is available at http://www.law.upenn.edu/bll/ulc/ure/evid1200.htm (06-03-2009).

411. Liability Insurance.
412. Sexual Behavior.

Article V

PRIVILEGES

501. Privileges Recognized Only as Provided.
502. Lawyer-Client Privilege.
503. [Psychotherapist] [Physician and Psychotherapist] [Physician and Mental Health Provider] [Mental Health Provider] -Patient Privilege.
504. Spousal Privilege.
505. Religious Privilege.
506. Political Vote.
507. Trade Secrets.
508. Secrets of State and Other Official Information; Governmental Privileges.
509. Identity of Informer.
510. Waiver of Privilege.
511. Comment upon or Inference from Claim of Privilege; Instruction.

Article VI

WITNESSES

601. General Rule of Competency.
602. Lack of Personal Knowledge.
603. Oath or Affirmation.
604. Interpreters.
605. Competency of Judge as Witness.
606. Competency of Juror as Witness.
607. Who May Impeach.
608. Evidence of Character and Conduct of Witness.
609. Impeachment by Evidence of Conviction of Crime.
610. Religious Beliefs and Opinions.
611. Mode and Order of Interrogation and Presentation.
612. Writing or Object Used to Refresh Memory.
613. Prior Statements of Witness.
614. Calling and Interrogation of Witnesses by Court.
615. Exclusion of Witnesses.
616. Bias of Witnesses.

Article VII

OPINIONS AND EXPERT TESTIMONY

701. Opinion Testimony by Lay Witnesses.
702. Testimony by Experts.
703. Basis of Opinion Testimony by Experts.
704. Opinion on Ultimate Issue.
705. Disclosure of Facts or Data Underlying Expert Opinion.
706. Court Appointed Expert Witness.

Article VIII

HEARSAY

801.   Definitions; Exclusions.
802.   Hearsay Rule.
803.   Hearsay Exceptions: Availability of Declarant Immaterial.
804.   Hearsay Exceptions: Declarant Unavailable.
805.   Hearsay Within Hearsay.
806.   Attacking and Supporting Credibility of Declarant.
807.   Statement of Child Victim.
808.   Residual Exception.

Article IX

AUTHENTICATION AND IDENTIFICATION

901.   Requirement of Authentication or Identification.
902.   Self-authentication.
903.   Subscribing Witness' Testimony Unnecessary.

Article X

CONTENTS OF WRITINGS, RECORDINGS, AND PHOTOGRAPHS

1001.   Definitions.
1002.   Requirement of Original.
1003.   Admissibility of Duplicates.
1004.   Admissibility of Other Evidence of Contents.
1005.   Public Records.
1006.   Summaries.
1007   Testimony, or Admission in Record of Party.
1008.   Functions of Court and Jury.

Article XI

MISCELLANEOUS RULES

1101.   Title.

Table of Cases

Abrambasic v. Ashcroft, 403 F. Supp. 2d 951, 958, 2005 U.S. Dist. LEXIS 31713 (D. S.D. 2005)   117

ACLU v. National Security Agency, 493 F.3d 644, 2007 U.S. App. LEXIS 16149 (6th Cir. 2007)   642

Addington v. Texas, 441 U.S. 418, 99 S. Ct. 1804, 60 L. Ed. 2d 323 (1979)   48, 51

Aguilar v. Texas, 378 U.S. 108, 84 S. Ct. 1509, 12 L. Ed. 2d 723 (1964)   373, 647

Ahmed v. Yates, 2006 U.S. Dist. LEXIS 18549 (N.D. Cal. 2006)   163

Ajaxo, Inc. v. E'Trade, 135 Cal. App. 4th 21, 51, 37 Cal. Rptr. 3d 221, 244, 2005 Cal. App. LEXIS 1950 (2005)   100

Alabama v. White, 496 U.S. 325 (1990)   655, 656

Aldridge v. Edmunds, 561 Pa. 323, 331, 750 A.2d 292, 296, 2000 Pa. LEXIS 1059 (2000)   534

Alfaro v. Florida, 837 So. 2d 429, 2002 Fla. App. LEXIS 13992 (2002)   496

Alfaro v. Terhune, 98 Cal. App. 4th 492, 120 Cal. Rptr. 2d 197, 2002 Cal. App. LEXIS 4116 (2002)   129

Allen v. Houston, 2008 U.S. Dist. LEXIS 72474 (D. Neb. 2008)   168

Allison v. Wall, 121 Ga. 822, 49 S.E. 831 (1905)   402

Al-Nayem v. Irving Independent School District, 159 S.W.3d 762, 764, 2005 Tex. App. LEXIS 1919 (2005)   513

Amador v. Dretke, 2005 U.S. Dist. LEXIS 6072 (W.D. Tex. 2005)   679

Ament v. Reassure America Life Insurance Co., 2009 Ohio 36, 2009 Ohio App. LEXIS 23 (Ohio 2009)   140

American National Water Mattress Corp. v. Manville, 642 P.2d 1330 (Alaska 1982)   354

Amos v. State, 896 N.E.2d 1163, 1170, 2008 Ind. App. LEXIS 2544 (Ind. 2008)   89

Andika v. State, 2005 Tex. App. LEXIS 4862 (2005)   561

Andrews v. Texas, 78 S.W.3d 13, 18, 2002 Tex. App. LEXIS 1056 (2002)   550

Angleton v. State, 686 N.E.2d 803 (Ind. 1997)   243

Apprendi v. New Jersey, 530 U.S. 466 at 483 (2000)   32

Arboleda v. Newland, Warden, 2003 U.S. Dist. LEXIS 513 (N.D. Cal. 2003)   344, 351

Arcement v. State, 2009 Tex. App. LEXIS 1096 (Tex. 2009)   247

Argersinger v. Hamlin, 407 U.S. 25 (1972)   680

Arizona ex rel. Thomas v. Schneider, 130 P.3d 991, 994, 2006 Ariz. App. LEXIS 44 (2006)   361

Arizona v. Evans, 514 U.S. 1, 1995 U.S. LEXIS 1806 (1995)   649

Arizona v. Fulminante, 499 U.S. 279 (1991)   57, 155, 237, 669, 670

Arizona v. Gant, _____ U.S. _____, 2009 U.S. LEXIS 3120 (2009)   651, 656

Arizona v. Harrod, 200 Ariz. 309, 26 P.3d 492, 498, 499, 2001 Ariz. LEXIS 104 (2001)   343

Arizona v. Harrod, 200 Ariz. 309, 315, 26 P.3d 492, 498, 2001 Ariz. LEXIS 104 (2001), *cert. granted*, 536 U.S. 953, 122 S. Ct. 2653, 153 L. Ed. 2d 830, 2002 U.S. LEXIS 4892 (2002), *remanded for resentencing*, 65 P.3d 948, 2003 Ariz. LEXIS 31 (2003)   341

Arizona v. Hicks, 480 U.S. 321, 1987 U.S. LEXIS 1056 (1987)   657

Arizona v. Sucharew, 66 P. 2d 59, 65, 2003 Ariz. App. LEXIS 61 (2003)   360

Arkansas v. Sullivan, 532 U.S. 769, 2001 U.S. LEXIS 4118 (2001)   662

Armstead v. State, 255 Ga. App. 385, 389, 565 S.E.2d 579, 582, 2002 Ga. App. LEXIS 633 (2002)   450

Armstrong v. Brown, 2002 Ohio App. LEXIS 6728 (2002), *appeal denied*, 98 Ohio St. 3d 1539, 2003 Ohio 1946, 786 N.E.2d 902, 2003 Ohio LEXIS 1076 (2003)   423, 424

Arnold v. Florida, 807 So. 2d 136, 2002 Fla. App. LEXIS 743 (2002)   591

Asplundh Manufacturing Company v. Benton Harbor Engineering, 57 F.3d 1190, 1201, 1202 (3d Cir 1995)   397

Atchison, T. & S. F. R. Co. v. Potter, 60 Kan. 808, 811, 58 P. 471, 1899 Kan. LEXIS 143 (1899)   264

Atlanta Journal-Constitution v. Jewell, 251 Ga. App. 808, 810, 555 S.E.2d 175, 179, 2001 Ga. App. LEXIS 1153 (2001)   334

Attaway v. Georgia, 259 Ga. App. 822, 826, 827, 578 S.E.2d 529, 533, 2003 Ga. App. LEXIS 270 (2003)   546

Atwell v. Lisle Park District, 286 F.3d 987, 2002 U.S. App. LEXIS 6775 (8th Cir. 2002)   167

Ayala v. Quarterman, 2009 U.S. Dist. LEXIS 13019 (S.D. Tex. 2009)   620

Bailey v. City of Atlanta, 2009 Ga. App. LEXIS 306 (2009)   128

Baker v. Commonwealth, 2009 Va. App. LEXIS 75 (Va. 2009)   28

Banks v. County of Allegheny, 2008 U.S. Dist. LEXIS 107544 (2008)   121

Banks v. Florida, 790 So. 2d 1094, 2001 Fla. LEXIS 1411 (2001)   496

Barfield v. State, 880 So. 2d 768, 770, 2004 Fla. App. LEXIS 8357 (2004), *reh'g denied*, 2004 Fla. App LEXIS 18629 (2004)   426

Barnes v. State, 460 So. 2d 126 (Miss. 1983)   361

Barnes v. Yoshikawa, 2002 Cal. App. Unpub. LEXIS 12095 (Cal. 2002)   145

Barrientos v. State, 1 So. 3d 1209, 2009 Fla. App. LEXIS 793 (Fla. 2009)   249

Bartholomew v. Wood, 34 F.3d 870 (9th Cir. 1994)   611

Bartman v. State, 2009 Alaska LEXIS 17 (Alaska 2009)   98

Bassett v. State, 795 N.E.2d 1050, 1053, 2003 Ind. LEXIS 750 (2003)   228

Baxter v. Baxter, 423 F.3d 363; 2005 U.S. App. LEXIS 19825 (3d Cir. 2005)   126

Bayou Liberty Association v. St. Tammany Parish Council, 2006 La. App. LEXIS 1378 (2006)   128

Bean v. State, 2007 Tex. App. LEXIS 8914 (Tex. 2007)   314

Beard v. Meridia Huron Hospital, 106 Ohio St. 3d 237, 239, 2005 Ohio 4787, 834 N.E.2d 323, 326, 2005 Ohio LEXIS 2077 (2005)   534

Behanna v. State, 985 So. 2d 550, 2007 Fla. App. LEXIS 19318 (Fla. 2007), *review denied*, 988 So. 2d 622, 2008 Fla. LEXIS 1338 (Fla. 2008)   213

Bell v. State, 847 So. 2d 558, 2003 Fla. App. LEXIS 8767 (Fla. 2003)   462

Bell v. State, 910 So. 2d 640, 2005 Miss. App. LEXIS 159 (2005)   409

Benavides v. State, 808 N.E.2d 708, 710, 2004 Ind. App. LEXIS 901 (2004)   578

Bennett v. State, 883 N.E.2d 888, 892, 2008 Ind. App. LEXIS 713 (Ind. 2008)   171

Benton v. Maryland, 395 U.S. 784, 1969 U.S. LEXIS 1167 (1969)   36

Bevan v. Bevan, 2006 Ohio 2775, 2006 Ohio App. LEXIS 2605 (2006)   351

Bieberle v. United States, 255 F. Supp. 2d 1190, 1206, 1207, 2003 U.S. Dist. LEXIS 5427 (D. Kan. 2003)   428

Bigby v. Dretke, 402 F.3d 551, 557, 2005 U.S. App. LEXIS 3815 (5th Cir. 2005)   216

Bitler v. A.O. Smith, 400 F.3d 1227, 2004 U.S. LEXIS 28000 (10th Cir. 2004)   443

Bittaker v. Woodford, 331 F.3d 715, 2003 U.S. App. LEXIS 11298 (9th Cir. 2003)   361

Bivens v. Six Unknown Named Agents of Federal Bureau of Narcotics, 403 U.S. 388, 1971 U.S. LEXIS 23 (1971)   641

Blanchard v. State, 104 Ark. 31, 35, 2008 Ark. App. LEXIS 775 (Ark. 2008)   203

Blanco v. Pan-American Life Ins. Co., 221 F. Supp. 219 (S.D. Fla. 1963)   116

Bland v. Fox, 172 Neb. 662, 111 N.W.2d 537 (1961)   100

Blank v. State, 2006 Alaska App. LEXIS 144 (2006)   596

Blau v. United States, 340 U.S. 332, 71 S. Ct. 301, 95 L. Ed. 306 (1950)   340

Blocker v. Burness, 2 Ala. 354, 355, 1841 Ala. LEXIS 357 (Ala. 1841)   264

Board of Education v. Earls, 536 U.S. 822, 2002 U.S. LEXIS 4882 (2002)   661

Bobo v. State, 102 Ark. 329, 334, 2008 Ark. App. LEXIS 427 (Ark. 2008)   506

Bohsancurt v. Eisenberg, 129 P.3d 471, 2006 Ariz. App. LEXIS 26 (2006)   468

Boim v. Quranic Literacy Inst., 340 F. Supp. 2d 885, 916, 2004 U.S. Dist. LEXIS 22745 (N.D. Ill. 2004)   288

Boldin v. State, 373 Ark. 295, 300, 2008 Ark. LEXIS 277 (Ark. 2008)   163

Bonilla v. Commercial Services of Perry, Inc., 900 N.E.2d 22; 2009 Ind. App. LEXIS 112 (Ind. 2009)   145

Bordenkircher v. Hayes 434 U.S. 357, 1978 U.S. LEXIS 56 (1978)   91

Bornstad v. Honey Brook Twp., 2005 U.S. Dist. LEXIS 19573 (E.D. Pa. 2006)   251

Borsarge v. State, 786 So. 2d 426, 430, 2001 Miss. App. LEXIS 227 (2001)   257

Bowlin v. Chrones, Warden, 2008 U.S. Dist. LEXIS (E.D. Cal. 2008)   140

Bowling v. State, 275 Ga. App. 45, 47, 619 S.E.2d 688, 689, 690, 2005 Ga. App. LEXIS 808 (2005)   402

Bradley v. O'Donoghue, 2005 U.S. Dist LEXIS 4716 (2005)   401

Bradley v. State ex rel. White, 990 S.W.2d 245, 248, 1999 Tex. LEXIS 33 (1999)   266

Bradley v. State, 2003 Ark. App. LEXIS 756 (2003)   528

Brady v. Maryland, 373 U.S. 83, 1963 U.S. LEXIS 1615 (1963)   92, 583, 611

Bram v. United States, 168 U.S. 532, 18 S. Ct. 187, 42 L. Ed. 568 (1897)   669

Branch v. Phillips Petroleum Co., 638 F.2d 873 (5th Cir. 1981)   378

Branzburg v. Hayes, 408 U.S. 665, 1972 U.S. LEXIS 132 (1972)   382

Brassfield v. State, 905 So. 2d 754, 760, 2004 Miss. App. LEXIS 1108 (2004)   291

Brattain v. Herron, 309 N.E.2d 150 (Ind. 1974)   594

Braun v. E.I. du Pont de Nemours & Co., 2006 U.S. Dist. LEXIS 37431 (D.S.D 2006)   114

Brendlin v. California, 551 U.S. 249, 2007 U.S. LEXIS 7897 (2007)   654

Breton v. Commissioner, 2006 Conn. Super. LEXIS 1240 (2006)   352

Briceno v. Scribner, 555 F.3d 1069, 2009 U.S. App. LEXIS 3524 (9th Cir. 2009)   143

Bridges v. Chambers, 447 F.3d 994, 997, 2006 U.S. App. LEXIS 11763 (7th Cir. 2006)   670

Brigham City v. Stuart, 547 U.S. 398, 2006 U.S. LEXIS 4155 (2006)   646

Bright v. United States, 698 A.2d 450 (D.C. App. 1997)   66

Broadhead v. State, 981 So. 2d 320,326, 2007 Miss. App. LEXIS 809 (Miss. 2007)   243

Brockenbrough v. Commonwealth, 2003 Va. App. LEXIS 243 (2003)   295

Brooks v. Tennessee, 406 U.S. 605 (1972)   17, 82

Brown v. Classic Inns, 2002 Wis. App 134, 255 Wis. 2d 832, 646 N.W.2d 854 (2002)   245

Brown v. Commonwealth, 2009 Va. App. LEXIS 226 (Va. 2009)   523

Brown v. Farwell, 525 F.3d 787, 796–97 (9th Cir. 2008)   120

Brown v. Hawai'i, 2009 U.S. Dist. LEXIS 10546 (D. Hawai'i 2009)   131

Brown v. Maryland, 368 Md. 320, 327, 793 A.2d 561, 565, 2002 Md. LEXIS 95 (2002)   306

Brown v. State, 182 Md. App. 138, 179, 2008 Md. App. LEXIS 121 (Md. 2008)   166

Brown v. State, 2007 Ala. Crim. App. LEXIS 111 (Ala. 2007)   524

Brown v. State, 270 Ga. App. 176, 605 S.E.2d 885, 2004 Ga. App. LEXIS 1381 (2004)   443

Brown v. State, 897 A.2d 748, 2006 Del. LEXIS 163 (Del. 2006)   87

Brown v. State, 958 A.2d 833, 2008 Del. LEXIS 468 (Del. 2008)   64, 65, 66

Bryant v. Burns-Hammond Const. Co., 197 N.C. 639, 1929 N.C. LEXIS 321 (1929)   148

Bryant v. City of New York, 404 F.3d 128, 2005 U.S. App. LEXIS 5376 (2d Cir. 2005)   675

Bryant v. State, 115 P.3d 1249, 1253, 2005 Alas. App. LEXIS 62 (2005)   224

Bryant v. United States, 859 A.2d 1093, 1106, 2004 D.C. App. LEXIS 526 (2004)   252, 464

Burch v. Louisiana, 441 U.S. 130 (1979)   32

Burkey v. State, 922 So. 2d 1033, 1035, 2006 Fla. App. LEXIS 2772 (2006)   496

Burnett v. State, 815 N.E.2d 201, 205, 2004 Ind. App. LEXIS 1864 (2004)   412

Burns v. State, 2005 Tex. App. LEXIS 1772 (Tex. 2005)   205

Burton v. CSX Transportation, 269 S.W.3d 1, 2008 Ky. LEXIS 236 (Ky. 2008)   231

Butler v. Principi, 244 F.3d 1337, 201 U.S. App. LEXIS 5270 (Fed. Cir. 2001)   173

Butler v. State, 294 Ga. App. 540, 2008 Ga. App. LEXIS 1228 (Ga. 2008)   151

Caballero v. State, 2005 Tex. App. LEXIS 1865 (2005)   471

Cage v. Louisiana, 498 U.S. 39, 111 S. Ct. 328, 112 L. Ed. 2d 339 (1990)   54

Calandra v. St. Agnes Med. Ctr., 2005 Phila. Ct. Com. Pl. LEXIS 254 (2005)   534

Caldron v. Ashcroft, 110 Fed. Appx. 789, 2004 U.S. App. LEXIS 19793 (9th Cir. 2004)   434

Calhoun v. State, 932 So. 2d 923, 2005 Ala. Crim. App. LEXIS 101 (2005), *cert. denied*, 2006 U.S. LEXIS 5233 (2006)   577, 580

California v. Acevedo, 500 U.S. 565 (1991)   655, 663

California v. Ciraolo, 476 U.S. 267, 106 S. Ct. 1809, 90 L. Ed. 2d 210 (1986)   566

California v. Funston, 2002 Cal. App. Unpub. LEXIS 3513 (2002)   603

California v. Greenwood, 486 U.S. 35, 1988 U.S. LEXIS 2279 (1988)   659

California v. Kurey, 88 Cal. App. 4th 840, 846, 847, 106 Cal. Rptr. 2d 150, 2001 Cal. App. LEXIS 319 (2001)   442

California v. Sanchez, 2002 Cal. App. Unpub. LEXIS 11068 (2002)   430

California v. Smith, 107 Cal. App. 4th 646, 131 Cal. Rptr. 2d 230, 2003 Cal. App. LEXIS 475 (2003), *petition for review denied*, 2003 Cal. LEXIS 3547 (2003)   627

California v. Tatum, 108 Cal. App. 4th 288, 133 Cal. Rptr. 2d 267, 2003 Cal. App. LEXIS 629 (2003)   549

Callen v. State, 2008 WY 107, 146, 192 P.3d 137, 2008 Wyo. LEXIS 111 (Wyo. 2008)   54

Campbell v. Rice, 408 F.3d 1166, 1171, 2005 U.S. App. LEXIS 9221 (9th Cir. 2005)   120

Carella v. California, 491 U.S. 263 (1989)   149, 179

Carmona v. Warden, 2007 Conn. Super. LEXIS 3425 (Conn. 2007)   124

Carpenter v. Lock, 257 F.3d 775, 2001 U.S. App. LEXIS 15918 (8th Cir. 2001), *cert. denied*, 534 U.S. 1091, 122 S. Ct. 834, 151 L. Ed. 2d 714, 2002 U.S. LEXIS 394 (2002)   375

Carrasco v. State, 154 S.W.3d 127, 128, 2005 Tex. Crim. App. LEXIS 76 (2005)   182

Carratelli v. Florida, 832 So. 2d 850, 861, 2002 Fla. App. LEXIS 17158 (2002)   426

Carroll v. United States, 267 U.S. 132, 161, 1925 U.S. LEXIS 361 (1925)   33, 654

Carter v. State, 275 Ga. App. 483, 486, 621 S.E.2d 503, 506, 2005 Ga. App. LEXIS 1003 (2005)   348

Cass v. County of Suffolk, 2005 U.S. Dist. LEXIS 8623 (E.D.N.Y. 2005)   661

Catina v. Maree, 498 Pa. 433, 447 A.2d 228 (1982)   410

Cavallaro v. United States, 153 F. Supp. 2d 52, 58, 2001 U.S. Dist. LEXIS 11232 (D. Mass. 2001)   335, 354

Cavallaro v. United States, 284 F.3d 236, 246, 2002 U.S. App. LEXIS 5366 (1st Cir. 2002)   354

Cavanagh v. Lentz, 2005 Conn. Super. LEXIS 2731 (Conn. 2005)   171

Chambers v. Maroney, 339 U.S. 42, 90 S. Ct. 1975, 26 L. Ed. 2d 419 (1970)   654

Chambers v. State, 924 So. 2d 975, 977, 2006 Fla. App. LEXIS 5058 (Fla. 2006)   290

Chandler v. State, 702 So. 2d 186 (Fla. 1997)   308

Chapell v. State, 710 S.W.2d 214 (Ark. 1986)   264

Chapman v. California, 386 U.S. 18, 23, 1967 U.S. LEXIS 2198 (1967)   165

Charleston Television, Inc. v. South Carolina Budget and Control Bd., 373 S.E.2d 890 (S.C. 1988)   173

Cheek v. United States, 498 U.S. 192, 199, 1991 U.S. LEXIS 348 (1991)   167

Chesek v. Jones, 406 Md. 446, 463, 2008 Md. LEXIS 609 (Md. 2008)   355

Chimel v. California, 395 U.S. 752, 89 S. Ct. 2034, 23 L. Ed. 2d 685 (1969)   649, 650

Choice Auto Brokers, Inc. v. Dawson, 274 S.W.3d 172, n. 1, 2008 Tex. App. LEXIS 7236 (Tex. 2008)   114

Christmas v. State, 2009 Miss. LEXIS 144 (Miss. 2009)   305

City of Chicago v. Lehmann, 262 Ill. 468, 104 N.E. 829 (1914)   393

City of Cleveland v. Tisdale, 2008 Ohio 2807, 2008 Ohio App. LEXIS 2372 (Ohio 2008)   621

City of Indianapolis v. Edmond, 531 U.S. 32 (2000)   236

City of Indianapolis v. Taylor, 707 N.E.2d 1047, 1051, 1999 Ind. App. LEXIS 456 (Ind. 1999)   160

City of North Ridgeville v. Stack, 2006 Ohio 1177, 2006 Ohio App. LEXIS 1063 (2006)   130

City of Parma Heights v. Nugent, 92 Ohio Misc. 2d 67, 700 N.E.2d 430, 1998 Ohio Misc. LEXIS 32 (1998)   237

Clanton v. United States, 488 F.2d 1069 (5th Cir. 1974)   358

Clark v. Arizona, 2006 U.S. LEXIS 5184 (2006)   156

Clark v. Arizona, 548 U.S. 735, 2006 U.S. LEXIS 5 (2006)   52, 53, 69, 201, 218

Clein v. State, 52 So. 2d 117 (Fla. 1951)   381

Clemmons v. State, 2006 Md. LEXIS 192 (2006)   437

Clemmons v. State, 392 Md. 339, 896 A.2d 1059, 2006 Md. LEXIS 192 (Md. 2006)   626, 631

Cleveland Heights v. Katz, 2001 Ohio App. LEXIS 5394 (2001)   620

Coles v. United States, 808 A.2d 485, 489, 2002 D.C. App. LEXIS 556 (2002)   310

Colorado v. Bertine, 479 U.S. 367, 107 S. Ct. 738, 93 L. Ed. 2d 739 (1987)   662

Colorado v. Caldwell, 43 P.3d 663, 667, 2001 Colo. App. LEXIS 1514 (2001)   395

Colorado v. Connelly, 479 U.S. 157, 1986 U.S. LEXIS 23 (1986)   673

Colorado v. Rogers, 68 P.3d 486, 2002 Colo. App. LEXIS 1627 (2002)   554

Colorado v. Trujillo, 49 P.3d 316, 2002 Colo. LEXIS 569 (2002)   306

Combs v. Kentucky, 74 S.W.3d 738, 744, 2002 Ky. LEXIS 98 (2002)   302

Commonwealth of Massachusetts v. Montalvo, 50 Mass. App. Ct. 85, 88, 735 N.E.2d 391, 394, 2000 Mass. App. LEXIS 763 (2000)   398

Commonwealth of Pennsylvania v. Tyson, 2002 Pa. Super. 168, 800 A.2d 327, 2002 Pa. Super. LEXIS 1071 (2002)   384

Commonwealth of Pennsylvania v. Weiss, 565 Pa. 504, 776 A.2d. 958, 2001 Pa. LEXIS 1574 (2001)   351

Commonwealth v. Allen, 269 Va. 262, 609 S.E.2d 4, 2005 Va. LEXIS 23 (2005)   52

Commonwealth v. Baumhammers, 960 A.2d 59, 2008 Pa. LEXIS 2078 (Pa. 2008)   87

Commonwealth v. Blasioli, 685 A.2d 151 (Pa. 1996)   629

Commonwealth v. Chiero, 24 Mass. L. Rep. 376, 2008 Mass. Super. LEXIS 245 (Mass. 2008)   156

Commonwealth v. Crork, 2009 Pa Super 24, 2009 Pa. Super LEXIS 31 (Pa. 2009)   552

Commonwealth v. Daye, 19 Mass L. Rep. 674, 2005 Mass. Super. LEXIS 368 (2005)   437, 626, 631

Commonwealth v. Edwards, 2006 Pa. LEXIS 1529 (2006)   548

Commonwealth v. Garmache, 35 Mass. App. 805, 626 N.E.2d 616 (1994)   249

Commonwealth v. Gaynor, 443 Mass. 245, 266, 820 N.E.2d 233, 251, 2005 Mass. LEXIS 7 (2005)   210, 628

Commonwealth v. Hanford, 2007 PA Super 345 (Pa. 2007)   171

Commonwealth v. Herring, 66 Mass. App. Ct. 360, 365, 2006 Mass. App. LEXIS 569 (Mass. 2006)   549

Commonwealth v. Hill, 52 Mass. App. 147, 153 (2001)   241

Commonwealth v. Inhabitants of Holliston, 107 Mass. 232 (1871)   545

Commonwealth v. Judd, 2006 Pa. Super. 84, 2006 Pa. Super. LEXIS 538 (2006)   86, 256

Commonwealth v. Kretchmar, 2009 PA Super 63, 2009 Pa. Super. LEXIS 79 (Penn. 2009)   625

Commonwealth v. Leneski, 66 Mass. App. Ct. 291, 294, 846 N.E.2d 1195, 1198, 2006 Mass. App. LEXIS 525 (2006)   523

Commonwealth v. Lugo, 63 Mass. App. Ct. 204, 824 N.E.2d 481, 2005 Mass. App. LEXIS 296 (2005)   443

Commonwealth v. Maddox, 955 S.W.2d 718 (Ky. 1997)   307

Commonwealth v. Morgan, 69 Va. Cir. 228, 232, 2005 Va. Cir. LEXIS 189 (Va. 2005)   481

Commonwealth v. Moss, 2004 Pa. Super 224, 852 A.2d 374, 2004 Pa. Super. LEXIS 1408 (2004)   442

Commonwealth v. Pallotta, 36 Mass. App. 669, 634 N.E.2d 915 (1994)   430

Commonwealth v. Patterson, 445 Mass. 626, 628 n. 2, 840 N.E.2d 12, 14 n.2, 2005 Mass. LEXIS 765 (2005)   439

Commonwealth v. Perryman, 55 Mass. App. Ct. 187, 193, 770 N.E.2d 1, 6, 2002 Mass. App. LEXIS 8 (Mass. 2002)   582

Commonwealth v. Ragland, 72 Mass. App. Ct. 815, 2009 Mass. App. LEXIS 1039 (Mass. 2008)   322

Commonwealth v. Rivera, 445 Mass. 119, 833 N.E.2d 1113; 2005 Mass. LEXIS 491 (2005)   576

Commonwealth v. Rogers, 444 Mass. 234, 344, 827 N.E.2d 669, 677, 2005 Mass. LEXIS 216 (Mass. 2005)   653

Commonwealth v. Salter, 2004 Pa. Super. 318, 858 A.2d 610, 614 2004 Pa. Super. LEXIS 2687 (Pa. 2004)   152

Commonwealth v. Salter, 2004 Pa. Super. 318, 858 A.2d 610, 615, 2004 Pa. Super. LEXIS 2687 (2004)   140

Commonwealth v. Serge, 896 A.2d 1170, 1178, 2006 Pa. LEXIS 561 (Pa. 2006)   443, 574

Commonwealth v. Statti, 16 Pa. Super. 577, 73 A.2d 688 (1950)   603

Commonwealth v. Vasquez, 20 Mass. L. Rep. 319, 2005 Mass. Super. LEXIS 656 (Mass. 2005)   456

Commonwealth v. Whitacre, 2005 Pa. Super. 221, 878 A.2d 96, 100, 2005 Pa. Super. LEXIS 1500 (2005)   444

Commonwealth v. Young, 73 Mass. App. Ct. 479, 484, 2009 Mass. App. LEXIS 15 (Mass. 2009)   328

Commonwealth v. Zimmermann, 70 Mass. App. Ct. 357, 2007 Mass. App. LEXIS 1050 (Mass. 2007)   624

Compan v. People, 121 P.3d 876, 882, 2005 Colo. LEXIS 873 (2005)   463

Conley v. Commonwealth, 2005 Va. App. LEXIS 516 (2005)   507

Conn v. Jack Does 1–40 et al., 2008 U.S. Dist. LEXIS 17733 (D.N.J.2008)   120

Connecticut v. Abernathy, 72 Conn. App. 831, 836, 837, 806 A.2d 1139, 1145, 1146, 2002 Conn. App. LEXIS 519 (2002)   307

Connecticut v. Beverly, 72 Conn. App. 91, 104, 805 A.2d 95, 104 (2002)   214

Connecticut v. Crnkovic, 68 Conn. App. 757, 793 A.2d 1139, 2002 Conn. App. LEXIS 159 (2002)   193, 215

Connecticut v. Cruz, 260 Conn. 1, 792 A.2d 823, 2002 Conn. LEXIS 127 (2002)   451

Connecticut v. Francis D., 75 Conn. App. 1, 17, 18, 815 A.2d 191, 203, 204, 2003 Conn. App. LEXIS 64 (2003)   323

Connecticut v. Johnson, 460 U.S. 73, 1983 U.S. LEXIS 131 (1983)   164

Connecticut v. Joly, 219 Conn. 234, 593 A.2d 96 (1991)   193

Connecticut v. Polanco, 69 Conn. App. 169, 797 A.2d 523, 2002 Conn. App. LEXIS 187 (2002)   473

Connecticut v. Vines, 71 Conn. App. 359, 371 A.2d 918, 926, 2002 Conn. App. LEXIS 406 (2002)   246

Cook v. Cook, 209 Ariz. 487; 104 P.3d 857; 2005 Ariz. App. LEXIS 6 (2005)   351

Cook v. State, 928 So. 2d 589; 2006 La. App. LEXIS 242 (La. 2006)   184

Corley v. United States, 129 S. Ct. 1558, 2009 U.S. LEXIS 2512 (2009)   198, 671

Cormier v. State, 955 S.W.2d 161 (Tex. 1997)   495

Correa v. Comm'r of Corr., 101 Conn. App. 554, 557, 2007 Conn. App. LEXIS 225 (Conn. 2007)   115

County of Orange v. Superior Court of Orange County, 155 Cal. App. 4th 1253, 2007 Cal. App. LEXIS 1649, n.1 (2007)   122

County of Riverside v. McLaughlin, 500 U.S. 44 (1991)   33

Cox v. Florida, 764 So. 2d 711, 713, 2000 Fla. App. LEXIS 7516 (2000)   115

Cox v. Miller, 296 F.3d 89, 2002 U.S. App. LEXIS 14398 (2d Cir. 2002)   370

Cox v. Mississippi, 2003 Miss. LEXIS 103 (2003)   363
Cox v. State, 774 N.E.2d 1025, 2002 Ind. App. LEXIS 1533 (2002)   463
Craft v. State, 274 Ga. App. 410, 2005 Ga. App. LEXIS 778 (Ga. 2005)   36
Crawford v. Washington, 541 U.S. 36, 2004 U.S. LEXIS 1838 (2004)   282, 349, 481, 492,
    498, 576
Crist v. Bretz, 437 U.S. 28, 36, 1978 U.S. LEXIS 107 (1978)   13
Crooks v. Lynch, 2009 U.S. App. LEXIS 4020 (8th Cir. 2009)   111
Cross v. Ledford, 161 Ohio St. 469, 120 N.E.2d 118 (Ohio 1954)   51
Crow v. Crawford, 259 S.W.3d 10, 2008 Mo. App. LEXIS 666 (Mo. 2008)   192
Culp v. State, 2005 Miss. LEXIS 828 (Miss. 2005)   174
Culver v. State, 2008 Ala. Crim. App. LEXIS 107 (Ala. 2008)   199
Cumbol v. State, 205 Tenn. 260, 326 S.W.2d 454 (1959)   123

D.F. v. Department of Revenue, 823 So. 2d 97, 98, 2002 Fla. LEXIS 1162 (2002)   149
D'Amico v. Delliquardri, 114 Ohio App. 3d 579, 683 N.E.2d 814 (1996)   362
Damitz v. State, 2005 Alaska App. LEXIS 26 (2005)   320
Daubert v. Merrell Dow Pharmaceuticals, 509 U.S. 579, 1993 U.S. LEXIS 4408 (1993)   230,
    239, 591
Daughtry v. Polk, 2006 U.S. App. LEXIS 17962 (4th Cir. 2006)   210
Davis v. Arkansas, 2003 Ark. App. LEXIS 386 (2003)   550
Davis v. District of Columbia, 247 A.2d 417 (D.C. Ct. App. 1968)   679
Davis v. State, 275 Ga. App. 714, 715–716, 2005 Ga. App. LEXIS 1099 (Ga. 2005)   151
Davis v. State, 350 Ark. 22, 35, 84 S.W.3d 427, 435, 2002 Ark. LEXIS 446 (2002)   563
Davis v. Washington, 547 U.S. 813, 2006 U.S. LEXIS 4886 (2006)   457
Dean v. Houston, 2006 U.S. Dist. LEXIS 2544 (D. Neb. 2006)   168
Dean v. State, 211 Iowa 143, 233 N.W. 36 (1930)   422
Deck v. Missouri, 544 U.S. 622, 628, 2005 U.S. LEXIS 4180 (2005)   549
Delaware v. Fensterer, 474 U.S. 15, 106 S. Ct. 292 (1985)   424
Department of Children's Services v. K.B., 2008 Tenn. App. LEXIS 122 (Tenn 2008)   51
Dermody v. State, 2002 Tex. App. LEXIS 6639 (2002)   351
DiBella v. Hopkins, 403 F.3d 102, 120, 2005 U.S. App. LEXIS 5332 (2d Cir. 2005)   356
Dick v. New York Life Ins. Co., 359 U.S. 437, 79 S. Ct. 921, 3 L. Ed. 2d 935 (1959)   160
Dickerson v. Cushman, 909 F. Supp. 1467 (M.D. Ala. 1995)   416
Dickerson v. United States, 530 U.S. 428, 2000 U.S. LEXIS 4305 (2000)   79, 324, 676
Disabato et al. v. State, 840 N.E.2d 1, 4, 2005 Ind. App. LEXIS 2390 (2005)   129
Dixon v. United States, 548 U.S. 1, 2006 U.S. LEXIS 4894 (2006)   63
Dobson v. Walker, 150 Fed. Appx. 49, 50, 2005 U.S. App. LEXIS 21294 (2d Cir. 2005)   679
Doe 2 v. Superior Court, 132 Cal. App. 4th 1504, 1516, 34 Cal. Rptr. 3d 458, 466, 2005 Cal.
    App. LEXIS 1537 (2005)   371
Doe Boy v. United States, 2006 U.S. Dist LEXIS 13503 (D. Del. 2006)   422
Doe v. Church of Jesus Christ of Latter-Day Saints, 122 Wash. App. 556, 568, 90 P.3d 1147,
    1154, 2004 Wash. App. LEXIS 1112 (2004)   370
Doe v. Oberweis Dairy, 2004 U.S. Dist. LEXIS 9204 (D. Ill. 2004)   364
Donnelly v. United States, 288 U.S. 243, 33 S. Ct. 449, 57 L. Ed. 820 (1913)   459
Doorbal v. State, 983 So.2d 464, 2008 Fla. LEXIS 215 (Fla. 2008)   546
Dowden v. Commonwealth, 260 Va. 459, 468, 536 S.E.2d 437, 441 (2000)   100
Doyle v. Ohio, 426 U.S. 610, 96 S. Ct. 2240, 49 L. Ed. 2d 91 (1976)   324
Dragani v. Bryant, 2005 U.S. Dist. LEXIS 38057, n. 7 (M.D. Fla. 2005)   496
Duckworth v. Eagan, 492 U.S. 195, 208 (1989)   644
Dunkle v. State, 2006 Okla. Crim. 29, 139 P.3d 228, 2006 Okla. Crim. App. LEXIS 29
    (2006)   574
Duran v. State, 881 S.W.2d 569 (Tex. 1994)   344

Easy Sportswear, Inc. v. Am. Econ. Ins. Co., 2008 U.S. Dist. LEXIS 51402 (W.D. Pa. 2008)   120

Edmonds v. State, 2006 Miss. App. LEXIS 311 (Miss. 2006)   479

Edwards v. Arizona, 451 U.S. 477 (1981)   673, 681

Edwards v. State, 762 N.E.2d 128, 136, 2002 Ind. App. LEXIS 50 (2002)   571

Eggers v. State, 914 So. 2d 883, 914, 2004 Ala. Crim. App. LEXIS 266 (2004)   565

Elias v. Pasmore, 2 K.B. 65 (1934)   640

Ellibee v. Fox, 2006 U.S. Dist. LEXIS 13351 (D. Kan. 2006)   419

Elliot v. Kiesewetter, 112 Fed. Appx. 821, 824, 2004 U.S. 821, 2004 U.S. App. LEXIS 21628 (3d Cir. 2004)   413

Ellis v. Wolfe-Shoemaker Motor Co., 227 Mo. 508, 55 S.W.2d 309 (1932)   26

Ellsberg v. Mitchell, 228 U.S. App. D.C. 225, 709 F.2d 51, 56 (D.C. Cir. 1983)   376, 379

El-Masri v. Tenet, et al., 2006 U.S. Dist. LEXIS 34577 (E.D. Va. 2006)   379

Elmore v. State, 13 Ark. App. 221, 227, 682 S.W.2d 758, 762, 1985 Ark. App. LEXIS 1735 (1985)   265

Elrod et al. v. J.C. Penny Life Insurance Company, 2000 Tenn. App. LEXIS 407 (Tenn. 2000)   160

Ervin v. State, 2006 Ark. App. LEXIS 95 (2006)   468

Escobedo v. Illinois, 378 U.S. 478, 1964 U.S. LEXIS 827 (1964)   680

Esguerra v. State, 2005 Alaska App. LEXIS 2 (2005)   281

Eshelman v. Orthoclear Holdings, 2009 U.S. Dist. LEXIS 19293 (N.D. Cal. 2009)   126

Esquibel v. Texas, 2005 Tex. App. LEXIS 6760 (2005)   435

Estate of Earl Wallace, Deceased, 2004 Phila. Ct. Com. Pl. LEXIS 134 (Pa. 2004)   475

Estate of Norman Holly v. American Family Life Assurance, 2005 Ohio 2281, 2005 Ohio App. LEXIS 2190 (2005)   159

Estate of Reiserer v. United States, 229 F.R.D. 172, 179, 2005 U.S. Dist. LEXIS 17597 (W.D. Wash. 2005)   356

Estate of Trentadue ex rel. Aguilar v. United States, 397 F.3d 840, 863, 2005 U.S. App. LEXIS 1811 (10th Cir. 2005)   159

Eta-Ndu v. Gonzales, 411 F.3d 977, 981, 982, 2005 U.S. App. LEXIS 12120 (8th Cir. 2005)   433

Everson v. State, 2008 Tex. App. LEXIS 4834 (Tex. 2008)   72

Ex parte Gillentine, 2006 Ala. Crim. App. LEXIS 107 (2006)   53, 54

Ex parte Malone, 2008 Ala. LEXIS 271 (2008)   89

Farrar v. Commonwealth, 2006 Va. App. LEXIS 301 (2006)   495

Fatemi v. Fatemi, 371 Pa. Super. 101, 537 A.2d 840 (Pa. Super. 1988)   116

Ferguson v. State, 2005 Ark. LEXIS 361 (Ark. 2005)   182

Ferguson v. State, 920 So. 2d 838, 840, 2006 Fla. App. LEXIS 2283 (2006)   163

Fields v. State, 998 So. 2d 1185, 2008 Fla. App. LEXIS 11871 (Fla. 2008)   63

Figueroa v. State, 250 S.W.3d 490, 504, 2008 Tex. App. LEXIS 2028 (Tex. 2008)   132

Finney v. Commonwealth, 277 Va. 83, 89, 2009 Va. LEXIS 12 (2009)   100

Fleenor v. State, 622 N.E.2d 140 (Ind. 1993)   67

Flippen Alliance v. Brannan, 267 Ga. App. 134, 136, 601 S.E.2d 106, 109, 2004 Ga. App. LEXIS 460 (2004)   128

Flora v. State, 925 So. 2d 797, 813, 2006 Miss. LEXIS 49 (2006)   551

Florida v. Farmiglietti, 817 So. 2d 901, 907, 908, 2002 Fla. App. LEXIS 6199 (2002)   364

Florida v. Jimeno, 500 U.S. 248, 1991 U.S. LEXIS 2910 (1991)   653

Florida v. Wells, 495 U.S. 1 (1990)   661, 662

Ford v. State, 158 S.W.3d 488, 2005 Tex. Crim. App. LEXIS (2005)   402

Foster v. California, 394 U.S. 440, 89 S. Ct. 1127, 22 L. Ed. 2d 402 (1969)   679

Frankenfield v. State, 2008 Tex. App. LEXIS 7920 (Tex. 2008)   230

Franklin v. Bradshaw, 2009 U.S. Dist. LEXIS 23715 (W.D. Ohio 2009)   192

Franklin v. State, 2006 Ga. App. LEXIS 1111 (2006)   543

Frazer v. El-Amin, 2004 Minn. App. LEXIS 1015 (2004)   279

Freeman v. Grubbs, 134 Fed. Appx. 233, 2005 U.S. App. LEXIS 10499 (10th Cir. 2005)   366

Freeman v. New York Central R. Co., 174 N.E.2d 550 (Ohio Ct. App. 1960)   613

Friends of Lagoon Valley v. City of Vacaville, 154 Cal. App.4th 807, 2007 Cal. App. LEXIS 1424 (Cal. 2007)   127

Frye v. United States, 54 App. D.C. 46, 293 F. 1013 (1923)   230, 556

Fuller v. State, 295 Ga. App. 349, 441, 2009 Ga. App. LEXIS 8 (Ga. 2009)   207

Funk v. United States, 290 U.S. 371, 54 S. Ct. 212, 78 L. Ed. 369 (1933)   28, 259

G.M.H. v. J.L.H., 700 S.W.2d 506 (Mo. Ct. App. 1985)   149

Gaddie v. Manlief (In re H.R. M.), 864 N.E.2d 442, 2007 Ind. App. LEXIS 775 (Ind. 2007)   205

Gage v. State, 2005 Tex. App. LEXIS 531 (2005)   224

Galbraith v. State, 2008 Texas App. LEXIS 8433 (Tex. 2008)   508

Gallo v. Gallo, 861 So. 2d 168, 173, 2003 La. LEXIS 3448, n.6 (2003)   12

Gamble v. Arkansas, 351 Ark. 541, 550, 95 S.W.3d 755, 761, 2003 Ark. LEXIS 44 (2003)   525

Gamble v. Ohio Department of Job and Family Services, 2006 U.S. Dist. LEXIS 968 (S.D. Ohio 2006)   129

Garcia v. Martinez, 2006 U.S. App. LEXIS 24199 (7th Cir. 2006)   589

Garcia v. State, 2005 Ark. LEXIS 559 (Ark. 2005)   567

Garcia v. State, 2005 Tex. App. LEXIS 4424 (2005)   395

Gardner v. Barney, 73 U.S. (6 Wall.)499, 18 L. Ed. 890 (1868)   125

Gault v. State, 878 N.E.2d 1260, 1263, 2008 Ind. LEXIS 43 (Ind. 2008)   297

Gavin v. Mississippi, 767 So. 2d 1072, 1077, 2000 Miss. App. LEXIS 454 (2000)   311

Gbur, Executrix v. Golio, 2009 Pa. LEXIS 177 (2009)   85

Gentry v. State, 443 S.E.2d 667 (Ga. Ct. App. 1994)   593

George v. Ellis, 2003 Pa. Super. 121, 820 A.2d 815, 2003 Pa. Super. LEXIS 441 (2003)   415

George v. Mississippi, 812 So. 2d 1103, 1105, 1106, 2001 Miss. App. LEXIS 436 (2001)   399

Georgia v. Randolph, 547 U.S. 103, 137, 2006 U.S. LEXIS 2498 (2006)   652, 657

Gerdes v. Kennamer, 155 S.W.3d 541, 548, 2004 Tex. App. LEXIS 10945 (2004)   127

Gichner v. Antonio Troiano Tile Co., 410 F.2d 238 (D.C. Cir. 1969)   485

Gideon v. Wainwright, 372 U.S. 335, 1963 U.S. LEXIS 1942 (1963)   680

Gilbert v. California, 388 U.S. 263, 265, 1967 U.S. LEXIS 1086 (1967)   432

Gilbert v. United States, 366 F.2d 923 (9th Cir. 1966)   594

Gillars v. United States, 182 F.2d 962 (D.C. Cir. 1950)   264

Gillespie v. State, 832 N.E.2d 1112, 1117, 2005 Ind. App. LEXIS 1505 (2005)   229

Glover v. State, 836 N.E.2d 414, 421, 2005 Ind. LEXIS 983 (2005)   262

Gonzalez v. State, 195 S.W.3d 114, 2006 Tex. Crim. App. LEXIS 1129 (Tex. 2006)   481

Gonzalez v. Texas, 2000 Tex. App. LEXIS 3032 (2000)   402

Goudeau v. Texas, 2002 Tex. App. LEXIS 5612 (2002)   289

Gould Electronics v. United States, 2002 U.S. Dist. LEXIS 262 (E.D. Pa. 2002)   117

Grace v. City of Cheyenne, 2006 U.S. App. LEXIS 15182 (10th Cir. 2006)   86

Gracia v. State, 2006 Tex. Crim. App. LEXIS 1284 (2006)   569

Graham v. State, 273 Ga. 187, 189, 614 S. E.2d 815, 818, 2005 Ga. App. LEXIS 442 (2005)   408

Granzer v. State, 2008 WY 118, 193 P.2d 266, 2008 Wyo. LEXIS 124 (Wyo. 2008)   59

Grayson v. King, 2006 U.S. App. LEXIS 21215 (11th Cir. 2006)   548

Green v. Commonwealth, 197 S.W.3d 76, 2006 Ky. LEXIS 140 (Ky. 2006)   565

Green v. Ransor, Inc. 175 S.W.3d 513, 516, 2005 Tex. App. LEXIS 8125 (2005)   145

Green v. State, 2006 Ark. LEXIS 167 (Ark. 2006)   542

Greenwald v. H & P 29th Street Associates, 659 N.Y.S.2d 473 (N.Y. 1997)   344

Grier v. Georgia, 273 Ga. 363, 541 S.E.2d 369, 2001 Ga. LEXIS 56 (2001)   567

Griffin v. California, 380 U.S. 609, 85 S. Ct. 1229, 14 L. Ed. 2d 106 (1965)   678

Griffin v. State, 230 Ga. App. 318, 496 S.E.2d 480 (1998)   668

Griffin v. State, 918 So. 2d 882, 884, 2006 Miss. App. LEXIS 12 (Miss. 2006)   526

Grimes v. Navigant Consulting, 185 F. Supp. 2d 906, 913, 2002 U.S. Dist. LEXIS 1708 (N.D. Ill. 2002)   116

Gross v. FBL Financial Services, Inc., 526 F.3d 356, 359, 2008 U.S. App. LEXIS 10355 (8th Cir. 2008)   145

Gross v. Jackson, 2008 U.S. Dist. LEXIS 37095 (S.D. Ohio 2008)   152

Gross v. United States, 394 F.2d 216 (8th Cir. 1968)   313

Gruzen v. State, 267 Ark. 380, 591 S.W.2d 342 (1979), *cert. denied*, 449 U.S. 852, 101 S. Ct. 144, 66 L. Ed. 2d 64 (1980)   367

Guerrier v. Florida, 811 So. 2d 852, 854, 2002 Fla. App. LEXIS 4087 (2002)   362

Gutman v. Industrial Comm., 71 Ohio App. 383, 50 N.E.2d 187 (1942)   547

Hager v. United States, 856 A.2d 1143, 1148, 2004 D.C. App. LEXIS (2004), *cert. denied*, 2006 U.S. LEXIS 2452 (2006)   412

Halkin v. Helms, 598 F.2d 1 (D.C. Cir. 1978)   378

Hall v. C.I.R., 729 F.2d 632 (9th Cir. 1984)   476

Hamilton v. Department of Social and Health Services, 109 Wash. App 718, 730, 37 P.3d 1227, 1233, 2001 Wash. App. LEXIS 2810 (2001)   336

Hamilton v. Jones, 2005 Ark. App. LEXIS 92 (2005)   427

Hamilton v. State, 293 Ga. App. 297, 298, 2008 Ga. App. LEXIS 926 (Ga. 2008)   150

Hampton v. Texas, 2003 Tex. App. LEXIS 3984 (2003)   307

Hanley v. Donoghue, 116 U.S. 1, 6 S. Ct. 242, 29 L. Ed. 535 (1885)   123

Hanna v. Price, 2005 U.S. Dist. LEXIS 30380 (W.D. Mich. 2005)   613

Hape v. State, 903 N.E.2d 977, 2009 Ind. App. LEXIS 637 (Ind. 2009)   245

Harrell v. City of Gastonia, 2009 U.S. Dist. LEXIS 6542 (W.D.N.C. 2009)   173

Harris v. New York, 401 U.S. 222 (1971)   248, 325, 674

Harrison v. Middleton, 52 Va. 527, 544 (1854)   295

Hartman et al. v. Moore, 126 S. Ct. 1695, 1705, 164 L. Ed. 2d 441, 456, 2006 U.S. LEXIS 3450 (2006)   146

Hasson v. Commonwealth, 2006 Va. App. LEXIS (2006)   440, 522

Hatcher v. State, 277 Ga. App. 611, 613, 627 S.E.2d 175, 177, 2006 Ga. App. LEXIS 164 (2005)   403

Havard v. State, 928 So. 2d 771, 2006 Miss. LEXIS 90 (Miss. 2006)   569

Hawai'i v. Jones, 98 Haw. 294, 2002 Haw. App. LEXIS 65 (2002)   279

Hawai'i v. Wong, 97 Haw. 512, 40 P.3d 914, 2002 Haw. LEXIS 100 (2002)   356

Hawkins v. Arkansas, 105 S.W.3d 397, 2003 Ark. App. LEXIS 334 (2003)   543

Hawkins v. United States, 358 U.S. 74, 75, 1958 U.S. LEXIS 115 (1958)   258, 339

Haycraft v. State, 760 N.E.2d 203, 209, 2001 Ind. App. LEXIS 2225 (2001)   254

Haynes Mall v. Central Carolina, 2006 N.C. App. LEXIS 175 (N.C. 2006)   110

Heartland Surgical Specialty Hosp., LLC v. Midwest Division, 2007 U.S. Dist. LEXIS 53216 (D. Kan. 2007)   315

Heath v. Rush, 259 Ga. App. 887, 578 S.E.2d 564, 2003 Ga. App. LEXIS 287 (2003)   402

Height v. State, 278 Ga. 592, 594, 595, 604 S.E.2d 796; 2004 Ga. LEXIS 958 (2004)   435

Heinzerling v. Goldfarb, 359 N.J. Super. 1, 8, 818 A. 2d 345, 349, 2002 N.J. Super. LEXIS 531 (2002)   531

Helena v. City of San Francisco, 2006 U.S. Dist. LEXIS 27 (N.D. Cal. 2006)   270

Helmig v. Kemna, 2006 U.S. App. LEXIS 22564 (8th Cir. 2006)   571

Henderson v. State, 2005 Tenn. Crim. App. LEXIS 667 (2005)   266

Hernandez v. Robles, 2005 N.Y. Slip Op. 9436, 805 N.Y.S.2d 354, 2005 N.Y. App. Div. LEXIS 13892 (2005)   344

Hernandez v. State, 4 So. 3d 642, 2009 Fla. LEXIS 149 (Fla. 2009)   287

Herring v. United States, _____ U.S. _____, 2009 U.S. LEXIS 581 (2009)   649

Hester v. United States, 265 U.S. 57 (1924)   658

Hicks v. Jones, 2008 U.S. Dist. LEXIS 104274, n.5 (N.D. Ok. 2008)   132

Hiibel v. Sixth Judicial District Court of Nevada, 542 U.S. 177, 194, 2004 U.S. LEXIS 4385 (2004)   433, 594, 663

Hill v. Geren, 2009 U.S. Dist. LEXIS 10237 (D.C. D.C. 2009)   173

Hill v. State v. State, 290 Ga. App. 140, 658 S.E.2d 863, 241, 2008 Ga. App. LEXIS 272 (2008)   64

Hill v. State, 2003 Fla. App. LEXIS 8327 (2003)   366

Hines v. State, 2006 Tex. App. LEXIS 3256 (2006)   396

Hinkle v. Cleveland Clinic, 159 Ohio App. 3d 351, 2004 Ohio 6853, 823 N.E.2d 945, 2004 Ohio App. LEXIS 6382 (2004)   424

Hinton v. State, 2006 Ala. Crim. App. LEXIS 72 (2006)   610, 619, 620

HLC Properties, Ltd. v. Superior Court, 35 Cal. 4th 54, 62, 105 P.3d 560, 565, 2005 Cal. LEXIS 1607 (2005)   360

Hoffman v. Gregory, 2005 Ark. LEXIS 135 (Ark. 2005)   36

Holloway v. State, 2005 Ark. LEXIS 497 (Ark. 2005)   563

Holt v. State, 2006 Tenn. Crim. App. LEXIS 107 (2006)   238

Holt v. United States, 218 U.S. 245, 31 S. Ct. 2, 54 L. Ed. 1021 (1910)   593

Hortman v. State, 293 Ga. App. 803, 807, 2008 Ga. App. LEXIS 1082 (Ga. 2008)   185

House v. Bell, 547 U.S. 518, 2006 U.S. LEXIS 4675 (2006)   629

Houston v. Schomig, 533 F.3d 1076, 1086, 2008 U.S. App. LEXIS 16251 (9th Cir. 2008)   183

Howard v. State, 2008 Miss. App. LEXIS 478 (Miss. 2008)   88

Hubanks v. Frank, 392 F.3d 926, 932, 2004 U.S. App. LEXIS 26791 (7th Cir. 2004)   594

Hubbert v. Mississippi, 759 So. 2d 504, 505, 506, 2000 Miss. App. LEXIS 196 (2000)   436

Huddleston v. United States, 485 U.S. 681, 108 S. Ct. 1496, 96 L. Ed. 2d 771 (1988)   227

Hudson v. Michigan, 547 U.S. 586, 2006 U.S. LEXIS 4677 (2006)   79, 641, 648

Hudson v. State, 95 Ark. 85, 102, 146 S.W.3d 380, 390, 2004 Ark. App. LEXIS 124 (2004)   556

Hull v. State, 172 S.W.3d 186, 189, 2005 Tex. App. LEXIS 6502 (2005)   514

Hutchins v. UPS, 2006 U.S. App. LEXIS 19885 (3d Cir. 2006)   581

Hyde v. Paskett, 383 F. Supp. 2d 1256, 2005 U.S. Dist. LEXIS 23165 (D. Idaho 2005)   115

Ibarrondo v. State, 2008 Fla. App. LEXIS 20619 (Fla. 2008)   142

Idaho v. Siegel, 137 Idaho 538, 541, 50 P.3d 1033, 1036, 2002 Idaho App. LEXIS 30 (2002)   225

Illinois v Caballes, 543 U.S. 405, 2005 U.S. LEXIS 769 (2005)   589

Illinois v. Diehl, 335 Ill. App. 3d 693, 704, 783 N.E.2d 640, 650, 2002 Ill. App. LEXIS 1060 (2003)   318

Illinois v. Gates, 462 U.S. 213, 103 S. Ct. 2317, 76 L. Ed. 2d 527 (1983)   373

Illinois v. Jennings, 252 Ill. 534, 96 N.E. 1077 (1911)   439

Illinois v. Krull, 475 U.S. 868, 107 S. Ct. 1160, 94 L. Ed. 2d 364 (1987)   644

Illinois v. Krull, 480 U.S. 340 (1987)   168

Illinois v. Lidster, 540 U.S. 419, 2004 U.S. LEXIS 656 (2004)   645

Illinois v. Millbratz, 323 Ill. App. 3d 206, 211, 751 N.E.2d 650, 2001 Ill. App. LEXIS 541 (2001)   303

Illinois v. Moore, 335 Ill. App. 3d 616, 781 N.E.2d 493, 2002 Ill. App. LEXIS 1058 (2002)   545

Illinois v. Rodriguez, 497 U.S. 177 (1990)   652

Illinois v. Sparks, 335 Ill. App. 3d 249, 253, 780 N.E.2d 781, 784, 2002 Ill. App. LEXIS 1132 (2002)   570

Illinois v. Thompson, 327 Ill. App. 3d 1061, 765 N.E.2d 1203, 2002 Ill. App. LEXIS 162 (2002)   455

Illinois v. Wardlow, 528 U.S. 119 (2000)   214

In re Aircraft Accident at Little Rock, Arkansas, June 1, 1999, 231 F. Supp. 2d 852, 2002 U.S. Dist. LEXIS 22881 (E.D. Ark. 2002)   427

In re Application of the United States of America for an Order Authorizing the Installation and Use of a Pen Register, 402 F. Supp. 2d 597 (D. Md. 2005)   667

In re Care and Treatment of Ward, 131 P.3d 540, 547, 2006 Kan. App. LEXIS 296 (Kan. 2006)   48

In re Chaing, 274 B.R. 295, 305, 2002 Bankr. LEXIS 170 (D. Mass. 2002)   116

In re Civil Commitment of Barber, 2005 Minn. LEXIS 355 (Minn. 2005)   48

In re Comair Air Disaster Litigation, 100 F.R.D. 350 (1983)   297

In re Crossley, 2003 Mich. App. LEXIS 327 (2003)   436

In re Directives Pursuant to Section 105b of the Foreign Intelligence Surveillance Act, 2008 U.S. App. LEXIS 27417 (Fed. Cir. 2008)   174

In re Estate of Bean, 2005 Tenn. App. LEXIS 754 (Tenn. 2005)   195

In re Estate of Doris Rosen, Deceased, 2003 Pa. Super. 96, 819 A.2d 585, 2003 Pa. Super. LEXIS 364 (2003)   475

In re Grand Jury Investigation, 918 F.2d 374 (3d Cir. 1990)   369

In re Grand Jury Proceedings, 445 F.3d 266, 274, 2006 U.S. App. LEXIS 10041 (2006)   357

In re Grand Jury Subpoena (Miller), 365 U.S. App. D.C. 13, 397 F.3d 964, 2005 U.S. App. LEXIS 2494 (2005)   386

In re Grand Jury Subpoenas, 2003 U.S. Dist. LEXIS 9022 (S.D.N.Y. 2003)   353

In re Inquest Subpoena (WCAX), 2005 Vt. 103, 890 A.2d 1240, 1241, 2005 Vt. LEXIS 244 (2005)   385

In re J.M., 2006 Ohio 1203, 2006 Ohio App. LEXIS 1088 (2006)   253, 254

In re Kentron D., 101 Cal. App. 4th 1381, 125 Cal. Rptr. 2d 260, 2002 Cal. App. LEXIS 4629 (2002)   450

In re Lott, 139 Fed. Appx. 658; 2005 U.S. App. LEXIS 12280 (2005)   360

In re Lott, 424 F.3d 446, 452, 2005 U.S. App. LEXIS 19429, 2005 Fed. Appx. 383P (6th Cir. 2005)   360

In re Loughran, 276 F. Supp. 393, 430, 1967 U.S. Dist. LEXIS 7589 (C.D. Cal. 1967)   250

In re Marriage Cases, 43 Cal. 4th 757, 2008 Cal. LEXIS 5247 (Cal. 2008)   344

In re New York County, 98 N.Y.2d 525, 779 N.E.2d 173, 178, 749 N.Y.S.2d 462, 467, 2002 N.Y. LEXIS 3140 (2002)   365

In re Roger W. Jordan, 913 So. 2d 775; 2005 La. LEXIS 2104 (2005)   93

In re Solis, 2008 Tex. App. LEXIS 7529 (Tex. 2008)   133

In re Swenson, 183 Minn. 602, 237 N.W. 589 (1931)   370

In re Winship, 397 U.S. 358 (1970)   49

In re Winship, 397 U.S. 358 (1970); State v. Sullivan, 34 Idaho 68, 199 P. 647 (1921)   57

In re Winship, 397 U.S. 358, 1970 U.S. LEXIS 56 (1970)   52, 53, 72

In the Interest of A. C., 263 Ga. App. 44, 45, 587 S.E.2d 210, 211, 2003 Ga. App. LEXIS 1087 (2003)   130

In the Interest of B.D.S., 269 Ga. App. 89, 90, 91, 603 S.E.2d 488, 489, 2004 Ga. App. LEXIS 1084 (2004), aff'd, 273 Ga. App. 576, 615 S.E.2d 627, 2005 Ga. App. LEXIS 579 (2005)   410

In the Interest of B.D.-Y., a Child under the Age of 18, 286 Kan. 686, 693, 187 P.3d 594, 599, 2008 Kan. LEXIS 343 (Kan. 2008)   50

In the Interest of F.P., 2005 Pa. Super. 220, 878 A.2d 91, 93, 2005 Pa. Super. LEXIS 1499 (2005)   521

In the Interest of J. D. S., a child, 273 Ga. App. 576, 615 S.E.2d 627, 2005 Ga. App. LEXIS 579 (2005)   623

In the Interest of J.P.B, 180 S.W.3d 570, 575, 2005 Tex. LEXIS 912 (Tex. 2005)   575

In the Interest of J.P.B., 2005 Texas App LEXIS 1159 (Tex. 2005)   575

In the Matter of Kassan D., 287 A.D.2d 564, 565, 566, 731 N.Y.S.2d 487, 2001 N.Y. App. Div. LEXIS 9594 (2001)   543

In the Matter of S.H., 2008 Tenn App. LEXIS 262 (Tenn. 2008)   51
In the Matter of the Care and Treatment of John W. Morgan v. State, 2009 Mo. App. LEXIS 8
    (Mo. 2009)   52
Indianapolis v. Edmond, 531 U.S. 32 (2000)   645
Ingram v. United States, 885 A.2d 257, 264, 2005 D.C. App. LEXIS 533 (2005)   489
Inoue v. Inoue, 118 Haw. 86, 101, 2008 Haw. App. LEXIS 50 (Hawai'I 2008)   149
Iowa v. Anderson, 636 N.W.2d 26, 32, 33, 2001 Iowa Sup. LEXIS 217 (2001)   350
Iowa v. Dullard, 2003 Iowa Sup. LEXIS 169 (2003)   450
Iowa v. Stevenson, 2001 Iowa App. LEXIS 752 (2001)   299
Isler v. United States, 2003 D.C. App. LEXIS 291 (2003)   299
Izac v. United States, 2008 U.S. Dist. LEXIS 80013 (N.D.W.VA. 2008)   281

J.L. v. Indiana, 789 N.E.2d 961, 963, 964, 2003 Ind. App. LEXIS 921 (2003)   468
J.R.T. II v. State, 783 N.E.2d 300, 2003 Ind. App. LEXIS 171 (2003)   435
Jackson v. City of Chicago, 2005 U.S. Dist. LEXIS 32538 (N. D. Ill. 2005)   361
Jackson v. State, 116 Nev. 334, 2000 Nev. LEXIS 35 (Nev. 2000)   183
Jackson v. State, 2005 Tex. App. LEXIS 3631 (2005)   347
Jackson v. United States, 856 A.2d 1111, 1114, 2004 D.C. App. LEXIS 413 (D.D.C. 2004)   225
Jackson v. Virginia, 443 U.S. 307, 99 S. Ct. 2781, 61 L. Ed. 2d 560 (1979)   56
Jaffee v. Richmond, 518 U.S. 1, 116 S. Ct. 1923 (1996)   362, 363
Jama Investments v. Los Alamos, 2006 U. S. Dist. LEXIS 29554 (E.D.N.M. 2006)   419
Jarrell v. Commonwealth of Virginia, 2002 Va. App. LEXIS 353 (2002)   318
Jefferson v. Roe, 2002 U.S. Dist. LEXIS 6153 (N.D. Cal. 2002)   416
Jenkins v. Commonwealth, 275 S.W.3d 226, 229, 2008 Ky. App. LEXIS 377 (Ky. 2008)   194
Johnson v. Commonwealth, 12 S.W.3d 258, 267, 1999 Ky. LEXIS 159 (1999)   121
Johnson v. Louisiana, 406 U.S. 356 (1972)   32
Johnson v. Quander, 370 U.S. App. D.C. 167, 440 F.3d 489, 499, 2006 U.S. App. LEXIS 6601
    (D.C. Cir. 2006)   630
Johnson v. State, 2008 Tex. App. LEXIS 5476 (Tex. 2008)   158
Johnson v. State, 878 S.W.2d 727 (Ark. 1994)   443
Johnson v. State, 929 So. 2d 4, 7, 2005 Fla. App. LEXIS 20 (2005)   469
Johnson v. Wilson, 2006 U.S. App. LEXIS 15479 (6th Cir. 2006)   144
Jones v. Bureau of Tennecare, 94 S.W.3d 495. 500, 501 (Tenn. 2002)   27
Jones v. Commonwealth, 277 Va. 171, 2009 Va. LEXIS 10 (Va. 2009)   242
Jones v. State, 2009 Ark. App. LEXIS 109 (Ark. 2009)   166
Jones v. State, 780 N.E.2d 373 at 376 (Ind. 2002)   86
Jones v. United States, 2003 D.C. App. LEXIS 434 (2003)   354
Joyner v. State, 2009 Fla. App. LEXIS 1492 (Fla. 2009)   194
Joyner v. United States, 818 A2d 166, 172, 2003 D.C. App. LEXIS 133 (2003)   311

K&K Leasing v. Tech Logistice, 2008 Iowa App. LEXIS 1107 (Iowa 2008)   126
Kaleta v. State, 2003 Tex. App. LEXIS 2677 (2003)   403
Kanani v. Phillips, 2004 U.S. Dist. LEXIS 20444 (S.D.N.Y. 2004)   590
Kansas Annotated Statutes, K.S.A. § 60–401 (2006)   194
Kansas v. Ventris, _____ U.S _____, 2009 U.S. LEXIS 3299 (2009)   325, 674
Kaufman v. Director of Revenue, 193 S.W.3d 300, 2006 Mo. App. LEXIS 215 (2006)   596
Kaufman v. United States, 350 F.2d 408 (8th Cir. 1965)   407
Kaupp v. Texas, 538 U.S. 626, 632, 2003 U.S. LEXIS 3670 (2003)   668
Kearney v. Savannah Foods, 350 F. Supp. 85 (S.D. Ga. 1972)   127
Kelly v. Florida, 843 So. 2d 223, 2003 Fla. App. LEXIS 4732 (2003)   306
Kentucky v. Whorton, 441 U.S. 786, 99 S. Ct. 2088, 60 L. Ed. 2d 640 (1979)   154
Kight v. State, 512 So. 2d 922 (Fla. 1987)   395
Killough v. State, 2008 Tex. App. LEXIS 1391, n.3 (Tex. 2008)   347

King v. State, 2008 Miss. App. LEXIS 765 (Miss. 2008)   309

Kline v. Lorillard, 878 F.2d 791 (4th Cir. 1989)   416

Knight v. Kerby Inland Marine, Inc., 363 F. Supp. 2d 859, 2005 U.S. Dist. LEXIS 10615 (2005)   119

Knowles v. Iowa, 525 U.S. 113, 1998 U.S. LEXIS 8068 (1998)   649

Kohlsaat v. Parkersburg & Marietta Sand Co., 266 F. 283 (4th Cir. 1920)   49

Kortum v. Johnson, 2008 ND 154, 2008 N.D. LEXIS 161 (N.D. 2008)   152

Krepps v. Government of the Virgin Islands, 2006 U.S. Dist. LEXIS 24904 (D.V.I. 2006)   568

Krinsky v. Doe, 159 Cal. App. 4th 1154, 2008 Cal. App. LEXIS 180 (Cal. 2008)   26

Kyllo v. United States, 533 U.S. 27 (2001)   566, 645

Lacaze v. Leger, 2008 U.S. Dist. LEXIS 37107 (W.D. La. 2008)   147

Lamar v. Georgia, 256 Ga. App. 567, 571, 568 S.E.2d 837, 2002 Ga. App. LEXIS 957 (2002)   569

Lamar v. Micou, 114 U.S. 218, 1885 U.S. LEXIS 274 (1885)   123

Lamkins v. State, 778 N.E.2d 1248, 1250, 2002 Ind. LEXIS 892 (2002)   289

Lampkins v. Indiana, 778 N.E.2d 1248, 1250, 2002 Ind. LEXIS 892 (2002)   291

Lancaster v. State, 294 Ga. App. 12, 17, 2008 Ga. App. LEXIS 1094 (Ga. 2008)   597

Lasalvia v. Johnson, 15 Mass. 622, 2003 Mass. Super. LEXIS 9 (2003)   535

Latimore v. City of Atlanta, 289 Ga. App. 85, 86, 2008 Ga. App. LEXIS 2 (Ga. 2008)   128

Lawrence v. State, 2005 Miss. App. LEXIS 552 (2005)   423

Lawrence v. Texas, 539 U.S. 558, 2003 U.S. LEXIS 5013 (2003)   344

Leary v. United States, 395 U.S. 6, 36, 1969 U.S. LEXIS 3271 (1969)   177

LeCroy v. Secretary, Florida Dept. of Corrections, 421 F.3d 1237, 1253, 2005 U.S. App. LEXIS 18570 (11th Cir. 2005)   361

Lee v. Martinez, 136 N.M. 166, 2004 N.M. LEXIS 378 (N.M. 2004)   184, 605

Leeper v. Texas, 139 U.S. 462 (1891)   594

Leeper v. Thornton, 344 P.2d 1101 (Okla. 1959)   427

Lego v. Twomey, 404 U.S. 477, 489, 1972 U.S. LEXIS 100 (1972)   669, 670

Leland v. Oregon, 343 U.S. 790 (1952)   64, 67

Leonard v. State, 100 Ohio St. 456, 127 N.E. 464 (1919)   24

Leppla v. State, 277 Ga. App. 804, 811, 627 S.E.2d 794, 800, 2006 Ga. App. LEXIS 75 (Ga. 2006)   219

Lewek v. State, 702 So. 2d 527 (Fla. 1997)   410

Lewis v. New York State Department of Civil Service, 2009 NY Slip Op 283, 2009 N.Y. App. LEXIS 415 (N.Y. 2009)   344

Lewis v. State, 2007 Ala. Crim. App. LEXIS 201 (Ala. 2007)   182

Lewis v. Virginia, 2004 Va. App. LEXIS 595 (2004)   420

Li v. State, 338 Or. 376, 110 P.3d 91, 2005 Or. LEXIS 490 (2004)   345

Liberty Mutual Ins. Co. v. Land, 186 N.J. 163, 169, 892 A.2d 1240, 1243, 2006 N.J. LEXIS 375 (N.J. 2006)   52

Liggett v. Superior Court, 260 Cal. Rptr. 161 (1989)   382

Linn v. State, 921 So. 2d 830, 2006 Fla. App. LEXIS 3040 (2006)   102

Livingston v. Texas, 2006 Tex. App. LEXIS 2234 (2006)   394

Logan v. United States, 144 U.S. 263, 1892 U.S. LEXIS 2080 (1892)   262

London v. State, 2008 Tex. App. LEXIS 9039 (Tex. 2008)   71

Long Lane Limited Partnership v. Bibb, 159 Fed. Appx. 189; 2005 U.S. App. LEXIS 26912 (Fed. Cir. 2005)   173

Long v. United States, 940 A.2d 87, 99, 2007 D.C. App. LEXIS 667 (D.C. Cir. 2007)   118

Longshore v. State, 399 Md. 486, 531, 532, 2007 Md. LEXIS 344 (Md. 2007)   246

Looney v. State, 2005 Ark. LEXIS 326 (Ark. 2005)   551

Looney v. State, 293 Ga. App. 639, 2008 Ga. App. LEXIS 1039 (Ga. 2008)   658

Lopez v. Texas, 990 S.W.2d 770, 777, 1999 Tex. App. LEXIS 871 (1999)   308

Lord Melville's Case, 29 How. St. Tr. 763 (1806)   31

Louisiana v. Nash, 821 So. 2d 678, 683, 684, 2002 La. App. LEXIS 1928 (2002)   351

Louisiana v. Scott, 823 So. 2d 960, 968, 2002 La. App. LEXIS 93 (2002), *remedial writ denied*, 843 So. 2d 1122, 2003 La. LEXIS 1653 (2003)   474

Louisiana v. Smith, 809 So. 2d 556, 565, 2002 La. App. LEXIS 221 (2002)   296

Lovelady v. State, 65 S.W.3d 810, 813, 2002 Tex. App. LEXIS 378 (2002)   118

Lumley v. State, 2006 Ga. LEXIS 755 (Ga. 2006)   526

Lynch v. Robertson, 2007 U.S. Dist. LEXIS 60835 (W.D. Pa. 2007)   114

Lyons v. State, 2008 Ark. App. LEXIS 430 (Ark. 2008)   255

Mack v. City of Abilene, 461 F.3d 547, 553 (5th Cir. 2006)   655

Mackey v. Russell, 148 Fed. Appx. 355, 2005 U.S. App. LEXIS 16933 (6th Cir. 2005)   247

Maddox v. Montgomery, 718 F.2d 1033 (11th Cir. 1983)   92

Maddox v. News Syndicate Co., 176 F.2d 897 (2d Cir. 1949)   28

Madisonville Boatyard, Ltd. v. Poole, 2001 U.S. Dist. LEXIS 20589 (E.D. La. 2001)   12

Maine v. Cookson, 2002 Me. Super. LEXIS 256 (2002)   619

Maine v. Irving, 2003 Me. 31, 818 A 2d 204, 2003 Me. LEXIS 36 (2003)   427

Makila Land Co. v. Kapu, 2006 Haw. App. LEXIS 181 (2006)   509

Malloy v. Hogan, 378 U.S. 1, 84 S. Ct. 1489, 12 L. Ed. 2d 653 (1964)   677

Malone v. ReliaStar Life Ins. Co., 2009 U.S. App. LEXIS 5106 (7th Cir. 2009)   172

Malutin v. State, 198 P.3d 1177, 2009 Alaska App. LEXIS 5 (Alaska 2009)   182

Mapp v. Ohio, 357 U.S. 643 (1961)   32, 79, 236, 641

Maranda v. State, 253 S.W.3d 762, 2007 Tex. App. LEXIS 9285 (Tex. 2007)   551

Marschke v. State, 185 S.W.3d 295, 307, 2006 Mo. App. LEXIS 280 (2006)   224

Marshall v. State, 2009 Ala. Crim. App. LEXIS 16 (Ala. 2009)   90

Marshall v. Williams, 153 N.C. 128, 134, 574 S.E.2d 1, 2002 N.C. App. LEXIS 1071 (2001)   401

Martin Marietta v. West Virginia, 227 F.R.D. 382, 2005 U.S. Dist. LEXIS 8379 (2005)   360

Martin v. Ohio, 480 U.S. 228 (1987)   50, 70

Maryland v. Buie, 494 U.S. 325, 110 S. Ct. 1093, 108 L. Ed. 2d 276 (1990)   651

Massachusetts v. Cintron, 435 Mass. 509, 522, 759 N.E.2d 700, 711, 2001 Mass. LEXIS 771 (2001)   311

Massachusetts v. Davis, 54 Mass. App. Ct. 756, 762, 767 N.E.2d 1110, 1116, 2002 Mass. App. LEXIS 674 (2002)   465

Massachusetts v. Ivy, 55 Mass. App. 851, 855, 774 N.E.2d 1100, 1104, 2002 Mass. App. LEXIS 1175 (2002)   463

Massachusetts v. Sheppard, 468 U.S. 981, 1984 U.S. LEXIS 154 (1984)   79, 644

Mata v. State, 46 S.W.3d 902, 910, 2001 Tex. Crim. App. LEXIS 45 (Tex. 2001)   119

Matos v. State, 899 So. 2d 403, 2005 Fla. App. LEXIS 4359 (2005)   427, 443, 624

Matter of Bennett, 2006 N.Y. Slip Op. 50889U (N.Y. 2006)   172

Matter of Infante v. Dignan, 865 N.Y.S.2d 167, 169 2008 N.Y. App. Div. LEXIS 7118 (N.Y. 2008)   160

Matter of Philip v. Lieberman, 851 N.Y.S.2d 141, 2008 N.Y. App. Div. LEXIS 57 (2008)   173

Mattox v. State, 191 P.3d 148, 2008 Alaska App. LEXIS 86 (Alaska 2008)   601

Mattox v. United States, 146 U.S. 140, 13 S. Ct. 50, 36 L. Ed. 917 (1892)   482

Mattox v. United States, 156 U.S. 237, 242, 15 S. Ct. 337, 339, 39 L. Ed. 409, 411, 1895 U.S. LEXIS 2131 (1895)   301

Maynard v. Government of the Virgin Islands, n.17, 2009 U.S. Dist. LEXIS 35132 (D.V.I. 2009)   323

McCall v. California, 542 U.S. 923, 2004 U.S. LEXIS 4451 (2004)   180

McCarter v. Commonwealth of Virginia, 38 Va. App 502, 506, 507, 566 S.E.2d 868, 869, 870, 2002 Va. App. LEXIS 393 (2002)   323

McCombs v. State, 2008 Ala. Crim. App. LEXIS 139 (Ala. 2008)   96

McCormick v. State, 2006 Tex. App. LEXIS 1619 (2006)   528

McCumber v. Texas, 202 Tex. App. LEXIS 7351 (2002)   471

McDowell v. Commonwealth, 48 Va. App. 104, 628 S.E.2d 542, 2006 Va. App. LEXIS 229 (2006)   472

McEwing v. State, 2006 Ark. LEXIS 332 (Ark. 2006)   65

McFarland v. United States, 150 F.2d 593 (D.C. Cir. 1945)   594

McGory v. City of New York, 2002 U.S. Dist. LEXIS 20177 (S.D.N.Y. 2002)   491

McGregor v. State, 2004 Tex. App. LEXIS 3365 (2004)   589

McHenry v. State, 820 N.E.2d 124, 128, 2005 Ind. LEXIS 4 (Ind. 2005)   571, 572

McIntosh v. State, 917 So. 2d 78, 84, 2005 Miss. LEXIS 754 (Miss. 2005)   568

McKeehan v. State, 838 So. 2d 1257, 1259, 2003 Fla. App. LEXIS 3367 (2003)   523

McKenny v. State, 967 So. 2d 951, 2007 Fla. App. LEXIS 15581 (Fla. 2007)   65

McMillin v. Davidson Industries, 2005 Ohio 224, 2005 Ohio App. LEXIS 221 (2005)   267

Meadows v. Commonwealth, 178 S.W.3d 527, 536, 2005 Ky. App. LEXIS 131 (2005)   211

Medina v. California, 505 U.S. 437, 449, 1992 U.S. LEXIS 3696 (1992)   157

Medina v. Diguglielmo, 373 F. Supp. 2d 526; 2005 U.S. Dist. LEXIS 10672 (E.D. Pa. 2005)   249

Mejia v. Garcia, 534 F.3d 1036, 1042, 2008 U.S. App. LEXIS 15933 (9th Cir. 2008)   146

Merriweather v. Commonwealth, 99 S.W.3d 448, 2003 Ky. LEXIS 39 (2003)   236

Michael v. State, 235 S.W.3d 723, 725, 2007 Tex. Crim. App. LEXIS 1267 (Tex. 2007)   327

Michell v. State, 689 So. 2d 1118 (Fla. 1997)   519

Michigan v. Allen, 466 Mich. 86, 87, n. 1, 643 N.W.2d 227, 229, n.1 (2002)   54

Michigan v. Harvey, 494 U.S. 344, 110 S. Ct. 1176, 108 L. Ed. 2d 293 (1990)   682

Michigan v. Jackson, 475 U.S. 625, 1986 U.S. LEXIS 91 (1986)   681

Michigan v. Long, 463 U.S. 1032, 103 S. Ct. 3469, 77 L. Ed. 2d 1201 (1983)   663

Michigan v. Sitz, 496 U.S. 444 (1990)   645

Microsoft v. Atek 3000 Computer, 2008 U.S. Dist. LEXIS 56689 (E.D.N.Y. 2008)   122

Miller v. Fenton, 474 U.S. 104, 106 S. Ct. 445, 88 L. Ed. 2d 405 (1985)   670

Miller v. Fenton, 474 U.S. 104, 112, 1985 U.S. LEXIS 144 (1985)   668

Miller v. State, 2004 Tex. App. LEXIS 11547 (Tex. 2004)   542

Mills v. Commonwealth, 95 S.W.3d 838, 840, 841, 2003 Ky. LEXIS 11 (2003)   286

Mills v. Oberg, 2005 Minn. App. LEXIS 106 (2005)   428

Mima Queen and Child v. Hepburn, 7 U.S. (3 Cranch) 290 (1813)   459

Mims v. Wright, 578 S.E.2d 606 (N.C. 2003)   337

Mincey v. Arizona, 437 U.S. 385, 1978 U.S. LEXIS 115 (1978)   325, 674

Minnesota v. Dickerson, 508 U.S. 366, 1993 U.S. LEXIS 4018 (1993)   664

Minnesota v. Gianakos, 644 N.W.2d 409, 418, 419, 2002 Minn. LEXIS 350 (2002)   350

Minnesota v. Martinez, 657 N.W.2d 600, 602, 603, 2003 Minn. App. LEXIS 252 (2003)   315

Minnesota v. Roman Nose, 667 N.W.2d 386, 2003 Minn. LEXIS 513 (2003)   556

Miranda v. Arizona, 384 U.S. 436, 16 L. Ed. 2d 694, 86 S. Ct. 1602 (1966)   32, 324, 672, 673, 680

Missouri v. Churchill, 98 S.W. 3d 536, 2003 Mo. LEXIS 37 (2003)   416

Missouri v. Dewey, 86 S.W.3d 434, 440, 2002 Mo. App. LEXIS 2055 (2002)   425

Missouri v. Mozee, 2003 Mo. App. LEXIS 940 (2003), State v. Bowens, 964 S.W. 2d 232, 240, 1998 Mo. App. LEXIS 383 (1998)   450

Missouri v. Pacheco, 101 S.W.3d 913, 2003 Mo. App. LEXIS 543 (2003)   559

Missouri v. Seibert, 542 U.S. 600, 2004 U.S. LEXIS 4578 (2004)   325

Mixon v. State, 179 S.W.3d 233, 235, 2005 Tex. App. LEXIS 9079 (2005)   357

Mixon v. State, 2007 Tex. App. LEXIS 4310 (Tex. 2007)   318

Moler v. Indiana, 782 N.E.2d 454, 2003 Ind. App. LEXIS 119, *transfer denied*, 2003 Ind. LEXIS 119 (2003)   406

Molerio v. FBI, 242 U.S. App. D.C. 137, 749 F.2d 815, 820–21 (D.C. Cir. 1984)   376

Moniz v. State, 933 A.2d 691, 696, 2007 R.I. LEXIS 100 (2007)   96
Montana v. Egelhoff, 518 U.S. 37, 56, 1996 U.S. LEXIS 3878 (1996)   220
Montana v. Kvislen, 2003 Mont. 27, 314 Mont. 176, 2003 Mont. LEXIS 26 (2003)   174
Montgomery Mutual v. Chesson, 399 Md. 314, 327, 2007 Md. LEXIS 331 (Md. 2007)   119
Montgomery v. State, 2006 Tex. App. LEXIS 3377 (2006)   423
Moon v. State, 22 Ariz. 418, 424, 198 P. 288 (Ariz. 1921)   615
Mooneyham v. State, 915 So. 2d 1102, 1104, 2005 Miss. App. LEXIS 989 (2005)   417
Moore v. Commonwealth, 634 S.W.2d 426 (Ky. 1982)   319
Moore v. Illinois, 408 U.S. 786, 92 S. Ct. 2562, 33 L. Ed. 2d 706 (1972)   583
Moore v. Illinois, 434 U.S. 220, 225, 1977 U.S. LEXIS 163 (1977)   683
Moore v. State, 2005 Ark. LEXIS 245 (2005)   290
Moran v. Ford Motor Co., 476 F.2d 289 (8th Cir. 1973)   416
Morrow v. State, 230 Ga. App. 137, 495 S.E.2d 609 (1998)   416
Moss v. Georgia, 274 Ga. 740, 559 S.E.2d 433, 2002 Ga. LEXIS 48 (2002)   540
Muhammad v. Commonwealth, 611 S.E.2d 537, 576, 2005 Va. LEXIS 39 (Va. 2005)   581
Mullin v. Brown, 210 Ariz. 545, 548, 115 P.3d 139, 142, 2005 Ariz. App. LEXIS 83 (2005)   151
Murray v. United States, 468 U.S. 796 (1984)   646
Murray v. United States, 487 U.S. 533 (1988)   642
Murrell v. State (In re Murrell), 215 S.W.3d 96, 2007 Mo. LEXIS 21 (Mo. 2007)   192
Myers v. State, 2009 Tex. App. LEXIS 8191 (Tex. 2008)   318

Neder v. United States, 527 U.S. 1 (1999)   59
Neder v. United States, 527 U.S. 1, 1999 U.S. LEXIS 4007 (1999)   53
Nehls v. Norris, 2008 U.S. Dist. LEXIS 101820 (E.D. Ark. 2008)   168
Neil v. Biggers, 409 U.S. 188, 1972 U.S. LEXIS 6 (1972)   208
Nester v. Jernigan, 908 So. 2d 145,149, 2005 Miss. LEXIS 467 (2005)   355
New Jersey v. Brown, 170 N.J. 138, 148, 784 A.2d 1244, 1251, 2001 N.J. LEXIS 1409 (2001)   486
New Jersey v. Nesbitt, 185 N.J. 504, 511, 888 A.2d 472, 478, 2006 N.J. LEXIS 7 (2006)   441
New Jersey v. Summers, 176 N.J. 306, 323, 324, 823 A.2d 15, 2003 N.J. LEXIS 567 (2003)   441
New Jersey v. Summers, 350 N.J. Super. 353, 365, 366, 795 A.2d 308, 2002 N.J. Super. LEXIS 195 (2002)   441
New Jersey v. T.L.O., 469 U.S. 325, 105 S. Ct. 733, 83 L. Ed. 2d 720 (1985)   661
New Jersey v. Velez, 329 N.J. Super. 128 at 134, 746 A.2d 1073 at 1077 (2000)   96
New Process Steel, L.P. v. Sharp Freight System, n.5, 2006 Tex. App. LEXIS 2967 (2006)   118
New York Times v. Gonzales, 382 F. Supp. 2d 457, 2005 U.S. Dist. LEXIS 2642 (2005)   386
New York v. Byrd, 303 A.D. 2d 184, 756 N.Y.S.2d 190, 2003 N.Y. App. Div. LEXIS 2223 (2003)   567
New York v. Lanza, 299 A.D.2d 649, 650, 749 N.Y.S.2d 618, 620, 2002 N.Y. App. Div. LEXIS 10780 (2002)   543
New York v. Quarles, 467 U.S. 649 (1984)   649, 675
New York v. Shinnecock Indian Nation, 523 F. Supp. 2d 185, 262, 2007 U.S. Dist. LEXIS 80443 (E.D N.Y. 2007)   117
Newport v. Commonwealth, 2005 Va. App. LEXIS 152 (Va. 2005)   179
Newsome v. State, 829 S.W.2d 260 (Tex. 1992)   290
Newton v. Kemna, 354 F.3d 776, 781, 2004 U.S. App. LEXIS 232 (8th Cir. 2004)   324
Nicholson v. Kane, 2009 U.S. Dist. LEXIS 21889 (N.D. Ga. 2009)   150
Nickleson v. State, 2005 Tex. App. LEXIS 6658 (2005)   223
Nimitz v. State, 2008 Tex. App. LEXIS 8341 (Tex. 2008)   139
Nix v. Williams, 467 U.S. 431 (1984)   642, 646
Noel v. Hendricks, 2006 U.S. Dist. LEXIS 41374 (D.N.J. 2006)   630

Norman v. Georgia, 269 Ga. App. 219, 223, 603 S.E.2d 737, 742, 2004 Ga. App. LEXIS 1120
    (2004)   249
North Carolina v. Beane, 146 N.C. App. 220, 225, 226, 552 S.E.2d 193, 196, 197, 2001 N.C.
    App. LEXIS 852 (2001)   281
North Carolina v. Boekenoogen, 147 N.C. App. 292, 297, 554 S.E.2d 848, 851, 2001 N.C. App.
    LEXIS 1143 (2001)   307
North Carolina v. Calloway, 2002 N.C. App. LEXIS 2438 (2002)   314
North Carolina v. Gregory, 154 N.C. App 718, 722, 572 S.E.2d 838, 840, 841, 2002 N.C. App.
    LEXIS 1534 (2002)   318
North Carolina v. Love, 576 S.E.2d 709, 712, 713, 2003 N.C. LEXIS 114 (2003)   299
North Carolina v. Riley, 54 N.C. App. 692, 695, 572 S.E.2d 857, 859, 2002 N.C. App. LEXIS
    1531 (2002)   466
North Carolina v. Robinson, 2002 N.C. App. LEXIS 2403 (2002)   291
North Dakota v. Stewart, 2002 N.D. 102, 646 N.W.2d 712, 715, 2002 N.D. LEXIS 140
    (2002)   316
North Dakota v. Stewart, 2002 N.D. 102, 646 N.W.2d 712, 715, 716, 2002 N.D. LEXIS 140
    (2002)   320

O'Brien v. Ed Donnelly Enterprises, 2007 U.S. Dist. LEXIS 92973 (S.D. Ohio 2007)   534
O'Daniel v. Messier 905 S.W.2d 182, 1995 Tenn App. LEXIS (Tenn 1995)   51
O'Grady v. Superior Court, 2006 Cal. App. LEXIS 802 (2006)   383
O'Neal v. Renico, 2005 U.S. Dist. LEXIS 31045 (E.D. Mich. 2005)   39
Ocean Mammal Inst. V. Gates, 2008 U.S. Dist. LEXIS 42068 (D.C. Haw. 2008)   358
Odum v. Georgia, 255 Ga. App. 70, 564 S.E.2d 490, 2002 Ga. App. LEXIS 478 (2002)   622
Ohio v. Boden, 2002 Ohio 5043, 2002 Ohio App. LEXIS 5060 (2002)   290
Ohio v. Bolling, 2001 Ohio App. LEXIS 3248 (2001)   407
Ohio v. Brennan, 2002 Ohio App. LEXIS 5788 (2002)   431
Ohio v. Bronner, 2002 Ohio 4248, 2002 Ohio App. LEXIS 4413 (2002)   222
Ohio v. Cotterman, 2001 Ohio App. LEXIS 3322 (2001)   249
Ohio v. Davis, 2002 Ohio App. LEXIS 7280 (2002)   403
Ohio v. DiBlasio, 2002 Ohio 2466, 2002 Ohio App. LEXIS 2691 (2002)   435
Ohio v. Doe, 433 F.3d 502, 2006 U.S. App. LEXIS 481 (6th Cir. 2006)   359
Ohio v. Linder, 2002 Ohio 5077, 2002 Ohio App. LEXIS 5113 (2002)   321
Ohio v. Mustafa, 2001 Ohio App. LEXIS 5661 (2001)   519
Ohio v. Payton, 2002 Ohio App. LEXIS 496 (2002)   506
Ohio v. Perry, 147 Ohio App. 3d 164, 170, 171, 768 N.E.2d 1259, 1264, 2002 Ohio App. LEXIS
    1169 (2002)   298
Ohio v. Roberts, 448 U.S. 56, 1980 U.S. LEXIS 140 (1980)   456
Ohio v. Robinette, 517 U.S. 33, 177 S. Ct. 417, 136 L. Ed. 2d 347 (1996)   653
Ohio v. Thomas, 2002 Ohio 7333, 2002 Ohio App. LEXIS 7226 (2002)   100
Ohio v. Turner, 105 Ohio St. 3d 331, 341, 2005 Ohio 1938, 826 N.E.2d 266, 278, 2005 Ohio
    LEXIS 961 (2005)   123
Ohio v. Zentner, 2003 Ohio App. LEXIS 2185 (2003)   394
Oliver v. United States, 466 U.S. 170, 104 S. Ct. 1735, 80 L. Ed. 2d 214 (1984)   658
Oregon v Bradshaw, 463 U.S. 1039, 103 S. Ct. 2830, 77 L. Ed. 2d 405 (1983)   681
Oregon v. Hass, 420 U.S. 714, 91 S. Ct. 1215, 43 L. Ed. 2d 570 (1975)   325, 674
Orion Ref. Corp. v. UOP, 259 S.W.3rd 749(Tex. 2007)   126
Orlenas v. United States, 517 U.S. 690 (1996)   655
Ortiz v. Texas, 2005 Tex. App. LEXIS 6721 (2005)   401
Osborne v. Salmon, 2006 Ark. App. LEXIS 266 (2006)   485
Osborne v. State, 2006 Miss. App. LEXIS 134 (2006)   293
Osbourn v. State, 92 S.W.3d 531, 537 (Tex. Crim. App. 2002)   392
Osbourn v. Texas, 92 S.W.3d 531, 537, 2002 Tex. Crim. App. LEXIS 236 (2002)   404

Oursbourn v. State, 259 S.W.3d 159, 180, 2008 Tex. Crim. App. LEXIS 686 (Tex. 2008)   247
Overton v. Mathes, 425 F.3d 518, 520, 2005 U.S. App. LEXIS 21885 (8th Cir. 2005)   549

Pacheco v. State, 698 So. 2d 393 (Fla. 1997)   305
Padilla v. State, 254 S.W.3d 585, 2008 Tex. App. LEXIS 2719 (Tex. 2008)   53, 202
Palmas y Bambu v. E.I Dupont, 881 So. 2d 565; 2004 Fla. App. LEXIS 7372 (Fla. 2004)   140
Panitz v. Behrend, 2001 Pa. Super. 93, 771 A.2d 803, 2001 Pa. Super. LEXIS 372 (2001)   416
Parker v. Allen, 2009 U.S. App. LEXIS 8275 (11th Cir. 2009)   613
Parker v. State, 2009 Ga. App. LEXIS 319 (Ga. 2009)   156
Parkinson v. Kelly, 2006 U.S. Dist. LEXIS 54661 (N.D.N.Y. 2006)   571
Parsons v. Honeywell, 929 F.2d 901, 907 (2d Cir. 1991)   491
Paschal v. State, 280 Ga. 430, 432, 628 S.E.2d 586, 589, 2006 Ga. LEXIS 202 (2006)   544
Patterson v. New York, 432 U.S. 197, 206 (1977)   50
Patterson v. New York, 432 U.S. 197, 97 S. Ct. 2319, 53 L. Ed. 2d 281 (1977)   67
Payne v. Commonwealth, 623 S.W.2d 867, 877 (Ky. 1981)   565
Payne v. Tennessee, 501 U.S. 808 (1991)   205
Pearce v. Commonwealth, 53 Va. App. LEXIS 113, 2008 Va. App. LEXIS 545 (Va. 2008)   301
Pennsylvania Board of Probation and Parole v. Scott, 524 U.S. 357, 1998 U.S. LEXIS 4037 (1998)   39
Pennsylvania v. Keys, 2003 Pa. Super. 5, 814 A.2d 1256, 1258, 2003 Pa. Super. LEXIS 4 (2003)   461, 465
Pennsylvania v. Zukauskas, 501 Pa. 500, 503, 462 A.2d 236, 237, 1983 Pa. LEXIS 620 (1983)   461
People v Wilkinson, 102 Cal. App. 4th 72, 125 Cal. Rptr. 2d 294 (2002)   91
People v. Acosta, 29 Cal. 4th 105 at 120, 52 P.3d 624 at 634, 124 Cal. Rptr. 2d 435 at 447 (2002)   132
People v. Alston, 24 A.D.3d 391, 806 N.Y.S.2d 208, 209, 2005 N.Y. App. Div. LEXIS 14894 (2005)   560
People v. Ayers, 125 Cal. App. 4th 988, 994, 23 Cal. Rptr. 3d 242, 245, 2005 Cal. App. LEXIS 50 (2005)   470
People v. Badgett, 30 Cal. Rptr. 2d 152 (1994)   343
People v. Bell, 2008 Mich. App. LEXIS 2307 (Mich. 2008)   265
People v. Benore, 2005 Mich. App. LEXIS 2718 (2005)   213, 568
People v. Bickham, 89 Ill. 2d 1, 431 N.E.2d 365 (1982)   367
People v. Bock, 357 Ill. App. 3d 160, 168, 827 N.E.2d 1089, 1095, 2005 Ill. App. LEXIS 386 (2005)   598
People v. Bostic, 2006 Colo. App. LEXIS 622 (2006)   657
People v. Bridges, 2003 Ill. App. LEXIS 888)   670
People v. Brooks, 2008 Mich. App. LEXIS 1581 (Mich. 2008)   204
People v. Brooks, 950 P.2d 649, 652, 1997 Colo. App. LEXIS 183 (1997)   592
People v. Brown, 2005 N.Y. Slip Op. 25303, 9 Misc. 3d 420, 423, 801 N.Y.S.2d 709, 711, 2005 N.Y. Misc. LEXIS 1556 (2005)   438
People v. Brown, 2006 Cal. App. Unpub. LEXIS 4196 (2006)   658
People v. Brown, 2009 Cal. App. Unpub. LEXIS 1600 (Cal. 2009)   169
People v. Brownridge, 225 Mich. App. 291, 570 N.W.2d 672 (1997)   490
People v. Bunyard, 2009 Cal. LEXIS 1102 (Cal. 2009)   90
People v. Carrasco, 163 Cal. App. 4th 978, 991, 2008 Cal. App. LEXIS 844 (Cal. 2008)   270
People v. Cazacu, 373 Ill. App. 3d 465, 2007 Ill. App. LEXIS 484 (Ill. 2007)   139
People v. Christmann, 3 Misc. 3d 309, 311, 776 N.Y.S.2d 437, 439, 2004 N.Y. Misc. LEXIS 45 (N.Y. 2004)   624
People v. Clark, 2009 Colo. App. LEXIS 365 (Colo. 2009)   209
People v. Clay, 361 Ill. App. 3d 310, 325, 836 N.E.2d 872, 885, 2005 Ill. App. LEXIS 994 (2005)   67, 68, 159

People v. Conner, 2005 Mich. App. LEXIS 653 (2005)   545

People v. Cook, 40 Cal. 4th 1334, 2007 Cal. LEXIS 5070 (Cal. 2007)   603

People v. Cotton, 2002 Cal. App. Unpub. LEXIS 421 (2002)   200

People v. Cumbee, 851 N.E.2d 934, 948, 2006 Ill. App. LEXIS 578 (2006)   555

People v. Dennis, 71 Cal. Rptr. 2d 680, 950 P.2d 1035 (1998)   422

People v. Diaz, 2005 Cal. App. Unpub. LEXIS 3559 (2005)   122

People v. Dicharry, 2007 Cal. App. Unpub. LEXIS 5538 (Cal. 2007)   529

People v. Dominguez, 39 Cal. 4th 1141, 1153, 47 Cal. Rptr. 3d 575, 2006 Cal. LEXIS 9977 (Cal. 2006)   570

People v. Driver, 62 Ill. App. 3d 847, 379 N.E.2d 840 (1978)   555

People v. Durio, 7 Misc. 3d 729, 731, 794 N.Y.S.2d 863, 685, 2005 N.Y. Misc. LEXIS 398 (N.Y. 2005)   482

People v. Echavarria, 362 Ill. App.3d 599, 607, 840 N.E.2d 815, 823, 2005 Ill. App. LEXIS 1284 (2005)   557

People v. Elie, 2006 Colo. App. LEXIS 1487 (2006)   327

People v. Esaw, 2002 N.Y. Slip Op. 40045U, 2002 N.Y. Misc. LEXIS 201 (N.Y. 2002)   250

People v. Farris, 130 Cal. App. 4th 773, 30 Cal. Rptr. 3d 426, 2005 Cal. App. LEXIS 1017 (Calif. 2005)   50, 67

People v. Flowers, 2009 Cal. App. Unpub. LEXIS 525 (Cal. 2009)   310

People v. Force, 170 Cal. App. 4th 797, 2009 Cal. App. LEXIS 85 (Cal. 2009)   49

People v. Forgione, 2008 NY Slip Op 28365, 2008 N.Y. Misc. LEXIS 5659 (N.Y. 2008)   279

People v. Garcia, 113 P. 3d 775, 2005 Colo. LEXIS 562 (2005)   428

People v. Garcia, 168 Cal. App. 4th 261, 292, 2008 Cal. App. LEXIS 2050 (Cal. 2008)   216

People v. Garcia, 36 Cal. 4th 777, 115 P.3d 1191, 31 Cal. Rptr. 3d 541, 2005 Cal. LEXIS 8226 (Cal. 2005)   561

People v. Garth, 353 Ill. App. 3d 108, 817 N.E.2d 1085, 2004 Ill. App. LEXIS 1192 (2004)   541

People v. Gilmore, 356 Ill. App. 3d 1023, 1031, 828 N.E.2d 293, 301, 2005 Ill. App. LEXIS 314 (2005)   483

People v. Givens, 384 Ill. App.3d 101, 2008 Ill. App. LEXIS 684 (Ill. 2008)   95

People v. Gomez, 134 Cal. App. 3d 874, 185 Cal. Rptr. 155 (1982)   346

People v. Gonzales, 35 N.Y. 49 (1866)   554

People v. Gonzales-Quevedo, 203 P.3d 609, 614, 615, 2008 Colo. App. LEXIS 1832 (Colo. 2008)   310

People v. Gonzalez, 275 Cal. Rptr. 729, 800 P.2d 1159 (1990)   63

People v. Grandberry, 2005 Mich. App. LEXIS 2099 (2005)   548

People v. Green, 2006 N.Y. Slip Op. 6014, 818 N.Y.S.2d 862, 2006 N.Y. App. Div. LEXIS 9719 (N.Y. 2006)   553

People v. Green, 2009 Mich. App. LEXIS 311 (Mich. 2009)   91

People v. Grenier, 200 P.3d 1062, 2008 Colo. App. LEXIS 356 (Colo. 2008)   157

People v. Grider, 246 Cal. App. 2d 149, 153, 54 Cal. Rptr. 497, 501, 1966 Cal. App. LEXIS 1013 (1966)   268

People v. Hammock, 2008 Mich. App. LEXIS 1982 (Mich. 2008)   515

People v. Handwerker, 2006 N.Y. Slip Op. 26119, 12 Misc. 3d 19, 816 N.Y.S.2d 824, 2006 N.Y. Misc. LEXIS 662 (2006)   57

People v. Harris, 2005 Mich. App. LEXIS 3264 (2005)   683

People v. Harris, 2009 Ill. App. LEXIS 118 (Ill. 2009)   249

People v. Harte, 131 P.3d 1180, 2005 Colo. App. LEXIS 1861 (2005)   366

People v. Herrera, 2007 Cal. App. Unpub. LEXIS 3965 (2007)   110

People v. Hickman, 470 Mich. 602, 684 N.W.2d 267, 2004 Mich. LEXIS 1544 (Mich. 2004)   683

People v. Hill, 2008 Cal. App. Unpub. LEXIS 3341 (Cal 2008)   209

People v. Hillsman, 362 Ill. App. 3d 623, 626, 839 N.E.2d 1116, 1120, 2005 Ill. App. LEXIS 1209 (2005)   553

People v. Hinton, 37 Cal. 4th 839, 887, 126 P.3d 981, 1018, 38 Cal. Rptr. 3d 149, 193, 2006 Cal. LEXIS 336 (Cal. 2006)   263

People v. Hogan, 114 P.3d 42, 51, 2004 Colo. App. LEXIS 2001 (Colo. 2004), *reh'g denied*, 2005 Colo. LEXIS 597 (Colo. 2005)   541

People v. Hooker, 253 Ill. App. 3d 1075, 625 N.E.2d 1081 (1993)   278

People v. Houseworth, 2008 Ill. App. LEXIS 1290 (Ill. 2008)   69

People v. Hudson, 655 N.Y.S.2d 219 (1997)   518

People v. Huerta, 2008 Cal. App. Unpub. LEXIS 2827 (Cal. 2008)   212

People v. Illinois, 2009 Ill. App. LEXIS 45 (Ill. 2009)   152

People v. Jack, 70 Cal. Rptr. 2d 676 (1997)   647

People v. Jaffarian, 799 N.Y.S.2d 733, 735, 2005 N.Y. Misc. LEXIS 1640 (2005)   366

People v. Jimenez, 796 N.Y.S.2d 232; 2005 N.Y. Misc. LEXIS 1114 (2005)   528

People v. Johnson, 199 Ill. Dec. 931, 634 N.E.2d 1285 (1994)   124

People v. Johnson, 2007 Mich. App. LEXIS 2858 (Mich. 2007)   611

People v. Johnson, 218 Ill. 2d 125, 140, 842 N.E.2d 714, 723, 2005 Ill. LEXIS 2072 (2005)   60

People v. Jurado, 38 Cal. 4th 72, 129, 131 P.3d 400, 438, 41 Cal. Rptr. 3d 319, 365, 2006 Cal. LEXIS 4391 (2006)   495

People v. K.S., 387 Ill. App. 3d 570, 2008 Ill. App. LEXIS 1333 (Ill. 2008)   252

People v. Laughlin, 137 Cal. App. 4th 1020, 1024, 40 Cal. Rptr. 3d 737, 739, 2006 Cal. App. LEXIS 388 (2006)   151

People v. Lee, 131 Cal. App. 4th 1413, 32 Cal. Rptr. 3d 745, 2005 Cal. App. LEXIS 1278 (2005)   69

People v. Lee, 2005 Mich. App. LEXIS 3186 (2005)   542

People v. Lee, 379 Ill. App. 3d 533, 538, 2008 Ill. App. LEXIS 117 (Ill. 2008)   181

People v. Lee, 868 N.Y.S.2d 453, 456, 2008 N.Y. App. Div. LEXIS 8768 (N.Y. 2008)   216

People v. Levy, 2008 NY Slip Op 51878U (N.Y. 2008)   469

People v. Loker, 80 Cal. Rptr. 3d 630, 2008 Cal. LEXIS 9275 (Cal. 2008)   169

People v. Lynn, 388 Ill. App.3d 272, 2009 Ill. App. LEXIS 82 (Ill. 2009)   597

People v. Madera, 112 P.2d 688, 2005 Colo. LEXIS 526 (2005)   352

People v. May, 2008 Cal. App. Unpub. LEXIS 7458 (Cal. 2008)   611

People v. McCall, 32 Cal. 4th 175, 179, 82 P.3d 351, 354, 8 Cal. Rptr. 3d 337, 340, 2004 Cal. LEXIS 8 (Cal. 2004)   180

People v. McKown, 226 Ill.2d 245, 2007 Ill. LEXIS 1163 (2007)   120

People v. Mead, 2006 Cal. App. Unpub. LEXIS 3150 (2006)   560

People v. Melendez, 102 P.3d 315; 2004 Colo. LEXIS 1006 (2004)   287

People v. Melski, 10 N.Y.2d 78, 176 N.E.2d 81 (1961)   346

People v. Michaels, 28 Cal. 4th 486, 541, 49 P.3d 1032, 122 Cal. Rptr. 2d 285 (2002)   112

People v. Miller, 164 Cal. App. 4th 653, 662. 2008 Cal. App. LEXIS 971 (Cal. 2008)   89

People v. Miller, 173 Ill. 2d 167, 670 N.E.2d 721 (1996)   415

People v. Miller, 295 A.D.2d 746, 747, 2002 N.Y. App. Div. LEXIS 6511 (2002)   250

People v. Monterroso, 34 Cal. 743, 22 Cal. Rptr. 3d 1, 101 P.3d 956 (2004)   483, 484

People v. Moreland, 226 Ill. Dec. 814, 686 N.E.2d 597 (1997)   57

People v. Muniz, 190 P.3d 774, 786, 2008 Colo. App. LEXIS 237 (Cal. 2008)   143

People v. Niccoli, 102 Cal. App. 2d 814, 228 P.2d 827 (1951)   172

People v. Nickson, 2006 Mich. App. LEXIS 2911 (Mich. 2006)   206

People v. Niene, 8 Misc. 3d 649, 652, 798 N.Y.S.2d 891, 894, 2005 N.Y. Misc. LEXIS 981 (N.Y. 2005)   152

People v. Nowicki, 385 Ill. App. 3d 53, 87, 88, 2008 Ill. App. LEXIS 869 (Ill. 2008)   252

People v. Owens, 183 P.3d 568, 574, 2007 Colo. App. LEXIS 884 (Colo. 2007)   195

People v. Panah, 35 Cal. 4th 395, 414, 107 P.3d 790, 803, 25 Cal. Rptr. 3d 672, 689, 2005 Cal. LEXIS 2712 (Cal. 2005)   604

People v. Parks, 485 P.2d 257 (Cal. 1971)   295

People v. Pomykala, 2003 Ill. LEXIS 7 (2003)   178

People v. Prentiss, 2008 Cal. App. Unpub. LEXIS 8119 (Cal. 2008)   283

People v. Reyes, 2007 Cal. App. Unpub. LEXIS 10300 (Cal. 2007)   319

People v. Richardson, 77 Cal. Rptr. 3d 163, 221, 2008 Cal. LEXIS 6208 (Cal. 2008)   185

People v. Rivera, 109 Cal. App. 4th 1241, 1244, 2003 Cal. App. LEXIS 903 (Cal. 2003)   25

People v. Rocafort, 2005 Mich. App. LEXIS 3274 (2005), appeal denied, 475 Mich. 870, 714 N.W.2d 322, 2006 Mich. LEXIS 1151 (Mich. 2006)   573

People v. Rodriguez, 133 Cal. App. 4th 545, 554, 34 Cal. Rptr. 3d 886, 892 2005 Cal. App. LEXIS 1628 (2005)   409, 431

People v. Rogelio, 2005 Cal. Unpub. LEXIS (Cal. 2005)   202

People v. Rogers, 39 Cal. 4th 826, 2006 Cal. LEXIS 9862 (Cal. 2006)   614

People v. Roraback, 666 N.Y.S.2d 397 (1997)   632

People v. Salas, 37 Cal. 4th 967; 127 P.3d 40, 38 Cal. Rptr. 3d 624, 2006 Cal. LEXIS 1900 (2006)   61

People v. Sallow, 100 Misc. 447, N.Y. Misc. LEXIS 809 (N.Y. 1917)   615

People v. Sanders, 2006 Mich. App. LEXIS 2 (2006)   664

People v. Sandoval, 56 A.D.3d 253, 866 N.Y.S.2d 656, 2008 N.Y. App. Div. LEXIS 8238 (NY 2008)   58

People v. Schoreck, 384 Ill. App.3d 904, 916, 2008 Ill. App. LEXIS 829 (Ill. 2008)   157

People v. Schoultz, 224 Ill. Dec. 885, 682 N.E.2d 446 (1997)   453

People v. Sinohui, 28 Cal. 4th 205, 210, 47 P.3d 629, 2002 Cal. LEXIS 3777 (2002)   258

People v. Smith, 168 Cal. App. 4th 7, 2008 Cal. App. LEXIS (Cal. 2008)   25

People v. Sneed, 2007 Cal. App. Unpub. LEXIS10270 (Cal. 2007)   392

People v. Souva, 2005 Colorado App. LEXIS 1615 (2005)   394

People v. Spry, 68 Cal. Rptr. 2d 691 (1997)   64

People v. Suehr, 2008 Cal. App. Unpub. LEXIS 2713 (Cal. 2008)   113

People v. Tabb, 12 A.D.3d 951, 952, 785 N.Y.S.2d 193, 194, 2004 N.Y. App. Div. LEXIS 14284 (N.Y. 2004), *appeal denied*, 4 N.Y.3d 768, 2005 N.Y. LEXIS 419 (2005)   178

People v. Tarver, 292 A.D.2d 110, 741 N.Y.S.2d 130, 2002 N.Y. App. Div. LEXIS 3631 (N.Y. 2002)   647

People v. Totten, 156 Cal. App. 4th 31, n.9, 2007 Cal. App. LEXIS 1697 (Ca. 2007)   127

People v. Urbano, 128 Cal. App. 4th 396, 26 Cal. Rptr. 3d 871, 2005 Cal. App. LEXIS 572 (2005)   352

People v. Valdez, 32 Cal. 4th 73, 84, 82 P.3d 296, 308, 8 Cal. Rptr. 3d 271, 2004 Cal. LEXIS 4 (Cal 2004)   616

People v. Vazquez, 2006 NY Slip Op 26225 (N.Y. 2006)   520

People v. Veren, 2005 Colo. App. LEXIS 1957 (2005), *reh'g denied*, 2006 Colo. App. LEXIS 112 (2006)   405

People v. Ward, 2009 Cal. App. Unpub. LEXIS 1023 (Cal. 2009)   211

People v. Wardell, 2005 Cal. App. Unpub. LEXIS 11539 (2005)   210

People v. Washington, 2009 Mich. App. LEXIS 308 (Mich. 2009)   218

People v. Washington, 363 Ill. App. 3d 13, 842 N.E.2d 1193, 1199, 2006 Ill. App. LEXIS 24 (2006)   184, 434

People v. Watson, 214 Ill. 2d 271, 825 N.E.2d 257, 2005 Ill. LEXIS 2 (Ill. 2005)   678

People v. Watson, 245 Mich. App. 572 at 583, 629 N.W.2d 411 at 420 (2001)   87

People v. West, 2007 Mich. App. LEXIS 1344 (Mich. 2007)   293

People v. Whicker, 2007 Cal. App. Unpub. LEXIS 5197 (Cal. 2007)   526

People v. Williams, 170 Cal. App. 4th 587, 2009 Cal. App. LEXIS 78 (Cal. 2009)   91

People v. Williams, 2008 Cal. App. Unpub. LEXIS 7807 (Cal. 2008)   290

People v. Williams, 284 A.D.2d 564, 726 N.Y.S.2d 740, 2001 N.Y. App. Div. LEXIS 11474, n.1 (N.Y. 2001)   647

People v. Williams, 43 Cal. 4th 584, 613, 2008 Cal. LEXIS 4818 (Cal. 2008)   335

People v. Wilson, 25 Cal. 2d 341, 153 P.2d 720 (1944)   421

People v. Wilson, 38 Cal. 4th 1237, 1245, 2006 Cal. LEXIS 8228 (Cal. 2006)   193

People v. Woodrum, 223 Ill. 2d 286, 308, 2006 Ill. LEXIS 1633 (Ill. 2007), *cert. denied*, Woodrum v. Illinois, 2007 U.S. LEXIS 4140 (2007)   139

People v. Woolcock, 2005 NY Slip Op 25045 (N.Y. 2005)   683

People v. Wooten, 283 A.D.2d 931, 933, 725 N.Y.S.2d 767, 770, 2001 N.Y. App. Div. LEXIS 4659 (N.Y. 2001)   555

People v. Young, 34 Cal. 4th 1149, 1171, 105 P.3d 487, 499, 24 Cal. Rptr. 3d 112, 126, 2005 Cal. LEXIS 1017 (2005)   110

People v. Young, 34 Cal. 4th 1149; 105 P.3d 487; 24 Cal. Rptr. 3d 112; 2005 Cal. LEXIS 1017 (2005)   124

People v. Zamudio, 43 Cal. 4th 327, 2008 Cal. LEXIS 4431 (Fla. 2008)   210

People v. Zunis, 134 Cal. App. 4th Supp. 1, 36 Cal. Rptr. 3d 489, 2005 Cal. App. 1873 (2005)   410

Pepper v. Triplet, 864 So. 2d 181, 189, 2004 La. LEXIS 151 (2004)   12

PepsiCo, Inc. v. Baird, Kurtz & Dobson LLP, 305 F. 3d 813, 815, 2002 U.S. App. LEXIS 192 (8th Cir. 2002)   336

Pereira v. United States, 347 U.S. 1, 74 S. Ct. 358, 98 L. Ed. 435 (1954)   351

Perez v. Department of Revenue, 778 P.2d 326 (Colo. Ct. App. 1989)   116

Perkins v. State, 2009 Ala. Crim. App. LEXIS 12 (Ala. 2009)   453

Perkins v. State, 441 S.E.2d 511 (Ga. 1994)   57

Perras v. Allstate Ins. Co. 2002 Conn. Super. LEXIS 3128 (2002)   337

Perrotti v. Meredith, 2005 PA Super 57, 868 A.2d 1240, 1243, 2005 Pa. Super. LEXIS 148 (2005)   343

Perry Lumber Company v. Durable Services, 271 Neb. 303, 310, 710 N.W.2d 854, 2006 LEXIS 47 (2006)   415

Perry v. State, 381 Md. 138, 848 A.2d 631, 2004 Md. LEXIS 246 (2004)   254

Persky v. Yeshiva University, 2002 U.S. Dist. LEXIS 23740 (S.D.N.Y. 2002)   335

Peters v. State, 2007 Alas. App. LEXIS 158 (Alaska. 2007)   595

Peters v. State, 984 So. 2d 1227, 2008 Fla. LEXIS 757 (Fla. 2008)   38

Peterson v. State, 274 Ga. 165, 167 (2001); State v. Stanley, 131 N.M. 368, 373, 37 P.3d 85, 91 (2001)   235

Phavixay v. State, 373 Ark. 168, 2008 Ark. LEXIS 234 (Ark. 2008)   226

Phillips v. State, 278 Ga. App. 439, 441 629 S.E.2d 130, 132 2006 Ga. App. LEXIS 350 (2006)   260

Phillips v. State, 550 N.E.2d 1290 (Ind. 1990)   564

Pierce County v. Guillen, 537 U.S. 129, 123 S. Ct. 720, 730, 154 L. Ed. 2d 610, 625, 626, 2003 U.S. LEXIS 747 (2003)   337

Pierce v. State, 937 A.2d 140, 2007 Del. LEXIS 497 (Del. 2007)   551

Pipitone v. Biomatrix, Inc., 288 F.3d 239, 244–45 (5th Cir. 2002)   592

Pless v. State, 2006 Ga. App. LEXIS 523 (2006)   470

Plouff v. State, 2006 Tex. App. LEXIS 2546 (2006)   400

Pointer v. Texas, 380 U.S. 400, 402 (1965)   301

Polk v. Indiana, 783 N.E.2d 1253, 1267, 1258, 2003 Ind. App. LEXIS 313 (2003)   322

Poole v. United States, 929 A.2d 413, 2007 D.C. App. LEXIS 470 (2007)   305

Pottorf v. Bray, 2003 Ohio 4255 (2003)   470

Poynter v. Murray, 964 F.2d 1404 (4th Cir.), *cert. denied*, 506 U.S. 958, 113 S. Ct. 419, 121 L. Ed. 2d 342 (1992)   681

Proffit v. State, 2008 WY 103 191 P.3d 974, 982, 2008 Wyo. LEXIS 108 (Wyo. 2008)   328

Pronesti v. Florida, 847 So. 2d 1165, 1166, 2003 Fla. App. LEXIS 9472 (2003)   497

Pulliam v. Mississippi, 2003 Miss. App. LEXIS 299 (2003)   519

Raffel v. United States, 271 U.S. 494, 46 S. Ct. 566, 70 L. Ed. 1054 (1926)   308

Ragland v. State, 385 Md. 706, 870 A.2d 609, 2005 Md. LEXIS 119 (2005)   404

Ramirez v. State, 2009 Fla. App. LEXIS 739 (Fla. 2009)   60

Randall v. Norfolk S. Ry. Co., 800 N.E.2d 951, 959, 2003 Ind. App. LEXIS 2406 (2003)   246
Rangel v. State, 2009 Tex. App. LEXIS 1555 (Tex. 2009)   514
Ransom v. State, 919 So. 2d 887, 888, 2005 Miss. LEXIS 595 (Miss. 2005), *cert. denied*, 2006 U.S. LEXIS 4985 (2006)   205
Ransome v. State, 2003 Md. LEXIS 39 (Md. Ct. App. 2003)   115
Rasul v. Bush, 215 F. Supp. 2d 55, 67, 2002 U.S. Dist. LEXIS 14031 (D.D.C. 2002)   115
Ratiff v. State, 110 P.3d 982, 2005 Alas. App. LEXIS 39 (2005)   440
Rawlings v. Kentucky, 448 U.S. 98, 111, 1980 U.S. LEXIS 142 (1980)   650
Reagan v. United States, 157 U.S. 301, 305 (1878)   15
Redmond v. Mississippi, 815 So. 2d 1241, 1245, 2002 Miss. App. LEXIS 123 (2002)   440
Reemer v. State, 835 N.E.2d 1005, 1007, 2005 Ind. LEXIS 955, n.4 (Ind. 2005)   515
Remor v. State, 991 So. 2d 957, 2008 Fla. App. LEXIS 14242 (Fla. 2008)   170
Requa v. Kent School District No. 415, 492 F. Supp. 1272, 2007 U.S. Dist. LEXIS 40920 (W.D. Wash. 2007)   122
Rex v. Watson, 2 Stark. 116 (1817)   31
Reynolds v. Florida, 837 So. 2d 1044, 2002 Fla. App. LEXIS 19140 (2002)   429
Richman v. Sheahan, 415 F. Supp. 2d 929, 2006 U.S. Dist. LEXIS 6667 (N.D. Ill. 2006)   421
Riley Hill General Contractor v. Tandey Corp., 757 P.2d 595 (Or. 1987)   52
Ring v. Arizona, 536 U.S. 584, 2002 U.S. LEXIS 4651 (2002)   53
Risher v. Texas, 85 S.W.3d 839, 842, 2002 Tex. App. LEXIS 6086 (2002)   487
Rivera v. Mueller, 596 F. Supp. 2d 1163, 2009 U.S. Dist. LEXIS 9308 (N.D. Ill. 2009)   630
Riverside v. McLaughlin, 500 U.S. 44 (1991)   671
Robbins v. State, 88 S.W.3d 256, 259, 2002 Tex. Crim. App. LEXIS 208 (2002)   235
Robinson v. State, 982 So. 2d 1260, 2008 Fla. App. LEXIS 8099 (Fla. 2008)   600
Robinson v. Texas, 2000 Tex. App. LEXIS 5792 (2000)   307
Robinson v. Woodford, 2006 U.S. App. LEXIS 6009 (9th Cir. 2006)   89
Rock v. Arkansas, 483 U.S. 44, 107 S. Ct. 2704, 97 L. Ed. 2d 37 (1987)   296
Rodgers v. State, 2006 Tex. Crim. App. LEXIS (2006)   443
Rodgers v. State, 2008 Ark. App. LEXIS 552 (Ark 2008)   207
Rodriguez v. Commonwealth, 107 S.W.3d 215, 219, 2003 Ky. LEXIS 138 (Ky. 2003)   213
Rogers v. State, 2006 Miss. LEXIS 226 (2006)   371
Roland v. State, 882 So. 2d 262, 265, 2004 Miss. App. LEXIS 911 (2004)   335
Roman Catholic Archbishop of Los Angeles v. Superior Court, 131 Cal. App. 4th 417, 421, 32 Cal. Rptr. 3d 209, 2005 Cal. App. LEXIS 1164 (2005)   371
Romanski v. Detroit Entertainment, L.L.C., 428 F.3d 629, 635, 2005 U.S. App. LEXIS 23336 (6th Cir. 2005)   661
Ronquillo v. Washington, 2001 Wash. App. LEXIS 2615 (2001)   619
Rosen v. United States, 245 U.S. 467, 1918 U.S. LEXIS 2150 (1918)   263
Ross v. State, 2006 Alaska App. LEXIS 41 (2006)   71
Ross v. State, 954 So. 2d 968, 988, 2007 Miss. LEXIS 235 (Miss. 2007)   147
Rothgery v. Gillespie County, _____ U.S. _____, 2008 U.S. LEXIS 5057 (2008)   680
Rothwell v. Yeager, 2008 Ark. Appl. LEXIS (Ark. 2008)   148
Rousan v. Roper, 436 F.3d 951, 959, 2006 U.S. App. LEXIS 3003 (8th Cir. 2006)   96
Roviaro v. United States, 353 U.S. 53, 77 S. Ct. 623, 1 L. Ed. 2d 639 (1957)   374
Rowe v. State, 276 Ga. 800, 582 S.E.2d 119, 2003 Ga. LEXIS 549 (2003)   567
Runnels v. State, 193 S.W.3d 105, 107, 2006 Tex. App. LEXIS 17 (Tex. 2006)   540
Rupert v. People, 429 P.2d 276 (Colo. 1967); McCall v. State, 408 N.E.2d 1218 (Ind. 1980)   406

Sabota v. State, 2006 Fla. App. LEXIS 12505 (2006)   469
Sadlier v. State, 2009 Tex. App. LEXIS 2962 (Tex. 2009)   484
Sakil v. State, 2008 Tex. App. LEXIS 4230 (Tex. 2008)   219
Sam v. State, 265 P. 609 (Ariz. 1928)   115

Samaniego-Hernandez v. State, 839 N.E.2d 798, 802, 2005 Ind. App. LEXIS 2450 (2005)   228
Samson Resources v. Wamsutter, 117 Fed. Appx. 641, 644, 2004 U.S. App. LEXIS 22795
    (10th Cir. 2004)   129
Samson v. California, 547 U.S. 843, 2006 U.S. LEXIS 4885 (2006)   653
San Martin v. State, 995 So. 2d 247, 2008 Fla. LEXIS 1460 (Fla. 2008)   2121
Sanchez v. State, 2005 Tex. App. LEXIS 5084 (2005)   576
Sanchez v. State, 2005 Tex. App. LEXIS 5084 n.2 (2005)   619
Sandstrom v. Montana, 176 Mont. 492, 497, 580 P.2d 106, 109 (1978)   164
Sandstrom v. Montana, 442 U.S. 510, 1979 U.S. LEXIS 113 (1979)   55, 62, 149, 163,
    164, 175
Sauerwin v. State, 2005 Ark. LEXIS 565 (2005)   421
Saunders v. Alabama, 2007 Ala. Crim. App. LEXIS 236 (Ala. 2007)   219
Saunders v. Commonwealth, 2003 Va. App. LEXIS 394 (2003)   495
Schmerber v. California, 384 U.S. 757, 1966 U.S. LEXIS 1129 (1966)   544, 593, 615
Schneckloth v. Bustamonte, 412 U.S. 218 (1973)   653
Schultz v. Ford Motor Co., 857 N.E.2d 977, 982 (Ind. 2006)   145
Schwab v. State, 969 So. 2d 318, 2007 Fla. LEXIS 2011 (Fla. 2007)   132
Scott v. State, 2008 Tex. App. LEXIS 6172 (Tex. 2008)   395
Scott v. United States, 953 A.2d 1082, 1092, 1093 (Dist. Col. 2008)   256
Sealed Party v. Sealed Party, 2006 U.S. Dist. LEXIS 28392 (2006)   358
Sec'y of Labor v. Keystone, 331 U.S. App. D.C. 422 (D.C. Cir. 1998)   148
Service Corporation of Westover Hills v. Guzzetta, 2007 Del. Ch. LEXIS 84 (Del. 2007)   122
Seymour v. State, 949 P.2d 881 (Wyo. 1997)   576
Shanks v. State, 185 Md. 437, 45 A.2d 85 (1945)   603
Sharp v. United States, 410 F.2d 969 (5th Cir. 1969)   308
Shepherd v. State, 690 N.E.2d 318 (Ind. 1997)   470
Sherman v. Arkansas, 2005 Ark. App. LEXIS 141 (2005)   546
Sherrod v. State, 280 Ga. 275, 275, 627 S.E.2d 36, 37, 2006 Ga. LEXIS 145 (Ga. 2006)   140
Siegert v. Gilley, 500 U.S. 226 at 236 (1991)   100
Siler v. Lucasfilm, Ltd., 979 F.2d 1504 (9th Cir. 1986)   523
Simmons v. State, 2006 Ark. App. LEXIS 276 (2006)   479
Simpson v. Florida Parole Commission, 2006 U.S. Dist. LEXIS 18068 (2006)   38
Singh v. Mukasey, 553 F.3d 207, 212, 2009 U.S. App. LEXIS 966 (2d Cir. 2009)   118
Singleton v State, 2009 Miss. App. LEXIS 169 (2009)   323
Slagle v. Bagley, 2006 U.S. App. LEXIS 20240, 2006 Fed. Appx. 0283P (6th Cir. 2006)   264
Slay v. Keller Industries, 823 So. 2d 623; 2001 Ala. LEXIS 439 (Ala. 2002)   591
Sloane v. State, 2004 Tex. App. LEXIS 6903 (2004)   402
Slwooko v. State, 2006 Alaska App. LEXIS 114 (2006)   672
Smallwood v. Commonwealth, 2005 Va. App. LEXIS 196 (2005)   421
Smallwood v. State, 296 Ga. App. 16, 2009 Ga. App. LEXIS 115 (Ga. 2009)   517
Smith v. Brown & Williamson Tobacco Corp., 2007 Mo. App. LEXIS 1144 (Mo. 2007)   114
Smith v. Cangieter, 2006 U.S. App. LEXIS 23085 (8th Cir. 2006)   592
Smith v. Commonwealth, 265 Va. 250, 576 S.E.2d 465, 2003 Va. LEXIS 36 (2003)   557
Smith v. Delaware, 2006 Del. LEXIS 340 (2006)   516
Smith v. Doe, 538 U.S. 84, 110, 2003 U.S. LEXIS 1949 (2003)   147
Smith v. Georgia, 254 Ga. App. 107, 108, 561 S.E.2d 232, 233, 2002 Ga. App. LEXIS 274
    (2002)   344
Smith v. Illinois, 390 U.S. 129, 131 (1968)   304
Smith v. Maryland, 442 U.S. 375 (1979)   667
Smith v. Ohio, 494 U.S. 541, 110 S. Ct. 1288, 108 L. Ed. 2d. 464 (1990)   650
Smith v. Secretary, 2007 U.S. Dist. LEXIS 57703 (M.D. Fla. 2007)   437
Smith v. Secretary, Department of Corrections, 2007 U.S. Dist. LEXIS 57703 (M.D. Fla.
    2007)   631

Smith v. State, 2004 Tex. App. LEXIS 11851 (2004)   554

Smith v. State, 2008 Tex. App. LEXIS 4779 (2008)   121

Smith v. State, 2009 Wyo. 2, 2009 Wyo. LEXIS 2 (Wyo. 2009)   541

Smith v. State, 284 Ga. 33, 2008 Ga. LEXIS 540 (Ga. 2008)   141

Smith v. State, 770 S.W.2d 70 (Tex. Ct. App. 1989)   360

Smith v. State, 839 N.E.2d 780, 785, 2005 Ind. App. LEXIS 2442 (2005)   522

Smith v. State, 898 So. 2d 907, 2004 Ala. Crim. App. LEXIS 93 (2004)   471

Smith v. State, 931 So. 2d 790, 2006 Fla. LEXIS 388 (Fla. 2006)   631

Smith v. United States, 966 A.2d 367, 2009 D.C. App. LEXIS 35 (D.C. App. 2009)   617

Sneed v. State, 876 So. 2d 1235, 1238, 2004 Fla. App. LEXIS 8390 (Fla. 2004)   167

Solorzano v. Bristow, 136 N.M. 658 N.M. 658, 662, 2004 NMCA 136; 103 P.3d 582, 586, 2004
    N.M. App. LEXIS 121 (2004)   159

Sony v. Soundview, 2001 U.S. Dist. LEXIS 23220 (D. Conn. 2001)   355

Soto v. New York City Transit Authority, 2006 N.Y. LEXIS 518 (2006)   410

South Carolina v. Mizzell, 349 S.C. 326, 563 S.E.2d 315, 2002 S.C. LEXIS 68 (2002)   301

South Dakota v. Neville, 459 U.S. 553, 1983 U.S. LEXIS 129 (1983)   602, 678

South Dakota v. Opperman, 328 U.S. 364, 96 S. Ct. 3092, 49 L. Ed. 2d 1000 (1976)   662

Spain v. Brown and Williamson Tobacco, 363 F.3d 1183, 1194, 2004 U.S. App. LEXIS 5792
    (11th Cir. 2004)   114

Sparrow v. Lindamood, 2006 U.S. Dist. LEXIS 9640 (M.D. Tenn. 2006)   101

Speybroeck v. State, 875 N.E.2d 813, 820, 2007 Ind. App. LEXIS 2408 (Ind. 2007)   510

St. Clair v. Commonwealth, 174 S.W. 2d 474, 480, 2005 Ky. LEXIS 334 (2005)   341

St. Petersburg v. Waller, 261 So. 2d 151 (Fla. 1972)   122

Stamper v. Griffin, 20 Ga. 312 (1856)   505

Stark v. Hickman, 455 F.3d 1070, 1077, 1078, 2006 U.S. App. LEXIS 19296 (9th Cir.
    2006)   165

Starr et al. v. Old Line Life Insurance Co., 104 Cal. App. 4th 487, 496, 128 Cal. Rptr. 2d 282,
    288, 2002 Cal. App. LEXIS 5174 (2002)   172

State ex rel. Juvenile Department v. Michael Spencer, 198 Or. App. 599, 604 108 P.3d 1189,
    1192, 2005 Or. App. LEXIS 346 (2005)   364

State ex rel. Verburg v. Jones, 211 Ariz. 413, 121 P.3d 1283, 1285, 2005 Ariz. App. LEXIS 148
    (2005)   678

State ex rel. Woods v. Cohen, 173 Ariz. 497, 501, 502, 844 P.2d 1147, 1151, 1152, 1992 Ariz.
    LEXIS 104 (1992)   343

State v. A.O., 2009 N.J. LEXIS 51 (N.J. 2009)   185

State v. Abd-Rahmaan, 154 Wash. 2d 280, 111 P.3d 1157, 2005 Wash. LEXIS 461 (2005)   38

State v. Aguilar, 218 Ariz. 25, 178 P.3d 497, 2008 Ariz. App. LEXIS 44 (Ariz. 2008)   50

State v. Aiken, 121 Ohio Misc. 2d 7, 2002 Ohio 6436, 779 N.E.2d 1105, 2002 Ohio Misc.
    LEXIS 44 (Ohio 2002)   113

State v. Ames, 950 P.2d 514 (Wash. 1998)   399

State v. Anglemyer, 269 Neb. 237, 243, 691 N.W.2d 153, 160, 2005 Neb. LEXIS 35 (2005)   506

State v. Anthony, 218 Ariz. 439, 2008 Ariz LEXIS 123 (Ariz. 2008)   30

State v. Arafat, 2006 Ohio 1722, 2006 Ohio App. LEXIS 15 (Ohio 2006)   572

State v. Arcia, 111 Conn. App. 374, 379,380, 2008 Conn. App. LEXIS 529 (Conn. 2008)   246

State v. Arita, 900 So. 2d 37, 44, 2005 La. App. LEXIS 501 (2005)   471

State v. Armstrong, 2007 Ohio 6405, 2007 Ohio App. LEXIS 5609 (Ohio 2007)   220

State v. Austin, 2005 Tenn. Crim. App. LEXIS 815 (2005)   619

State v. Ayers, 2005 Tenn. Crim. App. LEXIS 1108 (2005)   420

State v. Babers, 514 N.W.2d 79 (Iowa 1994)   61

State v. Baird, 195 S.W. 1010 (Mo. 1917)   115

State v. Baker, 287 Kan. 345, 363, 2008 Kan. LEXIS 694 (Kan. 2008)   197

State v. Baker, 956 S.W.2d 8 (Tenn. 1997)   320

State v. Ballon, 703 So. 2d 130 (La. 1997)   642

State v. Banks, 2004 Tenn. Crim. App. LEXIS 793 (2004)   200

State v. Barnhill, 166 N.C. 228, 601 N.E. 215. 204 N.C. App LEXIS 1607 (2004)   402

State v. Bates, 2003 Me. 67; 822 A.2d 1129; 2003 Me. LEXIS 77 (2003)   260

State v. Begley, 956 S.W.2d 471 (Tenn. 1997)   240

State v. Behn, 375 N.J. Super. 409, 868 A.2d 329, 2005 N.J. Super. LEXIS 73 (N.J. 2005)   631

State v. Bennett, 2008 Ohio 3969, 2008 Ohio App. LEXIS 3349 (2008)   664

State v. Bentley, 499 So. 2d 581 (La. 1987)   246

State v. Bergmann, 2009 Iowa App. LEXIS 54 (Iowa 2009)   362

State v. Berwald, 186 S.W.3d 349, 359, 2005 Mo. App. LEXIS 1917 (2005)   225

State v. Best, 2008 Tenn. App. LEXIS 744 (Tenn. 2008)   617

State v. Betha, 167 N.C. App. 215, 223, 605 S.E.2d 173, 179, 2004 N.C. App. LEXIS 2150 (2004)   570

State v. Black, 877 N.E.2d 1239, 1242, 2007 Ind. App. LEXIS 2762 (Ind. 2007)   149

State v. Black, 920 So. 2d 668, 670, 2006 Fla. App. LEXIS 48 (2006), *reh'g denied*, 2006 Fla. App. LEXIS 3673 (2006)   358

State v. Blackwell, 2009 Md. LEXIS 62 (Md. 2009)   601

State v. Bloomfield, 2004 Ohio 749, 2004 Ohio App. LEXIS 692 (2004)   201

State v. Blunt, 2008 ND 135, 2008 N.D. LEXIS 137 (N.D. 2008)   146

State v. Boston, 380 N.J. Super 487, 493, 882 A.2d 987, 991, 2005 N.J. Super. LEXIS 292 (2005)   416

State v. Bowman, 2009 Tenn. Crim. App. LEXIS 35 (Tenn. 2009)   479

State v. Bowman, 289 Conn. 809, 2008 Conn. LEXIS 565 (Conn. 2008)   192

State v. Boydston, 2006 Mo. App. LEXIS 1246 (2006)   552

State v. Boyer, 2006 Del. C.P. LEXIS 67 (Del. 2006)   598

State v. Bradley, 995 So. 2d 1230, 1235, 2008 La. App. LEXIS 1307 (La. 2008)   311

State v. Bradshaw, 195 N.J. 493; 950 A.2d 889; 2008 N.J. LEXIS 873 (N.J. 2008)   65

State v. Brady, 223 Or. 433, 354 P.2d 811 (1960)   123

State v. Braswell, 2008 Tenn. Crim. App. LEXIS 43 (Tenn. 2008)   222

State v. Brown, 2006 Wash. App. LEXIS 1092 (2006)   244

State v. Brown, 394 N.J. Super. 492, 507, 2007 N.J. Super. LEXIS 247 (N.J. 2007)   115

State v. Brownlow, 2003 Ohio 1819, 2003 Ohio App. LEXIS 1721 (2003)   96

State v. Buie, 671 S.E.2d 351, 353, 2009 N.C. App. LEXIS 48 (N.C. 2009)   222

State v. Bunn, 619 S.E.2d 918, 2005 N.C. App. LEXIS 2301 (2005)   425

State v. Burkhalter, 2006 Ohio 1623, 2006 Ohio App. LEXIS 1520 (2006)   118

State v. Burnes, 997 So. 2d 906, 2008 La. App. Unpub. LEXIS 715 (La. 2008)   619

State v. Burnice, 2006 Wash. App. LEXIS 45 (2006)   241

State v. Butcher, 2007 Ohio 5911, 2007 Ohio App. LEXIS 5203 (Ohio 2007)   292

State v. Butler, 2008 La. App. LEXIS 1388 (La. 2008)   58

State v. Butler, 2008 N.C. App. LEXIS 1645 (N.C. 2008)   217

State v. Campbell, 103 Wash. 2d 1, 691 P.2d 929, cert. denied, 471 U.S. 1094, 105 S. Ct. 2169, 85 L. Ed. 2d 526 (1984)   547

State v. Campbell, 2006 Tenn. Crim. App. LEXIS 584 (2006)   561

State v. Carlson, 559 N.W.2d 802 (N.D. 1996)   429

State v. Carpenter, 275 Conn. 785, 856, 882 A.2d 604, 648, 2005 Conn. LEXIS 396 (2005)   506

State v. Carter, 948 P.2d 1173 (Mont. 1997)   403

State v. Cassano, 96 Ohio St 3d. 94, 2002 Ohio 3751 (2002)   96

State v. Chapman, 359 N.C. 328, 352, 611 S.E.2d 794, 814, 2005 N.C. LEXIS 361 (2005)   553

State v. Charley, 2007 Ohio 1108, 2007 Ohio App. LEXIS 1029 (Ohio 2007)   210

State v. Chenette, 560 A.2d 365 (Vt. 1989)   367

State v. Childs, 257 S.W.3d 655, 658, 2008 Mo. App. LEXIS 975 (Mo. 2008)   84

State v. Cho, 2009 Haw. App. LEXIS 98 (Haw. 2009)   610

State v. Chomnarith, 654 N.W.2d 660, 666, 2003 Minn. LEXIS 2 (Minn. 2003)   566

State v. Clark, 136 S.W. 3d 582, 2004 Mo. App. LEXIS 904 (2004)   396

State v. Clark, 2007 Ohio 3777, 2007 Ohio App. LEXIS 3442 (Ohio 2007)   393

State v. Clark, 949 P.2d 1099 (Kan. 1997)   452

State v. Clay, 2009 Ohio 1204, 2009 Ohio App. LEXIS 1012 (Ohio 2009)   291

State v. Cobb, 295 N.C. 1, 243 S.E.2d 759 (1978)   398

State v. Cochrane, 897 A.2d 952, 955, 2006 N.H. LEXIS 48 (N.H. 2006)   600

State v. Coleman, 976 So. 2d 268, 2008 La. App. LEXIS 142 (2008)   69

State v. Cook, 2006 Kan. LEXIS 361, (2006)   89

State v. Cook, 2009 N.C. App. LEXIS 268 (N.C. 2009)   295

State v. Cortez, 935 F.2d 135 (8th Cir. 1991)   430

State v. Cousar, 660 S.E.2d 902, 905, 2008 N. C. App. LEXIS 1076 (N.C. 2008)   85

State v. Cowans, 336 Ill. App. 3d 173, 782 N.E.2d 779, 2002 Ill. App. LEXIS 1170 (2002), *appeal denied*, 2003 Ill. LEXIS 649 (2003)   542

State v. Craft, 149 Ohio App. 3d 176, 180, 776 N.E.2d 546, 548, 2002 Ohio App. LEXIS 4647 (2002)   304

State v. Crager, 116 Ohio St. 3d 369, 2007 Ohio 6840, 2007 Ohio LEXIS 3355 (Ohio 2007)   438

State v. Crager, 164 Ohio App. 3d 816, 826, 827, 2005 Ohio 6868, 844 N. E. 2d 390, 398, 399, 2005 Ohio App. LEXIS 6188 (2005), *cert. granted*, 109 Ohio St. 3d 1421, 2006 Ohio 1967, 2006 Ohio LEXIS 1037 (2006)   438

State v. Cruz, 218 Ariz. 149, 2008 Ariz. LEXIS 49 (2008), *cert. denied,* Cruz v. Arizona, 2009 U.S. LEXIS 428 (2009)   89

State v. Dale, 874 S.W.2d 446 (Mo. 1994)   306

State v. Dalluge, 2005 Wash. App. LEXIS 450 (2005)   561

State v. Damron, 151 S.W. 3d 510, 2004 Tenn. LEXIS 993 (2004)   436, 611

State v. Davis, 116 N.J. 341, 561 A.2d 1082 (1989)   360

State v. Davis, 2004 Ohio 5680, 2004 Ohio App. LEXIS 5144 (2004)   118

State v. Davlin, 272 Neb. 139, 158, 719 N.W.2d 243, 2006 Neb. LEXIS 123 (2006)   564

State v. Deases, 479 N.W.2d 597 (Iowa 1991)   453

State v. Delaney, 171 N.C. App. 141, 613 S.E.2d 699, 700, 701, 2005 N.C. App. LEXIS 1160 (2005)   425

State v. DeMarco, 275 N.J. Super 311, 646 A.2d 431 (1994)   354

State v. Detroy, 102 Haw. 13, 72 P.3d 485, 2003 Haw. LEXIS 314 (Haw. 2003)   566

State v. Dobrovich, 2005 Ohio 1441, 2005 Ohio App. LEXIS 1405 (2005)   523

State v. Domicz, 377 N.J. Super 515, 2005 N.J. Super. LEXIS 161 (N.J. 2005)   121

State v. Dougherty, 2009 N.C. App. LEXIS 485 (N.C. 2009)   284

State v. Duncan, 698 S.W.2d 63 (Tenn. 1985)   603

State v. Dunfee, 327 Mont. 335, 340, 114 P.3d 217, 221, 2005 Mont. LEXIS 225 (2005)   569

State v. Dunlap, 2007 Ohio 1624 (Ohio 2007)   610

State v. Eaton, 19 Ohio St.2d 145, 150, 2, 1969 Ohio LEXIS 348 (Ohio 1969)   214

State v. Edmon, 28 Wash. App. 98, 621 P.2d 1310 (1981)   430

State v. Engelhardt, 280 Kan. 113, 123, 119 P.3d 1148, 1159, 2005 Kan. LEXIS 462 (Kan. 2005)   561

State v. Escobido-Ortiz, 109 Haw. 359, 367, 126 P.3d 402, 410, 2005 Haw. App. LEXIS 520 (2005)   230

State v. Esse, 2005 Iowa App. LEXIS 1199 (Iowa 2005)   247

State v. Evans, 2006 Tenn. Crim. App. LEXIS 387 (2006)   347

State v. Everett, 630 S.E.2d 703, 2006 N.C. App. LEXIS 1302 (2006)   223

State v. Farrar, 2008 Tenn. Crim. App. LEXIS 825 (Tenn. 2008)   516

State v. Farrow, 2005 Ohio 3005, 2005 Ohio App. LEXIS 2799 (2005)   400

State v. Fernandez, 2008 N.C. App. LEXIS 1828 (N.C. 2008)   525

State v. Fernandez, 2008 N.C. LEXIS 1828 (N.C. 2008)   529

State v. Fichera, 2006 N.H. LEXIS 76 (N.H. 2006)   158

State v. Field, 2006 Idaho App. LEXIS 44 (2006)   465

State v. Finan, 275 Conn. 60, 63, 881 A.2d 187, 190, 2005 Conn. LEXIS 325 (2005)   421
State v. Flannel, 2008 Tenn. Crim. App. LEXIS 821 (Tenn. 2008)   244
State v. Flores, 2006 Minn. App. Unpub. LEXIS 390 (2006)   320
State v. Foley, 15 Nev. 64, 1880 Nev. LEXIS 16 (1880)   262
State v. Foulk, 2009 Tenn. Crim. App. LEXIS 16 (Tenn. 2009)   619
State v. Francis, 2003 Conn. Super. LEXIS 757 (2003)   375
State v. Francisco, 148 Wash. App. 168, 179, 2009 Wash App. LEXIS 22 (Wash 2009)   87
State v. Franklin, 956 So. 2d 823, 2007 La. App. LEXIS 901 (La. 2007), *writ denied*, 2008 La. LEXIS 86 (2008)   184
State v. Frasure, 323 Mont. 479, 100 P.3d 1013, 204 Mont. LEXIS 558 (2004)   401
State v. French, 2006 Haw. LEXIS 85 (2006)   421
State v. Garcia, 195 N.J. 192, 201, 2008 N.J. LEXIS 771 (N.J. 2008)   90
State v. Gardner, 490 N.W.2d 838 (Iowa 1992)   453
State v. Garrett, 188 S.W. 58 (Tenn. 1916)   115
State v. Georgekopoulos, 2005 Ohio 5106, 2005 Ohio App. LEXIS 4624 (2005)   619
State v. Germany, 2006 Wash. App. LEXIS (Wash. 2006)   141
State v. Gillespie, 710 N.W.2d 289, 298, 2006 Minn. App. LEXIS 24 (2006)   366
State v. Gilley 2008 Tenn. Crim. App. LEXIS 660 (Tenn. 2008)   556
State v. Glenn, 115 Wash. App. 540, 551, 62 P.3d 921, 927, 2003 Wash. App. LEXIS 161 (2003)   372
State v. Glover, 636 So. 2d 976 (La. 1994)   82
State v. Goff, 191 S.W.3d 113, 116, 2006 Mo. App. LEXIS 712 (2006)   541
State v. Gonzalez, 272 Conn. 515, 530, 864 A.2d 847, 857, 2005 Conn. LEXIS 20 (Conn. 2005)   214
State v. Gooden, 89 Conn. App. 307, 319, 873 A.2d 243, 251, 2005 Conn. App. LEXIS 202 (2005)   59
State v. Graves, 2003 Ohio 2359, 2003 Ohio App. LEXIS 2190 (Ohio 2003)   558
State v. Haines, 2008 Minn. Unpub. LEXIS 1479 (Minn. 2008)   245
State v. Hall, 940 A.2d 645, 2008 R.I. LEXIS 7 (R.I. 2008)   280
State v. Halls, 2006 Utah App. 142, 549 Utah Adv. Rep. 21, 2006 Utah App. LEXIS 136 (2006)   152
State v. Hancock, 108 Ohio St. 3d 57, 62, 2006 Ohio 160, 840 N.E.2d 1032, 1043, 2006 Ohio LEXIS 215 (2006)   50
State v. Hardesty, 2008 Ariz. App. LEXIS 121 (Ariz. 2008), review granted, 2009 Ariz. LEXIS 22 (Ariz. 2009)   121
State v. Hardin, 569 N.W.2d 517 (Iowa 1997)   362
State v. Hearns, 151 N.H. 226, 855 A.2d 549, 2004 N.H. LEXIS 129 (N.H. 2004)   678
State v. Hensley, 2005 Minn. App. LEXIS 233 (2005)   661, 662
State v. High Elk, 330 Mont. 259, 265, 127 P.3d 432, 436, 2006 Mont. LEXIS 6 (2006)   563
State v. Hill, 2006 Ohio 1408 (2006)   613
State v. Hofland, 151 N.H. 322, 327, 857 A.2d 1271, 1276, 2004 N.H. LEXIS 146 (N.H. 2004)   117
State v. Holland, 2008 Ohio 3450, 2008 Ohio App. LEXIS 2914 (Ohio 2008)   257
State v. Holly, 2009 NMSC 4, 2009 N.M. LEXIS 3 (N.M. 2009)   607
State v. Housley, 922 So.2d 659, 665, 2006 La. App. LEXIS 116 (2006)   542
State v. Howard, 2008 Wis. App. LEXIS 807 (Wis. 2008)   115
State v. Howell, 2008 Wash. App. LEXIS 799 (2008)   181
State v. Huehn, 53 P.3d 733, 737, 2002 Colo. App. LEXIS 21 (2002)   509
State v. Huff, 2004 Neb. App. LEXIS 117 (2004)   621
State v. Hupp, 2009 Ohio 1912, 2009 Ohio App. LEXIS 1622 (Ohio 2009)   521
State v. Ingram, 196 N.J. 23; 951 A.2d 1000, 2008 N.J. LEXIS 879 (N.J. 2008)   168
State v. J.G., 402 N.J. Super. 290, 293, 2008 N.J. Super. LEXIS 180 (N.J. 2008)   368
State v. Jackson, 112 Wash. 2d 867, 774 P.2d 1211 (1989)   141

State v. Jackson, 2005 Tenn. Crim. App. LEXIS 193 (2005)   579

State v. Jackson, 212 Wis. 2d 203, 567 N.W.2d 920 (1997)   303

State v. Jacobson, 87 Conn. App. 440, 450, 866 A.2d 678, 687, 2005 Conn. App. LEXIS 64 (2005)   546

State v. Johanesen, 319 Or. 128, 873 P.2d 1065 (1994)   306

State v. John L., 85 Conn. App. 291, 299, 856 A.2d 1032, 1038, 2004 Conn. App. LEXIS 407 (Conn. 2004)   521

State v. Johnson, 2006 Minn. App. Unpub. LEXIS 560 (Minn. 2006)   166

State v. Johnson, 2008 VT 135, 2008 Vt. LEXIS 200 (Vt. 2008)   306

State v. Johnson, 284 Kan. 18, 2007 Kan. LEXIS 328 (Kan. 2007)   213

State v. Just, 2007 ME 91, 2007 Me. LEXIS 92 (Me. 2007)   120

State v. K.N., 124 Wash. App. 875, 103 P.3d 844, 2004 Wash. App. LEXIS 3135 (2004)   115, 129

State v. Kelly, 2009 Conn. Super. LEXIS 98 (2009)   193, 242

State v. Kelly, 210 Ariz. 460, 112 P.3d 682, 2005 Ariz. App. LEXIS 70 (Ariz. 2005)   48

State v. Kemper, 158 Ohio App. 3d 185, 187, 2004 Ohio 4050, 814 N.E.2d 540, 541, 2004 Ohio App. LEXIS 3677 (2004)   354

State v. Kennedy, 85 S.C. 146, 150, 67 S.E. 152, 1910 S.C. LEXIS 219 (1910)   263

State v. Kim, 2008 Ohio 6928 (Ohio 2008)   120, 623

State v. King, 197 Neb. 729, 250 N.W.2d 655 (Neb. 1977)   328

State v. Klosterman, 114 Ohio App. 3d 327, 683 N.E.2d 100 (1996)   641

State v. Lane, 262 Kan. 373, 940 P.2d 422 (1997)   682

State v. Langholz, 2009 Kan. App. LEXIS 60 (Kan. 2009)   220

State v. Langley, 896 So. 2d 200, 207, 2004 La. App. LEXIS 3177 (2004)   88

State v. Lathim, 2006 Wash. App. LEXIS 936 (2006)   241

State v. Laveck, 2005 Ohio 62, 2004 Ohio App. LEXIS 6743 (2004)   290

State v. Lawson, 2002 Tenn. Crim. App. LEXIS 468 (2002)   281

State v. Lee, 2005 Tenn. Crim. App. LEXIS 399 (2005)   429

State v. Lente, 2005 NMCA 111, 119 P. 3d 737, 739, 740, 2005 N.M. LEXIS 105 (2005)   429

State v. Lerner, 308 A.2d 324 (R.I. 1973)   594

State v. Lewis, 2006 Tenn. Crim. App. LEXIS 237 (2006)   481, 487

State v. Lewis, 391 N.W.2d 726 (Iowa 1986)   65

State v. Lewis, 990 So. 2d 109, 116, 2008 La. App. LEXIS 1120 (La. 2008), *writ denied*, 2009 La. LEXIS 379 (La. 2009)   615

State v. Logan-Price, 197 P.3d 904, 2008 Kan. App. Unpub. LEXIS 976 (Kan. 2008)   598

State v. Long, 2005 Tenn. Crim. App. LEXIS 199 (2005)   559

State v. Lonsinger, 2005 Tenn. Crim. App. LEXIS 12 (2005)   407

State v. Lux, 2005 Wash. App. LEXIS 980 (2005)   519

State v. Lyles, 615 S.E.2d 890, 893, 894, 2005 N.C. App. LEXIS 1424 (2005)   413

State v. Maag, 2005 Ohio 3761, 2005 Ohio App. LEXIS 3461 (2005)   405

State v. Macdonald, 122 Wash. App. 804, 810, 95 P.3d 1248, 1251, 2004 Wash. App. LEXIS 1859 (Wash. 2004)   195

State v. Mack, 2006 Minn. App. Unpub. LEXIS 53 (2006)   528

State v. Martin, 137 Wash. 2d 774, 791, 975 P.2d 1020, 1029, 1999 Wash. LEXIS 287 (1999)   370

State v. Martinez, 149 N.C. App. 553, 560, 561 S.E.2d 528, 533 (2002)   235

State v. Mason, 271 Neb. 16, 709 N.W.2d 638, 2006 Neb. LEXIS 23 (2006)   412

State v. Matthis, 970 So. 2d 505, 2007 La. LEXIS 2389 (La. 2007)   562

State v. Mattson, 2005 S.D. 71, 698 N.W.2d 538, 552, 2005 S.D. LEXIS 73 (S.D. 2005)   678

State v. May, 210 Ariz. 452, 455, 112 P.3d 39, 42, 2005 Ariz. App. LEXIS 73 (2005)   476

State v. Mayes, 2004 Tenn. Crim. App. LEXIS 9 (2004)   481

State v. Mayo, 2006 Wis. App. 78, 713 N.W.2d 191, 2006 Wis. App. LEXIS 276 (Wis. 2006)   461

State v. McClain, 169 N.C. App. 657, 670, 610 S.E.2d 783, 792, 2005 N. C. App. LEXIS 804 (2005)   406

State v. McClellan, 2006 Md. App. LEXIS 103 (2006)   56

State v. McClure, 2006 N.C. App. LEXIS 47 (N.C. 2006)   541

State v. McCullough, 2008 Ohio 3055; 2008 Ohio App. LEXIS 2574 (Oh. 2008)   181

State v. McElroy, 29 Kan. App. 2d 990, 992–993, 35 P.3d 283, 286–287 (2001)   208

State v. McNeill, 360 N.C. 231, 249, 624 S.E.2d 329, 341, 2006 N.C. LEXIS 1 (2006)   50

State v. McVay, 620 S.E.2d 883, 2005 N.C. App. LEXIS 2402 (2005)   400

State v. Medeiros, 206 Haw. App. LEXIS 185 (2006)   439

State v. Menard, 844 So. 2d 1117 (La. Dist. Ct. App. 2003)   356

State v. Mendez, 2004 Ohio 3107, 2004 Ohio App. LEXIS 2755 (2004)   121

State v. Merida, 2008 R.I. LEXIS 118 (R.I. 2008)   307

State v. Miko, 2008 Ohio 1991, 2008 Ohio App. LEXIS 1703 (Oh. 2008)   120

State v. Miles, 211 Ariz. 475; 123 P.3d 669, 673, 2005 Ariz. App. LEXIS 161 (2005)   363

State v. Miller, 2003 Utah App. 76, 2003 Utah App. LEXIS 247 (2003)   57

State v. Miller, 208 S.W.3d 284, 2006 Mo. App. LEXIS 1737 (Mo. 2006)   192

State v. Miller, 754 N.W.2d 686, 706, 707, 2008 Minn. LEXIS 424 (Minn. 2008)   309

State v. Mitchel, 56 Wash. App. 610, 784 P.2d 568 (1990)   581

State v. Moley, 490 N.W.2d 764 (Wis. 1992)   659

State v. Monda, 198 P.3d 784, 2009 Kan. App. LEXIS 28 (Kan. 2009)   195

State v. Montgomery, 2006 Ala. Crim. App. LEXIS 36 (2006)   242

State v. Morehous, 97 N.J.L. 285, 117 A. 296, 1922 N.J. LEXIS 186 (1922)   368

State v. Moses, 107 Haw. 282, 285, 112 P.3d 768, 772, 2005 Haw. App. LEXIS 174 (2005)   368

State v. Mungroo, 104 Conn. App. LEXIS 668, 2007 Conn. App. LEXIS 436 (Conn. 2007)   193

State v. Nankoo, 2009 Minn. App. Unpub. 68 (Minn. 2009)   291

State v. Narron, 666 S.E.2d 860, 2008 N.C. App. LEXIS 1758 (N.C. 2008)   148

State v. Neeley, 2006 Ohio 418 2006 Ohio App. LEXIS 349 (2006)   296

State v. Nesbitt, 185 N.J. 504, 511, 888 A.2d 472, 476, 2006 N.J. LEXIS 7 (2006)   411, 420

State v. Newman, 208 Ariz. 507, 95 P.3d 950, 2004 Ariz. App. LEXIS 118 (2004)   181

State v. Nobach, 2002 Mont. 91, 309 Mont. 342, 46 P.3d 618, 2002 Mont. LEXIS 189 (2002)   395, 405

State v. Norman, 2006 Ohio 3362, 2006 Ohio App. LEXIS 3254 (2006)   599

State v. Nulf, 2008 Wash. App. LEXIS 2278 (Wash. 2008)   144

State v. Owings, 2006 Ohio 4281 (Ohio 2006)   566

State v. Palabay, 844 P.2d 1 (Wash. 1992)   453

State v. Palmer, 2009 Ida. App. LEXIS 17 (Ida. 2009)   227

State v. Palubicki,700 N.W.2d 476, 484, 2005 Minn. LEXIS 418 (2005)   347

State v. Parks, 245 Neb. 205, 511 N.W.2d 774 (1994)   141

State v. Pascal, 109 Conn. App. 45, 72, 2008 Conn. App. LEXIS 352 (Conn. 2008)   217

State v. Patel, 949 A.2d 401, 413 (R.I. 2008)   199

State v. Patterson, 2005 Ohio 6703; 2005 Ohio App. LEXIS 6050 (2005)   255

State v. Peay, 96 Conn. App. 421, 435, 900 A.2d 577, 2006 Conn. App. LEXIS 326 (2006)   516

State v. Perkins, 130 W. Va. 708, 45 S.E.2d 17 (1947)   35

State v. Phillips, 123 Wash. App. 761, 98 P.3d 838, 2004 Wash. App. LEXIS 2296 (2004), reh'g denied, 2005 Wash. LEXIS 492 (2005)   426

State v. Pitts, 116 N.J. 580, 625, 562 A.2d 1320, 1345, 1989 N.J. LEXIS 73 (N.J. 1989)   613

State v. Pollman, 286 Kan. 881, 2008 Kan. LEXIS 450 (Kan. 2008)   598

State v. Pona, 948 A.2d 941, 2008 R.I. LEXIS 69 (R.I. 2008)   202, 228

State v. Powers, 2002 Tenn. LEXIS 768 (2002), cert. denied, Powers v. Tennessee, 538 U.S. 1038, 2003 U.S. LEXIS 3797 (2003)   347

State v. Purvis, 2006 Ohio 1555, 2006 Ohio App. LEXIS 1493 (2006)   348

State v. Pusyka, 592 A.2d 850 (R.I. 1991)   453

State v. Quintana 2004 Utah App. 418, 103 P.2d 168, 169, 2004 Utah App. LEXIS 459 (2004)   439

State v. Ray, 290 Conn. 24, 37, 961 A.2d 947, 2009 Conn. LEXIS 5 (Conn. 2009)   63

State v. Reardon, 2009 N.C. App. LEXIS 306 (N.C. 2009)   619

State v. Rivet, 2008 ND 145, 2008 N.D. LEXIS 144 (N.D. 2008)   217

State v. Robbins, 986 So. 2d 828, 835, 2008 La. App. LEXIS 862 (La. 2008)   167

State v. Roberts, 2008 Ohio 5750, 2008 Ohio App. LEXIS 4821 (Ohio 2008)   99, 144

State v. Robinson, 2003 Iowa App. LEXIS 550 (Iowa 2003)   616

State v. Robinson, 653 S.E.2d 889, 2007 N.C. App. LEXIS 2556 (N.C. 2007)   660

State v. Rollins, 2009 N.C. LEXIS 348 (N.C. 2009)   338

State v. Roubideaux, 2008 S.D. 81, 2008 S.D. LEXIS 119 (S.D. 2008)   97

State v. Salters, 89 Conn. App. 221; 872 A.2d 933; 2005 Conn. App. LEXIS 200 (2005)   65

State v. Sarnowski, 2005 Wis. App 48, 280 Wis. 2d 243, 251, 694 N.W.2d 498, 502, 2005 Wis. App. LEXIS 150 (2005)   108

State v. Scheidel, 165 Ohio App. 3d 131; 2006 Ohio 195; 844 N.E.2d 1248; 2006 Ohio App. LEXIS 166 (2006)   322

State v. Scott, 20 Wash. 2d 696, 149 P.2d 152 (1944)   290

State v. Scott, 2008 Ohio 1862, 2008 Ohio App. LEXIS 1579 (Ohio 2008)   180

State v. Scott, 3 Ohio App. 2d 239, 32 Ohio Op. 2d 360, 210 N.E.2d 289 (1965)   130

State v. Seager, 571 N.W.2d 204 (Iowa 1997)   642

State v. Searcy, 288 Wis. 2d 804; 709 N.W.2d 497; 2005 Wis. App. LEXIS 1124 (2005)   269

State v. Seibert, 542 U.S. 600, 2004 U.S. LEXIS 4578 (2004)   237

State v. Selmon, 2006 Ohio 65, 2006 Ohio App. LEXIS 50 (2006)   397

State v. Serrano, 91 Conn. App. 227, 232, 880 A.2d 183, 188, 2005 Conn. App. LEXIS 390 (2005)   290

State v. Shanks, 640 A.2d 155 (Conn. 1994)   109

State v. Silva, 394 N.J. Super. 270, 2007 N.J. Super. LEXIS 200 (N.J. 2007)   113

State v. Sims, 272 Neb 811, 826, 827, 2006 Neb. LEXIS 185 (Neb. 2006)   266

State v. Singleton, 922 So. 2d 647, 650, 2006 La. App. LEXIS 115 (La. 2006)   103

State v. Slade, 2008 Mont. 341, 346 Mont. 271, 194 P.3d 677, 2008 Mont. LEXIS 574 (Mont. 2008)   62

State v. Sliwinski, 2004 Mont. 1221, 2004 Mont. Dist. LEXIS 2119 (2004)   475

State v. Smith, 2006 Del. C.P. LEXIS 34 (Del. 2006)   118

State v. Smith, 2006 Tenn. Crim. App. LEXIS 145 (2006)   599

State v. Smith, 289 N.C. 143, 221 S.E.2d 247 (1976)   292

State v. Snider, 168 N.C. App. 701, 706, 609 S.E.2d 231, 235, 2005 N.C. App. LEXIS 395 (2005)   570

State v. Sonya, 270 Neb. 870, 880, 708 N.W.2d 786, 795, 2006 Neb. LEXIS 5 (Neb. 2006)   52

State v. Spencer, 216 N.W.2d 131 (Minn. 1974)   436

State v. Stegman, 2009 Kan. App. LEXIS 124 (Kan. 2009)   144

State v. Stephens-Tun, 2008 Ohio 3491, 2008 Ohio App. LEXIS 2951 (Ohio 2008)   61

State v. Stewart, 265 S.W.3d 309, 316, 2008 Mo. App. LEXIS 1098 (Mo. 2008)   184

State v. Stoa, 2006 Haw. App. LEXIS 397 (2006)   622

State v. Stokes, 673 S.E.2d 434, 2009 S.C. LEXIS 35 (S.C. 2009)   226

State v. Stout, 2008 Mont. Dist. LEXIS 233 (Mont. 2008)   196

State v. Streckfuss, 171 N.C. App. 81; 2005 LEXIS 1190 (2005)   393

State v. Stribling, 2009 Ohio 1444, 2009 Ohio App. LEXIS 1240   214

State v. Stump, 254 Iowa 1181, 119 N.W.2d 210 (1963)   64

State v. Sutton, 450 P.2d 748 (Or. 1969)   300

State v. Taylor, 165 N.C. App. 750; 600 S.E.2d 483, 2004 N.C. App. LEXIS 1519 (2004)   443

State v. Taylor, 182 S.W. 159 (Mo. 1916)   114

State v. Taylor, 999 So. 2d 1262, 2009 La. App. Unpub. LEXIS 45 (La. 2009)   451

State v. Tetu, 2005 Haw. App. LEXIS 435 (Haw. 2005)   552

State v. Thomas, 158 S.W.3d 361, 2005 Tenn. LEXIS 135 (Tenn. 2005)   566

State v. Thompson, 950 P.2d 977 (Wash. 1998)   395

State v. Tody, 2009 Wisc. LEXIS 21 (Wis. 2009)   33

State v. Tolliver, 268 Neb 920, 921, 689 N.E.2d 567, 573, 2004 Neb. LEXIS 195 (2004)   413

State v. Toole, 640 A.2d 965 (R.I. 1994)   302

State v. Torres, 137 N.M. 607, 113 P.3d 877; 2005 N.M. App. LEXIS 56 (2005)   556

State v. Townshend, 2005 Ohio 6945, 2005 Ohio App. LEXIS 6239 (2005)   520

State v. Trevino, 132 Idaho 888, 980 P.2d 552, 1999 Idaho LEXIS 54 (1999)   609

State v. Tripathi, 226 Or. App. 552, 555, 2009 Or. App. LEXIS 147 (Or. 2009)   599

State v. Troisi, 2008 Ohio 6062, 2008 Ohio App. LEXIS (Ohio 2008)   58

State v. Trotman, 366 N.J. Super. 226, 234, 840 A.2d 952; 2004 N.J. Super. LEXIS 52 (N.J. 2004)   580

State v. Troutman, 2008 Tenn. Crim. App. LEXIS 899 (Tenn. 2008)   507

State v. Tucker, 215 Ariz. 298, 308, 2007 Ariz. LEXIS 64 (Ariz. 2007), *cert. denied*, Tucker v. Arizona, 128 S. Ct. 296, 2007 U.S. LEXIS 10884 (2007)   183

State v. Turner, 105 Ohio St. 3d 331, 2005 Ohio 1938, 826 N.E.2d 266, 2005 Ohio LEXIS 961 (2005)   125, 282

State v. Tyson, 658 S.E.2d 285, 287, 2008 N.C. App. LEXIS 652 (N.C. 2008)   112

State v. VanNguyen, 222 Ore. App. 55, 2008 Ore. App. LEXIS 1141 (Ore. 2008)   311

State v. Vejvoda, 231 Neb. 668, 438 N.W.2d 461 (1989)   112

State v. Vernes, 2006 Mont. 32, 331 Mont. 129, 132, 133, 130 P.3d. 169, 173, 2006 Mont. LEXIS 41 (2006)   413

State v. Vining, 645 A.2d 20 (Me. 1994)   443

State v. Virga, 2009 Tenn. Crim. App. LEXIS 161 (Tenn. 2009)   242

State v. Walker, 2006 N.J. Super. LEXIS 145 (2006)   421

State v. Washington, 664 N.W.2d 203, 2003 Mich. LEXIS1465 (Mich. 2003)   487

State v. Wasserman, 2008 Wis. App. 148, 2008 Wis. App. LEXIS 669 (Wis. 2008)   124

State v. Watson, 2007 Ohio 2804, 2007 Ohio App. LEXIS 2565 (Ohio 2007)   599

State v. Welch, 666 S.E.2d 826, 829, 830, 2008 N.C. App. LEXIS 1741 (N.C. 2008)   226

State v. Were, 118 Ohio St.3d 448, 2008 Ohio 2762, 890 N.E.2d, 2008 Ohio LEXIS 1615 (Ohio 2008)   66

State v. West, 2008 Ohio 1391, 2008 Ohio App. LEXIS 1210 (Ohio 2008)   51

State v. White, 259 S.E.2d 281 (N.C. 1979)   292

State v. Whitney, 889 N.E.2d 823, 2008 Ind. App. LEXIS 1344 (Ind. 2008)   598

State v. Wiggins, 2004 Del. Super. LEXIS 64 (Del. 2004)   678

State v. Williams, 2004 Tenn. Crim. App. LEXIS 191 (Tenn. 2004)   171

State v. Williams, 925 So. 2d 567, 573, 2006 La. App. LEXIS 593 (2006)   375

State v. Williamson, 144 Idaho 597, 602, 2007 Idaho App. LEXIS 43 (Ida 2007)   132

State v. Wilson, 2006 Ohio 2000; 2006 Ohio App. LEXIS 1860 (2006)   348

State v. Yamada, 116 Haw. 422, 2007 Haw. App. LEXIS 663 (Haw. 2007)   209

State v. Young, 378 S.C. 101, 106, 2008 S.C. LEXIS 153 (S.C. 2008)   222

State v. Young, 895 So. 2d 753, 757, 2005 La. App. LEXIS 536 (2005)   658

Steele v. State, 97 Wis. 2d 72, 294 N.W.2d 2 (1980)   430

Stein v. Bowman, 38 U.S. (13 Pet.)209, 223, 10 L. Ed. 129 (1839)   338

Stephenson v. State, 742 N.E.2d 463 (Ind. 2001)   60

Sterling v. Tenet, 416 F.3d 338, 341, 2005 U.S. App. LEXIS 15945 (4th Cir. 2005)   379

Sterner v. DEA, 2005 U.S. Dist. LEXIS 18467 (2005)   364

Stewart v. Maryland, 151 Md. App. 425, 827 A.2d 850, 2003 Md. App. LEXIS 75 (2003)   489

Stewart v. Southwest Foods, 688 So. 2d 733, 735, 1996 Miss. LEXIS 643 (1996)   268

Still v. Secretary of the Commonwealth, 73 Pa. D. & C. 106; 1950 Pa. D. & C. LEXIS 247 (1950)   123

Stimus v. State, 995 So. 2d 1149, 1151, 2008 Fla. App. LEXIS 18376 (Fla. 2008)   220

Stokes v. Commonwealth, 2008 Ky. LEXIS 321 (Ky. 2008)   122

Stokes v. Commonwealth, 2008 Ky. LEXIS 321 Ky. 2008)   109

Stoltie v. People, 501 F. Supp.2d 1252, 2007 U.S. Dist. LEXIS 53333 (C.D. Cal. 2007)   147

Stotler v. Florida, 834 So. 2d 940, 943, 2003 Fla. App. LEXIS 445 (2003)   303

Strickland v. Washington, 466 U.S. 668 at 683, 1984 U.S. LEXIS 79 (1984)   94

Strickler v. Greene, 527 U.S. 263, 281–282 (1999)   92, 583

Strong v. State, 372 Ark. 404, 416, 2008 Ark. LEXIS 112 (Ark. 2008)   216

Stubbs v. Colandrea et al., 154 Md. App. 673, 682, 841 A.2d 361, 366, 2004 Md. App. LEXIS 9 (Md. 2004)   146

Sulieman v. Roswell Park Cancer Inst., 2007 U.S. Dist. LEXIS 46599 (W.D. N.Y. 2007)   117

Sullivan v. Louisiana, 508 U.S. 275, 113 S. Ct. 2078, 124 L. Ed. 2d 182 (1993)   54, 57

Summum v. City of Ogden, 152 F Supp. 2d 1286, 2001 U.S. Dist. Lexis 12760, n. 10 (2001)   9

Swafford v. Florida, 828 So. 2d 966 at 967, 2002 Fla. LEXIS 789 (2002)   132

Swidler & Berlin v. United States, 524 U.S. 399, 1998 U.S. LEXIS 4214 (1998)   359

Tafoya v. Chapin, 2003 Neb. App. LEXIS 64 (2003)   246

Tank v. Comm'r of Internal Revenue, 270 F.2d 477 (6th Cir. 1959)   416

Taylor v. State, 640 So. 2d 1227 (Fla. 1994)   581

Taylor v. State, 77 Ark. App. 144, 150, 72 S.W.3d 882, 885 (Ark. 2002)   166

Tecom, Inc. v. United States, 66 Fed. Cl. 736, 768, 2005 U.S. Claims LEXIS 195 (2005)   173

Tenet Healthcare Corp. v. Gilbert, 277 Ga. App. 895, 627 S.E.2d 821, 2006 Ga. App. LEXIS 167 (2006)   428

Tenet v. Doe, 544 U.S. 1, 3, 2005 U.S. LEXIS 2202 (2005)   379

Tennessee v. Coleman, 2002 Tenn. Crim. App. LEXIS 84 (2002)   285

Tennessee v. Combs, 2002 Tenn. Crim. App. LEXIS 799 (2002)   429

Tennessee v. Neblett, 2003 Tenn. Crim. App. LEXIS 429 (2003)   313

Tennessee v. Pylant, 2003 Tenn. Crim. App. LEXIS 405 (2003)   297

Tennessee v. Woods, 2001 Tenn. Crim. App. LEXIS 797 (2001)   542

Terry v. Ohio, 392 U.S. 1, 88 S. Ct. 1868, 20 L. Ed. 2d 720 (1968)   663

Terry v. State, 2006 Ark. LEXIS 326 (2006)   47, 102

Thacker v. Commonwealth, 194 S.W.3d 287, 2006 Ky. LEXIS 174 (2006)   59

The Berkshires, L.L.C. v. Sykes, 2005 UT App 536, 2005 Utah App. LEXIS 552 (Utah 2005)   431, 432

The Termo Company v. Luther, 169 Cal. App. 4th 394, 404, 2008 Cal. App. LEXIS 2430 (Cal. 2008)   113

Thomas v. State, 197 Okla. 450, 172 P.2d 973 (1946)   434

Thomas v. State, 2009 Miss. App. LEXIS 192 (Miss. 2009)   317

Thompson v. Commonwealth, 177 S.W.3d 782, 783, 2005 Ky. LEXIS 370 (Ky. 2005)   599

Thompson v. Keohane, 516 U.S. 99 (1995)   672

Thompson v. State, 2006 Ark. App. LEXIS 364 (2006)   557

Thornburgh v. Commonwealth, 2006 Va. App. LEXIS 90 (Va. 2006)   166

Thornton v. State, 279 Ga. 676, 678, 620 S.E.2d 356, 360, 2005 Ga. App. LEXIS 634 (2005)   435

Thrasher v. Georgia, 2003 Ga. App. LEXIS 734 (2003)   440

Timm v. Reitz, 39 P.3d 1252, 1258, 2001 Colo. App. LEXIS 2019 (2001)   121

Tobin v. Liberty Mutual, 2007 U.S. Dist. LEXIS 23680 (D. Mass. 2007), *aff'd*, 553 F.3d 121, 2009 U.S. App. LEXIS 1278 (1st Cir. 2009)   114

Tolliver v. Greiner, 2005 U.S. Dist. LEXIS 32402 (N.D.N.Y. 2005)   549

Tome v. United States, 513 U.S. 150, 115 S. Ct. 696, 130 L. Ed. 2d 574 (1995)   454

Tomlinson v. State, 878 P.2d 311 (Nev. 1994)   528

Torres v. Texas, 2003 Tex. App. LEXIS 6580 (2003)   539

Tot v. United States, 319 U.S. 463, 1943 U.S. LEXIS 531 (1943)   141, 175, 176

Toth v. Grand Trunk Railroad, 306 F.3d 335, 2002 U.S. App. LEXIS 19169 (6th Cir. 2002)   128

Totten v. United States, 92 U.S. 105, 107, 1875 U.S. LEXIS 1732 (1875)   376, 379

Town of Suffolk v. Town of East Hampton, 406 F. Supp. 2d 227, 232, 2005 U.S. Dist. LEXIS 41036 (2005)   118

Townsend v. Sain, 372 U.S. 293, 83 S. Ct. 745, 768, 9 L. Ed. 2d 770 (1963)   612

Trammel v. United States, 445 U.S. 40, 44 (1980)   37, 258, 334, 336, 339, 362

Trevino v. Hardison, 2006 U.S. Dist. LEXIS 27294 (D. Idaho 2006)   609

Trotter v. State, 392 So. 2d 1045, 1048, 2006 Fla. LEXIS 940 (Fla. 2006)   113

Troxell v. Indiana, 778 N.E.2d 811, 814, 2002 Ind. LEXIS 888 (2002)   543

Trump v. O'Brien, 403 N.J. Super 281, 2008 N.J. Super. LEXIS 217 (N.J. 2008)   384

Turner v. Arkansas, 2005 Ark. App. LEXIS 237 (2005)   67

Turner v. City of Taylor, 412 F.3d 629, 2005 U.S. App. LEXIS 11233 (6th Cir. 2005)   675

Turner v. State, 181 Md. App. 477, 481, 2008 Md. App. LEXIS 106 (Md. 2008)   153

Turner v. United States, 396 U.S. 398, 1970 U.S. LEXIS 3146 (1970)   177

Twentieth Century Fox Film Corp. v. Marvel Enterprises, 155 F. Supp. 2d 1, 41, 2001 U.S. Dist. LEXIS 11568 (S. Dist. N.Y. 2001)   114

Ulmer v. State Farm, 897 F. Supp. 299, 302, 1995 U.S. Dist. LEXIS 13295 (W.D. La. 1995)   184

Underwood v. State, 708 So. 2d 18 (Miss. 1998)   567

United State v. Agurs, 427 U.S. 97, 1976 U.S. LEXIS 72 (1976)   583

United State v. Godinez, 110 F.3d 448 (7th Cir. 1997)   455

United State v. Nazemian, 748 F.2d 552 (9th Cir. 1991)   455

United States ex rel. Reed v. Gilmore, 1999 U.S. Dist. LEXIS 21525 (N.D. Ill. 1999)   422

United States v. 14.02 Acres of Land, 530 F.3d 883, 894, 2008 U.S. App. LEXIS 13309 (9th Cir. 2008)   125, 128

United States v. 60.14 Acres of Land, 362 F.2d 660 (3d Cir. 1966)   416

United States v. Abboud, 438 F.3d 554, 586, 2006 U.S. App. LEXIS 3797 (6th Cir. 2006)   421

United States v. Abdelaziz et al., 2008 U.S. Dist. LEXIS 49076 (W.D. Tex. 2008)   146

United States v. Abreu, 952 F.2d 1458 (1st Cir.), cert. denied, 503 U.S. 994, 112 S. Ct. 1695, 118 L. Ed. 2d 406 (1992)   548

United States v. Ali, 2006 U.S. Dist. LEXIS 21543 (E.D.N.Y. 2006)   652

United States v. Allen, 10 F.3d 405 (7th Cir. 1993)   279

United States v. Amanuel, 418 F. Supp. 2d 244, 2006 U.S. Dist. LEXIS 3890 (W.D.N.Y. 2006)   666

United States v. Amos, 803 F.2d 419 (8th Cir. 1986)   158

United States v. Anderson, 2006 U.S. App. LEXIS 11581 (8th Cir. 2006)   414

United States v. Anderson, 450 F.3d 294, 2006 U.S. App. LEXIS 14177 (7th Cir. 2006)   144

United States v. Anderson, 813 F.2d 1450 (9th Cir. 1987)   441

United States v. Andolschek, 142 F.2d 503 (2d Cir. 1944)   380

United States v. Antoon, 933 F.2d 200 (3d Cir.), cert. denied, 502 U.S. 907, 112 S. Ct. 300, 116 L. Ed. 2d 243 (1991)   666

United States v. Arellano-Ochoa, 2006 U.S. App. LEXIS 22466 (9th Cir. 2006)   649

United States v. Arhebamen, 2006 U.S. App. LEXIS 24564 (6th Cir. 2006)   314

United States v. Arroyo, 2009 U.S. App. LEXIS 4165 (7th Cir. 2009)   125, 131

United States v. Arvizu, 534 U.S. 266, 2002 U.S. LEXIS 490 (2002)   656

United States v. Ary, 2005 U.S. Dist. LEXIS 21958 (D. Kan. 2005)   360

United States v. Ash, 413 U.S. 300, 1973 U.S. LEXIS 45 (1973)   683

United States v. Aspinall, 389 F.3d 332, 344, 2004 U.S. App. LEXIS 23954 (2d Cir. 2004)   37

United States v. Avery, 2005 U.S. Dist. LEXIS 15979 (E.D. Pa. 2005)   491

United States v. Avila, 557 F.3d 809, 2009 U.S. App. LEXIS 4940 (7th Cir. 2009)   244

United States v. Ayala-Pizarro, 407 F.3d 25, 2005 U.S. LEXIS 8322 (1st Cir. 2005)   393

United States v. Bagley, 473 U.S. 667, 677, 1985 U.S. LEXIS 130 (1985)   583

United States v. Bailey, 169 Fed. Appx. 815, 821, 2006 U.S. App. LEXIS 3402 (5th Cir. 2006)   97

United States v. Banks, 556 F.2d 967, 981, 2009 U.S. App. LEXIS 3696 (9th Cir. 2009)   335

United States v. Banner, 442 F.3d 1310, 1315, 2006 U.S. App. LEXIS 5967 (11th Cir. 2006)   91

United States v. Barker, 735 F.2d 1280 (11th Cir. 1984)   409

United States v. Barnett, 398 F.3d 516, 522, 2005 U.S. App. LEXIS 2644 (6th Cir. 2005)   101

United States v. Barnett, 989 F.2d 546 (1st Cir.), cert. denied, 510 U.S. 850, 114 S. Ct. 148, 126 L. Ed. 2d 110 (1993)   651

United States v. Barrett, 8 F.3d 1296 (8th Cir. 1993)   460

United States v. Beck, 418 F.3d 1008, 2005 U.S. App. LEXIS 16713 (9th Cir. 2005)   393

United States v. Beck, 418 F.3d 1008; 2005 U.S. App. LEXIS 16713 (2005)   397

United States v. Begay, 2009 U.S. App. LEXIS 2577 (10th Cir. 2009)   203

United States v. Benally, 546 F.3d 1230, 1233, 2008 U.S. App. LEXIS 23555 (10th Cir. 2008)   267, 269

United States v. Benedetti, 433 F.3d 111, 116, 2005 U.S. App. LEXIS 28490 (1st Cir. 2005)   169, 215

United States v. Benjamin, 125 Fed. Appx. 438, 440, 2005 U.S. App. LEXIS 3943 (2005)   204

United States v. Bennafield, 287 F.3d 320, 202 U.S. App. LEXIS 8009 (4th Cir. 2002), cert. denied, 537 U.S. 961, 2002 LEXIS 7487 (2002)   200

United States v. Berber-Tinoco, 510 F.3d 1083, 1091, 2007 U.S. App. LEXIS 29301 (9th Cir. 2007)   112, 118, 266

United States v. Bisanti, 414 F.3d 168, 170, 2005 U.S. App. LEXIS 13575 (1st Cir. 2005)   336

United States v. Blackman, 2006 U.S. Dist. LEXIS 70147 (E.D.N.C. 2006)   287

United States v. Blanchard, 542 F.3d 1133, 2008 U.S. App. LEXIS 19151 (7th Cir. 2008)   266

United States v. Bledsoe, 70 Fed. Appx. 370, 2003 U.S. App. LEXIS 13312 (7th Cir. 2003)   514

United States v. Bonsu, 291 Fed. App. 505, 2008 U.S. App. LEXIS 17998 (4th Cir. 2008)   195

United States v. Boone, 437 F.3d 829, 839, 2006 U.S. App. LEXIS 3531 (8th Cir. 2006)   94

United States v. Booz, 451 F.2d 719 (3d Cir. 1971)   295

United States v. Bowman, 302 F.2d 1228, 1239, 1240, 2002 U.S. App. LEXIS 17165 (2002)   201

United States v. Bray, 445 F.2d 178 (5th Cir. 1971)   321

United States v. Brewer, 1 F.3d 1430 (4th Cir. 1993)   442

United States v. Brewer, 2002 U.S. Dist. LEXIS 6689 (N.D. Ill. 2002)   433

United States v. Brito, 427 F.3d 53, 61, 2005 U.S. App. LEXIS 22525 (1st Cir. 2006)   461

United States v. Broadwater, 2003 U.S. App. LEXIS 10873 (7th Cir. 2003)   320

United States v. Brooks, 589 F. Supp. 2d 618, 2008 U.S. Dist. LEXIS 102201 (E.D. Va. 2008)   241

United States v. Brown, 152 Fed. Appx. 59, 2005 U.S. App. LEXIS 22703 (2d Cir. 2005)   432

United States v. Bruce, 396 F.3d 697, 705, 2005 U.S. App. LEXIS 1712 (6th Cir. 2005)   660

United States v. Brudette, 86 Fed. Appx. 121, 2004 U.S. App. LEXIS 804 (6th Cir. 2004)   545

United States v. Buck, 324 F.3d 786, 791, 2003 U.S. App. LEXIS 4820 (5th Cir. 2003)   532

United States v. Bush, 405 F.3d 909, 2005 U.S. App. LEXIS 7114 (10th Cir. 2005)   397, 578

United States v. Camacho, 555 F.3d 695, 704, 2009 U.S. App. LEXIS 3592 (8th Cir. 2009)   270

United States v. Cano, 289 F.3d 1354, 1361, 1362, 2002 U.S. App. LEXIS 8590 (11th Cir. 2002), cert. denied, 2003 U.S. LEXIS 433 (2003)   396

United States v. Carr, 2006 U.S. Dist. LEXIS 6368 (D.D.C. 2006)   217

United States v. Carr, 362 U.S. App. D.C. 303, 373 F.3d 1350, 1353, 2004 U.S. App. LEXIS 14305 (D.C. Cir. 2004)   217

United States v. Carson, 455 F.3d 336, 2006 U.S. App. LEXIS 18361 (D.C. Cir. 2006)   478

United States v. Carter, 410 F.3d 942, 949, 2005 U. S. App. LEXIS 10830 (7th Cir. 2006)   414

United States v. Case, 2008 U.S. Dist. LEXIS 33891 (S.D. Miss. 2008)   146

United States v. Cedeno, 496 F. Supp. 2d 562, 2007 U.S. Dist. LEXIS 49631 (E.D. Pa. 2007)   355

United States v. Chan, 2002 U.S. Dist. LEXIS 1221 (S.D.N.Y. 2002)   313

United States v. Charles, 456 F.3d 249, 2006 U.S. App. LEXIS 19619 (1st Cir. 2006)   286

United States v. Chemical Foundation, Inc., 272 U.S. 1, 47 S. Ct. 1, 71 L. Ed. 131 (1926)   173

United States v. Chiquito, 175 Fed. Appx. 215, 2006 U.S. App. LEXIS 8724 (10th Cir. 2006)   571

United States v. Clintwood Elkhorn Mining Co., 128 S. Ct. 1511, 1518, 2008 U.S. LEXIS 3472 (2008)   147

United States v. Codrington, 2008 U.S. Dist. LEXIS 35859 (E.D.N.Y. 2008)   526

United States v. Conroy, 424 F.3d 833, 838, 2005 U.S. App. LEXIS 21080 (2005)   430

United States v. Conway, 53 Fed. Appx. 872, 876, 877, 2002 U.S. App. LEXIS 26341 (10th Cir. 2002)   320

United States v. Coutchavlis, 260 F.3d 1149, 2001 U.S. App. LEXIS 18363 (9th Cir. 2001)   119

United States v. Cowdin, 984 F. Supp. 1374 (D. Kan. 1997)   654

United States v. Crisp, 324 F.3d 261, 2003 U.S. App. LEXIS 6021 (4th Cir. 2003), *cert. denied*, 540 U.S. 888, 2003 U.S. LEXIS 6388 (2003)   439

United States v. Crosby, 294 F.2d 928 (2d Cir. 1961)   268

United States v. Cruz, 2006 U.S. App. LEXIS 18353 (10th Cir. 2006)   615

United States v. Curtin, 443 F.3d 1084, 1093, 2006 U.S. App. LEXIS 8071 (9th Cir. 2006)   194

United States v. Darling, 238 Fed. App. 258, 2007 U.S. App. LEXIS 15650 (9th Cir. 2007)   202

United States v. Davis, 2009 U.S. Dist. LEXIS 19404 (S.D. N.Y. 2009)   174

United States v. Davis, 41 Fed. Appx. 566, 571, 2002 U.S. App. LEXIS 15312 (3d Cir. 2002)   398

United States v. Davis, 602 F. Supp.2d 658, 2009 U.S. Dist. LEXIS 22514 (D. Maryland 2009)   438

United States v. Dedman, 527 F.3d 577, 587 (6th Cir. 2008)   109, 126, 131

United States v. Delatorre, 572 F. Supp. 2d 967, 2008 U.S. Dist. LEXIS 77787 (N. D. Ill. 2008)   268

United States v. deSoto, 885 F.2d 354 (7th Cir. 1989)   441

United States v. Deverso, 518 F.3d 1250, 1256, 2008 U.S. App. LEXIS 4629 (11th Cir. 2008)   513

United States v. Diaz, 2006 U.S. Dist. LEXIS 46315 (N.D. Ga. 2006)   174

United States v. DiCaro, 772 F.2d 1314 (7th Cir. 1985)   453

United States v. Dien Vy Phung, 127 Fed. Appx. 594, 2005 U.S. App. LEXIS 6146 (3d Cir. 2005)   593

United States v. Dingle, 2007 U.S. Dist. LEXIS (D. Conn. 2007)   299

United States v. Dionisio, 410 U.S. 1 (1973)   432

United States v. Doe, 128 Fed. Appx. 179, 2005 U.S. App. LEXIS 5707 (2d Cir. 2005)   594

United States v. Doe, 429 F.3d 450; 2005 U.S. App. LEXIS 25256 (3d Cir. 2005)   356

United States v. Drayton, 536 U.S. 194, 2002 U.S. LEXIS 4420 (2002)   654

United States v. Drury, 2003 U.S. App. LEXIS 18152 (11th Cir. 2003)   455

United States v. Dufresne, 58 Fed. Appx. 890, 2003 U.S. App. LEXIS 2126 (3d Cir. 2003), *cert. denied*, 538 U.S. 1064, 2003 U.S. LEXIS 4193 (2003)   153

United States v. Dukes, 242 Fed. Appx. 37, 2007 U.S. App. LEXIS 15961 (4th Cir. 2007)   531

United States v. Dunbar, 553 F.3d 48, 58, 2009 U.S. App. LEXIS 1639 (1st Cir. 2009)   339

United States v. Dunn, 480 U.S. 294, 107 S. Ct. 1134, 94 L. Ed. 2d 326 (1987)   659

United States v. Edelkind, 2006 U.S. Dist. LEXIS 41056 (W.D. La. 2006)   151

United States v. Edmo, 140 F.3d 1289 (9th Cir. 1998)   678

United States v. Edwards, 156 Fed. Appx. 954, 956, 2005 U.S. App. LEXIS 26786 (9th Cir. 2005)   318

United States v. Elashyi, 554 F.3d 480, 2008 U.S. App LEXIS 27088 (5th Cir. 2008)   109

United States v. Espino, 317 F.3d 788, 794, 2003 U.S. App. LEXIS 261 (8th Cir. 2003)   341, 346, 349, 350

United States v. Esxon, 328 F.3d 456, 459, 2003 U.S. App. LEXIS 8836 (8th Cir. 2003)   174

United States v. Etienne, 293 Fed. Appx. 977, 2008 U.S. App. LEXIS 20382 (4th Cir. 2008)   287

United States v. Evans, 431 F.3d 343, 347, 2005 U.S. App. LEXIS 27403 (8th Cir. 2005)   88
United States v. Evans-Martinez, 530 F.3d 1164, 2008 U.S. App. LEXIS 13972 (9th Cir. 2008)   143
United States v. Fasono, 2008 U.S. Dist. LEXIS 64055 (S.D. Miss. 2008)   629
United States v. Faust, 456 F.3d 1342, 2006 U.S. App. LEXIS 18366 (11th Cir. 2006)   589
United States v. Fendley, 522 F.2d 181 (5th Cir. 1975)   509
United States v. Figueroa, 548 F.3d 222, 227, 2008 U.S. App. LEXIS 23697 (2d Cir. 2008)   198, 307
United States v. Flores-Ocampo, 173 Fed. Appx. 688, 691, 2006 U.S. App. LEXIS 8367 (10th Cir. 2006)   653
United States v. Franklin, 415 F.3d 537, 547, 2005 U.S. App. LEXIS 14540 (5th Cir. 2005)   489
United States v. Frederick, 406 F.3d 754, 2005 U.S. App. LEXIS 7770 (6th Cir. 2005)   87
United States v. Freeman, 804 F.2d 1574 (11th Cir. 1986)   64, 158
United States v. Friday, 525 F.3d 938, 2008 U.S. App. LEXIS 9919 (2008), *cert. denied*, 2009 U.S. LEXIS 1548 (2009)   167
United States v. Fujii, 152 F. Supp. 2d 939 (N.D. Ill. 2000)   433
United States v. Fuller, 2006 U.S. App. LEXIS 14852 (5th Cir. 2006)   86
United States v. Fullwood, 342 F.3d 409, 2003 U.S. App. LEXIS 16309 (5th Cir. 2003), *cert. denied*, 540 U.S. 1111 (2004)   534
United States v. Gaines, 2006 U.S. App. LEXIS 22584 (7th Cir. 2006)   594
United States v. Gainey, 380 U.S. 63, 1965 U.S. LEXIS 1733 (1965)   176
United States v. Garcia, 117 Fed. Appx. 162, 2004 U.S. App. LEXIS 25480 (2d Cir. 2004)   478
United States v. Garcia, 2006 U.S. App. LEXIS 10555 (11th Cir. 2006)   423, 441
United States v. Garcia, 439 F.3d 363, 366, 2006 U.S. App. LEXIS 5032 (7th Cir. 2006)   441
United States v. Garcia, 474 F.3d 994, 2007 U.S. App. LEXIS 2272 (7thCir. 2007)   667
United States v. Garcia-Flores, 136 Fed. Appx. 685; 2005 U.S. App. LEXIS 12732 (5th Cir. 2005)   476
United States v. Gastfiaburo, 16 F.3d 582 (4th Cir. 1994)   655
United States v. Gates, 10 F.3d 765 (11th Cir. 1993)   249
United States v. Gianakos, 404 F.3d 1065 (2005), rev'd, 414 F.3d 912 (2005)   350, 587
United States v. Gipson, 446 F.3d 828, 2006 U.S. App. LEXIS 11040 (2006)   204
United States v. Goddard, 2006 U.S. App. LEXIS 6970 (D.C. Cir. 2006)   550
United States v. Goodson, 2009 U.S. App. LEXIS 6013 (4th Cir. 2009)   196
United States v. Grassi, 602 F.2d 1192 (5th Cir. 1979)   183
United States v. Green, 2008 U.S. App. LEXIS 18678 (2d Cir. 2008)   302
United States v. Green, 258 F.3d 683, 688, 2001 U.S. App. LEXIS 16770 (7th Cir. 2001)   299
United States v. Green, 405 F. Supp. 2d 104, 118, 2005 U.S. Dist. LEXIS 34273 n.26 (D. Mass. 2005)   619
United States v. Green, 428 F.3d 1131, 1134, 2005 U.S. App. LEXIS 24583 (8th Cir. 2005)   532
United States v. Gregoire, 425 F.3d 872, 880, 2005 U.S. App. LEXIS 21398 (10th Cir. 2005)   653
United States v. Gregory, 2009 U.S. App. LEXIS 1970 (11th Cir. 2009)   115
United States v. Gricco 2002 U.S. Dist. LEXIS 7564 (E.D. Pa. 2002)   433
United States v. Griffin, 440 F.3d 1138, 2006 U.S. App. LEXIS 6393 (9th Cir. 2006)   345
United States v. Grimes, 244 F.3d 375 (5th Cir. 2001)   200
United States v. Gutierrez-Casada, 553 F. Supp.2d 1259, 2008 U.S. Dist. LEXIS 39406 (D. Kan. 2008)   129
United States v. Haberek, 2006 U.S. Dist. LEXIS 44670 (N.D. Ill. 2006)   151
United States v. Hadley, 431 F.3d 484, 496, 2005 U.S. App. LEXIS 26526 (6th Cir. 2005)   463
United States v. Hamilton, 413 F.3d 1138, 1143–1144, 2005 U.S. App. LEXIS 12790 (10th Cir. 2005)   442
United States v. Hancock, 231 F.3d 557, 561, 2000 U.S. App. LEXIS 26827 (9th Cir. 2000)   167
United States v. Hand, 2006 U.S. App. LEXIS 17715 (11th Cir. 2006)   594

United States v. Haque, 2009 U.S. App. LEXIS 4231 (6th Cir. 2009)   109
United States v. Hardman, 2005 U.S. Dist. LEXIS 28923 (M.D. Tenn. 2005)   101
United States v. Harms, 442 F.3d 367, 375, 2006 U.S. App. LEXIS 6622 (5th Cir. 2006)   533
United States v. Harrison, 2005 U.S. Dist. LEXIS 6195 (E.D. Pa. 2005)   374, 375
United States v. Hart, 295 F.3d 451, 2002 U.S. App. LEXIS 11246 (2002)   533
United States v. Headbird, 461 F.3d 1074, 2006 U.S. App. LEXIS 22326 (8th Cir. 2006)   319
United States v. Hemphill, 514 F.3d 1350, 2008 U.S. App. LEXIS 2786 (D.C. Cir. 2008)   533
United States v. Herrera, 832 F.2d 833 (4th Cir. 1987)   432
United States v. Hicks, 389 F.3d 514, 523, 2004 U.S. App. LEXIS 22688 (5th Cir. 2004)   619
United States v. Hicks, 967 F. Supp. 242 (E.D. Mich. 1997)   672
United States v. Hildalgo, 229 F. Supp. 2d 961, 2002 U.S. Dist. LEXIS 21633 (D. Ariz. 2002)   433
United States v. Hitt, 981 F.2d 422 (9th Cir. 1992)   201
United States v. Hively, 202 F. Supp. 886, 889, 890 (E.D. Ark. 2002)   335
United States v. Howard, 51 Fed. Appx. 118, 2002 U.S. App. LEXIS 23711 (4th Cir. 2002)   582
United States v. Hutchings, 127 F.3d 1255 (10th Cir. 1997)   651
United States v. Ince, 21 F.3d 576 (4th Cir. 1994)   309
United States v. Jackson, 367 U.S. App. D.C. 320, 415 F.3d 88, 92, 2005 U.S. App. LEXIS 14951 (D.C. Cir. 2005)   655
United States v. Jamieson, 427 F.3d 394, 409, 2005 U.S. App. LEXIS 23337 (6th Cir. 2005)   531
United States v. Jett, 2006 U.S. Dist. LEXIS 27829 (N.D. Ind. 2006)   669
United States v. John Doe, 481 U.S. 102 (1987)   34
United States v. Johns, 2000 U.S. App. LEXIS 542 (6th Cir. 2000)   434
United States v. Johnson, 121 Fed. Appx. 912, 2005 U.S. App. LEXIS 2533 (2d Cir. 2005)   488
United States v. Johnson, 439 F.3d 947, 955, 2006 U.S. App. LEXIS 6040 (8th Cir. 2006), *motion to vacate denied*, Johnson v. United States, 2009 U.S. Dist. LEXIS 8363 (E.D. Mo. 2009)   211
United States v. Johnson, 445 F.3d 793, 2006 U.S. App. LEXIS 85, n.1 (5th Cir. 2006)   616
United States v. Jones, 2006 U.S. Dist. LEXIS 56473 (D.D.C. 2006)   580
United States v. Kaba, 999 F.2d 47 (2d Cir.), *cert. denied*, 510 U.S. 1002, 114 S. Ct. 577, 126 L. Ed. 2d 476 (1993)   669
United States v. Kane, 146 Fed. Appx. 912, 2005 U.S. App. LEXIS 22877 (9th Cir. 2005)   408
United States v. Kapp, 2003 U.S. Dist. LEXIS 4178 (N.D. Ill. 2003)   193
United States v. Kapp, 419 F.3d 666, 673, 2005 U.S. App. LEXIS 17606 (7th Cir. 2005)   415
United States v. Katz, 2006 U.S. App. LEXIS 11462 (8th Cir. 2006)   415
United States v. Kelly, 535 F.3d 1229, 2008 U.S. App. LEXIS 16572 (10th Cir. 2008), *cert. denied*, 2009 U.S. LEXIS 1053 (2009)   119
United States v. Kennedy, 427 F.3d 1136, 1143, 2005 U.S. App. LEXIS 23962 (8th Cir. 2005)   662
United States v. Kilgore, 151 Fed. Appx. 799, 802, 2005 U.S. App. LEXIS 20690 (11th Cir. 2005)   316
United States v. Kline, 112 Fed. Appx. 562, 2004 U.S. App. LEXIS 20759 (9th Cir. 2004), *cert. denied*, 544 U.S. 950, 2005 U.S. LEXIS 2818 (2005)   660
United States v. Kornegay, 410 F.3d 89, 94, 2005 U.S. App. LEXIS 10707 (1st Cir. 2005)   407
United States v. Laguerre, 119 Fed. Appx. 458, 2005 U.S. App. LEXIS 213 (4th Cir. 2005)   534
United States v. Laub Baking Co., 283 F. Supp. 217 (N.D. Ohio 1968)   615
United States v. Lentz, 2004 U.S. Dist. LEXIS 29650 (E.D. Va. 2004)   493
United States v. Lentz, 419 F. Supp. 2d 820, 826, 2005 U.S. Dist. LEXIS 41084 (E.D. Va. 2005)   357, 358, 361
United States v. Letner, 273 Fed. App. 491, 2008 U.S. App. LEXIS 8375 (6th Cir. 2008)   309
United States v. Lewis, 220 F. Supp. 2d 548, 2002 U.S. Dist. LEXIS 17062 (S.D. W.Va. 2002)   433

United States v. Lewis, 482 F.2d 632 (D.C. Cir. 1973)   313
United States v. Lewis, 833 F.2d 1380 (9th Cir. 1987)   112
United States v. Loften, 518 F. Supp. 839 (S.D.N.Y. 1981)   360
United States v. Logan, 121 F.3d 1172 (8th Cir. 1997)   308
United States v. Lohnes, 554 F.3d 1166, 1169 2009 U.S. App. LEXIS 3599 (8th Cir. 2009)   293
United States v. Lopez, 437 F.3d 1059, 1063, 2006 U.S. App. LEXIS 4052 (2006)   669, 670
United States v. Lopez, 443 F.3d 1026, 1030, 2006 U.S. App. LEXIS 9560 (8th Cir. 2006)   58
United States v. Lopez, 547 F.3d 397, 2008 U.S. App. LEXIS 23303 (2dCir. 2008)   652
United States v. Lopez-Lopez, 282 F.3d 1, 2002 U.S. App. LEXIS 2896 (1st Cir. 2002)   326
United States v. Love, 2003 U.S. App. LEXIS 10756 (8th Cir. 2003)   284
United States v. Lucarelli, 2006 U.S. Dist. LEXIS 39664 (D. Conn. 2005)   174
United States v. Lucas, 499 F.3d 769, 2007 U.S. App. LEXIS 20076 (8th Cir. 2007)   205
United States v. Madoff, 2009 U.S. App. LEXIS 5985 (2d Cir. 2009)   150
United States v. Marchand, 564 F.2d 983 (2d Cir. 1977)   454
United States v. Martinez, 3 F.3d 1191 (8th Cir. 1993)   124, 591
United States v. Martinez, 406 F.3d 1160, 1163, 2005 U.S. App. LEXIS 8624 (9th Cir. 2002)   675
United States v. Matlock, 415 U.S. 164, 94 S. Ct. 988, 39 L. Ed. 2d 242 (1974)   652
United States v. Matousek, 131 Fed. Appx. 641, 2005 U.S. App. LEXIS 9063 (10th Cir. 2005)   533
United States v. Matthews, 20 F.3d 358 (2d Cir. 1994)   460
United States v. McClintock, 2006 U.S. Dist. LEXIS 201 (E.D. Pa. 2006)   408
United States v. McConnet, 2006 U.S. App. LEXIS 23230 (10th Cir. 2006)   315
United States v. McCray, 437 F.3d 639, 2006 U.S. App. LEXIS 3116 (7th Cir. 2006)   284
United States v. McCuiston, 2006 U.S. App. LEXIS 16292 (5th Cir. 2006)   174
United States v. McGinnis, 2006 U.S. App. LEXIS 24451 (5th Cir. 2006)   592
United States v. McGlothen, 2009 U.S. App. LEXIS 3600 (10th Cir. 2009)   167
United States v. McKeever, 271 F.2d 669 (2d Cir. 1959)   295
United States v. McKeithan, 2002 U.S. App. LEXIS 23408 (3d Cir. 2002)   300, 302
United States v. McKnight, 17 F.3d 1139 (8th Cir. 1994)   662
United States v. McMurray, 20 F.3d 831 (8th Cir. 1994)   308
United States v. McMurrey, 827 F. Supp. 424 (S.D. Tex. 1993), *aff'd*, 48 F.3d 149 (1993)   320
United States v. Medina et al., 430 F.3d 869, 2005 U.S. App. LEXIS 26772 (2005)   152
United States v. Meza-Rodrigues, 2006 U.S. Dist. LEXIS 58619 (W.D. Mich. 2006)   616
United States v. Michel, 446 F.3d 1122, 1128, 2006 U.S. App. LEXIS 11665 (10th Cir. 2006)   141
United States v. Michigan, 680 F. Supp. 928 (W.D. Mich. 1987)   419
United States v. Miller, 2004 U.S. Dist. LEXIS 23299 (E.D. Pa. 2006)   316
United States v. Miller, 382 F. Supp. 2d 350 (N.D. N.Y. 2005)   649
United States v. Miller, 994 F.2d 441 (8th Cir. 1993)   548
United States v. Miranda-Lopez, 532 F.3d 1034, 1036, 2008 U.S. App. LEXIS 15200 (9th Cir. 2008)   143
United States v. Mirelez, 59 Fed. Appx. 286, 2003 U.S. App. LEXIS 2162 (10th Cir. 2003)   514
United States v. Molson, 2006 U.S. Dist. LEXIS 2292 (D. Neb. 2006)   126
United States v. Montague, 421 F.3d 1099, 1103, 2005 U.S. App. LEXIS 14593 (10th Cir. 2005)   261
United States v. Monteiro, 407 F. Supp. 2d 351, 2006 U.S. Dist. LEXIS 227 (D. Mass. 2006)   421
United States v. Montgomery, 152 Fed. Appx. 822, 826, 2005 U.S. App. LEXIS 21893 (11th Cir. 2005)   549
United States v. Montgomery, 377 F. 3d 582, 2004 U. S. App. LEXIS 15438 (6th Cir. 2004)   650
United States v. Montgomery, 384 F. 3d 1050, 1056, 2004 U. S. App. LEXIS 19322 (2004)   341, 345

United States v. Moon, 513 F.3d 527, 2008 U.S. App. LEXIS 879 (6th Cir. 2008)   531

United States v. Moore, 452 F.3d 382; 2006 U.S. App. LEXIS 14152 (5th Cir. 2006)   641, 666

United States v. More, 791 F.2d 566 (7th Cir. 1986)   464

United States v. Moreno, 68 U.S. 400 (1863)   515

United States v. Mornan, 413 F.3d 372, 380, 2005 U.S. App. LEXIS 13043 (3d Cir. 2005)   416, 432

United States v. Morrow, 374 F. Supp. 2d 51, 2005 U.S. Dist. LEXIS 8327 (D.D.C. 2005)   439

United States v. Morrow, 374 F. Supp. 42, 46 (D.D.C. 2005)   629

United States v. Murphy, 172 Fed. Appx. 461, 462, 2006 U.S. App. LEXIS 7827 (3d Cir. 2006)   317

United States v. Murry, 395 F.3d 712, 717, 2005 U.S. App. LEXIS 8 (7th Cir. 2005)   532

United States v. Nelson, 38 Fed. Appx. 386, 392 (9th Cir. 2002)   398

United States v. Nixon, 418 U.S. 683, 94 S. Ct. 3090, 41 L. Ed. 2d 1039 (1974)   335

United States v. Norman, 415 F.3d 466, 2005 U.S. App. LEXIS 13149 (5th Cir. 2005)   407

United States v. Olivares-Rangel, 2006 U.S. App. LEXIS 20595 (10th Cir. 2006)   641

United States v. Olofson, 2009 U.S. App. LEXIS 9433 (7th Cir. 2009)   286

United States v. One Parcel of Real Estate, 804 F. Supp. 319 (S.D. Fla. 1992)   435

United States v. One Star, 2006 U.S. App. LEXIS 25417 (8th Cir. 2006)   326

United States v. Ortiz, 447 F.3d 28, 32, 2006 U.S. App. LEXIS 10961 (1st Cir. 2006)   25

United States v. Owens, 484 U.S. 554, 108 S. Ct. 838, 98 L. Ed. 2d 951 (1988)   454

United States v. Ozuna, 561 F.3d 728, 2009 U.S. App. LEXIS 7034 (7th Cir. 2009)   431

United States v. Ozuna, 561 F.3d 728, 2009 U.S. App. LEXIS 7034 (7th Cir. 2009)   432

United States v. Padilla-Pena, 129 F.3d 457 (8th Cir. 1997)   667

United States v. Palermo, 410 F.2d 468 (7th Cir. 1969)   304

United States v. Parker, 553 F.3d 1309, 1314, 2009 U.S. App. LEXIS 359 (10th Cir. 2009)   227

United States v. Patane, 542 U.S. 630, 639, 2004 U.S. LEXIS 4577 (2004)   672

United States v. Payne, 119 F.3d 637 (8th Cir. 1997)   201

United States v. Peneaux, 432 F.3d 882, 891, 2005 U.S. App. LEXIS 28877 (8th Cir. 2005)   491

United States v. Percel, 553 F.3d 903, 912, 2008 U.S. App. LEXIS 26428 (5th Cir. 2008)   227

United States v. Perkins, 548 U.S. App. 510, 515, 2008 U.S. App. LEXIS 23678 (7th Cir. 2008)   132

United States v. Phibbs, 999 F.2d 1053 (6th Cir. 1993)   254

United States v. Place, 462 U.S. 696, 103 S. Ct. 2637, 77 L. Ed. 2d 110 (1983)   663

United States v. Pomranky, 165 Fed. Appx. 259, 260, 2006 U.S. App. LEXIS 2490 (4th Cir. 2006)   414

United States v. Ponds, 454 F.3d 313, 319, 2006 U.S. App. LEXIS 17718 (D.C. Cir. 2006)   677

United States v. Porter, 986 F.2d 1014 (6th Cir. 1993), *cert. denied*, 510 U.S. 933, 114 S. Ct. 347, 126 L. Ed. 2d 312 (1993)   300

United States v. Powell, 973 F.2d 885 (10th Cir. 1992), *cert. denied*, 507 U.S. 1161, 113 S. Ct. 1598, 123 L. Ed. 2d 161 (1992)   455

United States v. Pree, 408 F. 3d 855, 869, 2005 U.S. App. LEXIS 9222 (7th Cir. 2005)   431

United States v. Prieto, 549 F.3d 513, 524, 2008 U.S. App. LEXIS 24323 (7th Cir. 2008)   174

United States v. Prime, 431 F.3d 1147, 1153, 2005 U.S. App. LEXIS 27276 (2005)   431

United States v. Prince-Oyibo, 320 F.3d 494, 501, 2003 U.S. App. LEXIS 3568 (4th Cir. 2003)   121, 434

United States v. Ramos-Osequera, 120 F.3d 1028 (9th Cir. 1997)   341

United States v. Ray, 768 F.2d 991 (8th Cir. 1985)   300

United States v. Reneau, 390 F.3d 746, 2004 U.S. App. LEXIS 24837 (2d Cir. 2004), *cert. denied*, 544 U.S. 1007, 2005 U.S. LEXIS 3660 (2005)   397, 401

United States v. Reynolds, 2006 U.S. App. LEXIS 18115 (4th Cir. 2006)   263

United States v. Reynolds, 345 U.S. 1, 1953 U.S. LEXIS 2329 (1953)   377

United States v. Riley, 452 F.3d 160, 165, 2006 U.S. App. LEXIS 15584 (2d Cir. 2006)   114

United States v. Rios-Ramirez, 2004 U.S. Dist. LEXIS 26573 (D.P.R. 2004)   651

United States v. Rivera, 51 Fed. Appx. 47, 2002 U.S. App. LEXIS 24036 (2d Cir. 2002)   327

United States v. Robertson, 19 F.3d 1318 (10th Cir. 1994)   594

United States v. Robinson, 2008 U.S. Dist. LEXIS 102689 (S.D. Fla. 2008)   196

United States v. Robinson, 414 U.S. 218 (1973)   650

United States v. Rodriguez, 2009 U.S. App. LEXIS 4506 (9th Cir. 2009)   492

United States v. Rogers, 556 F.3d 1130, 1141, 2009 U.S. App. LEXIS 5236 (10th Cir. 2009)   264

United States v. Roman, 368 F. Supp. 2d 119, 2005 U.S. Dist. LEXIS 7772 (2005)   435

United States v. Romano, 382 U.S. 136, 1965 U.S. LEXIS 207 (1965)   176

United States v. Rose, 590 F.2d 232 (7th Cir. 1978), *cert. denied*, 442 U.S. 929 (1979)   529

United States v. Ross, 456 U.S. 798, 1982 U.S. LEXIS 18 (1982)   655

United States v. Roy, 2006 U. S. Dist. LEXIS 9583 (2006)   430

United States v. Ruiz Solorio, 337 F.3d 580, 592, 2003 U.S. App. LEXIS 14585 (6th Cir. 2003)   287

United States v. Rutland, 372 F.3d 543, 2004 U.S. App. LEXIS 12432 (3d Cir. 2004)   413

United States v. Rutland, 372 F.3d 543, 545, 2004 U.S. App. LEXIS 12432 (3d Cir. 2004)   421

United States v. Saddler, 538 F.3d 879, 2008 U.S. App. 17211 (8th Cir. 2008)   146

United States v. Saelee, 162 F. Supp. 2d 1097 (D. Alaska 2001)   408, 433

United States v. Salehi, 2006 U.S. App. LEXIS 16285 (3d Cir. 2006)   549

United States v. Sanchez-Garcia, 402 F.3d 175; 2005 U.S. App. LEXIS 4568 (8th Cir. 2006)   617

United States v. Santos, 131 F.3d 16 (1st Cir. 1997)   406

United States v. Santos, 201 F.3d 953, 963, 963, 2000 U.S. App. LEXIS 649 (7th Cir. 2000)   399

United States v. Sawyer, 607 F.2d 1191 (7th Cir. 1979)   300

United States v. Scheffer, 523 U.S. 303, 1998 U.S. LEXIS 2303 (1998)   608

United States v. Schmidt, 360 F. Supp. 339 (M.D. Pa. 1973)   353

United States v. Schussel, 291 Fed. Appx. 336, 2008 U.S. App. LEXIS 18836 (1st Cir. 2008)   351

United States v. Scott, 2006 U.S. App. LEXIS 14182 (9th Cir. 2006)   153

United States v. Scott, 267 F.3d 729 (7th Cir. 2001)   198

United States v. Scrushy, 2005 U.S. Dist. LEXIS 42127 (N.D. Ala. 2006)   270

United States v. Sczubelek, 402 F.3d 175, 2005 U.S. App. LEXIS 4568 (3d Cir. 2006)   630

United States v. Siegelman, 2009 U.S. App. LEXIS 5369 (11th Cir. 2009)   268

United States v. Sills, 120 F.3d 917 (8th Cir. 1997)   201

United States v. Singleton, 260 F.3d 1295, 1297, 1298, 2001 U.S. App. LEXIS 17694 (11th Cir. 2001)   342

United States v. Smaldone, 484 F.2d 311 (10th Cir. 1973)   304

United States v. Smith, 153 Fed. Appx. 187, 2005 U.S. App. LEXIS 23798 (4th Cir. 2005)   432

United States v. Smith, 2005 U.S. Dist. LEXIS 3782 (E.D. Pa. 2005)   374

United States v. Smith, 531 F.3d 1261; 2008 U.S. App. LEXIS 14797 (10th Cir. 2008)   156

United States v. Snow, 82 F.3d 935 (10th Cir. 1996)   615

United States v. Sosa, U.S. Dist. LEXIS 2254 (2006)   415

United States v. Spivey, 841 F.2d 799 (7th Cir. 1988)   303

United States v. Sprague, 134 Fed. Appx. 607, 2005 U.S. LEXIS 10127 (4th Cir. 2005)   434

United States v. Stackhouse, 2009 U.S. App. LEXIS 2760 (8th Cir. 2009)   144

United States v. Steiger, 318 F.3d 1039, 1048–49 (11th Cir. 2003)   580

United States v. Stifel, 433 F.2d 431 (6th Cir. 1970)   625

United States v. Stone, 222 F.R.D. 334, 2004 U.S. Dist. LEXIS 12873 (E.D. Tenn. 2004)   417

United States v. Street, 531 F.3d 703, 2008 U.S. App. LEXIS 14729 (2008), *cert. denied,* 129 S. Ct. 432, 2008 U.S. LEXIS 7688 (2008)   251

United States v. Stukes, 2004 U.S. Dist. LEXIS 21486 (S.D.N.Y. 2004), *aff'd*, 2006 U.S. App. LEXIS (2d Cir. 2006)   547

United States v. Sullivan, 246 F. Supp. 2d 696, 698, 2003 U.S. Dist. LEXIS 3015 (E.D. Ky. 2003)   412

United States v. Sullivan, 246 F. Supp. 2d 696, 698, 2003 U.S. Dist. LEXIS 3015 (E.D. Ky. 2003)   414

United States v. Taylor, 62 M.J. 636, 2006 CCA LEXIS 9 (2006)   347

United States v. Terry, 729 F.2d 1063 (6th Cir. 1984)   297

United States v. Thompson, 2006 U.S. App. LEXIS 12734 (3d Cir. 2006)   662

United States v. Toepfer, 2008 U.S. App. LEXIS 14811 (11th Cir. 2008)   143

United States v. Torres-Reyes, 46 Fed. Appx. 925 (2002)   520

United States v. Trenk, 2009 U.S. Dist. LEXIS 15333 (D.N.J. 2009)   336

United States v. Troupe, 2008 U.S. App. LEXIS 24941 (4th Cir. 2008)   129

United States v. Turcotte, 405 F.3d 515, 525, 2005 U.S. App. LEXIS 6710 (7th Cir. 2005)   167

United States v. Two Crow, 178 Fed. Appx. 610, 2006 U.S. App. LEXIS 11165 (8th Cir. 2006)   565

United States v. United Technologies Corp., 979 F. Supp. 108 (D. Conn. 1997)   354

United States v. Valuck, 286 F.3d 221 (5th Cir. 2002)   309

United States v. Vankesteren, 2009 U.S. App. LEXIS (4th Cir. 2009)   659

United States v. Varelli, 407 F.2d 735 (7th Cir. 1969)   304

United States v. Vazquez, 2009 U.S. App. LEXIS 2473 (10th Cir. 2009)   85

United States v. Vega-Figueroa, 234 F.3d 744, 755, 2000 U.S. App. LEXIS 32127 (1st Cir. 2000)   400

United States v. Ventura-Melendez, 275 F.3d 9, 14, 2001 U.S. App. LEXIS 26901 (1st Cir. 2001)   513

United States v. Villarman-Oviedo, 325 F.3d 1, 2003 U.S. App. LEXIS 5694 (1st Cir. 2003)   301

United States v. Vo, 413 F.3d 1010. 1016, 2005 U.S. App. LEXIS 12695 (9th Cir. 2005)   343

United States v. W.B., 452 F.3d 1002, 2006 U.S. App. LEXIS 17378 (8th Cir. 2006)   494

United States v. Wade, 388 U.S. 218, 223 (1967)   433

United States v. Wainwright, 351 F.3d 816, 2003 U.S. App. LEXIS 24731 (8th Cir. 2003)   531

United States v. Walker, 2006 U.S. App. 11280 (10th Cir. 2006)   441, 443

United States v. Walker, 2006 U.S. App. LEXIS 11289 (10th Cir. 2006)   412

United States v. Walker, 47 Fed. Appx. 639, 2002 U.S. App. LEXIS 19817 (4th Cir. 2002)   314

United States v. Ward, 989 F.2d 1015 (9th Cir. 1992)   282

United States v. Washington, 100 Fed. App. 39, 2004 U.S. App. LEXIS 11453 (2d Cir. 2004)   197

United States v. Washington, 417 F.3d 780, 783–784 (7th Cir. 2005)   284

United States v. Watson, 118 F.3d 1315 (9th Cir. 1997)   642

United States v. Wattleton, 296 F.3d 1184, 2002 U.S. App. LEXIS 13686 (11th Cir. 2002)   158

United States v. Webster, 442 F.3d 1065, 1066, 2006 U.S. App. LEXIS 8061 (8th Cir. 2006)   170, 215

United States v. Wesseh, 531 F.3d 633, 636 (8th Cir. 2008)   144

United States v. Westerhausen, 283 F.2d 844 (7th Cir. 1960)   67

United States v. Wiggins, 146 Fed. Appx. 437; 2005 U.S. App. LEXIS 19120 (11th Cir. 2005)   97

United States v. Williams, 2008 U.S. Dist. LEXIS 36623 (M.D. Fla. 2008)   203

United States v. Williams, 445 F.3d 724, 728 2006 U.S. App. LEXIS 9639 (4th Cir. 2006)   252

United States v. Williams, 506 F.3d 151, 2007 U.S. App. LEXIS 24726 (2d Cir. 2007), *cert. denied*, 2008 U.S. LEXIS 2859 (2008)   618

United States v. Williams, 506 F3d 151, 159, 159, 007 U.S. App. LEXIS 24726 (2d Cir. 2007)   619

United States v. Williams, 737 F.2d 594 (7th Cir. 1984)   453

United States v. Wilson, 281 Fed. Appx. 96, 2008 LEXIS 12302 (3rd Cir. 2008)   491

United States v. Winder, 2009 U.S. App. LEXIS, 3647 (10th Cir. 2009)   101
United States v. Woods, 2009 US. App. LEXIS 93 (4th Cir. 2009)   174
United States v. Yazzie, 976 F.2d 1252, 1256 (9th Cir. 1992)   397
United States v. Young, 2003 U.S. App. LEXIS 7432 (8th Cir. 2003)   215
United States v. Yukins, 444 F.3d 713, 719, 2006 U.S. App. LEXIS 8160 (6th Cir. 2006)   670
United States v. Zavala, 2006 U.S. App. LEXIS 15848 (3d Cir. 2006)   72
United States v. Zidar, 2006 U.S. App. LEXIS 11858 (9th Cir. 2006)   87
United States, 2009 U.S. App. LEXIS 4165 (7th Cir. 2009)   131
Unites States v. Dedman, 527 F.3d 577, 586, 2008 U.S. App. LEXIS 11407 (6th Cir. 2008)   123
Unites States v. Loma, 2006 U. S. App. LEXIS 24599 (9th Cir. 2006)   319
Unites States v. Ramirez-Robles, 386 F.3d 1234, 1248, 2004 U.S. App. LEXIS 21847 (9th Cir. 2004)   121
Upjohn Co. v. United States, 449 U.S. 383, 101 S. Ct. 677, 66 L. Ed. 2d 584 (1981)   352
USX Corp. v. Barnhart, 395 F.3d 161, 171, 2004 U.S. App. LEXIS 26868 (3d Cir. 2004)   148
Utah Gospel Mission v. Salt Lake City, 316 F. Supp. 2d 1201, 2004 U.S. Dist. LEXIS 12966 (2004)   114

Valle v. Texas, 109 S.W.3d 500, 2003 Tex. Crim. App. LEXIS 143 (2003)   475
Van Hook v. Anderson, 444 F.3d 830, 834, 2006 U.S. App. LEXIS 9628 (6th Cir. 2006)   673
Vanlandingham v. McGhee, 2008 U.S. Dist. LEXIS 67934 (E.D. Mich. 2008)   301
Varkonyi v. State, 276 S.W.3d 27, 2008 Tex. App. LEXIS 3353 (Tex. 2008)   522
Vasquez v. State, 2006 Tex. App. LEXIS 500 (2006)   280
Vaughn v. Shelby-Williams of Tenn., Inc., 813 S.W.2d 132 (Tenn. 1991)   112
Vazquez v. Rossnagle, 163 F. Supp. 2d 494, 2001 U.S. Dist. LEXIS 3974 (3d Cir. 2001)   436
Victor v. Nebraska, 511 U.S. 1, 114 S. Ct. 1239, 127 L. Ed. 2d 583 (1994)   55
Villa v. State, 2008 Tex. App. LEXIS 1025 (Tex. 2008)   211
Village Discount v. Department of Employment Security, 384 Ill. App.3d 522, 2008 Ill. App. LEXIS 757 (Ill. 2008)   523
Vinson v. State, 2006 Tex. App. LEXIS 1634 (2006)   559
Virginia v. Moore, _____ U.S. _____, _____, 2008 U.S. LEXIS 3674 (2008)   650

W.T. Rawleigh Co. v. Overstreet, 71 Ga. App. 873, 32 S.E.2d 574 (1944)   517
Waldorf v. Shuta, 916 F. Supp. 423 (D.N.J. 1996)   416
Walentukonis v. Florida, 2006 Fla. App. LEXIS 9766 (2006)   115, 133
Walker v. State, 2005 Ark. App. LEXIS 471 (2005)   345
Walker v. State, 896 So. 2d 712, 714, 2005 Fla. LEXIS 361 (Fla. 2005)   150
Walker v. State, 913 So. 2d 198, 232, 2005 Miss. LEXIS 216 (Miss. 2005)   171
Wallace v. Arkansas, 2003 Ark. App. LEXIS 15 (2003)   293
Ward v. Dretke, 420 F.3d 479, 494, 2005 U.S. App. LEXIS 16596 (5th Cir. 2005)   422
Warden v. Hayden, 387 U.S. 294 (1967)   649
Warner v. State, 2005 Ark. App. LEXIS 875 (2005)   282
Warner v. State, 2005 Ark. App. LEXIS 875 (Ark. 2005)   258
Warren v. Conway, 2008 U.S. Dist. LEXIS 106309 (E.D. N.Y. 2008)   305
Warren v. State, 164 Md. App. 153, 168, 882 A.2d 934, 943, 2005 Md. App. LEXIS 189 (2004)   402
Washington v. Bain, 2002 Wash. App. LEXIS 1863 (2002)   399
Washington v. Baker, 2002 Wash. App. LEXIS 2998 (2002)   552
Washington v. Cheatam, 112 Wash. App. 778, 785, 51 P.3d 138, 143, 2002 Wash. App. LEXIS 1832 (2002)   554
Washington v. Delgado, 2003 Wash. App. LEXIS 87 (2003)   545
Washington v. Dudley, 2003 Wash. App. LEXIS 1551 (2003)   530
Washington v. Fairbanks, 2003 Wash. App. LEXIS 2050 (2003)   539
Washington v. Fecuenco, 548 U.S. 212, 2006 U.S. LEXIS 5164 (2006)   60

Washington v. Fikre, 2003 Wash. App. LEXIS 191 (2003) 463

Washington v. Grzogorek, 2002 Wash. App. LEXIS 598 (2002) 462

Washington v. Hunotte, 2001 Wash. App. LEXIS 1941 (2001) 241

Washington v. Knott, 2002 Wash. App. LEXIS 392 (2002) 473

Washington v. Loucks, 98 Wash. 2d 563, 656 P.2d 480, 1983 Wash. LEXIS 1333 (1983) 241

Washington v. Olmedo, 112 Wash. App. 525, 531, 49 P.3d 960, 963, 2002 Wash. App. LEXIS 1705 (2002) 395

Wasserman v. Parciasepe, 377 N.J. Super. 191, 198, 871 A.2d 781, 784, 2004 N.J. Super. LEXIS 4 (N.J. 2004) 147

Webb v. State, 277 Ga. App. 355, 359, 626 S.E.2d 545, 549, 2006 Ga. App. LEXIS 85 (2006) 600

Webb v. State, 284 Ga. 122, 127, 2008 Ga. LEXIS 564 (Ga. 2008) 261

Webster v. Univ. of Tennessee, 2008 Tenn. App. LEXIS 413 (Tenn. 2008) 27

Weeks v. United States, 232 U.S. 383 (1914) 30

Weeks v. United States, 232 U.S. 383, 1914 U.S. LEXIS 1368 (1914) 641

Weems v. State, 485 S.E.2d 767 (Ga. 1997) 115

Wells v. Liddy, 37 Fed. Appx. 53, 2002 U.S. App. LEXIS 3356 (4th Cir. 2002) 244

Wells v. State, 2009 Ga. App. LEXIS 384 (Ga. 2009) 147

Wells v. State, 913 So. 2d 1053, 1057, 2005 Miss. App. LEXIS 434 (2005) 420

West Virginia v. Bohon, 211 W. Va. 277, 279, 565 S.E.2d 399, 401, 2002 W. Va. LEXIS 51 (2002) 345

Wheeler v. Commissioner of Social Services, 662 N.Y.S.2d 550 (1997) 367

White et al. v. The Pines Community Improvement Assn., 173 Md. App. 13, 2007 Md. App. LEXIS 23 (Md. 2007) 146

Wiley v. Commonwealth, 801 A.2d 644, 2002 Pa. Commw. LEXIS 510 (2002) 116

Wilkerson v. State, 2005 Ark. App. LEXIS 12 (Ark. 2005) 506

Williams v. McGinnis, 2006 U.S. Dist. LEXIS 29400 (E.D. N.Y. 2006) 155

Williams v. Price, 343 F.3d 223, 2003 U.S. App. LEXIS 18662 (3d Cir. 2003) 269

Williams v. Senkowski, 2001 U.S. Dist. LEXIS 10843 (S.D.N.Y. 2001) 292

Williams v. State, 2003 Alaska App. LEXIS 136 (2003) 470

Williams v. State, 2006 Tex. App. LEXIS 1687 (2006) 392

Williams v. State, 2008 Tex. App. LEXIS 2241 (Tex. 2008) 519

Williams v. State, 2009 Tex. App. LEXIS 1045 (Tex. 2009) 99

Williams v. State, 273 S.W.3d 200, 2008 Tex. Crim. App. LEXIS 692 (Tex. 2008) 219

Williams v. State, 733 N.E.2d 919, 922 (2000) 289

Wilson v. Ake, 354 F. Supp. 2d 1298; 2005 U.S. Dist. LEXIS 755 (2005) 345

Wilson v. Arkansas, 514 U.S. 927, 115 S. Ct. 1914, 131 L. Ed. 2d 976 (1995) 648

Wilson v. State, 2009 Tex. App. LEXIS 2954 (Tex. 2009) 298

Wilson v. State, 2009 Texas App. LEXIS 2954 (Tex. 2009) 569

Wilson v. State, 271 Ga. App. 359, 362, 609 S.E.2d 703, 706, 2005 Ga. App. LEXIS 41 (2005) 558, 590

Wilson v. State, 279 Ga. App. 459, 631 S.E.2d 391, 2006 Ga. App. LEXIS 483 (2006) 572

Wilson v. State, 950 A.2d 634, 2008 Del. LEXIS 263 (Del. 2008) 310

Wilson v. Wilkinson, 2009 U.S. Dist. LEXIS 31895 (S.D. Ohio 2009) 594

Wimberly v. State, 2005 Ala. Crim. App. LEXIS 103 (2005) 209

Wingfield v. State, 2005 Ark. 574 (2006) 530

Winkle v. State, 374 Ark. 128, 134, 2008 Ark. LEXIS 433 (Ark. 2008) 322

Winston v. Lee, 470 U.S. 753, 105 S. Ct. 1611, 84 L. Ed. 2d 662 (1985) 595

Witherspoon v. United States, 2008 U.S. Dist. LEXIS 94601 (W.D.N.C. 2008) 253

Wittenberg v. United States, 304 F. Supp. 744 (D. Minn. 1969) 321

Wong Sun v. United States, 371 U.S. 471 (1963) 79, 642, 646, 654

Wong-Wing v. State, 156 Md. App. 597, 847 A.2d 1206, 2004 Md. App. LEXIS 65 (2004) 345

Woodall v. Kentucky, 63 S.W.3d 104, 131, 2001 Ky. LEXIS 142 (2002) 327

Woods v. Lecureux, 110 F.3d 1215 (6th Cir. 1997)   292
Wyoming v. Houghton, 526 U.S. 295 (1999)   654, 655

Yancy v. State, 2009 Ala. Crim. LEXIS 38 (Ala. 2009)   24
Young v. Commonwealth, 47 Va. App. 616; 625 S.E.2d 691; 2006 Va. App. LEXIS 42 (2006)   236
Young v. Graham, 2005 U.S. Dist. LEXIS 20882 (2005)   114
Youngblood v. West Virginia, 547 U.S. 867, 2006 U.S. LEXIS 4884 (2006)   584
Younger v. State, 293 Ga. App. 20, 2008 Ga. App. LEXIS 898 (Ga. 2009)   206

Ziegler v. Crorfont, 516 P.2d 954 (Kan. 1973)   416

Index

Abbreviations, judicial notice of, 121–123
Absence, unexplained, 171–173
Abuse of discretion, 254
Accident reconstruction, 425–427
Accountant-client communication,
    336, 337
Accused
    burden of proof on, 60–63
    conduct of, 399–401, 450, 496
ACE-V (analysis, comparison, evaluation,
    and verification) methodology in
    fingerprint identification, 439
Adjudicative facts, judicial notice of,
    111–113, 130
Admissibility. *See also* Circumstantial
    evidence; Direct evidence; Hearsay;
    Material evidence; Opinion and expert
    testimony; Relevant evidence
    of confessions, 15. *See also Miranda*
        warnings
    of DNA evidence, 628
    of duplicate documents, 525
    of eyewitness testimony, 15
    of polygraph (lie detector) test, 143,
        183–185, 604–612
    proof via evidence and, 79–80
    of real evidence, 541–548
        chain of custody for, 542–545
        identification of, 547–548
        necessity for, 545–546
        relationship to crime of, 546–547
    of recorded recollections, 298
    of scientific evidence, 229–231
    trial judge decision on, 85
    of wiretap evidence, 15, 19, 237
Adultery, 347
Affirmations by witnesses, 281–283
Affirmative defenses, burden of proof in,
    61, 63–64
Age estimates, 397–398

Airplane crashes, expert testimony on,
    427–428
Alabama, Supreme Court of, 264
Alabama Court of Criminal Appeals, 242
Alcohol, driving under influence of. *See* DUI
    (driving under influence);
    Intoxication
Alcoholics Anonymous, 370
Alibi defense, 62–64, 217, 220
American Jurisprudence, 625
American Polygraph Association, 607
Ancient documents, 505, 508–509, 512
Anglican legal system, 12–14
Animations, computer-generated (CGA),
    442, 574
Annulments, 317
Appeals, 36–37, 84, 317. *See also* Courts of
    Appeals
Appearance, nonexpert opinion on, 398–399
Apple Computer Co., 383
Arizona Rules of Evidence, 468
Arkansas, Supreme Court of, 102, 562–563
Armed Forces, Court of Appeals for, 608
Arraignment, 671, 681–682
Arrest, searches after, 649–652
Atomic-absorption analysis, 626
Attorneys. *See* Defense attorneys; Privileges;
    Prosecution; Right-to-counsel provi-
    sions; Sixth Amendment to U.S.
    Constitution
Authentication. *See* Documentary evidence;
    Real evidence
Automobiles. *See also* Intoxication
    accident reports filed on, 470
    DUI and, 120
    expert testimony on accidents with,
        425–427
    real evidence of accidents with, 559–560
    searches of, 654–656
Autopsy results, 594

Ballistics analysis, 120, 443–444, 618–620

Bankruptcies, judicial notice and, 116

Best evidence rule, 522–525, 522–525

Beyond a reasonable doubt, proof, 46, 47, 49, 52–56

Bias, religious, 264

Bias of witnesses, 310–312

Bigamy, 347

Bill of Rights. *See* U.S. Constitution; individual amendments to the U.S. Constitution

"Black box" recorders, 427

Black's Law Dictionary, 24, 47, 193, 194, 245, 393

Bloggers, communication privilege and, 381

Blood comparison tests, 603–604

Blood spatter analysis, 556–557

Bloodstains, as real evidence of, 554–557

Blood tests for intoxication, 594–596

Breath tests for intoxication, 596–599

Burden of evidence, 48

Burden of going forward, 47–48, 67, 69

Burden of persuasion, 48–49

Burden of proof, 45–74

    on accused, 60–63

    alibi defense and, 63, 64–66

    all elements of crime in, 58–60

    beyond a reasonable doubt, 52–56

    clear and convincing evidence and, 50–52

    distinctions in, 46–49

    general affirmative defenses and, 63–64

    insanity defense and, 66–69

    Insanity Defense Reform Act of 1984 and, 158

    jury instructions on, 154–156

    preponderance of the evidence and, 49–50

    on prosecution, 56–58

    self-defense and, 69–71

    sufficiency of evidence and, 72–73

    of witness competency, 254

Burger, Chief Justice Warren, 51, 248, 335

Business and public records, as evidence, 466–473

California, Supreme Court of, 61, 162, 614

California Evidence Code, 363

California Rules of Evidence, 383

Caller ID, as evidence, 244

Case-in-chief, 81–82, 91, 222, 532, 534

Castro, Fidel, 116

Cellmark Diagnostics, 627

Cell phone messages, 579–580

Central Intelligence Agency (CIA), 378–380, 386

Certificate of Non-Existence of Record (CNER), 512

Chain of custody

    demonstrating, 560

    in drug cases, 557–559

    in examination and test result evidence, 590

    of photographs, 565–566

    of real evidence, 542–545

    strained, 552

Challenging evidence, procedure for, 83–85

Character evidence, 221–224

Child abuse, 347

Child pornography, 397, 442

Children as witnesses, 254–258, 292–293

Chinese legal system, 9

Circumstantial evidence

    for document authentication, 506, 515, 520

    as inference, 25

    weight in trials of, 100–103

Civil cases, 31–33, 138

Civil Rights Act, 378

Clear and convincing evidence, 50–52

Clergy, communication with, 368–372

Closing statements, 92

Code Napoleon, 12

CODIS (Combined DNA Index System), Federal Bureau of Investigation (FBI), 629–630

Coercion, as affirmative defense, 61

Collateral matters, as documentary evidence, 527

Collateral test of witness competency, 249

Colorado, Supreme Court of, 463

Comments on evidence, by trial judges, 87

Common law

    attorney-client communication privilege in, 352

    best evidence rule of, 528

    on clergy communication, 368

    development of, 13–14

    on documentary evidence, 508

    on flight of defendants, 213

    hearsay rule in, 458

    on illegally obtained evidence, 640

    knock and announce requirement of, 648–649

    marriage by, 343–345

    privileged communication in, 335, 336

    on summaries, 530

    on witness competency, 262–263

Common scheme or plan exception, 226

Communications. *See* Privileges

Competency, 233–272
  admissibility of evidence and, 80
  definition of, 236
  of evidence, 28, 236–248
    documentary, 238, 504
    of examination and test results, 590
    incompetent, 236–238
    negative, 245–247
    for some purposes, 247–248
    of telephone conversations,
      243–245
    test and experimental, 238–240
    of trained dogs, 240–242
  of judges as witnesses, 265–267
  of jurors as witnesses, 267–271
  of witnesses, 86–87, 248–251
    children as, 254–258
    convicted of crimes, 262–263
    general rule of, 248–251
    husband or wife of accused
      as, 258–262
    mental capacity in, 251–254
    nonexpert opinion of, 397–398
    religious beliefs for, 264–265
Comprehensive Crime Control
      Act of 1984, 157
Computer-generated animations (CGA),
      442, 574
Computer-generated documents, 472,
      509–510, 529
Concealment, inferences from, 168–171
Conclusive presumptions, 149
Conduct of accused, 399–401, 450, 496
Confederate States of America, 376
Confessions, 668–676
  admissibility of, 15
  delay in arraignment rule for, 671
  drug-induced, 613
  free and voluntary rule for, 668–671
  as hearsay rule exclusions, 487–490
  involuntary, 236
  Miranda rule for, 671–676
  of witnesses, 324–326
Confidentiality, duty of, 358
Confrontation, right of, 90, 286, 301–302.
      See also Right-to-counsel provisions;
      Sixth Amendment to U.S. Constitution
Confusion, exclusion of evidence because of,
      201–202
Connecticut, Supreme Court of, 165
Conspiracy, 349
Contempt of court, 262, 386
Contracts, freedom of, 12

Corpus Juris Civilis, in Roman legal
      system, 10
Corpus Juris Secundum, 193
Corroborative evidence, 27
Cosmopolitanization and Expansion, Period
      of, 12
Counsel, right to. *See* Right-to-counsel
      provisions; Sixth Amendment to U.S.
      Constitution
Counselor-client communication, 337
Court jurisdiction, 129–130
Courts of Appeals
  Alabama, 242
  Armed Forces, 608
  District of Columbia, 239, 377, 386,
      488–489, 609
  Eighth Circuit, 204, 216, 284, 319, 349,
      415, 430, 565
  Eleventh Circuit, 158, 409
  Fifth Circuit, 378, 532, 666
  First Circuit, 286
  Fourth Circuit, 72, 434, 609, 676
  Georgia, 260
  Hawai'i Intermediate, 509, 622
  Ninth Circuit, 194, 201, 361, 397, 408,
      523, 611, 672
  Oklahoma, 574
  Second Circuit, 401
  Seventh Circuit, 300, 303, 414, 514, 610
  Sixth Circuit, 421
  Tenth Circuit, 412, 419, 578
  Texas, 475
  Third Circuit, 369
Credibility, character evidence for, 222, 223
Crime
  advice in furtherance of, 356–357
  circumstances preceding, 211–213
  incriminating circumstances subsequent to,
      213–217
  real evidence of, 540–560
    bloodstains as, 554–557
    instruments as, 552–553
    narcotics as, 557–559
    relationship to, 546–547
    weapons as, 550–551
  of spouses against one another,
      348, 350
  witnesses convicted of, 262–263, 316–321
Crime laboratories, 443–444
Criminal evidence, 21–39
  in appeals, 36–37
  civil case evidence rules *versus,* 31–33
  definitions of, 24–28
  judicial notice of, 132–133

in parole hearings, 37–38
pretrial flow of, 33–35
in probation hearings, 37
reasons for excluding, 29–31
trial use of, 35–36
Cross-examination, 301–306
  as constitutional right, 301–302
  DNA identification and, 437
  doctrine of past recollection and, 301
  dying declarations and, 481, 483, 484
  of expert witnesses, 422–425
  in Federal Rules of Evidence, 300
  hearsay evidence and, 450, 460, 477–478
  of lay opinion witnesses, 395, 400
  overzealous, 86
  prosecution limitations on, 303–304
  re-, 305–306
  in Sixth Amendment to U.S. Constitution,
    493–494
  witness name and address in, 304
Cumulative evidence, 26, 204–205

Death
  attorney-client communication privilege
    after, 359
  declarations at, 32, 480–484
  presumption of, 171–173
Deductions. *See* Inferences
Defendants. *See also* Privileges
  case-in-chief of, 81–82
  case-in-rejoinder of, 82–83
  character evidence of, 221–224
  handwriting samples of, 432
  post-*Miranda* comments of, 216–217
  post-*Miranda* silence of, 325–326
  privacy expectation of, 554
  rebuttable presumption of
    innocence of, 152
  Sixth Amendment rights of, 90
  spouses as, 347–348
  testifying in own defense, 317
Defense attorneys, 94–97, 628
Defenses. *See also* Insanity Defense Reform
    Act of 1984
  alibi, 64–66
  burden of proof in, 61
  coercion as, 61
  against evidence, 217–220
  general affirmative, 63–64
  insanity, 66–69
  self-, 69–70
  in Sixth Amendment to U.S. Constitution,
    608–609

Delaware, Supreme Court of, 516
Delay in arraignment rule for
  confessions, 671
Delinquency, 646. *See also* Juvenile
  adjudication
Demonstrations and experiments, real
  evidence as, 582
Demonstrative real evidence, 539
Diagrams, as real evidence, 580–581
Dickey John machine
  (moisture content test), 582
Diodorus (ancient Greek historian), 8
Direct evidence, 24, 99–100, 506
Direct examination, 288–289
  as cross-examination basis, 301–302
  of experts, 419–422
  of lay opinion witnesses, 395
  overzealous, 86
Discovery, principles of, 583–584
Discretion, abuse of, 254
Discrimination, 378
Distance, nonexpert opinion on, 401–402
District of Columbia Court of Appeals
  on governmental privilege, 377–378
  on news media-informant privilege, 386
  on polygraph test, 609
  on scientific evidence, 239
  on statements against interest, 488–489
DNA Analysis Backlog Elimination Act of
  2000, 630
DNA (deoxyribonucleic acid) evidence
  bloodstains for, 555–556
  cases on, 627–630
  expert testimony on, 437–439
  judicial notice of, 109, 120
  polymerase chain reaction (PCR) test of,
    120, 438, 628
  Restriction Fragment Length
    Polymorphism (RFLP) test for, 438
  U.S. Supreme Court on, 556, 629
Doctor-patient privilege, 32
Documentary evidence, 25, 238, 501–536
  admissibility of, 503–504
  authentication of
    of ancient documents, 508–509
    of computer-generated documents,
      509–510
    direct or circumstantial
      evidence for, 506
    disputing, 507
    in Federal Rules of Evidence, 504–505
    methods of, 515–522
    nonexpert witnesses for, 507

authorship determination of, 431–433
best evidence rule for, 522–525
examples of, 517–522
learned treatises as, 534–535
as secondary evidence, 525–530
self-authentication of, 507, 510–515,
510–515, 519–520, 522
summaries as, 530–534
Dogs, trained, evidence of, 240–242
Doppler effect, in speed testing, 620
Douglas, Justice William O., 382
Drug use. *See also* Intoxication
expert testimony on, 440–442
nonexpert opinion on, 402–405
real evidence of, 557–559
Due process clause. *See also* Fifth
Amendment to U.S. Constitution;
Fourteenth Amendment to U.S.
Constitution
"beyond a reasonable doubt" requirement
and, 55
blood tests and, 595
evidence excluded by violations of, 79,
205–206, 676–679
information sharing requirements of,
93, 94
Insanity Defense Reform Act of
1984 and, 158
intoxication defense and, 219–220
mandatory presumptions and, 151
Sandstrom v. Montana (1979) and, 149
selective incorporation doctrine and, 641
self-defense and, 70
U.S. Supreme Court on, 17
witness separation and, 286
wrongfully obtained evidence and, 236
DUI (driving under influence), 120. *See also*
Automobiles; Intoxication
Duplicate documents, admissibility of, 525
Dying declarations, 32, 480–484

Eavesdropping, 237, 665–668
Egyptian legal system, 8
Eighth Circuit Court of Appeals
on admissibility of prior crime
convictions, 319
on conspiracy, 349
on cumulative evidence, 204
on expert testimony, 415, 430
on inferences from flights, 216
on judicial control of witnesses, 284
on photograph use, 565
Electronic Communications Privacy Act, 580

Eleventh Circuit Court of Appeals
Insanity Defense Reform Act
of 1984 and, 158
on nonexpert handwriting comparison,
408–409
on objection timeliness, 85
El-Masri, Khaled, 379–380
Endangered Species Act, 414
English language-limited witnesses,
292–293
"English Rule" on illegally obtained evidence, 640
Entrapment defense, 61, 217, 220
Errors
harmless standard of, 54, 84, 96
reversible, 84, 154, 302, 549, 569, 584
in rulings, 83
Event data recorders, 427
Examination and test results, 587–634
of ballistics experiments, 618–620
of blood comparisons, 603–604
of DNA analysis, 627–630
of fingerprint comparisons, 615–617
of Fourier Transform Infrared
Spectrophotometer, 632
of intoxication, 594–602
blood tests for, 594–596
breath tests for, 596–599
horizontal gaze nystagmus tests for,
600–601
implied consent statutes for, 601–602
urine tests for, 599
of neutron activation analysis, 625–626
overview of, 589–593
of person, 593–594
of Plasma Emission Spectroscopy, 630
polygraph (lie detector), 604–612
admissible if stipulated, 609–610
admissible under special
circumstances, 610
basis of, 604–605
New Mexico Supreme Court on,
605–607
U.S. Supreme Court on, 608–609
of speed detection, 620–624
from "truth serum," 612–614
Examination of witnesses. *See* Witnesses,
examination of
Excluding evidence. *See also* Hearsay
in pretrial motions, 78
reasons for, 28–30, 199–206
Exclusionary rule. *See* Fourth Amendment to
U.S. Constitution; Search and
seizure, unlawful

Exculpatory impeachment evidence, 92
Exigent or emergency circumstances, in
    searches, 645
Experimental evidence, 229–231,
    238–240, 582
Expert testimony. *See* Opinion and
    expert testimony
Extrinsic evidence, 321
Eyewitnesses, 15, 208, 414

Factfinding, 87, 137, 395
Facts
    judicial notice of, 111–113, 130, 131
    mistake of, 220
    presumption of, 147–148
    triers of, 143
Fairness, excluding evidence for,
    205–206, 679
Family. *See also* Privileges
    in Code Napoleon, 12
    conclusive presumptions to preserve,
        149–150
    history and records of, 473–476
Federal Bureau of Investigation (FBI)
    ballistics experts of, 626
    CODIS (Combined DNA Index System)
        of, 629–630
    fingerprint analysis of, 440
    Inductively coupled plasma-optical
        emission spectroscopy (ICP) and, 626
Federal Communications Act of 1934, 665
Federal laws, judicial notice of, 124–125
Federal Register, judicial notice of, 128
Federal Rules of Criminal Procedure, 33, 430, 580
Federal Rules of Evidence
    on admissibility of other evidence of
        contents, 527
    on admissibility of relevant evidence,
        196–198
    on admissibility questions, 78
    on authentication of articles connected to
        crimes, 550
    on authentication of evidence, 563
    on character and conduct of witnesses,
        312, 315
    on conviction of crime of witnesses,
        316–317, 328–320
    on court appointed experts, 417–418
    on cross-examination of experts, 422
    on documentary evidence authentication,
        504–505, 508
    on erroneous rulings, 83
    on exclusion of relevant evidence, 199

    on exclusion of witnesses, 285
    on expert opinion testimony, 411, 414
    on expert testimony, 419–420, 430,
        591–592
    on governmental privilege, 376
    on hearsay rule, 452, 455, 460, 461,
        466–467, 473–474, 477, 480, 484,
        485, 490
    on impeachment of witnesses, 306, 308
    on incompetent evidence, 237–238
    on interrogating witnesses, 283, 289, 300
    on judges as witnesses, 265–267
    on judicial notice of adjudicative facts,
        111, 130
    on jurors as witnesses, 267
    on lay opinion testimony, 394, 396–397
    on physician-patient privilege, 363
    on presumptions, 138
    on prior inconsistent statements of
        witnesses, 321
    on privileged communication, 333,
        336–337
    on recorded recollections, 297–298
    on relevant evidence, 192
    on religious beliefs, 264
    on requirement for original
        documents, 522
    on residual hearsay exception, 490,
        493–494
    on scientific evidence, 229–230, 238–240
    state interpretations of, 15–16
    on statements against interest, 484–485
    on summaries, 530, 581
    uniformity results of, 17
    on witness competency, 248
    on witness oaths, 281, 282
    on witness qualities, 278
    on writing to refresh memory, 293–294,
        297–298
Federal Tort Claims Act, 377
Federal Wiretap Act, 580, 666
Fifth Amendment to U.S. Constitution. *See
    also* Due process clause; Fourteenth
    Amendment to U.S. Constitution;
    Self-incrimination protection
    blood tests and, 596, 602
    compensation of expert witnesses and, 418
    evidence excluded by violations of,
        676–679
    examination of person and, 593–594
    excluding evidence based on, 79
    fingerprinting and, 615–617
    gunpowder residue test and, 436

on impeachment of witnesses, 308
Insanity Defense Reform Act of
    1984 and, 158
real evidence and, 540
self-incrimination protection in, 217,
    432, 488
Sullivan v. Louisiana (1993) on, 54
U.S. Supreme Court on, 17
on witness separation, 286
Fifth Circuit Court of Appeals, 378, 532, 666
Fingerprint comparisons, 439–440, 615–617
First Amendment to U.S. Constitution,
    281–282, 381–382, 386
First Circuit Court of Appeals, 286
Flight, inferences from, 168–171, 214–216
Florida, Supreme Court of, 496
Footprints, 616
Foreign countries' laws, judicial notice of,
    126–127
Foreign Intelligence Surveillance Act of
    1978, 19
Forum, law of, 124
Foster, Vincent W., Jr., 359
Fourier Transform Infrared
    Spectrophotometer, 632
Fourteenth Amendment to U.S. Constitution,
    94. *See also* Due process clause; Fifth
    Amendment to U.S. Constitution
blood tests and, 595
defense and, 70
excluding evidence based on, 79
Insanity Defense Reform Act of
    1984 and, 158
intoxication defense and, 219–220
mandatory presumptions and, 151
Sandstrom v. Montana (1979) and, 149
selective incorporation doctrine and, 641
U.S. Supreme Court on, 17
on witness separation, 286
Fourth Amendment to U.S. Constitution. *See
    also* Search and seizure, unlawful
blood tests and, 596
DNA samples and, 630
evidence excluded because of, 78–79
fingerprinting and, 615–617
real evidence and, 553–554, 566
wrongfully obtained evidence and, 236
Fourth Circuit Court of Appeals
on *Jackson v. Virginia* (1979), 72
on *Miranda* warnings, 676
on polygraph test, 434, 609
Free and voluntary rule for confessions,
    668–671

Freedom of Information Act, 377
Fruits of crime, possession of, 160–163

Gender, same, privileged communication
    and, 343
General affirmative defenses, 63–64
General Motors Company, 624
Geographical facts, judicial notice, 117–119
Georgia, Supreme Court of, 435, 540, 567
Georgia Bureau of Investigation, 440
Georgia Court of Appeals, 260
Good faith concept, 173, 174, 643–645
GPS tracking devices, 667
Grand jury, 34, 174
Graphic representations, judicial
    notice of, 122
Greek legal system, 9
Guilt or innocence, determining. *See* Rules of
    evidence, development of
Gunpowder residue tests, 436, 619–620

Habitual offender statutes, 91
Hammurabi (Mesopotamian king), 8
Handicapped witnesses, 292–293
Handwriting comparison, 408–409, 431–433.
    See also Documentary evidence
Harmless error standard, 54, 84, 96
Hawai'i, Intermediate Court of Appeals of,
    509, 620
Hawai'i Criminal Justice Data Center, 439
Hearsay, 28, 447–498. *See also* Recollections
definitions of, 452–458
development of rule on, 458–459
exceptions to, 459–460
    business and public records as, 466–473
    declarations against interest as, 484–490
    dying declarations as, 480–484
    family history and records as, 473–476
    former testimony as, 477–480
    residual, 490–494
    spontaneous or excited utterances as,
        460–466
    nontestimonial utterances as, 494–497
reasons for excluding, 450–451
summaries as, 533
Hebrew legal system, 9
Henry II of England, 13
HGN (horizontal gaze nystagmus test) for
    intoxication, 120, 600–601
Historical facts, judicial notice, 116–117
Hostile witnesses, 291–292
Husband-wife communication. *See* Privileges
Hypnosis, 296
Hypotheses, excluding, 102–103

Identity
    in attorney-client communication,
        355–356
    evidence of, 207–210
    of informants, 375
    nonexpert opinion on, 407–408
Illegally obtained evidence, 236–237. *See*
        also Confessions; Due process clause;
        Right-to-counsel provisions; Search and
        seizure, unlawful; Self-incrimination
        protection; Wiretap evidence
Illinois, Supreme Court of, 179, 647
Impeachment
    of defendants, 223
    exculpatory evidence for, 92
    of expert witnesses. *See* Opinion and
        expert testimony
    polygraph tests for, 610, 611
    religious beliefs and, 264
    of witnesses
        bias or prejudice in, 310–312
        on character and conduct, 312–316
        confession for, 324–326
        on crime conviction, 316–321
        on inconsistent statements,
            321–323
        own, 308–309
        on recollection defects, 323–324
Implied consent statutes for intoxication
        tests, 601–602
Impoundment, lawful, 661–662
Incompetent evidence, 236–238
Independent source rule, 646
Indictments, 45
Inductively coupled plasma-optical emission
        spectroscopy (ICP), 626
Inferences, 107. *See also* Presumptions;
        Stipulations
    constitutionality tests for, 175–180
    definition of, 140–143
    from flight or concealment, 168–171,
        213–216
    from intent, 163–167
    overview of, 137–138
    permissive, 150
    from possession of fruits of crime,
        160–163
    reasons for, 144–146
Informants
    confidential, 372–375
    independent source rule and, 646
    news media and, 337, 380–386

Innocence, presumption of, 147, 152–156.
        See also Rules of evidence,
        development of
Insanity defense
    burden of proof in, 50, 66–69
    expert testimony on, 428–430
    M'Naghten rule for, 218
    nonexpert opinion of, 405–407
    as waiver of physician-patient privilege,
        367–368
    witness competency and, 251–254
Insanity Defense Reform Act of 1984, 52,
        64, 67–69, 158
Instruments, as real evidence of, 552–553
Intelligence operations, 376
Intention of ordinary consequences,
        presumption of, 147, 163–167
Interest, statements against, 484–490
Internet, 381, 442
Intoxication, 594–602
    as affirmative defense, 219–220
    blood tests for, 594–596
    breath tests for, 596–599
    HGN (horizontal gaze nystagmus test) for,
        120, 600–601
    implied consent statutes for, 601–602
    nonexpert opinion on, 402–405
    urine tests for, 599
Inventory searches, 661
Involuntary confessions, 236

Judges, trial
    admissibility of evidence and, 205–206
    allowing visit of crime scene, 560–561
    jury instructions on, 154–156
    on lay opinion testimony, 395
    photograph use and, 562–563
    proof via evidence and, 85–88
    real evidence use and, 542, 544
    witness competency and, 248
    witness control by, 282–285
    as witnesses, 265–267
Judicial notice, 105–134
    in criminal cases, 132–133
    definition of, 108–111
    of facts, 111–113
    of geographical facts, 117–119
    of historical facts, 116–117
    of jurisdiction of courts, 129–130
    of language, abbreviations, and symbols,
        121–123
    of laws, 123–128

of matters of general knowledge, 113–116
process of, 130–132
of regulations, 128–129
of scientific facts, 119–121
Juries
court-appointed experts and, 418
instructions to, 130, 246, 302. *See also* Inferences; Judicial notice; Presumptions
jurors as witnesses and, 267–271
misleading, 203–204
proof via evidence and, 88–89
prosecution statements and, 92
scene of crime visits by, 561
tampering with, 268
trial judges assistance to, 88–89
Jurisdiction of courts, 129–130
Justinian (Roman ruler), 10
Juvenile adjudication, 317, 410, 494

Kansas, Supreme Court of, 264
Kennedy, Justice Anthony M., 100
Kentucky, Supreme Court of, 59, 154, 286
Knock-and-announce requirement, 648–649
Knowledge of law, presumption of, 167–168

Language, judicial notice of, 121–123
Law enforcement. *See* Police
Lawyers. *See* Defense attorneys; Privileges; Prosecution; Right-to-counsel provisions; Sixth Amendment to U.S. Constitution
Lay opinion testimony, 391. *See also* Opinion and expert testimony
Leading questions, 289–293
Legal evidence, 24
Lincoln, Abraham, 376
Lineups, 682–683
Logos, judicial notice of, 122
Louisiana, Supreme Court of, 93, 296, 471

Magnetic resonance imaging (MRI) systems, 576
Maine Revised Statutes, 259
Mandatory presumptions, 139, 150
Maps, as real evidence, 580–581
Marital harmony, promotion of, 18
Marriage, 258–262, 475. *See also* Privileges
Marshall, Chief Justice John, 459
Massachusetts, Supreme Judicial Court of, 628

Material evidence, 27. *See also* Relevant evidence
admissibility of, 80
definition of, 192–196
documentary evidence as, 504
examination and test results as, 590
exclusion of, 199–206
McCormick on Evidence, 306
Memories of witnesses, refreshing, 293–297. *See also* Recollections of witnesses
Mental capacity
attorney's statements on client, 358, 361
expert testimony on, 428–430
nonexpert opinion of, 405–407
witnesses' competency and, 251–254
Mesopotamian legal system, 8
Michigan Rules of Evidence, 574
Michigan Supreme Court, 54
Military Rules of Evidence, 608
Minnesota, Supreme Court of, 436
Minnesota Law Review, 458
Miranda warnings
confessions and, 671–676
custody requirement for, 672
defendant comments after, 216–217
defendant silence after, 325–326
violations of, 248, 641, 646
Mississippi, Supreme Court of, 551, 567
Mississippi Rules of Evidence, 526
Mistake, as affirmative defense, 61, 220
M'Naghten rule for insanity defense, 218
Models, as real evidence, 580–581
Montana, Supreme Court of, 164, 403
Motion pictures, as real evidence, 571–575
Motions, 78–79, 85, 95
Municipal ordinances, judicial notice of, 127–128

Narcotics, as real evidence, 557–559. *See also* Drug use; Intoxication
National Conference of Commissioners on Uniform State Laws, 16
National Institute of Justice, 627
Nebraska, Supreme Court of, 412, 415
Negative evidence, 245–247
Neutron activation analysis, 436–437, 625–626
Nevada, Supreme Court of, 528
New Hampshire, Supreme Court of, 158, 678
New Jersey, Supreme Court of, 416, 441
New Mexico, Supreme Court of, 605–607
News Gatherers Shield Laws (California), 383

News media-informant communication,
337, 380–386
Ninth Circuit Court of Appeals
on attorney-client privilege
exceptions, 361
on best evidence rule, 523
on hypnotically enhanced testimony, 296
on lay opinion testimony, 397, 408
on polygraph test, 611
on relevant evidence, 194
on *Thompson v. Keohane* (1995), 672
Nontestimonial utterances, 494–497
North Dakota, Supreme Court of, 320

Oaths or affirmations by witnesses, 281–283
Objections, 80, 79–80. *See also* Cross-
examination; Direct examination
O'Connor, Justice Sandra Day, 94
Offering evidence, procedure for, 83–85
Official acts, regularity of, 147, 173–174
Ohio Administrative Code, 129
Oklahoma Court of Criminal Appeals, 574
Omnibus Crime Control and Safe Streets Act
of 1968, 17, 19, 237, 675
Onboard diagnostics computer system
(OBD II), 624
Open fields, searches in, 658–659
Opening statements, 92, 97
Opinion and expert testimony, 389–445.
See also Documentary evidence
on ballistics, 618
on character of witnesses, 312, 314, 315
crime laboratories as sources of, 443–444
cross-examination of experts in, 422–425
distinctions between, 392–393
on document authentication, 520
examination of experts in, 419–422
expert opinions in, 411–415
expert opinion subjects in, 425–443
airplane crashes as, 427–428
automobile accidents as, 425–427
DNA identification as, 437–439
drug operations as, 440–442
fingerprint identification as, 439–440
handwriting as, 431–433
neutron activation analysis as, 436–437
physical and mental conditions as,
428–430
polygraph test results as, 434–436
summaries as, 430–431
typewriter comparisons as, 433–434
expert qualifications in, 415–417
expert selection in, 417–419

nonexpert opinion admissibility in,
394–397
nonexpert opinion subjects in, 397–410
age estimates as, 397–398
appearance as, 398–399
conduct as, 399–401
distance as, 401–402
handwriting as, 408–409
identification as, 407–408
intoxication and drug use as, 402–405
sanity or mental condition as, 405–407
speed as, 409–410
time and duration as, 402
Ordinances, judicial notice of, 127–128
Ordinary consequences, presumption of, 147,
163–167
Oregon, Supreme Court of, 300
Others, defense of, 220
Out-of-court statements, 28. *See also* Hearsay

Palm prints, 616
Pandects, in Roman legal system, 10
Pardons, 317, 320
Parental rights, termination of, 51
Parliament, British, 13
Parole
DNA samples and, 629–630
hearings for, 37–38, 116
search and seizure in, 653
Past recollections recorded, 297–300
Patient-physician communication, 362–368
Pecuniary interest, statements against,
485–487
Penal interest, statements against, 487–490
Pennsylvania, Supreme Court of, 140, 574
Pen registers and trap-and-trace devices, for
telephone numbers, 667
Pentateuch, in Hebrew legal system, 9
Perceptions, witness defects of, 323–324. *See
also* Recollections of witnesses
Perjury, 248
Permissive inferences, 150
Permissive presumptions, 150, 166
Personal digital assistants, messages on,
579–580
Persuasion, burden of, 48–49
Photographic arrays, for identification,
683–684
Photographs, as real evidence, 562–571
authentication of, 563
chain of custody and, 565–566
color, 569–570
enlargements and aerial, 570–571

gruesome, 567–568
posed, 566–567
time of taking of, 568–569
trial judge decision on, 562–563
unfair prejudicial effect of, 564–568
Physical conditions, expert testimony on, 428–430
"Physical" evidence, 26. *See also* Real evidence
Physician-patient communication, 362–368
Plain view doctrine, searches *versus*, 656–658
Plame, Valerie, 386
Plasma Emission Spectroscopy, 630
Plea bargains, 91
Police
  evidence wrongfully obtained by, 236–237
  search warrants and, 643–646, 649
  "steering" by, 208
  trial judges and, 86
Polygraph (lie detector) test, 604–612
  admissible if stipulated, 609–610
  admissible under special circumstances, 610
  basis of, 604–612
  expert testimony on, 434–436
  New Mexico Supreme Court on, 605–607
  reliability concerns on, 120
  stipulations on admissibility of, 143, 183–185
  U.S. Supreme Court on, 608–609
Polymerase chain reaction (PCR) test, of DNA evidence, 120, 438, 627, 628
Possession of fruits of crime, inferences from, 160–163
Posthumous revelations, as privilege exception, 359
Prejudice. *See* Unfair prejudice risk
Preponderance of the evidence, 46, 49–50
Presumptions, 107. *See also* Inferences; Stipulations
  of Acts of Congress, 511
  classes of, 148–151
  constitutionality tests for, 175–180
  of death, 171–173
  definition of, 138–140
  of fact, 147–148
  of guilt, 213–216
  of innocence, 152–156
  of intention of ordinary consequences, 163–167
  of knowledge of law, 167–168
  of law, 146–147

overview of, 137–138
reasons for, 144–146
of regularity of official acts, 173–174
of sanity, 156–159
situations of, 151–152
against suicide, 159–160
Pretrial flow of evidence, 33–35
Pretrial motions on evidence, 78–79
Prima facie evidence, 26
Privacy, expectation of, 554, 616, 659
Private individual, searches by, 660–661
Private property, in Code Napoleon, 12
Private writings, as documentary evidence, 520–522
Privileges, 331–388
  in attorney-client communication, 351–361
    assertion and waiver of, 360–361
    exceptions to, 355–359
    rules of, 351–353
    scope of, 353–355
  in clergy-congregant communication, 368–372
  in common law, 335, 336
  of confidential informants, 372–375
  Federal Rules of Evidence on, 333, 336–337
  in husband-wife communication, 338–351
    duration of, 350–351
    exceptions to, 345–350
    rules of, 339
    scope of, 339–345
  in news media-informant communication, 380–386
  in physician-patient communication, 362–368
    assertion and waiver of, 367–368
    exceptions to, 365–367
    rule of, 362–363
    scope of, 363–365
  reasons for, 337–338
  in state secrets and other official information, 376–380
  three categories of, 334–336
  valid claim of, 302
Probable cause
  evidence for, 34
  police proceeding without, 645
  Terry v. Ohio (1968) and, 663, 664
  for tracking vehicles, 667
  United States v. Leon (1984) and, 643
  warrantless search and, 649
Probation, DNA samples and, 629–630
Probation hearings, 37

Probation officers, searches and, 661
Proof via evidence, 26, 75–104. *See also*
    Burden of proof
    admissibility and, 79–80
    circumstantial evidence weight in,
        100–103
    defense attorney role in, 94–97
    direct evidence weight in, 97–100
    jury function in, 88–89
    offering and challenging, 83–85
    order of presenting, 81–83
    of other crimes, 224–229
    pretrial motions on, 78–79
    prosecuting attorney role in, 91–94
    trial judge role in, 85–88
    witness role in, 89–90
Property, shared, searches of, 652–654
Prosecution
    burden of proof on, 45, 56–58
    case-in-chief of, 81, 91
    case-in-rebuttal of, 82
    DNA evidence and, 628
    insanity defense and, 66
    proof via evidence and, 91–94
    rebuttal presumption of innocence
        and, 152
    relevance limitations on, 302–304
Psychologist-patient communication, 337,
    362–363
Public policy, presumptions of law and,
    145–146
Public records, as documentary evidence,
    518–520

Questions, leading, 289–293
Quintilian (Roman educator), 11

Radio Detection and Ranging (RADAR)
    speed testing, 620
Real evidence, 26, 537–585
    admissibility of, 541–548
        chain of custody for, 542–545
        identification of, 547–548
        necessity for, 545–546
        relationship to crime of, 546–547
    articles connected to crime as, 549–560
        bloodstains as, 554–557
        instruments as, 552–553
        narcotics as, 557–559
        weapons as, 550–551
    demonstrations and experiments as, 582
    demonstrative, 539
    diagrams, maps, and models as, 580–581

    exhibition of person as, 548–549
    motion pictures and videotapes as,
        571–575
    photographs as, 562–571
        authentication of, 563
        chain of custody of, 565–566
        color, 569–570
        enlargements and aerial, 570–571
        gruesome, 567–568
        posed, 566–567
        time of taking of, 568–569
        trial judge decision on, 562–563
        unfair prejudicial effect of, 564–567
    preservation and disclosure of, 583
    sound recordings as, 576–580
    unfair prejudice risk in, 540
    view of scene as, 560–562
    X-rays as, 575–576
"Reasonably effective assistance"
    standard, 94
Rebuttal, 82, 145, 150, 151, 152
Recollections of witnesses. *See also* Hearsay
    doctrine of past, 301
    Federal Rules of Evidence on, 297–298
    impeachment of witnesses on, 323–324
    recorded, 297–298
Recordings, 573, 575, 576–580
Redirect and recross-examination, 305–306
Refreshing memories of witnesses, 293–297
Regularity of official acts, 147, 173–174
Regulations, judicial notice of, 128–129
Rehabilitation, 317, 326–328
Rejection of Romanesque Law, Period of, 12
Rejoinder, case-in-, 82–83
Relationships, as reason for excluding
    evidence, 29
Relevancy
    in pretrial motions on evidence, 78
Relevant evidence, 27, 189–232. *See also*
    Material evidence
    admissibility of, 79–80, 196–198
    of character, 221–224
    of circumstances preceding crimes,
        211–213
    defenses against, 217–220
    definition of, 192–196
    documentary evidence as, 504
    examination and test results as, 590, 593
    exclusion of, 199–206
    experimental and scientific, 229–231
    of identity of persons, 207–210
    of identity of things, 210–211
    proof of other crimes as, 224–229

of subsequent incriminating circumstances, 213–217

witness competency and, 248–249

Religious beliefs for witness competency, 264–265

Reputation, 312, 315, 474

Residual exceptions to hearsay rule, 490–494

Restriction Fragment Length Polymorphism (RFLP) test for DNA identification, 438

Reversible errors, 84, 154, 302, 549, 568, 584

Right-to-counsel provisions. *See also* Sixth Amendment to U.S. Constitution

"reasonably effective assistance" standard in, 94

in state constitutions, 94

violations of, 79, 642, 680–684

Romanesque legal system, 11–12

Roman legal system, 10–11

Rules of evidence, development of, 5–20. *See also* Federal Rules of Evidence

in Anglican system, 12–14

court application of, 16–18

in early legal systems, 7–11

in future, 18–20

in Romanesque system, 11–12

in U.S., 14–16

Rules of Evidence for Federal Courts and Magistrates, 15, 336

Rules of Professional Conduct, of attorneys, 93

Sacramento (CA) Police Department, 439

Same-gender unions, 344–345

Sanity, presumption of, 147, 156–159

Scene of crime, as real evidence, 560–562

Scholarly writing, in expert testimony, 423

Scientific evidence, 229–231, 238–240. *See also* Examination and test results

Scientific facts, judicial notice of, 119–121

Search and seizure, unlawful, 665–668 *See also* Fourth Amendment to U.S. Constitution

citywide stops and brief searches as, 645

exigent or emergency circumstances *versus,* 645

independent source rule *versus,* 646

knock and announce requirement and, 648–649

lawful arrest exception to, 649–652

lawful impoundment exception to, 661–662

open fields exception to, 658–659

plain view doctrine exception to, 656–658

police "good faith" rationale *versus,* 643–645

private individual searches exception to, 660–661

on state and local level, 643

stop-and-frisk search *versus,* 662–664

USA PATRIOT Act and, 19

vehicle searches exception to, 654–656

waiver of constitutional right exception to, 652–654

Searches, sweep, 651–652

Search warrants, 616, 643–646, 649

Secondary evidence, documentary evidence as, 525–530

Second Circuit Court of Appeals, 401

Self-defense, 61, 69–71, 220, 565

Self-incrimination protection, 217. *See also* Due process clause; Fifth Amendment to U.S. Constitution

blood tests and, 595, 596

evidence excluded by violations of, 79, 676–679

examination of person and, 593–594

fingerprinting and, 615–617

handwriting sample requirements and, 432

hearsay rule and, 488

real evidence and, 540

Sensing diagnostic module (SDM), 624

September 11, 2001 attacks, 116

Seventh Circuit Court of Appeals

on cross-examination limitations, 303

on document authentication, 514

on expert testimony, 414

on polygraph test, 610

on recorded recollections, 300

Sexual assault, 348

Sexually Dangerous Persons Act (Illinois), 15

Sexual Offender Registration Act, 520

"Shield laws," 383–386

Short tandem repeat testing, of DNA evidence, 628

"Silent witness" authentication method, 573–574

Sister state laws, judicial notice of, 125–126

Sixth Amendment to U.S. Constitution, 90

attorney-client communication privilege in, 352

on cross-examination, 301–302, 349, 424

dying declarations and, 481, 483

excluding evidence by violations of, 79, 642, 680–684

hearsay evidence and, 460, 471, 477–478

right of confrontation in, 301–302, 438, 493–494
right-to-counsel requirements of, 94–97
right to defense of, 608–609
Sullivan v. Louisiana (1993) on, 54
on witness separation, 286
Sixth Circuit Court of Appeals, 421
Socrates, 10
Sodium amytal ("truth serum"), 612
Sound recordings, as real evidence, 576–580
Sources, news media. *See* News media-informant communication
South Dakota, Supreme Court of, 602
Speed, determination of, 409–410, 620–624
Spontaneous or excited utterances, 460–466
Spouses, as competent witnesses, 258–262. *See also* Privileges
Stalker Dual SL radar unit, 621
Standard Crash Reports, 470
Starr, Kenneth, 359
State secrets, privileges of, 376–380
State Supreme Courts. *See* individual state names
Statutory incompetency of evidence, 237
Statutory presumptions, 139–140, 175–180
Statutory reporters' privileges, 382–383
"Steering" by police, 208
Stipulations, 74. *See also* Inferences; Presumptions
  accepted, 108
  definition of, 143–144
  effect of, 180–183
  overview of, 137–138
  on polygraph (lie detector) test, 183–185, 609–610
Stop-and-frisk searches, 655, 662–664
Substitution of presumption for evidence, 152
Sufficiency of evidence, 72–73, 100–101, 103
Suicide, 159–160, 216, 359
Summaries, as evidence, 430–431, 530–534, 581
Suppression hearings, 35
Surveillance tapes, 571–572
Sweep searches, 651–652
Symbols, judicial notice of, 121–123

"Taint" hearing, 256
Tampering with evidence, 542–543, 558. *See also* Chain of custody
Telephone conversations, as evidence, 243–245, 505

Tenet, George, 379
Tenth Circuit Court of Appeals
  on court-appointed experts, 419
  on expert testimony, 412
  on sound recordings, 578
Termination of parental rights, 51
Terrorist activities, 19
Testimony, 25. *See also* Opinion and expert testimony
  evidence as, 100
  eyewitness, 15
  former, 477–480
  hypnotically enhanced, 296
Test results. *See* Examination and test results
Texas Court of Criminal Appeals, 475
Texas Rules of Evidence, 261
Texas Youth Commission, 475
Text messages, on cell phones, 579
Third Circuit Court of Appeals, 369
Thomas, Justice Clarence, 608
Time
  excluding evidence and, 31, 204–205
  nonexpert opinion on duration of, 401–402
  photographs taken, 568–569
  since convictions, admissibility and, 315
Tomography imaging systems, 575–576
Torah, in Hebrew legal system, 9
Totality of circumstances, 656
Trademarks, judicial notice of, 122
Trade secrets, 383
Trained dogs, evidence of, 240–242
Treatise or other scholarly writing, 423, 534–535
"Trial by battle," 13
Trial judges. *See* Judges, trial
Trials, criminal evidence used in, 35–36
"Truth serum," 612
Typewriter comparisons, 433–434

U.S. Air Force, 377
U.S. Congress
  Insanity Defense Reform Act of 1984, 52, 64, 67–69, 158
  Omnibus Crime Control and Safe Streets Act of 1968, 17, 675
  rules of evidence changes by, 15–16
  Rules of Evidence for United States Courts and Magistrates and, 15
  wiretapping regulations of, 665, 667
U.S. Constitution. *See also* individual amendments to the U.S. Constitution
  Congressional regulatory power in, 17
  evidence inadmissibility and, 197

excluding evidence violating, 30
inferences and, 175–180
law enforcement activities and, 86
presumptions and, 175–180
state judicial notice of, 125
U.S. Department of Health and Human
Services, 129
U.S. Department of the Navy, 513
U.S. Department of the Treasury, 436
U.S. Supreme Court
"all elements of crime" requirements, 59
attorney-client communication privilege,
352, 359
"beyond a reasonable doubt"
requirement, 53
burden of proof in affirmative defense,
63–64
confessions as evidence, 669
DNA evidence, 556, 629
document authentication methods, 505
duration of marital communication
privilege, 350
exhibition of persons, 548–549
expectation of privacy of convicts, 554
Fifth Amendment to U.S. Constitution, 17
Fourteenth Amendment to U.S.
Constitution, 17
governmental privilege, 376
habitual offender statutes, 91
handwriting sample requirements, 432
hypnotically enhanced testimony, 296
inferences, 141
insanity defense, 67
intoxication defense, 219–220
Jackson v. Virginia (1979), 72
judicial notice by, 123
Miranda warning violations, 642
moving vehicle searches, 654–656
parolees' expectations of privacy, 653
physician-patient privilege, 363
polygraph (lie detector) test, 608–609
presumption of sanity, 156–159
presumptions of ordinary
consequences, 166
privacy of personal phone numbers, 667
privileged communication, 336–338
proof of other crimes, 227
"reasonably effective assistance"
standard, 94
right to counsel at lineups, 682
*Rules of Evidence for United States Courts
and Magistrates* adoption by, 15
search warrants, 646–649

shared property authority and searches,
652–654
statutory presumption standards of, 175
stop-and-frisk searches, 662–664
Sullivan v. Louisiana (1993), 54
wrongfully obtained evidence, 236
"Ultimate issue" rule, 421
Unanticipated evidence, 205–206
Unexplained absence, 171–173
Unfair prejudice risk, 29
to accused, 29
exclusion of evidence because of,
199–201
by photographs, 564–567, 567–568
proof of other crimes as, 225–227
by real evidence, 540, 549
witnesses and, 310–312
Uniform Business Records Act, 467
Uniform Judicial Notice of Foreign
Law Act, 125
Uniform Rules of Evidence (National
Conference of Commissioners on
Uniform State Laws), 16, 128
Unreliable evidence, 30
Urine tests for intoxication, 599
USA PATRIOT Act, 19, 667
Utterances
nontestimonial, 494–497
spontaneous or excited, 460–466

Vehicle searches, 654–656
Venue, for trials, 57
Vermont, Supreme Court of, 367, 385
Victor v. Nebraska (1994), 55
Videotapes
authenticating, 517, 527–528
court discretion to use, 564
as real evidence, 548–549, 571–575
View of scene, as real evidence, 560–562
Voir dire, of juries, 269

Wall Street Journal, 116
Warrantless arrests, 33
Washington, Supreme Court of, 142
Weapons, as real evidence, 550–551
White, Justice Byron R., 382
Wigmore, Dean, 7, 524
William the Conqueror, 13
Wiretap evidence, 15, 19, 237, 665–668
Witnesses, examination of, 275–330. *See also*
Competency; Cross-examination;
Opinion and expert testimony
character evidence for, 221, 222, 223
cross-, 300–304

defendant confrontation in, 90
direct, 288–289
on documentary evidence, 507–508
impeachment in, 306–326
  bias or prejudice in, 310–312
  on character and conduct, 312–316
  confession for, 324–326
  on crime conviction, 316–321
  on inconsistent statements, 321–323
  of own witnesses, 308–309
  on recollection defects, 323–324
judicial control of, 283–285
judicial protection in, 86
leading questions in, 289–293
oaths or affirmations in, 281–282

proof via evidence and, 89–90
qualities of, 278–280
recorded recollections in, 297
redirect and recross-, 305–306
refreshing memories in, 293–297
rehabilitation of, 326–328
separation of, 285–288
Wrongfully obtained evidence, 236–237.
  See also Confessions; Due process
  clause; Right-to-counsel provisions;
  Search and seizure, unlawful; Self-
  incrimination protection; Wiretap
  evidence

X-rays, as real evidence, 575–576